Handbook of Research on the Illicit Drug Traffic

The **United Nations Research Institute for Social Development (UNRISD)** was established to promote in-depth research into the social dimensions of pressing problems and issues of contemporary relevance affecting development. Its work is inspired by the conviction that, for effective development policies to be formulated, an understanding of the social and political context is crucial, as is an accurate assessment of how such policies affect different social groups.

The Institute attempts to complement the work done by other United Nations agencies and its current research themes include the social impact of the economic crisis and adjustment policies; environment, sustainable development and social change; ethnic conflict and development; refugees, returnees and local society; the socioeconomic and political consequences of the international trade in illicit drugs; and the impact on participation of changes in the ownership of the means of production.

UNRISD, Palais des Nations, 1211 Geneva 10, Switzerland

Handbook of Research on the Illicit Drug Traffic

Socioeconomic and Political Consequences

LaMond Tullis

in cooperation with the United Nations Research Institute for Social Development

Foreword by Keith Griffin

Greenwood Press
New York • Westport, Connecticut • London

Library of Congress Cataloging-in-Publication Data

Tullis, LaMond.
   Handbook of research on the illicit drug traffic : socioeconomic
and political consequences / LaMond Tullis in cooperation with the
United Nations Research Institute for Social Development ; foreword
by Keith Griffin.
     p. cm.
   Includes bibliographical references and index.
   ISBN 0-313-27846-6 (alk. paper)
    1. Drug traffic. 2. Narcotics, Control of.   I. United Nations
Research Institute for Social Development.   II. Title.
HV5801.T78   1991
363.4'5—dc20   90-25218

British Library Cataloguing in Publication Data is available.

Library of Congress Catalog Card Number: 90-25218
ISBN: 0-313-27846-6

First published in 1991

Greenwood Press, 88 Post Road West, Westport, CT 06881
An imprint of Greenwood Publishing Group, Inc.

Printed in the United States of America

The paper used in this book complies with the
Permanent Paper Standard issued by the National
Information Standards Organization (Z39.48-1984).

10 9 8 7 6 5 4 3 2 1

Contents

Part II: Drug and Drug-Related Literature

Illustrations

Figures:

Flow Charts:

Tables:

Foreword

LaMond Tullis has written an excellent survey of the social and economic consequences of the production and consumption of narcotic drugs. The subject is highly controversial and fiercely debated. Prejudices abound; ignorance is widespread; the debate often is noisy and angry. One of the virtues of LaMond Tullis is that he does not allow himself to become distracted by the cacophony swirling around him: he keeps a cool head and speaks in a quiet, scholarly voice. His careful assessment of what we do and do not know about narcotic drugs is greatly to be welcomed.

His contribution is divided into two parts. The first half of the book consists of three sections that survey the published literature on the production and consumption of illicit drugs. Chapters are devoted to the global patterns of production and consumption of cocaine, heroin, and cannabis; to the consequences (positive and negative) of drug consumption and production; and to the policy measures that have been adopted, or might be adopted, in both consuming and producing countries. This half of the book will be of interest to readers who wish to obtain an overall view of the subject as well as to specialists who seek a guide to the literature outside their own particular area of knowledge.

The second half of the book contains an annotated bibliography of over 2,000 entries. The bibliography covers published works in English which have appeared in book form or in articles and press reports, as well as some in Spanish. This section will be invaluable to researchers working on the frontiers of the subject and to general readers who wish to pursue particular topics in greater depth.

The book is addressed to women and men everywhere, to anyone who wishes to become informed about this important subject. I hope it will be read by policymakers, legislators, law enforcement officials, judges, and social workers in both consuming and producing countries. It should also be read by teachers and students. The more that is known about narcotic drugs, and the more widely spread is the knowledge, the more likely we are to respond in a sensible way to the questions raised by drug consumption and production.

Illicit drugs are not of course the only drugs consumed in our societies. Alcohol and tobacco do more harm, cause more deaths and injury than does cocaine, heroin, or marijuana. Alcohol and tobacco however have been tamed or domesticated; they have been brought under control and absorbed into the culture. Marijuana, too, may be partially domesticated, but cocaine and heroine are wild, undomesticated substances that society has not yet learned to control. Indeed, as this book shows, there is little agreement about how one should go about trying to control illicit drugs.

Some place the emphasis on the supply side, on reducing substantially the production of drugs in the producing countries. Within this school of thought, at one extreme, are those who literally advocate a war on drugs. And war indeed there has been. Panama has been invaded and occupied by troops of the United States, with no effect so far on the supply of drugs. Colombia has experienced a nasty and extraordinarily violent war fought by its drug barons and the civil authority. Peasant cultivators of coca leaf in Peru have been shot and increasingly have sought the protection of the Shining Path, a Marxist guerilla group with revolutionary aspirations. Even in Bolivia, which so far has been relatively peaceful, military solutions are being urged and increasingly accepted.

At the other extreme of the supply-siders are those who seek alternatives to growing heroin poppies, coca leaf, or marijuana. Crop substitution programs have been tried in Thailand and Andean America. Grants (or bribes) have been offered to peasants to switch to other cash crops. Artisanal and small rural industries have been promoted. And in Peru and Bolivia, rural development in the altiplano has been advocated as a way of providing an alternative source of income to those who otherwise would migrate to the coca and cocaine producing regions. So far, however, these incentives have failed to work, primarily because at current drug prices there is no other crop or rural economic activity that can compete with coca, marijuana, and heroin poppies.

In between the stick of the military and the carrot of alternative development are programs to eradicate forcibly coca plants, to disrupt supplies of inputs needed to transform coca leaf into coca paste and ultimately cocaine, to intercept internal marketing channels in the producing countries, and to combat smuggling of drugs into the consuming countries. These efforts, too, have so far failed to produce the desired results. Consumption remains high despite vigorous efforts to cut off supplies at their source.

A number of analysts, perhaps a growing number, place the emphasis on the demand side, on reducing substantially the consumption of drugs in the importing countries. Here again, opinion is sharply divided as to how best this can be done. There are those who believe that the control of consumption should be seen primarily as a problem in the administration of criminal justice. That is, the focus is on law enforcement, the provision of an adequate number of police and drug agents, the destruction of networks of organized crime, and the construction of prisons. The experience so far in the United States, however, has shown the limitations of this approach. While the consumption of narcotic drugs crosses all class and social boundaries, those apprehended by the law have come disproportionately from the lower income classes and from racial and ethnic minorities, notably blacks and hispanics. The well connected (such as the mayor of Washington, D.C.), the rich, and the white seem to have escaped relatively unscathed.

Other analysts have argued that the best way to control demand in the long run is by creating conditions that lead people voluntarily to restrict their consumption. Emphasis is placed on public education and propaganda—analogous to the campaigns intended to discourage the use of tobacco—and on public health measures and the rehabilitation of drug users. Improved social conditions—a reduction in unemployment, a rise in living standards of the very poor, improved housing, and the provision of recreational facilities for the young (so that they will have an alternative to hanging out on the streets)—are seen as an important part of the solution. Still others have suggested that drugs be decriminalized and that their sale be regulated in a way similar to that of alcohol. It is argued that this would reduce many of the social costs that are a by-product of the illegal sale of drugs—the gang wars over turf and the robberies and muggings committed by addicts to raise money to pay for drugs. Decriminalization would also, it is argued, enable the authorities to exercise some quality control, to prevent the adulteration of drugs, and to sever the link between drugs and organized crime. Decriminalization, in other words, would help tame narcotic drugs rather than eliminate them.

Not all the policies mentioned are substitutes for one another. Some are complementary and can be combined to form a package of measures. Different consuming countries have relied on different packages, and much can be learned form a close study of the experiences of the major consuming countries. Equally, it is misleading, as I have done, to divide the drug problem between producing and exporting countries on the one hand and consuming and importing countries on the other. Some countries are both producers and consumers. Andean America, for example, has produced and consumed coca for many centuries and a small but growing part of the population recently has begun to consume cocaine. Similarly, the United States is by far the world's largest consumer of illegal drugs but it is also a major producer of marijuana.

Despite these qualifications it is generally true to say that the consuming countries tend to be rich whereas the producing countries tend to be poor. Moreover, a small proportion of total income in the consuming countries is devoted to expenditure on drugs whereas a high proportion of total income in some producing countries is derived from cultivation, processing, and transport of drugs. Suppression of illegal drugs would therefore severely damage the economies of some developing countries, and within many of those countries the burden would fall disproportionately on the very poor. While it is an exaggeration to say that narcotic drugs are a rich man's habit and a poor man's livelihood, elimination of the drug trade would accentuate income inequality both internationally and within the producing countries.

The social and economic consequences of the production, trade, and consumption of narcotic drugs are thus complex. Many of the complexities are raised in this book, and possible solutions are explored. The work was sponsored by the United Nations Research Institute for Social Development in Geneva, Switzerland, and it represents what we hope will be the first stage in a major research program. We are grateful to Professor Tullis for undertaking the study for us and to Brigham Young University for supporting the research and releasing Professor Tullis from some of his teaching commitments.

Paris
September 1990

Keith Griffin
Chairman of the Board
United Nations Research Institute
for Social Development

Preface

In the 1970s and 1980s, concerns about illicit drug production, trafficking, and consumption, and the public's response to all three, rose to the forefront of domestic and international policy issues. An intense scrutiny of illicit drug matters will likely characterize the 1990s. Can consumption be curtailed, supplies suppressed, and traffickers eliminated? Should they? Can the unintended economic, social, and political consequences of curtailing, suppressing, and eliminating somehow be mitigated? Can net producing and net consuming countries deal adequately with the social, economic, and political overhead costs of the drug traffic and with public efforts to suppress it? How? Should the whole policy debate be brought to closure by legalizing drugs? Would drug legalization produce its own array of unintended and largely unacceptable consequences?

The many-sided issues suggested by these questions involve moral, personal, economic, political, and social considerations. Hotly debated public issues usually do. In this volume we have tried to sort out most of the salient economic, social, and political themes currently discussed in the scholarly literature and in the responsible press. The review and the annotated bibliography (indexed by keywords) give students, researchers, and policymakers quick access to a substantial sample of the relevant literature.

This volume owes its inception to Keith Griffin and to the United Nations Research Institute for Social Development (UNRISD) whose governing board he chairs. We gratefully acknowledge UNRISD's financial support for this project.

The David M. Kennedy Center for International Studies at Brigham Young University has been generous in its support—supplying space, equipment, and research funding. Brigham Young University facilitated released time to allow me to spend a year's effort on the project, unencumbered by other university assignments. Princeton University's Center of International Studies afforded me office space, assistance, and collegial critiques during my stay as a visiting fellow, 1990-91.

Three Brigham Young University students contributed to this project: Melanie Larsen Jenkins (English), Scott McClesky (Economics), and Mark Freeman (Political Science). Jenkins' professional touch has graced the project from its inception, for which I am deeply indebted. McClesky was nearly indefatigable in his identifying likely entries for the annotated bibliography. Freeman paid particular attention to statistical matters.

Jason Alan and Lesley Jean helped prepare the bibliography and the index.

I have benefitted from, and am therefore also indebted to, several reviewers of the draft manuscript: Yusuf Bangura, Solon Barraclough, Cynthia Hewitt de Alcántara, Keith Griffin, Françoise Jaffré, Marta Morrill Tullis, and Jessica Vivian. To all these I give thanks.

Princeton, New Jersey
April 1991

Introduction

This *Handbook* surveys the literature on the social, economic, and political consequences of the illicit international drug trade. It examines information on the production, distribution, and consumption of those drugs and the policy instruments designed to deal with their effects. The volume also evaluates the intended, and sometimes unintended, consequences of various policies. It is organized so that the main text raises the relevant issues, which are then referenced to the literature and discussed in further detail in the endnotes.

The international illicit drug trade arises for reasons analogous to other international trading patterns. Demand, and therefore a market, exists; supply, and therefore a commodity, is available; traders, anxious to unite suppliers and consumers for a profit, abound.

Problems, liabilities, and even benefits from this illegal trade are therefore integrated into a world trading system. Observers are increasingly of the opinion that successful solutions to drug problems, whether in countries that produce more than they consume (net producers or exporters) or in countries that consume more than they produce (net consumers), will be found only in international cooperation that addresses demand, supply, trade, and the policy instruments that make all three illegal.

What are the significant social, economic, and political consequences of the modern illicit drug trade and the national and international responses to it? What has happened as the drug trade has collided with people, countries, and institutions? In an effort to answer these and related questions, and as a response to the growing international anxiety about illicit drugs, the United Nations Research Institute for Social Development (UNRISD), with financial support from Brigham Young University and its David M. Kennedy Center for International Studies, launched in 1989 a research effort to identify those consequences as discussed in the literature and to examine a range of policy instruments so far considered. Two phases of that work are reported in this *Handbook*—the literature survey and an accompanying annotated bibliography. The third phase, initiated in early 1991 and to be published later, makes a detailed examination of the illicit drug trade's impact on principal drug-producing countries.

The literature on illicit drugs is extensive and strikingly diverse. From more than 4,000 items that came to our attention—books, articles, and press reports—we selected 2,058 for inclusion in the annotated bibliography. These selections constitute the data base for this volume. We do not presume that the annotated bibliography is comprehensive; we do affirm that it is extensive, objectively annotated, and broadly representative of the diverse views on social, economic, and political consequences of the production and consumption of illicit drugs and the range of policy instruments currently in vogue or under discussion to deal with those consequences.

A significant portion of recent information on drug-related matters is topical and rapidly changing (e.g., production estimates, incidences of violence, law enforcement moves, implementation of new drug control policies, traffickers' activities). Much of it has not yet been sifted by scholars for significance and meaning. In looking into these fast-paced events, we have therefore found it necessary to turn to responsible journalists for contemporary on-site reports to supplement the scholarly literature that we have examined.

Most of the press reports included in this study come from *The New York Times, The Christian Science Monitor, The Miami Herald, The Los Angeles Times*, and occasionally from *The Wall Street Journal* and several international (e.g., *Financial Times*, London) and regional papers. In addition to placing this literature into a "consequence context," we have tried to examine it analytically. In areas currently informed mostly by journalists, readers will want to be alert to new thematic publications that will undoubtedly be forthcoming from the scholarly press or whose existence has escaped our attention in this survey.

Most of the literature reviewed here comes from the 1980–90 decade. It focuses on the drug traffic and its consequences both in net producing countries and in net consuming countries. As for net producing countries, the available literature in U.S. libraries deals mostly with Latin America, perhaps because cocaine and "crack" have so captured both American users and observers in recent years. Nevertheless, with respect to the opium industry, we have a good range of materials on Burma, Pakistan, Thailand, Afghanistan, and Laos. There is also a sampling of materials dealing with the cannabis trade in Latin America, the United States (a new cannabis exporter), the Caribbean, South Asia, and the Middle East.

As for net consuming countries, most of the available literature in U.S. libraries deals with the United States, although we do have literature for Latin America, the United Kingdom, Africa, Asia, Australia, Canada, Western Europe, and Russia. Because the United States is the largest consumer of illicit drugs, American drug use has been the most widely discussed and analyzed. Also, quite understandably, North America's major research libraries, which we have accessed through the Research Libraries Information Network,[1] have holdings that consist mostly of U.S.–produced materials.

Nevertheless, we have numerous research materials originating in Canada, Australia, Great Britain, Colombia, Bolivia, Peru, Mexico, and Thailand. We have reviewed the principal data bases.[2] We also have accessed a United Nations depository for its relevant holdings.

While numerous licit and illicit drugs are noted in the literature,[3] our discussion is confined to illicit drugs currently significant in international transactions—namely, cocaine and "crack,"[4] opium and heroin,[5] and several kinds of cannabis preparations,[6] including marijuana, ganja, and hashish. Even though in the principal drug consuming countries drug users increasingly choose illicit drugs other than those mentioned (e.g., synthetic opiates and "designer drugs"[7]), these fall outside the scope of this work except to note that their substitution for currently imported botanically based drugs in the United States and Western Europe would have substantial economic, social, and political consequences for countries that are net illicit drug producers. For example, a sudden collapse in demand for cocaine would throw more than a million people out of work in Colombia, Bolivia, and Peru, most of whom earn a substantial part if not all of their living as growers, couriers, hired field hands, property squatters or owners, members of private armies, coca-paste processors, hawkers, provisioners, petty merchants, sharks, or corrupt politicians and judges attached in some way to the cocaine trade. A sudden decline in income for all of these would produce substantial politically destabilizing events.[8]

During the past fifteen years, the illicit international drug trade has grown from cottage export production to highly organized, international economic exchanges employing hundreds of thousands of people and earning scores of billions of dollars annually.[9] A UN observer estimates the retail value of illicit drug trafficking to exceed the international trade in oil, and to be second only to the weapons trade.[10] Another study shows consumer expenditures in the United States alone likely to have exceeded the 1986 gross domestic product of eighty-eight different countries.[11] The huge volume and the vast sums of money and profits associated with the trade have imposed interesting, frequently serious, consequences on the political, economic, and social conditions of countries throughout the world as well as in their transnational relations.

The literature we survey on *consequences* is substantial, ranging through economic prosperity and enhanced employment opportunities, environmental degradation, distorted economies and social structures, troubled health care systems, subverted governments and national value systems, terrorized populations, and increasing human misery. Transnationally, the traffic affects international processes and institutions, as weak states and private actors become relatively more powerful.[12]

While understandable variations exist in production estimates, on four matters many observers agree: the production of marijuana, heroin, and cocaine/crack is increasing, especially cocaine/crack; cocaine traffickers, now finding their supply substantially exceeding current market demand in the United States,[13] are vigorously opening new markets in Canada, Great

Britain, and Western Europe (with Spain and Italy as principal ports of entry for Europe);[14] the increasing supply of illicit drugs relative to current demand contributes to additional violence as international cartels and domestic gangs war over market turf; and the policy instruments designed so far to curtail the demand for, suppress the traffic in, and control the supply of illicit drugs have not produced satisfactory conclusions.

Peru, Bolivia, and Colombia account for more than 98 percent of the world's cocaine supply.[15] The Golden Crescent (Pakistan, Afghanistan, Iran), the Golden Triangle (Burma, Laos, Thailand), Mexico, and Guatemala account for the vast majority of opiates (opium, morphine, heroin) traded internationally, although Lebanon's Bekaa Valley is fast becoming a producer.[16] Cannabis is produced in most parts of the world. Cannabis entering the U.S. market comes principally from Colombia, Mexico, Jamaica, and U.S. domestic crops.[17] Some worldwide exports emanate from Thailand, Morocco, Lebanon, and Iran.[18]

Production figures are, at best, gross estimates because of the clandestine nature of much of the drug trade itself, although considerable legitimate recorded trade for medical and scientific purposes is carried out.[19] Inasmuch as most countries have laws limiting production and also have drug-suppression programs with varying levels of application for illicit trade and use,[20] it is understandable that illicit traffickers would want to keep government authorities ignorant of their activities. Nevertheless, governments, private agencies, and the United Nations make estimates based on seizures, aerial and ground surveys, and consumption trends.[21]

With the exception of significant marijuana production in the United States, most illicit drugs destined for international trade originate in less developed countries (LDCs). Where are the illicit drugs consumed? Inasmuch as money and the prospects of more of it drive most of the illicit drug trade, presumably most of the trade would be directed to consumers in economically better off countries. So it is.

The United States is by far the largest single consumer of illicit drugs,[22] the principal rage now being cocaine/crack (perhaps declining somewhat in 1990–91, especially among the middle classes), although marijuana continues to be the most frequently used drug. Heroin consumption is an increasing problem, particularly in its association with the spread of the acquired immune deficiency syndrome (AIDS).[23] Nevertheless, cocaine/crack greatly concerns the United States, a worry that appears to be increasingly shared by the United Kingdom and other North Atlantic countries. While Great Britain, for example, has recently suffered a new heroin rage among thousands of young people,[24] in the late 1980s the country began to gear up for a cocaine/crack epidemic that, the authorities feared, could yet be the country's worst illicit drug experience.[25] The Colombians have been working diligently to open the European market to cocaine.[26]

Heroin has been a nominal problem in all Western European countries, but now cocaine is making substantial inroads there as well. Even the USSR has begun to lament its own drug problem. While, traditionally, the Soviet

Union's concern was heroin (made worse by returning veterans from the war in Afghanistan who had become addicted while in service there), now the USSR is noting the penetration of cocaine into its borderlands.[27] Canada and Australia have also noted increased consumption of illicit drugs.[28]

In the past, less developed countries have produced but tended not to consume drugs destined for the illicit international market; however, now the producers have also become consumers. The highly visible new consumption practice, especially in Peru, Bolivia, and Colombia, of smoking a mixture of coca paste (precursor to cocaine) and tobacco is producing unprecedented social ills. Some physicians, no doubt working on the medical profession's extreme margins, have resorted to controversial brain surgery, widely practiced among the Incas in ancient times, in an effort to cure the addicts.[29] Burma, Thailand, Laos, Iran, and Pakistan all note considerable problems with new waves of opium addiction,[30] and the addiction matter has once again cropped up as a public concern in China.[31] Africa is also in the news on this issue.[32] Consumption is no longer an exclusive "demand problem" of the "rich" countries.

Even though the production and consumption of illicit drugs have been part of the modern international scene for many decades, new and aggressive production and marketing efforts now affect the economic, social, personal, and political lives of millions of people. In this drama, cocaine and crack have increasingly made their presence felt. That, along with the growing consumption of heroin (increasingly used in conjunction with cocaine) is sure to present new public health and safety issues in the 1990s.

The current spectacle is not the first time the world or some part of it has been awash in drugs that are generally viewed as corrosive and destructive to individuals and society,[33] but our times are certainly significant in the history of drug use and abuse. Many people consider the international economy now to be engaged in a commerce of destruction. In some countries the public policy response has been frenetic.[34]

The balance of the literature survey is divided into three parts: patterns of production and consumption, consequences, and proffered new solutions. The first part—*Patterns of Production and Consumption*

Subject Outline
I. *PATTERNS OF PRODUCTION AND CONSUMPTION*
1. COCAINE
2. HEROIN
3. CANNABIS
II. *CONSEQUENCES*
4. RISE OF A NEW GENRE OF ORGANIZED TRAFFICKER
5. IMPLEMENTATION OF COUNTERVAILING INITIATIVES
6. DEMAND
III. *PROFFERED NEW SOLUTIONS*
7. LOCI OF ACTIVITIES TO REDUCE DEMAND
8. LOCI OF ACTIVITIES TO REDUCE SUPPLY
9. LOCI OF ACTIVITIES TO REDUCE CRIMINALITY AND THE SPREAD OF AIDS

of illicit drugs—sets the domestic and international arena in view so that an analysis of implications and consequences may be made. Here, as in these introductory pages, the main text offers a survey of the issues while the notes reference the literature and, in some cases, present bibliographical essays. Thus readers may move from the survey information in the main text to the notes for detailed discussions that are referenced to the annotated bibliography. An important caveat attends this method of presentation. The notes are not included so much to sustain a scholarly argument as to explore the breadth of issues associated with the illicit drug trade and to introduce the reader to the range of materials available about them. When the only available literature comes from press reports we point them out.

The second part—*Consequences*—focuses on the effects of production and consumption of the illicit drugs under review. It is developed in three chapters: Chapter 4 explores the rise of a new genre of organized trafficker; Chapter 5 examines the public's implementation of countervailing initiatives as a general response to market demand, ample product supply, and increasingly aggressive marketing techniques; and Chapter 6 discusses the consequences of demand independently of whether drugs are legal or illegal or whether law enforcement efforts do or do not exist.

The third part—*Proffered New Solutions*—reviews initiatives advanced in the literature that may yet be open to net producing and net consuming countries. It explores some of the likely intended and unintended consequences that could result from implementation of these initiatives.

NOTES

[1]RLIN (Research Libraries Information Network) is the automated information system of The Research Libraries Group, Inc. (RLG). It supports RLG's principal programs as well as the technical processing requirements of research libraries. RLIN has allowed us to scan the holdings of nearly one hundred research libraries in the United States and call, on interlibrary loan, for materials unavailable in Brigham Young University's or Princeton University's extensive holdings.

[2]The data bases searched, aside from Brigham Young University's and Princeton University's own holdings supplemented by RLIN, were the following: UNDOCS—University of Utah (a complete UN depository); UMI Dissertations Abstracts; UMI Newspaper Abstracts; UMI Periodical Abstracts; VU/TEXT; MELVYL—University of California; Applied Sciences and Technology Index (AST); General Sciences Index (GSI); Social Sciences Index (SSI); ABI/Inform; Economic Literature Index; National Newspaper Index (NNI); MEDLINE; PAIS International; Sociological Abstracts; AGRICOLA; and GPO Publications Reference File.

[3]Terrence C. Cox, et al. [*Drugs and Drug Abuse: A Reference Text*, 1983] classifies thirty-seven psychoactive drugs and twenty-nine "additional drugs of interest" in terms of how they affect the central nervous system. The listing ranges from "morning glory seeds" to heroin, and it includes a wide range of legally prescribed and illegal drugs. Carl Chambers et al. discuss numerous drugs in relationship to chemical dependencies [*Chemical Dependencies: Patterns, Costs, and Consequences*, 1987]. Edward Edelson examines the effects of both beneficial and potentially damaging psychoactive drugs on

the brain and summarizes their toxicology [*Drugs and the Brain*, 1987]. Ernest L. Abel has published at least two multiple-drug volumes focusing on psychoactive substances that affect sexuality [*Drugs and Sex: A Bibliography*, 1983; *Psychoactive Drugs and Sex*, 1985]. In the latter volume, fourteen drugs are surveyed, including tobacco and alcohol. Effects on hormones and reproductive tissue are reviewed, and clinical reports are referenced as are animal studies.

⁴Cocaine is an alkaloid derived from the leaves of the coca shrub. While the coca shrub in several varieties grows in many parts of the world, only those natural to South America are thought to contain commercially viable alkaloids that can be processed into cocaine [See, in general, Joseph Kennedy, *Coca Exótica: The Illustrated Story of Cocaine*, 1985]. Peter T. White gives a general overview of coca and cocaine production and trafficking and the many policy issues surrounding their illegality ["Coca," *National Geographic*, 1989]. A short but exceptionally competent look at the historical and epidemiological features of the recent upsurge in cocaine use (in a work concentrating on psychiatric complications of cocaine abuse) is made by Frank H. Gawin and Everett H. Ellinwood, Jr. ["Cocaine and Other Stimulants," *The New England Journal of Medicine*, 1988]. Katie A. Busch and Sidney H. Schnoll review the epidemiology, history, and pharmacology of cocaine ["Cocaine—Review of Current Literature and Interface with the Law," *Behavioral Sciences and the Law*, 1985]. Timothy Plowman ["Coca Chewing and Botanical Origins of Coca (*Erythroxylum spp.*) in South America," in *Coca and Cocaine: Effects on People and Policy in Latin America*, D. Pacini and C. Franquemont, eds., 1986] looks at the numerous varieties of the coca bush and their relative alkaloidal content. A Bolivian writer, in examining a waterfront of ideas about coca and cocaine, also examines coca's nutritional and medicinal properties [A. Gastón Ponce Caballero, *Coca, Cocaína, Tráfico*, 1983]. Crack is pure "alkaloidal cocaine" precipitated from cocaine hydrochloride (the commercial variety sold on the street) by simple chemical means. It is quick and powerful in its impact on the central nervous system ["Crack," *Medical Letter on Drugs and Therapeutics*, 1986]. James A. Inciardi discusses crack's appearance in the United States ["Beyond Cocaine: Basuco, Crack, and other Coca Products," *Contemporary Drug Problems*, 1987]. Note 1 in Chapter 1 of this handbook discusses cocaine bibliographies.

⁵Heroin is a narcotic drug synthesized from morphine, itself a derivative of opium which originates in the opium poppy. When originally produced in 1898 it was thought to be not only nonaddictive but also a useful aid in helping to cure people of opium and morphine addiction, mainly by removing withdrawal symptoms [see, in general, Charles F. Levinthal, "Milk of Paradise/Milk of Hell—The History of Ideas about Opium," *Perspectives in Biology and Medicine*, 1985]. Although morphine is used medically, heroin is not, except in cases where "heroin maintenance programs" are carried out. Judith Blackwell offers a review and critique of the British heroin maintenance medical practice ["The Saboteurs of Britain's Opiate Policy: Overprescribing Physicians or American-Style 'Junkies?'" *International Journal of the Addictions*, 1988]. Arnold S. Trebach, aside from giving a long historical analysis of public policy in the United States and Great Britain regarding heroin addiction, calls for heroin maintenance programs for U. S. addicts, to be supervised by medical doctors [*The Heroin Solution*, 1982]. Heroin provides more potency for less weight than does morphine, and it therefore lends itself to being the commodity of preference for smugglers who are able to conceal it more readily. Peter T. White, a journalist and photographer who visited all of the major poppy growing and transiting areas in Asia, the Middle East, and Mexico, depicts the entire range of poppy growing, opium refining, and narcotics trafficking ["The Poppy," *National Geographic*, 1985]. Note 1 in Chapter 2 of this handbook discusses heroin

bibliographies.

⁶Technically, the term refers to *Cannabis sativa L.*, a hemp plant that comes in a number of varieties [see Brian M. du Toit, *Cannabis in Africa*, 1980:6–18]. The plant's psychoactive narcotic—*tetrahydrocannabinol* (THC)—is consumed as hashish (resin extracted from the flower clusters and top leaves of hemp varieties grown in hot, moist climates) and marijuana (a cheaper, less concentrated substance obtained from the top flowers, leaves, and stems of plants usually grown in drier and colder climates) [William Harris and Judith Levey, eds., *The New Columbia Encyclopedia*, 1975]. The coarse fiber produced by the tall plant is used for cordage and in making paper, canvas, oakum (a caulking fiber), and other products. The plant is native to Asia, but it now grows in most parts of the world. Ernest L. Abel looks at its history [*Marihuana: The First Twelve Thousand Years*, 1980]. Du Toit [*Cannabis in Africa*] gives a historical perspective on Africa, and Anthony Henman and Osvaldo Pessoa, Jr., add medical, juridical, and anthropological observations in their historical treatment of cannabis in Brazil [*Diamba Sarabamba*, 1986]. Note 1 in Chapter 3 of this handbook discusses cannabis bibliographies.

⁷Roger Highfield discusses the kinds of drugs that are now being marketed from clandestine chemists' laboratories and the apparent difficulty in legislating against the expansion of "analogs" or varieties in this market ["Designer Drugs," *World Health*, 1986]. Methamphetamine is now coming strongly into the market in the United States [see Jane Gross, "Speed's Gain in Use Could Rival Crack, Drug Experts Warn," *The New York Times*, 1988]. A smokeable form of methamphetamine now available in Hawaii and thought to be penetrating the U.S. West Coast is known as "ice." It is apparently extremely addictive and gives a much greater "push" than crack cocaine, along with a commensurately fearsome impact on users' neurological systems ["Ice Overdose," *The Economist*, 1989]. Bob Baker and Eric Malnic speak of PEPAP, a synthetic heroin that is thirty-six times more powerful than pure heroin ["Potent New 'Designer Drug' Seized in Federal Raid on Simi Valley Lab," *The Los Angeles Times*, 1988]. Methaqualone, a synthetic sedative type drug that can be addictive and that can cause seizures is traded commercially internationally, but it is noted as having considerable "leakage" into illicit traffic [Gene R. Haislip, "International Traffic in Methaqualone," *Drug Enforcement*, 1982]. Phantom chemists appear to be ready to supply whatever market emerges, and these obscure laboratories can produce an enormous supply of fentanyl analogs in just a few months [Winifred Gallagher, "The Looming Menace of Designer Drugs," *Discover*, 1986].

⁸Absent the United States' addressing the situation head on with development aid, Bruce M. Bagley argues that the consequences will imperil the national security interests of this country ["The New Hundred Years War? US National Security and the War on Drugs in Latin America," *Journal of Interamerican Studies and World Affairs*, 1988]. A precipitous decline in prices paid to Bolivian peasant coca growers has caused much political unrest [James Painter, "Bolivia Tries to Break its Economic Addiction," *The New York Times*, 1990].

⁹As one might expect, the estimates vary widely, for they are just that—estimates. And these are subject to stretching in pursuit of agency or policy interests as, for example, law enforcement agencies' inflated estimates of the value of their seizures, based on retail street prices, when interdiction occurs in the country of origin (before export) or in transit wherein the actual value is much less. Peter Reuter explores this and related problems with drug estimates in three articles: ["The (Continued) Vitality of Mythical Numbers," *The Public Interest*, 1984; "Intercepting the Drugs: Big Cost, Small Results,"

The Washington Post, 1988; and, "Quantity Illusions and Paradoxes of Drug Interdiction: Federal Intervention into Vice Policy," *Law and Contemporary Problems*, 1988]. The *Economist* ["The Cocaine Economies," 1988] used National Narcotics Intelligence Consumers Committee (NNICC) estimates for the United States and undisclosed sources for Europe, concluding that the coca/cocaine economy was worth only $22 billion in 1987. This was "equivalent to world retail sales of diamonds in 1987, or Singapore's GDP, or all liquor sales in America." The *Economist* may have underestimated the value of the coca/cocaine economy. First, their data base may be flawed. Rensselaer Lee III is mentioned as criticizing the NNICC production estimates as being underreported. Of course, this would affect the estimates of retail sales volume, thus underestimating the value of the market at any price. Second, *Economist* estimates do not take into account retail sales of coca leaves (for chewing) and coca paste in Latin America or anywhere outside North America and Europe. This may be a minor point to the extent that very little of the total earnings come from these domestic markets. These caveats notwithstanding, the amount of money apparently being "laundered" from the drug trade certainly gives credence to the suggestion that multiple scores of billions of dollars are involved. Eighteen cities, worldwide, including Houston, Los Angeles, Miami, and New York in the United States, are the principal laundering centers ["Laundering Drug Money: Whitewash—or Crackdown?" *The Economist*, 1989]. From the United States alone, more than $100 billion a year having probable provenance in the cocaine trade is sent out via electronic transfer to accounts in foreign countries [Stephen Labaton, "Banking Technology Helps Drug Dealers Export Cash," *The New York Times*, 1989]. Since U.S. laws and enforcement on bank transactions have become quite stiff [see, for example, Charles W. Blau et al., *Investigation and Prosecution of Illegal Money Laundering: A Guide to the Bank Secrecy Act*, 1983; Paula Dwyer, "Getting Banks to Just Say 'No,'" *Business Week*, 1989], considerable drug money has moved into Canada (where banking laws are more lax) for laundering [Stephen Labaton, "Canada Seen as Major Haven for Laundering Drug Money," *The New York Times*, 1989]. From 1985–89 the Los Angeles Federal Reserve Bank experienced a 2,200-percent increase in its cash reserves; this is thought to confirm the region's emergence as a drug and money laundering center [Michael Isikoff, "Los Angeles Bank Surplus Linked to Drug Trade," *The Washington Post*, 1989]. Coincidentally, it was in Southern California where the largest cocaine bust in U.S. history occurred (September 1989), netting twenty tons [Stephen Loeper, "20 Tons of Cocaine Confiscated in Los Angeles," *Salt Lake Tribune*, 1989]. Europe is also now tightening up its banking laws ["Dirty Money: Closing Down the Launderette," *The Economist*, 1990].

[10]United Nations, Conference Room Paper No. 1, 13 October 1989, prepared for the Joint Meetings of the Committee for Programme and Co-ordination and the Administrative Committee on Co-ordination, 24th series, New York, 16–18 October 1989, 89-24360.

[11]See F. LaMond Tullis, "Cocaine and Food: Likely Effects of a Burgeoning Transnational Industry on Food Production in Bolivia and Peru," in *Pursuing Food Security*, W. Ladd Hollist and F. LaMond Tullis, eds., 1987:250.

[12]On this latter count, with illicit drugs as one agendum, Harvard University's Center for International Affairs has launched a multi-year project designed to "rethink our assumptions about processes of change in world politics, the conditions for a just and peaceful world order, and the implications for American foreign policy" [1989 statement from the center].

[13]The best evidence of a saturated market in 1988 was the continued decline in cocaine retail prices simultaneous with record seizures by law enforcement officials. In 1988 wholesale and retail cocaine prices in the United States fell to the lowest reported for any year [see National Narcotics Intelligence Consumers Committee, *The NNICC Report 1988*, 1989]. Jonathan A. K. Cave and Peter Reuter analyze these apparent anomalies within the context of a "smuggling model" [*The Interdictor's Lot: A Dynamic Model of the Market for Drug Smuggling Services*, 1988]. A departure from this trend, probably temporary, was noted in mid 1990. As a consequence of internal wars in Colombia and increased interdiction (and even in the face of a possible reduction in U.S. demand), the wholesale price of cocaine rose sharply, the first such rise in almost ten years. Prices in the U.S. market jumped nearly 40 percent, and heavily diluted cocaine was once again appearing on the market [see Joseph Treaster, "Cocaine Prices Rise, and Police Efforts May Be Responsible," *The New York Times*, 1990].

[14]Some argue that interdiction efforts in the United States pushed the Colombians to pursue market openings in Europe as early as 1985 ["U.S. Interdiction Efforts Forcing Coke Shipments to Europe, OC Commissioners Report," *Crime Control Digest*, 1985]. Whatever effect interdiction has had, with their new European experience the Colombians have both refined and expanded their operations as apparent market saturation in the United States, the price incentives in Spain (four times the Miami price) ["Colombia's Cocaine Overdose," *The Economist*, 1989], and relative ease of entry into Europe through Spain and Italy have made European traffic highly profitable [Alan Riding, "Colombian Cocaine Dealers Tap European Market," *The New York Times*, 1989].

[15]Total production for 1988 was estimated at between 348 and 454 metric tons, all of which was produced in the three countries mentioned with the exception of 1 ton which originated in Ecuador [National Narcotics Intelligence Consumers Committee, *The NNICC Report 1988*, 1989]. With processing efficiency on the rise, the three countries contributed to a sharp rise (to 776 metric tons) in the estimated amount of cocaine probably available for the wholesale market in 1989 [United States Department of State, Bureau of International Narcotics Matters, *International Narcotics Control Strategy Report*, 1990, p. 12]. The U.S. State Department continued its high cocaine yield estimates in its 1991 report [United States Department of State, Bureau of International Narcotics Matters, *International Narcotics Control Strategy Report*, 1991, p. 10], placing the metric tonnage between 700 and 890 from Bolivia, Peru, and Colombia. Small amounts are produced in isolated laboratories in Argentina [U.S. Congress, House Select Committee on Narcotics Abuse and Control, Report, "Latin American Study Missions Concerning International Narcotics Problems," 1986] and in Brazil [Alan Riding, "Brazil Acting to Halt New Trafficking in Cocaine," *The New York Times*, 1987; Riding, "Brazil Now a Vital Crossroad for Latin Cocaine Traffickers," *The New York Times*, 1988]. Elsewhere, mention is made of the seizure of three cocaine laboratories in Mexico, one in Canada, twenty-one in the United States, and major complexes in Panama and Venezuela. All this was indicative of the increased smuggling of coca paste to the United States and other countries where essential chemicals for cocaine refinement are more readily available [National Narcotics Intelligence Consumers Committee, *Narcotics Intelligence Estimate 1984*, 1985].

[16]For decades Hashish has been produced openly in the northern regions of the Bekaa, although opium-poppy growing was discouraged. Nevertheless, by 1987 it was reported that the Bekaa had become an export source for other narcotics. In a much publicized move, Syria's occupying troops decided to "put an end to the drug business" in the area [Jim Muir, "Syria Gets Tough on Lebanon's Drug Trade," *The Christian Science Monitor*, 1987], but the results were negligible [National Narcotics Intelligence

Consumers Committee, *The NNICC Report 1987*, 1988]. The problem still had not been resolved by mid 1990 [see, for example, Amy Kaslow, "New Lebanese Plan Would Fight Hashish in the Bekaa Valley," *The Christian Science Monitor*, 1990].

[17]Belize, which was a relatively significant contributor to the supply as late as 1986, now no longer figures significantly in production, the 1989 and 1990 figures having been cut in half from 1988 (down to sixty-six tons). See Elaine Sciolino, "World Drug Crop up Sharply in 1989 Despite U.S. Effort," *The New York Times*, 1990, and United States State Department, Bureau of International Narcotics Matters, *International Narcotics Control Strategy Report*, 1991, p. 136.

[18]U.S. and UN estimates show large increases in these areas as well as significant relative increases in several other countries. See National Narcotics Intelligence Consumers Committee, *The NNICC Report 1988* and United Nations, International Narcotics Control Board, *Report of the International Narcotics Control Board for 1988*, 1989. See also U.S. Department of State, Bureau of International Narcotics Matters, *International Narcotics Control Update*, November 1989, and U.S. Department of State, Bureau of International Narcotics Matters, *International Narcotics Control Strategy Report*, 1991.

[19]Governments furnish figures with respect to the licit trade for medical and scientific purposes in accordance with international treaties. These figures are reported annually in various publications of the United Nations' International Narcotics Control Board, Vienna, Austria [e.g., *Statistics on Narcotic Drugs*]. Characteristically, each report gives country-specific statistical data on legitimate opium production and on the manufacture and consumption of its derivative products, on legitimate coca leaf production and the manufacture of cocaine and its consumption, and on the legitimate consumption of other drugs, such as cannabis. Recognizing that opiates, cocaine, and marijuana have legitimate scientific and medical applications, the International Narcotics Control Board endeavors to limit drug supply and use to an adequate amount required for medical and scientific purposes and to ensure availability of these drugs for such purposes. This aside, the board, especially in recent years, has collaborated with governments to prevent illicit cultivation, production, and manufacture of and trafficking in and use of drugs. See its annual reports [*Report of the International Narcotics Control Board*].

[20]Member states of the United Nations periodically report to the UN any modifications to existing drug-enforcement laws or adoptions of new ones. These are published periodically under the title *United Nations Laws and Regulations*. In 1988 the UN Social Defence Research Institute published a comparative study of penal measures in Europe, Asia, Africa, and Latin America [*Drugs and Punishment: An Up-to-Date Interregional Survey on Drug-Related Offences*].

[21]Significant efforts at statistical estimates are to be found in the following governmental and international agency documents, usually published annually or semiannually: United Nations, International Narcotics Control Board, *Report of the International Narcotics Control Board*; U.S. Department of State, *International Narcotics Control Strategy Report*; and National Narcotics Intelligence Consumers Committee, *The NNICC Report*. Each gives a discussion, by region and country, on production, export, and transit of illicit drugs. The NNICC is a U.S. federal consortium of drug-related law enforcement, foreign and domestic policy, treatment, research, and intelligence agencies. Figures reported by NNICC are sometimes different from those reported by the U.S. Department of State [*International Narcotics Control Strategy Report*] because the NNICC subtracts in-country seizures and consumption from production totals, but therefore more accurately reflects export estimates. The UN report provides an excellent qualitative report on the regions it covers.

[22]The United Nations Secretariat has undertaken an effort to summarize national assessments of drug abuse and consequences, including demand factors ["Measures to Assess Drug Abuse and the Health, Social and Economic Consequences of Such Abuse: Summary of Information from 21 Countries," *Bulletin on Narcotics*, 1983]. International comparative statistics are difficult to obtain on a consistent basis, but the sense of the general trend and condition is found in the National Institute on Drug Abuse's *Patterns and Trends in Drug Abuse: A National and International Perspective*, 1985.

[23]New York City's projected AIDS epidemic, due in large part to heroin and cocaine addicts' sharing needles, threatens to break the city's health delivery system [Ernest Drucker, "AIDS and Addiction in New York City," *American Journal of Drug and Alcohol Abuse*, 1986]. Transfer of the virus from such people to non drug-using individuals (e.g., children, sexual partners) is alarming [Barry Stimmel, "AIDS, Alcohol and Heroin: A Particularly Deadly Combination," *Advances in Alcohol and Substance Abuse*, 1987]. Drug-related HIV transmission is noted in Great Britain [Roy Robertson, *Heroin, AIDS and Society*, 1987], and is spreading rapidly even among the clients of British drug-abuse clinics ["AIDS and Drugs: Shooting Up," *The Economist*, 1989]. A veritable alarm has been sounded in Italy [Roberto Suro, "Italy's Heroin Addicts Face New Challenge: AIDS," *The New York Times*, 1987].

[24]Karen DeYoung, "Britain Coming to Grips with Surge of Drug Abuse," *The Washington Post*, 1985. Howard Parker and his colleagues describe a community in the northwest of England that, "suddenly and unexpectedly," within the course of about three years, saw several thousand of its younger and poorest residents become regular heroin users. The effects on individuals, their families, the community, and the political decision makers (who were virtually paralyzed) are documented in *Living with Heroin*, 1988.

[25]See, in particular, Herbert D. Kleber, "Epidemic Cocaine Abuse: America's Present, Britain's Future?" *British Journal of Addiction*, 1988; Craig R. Whitney, "Crack Use Starts in Fearful Europe," *The New York Times*, 1989.

[26]Tom Mashberg, "Drugs in Europe: Signs of a Spreading Plague," *The New York Times*, 1990.

[27]In the general spirit of increasing openness that has characterized the Soviet Union since about 1986, one sees more and more public admission of the country's drug problem. Internal discussion developed enough to capture inclusion in various 1986–87 issues of the *Current Digest of the Soviet Press* [38(22):1, 38(32):1–7, and 38(34):1–20, 1986; 39(2):1–14, 1987]. By 1988 there was widespread discussion that the problem was far more serious than anyone had ever supposed [see, for example, John M. Kramer, "Drug Abuse in the Soviet Union, *Problems of Communism*, 1988; A. A. Gabiani, "Drug Addiction," *Soviet Sociology*, 1988], prompting the Soviets to propose formal law enforcement agreements with the United States [Michael Isikoff, "Soviets Suggest Trading Facts on Drug Traffic; U.S. Weighing Moscow's Unusual Proposal," *The Washington Post*, 1988], to prepare to make a formal bid to join Interpol [Thomas Land, "Soviet Drug War," *The New Leader*, 1988], and, in 1989, to launch a drug strike force against poppy growers in Soviet Turkmenia and surrounding border provinces [Esther B. Fein, "Soviets Confront Growers," *The New York Times*, 1989].

[28]Substantially increased heroin and cocaine supplies became available in Canada beginning in about 1983 [Rodney. T. Stamler, Robert C. Fahlman, and S.A. Keele, "Recent Trends in Illicit Drug Trafficking from the Canadian Perspective," *Bulletin on Narcotics*, 1983; Stamler, Fahlman, and Keele, "Illicit Traffic and Abuse of Cocaine," *Bulletin on Narcotics*, 1984]. By 1986 the Colombians were gaining great ascendancy in the increasing Canadian drug traffic [Marcus Gee, Ken Macqueen, and Michael Rose,

"Montreal's Deadly New Traffic in Cocaine," *Maclean's*, 1986]. Carl Robinson speaks of the Chinese Triads (traditional gangs) who have enhanced both quantity and distribution techniques in Australia ["The Day of the Triads: Hong Kong's Gangs Move in on Australia," *Newsweek*, 1988].

[29]There has been a striking amount of coverage on this issue. F. Raúl Jeri and his research team were giving scientific attention to health and medical complications and social science attention to social complications as early as 1978. They studied patients admitted to four hospitals in Lima, Peru, because of coca-paste smoking ["Further Experiences with the Syndromes Produced by Coca Paste Smoking," *Bulletin on Narcotics*, 1978]. He followed up with additional studies (refer to Jeri in the annotated bibliography). Michael Isikoff gives a journalist's view of the contemporary spread of both the habit and its consequences in Colombia ["Home-Grown Coca Plagues Colombia," *Washington Post*, 1989]. Even those who have considered cocaine the "prototypic recreational drug" have added a discussion in their revised book on findings regarding the "new and dangerous practice of smoking cocaine" [Lester Grinspoon and James B. Bakalar, *Cocaine: A Drug and Its Social Evolution*, 1985]. See also the listings in the annotated bibliography under the following authors: Flores Agreda, G. Aramayo and M. Sánchez, Tyler Bridges, Jonathan Cavanagh, Edmundo Morales ("Coca Paste and Crack"), R. M. Post and N. R. Contel, Ronald K. Siegel, and the special issue on cocaine of the *Bulletin on Narcotics* 36:2 (April-June 1984). The brain surgery episode was reported in *New Scientist* ["Peruvians Operate on Cocaine Addicts' Brains," 1983].

[30]See, as a representative example of some of the current coverage, Youssef M. Ibrahim, "Iran Puts Addicts in Its Labor Camps," *The New York Times*, 1989; Giancario Arnao, "Drug Enforcement Policy as a Factor in Trends of Trafficking and Use of Different Substances," *Journal of Psychoactive Drugs*, 1988; Pakistan Narcotics Control Board, *National Survey on Drug Abuse in Pakistan*, various years; Jamal Rasheed, "A Deadly Export Comes Home to Roost among the Youth of Pakistan," *Far Eastern Economic Review*, 1984; Terence White, "The Drug-Abuse Epidemic Coursing through Pakistan," *Far Eastern Economic Review*, 1985; C. P. Spencer and V. Navaratnam, *Drug Abuse in East Asia*, 1981; Joseph Westermeyer, "Treatment for Narcotic Addiction in a Buddhist Monastery," *Journal of Drug Issues*, 1980.

[31]Increased consumption in China appears largely to be a product of "leakage" from the new overland routes from the Golden Triangle into Hong Kong [Daniel Southerland, "Smugglers Using Routes in China to Move Heroin; Police Say Flow of Drug Is Increasing," *The Washington Post*, 1988; "China Cracks Big Drug Case," *Beijing Review*, 1988; "China Vows War on Drug Abuse," *Beijing Review*, 1988].

[32]In Africa, Nigeria has become a hot trafficking center [Michael T. De Sanctis, "Nigerians Becoming More Active in the Smuggling of Southwest Asian Heroin in the U.S., Europe," *Narcotics Control Digest*, 1985; James Brooke, "West Africa Becomes Route for Heroin Trade," *The New York Times*, 1987. See also the African section in United Nations Secretariat, Division of Narcotic Drugs, "Review of Drug Abuse and Measures to Reduce the Illicit Demand for Drugs by Region," *Bulletin on Narcotics*, 1987].

[33]For example, in America, frequent mention is made that the country is in the second, not the first, cocaine epidemic. Some ninety years ago episodes similar to today's were occurring. The two best historical analyses are by David I. Musto [*The American Disease: Origins of Narcotic Control*, 1987], and by David T. Courtwright [*Dark Paradise: Opiate Addiction in America Before 1940*, 1982]. Both authors call for a public memory of that era in order to understand both the limitations and the possibilities of

current and future public policies. A colorful pictorial display of the first drug wave is offered by Linda Gomez ["Cocaine: America's 100 Years of Euphoria and Despair," *Life*, 1984]. Within the context of this larger national experience, Patricia G. Erickson and her colleagues explore community case histories, with considerable focus on Canada [*The Steel Drug: Cocaine in Perspective*, 1987]. A technical, sociological, and politically referenced book that builds its discussion on these historical experiences from the vantage of observers who consider cocaine the prototypic recreational drug is authored by Lester Grinspoon and James B. Bakalar [*Cocaine: A Drug and Its Social Evolution*, 1985]. The *NOVA Law Review* ["Milestones in the War on Drugs"] in its 1987 special on drugs gave a chronological breakdown—1914 through October 1986—of the U.S. legal and statutory war on drugs. Daniel Kagan ["How America Lost Its First Drug War," *Insight*, 1989] reviews the history of drug epidemics and drug use in the United States and the official and public responses to those epidemics.

[34]An example of the concern at the highest levels and a mobilization of public opinion and resources is the U.S. *National Drug Control Strategy* promulgated by the U.S. White House in September 1989. It is an integrated strategy in the sense that it expands activity in at least seven areas: the criminal justice system; drug treatment programs; oversight and encouragement in education, community action, and the workplace; international initiatives; interdiction efforts; research; and an intelligence agenda. Further high-level initiatives were laid out in Cartagena, Colombia at an antidrug summit of the presidents of Bolivia, Peru, Colombia, and the United States [Andrew Rosenthal, "3 Andean Leaders and Bush Pledge Drug Cooperation," *The New York Times*, 1990] and in the United States [Joseph B. Treaster, "Bush Proposes More Anti-Drug Spending," *The New York Times* 1991].

PART I

SURVEY OF THE LITERATURE

A

Patterns of Production and Consumption

1

Cocaine

Cocaine,[1] or cocaine hydrochloride,[2] is a psychoactive alkaloid processed from the leaves of the coca shrub that thrives in several regions of the South American Andes.[3] As an agricultural crop, coca has had nominal commercial value in licit trade for many decades: it is used as a flavoring for soft drinks (the psychoactive alkaloids are now removed), as raw material in licit medical drug manufacturing, and—in spite of educational efforts to break a 2,000-year-old Andean South American habit—it is still chewed by over 3 million Peruvians and Bolivians who annually consume about 28,000 tons.[4] But it is with the exploding demand for illicit drugs that the planting and harvesting of coca have recently undergone dramatic expansion in Bolivia and Peru. Cultivation has now spread (although with an inferior genetic product[5]) into Colombia, Ecuador, Brazil's Amazon basin, and even Argentina.[6] At one time just a side cash crop for a peasant household, coca production has developed into a labor-intensive commercial crop amenable to the entrepreneurial spirit of scores of thousands of small-scale operators, many of whom are recent migrants to the coca growing regions.[7]

Although the coca bush is sensitive to climate, temperature, and rainfall, it does grow in a wide range of soils. Interestingly, in the proper climate, coca will grow in mineral-laden, infertile soils unsuitable for other cash crops.[8] And although the coca bush can be grown in many areas of the world, the only varieties yielding substantial cocaine alkaloids are not only natural to but are still located in the South American Andes. Peru and Bolivia, almost the only suppliers until the early 1980s when Colombia's and Ecuador's new plantings reached minimal maturity, still provide over 85 percent of the world's coca supply (see Figure 1).

Coca bushes mature sufficiently in three years for the leaves to be picked from three to six times annually—an excellent cash cropping pattern. After the bushes have matured, almost no cultivation is required, although initial planting and periodic harvesting are decidedly labor intensive. With hardly any additional labor requirements, the leaves render much more income per hectare than any other cash crop a small farmer could plant. A peasant family can easily work one or two hectares (roughly ten to twenty thousand square meters), earning several thousand dollars annually.

The U.S. State Department estimates that in 1990 over 120,000 hectares of coca were cultivated in Peru and an additional 50,000 in Bolivia (see Figure 2), from which over 235,000 metric tons of coca leaves were estimated to have been harvested (see Figure 3). From the traditional coca growing areas in

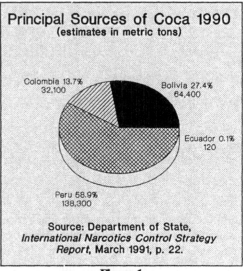

Principal Sources of Coca 1990
(estimates in metric tons)

Colombia 13.7%
32,100

Bolivia 27.4%
64,400

Ecuador 0.1%
120

Peru 58.9%
138,300

Source: Department of State,
International Narcotics Control Strategy Report, March 1991, p. 22.

Figure 1

the Bolivian Yungas and the Peruvian amazonic uplands near Cuzco, production has now expanded into the fertile lands of Bolivia's Chapare and Peru's Upper Huallaga Valley. In Bolivia, cocaine processing and now coca production have also entered the isolated Beni where it is said there are fewer roads and more airstrips per capita than perhaps anywhere else in the world—around 2,000 airstrips for 300,000 inhabitants.[9]

Of course, all these figures, as well as any others that could be cited, are only best estimates based on seizures, interdiction, aerial surveys, "guesstimates," and monitored trends. Whether high or low, all estimates are consistent in their judgment that production increased through the 1989 crop year.[10] Production may now have leveled off (see Figure 3) due, in part, to a drastic fall in prices paid to coca farmers.[11]

From the vantage of the peasant grower, a principal production risk is U.S.–sponsored coca eradication and cocaine interdiction efforts. While it takes three years from the first planting to begin harvesting coca, bushes can, and are, chopped down by teams of eradication workers who concentrate on the most accessible plots. Moreover, efforts are afoot to develop a satisfactory coca herbicide that can be sprayed

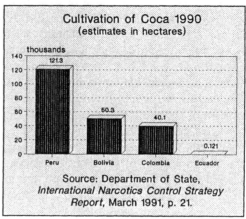

Cultivation of Coca 1990
(estimates in hectares)

thousands
140
120   121.3
100
80
60
40   50.3
20   40.1
0   0.121
    Peru Bolivia Colombia Ecuador

Source: Department of State,
International Narcotics Control Strategy Report, March 1991, p. 21.

Figure 2

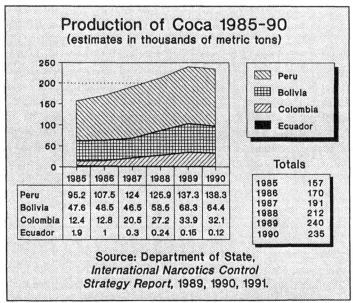

Figure 3

from aircraft. Despite heavy criticism, in 1989, Peru collaborated with the United States in testing "Spike" on a forty acre ravine near Tingo María in the country's Upper Huallaga Valley. Spike destroys not only coca but everything else that photosynthesizes.[12]

The peasants, in response to manual eradication and potential widespread aerial spraying, maintain a resolute posture against drug control officers and continue to expand their crops whenever coca prices have given them an incentive.[13] They have formed coca-growers' unions to resist government intervention,[14] have embraced antigovernment insurgent or terrorist groups for protection,[15] have moved further into isolated regions of the jungle,[16] and have brought out women, children, and the elderly to confront government troops and to protest their drug control presence in the villages (and in coca growing fields).[17] Peasant livelihood is at stake.

The coca leaves must be processed or refined. Most laboratory refining of cocaine has been done by Colombians in Colombia. Now, however, Peru and Bolivia are increasing their share of the production market for refined cocaine hydrochloride.[18] For one thing, Peruvians, in particular, are getting more experienced and able; for another, the Colombian drug lords are decentralizing and scaling down the size of their individual operations in the wake of fierce internal battles in their own country.[19] Many small, scattered laboratories are more difficult for the authorities either to find or, once found, to permanently put out of business. Laboratories are also being set up in other countries.[20]

The Colombians have been particularly adept not only at setting up refining operations but also in organizing suppliers (for coca leaf, coca paste, acetone, ether, hydrochloric acid) and in developing a highly sophisticated marketing network. Two main drug cartels operate out of Medellín and Cali, but others blossom from time to time to enhance the competition. The turf wars create conditions of violence that build on Colombia's historical "*la violencia.*"[21]

Once refined—mostly in Colombia but increasingly elsewhere—cocaine is transported clandestinely to major markets by every conceivable means, from flower pots to hollowed-out bricks, containers held within the intestines of human couriers, false-compartment trucks, small aircraft, ocean-going "mother ships," diplomatic pouches, U.S. army planes, and U.S. military personnel. The literature and press descriptions of the routes and the conveyances are quite extensive.[22] Sometimes several countries become involved as "transshippers"—Cuba, Nicaragua, Jamaica, the Bahamas, Mexico.[23]

Once cocaine reaches major consumption centers, it is usually adulterated to a greater or lesser degree to increase its volume[24] and then, through formal and informal distribution networks, it is placed in the hands of users, to snort, to inject, or to further modify chemically and then smoke.

Who are the users? Focusing on the United States, at the turn of the century, before cocaine became illegal and a prohibition culture developed, virtually every city dweller who had a spare coin consumed it (in soft drinks or in any one of several hundred patent medicines readily available).[25] Then, serious users had their champions in luminaries such as Sigmund Freud—until he had a radical change of mind and turned against the drug.[26] After 1914, when cocaine became illegal, stage and cinema

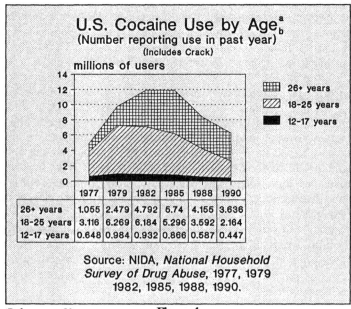

U.S. Cocaine Use by Age[a][b]
(Number reporting use in past year)
(Includes Crack)

millions of users

	1977	1979	1982	1985	1988	1990
26+ years	1.055	2.479	4.792	5.74	4.155	3.636
18-25 years	3.116	6.269	6.184	5.296	3.592	2.164
12-17 years	0.648	0.984	0.932	0.866	0.587	0.447

Legend: 26+ years, 18-25 years, 12-17 years

Source: NIDA, *National Household Survey of Drug Abuse*, 1977, 1979 1982, 1985, 1988, 1990.

[a]Refer to note 29   **Figure 4**
[b]Refer to note 30

personalities and other celebrities picked it up as a glamour drug. In the 1970s usage moved "down" the social pyramid to the middle class and increasingly became a recreational drug of choice for some adults and many adolescents. Lately, it is generally believed that cocaine and its derivative, crack, have taken on widespread use among the economic underclass of America's inner cities, many of whom also happen to be ethnic minorities.[27] On the other hand, by 1988 cocaine and even crack, showed signs of losing appeal among non–inner-city populations of all races[28] and among all age groups (see Figure 4).[29, 30] When the population segments are shown individually (Figures 5, 6, and 7), the decline in use appears quite striking. Law enforcement agencies, educators, politicians, and drug control policy makers all take credit; each notes, however, that more funding is required for his or her particular line of activity because the downtrends are insufficient.

As with the production statistics discussed earlier, consumption statistics are also "soft" for quite obvious reasons, as noted in the discussion in the appendix to this chapter. Nevertheless, it is widely believed that the trends indicated by these figures represent the real world reasonably well.

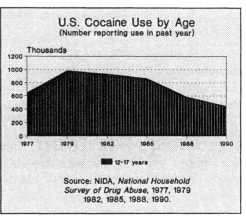

Figure 5

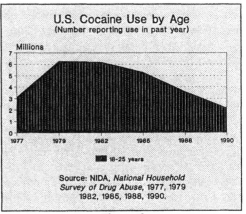

Figure 6

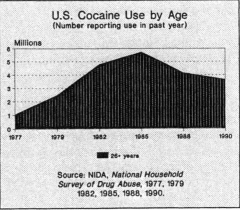

Figure 7

Cocaine consumption is apparently increasing in Western Europe,[31] enough so that some observers fear an impending epidemic,[32] although Europeans seem to be less concerned than the Americans.[33] Concerns were raised about increasing use in Eastern Europe many months before political liberalization in 1989 further opened the countries' borders to illicit drugs.[34]

Cocaine consumption is increasing in Latin America, principally in the form of cocaine paste (called *basuco* in Colombia) which is mixed with tobacco and smoked. This practice is widespread in Peru, Bolivia, and Colombia, particularly among teenagers and even children. Frequently the "wages" of young couriers are paid in cocaine paste, a portion of which the children use—having become addicted—and the rest of which they try to sell. Internal surveys in Peru show that perhaps 37 percent of the secondary school students use drugs. Over a quarter of the students first got involved by smoking cocaine paste.[35] This coincides with the dramatic increase in the cultivation of coca and the production of its alkaloid derivatives for international markets. All social classes are involved. The smoking of cocaine paste has aroused increasing concern among governmental authorities, forcing them now to be concerned with an internal drug consumption problem, not just an export problem driven by consumer habits in the United States and Western Europe.[36]

One must also mention the continuation of traditional coca consumption in the South American Andes, which accounts for approximately 28,000 tons of coca leaves each year. When masticated and mixed with lime, the leaves release small amounts of cocaine alkaloids that are absorbed through users' mouths. A resulting mild "narcotic" effect is said to bolster users against the ills of strenuous work at high altitudes, bitter-cold winter nights, and chronic hunger.[37] Coca chewing is seen as so intertwined with traditional culture that doing away with it would destroy what precious little is left of Andean native societies.[38] Some ethnographers and anthropologists, keen on preserving native cultures, therefore argue vigorously for Andean peoples' right to continue their traditional consumption practices.[39] Consumption levels appear to be quite stable. No one argues that traditional coca chewing poses consequences as serious as does the actual consumption of cocaine.

In sum, even though the number of cocaine users appears to be declining in the United States (still, however, cocaine's principal market) worldwide consumption may well be increasing.

How does one account for a history of such frenetic consumer activity? Cocaine acts as both an anesthetic (when applied topically) and as a stimulant to the central nervous system (when taken or injected internally or inhaled). When acting on the central nervous system, it produces, in humans, euphoric effects, hallucinatory experiences, and spurts—although temporary—of energy.[40] To be sure, this is sufficient attraction for some people. The literature attempts to explain variations in this attraction as a function of general biological, psychological, and environmental factors;[41] of certain personality types;[42] of specific life traumas such as physical or sexual abuse, broken homes, or child neglect;[43] of systemic or social/psychological conditions or societal anomie that bias people toward being persuaded to join a new crowd or to seek relief from psychological and perhaps physical pain in the comfort of a drug;[44] of cultural determinants;[45] of the absence of religiosity;[46] of the effect of drug pushers who establish market expansion by aggressive means;[47] of inner-city economic and social despair from which drugs (or drug dealing) offer one of the precious few respites in a life otherwise "nasty, brutish, and short;"[48] of the reinforcing effects of the drugs themselves.[49]

While apparently not addictive in the sense that narcotics (e.g., opium, morphine, heroin) or nicotine are addictive, cocaine's stimulatory effects nevertheless make it psychologically habit-forming.[50] The body does not appear to develop tolerance to the drug, requiring heavier and heavier doses to maintain a desired effect such as is the case with opiates. But severe depression frequently accompanies lack of use, and so users are heavily motivated to continue consuming the drug, sometimes to the exclusion of almost every other activity, including those involving sleep, sex, and food. This is particularly true with crack.[51]

Contemporary chronic users have increasingly sought less expensive and more effective ways to get cocaine into their bodies for the "rush" and the "high" that produces either interest in or a substitute for sensual delights.[52] From this search came crack, a highly psychologically if not physically addictive drug that is rampaging through North America's ghettos and its school yards and now is migrating to Europe.[53]

From the traditional practice of masticating coca leaves, users are now provided with increasingly sophisticated ways to absorb the potent psychoactive alkaloids of the coca bush into their bodies. While demand may have peaked in the United States, Europe appears increasingly poised for an epidemic.

Rapidly increasing consumer demand has provided income and sustenance to hundreds of thousands of coca producers and vast wealth to many refiners and traffickers. Later we address the consequences to societies, institutions, and countries, both in producing and exporting countries and in those that specialize in consumption.

Heroin, to which we now turn, maintains a steady clientele of users, although some increases are noted in several countries and among certain age groups.

APPENDIX

Two basic sources of statistics on cocaine use in the United States exist: a yearly report produced by the University of Michigan titled *Illicit Drug Use, Smoking, and Drinking by America's High School Students, College Students, and Young Adults* and the National Institute of Drug Abuse's (NIDA) *National Household Survey on Drug Abuse*. Both follow the same approach, asking three different questions about proximity of drug use: Have you ever used? Have you used in the past year? Have you used in the past month?

No direct empirical data are available to assess economic status and cocaine use, at least in the two surveys mentioned. However, race and education may serve as useful proxy variables for economic status, with minorities and those less educated more likely to be poor and therefore more likely to fall into what some have called the "economic underclass."

Although the University of Michigan data do not evaluate use by race, they do assess cocaine use among high school seniors according to college aspirations. College aspirations might reasonably reflect parents' education, which is clearly associated with economic status. Seniors not aspiring to college graduation seem more likely to use cocaine, although circumstances vary. Among non-college aspirants, 8.1 percent used cocaine at least once in 1977 compared to 5.5 percent for aspirants. In 1979, the difference was 13.7 percent to 9.5 percent; in 1982, 12.5 percent to 9.9 percent; in 1985, 14.7 percent to 11.4 percent; and in 1988, 9.7 percent to 6.7 percent. Beginning in 1987, the reports differentiated crack from cocaine use. Among non-college aspirants, 5.5 percent used crack compared to 2.8 percent of the aspirants; in 1988, the difference was 4.2 percent to 2.3 percent.

The 1988 report also assessed differences in cocaine and crack use, directly assessing parents' education on a six-point scale. The data on cocaine do not confirm the college aspiration conclusions noted above. The highest proportion of cocaine users (8.7 percent) were children of parents scoring between 4.5 and 5.0 on the education scale; the lowest proportion (7.2 percent) were children of parents scoring between 3.5 and 4.0 on the education scale. Among children whose parents scored the lowest, 7.6 percent had used cocaine at least once in the past year. On the other hand, the crack data do loosely support the college aspiration conclusions. Among children with parents scoring in the lowest cohort, 3.4 percent used crack at least once in the past year, compared to 2.1 percent of children with parents scoring in the highest cohort. However, the highest proportion of crack users (3.5 percent) were children whose parents scored in the middle cohort, and children (3.1 percent) whose parents scored in the second to highest cohort.

The preliminary news release of data from the University of Michigan (January 23, 1991) from its 1990 survey does not include college aspiration categories. Nevertheless, the press reporters note what they consider to be significant trends among minorities [Joseph B. Treaster, "Drop in Youths' Cocaine Use May Reflect a Societal Shift," *The New York Times*, 1991; Richard L. Berke, "Survey Shows Use of Drugs by Students Fell Last Year," *The New York Times*, 1990; "Bush Sees Anti-Drug Gain, Others See Flawed Data," *The New York Times*, 1990].

There is no indication of statistical significance in the various University of Michigan reports. Overall, it is difficult to evaluate the relationship between cocaine and crack use with the University of Michigan data.

NIDA's survey does not assess cocaine use by race or education until 1982. In terms of race, the 1982 data are only for young adults—those aged from 18 to 25. In this age group, 20 percent of whites compared to 10 percent of blacks and other minorities used cocaine at least once in 1982, with 17.7 percent to 10.6 percent (blacks) to 12.4 percent (hispanics) in 1985, and 12.6 percent to 8.1 percent to 12.6 percent in 1988. Data for all age cohorts are available beginning in 1985. Among these, 6.4 percent of whites, 6.2 percent of blacks, and 5.1 percent of hispanics used cocaine at least once in 1985; 4.0 percent of whites, 4.4 percent of blacks, and 5.7 percent of hispanics in 1988. This indicates an increased relative prevalence among minorities between 1985 and 1988, possibly reflecting an increasing movement of cocaine use to poorer classes.

NIDA's 1988 and 1990 surveys report separate data for crack use. In 1988, 0.4

percent of whites used crack at least once compared to 1.1 percent of blacks and 1.1 percent of hispanics. In 1990 the figures were 0.4 percent of whites and 1.7 percent of blacks. Data for crack use among hispanics was flawed and therefore not reported. The difference between whites and minorities may indicate more prevalent crack consumption among poorer classes. No differences between race cohorts in 1985 and 1988 are statistically significant ($p < .05$), although differences in 1988 crack use approach significance. In terms of education, data from NIDA are available for 1982 and 1985.

Among college graduates, 14 percent used cocaine at least once in 1982 compared to 11 percent of high school dropouts. This is dramatically reversed in 1985, indicating some association of cocaine use and economic status: 3.2 percent of college graduates used cocaine at least once in 1985 compared to 9.5 percent of high school dropouts. Statistical significance is not reported.

NIDA's 1985 survey also reports cocaine use by employment status. Among unemployed, 12.4 percent used cocaine at least once in 1985 compared to 8.5 percent of the full-time employed. This difference may further suggest more prevalent cocaine use among the poor. Again, statistical significance is not reported.

Of course, these data are subject to all the pitfalls of survey research, compounded in this case by the survey's subject being "illegal" and therefore understandably probably invoking a reporting bias among respondents. See the discussion in notes 28 and 29 of this chapter.

NOTES

[1]For the more casual as well as the serious reader, Peter T. White's colorful description of producers, traffickers, and consumers ["Coca," *National Geographic*, 1989] is both interesting and informative. Useful extensive bibliographies on coca and cocaine are found as bibliographical supplements to specialized treatises. These are indexed under the keyword ^*Bibliographies* in the bibliography. Several review essays are of note and are indexed under the keyword ^*Reviews*. As for stand-alone bibliographies, Lise Anglin [*Cocaine: A Selection of Annotated Papers from 1980 to 1984 Concerning Health Effects*, 1985] includes in her annotated bibliography papers in English, French, and German dealing with health effects of recreational cocaine use. History, chemistry, and botany may be mentioned in passing but are not discussed at length in the annotations. Most entries are from scientific journals, but several have been published as book chapters or separate reports. There are 277 entries and an author and a subject index. Joel L. Phillips and Ronald D. Wynne [*A Cocaine Bibliography—Nonannotated*, 1975] include in their bibliography over 1,800 references from 350 scientific journals and other sources gleaned from around the world. Theirs deals with sociopsychological, biomedical, political, and economic aspects of cocaine use and, to a lesser extent, coca, from 1585 to 1974. Morton Schatzman, Andrea Sabbadini, and Laura Forti ["Coca and Cocaine: A Bibliography," *Journal of Psychedelic Drugs*, 1976] give attention in their review essay to an often ignored yet vast literature published between 1880 and 1940, often in languages other than English, and also to more current literature dealing with the history of coca use among the Incas and Spaniards and the origins of cocaine use in Europe and North America. Their emphasis is more on sociology, psychology, and clinical features than on pharmacology and biochemistry. The bibliography appended to their review article is divided into two sections, "Coca" and "Cocaine," and contains twenty-seven pages of references, some of which are annotated. Additionally, based on their review of the literature, the authors were under the impression that most regular cocaine users—if

ingesting by nose or mouth—have been able to stop their use easily when they chose to, without returning to it. The authors believe that those who inject cocaine will find it harder to stop using the drug than will those who employ other routes of administration, and that injection of high doses is most likely to produce dangerous effects such as violence, paranoia, and psychosis. In the U.S. Department of Health, Education, and Welfare's 1976 bibliography [*Cocaine—Summaries of Psychosocial Research*] sixty-nine studies, ranging from Richard Ashley's general treatise on cocaine [*Cocaine: Its History, Uses and Effects*, 1975] to more specialized works on the psychopharmacology of cocaine, are reviewed. Selections are included from both the scientific and popular literature on the psychosocial aspects of cocaine use and, to a lesser extent, coca. The documents represent a time span from the turn of the century to the mid 1970s. Edgar Adams and his colleagues ["Trends in Prevalence and Consequences of Cocaine Use," *Advances in Alcohol and Substance Abuse*, 1986] survey some of the literature on the health consequences of cocaine abuse. Katie A. Busch and Sidney H. Schnoll ["Cocaine—Review of Current Literature and Interface with the Law," *Behavioral Sciences and the Law*, 1985] review the literature on the epidemiology, history, and pharmacology of cocaine as well as the relationship between cocaine and violence and the forensic and psychiatric issues surrounding its use. Donald J. Egan and David Owen Robinson ["Cocaine: Magical Drug or Menace?" *International Journal of the Addictions*, 1979] reviewed the evidence available as of the late 1970s concerning cocaine's physiological and psychological safety. John Grabowski and Steven I. Dworkin ["Cocaine: An Overview of Current Issues," *International Journal of the Addictions*, 1985] review a respectable body of medical literature in areas dealing with behavioral and neurobiological effects of cocaine use, in risks, dosage, routes of administration, and treatment. The three most cited companion treatises, particularly by those who are inclined to desire a change in current U.S. drug laws, appear to be Richard Ashley's *Cocaine*; Lester Grinspoon and James Bakalar's *Cocaine: A Drug and Its Social Evolution*, rev. ed., 1985; and Steven Wisotsky's *Breaking the Impasse in the War on Drugs*, 1987. All three include extensive bibliographies.

²Cocaine alkaloids are usually precipitated from solution by using hydrochloric acid. The tons of "cocaine" exported from South America are usually a salt of cocaine or "cocaine hydrochloride." H. L. Schlesinger reviews substantial literature on the taxonomy and alkaloid contents of coca plants, how cocaine alkaloids are extracted from the plants, and what chemical processes are involved ["Topics in the Chemistry of Cocaine," *Bulletin on Narcotics*, 1985]. These include discussions of the semirefined paste (marketed principally to local consumers in producing countries or to national or extranational drug laboratories), of cocaine hydrochloride (which is snuffed or injected intravenously), and of the chemically transformed crack (smoke of which is inhaled).

³With extensive reference to the literature, Timothy Plowman discusses the origin and dissemination of the *huánuco* and *ipadú* varieties of coca ["The Origin, Evolution and Diffusion of Coca, *Erythroxylum spp.* in South and Central America," *Pre-Columbian Plant Migration*, 1984]. A special "coca and cocaine" issue of the *Journal of Ethnopharmacology* [3:2&3 (1981)] gives a 200-page historical and scientific survey of coca and cocaine, including a chapter on the therapeutic value of coca in contemporary medicine.

⁴The consumption figures come from the U.S. Department of State, Bureau of International Narcotics Matters, *International Narcotics Control Strategy Report 1985*, 1985, pp. 52, 53, 117, and 118. The report lists Peru with 3 million coca chewers, Bolivia with 450,000. There is a large body of literature in the ethnographic tradition of contemporary anthropologists showing the integration that coca and its associated rituals have with cultural identity in the Peruvian and Bolivian Andes. See, for example,

Catherine J. Allen, *The Hold Life Has: Coca and Cultural Identity in an Andean Community*, 1988; William E. Carter, *Ensayos Científicos Sobre la Coca, 1983*; and Edmundo Morales, *Cocaine: White Gold Rush in Peru*, 1989.

⁵There are at least twenty-six varieties of coca with an alkaloid content ranging from 0.5 to 2.5 percent. The varieties in Peru and Bolivia are the best quality; those in Colombia and Ecuador render fewer alkaloids per given weight. The *ipadú* plant, suitable for the Amazon River basin of Colombia and Brazil, renders even less [U.S. House of Representatives, "International Narcotics Control Study Missions to Latin America and Jamaica . . . ," *A Report of the Select Committee on Narcotics Abuse and Control*, 1984, p. 18].

⁶Drug expansion in Argentina has predominately been for export. Argentina records lower drug abuse per capita than does either the United States or Europe, and there is widespread revulsion there regarding illicit drug use. See U.S. Department of State, Bureau of International Narcotics Matters, *International Narcotics Control Strategy Report, Midyear Update,"* 1985, p. 35. Right-wing Argentine military interests are accused of having links with the international drug trade [see Arthur M. Shapiro, "Drugs and Politics in Latin America: The Argentine Connections," *New Leader*, 1988].

⁷The economic incentives have not only been strong but have increased with each successful migration/colonization venture [D. A. Eastwood and H. J. Pollard, "Colonization and Cocaine in the Chapare, Bolivia: A Development Paradox for Colonization Theory," *Tijdschrift Voor Economishe en Sociale Geografie*, 1986; Eastwood and Pollard, "The Accelerating Growth of Coca and Colonisation in Bolivia," *Geography*, 1987]. Drug-traffic-induced migration offers opportunities for social mobility that otherwise would not exist [see Federico Aguiló's contribution in *Efectos del Narcotráfico: Temas de Política Social*, 1988]. One problem for areas that export humanity to the coca-growing regions is a shortage of manpower to engage in traditional food planting and food production routines. Thus nutritional deficiencies mount for women and children either unable (because of location) or unwilling (because of social or moral constraints) to enter into the coca/cocaine trade at whatever level [Jack M. Weatherford, *Narcóticos en Bolivia y los Estados Unidos*, 1987]. See also Harry Sanabria, "Coca, Migration, and Differentiation in the Bolivian Lowlands," *Studies in Third World Societies*, 1988; and Sanabria, "Social and Economic Change in a Bolivian Highland Valley Peasant Community: The Impact of Migration and Coca," 1989.

⁸The point is made in the U.S. Department of State, Bureau of International Narcotics Matters, *International Narcotics Control Strategy Report 1985*, pp. 71 and 111. The significance, of course, in light of population pressures on rural lands, should not escape the observer. The frequent query: "If one does not grow coca, then what does one grow?"

⁹Everett G. Martin describes the role of small aircraft in the transit of cocaine ["A Little Cattle Town in Bolivia is Thriving as a Financial Center," *The Wall Street Journal*, 1983].

¹⁰While many observers criticize the validity of U.S. drug use and drug control statistics [see Deborah M. Barnes, "Drugs: Running the Numbers," *Science*, 1989; Peter Reuter, "Quantity Illusions and Paradoxes of Drug Interdiction: Federal Intervention into Vice Policy," *Law and Contemporary Problems*, 1988; Reuter, "The (Continued) Vitality of Mythical Numbers," *Public Interest*, 1984], few focus their criticism specifically on source country production estimates. Nevertheless, undoubtedly there are problems with the production estimates: "Cultivation estimates rely on aerial surveys which cannot hope to home in on all coca-producing areas ["The Cocaine Economies; Latin America's

Killing Fields," *Economist*, p. 21]. Many nongovernment observers claim the estimates are low. Rensselaer Lee III, for instance, points out the discrepancies in U.S. and Peruvian estimates in 1987: Peru claimed 300,000 hectares were planted in coca, while the United States estimated cultivation to be between 98,000 and 121,000 hectares. Because coca leaf yields are based on these cultivation estimates, all estimates of coca leaf and eventual cocaine production may be significantly distorted. New data constantly provoke revisions. Thus official estimates for one year may appear as revised figures in subsequent publications. Compare, for example, the 1989 coca production estimates for Peru and Bolivia in U.S. Department of State, Bureau of International Narcotics Matters, *International Narcotics Control Strategy Report*, 1990, 1991. For a general discussion of the reliability of these estimates, and of the position that the Department of State may be underestimating the coverage, refer to the discussion in note 9 in the Introduction].

[11]James Painter, "Bolivia Tries to Break its Economic Addiction," *The Christian Science Monitor*, 1990; James Brooke, "Peru, Its U.S. Aid Imperiled, Plots a New Drug Strategy," *The New York Times*, 1991.

[12]"Peru Begins Spraying of Aerial Coca Killer," *Latinamerica Press*, 1989.

[13]Expansion has occurred in spite of U.S. directed and financed efforts to thwart it. Some violence, especially in Peru, has accompanied these efforts. Samuel Doria Medina gives production tables for coca in Bolivia's Chapare area [*La Economía Informal en Bolivia*, 1986] as do D. A. Eastwood and H. J. Pollard ["The Accelerating Growth of Coca and Colonisation in Bolivia," *Geography*, 1987]. More than a dozen peasants in the Chapare have been killed resisting drug control operations there ["Bolivia under Paz Estenssoro," *Latinamerica Press*, 1988]. Alan Riding reports on the continuing surges of violence in Peru's Upper Huallaga Valley ["Rebels Disrupting Coca Eradication in Peru," *New York Times*, 1989] as does Merrill Collett ["Maoist Guerrilla Band Complicates Antidrug War in Peru," *The Washington Post*, 1988]. Themes of production increases and violence in both Bolivia and Peru are picked up by Richard B. Craig ["Illicit Drug Traffic: Implications for South American Source Countries," *Journal of Interamerican Studies and World Affairs*, 1987].

[14]Kevin Healy notes the effective opposition to coca leaf eradication programs from well-organized Bolivian peasant unions tied closely to the national labor movement ["Bolivia and Cocaine: A Developing Country's Dilemmas," *British Journal of Addiction*, 1988]. *Latin America Regional Reports* ["Riding High on Cocaine"] noted as early as 1983 that Bolivian peasant unions had forced the government to reassess its U.S.-backed coca eradication programs then under way. See also Kevin Healy, "Coca, the State, and the Peasantry in Bolivia, 1982–1988," *Journal of Interamerican Studies and World Affairs*, 1988; James Painter, "Bolivia Resists Drug Role for Army," *The Christian Science Monitor*, 1990; Shirley Christian, "Bolivians Fight Efforts to Eradicate Coca," *The New York Times*, 1987; Lesley Gill, *Peasants, Entrepreneurs, and Social Change*, 1987; Michael Isikoff, "DEA in Bolivia: 'Guerrilla Warfare,' Coca Traffic Proves Resistant," *The Washington Post*, 1989; William R. Long, "Bolivia's U.S.–Aided Attack on Cocaine; an Uphill Struggle," *The Los Angeles Times*, 1988; and Dave Miller, "Drug Mafia Arms Campesinos," *Latinamerica Press*, 1988.

[15]This is especially true in Peru [see Kathryn Leger, "Peru Rebels Flourish in Drug Zone," *The Christian Science Monitor*, 1989]. David P. Werlich discusses a captured August 1986 document that establishes a clear linkage between the Shining Path [*Sendero Luminoso*] and the peasantry on this point. *Sendero* builds support among coca farmers, who deeply resent the government's program to eradicate their coca, by protecting the peasantry from local police and urban "carpetbaggers" functioning as drug traffickers

["Peru: García Loses His Charm," *Current History*, 1988]. Cynthia McClintock ["The War on Drugs: The Peruvian Case," *Journal of Interamerican Studies and World Affairs*, 1988] discusses how drug politics and economics have contributed to an alliance of drug traffickers and *Sendero*. For a short discussion of various insurgent groups that work in Colombia and Peru hand in hand with the drug industry, see David L. Westrate, "Drug Trafficking and Terrorism," *Drug Enforcement*, 1985. See also Elliott Abrams, "Drug Wars: The New Alliance against Traffickers and Terrorists," *Department of State Bulletin*, 1986; James Adams, *The Financing of Terror*, 1986; and James Brooke, "Colombia Presses Drive on Rebels, Smashing Base," *The New York Times*, 1990.

[16]U.S. congressional hearings in 1986 noted the move progressing even into the deep Amazon of Brazil where "wild" coca was being cultivated [U.S. Congress, House Select Committee on Narcotics Abuse and Control, Report, "Latin American Study Missions Concerning International Narcotics Problems," 1986].

[17]William P. Long describes a Bolivian antidrug raid on a village market where cocaine paste was being sold. Hundreds of peasants of all ages swarmed to pelt the raiders with rocks and sticks of dynamite (with burning fuses). Government forces beat a hurried retreat ["Bolivia's U.S.–Aided Attack on Cocaine; an Uphill Struggle," *The Los Angeles Times*, 1988]. Michael Isikoff also notes peasant resistance to the destruction of their coca operations ["DEA in Bolivia: 'Guerrilla Warfare', Coca Traffic Proves Resistant," *The Washington Post*, 1989].

[18]René Bascope highlights the refining operations in some Bolivian villages that began in the early 1980s [*La Veta Blanca: Coca y Cocaína en Bolivia*, 1982]. The Department of State, in its 1989 worldwide review, offers additional evidence of the decentralization trend [U.S. Department of State, Bureau of International Narcotics Matters, *International Narcotics Control Strategy Report*, 1989].

[19]The Colombian lords first moved into Peru and Bolivia when strong antidrug campaigns were under way in Colombia in the early 1980s. When, by 1984, campaigns were increasing in both intensity and temporary effectiveness in Bolivia and Peru, the lords moved on into Brazil [Richard House, "Mafia Boss' Arrest Reveals Brazilian Cocaine Connection," *The Washington Post*, 1984]. The Colombian government's heightened pressure on drug traffickers during 1989 and 1990 further discomforted them [Joseph B. Treaster, "Colombia Turns Drug War into a Long Chase," *The New York Times*, 1989; Treaster, "Drug Traffickers Peace Offer Divides Colombians," *The New York Times*, 1990; Treaster, "Surrender of Cocaine Smugglers Isn't Expected to Have Large Effect," *The New York Times*, 1990].

[20]The literature mentions the existence of cocaine laboratories in the northeast section of Argentina [U.S. Congress, House Select Committee on Narcotics Abuse and Control, Report, "Latin American Study Missions Concerning International Narcotics Problems," 1986] and in Brazil [Alan Riding, "Brazil Acting to Halt New Trafficking in Cocaine," *The New York Times*, 1987; Riding, "Brazil Now a Vital Crossroad for Latin Cocaine Traffickers" *The New York Times*, 1988]. In "Brazil Acting," Riding shows that Brazil is attractive to refiners because it is the only country in South America where two critically required processing chemicals—ether and acetone—are manufactured in industrial quantities. Elsewhere, reports mention the seizure of three cocaine laboratories in Mexico, one in Canada, twenty-one in the United States, and major complexes in Panama and Venezuela. All this was indicative of increased smuggling of cocaine base to the United States and other countries where essential chemicals for cocaine refinement are more readily available. It also suggests that a number of smugglers were trying to bypass the Colombians in their trafficking operations [National Narcotics Intelligence Consumers

Committee, *Narcotics Intelligence Estimate 1984*, 1985].

[21]*La Violencia* has been endemic for half a century in Colombia, claiming hundreds of thousands of lives. The social process and contributing factors are presented by the highly respected Colombian sociologists Germán Guzmán Campos, Orlando Fals Borda, and Eduardo Umana Luna [*La violencia en Colombia: estudio de un proceso social*, 8 ed., 1977)]. See, also, Herbert Braun, *The Assassination of Gaitán: Public Life and Urban Violence in Colombia*, 1985; Jonas Bernstein, "Bitter Convulsions in a Nation under the Influence of Drugs," *Insight*, 1989; and Alan Riding, "Colombia's Drugs and Violent Politics Make Murder a Way of Life, *The New York Times*, 1987.

[22]See, for example, Peter T. White, "Coca," *National Geographic*, 1989. The scandal over Colombia's diplomatic pouch is covered in *Latin American Weekly Report* ("Heads Roll in Trafficking Saga," 1988]. U.S. Army planes are covered by Michael Isikoff, "Drugs Allegedly Shipped in Army Planes' Mail," *The Washington Post*, 1988. The general air traffic issue is taken up by William Carley, "Losing Battle: U.S. Air War on Drugs so Far Fails to Stem Caribbean Smuggling," *The Wall Street Journal*, 1988.

[23]For documentary evidence regarding the drug links between the U.S.-backed Contras involved in the Nicaraguan civil war, see U.S. Congress, Senate Subcommittee on Terrorism, Narcotics and International Operations of the Committee on Foreign Relations, "Drugs, Law Enforcement and Foreign Policy," 1988. On Nicaragua as a transit country, see U.S. Department of State, Bureau of International Narcotics Matters, *International Narcotics Strategy Report*, 1989. Jonathan Kwitny makes particularly strong allegations about Nicaragua ["Money, Drugs and the Contras," *Nation*, 1987]. The evidence and the allegations regarding Mexico are legion. See, for example, Dan Williams, "2 Nations Stymied in Efforts to Shut off Flow: Mexico a Funnel for U.S.-Bound Cocaine," *The Los Angeles Times*, 1985; and U.S. Department of State, *International Narcotics Strategy Report*. On the Bahamas, considerable evidence was amassed in a 1987 U.S. congressional hearing [U.S. Congress, House Committee on Foreign Affairs, Hearing, "Narcotics Issues in the Bahamas and the Caribbean"], in which issues were discussed that had caused the Bahamas to convene a commission of inquiry in 1984 [Bahamas Commission of Inquiry, *Report*]. Transshipment continued to plague the Bahamas' political processes much later [Don A. Schanche, "Bahamas Leader Denies Drug Ties," *The Los Angeles Times*, 1989]. The transiting has been so pervasive in Jamaica that legitimate shipping has become a target for smuggling, aided in part by organized narcotics criminals, but also by shipping lines' employees and dock guards who have become corrupted. Signaled out for particular notice is the port at Kingston. Some companies, fearing U.S. sequestration laws, have boycotted deliveries of legitimate merchandise from Kingston to the United States out of fear that their vessels will become "contaminated" [Daniel Machalaba, "Shipping Lines Fall Prey to Drug Dealers," *The Asian Wall Street Journal*, 1989]. Cuba presents, perhaps, the most interesting case of a "transiting country." After repeated allegations beginning as early as 1983 alleging the Castro government's involvement in smuggling of illegal narcotics into the United States [e.g., Cuban-American National Foundation, *Castro's Narcotics Trade*, 1983; and James H. Michel, "Cuban Involvement in Narcotics Trafficking," *Department of State Bulletin*, 1983], Castro finally acknowledged the problem within the highest levels of his government, but denied he had any earlier knowledge. He had the principals tried and executed [Don Bohning, "Cuba Ties Officers to Drug Ring," *The Miami Herald*, 1989; Pablo Alfonso, "Expertos Sobre Cuba Dudan que Castro Desconociera Narcotráfico," *El Nuevo Herald* (Miami), 1989; David Brock, "Drug Smuggling Runs Deep in Official Cuban Connection," *Insight*, 1989; Don Shannon, "High-Level Drug Case Rocks Cuba," *The Los Angeles Times*, 1989; Robert Pear, "Cubans Disclose a Drug Network," *The New*

York Times, 1989; and Guy Gugliotta, "Castro Learns Tough Lesson about the Business of Drugs," *The Miami Herald*, 1989] and then offered to collaborate with the United States government in drug interdiction efforts [Michael Isikoff, "Cuba Seeks U.S. Cooperation in Curbing Drug Flights," *The Washington Post*, 1989]. See also Guy Gugliotta and Jeff Leen, *Kings of Cocaine*, 1989.

[24]The chemicals used to adulterate cocaine on the street, their pharmacology, and health-related impacts are discussed in the following articles: Gilbert J. Olivares et al., "Street Cocaine 1971–1975: Nature, Cost and Effects," *Veterinary and Human Toxicology*, 1977; Mercedes Morales-Vaca, "A Laboratory Approach to the Control of Cocaine in Bolivia," *Bulletin on Narcotics*, 1984; and David E. Smith and D. R. Wesson, "Cocaine," *Journal of Psychedelic Drugs*, 1978.

[25]A special issue of the *Journal of Ethnopharmacology* (1981) edited by L. Rivier and J. G. Bruhn, entitled "Coca and Cocaine 1981," gives extensive coverage (200 pages) of what was known in the early 1980s about coca and cocaine from both a historical and a scientific orientation. Among the historical reports are sundry episodes of the use of coca and cocaine as medicines. John Dillin describes how the drug was found in stores, taverns, in patent medicines and soft drinks ["Addiction in America: Roots of U.S. Drug Crisis Run Deep," *The Christian Science Monitor*, 1989]. Donald J. Egan and David Owen Robinson raise a similar historical discussion ["Cocaine: Magical Drug or Menace?" *International Journal of the Addictions*, 1979].

[26]In the early years, Sigmund Freud used cocaine and described its beneficial effects as curing indigestion, increasing strength, and treating alcoholism, asthma, and addiction to morphine [Joseph J. Forno, Richard T. Young, and Cynthia Levitt, "Cocaine Abuse—The Evolution from Coca Leaves to Freebase," *Journal of Drug Education*, 1981]. Lester Grinspoon and James B. Bakalar discuss not only the views of Freud but also those of Thomas Szasz, Nils Bejerot, and the individuals in their own sample of seventeen users [*Cocaine: A Drug and Its Social Evolution*, 1985].

[27]The appendix to this chapter discusses the two basic sources of statistics on which such projections may rest.

[28]See the statistical discussion in the appendix to this chapter. See also John Dillin, "Drug Use Dropping in Spite of City Woes, Studies Say," *The Christian Science Monitor*, 1989; and Joseph B. Treaster, "Cocaine Prices Rise, and Police Efforts May Be Responsible," *The New York Times*, 1990.

[29]Refers to [a] in Figure 4. NIDA conducts a survey of households every two or three years to assess the extent of drug use in the United States. The survey methodology is essentially identical for all surveys conducted: "A national probability sample of households in the coterminous United States was selected from 100 primary sampling units. The household population includes more than 98 percent of the U.S. population. It excludes persons living in group quarters or institutions; such as military installations, college dormitories, hotels, hospitals, and jails; and transient populations such as the homeless. Alaska and Hawaii have not been included in the sample since the first National Household Survey because of logistic and cost considerations" [NIDA, *National Household Survey on Drug Abuse*, 1988]. Estimates are reported in basically three different age groups: 12–17, 18–25, and 26 and older. In 1985 and 1988, the 26 and older category was further broken down to include two different age groups: 26–35, and 36 and older. These were combined using the methodology explained in note 30 below. The results of the survey should be interpreted with caution. First, "the value of self-reports obviously depends upon the honesty and memory of sampled respondents . . . . Some under- or over-reporting may occur." Second, total U.S. population estimates may

be biased as time from the last census increases, subsequently biasing the probability sample. Third, "the population surveyed is the noninstitutionalized population living in households, and therefore does not include some segments of the U.S. population which may contain a substantial proportion of drug users, such as college students living in dormitories, transients and those incarcerated" [NIDA, *National Household Survey on Drug Abuse*, 1988].

[30]Refers to note [b] in Figure 4. NIDA reports parameters in percentages. We consider the number of users to be a more relevant parameter when trying to illustrate possible relationships between illicit drug production and consumption. Consequently, the reported percentages were multiplied with the reported total population estimates to produce the total number of users in each age cohort in the population. Because of rounding in the reported numbers, there will be a degree of error in our population total estimates, but this is not significant. Also, only respondents reporting any use in the past year are included in the numbers above. This excludes cohorts reporting lifetime use, but not in the past year.

[31]National Institute on Drug Abuse, *Patterns and Trends in Drug Abuse: A National and International Perspective*, 1985; United Nations Secretariat, Division of Narcotic Drugs, "Review of Drug Abuse and Measures to Reduce the Illicit Demand for Drugs by Region," *Bulletin on Narcotics*, 1987; R. L. Hartnoll, "Current Situation Relating to Drug Abuse Assessment in European Countries," *Bulletin on Narcotics*, 1986.

[32]See the discussion by J. Camí and M. E. Rodríguez about Spain ["Cocaína: La epidemia que viene," *Medicina Clínica*, 1988. Cathy Booth ["Tentacles of the Octopus; The Mafia Brings Europe's Worst Drug Epidemic Home," *Time*, 1988] describes the extraordinary drug epidemic in Italy. Craig R. Whitney ["Crack Use Starts in Fearful Europe," *The New York Times*, 1989] discusses fears that the "American Disease" will spread to Europe's shores.

[33]Tom Mashberg, "Drugs in Europe: Signs of a Spreading Plague," *The New York Times*, 1990.

[34]See, for example, Jennifer Hull, "Shooting up under a Red Star," *Time*, 1987.

[35]Flores R. Agreda discusses the Peruvian evidence in "Drug Abuse Problems in Countries of the Andean Subregion," *Bulletin on Narcotics*, 1986.

[36]The health consequences appear to be severe and are discussed later in this handbook. The general phenomenon is detailed by Michael Isikoff of the *Washington Post* ["Home-Grown Coca Plagues Colombia," 1989] and Tyler Bridges ["Colombia: Drug Problems at Home," *The Washington Post*, 1986]. For general commentaries as well as specific applications see James Inciardi, "Beyond Cocaine: Basuco, Crack, and Other Coca Products," *Contemporary Drug Problems*, 1987; Carlos Briceño, *Las Drogas en el Perú*, 1983; Tyler Bridges, "Colombian Antidrug Plan," *The Christian Science Monitor*, 1987; Clara Germani, "Coca Addiction Hits Home—Among Rural Children of Drug-Producing Bolivia," *The Christian Science Monitor*, 1988; F. Raúl Jeri, "Further Experiences with the Syndromes Produced by Coca Paste Smoking, *Bulletin on Narcotics*, 1978 as well as Jeri's additional articles cited in the annotated bibliography; Kathryn Leger, "Bolivians Awaken to Tragedy of Child Drug Addiction," *The Christian Science Monitor*, 1986; and Edmundo Morales, "Coca Paste and Crack: A Cross-National Ethnographic Approach," *Studies in Third World Societies*, 1986. Of some interest to coca-paste observers is the following: Captured documents from Shining Path guerrillas (*Sendero Luminoso*), who have placed much of Peru's coca growing Upper Huallaga valley under their control, specify punishments for smoking coca paste [Jonathan Cavanagh, "Peru Rebels Threaten U.S. Drug Program," *The Wall Street Journal*, 1984].

[38]See, for example, the community study conducted by Catherine J. Allen [*The Hold Life Has: Coca and Cultural Identity in an Andean Community*, 1988)].

[39]Numerous contributors to *Coca and Cocaine: Effects on People and Policy in Latin America* [edited by Deborah Pacini and Christine Franquemont, 1986] are of this persuasion.

[40]The literature on the psychopharmacologic and health-related aspects of cocaine use is substantial. Mentioned in this note are six review articles giving extensive coverage of the diversity of this vast literature. Edgar H. Adams and his colleagues ["Trends in Prevalence and Consequences of Cocaine Use," *Advances in Alcohol and Substance Abuse*, 1986] focus on the health-related consequences of cocaine abuse. Katie A. Busch and Sidney H. Schnoll ["Cocaine—Review of Current Literature and Interface with the Law," *Behavioral Sciences and the Law*, 1985] review the epidemiology, history, and pharmacology of cocaine and discuss knowledge of the relationship between cocaine and violence and the forensic and psychiatric issues surrounding cocaine's use. Frank H. Gawin and Everett H. Ellinwood, Jr. ["Cocaine and Other Stimulants," *The New England Journal of Medicine*, 1988] review the literature on cocaine from the vantage of psychiatry, methods of treatment, and new avenues of theory and research. John Grabowski and Steven I. Dworkin ["Cocaine: An Overview of Current Issues," *The International Journal of the Addictions*, 1985] review a respectable body of literature in areas of behavioral and neurobiological effects of cocaine use, in risks, dosage, routes of administration, and in treatment. Lester Grinspoon and James B. Bakalar ["Adverse Effects of Cocaine: Selected Issues," *Annals of the New York Academy of Sciences*, 1981] discuss controlled experimental work on human beings from the mid 1970s through 1981. John B. Murray ["An Overview of Cocaine Use and Abuse," *Psychological Reports*, 1986], aside from tracing cocaine use from South American Indians through nineteenth-century European patterns into the twentieth-century United States, reviews route-specific literature with respect to differential psychopharmacologic effects with different potencies. All the review articles, including Grinspoon and Bakalar's, discuss the physical and psychiatric dangers of cocaine abuse.

[41]See, for example, Mark Galizio and Stephen A. Maisto, *Determinants of Substance Abuse: Biological, Psychological, and Environmental Factors*, 1985.

[42]Robert B. Carlson and William H. Edwards ["Human Values and Cocaine Use," *Journal of Drug Education*, 1987] noted that dominant value orientations differ between drug users and nonusers. Personal values are more important to drug users, whereas social values are more important to nonusers. A branch of "existential sociology" suggests that hedonism is a motivation for deviance, specifically played out at elite levels of drug taking and dealing. Such dealers and users do not remove themselves from conventional society and enter a life of deviance because of blockage of any legitimate opportunities for alternative activities, as others have claimed (e.g., the "social deprivation" model). Nor do they do so because of being failures within their conventional reference groups. They become deviants because of personality characteristics that crave pleasure and gratification that conventional society represses through its bureaucratization and impersonality. For an explication of this argument and considerable ethnographic data on a specific group, see Patricia A. Adler, *Wheeling and Dealing: An Ethnography of an Upper-Level Drug Dealing and Smuggling Community*, 1985. See also Patricia A. Adler and Peter Adler, "Shifts and Oscillations in Deviant Careers: The Case of Upper-Level Drug Dealers and Smugglers," *Social Problems*, 1983.

of an Upper-Level Drug Dealing and Smuggling Community, 1985. See also Patricia A. Adler and Peter Adler, "Shifts and Oscillations in Deviant Careers: The Case of Upper-Level Drug Dealers and Smugglers," *Social Problems*, 1983.

[43]See, for example, Richard Dembo et al., "The Relationship between Physical and Sexual Abuse and Tobacco, Alcohol, and Illicit Drug Use among Youths in a Juvenile Detention Center," *International Journal of the Addictions*, 1988.

[44]Herbert D. Kleber ["Epidemic Cocaine Abuse: America's Present, Britain's Future?" *British Journal of Addiction*, 1988] reviews the historical setting in which cocaine first became prevalent in America in the late nineteenth century as well as its recent reemergence. Possible reasons for this reemergence are reviewed and explained, including counter productive myths (exaggerations) as to drug use safety, relationship to prior marijuana use, celebrity endorsements and the role of the media, changes in the routes of administration, and the reenforcing effects of the drug itself. Delbert S. Elliot, David Huizinga, and Suzanne S. Ageton, [*Explaining Delinquency and Drug Use*, 1982] present an explanatory model that builds upon and synthesizes traditional "strain, social control, and social learning" perspectives, bringing them together into a single model that the authors believe accounts for delinquent behavior and drug use. Ralph W. Larkin's book [*Suburban Youth in Cultural Crisis*, 1979] reads as a composite ethnography of an American middle-class suburb and its high school. While drug-related issues are only a part of the focus, drug use is shown to occur as a construct of "routinization of pleasure" within the social fabric and social interaction of young people. Denise B. Kandel et al. ["Antecedents of Adolescent Initiation into Stages of Drug Use: A Developmental Analysis," in *Longitudinal Research on Drug Use*, 1978] illustrate the role of social context of adolescent drug involvement.

[45]Joseph Westermeyer ["Cultural Patterns of Drug and Alcohol Use: An Analysis of Host and Agent in the Cultural Environment," *Bulletin on Narcotics*, 1987] points out cross-cultural studies of drug problems that show that certain social strategies concerning drug use hinder the development of such problems and help to reduce and prevent the abuse of drugs and alcohol, while certain other strategies are liable to add to drug problems, and these are culturally specific in their effects. Griffith Edwards and Awni Arif, eds. [*Drug Problems in the Sociocultural Context: A Basis for Policies and Programme Planning*, 1980] offer case studies of sociocultural patterns of drug use and an analysis of the commonalities and diversity among drug use patterns in different countries. Studies come from the Middle East, Africa, Latin America, the Far East, and South East Asia.

[46]See the study of nearly 5,000 respondents conducted by Khalil Akhtar Khavari and Teresa McCray Harmon ["The Relationship Between the Degree of Professed Religious Belief and Use of Drugs," *International Journal of the Addictions*, 1982]. In general, those who viewed themselves as "very religious" drank less and used fewer psychoactive drugs than those who considered themselves "not religious at all." Significantly elevated use of drugs was noted among those with "not religious at all" preferences.

[47]The *Economist* ["Does This War Make Sense?," 1989] speaks of drug dealers battling each other over market shares while at the same time working to expand their markets. Drug supply appeared to exceed a level of demand convenient for dealers.

[48]Playing on a Hobbesian phrase, poverty and economic deprivation are frequently advanced as important precursors to hard drug use. See, for example, Armando Morales, "Substance Abuse and Mexican American Youth: An Overview," *Journal of Drug Issues*, 1984; and Robert Marquand, "Fatal Attraction for Inner-City Teens: An Honor Student Done in by Drugs," *The Christian Science Monitor*, 1989. A popular explanation of drug

use among lower classes (but not middle or upper classes) is to be found in economic, social, and environmental deprivation [e.g., see Carlos Harrison, "Kids on Crack: 880 Crimes Each in a Year," *The Miami Herald*, 1989].

[49]Marian W. Fischman and Charles R. Schuster's study ["Cocaine Self-Administration in Humans," *Psychopharmacology Bulletin*, 1983] showed cocaine to be a potent reinforcer for humans as well as animals. Frank Gawin and Herbert Kleber's studies ["Pharmacologic Treatments of Cocaine Abuse," *Psychiatric Clinics of North America*, 1986] present increasing clinical evidence of intractable addiction—not just psychological attraction—being involved with chronic cocaine use. Sidney Cohen ["Recent Developments in the Abuse of Cocaine," *Bulletin on Narcotics*, 1984] speaks of the strong desires cocaine users have to return to the momentary ecstatic experience because of the cyclical depression that chronic users experience. Pre-1980 contributors tended to downplay dependency and reinforcing phenomena [e.g., Donald J. Egan and David Owen Robinson, "Cocaine: Magical Drug or Menace?" *International Journal of the Addictions*, 1979]. John B. Murray reviews considerable pharmacological literature ["An Overview of Cocaine Use and Abuse," *Psychological Reports*, 1986].

[50]One ought to urge caution here, I suppose, considering Frank Gawin and Herbert Kleber's studies ["Pharmacologic Treatments of Cocaine Abuse," *Psychiatric Clinics of North America*, 1986], which present increasing clinical evidence of intractable addiction—not just psychological attraction—with chronic cocaine use. See also entries in the previous note.

[51]As reported by Gina Kolata ["Experts Finding New Hope on Treating Crack Addict," *The New York Times*, 1989], there is a research line that assumes that crack addiction is more a relationship to the setting and circumstances of the users than to the biochemical reaction that the drug produces. On the other hand, the severe biochemical model is suggested by James A. Inciardi ["Beyond Cocaine: Basuco, Crack, and other Coca Products," *Contemporary Drug Problems*, 1987]; Michael Isikoff, ["Users of Crack Cocaine Link Violence to Drug's Influence," *The Washington Post*, 1989]; and numerous contributors to a U.S. congressional hearing [U.S. Congress, House Select Committee on Narcotics Abuse and Control, Hearing, "The Crack Cocaine Crisis," 1986]. In particular, it is hard to square the "setting and circumstance" thesis with what happens to infants born of crack-using women (unless, of course, one assumes that it is the setting and circumstance that cross the placental barrier rather than the crack itself). See Peter Kerr, "Crack Addiction: The Tragic Toll on Women and Their Children," *The New York Times*, 1987.

[52]Reference is made to the dose-related effect of cocaine on sexuality. As dose increases, previous experiences of enhanced libido and sexual performance are reversed. See Ernest L. Abel's *Psychoactive Drugs and Sex*, 1985, which includes a substantial bibliography for each drug discussed.

[53]See Craig R. Whitney, "Crack Use Starts in Fearful Europe," *The New York Times*, 1989; David Broder, "Fearing Crack Invasion, Europe Steps up Antidrug Efforts," *The Washington Post*, 1989; and Tom Mashberg, "Drugs in Europe: Sign of a Spreading Plague," *The New York Times*, 1990.

2

Heroin

Heroin[1] alkaloids are derived from morphine through a simple chemical process. Morphine, in turn, is obtained from opium. All originate in the agronomic chemistry of the opium poppy. The poppy itself is grown in many parts of the world, but principally in Burma, Afghanistan, Pakistan, Mexico, Thailand, Iran, and Laos (see Figures 8 and 9). For centuries opium poppies were a crop of significance in Turkey but declined in the 1970s in the face of vigorous crop eradication efforts there.[2] Mexico and Pakistan happily made up the production shortfalls by dramatically increasing their own poppy cultivation.[3] It appears that poppy growing has increased in Lebanon's Bekaa Valley[4] and has now begun in Guatemala.[5]

Most opium originates as a sticky brown gum (dried from emissions oozing from the base of the mature poppy bulb through slits made by harvesters' knives and which are then aggregated and compacted). Some opium is collected from "poppy straw," e.g., the dried plant itself. However, extraction of the alkaloids from the dried plant is complex and costly, requiring capital intensive procedures.

Opium (from which morphine, heroin, and

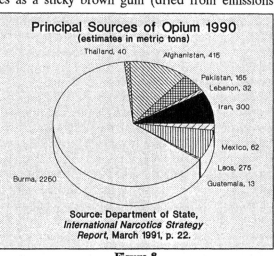

Principal Sources of Opium 1990
(estimates in metric tons)

Thailand, 40
Afghanistan, 415
Pakistan, 165
Lebanon, 32
Iran, 300
Mexico, 62
Laos, 275
Guatemala, 13
Burma, 2260

Source: Department of State,
International Narcotics Strategy Report, March 1991, p. 22.

Figure 8

other alkaloids derive)[6] has, as has coca, a long history of use. From the earliest times—certainly long before 4,000 B.C.—opium was known for its medicinal qualities; it was used as a narcotic in Sumerian and European cultures 6,000 years ago. Opium was introduced into India by Muslims; from there it spread to China where people learned to smoke it, a practice that was thereafter adopted in many parts

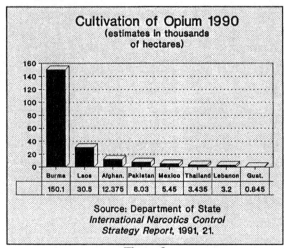

Figure 9
(Cultivation information unavailable for Iran)

of the world.[7] It was a significant point of contention in at least one war (the Opium War between Great Britain and China, 1840–1842) and thereafter became an important Indian export commodity in British controlled trade with the Chinese.[8]

Morphine was first produced in 1803, heroin in 1898.[9] Heroin provides more potency for less bulk and weight than does morphine or opium, and so therefore lends itself to being the commodity of preference for smugglers who are able to conceal it more readily.

Having a relatively high value to weight ratio, the marketing of opium, morphine, and heroin does not require roads and motorized transport as do most conventional commercial agricultural crops or products derived from them. Profitable production and refining can therefore occur in remote areas. Inasmuch, therefore, as heroin can be, and is, produced in village laboratories that service nearby opium growers,[10] opium poppies have understandably become a cash crop of preference among peasants in remote areas badly served by the states in which they live.[11]

Relative ease of marketing under conditions of fairly primitive transport services (e.g., pack animals), physical remoteness of opium growing communities and their distance from state services (including law enforcement), and the attractive financial returns frequently associated with the narcotics trade have induced many rural farmers to engage in opium poppy production,[12] either as a side cash crop or as a principal cultivation engaging the labor of an entire peasant family. Pan-village organizations—sometimes operating as a state within a state[13]—as well as local village groups or freelance village-based entrepreneurs collect the opium and move it through a refining process and then on to market. They use long-established routing and trafficking procedures or develop new ones when the need arises (e.g., when patterns are disrupted by law enforcement agents, civil wars, or robber barons).

A recent route change involves mainland China. As Hong Kong police have become more effective in interdicting drug shipments out of the Golden Triangle arriving by sea, smugglers have secured land routes through China to Hong Kong. Drug smuggling became a problem for China following the country's opening of its borders to tens of thousands of tourists and businessmen in 1981. All this follows a 1988 bumper crop of opium in the Golden Triangle for which traffickers vigorously sought market outlets.[14] These conditions, resources, and opportunities combined to promote a dramatic increase in opium production from 1985 to 1989, especially in Burma (see Figure 10), and have even induced an incipient major contribution from Lebanon and Guatemala (see Figure 11). In 1990 there was about a 15 percent drop in production due, in part, to poor weather and political disturbances in Afghanistan and Burma (now Myanmar).

Opiate addiction has occurred wherever and whenever opiates have been available. In America, opiate addiction moved from a nineteenth-century habit of some middle- and numerous upper-class women to a twentieth-century practice involving lower-class urban males, social misfits, hustlers, and other marginalized segments of society. The underlying transformation in social-class usage was well under way before the early twentieth-century initiation of legislation criminalizing opiate use. This social-class change in predominant use is thought by some to be one of the principal reasons that prohibition legislation was passed.[15] Underlying U.S. heroin control policies was the assumption that normal or useful functioning in society and drug use were incompatible. It was therefore thought that legislation to criminalize use was required as a drug control measure.

The social-class transformation of heavy use in America appears to have

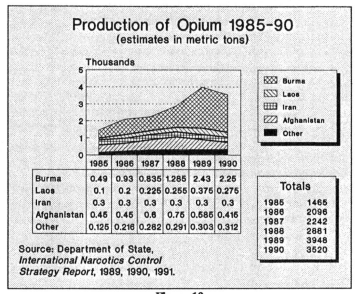

Figure 10

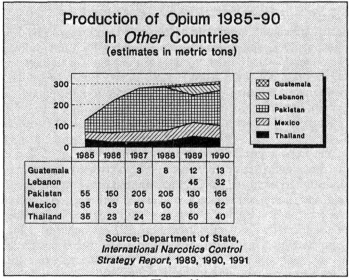

Figure 11

been associated with prevailing medical practices that moved away from maintenance medication—some physicians appeared to be frightened by their experience in prescribing heroin—to viewing addiction as criminal behavior that ought to receive appropriate sanctions. Such a shift in the informed medical view of opium, morphine, and heroin helped to change American society's views on the acceptability of any of the opiates for routine treatment or maintenance[16] and ultimately for general use. Except under controlled medical supervision, opiate distribution and use remains a criminal activity in the United States.

Elsewhere, other assumptions oriented drug policy developments. Nevertheless, of considerable interest to historians of comparative drug control policies is that several other countries have taken a noncriminal orientation to heroin use but are still experiencing an increase in user addicts and a frightening change in their accorded if not real social-class status. In the United Kingdom, for example, between the mid 1920s until the early 1960s, heroin maintenance policies were in effect (allowing physicians to prescribe heroin for those addicted to it). It was assumed that a "stabilized" addict could function tolerably well in society while on opiates, and that this was less costly than attempts to remove addicts from the source of their dependency.[17] However, just as in the United States, the number of users increased, and their accorded social status underwent unwelcome changes, from the "repentant" deviant tolerated by society to the "junkie" feared and detested by society.[18] The alarming increase in the number of users, as well as the transformation in their social type, was made possible, in part, by overprescribing physicians.[19]

A new social class of addicts developed—people who had a substantial disdain for conventional values or pursuits, were enamored with a lifestyle offensive to the larger population, and were thought to participate in demonstrable criminal activities. All this prompted a reevaluation of the British drug control policy, with debates continuing to the present day,[20] particularly in light of the spectacular increase in heroin addiction in several English communities.[21] "Heroin maintenance" in the United Kingdom suffered a crisis of credibility and has now been much reduced.

The Netherlands, also noted for its noncriminalizing consumption policies, has begun an internal political reassessment of them, not only for reasons analogous to those of the United Kingdom but also because Amsterdam has become a heavy drawing card for many of the world's "social deviants."[22] On these policy issues there is considerable disagreement and political conflict, with persuasive arguments raised on all sides.[23]

Other countries are experiencing an upsurge in heroin use. For example, India—once largely free from opium addiction even though the country, while under the British Raj, cultivated the poppy for export and still has a sizeable annual production for licit medical use—is witnessing a swiftly growing number of its citizen's becoming addicted. It is estimated that between 1982 and 1987 from a half million to one million Indians developed a heroin dependency. All of this is challenging cultural traditions and family life and, it is said, is fragmenting the social fabric of India's cities. Addiction has moved beyond the affluent neighborhoods to rootless migrants. The drug is now easily available in New Delhi and in other Indian cities.[24]

Addiction rates have increased elsewhere. Since 1979 there has been an alarming increase—perhaps six fold—among young people in Ireland in the abuse of drugs, heroin included. One study of north Dublin suggested that as many as ten percent of people age 15–20 were addicted to heroin.[25] Addiction among Vietnamese youth is increasing,[26] as well as among U.S. crack users.[27] A highly addictive mixture of cocaine/crack and smokeable heroin has now emerged as a drug of choice among some New York chronic drug abusers,[28] precisely at a time when it was thought that heroin use in America was declining, as it appears to be among 18–25 year olds (see the data table in Figure 12). However, since about 1988, heroin use appears to have been increasing among 12–17 year olds (see Figure 12).[29, 30] Malaysia, Thailand, and Pakistan all note startling increases in spite, in Malaysia's case, of strong drug-control policies.[31] Heroin, smuggled into Sri Lanka by tourists, is now the most widely abused drug there.[32] While marijuana has long been used in Nepal, harder drugs have only recently come into the country and are now responsible for the widespread addiction of Nepalese school children to heroin.[33]

The United Nations Commission on Narcotic Drugs noted at its February 1987 session that the drug-abuse situation continued to deteriorate in most parts of the world, and that the use of heroin and cocaine had escalated. The age group of first-time users had fallen from adolescents to preadolescents. In most countries, drug abuse had spread to all social strata, and the proportion of female users was rising.[34]

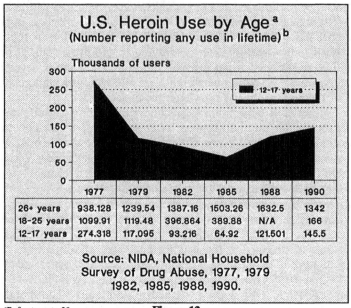

U.S. Heroin Use by Age[a]
(Number reporting any use in lifetime)[b]

Thousands of users

	1977	1979	1982	1985	1988	1990
26+ years	938.128	1239.54	1387.16	1503.26	1632.5	1342
18-25 years	1099.91	1119.48	396.864	389.88	N/A	166
12-17 years	274.318	117.095	93.216	64.92	121.501	145.5

Source: NIDA, National Household
Survey of Drug Abuse, 1977, 1979
1982, 1985, 1988, 1990.

[a]Refer to note 29
[b]Refer to note 30

Figure 12

Some of the new heroin addiction is attributable to drug control policies. When opium use and sale were prohibited in Burma, Hong Kong, Malaysia, Singapore, and Thailand, many opium addicts switched to heroin, starting a trend that has accelerated heroin abuse and spread it geographically, involving countries such as India and Sri Lanka, which had no prior experience with the problem.[35]

Why are some people in all parts of the world so attracted to heroin? As with cocaine, the psychopharmacological properties of heroin, coupled with subjective effects, produce pleasurable alterations in mood, perception, and sense of being. Street users speak of a "rush" and a "high." The rush appears to come almost immediately after intravenous injection and lasts for a minute or two. It is usually described as a "violent, orgasmic experience, somewhat like a sexual orgasm, only vastly more so."[36] Then comes a four- or five-hour high, usually described as an extremely pleasant drowsy state in which neither the users' critical needs nor wants seem terribly burdensome to them. The effect appears to be differentiated somewhat on the basis of the genetic makeup of the users and the total ambience in which they do their drug taking.

Frequent use induces extreme dependency on or addiction to the drug as well as increasing levels of tolerance. Habitual takers desperately require increasing quantities to produce the same pharmacological/psychological effect. Heroin addicts find it necessary to "shoot up" three or more times a day.

In the United States, heroin and cocaine were widely used at the turn of this century. Cocaine use then fell out of style, no doubt due in major part to official and unofficial propaganda against it and the passage of anti-cocaine laws. Heroin got the same official and unofficial treatment, but its users appeared either less able or less willing to abandon the drug.

In time, heroin use took on social connotations associated with junkies, "down and outs," and other social undesirables. While it became "mother, father, lover, and friend" to those who consumed it, nonusers grew to fear and abhor both it and its users.

Accordingly, while cocaine in recent years was the recreational drug of choice for the economic upper class before the drug migrated to lower realms, heroin has not enjoyed such a reputation. Coincidentally, there are far fewer users of heroin than of cocaine, but its users appear to be more implacably attached to it.

NOTES

[1]For the more casual as well as the serious reader, Peter T. White, a journalist who visited all major poppy growing and transiting areas in Asia, the Middle East, and Mexico, depicts the entire range of poppy growing, opium refining, and narcotics trafficking in "The Poppy," *National Geographic*, 1985. As for sources with extensive bibliographies, the 1987 update of David I. Musto's notable 1973 work on the history of opiates in America is worthy of attention [*The American Disease: Origins of Narcotic Control*] as is David T. Courtwright's *Dark Paradise: Opiate Addiction in America Before 1940*, 1982. Sociological literature on heroin and deviance is reviewed by Charles W. Lidz and Andrew L. Walker [*Heroin, Deviance, and Morality*, 1980]. Surprisingly, except for a short bibliography by J. C. Kramer on the scientific research of opiates ["Opiates: Two Centuries of Scientific Research," *Journal of Psychedelic Drugs*, 1989], from our survey of the literature (see note 2 in the Introduction to this handbook), we were unable to identify a single stand-alone bibliography on heroin, even after a supplemental search of *Bibliographic Index*.

[2]James W. Spain ["The United States, Turkey, and the Poppy," *Middle East Journal*, 1975] gives a synoptic history of the poppy in Turkey, of U.S. pressure on Turkey to curtail cultivation, and of Turkey's reaction in the mid-1970s, which was to reject U.S. pressure.

[3]The "French Connection" supplied heroin to American addicts from the 1930s until 1973, principally from opium sources in Turkey. Its operations were terminated by an international law enforcement effort that included the suppression of opium poppy cultivation in Turkey. The resulting shortage of heroin enabled Mexican and Asian traffickers to penetrate the American market, boosting opium poppy production in the Golden Triangle (Burma, Laos, Thailand) and in Mexico [see James Van Wert, "U.S.–Mexican Aerial Opium Eradication Program: A Summative Evaluation," 1982; John Bacon, "Is the French Connection Really Dead?" *Drug Enforcement*, 1981]. By the mid-1970s Mexican heroin accounted for 87 percent of the U.S. market. With subsequent suppression in Mexico, Pakistan filled the market demand and thereafter became the world's biggest heroin exporter ["Heroin Brings More Trouble," *The Economist*, 1986]. See also David Kline, "The Khyber Connection," *The Christian Science Monitor*, 1982; and Lawrence Lifschultz, "Inside the Kingdom of Heroin," *Nation*, 1988.

⁴Jim Muir, "Syria Gets Tough on Lebanon's Drug Trade," *The Christian Science Monitor*, 1987.

⁵A startling note by Wilson Ring ["Opium Production Rises in Guatemala Mountains," *The Washington Post*, 1989] alleges a meteoric rise in opium production in the mountains along the Mexican border with, it is alleged, production possibilities to supply three times the yearly need of the estimated 500,000 U.S. addicts. According to the U.S. Department of State, supplying those needs would have to be done with thirteen tons of opium, Guatemala's estimated production in 1990 (see Figure 8). The eastern part of the country is used for cocaine transshipments and marijuana production, and now the western for poppy growing. Aerial spraying has been suspended because of ground fire. Leftist insurgents are protecting the growing as a way to earn operating funds. See also Brook Larmer, "US Targets Guatemalan Opium," *The Christian Science Monitor*, 1990; and "Guatemala: International Pressure on Drug Traffickers Opens a New Frontier," *Latinamerica Press, 1989*.

⁶The principal psychoactive alkaloid in opium is morphine, from which heroin is synthesized. Other alkaloidal constituents are codeine, papaverine, and narcotine. Morphine, heroin, and codeine are addictive; papaverine and narcotine are not [William Harris and Judith Levey, eds., *The New Columbia Encyclopedia*, 1975, p. 2009]. The pure heroin alkaloid is not marketed because, being insoluble in water, it is useless for injection. Just as with cocaine alkaloids, heroin alkaloids are turned into a hydrochloride salt in the refining process [see John Kaplan, *The Hardest Drug: Heroin and Public Policy*, 1983, p. 7].

⁷Harris and Levey, eds., *The New Columbia Encyclopedia*, 1975, p. 2009.

⁸Geoffrey Harding [*Opiate Addiction, Morality and Medicine*, 1988)] devotes a chapter to the Opium Wars and to the international trade that precipitated them. Tan Chung, from an odyssey that began at Delhi University and included a sojourn at Harvard University, advances revisionist historical views on the subject [*China and the Brave New World*, 1978]. The blow-by-blow events are chronicled by Jack Beeching [*The Chinese Opium Wars*, 1975]. See also Peter Ward Fay, *The Opium War 1840–42*, 1975.

⁹For explication of the science behind these discoveries, along with some of the drama and excitement that discoverers must have experienced, see Walter Sneader, *Drug Discovery: The Evolution of Modern Medicines*, 1985.

¹⁰Peter T. White's text is interesting and highly informative, and Steve Raymer's photographs are remarkable on this point ["The Poppy," *National Geographic*, 1985].

¹¹Most states in these areas are characterized as weak with only limited credible authority in their own hinterlands even when they desire to exercise authority there. See, for example, the short discussion by Rensselaer W. Lee III, "The Drug Trade and Developing Countries," *Policy Focus*, 1987.

¹²It must be acknowledged, of course, that as organized traffickers assume control in a given area they may force peasants to grow opium poppies, coca bushes, or cannabis plants against their will and for which, given the circumstances, they may receive relatively little economic gain. Such appears to be the case in Burma's Shan state with respect to opium poppies [Edith T. Mirante, "The Shan Frontier: Exploitation and Eradication," 1989].

¹³Of particular note are the operations of Khun Sa on the Burma-Thailand border. See, for example, Kim Gooi and John McBeth, "High-Priced High," *Far Eastern Economic Review*, 1986; Vichai S., "Warlords of the Poppy Fields," *Bangkok Post*, 1983 [this author is listed in the bibliography as S., Vichai]; Daniel Burstein, "The Deadly Politics of Opium," *Maclean's*, 1982; Barbara Crossette, "An Opium Warlord's News

Conference Spurs Burma and Thailand to Battle Him," *The New York Times*, 1987; and Denis D. Gray, "A Deluge from the Golden Triangle," *Nation*, 1989.

[14]Daniel Southerland, "Smugglers Using Routes in China to Move Heroin; Police Say Flow of Drug is Increasing," *The Washington Post*, 1988.

[15]This follows a "fear of the undesirables" thesis which has gained approval in the literature as an explanation of drug-repression measures. A portion of this literature is discussed by Charles W. Lidz and Andrew L. Walker [*Heroin, Deviance, and Morality*, 1980].

[16]The best discussion on these points is found in David T. Courtwright's *Dark Paradise: Opiate Addiction in America before 1940*, 1982.

[17]A good source on the history of ideas about opium use in England and in America is found in Charles F. Levinthal's "Milk of Paradise/Milk of Hell—The History of Ideas about Opium," *Perspectives in Biology and Medicine*, 1985. A lengthy historical analysis of U.S. and British public policy regarding heroin is found in Arnold Trebach's *The Heroin Solution*, 1982. Trebach proposes a heroin maintenance or opium maintenance program for addicts but one with sufficient controls to avoid the problem of overprescribing physicians.

[18]Carol Smart reviews some of the social-class determinants of British concern ["Social Policy and Drug Addiction: A Critical Study of Policy Development," *British Journal of Addiction*, 1984].

[19]Judith Blackwell claims the social-class transformation of United Kingdom users resulted from overprescribing physicians who nourished the new subculture by their generous prescribing practices ["The Saboteurs of Britain's Opiate Policy: Overprescribing Physicians or American Style 'Junkies'?" *The International Journal of the Addictions*, 1988].

[20]Among the debaters are S. J. Appavoo ["Addiction—Plague of the Nation," *The Police Journal*, 1985] who argues for heavier sentences, greater public awareness, and a revamping of the laws to deal more effectively with drug pushers. Long mandatory sentences are required as well as asset seizures. There must be a presumption that all property held by people involved in drug trafficking has arisen from their criminal activity. Trevor Bennett ["The British Experience with Heroin Regulation," *Law and Contemporary Problems*, 1988] sees Britain's rapidly changing drug policies giving mixed messages both to users and to nonusers—the government is seen as neither having developed a philosophically and morally sound system for controlling addiction nor created a rational pragmatic approach in its place. Nicholas Dorn and Nigel South ["Criminology and Economics of Drug Distribution in Britain: Options for Control," *Journal of Drug Issues*, 1986], in a severe attack on current assumptions governing British drug policies, want us to look at the "irregular economy" as the primary motor behind recent expansions in heroin use in the country. Marek Kohn [*Narcomania on Heroin*, 1987] adds a polemic about perceptions of the British drug epidemic and the panic associated with it. He is neither in favor of punishment of drug users by the criminal law nor of the free availability of drugs, but he holds that drugs must, in the final analysis, be controlled by culture, customs, and conventions for which the law weighs as a "recourse of last resort."

[21]See, for example, Howard Parker, Keith Bakx, and Russel Newcomb, *Living with Heroin*, 1988; Geoffrey Pearson, Mark Gilman, and Shirley McIver, *Young People and Heroin: An Examination of Heroin Use in the North of England*, 1987; and, Justine Picardie, and Dorothy Wade, *Heroin: Chasing the Dragon*, 1985.

[22]The point is made by Edward Cody in "Dutch Pull Welcome Mat away from Drug Users; Crackdown Intended to Alter Image That Attracts Tourists Seeking Trouble-free High," *The Washington Post*, 1988. See also Martien Kooyman, "The Drug Problem in the Netherlands," *Journal of Substance Abuse Treatment*, 1984. It is well to keep in mind that in 1983 Amsterdam's political authorities petitioned the Dutch government for permission to dispense free heroin to addicts in order to combat the then rising tide of drug addiction in the city [Peter Lewis, "Legal Heroin in Holland?" *Maclean's*, 1983]. By 1988, in addition to more vigorous control of heroin as discussed by Cody ("Dutch Pull Welcome Mat," 1988), Amsterdam had introduced a needle exchange program to try to arrest transmission of the HIV virus (AIDS) which affected about one third of the city's estimated 3,000 intravenous drug users [Janet Mohun, "Amsterdam Targets Its Drug Users, *New Scientist*, 1988]. See also Burton Bollag, "Swiss-Dutch Drug Stance: Tolerance," *The New York Times*, 1989.

[23]Dutch policies have, on the whole, been diametrically opposed to policies in other countries that advocate a "war on drugs." Two basic elements of the Dutch policy are decriminalization of use and retail trade in marijuana and hashish as a means to keep young people from experimenting with drugs such as heroin and cocaine. This "separation of the markets" policy is viewed as having been quite successful. Recently, the Dutch have attempted to "normalize" their drug problems by reducing recrimination across the board. Some feel that this minimizes harm to users and to the Dutch society, aside from also helping to prevent the spread of AIDS. See Henk Jan van Vliet, "Separation of Drug Markets and other Normalization of Drug Problems in the Netherlands: An Example for Other Nations?" *The Journal of Drug Issues* 30:3(Summer): 463-71.

[24]Sanjoy Hazarika discusses these points ["Heroin Addiction Big New Problem in India," *The New York Times*, 1987]. See also D. Mohan et al., "Changing Trends in Heroin Abuse in India: An Assessment Based on Treatment Records," *Bulletin on Narcotics*, 1985.

[25]D. Corrigan, "Drug Abuse in the Republic of Ireland: An Overview," *Bulletin on Narcotics*, 1986.

[26]Barbara Crossette, "Addiction Rising among Vietnamese Youth," *The New York Times*, 1988.

[27]Patrice Gaines-Carter, "Crack Sends Some Drug Users Backsliding into Arms of Heroin," *The Washington Post*, 1989.

[28]Michel Marriott, "Latest Drug of Choice for Abusers Brings New Generation to Heroin," *The New York Times*, 1989.

[29]Refers to note [a] in Figure 12. The general caveats for all these NIDA-based tables (derived from NIDA, *National Household Survey on Drug Abuse*, annually) are to be found in note 29 in Chapter 1 of this handbook. Additionally, please observe that the exclusion of nonhousehold populations is a particularly acute problem with heroin use data, as many heroin users would be found among transients. Consequently, the survey probably underestimates heroin use. Another problem particularly affecting these estimates is sampling error caused by small numbers of respondents reporting heroin use .

[30]Refers to note [b] in Figure 12. In addition to the general considerations for all these NIDA graphs discussed in note 30 of Chapter 1, consider the following: Ideally, only respondents reporting use in the past year are used to indicate trends of use. However, the small sample size prevents any accurate estimation of heroin use frequency. Consequently, the above numbers are estimates of those who have ever used heroin, which may or may not reflect the number of current users. In fact, decreases in the household population of lifetime users may conceivably reflect increases in the transient population

currently using heroin.

[31]Lloyd Garrison, "Let Them Shoot Smack," *Time*, 1984; and Steven Erlanger, "In Malaysia and Singapore, A Mixed Drug Picture," *The New York Times*, 1989. Before 1980, heroin was virtually unknown and unavailable in Pakistan. By 1985 Pakistan was recognized as the world's leading heroin exporter [Terence White, "The Drug-Abuse Epidemic Coursing through Pakistan," *Far Eastern Economic Review*, 1985].

[32]D. P. Kumarasingha, "Drugs—A Growing Problem in Sri Lanka," *Forensic Science International*, 1988; and N. Mendis, "Heroin Addiction among Young People: A New Development in Sri Lanka," *Bulletin on Narcotics*, 1985.

[33]Kedar Man Singh, "A Taste of Smack," *Far Eastern Economic Review*, 1986. The Kingdom of Nepal has also been rocked by the arrest of high-ranking aids and authorities, including a national police superintendent, on charges of corruption and drug smuggling. The integrity of the famed Gurkha troops is also thought to have been impinged [Rone Tempest, "Drugs, Murder Attempt, Corruption Rob Peaceful Nepal of Its Innocence," *The Los Angeles Times*, 1987]. All this has facilitated the spread of illicit drugs in Nepal, even to school children.

[34]United Nations Secretariat, Division of Narcotic Drugs," Review of Drug Abuse and Measures to Reduce the Illicit Demand for Drugs by Region, *Bulletin on Narcotics*, 1987. In addition, Arnold S. Trebach documents "The Enigmatic Epidemic" worldwide in his 1982 volume [*The Heroin Solution*].

[35]Charas Suwanela and Vichai Poshyachinda, "Drug Abuse in Asia," *Bulletin on Narcotics*, 1986. For additional discussion of this controversial matter, see Joseph Westermeyer, "The Pro-Heroin Effects of Anti-Opium Laws in Asia," *Arch. Gen. Psychiatry*, 1976.

[36]The citation comes from John Kaplan, *The Hardest Drug*, 1983, p. 22.

3

Cannabis

Cannabis[1] (*Cannabis sativa L.*) is a hemp plant that appears in several wild and cultivated varieties. The plant's psychoactive narcotic—tetrahydrocannabinol (THC)—is consumed as hashish (resin extracted from the flower clusters and top leaves of hemp varieties grown generally in hot, moist climates) and marijuana (a cheaper and less concentrated substance obtained from the top flowers, leaves, and stems of plants usually grown in drier and colder climates). The coarse fiber produced by the tall plant is used for cordage and in making paper, canvas, oakum (a caulking fiber), and other products. The plant is native to Asia, but now grows in most parts of the world.[2]

Most of the world's marijuana is grown in the Western Hemisphere, mostly in Mexico (see Figure 13),[3] in part because of easier access to the U.S. market. Aside from its own significant domestic production (California and Kentucky), marijuana entering the U.S. market comes principally from Mexico, followed by Colombia and Jamaica. Jamaica's relative contribution of 835 tons in 1990 is not significant. But it may become so. Although Jamaica met its 1989 goal of eradicating more than 1,500 hectares of cannabis plants, production then soared in 1990, from 190 tons to 835 tons. Belize continues to experience

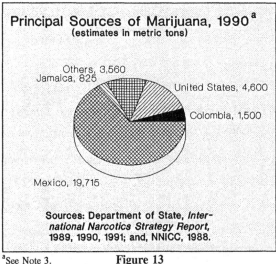

Principal Sources of Marijuana, 1990[a]
(estimates in metric tons)

Others, 3,560
Jamaica, 825
United States, 4,600
Colombia, 1,500
Mexico, 19,715

Sources: Department of State, *International Narcotics Strategy Report*, 1989, 1990, 1991; and, NNICC, 1988.

[a]See Note 3.   **Figure 13**

production declines; its current estimated annual production of 60 tons is not significant in the international market.

Production increased dramatically in Colombia and in the United States between 1986 and 1988 (see Figure 14), and it may still be increasing in the United States although the statistics we have reviewed are inconclusive. Between 1988 and 1989 large tracts of Colombian marijuana fields were eradicated by aerial spraying programs. By 1990 the Colombian contribution to the world's marijuana supply had declined substantially.

Mexico is the striking anomaly; its 1989 production estimates are nearly six times those of 1988. While real production may well have increased in Mexico, it is more likely that the United States has previously underestimated Mexico's marijuana production.[4] The revised Mexican estimates highlight the impreciseness of production statistics regarding all illicit drugs. All this aside, in 1990 Mexico carried out an aggressive marijuana eradication program that reduced marijuana cultivation by perhaps 15 percent. This appeared to account for a production decrease during the 1990 crop year.

Lebanon, Pakistan, Afghanistan, and Morocco are the principal producers of hashish (see Figure 15). As with marijuana, hashish production increased between 1988 and 1989, but then fell precipitously (see Figure 16). Lebanon's contribution was cut drastically. Weather and civil strife are thought to have contributed to the reduction. Significant stockpiling from the previous year is also thought to have depressed the 1990 crop. However, as drug-control observers have not been given access to Lebanese ports, all the estimates are subject to a wide margin of error, which emphasizes, once again, their tenuous nature.

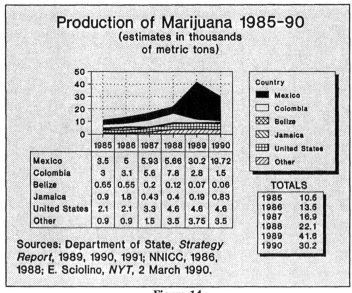

Figure 14

Cannabis in its many prepared forms has been used for thousands of years.[5] Marijuana, ganja,[6] hashish, and hashish oil[7] are all used now. The multipurpose hemp plant itself has accompanied the migrations of peoples over oceans and across continents, resulting in a nearly universal distribution. Recent genetic developments have both reduced its climatic limitations and increased

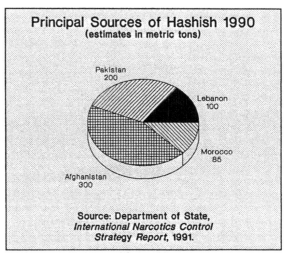

Figure 15

the potency of its psychoactive properties.[8] As it now finds its home, both as grown and as consumed, in most countries of the world, and, as it continues to be valued for its pharmacological effects, it has widespread use. The 1990 household survey in the United States, for example, showed that 10.2 percent of the population had used the drug within the past year[9] even though overall consumption of cannabis in America has been declining in recent years (see Figure 17).[10] Cannabis production appears to have

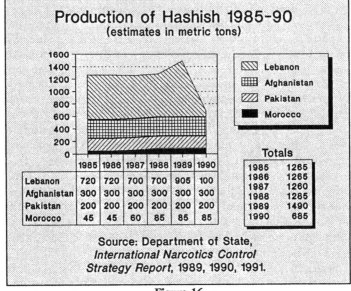

Figure 16

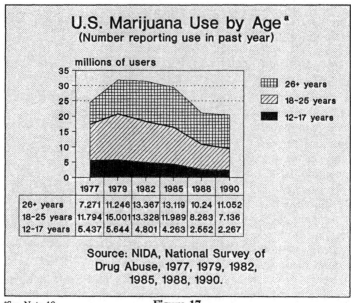

U.S. Marijuana Use by Age[a]
(Number reporting use in past year)

millions of users

	1977	1979	1982	1985	1988	1990
26+ years	7.271	11.246	13.367	13.119	10.24	11.052
18-25 years	11.794	15.001	13.328	11.989	8.283	7.136
12-17 years	5.437	5.644	4.801	4.263	2.552	2.267

Source: NIDA, National Survey of
Drug Abuse, 1977, 1979, 1982,
1985, 1988, 1990.

[a]See Note 10   **Figure 17**

fallen (see Figures 14 and 16) consistent with a reduced U.S. market. This
may be compelling evidence that new markets in other countries are not
being opened rapidly, or that crop eradication practices are taking their toll.

Whether cannabis use is beneficial, prejudicial, or simply benign with
respect to individuals and society is an ever-continuing debate. Thus the
cannabis use literature is highly diverse. Some of it points to historical use
patterns in given cultural or subcultural settings, thereby raising arguments
that may be specific to history and culture. For example, cannabis use in
Jamaica, in Costa Rica among some of the country's lower classes, and
among some groups in Greece, Africa, and India has long been sanctioned
by attitudes about ritual, social exchange, or empirical medicine that are
strongly imbedded in the cultural psyche of the respective peoples.[11] By
contrast, although some countries have exhibited a more subdued embrace
of cannabis, their social fabric has nevertheless exhibited a "culture of tolerance" which, while not as tenacious as drug use encouragement deriving
from religio-cultural symbolism, has nevertheless encouraged the use of
cannabis and perhaps other illicit drugs. For example, in the United States,
some drug use has been culturally sanctioned. Until recently, tobacco smoking was a cultural practice of widespread acceptance; it continues to be so
in Mexico and Russia. In all three countries alcohol consumption is generally
legal, although of an increasing public concern. Such "cultural allowances"
blur the boundaries under discussion here.

In cultures that disapprove of mind-altering drugs, chronic cannabis users
are viewed negatively and take on the social status of cultural outcasts.[12]
When social attitudes are less critical of drug use, negative perceptions of

cannabis users are also less.[13] The same relationship apparently holds when social perceptions are in a state of flux or transformation. Current trends, somewhat contradictory, are instructive. Whether the Dutch, on the whole, give cultural approval to drug use is not known to this reviewer, but the Netherlands now permits nearly unfettered use of cannabis; people flock there in droves to satisfy their curiosity about the drug if not to become chronic consumers.[14] In the United States, where cannabis use has had a strong negative appeal to the majority of citizens, several states nevertheless have, for a time, decriminalized its use.[15] A major observer of the cannabis scene predicts that the future of cannabis in America "will inevitably be that of decriminalization and eventual legalization, subject no doubt to the same regulatory measures as those that apply to alcohol."[16]

With respect to cocaine and heroin, their psychopharmacological (and perhaps associated cultural) effects appear to account for the frenetic desire some people have for them. What is so attractive about cannabis? The attractiveness is euphoria—a feeling of great happiness or well-being. Users report a heightened sensitivity to colors, shapes, and other external stimuli such as music and the pleasurable company of friends, including, some have thought, sexual partners.[17] There is a considerable distortion in the sense of time. Some observers note that chemically induced euphoria may be particularly attractive—thereby leading to sustained or chronic use—to individuals and groups for whom normal life does not offer nonchemically induced conditions for such enjoyment.[18] One former male user expressed his first experience with marijuana this way:

> The music seemed more beautiful. Everything just seemed so happy and mellow. It was very comforting. Colors seemed more vibrant. It seemed, in a sense, as if maybe it was free from the sort of grimness and painfulness of normal life . . . I mean it was a different, different world. All more vivid and glowing and what not. . . . In many ways, life today is so unpleasant and so full of hassles, so full of many negative things—lots of pressures and stresses—and so ugly in so many ways, that it's hard to blame somebody if they all of a sudden think that they have found something that is much more beautiful and gives them this kind of pleasure that is so different from anything they've ever seen before, where everything seems so nice and harmonious. Gosh—it's pretty tempting![19]

Insofar as life's sadness, disappointments, structural impediments to goal realization, influence of peer groups, upbringing, personal tragedies, personality, or genetic makeup may be contributory to peoples' attraction to cannabis, there are hardly any convincing theories that would adequately take all these factors into consideration. Most studies therefore speak only in "personality-specific" and "social-specific" variables that seem to correlate with cannabis use but which, of themselves, may offer little causal explanation.[20] Moreover, as already pointed out, the variables themselves may be culture specific to some extent. In some countries marijuana is used because it is the custom to use marijuana (see the cross-cultural discussion in note 11).

While cannabis use poses problems for societies regardless of its legality, the social consequences associated with its use, as we will see in Section B, are of small magnitude compared to those of heroin and cocaine.

NOTES

[1]Ernest L. Abel appears to be the most prolific bibliographer of drugs, cannabis included [i.e., *A Comprehensive Guide to the Cannabis Literature*, 1979; *Drugs and Sex: A Bibliography*, 1983; and, *Narcotics and Reproduction: A Bibliography*, 1983]. Meyer D. Glantz has edited a volume [*Correlates and Consequences of Marijuana Use*, 1984] intended to provide researchers with a survey of literature through the early 1980s on the psychological and social correlates and consequences of marijuana use, excluding, on the whole, biomedical literature. Following his review essay, abstracts of 127 articles of representative and significant research and theory on the topic are reproduced. Oriana Josseau Kalant et al. present 1,718 annotated entries cross-referenced in numerous categories [*Cannabis: Health Risks. A Comprehensive Annotated Bibliography (1844-1982)*, 1983]. Criteria for including articles in their bibliography were simply that they "dealt with, claimed, or clearly demonstrated adverse effects of cannabis on health." Papers from the social sciences and those dealing with legal or political issues are not included. Coy Waller and others have produced a series of volumes that include the pharmacology of marijuana and related pharmaceutical issues [*Marijuana: An Annotated Bibliography*, 1971, 1972, 1976, 1982, 1983)].

[2]William Harris and Judith Levey, eds., *The New Columbia Encyclopedia*, 1975.

[3]Refers to Figure 13. The U. S. Department of State's *International Narcotics Control Strategy Report* does not include, in its "Worldwide Production Totals" any marijuana grown in the United States. The National Narcotics Intelligence Consumers Committee Report of 1988 [*The NNICC Report of 1988: The Supply of Illicit Drugs to the United States*] gives U.S. production at 4,600 tons, which may have increased, but most probably not declined, in later years [see "Marijuana Crop: Moonshine Again," *The Economist*, 1990]. We have carried the 1988 estimates on.

[4]The U.S. Department of State, Bureau of International Narcotics Matters, *International Narcotics Control Strategy Report*, 1990, p. 13 states: "In 1989, approximately 58,000 hectares of marijuana were estimated to be under cultivation in Mexico. New analytic methodologies have enabled the U.S. Government to assess more accurately the extent of marijuana cultivation, and to revise upward the amount of marijuana believed under cultivation during the past several years." The 1991 report shows a 1990 crop-year figure of 35,050 hectares.

[5]Ernest L. Abel looks at its history [*Marijuana: The First Twelve Thousand Years*, 1980]; Brian M. du Toit [*Cannabis in Africa*, 1980] gives a historical perspective on Africa; and Anthony Henman and Osvaldo Pessoa, Jr., add medical, juridical, and anthropological observations in their historical treatment of cannabis in Brazil [*Diamba Sarabamba*, 1986].

[6]Ganja is a variety of cannabis used in Jamaica. See, for example, the discussions by Melanie C. Dreher, "Poor and Pregnant: Perinatal Ganja Use in Rural Jamaica," *Advances in Alcohol and Substance Abuse*, 1989; Vera Rubin and Lambros Comitas, *Ganja in Jamaica: Medical Anthropological Study of Chronic Marihuana Use*, 1975; Gabriel G. Nahas, "Critique of a Study on Ganja in Jamaica," *Bulletin on Narcotics*, 1985 (Nahas criticizes the methodological limitations in the sampling technique in the

Rubin and Comitas study, the small number in the sample, and the philosophical premises that dispose the authors to view cannabis smoking as having socially beneficial properties); and Jeff Stein, "Free-Market Magic: Jamaica Has Gone to Ganja," *The Washington Post*, 1984.

[7]Hashish oil is a concentration of the basic active ingredient in cannabis—tetrahydrocannabinol (THC). The basic production principle appears to be similar to that of percolating coffee. Only simple equipment is required. The THC concentration in this oil may be as high as 90 percent [U.S. Department of Justice, *Liquid Hashish*, 1986]. Hashish oil has made a substantial penetration of the cannabis market in Canada [Rodney T. Stamler, Robert C. Fahlman, and S. A. Keele, "Illicit Traffic and Abuse of Cannabis in Canada," *Bulletin on Narcotics*, 1985] as well as in the United States where it first appeared in the early 1970s.

[8]For a discussion of the improvements in plant genetics and horticultural techniques that have permitted marijuana to be produced as a commercial crop in the majority of states in America, where it has exceeded commercial food crops in cash value in many agricultural areas, see U.S. Congress, House Committee on Government Operations, "Commercial Production and Distribution of Domestic Marijuana," 1983.

[9]National Institute on Drug Abuse, *National Household Survey on Drug Abuse: Population Estimates*, 1990.

[10]The same caveats addressed in notes 29 and 30 of Chapter 1 on cocaine also apply to this NIDA-based graph.

[11]In Costa Rica, one study found significant differences in behavior between users and nonusers of cannabis to be highly correlated with different ki..ds of socialization experiences. The differences did not appear to be adequately explained by marijuana use alone [William E. Carter and Paul L. Doughty, "Social and Cultural Aspects of Cannabis Use in Costa Rica," *Annals of the New York Academy of Sciences*, 1976; and also William E. Carter, ed., *Cannabis in Costa Rica: A Study of Chronic Marihuana Use*, 1980]. However, a follow-up study showed that Costa Rican marijuana smokers, on the whole, are lodged in the bottom strata of a society that has a pervasive disapproval of marijuana smoking. This poses problems for lower strata marijuana smokers who, aside from problems derived from smoking the drug, have greater problems with kin and family, are more vulnerable to arrest and imprisonment, are viewed as being untrustworthy and undesirable, and have difficulty both in obtaining and in retaining employment [J. Bryan Page, Jack Fletcher, and William R. True, "Psychosociocultural Perspectives on Chronic Cannabis Use: The Costa Rican Follow-Up," *Journal of Psychoactive Drugs*, 1988]. In Jamaica it was found that the use of ganja in reducing the physiological symptoms of pregnancy and associated psychological stress had cultural reinforcements that may actually mitigate ganja's potentially harmful effects [Melanie C. Dreher, "Poor and Pregnant: Perinatal Ganja Use in Rural Jamaica," *Advances in Alcohol and Substance Abuse*, 1989]. In any event, in Jamaica, marijuana use in pregnancy carries social overtones of reenforcement, mutual aid and help, and conviviality. Newborn babies are cared for and are stimulated. Some think that marijuana used in pregnancy under these cultural and social-environmental conditions must be viewed differently from marijuana used under other circumstances when examining newborn outcomes. The care-giving environment may have a greater effect on the positive development of the infant than the single effects of marijuana use during pregnancy [Janice S. Hayes, Melanie C. Dreher, and J. Kevin Nugent, "Newborn Outcomes with Maternal Marihuana Use in Jamaican Women," *Pediatric Nursing*, 1988]. Many Black African students in South Africa use cannabis in ways that evoke strong continuities of ritual, medicinal, and contextual uses

of the drug that appear to mitigate many adverse social effects experienced by other ethnic groups [Brian M. du Toit, *Drug Use and South African Students*, 1978]. Other studies of interest on this cultural topic include Jerome L. Himmelstein, *The Strange Case of Marijuana: Politics and Ideology of Drug Control in America*, 1983; Patricia J. Morningstar, "Thandai and Chilam: Traditional Hindu Beliefs about the Proper Uses of Cannabis," *Journal of Psychoactive Drugs*, 1985; Vera Rubin, *Cannabis and Culture*, 1975; Vera Rubin and Lambros Comitas, *Ganja in Jamaica: Medical Anthropological Study of Chronic Marihuana Use*, 1975; and, Costas Stefanis, Rhea Dornbush, and Max Fink, eds., *Hashish: Studies of Long-Term Use* [in Greece], 1977.

[12]On this point, see John Auld's study of the U.S. social reaction in the early 1970s to marijuana use [*Marijuana Use and Social Control*, 1981].

[13]For example, Jerome L. Himmelstein ["From Killer Weed to Drop-out Drug: The Changing Ideology of Marihuana," *Contemporary Crises*, 1983; and, Himmelstein, "The Continuing Career of Marijuana: Backlash . . . Within Limits, *Contemporary Drug Problems*, 1986] documents the early 1980s' shift in public attitude about marijuana in the United States which saw it gain more acceptance and less opprobrium within American society. The social status of the actor appears to determine the moral status of the act. Marijuana, increasingly used by middle- and upper-class citizens, began to be associated with a decrease in the intensity of the attacks against it. Nevertheless, there has now been a small backlash; American tolerance is apparently declining. Several states that had decriminalized marijuana use are now reversing their stand, including Oregon, which pioneered marijuana use decriminalization in 1973 [Mark A. Stein, "Recriminalization: Lenient Pot Laws Going up in Smoke," *The Los Angeles Times*, 1989].

[14]The best short review coming to our attention is Govert F. Van de Wijngaart's, "A Social History of Drug Use in the Netherlands: Policy Outcomes and Implications," *Journal of Drug Issues*, 1988. See also Henk Jan van Vliet, "Separation of Drug Markets and the Normalization of Drug Problems in the Netherlands: An Example for Other Nations?" *The Journal of Drug Issues*, 1990.

[15]In the 1970s, eleven states decriminalized the possession of small amounts of marijuana for personal use (that is, the laws that required jail sentences and a permanent criminal record were repealed and simple possession became punishable by a fine only). Every state maintained stiff penalties for commercial growers and traffickers. Extended discussion on this issue may be found in Paul H. Blachly, "Effects of Decriminalization of Marijuana in Oregon," *Annals of the New York Academy of Sciences*, 1976; Eric Josephson, "Marijuana Decriminalization: The Processes and Prospects of Change," *Contemporary Drug Problems*, 1981; and David L. Suggs, "A Qualitative and Quantitative Analysis of the Impact of Nebraska's Decriminalization of Marijuana," *Law and Human Behavior*, 1981. One ought to temper any academic observations by the political fact that recriminalization efforts have begun or have been successful in seven states (California, Oregon, Alaska, Colorado, Maine, Nebraska, and North Carolina) [Mark A. Stein, "Recriminalization: Lenient Pot Laws Going up in Smoke," *The Los Angeles Times*, 1989].

[16]Ernest L. Abel, *Marihuana, The First Twelve Thousand Years*, 1980, p. 271.

[17]Ernest L. Abel [*Marijuana, Tobacco, Alcohol, and Reproduction*, 1983] affirms that marijuana consumption is unquestionably associated with increased sexual activity for many individuals, but increased sex may have less to do with marijuana than with the expectations associated with its use. The evidence either way appears to be somewhat inconclusive. Abel's bibliography [*Drugs and Sex: A Bibliography*, 1983] includes a section on marijuana. See also the discussions by James A. Halikas et al., "A

Longitudinal Study of Marijuana Effects," *The International Journal of the Addictions*, 1985; and Helen C. Jones and Paul W. Lovinger, *The Marijuana Question and Science's Search for an Answer*, 1985.

[18]It is this presumption that drives much of the "development" literature dealing with America's inner cities. Remove the "causes" of despair (through economic development) and drug use will decline. It is also a presumption consistent with the research findings of several authors; however, the correlations seem to be most persuasive with heroin. See, for example, Geoffrey Pearson, "Social Deprivation, Unemployment, and Patterns of Heroin Use," in *A Land Fit for Heroin? Drug Policies, Prevention and Practice*, Nicholas Dorn and Nigel South, eds., 1987.

[19]Cited in Helen C. Jones and Paul W. Lovinger, *The Marijuana Question and Science's Search for an Answer*, 1985, p. 1.

[20]In an important review of the literature, Margaret Penning and Gordon E. Barnes ["Adolescent Marijuana Use: A Review," *International Journal of the Addictions*, 1982] identified personality-specific and social-specific variables that might account for the increased use of marijuana among some American high school students and high school dropouts; special notes consider the increasing number of female users. As for social-specific variables, mixed support has been found for family situations that are predictive. Parents of U.S. marijuana users are generally characterized as being less loving and supportive and more inclined toward the use of drugs themselves. They also tend to be more permissive. Peer and sibling use of marijuana also seem to be particularly important predictors of adolescent marijuana use. Findings on personality characteristics of marijuana users are not extensive and are somewhat contradictory. Richard H. Schwartz ["Frequent Marijuana Use in Adolescence: What Are the Signs, Stages?" *NASSP Bulletin*, 1985] found the precursor signs that placed adolescents at risk to be estrangement from family, moodiness, deterioration in moral values, apathy, shift in peer group allegiance to a drug using clique, academic underachievement, school attendance problems, and defense of drugs and drug culture. As is readily apparent, much of the "precursor" literature is "soft" and inconclusive.

B

Consequences

A substantial international demand for psychoactive drugs, coupled with their illegality, present compelling incentives on two fronts. The first is to supply the market; the second is to suppress it or at least to prevent its being provisioned. Money drives the incentive to supply the market; moral, utilitarian, political, ideological, and pragmatic views drive the incentive to suppress it. In the supply category, drug traffickers invoke their profit imperatives. In the suppression category, national governments, international and regional organizations, drug-enforcement agencies, law-enforcement personnel, national guards, religious leaders, militaries, politicians, educators, media experts, employers, and parents struggle to exercise countervailing influences that combine moderate to severe sanctions, drug education, and social and parental pleading. All the measures are designed to reduce demand, to control supply, to suppress traffic, and to deal in some reasonable way with drug addicts.

The countervailing efforts are sometimes logical, sometimes irrational, sometimes frenzied—but nearly always intense. In producer countries, international and domestic efforts invoke the full spectrum of law enforcement and drug control strategies, including crop eradication, control of precursor chemicals, crop substitution, disruption of major trafficking networks, asset forfeitures, techniques of controlled delivery, facilitation of extradition of drug traffickers, controls over ships and aircraft in international space, and surveillance of land, water, and air approaches to the frontier. Sometimes economic incentives are included to encourage producer-country growers to abandon their coca bushes, opium poppies, and cannabis plants. On occasion, these economic incentives are coupled with integrated rural development strategies.

All internationally invoked strategies within producer countries are directed toward controlling illicit drug supply and suppressing illicit international trafficking before the products ever reach the principal consuming nations. Of course, principal producer countries are also experiencing increasing domestic psychoactive drug use, and many producer nations have therefore devised internal policies to deal with this trend.

In the principal consuming countries, law enforcement efforts are expended to heighten trafficker and user risk—through network disruption, interdiction, asset forfeiture, "stings," surveillance, criminal prosecution, detention—and to implement educational and other programs to convince people voluntarily to reduce their illicit drug use. These "negative" and "positive" sanctions are intended to reduce supply and demand.

The intense efforts to supply drugs and vigorous efforts to control drug supply and consumption in most parts of the world would not exist without, on the one hand, consumer demand for psychoactive drugs and, on the other, policies that illegalize consumption. The rise of a new genre of organized trafficker to service demand, and the increased implementation of countervailing initiatives to suppress demand and supply, constitute, therefore, the first round of consequences of the twin factors of drug demand and drug illegality.

The imperatives: An illegal market must be supplied; it must be suppressed. The effects infiltrate the social, economic, and political fabric of nations, course the environment, and affect personal lives throughout most of today's world. Flow Chart 1 suggests the causal sequence this discussion implies.

Flow Chart 1
Consequences of Psychoactive Drug Demand,
Supply, and Illegalizing Policies

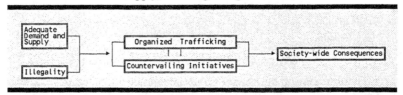

Supply efforts and suppression policies create notable intended and unintended effects. However, as we explore in Chapter 6, demand or consumption—illegality aside—independently leads to several society-wide consequences.

Some of the numerous possible "consequence permutations" of these relationships among demand, supply, and supplier are intimated in Tables 1 and 2. The tables distinguish effects in net producer from net consumer countries. They focus on consequences from market demand, drug control policies, and traffickers' activities. In the drug control policy categories they require us to distinguish between intended and unintended consequences of control policies designed for domestic application. They encourage us to reflect on the consequences of proffered consumer-country policies to control supplies and to suppress traffic at the drug trails' origins in producer countries (Table 1). In those net producer countries, drug control policies must be distinguished as to their domestic effects and their impact on supplies for the international market (Table 2).

As illustrations, among the many likely candidates for cell 25, Table 2 (which represents the unintended, unforseen consequences of international drug-control policies applied in drug-producing countries), is a substantial incentive for organized crime to take over the drug supplying business. Small-scale smuggling of the product into principal consumer countries cannot meet the demand. Prices thus rise, therefore attracting the attention of existing crime syndicates and motivating others to devise ways by which the lucrative trade can be undertaken. On the other hand, cell 1 in both tables focuses on the social consequences of market demand independent of the effects of drug control policies. Likely candidates for cell 11 include effects of drugs on fetuses, changes in social values, and declining school attendance.

Table 1
Predominant Consequences of Illicit Drug Trade in Net Consumer Countries

| | From Market Demand | From Drug Control Policies | | | | From Drug Traffickers |
| | | For Domestic Applictn | | For Internatl Applictn^ | | |
		In*	Un+	In*	Un+	
Social	1	6	11	16	21	26
Economic	2	7	12	17	22	27
Political	3	8	13	18	23	28
Environmental	4	9	14	19	24	29
Personal	5	10	15	20	25	30

^Consumer country intentions to control supplies and suppress traffic in producer countries.
*Intended Consequences.
+Unintended Consequences.

Table 2
Predominant Consequences of Illicit Drug Trade in Net Producer Countries

| | From Market Demand | | From Drug Control Policies | | | | From Drug Traffickers |
| | Domestic | Internatl | For Domestic Market | | For Internatl Market^ | | |
			In*	Un+	In*	Un+	
Social	1	6	11	16	20	25	30
Economic	2	7	12	17	21	26	31
Political	3	8	13	18	22	27	32
Environmental	4	9	14	19	23	28	33
Personal	5	10	15	20	24	29	34

^Application at behest of consumer countries to control supplies and suppress traffic.
*Intended Consequences.
+Unintended Consequences.

Cell 6 of Table 1 focuses on the *intended* effects of domestic drug control policies in net user countries (e.g., demand reduction, traffic suppression), and cell 11 on the *unintended* consequences. Issues advanced for this cell include AIDS, street crime, and user victimization.

Moving to net producer countries, cell 6, Table 2 (focusing on the social consequences in net producer countries of international market demand) calls our attention to topics such as new role models, social mobility, the new rich, and migration; cell 16 to organized crime, illegally derived fortunes and their subsequent use, and corruption. Among unintended social consequences of *international* drug control policies (cell 25, Table 2) are the creation of an international narcotics mafia; a developing alliance of political insurgents, terrorists, and peasant growers into an antistate; and selective retention of criminal elements in the wake of regional and national flight from drug-related violence.

As these tables suggest, the literature on illicit drugs not only advances assorted interpretations of the ills of demand, it also focuses on the ills and benefits deriving from illegalizing drugs, from ensuing drug control initiatives, and from the behavior of traffickers themselves. Accordingly, Tables 1 and 2 offer helpful matrices to sort out some of the literature on the consequences that derive from drug demand, the domestic and international control strategies being applied in net consumer and producer countries, and the way in which the market is supplied. The tables also encourage us to examine unintended as well as intended consequences of drug control policies and to be cognizant as to whether the policies are failing or are successful in their intended functions. All these consequences are inexorably intertwined in the linkages among demand, supply, illegality, and public policy.

In Section B we focus on the social, political, and economic consequences deriving from meeting and disrupting supply—that is, on the rise of new organized traffickers and on the implementation of drug control policies intended to thwart their business—and on society-wide consequences deriving from demand. We make incidental mention of environmental and personal consequences when these drive other aggregate dimensions suggested in Table 1. The information is therefore developed around traffickers, drug control response (countervailing initiatives), and market demand.

4

Rise of a New Genre
of Organized Trafficker

The illegal drug trade has attracted dissimilar people driven by paramount commonalities—money and power. Although their goals are the same, their operations are not, and these have produced divergent drug-distribution patterns. These divergent patterns impose contrasting effects on the economies and societies of nations. It is therefore useful to describe current patterns so that subsequently we may more adequately address their consequences.

We repeat an important caveat. Although scholarly works on traffickers are increasingly available, because of fast-paced recent events information on current traffickers comes mostly from the responsible press. The discussion below is intended to examine the range of issues surrounding traffickers as reported in the press and in scholarly works that are now appearing. By its nature, the press tends to focus on the spectacular, and frequently the reports tend not to be analytically integrated into countries' larger political, social, and economic issues. (Several correspondents for *The New York Times*, *The Christian Science Monitor*, and other major papers are exceptions to this observation). Nevertheless, the press does report events, and these become an important "data set"—sometimes the only one—from which an analysis may derive. The following review should therefore not be read as an attempt to develop a systematic view on the referenced countries' global social, economic, and political states of affairs. It is an exploration of drug-related events as reported in the responsible press and scholarly literature, developed within the context of considering political, economic, and social consequences that appear to derive from traffickers' movement of illicit drugs. These consequences, and their classification in this chapter, do signal areas for considerable scholarly research. Much of that research is now underway by scholars throughout the world and will be reported in journals and books in due course.

Drug trafficker patterns considered important to this handbook are both significant and distinguishable in five areas: first, the level of activity (whether traffickers are wholesalers, middlemen, or retailers); second, the degree of organization (e.g., whether they have payrolls or enforceable "personnel policies," develop specialized departments, have vertical integration, build or struggle over regional or countrywide market shares); third, the type of drug being dealt; fourth, the existence of any alliance of the traffickers with insurgent or terrorist groups; and, fifth, the way in which organized traffickers approach market competition over market shares.

Early in the current drug use wave, much drug distribution was akin to a cottage industry—small-time traffickers, including tourists, picking up a few hundred grams of heroin or cocaine or a kilo of marijuana from a producer and distributing the product directly to casual but trusted contacts and personal friends, who in turn passed along small amounts, some of it for financial gain. Some of the traffic is still carried out that way. However, trafficking is increasingly organized, particularly at the production, wholesale, and middleman levels, pronouncedly so for cocaine and heroin (apparently less so for marijuana). This appears to have pushed most of the small-time dealers into strictly retail street sales. Even here there is evidence that organization is taking place, at least in the United States, where isolated cottage industry street vendors, who buy from a wholesaler and then peddle their wares, may be in decline in favor of more elaborate distribution networks. For example, some dealers now use children as fronts in order to take advantage of lenient juvenile crime laws, even when children are heavily and purposefully engaged in adult crimes.[1]

Some large, vertically integrated, multinational, illicit drug-distribution organizations existed as early as the 1930s. For example, the French Connection (between refiners and traffickers headquartered in Marseilles and opium growers in Turkey) supplied heroin to American addicts from the 1930s until 1973, when the connection was terminated by an international law enforcement effort that not only destroyed the French laboratories but ultimately also put Turkish opium growers out of business.[2] The resulting shortage of heroin enabled Mexican, Pakistani, and Asian traffickers to penetrate the American market as well as to increase production in order to cover supply shortages elsewhere.[3]

Other early drug-pushing organizations that met their demise or fell on hard times can be mentioned. The Sicilian "Pizza Connection" fell in 1984 as a consequence of law enforcement efforts. The participants were obscure Sicilian pizza men, bakers, and contractors operating in the United States independently of their American mob counterparts. They masterminded the flow of heroin into the United States and laundered money through their pizza parlors for Swiss bank accounts.[4]

One loose-knit group making money from smuggling marijuana into the United States was "The Company." As of 1984, law enforcement penetration of this group was the largest ever in terms of the number of indicted defendants, the size of asset forfeitures to the government, and the area covered by law enforcement covert operations.[5]

Of course, the main American Sicilian mafia dealing in drugs continues on, damaged from time to time, but nevertheless highly effective, particularly in the heroin market where it controls a worldwide network. The Sicilian mafia is also trying to carve out territorial control for itself in several cocaine markets.[6]

While the French, Pizza, Company, and other connections have been put out of business by law enforcement efforts or were eclipsed by later comers—there being no shortage of people willing to organize to meet market demand[7]—the old Sicilian mafia lives on. So also do a good many later comers: the Chinese Triads,[8] which are beginning to replace traditional organized crime networks in the Asian heroin market;[9] the Mexican mafia, which specializes in cocaine, marijuana, and Mexican heroin;[10] the Colombian cocaine cartels, which, although somewhat loosely structured, nevertheless export violence along with their product and efficient organization wherever they operate;[11] the Japanese Yakuza, which are now pushing narcotics (heroin, principally), with networks in Hawaii and the western United States;[12] the Jamaican Posses, who have a high propensity for violence and like to traffic in large volumes of drugs (wholesale and retail) and firearms throughout the United States and the Caribbean;[13] the Aryan brotherhood and the Texas syndicate;[14] and additional statewide as well as many small regional groups. The first U.S. federal reports on the corporate structure of the illegal drug trade identified forty-three major groups operating in the United States.[15] Organized groups now involve rural operatives and Los Angeles street gangs.[16] These later comers are increasingly gravitating to sophisticated organization and distribution techniques, using all the high technology that is currently available to law enforcement agencies as a protective counter-measure to increasingly refined law enforcement efforts.[17]

North America, as a consuming society, appears to be well laced with organized traffickers, both large and small. Heavy consuming societies elsewhere also appear to be undergoing increasing tendencies toward drug traffic organization. One encounters references to Australia where the Chinese Triads are setting up their heroin network,[18] to the United Kingdom where the Triads are also thought to be at work,[19] to Spain and Italy where the Colombians have established "ports of entry" for the rest of Europe and work in collaboration with conventional Italian *mafiosi*,[20] to Holland where pushers in Amsterdam's booming drug market now offer free home delivery,[21] to the Soviet Union whose own peculiar regime of denial and forceful "curtain" vis-à-vis unwanted Western entrants were nevertheless no match for determined drug trafficking organizations, even before the Soviet Union's economic crises weakened its ability at internal control.[22]

Aside from the trafficking organizations that extend into or are based in principal consumer countries, evidence—both hard and soft—of substantial organized production and marketing networks is advanced in the literature for most of the "producer" or "transiting" countries not discussed above—Peru,[23] Bolivia,[24] Burma,[25] Pakistan,[26] Afghanistan,[27] Thailand,[28] and Laos.[29] Sophisticated organizations have either existed or appear to be cropping up in countries "peripheral" to the drug trade—Cuba,[30] Honduras,[31] Venezuela,[32] Brazil,[33] the Bahamas,[34] Paraguay,[35] Costa Rica,[36] West

Africa,[37] Turkey,[38] Canada,[39] Turks and Caicos Islands,[40] Panama,[41] Bulgaria,[42] El Salvador,[43] Argentina,[44] and Haiti.[45]

Given the nearly universal illegality of current trafficking in drugs, it is understandable that the descriptor for organized drug groups is organized crime. The bibliography that constitutes the data set for this handbook includes over one hundred entries with keyword retrieval under "organized crime." Twenty-eight deal with cocaine traffic;[46] twenty are associated with heroin traffic;[47] five concern the distribution of cannabis.[48] The remainder focus generally on the drug traffic and its consequences. Currently, it is difficult to imagine any organized criminal group not having at least a portion of its operations dedicated to drug trafficking; the income is enormous and, at least until recently, additional prospects have been staggering.

As of 1990 there appeared to be a growing tendency for some organized groups (when they were not fighting each other over market shares) to collaborate in cooperative arrangements to facilitate their work. It is reported that New York mafia "families" have strong ties to Colombian and Cuban dealers in the Miami area; they also work with Asian groups, some motorcycle gangs,[49] and the Italian mafia.[50] The so-called Jamaican Posses, with around 10,000 members, traffic not only in marijuana but also in Colombian cocaine; they appear to be developing relationships with Los Angeles street gangs, who are themselves on the move into America's heartland because of increased competition and apparent market saturation in Southern California.[51] The largest and best-known Colombian groups have developed important facilitating arrangements with "five Mexican families" and have a considerable distribution network (involving many Colombian nationals) in the United States and in Western Europe.[52]

Frequently questioned is whether terrorist or insurgent groups are really allied with any of these organizations (or whether the organizations themselves are involved in terrorist activities), to finance their operations, to prosecute an ideological position, to gain political support, or to undermine an existing government. This seems particularly important to sort out, given that the U.S. government has long argued that such links and activities do indeed exist.[53]

A number of terrorist or insurgent organizations—whatever else drives them—deal in drugs for pragmatic reasons.[54] Several, particularly in the coca growing regions of South America, use their support of the cocaine trade to bolster political positions and to acquire operating funds even though they may be ideologically opposed to the drug trade itself.[55] A not-so-ideologically motivated group is protecting the new surge of opium poppy growing in Western Guatemala.[56] Colombian political terrorists are now said to be financing much of their operations through the drug trade, which has caused some "conventional" drug barons to explode in retribution.[57] This has contributed to the "drug terrorism" spawned by the Colombian drug cartels themselves in an effort to find a secure position for themselves in Colombian society.[58] An Ecuadorian terrorist group, which is said to be working in coordination with groups in Colombia and Peru, is also reported to be cooperating with regional drug traffickers.[59] Separatist terrorists in Sri Lanka are said to have become engaged in drug traffic in order to finance their arms and ammunition purchases.[60] The U.S.-supported Contras in Central America were repeatedly accused of linking with drug traffickers in order to supplement their U.S. subsidies,[61] just as the rebels of Afghanistan did during the Soviet Union's occupation of their homeland.[62]

Some Colombian drug cartels are arming peasants in Bolivia in an effort to keep drug production sources open[63] and are even paying Colombian rebel groups, such as M-19 guerrillas, to protect cartel laboratories and to eliminate domestic opposition.[64]

Some insurgent groups, particularly in Burma (Myanmar) and Thailand, are involved in a civil war.[65]

There are even allegations that one government—Bulgaria—has dealt in drugs, weapons, and terrorism in an effort to subvert Western governments in ways that allegedly were orchestrated in Moscow. The matter prompted one U.S. senator to introduce a bill in congress that would direct the U.S. president to conduct a comprehensive review of U.S. policy toward Bulgaria.[66] One author attempts to place the connection of drugs and terrorism into an international perspective that takes into account various kinds of terrorist activities—official, unofficial, and counter-official.[67]

There is fear that the enormous profits from the drug trade will attract terrorist groups into the principal consuming countries, such as the United States.[68] Thus there is concern that the drug/terrorism connection will increasingly encourage such groups to force agendas on governments, destabilize democracies, spawn anarchy, and export revolution.[69]

Those fears notwithstanding, most drug-related terrorist acts in the principal consuming countries still seem to be conducted among and between drug organizations and pushers. They are struggling for market shares and are experiencing heightened internal "leadership challenges" within their ranks.[70] The better organized and perhaps more vertically integrated a group is, the more likely it is to be able to prosecute its interests vigorously. This is particularly so when societies take strong countermeasures to protect their own affairs.

These trafficker activities must be cast against the political fabric of a nation in order to understand their consequences. Where political institutions are relatively strong, traffickers appear to be a troubling but not strongly disrupting influence on national life. In institutionally weak countries, drug traffickers are on center stage and impose a struggle for a nation's institutional life, for discrete subnational territory, and for control over the lives of many citizens. It therefore appears that criminal power resides best with those who can organize and fund the activity of crime and who operate in institutionally weak states.

All this notwithstanding, while currently the cocaine cartels seem to be the most efficient and profitable in their activities, this may derive not so much from impressive marketing organization (the heroin groups likely get the nod here) as from the product they peddle riding waves of increased demand. Moreover, owing to accidents of history and geography, cocaine production is relatively localized (Colombia, Peru, Bolivia), not spread over various regions throughout the world. Vertical integration is therefore more possible, and control, even from "loose cartels," is more easily accomplished. Should the demand for cocaine subside, Colombia's cartels—their profits notwithstanding—would fall on abundantly hard times. In the meantime, however, they are strong enough to be more than just a "troubling influence" on Colombia's national life.

Marijuana traffickers are the least globally organized (even though marijuana is more widely used) which, coincidentally, is associated with marijuana's worldwide production geography ("anybody can grow it") and with what looks to be marijuana traffickers' relatively reduced power against and threat to societies that have criminalized their work.

Drug demand produced the drug marketers; illegality turned them into national and international criminals who have copied the behavior of age-old secret combinations. The social, economic, and political havoc they have heaped on producer and consumer societies has few parallels; in the process, their chiefs and numerous subalterns have become fabulously rich. The secret drug combinations' success lies in part in the relative failure, at least through 1989, of drug control policies intended to cripple their abilities and incapacitate their criminal offshoots.

Consider, again, the cells in Tables 1 and 2 as a point of departure. The intended social effects (cells 6 and 16 in Table 1; cells 11 and 20 in Table 2) of national and international drug control policies are to deprive the traffickers of their base of support by curtailing demand, reducing consumption, and giving growers economic options. The intended political effects (cells 8 and 18 in Table 1; cells 13 and 22 in Table 2) are to orchestrate international agreements to decapitate the organizations' leadership by incarcerating their principals in relatively incorruptible prisons (U.S.) or by hunting them down and destroying or extraditing them (e.g., as in Colombia). The intended economic effects (cells 7 and 17 in Table 1; cells 12 and 21 in Table 2) are to invoke a combination of policies that lower prices and therefore profits, give incentives for alternative grower pursuits, and sequester whatever illegally gotten gains remain. Activities suggested in cells 20, 21, and 22 (Table 2) entail considerable bilateral and even multilateral cooperation. However, despite all the cooperative efforts, the drug trade, with a temporary hiatus now and again, has performed quite well for those who push it.

That the secret combinations continue to flourish is testament to their resiliency, to the relative incapacity of law enforcement and drug control agencies, to the inadequacy of international agreements, to the inappropriateness of present drug control policies, or to the difficulties democracies and even some dictatorships have in implementing scorched-earth responses against corrosive enemies, particularly when the enemies are their own citizens. Unless the international demand for illicit drugs declines substantially, these problems will likely remain.

In Chapter 5 we detail the general failure of antidrug policies to control the traffickers. Here we note some people's view that the Colombian cartels' disarray in the early part of 1990—even employing, apparently, a public relations firm—are a sign that increased international cooperation, greater domestic and international vigilance, and more effective interdiction and drug network disruption are beginning to pay off.[71] This conclusion is, of course, not shared by all as having long-term durability. Nevertheless, important Colombian drug barons have now surrendered to the authorities.[72]

We have discussed the rise of organized traffickers as one consequence of the current interplay among demand, supply, illegality, and antidrug public policy. We now turn our attention to specific effects of this consequence beyond traffickers' simply supplying an illegal market and reaping rewards for so doing.

Most of the literature concentrates on the devastating upheaval the traffickers create, especially in producer countries where they are relatively more powerful vis-à-vis the state. However, aside from reflecting on the traffickers themselves, some of the literature converges on benefits—economic, social, and political—derived by segments of society otherwise outside the pale of power, prestige, and economic security. And, some of the literature notes the general economic boom filtering throughout a nation as a new export commodity gains rapid ascendancy. There are, in short, both beneficiaries and victims, and national benefits and liabilities (see Flow Chart 2).

Flow Chart 2
Traffickers Produce
Both Beneficiaries and Victims

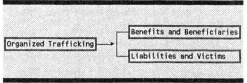

BENEFITS AND BENEFICIARIES

The most vaunted beneficiaries are, of course, the traffickers themselves. Their sudden rise to fortune, their conspicuous consumption, their multiple villas, ranches, retreats, estates, bunkers, hotels, apartment complexes, money-laundering institutions, legitimate businesses, private armies, aircraft, ships, communications equipment, and personal toys (e.g., private zoos) have all been discussed. Sometimes entire communities are beneficiaries. However, what else the traffickers do with their wealth is of increasing concern (e.g., bribing judges and subverting legitimate businesses), a matter we raise later.

Khun Sa, one of the opium warlords of the Golden Triangle, even holds news conferences to boast of his large fortune.[73] Roberto Suárez was, before his capture and incarceration in Bolivia,[74] sufficiently endowed economically to offer to pay off two-thirds of his country's foreign debt (then running at $3,000,000,000) in exchange for government leniency.[75] The Colombians from the Medellín cartel—Pablo Escobar Gaviria, Jorge Ochoa, José Rodríguez Gacha (now deceased), Gilberto Rodríguez Orejuela—have all been particularly conspicuous about their consumption.[76] Carlos Lehder (now serving a multiple life sentence in a Miami jail) was among the first not only to flaunt his wealth but to employ it for power.[77] And, in Mexico, Caro Quintero lavished on friends the kind of money that almost every Mexican appeared to covet.[78]

The major traffickers like to see themselves—and wish others would, too—as local entrepreneurs who create jobs and generate wealth for their countrymen.[79] It is true that communities have sometimes benefitted immensely from the barons' largesse. The traffickers thereby win over the people in patterns of loyalty and dedication that protect them from the authorities.[80]

Money draws people like honey draws ants; thousands seek a share of the drug lucre. Thus lesser traffickers in net consuming countries have also become immense beneficiaries of the trade, although they are less well known.[81] On down the trafficking line, many are recognized by their public display of gold, from adorned teeth to pharaoh-style head dresses. Then, of course, come the money launderers and the unsuspecting banks that nevertheless earn valuable profits on drug-money deposits. In specific instances, some people are making monstrous incomes from this business.[82] In a perverse way these are, we suppose, "beneficiaries."

There are reports of more conventional beneficiaries in consuming countries. Some single inner-city mothers, largely formally uneducated and economically disadvantaged, have entered the drug trade with more long-term objectives in mind than many of their male counterparts. From the trade they acquire a certain business acumen and are investing their drug money in legitimate businesses. Some have become rather successful.[83] Then, also, in some communities one finds merchants and politicians much in favor of the trade.[84]

More widely diffused benefits appear to be confined mostly to producer countries—foreign exchange earnings,[85] growers' income within those countries, multiplier employment effects, more buoyant (or perhaps just less catastrophic) national economies, and, of course, stunning opportunities for local politicians to enjoy the Midas touch by turning their public trusts into private gain.

Peru's immediate past president, Alan García, has spoken of his country's coca exports as "the only raw material that has increased in value" and that "the most successful effort to achieve Andean integration has been made by the drug traffickers."[86] The volatility of such benefits is amply seen in the 1990–91 crash of the coca markets which has left many Bolivian and Peruvian peasants impoverished once again.[87] Nevertheless, when the market is "up," successes imply benefits for the entire country. Still, García generally favored the antidrug war but wanted the United States to pursue a course of demand reduction and income replacement for peasant growers rather than emphasize crop suppression and law enforcement strategies.[88]

Until the February 1990 Andean drug conference in Cartagena, Colombia (attended by the presidents of Bolivia, Peru, Colombia, and the United States), the United States appeared to view almost all the benefits filtering down to agricultural growers as illegitimate, "unintended," and therefore of small public policy consideration for replacement should the antidrug war actually succeed. Producer countries' obligations were to control drug supply and suppress traffic. The economic fallout was largely their problem. However, the Latin Americans impressed President George Bush with the need to work more vigorously on demand in his own country and to help them with income replacement opportunities for their coca growing peasantry.[89]

In spite of occasional largesse, the same disinterest in the economic effects of a rise and fall in the illicit drug trade on people distanced from power, prestige, and economic security in net producer countries has characterized the traffickers who facilitated peasant farmers' drug growing in the first place. Being driven by money and the people and things money buys, traffickers have been mostly interested in securing a stable supply of raw product, not in providing social services for an impoverished peasantry.

Increased Income and Employment

All this notwithstanding, the drug boom did occur, and some of the profits have filtered down in the form of enhanced income and expanded employment opportunities for some of societies' lower echelons. That such benefits have now been widely experienced, however illegitimate or unintended, presents strong political incentives for their continuation in spite of the play and counter-play between the chief prodrug and antidrug protagonists.

At the producer level, the illicit drug industry is labor intensive, decentralized, growth-pole oriented, cottage-industry promoting, and foreign exchange earning—desirable features of rural development in economically stagnating areas. Even under illicit marketing conditions, the drug traffic heavily infuses capital into backwater areas, turning frontier towns into regional shopping centers and improving employment at many levels.[90]

There is an odd economic back flow into producer countries' urban areas, an irony of considerable visibility. For centuries many nations have disproportionately taxed their rural populations in favor of urban dwellers. For example, prices paid to peasant producers for basic foodstuffs have usually been fixed or controlled at artificially low levels. Now, however, bankers fly to backwater areas to, in effect, beg for "drug dollars" for their foreign exchange starved banks so that urban customers may continue to import their accustomed consumer goods.[91] More than just peasants are benefitting from illicit drugs.

Income linkages develop among the lower classes which spread the drug trade's benefits throughout many rural societies. For example, food produced in South America's Andean villages finds its way into coca growing regions in exchange for money, coca, and cocaine. Impoverished villages thereby become commercial providers of the foodstuffs required for the specialized coca growing labor to continue. While the "caloric exchange ratio," that is, the ratio of food exported to benefits received, is relatively exploitative of the highland peasants,[92] it appears to be less than the alternative exploitation that highlanders have historically suffered. In any event, villagers now engage in the trade with abandon.

This array of economic benefits from supplying an international market has become quite substantial in some areas. If the benefits originated in a legitimate economic development model, the world would herald them as a positive sign of progress and improvement in the lesser developed regions of countries such as Peru, Bolivia, Colombia, Mexico, Guatemala, Jamaica, Burma, Thailand, Laos, Afghanistan, Pakistan, and Lebanon.

Although the income source is criticized, aside from many of the traffickers themselves becoming unbelievably wealthy, several million people heretofore marginalized from their countries' national societies, economies, and polities, have benefitted. As a consequence, they have earned more money, experienced more social mobility, and exercised more power over their destiny and that of their children than perhaps at any time in this century.

Consider Pakistan. The country's hill tribes have imported chemists from Asia to teach them how to convert opium into heroin; opium, itself, is undesirable for illicit international trade. The tribes now produce enough heroin to make their country one of the world's leading drug exporters; and Pakistan is now the principal provider for the North American market.[93] The tribes also supply a rapidly growing domestic market.[94] They operate a sufficiently good intelligence program to rebound from their central government's unevenly applied tough suppression measures,[95] in part because they are successful in corrupting some of Pakistan's military officers assigned to drug duty.[96]

It might seem unusual that the tribes could orchestrate all this on their own. Yes, they needed a link to international markets, a service provided by what Yev Yelin describes as the "International Narcotics Mafia."[97] The result? By anyone's standards the incomes of tens of thousands of these people have become relatively substantial, made possible by the confluence of demand, supply, illegality, ready traffickers, and international drug control policies.

In the neighboring hill country that divides Pakistan from Afghanistan, opium poppies have proven to be a quick, reliable source of money for rural Afghans. Poppies are particularly attractive owing to the relative absence of alternative income sources in the region.[98] The economic facts are quite simple. With an illicit trafficker–serviced market, peasants and isolated villagers can usually earn more cash income than with any other cash crop they could plant or any other product they could produce.

As we have seen, until early 1990 when the effects—probably temporary—of the Colombian internal wars between government and traffickers were finally felt in Bolivia in the form of reduced coca markets, the economic returns in the coca industry were quite attractive for every involved Bolivian. Not surprisingly, therefore, the export value of the coca trade rose to exceed the value of all other exports combined.[99] While the traffickers have kept much of their earnings outside the country, they have returned enough to make coca growing a relatively lucrative farming operation. Some people now conclude that the principal problem for the Bolivian authorities is not the suppression of coca production and the criminal activities associated with it, but rather the recognition that coca cultivation is the peasantry's principal source of income.[100] Currently, there is hardly any other viable income replacement for tens of thousands of people.[101] Small wonder that peasant growers have vigorously resisted the involuntary eradication of their crops. More than a dozen peasants in Bolivia's Chapare have been killed defying drug control operations there.[102] Similar encounters have taken place in Peru.[103] However, with the depressed coca prices in 1990 and 1991, more peasants have voluntary eradicated their crops in exchange for cash incentives from the government (financed by the United States).[104]

If wholesale suppression activities are successful, or if the market precipitously and permanently collapses, what will net producer country governments and their international sponsors do with an angry, hungry peasantry or with other small-scale producers? The poignancy is best understood by reflecting on the international political implications if this were to occur without people being able to turn to alternative economic pursuits. The loss of benefits to the net producer societies' underclasses would probably unleash events that the consumer countries' sworn political enemies would exploit. Quite aside from the drug industry being a substantial source of employment and producer income, in several countries it has developed a large popular political base.[105] That base is already reflected in insurgent movements in Peru, Colombia, and Burma. Thus absent the United States' addressing the situation head on with development aid, it is often argued that the consequences would imperil America's national security interests.[106]

There is precedent: In spite of substantial help from the United States and United Nations Fund for Drug Abuse Control (UNFDAC), the Thai government has been wary to move against some of its more recalcitrant opium poppy growers, remembering that it was an earlier destruction of opium fields that allowed Communist cadres to infiltrate and win over many hill tribesmen to an antigovernment cause.[107] The result continues to tax Thai authorities and to contribute to political stress within the country.

If the nexus of illicit drug demand, supply, ready traffickers, and international drug control policies has boosted rural incomes, the increased income itself has produced its own consequences. Among these are peasant and labor migration to open up frontier lands and social mobility for some rural families. Internal migration and social mobility have returned to further enhance rural people's incomes and begin to increase their political power (usually through unionizing or by joining insurrectionist groups). The logic of the process could lead eventually to a restructuring of the economic and political power bases in net producer countries in ways that open them for expanded leadership recruitment and greater involvement of their citizens in the use of productive resources (see Flow Chart 3). The process could

Flow Chart 3
Further Beneficial Consequences
for Producer Countries' Peasantry

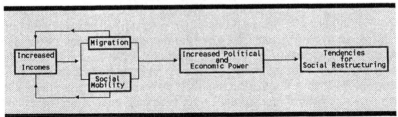

occur benignly if income growth continues, but it will probably turn violent if it is suddenly withdrawn.[108] In many cases, some sort of change is centuries overdue. It is ironic that illicit drugs may force the issue before the close of this century.

Migration and Social Mobility

Migrations of peoples have been fundamental to the history of humankind, having occurred for millennia and for multiple reasons. Sometimes people are driven by war, pestilence, governments, overcrowding, poverty. For example, in a program sponsored by the United States, the Burmese government has attempted to eradicate poppy fields by aerial spraying in its sector of the Golden Triangle. As a consequence of crop destruction, a massive influx of hill tribe refugees into Thailand has alarmed human rights organizations.[109] Yet, replacement opium poppy fields are being planted, both in Burma and in Thailand. On the other hand, people sometimes migrate in response to resource finds—land, gold, climate, economic opportunity—and all the anticipation and hope accompanying such news. In Bolivia, some 1,000 unemployed tin miners and their families marched en masse 120 kilometers from La Paz to the coca growing region of Chulumani where they threatened to take up the illicit activity if the government declined to assist them.[110] In a practical sense, "Push" and "pull" factors that work in tandem are not uncommon.

Coca migrations combine both push and pull. True, migrations into recently settled South American drug growing areas began before their utility as coca incubators became widely known.[111] And, existing colonists turned to the drug trade when it became profitable. However, as the profits derived from the trade became well known, increased colonization and further coca production resulted as people fled impoverished highland villages and city slums, drawn to the prospects of relative fortunes in what Edmundo Morales has called a "white gold rush,"[112] particularly in Peru and Bolivia.[113]

In the latter half of this century resource-poor ancestral villages have generally disgorged their surplus populations to regional and primate cities, turning these into burgeoning shanty towns and slums. In recent years, the cities have become less and less attractive to rural migrants. Many of the more recent village émigrés are therefore turning to frontiers, forests, and jungles, still driven by poverty but now also by the prospects of relative wealth. Where potential suitable land resources exist as, for example, in South America's western Amazonic basin, wholesale migration is occurring. Bolivia's Yungas and Chapare areas have blossomed, as has Peru's upper Huallaga Valley.

Market transport costs are irrelevant in drug-related migrations because of the high unit value per weight of the product sold. While growers' incomes are but a fraction of the total drug trade value, the economic incentives, and therefore the "pull" factor in migration, are relatively strong.

The economic incentives are not only strong but increase with each successful migration. On the frontier, land is available for purchase or for the taking. With hard work, a trafficker-serviced market, and some luck, family income increases substantially. Consumption rises, with commensurate investment in self-pride and self-assurance, both of which combine to limit the degree to which governments, traditional land barons, and a regional economic elite can successfully intimidate the new colonists and, more particularly, their children.

Colonists send money back to their villages. This and increased emphases on educational opportunities for children who migrate and those who stay combine to offer the successful agrarian entrepreneur a kind of social mobility—a rise in social and eventual occupational status—that heretofore only others could dream of. Some even become traffickers themselves, thereby completing the round of new social mobility. This effect has been particularly noted in Bolivia.[114]

Power and Social Restructuring

Whether migration is required for increased income (as in Peru and Bolivia), or whether drug crops are substituted for food crops on old lands (as is done by the hill tribes of the Golden Crescent and Golden Triangle), success breeds a heady optimism. This encourages people to struggle against alleged oppressors. In the cases under study, this usually means central governments. More ominously, even temporary success creates opportune conditions for credible demands to be made on governments should the bottom fall out of the drug market.

The best indicators known to this reviewer of the event-sequencing outcome suggested in Flow Chart 3 are the insurgent activities of Khun Sa (discussed in notes 25 and 28 of this chapter) in Burma and Thailand and the coca growers' unions in South America. One might include the *Sendero Luminoso* (see note 55, this chapter), but this organization has imposed itself on the peasantry as much as the peasantry has embraced it. So we will discuss it later in a different context.

Coca grower unions have become so powerful and their demands so convincing that Peru's past president, Alan García, even tried to introduce one peasant leader to President George Bush at the Drug Summit in Cartagena. Bush refused the proffered meeting, a disappointment to more than 200,000 peasants of Peru's growers' union.[115] In the afterglow of hindsight, the refusal will likely be seen as a diplomatic mistake, even if García's principal intent was to embarrass Bush.

In Bolivia, the most effective opposition to coca leaf eradication comes from the peasant unions, most of which are closely tied to the national labor movement.[116] In fact, in 1983 the unions forced the Bolivian government to reassess its U.S.–backed coca eradication programs in the Andes,[117] and the unions have since imposed an entirely new agenda on the Bolivian government.

Peasants who can force agendas and negotiations on national governments may likely, in time, oblige their societies to an involuntary restructuring. Migration and social mobility have contributed to this possibility, and both have been facilitated by the increased income, functional integration, and social cohesion derived from provisioning the drug market. All, ultimately, is made possible by the illicit drug demand and by the traffickers who link supplier with user, however high the risk.

LIABILITIES AND VICTIMS

As suggested in Flow Chart 1, traffickers arose from a confluence of adequate demand and supply, illegalizing policies, and countervailing initiatives (e.g., antidrug law enforcement). Drug demand, illegalizing policies, and countervailing initiatives have produced their own consequences, to which we turn in due course.

Here we continue to focus on traffickers. Flow Chart 2 and its accompanying discussion indicate that traffickers can produce benefits and beneficiaries as well as liabilities and victims. As we saw above, some of the literature looks into benefits, particularly into their needed replacement in net producer countries should drug control policies aimed at suppression of supply and demand be successful. However, most of the trafficker-related literature on consequences is of a contrary persuasion, being entirely negative.

The literature examines widespread trafficker-induced ills in net consumer and net producer countries. However, although both producer and consumer nations suffer from the drug trade and all its constituent parts (demand, supply, ready suppliers, drug control laws, and antidrug policies themselves), the bulk of the literature points to the liabilities and suggests that most of them probably occur in net producer countries.

While net producer countries characteristically receive some benefits as well as the many liabilities from trafficker-facilitated trade, it is hard to imagine many *consumer* country benefits from the traffic, although some U.S. inner-city single mothers appear to be making drug-money investments in profitable legitimate businesses, which is allowing social mobility within and out of the ghettos.

Net consumer countries do suffer trafficker-induced ills (e.g., drug trading gangs, turf wars, indiscriminate homicides, unsafe streets and neighborhoods, frequent assassinations, and the occasional intimidation, bribery, or other corruption of members of law enforcement agencies and the judiciary). These ills notwithstanding, it is the net producer countries that suffer heavily detrimental, trafficker-induced consequences. Most observers argue that these ills far outweigh any commensurate benefits in income and supplemental employment—for the peasantry or anyone else.

Principal among the political liabilities and casualties are traffickers' assaults on government institutions through infiltration, corruption, intimidation and violence and, in general, an undermining of the legitimate affairs of state. Frequently, traffickers or their spin-off gangs exercise territorial control over streets, ghettos, regions, and whole departments by creating an antistate wholly outside the rule of law. Understandably, fears for the national integrity of the state itself are often raised. These consequences cut across social, political, and economic dimensions.

More specifically, in the economy, traffickers exploit, corrupt, foster illegal markets, help sustain a nontaxed underground or parallel economy, require the expenditure of hundreds of millions of dollars on law enforcement activities and prosecutions, undermine banking institutions, assault the environment, shrink credit pools for legitimate lending, inflate values of land and property, hurt manufacturing, lower the quality of investments, undermine a nation's ability to compete internationally, build economic empires on terror and bribery, and finance businesses that compete with, undermine, and frequently destroy legitimate enterprises.

In the social sphere, traffickers corrupt a population by attracting new generations to the drug trade, glamorizing gangs, and glorifying role models of the conspicuously consuming new rich, thereby detracting from social values on which a legitimate state and its people may be built or maintained. They thereby contribute to social disorganization and to a certain amount of social and value anarchy. None of this yet mentions the children attracted to their trade who become pitiably addicted, roaming as homeless street urchins, or the traffickers' indiscriminate murder of uninvolved bystanders.

The above incomplete list summarizes an astonishing array of "impacts" encountered in the literature. We begin by examining a sample on traffickers' effects on public affairs and on the governmental, judicial, and political institutions that sustain them.

Traffickers' Assaults on Government and Law

We are quite willing to allow that in theory and even in practice some governments ought to be assaulted, that some laws ought to be subverted, and that some politicians ought to change occupations. They serve privileged cliques and their foreign supporters, oppress citizens of contrary mind or ability, and perpetuate institutionalized violence. However, even under these extreme conditions, the literature generally points to drug traffickers' being undesirable agents of structural change. They assault and undermine without building replacements that are either desirable or survivable. Thus traffickers offer hardly anything of social or political value in return for undermining even "evil" governments and "corrupt" laws. The general consequence of their labors is therefore considerable social and economic overhead and institutional waste and debris. This effect is even more pronounced in countries enjoying a modicum of legitimate government and rule of law.

Flow Chart 4
How Traffickers Facilitate Their Work

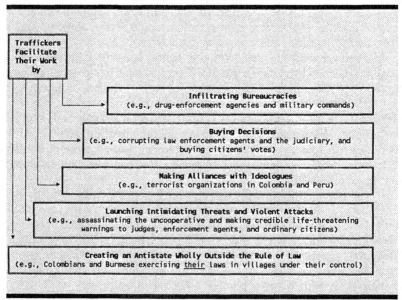

While traffickers appear to have few social, political, or economic plans that extend beyond their own immediate wants and needs, they do have plans for exploitation and waste. Traffickers' plans are a natural consequence of their methods—infiltrating bureaucracies, buying public and private decisions, launching intimidating threats and violent attacks, making alliances with ideologues, and creating anti-states wholly outside the rule of law. Flow Chart 4 summarizes the methods and offers relevant illustrations. We address each in turn.

Infiltrating Bureaucracies

One difficulty noted by international drug-enforcement agents is the degree to which the implementation of net producer country antidrug policies is routinely compromised—raids, for example, being made known to traffickers well before being staged. One way is through insiders who, by selling information for private gain, act as free-lance "criminal informants." Apparently, however, trafficker operatives also work inside the bureaucracies for reasons of economic security, ideological sympathy, or out of fear and intimidation. Agency efforts to control supply and suppress traffic, particularly in net producer countries, are therefore highly compromised, as are other instrumental bureau ends.

Some observers speak of "moles" at work in various bureaucratic agencies, including, in Colombia, the U.S. embassy. This mole (or moles) works in collaboration with infiltrators into the most important Colombian state agencies. Working in a network tied to and secured by the traffickers, the infiltrators have given the drug barons access to the decisions of Colombia's National Council of Security, the supreme court, the armed forces, the secret police, and even the U.S. Embassy.[118] Similar allegations are raised for Pakistan,[119] Peru,[120] and Honduras.[121]

The Peruvian administration of Fernando Belaúnde was thought to be so infiltrated with Traffickers' operatives that some observers accused many of the administration's higher officials of actually being traffickers themselves.[122] The same has apparently been true of the government of the Bahamas,[123] although the country's prime minister was incensed over suggestions that he might be indicted on drug charges in the United States. He launched a counter-diplomatic campaign.[124]

Traffickers actually took over the Bolivian government in the early 1980s[125] and have, to some extent, maintained a high level of infiltration since. A former Bolivian naval officer gave extensively documented testimony of widespread police and military protection of the country's illegal drug manufacturers and traffickers.[126]

Nepal, usually thought to be a peaceful kingdom, was startled by a 1987 drug scandal. High-ranking government aids and authorities, including a national police superintendent, were arrested. All were charged with "corruption and drug smuggling." Even the sterling reputation of the Gurkha troops was sullied.[127]

Mexico may be the most "infiltrated" country in the world. Corruption is not only expected but has become a national trait[128] which, in the case of drugs, is thought to have involved the highest levels of the federal police force and drug-enforcement agencies. Drug interests therefore have on occasion apparently commanded the very agencies charged with controlling them.[129]

The regular Mexican agencies have been so compromised that the Salinas government has trained some twelve hundred police officers, engineers, doctors, teachers, and former soldiers to be deployed across the country in "special shock troops" commanded by the Mexican attorney general's newly created antinarcotics investigation and operations division. Kept outside regular infiltration and graft channels, and being more highly trained, more professional, and better paid, it is hoped that the "troops" can break out of the country's traditional mold.[130]

Other cases of infiltration that subvert a whole bureaucracy and place it in the hands of the traffickers involve drug transit countries. One of the most bizarre is Cuba. Although Cuba is not a drug producer country, it has been an important rest and security station for traffickers. The traffickers' infiltration of the Cuban government was remarkable; it occurred right under Fidel Castro's eyes and involved some of his most trusted *compadres*. After repeated allegations beginning as early as 1983 about the Cuban government's involvement in drug smuggling into the United States,[131] Castro finally acknowledged the problem within the highest levels of his government (earlier knowledge of which he denied). He had the principals tried and executed[132] and then offered to collaborate with the United States government in drug interdiction efforts.[133] Nevertheless, drug smuggling flights continue unabated over Cuba, leading some to conclude that a complicity between Colombian drug traffickers and Cuban officials extends well beyond those who were executed.[134]

As in the case of Cuba, Colombia has made strident efforts to root out infiltrators. It is probably a losing task because the people are so highly placed within the bureaucracies.[135]

In 1987 an internal report from the government of Trinidad and Tobago (bureaucrats investigating fellow bureaucrats) disclosed top governmental officials being linked to drug transiting operations.[136]

The infiltration chain goes even higher. The arrest in 1989 of Edward K. O'Brian raised, for the first time, the possibility that the traffickers had even penetrated the U.S. Drug Enforcement Administration's headquarters in Washington, D.C.[137]

Oddly, certain self-described well-meaning individuals attached to the U.S. CIA apparently promoted infiltration in Honduras as they facilitated U.S. flight crews' covertly ferrying arms to the Nicaraguan rebels and smuggling cocaine and other drugs on their return trips to the United States. One crew member, when confronted, argued that he had White House protection.[138] While Honduras was supporting U.S. foreign policy vis-à-vis the Nicaraguan Contras, the United States ignored the cocaine connections that were developing in the highest levels of the country's military and civilian leaders.[139]

Some authors now view the drug trade as being at the heart of a number of social, economic, and political processes affecting net producer societies, all magnified by traffickers' infiltration of governmental institutions. Infiltration has increased levels of simple and gross corruption and has diverted political power and attention away from normal institutional activities, thereby decreasing agencies' abilities to carry out their prescribed functions.[140] In some quarters, arguments are advanced that an indulgent or even venal U.S. government is actually part of the conspiracy.[141]

The consequences of infiltration are quite clear. Insofar as the traffickers' assault on government via infiltration turns government and agency decision making away from the ends of government to the ends of the traffickers, a whole population ultimately may suffer. Certainly, governments' prospects of addressing questions of political legitimacy—assuming a desire exists—are compromised.

Buying Public Decisions

For drug interests, either infiltrating or corrupting governmental institutions produces the same outcomes. It enhances profits and lowers risks. However, infiltration and corruption also undermine, delegitimize, and ultimately may destroy a country's governmental and political institutions. But whereas infiltration is, in effect, traffickers' agents directly compromising legitimate government, corruption is part-time, sometimes highly placed income seekers, selling both their honor and their public office for occasional or sustained private gain. Aside from compromising a government's ability to function, both infiltrators and "corruptors" diminish the respect a population may have for a country's system of laws and its administration of justice. In some sense diminished respect converts people in wholesale lots to "join up" with underground economies, tax evaders, and anyone advocating alternative employment and political standards. Such disrespect and the lack of legitimacy that accompanies it make affected countries exceedingly difficult to govern.[142]

Perhaps the biggest sense of assault is associated with a compromised judiciary. In Costa Rica there was general dismay over a highly influential Argentine national living there who was arrested and extradited to France on heroin trafficking. Many Costa Ricans had fallen with him, in fact or by reputation, including three supreme court justices, numerous lower justices, one leading presidential contender, the homicide chief of the judicial police, and one ambassador, all of whom had protected the trafficker and his operators. Other reputations were put in question.[143]

In Bolivia a view appears to prevail that most judges have their price,[144] a perception reinforced when several of the country's best-known names in the drug trade were acquitted in Santa Cruz. Serious questions were raised as to the fundamental ability of the criminal justice system to regularize any predictable behavior in the face of the drug barons.[145] Unremarkably, therefore, the cocaine business booms in Riberalta, Bolivia, although the area has three military bases built at U.S. instigation and has U.S. army personnel and DEA agents frequently on location. The Colombian cartel that sets the area's coca prices appears to have its stable of judges.[146]

Judges have also been bought off in the Bahamas,[147] Ireland,[148] Venezuela,[149] and Mexico[150] and have been compromised in many other countries.[151]

In the United States, one would probably expect corruption to begin in the Customs Services, and apparently it did. Now it has begun to impinge on other U.S. agencies.[152] Law enforcement agents in New York City, Miami, and Los Angeles have been implicated in drug-dealer shakedowns,[153] and drug-enforcement agents in New York, Washington, and Miami have been targeted for investigation or have been arrested, as have rural sheriffs in Georgia, federal prosecutors in Boston, and government agents and customs officials in California.[154] In California, three former federal drug agents were charged in a cocaine corruption case in which they allegedly gave tips to dealers and helped to work money-laundering schemes.[155]

Perhaps the ultimate corrupting assault is drug barons' buying votes in elections that otherwise are free and open.[156]

Making Alliances with Ideologues

Political ideologues, if not themselves in political power, usually have one thing in mind—obtaining it. Some are circumspect and prefer powers of persuasion in a legitimate electoral process. Others resort to any means, including insurgency, terrorism, and indiscriminate violence. Insurgents are at work in Peru, Colombia, Burma, and Sri Lanka. Some of them have forged an alliance of convenience with drug traffickers.

For a share of the illicit drug profits as a means to pursue their own political ends,[157] insurgent ideologues police the peasantry through intimidation and violence or, alternatively, by protecting them from central governments' drug control agents[158] even, in the case of Bolivia, to the extent of arming them[159] or, in the case of Burma, conscripting them into a guerrilla army.[160] The traffickers, in turn, pay to keep their supply lines open at an affordable cost. Traffickers and insurgents both operate to undermine government institutions and to assault the existing institutions of power.[161]

The alliance that produces these consequences is pragmatic and dissolvable, either as the insurgents try to take over the drug trade directly or as the ideologues have a political change of heart. For example, in Colombia when traffickers tried to gouge the peasantry "too much" by lowering the price paid for coca paste in regions under guerrilla control, the insurgents struck with a fury and vengeance that startled even seasoned observers there.[162] This caused one reporter to wonder whether trafficker-insurgent alliances even existed.[163] On the other hand, drug control agents in Peru find it necessary to construct fortified bases to protect their personnel from insurgent assaults in defense of territory and income that are attached to the coca trade.[164]

Quite aside from imposing considerable operations' overhead costs on a country, drug traffickers, all on their own, are able to undermine governments. In alliance with insurgents, the havoc they impose on institutions and individual lives is considerable.

Launching Intimidating Threats and Violent Attacks

With the income from the drug trade, insurgents and traffickers are able to import or otherwise obtain weapons, which they freely employ in pursuit of their disparate ends. They are able to force agendas on friends and foes alike, appealing to the former with money, to the latter with threats to life and property.[165]

They finance paramilitary death squads to assassinate judges, politicians, and reporters judged to be against their cause,[166] even turning some communities into "hit" towns.[167] They kill police and soldiers sent to enforce the law.[168] They kidnap and extort.[169] And, they indiscriminately abuse innocent bystanders.[170] Planting bombs is the newest rage, a "step up" from random one-on-one killings. In December, 1989, Colombian drug traffickers set off a "truck bombing" in Bogotá that killed fifty-two people, wounded hundreds of others, and left a twenty-foot-deep crater in front of the country's central police offices.[171] In Peru, however, the old practices continue unabated. In true form, rebels stepped up their random killings of politicians in an effort to disrupt the country's 1989 elections.[172]

Understandably, the press sometimes notes a declining "will" among the judicial and law enforcement officials subjected to this kind of intimidation,[173] particularly in light of their families' exposure through carefully planned kidnappings, rapes, and tortures.[174] A kind of self-censorship permeates at-risk institutions in order to lower the potential exposure of their personnel. Arrests that ought to be made are not ordered; prosecutions that ought to be carried out are deferred; sentences that ought to be handed down are avoided or reversed; articles that ought to be written are avoided or completed ones shelved; citizens who ought to inform authorities about traffickers do not. Only the more courageous individuals and institutions continue to place themselves at risk, frequently at profuse personal and institutional cost. In Colombia, one newspaper launched investigative efforts into police corruption, reporting on a police captain who assigned his whole small-town force to protect cocaine barons as they attended a party. The paper's owner was quickly assassinated.[175] The marvel is that so many people continue to step forward to take such extreme personal risks.

Creating an Antistate Wholly Outside the Rule of Law

Where either traffickers or ideologues in alliance with them have grown powerful enough to neutralize governmental institutions and to intimidate the local citizenry, they have, in effect, taken over a territory. Their will supplants law, government, tradition, and conventional honor. The infamous Rodríguez Gacha, for example, controlled his Colombian community from the scaffold of the highly visible gallows he had constructed in his front yard, defying any law other than his own will to prevail.[176] Khun Sa operates his own system of justice in the Burmese hills where his guerrillas control not only the opium trade but also the villages and transit routes on which it is carried out.[177] *Sendero Luminoso*, the Peruvian insurgent group espousing a strange brand of Maoism and the revanchist ideology of ancient Incan lords, tells peasants what they can cultivate,[178] "cleans up streets, improves public services and imposes a bloody but effective brand of justice in a region that the central government, as far as municipal services and government are concerned, has largely abandoned."[179]

It is true that some of these consequences ought probably to be classified as improvements,[180] but improvements at what long-term cost?

Traffickers' Sundry Economic and Social Effects

Aside from their assaults on government and the law, traffickers also impose sundry economic and social consequences. One of the most discussed of these is the traffickers' impetus to the vitality of the non-taxed underground or parallel economies in net producer countries.[181]

These economies are technically "hidden" from national income accounts, from tax collectors, and from national planning considerations. Some sources show that important macroeconomic variables are therefore biased in a country's official statistics. Unemployment, for example, may be highly overestimated while production indicators may incorporate barely half the country's real economic activity.[182]

In fact, the underground or parallel economies may provide the bulk of a country's employment, making no small contribution to containing political instability, which would be driven to considerable levels if those employed in the underground economy were without income sources.

Certainly, underground or parallel economies would exist independently of the drug traffickers, as Hernando de Soto's widely read treatise persuasively points out.[183] All the institutional logic for such economies rests squarely with the way in which many governments carry out their economic policies. Endless government red tape forces up to as many as half of a country's merchants into the "informal sector" in order to carry out any kind of productive business. Thus there are side benefits. Aside from facilitating economic growth, the illegal or parallel economy may, under some conditions, provide opportunities for capital accumulation and investment in licit productive enterprises beyond what otherwise would be possible.[184]

But the traffickers distort both the economy and economic policies by, on the one hand, importing hordes of cash and, on the other, developing every clandestine and secretive way they can to disguise its origins. The economies themselves become "addicted," and, it is said, suffer both the traumatic cycles and disjointed behavior of individual addicts.[185] Quite aside from governments' being misled to choose inadequate fiscal and monetary policies because of distorted information about their economies, traffickers independently affect tax collection and tax morale, and they promote the idea that some types of criminal economic behavior are normal.

If, on balance—given the institutional settings out of which they emerge—parallel economies are "good," it might be argued that traffickers "help." If, on the other hand, such economies are "bad," traffickers heap additional burdens on net producer countries because they certainly do accentuate all the features of the hidden or parallel economy.

Considerable evidence points to traffickers' directly and indirectly causing substantial increased institutional overhead costs in law enforcement and judicial functions, problems we review in Chapter 5. However, there is no necessary "zero-sum" relationship between traffickers' activities and all drug control costs, although the tendency is certainly clear. Consider, for example, the costs of using the military in the drug war. Sunken costs in materiel, equipment, and facilities and the ongoing costs of administration and man-power, upkeep and training exist regardless of the military's being deployed for drug control operations. Most countries have armies; they cost whether at rest or at war. Of course, whenever at work—on the drug war or whatever else—supplemental costs are incurred.

On the other hand, law enforcement and judicial costs increase in direct proportion to the number of traffickers and a country's will to fight them. Costs to Colombia are fierce on this count: more police, more judges, more costs to protect them, more jails.

Traffickers undermine legitimate banking institutions through their money-laundering schemes[186] at the same time they promote unscrupulous financial institutions as legitimate competitors.[187] They build economic empires on terror and bribery—hardly any of which are associated with legitimate competitive business practices. Insofar as traffickers are successful in converting funds to, for example, legitimate manufacturing, they therefore undermine the ability of their country to position itself competitively in world commerce.[188] Business protected internally by terror and bribery hardly ever develops an ability to survive competitively in an international market.

By their extravagant expenditures, traffickers inflate land and property values beyond any conceivable economic utility, thereby depriving others of resources that could be used for economic development and legitimate personal gain based on normal economic competition.[189] Moreover, traffick-ers shrink credit pools for legitimate lending, particularly with lending for employment-producing investments.[190]

Of increasing concern is traffickers' assault on the environment with attendant long-term economic implications.[191] They have encouraged slash-and-burn farming in Peru's upper Huallaga Valley, which contributes to severe soil erosion, heightening the risk of massive landslides in the region.[192] They have polluted rivers by dumping used precursor chemicals, and they have damaged rain forests,[193] a problem of increasing note in Mexico.[194]

In the United States, traffickers dump chemical waste from illegal drug laboratories in school playgrounds, down bathtub drains, and along roads and creeks, thereby contaminating underground water supplies and top-soil.[195] There is even concern about the environmental contamination that marijuana growers and traffickers are heaping on U.S. national forests.[196]

If the deleterious effects on politics and economics were not of considerable concern, particularly in net producer countries, trafficker-related social impacts would be. Principal among these is the corruption of a whole generation of young people attracted to the glamour of drug-money income in ways that glorify the conspicuous consumption of the new trafficker rich.[197] There is concern that such values are dysfunctional to the long-term social interests of a state that needs to compete economically internationally, ultimately in legitimate trade, or to values consistent with the maintenance of democratic traditions or aspirations.[198] Equally as bad, it is now surmised that in Colombia the newly rich drug barons have replaced the coffee oligarchy of the late nineteenth century, with the perverse consequence of reenforcing the old social order rather than destabilizing it.[199]

As we mentioned before and explore in detail in Chapter 6, none of this discussion yet explores the personal losses imposed on the children whom traffickers attract to their trade—pitiably addicted,[200] roaming, homeless street urchins[201]—or the traffickers' indiscriminate murder of uninvolved bystanders and the attendant loss to families (income and nurturing) and to society (intellect and energy).

We have identified three main categories of drug trade "consequences" distributed in social, economic, political, environmental, and personal dimensions: market demand, drug control policies, and drug traffickers themselves (see Tables 1 and 2). In this chapter we discussed traffickers, noting that the principal consequences of their activities, both beneficial and deleterious, appear to have fallen on net producer countries.

In Chapter 5 we examine the consequences derived from drug control policies. These policies have a profound effect on both net producer and net consumer nations. In Chapter 6 we find, as one would expect, that most of the demand-related deleterious consequences, with few redeeming ones, fall on consuming countries, be they net producers or net exporters of the illicit commodities that plague them. The impact of these demand-driven consequences is being felt more and more in net producer countries because their own drug consumption habits have been growing exponentially.

NOTES

[1]See Gina Kolata, "In Cities, Poor Families Are Dying of Crack," *The New York Times*, 1989.

[2]John Bacon discusses the French Connection and those who dominated it and speculates about a possible resurrection of the French criminal underworld ["Is the French Connection Really Dead?" *Drug Enforcement*, 1981]. The negotiations between the United States and Turkey, and the effectiveness of the opium-ban laws in Turkey following the demise of the French Connection, are discussed in two U.S. congressional hearings [U.S. Congress, House Committee on International Relations, Subcommittee on Future Foreign Policy Research and Development, "The Effectiveness of Turkish Opium

Control," 1975; and U.S. Congress, House Committee on Foreign Affairs, "Turkish Opium Ban Negotiations," 1974].

[3]James Van Wert ["U.S.–Mexican Aerial Opium Eradication Program: A Summative Evaluation," Ph.D. diss., 1982] gives a helpful overview of the development of Mexico's capacity to address market demand in the United States. As of 1986 Pakistan had developed into the world's biggest exporter of heroin ["Heroin Brings More Trouble," *The Economist*, 1986], more than half of which ends up in the U.S. market ["Pakistan Tribes a Big Hurdle in Drive to Limit Heroin Trade," *Narcotics Control Digest*, 1985]. See also Cait Murphy, "High Times in America; Why Our Drug Policy Can't Work," *Policy Review*, 1987.

[4]See Ralph Blumenthal, *Last Days of the Sicilians*, 1988.

[5]See Wayne Greenhaw, *Flying High: Inside Big-Time Drug Smuggling*, 1984.

[6]Sean M. McWeeney ["The Sicilian Mafia and Its Impact on the United States," *FBI Law Enforcement Bulletin*, 1987] reviews the Sicilian mafia's relationship to heroin and cocaine trafficking. Paul Houston ["201 in U.S., Italy Charged in Drug Trade," *Los Angeles Times*, 1988] describes one of the recent "busts" involving several individuals in the Sicilian mafia.

[7]A recent example on the heroin/cocaine/marijuana trail involves Mexico. In 1989 two notorious drug barons were arrested (Rafael Caro Quintero and Ángel Félix Gallardo). As soon as they were removed from circulation, their lieutenants and others shifted drug operations to other locations, encompassing a different set of people but servicing the same market [see Larry Rohter, "As Mexico Moves on Drug Dealers, More Move In," *The New York Times*, 1989].

[8]Frank Robertson [*Triangle of Death: The Inside Story of the Triads—The Chinese Mafia*, 1977] characterizes the Chinese Triads as criminal offshoots of a once vast patriotic organization formed to rid China of its despotic overlords and to establish a republic. The original triad society still exists, the author says, in fragmented form in Hong Kong and in almost every sizeable Chinese overseas community. Although the overwhelming majority of its members are lawful, hard-working citizens, there is a criminal minority, organized into some 1,500 gangs worldwide. The criminal offshoots from Hong Kong—extremely closely knit brotherhoods, difficult to penetrate—are specializing in heroin distribution in Great Britain, all of Europe, and the United States [Fenton Bresler, *The Trail of the Triads: An Investigation into International Crime*, 1980]. See also Stephen Brookes, "Chinese Mafia Takes Vice Abroad," *Insight*, 1989; Ian Buruma and John MacBeth, "Asia's Organized-Crime Jigsaw and the Western Connection; An East-Side Story," *Far Eastern Economic Review*, 1984; Emily Lau, "Brotherhood of Extortion," *Far Eastern Economic Review*, 1984; William Overend, "Violence Feared as Asian Heroin Influx Soars," *The Los Angeles Times*, 1988; President's Commission on Organized Crime, *Organized Crime of Asian Origin*, 1984; and Keith B. Richburg, "More Heroin Said to Enter U.S. from Asia; Chinese Gangs Replacing Traditional Organized Crime Networks," 1988. The triads are moving into Australia along with their heroin network and have hurt the Chinese community's image there. The resident Chinese have nevertheless been unwilling to inform on gang members [Carl Robinson, "The Day of the Triads; Hong Kong's Gangs Move in on Australia," *Newsweek*, 1988]. They are said, now, to dominate the New York heroin trade with their connection known as the "China White Trail" [Peter Kerr, "Chinese Now Dominate New York Heroin Trade," *The New York Times*, 1987; Peter Kerr, "Chasing the Heroin from Plush Hotel to Mean Streets," *The New York Times*, 1987].

[9]Keith B. Richburg, "More Heroin Said to Enter U.S. from Asia; Chinese Gangs Replacing Traditional Organized Crime Networks," *The Washington Post*, 1988. These Chinese groups now dominate the New York heroin trade, made possible not only by their own aggressive marketing strategies but also by the weakening of traditional organized crime there through generational divisions and a series of major prosecutions. A vacuum developed, and the Triads filled it [Peter Kerr, "Chinese Now Dominate New York Heroin Trade," *The New York Times*, 1987].

[10]In general, in Mexico, organizations are mentioned by their leaders' names or simply as "families." For example, William Overend speaks of "seven major drug families of Mexico" who are developing a partnership with Colombian cartels to use Mexico as a transshipment point for cocaine in transit to the United States and Canada ["Cocaine Floods Southland via Colombia-Mexico Link," *The Los Angeles Times*, 1987]. One of these is the Herrera Family [see Peter A. Lupsha, "Drug Trafficking: Mexico and Colombia in Comparative Perspective," *Journal of International Affairs*, 1981]. Of named organizations, there is the Caro Quintero group (responsible for the torture murder of DEA agent Enrique Camarena), whose maximum leader has just been sentenced to over forty years in a Mexican jail. Perhaps hundreds of articles, journalistic and academic, have been written about this man, Rafael Caro Quintero, and his organization. Representative are two articles by John J. Fialka ["Death of U.S. Agent in Mexico Drug Case Uncovers Grid of Graft," *The Wall Street Journal*, 1986; and "How the Mexican Trail in Drug Agent's Death Yields Cache of 'Crack,'" *The Wall Street Journal*, 1986], and one by Michael Isikoff ["Informer Ties Top Mexican to Drug Deals: Allegations Revealed in DEA Affidavit, *The Washington Post*, 1988], which emphasize the endemic corruption among Mexican authorities; a Caro Quintero on-the-drug-trail biography, of sorts, by Luís Méndez [*Caro Quintero al Trasluz*, 1985]; and a description of popular ballads and films glorifying Caro Quintero, who appears to have become a legitimate "antihero" for Mexico's impoverished masses [John Ross, "Mexican Youth Make Folk Hero out of Drug Lord," *Latinamerica Press*, 1987]. Ángel Félix Gallardo's group is also placed among the highly active Mexican operators [see William Branigin, "Mexicans Arrest Prime Drug Suspect: Félix Gallardo Led DEA's Wanted List," *The Washington Post*, 1989; Brook Larmer, "Mexico's Corruption Clampdown: Arrest of Corrupt Officials Along with Drug Baron May Root out Graft," *The Christian Science Monitor*, 1989; and Larry Rohter, "Mexicans Arrest Top Drug Figure and 80 Policemen" *The New York Times*, 1989]. Mexico became a funnel for South American cocaine [see Dan Williams, "2 Nations Stymied in Efforts to Shut off Flow: Mexico a Funnel for U.S.-Bound Cocaine," *The Los Angeles Times*, 1985; and William Branigin, "The Mexican Connection," *The Washington Post*, 1988] long before the Colombians moved to Mexico to personally take over much of the cocaine operations there [see Brook Larmer, "Colombians Take over 'Coke' Trade in Mexico," *The Christian Science Monitor*, 1989].

[11]Discussions of the Colombian cartels are applied (e.g., examination of their impact on society and on both supply-side and demand-side drug traffic), and theoretical (e.g., whether they are vertically integrated in a conventional business sense or by intimidation and terror—there being hardly any disagreement that some kind of vertical integration exists). Discussions concern how many cartels there are, what their international characteristics are, how much legitimate business enterprise they are taking over, the degree to which they are corrupting the judicial and political systems (particularly of Colombia), their economic impact on the larger society, who their principals are, how powerful and rich they are, and so forth. For example, in two articles, Merrill Collett describes the way in which the Medellín cartel, in particular, has used its "business wizardry" to

create an economic boom in Colombia and how the cocaine barons have made vigorous efforts to become accepted as successful entrepreneurs rather than as criminals. Unsuccessful here, the lords have amassed a state-within-a-state organizational apparatus complete with narcoarmies that are, in many instances, better equipped than the Colombian military ["Colombia's Sophisticated Drug Traffickers Trigger Economic Boom, Political Violence," *Latinamerica Press*, 1988; and "Colombia's Losing War with Drug Kings," *The Christian Science Monitor*, 1988]. The cartels' sanguinary assaults are reminiscent of prior chapters in a turbulent history of violence in the country [Jonas Bernstein, "Bitter Convulsions in a Nation under the Influence of Drugs," *Insight*, 1989]. Fabio Castillo looks into the way in which the cartels have infiltrated the law enforcement and judicial administrations [*Los Jinetes de la Cocaína*, 1987]. There appear to be four Colombian cartels ["U.S. Has 43 Big Drug Groups," *The Miami Herald*, 1989] of which Medellín and Cali are the best known. Their murderous assault on each other is described by James Brooke ["A Report from the Front Lines in Colombia: The Drug War Will Be Long," *The New York Times*, 1989], *The Economist* ["Colombia: All Fall Down," 1988], Heather Dewar and Lori Rozsa ["Cartel Figure Arrested," *The Miami Herald*, 1989], and Pedro Pablo Camargo, ["Luchan los Narcos por el Control de las Plazas; Destruyen Centro Comercial y Matan un Alcalde," *Excelsior*, 1989]. Jeff Leen chronicles the cartels' prominent murders and their intimidation of politicians and rivals ["Bush Lauds Colombia Drug Battle," *The Miami Herald*, 1989], a theme he developed further with Guy Gugliotta [*Kings of Cocaine: Inside the Medellín Cartel*, 1989]; and Joseph B. Treaster ["Colombia's Cali Drug Cartel: The Less Flamboyant Competitor of Medellín," *The New York Times*, 1989] analyses the social psychology and social history of the respective members. The U.S. Senate examined a host of these and related issues in one of its committee reports [U.S. Congress, Senate Caucus on International Narcotics Control and the Congressional Research Service, Report, "Combating International Drug Cartels: Issues for U.S. Policy," 1987]. See also "Colombia Cartels Tied to Bombing," *The New York Times*, 1989; Jeff Gerth, "Report Says Mercenaries Aided Colombian Cartels," *The New York Times*, 1991; and Joseph B. Treaster, "'Arsenal' in Trunks Linked to a Colombian Drug Gang," *The New York Times*, 1990.

[12]There is some redundancy in the term inasmuch as the word Yakuza means Japanese organized criminals. They have a mafia-like drug trafficking organization which operates outside Japan (the unwavering Japanese police force and a closely knit Japanese society that readily cooperates with the police act as deterrents to any extensive drug operations on home soil [see Daniel Sneider, "How the Eliot Ness of Japan's Drug World Gets the Job Done," *The Christian Science Monitor*, 1987]. The President's Commission on Organized Crime [*Organized Crime of Asian Origin, Record of Hearing III*, 1984] received testimony of these groups, which are creating enclaves of terror in various parts of the United States. Much of the extortion, corruption, and protection rackets fostered by these groups were said to be associated with illegal narcotics. In 1985, the U.S. Drug Enforcement Agency picked up top leaders of the Yakuza who are operating in Hawaii and the western United States, but it was not thought that they would be leaderless for long ["DEA Smashes Leadership of Yakuza: New Wars Predicted," *Organized Crime Digest*, 1985]. Ian Buruma and John MacBeth also discuss the Yakuza (along with the Chinese Triads) ["Asia's Organized-Crime Jigsaw and the Western Connection: An East-Side Story," *Far Eastern Economic Review*, 1984]. See also "Japan's Gangsters: Honourable Mob," *The Economist*, 1990.

[13]See Phillip C. McGuire, "Jamaican Posses: A Call for Cooperation among Law Enforcement Agencies," *The Police Chief*, 1988. Bernard D. Headly ["War in 'Babylon': Dynamics of the Jamaican Informal Drug Economy," *Social Justice*, 1988] argues that

"dependent development" in Jamaica has produced such a scarcity of socially acceptable work that a substantial part of the Jamaican population has been economically marginalized. To extricate itself from that marginalization, some Jamaicans join gangs, emigrate to the United States, and become involved in the international drug traffic. It is thought that the Posses working in the United States have about 10,000 members ["U.S. Has 43 Big Drug Groups," *The Miami Herald*, 1989]. The gangs deal in cocaine (through contacts with the Medellín cartel) and in marijuana, some of which is transshipped from Jamaica. Marshall Ingwerson ["Jamaican Drug Gangs Stake out Turf in US," *The Christian Science Monitor*, 1987] describes the groups as being closely knit and heavily armed; they reside mostly in south Florida but now extend their operations to such unlikely cities as Kansas City, Missouri, and Newport News, Virginia. The Posses have extended their operations and coverage into other southern cities. They appear to be particularly adept at moving crack into northern cities. They appear to make higher profits than other drug distributors because they cut out the middlemen [George Volsky, "Jamaican Drug Gangs Thriving in U.S. Cities," *The New York Times*, 1987].

[14]The Aryan brotherhood and the Texas syndicate, along with many other groups, are discussed in the President's Commission on Organized Crime, *The Impact: Organized Crime Today*, 1986.

[15]Reported in "U.S. Has 43 Big Drug Groups," *The Miami Herald*, 1989.

[16]Rural areas in Ohio and Wyoming are particularly noted for expansion activities of drug trafficking organizations; increasing attention is being paid to rural Georgia and South Carolina [Julie Johnson, "Drug Gangs Are Now Operating in Rural States, Justice department Says," *The New York Times*, 1989]. Mention is also made in *The Miami Herald* of the organizations' establishing rural operatives ["U.S. Has 43 Big Drug Groups," 1989]. As for street gangs, the most frequently mentioned are Los Angeles gangs, particularly because they have now taken their activities nationwide [Scott Armstrong, "Los Angeles Gangs Go National," *The Christian Science Monitor*,1988], even into rural U.S. states which had appeared to be somewhat immune to the excesses of organized drug trafficking. See also Tom Morganthau, et al. "The Drug Gangs," *Newsweek*, 1988; and William Overend, "Violence Feared as Asian Heroin Influx Soars," *The Los Angeles Times*, 1988.

[17]See, for example, Michael Mecham, "Drug Smugglers Prove Elusive Targets for Interdiction Forces," *Aviation Week and Space Technology*, 1989; and William Carley, "Losing Battle: U.S. Air War on Drugs So Far Fails to Stem Caribbean Smuggling," *The Wall Street Journal*, 1988.

[18]See Carl Robinson, "The Day of the Triads: Hong Kong's Gangs Move in on Australia," *Newsweek*, 1988; and Stephen Brookes, "Chinese Mafia Takes Vice Abroad," *Insight*, 1989. See also U.S. Department of State, Bureau of International Narcotics Matters, *International Narcotics Control Strategy Report*, 1989.

[19]Fenton Bresler, *The Chinese Mafia: An Investigation into International Crime*, 1981.

[20]Cathy Booth ["Tentacles of the Octopus; The Mafia Brings Europe's Worst Drug Epidemic Home," *Time*, 1988] and Karen Wolman ["Europe's Cocaine Boom Confounds Antidrug War," *The Christian Science Monitor*,1989] describe the extraordinary drug epidemic in Italy which is thought to derive from the mafia's lucrative drug trade which it has shared with crime families and drug cartels in the United States and South America. The mafia is characterized as being strong enough to be an antistate. It is thought that as much as fifty tons of cocaine a year may be entering Europe through Spain, orchestrated by the Colombians [Alan Riding,"Colombian Cocaine Dealers Tap European

Market," *The New York Times*, 1989]. See also "U.S. Interdiction Efforts Forcing Coke Shipments to Europe, OC Commissioners Report," *Crime Control Digest*, 1985.

[21]"Dutch Drug Sellers Getting Too Pushy," *The Los Angeles Times*, 1987. See also Burton Bollag, "Swiss-Dutch Drug Stance: Tolerance," *The New York Times*, 1989.

[22]Thomas Land ["Soviet Drug War," *The New Leader*, 1988] notes that the Soviet Union, having long denied that it had a problem with drugs, was expected to make a formal bid to join Interpol in order to deal more effectively with the crime syndicates that are invading the country. While in the Asian regions of the USSR opium poppies have been used for many generations, now heroin is being smuggled in from Pakistan, Afghanistan, and Iran.

[23]The evidence for organization and networks come from a wide range of sources: Marcial Barrón identifies the principal Peruvian traffickers [*El Infierno Blanco*, 1984]; Tyler Bridges claimed that in 1987 Colombian traffickers controlled the entire northern part of the upper Huallaga Valley, where most of the country's coca production is carried out ["Drug Traffickers, Guerrillas Curtail Peru's Antidrug Efforts," *The Christian Science Monitor*, 1987]; some of the highest officials in the Belaúnde administration were involved in 1985 ["Cocaine Scandal Hits Lima," *Latin America Weekly Report*, 1985]; Peruvian traffickers are organized enough to launch a full-scale attack on a principal Peruvian drug-enforcement agency ["Cocaine Traffickers Kill 17 in Peru Raid on Antidrug Team," *The New York Times*, 1984]; and Edmundo Morales reports not only the existence of organization but also a fairly rigid hierarchy among even low-level producers ["Coca Culture: The White Cities of Peru," *Thesis* (CUNY Graduate School Magazine), 1986]. See also Cynthia McClintock, "The War on Drugs: The Peruvian Case," *Journal of Interamerican Studies and World Affairs*, 1988; and U.S. Congress, House Select Committee on Narcotics Abuse and Control, *Drugs and Latin America: Economic and Political Impact and U.S. Policy Options*, 1989.

[24]The strength of the networks vis-à-vis the Bolivian judiciary is discussed by Shirley Christian ["Drug Case Raises Doubts in Bolivia," *The New York Times*, 1988], and the ability of the networks to launch "contract killings" is described in "Colombianization," *World Press Review*, 1989.

[25]Vichai S. ["Warlords of the Poppy Fields," *Bangkok Post*, 1983] describes them simply as "warlords" of the type abundant in the China of old and as being alive and well in the hills of Burma. Khun Sa and others are discussed. They have the ability to engage an entire military establishment. Described here are the Thai armies forcing Khun Sa from his mountain stronghold [Paisal Sricharatchanya, "Beating a Retreat," *Far Eastern Economic Review*, 1987]. See also the discussion in note 28.

[26]The Pakistani hill tribes are organized enough to import chemists from Asia to teach them how to convert opium into heroin, to set up their laboratories, and now to turn out enough product to become the world's leading heroin exporter as well as to supply a rapidly growing domestic market [Terence White, "The Drug-Abuse Epidemic Coursing through Pakistan," *Far Eastern Economic Review*, 1985] and to supply most of the heroin entering the North American market [David Kline, "From a Smugglers' Paradise Comes Hell," *Maclean's*, 1982]. The tribes operate a sufficiently good intelligence program to rebound from tough suppression measures undertaken by Pakistan's central government ["Pakistan Tribes a Big Hurdle in Drive to Limit Heroin Trade," *Narcotics Control Digest*, 1985]. The tribes have been able to corrupt some Pakistani military officers in order to facilitate their exports [Richard M. Weintraub, "Pakistani Drug Drive Seen in 2 Major Hauls; Military Officers Held in Seizure of Heroin," *The Washington Post*, 1986]. It might seem a little much that the tribes could orchestrate all this on their own.

Yev Yelin ["Why the 'Golden Crescent' Still Flourishes," *The New York Times*, 1985] traces their success to the country's having been infiltrated by the international narcotics mafia.

[27]When the Soviet Union invaded Afghanistan, opium and heroin production appeared to increase (opium poppies being a cash "war crop" less easily destroyed by an occupying force bent on pacifying a rebellious countryside). Enough "freedom for maneuver" existed that, when Pakistan began a large interdiction effort in 1985, a number of Pakistani heroin labs moved to Afghanistan, thereby helping that country increase its drug making technology and productivity ["Pakistan Tribes a Big Hurdle in Drive to Limit Heroin Trade," *Narcotics Control Digest*, 1985]. The bibliography on which this handbook is based does not contain further evidence of organized trafficking in Afghanistan, but one must suppose, no doubt, that the highly effective pan-village organizations created to prosecute a sustained war against the Soviets would have given villagers sufficient expertise to produce and market drugs. In any event, Afghanistan certainly has a significant and relatively stable opium production industry (see Figures 8 and 10, Chapter 2).

[28]Aside from basing much of his operation in Burma, Khun Sa operates in Thailand [Daniel Burstein,"The Deadly Politics of Opium," *Maclean's*, 1982; Barbara Crossette, "An Opium Warlord's News Conference Spurs Burma and Thailand to Battle Him," *The New York Times*, 1987; Rodney Tasker, "Chasing the Red Dragon," *Far Eastern Economic Review*, 1987]. Bertil Lintner ["Orchards and Opium," *Far Eastern Economic Review*, 1984] describes how remnants of the Chinese Kuomintang, who entered Thailand as a defeated army in 1946, are now much less interested in practicing military matters than in doing business in opium in the Thai mountains. Hong Kong crime syndicates are believed to be operating in Thailand, just as they are in Burma [David Clark Scott, "Surging Sales for Golden Triangle: Many Drug-Enforcement Officials Believe Hong Kong Crime Syndicates Are Responsible," *The Christian Science Monitor*, 1989].

[29]The United States has considered the Laotion government itself to be heavily involved in the production and export of heroin [Peter Kerr, "U.S. Says Laos Government Is Deeply Involved in Drugs," *The New York Times*, 1988] or, at the very least, is condoning it [Rodney Tasker, "Chasing the Red Dragon," *Far Eastern Economic Review*, 1987]. Hong Kong crime syndicates are thought to be operating in Laos as well as in Burma [David Clark Scott, "Surging Sales for Golden Triangle," *The Christian Science Monitor*, 1989]. However, friendlier relations were noted in January, 1990 [Henry Kamm, "U.S. and Laos Are Getting Friendlier," *The New York Times*, 1990]. Laos initiated moves for better relations (and economic aid), and the United States' initial response was favorable. The principal agreement is to coordinate efforts to fight the narcotics trade. See also Stephen Brookes, "The Perilous Swim in Heroin's Stream," *Insight*, 1990.

[30]In Cuba the trafficking organization, with or without Fidel Castro's official blessing (and this is arguable), operated at the highest levels of government and used whatever portion of the governmental apparatus was required for its activities. In any event, after repeated allegations, beginning as early as 1983, of the government's involvement in the smuggling of illegal narcotics into the United States [e.g., *Castro's Narcotics Trade* (Cuban American National Foundation, Inc., 1983), and James H. Michel, "Cuban Involvement in Narcotics Trafficking," *Department of State Bulletin*, 1983], Castro finally acknowledged the problem within his government (earlier knowledge of which he denied), had the principals tried and executed [Don Bohning,"Cuba Ties Officers to Drug Ring," *The Miami Herald*, 1989; Pablo Alfonso, "Expertos Sobre Cuba Dudan que

Castro Desconociera Narcotráfico," *El Nuevo Herald* (Miami), 1989; David Brock, "Drug Smuggling Runs Deep in Official Cuban Connection," *Insight*, 1989; Don Shannon, "High-Level Drug Case Rocks Cuba," *The Los Angeles Times*, 1989; Robert Pear, "Cubans Disclose a Drug Network," *The New York Times*, 1989; Guy Gugliotta, "Castro Learns Tough Lesson about the Business of Drugs," *The Miami Herald*, 1989], and then offered to collaborate with the U.S. government in drug interdiction efforts [Michael Isikoff, "Cuba Seeks U.S. Cooperation in Curbing Drug Flights," *The Washington Post*, 1989].

[31]In Honduras the organized trafficking appears to occur within the higher officer levels of the military [Thomas P. Anderson, "Politics and the Military in Honduras," *Current History*, 1988; Robert Collier, "Honduras: Mounting Evidence Implicates Armed Forces in Cocaine Trafficking," *Latinamerica Press*, 1988] or to be closely tied to those military officers [Brook Larmer, "Honduran Drug Kingpin Poses Dilemma for US Pursuers," *The Christian Science Monitor*, 1988; Mark B. Rosenberg, "Narcos and Politicos: The Politics of Drug Trafficking in Honduras," *Journal of Interamerican Studies and World Affairs*, 1988]. See also the country discussion in U.S. Department of State, Bureau of International Narcotics Matters, *International Narcotics Control Strategy Report*, 1989.

[32]Venezuela appears to have a home grown mafia that is tied to the drug trade, helping the Colombians use Venezuelan ports for export ["'Anti-Mafia' Law Follows Exposés," *Latin America Regional Reports*, 1984; Germán Carias, *La Mafia de la Cocaína*, 1986; "Increased Concern over Trafficking," *Latin American Weekly Report*, 1986; and Alan Riding, "Cocaine Finds a New Route in Venezuela," *The New York Times*, 1987].

[33]Vittoria Bacchetta ["Brazil: Drug Trafficking Gangs Vie for Control of Rio's Impoverished Favelas," *Latinamerica Press*, 1987] describes the movement of organized drug lords into the outskirts of São Paulo, where the residents defend their new benefactors from the police (for playing a "Robin Hood" role). Brazil has become vital in the cocaine trade as a transit country for Andean traffickers, as a producer of precursor chemicals, and, we can add, as an emerging coca cultivator [U.S. Department of State, Bureau of International Narcotics Matters, *International Narcotics Control Strategy Report*, 1989].

[34]Aside from transit, the Bahamas is believed to have developed a highly sophisticated money-laundering infrastructure [U.S. Congress, House Committee on Foreign Affairs, Hearing, "Narcotics Issues in the Bahamas and the Caribbean, 1987"].

[35]For several years, reports have been surfacing about Paraguay as a transshipment point for ether, acetone, and hydrochloric acid to be used in refining cocaine, with allegations that high-level officials in the Stroessner administration were implicated, as also were members of the present administration. See Kai Bird and Max Holland, "Paraguay: The Stroessner Connection," *Nation*, 1985; Joel Brinkley, "Paraguay Pledges Action on Cocaine," *The New York Times*, 1985; "Cocaine Route Turns North," *Latin American Weekly Report*, 1985; "Paraguay Refuses to Destroy Cocaine Production Chemicals," *Narcotics Control Digest*, 1985; Alan Riding, "Paraguay's Leader Denies Ties to Drugs," *The New York Times*, 1989; and U.S. Congress, House Committee on Foreign Affairs, Hearing, "Narcotics Review in South America, 1988".

[36]See Richard Bordreaux, "Scandal Spotlights Costa Rica's Battle on Drugs," *The Los Angeles Times*, 1989; J. D. Gannon, "Tiny Costa Rica Gamely Tackles Drug Trafficking," *The Christian Science Monitor*, 1989; Guy Gugliotta, "Costa Rica Drug Probe Taints Elite with Scandal," *The Miami Herald*, 1989; Tina Rosenberg," Miami South,"

The New Republic, 1986; and U.S. Congress, House Committee on Foreign Affairs, Hearing,"Narcotics Review in South America, 1988. "

[37]The references in our bibliography implicate Nigeria, speaking even of a "Nigerian Connection" [James Brooke, "West Africa Becomes Route for Heroin Trade," *The New York Times*, 1987]. See also Michael T. De Sanctis, "Nigerians Becoming More Active in the Smuggling of Southwest Asian Heroin in the U.S., Europe," *Narcotics Control Digest*, 1985; and the African section in United Nations Secretariat, Division of Narcotics Drugs, "Review of Drug Abuse and Measures to Reduce the Illicit Demand for Drugs by Region," *Bulletin on Narcotics*, 1987.

[38]Whereas Turkey used to be a major producer tied to the French Connection, it now facilitates the explosion in the heroin traffic moving west from eastern sources. One must presume, we suppose, the existence of a fairly sophisticated organization to accomplish this [Alan Cowell, "For Heroin, Turkey Is Land Bridge to West," *The New York Times*, 1987].

[39]Asian triads, with a fairly sophisticated hierarchical organization, are alleged to have much of the Canadian heroin trade [Fenton Bresler, *The Chinese Mafia*, 1981]. The Colombians have acquired a substantial ascendancy in the cocaine trade [Marcus Gee, Ken Macqueen, and Michael Rose, "Montreal's Deadly New Traffic in Cocaine," *Maclean's* 1986]. See also the discussions by Rodney T. Stamler, Robert C. Fahlman, and S. A. Keele, "Recent Trends in Illicit Drug Trafficking from the Canadian Perspective," *Bulletin on Narcotics*, 1983; Rodney T. Stamler, Robert C. Fahlman, and S A. Keele, "Illicit Traffic and Abuse of Cocaine," *Bulletin on Narcotics*, 1984; Rodney T. Stamler, and Robert C. Fahlman, editors, *RCMP National Drug Intelligence Estimate 1984/85 with Trend Indicators through 1987*; U.S. Congress, House Committee on Foreign Affairs, Hearing, "Narcotics Review in South America," 1988; and George Volsky "Jamaican Drug Gangs Thriving in U.S. [and Canadian] Cities," *The New York Times*, 1987.

[40]Some government personnel have organized to carry out the traffic [see, for example, "Island in a Stew," *The Economist*, 1985; and "Open Palms among the Palm Trees," *The Economist*, 1986]. By 1986 the matter had become so grave that Britain virtually reimposed direct rule on these dependencies.

[41]Vigorous denunciations of the now infamous General Manuel Noriega, nominal dictator of Panama until December, 1989, began in the early 1980s. See, for example, Linda Feldmann, "Hearings Tie Noriega to Contras and Drugs; Panamanian Bases Used for Contra Training," *The Christian Science Monitor*, 1988; "Panama: Corruption, Drug Charges Hurt but Fail to Unseat Noriega," *Latinamerica Press*, 1988; Steve Ropp, "General Noriega's Panama," *Current History*, 1986; U.S. Congress, House Committee on Foreign Affairs, Hearing, "Issues in United States Panamanian Anti-narcotics Control," 1986; U.S. Congress, House Select Committee on Narcotics Abuse and Control, Hearing, "Panama," 1986; U.S. Congress, House Committee on Foreign Affairs, Hearing, "Narcotics Review in Central America," 1988; U.S. Congress, Senate Permanent Subcommittee on Investigations of the Committee on Governmental Affairs, Hearing, "Drugs and Money Laundering in Panama," 1988; and U.S. Department of State, Bureau of International Narcotics Matters, *International Narcotics Control Strategy Report*, 1989.

[42]Juliana Geran Pilon ["The Bulgarian Connection: Drugs, Weapons and Terrorism," *Terrorism*, 1987] advances evidence to support her thesis that the Bulgarian government, intent on subverting Western governments in ways that appeared to have been orchestrated in Moscow, dealt in drugs, weapons, and terrorism. See also U.S. Department of State, Bureau of International Narcotics Matters, *International Narcotics Control Strategy*

Report, 1989.

[43]Right-wing business circles attached to Roberto d'Aubuisson are discussed as having attachments to the cocaine trade within El Salvador [Craig Pyes and Laurie Becklund, "Inside Dope in El Salvador," *The New Republic*, 1985].

[44]Arthur M. Shapiro ["Drugs and Politics in Latin America: The Argentine Connections," *The New Leader*, 1988] makes a connection between right-wing military and allied interests and the international drug trade. The former military dictatorship in Argentina helped to install the drug trafficking García Mesa regime in Bolivia in return for an agreement that García would not sell cocaine in Argentina. In 1988, however, the political right (very much on the defensive in Argentina) appeared to be financing itself through drug dealing and therefore using its good organizational offices to facilitate drug movements. See also U.S. Department of State, Bureau of International Narcotics Matters, *International Narcotics Control Strategy Report*, 1989, which expresses increasing concern that Argentina is becoming a refining and transit center for cocaine.

[45]There has been much official complicity in drug transshipments from Latin America destined for markets in the United States [Jim Hodgson, "Dominican Republic, Haiti Struggle Against Smuggling of Basic Food Items, Narcotics," *Latinamerica Press*, 1988]. However, by 1989 Haiti's new president was receiving praise for his efforts to combat narcotics—"an effort that may have been a factor in recent coup attempts against him" [Robert Pear, "U.S. Praises Haitian on Drug Efforts," *The New York Times*, 1989]. See also U.S. Department of State, Bureau of International Narcotics Matters, *International Narcotics Control Strategy Report*, 1989.

[46]Mario Arango and Jorge Child, *Narcotráfico: Imperio de la Cocaína*, 1987; William Branigin, "The Mexican Connection," *The Washington Post*, 1988; Tyler Bridges, "Drug Traffickers, Guerrillas Curtail Peru's Antidrug Efforts," *The Christian Science Monitor*, 1987; Fabio Castillo, *Los Jinetes de la Cocaína*, 1987; Shirley Christian, "Drug Case Raises Doubts in Bolivia," *The New York Times*, 1988; "Cocaine: The Military Connection," *Latin America Regional Reports*, 1980; Merrill Collett, "Drug Barons' Tentacles Run Deep in Colombian Society," *The Christian Science Monitor*, 1987; Merrill Collett, "Colombia's Sophisticated Drug Traffickers Trigger Economic Boom, Political Violence," *Latinamerica Press*, 1988; Merrill Collett, "Colombia's Losing War with Drug Kings," *The Christian Science Monitor*, 1988; Merrill Collett, "Collision Course in Colombia: Traffickers Threaten Land Reform," *The Christian Science Monitor*, 1989; "Colombia; All Fall Down," *The Economist*, 1988; "Colombianization," *World Press Review*, 1989; "Drug Mafia Could Have Killed Pardo," *Latin American Weekly Report*, 1987; George Hackett and Michael A. Lerner, "L.A. Law: Gangs and Crack," *Newsweek*, 1987; Michael Isikoff and Eugene Robinson, "Colombia's Drug Kings Becoming Entrenched; Cocaine Profits Penetrating Economy," *The Washington Post*, 1989; Brook Larmer, "Colombians Take over 'Coke' Trade in Mexico," *The Christian Science Monitor*, 1989; Brook Larmer, "Mexico's Corruption Clampdown; Arrest of Corrupt Officials Along with Drug Baron May Root out Graft," *The Christian Science Monitor*, 1989; Ruth Marcus, "Assault on Cartel Fails to Halt Drugs; Prosecutors Say Leader of Colombian Group Smuggled Tons of Cocaine into the U.S.," *The Washington Post*, 1988; President's Commission on Organized Crime, *Organized Crime and Cocaine Trafficking*, 1984; Selwyn Raab, "Links to 200 Murders in New York City Last Year; The Ruthless Young Crack Gangsters," *The New York Times*, 1988; Warren Richey,"Cocaine Connection: Wealth, Violence, Drugs and Colombia," *The Christian Science Monitor*, 1985; Alan Riding, "Cocaine Billionaires: The Men Who Hold Colombia Hostage," *The New York Times*, 1987; Alan Riding, "Colombian Cocaine Dealers

Tap European Market," *The New York Times*, 1989; Norman Riley, "The Crack Boom is Really an Echo," *Crisis*, 1989; William E. Schmidt, "Crack Epidemic Missing Chicago in Urban Sweep," *The New York Times*, 1989; and Karen Wolman, "Europe's Cocaine Boom Confounds Antidrug War," *The Christian Science Monitor*, 1989.

⁴⁷John Bacon, "Is the French Connection Really Dead?" *Drug Enforcement*, 1981; Ralph Blumenthal, *Last Days of the Sicilians*, 1988; Fenton Bresler, *The Trail of the Triads*, 1980; Fenton Bresler, *The Chinese Mafia*, 1981; Stephen Brookes, "Chinese Mafia Takes Vice Abroad," *Insight*, 1989; Steven Brookes, "The Perilous Swim in Heroin's Stream," *Insight*, 1990; Peter Kerr, "Chasing the Heroin from Plush Hotel to Mean Streets," *The New York Times*, 1987; Peter Kerr, "Chinese Now Dominate New York Heroin Trade," *The New York Times*, 1987; Matt Lait, "Heroin Traffic Shifts to the West; Mexican, Asian Smugglers Dominate; Seizures Rise Dramatically," *The Washington Post*, 1989; Emily Lau, "Brotherhood of Extortion," *Far Eastern Economic Review*, 1984; Robert B. McBride, "Business as Usual: Heroin Distribution in the United States," *Journal of Drug Issues*, 1983; Sean M. McWeeney, "The Sicilian Mafia and Its Impact on the United States," *FBI Law Enforcement Bulletin*, 1987; William Overend, "Violence Feared as Asian Heroin Influx Soars," *Los Angeles Times*, 1988; President's Commission on Organized Crime, *Organized Crime and Heroin Trafficking*, 1985; Keith B. Richburg, "More Heroin Said to Enter U.S. from Asia; Chinese Gangs Replacing Traditional Organized Crime Networks," *The Washington Post*, 1988; Carl Robinson, "The Day of the Triads," *Newsweek*, 1988; Michael De Sanctis, "Nigerians Becoming More Active in the Smuggling of Southwest Asian Heroin in the U.S., Europe, *Narcotics Control Digest*, 1985; David Clark Scott, "Surging Sales for Golden Triangle: Many Drug Enforcement Officials Believe Hong Kong Crime Syndicates Are Responsible," *The Christian Science Monitor*, 1989; Rodney T. Stamler, Robert C. Fahlman, and S. A. Keele, "Recent Trends in Illicit Drug Trafficking from the Canadian Perspective," *Bulletin on Narcotics*, 1983; and Yev Yelin, "Why the 'Golden Crescent' Still Flourishes," *The New York Times*, 1985.

⁴⁸Frances A. Hunt, "Are the National Forests Going to Pot?" *American Forests*, 1987; James B. Slaughter, "Marijuana Prohibition in the U.S.: History and Analysis of a Failed Policy," *Columbia Journal of Law and Social Problems*, 1988; Rodney .T. Stamler, Robert C. Fahlman, and S. A. Keele, "Recent Trends in Illicit Drug Trafficking from the Canadian Perspective," *Bulletin on Narcotics*, 1983; U.S. Congress, House Committee on Government Operations, "Commercial Production and Distribution of Domestic Marijuana, 1983;" and U.S. Department of Justice, Cannabis Investigations Section, Drug Enforcement Administration, *1987 Domestic Cannabis Eradication/Suppression Program*, 1987.

⁴⁹See "U.S. Has 43 Big Drug Groups," *The Miami Herald*, 1989; and Rachel Ehrenfeld, "Narco-Terrorism and the Cuban Connection," *Strategic Review*, 1988.

⁵⁰Cathy Booth, "Tentacles of the Octopus; The Mafia Brings Europe's Worst Drug Epidemic Home," *Time*, 1988.

⁵¹"U.S. Has 43 Big Drug Groups," *The Miami Herald*, 1989.

⁵²See Brook Larmer, "Colombians Take over 'Coke' Trade in Mexico," *The Christian Science Monitor*, 1989; and William Overend, "Cocaine Floods Southland via Colombia-Mexico Link," *The Los Angeles Times*, 1987.

⁵³Elliott Abrams, in an address before the Council on Foreign Relations, made the Reagan administration's brief for the existence of an alliance between drug traffickers and terrorists ["Drug Wars: The New Alliance against Traffickers and Terrorists," *Department of State Bulletin*, 1986]. See also Clyde Taylor, "Links between

International Narcotics Trafficking and Terrorism," *Department of State Bulletin*, 1985. Affirming the connection was the general tenor of several U.S. congressional hearings [e.g., U.S. Congress, Senate Committee on Labor and Human Resources, Subcommittee on Alcoholism and Drug Abuse of the Committee on Labor and Human Resources, Hearing, "Drugs and Terrorism, 1984"; U.S. Congress, Senate Committee on Foreign Relations and the Committee on the Judiciary, Joint Hearing, "International Terrorism, Insurgency, and Drug Trafficking: Present Trends in Terrorist Activity," 1985; and U.S. Congress, Senate Subcommittee on Terrorism, Narcotics and International Operations of the Committee on Foreign Relations, "Drugs, Law Enforcement and Foreign Policy," 1988]. See also Cynthia McClintock, "The War on Drugs: The Peruvian Case," *Journal of Interamerican Studies and World Affairs*, 1988.

[54]See, for example, James Adams, *The Financing of Terror*, 1986. Robert Cribb shows how the Indonesian independence movement (1945–1949) was financed in large part through the sale of opium when the Dutch trade blockade suppressed normal commerce in rubber and sugar ["Opium and the Indonesian Revolution," *Modern Asian Studies*, 1988]. Grant Wardlaw argues strongly against the linkages being understood in political or ideological terms. Drug connections exist, on the whole, for practical economic reasons rather than ideological ones ["Linkages between the Illegal Drugs Traffic and Terrorism," *Conflict Quarterly*, 1988].

[55]The best example is *Sendero Luminoso* (Shining Path) in Peru. This band of guerrillas entered the upper Huallaga Valley, Peru's principal coca growing region, as early as 1984 and successfully turned regional opinion against a U.S.-backed coca eradication program into a campaign of antigovernment violence. In the process, the guerrillas have gained something of a sanctuary and considerable peasant support [Jonathan Cavanagh, "Peru Rebels Threaten U.S. Drug Program," *The Wall Street Journal*, 1984]. It is of considerable interest that whenever Shining Path takes over a village, it cleans up streets, improves public services, and imposes a bloody but effective brand of justice in a region that the central government, as far as municipal services and government are concerned, has largely abandoned. The guerrillas, by protecting the peasants, facilitate the production of drugs, but they prohibit their use in the areas they control [Merrill Collett, "Maoist Guerrilla Band Complicates Antidrug War in Peru," *The Washington Post*, 1988; and Collett, "Peruvians Flock to Upper Huallaga Valley to Cash in on Expanding Coca Bonanza," *Latinamerica Press*, 1988]. Collett, who shows Shining Path to be involved in coca growing regions to produce income and expand their ideological influence, decries arguments attempting to show a collaborative relationship between the guerrillas and actual drug traffickers [Merrill Collett, "The Myth of the Narco-Guerrillas," *The Nation*, 1988]. Richard B. Craig, who takes a slightly different view on Shining Path, suggests a more explicit connection ["Illicit Drug Traffic: Implications for South American Source Countries," *Journal of Interamerican Studies and World Affairs*, 1987]. Monte Hayes ["Peru Rebels Profit from Drug Ties," *The Los Angeles Times*, 1987] argues that Shining Path has worked since 1987 in a "deadly alliance" with drug dealers and peasants involved in the drug trade and that the coca trade has become a principal source of income for the terrorists. See also Ronald Berg, "Sendero Luminoso and the Peasantry of Andahuaylas," *Journal of Interamerican Studies and World Affairs*, 1987; Michael Isikoff, "U.S. Suffering Setbacks in Latin Drug Offensive; Violence Mounting as Coca Production Soars," *The Washington Post*, 1989; Cynthia McClintock, "The War on Drugs: The Peruvian Case," *Journal of Interamerican Studies and World Affairs*, 1988; Cynthia McClintock et al., "Peru's Harvest of Instability and Terrorism," *The Christian Science Monitor*, 1989; Alan Riding, "Peru's Two Complex Battles: Drugs and Terror," *The New York Times*, 1987; Alan Riding, "Rebels Disrupting Coca Eradication

in Peru," *The New York Times*, 1989; James F. Smith, "Peruvian Guerrillas Unite Peasants, Set Social Order," *The Los Angeles Times*, 1989; and, David Werlich, "Debt, Democracy and Terrorism in Peru," *Current History*, 1987. Robin Kirk ["Peru: Ayacucho Relief Work Faces Multiple Obstacles," *Latinamerica Press*, 1987] describes the "home country" of Shining Path (its abode before it got into the drug trade).

⁵⁶Wilson Ring, "Opium Production Rises in Guatemala Mountains," *The Washington Post*, 1989.

⁵⁷Scott B. MacDonald, *Mountain High, White Avalanche: Cocaine and Power in the Andean States and Panama*, 1989. The never-ending spiral of violence has caused some peasant growers to conclude that the economic returns are simply not worth the risks [Mark A. Uhlig, "Colombia's War on Cocaine: Farmers' Fears Help Cause," *The New York Times*, 1989].

⁵⁸See, for example, Leslie Wirpsa, "Colombian Mafia Hurt by Testimony of Key Deserter," *The Miami Herald*, 1989.

⁵⁹Robert Thomas Baratta, "Political Violence in Ecuador and the AVC," *Terrorism*, 1987.

⁶⁰See D. P. Kumarasingha, "Drugs—A Growing Problem in Sri Lanka," *Forensic Science International*, 1988.

⁶¹Jonathan Kwitny, "Money, Drugs and the Contras," *The Nation*, 1987.

⁶²See Mary Thornton, "Sales of Opium Reportedly Fund Afghan Rebels, *The Washington Post*, 1983.

⁶³See Dave Miller, "Drug Mafia Arms Campesinos," *Latinamerica Press*, 1988; and "Probing into the Underworld," *Latin America Regional Reports*, 1983.

⁶⁴Timothy Ross, "Colombia Goes after Drug Barons," *The Christian Science Monitor*, 1987.

⁶⁵See Barbara Crossette, "An Opium Warlord's News Conference Spurs Burma and Thailand to Battle Him," *The New York Times*, 1987; and Lucy Komisar, "Solving Burma's Guerrilla War Would End the Opium Trade," *The Christian Science Monitor*, 1988. Edith T. Mirante ["Burma—Frontier Minorities in Arms," *Cultural Survival Quarterly*, 1987] shows that the opium trade has allowed insurgent groups to obtain better weapons than those of the Burmese army. There has been considerable discussion that the civil war in Burma is drug driven rather than equity driven, that is, that insurgency exists because drugs exist as an end rather than as a means. The contrary view is expressed by Josef Silverstein ["Foreign Mediation Could Help End Burma's Civil War," *Far Eastern Economic Review*, 1988]. With still another view, David L. Westrate ["How Are Drug Trafficking and Terrorism Related?" *Narcotics Control Digest*, 1985] compares Burma with Colombia. One of the fallouts in Thailand is a considerable official attack on the Hmong and other minorities, all justified on the basis of the Hmong being "opium producers," "insurgents," and "destroyers of the environment," accusations to which Nicholas Tapp takes strong exception [*The Hmong of Thailand: Opium People of the Golden Triangle*, 1986].

⁶⁶See Juliana Geran Pilon, "The Bulgarian Connection: Drugs, Weapons and Terrorism," *Terrorism*, 1987.

⁶⁷John H. Langer, "Recent Developments in Drug Trafficking: The Terrorism Connection," *The Police Chief*, 1986.

⁶⁸As of 1987 the FBI concluded that no linkages between narcotics traffickers and terrorist groups in the United States appeared to exist. The agency's representative did allow, however, for the development of such linkages in view of events elsewhere in the

world [Daniel Boyce, "Narco-Terrorism," *FBI Law Enforcement Bulletin*,1987]. Patricia A. Jones ["Cocaine and Violence: A Marriage Made in Hell!" *Crisis*, 1989] says that the worst fears have now come to pass, because the terrorist organizations connected with the drug industry, if not terrorist activities by drug organizations, are taking place both in the United States and in South America.

[69]This point is advanced by Michael Satchell, "Narcotics: Terror's New Ally," *U.S. News and World Report*, 1987. Mark S. Steinitz ["Insurgents, Terrorists, and the Drug Trade," *The Washington Quarterly*, 1985] examines the evidence of involvement of terrorists in the drug trade with respect to Latin America, Southeast Asia, the Middle East, and Europe, examining the factors behind the linkages and, in particular, the changing patterns of the international drug scene that have brought insurgency, terrorism, and the drug trade into closer geographical proximity.

[70]See, for example, "Slaughter in the Streets; Crack Touches off a Homicide Epidemic," *Time*, 1988; and George Hackett and Michael A. Lerner, "L.A. Law: Gangs and Crack," *Newsweek*, 1987. Sometimes the struggles are played out in the producer countries themselves. Pedro Camargo reports the veritable destruction of the central plaza in the city of Armenia, Colombia, as warring gangs attached to the Medellín and Cali cartels struggled for the New York cocaine market [Pedro Pablo Camargo, "Luchan los Narcos por el Control de las Plazas; Destruyen Centro Commercial y Matan un Alcalde," *Excelsior*, 1989]. Peter Reuter appears to argue that under conditions of market imbalance (supply exceeding demand) of goods in an illicit traffic, carnage would result whether the traffic was "organized" or not ["An Economist Looks at the Carnage," *The Washington Post*, 1989].

[71]See, for example, Joseph B. Treaster, "Drug Traffickers' Peace Offer Divides Colombians," *The New York Times*, 1990; and Treaster, "Eager for Good Press, Drug Bosses Sacrifice Laboratory in Colombia," *The New York Times*, 1990. Earlier, hope was raised but quickly dashed. See Michael Isikoff, "Medellín Cartel Leaders Offered U.S. a Deal; Officials Rebuffed Plan That Sought Amnesty for Ending Drug Trade, Providing Data on Leftists," *The Washington Post*, 1988.

[72]"Suspect Tied to Medellín Cartel Leadership Becomes 3rd to Surrender," *The New York Times*, 1991; and Joseph B. Treaster, "Surrender of Cocaine Smuggler Isn't Expected to Have Large Effect," *The New York Times*, 1991.

[73]Barbara Crossette, "An Opium Warlord's News Conference Spurs Burma and Thailand to Battle Him," *The New York Times*, 1987. See also Kim Gooi and John McBeth, "High-Priced High," *Far Eastern Economic Review*, 1986; Vichai S., "Warlords of the Poppy Fields," *Bangkok Post*, 1983; Paisal Sricharatchanya, "Beating a Retreat," *Far Eastern Economic Review*, 1987; Daniel Burstein,"The Deadly Politics of Opium," *Maclean's*, 1982; Rodney Tasker, "Chasing the Red Dragon," *Far Eastern Economic Review*, 1987; Bertil Lintner, "Orchards and Opium," *Far Eastern Economic Review*, 1984; David Clark Scott, "Surging Sales for Golden Triangle: Many Drug-Enforcement Officials Believe Hong Kong Crime Syndicates Are Responsible," *The Christian Science Monitor*, 1989; and Denis D. Gray, "A Deluge from the Golden Triangle," *Nation*, 1989.

[74]"Now Let's Slay the Other Dragon," *The Economist*, 1988.

[75]"Bolivian Leader Starts a Fast," *The New York Times*, 1984. See also the discussion by Warren Hoge, "Bolivians Find Patron in Reputed Drug Chief," *The New York Times*, 1982.

[76]See Jeff Leen, "Bush Lauds Colombia Drug Battle," *The Miami Herald*, 1989; Jonas Bernstein, "Bitter Convulsions in a Nation under the Influence of Drugs," *Insight*, 1989; and Miguel Varon, "Drug Trade Brings in $2 Billion Annually: Despite Crackdown, Colombian Drug Barons Control Economy," *Latinamerica Press*, 1987.

[77]Alan Riding, "Cocaine Billionaires: The Men Who Hold Colombia Hostage," *The New York Times*, 1987.

[78]Luís Méndez, *Caro Quintero al Trasluz*, 1985.

[79]Merrill Collett, "Colombia's Sophisticated Drug Traffickers Trigger Economic Boom, Political Violence," *Latinamerica Press*, 1988.

[80]See, for example, William R. Long, "Drug Lords Rule over Rio's Slums," *The Los Angeles Times*, 1987; Warren Hoge, "Bolivians Find Patron in Reputed Drug Chief," *The New York Times*, 1982; Vittoria Bacchetta, "Brazil: Drug Trafficking Gangs Vie for Control of Rio's Impoverished Favelas," *Latinamerica Press*, 1987; and John Ross, "Mexican Youth Make Folk Hero out of Drug Lord," *Latinamerica Press*, 1987.

[81]See, for example, Leon Dash, "A Dealer's Rule: Be Willing to Die," *The Washington Post*, 1989; Wayne Greenhaw, *Flying High: Inside Big-Time Drug Smuggling*, 1984; and Patricia A. Adler, *Wheeling and Dealing: An Ethnography of an Upper-Level Drug Dealing and Smuggling Community*, 1985.

[82]On the general issue, see Charles W. Blau et al., *Investigation and Prosecution of Illegal Money Laundering: A Guide to the Bank Secrecy Act*, 1983; Paula Dwyer, "Getting Banks to Just Say 'No.'" *Business Week*, 1989; Allan Dodds Frank, "See No Evil," *Forbes*, 1986; Stephen Labaton, "Unassuming Store Fronts Believed to Launder Drug Dealer's Profits," *The New York Times*, 1989; U.S. Congress, House Committee on the Judiciary, Subcommittee on Crime, Hearings, "Use of Casinos to Launder Proceeds of Drug Trafficking and Organized crime, 1984;" U.S. Department of Justice, Federal Bureau of Investigation, *Financial Investigative Techniques: Money Laundering*, 1984; and Karen Wolman, "Italy Takes Aim at Money Laundering," *The Christian Science Monitor*, 1989.

[83]We have no published reports on this phenomenon. The coverage was carried on CNN in February 1990.

[84]For example, when a drug-fueled economic boom came to several south Texas communities, one auto dealer was heard to say: "This is an amazing place. They'll come in with paper sacks filled with money, almost always in $20 bills, and buy a car. I don't condone drug smuggling, but I tell you, I love these guys . . . the hardest part is counting out $40,000 in 20s" [John Dillin, "Narco Economy: Drug Traffic Thrives along Border," *The Christian Science Monitor*, 1989]. In the same community, while trying to establish whether drug-money laundering was occurring, Internal Revenue Service agents were "actually lectured by bank officials that investigations were bad for business" [Dillin, "Narco Economy"]. When California implemented its antimarijuana drive known as CAMP, local residents in Humbolt County turned down federal antinarcotics money in the late 1970s because of the extraordinary economic boom from the marijuana trade. Residents did not want the boom disturbed [Mark Beauchamp, "Getting Straight," *Forbes*, 1987].

[85]The hard-currency returns entering a country are of some obvious assistance if there is a shortage. Allegations have been made that the government of Laos promotes the cultivation and export of marijuana in order to earn desperately needed foreign exchange [Barbara Crossette, "Thai Officials Say Laos Turns to Marijuana to Help Budget," *The New York Times*, 1987]. Debt is said to drive the pursuit of drug-related foreign exchange earnings [Peter Hakim, "Debt and Drugs: Deadly Partnership," *The Christian*

Science Monitor, 1987]. See also Kevin Healy, "Bolivia and Cocaine: A Developing Country's Dilemmas," *British Journal of Addiction*, 1988; and Rensselaer Lee III, "The Drug Trade and Developing Countries," *Policy Focus*, 1987.

[86]William D. Montalbano, "Latins Push Belated War on Cocaine," *The Los Angeles Times*, 1985.

[87]James Painter, "Bolivia Tries to Break Its Economic Addiction," *The Christian Science Monitor*, 1990; and James Brooke, "Peru, Its U.S. Aid Imperiled, Plots a New Drug Strategy," *The New York Times*, 1991.

[88]See Andrew Rosenthal, "3 Andean Leaders and Bush Pledge Drug Cooperation: 'First Anti-Drug Cartel,'" *The New York Times*, 1990.

[89]See Joseph B. Treaster, "A Peruvian Peasant Fails to See Bush," *The New York Times*, 1990.

[90]F. LaMond Tullis, "Cocaine and Food: Likely Effects of a Burgeoning Transnational Industry on Food Production in Bolivia and Peru," in *Pursuing Food Security*, 1987, pp. 257-58. See also Marlise Simons, "Cocaine Means Cash in Bolivia Bank," *The New York Times*, 1984.

[91]Everett Martin, "A Little Cattle Town in Bolivia Is Thriving as a Financial Center," *The Wall Street Journal*, 1983.

[92]Edmundo Morales, "Land Reform, Social Change, and Modernization in the National Periphery: A Study of Five Villages in the Northeastern Andes of Peru," Ph.D. diss., 1983. Morales holds, nevertheless, that "the direct economic relationship between peasants, the urban poor and the underworld brings a plethora of negative effects that disturb the traditional life in the countryside" (p. 136).

[93]David Kline, "From a Smugglers' Paradise Comes Hell," *Maclean's*, 1982; David Kline, "The Khyber Connection," *The Christian Science Monitor*, 1982; U.S. Department of State, Bureau of International Narcotics Matters, *International Narcotics Control Strategy Report*, annuals of 1989, 1990, 1991.

[94]Terence White, "The Drug-Abuse Epidemic Coursing through Pakistan," *Far Eastern Economic Review*, 1985.

[95]"Pakistan Tribes a Big Hurdle in Drive to Limit Heroin Trade," *Narcotics Control Digest*, 1985.

[96]Richard Weintraub, "Pakistani Drug Drive Seen in 2 Major Hauls; Military Officers Held in Seizure of Heroin," *The Washington Post*, 1986.

[97]Yev Yelin, "Why the 'Golden Crescent' Still Flourishes," *The New York Times*, 1985.

[98]Henry Kamm, "Afghan Opium Yield up as Pakistan Curbs Crop," *The New York Times*, 1988.

[99]F. LaMond Tullis, "Cocaine and Food," in *Pursuing Food Security*, p. 253.

[100]Carlos Norberto Cagliotti, "La Economía de la Coca en Bolivia," *Revista de la Sanidad de las Fuerzas Policiales*, 1981.

[101]Clara Germani, "In Bolivia, The Hard Reality of Coca; Even Bold Antidrug Measures Can't Beat the Economic Facts," *The Christian Science Monitor*, 1988. See also Peter Hakim, "Debt and Drugs: Deadly Partnership," *The Christian Science Monitor*, 1987; and Kevin Healy, "Bolivia and Cocaine: A Developing Country's Dilemmas," *British Journal of Addiction*, 1988.

[102] "Bolivia under Paz Estenssoro," *Latinamerica Press*, 1988.

[103]Alan Riding reports on the continuing surges of antigovernment/anti–U.S. violence in Peru's upper Huallaga Valley ["Rebels Disrupting Coca Eradication in Peru," *New York Times*, 1989] as does Merrill Collett ["Maoist Guerrilla Band Complicates Antidrug War in Peru," *The Washington Post*, 1988]. Themes of production increases and violence in both Bolivia and Peru are picked up by Richard B. Craig ["Illicit Drug Traffic: Implications for South American Source Countries," *Journal of Interamerican Studies and World Affairs*, 1987].

[104]James Painter, "Bolivia Tries to Break Its Economic Addiction," *The Christian Science Monitor*, 1990.

[105]Rensselaer W. Lee III, "Why the U.S. Cannot Stop South American Cocaine," *Orbis*, 1988.

[106]Bruce M. Bagley, "The New Hundred Years War? US National Security and the War on Drugs in Latin America," *Journal of Interamerican Studies and World Affairs*, 1988.

[107]John McBeth, "The Opium Laws," *Far Eastern Economic Review*, 1984.

[108]The early theoretical literature on these points is reviewed in F. LaMond Tullis, *Politics and Social Change in Third World Countries*, 1973; and Tullis, *Lord and Peasant in Peru*, 1970.

[109]Bertil Lintner, "The Deadly Deluge," *Far Eastern Economic Review*, 1987.

[110]"Bolivia: Laid-off Miners Survive by Growing Coca," *Latinamerica Press*, 1988.

[111]See, for example, Ray Henkel, "The Move to the Oriente: Colonization and Environmental Impact," in *Modern-Day Bolivia: Legacy of the Revolution and Prospects for the Future*, J. R. Ladman, ed., 1982; and D. A. Eastwood and H. J. Pollard, "Colonization and Cocaine in the Chapare, Bolivia: A Development Paradox for Colonization Theory," *Tijdschrift Voor Economishe en Sociale Geografie*, 1986.

[112]Edmundo Morales, *Cocaine: White Gold Rush in Peru*, 1989.

[113]D. A. Eastwood and H. J. Pollard, "The Accelerating Growth of Coca and Colonisation in Bolivia," *Geography*, 1987.

[114]*Efectos del Narcotráfico: Temas de Política Social*, 1988, with particular attention to the contributions by Federico Aguiló.

[115]Joseph B. Treaster, "A Peruvian Peasant Fails to See Bush, *The New York Times*, 1990. See also David P. Werlich, "Peru: García Loses His Charm," *Current History*, 1988.

[116]See, for example, the observations by Shirley Christian ["Bolivians Fight Efforts to Eradicate Coca," *The New York Times*, 1987], Lesley Gill [*Peasants, Entrepreneurs, and Social Change*, 1987], Kevin Healy ["Bolivia and Cocaine: A Developing Country's Dilemmas," *British Journal of Addiction*, 1988; "Coca, the State, and the Peasantry in Bolivia, 1982–1988," *Journal of Interamerican Studies and World Affairs*, 1988; and "The Political Ascent of Bolivia's Peasant Coca Leaf Producers," paper presented at the fifteenth International Congress of the Latin American Studies Association, 1989], Michael Isikoff ["DEA in Bolivia: 'Guerrilla Warfare,' Coca Traffic Proves Resistant," *The Washington Post*, 1989], Dave Miller ["Drug Mafia Arms Campesinos," *Latinamerica Press*, 1988], James Painter ["Bolivia's New President Faces an Old Problem: How to Control Coca Growing," *Latinamerica Press*, 1989], and Susanna Rance ["Bolivia: New Coca Control Law Aggravates Tense Situation," *Latinamerica Press*, 1988].

[117]"Riding High on Cocaine," *Latin America Regional Reports*, 1983.

[118]See the discussion by Fabio Castillo, *Los Jinetes de la Cocaína*, 1987, and "Narcoespías Infiltran Gobierno Colombiano," *El Nuevo Herald*, 1989.

[119]Yev Yelin, "Why the 'Golden Crescent' Still Flourishes," *The New York Times*, 1985. Richard M. Weintraub ["Pakistani Drug Drive Seen in 2 Major Hauls; Military Officers Held in Seizure of Heroin," *The Washington Post*, 1986] avers that with obvious complicity and evidence of corruption, two officers were detained and placed under arrest.

[120]Marcial Barrón, *El Infierno Blanco*, 1984.

[121]Robert Collier, "Honduras: Mounting Evidence Implicates Armed Forces in Cocaine Trafficking," *Latinamerica Press*, 1988.

[122]"Cocaine Scandal Hits Lima," *Latin America Weekly Report*, 1985.

[123]Clara Germani, "Drug Corruption Is Main Issue in Bahamian Election," *The Christian Science Monitor*, 1987; Joel Brinkley, "Drugs and Graft Main Issue in Bahamas Vote," *The New York Times*, 1987.

[124]Don A. Schanche, "Bahamas Leader Denies Drug Ties," *The Los Angeles Times*, 1989.

[125]See "Cocaine: The Military Connection," *Latin America Regional Reports*, 1980; Gregorio Selser, *Bolivia: El Cuartelazo de los Cocadólares*, 1982; Richard B. Craig, "Illicit Drug Traffic: Implications for South American Source Countries," *Journal of Interamerican Studies and World Affairs*, 1987; Gerdo Irusta and J. Poirot, *Los Adoradores de la Diosa Blanca: Relatos Verídicos del Narcotráfico en Bolivia*, 1986; *Narcotráfico y Política: Militarismo y Mafia en Bolivia*, 1982.

[126]Three days later, six unidentified persons machine gunned the man's home. While it was said that for the first time the Bolivian congress had the documents it needed "to lift the veil that so generously has been provided to protect the drug trafficker's network," owing to infiltration it is entirely uncertain whether the government can actually muster enough resolve to do so [Erick Foronda, "Bolivia: Military Expose Attests Official Protection of Druglords," *Latinamerica Press*, 1988].

[127]Rone Tempest, "Drugs, Murder Attempt, Corruption Rob Peaceful Nepal of Its Innocence," *The Los Angeles Times*, 1987.

[128]The phenomenon is widely recognized. See, for example, the short treatise by Mary Williams Walsh, "Many Mexican Police Supplement Low Pay with 'Tips' and 'Fines,'" *The Wall Street Journal*, 1986.

[129]See the Mexican entries in note 10 of this chapter, observing, in particular, John J. Fialka's account of how police at all levels profit from the trade in marijuana, accumulating huge assets ["Death of US Agent in Mexico Drug Case Uncovers Grid of Graft," *The Wall Street Journal*, 1986]. See also Brook Larmer, "Mexico's Corruption Clampdown," *The Christian Science Monitor*, 1989.

[130]Larry Rohter, "Mexico Using Special Squad in Drug War," *The New York Times*, 1989.

[131]See, for example, Cuban-American National Foundation, Inc., *Castro's Narcotics Trade*, 1983 and James H. Michel, "Cuban Involvement in Narcotics Trafficking," *Department of State Bulletin*, 1983.

[132]Don Bohning, "Cuba Ties Officers to Drug Ring," *The Miami Herald*, 1989; Pablo Alfonso, "Expertos Sobre Cuba Dudan que Castro Desconociera Narcotráfico," *El Nuevo Herald*, 1989; David Brock, "Drug Smuggling Runs Deep in Official Cuban Connection," *Insight*, 1989; Don Shannon, "High-Level Drug Case Rocks Cuba," *The Los Angeles Times*, 1989; Robert Pear, "Cubans Disclose a Drug Network," *The New York Times*, 1989; and Guy Gugliotta, "Castro Learns Tough Lesson about the Business of Drugs," *The Miami Herald*, 1989.

[133]Michael Isikoff, "Cuba Seeks U.S. Cooperation in Curbing Drug Flights," *The Washington Post*, 1989.

[134]Michael Isikoff, "Drug Flights Unabated over Cuba," *The Washington Post*, 1989.

[135]"Purga en la Policía Colombiana, *El Nuevo Herald*, 1989.

[136]"Secret Report on Drugs Is Leaked," *Latin American Weekly Report*, 1987.

[137]"Arrested DEA Agent May Have Tipped off Major Cocaine Ring," *The Miami Herald*, 1989.

[138]Joel Brinkley, "Contra Arms Crews Said to Smuggle Drugs," *The New York Times*, 1987; Robert Collier, "Honduras: Mounting Evidence Implicates Armed Forces in Cocaine Trafficking," *Latinamerica Press*, 1988; Michael Isikoff, "Reagan Aides Accused of Hampering Drug War; Contra Aid Had Priority over Fighting Traffickers, Hill Report Says," *The Washington Post*, 1989; and U.S. Congress, Senate Subcommittee on Terrorism, Narcotics and International Operations of the Committee on Foreign Relations, "Drugs, Law Enforcement and Foreign Policy, 1988."

[139]Brook Larmer, "Honduran Drug Kingpin Poses Dilemma for US Pursuers," *The Christian Science Monitor*, 1988.

[140]The discussion is raised most vigorously for Colombia. See Alvaro Camacho, *Droga, Corrupción y Poder: Marijuana y Cocaína en la Sociedad Colombiana*, 1981; Fabio Castillo, *Los Jinetes de la Cocaína*, 1987; and Michael Flatte and Alexei J. Cowett, "Drugs and Politics: An Unhealthy Mix," *Harvard International Review*, 1986. For a general discussion, see Ethan Nadelmann, "The DEA in Latin America: Dealing with Institutionalized Corruption," *Journal of Interamerican Studies and World Affairs*, 1987.

[141]See, for example, James Mills, *The Underground Empire: Where Crime and Governments Embrace*, 1986. Jonathan Kwitny [*The Crimes of Patriots: A True Tale of Dope, Dirty Money, and the CIA*, 1987] exposes, by the author's claim, "crimes committed against American citizens in pursuit of [our anticommunist foreign] policy." In exposing the workings of a small Australian bank, the author draws in a network of U.S. generals, admirals, and CIA operatives, including a former director of the CIA, into operations that promoted the heroin trade, tax evasion, and gun running. Lawrence Lifschultz ["Inside the Kingdom of Heroin," *The Nation*, 1988] discusses President Zia of Pakistan and President George Bush.

[142]See, in general, Herbert E. Alexander and Gerald E. Caiden, eds., *The Politics and Economics of Organized Crime*, 1985; Marcial Barrón, *El Infierno Blanco*, 1984; Barbara Bradley, "Cracking the Drug Menace," *The Christian Science Monitor*, 1988; Alvaro Camacho, *Droga, Corrupción y Poder: Marijuana y Cocaína en la Sociedad Colombiana*, 1981; Richard Craig, "Human Rights and Mexico's Antidrug Campaign," *Social Science Quarterly*, 1980; Richard B. Craig, "Illicit Drug Traffic: Implications for South American Source Countries," *Journal of Interamerican Studies and World Affairs*, 1987; Michael Flatte and Alexei J. Cowett, "Drugs and Politics: An Unhealthy Mix," *Harvard International Review*, 1986; Bradley Graham, "Impact of Colombian Traffickers Spreads: Corrupted Officials Said to Undercut Hemispheric Security," *The Washington Post*, 1988; Ray Henkel, "The Bolivian Cocaine Industry," *Studies in Third World Societies*, 1988; Michael Isikoff, "Warriors against Cocaine: It's Guerrilla Warfare for DEA Agents on the Bolivian Front Lines," *The Washington Post*, 1989; David Kline, "How to Lose the Coke War," *The Atlantic*, 1987; Ethan Nadelmann, "The DEA in Latin America: Dealing with Institutionalized Corruption," *Journal of Interamerican Studies and World Affairs*, 1987; *Narcotráfico y Política: Militarismo y Mafia en Bolivia*, 1982; William Overend and John Kendall, "Drug Agents' Tips to Dealers

Alleged," *The Los Angeles Times*, 1988; President's Commission on Organized Crime, *Organized Crime and Cocaine Trafficking*, 1984; Jim Schachter, "Customs Service Cleans House in a Drive on Drug Corruption," *Los Angeles Times*, 1987; and Steven Wisotsky, "Introduction: In Search of a Breakthrough in the War on Drugs," *NOVA Law Review*, 1987.

[143]Richard Bordreaux, "Scandal Spotlights Costa Rica's Battle on Drugs," *The Los Angeles Times*, 1989; Guy Gugliotta, "Costa Rica Drug Probe Taints Elite with Scandal," *The Miami Herald*, 1989.

[144]Fabio Castillo, *Los Jinetes de la Cocaína*, 1987.

[145]Shirley Christian, "Drug Case Raises Doubts in Bolivia," *The New York Times*, 1988.

[146]Penny Lernoux, "Playing Golf While Drugs Flow," *The Nation*, 1989.

[147]Bahamas Commission of Inquiry, *Report of the Commission of Inquiry*, 1984.

[148]Sean Flynn and Padraig Yeates, *Smack: The Criminal Drugs Racket in Ireland*, 1985.

[149]Alan Riding, "Cocaine Finds a New Route in Venezuela," *The New York Times*, 1987.

[150]U.S. Congress, House Committee on Foreign Affairs, Hearing, *Narcotics Review in South America*, 1988.

[151]U.S. Department of State, Bureau of International Narcotics Matters, *International Narcotics Control Strategy Report*, 1989.

[152]Jim Schachter, "Customs Service Cleans House in a Drive on Drug Corruption," *The Los Angeles Times*, 1987.

[153]Victoria Irwin, "Drugs and Police: Cities Probe the Corruption Connection," *The Christian Science Monitor*, 1986; and Seth Mydans, "6 Los Angeles Officers Charged in Drug Cases," *The New York Times*, 1991.

[154]John Kendall, "Drugs, Money Add up to Temptation for Police," *The Los Angeles Times*, 1988. See also "Slice of Vice: More Miami Cops Arrested," *Time*, 1986.

[155]See William Overend and John Kendall, "Drug Agents' Tips to Dealers Alleged," *The Los Angeles Times*, 1988; and William Overend, "Chaotic DEA Office Ripe for Problems in the Early 1980s," *The Los Angeles Times*, 1988.

[156]Merrill Collett, "Rumors of Drug Money Taint Vote," *The Christian Science Monitor*, 1989.

[157]See Monte Hayes, "Peru Rebels Profit from Drug Ties," *The Los Angeles Times*, 1987.

[158]See, for example, Merrill Collett, "Peruvians Flock to Upper Huallaga Valley to Cash in on Expanding Coca Bonanza," *Latinamerica Press*, 1988.

[159]Dave Miller, "Drug Mafia Arms Campesinos," *Latinamerica Press*, 1988.

[160]See, for example, Lucy Komisar, "Solving Burma's Guerrilla War Would End the Opium Trade," *The Christian Science Monitor*, 1988; Josef Silverstein, "Foreign Mediation Could Help End Burma's Civil War," *Far Eastern Economic Review*, 1988; and Denis D. Gray, "A Deluge from the Golden Triangle," *The Nation*, 1989.

[161]See the following for relevant discussions and important general coverage on Peru, Colombia, Burma, and Sri Lanka: Elliott Abrams, "Drug Wars: The New Alliance against Traffickers and Terrorists," *Department of State Bulletin*, 1986; Marcial Barrón, *El Infierno Blanco*, 1984; Tyler Bridges, "Drug Traffickers, Guerrillas Curtail Peru's Antidrug Efforts," *The Christian Science Monitor*, 1987; Jonathan Cavanagh, "Peru

Rebels Threaten U.S. Drug Program," *The Wall Street Journal*, 1984; Merrill Collett, "Maoist Guerrilla Band Complicates Antidrug War in Peru," *The Washington Post*, 1988; Merrill Collett, "Peruvians Flock to Upper Huallaga Valley to Cash in on Expanding Coca Bonanza," *Latinamerica Press*, 1988; Richard B. Craig, "Illicit Drug Traffic: Implications for South American Source Countries," *Journal of Interamerican Studies and World Affairs*, 1987; Barbara Crossette, "An Opium Warlord's News Conference Spurs Burma and Thailand to Battle Him," *The New York Times*, 1987; Rachel Ehrenfeld, "Narco-Terrorism and the Cuban Connection," *Strategic Review*, 1988; Monte Hayes, "Peru Rebels Profit from Drug Ties," *The Los Angeles Times*, 1987; Michael Isikoff, "U.S. Suffering Setbacks in Latin Drug Offensive," *The Washington Post*, 1989; D. P. Kumarasingha, "Drugs—A Growing Problem in Sri Lanka," *Forensic Science International*, 1988; Charles Lane, "Coke Basket of America," *The New Republic*, 1985; Kathryn Leger, "Peru Rebels Flourish in Drug Zone," *The Christian Science Monitor*, 1989; Cynthia McClintock, Abraham Lowenthal, and Gabriela Tarazona-Sevillano, "Peru's Harvest of Instability and Terrorism," *The Christian Science Monitor*, 1989; Scott B. MacDonald, *Mountain High, White Avalanche: Cocaine and Power in the Andean States and Panama*, 1989; Alan Riding, "Peru's Two Complex Battles: Drugs and Terror," *The New York Times*, 1987; Alan Riding, "Rebels Disrupting Coca Eradication in Peru," *The New York Times*, 1989; Wilson Ring, "Opium Production Rises in Guatemala Mountains," *The Washington Post*, 1989; James F. Smith, "Peruvian Guerrillas Unite Peasants, Set Social Order," *The Los Angeles Times*, 1989; Mark S. Steinitz, "Insurgents, Terrorists, and the Drug Trade," *The Washington Quarterly*, 1985; U.S. Congress, Senate Committee on Labor and Human Resources, Subcommittee on Alcoholism and Drug Abuse, Hearing, "Drugs and Terrorism 1984," 1985; U.S. Congress, Senate Committee on Foreign Relations and the Committee on the Judiciary, Joint Hearing, "International Terrorism, Insurgency, and Drug Trafficking: Present Trends in Terrorist Activity, 1985; Grant Wardlaw, "Linkages between the Illegal Drugs Traffic and Terrorism," *Conflict Quarterly*, 1988; David L. Westrate, "Drug Trafficking and Terrorism," *Drug Enforcement*, 1985; and David Westrate, "How Are Drug Trafficking and Terrorism Related?" *Narcotics Control Digest*, 1985.

[162]See Merrill Collett, "Colombia's Sophisticated Drug Traffickers Trigger Economic Boom, Political Violence," *Latinamerica Press*, 1988.

[163]Merrill Collett, "The Myth of the Narco-Guerrillas," *The Nation*, 1988.

[164]Mark Day, "Peru: Battle Intensifies over Renewed Drug Eradication Plan," *Latinamerica Press*, 1989.

[165]Michael Satchell, "Narcotics: Terror's New Ally," *U.S. News and World Report*, 1987.

[166]See "Drug Mafia Could Have Killed Pardo," *Latin America Weekly Report*, 1987; "President Turns Right for Support," *Latin America Weekly Report*, 1984; Alan Riding, "Shaken Colombia Acts at Last on Drugs," *The New York Times*, 1984; Alan Riding, "Colombia's Drugs and Violent Politics Make Murder a Way of Life," *The New York Times*, 1987; John Ross, "Colombia: Judge's Murder Linked to Drug Mafias," *Latinamerica Press*, 1986; Melinda Beck, "The Evil Empire," *Newsweek*, 1985; Tina Rosenberg, "Murder City," *The Atlantic*, 1988; William R. Long, "Colombia Girds to Face Drug Lords' Hired Guns," *The Los Angeles Times*, 1989; William D. Montalbano, "Colombia's Press Pays in Blood for Anti-Drug Stand," *The Los Angeles Times*, 1987; Mark A. Uhlig, "As Colombian Terror Grows, the Press Becomes the Prey, *The New York Times*, 1989; Miguel Varon, "Colombia: Drug Bosses Wage War against Extradition," *Latinamerica Press*, 1988; Miguel Varon, "Colombia: Many Flee Abroad as

Violence, Death Threats Increase," *Latinamerica Press*, 1988; Miguel Varon, "Uncontrolled Violence Embroils Smugglers, Narcos, Army in Colombian Emerald Fields," *Latinamerica Press*, 1988; and Leslie Wirpsa, "Colombians Brace for Drug War," *The Christian Science Monitor,* 1989.

[167]"Colombianization," *World Press Review*, 1989.

[168]"Colombians Blame Drug Traffickers," *Latin American Weekly Report*, 1987.

[169]Penny Lernoux, "Colombia Can't Kick Drugs Alone," *The Nation*, 1988.

[170]See A. Patricia Jones, "Cocaine and Violence: A Marriage Made in Hell!" *Crisis*, 1989.

[171]"Colombia Cartels Tied to Bombing," *The New York Times*, 1989.

[172]Joseph B. Treaster, "Rebels in Peru Step up the Killings of Politicians to Disrupt the Elections," *The New York Times*, 1989.

[173]Alan Riding, "Colombia Effort against Drugs Hits Dead End," *The New York Times*, 1987; James Brooke, "A Report from the Front Lines in Colombia: The Drug War Will Be Long," *The New York Times*, 1989; James Brooke, "In the Drug War, Medellín is a Reluctant Fighter," *The New York Times*, 1989; and Merrill Collett, "Colombia's Losing War with Drug Kings," *The Christian Science Monitor*, 1988.

[174]The most poignant example of the effect of these operations is Colombia's former Minister of Justice, Mónica de Greiff, who fled to exile in the United States with her husband and child when traffickers' threats on the child's life became credible. See Joseph B. Treaster, "Uneasy Exile for Ex-Aide of Colombia," *The New York Times*, 1989.

[175]William D. Montalbano, "Colombia's Press Pays in Blood for Anti-Drug Stand," *The Los Angeles Times*, 1987.

[176]Jonas Bernstein, "Bitter Convulsions in a Nation under the Influence of Drugs," *Insight*, 1989. See also Jeff Leen, "Bush Lauds Colombia Drug Battle," *The Miami Herald*, 1989; and Joseph B. Treaster, "Colombia Turns Drug War into a Long Chase," *The New York Times*, 1989.

[177]See the references in notes 25 and 28, this chapter.

[178]Jonathan Cavanagh ["Peru Rebels Threaten U.S. Drug Program," *The Wall Street Journal*, 1984] and Merrill Collett ["Maoist Guerrilla Band Complicates Antidrug War in Peru," *The Washington Post*, 1988] describe how the guerrillas encourage the peasants under their jurisdiction to grow coca (to which they are ideologically opposed but for which they as well as the peasants are in economic bondage or dependency) but demand that they not avoid their duty to "grow food for the revolution."

[179]Merrill Collet, "Maoist Guerrilla Band Complicates Antidrug War in Peru," *The Washington Post*, 1988.

[180]James F. Smith, "Peruvian Guerrillas Unite Peasants, Set Social Order," *The Los Angeles Times*, 1989.

[181]"Dutch disease" is sometimes used to describe the ensuing conditions and their effects. See Michael Gillgannon, "Drugs, Debt and Dependency," *America*, 1988; Linda Kamas, "Dutch Disease Economics and the Colombian Export Boom," *World Development*, 1987; and Francisco Thoumi, "Some Implications of the Growth of the Underground Economy in Colombia," *Journal of Inter-American Studies and World Affairs*, 1987.

[182]See Wulf Gaertner and Alouis Wenig, eds., *Studies in Contemporary Economics: The Economics of the Shadow Economy*, 1983; Michael Gillgannon, "Drugs, Debt and Dependency," *America*, 1988; J. Gomez, "The Colombian Illegal Economy: Size,

Evolution, Characteristics and Economic Impact," in *State and Society in Contemporary Colombia: Beyond the National Front*, Bruce Bagley, Francisco Thoumi, and J. Tokatlian, eds., 1987; Vito. Tanzi, ed., *The Underground Economy in the United States and Abroad*, 1982; Hernando Larrazábal et al., *El Sector Informal en Bolivia*, 1986; Peter A. Lupsha, "Drug Trafficking: Mexico and Colombia in Comparative Perspective," *Journal of International Affairs*, 1981; Robert B. McBride, "Business as Usual: Heroin Distribution in the United States," *Journal of Drug Issues*, 1983; Edmundo Morales, "Land Reform, Social Change, and Modernization in the National Periphery," 1983; Ernesto Samper, *La Legalización de la Marihuana*, 1980; Carl P. Simon and Ann D. Witte, *Beating the System: The Underground Economy*, 1982; Vito Tanzi, "The Underground Economy," *Finance and Development*, 1983; Francisco E. Thoumi, "Colombian Laws and Institutions, Money Dirtying, Money Laundering, and Narco-Businessmen's Behavior," unpublished manuscript, 1989; Francisco Thoumi, "Some Implications of the Growth of the Underground Economy in Colombia," *Journal of InterAmerican Studies and World Affairs*, 1987; and Miguel Varon, "Colombia: Labyrinthine Bureaucracy Generates Burgeoning Informal Sector," *Latinamerica Press*, 1987.

[183]Hernando de Soto, *The Other Path: The Invisible Revolution in the Third World*, 1989.

[184]Doug Timmer, "The Productivity of Crime in the United States: Drugs and Capital Accumulation," *Journal of Drug Issues*, 1982.

[185]Michael Flatte and Alexei J. Cowett, "Drugs and Politics: An Unhealthy Mix," *Harvard International Review*, 1986.

[186]See Paula Dwyer, "Getting Banks to Just Say 'No.'" *Business Week*, 1989; Stephen Labaton, "Canada Seen as Major Haven for Laundering Drug Money," *The New York Times*, 1989; Stephen Labaton, "US, in Drug Drive, to Regulate Shift of Funds Abroad," *The New York Times*, 1989; "Money Laundering: Who's Involved, How It Works, and Where It's Spreading," *Business Week*, 1985; National Narcotics Intelligence Consumers Committee, *Narcotics Intelligence Estimate*, 1983; President's Commission on Organized Crime, *Organized Crime and Money Laundering*, 1984; Ariel Remos, "Cuba's Drug-Trafficking Bank," *The Washington Times*, 1985; U.S. Congress, House Subcommittee on Financial Institutions Supervision, Regulation and Insurance of the Committee on Banking, Finance and Urban Affairs, Hearing, "Tax Evasion, Drug Trafficking and Money Laundering as They Involve Financial Institutions," 1986; and Karen Wolman, "Italy Takes Aim at Money Laundering," *The Christian Science Monitor*, 1989.

[187]Stephen Labaton, "Unassuming Store Fronts Believed to Launder Drug Dealer's Profits," *The New York Times*, 1989.

[188]Francisco Thoumi, "Some Implications of the Growth of the Underground Economy in Colombia," *Journal of InterAmerican Studies and World Affairs*, 1987.

[189]Richard B. Craig, "Illicit Drug Traffic: Implications for South American Source Countries, *Journal of Interamerican Studies and World Affairs*, 1987.

[190]Ibid.

[191]Richard A. Crooker, "Forces of Change in the Thailand Opium Zone," *The Geographical Review*, 1988; and Tamar Jacoby, Mark Miller, and Richard Sandza, "A Choice of Poisons," *Newsweek*, 1988.

[192]Jacoby, Miller, and Sandza, "A Choice of Poisons," *Newsweek*, 1988.

[193]Mark Mardon, "The Big Push," *Sierra*, 1988.

[194]John Ross, "Mexico: Chimalapas Forest Falls to Loggers, Oil Pipelines, Poppy and Marijuana Fields," *Latinamerica Press*, 1988.

[195]Gordon Witkin, "The New Midnight Dumpers," *U.S. News and World Report*, 1989.

[196]Frances A. Hunt, "Are the National Forests Going to Pot?" *American Forests*, 1987; and U.S. General Accounting Office, *Additional Actions Taken to Control Marijuana Cultivation and Other Crimes on Federal Lands*, 1984.

[197]Bruce M. Bagley, "The Colombian Connection: The Impact of Drug Traffic on Colombia," *Coca and Cocaine: Effects on People and Policy in Latin America*, Deborah Pacini and Christine Franquemont, eds., 1986; John McCoy, "The Cocaine Boom: A Latin American Perspective," *Latinamerica Press*, 1988.

[198]Rushworth M. Kidder, "Drug Strategy within an 'Ethical Fairyland,'" *The Christian Science Monitor*, 1989; David Mutch, "To the Heart of the Drug Problem," *The Christian Science Monitor*, 1989; Francisco E. Thoumi, "Colombian Laws and Institutions, Money Dirtying, Money Laundering, and Narco-Businessmen's Behavior," 1989; and Cynthia McClintock, Abraham F. Lowenthal, and Gabriela Tarazona-Sevillano, "Peru's Harvest of Instability and Terrorism," *The Christian Science Monitor*, 1989.

[199]John McCoy, "The Cocaine Boom: A Latin American Perspective," *Latinamerica Press*, 1988.

[200]Carlos Briceño, *Las Drogas en el Perú*, 1983; Kedar Man Singh, "A Taste of Smack," *Far Eastern Economic Review*, 1986; and Gina Kolata, "In Cities, Poor Families Are Dying of Crack," *The New York Times*, 1989.

[201]Clara Germani, "Coca Addiction Hits Home—Among Rural Children of Drug-Producing Bolivia," *The Christian Science Monitor*, 1988.

5

Implementation of Countervailing Initiatives

We turn now to the implementation and consequences of drug control, law enforcement, and other countervailing initiatives. This constitutes the second of the major categories of effects discussed in this handbook which are distributed along social, economic, political, and personal dimensions (see Tables 1 and 2). In the next chapter we turn to the third major consequence-producing category—demand.

Given the extensive production and distribution of illicit drugs, and given that most people view this with alarm, it is to be expected that reactions—private as well as those translated into public policies—would be forthcoming. Thus multiple and frequently conflicting responses to the existing illicit drug traffic are noted. At a personal level, they range from some merchants' near euphoria for the traffic's economic boom to their communities[1] to the despair some family members feel for disordered or lost lives of loved ones.[2] At a public policy level, one hears with increasing frequency a range of responses from "get tough" to "legalization." We address some of these in Section C.

What is certain is that numerous laws and policies worldwide have already been set in place. Just as a new genre of traffickers arose in response to a substantial drug demand and an adequate supply within the context of illegalizing drug policies (see Flow Chart 1), nations and international organizations have set countervailing initiatives in force to deal with them. Both organized trafficker and countervailing initiative—themselves being initial consequences of demand, supply, and illegalizing policies—have in turn produced their own rounds of economic, social, and political consequences.

In most nations, fear, concern, disgust, dismay, moral outrage, ideology, and sometimes political opportunism have fostered political action culminating in national drug control policies and international agreements designed to reduce (if not prevent) production and consumption of and traffic in the drugs under review in this handbook. In addition, in recent years, more attention has been given to public treatment and rehabilitation of consumers for whom the laws and policies obviously have had little preventive effect.[3]

MULTILATERAL AND BILATERAL AGREEMENTS

The diversity of response to the drug traffic is probably exceeded only by the variety of national laws and policies designed to address it.[4] For example, Bolivia recently made coca growing illegal, but only in designated areas.[5] The country thereby not only acceded to the demands of the local coca chewing market (which is not illegal but which is controlled and taxed to some extent) but also created conditions of windfall profits for favored regions. As long as demand is high and profits are appealing, it is almost certain that peasants with coca growing licenses will not dedicate all their production to licit trade. The Soviet Union, on the other hand, makes no provision for allowing poppy growing to satisfy the long-standing opium consumption habits of some of its southern ethnic groups.[6] The United States, for its part, makes any consumption illegal (except small amounts of marijuana in some states (see p. 39). The Netherlands has a fairly permissive drug consumption policy, especially for marijuana (see p. 39), as also does Switzerland.[7]

Regardless of such diversity in national laws and policies, it appears that every country has declared the *indiscriminate* public consumption of coca-, opium-, and cannabis-derived drugs to be illegal. At a minimum, drug use limitations are in place virtually worldwide. The enforcement ranges from an outright ban on consumption to an array of policies designed to control (and tax) authorized consumption under specified conditions. With respect to unfettered use, the principal public response to drugs so far has therefore been "illegality."

National laws and drug control policies notwithstanding, we have already seen that the illicit traffic persists; the drugs continue to be produced, shipped, stored, and consumed. Part of the difficulty is that drugs have no national boundaries, either as produced, marketed, or consumed. There has thus been considerable impetus toward international cooperation not only to enact but also to implement more effective national drug control policies and international agreements to give them increased efficacy. In recent years these national and international efforts have increased both in volume and intensity.

The prelude to modern international drug control cooperation began over eighty years ago when opium, then progressively viewed as a scourge to humanity, was brought under international jurisdiction. In 1909, thirteen nations met at Shanghai in what became known as the first international conference on narcotic drugs. It set up the Opium Commission, a constituent body which, after deliberating for several years, produced the first international drug control treaty—the International Opium Convention, signed at the Hague, the Netherlands, in 1912. Constituent member parliaments finally ratified it in 1915.

A later international body, the League of Nations, followed with virtually standing committee discussions after 1920 and produced conventions in

1925, 1931, and 1936. The resulting international agreements were designed to supervise statistical control over opium production (the previous International Opium Convention had called for statistics), to limit drug production to amounts needed for medical and other licit use, and to provide for severe punishment of illicit drug traffickers.[8] Subsequently, the United Nations worked for cooperative agreements that would, in effect, expand signatories' criminal jurisdiction (by convention and treaty) and encourage national policies aimed to reduce both supply and demand of illicit drugs.

Since the 1936 League of Nations' Convention for the Suppression of the Illicit Traffic in Dangerous Drugs, the United Nations (UN), through conventions and protocols[9] and the work of its various subagencies, which carry out drug-related agenda,[10] has attempted to make law enforcement efforts more possible across national boundaries and to encourage member states to cooperate in all areas of illicit drug control, including treatment and rehabilitation. The most frequently cited UN initiatives are the 1961 Single Convention on Narcotic Drugs, which consolidated most of the earlier international instruments, and the 1972 Protocol amending the Single Convention, which strengthened provisions for suppressing production and distribution of drugs but also called for rehabilitation and social reintegration policies for drug offenders as possible alternatives to imprisonment.

Other milestones in UN–orchestrated agreements are the 1971 Convention on Psychotropic Substances, the 1981 International Drug Abuse Control Strategy, the 1984 Declaration on the Control of Drug Trafficking and Drug Abuse, a 1987 Draft Convention against Illicit Traffic in Narcotic Drugs and Psychotropic Substances (see note 8), and a 1987 international conference on Drug Abuse and Illicit Trafficking, the first ever meeting of UN–member states to discuss and assess both the supply and demand sides of the drug abuse chain. A practical handbook of recommended steps for governmental and nongovernmental organizations to use in combating drug abuse in all of its spectra emerged from the conference.[11]

In 1990 the General Assembly held high-level special sessions to expand the scope and effectiveness of current antidrug efforts, declaring, at the close of the sessions, the 1990s the "UN Decade against Drug Abuse." The sessions dealt with tightening legal and practical cooperation among member states. The urgency was highlighted by Colombia's mortal struggle with its drug barons. Significantly, net consuming nations were obligated to address more vigorously the need to reduce their demand for illicit drugs.[12] A consensus thus emerged that all affected countries, whether net consumers or net producers, collectively shared in the blame for the traffic's existence. They would therefore have to mutually direct their attention to all facets of the trade—consumption, trafficking, and production. At the same time, a new urgency arose about deleterious socioeconomic consequences of illicit drug production, trade, and consumption.[13]

In general, beyond all these activities, the United Nations works to give added direction to each member state's obligation to enact appropriate antidrug legislation and to establish administrative offices and law enforcement agencies dedicated to reducing drug-related transactions within their borders. As currently developed, these conventions, protocols, and UN–orchestrated treaties, agreements, and resolutions are designed to reduce supply of, demand for, and distribution of drugs currently deemed illegal, and to enhance treatment and rehabilitation of offenders.

There is other international cooperation.[14] The Colombo Plan, organized in 1950 as a regional intergovernmental organization for cooperative economic and social development in Asia and the Pacific, comprises twenty-six member states. The Drug Advisory Programme of the Colombo Plan Bureau is active in strengthening cooperation among agencies and member states dealing with drug problems.[15]

The Cooperation Group to Combat Drug Abuse and Illicit Trafficking in Drugs of the Council of Europe, known as the Pompidou Group, set up in 1971 to exchange views in Western Europe in response to the growing drug problem, in 1980 became part of the Council of Europe. It has sixteen members. The group deals with all areas of drug control, including suppression, prevention, treatment and rehabilitation. It also has shown interest in physiological and other health-related effects of drug use.[16]

In order to achieve their common goal of suppressing illicit drug traffic, the member states of the Association of Southeast Asian Nations (ASEAN) have adopted various legislative and administrative measures aimed at establishing uniform methods. This activity derives from the association's view that drug trafficking is a threat to the national security, stability, and integrity of all its member states.[17]

There is a Permanent Secretariat of the South American Agreement on Narcotic Drugs and Psychotropic Substances (ASEP), which came into force in 1976 and is generally targeted for eradicating coca crops and suppressing illicit drug trafficking. It encourages the establishment of national drug control coordinating bodies, urges legislative cooperation among states in measures conducive to drug control, and operates a computerized system designed to facilitate contacts between the various drug law-enforcement agencies of ASEP member states.[18]

In 1988, the Inter-Parliamentary Union, in cooperation with the United Nations and with the support of the World Health Organization and the Latin American Parliament, held a conference in Venezuela, which was attended by twenty-four Western Hemispheric nations, including the United States. After addressing the standard categories of suppression of supply and consumption, prevention, and treatment and rehabilitation, the delegates raised a substantial discussion about the need to reduce illicit demand, no doubt for the ears of the U.S. delegation.[19]

Further multilateral cooperative efforts in Latin America include initiatives of the Organization of American States. It has adopted resolutions and has held conferences focusing on drug trafficking and on ways to deal with it, including emphasizing a role for public education (again, the demand problem) and on procedures to reduce traffickers' profits.[20]

Through its secretariat, the British Commonwealth has formulated ways to create greater mutual judicial assistance in criminal matters and thereby strengthen national authorities' ability to investigate, prosecute, and convict international drug traffickers. They have worked on model legislation.[21]

Other multilateral organizations work in drug control areas: the South Pacific Commission, the Pan-Arab Bureau for Narcotic Affairs of the League of Arab States,[22] and the Customs Co-operation Council.[23] The enthusiasm for international cooperation now even involves China, which is collaborating with Interpol.[24]

Aside from the many multilateral arrangements developed in response to drug trafficking, bilateral agreements—or at least working promises—are in force, too. Most appear to be between the United States and principal source countries, first with Turkey,[25] lately with countries such as Pakistan,[26] Peru, Bolivia, Colombia, Mexico,[27] and Italy.[28] The intent, through provision of money and materiel, is to suppress the drug traffic at its origin.

The net producing countries' agreements with the United States have not always brought out the best in understanding; the other countries usually complain of being pushed around, and the United States usually raises the specter of incompetency and corruption,[29] perhaps as a detraction from its own frustration in attempting to reduce illicit drug demand at home. All this notwithstanding, the USSR—both a producing and a consuming country—has proposed a formal agreement with the Drug Enforcement Administration (DEA) of the United States—also a producing and consuming nation—to cooperate against international drug traffickers.[30] Jamaica's prime minister, Michael Manley, once proposed an international anti-narcotics strike force that would interdict drugs, eradicate crops, and mount paramilitary-style attacks against traffickers.[31] In practice this would license the United States to carry out the activities. The proposal has therefore evoked considerable commentary; Manley has now backed away,[32] particularly since the U.S. invasion of Panama in December 1989, which he roundly criticized.[33]

The urgency that draws nations together on the drug issue and that drives their multilateral and bilateral agenda is widely felt. A probable outcome will be more effective and more efficient national and international efforts to reduce supplies and to interdict traffic in net producer countries, perhaps even to reduce demand in net consumer nations. Large consuming nations such as the United States will probably be more sensitive regarding the burdens that producer nations bear as suppliers of a market mostly dictated outside their borders. Producer nations will continue to demand a quid-pro-quo exchange (e.g., foreign aid, debt forgiveness) for their redoubled efforts at controlling supply and suppressing traffic.

In the February 1990 UN session that plotted a global antidrug strategy, net producer countries were clearly pleased to see the shift in emphasis from suppression and interdiction to demand reduction. This was accomplished not without foot dragging. The United States and Britain had wanted the discussions to be held in the Security Council where they had a disproportionately powerful voice, thereby forcing the agenda to remain on drug production and interdiction. Brazil succeeded in moving the session out of the Security Council into the General Assembly, where each nation has an equal vote. The result was to oblige net consumer countries to work on their own consumption trends as much as they want to work on others' production and trafficking problems.[34]

There is a danger, however, in greater effectiveness which results from frustration, fear, moral outrage, some political opportunism, and all that goes with it, particularly for those concerned with sovereignty and human rights. When pressed to the wall, nations become more willing to concede sovereign rights, in part because the drug problem is much too vast for any country, no matter how powerful, to take on alone.[35] However, dealing with nationalism and internal political maneuvering will be a struggle for states whose nationality becomes viewed as having been heavily compromised. We have already seen how Colombia, in spite of the gravity of its own internal struggles, found it politically necessary to refuse proffered U.S. assistance in the form of a sea armada stationed off its coast.

Constitutional and ideological restraints on the abuse of human rights could ultimately be one of the casualties of increased international cooperation. All this is complicated by a 28 February 1990 U.S. Supreme Court ruling that the U.S. Constitution does not prohibit unreasonable searches and seizures by American law enforcement agencies against non–U.S. citizens and their property in foreign countries.[36] The way was clearly open for General Manuel Noriega's seized financial records to be used against him in his U.S. trial. The way is apparently open for U.S. unilateral activity—clandestine and military—to unfold elsewhere. Restraint and judicial protection may be withdrawn to more than "foreigners" on their own soil. Excesses will likely increase; the incidence of "mistakes" will most likely rise.

This is not a brief against cooperation, effectiveness, and efficiency. It is, rather, a voice of concern that, if wise men and women are not at the helm, the consequences of the international drug cure could exceed the current drug-related social, political, and economic damage.

Strong states (mostly net consumers), while tempered from time to time as in the recent UN sessions described above, will nevertheless probably continue to drive much of the international agenda from the vantage of their national policies and political needs, however congruent these may be with international cooperative agreements.

NATIONAL POLICIES

Most multilateral and bilateral agreements appear to have originated on two fronts: first, in net user countries' pressure on net producer countries to *control the supply* of illicit narcotic drugs and psychotropic substances within their borders; second, to *interdict drug traffic* escaping the supply-reduction net. The principal objective is to reduce the supply of drugs securable for the international market.

As the international traffic has increased dramatically in spite of these efforts, and as producer countries have become user countries themselves, the issue of who was at fault for the traffic has been raised ever more frequently. Production occurs to meet demand, producer countries have long argued. As we have seen, principal user countries, such as the United States, have been forced by crop control, traffic suppression, and interdiction failures to begin to take heed of *demand* in the international traffic in illicit drugs.

Control, interdiction, and demand, and the political interplay among and between them, have given rise to national policies in line with multilateral agreements. Not surprisingly, therefore, one of the consequences of nationally and internationally orchestrated responses to the drug traffic has been the development of a series of conventions and national laws that are quite complementary to each other.[37]

Now that the net producer countries are increasingly willing to talk about the problems of supply, and now that the net consumer countries are increasingly willing to address the issues of demand, it is to be expected that international agreements would focus on the whole package. In a recent UN multilateral agreement,[38] for example, prevention and reduction of illicit demand are not only prominent in the discussion, they are listed first. Thereafter, control of supply, suppression of illicit trafficking, and treatment and rehabilitation of drug abusers are addressed.

Classifying the national countervailing response literature so that it aligns with the above categories—demand reduction, supply control, traffic suppression, treatment and rehabilitation—and several subsections of the UN Comprehensive Multidisciplinary Outline (referenced in note 37) helps in two ways: First, the categories are a useful way to consider further multilateral and bilateral responses to the drug traffic. Second, the categories help us review the range of antidrug policies that many consuming and producing nations have adopted and some of the consequences of their having done so.

Prevention and Reduction of Illicit Demand

Current policies aimed at preventing and reducing illicit demand for drugs include general law enforcement activities, education programs, initiatives in the work place, civic action, and appropriation of the general powers of persuasion of the mass media (see Flow Chart 5). While most countries with internal drug consumption problems employ all these activities to a greater or lesser degree, the net consumer countries have honed them to a relative precision.

General Law Enforcement Activities

Law enforcement activities are designed to accomplish many tasks—order, safety, punishment, deterrence, control, protection, and retribution.[39] As a subset of a nation's drug control policies, they are intended to reduce demand, control supply, and suppress traffic in illicit drugs—mostly through negative sanctions. We consider control of supply and suppression of illicit traffic (e.g., crop eradication, asset forfeiture, extradition) and their consequences in subsequent sections of this chapter. Here we turn to the relationship of law enforcement to drug demand and to the consequences that derive therefrom. Table 3, adapted from the categories laid out in Tables 1 and 2, illustrates the intended and unintended permutations distributable as social, economic, political, environmental, and personal consequences.

General drug law enforcement aimed at reducing demand has sought to raise the costs and risks associated with trafficking in and using illicit drugs. Principally, this has been carried out through powers of arrest and referrals to countries' penal systems. The intent of "negative sanctions" is to prevail on people's fears of being caught—with attendant risks of detention, loss of assets, public embarrassment, forced treatment, or execution—to discourage them from using illicit drugs.

In the application of negative sanctions, some countries focus on traffickers but are relatively lenient on users; others treat individual users and traffickers in about the same degree of severity, which may range from relatively benign sanctions to draconian intervention. Almost all countries appear to have experimented through time with varying levels of tough and lenient sanctions on users depending on the generalized consumption of drugs within their borders and their governments' political will to exercise authority on drug-related issues, whether for political or ideological reasons.

The degree of severity of law enforcement applications—almost

Flow Chart 5
Foci of Activities to Reduce Demand

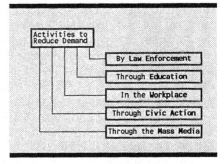

Table 3
Distribution of Intended and Unintended Consequences of Law Enforcement Action

	From Drug Control Policies			
	To Suppress Demand		To Suppress Supply & Traffic	
	In*	Un+	In*	Un+
Social	1	6	11	16
Economic	2	7	12	17
Political	3	8	13	18
Environmental	4	9	14	19
Personal	5	10	15	20

always when applied to individual users but sometimes also to traffickers—is usually much less with cannabis than with opium and coca. With this caveat, and with the allowance that no country fits perfectly in a 2 x 2 table, one might nevertheless consider Table 4 a useful delineation of several types of country-specific law enforcement practices, at least to illustrate tendencies.[40] In table 4, Iran is listed as having a "tough" policy on users *and* traffickers: both are readily executed or sent to forced labor camps.

Table 4
Comparative Law Enforcement Policies

		POLICY FOCUS	
		Individual Users	Traffickers
S A N C T I O N S	Tough	Iran Malaysia Singapore China United States (Cocaine/Heroin)	Iran Malaysia Singapore China Colombia USSR Finland United States
	Lenient	Netherlands Switzerland Spain Peru Bolivia Jamaica United States (Cannabis)	Pakistan Panama (Pre 1990) Laos

Iran has had the death penalty for drug traffickers, which is sometimes applied to users, at least since the Islamic revolution that deposed the Shah.[41] Enforcement measures apparently quickened in 1989, due, in part, to neighborhood Islamic revolutionary committees having taken over drug fighting from the police, most certainly with national approval. Clerical and civil tribunals sent over 55,000 drug addicts to labor camps in several provinces, with prospects that 150,000 more would follow. In January 1989 a drug sweep through Iranian cities resulted in the arrest of nearly 1,000 people, of whom 17 were given public hangings. The country has a mandatory death sentence for anyone caught with more than an ounce of heroin, morphine, codeine, or methadone in his or her possession.[42] By July 1989 it was reported that nearly 1,000 "smugglers" had been executed, although some observers say they were little more than political opponents of the existing regime.[43] In spite of these measures, the country continues to have serious drug use and drug trafficking problems.

Malaysia presents greater civil and legal rationality but no less severe judgment on traffickers. Against the protests of Australia, the United Kingdom, and the United States, in 1986 the Malaysian government hung two Australians—the first caucasians to die under the country's Dangerous Drugs Act—just as it has hung a number of its own citizens. In short, to be convicted of drug trafficking in Malaysia is to be jailed and perhaps hanged. This draconian net extends to some classes of drug users as well.[44]

Singapore applies similarly tough sanctions on traffickers and on individual users.[45] Following a sudden and precipitous increase in 1975 in heroin use (thought to involve as many as 3% of the country's male youth), in 1977 the government responded with an aggressive enforcement strategy aimed at rapid reduction in consumption. Large-scale sweeps were implemented to arrest suspected users and to commit those with positive tests (which were compulsory) to mandatory rehabilitation centers.[46] However, matters were still under insufficient control in 1985. The authorities launched another large-scale arrest and detention operation. As of July of that year, twenty-one people, including two women, had been convicted and sentenced to death for drug trafficking; eighteen had been hanged.[47] The country's immigration department maintains a register of drug offenders and refuses to issue passports to people who have a drug offense—another effort designed to curtail illicit drug trafficking given that Singaporians like to travel beyond their country's borders.[48]

Although light-years away from Iran, Malaysia, and Singapore, several of the Nordic countries take a no-nonsense approach to drug trafficking. Finland, in particular, has little patience with traffickers. Of all the Nordic countries, Finland has developed the most "subjugating" penal traditions. Norway, on the other hand, has the most vigorous drug control policies, with considerable moralistic drives against drug use and abuse having become part of the cultural fabric. Neither Finland nor Norway, whether for reasons of vigorous negative deterrence or broader considerations, really has much of a drug problem.[49]

The United States presents a special case. National political policy is aggressive with respect to traffickers; high-level Bush administration officials have called for the death penalty whether or not traffickers have committed homicides.[50] United States policy now also involves the military in antidrug law enforcement activities.[51] Moreover, for the most part, the country's fifty state law-enforcement agencies and thousands of local units appear to concur with this increasingly aggressive national posture. However, an independent U.S. judiciary renders highly diverse decisions, some tough, some lenient.[52]

As for individual drug use, U.S. judicial decisions appear to be on the lenient side of the negative sanction equation, particularly for cannabis use. Even for hard drug use, some observers have suggested that hiring a clever lawyer will give one a better than even chance of beating the U.S. system, even for substantial traffickers. However, this idea has been given a serious setback by a 1989 U.S. Supreme Court decision which narrowly ruled that the government can freeze a defendant's assets intended for legal fees in cases involving drugs. It is thought that this will deter some lawyers from wanting to represent clients accused of drug-related activities.[53]

Nevertheless, in the United States, enforcement against drug use appears to have tightened up among some classes of users,[54] and progressively credible negative sanctions have been forthcoming, facilitated, in part, by recent Supreme Court decisions in favor of tough measures not only on traffickers but on some consumers.[55] National, state, and local political administrations are beefing up their law enforcement efforts, and some federal and state courts seem to be handing down tougher sentences and decisions, all with the idea that negative sanctions, if credible and sure, will indeed reduce demand.[56] Following a fifteen-year hiatus, this trend now is also visible for users of cannabis who, for a time, enjoyed relative immunity from severe difficulties with the law.[57] Nevertheless, for the most part, U.S. negative sanctions applied to individual cannabis users are still in the lenient category.

Somewhere in between countries such as Finland and the United States, on the one hand, and Iran, Malaysia, and Singapore, on the other, lie countries such as China, Colombia, and the USSR which also are tough on traffickers. Under Mao Zedong, China eliminated traffickers and unrepentant users through harsh measures, reducing drug use to a negligible social problem.[58] Recently, overland traffic from the Golden Triangle to Hong Kong has caused a resurgence of trafficking problems. The current Chinese regime has been swift to act with broad detention sweeps that may have been uncluttered by judicial safeguards, even by the standards of the country's neighborhood people's tribunals.[59]

The USSR makes sweeping raids from time to time. While loss of personal assets is not such an intimidating deterrence in the Soviet Union as in capitalist countries, jail sentences are routinely tough and treatment equally so for traffickers.[60] However, there are efforts in the Soviet Union to decriminalize the casual use of drugs, especially nonnarcotic ones.[61]

Colombia is in an all-out war with traffickers, with no holds barred. Since 1988, the country's armed forces have been involved in raids on cocaine processing complexes and in tracking down drug traffickers.[62] This may have less to do with drugs per se than with the threat that the country's drug barons may actually take over the Colombian state as earlier they took over, temporarily, the Bolivian one.[63]

In the case of Colombia and countries like it, one must make a distinction between what a country's law enforcement system is trying to do and what it is able to do. States relatively weak institutionally—and subject to the persuasive influence of antistate financial incentives (bribes) such as are prevalent in the drug trade—have a limited capacity to sustain a lengthy conflict with drug traffickers. Already there are serious calls in Colombia to abandon the war if not to legalize drugs.[64] These voices have not had a significant impact on Colombia's drug control policies except in the country's efforts to entice drug traffickers to surrender in exchange for relatively lenient penalties.[65]

Bolivia, Peru, Ecuador, Mexico—all are institutionally weak even though each is investing substantial efforts to control the drug trade. Detainees who cannot either buy themselves out of prison or afford a luxury suite while in it receive quite severe negative incentives.

For analogous reasons we place Pakistan in the lenient cell of Table 4. Although its antinarcotics laws for traffickers are as tough as Colombia's, the laws are not systematically—indeed, hardly ever—vigorously implemented, former Prime Minister Benazir Bhutto's assurances notwithstanding.[66] This sets Pakistan apart from countries such as Colombia, which, however weak institutionally, nevertheless have greater consistency between the drug laws and their implementation.

We place Laos in the traffickers' lenient cell, in part because in 1987 the government actually appeared to be championing traffickers' interests by promoting cultivation and export of marijuana and heroin in order to earn desperately needed foreign exchange.[67] In January 1990, however, Laos initiated moves for better relations with the United States and received a favorable response—meaning that the country has accepted foreign aid in exchange for a plan to work on its drug production and distribution problem.[68] The position of Laos may therefore be in flux.

The lower left-hand cell of Table 4 suggests that some countries, either by design or by default, are relatively lenient with individual users. The Netherlands and Switzerland come to mind as, perhaps, archetypes.[69] On the other hand, in 1983 Spain legalized marijuana,[70] and the country has liberal policies on other drugs.

Peru and Bolivia are listed in the lenient-on-individual-users cell, not because the countries officially tolerate illicit drug use but because their drug control and law enforcement efforts are mostly spent on drug traffickers, probably nearly to the maximum institutionally possible. Little energy or political will is left for simple drug users. Of course, the countries are the ancestral home of the original coca chewers. The practice is still widely shared in the Andean highlands, which probably evokes a degree of cultural tolerance for a variety of coca derivatives.

As for Jamaica, ganja (marijuana) is unreservedly integrated into the social fabric of the land; as many as half the adults consume the drug.[71] While authorities have cracked down from time to time on traffickers,[72] individual users pass with impunity.[73]

Finally, the United States occupies a relatively lenient position on individual use (for marijuana) because several states have decriminalized its consumption[74]—although they are rethinking their positions[75]—and because, in any event, simple possession generally does not carry severe penalties, frequently only misdemeanor charges.[76]

We have the impression that the severity of negative sanctions is increasing in some nations otherwise lenient on traffickers, while at the same time calls for legalization abound in countries such as the United States, a matter to which we turn in Section C. The literature does not lack for strong advocates both for and against this policy initiative.[77]

Having now described the differential array of law enforcement practices in vogue, it is useful to ask two questions: Are they effective? Are they justified? The first focuses on the intended consequence of reducing demand, the second on unintended consequences that may be quite deleterious to

Table 5
Effective vs. Deleterious Consequences of Law Enforcement Practices

| | | UNINTENDED DELETERIOUS CONSEQUENCES | |
		Negligible	Substantial
E F F E C T I V E N E S S	H I G H	1 Admirable	2 Discussible
	L O W	3 Questionable	4 Unacceptable

individuals, society, and conventional institutions. Practices that are effective and produce no negligible deleterious consequences (cell 1 of Table 5) might be considered *admirable*. Practices that are ineffective in reducing demand but produce substantial deleterious consequences (cell 4) would be *unacceptable*; the unintended consequences in this case are considerably worse than the proffered cure. Practices that produce substantial deleterious consequences and are highly effective in reducing demand (cell 2) would at least be *discussible*. Practices that are both ineffective and produce negligible deleterious consequences would, at the best, be *questionable*. The "admirable," "discussible," "questionable," and "unacceptable" conclusions are, of course, based on value judgments between the relative importance of any deleterious consequences of law enforcement efforts and the deleterious consequences of widespread drug use that the efforts are intended to curtail.

With these caveats in mind, let us examine what the literature says about effectiveness. That is, do law enforcement activities really reduce demand?

Effectiveness of Policies. Oddly, the literature we have reviewed offers precious little systematic evidence, although anecdotal information supports the view that asset forfeiture is a greater deterrence to people with property than incarceration is to people without it.[78] We might deduce that credible law enforcement practices, whether moderate or severe, will likely deter people from drug use who have a lot to lose in terms of personal or business possessions. For others, severe sanctions seem to act as no greater deterrence than less severe ones, and neither is particularly effective unless it is manifestly credible (i.e., punishment is swift and sure).[79] For some, greater law enforcement severity may in fact induce more involvement with drug taking, the drug culture, and the criminal activities associated with them.[80]

The literature does address the relationship of *criminality* to drug abuse, and this may offer indirect evidence on the degree to which law enforcement efforts may reduce demand, at least among population segments inclined toward criminality.[81] For individuals who consume or traffic in drugs and are involved in crime, sanctions, whether moderate or severe, appear to make no difference. If law enforcement makes no difference with the criminality of these people, it seems unlikely that it would deter their drug use. In a comparative study of experimental and controlled subjects in Argentina, Brazil, Costa Rica, Japan, Jordan, Italy, Malaysia, Singapore, and the United States (state of New York), with inclusion of independent studies conducted in Sweden and the United Kingdom, a close association was found to exist among drug abuse, criminal behavior, and social attitudes alien to being influenced by law enforcement. No correlation was found between the severity of drug laws and the extent of drug abuse and its associated criminality.[82]

The U.S. National Academy of Sciences found a negative correlation between crime rates of all kinds, including those related to drugs, and non-capital sanctioned risks. On capital sanctions, the academy's panel concluded that the evidence available did not provide any usable evidence on the deterrent effect of capital punishment.[83] A Canadian study concluded that severe penalties do not, of themselves, discourage drug use but that the credible application of penalties did have an effect on certain population groups.[84]

Interestingly, populations least deterred by law enforcement efforts took arrests that disrupted interpersonal networks quite seriously. They viewed other arrests rather casually. When police concentrated on disrupting traffickers' and users' interpersonal networks by their arrests, these populations avoided arrest nearly at all costs. The perceived severity of law enforcement practices was tied to the degree to which they disrupted social networks. Placing criminal sanctions into a social complex and noting network tolerance appeared to result in an improved way of analyzing appropriate law enforcement policies and priorities. Forcing "network closure" reduced some drug-related criminal activity that otherwise would have occurred.[85] Among these populations, such a strategy might also reduce drug demand, but we are not aware of any evidence supporting this view.

Others are quite pessimistic about the ability of law enforcement activities to reduce demand among those really dedicated to the drug culture.[86] Not even the famed efficiency of the Soviet police force has made much of a dent in drug use in the USSR's southern republics.[87]

Aside from arrests, countries' sentencing policies are also considered part of deterrence. No conclusive evidence appears to exist on the effectiveness of sentencing policies in some countries with respect to drug-related infractions.[88] On the other hand, harsh mandatory laws apparently are not an effective deterrent in common law countries because getting convictions on harsh penalties is exceedingly difficult. The tougher the laws are in some countries, the more likely juries are to acquit a defendant.[89] At the very least, rulings are frequently contradictory, even on the utilization of evidence.[90] And the occasional harsh sentence sometimes appears, on the surface, to be so bazaar that it evokes no generalized credibility.[91]

Perhaps Malaysia offers evidence on law enforcement effectiveness. To be caught trafficking in drugs in Malaysia is to be jailed and hanged. The question is, do such draconian measures work to suppress or subdue drug demand there? There is controversial evidence as to whether the measures taken, including public whippings, are reducing drug demand.[92] One author opines that the harsh measures, in turn driven by severe laws, have had an impoverishing effect on the country's democratic institutions without appreciably affecting drug demand.[93]

On the other hand, in the United States, it has been noted that law enforcement efforts to curtail demand (insofar as driving out traffickers is an indicator) are considerably improved when communities, citizens, and police officers collaborate and cooperate.[94] And, in Singapore, the large-scale police maneuvers in the late 1970s implemented to arrest suspected heroin users and commit those with positive tests to mandatory rehabilitation centers appeared to reduce demand somewhat.[95]

On balance, judgment is mixed on the effectiveness of law enforcement actions in deterring drug-related crime, and probably drug demand as well.

Nevertheless, demand is probably reduced among people who have assets to lose (property or social networks), but law enforcement probably has little effect on hard core users not classified as having property or networks at risk. This observation appears to hold true regardless of the severity of the law enforcement policies.

Unintended Consequences. If the intended law enforcement effects of reducing demand get a mixed review, what of the unintended consequences of the effort as distributed along social, economic, political, and personal dimensions (see Table 3)? And, are the consequences "questionable," "unacceptable," "discussible," or "admirable" (see Table 5)?

In our data set, four themes emerge paramount with respect to the unintended consequences of a law enforcement response to the drug traffic. These themes deal less with economics and politics (although much concern over consequences is raised here, too) than with society and the individual. They are *corruption, crime, AIDS,* and *human rights.* We review these before turning to the less frequently cited concerns.

Much of the literature focusing on the deleterious effects of antidrug law enforcement measures appears to assume demand as a given. Drug consumption per se is acknowledged to have many wide-ranging problems. But, many of these allegedly are exacerbated and additional ones are created by illegalizing laws and their accompanying enforcement strategies. Thus, according to this literature, corruption of the police would not exist if dealer incentives were not so high, themselves made possible by illegalizing policies that create a windfall "crime tax" for the traffickers. Drug-related crime would not exist—at least the systemic and economically driven crime thought to be associated with drug use—if drug users were not forced to obtain their drugs from illegal sources and to engage in illegal pursuits in order to afford the drugs' artificially high price. The incidence of Acquired Immune Deficiency Syndrome (AIDS), widely transmitted by intravenous heroin and cocaine users who share contaminated hypodermic needles and then move along to infect their sexual partners, would be greatly reduced if users could easily obtain clean needles and legally enjoy their drugs. Human rights would not be abused if the war against drugs did not exist. These are controversial assumptions, of course; they appear generally to be associated with many of the discussions about law enforcement consequences, particularly in light of a belief in law enforcement's mixed record at reducing demand. Below we examine a range of literature in each category, beginning with corruption.

In Chapter 4 we reviewed the ample corruption that traffickers generate in net producer countries, principally as they buy public decisions as part of their general assault on government and law. Less manifest but equally deleterious consequences are noted regarding corruption in net importing or consuming countries. Referenced are the "purchase" of police, drug agents, bureaucrats, and the judiciary and the fear that more of it will occur.

It would be expected that the corruptibility of police and drug agents would occur in areas of highest traffic and greatest market demand. Miami, Washington, D.C., New York City, and Los Angeles have been noted most frequently in the United States,[96] although some mention is made of political corruption in small, machine-run cities and among rural sheriffs in Georgia, federal prosecutors in Boston, and customs officials in California.[97] It appears that even the reputation of the Drug Enforcement Administration headquarters in Washington, D.C., has been slightly marred.[98]

The drug traffic, particularly in cocaine, is viewed as one of the most corruptive and corrosive forces in American society.[99] Given the mixed record of law enforcement's success in reducing demand and therefore the traffic, there is increasing concern about some of the unintended consequences. Corruption is one; crime is another.

Extensive literature exists on the relationship of *crime* to drugs.[100] We reviewed some of it above when we indirectly attempted to assess whether law enforcement efforts were reducing demand. With respect to crime, some arguments are raised that drug use does not increase criminality; some, that it does. There is undeniable evidence that crime and drugs go hand in hand[101] and that drug-related crime is either increasing rapidly[102] or has always been considerably more than anyone had guessed.[103] But there is contradictory evidence as to whether criminals gravitate to drug use or drug use produces criminals.[104] There are increasing efforts to try to determine the nature of the connection.[105] Regardless, there is widespread acceptance that in principal consuming countries with illegalizing laws, heroin addicts, and perhaps crack addicts, too, are driven to property crimes to support their habits.[106]

The most discriminating discussions suggesting that drug use increases criminal behavior tend to make distinctions about kinds of crime. For example, James Inciardi distinguishes drug-related crimes or violence that are economically driven (acquiring money to buy drugs) and systemically driven (drug networks trying to outrun law enforcement and drug enforcement agents) from the crime and violence associated with the psychopharmacological properties of the drugs themselves.[107]

Further distinctions are made as to whether the drug involved is heroin, cocaine, or marijuana. It is widely assumed that heroin users (and now crack users, too,[108]) are driven economically to engage in crime to support their habit whereas it may be that many users of other drugs simply opt out of consumption when prices rise beyond their purchasing abilities. Some authors are scathingly critical of "paranoid public ideas" that marijuana use causes criminal behavior.[109] Nevertheless, some studies show that marijuana users have higher delinquency rates than nonusers or even alcohol users. While the causal link is discussible, there is a significant statistical relationship between social deviance and marijuana use.[110]

Additional distinctions are made even with heroin users. Even though there is a general association between crime and heroin addiction, in order to detect causal relationships addicts must be classified according to whether they were involved in crime before becoming addicted. Significantly, in treatment programs, extensive prior criminal involvement is associated with negative treatment outcomes.[111] Also, those previously involved in crime increase their criminal activities when they become addicted; those not so involved in crime become sharply involved in criminal behavior as they become addicted.[112]

One review study, admitting to no definitive resolution of the controversy as to whether narcotics use causes crime, crime causes narcotics use, or narcotics use and crime are simply spuriously related as a consequence of common causes, does post interesting findings: "both arrest and minor property crime precede addiction for most addicts;" "narcotics-use levels facilitate and multiply the amount of property crime activity;" "there is a qualitative shift in the types of crime as addiction levels increase;" "dealing in illicit narcotics is a major intervening factor in narcotics use;" "there is an inverse relationship between dealing and property crime." This source allows that law enforcement interventions "can reduce criminality of most addicts by making 'choice' of addiction, and the crime required to support it, less desirable." These researchers would therefore argue against either abandoning law enforcement or relying excessively on a medical model for treatment.[113]

While the discussions on causation continue, but with considerable agreement that heroin and perhaps crack users really are driven to crime, there is a growing body of evidence suggesting that drug abusers—especially crack users—are at high risk for violence,[114] one outcome of which is increased homicides.[115]

One certain consequence of the *belief* of a causal connection between drug use and crime, especially heroin, is a burgeoning of private anticrime efforts, including security guards, guard dogs, bars and alarm systems, self-defense classes, and handgun purchases.[116]

A certain amount of property crime is caused by opiate addiction, and crimes of violence are clearly attached to crack cocaine use. Are both "caused" by illegalizing laws and the law enforcement strategies selected to implement them? Some of the crimes, and some of the violence, clearly appear to be. But all this leaves unsaid any speculations about increased addiction that might occur if the illegalizing laws and antidrug law enforcement tactics were removed. Perhaps property crimes would decline and heroin prices would drastically fall if the "crime tax" of illegality were removed, even if increased consumption occurred. Present trends suggest that increased consumption of crack would take place, and with it increasing levels of crack- and cocaine- related violence regardless of changes in laws or law enforcement strategies. Observing that laws and their enforcement create undesirable consequences does not argue necessarily that the consequences would be any less undesirable were the laws and implementing strategies removed.

The incidence of AIDS has been increasing worldwide.[117] Whereas in the past the HIV virus that causes AIDS was spread mostly by homosexual men, now it is rampant among intravenous drug users. The rate of new infections in homosexual men has dropped sharply since 1983, but it is steadily rising among needle-using addicts at the rate of about three percent per year,[118] especially among those who inject cocaine (more so than among those who inject heroin), apparently because cocaine users often inject several times an hour.[119] AIDS is also rising among crack users, who seem to have rushed into commercial sex in order to raise money for their purchases. (Accompanying the HIV increase among this group has been an alarming increase in syphilis and gonorrhea.)[120] While crack is inexpensive, its addictive nature quickly causes users to run out of money to support their massive habits.

It is now incontrovertible that intravenous drug users are rapidly spreading the AIDS virus,[121] among themselves as they share needles, to sexual partners who may be unaware of[122] or unconcerned about the hazards, and to unborn children[123] who begin life not only with an unfortunate legacy but who usually become wards of the state, with accompanying enormous financial costs to the public.[124] There is an alarming increase of AIDS among minorities and women.[125] Even conservative projections based on demographic variables and imputed behavioral characteristics suggest a complete breakdown in the delivery of health services in New York City as AIDS patients overwhelm the system.[126] All this presents, of course, enormous policy issues in such areas as minorities, prostitutes, methadone maintenance programs, needle-giveaway programs, drug users' organizations, HIV infections in prisons, women, and social overhead costs.[127]

We discuss treatment procedures (e.g., methadone maintenance, needle-exchange programs, and heroin maintenance) later in this chapter. Here we face the following question: As an unintended consequence, do current illegalizing policies and law enforcement practices enhance the spread of AIDS? If one assumes that sharing contaminated needles is the principal culprit, and that this occurs because of users' required clandestine behavior to avoid detection, a case can be made. It is true that the incidence of new infections in Amsterdam, which has a needle-exchange program, is less than, say, in New York,[128] a comparison that has sparked conventional arguments and counterarguments regarding needle-sharing programs.[129] Studies in three U.S. cities reported that needle-exchange programs reduced needle sharing and therefore the risk of transmitting the AIDS virus.[130] The U.S. secretary of health and human services at one time announced that the U.S. government would be "supportive" of local communities wanting to institute a needle-exchange program to help stop the spread of AIDS by drug addicts.[131] If these assumptions and apparent outcomes of needle-exchange programs are true, then less law enforcement is called for if AIDS is viewed as a harm greater than others that would occur in the absence of antidrug laws and their enforcement.[132]

On the other hand, studies show that addicts share needles not simply to hide their behavior but also because they participate in a social economy that likely would exist independently of legalizing policies or a reduced level of law enforcement.[133] Moreover, while evidence from Europe shows that needle-exchange programs do not increase drug use, the same evidence disputes how effective these programs are in controlling AIDS infections.[134]

Beyond these considerations, "AIDS is out," having moved from homosexuals to drug users to larger populations, mostly by illegitimate and legitimate heterosexual contact and the occasional contaminated blood transfusion. If the unintended contribution of law enforcement to the spread of AIDS could be eliminated overnight, it is unclear what the total impact of this would be on the continued spread of this horrendous disease.

The fourth principal concern on unintended consequences of law enforcement responses to the drug traffic appearing in our data set deals with the actual and probable violation of *human, civil, and constitutional rights*. The concern is not law enforcement per se or even societies' needs to legitimately exercise restraint on a drug using public, but rather the tendency toward excesses. How many civil rights should be abridged, human rights abrogated, and constitutional restraints in democratic countries abused in the war on drugs? Where should the line be drawn? And, at whatever point, how does one trade off the social, economic, and political ills of abuse against the abrogation of individual human, civil, and constitutional rights? Differing perspectives based on disparate value premises and personal experiences promote differential responses.

In a practical way, does it seem right that drug sweeps should be made in which tens of thousands of people are arrested, dozens hanged, and thousands sent to labor camps—all with minimal attention to anything remotely resembling due process? Drug use would have to present a fairly severe threat to the social order to justify such measures. Clearly, they would not be tolerated in many countries; they are a matter of course in Iran.[135]

Many human rights charges have been leveled against Mexico in its antidrug campaigns, particularly during arrest, detention, and imprisonment for narcotics violations and for the wholesale abuse of peasants during drug-related maneuvers in the countryside.[136] In Bolivia antidrug police squads in coca growing regions have attacked peasants and robbed them of money and goods, sometimes killing them.[137] Severe sanctions exist in Asia,[138] and abuses have been reported in France[139] and in the United States.[140] The potential exists for more.

For example, in the United States, much discussion has arisen over "drug courier profiles," which have been developed to aid antidrug agents to curb drug smuggling on airlines. The profiles consist of characteristics thought to indicate whether a particular airline passenger is carrying drugs. Relying on this profile, airport agents have questioned, detained, and searched such individuals with considerable inconsistency and empirical inadequacy.[141] Regardless, the courts appear to be willing to accept the profile's validity even in light of numerous errors, which has caused U.S. Supreme Court justices Brennan and Marshall to declare use of the list of traits a dangerous method.[142] Obviously a fine line must be walked to balance the constitutional rights of the travelling public against any legitimate need to fight narcotics trafficking. Some people are trying to discover that line.[143]

Aside from the outrages committed when law enforcement forces act against their own institutional principles, and aside from constitutional difficulties in trying to find the right balance, there is concern about the probable occurrence of numerous human and civil rights violations when wholesale law enforcement sweeps occur, in Iran or anywhere else. Particularly is this fear justified as military organizations become more and more involved in law enforcement efforts. With some exceptions, militaries are generally trained to kill and destroy; neither outcome is consistent with the maintenance of human, civil, and constitutional rights.[144]

Many of these unintended consequences occur, of course, with the criminalization of users and the associated stigma that largely remove them from an ability to function in normal society,[145] frequently forcing them into multiple kinds of crime. Criminalization and stigmatization are seen to contribute to family breakdown and mistrust, with children turning in their parents to authorities, and parents their children.[146]

Aside from law enforcement consequences regarding corruption, crime, AIDS, and human rights, numerous additional "consequence concerns" are detected in the literature. Among the political ones are dysfunctional nationalism in net producer countries arising when nations such as the United States take a high-profile law enforcement and drug enforcement role in them, particularly when this entails "colonial extradition" measures against local citizens.[147] In the past the resulting "negative nationalisms" have produced highly unstable political consequences in Latin America.

As we have seen, law enforcement measures to reduce demand in net consumer countries tend to produce a sophisticated opposition in traffickers, gangs, and their cohorts. That opposition is increasingly armed. Throughout the United States, drug pushers and their allies frequently have far more effective guns than do the police who are trying to control them.[148] In effect, a "counter-army" is being created, producing conditions for further societal militarization as desperate policymakers mobilize resources to counterattack. In democratic countries, always in view is the threat this poses for the institutions of freedom and liberty which sustain democratic practices.[149]

Finally, in the political category, "political will" is discussed, which has been thought to be on the decline in Colombia as the cocaine mafia responded to law enforcement efforts with a savage fury that indiscriminately destroyed, maimed, and killed.[150] A change of political heart is unremarkable. Countries do it all the time. In the drug war, however, "throwing in the towel" will not necessarily reduce the institutional threat from the drug barons. Mafias, once created, tend to maintain a continued reason for existence long after the utility of initial justifications has expired. It would indeed be ironic if, in deciding to make peace with the drug mafia, an exhausted Colombia continued to suffer from a counterstate that its vigorous law enforcement efforts had indirectly caused to exist.

The unintended law enforcement consequences in the *economy* are, as one might imagine, largely attached to costs. Aside from increased law enforcement and military operations costs, huge prison systems must be erected and maintained to handle the increased load from drug arrests. In the United States, for example, the administration has been asked to double the projected expenditures for new prisons, increasing federal expenditures on jails to $1.2 billion in 1990.[151] Court costs are up considerably; new judges must be hired to work through the large backlog of cases, most of which are drug related. The economic costs are not all that is felt here. Many civil matters are being squeezed out of any consideration as a result of the surge in the number of drug cases, which have increased nearly 300 percent in the last several years.[152]

Costs of all kinds skyrocket, a situation that has provoked some to begin cost-benefit analyses on the effectiveness of law enforcement strategies vis-à-vis certain kinds of trade-offs.[153] While we do not have an estimated global figure for all imagined direct and indirect costs, they must truly be substantial.

As for unintended *social* consequences of law enforcement policies, the literature notes a number deriving from illegalizing policies and the law enforcement efforts to sustain them. Among these is a promotion of more dangerous drug use by forcing, for convenience of clandestine smuggling, the development of more potent drugs that weigh less, are less bulky, and are therefore more easily hidden. Pakistan, for example, where heroin addiction was unknown until 1979 but opium was widely used, now has a major heroin addiction problem since the banning of opium.[154] A similar phenomenon is noted in several other Asian countries. When antiopium laws were enacted in countries where opium use was traditional, heroin suddenly appeared. Within a decade, heroin addiction surpassed opium addiction.[155] Despite more than 500 million dollars spent by New York City in 1988 on drug-related enforcement alone, more than twice the amount than in 1986 (and perhaps half that in 1989), crack is more pervasive and prevalent than ever before, and its effects are more violent and insidious on the impoverished citizens the city has spent so many hundreds of millions of dollars trying to help.[156]

Court congestion deriving from drug cases not only increases costs, as noted above, it also denies due process in countries whose very legal foundation rests on its presumption.[157] Congestion also enhances the level of "counter-socialization" that inmates give each other, particularly young ones (predominately held on drug-related charges), which increases the likelihood that they will not function well in society when released. Then, to accommodate some of the court-mandated reduction in overcrowding, early prison releases must be negotiated. In some U.S. states, for example, serving from one-third to one-half a sentence places one in line for an early release, creating a sham of the sentencing process[158] or of the laws themselves. The backup in the judicial system and the overcrowded prisons cause judges to be reluctant to incarcerate some categories of convicted felons.[159] The felons therefore roam through society with virtual impunity.

Seedy neighborhoods laced with crack houses, endemic crime, and terrorized residents are commonplace.[160] Pushed from a given area by law enforcement efforts, angry residents, or visiting vigilantes, the criminals simply migrate to other neighborhoods or countries and set up shop,[161] creating in the inner cities the extraordinary analogy of slash-and-burn agriculture in the tropics. After laying an area to waste, the principals move on to lay claim to another. Less likely is that the passage of time will heal the wounds.

More troubling to some, however, is that drug trafficking, fueled by what some have thought to be an insatiable demand in net consumer countries, is literally overwhelming law enforcement agents. "Swamped" is the word most frequently encountered.[162] As the situation becomes more desperate, calls increase for additional trained manpower. It is this situation in net consumer countries, more than anything else, that has swung the military into becoming involved in the drug war, with the attendant dangers we have already noted.[163]

The inconsistencies and philosophical anomalies are seen to promote a disrespect for the law[164] and to place police officers in circumstances of excessive risk for little gain.[165]

Adequate international demand for psychoactive drugs, combined with their general illegality, has given rise to organized trafficking and countervailing initiatives directed both at traffickers and at users in order to reduce demand and supply. Both have combined to produce society-wide consequences (Flow Chart 1). When considering law enforcement effectiveness, along with its unintended deleterious consequences, has the outcome been "admirable," "discussible," "questionable," or "unacceptable?" (Table 5). The literature in our data set would appear to opt for "questionable" or "unacceptable." This does not mean, of course, that the consequences truly should be so judged, only that the preponderant literature reviewed for this handbook appears to do so.

Education

Aside from law enforcement sanctions, most nations have implemented educational endeavors to reduce illicit drug demand. Early programs focused on "factual approaches" and "risk-oriented teaching methods" to drug education (i.e., teaching young people about the psychopharmacological properties of drugs to produce aversion, fear, and anxiety about using them).[166]

There is an inordinately small correlation between youths' knowledge of the drugs' psychopharmacological properties and their conviction not to use them.[167] In fact, simply giving information, particularly if deleterious pharmacological properties are exaggerated, frequently heightens drug use.[168]

Most current literature therefore focuses not on whether antidrug education is desirable but whether it is effective (i.e., "what works and what doesn't work in terms of education's being a deterrent to drug taking"). The programs vary widely in theory, scope, and application. Their promoters strive to give each an "effectiveness ascendancy." All acknowledge that beyond facts and even legitimate scare tactics something additional is required to make the programs effective. In a macro sense this addition is an ethos of antidrug values. But this seems to work only if educational programs also integrate into their efforts support groups such as family, peers, "reasoning skill groups," religions, community, and/or volunteer groups, with the general acknowledgment that no single method is likely to work under all conditions.[169]

Testing in the Workplace

From the vantage of political authorities who create public policy, screening for drug use in the workplace is desirable—other people must face employee wrath even though public policy or law mandates testing. Regardless, the impact on the reduction of illicit demand will likely be positive. After all, people's jobs are at stake. To "sequester" a job is somewhat like "sequestering assets," and there is evidence that asset forfeiture has a considerable deterrence on drug trafficking.[170]

Initially, American business was a reluctant, often highly skeptical partner in using the workplace to reduce illicit demand. That was before employers began to weigh the impact of their employees' drug use on business profits. The costs are now readily apparent, observable, and, to some extent, calculable. They are substantial.

A 1980 report shows that, spread out over the entire work force, drug abuse in the United States cost $472 per employee (averaged over 100 million employees). Of this, 81 percent was attributed to lost productivity, 12 percent to crime costs, 3 percent to medical expenses, 2 percent to victims' costs, and 1 percent to social programs. Property damage was 0.2 percent of the total cost.[171] More than 80 percent of the organizations surveyed in a 1983 study reported they had to deal directly with drug problems, with the added insult that antidrug efforts in the workplace of the previous five to ten years had largely been ineffective.[172] In Canada, cocaine has seduced ambitious executives and has contributed to costly absenteeism from the workplace.[173] Economic losses, impacts on careers, added economic and social externalities on business enterprises—all are now part of the business landscape in North America and increasingly in much of the world. But even to discuss this within an employee-employer relationship is fraught with difficulties.[174]

In the wake of the perception that drug use in the workplace costs billions of dollars annually to American businesses (decreased productivity and increased error, theft, absenteeism, and accident rates), the U.S. federal government in 1986 mandated a "drug-free federal workplace" in order to set the pace for drug-free workplaces everywhere.[175] The government appeared to be serious, and for good reasons. In one 1989 random drug test, 203 federal officials were caught using illegal drugs. Among these were 60 air traffic controllers and 42 workers employed in the nuclear and chemical weapons security program.[176]

The fear of detection and possible loss of employment are deterrents to illicit drug use. Although this is an effective negative sanction, it usually does not create harmonious employer-employee relations,[177] except under conditions in which employees believe that other employees' drug use may contribute to accidents in the labor force, including their own. Regardless, negative deterrence is a response that many enterprises exploit. Other employers, however, have established approaches that do not place employment in jeopardy initially, but rather they approach individuals, their families, and associated "situational matters" in ways to help valued employees overcome a debilitating practice.[178]

Whether positive or negative sanctions, with few notable exceptions the principal means of detection is a random urine test, a drug-sniffing dog, or unannounced desk searches. Controversy surrounding all these practices has escalated.[179] Aside from the constitutional issues involved in U.S. society,[180] the accuracy of urine tests themselves has provoked considerable discussion.[181]

The controversies notwithstanding, mandatory urine testing has been instituted in U.S. air and rail travel industries and in public health and safety agencies. The constitutionality of these provisions has been upheld by U.S. appellate courts and the U.S. Supreme Court.[182] Increasingly, state agencies and business enterprises are turning to mandatory practices in an effort to cut their productivity losses.[183]

Civic Action

Communities tend to know what their difficulties are and frequently have some of the best ideas on how to resolve them. It becomes more evident that, without instrumental community attention to the problems, outside agencies are unlikely to deal with them successfully. Eliciting concerted community involvement in drug-abuse problems is therefore thought to offer opportunities to reduce illicit drug demand. Support from diverse community organizations in a "civic action" effort to reduce demand is thought to help. It is usually acknowledged that collaboration with law enforcement officials, to continue to increase individual risks to traffickers and users, is required.

Much current literature therefore calls for community involvement in reducing drug demand. We are told that no national or federal agency ought to assume that it can step into a community with demand reduction, traffic suppression, or treatment and rehabilitation schemes without prior community consultation—if it hopes to be successful. Community perspectives, it is affirmed, must be included in policy decisions, and key opinion leaders ought to be relied on as a source of appropriate policy information.[184]

Raising the élan of a community for voluntary antidrug service is decisive, but effective coordination is required in order to assure that acceptable goals are pursued in noncounter-productive ways. Some communities are attempting to orchestrate this coordination. One interesting example comes from Detroit.[185] In one of the city's abandoned-house districts, the community has launched an effort to purchase "crack houses," renovate them, and sell them at low cost (for an average of $18,000 in 1988) to senior citizens and single parent families who need housing the most and who can be relied upon not to participate in the drug trade. Considerable volunteerism exists, including church workers who, along with unemployed neighbors hired temporarily, do most of the renovation work.

Many buyers get their down payments through "sweat equity" and at the same time learn valuable construction and maintenance skills. They thereby acquire both a financial stake and a "pride" stake in their new homes, and they present a natural resistance to "drug demand."

On the other side, sometimes people in small neighborhoods, impatient with a community's attention to their problems or despairing that the police can adequately protect them, prosecute their interests independently of any official blessing. The illustrations are always poignant; in many cases, also productive. One pipeline entrepreneur hired neighborhood gang members as bona fide employees. He has been successful in reforming some of them.[186] Self-help groups for addicts are blossoming everywhere. Some, such as Cocaine Anonymous, are patterned after "holistic" rehabilitation programs having a long history of success in alcohol dependency.[187] Youth "networks for abstinence" groups are forming all over the United States at a "rather astonishing rate."[188] Another group runs an anonymous hotline. Neighborhood residents, who may be fearful to call police (lest their identity be betrayed) appear willing to use the anonymous hotline to report drug activities in their heavily drug-infested neighborhoods. Information is then passed on to the police. Police investigate and report to "Drop-a-Dime." The feedback is then circulated around the community in informal information networks.[189] And, beyond all this, parent groups have been forming in support of information networks.[190]

Sometimes citizens, on their own, simply stand up and fight,[191] a phenomenon increasingly noted in public (subsidized) housing projects in the United States.[192] It may well be for this reason that the U.S. government and several cities have taken renewed interest in the environment of their public housing, making efforts to remove drug traffickers, or the families of those involved in drug trafficking, from the projects.[193]

Usually, law enforcement organizations object to citizens' acting on their own in such matters, particularly if injury is likely, not only because their own inability to deal with citizens' concerns is made manifest, but also because the exercises sometimes take on the specter of vigilantism.[194] It is fair to say that when citizens move this far in their drug fight they are not only involved but concerned, frightened, despairing, and wholly disinclined to have much faith in their government.[195] Sadly, sometimes even the citizens simply give up.[196]

The Mass Media

United States congressional representatives have urged their country's television networks to campaign against illegal drug use.[197] The U.S. Congress has held hearings for "influencers of American perceptions" to present testimony about what they were prepared to do to help lower illicit drug demand.[198] There is widespread belief that appropriate mass media campaigns could produce respectable results.

It seems quite uncontroversial to suggest that the mass media could effectively help reduce drug-abuse demand; however, the media could also be a dangerous friend. Assuming that the media include cinema as well as television, newsprint, and radio and that the publicly known social mores of "trend setters"—particularly in cinema and television—also produce consequential emotive images, it could be said that the media have so far produced more harm than good. Indeed, suggestions are raised that any media campaign would probably find it necessary to somehow undermine some media personalities' own drug mores if its antidrug message were to be credible.[199]

While during prime time viewing in 1985 the U.S. television media rather uniformly portrayed illegal drug users to be abusers, the most startling finding of one study was the phenomenal amount of drug use shown, most of it inconsequential to the plots, however weak these were. Nevertheless, with respect to illicit drugs, the portrayals were shown as almost always producing negative consequences, frequently with dire results.[200] However, one literature review on mass media's role in drug-abuse prevention revealed that audiences would need to be segmented and presentations custom-designed if demand reduction results were to be expected.[201]

Yet, the appeal to use the mass media in some constructive way will not subside. Perhaps this derives from the underlying reality of its potential usefulness. The media's effectiveness, at least in Colombia, is attested by how frequently its antidrug advocates and their organizations have been subjected to vicious life-wasting attacks.[202] Traffickers certainly think the Colombian mass media are credible and effective, so much so, in fact, that they have purchased their own newspapers, television stations, and radio stations and do their own work to affect public opinion.[203]

In the United States a volunteer group of advertising executives has persuaded a diversity of product manufacturers (of toy cars and trucks, videos that play as motorists pump gasoline, television dramas, and school supplies) to join them in an antidrug crusade—albeit subtle—using the mass media. In 1990 the executives' advertising agencies contributed thousands of hours in creating what they hoped would be influential spots for newspapers, magazines, radio, and television. In turn, TV networks, independent stations, and other media gave $365 million worth of advertising space and time to carry the agencies' donated work. A scholarly assessment of the effectiveness of this campaign has not been done. However, the assumption is that if a clever advertisement can persuade one to buy a specific product, an equally clever advertisement may persuade one to avoid illegal drugs.[204]

We have reviewed the principal options intended to reduce the demand for illicit drugs—law enforcement, education, the workplace, civic action, and the mass media. Of these, the most troubling unintended consequences appear to involve law enforcement. New approaches under way and probable ones forthcoming appear to hold demand-reduction promise in the other categories, although each is fraught with the potential for crisis and failure. We noted, for example, some troubling employee morale and constitutional issues associated with mandatory drug testing.

We turn now to a consideration of the second category of activities intended to implement national policies aimed at reducing drug consumption: control of supply.

Control of Supply

Until recently, the international community placed considerable faith in supply-control policies as the principal way to reduce illicit drug consumption. Many nations and international agencies still place effusive trust in this policy, which is usually translated into the eradication of the crops from which the drug alkaloids are derived. Countries now recognize, however, that the eradication of illicitly cultivated opium poppy, coca bush, and cannabis plants is a highly complex and difficult undertaking, one which so far has produced unsatisfactory results.

Part of the eradication difficulty is the growers' reluctance to acquiesce voluntarily to the destruction of their valuable cash crops. But it is not just income considerations that drive resistance to eradication. As we saw from the literature reviewed on drugs and culture,[205] the plants are apparently inextricably intertwined with some indigenous cultures, making eradication policies more difficult to implement. However, beyond economic and cultural considerations attached to growers' lives lie the political and paramilitary organizations that protect them. Thus, in response to market demand, huge plantings of opium poppy, coca bush, and cannabis plants continue successfully to be made, with an accompanying increase in the availability of illicit drugs on the international market.[206] With renewed energy, consuming nations have reasserted their efforts to destroy, reduce, or eliminate the need for the crops. The tactics, employing negative sanctions and positive incentives, are principally four: continued crop eradication, control of precursor chemicals, crop substitution, and rural economic development.

Crop Eradication

Opium poppy, coca bush, and cannabis plants are destroyed either by physically uprooting them or by spraying them with an herbicide.[207] In late 1989 considerable eradication efforts had been targeted for or were under way in Peru and Bolivia (coca bush), the United States (cannabis), Mexico (cannabis and opium poppy), and Burma and Guatemala (opium poppy). Other countries also have eradication programs. In 1981, only two countries were eradicating illicit drug crops; by 1985, fourteen countries had eradication programs.[208]

It is probably fair to say that a 1986 U.S. State Department release,[209] which gave the reduction of these plants the highest U.S. government priority, accurately reflected U.S. official consensus through 1987. Thereafter, with a preponderant emphasis on Latin America (see Figure 18), everything began to take a back seat to drug law enforcement and interdiction (see Figure 19).[210] Nevertheless, crop eradication efforts continue. In exchange for U.S. material help and other incentives, both public and private, producer countries as well as several U.S. states have uprooted and sprayed thousands of hectares of plants and have engaged in other activities designed to reduce the supply of the agricultural precursor crops for cocaine and crack, heroin and morphine, and marijuana and hashish.

International interest in eradicating coca was facilitated by the South American agreement on Narcotic Drugs and Psychotropic Substances (ASEP).[211] Bilateral crop eradication agreements have been struck with Bolivia, Peru, and Mexico.[212] The United States has offered both money and military assistance and, in a few cases, has supplied operational personnel for eradication efforts.[213]

In Peru, agreements with the national government notwithstanding, peasants have resisted the program so intensely that, in order to save their crops, they have become ready allies with insurgent groups.[214] Indeed, because of this, on-site U.S. Drug Enforcement Administration officials have come under serious risk and have found it necessary to construct a Vietnam-type "secure base" in Santa Lucía in the upper Huallaga Valley in order to carry out their work. The base can be supplied and staffed safely only by air transport.[215]

Peasant resistance is also strong in Bolivia.[216] Consequently, the new Bolivian government is rethinking its whole position on eradication, aided by a huge, lengthy, and volatile national debate over the eradication issue.[217] In Burma, a civil war continues, complicated by moves and countermoves over opium poppy production.[218]

Because of the magnitude of the eradication task, and because of the frequently effective resistance against ground eradication teams, including, in a few cases, the killing of eradication team members,[219] attention has turned to aerial spraying. Cannabis plants have been sprayed in the United States[220] and in Mexico,[221] opium poppy plants in Burma,[222] Mexico, and Guatemala,[223] and the search has been under way for a safe

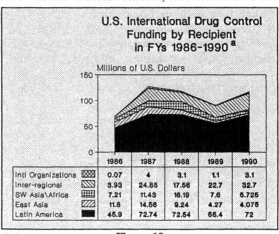

U.S. International Drug Control Funding by Recipient in FYs 1986-1990 [a]

Millions of U.S. Dollars

	1986	1987	1988	1989	1990
Intl Organizations	0.07	4	3.1	1.1	3.1
Inter-regional	3.93	24.85	17.56	22.7	32.7
SW Asia\Africa	7.21	11.43	16.19	7.6	5.725
East Asia	11.8	14.56	9.24	4.27	4.075
Latin America	45.9	72.74	72.54	55.4	72

[a]Refer to note 210   **Figure 18**

herbicide for the hearty coca bush. Some test applications have now been carried out in Bolivia and Peru.

In Bolivia, experiments were conducted in Villa Tunari, a town where a confrontation between small coca growers and police claimed several lives in June 1988.[224] Then, astonishing virtually everyone, Peru's previous president, Alan

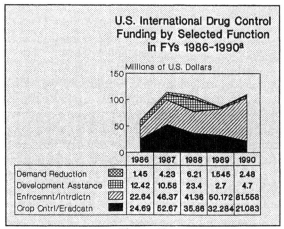

U.S. International Drug Control Funding by Selected Function in FYs 1986-1990[a]

Millions of U.S. Dollars

	1986	1987	1988	1989	1990
Demand Reduction	1.45	4.23	6.21	1.545	2.48
Development Asstance	12.42	10.58	23.4	2.7	4.7
Enfrcemnt/Intrdlctn	22.64	46.37	41.36	50.172	81.558
Crop Cntrl/Eradcatn	24.69	52.67	35.86	32.284	21.083

[a]Refer to note 210   **Figure 19**

García, said he was willing to use herbicides to eradicate the coca leaf if UN scientists certified that the ecological impact would be minimal.[225] Whether that certification was received is not known to this reviewer, but a seventy-acre test, the final one before massive aerial eradication was scheduled to begin, was carried out in March 1989.[226] New reports in early 1990 indicated that all spraying in Peru had been halted. The opposition to it was too strong.

Aerial spraying has been accompanied by national and international commentary that, it is fair to say, has limited the spraying applications. One author describes how environmental groups sued the DEA and prevented its continuing a spraying program in Mexico until environmental-impact statements were prepared and the product being used—paraquat—had its label amended. The movement showed that the DEA paraquat program was potentially hazardous to both the public (especially marijuana users) and the environment, and that it also violated two federal environmental acts. It has been a long struggle for the U.S. State Department in its international paraquat spraying efforts. Smokers mobilized political support because of the health dangers associated with smoking contaminated marijuana from Mexico.[227] In the late 1970s over one-fifth of the marijuana samples from the southwestern United States were contaminated with paraquat.[228] In 1983, U.S. officials were saying that it was "unlikely that paraquat spraying endangers the health of marijuana smokers in the United States."[229] However, when the plans for resumption of spraying were announced in 1988, environmentalists struck with vigorous objections.[230]

Another author, in a show of informational entrepreneurship, reported that the herbicidal spraying program in Burma killed a number of elderly women, and that children and many old people were made sick and their food crops and animals were destroyed.[231] California officials refused to let the federal government spray on public lands within its borders,[232] and the U.S. Congress, alarmed at the controversy, held two highly charged hearings[233] and issued a final report.[234] One U.S. company has even refused to sell the spray to the U.S. government, fearing retribution on its physical facilities in the countries of application.[235] Nevertheless, the efforts go on, although the effectiveness is continually under question.[236]

As for the coca bush, some observers now place hope in swarms of an unusual butterfly that is a voracious eater and feeds exclusively on coca plant leaves. In 1988 the creatures had destroyed almost 20,000 hectares of illegally grown coca in Peru. Growers were looking for effective insecticides, and antidrug experts were investigating ways to propagate the butterflies. Interestingly, entomologists seemed to know little about them.[237]

The intended consequence of eradication is to reduce the supply of drugs, the rationale being that a reduced supply will limit consumption. Neither crop uprooting nor herbicidal spraying has been successful in reducing supply. From 1985 through 1989 coca leaf production increased every year, from an estimated 157,000 to 240,000 metric tons. A slight reduction of 5,000 metric tons in 1990 is almost wholly accounted for by Bolivia (see Figure 3), where coca leaf prices have fallen drastically. One suspects that it is more the economics of the matter than eradication that accounts for the Bolivian reduction. In spite of the drug wars in Colombia that have so affected the Bolivian coca leaf market, Colombia's fledgling production increased more than 2.6 times between 1985 and 1990 (see Figure 3) and held quite steady from 1989 to 1990 when most of the internal disruption in Colombia was taking place and Bolivian production was falling off slightly.

As for opium production, increases were noted for every producing country from 1985 through 1988, from a global metric tonnage of 1,465 to 2,881. A substantial increase in Burma (from 1,285 to 2,430 metric tons) occurred between 1988 and 1989, although 1990 production fell to 2,250 metric tons (see Figure 10). Significantly, the decline in Burma occurred simultaneously with the country's virtual abandonment of its eradication program, making quite difficult any assertion that eradication was the cause.[238] Lebanon and Guatemala sport a sufficient increase to now merit notation in the U.S. Department of State's worldwide production estimates (see Figure 11).[239]

The most remarkable reported production increase is marijuana in Mexico, from a 1988 estimate of 5,655 tons to a 1989 estimate of 30,200[240] (see Figure 14). Much of the increase probably reflects a realization of substantial production underestimates in prior years; much of it may well be a real increase.

Both crop uprooting and herbicidal spraying to eradicate drug production have galvanized peasant resistance and, as we have seen, have forced the Bolivian and Peruvian governments to take a less aggressive posture on crop destruction. Fatalities have been noted and will likely increase. Political unrest is substantial. The reasons are simple enough. Just as drug production has enhanced the economic position of the peasantry involved, the prospects of its sudden destruction create social despair and anger. An actual sudden destruction would produce an economic and political catastrophe.

Thus the information above and in Chapter 4 on how crop eradication programs have motivated peasant growers to become allied with insurgent forces ought to come as no surprise. The results have certainly become a matter of substantial concern in Peru where the *Sendero Luminoso* now controls large sectors of the country.

In reflecting on the "consequence permutations" of drug control policies in Table 3 (of which demand reduction, supply control, traffic suppression, and treatment and rehabilitation are constituent parts), one readily gets the impression that the "unintended" consequences of controlling supply are of substantial political and economic concern to national governments and ought also to be of concern to the United States.

Control of Precursor Chemicals

In spite of crop eradication, ample supplies of opium poppy resin, coca leaves, and cannabis plants remain for domestic and international markets. But the plants need processing. In particular, opium poppy resin and coca leaves require industrial chemicals to liberate the psychoactive alkaloids to be commercialized as heroin and cocaine. Sulfuric acid, hydrochloric acid, acetone, and ether are mentioned for cocaine processing. Hydrochloric acid and other chemicals (e.g., ecgonine and thebaine) are mentioned as being required for opium poppy resin. While sulfuric acid, hydrochloric acid, acetone, and ether are industrial compounds available in most countries on the open market, ecgonine and thebaine are subject to the control provisions of the 1961 Single Convention on Narcotic Drugs and Psychotropic Substances.[241] They ought, therefore, to be more easily controlled.

The call is out for national governments to report promptly significant movements of any of these precursor chemicals,[242] particularly if the chemicals are likely to be transported into areas known to have illicit drug processing laboratories. The monitoring of such chemicals also helps to identify "transiting" countries whose governmental officials may be giving tacit or explicit approval to the drug traffic.

The apparent first flurry of international interest in precursor chemicals involved Paraguay in 1985. Large quantities of the chemicals were moving openly through the country's customs offices. Moreover, high-level officials in the Stroessner administration were implicated in traffic quite openly destined to support cocaine processing laboratories.[243]

In early January 1985 the United States publicly urged Paraguay to increase its control over precursor chemical traffic. The Stroessner administration, perhaps embarrassed by the notoriety of high-level connections with the cocaine industry, by 9 January 1985 had seized nearly 50,000 gallons of ether, acetone, and hydrochloric acid obviously destined for cocaine processors whose principal market was the United States.[244] The quantities seized—probably not including the entire stock then within Paraguay's borders—were not insignificant. It was estimated they were sufficient to process about 10 percent of the total 1985 U.S. demand for cocaine.[245]

Paraguayan officials refused a U.S. solicitation to destroy the chemicals on the grounds that they could be redirected to a useful and licit end. In any event, President Stroessner himself would have to be consulted, officials said.[246]

The United States mounted considerable pressure, however, and by 23 January, when members of the U.S. Congress visited Paraguay, Stroessner's government promised it would destroy the chemical cache.[247]

The Paraguayan seizure hardly put a dent in operations. Indeed, by 1989 government authorities in Colombia could seize nearly half a million gallons of precursor chemicals and still not materially affect the drug traffic.[248]

Colombia's efforts against common industrial chemicals may have produced counterproductive consequences. Underground cocaine "cooks" simply began using more dangerous chemicals which created new, major health hazards (benzene, a carcinogen, was noted) while at the same time reducing the costs of production because the more dangerous chemicals were also less expensive.[249]

In the United States, efforts are being made to compel chemical companies to keep closer track of compounds required to make illegal drugs.[250] Moreover, international treaties have been negotiated requiring industrial as well as "industrial transit" countries to keep detailed records of precursor chemicals within their national jurisdictions.[251] Among other consequences, this might force Hong Kong's industrialists to restrain the movement of precursor chemicals into the Golden Triangle.[252]

The United Nations, in a February 1990 special session dedicated to finding an effective way to expand its antidrug efforts, called for national and international vigilance over precursor chemicals as part of its supply-reduction strategy.[253] Although the UN has clearly shifted away from a near exclusive attachment to supply reduction in favor of incorporating demand-reduction policies in its agenda, its position on precursor chemicals is likely to foster additional disruption of the drug trade.

The clampdown on precursor chemicals has motivated major cocaine processors to move some of their operations. Under some circumstances, it is easier to smuggle cocaine paste than it is to smuggle the chemicals required to process it. Mexico, where industrial chemicals are easily obtained, has become a country of new cocaine factories,[254] as has Brazil.[255] Argentina, Venezuela, Panama, Canada, and even the United States have seen cocaine processing laboratories spring up within their borders.[256]

Interestingly, Brazil is the only South American country where two of the required chemicals for cocaine—ether and acetone—are manufactured in industrial quantities. Brazil has hardly any control over the chemicals, although the country is trying to ferret out the cocaine producing laboratories.[257] Small wonder, however, that some drug barons in Colombia have found Brazil to be so attractive.

Precursor chemical seizures have been significant; however, they have not dented production much, in part because traffickers have begun to utilize alternative (and more dangerous) chemicals and in part because they have moved their paste processing to countries where chemicals are readily available on the market.

Crop Substitution

With the failure of crop eradication nearly everywhere, and with the control of precursor chemicals, so far, having rather inconsequential results in affecting drug production, renewed energy has been directed to crop substitution, the third principal policy initiative to control the supply of illicit drugs. Crop substitution seeks to motivate farmers away from growing opium poppy, coca bush, and cannabis plants to cultivating domestic food crops for the commercial market. Crop substitution programs have been applied vigorously in Thailand[258] and in Colombia's Cauca province,[259] both with some success. Some success has even been noted recently in Pakistan.[260] However, efforts to apply the program elsewhere have left observers quite pessimistic about the prospects for success. Notable examples are Peru,[261] Bolivia,[262] and Burma.[263]

Accordingly, much of the crop substitution literature concentrates on its failures.[264] Failure exists not only because economic incentives favor coca and opium poppies over food crops by a margin of as much as fifty to one,[265] but also because the crop substitution programs have generally lacked an integrated development agenda or have failed to produce proffered governmental incentives.[266]

On the whole, therefore, crop reduction control strategies—crop eradication and crop substitution—are in trouble in most parts of the drug growing world. In the meantime, drug enforcement officials in the United States, which appears to be the principal backer of these programs (although the UN is heavily involved in Thailand and Colombia[267]), are attempting to persuade the country's politicians to fund an integrated aid program in Latin America—of which crop substitution would be a part. By an overall rural development approach they hope to persuade farmers to grow alternative crops and thereby cut back on supplies of coca.[268]

Rural Economic Development

Opium poppy, coca bush and cannabis plants can be, and often are, cultivated on lands that are both marginal and remote. The higher the level of law enforcement measures directed against growers, the more the growers tend to move their cultivations to isolated areas relatively free from state authority. The quality of growers' social life may decline, but by staying in the coca trade as long as prices are attractive their prospects of continued income dramatically remain. Money and security (along with opportunity) drive most migrations associated with the movement of coca cultivation to relatively remote areas.[269]

Market transport costs are irrelevant in these migrations because of the drugs' high unit value per weight. Moreover, while growers' income is only a small fraction of total drug trade value, the economic incentives are relatively significant, as we saw in the discussion on *crop substitution*.

Crop substitution is most effective when integrated with an overall rural development program. This small conclusion has been a long time seeing the light of day, at least as far as being part of an international drug control strategy. Nevertheless, *integrated rural development* is now riding a wave of considerable enthusiasm among those who hope to find an effective formula to control the supply of illicit drugs. It appears that significant efforts are underway in Bolivia to induce reverse migration from the Chapare and to promote rural development there and in alternative magnet villages.[270]

The literature on applying integrated rural development strategies for controlling illicit drug supply is quite sparse, in part, no doubt, because the strategies are relatively recent and do not have a long track record. Nevertheless, reports have been coming in from the Cauca province in Colombia and from Thailand.[271] An integrated rural development focus is a long-awaited move.[272]

We have seen how the public has responded to contemporary patterns of production and consumption of cocaine, heroin, and cannabis with multilateral and bilateral agreements and national policies designed to reduce demand and control supply. We now turn to the third category of activities intended to implement national and international policies aimed at reducing drug production and consumption—suppressing the traffickers who move the drugs.

Suppression of Illicit International Trafficking

Earlier we reviewed some of the sophisticated and complex ways illicit trafficking is carried out.[273] Traffickers have employed—indeed, continue to employ—every conceivable organizational, strategic, and tactical means to facilitate moving their product to market and to conceal the proceeds derived from its sale. Thus they have conspired to corrupt if not take over law enforcement agencies.[274] They have infiltrated financial institutions in order to launder their money.[275] They have moved to subvert the integrity and stability of certain national governments and to intimidate their judiciaries;[276] to browbeat if not assassinate governmental officials, citizens, and would-be informers; and to engage indiscriminately in crimes of violence, including terrorism.[277] All this is done to facilitate a freer, less risky movement of psychoactive drugs into the international market. Indeed, in some areas, organized drug traffickers have gone so far as to gain virtual control over large sections of countries' real estate in order to accomplish their ends. Here their idiosyncratic preferences become law.[278] They controlled the Bolivian government from 1980 to 1982,[279] appeared to have considerable sway in Panama from about 1980 to 1989,[280] and, more recently, were said to control Laos.[281]

How may international traffickers' efforts be thwarted? The literature suggests five major strategies: disruption of major trafficking networks; forfeiture of assets; technique of controlled delivery; facilitation of extradition; and surveillance of land, water, and air approaches to an importing country's frontier, and controls over ships and aircraft in international space.

Disruption of Major Trafficking Networks

Disrupting the major trafficking networks not only interdicts drugs directly, it makes life difficult for leading drug distributors, at least to the extent of increasing their inconveniences, risks, and costs.

One thing prominent traffickers dearly detest is prolonged inconveniences. Putting such people on the run and removing them from their accustomed amenities is highly psychologically destabilizing[282] because it drastically reduces much of their pleasure of being rich. At some point such people tire and may even sue for peace. For example, Colombia's Medellín "extraditables"—drug barons who in early 1990 had been on the run for half a year—have once again pled with their government to be allowed to return to their families and communities. In exchange, they would suspend the shipment of drugs and surrender the weapons, explosives, laboratories, hostages, and clandestine landing strips and other effects related to their activities "at such a time as we are granted constitutional and legal guarantees."[283] A similar offer was made by the grand drug smuggler of the Golden Triangle, Khun Sa, who has been pursued relentlessly by the Thai and Burmese authorities.[284]

The Colombian offer has been heard before.[285] While the traffickers have not proposed to disband their organizations or surrender their stockpiled cocaine or massive bank accounts, some people think that pressing the traffickers this far with a terribly inconvenient lifestyle—always with the risk of capture and extradition to the United States—helps disrupt their ability to move drugs across international frontiers.

The advantage of the "inconveniencing" tendency, the literature suggests, is not so much that drug barons tire but that under pressure they make mistakes, thereby giving governments an increased opportunity to capture them. If the traffickers view capture as a generally credible threat, their perception of personal risk is raised, and this perception may well reduce their drug-related activities. This seemed to happen temporarily in Colombia after one kingpin, José Rodríguez Gacha, was gunned down following his "exposure" after he personally took charge of a large shipment of cocaine with a U.S. destination. He was, as they say, between a rock and a hard place. His shipping specialist had been captured earlier and had been extradited. Rodríguez Gacha had no one else who could readily engineer the shipment. In some desperation he took the risk, and he lost.[286]

One drawback with a policy of inconvenience and heightened risk is that events such as occurred with Rodríguez Gacha must occur quite regularly. Otherwise, the traffickers' sense of invulnerability returns.

But credible fear of increased risk aside, when a kingpin does happen to fall, it is widely observed that someone almost invariably steps forward to take his place. This may not be entirely propitious, especially in Latin America where almost all organizations, not just clandestine or informal ones, are built on a central figure's "personal" control.[287] Such organizations appear to recover more slowly, and they are more prone to internal leadership struggles after the removal of a principal chief than happens when more institutionalized groups suffer internal leadership disruptions. Being thus weakened, drug organizations may be less able to move their product to market.

Thus the fall of a central figure may do more than simply disrupt traffic temporarily. It may slow it down for an extended period. For example, the U.S. invasion of Panama notwithstanding, it was thought that removing Manuel Noriega from Panama would materially alter that country's "safe haven" function for cocaine shipments and money laundering. At the least, traffickers would be required to find alternative routes and networks. Never mind that they *do* tend to find them, the optimists say; the very act of disrupting the traffic through inconvenience and heightened risk increases traffickers' costs while weakening their organizations. This, coupled with other cost-increasing measures, is thought to be helpful.

Thus much of the literature implicitly focuses on increasing the costs (or, on the other hand, the futility of increasing the costs sufficiently[288]) that traffickers must bear. Not only are costs increased through such measures as interdiction of shipped drug supplies[289]—now with greater involvement of countries' militaries[290]—but also in closing down access to conveyances and ports,[291] putting pressure on transport firms to be vigilant and penalizing them through asset-forfeiture laws if they are not (see next section), and checking on large movements of cash to ascertain whether it has provenance in the drug trade. Banks and bank executives who either are in complicity with or insufficiently vigilant of drug-related financial transactions are being fined or sued.[292] This is thought to have a dampening effect on their enthusiasm for readily accepting drug-related deposits. It also raises costs to traffickers, for they must continually struggle to find places where they can productively and safely place their liquid assets.

To complete our discussion of the strategy of disrupting networks by increasing costs and risks, we mention the psychological costs if not actual economic ones associated with a new U.S. law that prohibits lawyers' fees being paid with funds of illicit provenance. Not surprisingly, lawyers have vigorously objected to this provision.[293]

The challenge facing national governments and international agencies, if their suppression of traffic policies is to bear fruit, is how to raise inconvenience and heighten risk to a satisfactory threshold and then have the political will to sustain them. It is not clear that such political will exists. The problem is that traffickers do not give up easily and have, in the case of Burma and Colombia, responded with such life-wasting and property-destroying tactics as to implant fear in the most resolute and hardy government.

Traffic may be disrupted; supplies nevertheless seem somehow to continue to get to the final consumer. Along the way, however, as we saw in the previous chapter, some of the unfortunate side effects of traffic suppression are destruction and death and perhaps governmental decay.

Forfeiture of Assets

The increased volume of illicit drug money may not be drug-enforcement agencies' principal challenge. The principal challenge may derive from the increasingly complex ways in which traffickers transfer their cash and property, availing themselves of multifarious corporate structures and business transactions involving banks, trusts, real estate, and legitimate enterprise. How to respond? One policy has been asset forfeiture—a device to deprive drug criminals of the fruits of their labors.[294]

Some countries confiscate only property and goods directly involved in an illicit drug transaction for which a criminal conviction is obtained; other countries extend the forfeiture net to include everything that appears to have been acquired by illegitimate means.[295] Recent international discussion would include provisions for a government to pursue extraterritorial sequestration of an offender's assets.[296]

In the United States, courts have given wide interpretation to forfeiture laws. For example, in a California case, the appellate courts upheld the forfeiture of a marijuana grower's entire property even though he used only a small portion of it for illegal activities. Reversed was a lower court's judgment that only the land on which the marijuana had actually been grown was subject to forfeiture. The court's ruling startled many observers.[297] Beyond this, a new 1988 U.S. law allows the Justice Department to seize all funds and assets funneling through operations intended to disguise the source of ill-gotten money, not just the profits as allowed by a 1986 law. Nearly a half billion dollars were seized during a few months in 1989.[298]

Abundant optimism is attached to asset-forfeiture provisions in many countries' laws. One may not have much success with crop substitution and eradication policies or with drug interdiction efforts, or even with the surety of a jail sentence for convicted traffickers. Traffickers seem to fear imprisonment only second to losing their assets,[299] a matter that has led some observers to speak of asset-forfeiture policies being "a final solution to international drug trafficking."[300]

Law enforcement agencies at all levels are motivated. The proceeds are divided among the agencies making a "bust"—additional equipment, organizational perquisites, and a certain enjoyment of the "spoils" of war, which may include high-tech equipment.[301] For an added push, one columnist calls not only for splitting the "profits" among law enforcement agencies but also sharing them with those who "turn drug dealers in . . . . The point is, if greed is what makes people deal drugs, why not use that same greed to bust up the drug traffic?"[302] The December 1989 U.S. placement of a $1-million bounty on General Manuel Noriega may be an extended case in point.

For a time the United States instituted a "zero-tolerance" policy, meaning, principally, that conveyances on which any amount of illegal drug was carried would be sequestered.[303] Owners of fishing vessels, whose crews sometimes carried "an ounce or more," thought this policy to be quite onerous. They complained bitterly about the 113 vessels seized under zero-tolerance policies. Owners claimed they were being punished for violations over which they had no control. Among commercial fishermen, concern was raised that the livelihood of an entire crew was being endangered by one crew member.

The United States soon ended this draconian measure,[304] a decision that some legal philosophers had long advocated.[305] The rescinding was hastened, perhaps, by the notoriety of cases of property being forfeited with no crime having been established.[306]

The effort, of course, was to make users accountable for the social overhead consequences their drug demand created.[307] But, in the United States, there was a larger concern. While the law on zero tolerance was in effect, judges frequently refused to impose its full measure because they considered it too severe.[308]

While zero tolerance has gone by the wayside, asset forfeitures nevertheless continue. Banks, in particular, have now been put on notice to select their customers carefully.[309]

Technique of Controlled Delivery

Controlled delivery is a scheme within a larger law enforcement strategy to destabilize if not capture major traffickers. A recent UN document identifies it as "allowing a delivery of illicit drugs, once detected, to proceed, under constant and secret surveillance, to the ultimate destination envisaged by the traffickers, the object of the surveillance being to lead to the discovery and eventual arrest of the trafficking ringleaders."[310] There is evidence of such operations—some even successful—in major consuming countries.[311]

One of the scheme's major drawbacks as well as virtues is related to exposure time. The longer an effort targeted to a specific surveillance operation goes on and the more involved it becomes, the greater the chance that it will be compromised either through accidental or corrupting information leakages. Corruption is particularly noticed in some producing countries. Accordingly, it is quite unusual for target-specific long-term surveillance to be successful in a major producing country.

Facilitation of Extradition

Principal consuming countries, such as the United States (and now France[312]), have long had a keen interest in bringing to justice accused criminals who have found sanctuary in foreign lands. Traffickers, when they have become wealthy, habitually seek haven in a state having no extradition treaty with a principal consuming nation, or one having laws and a standard of justice sufficiently lax that a proper display and modest sharing of drug proceeds will buy a safe haven. The struggle is to devise an acceptable way to lay hands on such people.

One device is to enlist the cooperation of countries in elaborating bilateral or multilateral *extradition treaties*.[313] These make provisions for removing people in one country to the judicial processes of another, a matter that has become particularly important since extralegal measures (including abductions and irregular detentions) have become increasingly unacceptable.[314]

In 1984 the United States signed drug-focused extradition treaties with Costa Rica, Jamaica, Thailand, and Italy.[315] Earlier, it had negotiated one with Colombia, but this became an on-again, off-again arrangement coinciding with the ebb and flow of drug-related violence and judicial intimidation in that country. As of 1990, the treaty was back in force.[316]

Over time, numerous arguments have been raised to broaden the scope of extraditable offenses by allowing extradition for attempts and conspiracies, not just acts,[317] and there has been ample discussion about cultivating multilateral agreements on all these counts. Multilateral agreement was given impetus in 1988 when forty-three nations signed a UN pact that would better enable them to freeze and to confiscate bank accounts and to extradite suspects.[318] As one might imagine, drug traffickers and their lawyers vigorously resist all these arrangements.[319]

Extradition treaties appear to be a strong deterrent to some traffickers; among others, they create conditions of reactive violence and carnage. Citizens of producer countries suffer these events disproportionately. The Medellín cartel seems to be appropriately classified in the reactive-violence-and-carnage category; it is certain that Colombia has suffered a great deal. As a condition of reducing the carnage, Colombian traffickers have demanded an ironclad promise that no drug baron will be extradited to the United States.[320]

It is fair to say that Colombia's Medellín cartel members were traumatized when one of their principals, Carlos Lehder, became the first to be successfully extradited to the United States.[321] While the cartel's violence unleashed indiscriminately on Colombians has caused the Colombian state to falter from time to time, the country has recommitted its resolve to continue with extraditions,[322] with reaffirmations as late as January 1990.

National resentments frequently accompany extraditions, even among people who have little sympathy with those extradited.[323] This appears mostly when a society is under abundant internal political stress. From whatever source, "antiextradition nationalism" is counterproductive for the treaties' purposes. In such societies excessive reliance on extradition as a means to acquire prosecutional control over illicit drug traffickers may thus be shortsighted if it puts national leaders in exporting countries, who would like to be cooperative, in a political bind. Accordingly, some observers have called for a policy of "expulsion" through existing diplomatic channels, but under conditions of no safe haven. A country such as the United States might accomplish the ends of extradition without paying the attendant political price[324]

Surveillance of Land, Water and Air Approaches to the Frontier, and Controls over Ships and Aircraft in International Space—Interdiction

The descriptor, both symbolic and real, is *interdict*—"to cut or destroy (an enemy line of communication) by firepower so as to halt an enemy's advance."[325] National, binational, and international interdiction policies and conventions have been designed to permit states to stop the entry of illicit drugs into their national boundaries by, if necessary, extraterritorial, and even extraordinary means.[326] Thus, aside from "military cooperation agreements" that see militaries of one state working on drug control matters in another,[327] states may even exercise control over ships and aircraft in international space independently of registered countries' acquiescence.[328]

Surveillance and control, it is assumed, heighten traffickers' risks because they facilitate interdiction and drug seizures. It is thought that fewer drugs will move into high-risk traffic. Regardless, by removing large quantities of drugs from circulation—reducing the aggregate amount available either by smugglers' risk-conscious restraint or by seizure—it is thought that total supply ought to decline and, assuming constant or increasing demand, prices rise.[329] As prices rise, it is thought that users sensitive to price increases would eventually curtail consumption.[330] This would benefit an overall drug control program.

Accordingly, the call is for coast guards, militaries, navies, air forces, and national guards to coordinate their activities with regular civilian agencies (e.g., customs,[331] border patrols[332]) to track, stop, search, and detain suspected carriers and, in the case of aircraft, to alert ground-based law enforcement officials of locations of touchdown.[333] The United Nations has elaborated brief, but quite comprehensive, guidelines with recommendations for regional and international levels of activity.[334] In 1988 the United States and twenty-nine other countries in Latin America and Europe secretly coordinated military and police operations aimed at destroying clandestine cocaine laboratories and disrupting the operations of Colombian drug cartels.[335]

From the information in our bibliography, the biggest flurry of interdiction discussion has been within U.S. political organizations and governmental agencies. Within these circles, sustained arguments for and against military involvement began before 1986.[336] However, regardless of increasing militarization, and despite a doubling of federal interdiction expenditures over a five-year period (1982–1987), observers soon noted that the quantity of drugs smuggled into the United States was increasing. No clear correlation between the level of interdiction expenditures and the availability of illegally imported drugs in the domestic market appeared to exist. The fault, it was concluded, was in the fragmentation of interdiction agencies and in their lack of overall direction. Many considered the matter beyond squabbling civilians' ability to address.[337]

Accordingly, in 1988 quite radical discussions were heard. For example, a U.S. House bill under consideration contained a broad, sweeping mandate to the military to substantially halt the flow of drugs into the United States "within 45 days." Under the House bill the military would seal the borders to drug traffickers, using whatever search, seizure, and arrest powers that were necessary. A Senate companion bill, less flamboyant, would have the Department of Defense detect and monitor all potential aerial and maritime threats to national security and carefully designate certain armed forces personnel to use civil law enforcement powers beyond the country's borders.[338] Clearly, there was considerable optimism. One of the more interesting outcomes was the deployment of a band of radar-detecting blimps on the southern border of the United States.[339]

Neither the Senate nor the House got its way exactly, but, after several organizational starts and stops, the U.S. Department of Defense did establish a command network to coordinate military surveillance of drug smuggling. Two top-level coast guard officials were given major responsibilities.[340] In 1989 an integrated agency task force, headed by Coast Guard admirals, was formed to lead joint military efforts to stop drug smuggling on the Atlantic and Pacific coasts of the United States.[341] However reluctant the military had been—and it had been[342]—it was now clearly on board, including several state national guard units.[343]

Aside from the tactical and programmatic "should-we-or-shouldn't-we" discussions reviewed above, abundant commentary has been raised about whether involving the military in drug-related operations is constitutional, whether it is likely to provoke a violation of people's civil rights, and whether it subordinates U.S. laws and institutions to international jurisdiction.[344]

We have discussed some of the consequences of the illicit drug trade, including the rise of a new genre of organized trafficker and the implementation of countervailing initiatives to deal with consumption, production, and supply. Multilateral and bilateral agreements have been adopted to this end as have national policies relating to the prevention and reduction of illicit demand, control of supply, suppression of illicit international trafficking, and interdiction.

We turn now to a fourth category of national policies aimed at reducing consumption and therefore the incentives for producers and traffickers to supply the market, namely, treatment and rehabilitation.

Treatment and Rehabilitation

Drug addiction is now a worldwide phenomenon, which gives no quarter to culture, social class, or age; it is more extensive now than perhaps at any other historical epoch, even after taking into consideration drugs' traditional use for ritualistic, initiatory, diagnostic, ecstatic, and orgiastic purposes.

Most modern societies' treatment and rehabilitation goals are to reclaim addicted users who either have been captured in a network of traditional drug use or who have succumbed to its modern permutations. The addict, society judges, is not only a personal failure but constitutes a loss—economic and social—as well as a threat to the larger community. Inasmuch as punitive policies and negative sanctions have failed either to deter some people's drug use or to cause them to refrain from becoming addicted, can addicts be reclaimed so as to become more useful and less threatening socially and economically? It is also thought that adequate treatment and rehabilitation programs will help to reduce demand. With these ends in mind, most countries try to treat and to rehabilitate, but the variations are immense and the success rate appears to be equally as diverse.

All major consuming countries have local, regional, and sometimes even national drug-treatment programs. The country-specific treatment issues revealed in our bibliography vary. In the United States, the applied and practical discussions are in relationship to treatment theories and program effectiveness,[345] AIDS,[346] women,[347] methadone maintenance,[348] heroin maintenance,[349] the homeless,[350] support groups,[351] culture,[352] compulsion,[353] and costs.[354] In the United Kingdom, they concern effectiveness,[355] social reintegration,[356] and heroin maintenance.[357] In Scandinavia, there are institutional issues such as the use of psychiatric clinics and hospitals, new types of out-patient clinics,[358] and even the development of drug-treatment collectives;[359] there are topical issues relating to coercive treatment measures and to the use of methadone.[360]

In the bibliography there is a generic entry for Africa,[361] another for Southeast Asia,[362] and specific notes on Malaysia,[363] Thailand,[364] Laos,[365] Burma,[366] Hong Kong,[367] and Singapore.[368] West Germany is also brought up for review.[369]

Addiction views derive from multiple disciplines and orientations: history, political science, economics, sociology, psychology, medicine, physiology, pharmacology, philosophy, law enforcement, religion, and even witchcraft. Each offers explanations as to why people become addicted; each advances corresponding answers about treatment programs for them. Howard Shaffer observes that some physicians offer a theory of opiate addiction based on metabolic deficiency; some sociologists contribute perspectives dealing with social/cultural environmental influences; several psychoanalysts present evidence regarding functioning of the mind; the behavioralists offer a behavioral orientation. Various authors offer perspectives on history and related social policy, on the psychodynamics of addiction, on psychosocial perspectives on addiction, on behavioral approaches to addiction, and on physiological formulations of addiction.[370]

Not surprisingly, one encounters diverse treatment models, ranging from the bizarre to empirically based psychological and medical approaches:[371] the "abstinence model,"[372] acupuncture,[373] compulsion,[374] the therapeutic community (inspired by Alcoholics Anonymous),[375] hospitalization,[376] detoxification,[377] methadone maintenance (for heroin),[378] methadone-to-abstinence,[379] heroin maintenance,[380] "cold turkey" withdrawal,[381] education,[382] family involvement,[383] chemical antagonists or pharmacological therapy,[384] and various kinds of holistic programs.[385]

Three divergent continua mark much of the literature on treatment; they identify treatment foci circumscribed by a particular treatment model. These continua represent *a priori* as well as empirically derived assumptions relating to punishment–rehabilitation, single variable–holistic orientations, and social/psychological–biological perspectives.

How is society best served? By prescribing treatments that punish addicts (deterrence effects intended) prior to their reintegration into normal society, or by prescribing treatments that therapeutically rehabilitate addicts on the assumption that a cure-a-disease model rather than a crime model best reclaims lost folk?

The prevailing view among treatment practitioners holds punishment and rehabilitation approaches to be mutually antagonistic. Given, this view holds, that the reasons for drug addiction are global in scope (affected by economic, political, and social factors), individual punishment within the context of a criminal justice system or individual treatment excised from the patients' relationship to society cannot succeed.[386] Accordingly, a growing tendency exists toward benign rehabilitation treatment programs; more rapid social reintegration of offenders is thought to occur.[387]

In many ways, the opposing poles of the punishment–rehabilitation continuum exemplify a struggle between politicians and practitioners. Politicians focus on interdiction and law enforcement models (giving considerable credence to the deterrence effect of negative sanctions) whereas treatment practitioners advocate therapeutic rehabilitation (assuming that approaches involving exclusive negative sanctions are, for the most part, counterproductive).[388]

With respect to the independent–holistic continuum, there is a clear tendency away from treating individuals outside the context of their actual lives as social human beings. Aside from integrating the resources of family, community, and church, holistic approaches may involve, by modern standards, curious particulars. For example, herbal therapy, although practiced for centuries before its decline in the twentieth, is making a return with an integrated support system reminiscent of traditional religion.[389] For the same reasons, traditional medicine, as practiced in Malaysia and Thailand, is used to treat some heroin abusers when their personalities and perceived needs so dictate. For these people, traditional medicine approaches have been more effective than normal institutional treatment.[390] In New York City's Lincoln Hospital, even acupuncture is used[391] to relieve withdrawal symptoms, prevent drug craving, and increase the participation rate in long-term treatment programs.

As for the psychological–biological continuum, one sees a struggle between practical medicine on the one hand and social workers and psychologists on the other. If the causes of addiction are strictly biological, then detoxification and pharmacological therapy are called for. If, on the other hand, the causes are strictly psychological, an individual counselling model is called for. But if they are social-psychological, or social-psychological-biological, the treatment orientation must adjust if it is to be successful.[392]

In Chapters 4 and 5 we examined the rise of a new genre of organized trafficker and the implementation of countervailing initiatives to deal with traffickers and the drug traffic they facilitate. In Chapter 4 we saw how their work produced benefits and beneficiaries as well as liabilities and victims. Among the former were increased incomes for growers, accompanied by prospects of migration, social mobility, and more access to political power. As for liabilities and victims, we reviewed literature on traffickers' assaults on government and law through infiltrating bureaucracies, buying public decisions, making alliances with ideologues, launching intimidating threats and violent attacks (thereby undermining government and society), and creating an antistate wholly outside the rule of law. We also reviewed sundry economic and social effects of traffickers' activities.

In Chapter 5 we looked into multilateral and bilateral agreements and to the development of national drug control policies and laws. Focus was on the prevention and reduction of illicit demand, control of supply, suppression of illicit international trafficking, and treatment and rehabilitation. Within the discussion on prevention and reduction of illicit demand, we reviewed the development and consequences of law enforcement activities,

Subject Outline

I. PATTERNS OF PRODUCTION AND CONSUMPTION

   A. COCAINE
   B. HEROIN
   C. CANNABIS

II. CONSEQUENCES

   A. RISE OF A NEW GENRE OF ORGANIZED TRAFFICKER
      1. Benefits and Beneficiaries
         a. Increased Income and Employment
         b. Migration and Social Mobility
         c. Power and Social Restructuring
      2. Liabilities and Victims
         a. Traffickers' Assaults on Government and Law
           (1) Infiltrating Bureaucracies
           (2) Buying Public Decisions
           (3) Making Alliances with Ideologues
           (4) Launching Intimidating Threats and Violent Attacks
           (5) Creating an Antistate Wholly Outside the Rule of Law
         b. Traffickers' Sundry Economic and Social Effects

   B. IMPLEMENTATION OF COUNTERVAILING INITIATIVES
      1. Multilateral and Bilateral Agreements
      2. National Policies
         a. Prevention and Reduction of Illicit Demand
           (1) General Law Enforcement Activities
           (2) Education
           (3) Testing in the Workplace
           (4) Civic Action
           (5) The Mass Media
         b. Control of Supply
           (1) Crop Eradication
           (2) Control of Precursor Chemicals
           (3) Crop Substitution
           (4) Rural Economic Development
         c. Suppression of Illicit International Trafficking
           (1) Disruption of Major Trafficking Networks
           (2) Forfeiture of Assets
           (3) Technique of Controlled Delivery
           (4) Facilitation of Extradition
           (5) Surveillance of Land, Water and Air Approaches to the Frontier, and Controls over Ships and Aircraft in International Space—Interdiction
         d. Treatment and Rehabilitation

   C. DEMAND

III. PROFFERED NEW SOLUTIONS

education efforts, drug testing in the workplace, civic action, and appeals by the mass media.

In the section on control of supply we dealt with crop eradication, control of precursor chemicals, crop substitution, and rural economic development. In discussing the section on suppression of illicit international trafficking, we looked into literature on disrupting major trafficking networks, asset forfeitures, techniques of controlled delivery, extradition, and surveillance of land, water, and air approaches to the frontier, and controls over ships and aircraft in international space.

We turn now to the third major arena of consequences, that which derives from *demand*. Here we consider literature germane to a discussion of consequences independent of whether drugs are legal or illegal or law enforcement efforts exist or do not. The outline on the previous page graphically reviews the terrain covered and that which remains.

NOTES

[1] See note 84, Chapter 4.

[2] Jerry Adler et al., present poignant anecdotes of family disintegration in "Hour by Hour Crack," *Newsweek*, 1988. Gina Kolata ["In Cities, Poor Families Are Dying of Crack," *The New York Times*, 1989] considers similar themes.

[3] The bibliography in this handbook contains 217 entries cross-referenced to "Treatment." Of these, 34 are review essays, and 7 are either annotated bibliographies or contain extensive bibliographies. The treatment literature is reviewed later in this chapter. Mention here is made only of the seven bibliographies. Susan J. Christensen and Alice Q. Swanson ["Women and Drug Use: An Annotated Bibliography," *Journal of Psychedelic Drugs*, 1974] include extensive annotations of the pre-1971 literature on women and drugs. James R. Cooper et al., editors [*Research on the Treatment of Narcotic Addiction: State of the Art*, 1983] focus specifically on methadone as a drug maintenance strategy and as a detoxification treatment. Mark H. Pollack, Andrew W. Brotman, and Jerrold F. Rosenbaum ["Cocaine Abuse and Treatment," *Comprehensive Psychiatry*, 1989] alert clinicians to the problems of dual diagnosis and dual dependence and to the effects of drug use on family, employment, and social systems. Marsha Rosenbaum [*Women on Heroin*, 1981] includes an extensive bibliography on how women have fared in treatment programs historically. Howard Shaffer and Milton Earl Burglass have edited a multidisciplinary volume that brings together the major contributions to the addiction treatment theory literature; they have provided a fine bibliography in *Classic Contributions in the Addictions*, 1981. M. Duncan Stanton, Thomas C. Todd, et al. [*The Family Therapy of Drug Abuse and Addiction*, 1982] provide an extensive bibliography premised on the assumption that drug-abuse therapy should be a subset of family psychotherapy. Finally, Nancy S. Tobler, in identifying the most effective programs for reducing teenage drug use, includes a substantial bibliography with her article ["Meta-Analysis of 143 Adolescent Drug Prevention Programs: Quantitative Outcome Results of Program Participants Compared to a Control or Comparison Group," *Journal of Drug Issues*, 1986].

[4] Exemplary is the fact that over 500 of the bibliographical entries constituting the data set for this handbook are coded under "Drug Control Policies" or a subset thereof (e.g., "Drug Control Policies, Effectiveness").

⁵The particulars are discussed in Susanna Rance, "Bolivia: New Coca Control Law Aggravates Tense Situation," *Latinamerica Press*, 1988. See also Maria Laura Avignolo, "Bolivia: Coca Control Law Feeds Anti–U.S. Sentiment," *Latinamerica Press*, 1988; and Kevin Healy, "Coca, the State, and the Peasantry in Bolivia, 1982–1988," *Journal of Interamerican Studies and World Affairs*, 1988.

⁶"Some Plain Talk about Drug Addiction," *The Current Digest of the Soviet Press*, 1986. See also the discussion in note 27 of the *Introduction* and note 60, this chapter.

⁷Burton Bollag, "Swiss-Dutch Drug Stance: Tolerance," *The New York Times*, 1989. See also Richard J. Bonnie, *Marijuana Use and Criminal Sanctions: Essays on the Theory and Practice of Decriminalization*, 1980.

⁸Useful historical summaries and analyses of these international cooperative efforts may be found in S. D. Stein, *International Diplomacy, State Administrators, and Narcotics Control: The Origins of a Social Problem*, 1985; United Nations, *The United Nations and Drug Abuse Control*, 1987; L. E. S. Eisenlohr, *International Narcotics Control*, 1981; Hsien Chou Liu, *The Development of a Single Convention on Narcotic Drugs: A Historical Survey for the International Cooperation in Solving the Crucial Problem of Narcotic Drugs*, 1979; and S. K. Chatterjee, *Legal Aspects of International Drug Control*, 1981.

⁹Mentioned are the 1946 Protocol, which legally transferred the League of Nations' drug control functions to the United Nations; the 1948 Protocol, which included synthetic mind-altering drugs within the mantle of international law and control; the 1953 Opium Protocol, which dealt with limiting opium use and trade to medical and scientific needs; the Single Convention on Narcotic Drugs of 1961 (mentioned in the text); the 1972 Protocol amending the Single Convention, which emphasized the need for additional efforts to prevent illicit production of, traffic in, and use of narcotics and to provide treatment and rehabilitation services to drug abusers; the 1971 Convention on Psychotropic Substances, which placed under international law additional man-made drugs capable of altering behavior and mood and of creating harmful dependency effects (including hallucinogens, such as LSD [lysergic acid diethylamide] and mescaline); stimulants, such as amphetamines; and sedative-hypnotic drugs, such as barbiturates; the 1981 International Drug Abuse Control Strategy, a kind of master plan for international cooperation that included numerous aspects of drug control—abuse, trafficking, treatment, rehabilitation, and crop substitution—and proposals for action in these areas by member states; a Convention against Illicit Traffic in Narcotic Drugs and Psychotropic Substances (drafted in 1984, signed in 1988) to cope with the expansion of illicit drug trafficking by better enabling nations to freeze and confiscate bank accounts and extradite suspects; and the 1987 International Conference on Drug Abuse and Illicit Trafficking. Information about these protocols, conventions, conferences, and agreements may be found in United Nations, *The United Nations and Drug Abuse Control*, 1987; United Nations, Division of Narcotic Drugs, *Declaration of the International Conference on Drug Abuse and Illicit Trafficking and Comprehensive Multidisciplinary Outline of Future Activities in Drug Abuse Control*, 1988; Victoria Kaufman, "United Nations: International Conference on Drug Abuse and Illicit Trafficking," *Harvard International Law Journal*, 1988; "43 Nations Sign U.N. Pact on Fighting Drugs," *The Los Angeles Times*, 1988; David D. Brown, "UN Antidrug Conference Chalks up Significant Firsts," *The Christian Science Monitor*, 1987; U.S. Congress, Senate Caucus on International Narcotics Control, Report, "The U.N. Draft Convention against Illicit Traffic in Narcotic Drugs and Psychotropic Substances," 1987; United Nations, *International Strategy and Policies for Drug Control*, 1982; and Lucia Mouat, "UN Session Plots Global Antidrug Strategy,"

The Christian Science Monitor, 1990.

[10]Numerous UN agencies have drug-abuse and illicit trafficking agenda, the principal ones being the Commission on Narcotic Drugs (CND) (established in 1946 as one of the six functional commissions of the Economic and Social Council (ECOSOC), which is the United Nations' central policymaking body charged with in-depth review of drug-abuse controls for which the UN assumes some purview) and, through 1990, three Vienna-based units in the UN Secretariat: the Division of Narcotic Drugs (DND), the United Nations Fund for Drug Abuse Control (UNFDAC), and the International Narcotics Control Board (INCB). DND carried out multiple supporting roles for member governments and specialized agencies dealing with treaty implementation, scientific research and technical information, supply and demand reduction, and information coordination. UNFDAC aided governments in practical ways in combating the production, trafficking, and use of illicit drugs (including carrying out activities in rural development). INCB supplemented statistical estimates and controls on illicit drugs as it worked to ensure that member governments were in compliance with treaty provisions (working to ensure the availability of drugs for medical and scientific purposes and providing statistical information to limit the cultivation, production, and manufacture of drugs beyond those needs). These agencies and others are described in United Nations, *The United Nations and Drug Abuse Control,* 1987. In late 1990 and continuing into June 1991 (following a mandate from the UN General Assembly), the above three organizations began the process of merging into a new super-agency—the United Nations Drug Control Program—also headquartered in Vienna. As of this writing the organizational outcome was still in flux.

[11]David D. Brown, "UN Antidrug Conference Chalks up Significant Firsts," *The Christian Science Monitor,* 1987.

[12]Lucia Mouat, "UN Session Plots Global Antidrug Strategy," *The Christian Science Monitor,* 1990.

[13]For example, following a General Assembly resolution (44/142) on 15 December 1989 regarding international action to combat drug abuse and illicit trafficking, the secretary general convened an intergovernmental expert group to study the economic and social consequences of the illicit traffic in drugs. The report was made available to member states on 18 December 1990 (A/C.3/45/8).

[14]Our data set contains the following references not cited elsewhere: Robert L. Pisani, "International Efforts to Reform Cannabis Laws," *Journal of Drug Issues,* 1983; and U.S. Congress, House Committee on Foreign Affairs, Report, "Compilation of Narcotics Laws, Treaties, and Executive Documents," 1986.

[15]P. A. Abarro ["The Role of the Drug Advisory Programme of the Colombo Plan Bureau in the Fight against Illicit Drug Traffic," *Bulletin on Narcotics,* 1983] describes the role of the Drug Advisory Programme in helping member states to update their drug legislation and promote drug law enforcement actions. See also Abarro's "The Role of an Intergovernmental Regional Organization in Combating Drug Trafficking: A Perspective of the Colombo Plan Bureau," *Bulletin on Narcotics,* 1987.

[16]C. Brule ["The Role of the Pompidou Group of the Council of Europe in Combating Drug Abuse and Illicit Drug Trafficking," *Bulletin on Narcotics,* 1983] describes the political and technical activities of the Pompidou Group, illustrating how it operates to combat drug abuse at the international level. N. A. Nagler ["The Council of Europe Co-operation Group to Combat Drug Abuse and Illicit Trafficking in Drugs (The Pompidou Group)," *Bulletin on Narcotics,* 1987] describes some of the topics the Pompidou Group raises for consideration—dealing with drug trafficking on the high seas, the role of the criminal justice system in responding to the needs of drug misusers, methods of reaching

young people particularly at risk, problems concerning women and drugs, control services at major airports, and AIDS.

[17]Two senior advisers in the Attorney General's office of Malaysia describe some of the relatively recent developments in the adoption of common measures within ASEAN. See J. L. O'Hara and M. Zawawi Salleh, "Recent Developments in Legislative and Administrative Measures in Countries of the Association of Southeast Asian Nations to Counter the Illicit Trafficking in Drugs," *Bulletin on Narcotics*, 1987. Chavalit Yodmani ["The Role of the Association of South-East Asian Nations in Fighting Illicit Drug Traffic," *Bulletin on Narcotics*, 1983] views member states' roles in combatting illicit drug traffic.

[18]The best descriptive coverage on ASEP is found in two articles by Carlos Norberto Cagliotti ["The Role of the South American Agreement on Narcotic Drugs and Psychotropic Substances in the Fight against Illicit Drug Trafficking," *Bulletin on Narcotics*, 1983; and, "Co-operation between South American Countries in the Struggle against Drug Abuse and Illicit Drug Trafficking," *Bulletin on Narcotics*, 1987].

[19]See "Inter-Parliamentary Conference on Drug Abuse and Illicit Trafficking in the Western Hemisphere," *Inter-Parliamentary Bulletin*, 1988.

[20]I. G. Tragen, "Co-operation of Countries within the Organization of American States to Combat Drug Problems," *Bulletin on Narcotics*, 1987.

[21]See D. A. Chaiken, "Commonwealth Initiative in the Tracing, Seizing, Freezing and Forfeiture of Drug Proceeds," *Bulletin on Narcotics*, 1984. In criticizing the lack of forfeiture provisions in the "commonwealth perspective," S. K. Chatterjee reviews general commonwealth provisions on drugs ["Forfeiture of Proceeds of Drug-Related Crimes: A British Commonwealth Perspective," *Bulletin on Narcotics*, 1983]. The failure of forfeiture provisions within British Commonwealth legislative models is driven home by N. Liverpool ["The Seizure and Forfeiture of Property Associated with Criminal Activity," *Bulletin on Narcotics*, 1983].

[22]Although these are not referenced in the bibliography in this handbook, they are mentioned in United Nations, *The United Nations and Drug Abuse Control*, 1987, p. 81.

[23]G.D. Gotschlich, "Action by the Customs Co-Operation Council to Combat Illicit Drug Trafficking," *Bulletin on Narcotics*, 1983.

[24]"China Cracks Big Drug Case," *Beijing Review*, 1988. One hundred and fifty-three countries are members of Interpol. It has a drugs subdivision that responds to incoming communications on drug-enforcement matters; it conducts intelligence analysis of information; and it produces tactical and strategic intelligence reports [W. J. Leamy, "International Co-Operation through the Interpol System to Counter Illicit Drug Trafficking," *Bulletin on Narcotics*, 1981].

[25]James W. Spain ["The United States, Turkey and the Poppy," *Middle East Journal*, 1975] chronicles Turkey's early agreements with the United States.

[26]Our latest entry on the on-going saga in Pakistan is Sheila Tefft's "Bhutto Battles the Drug Trade," *The Christian Science Monitor*, 1989; and U.S. Department of State, Bureau of International Narcotics Matters, *International Narcotics Control Strategy Report*, 1991.

[27]The 1986 implementation of the agreements were the subject of a congressional hearing [U.S. Congress, House Committee on Foreign Affairs, Hearing, "The Role and Activities of the National Drug Enforcement Policy Board," 1986], as was the case in 1987 [U.S. Congress, House Committee on Foreign Affairs, Hearing, "Review of Latin American Narcotics Control Issues," 1987] and 1988 [U.S. Congress, House Committee on Foreign Affairs, Hearing, "Narcotics Review in South America," 1988]. Mary Ellen

Welch discusses the nature of the agreements in Colombia and Bolivia from the vantage of an "extraterritorial war" ["The Extraterritorial War on Cocaine: Perspectives from Bolivia and Colombia," *Suffolk Transnational Law Journal*, 1988]. Cynthia McClintock ["The War on Drugs: The Peruvian Case," *Journal of Interamerican Studies and World Affairs*, 1988] analyzes the antidrug efforts undertaken by the United States and Peruvian governments under bilateral agreements; Richard B. Craig ["Illicit Drug Traffic and U.S.–Latin American Relations," *Washington Quarterly*, 1985] examines the international relations implications of the agreements. See also Andrew Rosenthal, "3 Andean Leaders and Bush Pledge Drug Cooperation," *The New York Times*, 1990; James Brooke, "Peru Develops Plan to Work with U.S. to Combat Drugs," *The New York Times*, 1991.

[28]Roberta Louise Rubin, "International Agreements: Two Treaties between the U.S. and Italy," *Harvard International Law Journal*, 1985.

[29]See Shirley Christian, "Bolivians Fight Efforts to Eradicate Coca," *The New York Times*, 1987; Richard B. Craig, "Illicit Drug Traffic and U.S.–Latin American Relations," *Washington Quarterly*, 1985; Mark Day, "Peru: Battle Intensifies over Renewed Drug Eradication Plan," *Latinamerica Press*, 1989; John S. DeMott, "Striking at the Source," *Time*, 1986; Alejandro Deustua, *El Narcotráfico y el Interés Nacional: Un Análisis en la Perspectiva Internacional*, 1987; John J. Fialka, "Death of US Agent in Mexico Drug Case Uncovers Grid of Graft," *The Wall Street Journal*, 1986; Robert P. Hey, "Nations Unite to Fight Drugs: Combating Foreign Supply and US Demand," *The Christian Science Monitor*, 1986; Michael Isikoff, "DEA in Bolivia: 'Guerrilla Warfare,' Coca Traffic Proves Resistant," *The Washington Post*, 1989; U.S. Congress, House Committee on Foreign Affairs, Hearing, "United States-Mexican Cooperation in Narcotics Control Efforts, 1986;" U.S. Congress, House Committee on Foreign Affairs, Hearing, "Review of Latin American Narcotics Control Issues," 1987; and U.S. Congress, House Committee on Foreign Affairs, Hearing, "Narcotics Review in South America, 1988."

[30]Michael Isikoff, "Soviets Suggest Trading Facts on Drug Traffic; U.S. Weighing Moscow's Unusual Proposal," *The Washington Post*, 1988.

[31]Michael Isikoff, "Jamaican Urges Anti-Drug Force," *The Washington Post*, 1989.

[32]Richard L. Berke, "Jamaican Backs off Proposal for Anti-Drug Force," *The New York Times*, 1989.

[33]Robert Pear, "Jamaican Criticizes Panama Invasion," *The New York Times*, 1990.

[34]Lucia Mouat, "UN Session Plots Global Antidrug Strategy," *The Christian Science Monitor,* 1990.

[35]Lucia Mouat, "Nations More Willing to Concede 'Rights' to Fight International Drug War," *The Christian Science Monitor*, 1990.

[36]Linda Greenhouse, "Justices Back Property Searches of Foreigners in Foreign Nations," *The New York Times*, 1990.

[37]An examination of specific laws may be found in the following: Mark J. Barnes, Carrol H. Kinsey, and Ellice A. Halpern, "A Question of America's Future: Drug-Free or Not?" *Kansas University Law Review*, 1988; C. Jacquemart, "An Assessment of Legal Measures to Trace, Freeze and Confiscate the Proceeds of Drug Crimes in France: The Customs Viewpoint," *Bulletin on Narcotics*, 1984; Douglas Jehl, "U.S. Ends Seizures of Vessels under 'Zero Tolerance' Policy," *The Los Angeles Times*, 1989; Mark J. Kadish, Rosalyn Suna Kadish, and Alan J. Baverman, "A Powerful Weapon for Federal Prosecutors," *Trial*, 1983; U. Khant, "Measures to Prevent and Reduce Drug Abuse Among Young People in Burma," *Bulletin on Narcotics*, 1985; George A. Kurisky, Jr., "Civil Forfeiture of Assets: A Final Solution to International Drug Trafficking?,"

Houston Journal of International Law, 1988; Michael D. Lyman, *Narcotics and Crime Control*, 1987; "Milestones in the War on Drugs," *Nova Law Review*, 1987; Edgar Oblitas, *Narcotráfico, Decreto Ley No. 18714 de Control y Lucha Contra Sustancias Peligrosas*, 1982; President's Commission on Organized Crime, *The Cash Connection: Organized Crime, Financial Institutions, and Money Laundering*, 1984; Charles S. Saphos, et al., *Handbook on the Anti-Drug Abuse Act of 1986*, 1987 (includes bibliographies); Maria E. Sokalska, "Legal Measures to Combat Drug-Related Problems in Poland," *Bulletin on Narcotics*, 1984; Gerald F. Uelmen, "Punishing Drug Offenders: An International and Comparative Perspective," *Journal of Drug Issues*, 1983; U.S. Congress, House Committee on Foreign Affairs, Report, "Compilation of Narcotics Laws, Treaties, and Executive Documents," 1986; U.S. Congress, Senate Caucus on International Narcotics Control, Report, "Legislation Aimed at Combating International Drug Trafficking and Money Laundering," 1986; Joseph Westermeyer, "The Pro-Heroin Effects of Anti-Opium Laws in Asia," *Arch. Gen. Psychiatry*, 1976; Michael Wines, "Law Enabled U.S. to Seize Proceeds of Drug Money Scheme," *The New York Times*, 1989; M. S. Zaki, "Egyptian Law on the Sequestration and Confiscation of Property Acquired through Smuggling and Trafficking in Drugs," *Bulletin on Narcotics*, 1983.

[38]United Nations, Division of Narcotic Drugs, *Declaration of the International Conference on Drug Abuse and Illicit Trafficking and Comprehensive Multidisciplinary Outline of Future Activities in Drug Abuse Control*, 1988.

[39]Review essays or works worthy of note that survey considerable literature on law enforcement issues are the following: Katie A. Busch and Sidney H. Schnoll ["Cocaine—Review of Current Literature and Interface with the Law," *Behavioral Sciences and the Law*, 1985] discuss knowledge of the relationship between cocaine and violence and explore the forensic-psychiatric issues surrounding cocaine's use. Karlene Faith [*Drug Addiction: From a Study of Women and Criminal Justice*, 1981] spent three years interviewing prisoners in the California Institution for Women and concludes that punishment and rehabilitation are mutually antagonistic approaches to the drug problem. B. Muller ["The Drug Problem in the Federal Republic of Germany," *Drug and Alcohol Dependence*, 1985] analyzes West Germany's narcotic drugs law from the viewpoint of punishment versus treatment. Adam Wagstaff and Alan Maynard [*Economic Aspects of the Illicit Drug Market and Drug Enforcement Policies in the United Kingdom*, 1988] review the international economics literature on the cost effectiveness of law enforcement strategies on drug issues.

[40]For a survey of drug-related penal measures in Europe, Asia, Africa, and Latin America, see United Nations Social Defense Research Institute, *Drugs and Punishment: An Up-to-Date Interregional Survey on Drug-Related Offences*, 1988.

[41]D.C. Jayasuriya, "Penal Measures for Drug Offences: Perspectives from some Asian Countries," *Bulletin on Narcotics*, 1984.

[42]"17 Reported Hanged in Iran Anti-Drug Campaign," *The New York Times*, 1989.

[43]Youssef M. Ibrahim, "Iran Puts Addicts in Its Labor Camps," *The New York Times*, 1989.

[44]Suhaini Aznam and Emily Lau ["Equal under the Law," *Far Eastern Economic Review*, 1986] discuss the hanging of the two Australians. Michael Schwarz ["Deadly Traffic," *The New York Times*, 1987] questions whether such draconian measures, which in turn derive from draconian laws, really reduce use of or traffic in illicit drugs. C. P. Spencer and V. Navaratnam [*Drug Abuse in East Asia*, 1981] discuss the legal basis for the measures and offer a country-specific bibliography for Malaysia (and other East Asian countries). Summaries and comparisons of penal measures that include Malaysia

are the following: T. Asuni and F. Bruno, "Summary of an Eleven-Country Study of Socio-Legal Measures to Combat Drug Abuse and Related Crime," *Bulletin on Narcotics*, 1984; Francesco Bruno, *Combatting Drug Abuse and Related Crime: Comparative Research on the Effectiveness of Socio-Legal Preventive and Control Measures in Different Countries on the Interaction between Criminal Behaviour and Drug Abuse*, 1984; and, D. C. Jayasuriya, "Penal Measures for Drug Offences: Perspectives from Some Asian Countries," *Bulletin on Narcotics*, 1984.

[45]In addition to the citations in notes below, the comparative studies by T. Asuni and Francesco Bruno, D. C. Jayasuriya, and C. P. Spencer and V. Navaratnam cited in note 44, above, should be consulted.

[46]See W. H. McGlothlin, "The Singapore Heroin Control Programme," *Bulletin on Narcotics*, 1980.

[47]"Singapore Declares War on International Drug Traffickers," *Narcotics Control Digest*, 1985.

[48]Poh Geok Ek, "Denial of Passports to Drug Offenders in Singapore," *Bulletin on Narcotics*, 1984.

[49]Francesco Bruno compares Sweden's policies with those of ten other countries (Argentina, Brazil, Costa Rica, Italy, Japan, Jordan, Malaysia, Singapore, the United Kingdom, and the United States) in an attempt to assess the relative effectiveness of their socio-legal prevention and control measures on criminal behavior [*Combatting Drug Abuse and Related Crime*, 1984]. Kettil Bruun and Pia Rosenqvist ["Alcohol and Drug Control Policies in the Nordic Countries," *Journal of Drug Issues*, 1980] give a comparative analysis of Nordic countries regarding their governments' policies aimed at influencing the availability of alcohol and drugs. Denmark appears to be most out of step with the other Nordic countries, especially in alcohol control. Nevertheless, the countries' narcotics policies tend to support existing international agreements with respect to criminal-political measures. It is worth saying, at this point, that the Nordic countries appear to have little confidence in "easy" treatment programs such as methadone maintenance for heroin addicts [see, for example, Olafur Hallgrimsson, "Methadone Treatment: The Nordic Attitude," *Journal of Drug Issues*, 1980]. No doubt this biases the countries toward "unconventional" treatment models that others might view as a bit radical (e.g., the development of treatment collectives that vigorously promote useful social interaction and dependence on others' adequately functioning) [Helge Waal, "Unconventional Treatment Models for Young Drug Abusers in Scandinavia," *Journal of Drug Issues*, 1980]. Some of the Nordic debate on drug problems and law enforcement measures is captured in Ragnar Hauge's "Trends in Drug Use in Norway," *Journal of Drug Issues*, 1985. S. Riberdahl ["Forfeiture of the Proceeds of Drug-Related Crimes: A Swedish Point of View," *Bulletin on Narcotics*, 1984] looks into Sweden's punitive sequestration laws as a means of deterring traffickers.

[50]On 11 January 1990, the CBS radio network reported that William Bennett, President George Bush's "drug czar," had called for such legislation. Bennett also asked the Bush administration to double the projected expenditures for new prisons, increasing to $1.2 billion in 1990 [Richard Berke, "Drug Chief Calls for a Vast Prison Plan," *The New York Times*, 1989]. Even after Bennett left the administration, Bush continued to call for increased spending, with the proportion dedicated for domestic enforcement actually having increased relative to treatment, prevention, and interdiction [Joseph B. Treaster, "Bush Proposes More Anti-Drug Spending," *The New York Times*, 1991].

[51]Initially, the military was extremely reluctant to take on drug operations [Chris Adams, "Second Thoughts on the Military as Narcs; Hearings Stress Doubts on Pentagon's Drug-Interdiction Role," *The Washington Post*, 1988; Angus Deming and John Barry, "Reluctant Recruits: Drugs and the Military," *Newsweek*, 1986; Peter Grier, "Congress, Pentagon Dispute Armed Forces' Role in Drug Fight," *The Christian Science Monitor*, 1988; and George C. Wilson and Molly Moore, "Pentagon Warns of a No-Win Mission; Military Says Offensive against Drugs Would Overstretch Resources," *The Washington Post*, 1988]. However, given that drug traffickers were clearly overwhelming existing law enforcement capabilities, the political system continued to insist that military involvement was both necessary and justified [Richard L. Berke, "Panel Said to Seek New Military Role in Fight on Drugs," *The New York Times*, 1989; Sara Fritz and John Broder, "Urban Blood Baths Spur Plan for Pentagon War on Drugs," *The Los Angeles Times*, 1988], and this even in the face of continued anxieties about the matter [Sara Fritz, "Cheney, Nunn at Odds Over Military's Drug Role," *The Los Angeles Times*, 1989]. Lately, the military has showed considerably more enthusiasm due, some have alleged, to its need to avoid budget cuts at a time when strong evidence is being presented that the East-West cold war is winding down. For extended discussions, refer to the following: Alan Dixon et al., "Should U.S. Armed Forces Play a Major Role in Interdicting Drug Traffic into the U.S.?" *Congressional Digest*, 1986; Irving Kristol, "War on Drugs? Then Get Serious and Use the Military," *The Washington Post*, 1988; Eliot Marshall, "A War on Drugs with Real Troops?" *Science*, 1988; David C. Morrison, "The Pentagon's Drug Wars," *National Journal*, 1986; Peter Reuter, Gordon Crawford, and Jonathan Cave, *Sealing the Borders: The Effects of Increased Military Participation in Drug Interdiction*, 1988; U.S. Congress, Senate Committee on Armed Services, Hearing, "Role of the Department of Defense in Drug Interdiction," 1988; U.S. General Accounting Office, Report to Congressional Requesters, *Drug Control: Issues Surrounding Increased Use of the Military in Drug Interdiction*, 1988; and U.S. General Accounting Office, Report to Congressional Requesters, *Drug Interdiction: Operation Autumn Harvest: A National Guard—Customs Anti-Smuggling Effort*, 1988. See also the items listed in "Literature on the Drug Issue," *Journal of Interamerican Studies and World Affairs*, 1988.

[52]Patricia Davis ["Uneven Scales of Justice Tilt Drug War in Dealers' Favor; Sentences in Fairfax Case Vary Widely," *The Washington Post*, 1989] discusses how some judges are lenient and others severe in their sentences on drug dealers even within one county (Fairfax, Virginia), and how the sentencing disparity is causing problems for law enforcement agencies.

[53]See Donna Gehrke and Aaron Epstein, "Lawyers Dealt Setback in Drug-Case Defenses," *The Miami Herald*, 1989; and Al Kamen, "Court Curbs Use of Criminals' Assets to Pay Lawyers," *The Washington Post*, 1989.

[54]See, for example, Barbara Bradley's discussion of the U.S. Custom Service's 1988 zero-tolerance program (later relaxed), which allowed confiscation of anyone's property who had even a trace of illegal drugs. Law enforcement officials in Miami and New Jersey were quite enthusiastic about the program ["Users Now Prime Targets in U.S. Antidrug Offensive," *The Christian Science Monitor*, 1988].

[55]For example, the U.S. Supreme Court has upheld the drug testing programs that have begun in the railroad industry [Linda Greenhouse, "Court Backs Tests of Some Workers to Deter Drug Use," *The New York Times*, 1989; Al Kamen, "Court Upholds Conrail Policy on Drug Tests," *The Washington Post*, 1989] and allows mandatory testing of employees in law enforcement and public safety occupations [Judith Havemann,

"Rulings Force Agencies to Reevaluate Test Policies," *The Washington Post*, 1989].

[56]An unusual application, with heavy economic overtones and potential disincentives to dealers, was handed down by a Brooklyn judge who ordered a convicted heroin dealer to pay more than $2 million in restitution to support drug rehabilitation programs in New York City. The judge had calculated a direct "harm to victims" formula. He clearly hoped his decision would set a precedent [Leonard Buder, "Dealer Must Pay to Treat Addicts," *The New York Times*, 1988]. The Virginia Supreme Court upheld a lower court's decision that a defendant who had supplied cocaine to a woman who died as a result of an overdose was properly found guilty of second degree felony murder ["Drug Traffickers Guilty of Felony-Murder," *The Criminal Law Report*, 1985]. The California Supreme Court has upheld the constitutionality of warrantless aerial surveillance over open fields as police search for illegal marijuana cultivations [Philip Hager, "Air Searches for Marijuana in Open Fields Ruled Legal," *The Los Angeles Times*, 1987].

[57]See the bibliographical discussion in note 15, Chapter 3.

[58]Shen Chenru, "Keeping Narcotics under Strict Control: Some Effects in China," *Impact of Science on Society*, 1984; Paul Lowinger, "The Solution to Narcotic Addiction in the People's Republic of China," *American Journal of Drug and Alcohol Abuse*, 1977; C. P. Spencer and V. Navaratnam, *Drug Abuse in East Asia*, 1981; Charas Suwanela and Vichai Poshyachinda, "Drug Abuse in Asia," *Bulletin on Narcotics*, 1986.

[59]"China's Attitude towards Narcotics Control," *Beijing Review*, 1987; "China Cracks Big Drug Case," *Beijing Review*, 1988; "China Vows War on Drug Abuse," *Beijing Review*, 1988.

[60]While the entries on this subject in this handbook's bibliography are relatively sparse, they uniformly indicate considerable soul-searching in the USSR: "4000 Held in Soviet Union in Drug Crackdown," *The New York Times*, 1987; T. A. Bogoliubova and K. A. Tolpekin, "Narcotism and Narcomania: Basic Directions of Control and Prevention," *Soviet Law and Government*, 1988; Nancy Cooper and Steven Strasser, "We Closed Our Eyes to it," *Newsweek*, 1986; Ester B. Fein, "Soviets Confront Growers," *The New York Times*, 1989; A. A. Gabiani, "Drug Addiction," *Soviet Sociology*, 1988; "Growing Concern over the Drug Scene," *The Current Digest of the Soviet Press*, 1986; "Kremlin Admits Drug Use Is Spreading in USSR," *The Christian Science Monitor*, 1987; "Soviet Drug Scene Gets Heavy Coverage," *The Current Digest of the Soviet Press*, 1987; "Who Are Soviet Drug Users, Dealers?" *The Current Digest of the Soviet Press*, 1986.

[61]John M. Kramer, "Drug Abuse in the Soviet Union," *Problems of Communism*, 1988.

[62]Alan Riding, "Colombia Uses Army in Cocaine Raids," *The New York Times*, 1988. The country's "official white paper" regarding its aspirations and efforts is *The Fight against the Drug Traffic in Colombia*, 1988. Copious notes are provided by Mary Ellen Welch, "The Extraterritorial War on Cocaine: Perspectives from Bolivia and Colombia," *Suffolk Transnational Law Journal*, 1988.

[63]Regarding Colombia, two perceptive articles by Merrill Collett reveal the nature of this threat: "'Drug Barons' Tentacles Run Deep in Colombian Society," *The Christian Science Monitor*, 1987; and "Colombia's Losing War with Drug Kings," *The Christian Science Monitor*, 1988. Fabio Castillo [*Los Jinetes de la Cocaína*, 1987] chronicles the drug trade and, by implication, demonstrates the degree to which the traffickers have infiltrated his country's law enforcement and judicial administrations. For Bolivia, see Scott Armstrong and Karia Vallance, "U.S.–Bolivia Relations Further Strained as Cocaine Smuggling Charges Fly," *The Christian Science Monitor*, 1980; "Cocaine: The

Military Connection," *Latin American Regional Reports*, 1980; Richard B. Craig, "Illicit Drug Traffic: Implications for South American Source Countries," *Journal of Interamerican Studies and World Affairs*, 1987; Michael Flatte and Alexei J. Cowett, "Drugs and Politics: An Unhealthy Mix," *Harvard International Review*, 1986; Scott B. MacDonald, *Mountain High, White Avalanche: Cocaine and Power in the Andean States and Panama*, 1989; and Gregorio Selser, *Bolivia: El Cuartelazo de los Cocadólares*, 1982.

[64]See James Brooke, "In the Drug War, Medellín Is a Reluctant Fighter," *The New York Times*, 1989.

[65]Clifford Krauss, "Colombian Leader is Hailed by Bush," *The New York Times*, 1991; and Joseph B. Treaster, "Surrender of Cocaine Smuggler Isn't Expected to Have Large Effect," *The New York Times*, 1991.

[66]British drug laws were on Pakistan's books until 1979, when more severe penalties were prescribed for violators of laws concerning the importation, exportation, and manufacturing or processing of any intoxicants—referring mainly to products of cannabis, opiates, and cocaine. In 1983 even more punitive sanctions were instituted. M. Husain ["Provisions in the Laws of Pakistan to Combat Serious Drug-Related Offences," *Bulletin on Narcotics*, 1984] describes these measures. In 1984 Pakistan tried to step up the implementation of these laws by rounding up suspected dealers [William Claiborne, "Pakistan Steps up Antidrug Campaign," *The Washington Post*, 1984]. Little came of this, and the effort was not sustained. On her first day in office, Pakistan's former prime minister, Benazir Bhutto, vowed to fight the growth of illicit narcotics distribution and production in her country [Richard M. Weintraub, "Bhutto Says Drug Fight Is Top Priority," *The Washington Post*, 1988]. Although her statement pleased the United States, her "war" remained little more than a skirmish. Pakistani authorities said they were doing all they could. In the meantime, Pakistan continued to be the world's biggest heroin exporter ["Heroin Brings More Trouble," *The Economist*, 1986].

[67]See Barbara Crossette, "Thai Officials Say Laos Turns to Marijuana to Help Budget," *The New York Times*, 1987; Henry Kamm, "U.S. and Laos Are Getting Friendlier," *The New York Times*, 1990; Peter Kerr, "U.S. Says Laos Government Is Deeply Involved in Drugs," *The New York Times*, 1988; Rodney Tasker, "Chasing the Red Dragon," *Far Eastern Economic Review*, 1987; and Jon A. Wiant, "Narcotics in the Golden Triangle," *The Washington Quarterly*, 1985.

[68]Henry Kamm, "U.S. and Laos Are Getting Friendlier," *The New York Times*, 1990.

[69]Martien Kooyman ["The Drug Problem in the Netherlands," *Journal of Substance Abuse Treatment*, 1984] gives a historical backdrop to the drug problem in the Netherlands, including a number of assumptions that underlie the country's permissive policy. Richard J. Bonnie [*Marijuana Use and Criminal Sanctions: Essays on the Theory and Practice of Decriminalization*, 1980] offers a comparative drug-policy study of the Netherlands and other European countries, including France, Italy, Switzerland, and the United Kingdom. See also Govert F. Van de Winjgaart, "A Social History of Drug Use in the Netherlands: Policy Outcomes and Implications," *Journal of Drug Issues*, 1988. Burton Bollag ["Swiss-Dutch Drug Stance: Tolerance," *The New York Times*, 1989] also makes a comparative analysis. Refer also to the bibliographical discussion in notes 22 and 23, Chapter 2.

[70]"Guess Which Country Has Legalized Pot," *Newsweek*, 1983.

[71]Joseph B. Treaster, "Jamaica, Close U.S. Ally Does Little to Halt Drugs," *The New York Times*, 1984.

[72]See, for example, Edward Cody, "Drug Raid Proves Bust; Villagers Lament Jamaican Drive on 'Ganja,'" *The Wall Street Journal*, 1986.

[73]The widespread use among pregnant women is discussed by Janice S. Hayes, Melanie C. Dreher, and J. Kevin Nugent ["Newborn Outcomes with Maternal Marihuana Use in Jamaican Women," *Pediatric Nursing*, 1988]. See also Bernard D. Headley, "War in 'Babylon': Dynamics of the Jamaican Informal Drug Economy," *Social Justice*, 1988; Gabriel G. Nahas, "Critique of a Study on Ganja in Jamaica," *Bulletin on Narcotics*, 1985; and Vera Rubin and Lambros Comitas, *Ganja in Jamaica: Medical Anthropological Study of Chronic Marihuana Use*, 1975.

[74]See the bibliographical discussion in note 15, Chapter 3.

[75]Mark A. Stein, "Recriminalization: Lenient Pot Laws Going up in Smoke," *The Los Angeles Times*, 1989.

[76]See Eric Josephson, "Marijuana Decriminalization: The Processes and Prospects of Change," *Contemporary Drug Problems*, 1981; Peat, Marwick, Mitchell and Company, *Marijuana: A Study of State Policies and Penalties*, 1977.

[77]For arguments within the United States, see Arnold S. Trebach, *The Heroin Solution*, 1982; Lester Grinspoon, *Marihuana Reconsidered*, 1977; Lester Grinspoon, "A Proposal for Regulation and Taxation of Drugs," *Nova Law Review*, 1987; and Ethan Nadelmann, "U.S. Drug Policy: A Bad Export," *Foreign Policy*, 1988. For tempering counterarguments see Charles B. Rangel, "Legalize Drugs? Not on Your Life," *The New York Times*, 1988; Jerome H, Skolnick, "Drugs: More or Fewer Controls?" *The Los Angeles Times*, 1988; U.S. Congress, House Select Committee on Narcotics Abuse and Control, "Drug Legalization—Catastrophe for Black Americans," 1988; Margaret Y. K. Woo, "Drug Delusions," *The Christian Science Monitor*, 1988; James A. Inciardi, "Editor's Introduction: Debating the Legalization of Drugs," *American Behavioral Scientist*, 1989; and James A. Inciardi and Duane C. McBride, "Legalization: A High-Risk Alternative in the War on Drugs," *American Behavioral Scientist*, 1989.

[78]There is indirect evidence that this relationship holds in India [B. B. Gujral, "Forfeiture of Illegally Acquired Assets of Drug Traffickers: The Position in India," *Bulletin on Narcotics*, 1983] and in the United States [George A. Kurisky, Jr., "Civil Forfeiture of Assets: A Final Solution to International Drug Trafficking?" *Houston Journal of International Law*, 1988]. N. Liverpool makes the case for the British Commonwealth ["The Seizure and Forfeiture of Property Associated with Criminal Activity," *Bulletin on Narcotics*, 1983]. See also U.S. Congress, House Committee on the Judiciary, Subcommittee on Crime, Hearing, "Forfeiture in Drug Cases," 1982.

[79]Patricia G. Erickson, et al., *The Steel Drug: Cocaine in Perspective*, 1987.

[80]Francesco Bruno, *Combatting Drug Abuse and Related Crime: Comparative Research on the Effectiveness of Socio-Legal Preventive and Control Measures in Different Countries on the Interaction between Criminal Behaviour and Drug Abuse*, 1984.

[81]Crime associated with drug use has risen sharply in recent years ["Crime's Link to Drugs up Steeply in 12 Years," *The New York Times*, 1988]. A considerable body of literature makes the case that, although drug use and criminality are seen to correlate, drug use does not make the criminal. Criminal behavior exists before drug involvement. See, for example, Richard R. Clayton, "The Delinquency and Drug Use Relationship among Adolescents: A Critical Review," in *Drug Abuse and the American Adolescent*, Dan J. Lettieri and Jacqueline P. Ludford, eds., 1980; and George Speckart, "Narcotics and Crime: A Multisample Multimethod Approach," Ph.D. diss., 1984. The alternative thesis, or evidence supporting an alternative thesis, is advanced by Jan Chaiken and Marcia R. Chaiken, with Joyce E. Peterson, *Varieties of Criminal Behavior: Summary*

and Policy Implications, 1982; David T. Courtwright, *Dark Paradise: Opiate Addiction in America before 1940*, 1982; and Bernard A. Gropper, "Probing the Links between Drugs and Crime," *Research in Brief*, 1985. General treatises include Carl Chambers et al., *Chemical Dependencies: Patterns, Costs, and Consequences*, 1987; Richard R. Clayton, "Federal Drugs-Crime Research: Setting the Agenda," in *The Drugs-Crime Connection*, James A. Inciardi, ed., 1981; Richard R. Clayton and Harwin L. Voss, *Young Men and Drugs in Manhattan: A Causal Analysis*, 1981; Robert P. Gandossy et al., *Drugs and Crime: A Survey and Analysis of the Literature*, 1980; James A. Inciardi, *The Drugs-Crime Connection*, 1981; Duane C. McBride and Clyde B. McCoy, "Crime and Drugs: The Issues and Literature, *Journal of Drug Issues*, 1982; and James C. Weissman and Robert L. DuPont, eds., *Criminal Justice and Drugs: The Unresolved Connection*, 1981. See also James Q. Wilson and Richard J. Herrnstein, *Crime and Human Nature*, 1985.

[82]T. Asuni and F. Bruno, "Summary of an Eleven-Country Study of Socio-Legal Measures to Combat Drug Abuse and Related Crime," *Bulletin on Narcotics*, 1984.

[83]Alfred Blumstein, Jacqueline Cohen, and Daniel Nagin, eds., *Deterrence and Incapacitation: Estimating the Effects of Criminal Sanctions on Crime Rates*, 1978.

[84]Patricia G. Erickson, et al., *The Steel Drug: Cocaine in Perspective*, 1987.

[85]Sheldon Ekland-Olson, John Lieb, and Louis Zurcher, "The Paradoxical Impact of Criminal Sanctions: Some Microstructural Findings," *Law and Society Review*, 1984.

[86]See, for example, Karlene Faith, "Drug Addiction: From a Study of Women and Criminal Justice," Ph.D. diss., 1981; Mark Fraser and Nance Kohlert, "Substance Abuse and Public Policy," *Social Service Review*, 1988; Arnold S. Trebach, "The Lesson of Ayatollah Khalkhali," *Journal of Drug Issues*, 1983; Gerald F. Uelmen, "Punishing Drug Offenders: An International and Comparative Perspective," *Journal of Drug Issues*, 1983; and Grant Wardlaw, "The Realities of Drug Enforcement," *Journal of Drug Issues*, 1986.

[87]Ester B. Fein, "Soviets Confront Growers," *The New York Times*, 1989.

[88]H. Hanreich, "Drug-Related Crime and Sentencing Policies from the Perspective of the United Nations Crime Prevention and Criminal Justice Programme," *Bulletin on Narcotics*, 1984.

[89]Richard Moran, "When Drug Laws Are Too Harsh to Work," *The Christian Science Monitor*, 1988.

[90]William M. Fitzgerald, "The Constitutionality of the Canine Sniff Search: From Katz to Dogs," *Marquette Law Review*, 1984.

[91]"Heroin Sale That Results in Death May Constitute Murder, Manslaughter," *The Criminal Law Reporter*, 1984. The "unbelievability" appears to exist in spite, in this case, of the Tennessee Supreme Court's holding that "a heroin seller who is shown to have acted with such indifference to the consequences of his unlawful actions as to constitute malice may be liable for murder when a customer dies from the effects of the heroin."

[92]Michael Schwarz, "Deadly Traffic," *The New York Times*, 1987.

[93]Ibid.

[94]Kirsten A. Conover, "Defeating Drug Dealers: Drop-a-Dime Project Pays Off," *The Christian Science Monitor*, 1989; George Hackett, "Saying 'No' to Crack Gangs," *Newsweek*, 1988; "How to Oust a Drug Dealer: Ideas for Embattled Tenants," *The New York Times*, 1987; and Andrew Malcolm, "Weapon in Drug War: Imagination," *The New York Times*, 1990.

[95]W. H. McGlothlin, "The Singapore Heroin Control Programme," *Bulletin on Narcotics*, 1980.

[96]Victoria Irwin, "Drugs and Police: Cities Probe the Corruption Connection," *The Christian Science Monitor*, 1986; John Kendall, "Drugs, Money Add up to Temptation for Police," *The Los Angeles Times*, 1988; Seth Mydans, "6 Los Angeles Officers Charged in Drug Cases," *The New York Times*, 1991.

[97]Herbert E. Alexander and Gerald E. Caiden, eds., *The Politics and Economics of Organized Crime*, 1985; John Kendall, "Drugs, Money Add up to Temptation for Police," *The Los Angeles Times*, 1988; William Overend and John Kendall, "Drug Agents' Tips to Dealers Alleged," *The Los Angeles Times*, 1988; Jim Schachter, "Customs Service Cleans House in a Drive on Drug Corruption," *The Los Angeles Times*, 1987; and "Slice of Vice: More Miami Cops Arrested," *Time*, 1986.

[98]"Arrested DEA Agent May Have Tipped off Major Cocaine Ring," *The Miami Herald*, 1989; and William Overend, "Chaotic DEA Office Ripe for Problems in the Early 1980s," *The Los Angeles Times*, 1988.

[99]James Lieber, "Coping with Cocaine," *Atlantic*, 1986; Steven Wisotsky, "Introduction: In Search of a Breakthrough in the War on Drugs," *Nova Law Review*, 1987.

[100]The U.S. federal government has moved to stimulate drugs-crime research, which has produced a voluminous response [Richard R. Clayton, "Federal Drugs-Crime Research: Setting the Agenda," in *The Drugs-Crime Connection*, James A. Inciardi, ed., 1981]. The National Institute of Justice has produced a survey of the literature as of 1979 [Robert P. Gandossy et al., *Drugs and Crime: A Survey and Analysis of the Literature*, 1980]. For an excellent review of the literature as of the early 1980s see James A. Inciardi, ed., *The Drugs-Crime Connection*, 1981. See also the literature reviews by Carl G. Leukefeld ["The Clinical Connection: Drugs and Crime," *The International Journal of the Addictions*, 1985] and Duane C. McBride and Clyde B. McCoy ["Crime and Drugs: The Issues and Literature," *Journal of Drug Issues*, 1982]. Louise Greene Richards ["Drugs and Crime: Theory Engagement after a Forced Marriage," *Contemporary Drug Problems*, 1980] attempts to describe and account for the dissatisfaction associated with generalizations about the drug-crime connection. See also the bibliographical discussion in note 81, this chapter.

[101]John C. Ball, et al., "Lifetime Criminality of Heroin Addicts in the United States," *Journal of Drug Issues*, 1982; Ronald Bayer, "Heroin Addiction, Criminal Culpability, and the Penal Sanction," in *Criminal Justice and Drugs: The Unresolved Connection*, James C. Weissman and Robert L. DuPont, eds., 1981; George Beschner, ed., *Teen Drug Use*, 1986; Scott Bronstein, "Study Shows Sharp Rise in Cocaine Use by Suspects in Crimes," *The New York Times*, 1987; William E. Carter, ed., *Cannabis Use in Costa Rica: A Study of Chronic Marihuana Use*, 1980; Jan Chaiken and Marcia R. Chaiken with Joyce E. Peterson, *Varieties of Criminal Behavior: Summary and Policy Implications*, 1982; Richard R. Clayton and Harwin L. Voss, *Young Men and Drugs in Manhattan: A Causal Analysis*, 1981; Dana E. Hunt, Douglas S. Lipton, and Berry Spunt, "Patterns of Criminal Activity among Methadone Clients and Current Narcotics Users Not in Treatment," *Journal of Drug Issues*, 1984; Bruce Johnson, Kevin Anderson, and Eric D. Wish, "A Day in the Life of 105 Drug Addicts and Abusers: Crimes Committed and How the Money Was Spent," *Sociology and Social Research*, 1988; J. Kraus, "Juvenile Drug Abuse and Delinquency: Some Differential Associations," *British Journal of Psychiatry*, 1981; U.S. Congress, Senate Committee on Labor and Human Resources, Subcommittee on Alcoholism and Drug Abuse, Hearing, "Impact of Drugs on Crime," 1984; and U.S. Department of Commerce, *Drug Use and Crime: Report of the Panel on*

Drug Use and Criminal Behavior, 1976.

[102]"Crime's Link to Drugs up Steeply in 12 Years," *The New York Times*, 1988. Report on the U.S. Justice Department's Bureau of Justice Statistics report issued 10 July 1988.

[103]B. Bower, "Heroin and Crime: A Stronger Link," *Science News*, 1984.

[104]See T. Asuni and F. Bruno, "Summary of an Eleven-Country Study of Socio-Legal Measures to Combat Drug Abuse and Related Crime," *Bulletin on Narcotics*, 1984; Francesco Bruno, *Combatting Drug Abuse and Related Crime: Comparative Research on the Effectiveness of Socio-Legal Preventive and Control Measures in Different Countries on the Interaction Between Criminal Behaviour and Drug Abuse*, 1984; Angela Burr, "Chasing the Dragon," *The British Journal of Criminology*, 1987; Cheryl Carpenter et al., *Kids, Drugs, and Crime*, 1988; Charles E. Faupel and Carl B. Klockars, "Drugs-Crime Connections: Elaborations from the Life Histories of Hard-Core Heroin Addicts," *Social Problems*, 1987; George Speckart, "Narcotics and Crime: A Multisample Multi-method Approach," Ph.D. diss., 1984; and, Harwin L. Voss, "Drugs, Crime, and Occupational Prestige," *Journal of Psychoactive Drugs*, 1981.

[105]Richard R. Clayton, "The Delinquency and Drug Use Relationship among Adoles-cents: A Critical Review," in *Drug Abuse and the American Adolescent*, Dan J. Lettieri and Jacqueline P. Ludford, eds., 1980.

[106]M. Douglas Anglin et al., "Consequences and Costs of Shutting off Methadone," *Addictive Behaviors*, 1989; John Ball, "A Selective Review of the Crime-Drug Literature with Reference to Future Research Implications," in *Drug Use and Crime: Report of the Panel on Drug Use and Criminal Behavior*, Robert Shellow, ed., 1976; John C. Ball, John W. Shaffer, and David N. Nurco, "The Day-to-Day Criminality of Heroin Addicts in Baltimore: A Study in the Continuity of Offense Rates," *Drug and Alcohol Depen-dence*, 1983; John C. Ball et al., "The Criminality of Heroin Addicts When Addicted and When off Opiates," in *The Drug-Crime Connection*, James A. Inciardi, ed., 1981; Bernard Godwin, "An Economic Analysis of the Illicit Drug Market," *The International Journal of the Addictions*, 1983; Roger D. Blair and Ronald J. Vogel, "Heroin Addiction and Urban Crime," *Public Finance Quarterly*, 1973; Carl Chambers, et al., *Chemical Dependencies: Patterns, Costs, and Consequences*, 1987; James J. Collins, Robert L. Hubbard, and J. Valley Rachal, "Expensive Drug Use and Illegal Income: A Test of Explanatory Hypotheses," *Criminology*, 1985; Rosa Del Olmo, "Female Criminality and Drug Trafficking in Latin America: Preliminary Findings," *Studies in Third World Societies*, 1986; Charles E. Faupel, "Heroin Use, Street Crime, and the 'Main Hustle': Implications for the Validity of Official Crime Data," *Deviant Behavior*, 1986; James A. Inciardi, "Heroin Use and Street Crime," *Crime and Delinquency*, 1979; Bruce D. Johnson, "If You Can Incarcerate Local Heroin Abusers, You Can Cut Back on Property Crimes," *Crime Control Digest*, 1984; Bruce D. Johnson et al., *Taking Care of Business: The Economics of Crime by Heroin Users*, 1985; Howard Kurtz, "Across the Nation, Rising Outrage," *The Washington Post*, 1989; David Lees, "Executive Addicts," *Canad-ian Business*, 1986; Edmundo Morales, "Land Reform, Social Change, and Moderniza-tion in the National Periphery," Ph.D. diss., 1983; David N. Nurco and Robert L. DuPont, "A Preliminary Report of Crime and Addiction within a Community-wide Population of Narcotic Addicts," *Drug and Alcohol Dependence*, 1977; Lester P. Silver-man and Nancy L. Spruill, "Urban Crime and the Price of Heroin," *Journal of Urban Economics*, 1977; Rodney T. Stamler, Robert C. Fahlman, and S. A. Keele, "Recent Trends in Illicit Drug Trafficking from the Canadian Perspective," *Bulletin on Narcotics*, 1983; and James C. Weissman and Karen N. File, "Criminal Behavior Patterns of

Female Addicts: A Comparison of Findings in Two Cities," *International Journal of the Addictions*, 1976.

[107]James A. Inciardi, "Editor's Introduction: Debating the Legalization of Drugs," *American Behavioral Scientist*, 1989; and James A. Inciardi and Duane C. McBride, "Legalization: A High-Risk Alternative in the War on Drugs," *American Behavioral Scientist*, 1989.

[108]Carlos Harrison, "Kids on Crack: 880 Crimes Each in a Year," *The Miami Herald*, 1989.

[109]See, for example, Lester Grinspoon, *Marihuana Reconsidered*, 2d ed., 1977.

[110]Michael Lamanna, "Marijuana: Implications of Use by Young People," *Journal of Drug Education*, 1981.

[111]David N. Nurco et al., "A Comparison by Race/Ethnicity of Narcotic Addict Crime Rates in Baltimore, New York, and Philadelphia," *American Journal of Drug and Alcohol Abuse*, 1986.

[112]David Nurco et al., "Differential Criminal Patterns of Narcotic Addicts over an Addiction Career," *Criminology*, 1988.

[113]George Speckart and M. Douglas Anglin, "Narcotics Use and Crime: An Overview of Recent Research Advances," *Contemporary Drug Problems*, 1986.

[114]Bernard A. Gropper, "Probing the Links between Drugs and Crime," *National Institute of Justice: Research in Brief*, 1985; Michael Isikoff, "Users of Crack Cocaine Link Violence to Drug's Influence," *The Washington Post*, 1989.

[115]Ronald Hefferman, John M. Martin, and Anne T. Romano, "Homicides Related to Drug Trafficking," *Federal Probation*, 1982; Michel Marriott, "After Three Years, Crack Plague in New York Only Gets Worse," *The New York Times*, 1989; Selwyn Raab, "Links to 200 Murders in New York City Last Year; The Ruthless Young Crack Gangsters," *The New York Times*, 1988; Jonathan C. Randal, "In Britain, Drug Kills Are Rarity," *The Washington Post*, 1980; "Slaughter in the Streets; Crack Touches off a Homicide Epidemic," *Time*, 1988; and Isabel Wilkerson, "Urban Homicide Rates in U.S. Up Sharply in 1986," *The New York Times*, 1987.

[116]Courtland Milloy and Edward D. Sargent, "U.S. Crime Wave Linked to Flood of Heroin, Cocaine," *The Washington Post*, 1983.

[117]U.S. General Accounting Office "AIDS: Information on Global Dimensions and Possible Impacts," 1987.

[118]"AIDS Watch: Mapping the Epidemic," *Discover*, 1988. Gives worldwide statistics on AIDS in relationship to geographical concentrations. For an epidemiological discussion, see Jeffrey P. Koplan, Ann M. Hardy, and James R. Allen, "Epidemiology of the Acquired Immunodeficiency Syndrome in Intravenous Drug Abusers," *Advances in Alcohol and Substance Abuse*, 1985; and C. Schuster and R. Pickens, "AIDS and Intravenous Drug Abuse," in *Problems of Drug Dependence, 1988*, Louis S. Harris, ed., 1988.

[119]Bruce Lambert, "AIDS Danger Rises for Cocaine Users; Virus Is Spreading Faster than with Heroin—Peril Is in Contaminated Needles," *The New York Times*, 1988.

[120]"The AIDS Plague Spreads," *The Economist*, 1989.

[121]Richard Conviser and John H. Rutledge, "Can Public Policies Limit the Spread of HIV among IV Drug Users," *Journal of Drug Issues*, 1989; Ernest Drucker, "AIDS and Addiction in New York City," *American Journal of Drug and Alcohol Abuse*, 1986.

[122]Ernest Drucker ["The Disease of Ignorance," *New York News Day*, 1988] shows that the most serious AIDS risk to the adolescent population in New York City, especially to young women, is related to their heterosexual behavior. Adolescents with AIDS are twice as likely as adults to be female and to have acquired the disease through heterosexual intercourse. This appears to be related to their inability to make prudent choices about their sexual partners or to gain some control over their sexual behavior.

[123]Harry W. Haverkos, "Overview: HIV Infection among Intravenous Drug Abusers in the United States and Europe," in *Needle Sharing among Intravenous Drug Abusers: National and International Perspectives*, Robert J. Battjes and Roy W. Pickens, eds., 1988.

[124]Ernest Drucker, "AIDS and Addiction in New York City," *American Journal of Drug and Alcohol Abuse*, 1986; Ernest Drucker et al., "IV Drug Users with AIDS in New York: A Study of Dependent Children, Housing and Drug Addiction Treatment," unpublished paper, 1988.

[125]Harold M. Ginzburg, Mhairi Graham MacDonald, and James William Glass, "AIDS, HTLV-III Diseases, Minorities and Intravenous Drug Abuse," *Advances in Alcohol and Substance Abuse*, 1987; Rand L. Stoneburner, "A Larger Spectrum of Severe HIV-1–Related Disease in Intravenous Drug Users in New York City," *Science*, 1988.

[126]Michael H. Alderman et al., "Predicting the Future of the AIDS Epidemic and its Consequences for the Health Care System of New York City," *Bulletin of the New York Academy of Medicine*, 1988.

[127]Don des Jarlais, "Policy Issues Regarding AIDS Among Intravenous Drug Users: An Overview," *AIDS and Public Policy Journal*, 1988.

[128]Janet Mohun, "Amsterdam Targets Its Drug Users," *New Scientist*, 1988.

[129]"Pro and Con: Free Needles for Addicts, to Help Curb AIDS?" *The New York Times*, 1989.

[130]Lawrence K. Altman, "Needle Exchange Programs Hint a Cut in AIDS Virus Transmission," *The New York Times*, 1989.

[131]Spencer Rich, "Aiding Needle Exchange Is Illegal, Rangel Says: Experts Dispute Drug Panel Chairman," *The Washington Post*, 1989.

[132]Richard Conviser and John H. Rutledge, "Can Public Policies Limit the Spread of HIV among IV Drug Users?," *Journal of Drug Issues*, 1989.

[133]John K. Watters, "Observations on the Importance of Social Context in HIV Transmission Among Intravenous Drug Users," *Journal of Drug Issues*, 1989; Sheigla Murphy, "Intravenous Drug Use and AIDS: Notes on the Social Economy of Needle Sharing," *Contemporary Drug Problems*, 1987.

[134]Ellen Goodman, "Needles for Addicts? No." *The Washington Post*, 1988.

[135]"17 Reported Hanged in Iran Anti-Drug Campaign," *The New York Times*, 1989; Youssef M. Ibrahim, "Iran Puts Addicts in Its Labor Camps," *The New York Times*, 1989.

[136]Richard B. Craig, "Human Rights and Mexico's Antidrug Campaign," *Social Science Quarterly*, 1980; and Lucy Conger, "Mexico: Rights Violations Are on the Rise," Latinamerica Press, 1990.

[137]"Human Rights Watch—August," *Latinamerica Press*, 1988.

[138]D.C. Jayasuriya, "Penal Measures for Drug Offences: Perspectives from Some Asian Countries," *Bulletin on Narcotics*, 1984.

[139]C. Jacquemart, "An Assessment of Legal Measures to Trace, Freeze and Confiscate the Proceeds of Drug Crimes in France: The Customs Viewpoint," *Bulletin on Narcotics*, 1984.

[140]Dale Gieringer, "Inside the DEA," *Reason*, 1986; and Seth Mydans, "6 Los Angeles Officers Charged in Drug Cases," *The New York Times*, 1991.

[141]Charles L. Becton, "The Drug Courier Profile: 'All Seems Infected to th' Infected Spy, as All Looks Yellow to the Jandic'd Eye,'" *North Carolina Law Review*, 1987.

[142]Linda Greenhouse, "High Court Backs Airport Detention Based on 'Profile,'" *The New York Times*, 1989.

[143]Abraham Abramovsky, "Money-Laundering and Narcotics Prosecution," *Fordham Law Review*, 1986.

[144]Chris Adams, "Second Thoughts on the Military as Narcs," *The Washington Post*, 1988. See also Morris J. Blachman and Kenneth E. Sharpe, "The War on Drugs: American Democracy Under Assault, *World Policy Journal*, 1989-90.

[145]Patricia G. Erickson et al., *The Steel Drug: Cocaine in Perspective*, 1987.

[146]Ann Levin, "Some Children, Turned off to Drugs, Turn in Their Parents," *The Christian Science Monitor*, 1987.

[147]See, for example, Mario Arango and Jorge Child, *Los Condenados de la Coca: El Manejo Político de la Droga*, 1985; Maria Laura Avignolo, "Bolivia: Coca Control Law Feeds Anti–U.S. Sentiment," *Latinamerica Press*, 1988; Lupe Cajias, "Increased Presence of U.S. Troops Worries Bolivians," *Latinamerica Press*, 1989; "Honduras: Et Tu?" *The Economist*, 1988; and Michael Isikoff, "Warriors against Cocaine: It's Guerrilla Warfare for DEA Agents on the Bolivian Front Lines," *The Washington Post*, 1989.

[148]Robert P. Hey, "Drug Traffickers Outgunning Police, A Mayor Laments," *The Christian Science Monitor*, 1989.

[149]Morris J. Blachman and Kenneth E. Sharpe, "The War on Drugs: American Democracy Under Assault," *World Policy Journal*, 1989–90.

[150]Alan Riding, "Colombia Effort against Drugs Hits Dead End," *The New York Times*, 1987; Joseph B. Treaster, "Colombians, Weary of the Strain, Are Losing Heart in the Drug War," *The New York Times*, 1989; and "Release of Trafficker Shakes Hope in Colombian Drug Plan," *The New York Times*, 1991.

[151]Richard L. Berke, "Drug Chief Calls for a Vast Prison Plan," *The New York Times*, 1989.

[152]Richard L. Berke, "Criminals' Cases Clog U.S. Courts," *The New York Times*, 1989.

[153]Adam Wagstaff and Alan Maynard, *Economic Aspects of the Illicit Drug Market and Drug Enforcement Policies in the United Kingdom*, 1988.

[154]Giancario Arnao, "Drug Enforcement Policy as a Factor in Trends of Trafficking and Use of Different Substances," *Journal of Psychoactive Drugs*, 1988.

[155]Joseph Westermeyer, "The Pro-Heroin Effects of Anti-Opium Laws in Asia," *Arch. Gen. Psychiatry*, 1976.

[156]Michel Marriott, "After Three Years, Crack Plague in New York Only Gets Worse," *The New York Times*, 1989.

[157]Richard L. Berke, "Criminals' Cases Clog U.S. Courts," *The New York Times*, 1989.

[158]Marshall Ingwerson, "Rise in Drug Offenses Crams Prisons; Inmates Getting Released Earlier," *The Christian Science Monitor*, 1988.

[159]Peter Kerr, "War on Drugs Puts Strain on Prisons, U.S. Officials Say," *The New York Times*, 1987.

[160]Lee P. Brown, "Strategies for Dealing with Crack Houses," *FBI Law Enforcement Bulletin*, 1988.

[161]For inner-city migrations, see "Supply-Side Failures," *The Economist*, 1988. For comparative and international perspectives, see "Clean-up Campaign Gives Poor Results," *Latin American Weekly Report*, 1984; Edward Cody, "Dutch Pull Welcome Mat away from Drug Users," *The Washington Post*, 1988; "Iran's Drug Crackdown Stirs Concern in Gulf," *The Christian Science Monitor*, 1989; and Tina Rosenberg, "Miami South," *The New Republic*, 1986.

[162]David E. Pitt, "Surge in New York Drug Arrests Sets off Criminal-Justice Crisis," *The New York Times*, 1989; Niel Proto, "Illicit Plans Threatening Sovereignty at Home and Abroad," *The Christian Science Monitor*, 1989.

[163]See also Joel Brinkley, "Bolivia Drug Crackdown Brews Trouble," *The New York Times*, 1984; Mark Day, "Peru: Battle Intensifies over Renewed Drug Eradication Plan," *Latinamerica Press*, 1989; "Losing the War against 'Narcos,'" *Latin American Regional Reports*, 1983; and U.S. Congress, House Committee on the Judiciary, Subcommittee on Crime, Hearing, "Military Cooperation with Civilian Law Enforcement," 1985.

[164]Patricia Davis, "Uneven Scales of Justice Tilt Drug War in Dealers' Favor," *The Washington Post*, 1989; Dale Gieringer, "Inside the DEA," *Reason*, 1986; Nicholas C. McBride, "'Zero Tolerance': Zero Effect?" *The Christian Science Monitor,* 1988; and Susanna Rance, "Bolivia: New Coca Control Law Aggravates Tense Situation," *Latinamerica Press*, 1988.

[165]John J. Fialka, "Death of US Agent in Mexico Drug Case Uncovers Grid of Graft," *The Wall Street Journal*, 1986; Peter Kerr, "Anti-Drug Agents Castigate U.S. Policy as Inadequate," *The New York Times*, 1990.

[166]See P. Schioler, "Information, Teaching and Education in the Primary Prevention of Drug Abuse among Youth in Denmark," *Bulletin on Narcotics*, 1981; William J. Serdahely, "A Factual Approach to Drug Education and Its Effects on Drug Consumption," *Journal of Alcohol and Drug Education*, 1980.

[167]In a controlled study of two junior high schools, an intervention educational program produced positive effects for females on several drug-related variables, but few effects on males. Studies that do not focus on social and psychological factors influencing drug use and do not train students in relative resistive competencies appear to have no effect [Joel M. Moskowitz et al., "Evaluation of a Junior High School Primary Prevention Program," *Addictive Behaviors*, 1983]. Four large-scale surveys were conducted at three-year intervals beginning in 1977; the most recent one was implemented in 1986. The standard demographic variables were employed. The analysis confirmed some of the speculations found elsewhere in the literature—that, although education appears to increase a student's drug-related knowledge, it does little to change his or her attitudes about substance abuse [Pietro J. Pascale, "Trend Analyses of Four Large-Scale Surveys of High School Drug Use 1977–1986," *Journal of Drug Education*, 1988]. On the other side, August Pérez, a Colombian national who was educated in Belgium and holds advanced degrees in psychology, places almost absolute confidence in information as supplied through an educational program to reduce demand [*Cocaína: Surgimiento y Evolución de un Mito*, 1987]. See also John Kaplan, "Taking Drugs Seriously," *The Public Interest*, 1988.

[168]See Keith Pickens, "Drug Education: The Effects of Giving Information," *Journal of Alcohol and Drug Education*, 1985; and William J. Serdahely, "A Factual Approach to Drug Education and Its Effects on Drug Consumption," *Journal of Alcohol and Drug Education*, 1980.

[169]One study found that the most effective educational programs created an atmosphere of intolerance toward drugs within the school, educated teachers about the effects of habitual drug use on adolescents and assisted them in recognizing symptoms, and gave students opportunities to help each other and themselves through positive peer counseling programs—all beginning as early as the seventh grade [*Marijuana: The National Impact on Education*, 1982]. The development of reasoning skills within social settings through the examination of complex and competing materials is viewed as being effective [Gary E. McCuen, *The International Drug Trade*, 1989]. Margaret E. Mitchel and her colleagues ["Cost Effectiveness Analysis of an Educational Drug Abuse Prevention Program," *Journal of Drug Education*, 1984] found, from a reasonably well-controlled experimental research design in which students were more or less randomly assigned to specific courses in their school designed to influence their drug taking behavior, that only the religion course appeared to alter significantly subsequent drug taking behavior. Courses in health and social studies had no effect. Pietro J. Pascale's study ["Trend Analyses of Four Large-Scale Surveys of High School Drug Use 1977–1986," *Journal of Drug Education*, 1988] showed that, when peer groups are the primary sources of instruction about drug abuse, larger attitude changes are more likely to take place than when an educational program focuses principally on information. Therefore, combine positive peer influence with accurate information. Glenn E. Rohrer and his collaborators describe a crack cocaine education project carried out in a Florida school system ["Crack Cocaine Education in the Public Schools," *Journal of Alcohol and Drug Education*, 1987]. Ten patients being treated for cocaine addiction were used as members of a "crack awareness" team to present information to Florida school students. Their experiment showed that seven of the ten patients being treated for cocaine addiction improved, and also that they had a constructive impact on the students. See also the discussions in and studies reported by the following: Herb Roehrich and Mark S. Gold, "800-COCAINE: Origin, Significance, and Findings," *Yale Journal of Biology and Medicine*, 1988; Meir Teichman, Giora Rahav, and Zipora Barnea, "A Comprehensive Substance Prevention Program: An Israeli Experiment," *Journal of Alcohol and Drug Education*, 1988; U.S. Congress, House Select Committee on Narcotics Abuse and Control, Hearing, "Drug Abuse Prevention in America's Schools," 1987; U.S. Congress, Senate Committee on Labor and Human Resources, Subcommittee on Children, Family, Drugs, and Alcoholism, Hearing, "Drug Abuse—Prevention, Education, and Treatment, 1988; U.S. Congress, Senate Committee on Labor and Human Resources, Hearing, "Impact of Drug Education," 1987; and Chudley E. Werch, "Rethinking Critical Issues in Drug Programming," *Journal of Alcohol and Drug Education*, 1987.

[170]See, for example, P. Arlacchi, "Effects of the New Anti-Mafia Law on the Proceeds of Crime and on the Italian Economy," *Bulletin on Narcotics*, 1984; Lee P. Brown, "Strategies for Dealing with Crack Houses," *FBI Law Enforcement Bulletin*, 1988; B. B. Gujral, "Forfeiture of Illegally Acquired Assets of Drug Traffickers: The Position in India," *Bulletin on Narcotics*, 1983; and George A. Kurisky, Jr., "Civil Forfeiture of Assets: A Final Solution to International Drug Trafficking?" *Houston Journal of International Law*, 1988.

[171]Robert E. Hosty and Francis J. Elliott, "Drug Abuse in Industry: What Does It Cost and What Can Be Done?" *Security Management*, 1985.

[172]James W. Schreier, "A Survey of Drug Abuse in Organizations," *Personnel Journal*, 1983. See also Cheryl Sullivan, "Cocaine in the Workplace Alarms Silicon Valley," *The Christian Science Monitor*, 1986.

[173]David Lees, "Executive Addicts," *Canadian Business*, 1986.

[174]Obviously, the industrial relations issues are myriad. Tia and R. V. Denenberg help sort them out [*Alcohol and Drugs: Issues in the Workplace*, 1983]. When there were no uniform U.S. federal guidelines available to deal with urine testing, many American companies formulated their own. A congressional hearing took place in 1987, motivated by the need to find out how the public and private sectors were dealing with drug abuse in the workplace, especially as it related to the controversial issue of urine testing [U.S. Congress, House Select Committee on Narcotics Abuse and Control, Hearing, "Drug Abuse in the Workplace," 1987]. The U.S. Chamber of Commerce responded with a study to assist business enterprises in practical compliance with federal and state drug-abuse regulations, emphasizing drug testing within the context of a larger comprehensive drug prevention program [Mark A. de Bernardo, *Drug Abuse in the Workplace: An Employer's Guide for Prevention*, 1986]. See also U.S. General Accounting Office, Report to the Honorable Charles Schumer, House of Representatives, *Employee Drug Testing: Information on Private Sector Programs*, 1988; and Michael D. Lyman, *Narcotics and Crime Control*, 1987.

[175]See Carita Zimmerman, "Urine Testing: Testing-Based Employment Decisions and the Rehabilitation Act of 1973," *Columbia Journal of Law and Social Problems*, 1989.

[176]Judith Havemann, "Drug Tests Catch 203 In Sensitive Jobs," *The Washington Post*, 1989.

[177]See Diane Wagner, "The Drug Dependency Dilemma: Managers Weigh Privacy versus Productivity in the Quest for a Drug Free Work Place," *California Business*, 1986. L. Camille Hebert ["Private Sector Drug Testing: Employer Rights, Risks, and Responsibilities," *Kansas University Law Review*, 1988] discusses the methods that private employers use and the issues such methods raise with respect to invasion of privacy, defamation, infliction of emotional distress, wrongful discharge, discrimination against the handicapped, and so forth. In the final analysis, Richard J. Hirn ["Drug Tests Threaten Employers, Too," *The New York Times*, 1988] notes that employees may sue employers for invasion of privacy and, in any event, expose the employers to considerable costs. All this says nothing about the general morale problem that random drug testing generally imposes, a matter amply illustrated by one company in Albuquerque, New Mexico, which conducted a private raid on its employees [Chris Spolar, "When Privacy and Company Prerogatives Clash," *The Washington Post*, 1988]. There are ways around these problems, however. J. Alan Lips and Michael C. Lueder ["An Employer's Right to Test for Substance Abuse, Infectious Diseases, and Truthfulness versus an Employee's Right to Privacy," *Labor Law Journal*, 1988] comment that, although an employer is justified in testing employees, the prudent employer will base testing decisions on reasonable needs, rather than on economic power to require it, and will keep the information confidential. Andrew Kupfer ["Is Drug Testing Good or Bad," *Fortune*, 1988] calls for executives to train their supervisors to spot problems, or to promote employee assistance programs, or to communicate clearly and sympathetically with employees about drug problems—on the assumption that companies then will not have the problems—before joining the burgeoning ranks of drug testers. He advanced two companies—Perkin-Elmer and Hewlett-Packard—as illustrations of successful drug control programs not involving intrusive urine testing. Robert E. Willette ["Drug-Testing Programs," in *Urine Testing for Drugs of Abuse*, Richard L. Hawks and C. Nora

Chiang, eds., 1986] surveys programs already introduced into various government agencies, public utility companies, large industrial corporations, and even some small companies. Successful programs are noted for clearly communicating to all employees and applicants the nature of the drug programs and the consequences of detected drug use. Reasonableness and fairness are emphasized as important variables contributing to a successful program.

[178]Early on, Herbert J. Freudenberger advocated such an approach ["Substance Abuse in the Workplace," *Contemporary Drug Problems*, 1982].

[179]See, for example, Craig Reinarman, Dan Waldorf, and B. Murphy, "Scapegoating and Social Control in the Construction of a Public Problem: Empirical and Critical Findings on Cocaine and Work," *Research in Law, Deviance and Social Control*, 1988. This article presents empirical findings against cocaine's having as deleterious a role in the workplace as alleged. The data base consists of sixty users who reported using cocaine at work. The authors survey a modest body of literature. Steven Wisotsky ["Exposing the War on Cocaine: The Futility and Destructiveness of Prohibition," *Wisconsin Law Review*, 1983] argues for respecting privacy of the home but disallowing public use of drugs. Laws should punish individuals for specific acts of wrong-doing not for drug use per se. Carita Zimmerman ["Urine Testing: Testing-Based Employment Decisions and the Rehabilitation Act of 1973," *Columbia Journal of Law and Social Problems*, 1989] outlines the inaccuracy rate of the tests and sifts through arguments for their irrelevance. She examines problems commonly involved in the implementation of mass employee urine testing programs, discusses objections to employee drug screening (as an unreasonable invasion of privacy), and advances the argument that positive drug testing results as the sole basis for employment decisions, without regard to an individual's actual capabilities, constitutes a violation of the 1973 U.S. Rehabilitation Act. James Felman and Christopher J. Petrini ["Drug Testing and Public Employment: Toward a Rational Application of the Fourth Amendment," *Law and Contemporary Problems*, 1988] consider that, with mandatory testing, individual interests are subordinated to social interests to a greater degree than ever before. Drug testing is a highly intrusive bodily search that invades reasonable privacy rights.

[180]See, for example, Sami M. Abbasi, Kenneth W. Hollman, and Joe H. Murey, Jr., "Drug Testing: The Moral, Constitutional, and Accuracy Issues," *Journal of Collective Negotiations*, 1988; Chris Spolar, "An Off-Duty User's Fate; Firing Reflects Reach of Company Policies," *The Washington Post*, 1988.

[181]Eliot Marshall ["Testing Urine for Drugs," *Science*, 1988] claims that urine tests are not only fast but reasonably accurate. Lawrence Miike and Maria Hewitt, on the other hand ["Accuracy and Reliability of Urine Drug Tests," *Kansas University Law Review*, 1988], might allow for the tests' quickness but still not appreciate the physical intrusion increasingly required to collect reliable urine samples. Beyond this, there is considerable chance for error in mass testing, and even a small error rate will represent large numbers of people. John P. Morgan ["The 'Scientific' Justification for Urine Drug Testing," *Kansas University Law Review*, 1988] adds that the rationale for drug testing via urinary analysis is justified more from religious than scientific language. Chris Spolar ["How Lab Results Can Change Lives; Technology and Accuracy Improve, but Growing Pains Apparent," *The Washington Post*, 1988] allows that high accuracy rates are noted but that they nevertheless do not avoid the substantial problems created when errors are made. There must be safeguards for employees so that procedures for finding and acknowledging testing errors may be institutionalized.

[182]Linda Greenhouse, "Court Backs Tests of Some Workers to Deter Drug Use," *The New York Times*, 1989; Judith Havemann, "Rulings Force Agencies to Reevaluate Test Policies," *The Washington Post*, 1989; Al Kamen, "Court Upholds Conrail Policy on Drug Tests," *The Washington Post*, 1989; and Tracy Thompson, "Ruling Clears Way for Drug Tests of Workers with Top Clearances," *The Washington Post*, 1989.

[183]Shala Mills Bannister, "Drug Testing Legislation: What Are the States Doing?" *Kansas University Law Review*, 1988.

[184]These points are pervasive in the literature. See, for example, Ann F. Brunswick, "Dealing with Drugs: Heroin Abuse as a Social Problem," *The International Journal of the Addictions*, 1986. Gina Kolata ["Community Program Succeeds in Drug Fight," *The New York Times*, 1989] reports on a new study—not yet available to this reviewer—showing that a comprehensive community program that encourages teenagers to avoid drugs, including cigarettes and alcohol, has been much more successful than programs relying only on the schools. K. A. Mufti ["Community Programme in Pakistan Aimed at Preventing and Reducing Drug Abuse," *Bulletin on Narcotics*, 1986] chronicles the growth and development of the Green December Movement in Pakistan, established in 1983, to catalyze community and provincial resources in northwestern Pakistan to treat and rehabilitate drug addicts. Emphasis is placed on the involvement of religious leaders in prevention strategies, particularly in an educational sense for the broad population not yet addicted. This movement appears to have produced positive results. Community projects have been carried out in Hong Kong in a "Youth against Drugs Scheme," which, with community support, provides youths an opportunity to develop and implement antinarcotics publicity projects in their own way with limited supervision [Handrick W. K. Ng, "Drug Demand Reduction Programmes for Young People in Hong Kong," *Bulletin on Narcotics*, 1985]. In Denmark [P. Schioler, "Information, Teaching and Education in the Primary Prevention of Drug Abuse among Youth in Denmark," *Bulletin on Narcotics*, 1981], the call is to integrate education and prevention programs into the very heart and soul of the community. Yugoslavia's comprehensive approach involves community, parents, other members of families, schools, and work-places. True, the Yugoslavian police are intensifying their efforts in order to raise negative deterrence perceptions, but community services agencies are also trying to create "healthy alternative activities" for youth [M. Skrlj, "Programme Base for the Prevention of Drug Abuse in Yugoslavia," *Bulletin on Narcotics*, 1986]. In the Philippines a government coordinating body has facilitated efforts with nongovernmental organizations to make drug-abuse prevention programs more viable and relevant [S.Q. Quejas, "The Role of Non-Governmental Organizations in the Prevention and Reduction of Drug Abuse: The Philippine Experience," *Bulletin on Narcotics*, 1983]. Most of these appear to assume that systemic and integrationalist strategies are called for because drug use is promoted or deterred by conditions in family, school, and peer group, and it cannot be understood simply as a result of individual intrapsychic processes. Inasmuch as these "situational conditions" can only be approached from a systemic community involvement, the rationale for the larger community's involvement is viewed not only as being justified but highly productive [See Martin Shain, William Riddell, and Heather Lee Kilty, *Influence, Choice, and Drugs: Towards a Systematic Approach to the Prevention of Substance Abuse*, 1977].

[185]Isabel Wilkerson, "Detroit Citizens Join with Church to Rid Community of Drugs," *The New York Times*, 1988.

[186]Bob Baker, "Tough Boss Shows Gang Members New Way of Life," *The Los Angeles Times*, 1988.

[187]Celestine Bohlen, "Support Groups Are Offering Embrace to Cocaine's Victims," *The New York Times*, 1989.

[188]Diane Broughton, "Youth Peer Programs Springing up across Country," *Alcoholism and Addiction*, 1986.

[189]Kirsten A. Conover, "Defeating Drug Dealers: Drop-a-Dime Project Pays Off," *The Christian Science Monitor*, 1989.

[190]See R. A. Lindblad, "A Review of the Concerned Parent Movement in the United States of America," *Bulletin on Narcotics*, 1983; Marsha Manatt, *Parents, Peers and Pot II: Parents in Action*, 1983.

[191]See, for example, Eric Pooley's description ["Fighting Back against Crack," *The New York Times*, 1989] of how a number of groups in New York City took on crack dealers in their neighborhoods.

[192]Michel Marriott, "And in the Streets, Citizens Fight Dealers," *The New York Times*, 1989; "How to Oust a Drug Dealer: Ideas for Embattled Tenants," *The New York Times*, 1987.

[193]See Gwen Ifill, "Cities Seek to Emulate Alexandria on Evictions," *The Washington Post*, 1989; Douglas Jehl, "U.S. Waives Tenant Laws to Aid Virginia Battle against Drugs in Public Housing," *The Los Angeles Times*, 1989; Emmanuel P. Popolizio, "At Long Last, A Victory over the Drug Dealers," *The New York Times*, 1988; and Martin Tolchin, "Kemp Vows to Oust Tenants Over Drugs," *The New York Times*, 1989. All this raises problems of due process in the United States. See Jay Mathews, "Cities Target Drug Dealers for Eviction; N.Y. Renters Ousted before Criminal Trial," *The Washington Post*, 1989.

[194]See Peter Kerr, "Citizen Anti-Crack Drive: Vigilance or Vigilantism?" *The New York Times*, 1988; Carl T. Rowen, "The New Lynch Mobs: Drug Vigilantes," *The Washington Post*, 1988; Kenneth T. Walsh, Ronald A. Taylor, and Ted Gest, "The New Drug Vigilantes," *U.S. News and World Report*, 1988; and, Linda Wheeler, "Crack Houses Are Torched in NW Area; Neighborhood Official Doubts Vigilantism," *The Washington Post*, 1989.

[195]See Larry Martz et al., "Trying to Say No," *Newsweek*, 1986.

[196]James C. McKinley, Jr., "Friendships and Fear Erode a Will to Fight Drugs in Brooklyn," *The New York Times*, 1989.

[197]Mary Thornton and Zeynep Alemdar, "Lawmakers Ask TV Networks to Aid Drug Fight," *The Washington Post*, 1986.

[198]See, for example, U.S. Congress, Senate Committee on Labor and Human Resources, Subcommittee on Alcoholism and Drug Abuse, Hearing, "Role of the Media in Drug Abuse Prevention and Education," 1984.

[199]Tom Morganthau and Michael Reese, "Going after Hollywood: Critics Call for the Deglamorization of Drugs," *Newsweek*, 1986.

[200]Patrick T. Macdonald, "Prime Time Drug Depictions," *Contemporary Drug Problems*, 1985.

[201]Patricia Bandy and Patricia Alford President, "Recent Literature on Drug Abuse Prevention and Mass Media: Focusing on Youth, Parents, Women and the Elderly," *Journal of Drug Education*, 1983.

[202]See, for example, William D. Montalbano, "Colombia's Press Pays in Blood for Anti-Drug Stand," *The Los Angeles Times*, 1987; Alan Riding, "Colombia's Press Unites to Fight Drugs," *The New York Times*, 1987; Timothy Ross, "Colombian Media Take on the Drug Lords," *The Christian Science Monitor*, 1987; and, Mark A. Uhlig, "As

Colombian Terror Grows, the Press Becomes the Prey," *The New York Times*, 1989; James Brooke, "Colombia Abductions Signal Escalation of Drug War," *The New York Times*, 1990; and James Brooke, "Colombian Kidnappings Are Gagging the Press," *The New York Times*, 1991.

[203]U.S. Congress, House Select Committee on Narcotics Abuse and Control, *Drugs and Latin America: Economic and Political Impact and U.S. Policy Options*, 1989.

[204]Joseph B. Treaster, "On Toys to TV Shows, Stepping up Drug Fight," *The New York Times*, 1991.

[205]See the references and the text discussions associated with notes 37 and 38, p. 8.

[206]Elaine Sciolino, "World Drug Crop up Sharply in 1989 Despite U.S. Effort," *The New York Times*, 1990. See also Figures 3, 10, 15, and 17.

[207]The methods the United States pursues are described in "Peru: Meese Visit Signals New U.S. Resolve to Eradicate Coca Plant," *Latinamerica Press*, 1988.

[208]See John Whitehead, "U.S. International Narcotics Control Programs and Policies," *Department of State Bulletin*, 1986.

[209]Ibid.

[210]Data for Figures 18 and 19 come from U.S. Department of State, Bureau of International Narcotics Matters, *International Narcotics Control Strategy Report*, 1987; 1988; 1989; 1990; 1991; and "Agency Intensifies Effort in Anti-Drug Fight," *USAID Highlights*, 1988. Most international narcotic control funding seems to be disbursed by the Department of State's Bureau of International Narcotics Matters and the Agency for International Development. The U.S. Information Agency is also involved in international narcotics control ["Agency Intensifies Effort," *USAID Highlights*, 1988], but funding information is not reported for its programs. Overall, the figures reported are probably reasonable estimations of U.S. international narcotic control funding for the years considered.

[211]See note 17 and the accompanying text for a general discussion of ASEP.

[212]See the discussion in note 27.

[213]See, for example, Michael Isikoff, "Warriors against Cocaine: It's Guerrilla Warfare for DEA Agents on the Bolivian Front Lines," *The Washington Post*, 1989; Shirley Christian, "Bolivians Fight Efforts to Eradicate Coca," *The New York Times*, 1987.

[214]The current literature is discussed in note 55, Chapter 4.

[215]Mark Day, "Peru: Battle Intensifies over Renewed Drug Eradication Plan," *Latinamerica Press*, 1989; Michael Massing, "In the Cocaine War the Jungle is Winning, *The New York Times Magazine*, 1990.

[216]In addition to the bibliographical discussion in note 14, Chapter 1, regarding labor union organization to resist eradication, see Graham Bradley, "Bolivian Barometer: Coca Price Falls," *The Washington Post*, 1986; James Painter's two articles ["Bolivia to Crack Down on Coca," *The Christian Science Monitor*, 1989; and "Bolivia's New President Faces an Old Problem: How to Control Coca Growing," *Latinamerica Press*, 1989]; and "Peasants Protest at Coca Plan," *Latin American Weekly Report*, 1987.

[217]Synopses of much of the debate are contained in Instituto Latinoamericano de Investigaciones Sociales, "La Economía Campesina y el Cultivo de la Coca," *Debate Agrario*, 1987.

[218]The bibliography is discussed in note 65, Chapter 4.

[219]"Cocaine Traffickers Kill 17 in Peru Raid on Antidrug Team," *The New York Times*, 1984.

[220]Apparently, the spraying of U.S. public lands has been under way since the mid-1970s. The first involuntary spraying of private U.S. land that involved the DEA occurred in 1988 ["Paraquat Is Sprayed on Marijuana in Texas," *The New York Times*, 1988].

[221]See John Whitehead, "U.S. International Narcotics Control Programs and Policies," *Department of State Bulletin*, 1986; and Mexico's own white paper on the subject [*Mexican Topics: Questions Involving Mexico That Have Aroused International Public Interest*, 1986]. James Van Wert's Ph.D. dissertation is a good source for early efforts ["U.S.–Mexican Aerial Opium Eradication Program: A Summative Evaluation," 1982].

[222]See Bertil Lintner, "The Deadly Deluge," *Far Eastern Economic Review*, 1987; Denis D. Gray, "Hailed US Herbicide Campaign Comes under Attack," *Nation*, 1987.

[223]U.S. Department of State, Bureau of International Narcotics Matters, *International Narcotics Control Strategy Report*, 1989; Brook Larmer, "US Targets Guatemalan Opium," *The Christian Science Monitor*, 1990.

[224]"Bolivia: Herbicides Used against Coca, Report Says," *Latinamerica Press*, 1988.

[225]Michael L. Smith, "Peru Calls for U.S. to Join in Tougher Anti-Coca Effort," *The Washington Post*, 1988.

[226]Michael Isikoff, "Peruvian Coca Fields Sprayed in Test of Plan," *The Washington Post*, 1989; "Peru Begins Spraying of Aerial Coca Killer," *Latinamerica Press*, 1989.

[227]Kathy Smith Boe, "Paraquat Eradication: Legal Means for a Prudent Policy?" *Environmental Affairs*, 1985.

[228]Philip J. Landrigan et al., "Paraquat and Marijuana: Epidemiologic Risk Assessment," *American Journal of Public Health*, 1983.

[229]L. Garmon, "Pot-Smokers May Be Imperiled by Paraquat-Spraying Program," *Science News*, 1983.

[230]Michael Isikoff, "Paraquat Spraying to Resume at Suspected Marijuana Fields; Opponents Threaten to Block DEA Plan in Court," *The Washington Post*, 1988.

[231]Edith T. Mirante, "A Rare Look at America's Opium War—From the Ground Up," *Earth Island Journal*, 1989.

[232]Amy Stevens, "State Balks at Paraquat Use on Marijuana Fields," *The Los Angeles Times*, 1988.

[233]U.S. Congress, House Select Committee on Narcotics Abuse and Control, Hearing, "Is Paraquat-Sprayed Marihuana Harmful or Not?," 1980; U.S. Congress, House Select Committee on Narcotics Abuse and Control, Hearing, "Health Implications of Paraquat-Contaminated Marihuana," 1979.

[234]U.S. Congress, House Select Committee on Narcotics Abuse and Control, Report, "The Use of Paraquat to Eradicate Illicit Marihuana Crops and the Health Implications of Paraquat-Contaminated Marihuana on the U.S. Market," 1980.

[235]Malcolm Gladwell, "Plan to Curb Drug Trade in Peru Set Back: Eli Lilly Refuses to Sell Herbicide," *The Washington Post*, 1988.

[236]One radical source claims that the spraying has less to do with drug control than with counter-insurgency tactics [Mary Jo McConahay and Robin Kirk, "Over There," *Mother Jones*, 1989]. This point aside, the U.S. Government Accounting Office (GAO) concluded that maintaining aerial eradication at current levels would not eliminate Mexico as a major source of heroin and marijuana [U.S. General Accounting Office, Report to the Congress, *Drug Control: U.S.-Mexico Opium Poppy and Marijuana Aerial Eradication Program*, 1988]. Peter A. Lupsha ["Drug Trafficking: Mexico and Colombia in Comparative Perspective," *Journal of International Affairs*, 1981] holds that, regard-

less of any success in Mexico, one ought not to look toward applying an herbicide program in Colombia because it would not work in that country. On the other hand, James Van Wert ["U.S.–Mexican Aerial Opium Eradication Program: A Summative Evaluation," Ph.D. diss., 1982] argues that the Mexican program on opium was quite successful.

[237]Mary Dempsey, "Butterflies Thwart Cocaine Barons," *New Scientist*, 1988.

[238]United States Department of State, Bureau of International Narcotics Matters, *International Narcotics Control Strategy Report*, 1991, p. 229.

[239]U.S. Department of State, Bureau of International Narcotics Matters, *International Narcotics Control Strategy Report*, 1990, 1991.

[240]Ibid. Note that the 1991 report revises the figures downward, from 47,590 to 30,200 metric tons. See also Elaine Sciolino, "World Drug Crop Up Sharply in 1989 Despite U.S. Effort," *The New York Times*, 1990.

[241]United Nations, Division of Narcotic Drugs, *Declaration of the International Conference on Drug Abuse and Illicit Trafficking and Comprehensive Multidisciplinary Outline of Future Activities in Drug Abuse Control*, 1988, p. 40. See also the bibliographic discussion in note 9.

[242]The 1987 UN conference on drug abuse and illicit trafficking (Vienna) suggested action at national, regional, and international levels, calling, in particular, for states to "observe and give full effect to the principles embodied in the 1961 and 1971 Conventions" [United Nations, Division of Narcotic Drugs, *Declaration of the International Conference on Drug Abuse and Illicit Trafficking and Comprehensive Multidisciplinary Outline of Future Activities in Drug Abuse Control*, p. 41].

[243]See, for example, Kai Bird and Max Holland, "Paraguay: The Stroessner Connection," *Nation*, 1985; "Cocaine Route Turns North," *Latin American Weekly Report*, 1985; and "The Guaraní Connection," *Latin American Regional Reports*, 1985.

[244]John M. Goshko, "U.S. Prods Paraguay on Cocaine," *The Washington Post*, 1985.

[245]Joel Brinkley, "Paraguay Pledges Action on Cocaine," *The New York Times*, 1985.

[246]"Paraguay Refuses to Destroy Cocaine Production Chemicals," *Narcotics Control Digest*, 1985.

[247]Joel Brinkley, "Paraguay Pledges Action on Cocaine," *The New York Times*, 1985.

[248]William R. Doerner, "The Chemical Connection," *Time*, 1989.

[249]Timothy Ross, "Colombia's Bid to Cut off Drug-Processing Chemicals Backfires," *The Christian Science Monitor*, 1987.

[250]Janice Long, "House Approves Chemical Diversion Bill," *Chemical and Engineering News*, 1987.

[251]Robert Pear, "Draft Treaty Seeks to Take the Profit out of Drugs," *The New York Times*, 1988.

[252]This subject is one of many raised in U.S. Department of State, Bureau of International Narcotics Matters, *International Narcotics Control Strategy Report*, 1989.

[253]Lucia Mouat, "UN Session Plots a Global Antidrug Strategy," *The Christian Science Monitor*, 1990.

[254]Camille Groedidler ["Mexico Becoming Center of Drug Traffic Despite Anti-Drug Drive," *The Christian Science Monitor*, 1984] describes how, as early as 1984, Mexico was becoming a key transhipment state for drugs from Latin America to the United States. Cocaine factories—never before seen in Mexico—were moving into the country and were processing coca paste from South America. The needed petrochemical ingredients were more available and less controlled in Mexico than in conventional countries of

narcotics origin.

[255]Alan Riding ["Brazil Acting to Halt New Trafficking in Cocaine," *The New York Times*, 1987] describes how South American drug trafficking rings have moved into Brazil, which has good airline connections and easier access to the vital chemicals required to process coca and coca paste into cocaine.

[256]See U.S. Congress, House Select Committee on Narcotics Abuse and Control, Report, "Latin American Study Missions Concerning International Narcotics Problems," 1986; U.S. Department of State, Bureau of International Narcotics Matters, *International Narcotics Control Strategy Report*, 1989; and, note 15 of the *Introduction* to this handbook.

[257]Alan Riding, "Brazil Acting to Halt New Trafficking in Cocaine," *The New York Times*, 1987. See also the bibliographic discussion in note 15 of the *Introduction*.

[258]Since the early 1980s Kasetsart University, Bangkok, Thailand, has carried out more than a dozen agronomic feasibility studies for opium poppy substitution, which it has published in its Highland Agricultural Project series. Chiang Mai University in Chiang Mai, Thailand, published in 1981 a two-volume work on medicinal plants as economic replacement crops for the opium poppy in northern Thailand, and, in 1984, the Maejo Institute of Agricultural Technology, Chiang Mai, worked on cultivars of tomato, lettuce, and cucumber. Crop substitution feasibility seemed an open enough possibility. But the problem was deeper than simple agronomic considerations; it involved the economic and political fabric of the nation. Some of the difficulties are discussed by John McBeth ["The Opium Laws," *Far Eastern Economic Review*, 1984]; and some of the successes are described by *The Christian Science Monitor* ["Thailand: Antidrug Success Story, 1988] and the *Far Eastern Economic Review* ["Where Poppies Once Stood," 1984].

[259]The success in Cauca is reported by Tyler Bridges ["Colombian Farmers Start Anew after Coca 'Bonanza,'" *The Christian Science Monitor*, 1986] and Timothy Ross ["UN Aid Helps Some Colombians Shake Free of Coca Dependency," *The Christian Science Monitor*, 1988]. Mark A. Uhlig ["Colombia's War on Cocaine: Farmers' Fears Help Cause," *The New York Times*, 1989] describes some of the negative forces that help account for the success.

[260]Edward Girardet, "Helping Farmers Shake Poppy Habit," *The Christian Science Monitor*, 1989.

[261]Joel Brinkley ["In the Drug War, Battles Won and Lost," *The New York Times*, 1984] reports pessimistically on Peru's crop substitution program, as does Everett G. Martin ["High Drama in the Jungles of Peru: Fight against Cocaine Is a Tangled-up Affair," *The Wall Street Journal*, 1984].

[262]Shirley Christian ["Bolivian Peasants Pin Hopes on Coca; Despite Government Program to Eradicate Plants, Poor Are Increasing Crops," *The New York Times*, 1988; and "Bolivia Shifts Tactics in Drug Fight," *The New York Times*, 1989] lays failure on the severe shortage of money for the government to carry out its crop substitution and relocation programs and the inability of the military otherwise to coerce the desired behavior. D. A. Eastwood and H. J. Pollard ["Colonization and Cocaine in the Chapare, Bolivia: A Development Paradox for Colonization Theory," *Tijdschrift Voor Economishe en Sociale Geografie*, 1986] lay failure strictly on economics—peasants make more money growing coca. The same point is raised by Michael Isikoff, "DEA in Bolivia: 'Guerrilla Warfare,' Coca Traffic Proves Resistant," *The Washington Post*, 1989. It should be noted that the Associated Press put out a release in January 1988 quoting the Bolivian program's director, Anibal Aguilar, as saying that the crop substitution program

sponsored by the United States had met with unprecedented success [reported in a U.S. regional newspaper, the *Herald*, under the heading of "Bolivian Farmers Persuaded to Destroy Coca," 1988]. As of 1990 matters may have materially changed in Bolivia because of the economic crisis brought on by depressed coca leaf prices [James Painter, "Bolivia Tries to Break Its Economic Addiction," *The Christian Science Monitor*, 1990].

[263]Bertil Lintner ["Tax Revenue from Opium Helps Finance the Party," *Far Eastern Economic Review*, 1987] describes the travails of rural peasants who find that governmental crop substitution programs have produced only famine and crisis for them. So they have reverted to growing opium poppies. A dominant Burmese political party helps to finance itself by taxing the opium trade. In areas dominated by the Chinese-sponsored CPB party, opium is the only cash crop.

[264]Aside from the country-specific illustrations of Bolivia, Peru, and Burma noted in the main text, see the country reports on Burma, Pakistan, Mexico, and Peru mentioned by Joel Brinkley ["In the Drug War, Battles Won and Lost," *The New York Times*, 1984].

[265]This line of economic analysis is pursued by René Bascope Aspiazú, *La Veta Blanca: Coca y Cocaína en Bolivia*, 1982; Carlos Norberto Cagliotti, "La Economía de la Coca en Bolivia," *Revista de la Sanidad de las Fuerzas Policiales*, 1981; Amado Canelas-Orellana and Juán Carlos Canelas Zannier, *Bolivia, Coca, Cocaína: Subdesarrollo y Poder Político*, 1983; Richard B. Craig, "Illicit Drug Traffic: Implications for South American Source Countries," *Journal of Interamerican Studies and World Affairs*, 1987; Jorge Dandler, "El Desarrollo de la Agricultura, Políticas Estatales y el Proceso de Acumulación en Bolivia," *Estudios Rurales Latinoamericanos*, 1984; Samuel Doria Medina, La Economía Informal en Bolivia, 1986; D. A. Eastwood and H. J. Pollard, "Colonization and Cocaine in the Chapare, Bolivia: A Development Paradox for Colonization Theory," *Tijdschrift Voor Economishe en Sociale Geografie*, 1986; Instituto Latinoamericano de Investigaciones Sociales, "La Economía Campesina y el Cultivo de la Coca," *Debate Agrario*, 1987; Andre McNicoll, *Drug Trafficking: A North-South Perspective*, 1983; and James Painter, "Bolivia's New President Faces an Old Problem: How to Control Coca Growing," *Latinamerica Press*, 1989. Painter notes that the peasants are reluctant to accept positive economic incentives in Bolivia of almost $2,000 a hectare (about $800 an acre) to enter crop substitution programs.

[266]A general perspective on this issue is developed by Andre McNicoll, *Drug Trafficking: A North-South Perspective*, 1983. In Bolivia's case, part of the problem has been a lack of institutional support for alternative crops, including financial credit for a reasonable length of time [see James Painter, "Bolivia's New President Faces an Old Problem," *Latinamerica Press*, 1989].

[267]For years the United Nations Fund for Drug Abuse Control (UNFDAC) has carried out a substitution and demonstration project in Thailand's hill country [John McBeth, "The Opium Laws," *Far Eastern Economic Review*, 1984]. It has also given assistance to Colombia's Cauca province (See the bibliographical discussion in note 258).

[268]Guy Gugliotta, "Bennett Urges Aid to Divert Coca Economy," *The Miami Herald*, 1989.

[269]See the bibliographic discussion in note 7, Chapter 1.

[270]The U.S. ambassador to Bolivia, Robert Gelbard, explained his program during an October 1989 visit to Brigham Young University's David M. Kennedy Center for International Studies.

[271]Refer to notes 258 and 259 for a bibliographic discussion.

[272]As early as 1983 Andre McNicoll [*Drug Trafficking: A North-South Perspective*, 1983] tried to shed light on this problem in a straightforward study on the relative roles of supply and demand in the drug trade. Until McNicoll's publication, most discussions tended to concentrate on negative sanctions (e.g., crop eradication) as opposed to demand and prevention as a means to reduce illicit drug problems. But, if one desires control of supply to be part of an overall drug-reduction strategy, one must focus, he said, on the economies of producer societies as contributors to the international flow of illegal narcotics. Because it is a huge economic factor in some developing countries, the drug trade must be addressed in economic terms. One of the antidotes he laid out was *rural development*. Of course, rural development within the context of an overall economic development plan has been advanced vigorously for some time. [See, for example, an article and two books in which this reviewer has discussed some of them: F. LaMond Tullis, "The Current View on Rural Development: Fad or Breakthrough in Latin America?" in *An International Political Economy*, vol. 1 of *International Political Economy Yearbook*, 1985; F. LaMond Tullis and W. Ladd Hollist, eds., *Food, the State, and International Political Economy*, 1986; and Ladd Hollist and LaMond Tullis, eds., *Pursuing Food Security: Strategies and Obstacles in Africa, Asia, Latin America, and the Middle East*, 1987]. That rural development should be a principal focus for anyone interested in doing something about illicit narcotics is a theme increasingly heard, as evidenced, for example, by Charles Stuart Park's ["The Coke War," *Atlantic*, 1987] brief letter to the editor of *Atlantic*. He argued vigorously and persuasively against David Kline's prior *Atlantic* article, in 1987, on "How to Lose the Coke War." Park sees the solution to failures in coca eradication not to be in high-visibility, high-speed strikes, but rather in long-term programs of essential rural development accompanied by appropriate economic incentives for crop substitution. This is the position taken by Edmundo Morales ["Comprehensive Economic Development: An Alternative Measure to Reduce Cocaine Supply," *The Journal of Drug Issues*, 1990].

[273]Refer to Chapter 4.

[274]Notable mention of corrupting influences are made for the Bahamas [Bahamas Commission of Inquiry, *Report of the Commission of Inquiry*, 1984]; Peru [Marcial Barrón, *El Infierno Blanco*, 1984]; Paraguay [Kai Bird and Max Holland, "Paraguay: The Stroessner Connection," *Nation*, 1985]; Costa Rica [Richard Bordreaux, "Scandal Spotlights Costa Rica's Battle on Drugs," *The Los Angeles Times*, 1989]; Colombia [Alvaro Camacho-Guizado, *Droga, Corrupción y Poder: Marijuana y Cocaína en la Sociedad Colombiana*, 1981]; Honduras [Robert Collier, "Honduras: Mounting Evidence Implicates Armed Forces in Cocaine Trafficking," *Latinamerica Press*, 1988]; Bolivia [Michael Flatte and Alexei J. Cowett, "Drugs and Politics: An Unhealthy Mix," *Harvard International Review*, 1986]; Cuba [Michael Isikoff, "Drug Flights Unabated over Cuba," *The Washington Post*, 1989]; Burma [Suzanne McBee, "Flood of Drugs—A Losing Game," *U.S. News and World Report*, 1985]; El Salvador [Craig Pyes and Laurie Becklund, "Inside Dope in El Salvador," *The New Republic*, 1985]; Nigeria [Michael T. De Sanctis, "Nigerians Becoming More Active in the Smuggling of Southwest Asian Heroin in the U.S., Europe," *Narcotics Control Digest*, 1985]; the United States [Jim Schachter, "Customs Service Cleans House in a Drive on Drug Corruption," *The Los Angeles Times*, 1987; "Slice of Vice: More Miami Cops Arrested," *Time*, 1986]; Trinidad and Tobago ["Secret Report on Drugs Is Leaked," *Latin American Weekly Report*, 1987]; Brazil [Percival de Souza, *Society-Cocaína*, 1981]; Nepal [Rone Tempest, "Drugs, Murder Attempt, Corruption Rob Peaceful Nepal of Its Innocence," *The Los Angeles Times*, 1987]; and Pakistan [Richard M. Weintraub, "Pakistani Drug Drive Seen in 2 Major Hauls," *The Washington Post*, 1986; Yev Yelin, "Why the 'Golden Crescent'

Still Flourishes," *The New York Times*, 1985].

[275]One of the most striking cases involves two principal units of the Luxembourg-based Bank of Credit and Commerce International. In the first U.S. federal case of money laundering against a large international bank, this one pleaded guilty to reduced charges and agreed to forfeit $14 million. See Jeff Gerth, "2 Foreign Bank Units Plead Guilty to Money Laundering," *The New York Times*, 1990.

[276]The most striking case is the traffickers' (in apparent alliance with the Colombian M-19 insurgency group) assassination of over one-half the justices of the Colombian Supreme Court, all in one fell swoop [John Ross, "Colombia: Judge's Murder Linked to Drug Mafias," *Latinamerica Press*, 1986; Miguel Varon, "Colombia: Drug Bosses Wage War against Extradition," *Latinamerica Press*, 1988]. For an analysis of *Sendero Luminoso* and *Túpac Amaru* in Peru, see Cynthia McClintock, "The War on Drugs: The Peruvian Case," *Journal of Interamerican Studies and World Affairs*, 1988.

[277]The best examples appear to be the indiscriminate terrorism waged in Burma, Colombia, and Peru [see, respectively, David L. Westrate, "Drug Trafficking and Terrorism," *Drug Enforcement*, 1985; Leslie Wirpsa, "Colombian Mafia Hurt by Testimony of Key Deserter, *The Miami Herald*, 1989; and Alan Riding, "Peru's Two Complex Battles: Drugs and Terror," *The New York Times*, 1987].

[278]The archetypical example is *Sendero Luminoso*, which now effectively controls much of Peru's principal coca producing area, the upper Huallaga Valley. See Merrill Collett, "Maoist Guerrilla Band Complicates Antidrug War in Peru," *The Washington Post*, 1988. Refer also to the bibliographic discussion in note 55, Chapter 4.

[279]See Scott Armstrong and Karia Vallance, "U.S.–Bolivia Relations Further Strained as Cocaine Smuggling Charges Fly," *The Christian Science Monitor*, 1980; "Cocaine: The Military Connection," *Latin American Regional Reports*, 1980; and Gregorio Selser, *Bolivia: El Cuartelazo de los Cocadólares*, 1982.

[280]See, for example, Steve Ropp, "General Noriega's Panama," *Current History*, 1986.

[281]See, for example, Barbara Crossette, "Thai Officials Say Laos Turns to Marijuana to Help Budget," *The New York Times*, 1987; Peter Kerr, "U.S. Says Laos Government Is Deeply Involved in Drugs," *The New York Times*, 1988; Rodney Tasker, "Chasing the Red Dragon," *Far Eastern Economic Review*, 1987; U.S. Department of State, Bureau of International Narcotics Matters, *International Narcotics Control Strategy Report*, 1989; E. A. Wayne, "US Dilemma with Laos: Protect the Living—or Dead?" *The Christian Science Monitor*, 1988; and Ann B. Wrobleski, "Presidential Certification of Narcotics Source Countries," *Current Policy*, 1988.

[282]A supporting discussion dealing with the social psychology of members of the Colombian Medellín cartel and the apparent representative smugglers operating in the United States is given by Joseph B. Treaster, "Colombia's Cali Drug Cartel: The Less Flamboyant Competitor of Medellín," *The New York Times*, 1989; and by Patricia A. Adler, *Wheeling and Dealing: An Ethnography of an Upper-Level Drug Dealing and Smuggling Community*, 1985. The "normal" trafficker (Cali cartel members excepted) appears to have a relatively low time horizon and finds deferring gratification an extremely unsettling experience.

[283]Discussed by Tom Wells, Associated Press writer, and reported in a U.S. regional newspaper ["Cocaine Cartel Cries Uncle, Asks Colombia for Pardon," *Salt Lake Tribune*, 18 January 1990]. More recently some cartel leaders are surrendering under government guarantees of reduced sentences and no extradition to the United States [Clifford Krauss, "Colombian Leader is Hailed by Bush," *The New York Times*, 1991]. An analysis of

political perspectives on this issue is given by Juan Gabriel Tokatlián ["National Security and Drugs: Their Impact on Colombian–U.S. Relations," *Journal of Interamerican Studies and World Affairs*, 1988].

[284]Denis D. Gray ["A Deluge from the Golden Triangle," *Nation*, 1989] discusses an apparent pact between Khun Sa and the Burmese government.

[285]In the fall of 1986 Colombia's Medellín drug cartel, the world's largest, offered to abandon its trade and to provide sensitive intelligence about guerrilla movements in Colombia in return for amnesty from prosecution [Michael Isikoff, "Medellín Cartel Leaders Offered U.S. a Deal," *The Washington Post*, 1988].

[286]Background on the enigmatic José Rodríguez Gacha is provided by Jonas Bernstein, "Bitter Convulsions in a Nation under the Influence of Drugs," *Insight*, 1989; Jeff Leen, "Bush Lauds Colombia Drug Battle," *The Miami Herald*, 1989; and Joseph B. Treaster, "Colombia Turns Drug War Into a Long Chase," *The New York Times*, 1989.

[287]The reference is to the Latin American phenomenon of *personalismo*. While the term has wide application in social interaction, in an organizational sense it is a condition of exaggerated importance of a leader who purposefully maintains weak institutional structures in order to enhance the appearance of his indispensability. See, in general, the discussion by Glen Caudill Dealy, *The Public Man*, 1977.

[288]Peter Reuter has pursued this argument. See, for example, Jonathan A. K. Cave and Peter Reuter, *The Interdictor's Lot: A Dynamic Model of the Market for Drug Smuggling Services*, 1988; G. B. Crawford and Peter Reuter, *Simulation of Adaptive Response: A Model of Drug Interdiction*, 1988; and Peter Reuter, "Eternal Hope: America's Quest for Narcotics Control, *The Public Interest*, 1985.

[289]International interdiction efforts range all the way from increasing U.S. Coast Guard activities [e.g., Paul A. Yost, "Coast Guard Activities, Performance Increase Despite Budget Difficulties," *Sea Technology*, 1988] to supplying high-tech speedboats to the Bolivian navy to patrol its own rivers [U.S. General Accounting Office, Fact Sheet, *Drug Control: River Patrol Craft for the Government of Bolivia*, 1988], which some Bolivian officers promptly proceeded to use in collusion with the traffickers! [Erick Foronda, "Bolivia: Military Exposé Attests Official Protection of Drug-lords," *Latinamerica Press*, 1988]. The efforts include tethered balloons along the U.S. southwestern border, which Peter Reuter compares to the Maginot Line [Michael Isikoff, "Fighting the Drug War: From Arizona to Fairfax," *The Washington Post*, 1988], and a four-mile-long ditch along a stretch of the U.S.–Mexican border [Matt Lait, "At the Border, Deep Concern about a Shallow Ditch," *The Washington Post*, 1989], which some have called "our buried Berlin Wall" ["U.S. Plans 4-Mile Ditch on Border to Stem Drug Flow to California," *The New York Times*, 1989]. Clearly, much of the "interdiction literature" offers a variety of views regarding appropriateness if not "effectiveness." See, for example, Richard B. Craig, "La Campaña Permanente: Mexico's Antidrug Campaign," *Journal of Interamerican Studies and World Affairs*, 1978; J. Michael Kennedy, "Aerial Drug War Has Its Ups, Downs," *The Los Angeles Times*, 1989; Patrick McDonnell, "Odds Still with Smugglers in U.S. Air War against Drugs," *The Los Angeles Times*, 1988; Peter Reuter, "Intercepting the Drugs: Big Cost, Small Results," *The Washington Post*, 1988; Peter Reuter, *Can the Borders Be Sealed?*, 1988; U.S. Congress, Office of Technology Assessment, *The Border War on Drugs*, 1987; U.S. Government Accounting Office, Report to Congressional Requesters, *Drug Smuggling: Capabilities for Interdicting Private Aircraft Are Limited and Costly*, 1989; and Mary Welch, "The Extraterritorial War on Cocaine: Perspectives from Bolivia and Colombia," *Suffolk Transnational Law Journal*, 1988. A general evaluation of interdiction (and other traffic-suppression

policy options) is given by Mark Fraser and Nance Kohlert ["Substance Abuse and Public Policy," *Social Service Review*, 1988]. Some mention is made of U.S. interagency rivalry associated with interdiction efforts [e.g., Michael Isikoff, "Drug Fighters Resist Unifying, Senators Say," *The Washington Post*, 1988].

290See note 50 for a bibliographic discussion of the controversy surrounding the involvement of U.S. military forces. The decision having been made to involve the U.S. Navy in substantial operations off the Colombian coast, the new controversy is that the Colombians do not want them. See Michael Gordon, "U.S. Delays Plan to Station Ships Close to Colombia," *The New York Times*, 1990. The never-ending discussion as to the appropriateness of military intervention in the drug war is exemplified by John P. Coffey, "The Navy's Role in Interdicting Narcotics Traffic: War on Drugs or Ambush on the Constitution?" *The Georgetown Law Journal*, 1987. See also Morris J. Blachman and Kenneth E. Sharpe, "The War on Drugs: American Democracy under Assault," *World Policy Journal*, 1990.

291Perhaps the most striking example is the port at Kingston, Jamaica. Legitimate shipping out of that port had become a target for smuggling, aided, in part, by organized narcotics criminals, but also by shipping-lines employees and dockyard guards. Consequently, some companies boycotted making further deliveries from Kingston to the United States, a factor that caused port business to fall by 50 percent in less than a year [Daniel Machalaba, "Shipping Lines Fall Prey to Drug Dealers," *The Asian Wall Street Journal*, 1989].

292See, for example, Jeff Gerth, "2 Foreign Bank Units Plead Guilty to Money Laundering," *The New York Times*, 1990; Paula Dwyer, "Getting Banks to Just Say 'No,'" *Business Week*, 1989; and Andrea M. Grilli, "Preventing Billions from Being Washed Offshore; A Growing Approach to Stopping International Drug Trafficking," *Syracuse Journal of International Law and Commerce*, 1987.

293See, for example, John Dombrink and James W. Meeker, "Beyond 'Buy and Bust': Nontraditional Sanctions in Federal Drug Law Enforcement," *Contemporary Drug Problems*, 1986; John Dombrink, James W. Meeker, and Julie Paik, "Fighting for Fees—Drug Trafficking and the Forfeiture of Attorney's Fees," *Journal of Drug Issues*, 1988; Donna Gehrke and Aaron Epstein, "Lawyers Dealt Setback in Drug-Case Defenses," *The Miami Herald*, 1989; Al Kamen, "Court Curbs Use of Criminals' Assets to Pay Lawyers," *The Washington Post*, 1989; and Gordon Witkin, "Hitting Kingpins in Their Assets," *U.S. News and World Report*, 1988.

294One of the best early reviews is by Rodney T. Stamler ["Forfeiture of the Profits and Proceeds of Drug Crimes," *Bulletin on Narcotics*, 1984]. An excellent later review is by Andrea M. Grilli ["Preventing Billions from Being Washed Offshore: A Growing Approach to Stopping International Drug Trafficking," *Syracuse Journal of International Law and Commerce*, 1987].

295See the bibliographic entries in note 170 for mention of provisions in Italy, India, and the United States. Additionally, for the United States, see U.S. General Accounting Office, Report to the Subcommittee on Crime, Committee on the Judiciary, House of Representatives, *Seized Conveyances: Justice and Customs Correction of Previous Conveyance Management Problems*, 1988; and also "State Asset Forfeiture Laws Can Help Stop Drug Traffic, Beef up Police Budgets," *Crime Control Digest*, 1985. A legal review of the early 1970 laws and their successors is offered by William J. Corcoran and Martin C. Carlson ["Criminal Prosecution of Drug Traffickers under the Continuing Criminal Enterprises Statute in Federal Courts of the United States of America," *Bulletin on Narcotics*, 1983]. For France, see C. Jacquemart, "An Assessment of Legal Measures to Trace, Freeze and Confiscate the Proceeds of Drug Crimes in France: The Customs Viewpoint," *Bulletin on Narcotics*, 1984. For Australia, see M. Moynihan, "Law Enforcement and Drug Trafficking Money: Recent Developments in Australian Law and Procedure," *Bulletin on Narcotics*, 1983. For Sweden see S. Riberdahl, "Forfeiture of the Proceeds of Drug-Related Crimes: A Swedish Point of View," *Bulletin on Narcotics*, 1984. For Malaysia, see K. C. Vohrah, "Forfeiture of the Profits and Proceeds Derived from Drug Trafficking: Thoughts on Future Action in Malaysia," *Bulletin on Narcotics*, 1984. For Egypt see M. S. Zaki, "Egyptian Law on the Sequestration and Confiscation of Property Acquired through Smuggling and Trafficking in Drugs," *Bulletin on Narcotics*, 1983. There is a problem of depriving innocent transporters interest in their property [Bruce C. Conybeare, Jr., "Federal Civil Forfeiture: An Ill-Conceived Scheme Unfairly Deprives an Innocent Party of Its Property Interest," *University of Detroit Law Review*, 1984].

[296]Lucia Mouat, "UN Session Plots Global Antidrug Strategy," *The Christian Science Monitor*, 1990.

[297]Kim Murphy, "Seizure of Pot Grower's Property Upheld," *The Los Angeles Times*, 1987.

[298]Michael Wines, "Law Enabled U.S. to Seize Proceeds of Drug Money Scheme," *The New York Times*, 1989.

[299]See the vigorous discussion by N. Liverpool, "The Seizure and Forfeiture of Property Associated with Criminal Activity," *Bulletin on Narcotics*, 1983.

[300]George A. Kurisky, Jr., "Civil Forfeiture of Assets: A Final Solution to International Drug Trafficking?" *Houston Journal of International Law*, 1988.

[301]See, for example, William Overend, "Failure to Share Funds Could Cripple War on Drugs, Gates Says," *The Los Angeles Times*, 1987; Steven Zimmerman, "A Windfall in Recovered Assets," *Drug Enforcement*, 1984;" and State Asset Forfeiture Laws Can Help Stop Drug Traffic, Beef Up Police Budgets," *Crime Control Digest*, 1985.

[302]William Raspberry, "Sharing the Drug Peddlers' Profits," *The Washington Post*, 1988.

[303]Barbara Bradley, "Users Now Prime Targets in U.S. Antidrug Offensive," *The Christian Science Monitor*, 1988.

[304]Douglas Jehl, "U.S. Ends Seizures of Vessels under 'Zero Tolerance' Policy," *The Los Angeles Times*, 1989.

[305]See, for example, Bruce C. Conybeare, Jr., "Federal Civil Forfeiture: An Ill-Conceived Scheme Unfairly Deprives an Innocent Party of Its Property Interest," *University of Detroit Law Review*, 1984.

[306]Marshall Ingwerson, "Authorities Target the Profits of Crime," *The Christian Science Monitor*, 1987.

[307]See the political discussion in U.S. Congress, House Subcommittee on Coast Guard and Navigation of the Committee on Merchant Marine and Fisheries, Hearing, "'Zero Tolerance' Drug Policy and Confiscation of Property," 1988.

[308]Nicholas C. McBride, "'Zero Tolerance': Zero Effect? Prosecutors See Few Results from Crackdown on Drug Users," *The Christian Science Monitor*, 1988.

[309]See, for example, Paula Dwyer, "Getting Banks to Just Say 'No.'" *Business Week*, 1989; and Andrea M. Grilli, "Preventing Billions from Being Washed Offshore: A Growing Approach to Stopping International Drug Trafficking," *Syracuse Journal of International Law and Commerce*, 1987.

[310]United Nations, Division of Narcotic Drugs, *Declaration of the International Conference on Drug Abuse and Illicit Trafficking and Comprehensive Multidisciplinary Outline of Future Activities in Drug Abuse Control*, 1988, p. 55.

[311]Paul Houston ["201 in U.S., Italy Charged in Drug Trade," *The Los Angeles Times*, 1988] describes a massive international operation resulting in the arrest of 68 persons in the United States and 133 in Italy, including several in the Sicilian mafia. Stephen Loeper ["20 Tons of Cocaine Confiscated in Los Angeles," *The Salt Lake Tribune*, 1989] describes a lengthy surveillance that ended at a warehouse in a quiet section of the city. It was the largest U.S. cocaine seizure in history. A lengthy Chinese scheme produced the arrest of numerous drug traffickers in 1988 ["China Cracks Big Drug Case," *Beijing Review*, 1988].

[312]Richard Bordreaux ["Scandal Spotlights Costa Rica's Battle on Drugs," *The Los Angeles Times*, 1989] discusses France's insistence that Costa Rica extradite a highly influential resident Argentine national on heroin trafficking. He was.

[313]Robert Linke [*Extradition for Drug-Related Offenses: A Study of Existing Extradition Practices and Suggested Guidelines for Use in Concluding Extradition Treaties*, 1985] provides, in addition to a nice bibliography, a document to assist government officials and jurists in interpreting existing laws and regulations governing extradition cases. The volume may also be of assistance to drafters of domestic legislation in matters relating to extradition and mutual assistance in criminal matters. Steven A. Bernholz, Martin J. Bernholz, and G. Nicholas Herman ["International Extradition in Drug Cases," *North Carolina Journal of International Law and Commercial Regulation*, 1985] review the whole matter from the standpoint of the criminal defense bar, focusing on drug defendants and their rights.

[314]Sometimes the treaties have not worked (failure of bilateral cooperation in implementing their provisions) or, in some cases, aggrieved states have not had treaties. In the mid-1970s the United States resorted to extraordinary means to circumvent the limitations, including abductions (unilateral seizures of alleged offenders) and irregular detentions (law enforcement agent bilateral collaboration, independent of judicial processes, to move alleged offenders into its hands). Abraham Abramovsky and Steven J. Eagle ["U.S. Policy in Apprehending Alleged Offenders Abroad: Extradition, Abduction, or Irregular Detention?," *Oregon Law Review*, 1977] lay out the accusations and legal issues. A 1988 article in *The Economist* ("Honduras: Et Tu?") noted a notorious drug trafficker's abduction—apparently by Americans—in Honduras and his transfer to the United States for incarceration. Wide-eyed protests resulted in Honduras.

[315]See Richard J. Barnett, "Extradition Treaty Improvement to Combat Drug Trafficking," *Georgia Journal of International and Comparative Law*, 1985; Roberta Louise Rubin, "International Agreements: Two Treaties Between the U.S. and Italy," *Harvard International Law Journal*, 1985.

[316]In addition to listings on Colombia cited elsewhere in this subsection, the relevant entries in this handbook's data base include the following: Mario Arango and Jorge Child, *Los Condenados de la Coca: El Manejo Político de la Droga*, 1985; James Brooke, "A Report from the Front Lines in Colombia: The Drug War Will Be Long," *The New York Times*, 1989; Merrill Collett, "Colombia's Losing War with Drug Kings," *The Christian Science Monitor*, 1988; "Colombian Court Backs Extradition," *The New York Times*, 1989; Jeff Leen, "Bush Lauds Colombia Drug Battle," *The Miami Herald*, 1989; M. Niedergang, "Some See Answer to Colombia's Problems in Legal Drugs," *LeMonde/Manchester Guardian Weekly*, 1987; Warren Richey, "Despite Treaty Most Colombian Drug Dealers Escape US Hands," *The Christian Science Monitor*, 1986; Alan

Riding, "Shaken Colombia Acts at Last on Drugs," *The New York Times*, 1984; John Ross, "Colombia: Judge's Murder Linked to Drug Mafias," *Latinamerica Press*, 1986; Juan G. Tokatlian, "National Security and Drugs: Their Impact on Colombian–US Relations," *Journal of Interamerican Studies and World Affairs*, 1988; and Miguel Varon, "Colombia: Drug Bosses Wage War against Extradition," *Latinamerica Press*, 1988.

[317]See J. Richard Barnett, "Extradition Treaty Improvement to Combat Drug Trafficking," *Georgia Journal of International and Comparative Law*, 1985.

[318]"43 Nations Sign U.N. Pact on Fighting Drugs," *The Los Angeles Times*, 1988.

[319]See, for example, the discussion by M. Niedergang, "Some See Answer to Colombia's Problems in Legal Drugs," *LeMonde/Manchester Guardian Weekly*, 1987; Miguel Varon, "Colombia: Drug Bosses Wage War against Extradition," *Latinamerica Press*, 1988.

[320]Merrill Collett, "Colombia's Losing War with Drug Kings," *The Christian Science Monitor*, 1988.

[321]The anxiety extended to American citizens who were living in Colombia and feared becoming indiscriminate terrorist targets in reprisal for Lehder's capture and extradition to the United States ["Americans in Colombia Fear Reprisals for Lehder's Capture," *The Los Angeles Times*, 1987].

[322]The official White Paper on this is the following: *The Fight against the Drug Traffic in Colombia*, Office of the President of the Republic, 1988.

[323]See, for example, the outburst by Mario Arango and Jorge Child, *Los Condenados de la Coca: El Manejo Político de la Droga*, 1985.

[324]See, for example, R. S. Lockwood, "The United States Drug Problem and International Trafficking, Part II, Denial of Safe-Havens to Illicit Drug Traffickers," *International Journal of the Addictions*, 1977.

[325]From *The American Heritage Dictionary*, 2d ed., 1982.

[326]G. B. Crawford et al. have developed a simulation model on interdiction that takes into account smugglers' adaptations to interdiction agencies' strategies [*Simulation of Adaptive Response: A Model of Drug Interdiction*, 1988].

[327]Such arrangements exist, for example, between Bolivia and the United States [Robert P. Hey, "Nations Unite to Fight Drugs: Combating Foreign Supply and US Demand," *The Christian Science Monitor*, 1986].

[328]U.S. Congress, House Committee on the Judiciary, Subcommittee on Crime, Hearing, "Defining Customs Waters for Certain Drug Offenses," 1985. Discussed were provisions of the Marijuana on the High Seas Act, which enables the U.S. Coast Guard to interdict vessels trafficking in drugs even if outside territorial waters.

[329]In reality, prices have fallen drastically while aggregate demand appears not to have fallen much. This suggests greater availability of supply even in the face of increased interdiction and seizure. Peter Reuter consistently points this out [e.g., "Quantity Illusions and Paradoxes of Drug Interdiction: Federal intervention into Vice Policy," *Law and Contemporary Problems*, 1988; *Can the Borders Be Sealed?*, 1988; "Intercepting the Drugs: Big Cost, Small Results," *The Washington Post*, 1988].

[330]Observers point out that heroin demand appears to be quite inelastic with respect to price—prices could skyrocket without a proportionate decrease in demand. See James V. Koch and Stanley E. Grupp, "The Economics of Drug Control Policies," *The International Journal of the Addictions*, 1971; Lester P. Silverman and Nancy L. Spruill, "Urban Crime and the Price of Heroin," *Journal of Urban Economics*, 1977; and

Michael D. White and William A. Luksetich "Heroin: Price Elasticity and Enforcement Strategies," *Economic Inquiry*, 1983. Crack cocaine may be equally inelastic. There is probably greater price elasticity of demand with regular cocaine and with marijuana.

[331]Representative activities are discussed in U.S. General Accounting Office, Report to Congressional Requesters, "Drug Interdiction: Operation Autumn Harvest: A National Guard–Customs Anti-Smuggling Effort," 1988.

[332]See, for example, the discussions in U.S. Congress, House Select Committee on Narcotics Abuse and Control, Hearing, "Drug Abuse and Trafficking along the Southwest Border (Tucson)," 1986. A history of Border Patrol policies and procedures may be found in U.S. Congress, Senate Committee on Governmental Affairs, "Border Management Reorganization and Drug Interdiction," 1988.

[333]Many observers judge that a pilot experienced in smuggling is unlikely to be caught entering the United States from Mexico or the Caribbean [e.g., Patrick McDonnell, "Odds Still with Smugglers in U.S. Air War against Drugs," *The Los Angeles Times*, 1988; Michael Mecham, "Drug Smugglers Prove Elusive Targets for Interdiction Forces," *Aviation Week and Space Technology*, 1989]. There has been some discussion about shooting down suspected aircraft that ignore signals to land.

[334]United Nations, Division of Narcotic Drugs, *Declaration of the International Conference on Drug Abuse and Illicit Trafficking and Comprehensive Multidisciplinary Outline of Future Activities in Drug Abuse Control*, 1988, pp. 68-71. Philosophical discussions, from the U.S. vantage, may be found in U.S. Congress, Senate Permanent Subcommittee on Investigations of the Committee on Governmental Affairs, Hearing, "Federal Drug Interdiction: Command, Control, Communications, and Intelligence Network," 1987.

[335]Michael Isikoff, "30 Nations Join in Attacks on Drug Cartels," *The Washington Post*, 1988.

[336]See the discussion by Alan Dixon et al., "Should U.S. Armed Forces Play a Major Role in Interdicting Drug Traffic into the U.S.?," *Congressional Digest*, 1986.

[337]Michael Isikoff ["Drug Fighters Resist Unifying, Senators Say," *The Washington Post*, 1988] describes how the two-year-old Customs Service program set up to centralize federal drug interdiction efforts has become hamstrung by agency rivalries and other problems. Questions were raised as to whether Congress should even continue to fund it.

[338]U.S. Congress, Senate Committee on Armed Services, Hearing, "Role of the Department of Defense in Drug Interdiction," 1988.

[339]See Michael Isikoff, "Fighting the Drug War: From Arizona to Fairfax," *The Washington Post*, 1988; and Michael J. Kennedy, "Aerial Drug War Has Its Ups, Downs," *The Los Angeles Times*, 1989.

[340]Molly Moore, "Coast Guard to Coordinate Drug Interdiction Effort," *The Washington Post*, 1989. The U.S. Customs Service complained that it had been bypassed.

[341]Richard L. Berke, "Two Admirals Named to Combat Drugs: Pentagon to Be Main Agency in Bid to Stop Smugglers," *The New York Times*, 1989. Customs' earlier competing position is discussed in U.S. General Accounting Office, Report to Congressional Requesters, *Drug Interdiction: Should the Customs Command and Control Program be Continued as Currently Evolving?*, 1988. See also U.S. General Accounting Office, Report to Congressional Requesters, *Drug Control: Issues Surrounding Increased Use of the Military in Drug Interdiction*, 1988.

[342]See Chris Adams, "Second Thoughts on the Military as Narcs; Hearings Stress Doubts on Pentagon's Drug-Interdiction Role," *The Washington Post*, 1988; and Angus Deming and John Barry, "Reluctant Recruits: Drugs and the Military," *Newsweek*, 1986.

[343]See Douglas Jehl, "U.S. Enlisting Guard in Drug Fight; California among 12 States Involved in New Border Patrol Roles," *The Los Angeles Times*, 1981; and, R. H. Melton, "Virginia National Guard Enlisted in Drug War," *The Washington Post*, 1989; and U.S. General Accounting Office, Report to Congressional Requesters, *Drug Interdiction: Operation Autumn Harvest*, 1988.

[344]See John P. Coffey, "The Navy's Role in Interdicting Narcotics Traffic: War on Drugs or Ambush on the Constitution?" *The Georgetown Law Journal*, 1987; Nadine Epstein, "US Border Agents Charged with Rights Abuse: Customs, INS Forces Walk Legal Tightrope in Bid to Catch Illegals and Drug Smugglers," *The Christian Science Monitor*, 1988; Enrique Rodríguez, "La Persecución de Narcóticos en Alta Mar: Su Efecto sobre los Principios Jurisdiccionales del Derecho Internacional," *Revista Jurídica de la Universidad Interamericana*, 1985. Also see Morris J. Blachman and Kenneth E. Sharpe, "The War on Drugs: American Democracy Under Assault," *World Policy Journal*, 1989-90.

[345]See Bruce Bullington, *Heroin Use in the Barrio*, 1977; John Horgan, "Ignorance in Action," *Scientific American*, 1988. In a wide-ranging critique on numerous drug-related issues, James Lieber ["Coping with Cocaine," *Atlantic*, 1986] discusses drug treatment programs.

[346]AIDS has become epidemic in some U.S. cities (e.g., New York City), and a desperate call is out to treat it in relation to the overall heroin and cocaine problem [Ernest Drucker et al., "IV Drug Users with AIDS in New York: A Study of Dependent Children, Housing and Drug Addiction Treatment," 1988]. Two government studies made public in 1989 said that a plan to give heroin addicts greater access to methadone would probably not ease the spread of AIDS; the reports questioned the effectiveness of current treatment programs ["AIDS Benefit in Methadone Use Is Questioned," *The New York Times*, 1989]. An earlier report had urged methadone maintenance programs for heroin addicts in order to halt the spread of AIDS [Lawrence K. Altman, "U.S. to Ease Methadone Rules for Addicts to Combat AIDS," *The New York Times*, 1989]. "Drug normalization" or "drug leniency" policies in the Netherlands are advanced as playing a significant role in the prevention of AIDS [Henk Jan van Vliet, "Separation of Drug Markets and the Normalization of Drug Problems in the Netherlands: An Example for Other Nations?" *The Journal of Drug Issues*, 1990]. However, as a group, U.S. intravenous drug users have not responded well to AIDS prevention messages [James A. Inciardi, "HIV, AIDS and Intravenous Drug Use: Some Considerations," *The Journal of Drug Issues*, 1990]. For an extended discussion, see C. Drummond et al., "Rethinking Drug Policies in the Context of the Acquired Immunodeficiency Syndrome," *Bulletin on Narcotics*, 1987.

[347]One bibliography and an extensive review of the literature are of note: Susan J. Christensen and Alice Q. Swanson, "Women and Drug Use: An Annotated Bibliography," *Journal of Psychedelic Drugs*, 1974; Marsha Rosenbaum, *Women on Heroin*, 1981. Studies arguing for gender-specific treatment (not necessarily confined to the United States) are found in Margaret L. Griffin and Steven M. Mirin, "A Comparison of Male and Female Cocaine Abusers," *Archives of General Psychiatry*, 1989; Jeanne C. Marsh and Nancy A. Miller, "Female Clients in Substance Abuse Treatment," *The International Journal of the Addictions*, 1985; Josette Mondanaro, *Chemically Dependent Women: Assessment and Treatment*, 1989, and Kerstin Tunving and Kerstin Nilsson,

"Young Female Drug Addicts in Treatment: A Twelve Year Perspective," *Journal of Drug Issues*, 1985. The counter gender-specific argument is raised by Glenda Kaufman Kantor, "Treatment Outcomes of Narcotic-Dependent Women: A Study of the Effects of Affiliations, Support Systems, Presence of Children and Sex-Role Perceptions," master's thesis, 1984. William Bennett called for forced treatment of cocaine addicted pregnant women to avoid a generation of offspring with severe learning disabilities ["Bennett Studying Drug Babies," *The Miami Herald*, 1989]. The increasing incidence of drug-addicted incarcerated women is a concern [Karlene Faith, "Drug Addiction: From a Study of Women and Criminal Justice," Ph.D. diss., 1981].

[348]The advent of AIDS stimulated a new interest in using methadone—bringing addicts into clinics for maintenance in order to reduce their needle sharing. Ample controversy ensued [Michael Abramowitz, "AIDS Stimulates New Interest in Methadone; Controversial Drug Called a Lifesaver—and a Crutch for Addicts," *The Washington Post*, 1989]. In March 1989 the Food and Drug Administration (FDA) had urged that methadone be made available to thousands of heroin addicts regardless of their being involved in a comprehensive treatment program, principally because over 50 percent of intravenous drug users who seek methadone treatment are infected with the AIDS virus. Relaxation of methadone requirements would halt the spread of AIDS into the remaining 50 percent of the heroin-addicted population [Lawrence K. Altman, "US to Ease Methadone Rules for Addicts to Combat AIDS," *The New York Times*, 1989]. However, this position was countered in August 1989 by two government-sponsored studies which argued that the methadone maintenance plan would probably not ease the spread of AIDS because the addicts will go right on sharing needles ["AIDS Benefit in Methadone Use is Questioned, *The New York Times*, 1989]. Issues surround methadone-maintained children [Tove S. Rosen and Helen L. Johnson, "Long-Term Effects of Prenatal Methadone Maintenance," in *Current Research on the Consequences of Maternal Drug Abuse*, 1985]. No uniform, long-term effects of prenatal methadone maintenance on the children were revealed in this study. In the short term (the first thirty-six months of life), however, methadone-maintained children have a higher incidence of minor neurological abnormalities and lower scores on developmental evaluations.

[349]Physicians in the United States, as opposed to those in England, are highly constrained in treating narcotic addiction by prescribing narcotics. They want more freedom [Donald R. Wesson, "Revival of Medical Maintenance in the Treatment of Heroin Dependence," *Journal of the American Medical Association*, 1988]. See also Michael Cross, "A Case for Legal Heroin," *New Scientist*, 1984.

[350]Gina Kolata ["Twins of the Streets: Homelessness and Addiction," *The New York Times*, 1989] discusses new policies that some agencies for the homeless have begun to adopt to try to impose greater responsibility on addicts in exchange for treatment privileges.

[351]Celestine Bohlen, "Support Groups Are Offering Embrace to Cocaine's Victims," *The New York Times*, 1989.

[352]Treatment (as well as other programs) must be culturally specific if success is to be expected [Bruce Bullington, *Heroin Use in the Barrio*, 1977].

[353]The present lack of knowledge about the effectiveness of compulsory treatment raises ethical as well as practical questions regarding potential success [Jerome J. Platt et al., "The Prospects and Limitations of Compulsory Treatment for Drug Addiction," *Journal of Drug Issues*, 1988]. On the other hand, because it is difficult to get young people to realize that they have a drug problem, let alone get them into treatment centers, it must be the responsibility of others to intervene on their behalf. Family members are

not reliable in referring their own youngsters. Community resources must take charge [Barry S. Brown et al., "Kids and Cocaine—A Treatment Dilemma," *Journal of Substance Abuse Treatment*, 1989]. But when is legal coercion therapeutically useful? What is legal coercion's value in reducing the "contagious" aspects of the drug-using life-style? And, where and how have compulsory treatment and civil commitment/legal coercion worked in the past? [Carl G. Leukefeld and Frank M. Tims, eds., *Compulsory Treatment of Drug Abuse: Research and Clinical Practice*, 1988].

[354]Jean Seligmann ["Crack: The Road Back," *Newsweek*, 1986] describes how rehabilitation centers are straining under the load that the new drug epidemic has caused. Detoxification runs about $15,000 a month per addict [Michael Abramowitz, "Need for Hospital Stays by Addicts Questioned," *The Washington Post*, 1989], a matter leveraged many times because of increased treatment traffic [National Institute on Drug Abuse, *Trends in Demographic Characteristics and Patterns of Drug Use of Clients Admitted to Drug Abuse Treatment Programs for Cocaine Abuse in Selected States: Cocaine Client Admissions 1979–1984*, 1987]. All this is aggravated further by increasing numbers of "crack babies" whose hospital treatment stay costs tens of thousands of dollars for each one [Bill Barol et al., "Cocaine Babies: Hooked at Birth," *Newsweek*, 1986].

[355]See, for example, the lessons of history advanced by Gerry V. Stimson and Edna Oppenheimer, *Heroin Addiction: Treatment and Control in Britain*, 1982.

[356]H. Hanreich, "Drug-Related Crime and Sentencing Policies from the Perspective of the United Nations Crime Prevention and Criminal Justice Programme," *Bulletin on Narcotics*, 1984; "Getting Britain off the Heroin Hook," *The Economist*, 1984.

[357]Jeremy Laurance, "Shooting up the Desperate," *New Statesman and Society*, 1988; Angela Burr, "A British View of Prescribing Pharmaceutical Heroin to Opiate Addicts: A Critique of the 'Heroin Solution' with Special Reference to the Piccadilly and Kensington Market Drug Scenes in London," *International Journal of the Addictions*, 1986.

[358]Nils Retterstol, "Models for the Treatment of Young Drug Dependents in Scandinavia," *Journal of Drug Issues*, 1980.

[359]Helge Waal, "Unconventional Treatment Models for Young Drug Abusers in Scandinavia," *Journal of Drug Issues*, 1980.

[360]Olafur Hallgrimsson, "Methadone Treatment: The Nordic Attitude," *Journal of Drug Issues*, 1980.

[361]Patrick Edobar Ibginovia, "The Prevention, Treatment and Rehabilitation of Drug-Dependent Persons in Africa," *International Journal of Offender Therapy and Comparative Criminology*, 1983; and, Griffith Edwards and Awni Arif, eds., *Drug Problems in Sociocultural Context, A Basis for Policies and Programme Planning*, 1980.

[362]Griffith Edwards and Awni Arif, eds., *Drug Problems in the Sociocultural Context*, 1980; D. C. Jayasuriya, "Law and the Treatment of Alcohol- and Drug-Dependent Persons in South-East Asia," *Medicine and Law*, 1985.

[363]Sally Hope Johnson, "Treatment of Drug Abusers in Malaysia: A Comparison," *The International Journal of the Addictions*, 1983; James F. Scorzelli, "Assessing the Effectiveness of Malaysia's Drug Prevention Education and Rehabilitation Programs," *Journal of Substance Abuse Treatment*, 1988.

[364]Vichai Poshyachinda, "Indigenous Treatment for Drug Dependence in Thailand," *Impact of Science on Society*, 1984; Joseph Westermeyer, "Treatment for Narcotic Addiction in a Buddhist Monastery," *Journal of Drug Issues*, 1980.

[365]Joseph Westermeyer, "Treatment for Narcotic Addiction in a Buddhist Monastery," *Journal of Drug Issues*, 1980.

[366]Philip Zealey, "United Nations/Burma Programme for Drug Abuse Control, the First Phase: 1976-1981," *Bulletin on Narcotics*, 1981; U. Khant, "Measures to Prevent and Reduce Drug Abuse among Young People in Burma," *Bulletin on Narcotics*, 1985.

[367]Nicholas D. Kristof, "Hong Kong Program: Addicts without AIDS," *The New York Times*, 1987.

[368]W. H. McGlothlin, "The Singapore Heroin Control Programme," *Bulletin on Narcotics*, 1980; B. C. Ng, "Treatment and Rehabilitation of Drug Addicts in Singapore 1977-1982," *The Annals of the Academy of Medicine*, 1984.

[369]B. Muller, "The Drug Problem in the Federal Republic of Germany," *Drug and Alcohol Dependence*, 1985; Jerome J. Platt et al., "The Prospects and Limitations of Compulsory Treatment for Drug Addiction," *Journal of Drug Issues*, 1988.

[370]Howard Shaffer and Milton Earl Burglass, eds., *Classic Contributions in the Addictions*, 1981, p. 483. They have an extensive bibliography.

[371]Irving Silverman ["Addiction Intervention: Treatment Models and Public Policy," *International Journal of the Addictions*, 1985] and Sidney Cohen ["Recent Developments in the Abuse of Cocaine," *Bulletin on Narcotics*, 1984] block out several of those listed in this paragraph. Silverman briefly discusses the successes and failures of some of the models and argues for the movement toward a more coherent holistic system. Cohen, mentioning that there is no specific way to treat dysfunctional cocaine use, offers helpful notes on several models.

[372]Reviewed by Sidney Cohen, "Recent Developments in the Abuse of Cocaine," *Bulletin on Narcotics*, 1984; Irving Silverman, "Addiction Intervention: Treatment Models and Public Policy, *International Journal of the Addictions*, 1985; and Arnold M. Washton and Nannette S. Stone, "The Human Cost of Chronic Cocaine Use," *Medical Aspects of Human Sexuality*, 1984.

[373]M. O. Smith and I. Khan, "An Acupuncture Programme for the Treatment of Drug-Addicted Persons, *Bulletin on Narcotics*, 1988.

[374]The model and its many issues are raised by Henrick J. Harwood et al., "The Costs of Crime and the Benefits of Drug Abuse Treatment," in *Compulsory Treatment of Drug Abuse, Research and Clinical Practice*, 1988; D.C. Jayasuriya, "Penal Measures for Drug Offences: Perspectives from Some Asian Countries," *Bulletin on Narcotics*, 1984; U. Khant, "Measures to Prevent and Reduce Drug Abuse among Young People in Burma," *Bulletin on Narcotics*, 1985; Carl G. Leukefeld and Frank M. Tims, eds., *Compulsory Treatment of Drug Abuse: Research and Clinical Practice*, 1988; and, Jerome J. Platt et al., "The Prospects and Limitations of Compulsory Treatment for Drug Addiction," *Journal of Drug Issues*, 1988.

[375]Lewis Yablonsky [*The Therapeutic Community: A Successful Approach for Treating Substance Abusers*, 1989] traces the history and development of therapeutic communities as a treatment orientation and delineates the concepts and methods that are thought to make such communities work across various cultures. George De Leon [*The Therapeutic Community: Study of Effectiveness*, 1984] presents research findings showing that the success—in terms of removing people from crime and drug use—of the therapeutic community approach toward rehabilitation has been rather impressive. After a lengthy longitudinal study, 31 percent of dropouts from the program were found to be free from crime and drug use compared with 75 percent of the graduates; 56 percent of the dropouts and 93 percent of the graduates had improved over their pretreatment status. The author contrasts a drug-free residential therapeutic community with other modalities of treatment, including detoxification, methadone maintenance, and drug-free outpatient treatment. See also Richard C. Page and Sam Mitchell, "The Effects of Two Therapeutic

Communities on Illicit Drug Users between 6 Months and 1 Year after Treatment," *International Journal of Addictions*, 1988; and D. Dwayne Simpson and S. B. Sells, "Effectiveness of Treatment for Drug Abuse: An Overview of the DARP Research Program," *Advances in Alcohol and Substance Abuse*, 1982. See also Henry Nichols, "Narcotics Anonymous," *Journal of Substance Abuse Treatment*, 1988; David N. Nurco et al., *Ex-Addicts' Self-Help Groups: Potentials and Pitfalls*, 1983; Mark Peyrot, "Narcotics Anonymous: Its History, Structure, and Approach," *International Journal of the Addictions*, 1985; Vichai Poshyachinda, "Indigenous Treatment for Drug Dependence in Thailand," *Impact of Science on Society*, 1984; and Helge Waal, "Unconventional Treatment Models for Young Drug Abusers in Scandinavia," *Journal of Drug Issues*, 1980.

[376]Hospitalization as a treatment procedure for addicts has fallen on hard times, partly because of costs, partly because of failure of effectiveness. See the brief notes by Christopher D. Webster, "Compulsory Treatment of Narcotic Addiction," *International Journal of Law and Psychiatry*, 1986; Michael Abramowitz, "Need for Hospital Stays by Addicts Questioned," *The Washington Post*, 1989.

[377]Comments may be found in Sidney Cohen, "Recent Developments in the Abuse of Cocaine," *Bulletin on Narcotics*, 1984; James Cooper et al., eds., *Research on the Treatment of Narcotic Addiction: State of the Art*, 1983; Edwin T. Fujii, "Public Investment in the Rehabilitation of Heroin Addicts," *Social Science Quarterly*, 1979; George De Leon, *The Therapeutic Community: Study of Effectiveness*, 1984; B. C. Ng, "Treatment and Rehabilitation of Drug Addicts in Singapore 1977–1982," *The Annals of the Academy of Medicine*, 1984; and Irving Silverman, "Addiction Intervention: Treatment Models and Public Policy," *International Journal of the Addictions*, 1985. Not much hope is given for detoxification programs [see, for example, D. Dwayne Simpson and S. B. Sells, "Effectiveness of Treatment for Drug Abuse," *Advances in Alcohol and Substance Abuse*, 1982; and Douglas S. Lipton and Michael J. Maranda, "Detoxification from Heroin Dependency: An Overview of Method and Effectiveness," *Advances in Alcohol and Drug Abuse*, 1982]. Lipton and Maranda assert that detoxification fails as a treatment procedure because it does not produce satisfactory retention rates of detoxified conditions. Detoxification should be viewed only as a preliminary step.

[378]See notes 348 and 360 for references to methadone treatment in the United States and Scandinavia. Edward C. Senay ["Methadone Maintenance Treatment," *The International Journal of the Addictions*, 1985] reviews the world literature on methadone. Other references include the following: Margaret Allison and Robert L. Hubbard, "Drug Abuse Treatment Process: A Review of the Literature," *International Journal of the Addictions*, 1985; M. Douglas Anglin et al., "Consequences and Costs of Shutting off Methadone," *Addictive Behaviors*, 1989; James R. Cooper et al., eds., *Research on the Treatment of Narcotic Addiction: State of the Art*, 1983; Edwin T. Fujii, "Public Investment in the Rehabilitation of Heroin Addicts," *Social Science Quarterly*, 1979; Dana E. Hunt, Douglas S. Lipton, and Barry Spunt, "Patterns of Criminal Activity among Methadone Clients and Current Narcotics Users Not in Treatment," *Journal of Drug Issues*, 1984; George De Leon, *The Therapeutic Community: Study of Effectiveness*, 1984; J. A. Liappas, F. A. Jenner, and B. Vincente, "Literature on Methadone Maintenance Clinics," *International Journal of the Addictions*, 1988; Tove S. Rosen and Helen L. Johnson, "Long-Term Effects of Prenatal Methadone Maintenance," in *Current Research on the Consequences of Maternal Drug Abuse*, Theodore M. Pinkert, ed., 1985; Irving Silverman, "Addiction Intervention: Treatment Models and Public Policy," *International Journal of the Addictions*, 1985; and D. Dwayne Simpson and S. B. Sells, "Effectiveness

of Treatment for Drug Abuse," *Advances in Alcohol and Substance Abuse,* 1982. According to David P. Ausubel ["Methadone Maintenance Treatment: The Other Side of the Coin," *International Journal of the Addictions,* 1983], methadone maintenance treatment for heroin addiction leaves much to be desired. He discusses the unsatisfactory factors, and he asserts that official evaluation studies have grossly exaggerated the clinical effectiveness of methadone treatment. Among other problems, the maintenance program has inadvertently created many more methadone addicts than it has cured heroin addicts. In any event, much of the methadone provided on treatment programs is apparently being diverted to street usage [Barry Spunt et al., "Methadone Diversion: A New Look," *Journal of Drug Issues,* 1986].

[379]Irving Silverman, "Addiction Intervention: Treatment Models and Public Policy," *International Journal of the Addictions,* 1985.

[380]The goal with heroin maintenance is to provide addicts with all the legitimate heroin they need in order to remove them from having to deal with—and therefore to support—the criminal underworld. Policy discussion by Donald R. Wesson, "Revival of Medical Maintenance in the Treatment of Heroin Dependence," *Journal of the American Medical Association,* 1988.

[381]Enforced incarceration to detoxify users is the usual definition of "cold turkey." Its use in Singapore, and its lack of appropriateness elsewhere, is discussed by Scott B. MacDonald, *Dancing on a Volcano: The Latin American Drug Trade,* 1988.

[382]See the discussions on using education as a treatment mode by Sidney Cohen, "Recent Developments in the Abuse of Cocaine," *Bulletin on Narcotics,* 1984; Don Colburn et al., "Health: Getting Hooked, Getting Helped," *The Washington Post,* 1988; and Glenn E. Rohrer et al., "Crack Cocaine Education in the Public Schools," *Journal of Alcohol and Drug Education,* 1987.

[383]A growing body of literature looks at how immediate family and close friends may help in drug abuser treatment and rehabilitation [Marc Galanter, "Social Network Therapy for Cocaine Dependence," *Advances in Alcohol and Substance Abuse,* 1986]. A widespread impression has developed among drug-treatment officials that involving family in programs tends to produce positive results. See, for example, Edward Kaufman, "A Contemporary Approach to the Family Treatment of Substance Abuse Disorders," *American Journal of Drug and Alcohol Abuse,* 1986; H. Charles Fishman, "A Family Approach to Marijuana Use," in *Marijuana and Youth: Clinical Observations on Motivation and Learning,* 1982. Even so, there are at least nine models of "best" strategies [Brenna H. Bry, "Family-Based Approaches to Reducing Adolescent Substance Use: Theories, Techniques, and Findings," in *Adolescent Drug Abuse: Analyses of Treatment Research,* Elizabeth R. Rahdert and John Grabowski, eds., 1988; Emily F. Garfield and Jeanne Gibbs, "Fostering Parent Involvement for Drug Prevention," *Journal of Drug Education,* 1982; and Edward Kaufman, "Family Systems and Family Therapy of Substance Abuse: An Overview of Two Decades of Research and Clinical Experience," *International Journal of the Addictions,* 1985]. One group views drug abuse therapy as a subset of family psychotherapy [M. Duncan Stanton et al., *The Family Therapy of Drug Abuse and Addiction,* 1982; includes extensive bibliography]. How-to books for families are also available [e.g., Robert L. Du Pont, *Getting Tough on Gateway Drugs: A Guide for the Family,* 1984].

[384]It has usually been thought that cocaine dependency is a minor "psychological" addiction without a "physiological" withdrawal syndrome. Thus treatments for cocaine abuse have usually involved psychological, therapeutic efforts aimed at altering addictive behaviors. There is now increasing clinical evidence of intractable addiction and profound

deleterious physiological effects of chronic cocaine abuse, justifying, therefore, intervention with pharmacological agents just as is done with heroin [Frank Gawin and Herbert Kleber, "Pharmacologic Treatments of Cocaine Abuse," *Psychiatric Clinics of North America*, 1986; Herbert D. Kleber, "Epidemic Cocaine Abuse: America's Present, Britain's Future?" *British Journal of Addiction*, 1988]. Some psychiatrists now prescribe antidepressants and amino acids to cocaine addicts to relieve their craving [Robert Wilbur, "A Drug to Fight Cocaine," *Science*, 1986]. Other medical practitioners argue that cocaine abuse can be controlled effectively and inexpensively by employing phenelzine—thought to correct any biochemical defects caused by chronic cocaine use and to produce very disagreeable results after any subsequent cocaine intake. Some think that other pharmacological agents appear not to work well [Daniel H. Golwyn, "Cocaine Abuse Treated with Phenelzine," *International Journal of the Addictions*, 1988]. That claim notwithstanding, other chemical agents are advanced as being useful in fighting cocaine abuse [Mark H. Pollack, Andrew W. Brotman, and Jerrold F. Rosenbaum, "Cocaine Abuse and Treatment," *Comprehensive Psychiatry*, 1989; includes an extensive bibliography]; one author advances a case for desipramine and lithium [Deborah M. Barnes, "Breaking the Cycle of Addiction," *Science*, 1988]. Buprenorphine has been advocated as a good antiheroin and anticocaine pharmacologic agent [Thomas H. Maugh, II, "Drug Seems to Block Users Cocaine Need," *Los Angeles Times*, 1989]. Naltrexone as an opiate antagonist is said to be based on the same principles as disulfiram in the management of alcohol abuse [Colin Brewer, "The Management of Opiate Abuse: Learning from Other Addictions," *Journal of Drug Issues*, 1988].

[385]Celestine Bohlen ["Support Groups Are Offering Embrace to Cocaine's Victims," *The New York Times*, 1989] describes how cocaine addicts and their families find solace in self-help groups, which are blossoming virtually everywhere in the United States. Some, such as Cocaine Anonymous, are patterned after holistic rehabilitation programs having a long history of success in alcoholic dependence. The effort is to deal with mental, physical, emotional, and spiritual problems accompanying substance abuse. Irving Silverman ["Addiction Intervention: Treatment Models and Public Policy," *International Journal of the Addictions*, 1985] calls for a movement toward a more coherent and holistic system. See also Jeanne C. Marsh and Nancy A. Miller, "Female Clients in Substance Abuse Treatment," *The International Journal of the Addictions*, 1985; Ethan Nebelkopf, "Herbal Therapy in the Treatment of Drug Use," *The International Journal of the Addictions*, 1987; and Arnold M. Washton, "Preventing Relapse to Cocaine," *Journal of Clinical Psychiatry*, 1988.

[386]See Karlene Faith, "Drug Addiction: From a Study of Women and Criminal Justice," Ph.D. diss., 1981.

[387]See H. Hanreich, "Drug-Related Crime and Sentencing Policies from the Perspective of the United Nations Crime Prevention and Criminal Justice Programme," *Bulletin on Narcotics*, 1984.

[388]See John Horgan, "Ignorance in Action," *Scientific American*, 1988; B. Muller, "The Drug Problem in the Federal Republic of Germany," *Drug and Alcohol Dependence*, 1985.

[389]See Ethan Nebelkopf, "Herbal Therapy in the Treatment of Drug Use," *The International Journal of the Addictions*, 1987.

[390]See Sally Hope Johnson, "Treatment of Drug Abusers in Malaysia: A Comparison," *The International Journal of the Addictions*, 1983; Vichai Poshyachinda, "Indigenous Treatment for Drug Dependence in Thailand," *Impact of Science on Society*, 1984.

[391]M. O. Smith and I. Khan, "An Acupuncture Programme for the Treatment of Drug-Addicted Persons, *Bulletin on Narcotics*, 1988.

[392]Literature germane to this continuum includes the following: Colin Brewer, "The Management of Opiate Abuse: Learning from Other Addictions," *Journal of Drug Issues*, 1988; Anna Rose Childress, A. Thomas McLellan, and Charles P. O'Brien, "Behavioral Therapies for Substance Abuse," *The International Journal of the Addictions*, 1985; Frank Gawin and Herbert Kleber, "Pharmacologic Treatments of Cocaine Abuse," *Psychiatric Clinics of North America*, 1986; Gina Kolata, "Experts Finding New Hope on Treating Crack Addict," *The New York Times*, 1989; Roger E. Meyer, "Psychobiology and the Treatment of Drug Dependence: The Biobehavioral Interface," *American Journal of Drug and Alcohol Abuse, 1986;* Henry Nichols, "Narcotics Anonymous," *Journal of Substance Abuse Treatment*, 1988; "Peruvians Operate on Cocaine Addicts' Brains," *New Scientist*, 1983; Mark H. Pollack, Andrew W. Brotman, and Jerrold F. Rosenbaum, "Cocaine Abuse and Treatment," *Comprehensive Psychiatry*, 1989; Richard Restak, "Drug Deaths and Pavlov's Dogs," *The Washington Post*, 1988; and Donald R. Wesson, "Revival of Medical Maintenance in the Treatment of Heroin Dependence," *Journal of the American Medical Association*, 1988.

6

Demand

Illicit drug demand—the amount consumers are ready and able to buy at a given time for a given price at a given level of risk—drives the illicit drug market. Efforts to reduce demand by striking at the source of supply through programs of crop eradication (thereby raising prices as supply is reduced) or at distribution through programs of suppression, interdiction, and asset forfeitures aimed at traffickers and users (for the same intended effect) have not appeared to affect prices materially over the long run.[1] The efforts have therefore not interfered with most consumers' ability to continue to purchase drugs consistent with their willingness to run the risk.

Law enforcement efforts designed to heighten user risks—fines, incarceration, forfeiture of assets—may well have deterred large numbers of people from experimenting with illicit drugs in the first place. This is, of course, a conjecture. Law enforcement does appear to have had a slight to moderate deterring effect on demand among some conventional population groups classified as "recreational users." However, the efforts appear not to have reduced materially other types of users' consumption habits.[2]

Drug testing in the workplace has certainly been a deterrent to many people, as have certain kinds of educational programs in the schools that incorporate peer influences, antidrug values, and penalties for the noncompliant who have much to lose (e.g., high school athletes being dropped from teams as a consequence of failed mandatory urine tests). Advertisements over the mass media may also have contributed to some people's making a personal decision to stay off drugs or to abandon using them.

All that notwithstanding, illicit drug consumption remains high in the United States (although it may now be declining) and is expanding in many other countries. As we have seen, the United Kingdom, Western Europe, Canada, Australia, the Soviet Union and numerous net drug producing countries have all noted upsurges in occasional and chronic consumption as well as outright addiction.

As we saw in Chapter 5 of this handbook, illegalizing laws and antidrug policies in response to demand have given rise to numerous consequential effects—some positive, many negative—for countries, societies, and peoples. What may we say about the consequences of demand (assuming constant or declining prices) independent of whether drugs are legal or illegal or law enforcement efforts exist or do not? In what way or ways do individuals' consumption of cocaine, heroin, and cannabis produce significant social, economic, or political consequences independent of illegalizing laws and policies?

Answers to these questions must first identify the personal consequences of drug taking independent of illegalizing laws and policies and then determine whether those consequences have externalities of any social, economic, or political significance. We have no expectation of advancing a definitive response in the categories implied by this reasoning but rather have organized a discussion of the literature around relevant categories that stand in a logical relationship with the question. Tables 6 and 7 give us a good place to start.

Table 6 alerts us to the considerable inconclusiveness of the personal consequences of drug use by warning that many "conclusions" are disputed, some heatedly so. While mention will be made of disputed as well as generally accepted conclusions regarding personal consequences of acute and chronic consumption of cocaine, heroin, and cannabis, we have tried to organize the "consequence" literature around externalities deriving from generally *accepted* conclusions of the drugs' effects on individual users. The entries in the various cells of Table 6 illustrate the diversity of conclusions offered by the drug literature.

For example, as the discussion below on cannabis shows, it is generally agreed that acute and chronic consumption of marijuana and hashish produce marked impairment of short-term memory and other mental functions. However, disputed is whether these impairments last beyond the intoxication phase of the drug. Additionally, there is contradictory literature on the degree to which chronic use may affect fetuses' well-being or adult users'

Table 6
Generally Accepted and Disputed Conclusions about
Personal Consequences of Acute and Chronic Consumption

	Generally Accepted Conclusions	Disputed Conclusions
Cocaine	e.g., Overdose death; Violence; Serious psychobiological and neurobiological problems. 1	e.g., Non crack-cocaine induced violence; Cocaine psychosis. 4
Heroin	e.g., Overdose death; Damaged fetuses; Reduced control over impulses; Reduced concentration 2	e.g., Criminality 5
Cannabis	e.g., Marked impairment of short-term memory and other mental functions. 3	e.g., Cannabis psychosis; Adverse effects on fetuses; Long-term impairment of short-term memory 6

Table 7
Generally Accepted Consequences of Acute and
Chronic Drug Consumption Likely to Produce
Significant Externalities

	Cannabis	Heroin	Cocaine
Social	e.g., Marked impairment of short-term memory and other mental functions; Probable damaged fetuses.	e.g., Impaired fetuses; Reduced control of impulses; Reduced social and family bonding; Reduced productivity.	e.g., Impaired fetuses; Compulsiveness; Poor parent-child bonding; "Crack neighborhoods."
Economic	e.g. Impaired sensory and perceptual functions.	e.g., Neurobiological collapse from overdose; Reduced worker productivity	e.g., Neurobiological collapse from overdose; Impaired fetuses; Hospital, welfare, and general social services costs.
Political	e.g. Adverse effect on classroom performance and psychological and emotional development of adolescents.	e.g., Treatment models and costs; Welfare costs.	e.g., Public policy initiatives on welfare and social services costs.

psychological stability. Further illustrations for cannabis and the other drugs as well as likely significant externalities that derive from these personal consequences are discussed in following sections.

Table 7 illustrates the generally accepted consequences of acute and chronic drug consumption that are likely to produce significant externalities in social, economic, and political categories. For example, any marked mental impairments that contribute to highway, air, rail, or industrial accidents produce economic loss for governments, companies, and families. They create social distortions insofar as the responsibilities of key actors or their victims must necessarily be picked up by others (e.g., orphaned children cared for by the state or by relatives). Political fallout is seen as governments mobilize to deal with a perceived deterioration in national well-being such as may derive from drugs' adverse effects on the academic performance of students or the emotional and psychological well-being of adolescents. People get the view that the future of their country may be at stake.

Table 8 further exemplifies practical consequences, illustrating the need to consider whether the generally accepted conclusions about the consequences of individual use produce no significant externalities and are therefore "victimless," or whether they are "victimizing" of other individuals or produce other externalities of social, economic, or political significance. While victimless overtones may have political, social, and economic consequences for a country, there is a presumption that victimizing consequences would be much more significant.

The greatest impact in any of the categories occurs, of course, in the principal consuming countries, but the trends indicated are increasingly relevant for net exporting countries because of their citizens' current

Table 8
Externalities of Acute and Chronic Consumption
Independent of Criminalizing Drug Control Policies

	Victimless	Victimizing	Other Externalities
Cocaine	e.g. Overdose deaths? 1	e.g. Crack babies; Violence; severe family disorders. 4	e.g. School dropouts; Low productivity; Treatment programs; Hospital costs. 7
Heroin	e.g. Overdose deaths? 2	e.g. Collapsed love relationships; Petty property crime; Severe family disorders; Damaged fetuses. 5	e.g. Hospital costs; Methadone maintenance costs; Other treatment costs; Reduced worker productivity. 8
Cannabis	e.g. Workers in low tech and low safety related employment. 3	e.g. Airline, rail, automobile, and industrial accidents. 6	e.g. Lost worker productivity in technologically advanced societies. 9

tendency to consume more of their own domestic product.

Whatever consequences the literature does address are most evident when use is chronic (e.g., several times a week at whatever dosage) or is high enough to produce intoxication even if used only rarely. The occasional drinking of a moderate amount of alcohol or smoking a like amount of cannabis may produce self harm but little social harm. Sufficient consumption of either to produce intoxication may lead to disasters for others as well as self. With "harder" drugs—heroin, cocaine, crack cocaine—the public implications are potentially more severe but not necessarily so. One person snorting a line of cocaine will hardly lead to the kinds of public burdens that five, ten, or twenty percent of a country's chronically using population could produce. By the same token, large numbers of people might use a small amount of a psychoactive drug infrequently and produce little social harm, whereas a small number of people *abusing* the same drug could create socio-economic and political harms totally unacceptable to modern society. Thus, although public policy necessarily faces "continua," discussions dealing with the polar ends of each help to clarify relationships while also acknowledging their "softness." Table 9 illustrates several common-sense notions. External-ities, as shown, are thought to be highest in cell 1 where many people abuse drugs, lowest in cell 9 where a few people are no more than casual users. Cells 2, 4, 6, and 8 represent numerous possible conditions between the continua's hypothetical polar extremes.

Here we discuss public consequences stemming from dosage rates or usage frequency high enough to be "acute" or "chronic"—in other words, *abuse*. This does not, of course, necessarily rule out similar if not attenuated consequences deriving from occasional use. The manifestations, insofar as

Table 9
Common-Sense Categories of Drug Use and Abuse That
Impose Socioeconomic and Political Externalities on Society

		AMOUNT OF USE		
		Chronic, Intoxicating (Abuse)	Continua	Use (But not Abuse)
N U M B E R	M a n y	Large socio-economic and political externalities, probably nationwide **1**	<————> **2**	Some public costs, no doubt, but the matter is open to dispute as to how extensive **3**
O F	C o n t i n u a	↑ ⋮ ↓ **4**	↓ **5**	↑ ⋮ ↓ **6**
U S E R S	F e w	Public externalities may be significant in local areas but probably not nationwide **7**	<————> **8**	Few externalized costs **9**

they exist, are simply more obvious and less disputable when discussed in light of chronic or acute use.

Thus we reference literature on generally accepted *conclusions* that implicitly or explicitly suggest *victimization* or other *externalities* that appear to have significant economic, political, or social consequences.

CANNABIS

Perhaps more than any other abused drug, Cannabis has a diversity of experts whose research and opinion could justify almost any view. The positions start with claims that cannabis, at whatever dosage and whatever use frequency, almost inevitably produces harmful physiological, mental, psychological, and/or ethical consequences.[3] At the other extreme are arguments that cannabis consumption not only produces little or no personal harm[4] but actually contributes positive results to users' lives.[5] Most studies appear to camp more or less on middle ground, siding with cautionary admonishings or giving subdued refutations.[6] One conclusion from this diverse reporting is clear: The possibility of generalizing a given piece of cannabis research is highly circumscribed by nonpsychopharmacological variables—culture, situation, user expectations, ethical standards, other people, and, apparently, a large number of unknowns.

Clearly, some people have used cannabis with little apparent harmful effect to themselves. However, others have been devastated if not destroyed by the psychopharmacology of the drug or its effects as developed in combination with one or more of the above mentioned situational variables. Not clear is whether social, political, and economic externalities deriving from individual use are more pronounced among cannabis users who experience negligible if any personal harm or among those who have suffered mild to profound personal traumas. The presumption, in most cases, is that the more severe the personal effect the more substantial the social, economic, or political consequences are likely to be.

In Chapter 3 we discussed some of the reported pleasurable sensory experiences that marijuana users report. A host of other effects are reported in the literature—some generally accepted, some disputed—several of which are thought to produce social, economic, and political externalities. In Table 10, illustrations of the variations are presented, first as disputed and second as generally accepted; a separate section in the second column lists effects likely to have externalities of interest to readers of this handbook.

From the *with probable significant externalities* subsection of the tabulation in Table 10, one surmises social, political, and economic externalities on unborn children; on victims of accidents caused by cannabis-impaired drivers, pilots, and sea captains; on present educational accomplishments and future productivity of children and adolescents; and on adult users' current ability to contribute economically in a high-technology society. The consequence illustrations are, of course, not exhaustive. They are enough to show that these and perhaps other probable externalities deriving from generally accepted evidence have political, economic, and social significance.

Most of the literature of relevance to this section appears to focus on accidents caused, or likely to be caused, by impairment of cannabis users' mental functions and psychomotor skills when intoxicated or when post-intoxication impairment may exist. Some evidence is advanced showing impairment to be of longer duration than the intoxication phase and to be measurable at lower usage levels than those required to produce acute intoxication.

Robert Petersen reviewed considerable literature on this line of reasoning in a 1984 National Institute on Drug Abuse publication.[7] As early as 1944 studies found that hand steadiness was reduced, a matter generally confirmed in later studies. Reaction time in complex situations (as opposed to simple ones) is adversely affected, directly related to dosage levels. The reaction-time delays may be accounted for by subjects' inability to maintain continuous attention with complex information-processing needs. In fact, almost any test (e.g., tracking) that requires continuous rather than intermittent attention is adversely affected by cannabis intoxication. This raises, of course, the probable effect that cannabis intoxication has on safety-related complex tasks where continuous attention is required, such as operating heavy machinery, driving in traffic, flying airplanes, or piloting ships. Among some people, attention and psychomotor deficits have been measured for as

Table 10
Disputed and Generally Accepted Evidence
on the Personal Effects of Chronic or Acute
Consumption of Cannabis

Disputed	*Generally Accepted*
—Marked impairment of short-term memory persists long after intoxication ends.	—Preoccupation with the immediate present.[17]
	—Increased work load on the heart.[18]
—Cannabis psychosis[8] or psychological stress or panic disorder lasting a few days to a few weeks.	—Impaired blood circulation.[19]
—"Amotivational Syndrome."[9]	—Abnormalities in sperm count, motility, and structural characteristics.[20]
—Decreased serum testosterone levels.[10]	—Reduced aggressiveness (self acceptance and calmness).[21]
—Abnormal menstrual cycles and lower prolactin levels.[11]	*With Probable Significant Externalities*
—Chromosomal damage.[12]	—Marked impairment of short-term memory and other mental functions.[22]
—Assured adverse affects on fetuses.[13]	
—Impairment of the immune system.[14]	—Probable adverse affects on fetuses.[23]
—Atrophy of the brain.[15]	—Impaired tracking ability in sensory and perceptual functions.[24]
—Respiratory ills, including lung cancer.[16]	—Strong clinical evidence of adverse psychological, emotional, and social development of children and adolescents.[25]
	—Indirect scientific evidence and direct clinical observation that classroom performance is affected.[26]

long as ten hours after initial intoxication.[27]

These observations have given rise to a host of vehicle *driving studies*, which Petersen also reviews. In simulator exercises, nearly all participants show clear psychomotor deficits that could affect driving safety. The limiting factor has been less a subject's mechanical control over the vehicle than his or her perceptual ability to drive it safely. Under driving conditions more realistic than simple simulators, however, clear deficits are almost invariably noted in subjects' ability to handle curves, judge distances, maintain safe speeds, and negotiate tight traffic.[28]

A single intoxicated or post-intoxicated but nevertheless impaired automobile driver may be of small concern in the social aggregate; however, similar impairment of a train engineer, bus driver, or airline pilot would evoke considerable commentary. Flight simulator tests show pilots unable to judge safe distances and safely handle complex takeoff, landing, and emergency exercises, even after a single nominal dose of marijuana. Normal pilot performance does not return until several hours after initial cannabis consumption.[29]

The logic of this evidence would argue for a high probability of cannabis-related accidents under conditions of inherent danger requiring rapid responses to complex situations that demand continuous attention. Obviously, certain kinds of occupations and activities would be more vulnerable than others. Driving in congested traffic, piloting airplanes, safety officers responding to emergency calls, surgeons performing operations, generals implementing war preparations, and executives poised for the next merger or takeover would seem to qualify. "Mistakes" may destroy lives, squander the public's money, and create public policy dilemmas, suggesting that in a few critical areas, under specified circumstances, significant social, political, and economic consequences *could* follow.

But do they? The answer is probably yes, but our literature does not bring much direct evidence to bear on it. Attempts have been made to determine the role of marijuana in automobile accidents. However, detection techniques pioneered for alcohol—the preferred test because law enforcement training modules are already in place—have a difficult transferability. Blood cannabinoid levels drop within minutes of marijuana use. Within two hours or so they may not be readily measurable by blood sampling techniques, although urinalysis can detect cannabinoids for several days following ingestion. Nevertheless, the direct connection of cannabinoids to accidents has been a difficult one to make. Regardless, the studies indicate that cannabinoids are probably a significant factor in some kinds of accidents.[30] Insofar as they are, all the political, social, and economic implications of loss of life, property, and productivity fall upon users and nonusers alike. In these cases it is therefore incorrect to speak of cannabis consumption as a victimless activity.

Similar arguments are made with respect to the additional cannabis-related items listed in the *generally accepted evidence* column in the above tabulation that have probable externalities. For example, the literature cited in note 23 on probable adverse effects on fetuses detects numerous short-term impairments that are thought to be overcome within two years of an infant's birth. The nagging anxiety among some pediatricians, however, is whether the measurements and tests are adequate to assure a clean bill of health for the newborn whose mothers contaminated them in utero. Health costs are skyrocketing, and some of those may be associated with the care of infants born of cannabis-using parents.

The ultimate impact on adolescent users as they mature may never be entirely known. But the generally agreed-upon evidence cited in notes 25 and 26 are sufficient to cause concern: school studies unassimilated; marketable skills unacquired; a high time horizon unexamined; life's goals unarticulated. Generalized to an entire country, an economic system of a complex technological society (as opposed to a simple agrarian or labor-intensive society) must ultimately surely suffer if large numbers of its present and future workers are acute or chronic cannabis users.

But does it suffer? Will it suffer? Our data base does not offer direct corroborating evidence, although the circumstantial signs are highly incriminating, particularly if an "abusing threshold" were consistently maintained (large numbers of people chronically using or becoming intoxicated—cell 1, Table 9).

HEROIN

While disputes among the experts exist regarding the effects of acute and chronic consumption of heroin, on the whole, the opinions are not nearly as diverse nor the conclusions as ambiguous as with cannabis products.[31] Most reviewers consider that, under acute or chronic consumption, the drug produces serious adverse psychological and neurobiological effects. A principal concern is with overdoses that induce death at worst and substantial hospital emergency costs at best.[32] In the United States, since 1987, heroin has ranked second only to cocaine as a problem drug in hospital emergency rooms.[33] Our data do not indicate the proportion of hospital costs that heroin emergency room patients bear, but we presume that most costs are externalized to the general public in terms of welfare considerations. In these cases a clear economic consequence is therefore tied to heroin use regardless of whether the users die. Death is, of course, a personal loss of considerable magnitude to the heroin user.

Would not these externalities and tragedies be reduced if heroin were decriminalized, regulated, and taxed? Heroin overdoses caused by users' lack of knowledge of the purity[34] of the product they ingest would likely decline because purity rates would be posted, and an informed judgment about the quantity to inject could be made. However, while some reduction in overdose emergencies and deaths would no doubt be noted, it is unlikely that this would significantly reduce the rate of emergencies among addicts who are not just "maintaining" their addiction but are rather routinely injecting heroin to the margin, and even beyond, required for the intense euphoria the drug delivers, regardless of levels of the addictive tolerance. These margins appear to vary somewhat, depending on conditions of psyche, health, and circumstance. Purity differentials aside, overdoses are therefore still possible and likely as addicts misjudge their own condition prior to injecting heroin. Moreover, it is not certain that a liberal access policy for heroin would interfere much with illicitly manufactured heroin on the market, or that one would avoid a rapid and substantial increase in the number of "regulated" heroin users who would still be candidates for overdoses.[35]

Deaths, hospital costs, and related issues notwithstanding, it is widely believed, and there is considerable evidence to support the proposition, that when heroin comes into a person's life, "love flies out the window." Couples have more arguments over money, drugs, and sex (or its absence) resulting in bitterness, resentment, and despair. All this produces, on more than isolated occasions, severe stress within families, "spouse battering," and family dissolution. The combined circumstances are particularly hard on women addicts. One study concluded that the woman addict occasionally gives up men completely and, in so doing, relinquishes "one of the few roles open to her—that of homemaker."[36] This may, of course, simply be a sexist observation. It also may reflect the reality of the educational levels and the employability of heroin-using women.

As love departs and is accompanied by a decline in stable relationships, society is frequently left to pick up the pieces in welfare costs, aid to dependent children, and socialization and educational difficulties among the children belonging to drug-broken families.

A third issue of concern deals with children exposed in utero to narcotics. They score significantly lower on controlled tests designed to measure neuropsychological and behavioral functioning. The inferences from these and related tests are that "in utero narcotic exposure seems to cause pervasive neuropsychological and behavioral results, primarily in the domains of perceptual-motor, memory, spacial relations, concentration, impulse control, feeling of well being, and general competence to interact with the environment."[37] Insofar as these impairments persist through the individuals' maturation, heroin use cannot be judged a "self-harm" isolated from the victims it produces.

Do mothers who substitute official methadone maintenance for street heroin in an effort to extract themselves from a harmful addiction nevertheless continue to injure their fetuses? The evidence is contradictory.[38] However, there is a statistically significant relationship between mothers' being on methadone and their requiring more assistance in parenting, being more isolated socially, and being less likely to pursue vocational and educational activities.[39] One presumes that these conditions impose certain social overhead costs on society independent of whether methadone actually harms the children.

Children whose life chances are impaired in utero by their mothers are victims of drug demand; so also is society a victim. Society is deprived of the full complement of the children's potential contribution. Most societies can absorb a moderate number of such people; large numbers of these children present a different public policy issue. In any event, the tendency of heroin-addicted mothers to damage their offspring while in utero must be understood as contributing to externalities with political, social, and economic dimensions which, depending on numbers involved, can be significant. One must be reminded, perhaps, that the consequences discussed and implied here derive from demand, not from the unintended effects of law enforcement efforts.

Heroin addicts' social and work productivity is known to suffer, although disputed is whether it is the business of government to inquire into the social productivity of its citizens and to attempt to oblige them to conform to a "productive mold."[40] This moves the discussion of consequences to a consideration of their significance *and* to the ethical question of anyone's objecting to social deviations let alone trying to do anything about them. Perhaps, again, it is a matter of scale. Few people, little problem. Enough people to undermine the economic, social, and even political viability of a nation is reason for legitimate concern regardless of whether a proposed solution sustains the test of philosophical adequacy. Survival questions, real or alleged, hardly ever do.

Finally, whether legal or not, heroin addicts will either struggle to maintain their consumption or break their addiction. The further they move into heroin, the less able they are to hold high-technology jobs—sometimes any job at all—independent of a given society's depriving them of legitimate income earning opportunities by economic and social ostracism. Addicts' incomes decline and they likely turn to petty property crime to maintain their livelihood and addiction even with vastly reduced heroin prices.[41] The results obviously impose economic externalities on society.

On the other hand, those struggling to break their addiction do need and deserve assistance, thereby obligating society, for both practical and moral reasons, to continue to fund treatment centers or to find alternative means of assistance with proven success.[42] Either way there is an impact on the public treasury.

All this leaves unsaid, of course, whether the externalities deriving from demand are "better" or "worse" than those deriving from law enforcement efforts to reduce it. The point here is simply to explore the dimensions of demand-related externalities that have significant social, economic, and political consequences independent of illegalizing laws or the policies to implement them. Cannabis users produce nominal consequences on society, heroin users much more. Cocaine users, because of the sheer numbers involved if not the social chemistry of the drug itself, appear to be the greatest challenge.

COCAINE

As recently as 1975 one major connoisseur of the cocaine scene, in a heavily read and subsequently cited handbook on the history, use, and effects of the drug, wrote that cocaine is nonaddictive and relatively harmless and therefore should be legalized in order to be used for an enjoyment that is essentially victimless. He furthered his efforts by including in his publication appendices detailing how to refine, store, and use cocaine.[43] Other observers were taking similar positions as late as 1979.[44]

Discordant voices were heard, however. By the late 1970s disquieting evidence was accumulating about cocaine's physiological and psychological safety even though many deficiencies in the knowledge base of the drug's effects on the human organism were acknowledged to exist.[45] By the beginning of the 1980s the evidence was more disconcerting for chronic as well as acute users,[46] although it continued to be said that undesired effects on recreational (occasional) users were rare and not serious.[47]   Some held that, in any event, the positive rewards—the stimulation and the euphoria—overshadowed the negative consequences, even when such effects were dysfunctional to appetite, sleep, or sexual relations,[48] and that these dysfunctional aspects certainly did not merit illegalizing the drug.[49]

By about 1984—and certainly by 1985—virtually everyone writing on the effects of cocaine on human beings presented increasingly alarming information, even for recreational users.[50] By the late 1980s many subscribed to the idea that cocaine, at whatever dose and whatever usage frequency, is unsafe and potentially harmful.[51] Most of the literature in our data base views cocaine consumption with considerable alarm regarding its harmful personal effects,[52] especially on acute and chronic users, and especially on those who free base or who smoke crack cocaine or cocaine paste (*basuco*).[53]

The route of administration is viewed as important in understanding cocaine's psychobiological and neurobiological effects. Intranasal ingestion and even smoking cocaine hydrochloride is viewed as producing consequences much less malignant than injecting cocaine hydrochloride or smoking pure cocaine alkaloids ("free basing") or in smoking crack cocaine or cocaine paste.[54] By virtually unanimous vote, crack cocaine is the most deleterious.

The question is, does self-harm necessarily create significant social, economic, and political consequences? As with cannabis and heroin, we look first at generally agreed-upon self-harms and then try to determine which from among them would likely have significant consequences for societies and peoples.

Among examples of consequences not likely to produce significant social, economic, or political externalities (except insofar as the public must pick up hospital and treatment costs) are "cocaine panic disorders," which begin among some people during recreational cocaine use but continue after usage stops. These disorders are characterized, in part, by a rapid heartbeat, faintness, shortness of breath, and extreme nervousness.[55]

Another example of self-harm but with mixed probabilities of creating significant externalities is cocaine-related depression.[56] The depression, observed to accompany panic disorders as well as develop independently of them, is particularly noted among female users. More often than males, female users have experiences with major cocaine-related depression, a condition from which they improve less rapidly than do males. Thus they are more likely than cocaine-using males to experience more personal problems, have less stability in work situations, and find less satisfaction in any treatment programs they enter.[57] Of course, large numbers of psychologically depressed people anywhere, for whatever reason, be they female or male, are quite capable of producing social and economic costs—abandoned or inadequately cared-for children, hospital and welfare costs of indigent or economically vulnerable abusers, productivity losses in the work place, and so forth.

Nevertheless, panic disorders and many nominal personal health problems such as mild depression are examples, on the whole, of factors that produce unremarkable externalities. Not so, however, when the health problems, usually associated with cocaine overdoses,[58] land either the users or their offspring in hospital emergency wards or funerary parlors. If the users have ample economic resources and insurance policies, few costs may be externalized, except the usual increase in insurance premiums for everyone as actuaries work on the "pool" and as medical insurance plans weigh their profits. But, increasingly, cocaine-related emergency ward patients appear to come from social strata that have few economic resources and little medical insurance. The public, in large part, cares for them insofar as they are cared for at all. Social overhead costs increase, as do taxes to cover them. Insurance costs rise, as do everyone's premiums. At some point, political resistance is created. In the United States, some hospitals are refusing indigent cases, and the public is demanding a roll-back of insurance costs and taxes.

While these points are interesting and have the prospect of becoming more so, they are still mostly side issues. The cocaine-related events that produce the most troublesome externalities are the following: cocaine alkaloids that cross the placental barrier and produce "crack" babies and other deleterious newborn outcomes, and cocaine-related violence and aggression.

Fetuses

The most frequently discussed externality is cocaine's effects on a female user's fetus, on the newborn, and on pregnancy outcomes.[59] Popular descriptions abound of the hardships that newborns suffer when they enter life already addicted to cocaine.[60] Beyond these matters, however, researchers find that cocaine-using women not only tend to have a significantly higher rate of spontaneous abortion than nonusers, their infants have significant depression of interactive behavior and a relatively poor organizational response to environmental stimuli. All this suggests a potentially profound impact on the child's neurological behavior.[61] The newborn's birth weight is lower,[62] and, although it is not reported whether brain size catches up after the infants are weaned from cocaine, studies do show the intracranial hemidiameter of fetuses of cocaine-using women to be significantly smaller than those of fetuses of nonusers. Moreover, parent-child bonding between such infants and their mothers is adversely affected.[63]

Most of the above relate to cocaine-addicted infants' initial human suffering (withdrawal from addiction), their eventual life's chances, and the quality of human relationships between them and their mothers. These are important social considerations. However, it is the impact of placental barrier transfer of cocaine alkaloids on the public treasury that evokes the most political and economic discussion—a discussion complicated both by the rapid increase in the numbers of cocaine-addicted babies being seen in hospital intensive care units and by their staggering costs. For example, $100,000 is viewed as not being an unrealistic figure to cover a newborn cocaine-addicted child's intensive care costs, not to mention likely subsequent child abuse by cocaine-impaired parents. Such violence (the syndrome is discussed below) produces its own ultimate economic costs on society—family counseling, welfare, eventual additional overhead on educational institutions, and so forth.[64]

There is a ray of optimism coming from the Northwestern University Medical School for a conscientious pregnant woman: If she stops smoking cocaine soon after becoming pregnant she *might* be able to reduce the risk of physical or mental damage to her child.[65]

Violence and Aggression

Impaired newborns frequently are the target of the violence associated with the psychopharmacology of cocaine, especially in its crack form.[66] In one of the first studies clearly linking violent behavior and crack cocaine use, it was reported that nearly half of the callers to a nationwide cocaine hotline said they had committed violent crimes or aggressive acts, including—aside from child abuse—robbery, rape, murder and other physical assaults. Two-thirds of those reporting aggressive behavior indicated they did so while using crack rather than during withdrawal.[67]

It is thought that cocaine-related stress over money, sex, and violence contribute to family disintegration;[68] that cocaine-using parents neglect their offspring; that cocaine using offspring frequently abuse their parents or their siblings, impoverish their intellect, and remove themselves from productive social and economic integration;[69] and that many shootings among teenagers are associated with cocaine and crack.[70] If real, the economic and social costs are staggering. If believed, but nevertheless unreal, the political consequences are virtually the same. Policies are enacted to deal with a perceived social condition.

Aside from self-harm, crack cocaine produces victims, and the result in many cases is to create social, economic, and political externalities that the public must bear.[71] Mentioned in this section are damaged fetuses, children, adolescents, and families; psychopharmacologically related violence; transportation and workplace accidents; workplace and classroom inefficiencies; increased business and social overhead; and heightened social welfare costs. It is on these grounds that most writers judge cocaine demand to be a public, not a private, issue. It seems quite clear that these considerations apply quite aside from public laws and policies that illegalize cocaine and enforce its proscription.

We have now seen that supply, demand, and the efforts to disrupt or reduce both have all created externalities, both peculiar and expected, which have social, economic, and political consequences. Some are tolerable, some counterproductive, some inadmissable. Is anything yet to be done? Section C considers the literature dealing with *solutions* beyond those already raised in Chapter 5 in the discussions on countervailing initiatives.

NOTES

[1]A mid-1990 sharp price increase in the wholesale price of cocaine, the first such rise in almost ten years, may alter these observations [See Joseph B. Treaster, "Cocaine Prices Rise, and Police Efforts May Be Responsible," *The New York Times*, 1990]. The increase could have resulted from a sharp rise in consumption (unlikely), effective interdiction efforts that reduced supplies, therefore heralding extensive law enforcement efforts both in the United States and in its principal drug supplier countries (little corroborating evidence although a position favored by *The Economist* ["Drugs: Goodby, Cocaine," 1990]), or supply difficulties in Latin America. Supply difficulties, due to internal wars in Colombia, are the most likely reason. Colombia's drug barons are not able to move their cocaine. This condition decreases supplies in consumer countries and at the same time depresses prices for coca-leaf growers. Bolivian growers, for example, were, in mid-1990, in a crisis condition [see James Painter, "Bolivian Coca Growers Voluntarily Eradicate Crops as Price Drops," *The Christian Science Monitor*, 1990; and Painter, "Bolivia Tries to Break Its Economic Addiction," *The Christian Science Monitor*, 1990]. The coca-leaf depression was still severe in 1991 [James Brooke, "Peru, Its U.S. Aid Imperiled, Plots a New Drug Strategy," *The New York Times*, 1991].

[2]See the discussions on consumption in Ch. 1 (pp. 6-9), Ch. 2 (pp. 26-29), and Ch. 3 (pp. 38-40).

[3]See, for example, Lee I. Dogoloff, "Don't Legalize Marijuana," *The New York Times*, 1987; Roy Hanu Hart, *Bitter Grass: The Cruel Truth about Marijuana*, 1980; Donna J. Hymes, "New Reasons to 'Keep off the Grass,'" *Current Health*, 1987; Oriana Josseau Kalant et al., *Cannabis: Health Risks*, 1983; and Gabriel G. Nahas, *Keep off the Grass: A Scientific Enquiry into the Biological Effects of Marijuana*, 1979. Donald Ian Macdonald ["Marijuana Smoking Worse for Lungs," *Journal of the American Medical Association*, 1988] claims that smoking one marijuana "joint" is approximately four times more hazardous to health than smoking a single tobacco cigarette. On this theme see, also, "Marijuana more Harmful than Tobacco," *New Scientist*, 1987. Louis Lasagna ["Is the Social Use of Marijuana Dangerous or Addictive?," *Advances in Alcohol and Substance Abuse*, 1985] admonishes that, although marijuana and hashish are not innocent materials or harmless, the exaggeration of the risks of using them, and the loss of credibility that scientists and regulatory officials suffer when they fall into a "reefer madness" mode, does everyone a disservice. The best policy is to be both concerned and honest. In a similar vein, Tod H. Mikuriya and Michael R. Aldrich ["Cannabis 1988: Old Drug, New Dangers: The Potency Question," *Journal of Psychoactive Drugs*, 1988] decry the current "potency scare," which alleges that newly marketed varieties of cannabis are anywhere from four to ten times more potent than in the past. It is all a disinformation campaign, they allege, the net effect of which will be to reduce the legitimacy and credibility of drug counselors.

[4]A sampling of the literature in the "harmless" or "reduced risk" category includes the following: William E. Carter, ed., *Cannabis in Costa Rica: A Study of Chronic Marihuana Use*, 1980; Lambros Comitas, "Cannabis and Work in Jamaica: A Refutation of the Amotivational Syndrome," *Annals of the New York Academy of Sciences*, 1976; Lester Grinspoon, *Marihuana Reconsidered*, 2d ed., 1977; Leo E. Hollister, "Cannabis—1988," *Acta Psychiatrica Scandinavia, Supplement*, 1988; Paula H. Ikleinman et al., "Daily Marijuana Use and Problem Behaviors among Adolescents," *International Journal of the Addictions*, 1988; Shai Linn et al., "The Association of Marijuana Use with Outcome of Pregnancy," *American Journal of Public Health*, 1983; Roger E.

Meyer, "Psychiatric Consequences of Marihuana Use: The State of the Evidence," in *Marihuana and Health Hazards: Methodological Issues in Current Marihuana Research*, J. R. Tinklenberg, ed., 1975; Vera Rubin and Lambros Comitas, *Ganja in Jamaica: Medical Anthropological Study of Chronic Marihuana Use*, 1975; and Costas Stefanis, Rhea Dornbush, and Max Fink, eds., *Hashish: Studies of Long Term Use*, 1977.

[5]Refer to note 11, Chapter 3 for a discussion of the relationship of culture to cannabis use among Jamaican women.

[6]See, for example, Ernest L. Abel, *Marijuana, Tobacco, Alcohol, and Reproduction*, 1983; Ernest L. Abel and Robert J. Sokol, "Marijuana and Cocaine Use during Pregnancy," in *Drug Use in Pregnancy*, Jennifer R. Niebyl, ed., 1988; *Analysis of the Domestic Cannabis Problem and the Federal Response*, National Drug Enforcement Policy Board, 1986; B. Bower, "'Day After' Effects of Pot Smoking," *Science News*, 1985; Carl Chambers et al., *Chemical Dependencies: Patterns, Costs, and Consequences*, 1987; Sidney Cohen, "Cannabis: Effects upon Adolescent Motivation," in *Marijuana and Youth: Clinical Observations on Motivation and Learning*, 1982; Rhea L. Dornbush, Alfred M. Freedman, and Max Fink, eds., "Chronic Cannabis Use," *Annals of the New York Academy of Sciences*, 1976; Rhea Dornbush and A. Kokkevi, "Acute Effects of Cannabis on Cognitive, Perceptual, and Motor Performance in Chronic Hashish Users," *Annals of the New York Academy of Sciences*, 1976; P. A. Fried, "Postnatal Consequences of Maternal Marijuana Use," in *Current Research on the Consequences of Maternal Drug Abuse*, Theodore Pinkert, ed., 1985; A. Hamid Ghodse, "Cannabis Psychosis," *The British Journal of Addiction*, 1986; Meyer D. Glantz, ed., *Correlates and Consequences of Marijuana Use*, 1984; James A. Halikas et al., "A Longitudinal Study of Marijuana Effects," *The International Journal of the Addictions*, 1985; Herbert Hendin, *Living High: Daily Marijuana Use among Adults*, 1987; Ralph Hingson et al., "Maternal Marijuana Use and Neonatal Outcome: Uncertainty Posed by Self-Reports," *American Journal of Public Health*, 1986; Leo E. Hollister, "Marijuana and Immunity," *Journal of Psychoactive Drugs*, 1988; Les Leanne Hoyt, "Effects of Marijuana on Fetal Development," *Journal of Drug and Alcohol Education*, 1981; S. Husain and I. Khan, "An Update on Cannabis Research," *Bulletin on Narcotics*, 1985; Helen C. Jones and Paul W. Lovinger, *The Marijuana Question and Science's Search for an Answer*, 1985; Michael Lamanna, "Marijuana: Implications of Use by Young People," *Journal of Drug Education*, 1981; Ingrid L. Lanter, "Marijuana Abuse by Children and Teenagers: A Pediatrician's View," in *Marijuana and Youth: Clinical Observations on Motivation and Learning*, 1982; *Marijuana and Health*, National Academy of Sciences, 1982; Thomas H. Maugh, "Marijuana 'Justifies Serious Concern,'" *Science*, 1982; Madelaine O. Maykut, *Health Consequences of Acute and Chronic Marijuana Use*, 1984; Raphael Mechoulam, "Research on Cannabis: An Overview," *Impact of Science on Society*, 1984; Doris H. Millman, "Psychological Effects of Cannabis in Adolescence," in *Marijuana and Youth: Clinical Observations on Motivation and Learning*, 1982; Gabriel G. Nahas et al., *Marihuana in Science and Medicine*, 1984; National Institute on Drug Abuse, *Marijuana and Health*, 1982; Qutub H. Qazi et al., "Abnormalities in Offspring Associated with Prenatal Marihuana Exposure," *Developmental Pharmacology and Therapeutics*, 1985; M. I. Soueif, "Differential Association Between Chronic Cannabis Use and Brain Function Deficits," *Annals of the New York Academy of Sciences*, 1976; D. P. Tashkin et al., "Subacute Effects of Heavy Marihuana Smoking on Pulmonary Function in Healthy Men," *New England Journal of Medicine*, 1976; Katherine Tennes, "Effects of Marijuana on Pregnancy and Fetal Development in the Human," in *Marijuana Effects on the Endocrine and Reproductive Systems*, Monique Braude and Jacqueline Ludford, eds. 1983; K. Tunving, "Psychiatric Effects of Cannabis Use," *Acta*

Psychiatrica Scandinavica, 1985; U.S. Congress, Senate Committee on Labor and Public Welfare, Subcommittee on Alcoholism and Narcotics, Hearing, "Marihuana Research and Legal Controls," 1974; U.S. Congress, Senate Committee on the Judiciary, Subcommittee on Criminal Justice, Hearing, "Health Consequences of Marihuana Use," 1980; U.S. Congress, Select Committee on Narcotics Abuse and Control, "Health Questions About Marihuana," 1982; and Renee C. Wert and Michael L. Raulin, "The Chronic Cerebral Effect of Cannabis Use," *International Journal of the Addictions*, 1986.

[7]Robert C. Petersen, "Marijuana Overview," in *Correlates and Consequences of Marijuana Use*, Meyer D. Glantz, ed., 1984.

[8]Robert C. Petersen, "Marijuana Overview," in *Correlates and Consequences of Marijuana Use*, Meyer D. Glantz, ed., 1984, pp. 10-11; A. Hamid Ghodse, "Cannabis Psychosis," *The British Journal of Addiction*, 1986; Roger E. Meyer, "Psychiatric Consequences of Marihuana Use: The State of the Evidence," in *Marijuana and Health Hazards: Methodological Issues in Current Marijuana Research*, J. R. Tinklenberg, ed., 1975; and K. Tunving, "Psychiatric Effects of Cannabis Use," *Acta Psychiatrica Scandinavica*, 1985.

[9]Robert C. Petersen, "Marijuana Overview," in *Correlates and Consequences of Marijuana Use*, Meyer D. Glantz, ed., 1984, p. 11; See also Diana Baumrind and Kenneth A. Moselle, "A Developmental Perspective on Adolescent Drug Abuse," *Advances in Alcohol and Substance Abuse*, 1985; Sidney Cohen, "Cannabis: Effects upon Adolescent Motivation," in *Marijuana and Youth: Clinical Observations on Motivation and Learning*, 1982; Lambros Comitas, "Cannabis and Work in Jamaica: A Refutation of the Amotivational Syndrome," *Annals of the New York Academy of Sciences*, 1976; Rhea L. Dornbush, Alfred M. Freedman, and Max Fink, eds., "Chronic Cannabis Use," *Annals of the New York Academy of Sciences*, 1976; Herbert Hendin, *Living High: Daily Marijuana Use Among Adults*, 1987; Denise B. Kandel, ed., *Longitudinal Research on Drug Use: Empirical Findings and Methodological Issues*, 1978; Doris H. Millman, "Psychological Effects of Cannabis in Adolescence," in *Marijuana and Youth: Clinical Observations on Motivation and Learning*, 1982; Patricia J. Morningstar, "Thandai and Chilam: Traditional Hindu Beliefs about the Proper Uses of Cannabis," *Journal of Psychoactive Drugs*, 1985; and Vera Rubin and Lambros Comitas, *Ganja in Jamaica: Medical Anthropological Study of Chronic Marihuana Use*, 1975.

[10]Ernest L. Abel, *Psychoactive Drugs and Sex*, 1985; and Carl Chambers and Kathryn Pribble, "Gaining Some Understanding of Drugs and Their Effects," in *Chemical Dependencies: Patterns, Costs, and Consequences*, Carl Chambers et al., eds., 1987.

[11]Robert C. Petersen, "Marijuana Overview," in *Correlates and Consequences of Marijuana Use*, Meyer D. Glantz, ed., 1984.

[12]Ibid., and Vera Rubin and Lambros Comitas, *Ganja in Jamaica: Medical Anthropological Study of Chronic Marihuana Use*, 1975.

[13]Katherine Tennes ["Effects of Marijuana on Pregnancy and Fetal Development in the Human," in *Marijuana Effects on the Endocrine and Reproductive Systems*, Monique C. Braude and Jacqueline P. Ludford, eds., 1983] acknowledges that early studies on human pregnancies suggested that marijuana could alter the delivery process, reduce the infant's weight gain, or affect visual and neurological processes. However, she concludes that confirmation of these findings is lacking as is evidence for the effect of direct action of marijuana. Nevertheless, other authors maintain that marijuana has at least a highly probable impact in the categories. See the listings under *with probable externalities* in the right-hand column of the main text.

[14]Leo E. Hollister, "Marijuana and Immunity," *Journal of Psychoactive Drugs*, 1988; National Institute on Drug Abuse, *Marijuana and Health*, 1982; and Robert C. Petersen, "Marijuana Overview," in *Correlates and Consequences of Marijuana Use*, Meyer D. Glantz, ed., 1984.

[15]Robert C. Petersen, "Marijuana Overview," in *Correlates and Consequences of Marijuana Use*, Meyer D. Glantz, ed., 1984.

[16]William E. Carter, ed., *Cannabis in Costa Rica: A Study of Chronic Marihuana Use*, 1980; Lester Grinspoon, *Marihuana Reconsidered*, 2d ed., 1977; Donna J. Hymes, "New Reasons to 'Keep off the Grass,'" *Current Health*, 1987; Helen C. Jones and Paul W. Lovinger, *The Marijuana Question and Science's Search for an Answer*, 1985; Donald Ian Macdonald, "Marijuana Smoking Worse for Lungs," *Journal of the American Medical Association*, 1988; *Marijuana and Health*, National Academy of Sciences, 1982; "Marijuana More Harmful than Tobacco," *New Scientist*, 1987; National Institute on Drug Abuse, *Marijuana and Health*, 1982; and D. P. Tashkin et al., "Subacute Effects of Heavy Marihuana Smoking on Pulmonary Function in Healthy Men," *New England Journal of Medicine*, 1976.

[17]Carl Chambers and Kathryn Pribble, "Gaining Some Understanding of Drugs and Their Effects," in *Chemical Dependencies*, Carl Chambers et al., eds., 1987, p. 29; M. I. Soueif, "Differential Association between Chronic Cannabis Use and Brain Function Deficits," *Annals of the New York Academy of Sciences*, 1976.

[18]Donna J. Hymes, "New Reasons to 'Keep off the Grass,'" *Current Health*, 1987; Helen C. Jones and Paul W. Lovinger, *The Marijuana Question and Science's Search for an Answer*, 1985; *Marijuana and Health*, National Academy of Sciences, 1982; and National Institute on Drug Abuse, *Marijuana and Health*, 1982.

[19]*Marijuana and Health*, National Academy of Sciences, 1982; and Robert C. Petersen, "Marijuana Overview," in *Correlates and Consequences of Marijuana Use*, Meyer D. Glantz, ed., 1984.

[20]Carl Chambers and Kathryn Pribble, "Gaining Some Understanding of Drugs and Their Effects," in *Chemical Dependencies*, Carl Chambers et al., eds., 1987, pp. 34-35. See also Ernest L. Abel, *Marijuana, Tobacco, Alcohol, and Reproduction*, 1983; *Marijuana and Health*, National Academy of Sciences, 1982; National Institute on Drug Abuse, *Marijuana and Health*, 1982; and Robert C. Petersen, "Marijuana Overview," in *Correlates and Consequences of Marijuana Use*, Meyer D. Glantz, ed., 1984, p. 9.

[21]Robert Hendin, *Living High: Daily Marijuana Use among Adults*, 1987; Carl Chambers and Kathryn Pribble, "Gaining Some Understanding of Drugs and Their Effects," in *Chemical Dependencies*, Carl Chambers et al., eds., 1987.

[22]Carl Chambers and Kathryn Pribble, "Gaining Some Understanding of Drugs and Their Effects," in *Chemical Dependencies*, Carl Chambers et al., eds., 1987, pp. 32-33; Donna J. Hymes, "New Reasons to 'Keep off the Grass,'" *Current Health*, 1987; *Marijuana and Health*, National Academy of Sciences, 1982; M. I. Soueif, "Differential Association between Chronic Cannabis Use and Brain Function Deficits," *Annals of the New York Academy of Sciences*, 1976. See also Rhea L. Dornbush and A. Kokkevi, "Acute Effects of Cannabis on Cognitive, Perceptual, and Motor Performance in Chronic Hashish Users," *Annals of the New York Academy of Sciences*, 1976; Madelaine O. Maykut, *Health Consequences of Acute and Chronic Marijuana Use*, 1984; Sarbjit Mendhiratta et al., "Cannabis and Cognitive Functions: A Re-Evaluation Study," *British Journal of Addiction*, 1988; *Marijuana: The National Impact on Education*, American Council on Marijuana and Other Psychoactive Drugs, 1982; and National Institute on Drug Abuse, *Marijuana and Health*, 1982.

[23]Ernest L. Abel, *Marijuana, Tobacco, Alcohol, and Reproduction*, 1983; Ernest L. Abel and Robert J. Sokol, "Marijuana and Cocaine Use during Pregnancy," in *Drug Use in Pregnancy*, Jennifer R. Niebyl, ed., 1988; P. A. Fried, "Postnatal Consequences of Maternal Marijuana Use," in *Current Research on the Consequences of Maternal Drug Abuse*, Theodore Pinkert, ed., 1985; *Marijuana and Health*, National Academy of Sciences, 1982; and Katherine Tennes, "Effects of Marijuana on Pregnancy and Fetal Development in the Human," in *Marijuana Effects on the Endocrine and Reproductive Systems*, Monique C. Braude and Jacqueline P. Ludford, eds., 1983.

[24]Carl Chambers and Kathryn Pribble, "Gaining Some Understanding of Drugs and Their Effects," in *Chemical Dependencies*, Carl Chambers et al., eds., 1987, p. 32; Robert C. Petersen, "Marijuana Overview," in *Correlates and Consequences of Marijuana Use*, Meyer D. Glantz, ed., 1984, pp. 6-8. See also B. Bower, "'Day After' Effects of Pot Smoking," *Science News*, 1985; Rhea L. Dornbush and A. Kokkevi, "Acute Effects of Cannabis on Cognitive, Perceptual, and Motor Performance in Chronic Hashish Users," *Annals of the New York Academy of Sciences*, 1976; *Marijuana and Health*, National Academy of Sciences, 1982; and Jerome A. Yesavage et al., "Carry-over Effects of Marijuana Intoxication on Aircraft Pilot Performance; A Preliminary Report," *American Journal of Psychiatry*, 1985.

[25]Sidney Cohen, "Cannabis: Effects upon Adolescent Motivation," in *Marijuana and Youth: Clinical Observations on Motivation and Learning*, 1982; Denise B. Kandel, "Drugs and Drinking Behavior among Youth," *Annual Review of Sociology*, 1980; *Marijuana: The National Impact on Education*, American Council on Marijuana and Other Psychoactive Drugs, 1982; Doris H. Millman, "Psychological Effects of Cannabis in Adolescence," in *Marijuana and Youth: Clinical Observations on Motivation and Learning*, 1982; Margaret Penning and Gordon E. Barnes, "Adolescent Marijuana Use: A Review," *International Journal of the Addictions*, 1982; and Richard H. Schwartz, "Frequent Marijuana Use in Adolescence: What Are the Signs, Stages?" *NASSP Bulletin*, 1985.

[26]Robert C. Petersen, "Marijuana Overview," in *Correlates and Consequences of Marijuana Use*, Meyer D. Glantz, ed., 1984, p. 5.

[27]Petersen (Ibid.) cites H. Moskowitz, S. Sharma, and K. Zieman ["Duration of Skills Performance Impairment, *Proceedings of the 25th Conference of the American Association of Automotive Medicine*, 1981].

[28]In addition to Petersen's review, see Dale H. Gieringer, "Marijuana, Driving and Accident Safety," *Journal of Psychoactive Drugs*, 1988; Donna J. Hymes, "New Reasons to 'Keep off the Grass,'" *Current Health*, 1987; and *Marijuana and Health*, National Academy of Sciences, 1982.

[29]In addition to Petersen's review (Ibid.), see Jerome A. Yesavage et al., "Carry-over Effects of Marijuana Intoxication on Aircraft Pilot Performance: A Preliminary Report," *American Journal of Psychiatry*, 1985.

[30]See Robert C. Petersen, "Marijuana Overview," in *Correlates and Consequences of Marijuana Use*, Meyer D. Glantz, ed., 1984.

[31]A principal exception to this generalization is a paragraph in John Kaplan's *The Hardest Drug: Heroin and Public Policy*, 1983. Kaplan affirms that "surprisingly, the best estimates of the physical damage heroin does to its user, when used under conditions of free availability, indicate that the drug is a relatively safe one, at least as compared to alcohol and tobacco. While the long-term, heavy use of these legal drugs may cause serious, indeed fatal, tissue damage, heroin produces no analogy to the cirrhosis, peripheral neuritis, gastritis, and central nervous system damage caused by long-term, heavy

use of alcohol, or to the cardiovascular and lung impairment caused by tobacco use" (p. 127). On the whole, this is a scholarly book devoted to examining the costs and benefits of different public policies toward heroin. Any heroin policy will benefit some people while hurting others; the present U.S. policy hurts U.S. institutions of criminal justice, those who are addicted, and those upon whom addicts prey—at least to the extent of any additional depredation caused by their heroin addiction. After examining these consequences of heroin prohibition, the author explores a policy of "free availability." This policy would, in many ways, improve the lives of present addicts and of those they victimize, as well as the integrity of criminal justice processes. On the other hand, it would hurt those who would then become addicted and who would not otherwise have encountered heroin. It would also hurt those who, in one way or another, would suffer more from the public health and personal aspects of a greatly increased addiction rate than they do from the many ramifications of the present U.S. heroin policy. If free availability does not hold sufficient benefits to warrant implementation, what about heroin maintenance? Implementation of this policy in the United States would injure those who would have to pay the bill, those who live in the vicinity of a heroin distribution center, and those who become addicted through diversion from the system; it would improve the lot of prison addicts and those whom they victimize. Kaplan then presents an extensive discussion on the law and the user, arguing that decriminalizing use (as opposed to decriminalizing supply), if coupled with coerced treatment for those who cannot "handle their drug," would constitute a least offensive option and one that would produce greater benefits than any of the current policies extant or any of the variations that he examined.

[32]See Ronald Kesler, "Cheaper Heroin Resulting in More Deaths," *The Washington Post*, 1983; Matt Lait, "Heroin Traffic Shifts to the West," *The Washington Post*, 1989; and A. James Ruttenber and James L. Luke, "Heroin-Related Deaths: New Epidemiologic Insights," *Science*, 1984.

[33]Matt Lait, "Heroin Traffic Shifts to the West," *The Washington Post*, 1989.

[34]See Ronald Kesler, "Cheaper Heroin Resulting in More Deaths," *The Washington Post*, 1983; and U.S. Department of Justice, Drug Enforcement Administration, Office of Intelligence, *Black Tar Heroin in the United States*, 1986.

[35]Angela Burr, "A British View of Prescribing Pharmaceutical Heroin to Opiate Addicts," *International Journal of the Addictions*, 1986.

[36]Marsha Rosenbaum, "When Drugs Come into the Picture, Love Flies out the Window: Love Relationships Among Women Addicts," *International Journal of the Addictions*, 1981; Marsha Rosenbaum, *Women on Heroin*, 1981.

[37]See Don DeBoau Davis, "Neurobehavioral Functions among Children Exposed to Narcotics in Utero: A Multivariate Analysis," Ph.D. diss., 1985.

[38]Don Davis's subjects [cited in note 36] who were born of methadone-maintained mothers, scored in the more pathological direction on his scales than children exposed in utero to heroin. On the other hand, Tove S. Rosen and Helen L. Johnson ["Long-Term Effects of Prenatal Methadone Maintenance," in *Current Research on the Consequences of Maternal Drug Abuse*, Theodore M. Pinkert, ed., 1985] declare that there are no uniform long-term effects of prenatal methadone maintenance on the children in their study. They did acknowledge that, in the short term (first three years of life), "methadone maintained children have a higher incidence of minor neurological abnormalities and lower scores on developmental evaluations." See also David P. Ausubel, "Methadone Maintenance Treatment: The Other Side of the Coin," *International Journal of the Addictions*, 1983.

[39]Kathleen B. Fiks, Helen L. Johnson, and Tove S. Rosen, "Methadone-Maintained Mothers: 3-Year Follow-up of Parental Functioning," *International Journal of the Addictions*, 1985.

[40]John Kaplan, *The Hardest Drug: Heroin and Public Policy*, 1983, p. 131.

[41]See, for example, John Ball, "A Selective Review of the Crime-Drug Literature with Reference to Future Research Implications," in *Drug Use and Crime: Report of the Panel on Drug Use and Criminal Behavior*, Robert Shellow, ed., 1976; John Ball, John W. Shaffer, and David N. Nurco, "The Day-to-Day Criminality of Heroin Addicts in Baltimore: A Study in the Continuity of Offense Rates," *Drug and Alcohol Dependence*, 1983; John Ball et al., "Lifetime Criminality of Heroin Addicts in the United States," *Journal of Drug Issues*, 1982; and Bruce Johnson, Kevin Anderson, and Eric D. Wish, "A Day in the Life of 105 Drug Addicts and Abusers: Crimes Committed and How the Money Was Spent," *Sociology and Social Research*, 1988.

[42]One alternative is presented by Patrick Biernacki, *Pathways from Heroin Addiction: Recovery without Treatment*, 1986. See also Colin Brewer, "The Management of Opiate Abuse: Learning from Other Addictions," *Journal of Drug Issues*, 1988; Ann F. Brunswick, "Dealing with Drugs: Heroin Abuse as a Social Problem," *The International Journal of the Addictions*, 1986; Angela Burr, "A British View of Prescribing Pharmaceutical Heroin to Opiate Addicts," *International Journal of the Addictions*, 1986; Philip Connell, "'I Need Heroin.' Thirty Years' Experience of Drug Dependence and of the Medical Challenges at Local, National, International and Political Levels. What Next?" *British Journal of Addiction*, 1986; and Douglas S. Lipton and Michael J. Maranda, "Detoxification from Heroin Dependency: An Overview of Method and Effectiveness," *Advances in Alcohol and Drug Abuse*, 1982.

[43]Richard Ashley, *Cocaine: Its History, Uses, and Effects*, 1975.

[44]See, for example, J. L. Phillips and R. W. Wynne, *Cocaine: The Mystique and the Reality*, 1980.

[45]Donald J. Egan and David Owen Robinson, "Cocaine: Magical Drug or Menace?" *International Journal of the Addictions*, 1979. Ronald K. Siegel ["Cocaine Smoking," *New England Journal of Medicine*, 1979], asserted in 1979 that smoking coca leaf, cigars, and cigarettes and even mixing cocaine hydrochloride with tobacco or marijuana cigarettes seemed to provoke little or no intoxication except for large doses, which, in any event, seemed not to result in any serious consequences. However, smoking cocaine alkaloid or base (free base) presented conditions highly deleterious to one's health, producing anomalies such as "manic-like euphoria, depressive-like dysphoria, or schizophrenic-like paranoid psychosis." No doubt he would be equally alarmed at the consequences of smoking present-day crack.

[46]See, for example, C. Carbajal, "Psychosis Produced by Nasal Aspiration of Cocaine in Hydrochloride," in *Cocaine 1980*, F. R. Jeri, ed., 1980; Sidney Cohen, *Cocaine Today*, 1981; R. B. Millman, "Adverse Effects of Cocaine," *Hospital and Community Psychiatry*, 1982; and Ronald K. Siegel, "Long-Term Effects of Recreational Cocaine Use: A Four Year Study," in *Cocaine 1980*, F. R. Jeri, ed., 1980;

[47]Lester Grinspoon and James G. Bakalar, "Adverse Effects of Cocaine: Selected Issues," *Annals of the New York Academy of Sciences*, 1981.

[48]Ronald K. Siegel, "Cocaine and Sexual Dysfunction: The Curse of Mama Coca," *Journal of Psychoactive Drugs*, 1982.

[49]C. Van Dyke and R. Byck, "Cocaine," *Scientific American*, 1982.

[50]See, for example, John Grabowski and Steven I. Dworkin, "Cocaine: An Overview of Current Issues," *The International Journal of the Addictions*, 1985; Jerry M. Isner et al., "Acute Cardiac Events Temporally Related to Cocaine Abuse," *The New England Journal of Medicine*, 1986. See also Sidney Cohen, "Recent Developments in the Abuse of Cocaine," *Bulletin on Narcotics*, 1984; and John Murray "An Overview of Cocaine Use and Abuse," *Psychological Reports*, 1986. It should be noted that an alarm for recreational users had been sounded as early as 1979 by C. V. Wetli and R. K. Wright ["Death Caused by Recreational Cocaine Use," *Journal of the American Medical Association*, 1979].

[51]Gina Maranto, "Coke: The Random Killer," *Discover*, 1985.

[52]Specific and general overviews of all concerns may be found in the following: Ernest L. Abel and Robert J. Sokol, "Marijuana and Cocaine Use during Pregnancy," in *Drug Use in Pregnancy*, Jennifer R. Niebyl, ed., 1988; Michael Abramowitz, "Pregnant Cocaine Users Reduce Risk by Stopping," *The Washington Post*, 1989; Edgar H. Adams et al., "Trends in Prevalence and Consequences of Cocaine Use," *Advances in Alcohol and Substance Abuse*, 1986; Jerry Adler et al., "Hour by Hour Crack," *Newsweek*, 1988; Lise Anglin, *Cocaine: A Selection of Annotated Papers from 1980 to 1984 concerning Health Effects*, 1985; A. Arif, ed., *Adverse Health Consequences of Cocaine Abuse*, 1987; Thomas A. Aronson and Thomas J. Craig, "Cocaine Precipitation of Panic Disorder," *The American Journal of Psychiatry*, 1986; Bill Barol, et al., "Cocaine Babies: Hooked at Birth," *Newsweek*, 1986; B. Bower, "Cocaine Smoking May Cause Lung Damage," *Science News*, 1984; Tyler Bridges, "Colombia: Drug Problems at Home," *The Washington Post*, 1986; Katie A. Busch and Sidney H. Schnoll, "Cocaine—Review of Current Literature and Interface with the Law," *Behavioral Sciences and the Law*, 1985; Carl Chambers et al., *Chemical Dependencies: Patterns, Costs, and Consequences*, 1987; Ira J. Chasnoff et al., "Cocaine Use in Pregnancy," *New England Journal of Medicine*, 1985; Calvin Chatlos and Lawrence D. Chilnick, *Crack: What You Should Know about the Cocaine Epidemic*, 1987; Sidney Cohen, "Adverse Effects of Cocaine," *Consumer's Research Magazine*, 1985; "Crack," *Medical Letter on Drugs and Therapeutics*, 1986; Louis L. Cregler and Herbert Mark, "Medical Complications of Cocaine Abuse," *New England Journal of Medicine*, 1986; Frank H. Gawin and Herbert D. Kleber, "Abstinence Symptomatology and Psychiatric Diagnosis in Cocaine Abusers," *Archives of General Psychiatry*, 1986; John Grabowski and Steven I. Dworkin, "Cocaine: An Overview of Current Issues," *The International Journal of the Addictions*, 1985; Margaret L. Griffin and Steven M. Mirin, "A Comparison of Male and Female Cocaine Abusers," *Archives of General Psychiatry*, 1989; Lester Grinspoon and James B. Bakalar, *Cocaine: A Drug and Its Social Evolution*; rev. ed., 1985; Signe Hammer and Lesley Hazleton, "Cocaine and the Chemical Brain," *Science Digest*, 1984; Michael Isikoff, "Users of Crack Cocaine Link Violence to Drug's Influence," *The Washington Post*, 1989; Douglas Jehl, "Surge Reported in Health Emergencies Tied to Cocaine," *The Los Angeles Times*, 1989; John B. Murray, "An Overview of Cocaine Use and Abuse," *Psychological Reports*, 1986; Charles P. O'Hara III, "Behavioral Effects of Phencyclidine and Cocaine on Infants Exposed in Utero, as Measured by the Neonatal Behavioral Assessment Scale," Ph.D. diss., 1987; Peter T. Pasternack, Stephen B. Colvin, and I. Gregory Baumann, "Cocaine-Induced Angina Pectoris and Acute Myocardial Infarction in Patients Younger than 40 Years," *The American Journal of Cardiology*, 1985; M. E. Pasto et al., "Ventricular Configuration and Cerebral Growth in Infants Born to Drug-Dependent Mothers," *Pediatric Radiology*, 1985; R. M. Post and N. R. Contel, "Human and Animal Studies of Cocaine: Implications for Development of Behavioral Pathology," in *Stimulants: Neurochemical, Behavioral, and Clinical*

Perspectives, I. Creese, ed., 1983; Richard B. Resnick and Elaine B. Resnick, "Cocaine Abuse and Its Treatment," *The Psychiatric Clinics of North America*, 1984; Jeffrey S. Rosecan and Barbara F. Gross, "Newborn Victims of Cocaine Abuse," *Medical Aspects of Human Sexuality*, 1986; Reginald Smart, "Cocaine Use and Problems in North America," *Canadian Journal of Criminology*, 1986; U.S. Congress, House Select Committee on Narcotics Abuse and Control, Hearing, "Cocaine Babies," 1987; Arnold M. Washton and Mark S. Gold, "Chronic Cocaine Abuse: Evidence for Adverse Effects on Health and Functioning," *Psychiatric Annals*, 1984; Arnold M. Washton and Mark S. Gold, *Cocaine: A Clinician's Handbook*, 1987; and Arnold Washton and Nannette Stone, "The Human Cost of Chronic Cocaine Use," *Medical Aspects of Human Sexuality*, 1984.

[53]See, for example, G. Aramayo and M. Sanchez, "Clinical Manifestations Using Cocaine Paste," in *Cocaine 1980*, F. R. Jeri, ed., 1980; A. Arif, ed., *Adverse Health Consequences of Cocaine Abuse*, 1987; B. Bower, "Cocaine Smoking May Cause Lung Damage," *Science News*, 1984; Joseph J. Forno, Richard T. Young, and Cynthia Levitt, "Cocaine Abuse—The Evolution from Coca Leaves to Freebase," *Journal of Drug Education*, 1981; Lester Grinspoon and James B. Bakalar, *Cocaine: A Drug and Its Social Evolution*; rev. ed., 1985; James A. Inciardi, "Beyond Cocaine: Basuco, Crack, and Other Coca Products," *Contemporary Drug Problems*, 1987; Michael Isikoff, "Home-Grown Coca Plagues Colombia," *The Washington Post*, 1989; R. B. Millman, "Adverse Effects of Cocaine," *Hospital and Community Psychiatry*, 1982; Ronald K. Siegel, "Cocaine Smoking," *New England Journal of Medicine*, 1979; Ronald K. Siegel, "Long-term Effects of Recreational Cocaine Use: a Four Year Study," in *Cocaine 1980*, F. R. Jeri, ed., 1980; and J. Thomas Ungerleider and Therese Andrysiak, "Changes in the Drug Scene: Drug Use Trends and Behavioral Patterns," *Journal of Drug Issues*, 1984.

[54]See, for example, John Grabowski and Steven I. Dworkin, "Cocaine: An Overview of Current Issues," *The International Journal of the Addictions*, 1985; Nicholas J. Kozel and Edgar Adams, eds., *Cocaine Use in America: Epidemiologic and Clinical Perspectives*, 1985; and Richard B. Resnick and Elaine B. Resnick, "Cocaine Abuse and Its Treatment," *The Psychiatric Clinics of North America*, 1984.

[55]Thomas A. Aronson and Thomas J. Craig, "Cocaine Precipitation of Panic Disorder," *The American Journal of Psychiatry*, 1986.

[56]Lester Grinspoon and James B. Bakalar ["Adverse Effects of Cocaine: Selected Issues," *Annals of the New York Academy of Sciences*, 1981] allow that in high doses cocaine can cause depression (and even death). For diverse disciplinary points of view, see Frank H. Gawin and Herbert D. Kleber, "Abstinence Symptomatology and Psychiatric Diagnosis in Cocaine Abusers," *Archives of General Psychiatry*, 1986; R. B. Millman, "Adverse Effects of Cocaine," *Hospital and Community Psychiatry*, 1982; Richard B. Resnick and Elaine B. Resnick, "Cocaine Abuse and Its Treatment," *The Psychiatric Clinics of North America*, 1984; and Ronald K. Siegel, "Cocaine Smoking," *New England Journal of Medicine*, 1979.

[57]Margaret L. Griffin and Steven M. Mirin, "A Comparison of Male and Female Cocaine Abusers," *Archives of General Psychiatry*, 1989.

[58]See "Crack," *The Medical Letter on Drugs and Therapeutics*, 1986; Patrice Gaines-Carter, "Crack Sends Some Drug Users Backsliding into Arms of Heroin," *The Washington Post*, 1989; Douglas Jehl, "Surge Reported in Health Emergencies Tied to Cocaine," *The Los Angeles Times*, 1989; R. B. Milman, "Adverse Effects of Cocaine," *Hospital and Community Psychiatry*, 1982; R. M. Post and N. R. Contel, "Human and Animal

Studies of Cocaine: Implications for Development of Behavioral Pathology," in *Stimulants: Neurochemical, Behavioral, and Clinical Perspectives*, I. Creese, ed., 1983; and Arnold M. Washton and Mark S. Gold, "Chronic Cocaine Abuse: Evidence for Adverse Effects on Health and Functioning," *Psychiatric Annals*, 1984.

[59]Ernest L. Abel and Robert J. Sokol ["Marijuana and Cocaine Use during Pregnancy," in *Drug Use in Pregnancy*, Jennifer R. Niebyl, ed., 1988] review and summarize information on cocaine and marijuana use during pregnancy. They offer suggestions for the clinical management of pregnant patients who use drugs, and they note many studies with inconclusive correlations about the drugs' effects on fetuses.

[60]See, for example, Jerry Adler et al., "Hour by Hour Crack," *Newsweek*, 1988; Bill Barol et al., "Cocaine Babies: Hooked at Birth," *Newsweek*, 1986; and Louis Kraar, "How to Win the War on Drugs," *Fortune*, 1990.

[61]Ira J. Chasnoff et al., "Cocaine Use in Pregnancy," *The New England Journal of Medicine*, 1985.

[62]Jeffrey S. Rosecan and Barbara F. Gross, "Newborn Victims of Cocaine Abuse," *Medical Aspects of Human Sexuality*, 1986.

[63]Charles P. O'Hara III, "Behavioral Effects of Phencyclidine and Cocaine on Infants Exposed in Utero, as Measured by the Neonatal Behavioral Assessment Scale," Ph.D. diss., 1987.

[64]See the testimony given in U.S. Congress, House Select Committee on Narcotics Abuse and Control, Hearing, "Cocaine Babies," 1987.

[65]Michael Abramowitz, "Pregnant Cocaine Users Reduce Risk by Stopping," *The Washington Post*, 1989.

[66]Katie A. Busch and Sidney H. Schnoll ["Cocaine—Review of Current Literature and Interface with the Law," *Behavioral Sciences and the Law*, 1985] include in their discussion extant knowledge of the relationship between cocaine and violence as well as the forensic-psychiatric issues surrounding its use. See also Scott Armstrong, "Crack Reasserts Itself across US," *The Christian Science Monitor*, 1988. In 1981 Lester Grinspoon and James B. Bakalar ["Adverse Effects of Cocaine: Selected Issues," *Annals of the New York Academy of Sciences*, 1981] argued that cocaine tends not to produce aggressive behavior; however, crack cocaine had not yet been invented.

[67]See Michael Isikoff, "Users of Crack Cocaine Link Violence to Drug's Influence," *The Washington Post*, 1989.

[68]See, for example, Jerry Adler et al., "Hour by Hour Crack," *Newsweek*, 1988; Gina Kolata, "In Cities, Poor Families Are Dying of Crack," *The New York Times*, 1989.

[69]See, for example, Calvin Chatlos and Lawrence D. Chilnick, *Crack: What You Should Know about the Cocaine Epidemic*, 1987; Sidney Cohen, "Adverse Effects of Cocaine," *Consumer's Research Magazine*, 1985.

[70]Isabel Wilkerson, "Urban Homicide Rates in U.S. up Sharply in 1986," *The New York Times*, 1987.

[71]Social overhead costs are discussed by Louis L. Cregler and Herbert Mark, "Medical Complications of Cocaine Abuse," *New England Journal of Medicine*, 1986; Nicholas J. Kozel and Edgar H. Adams, eds., *Cocaine Use in America: Epidemiologic and Clinical Perspectives*, 1985; and Arnold M. Washton and Nannette S. Stone, "The Human Cost of Chronic Cocaine Use," *Medical Aspects of Human Sexuality*, 1984.

C

Proffered New Solutions

Most people in principal drug consuming countries, and perhaps most people almost everywhere, do not approve of mind-altering drugs other than perhaps alcohol. Quite certainly, most do not esteem the criminality associated with drug traffic or the social, political, and economic consequences that users impose on their communities and countries. Therefore, with the exception of a minority of people who advocate unfettered consumption of their drugs of choice, most newly proffered solutions to the dilemmas addressed in this handbook—even liberalizing ones—are not motivated by desires for drugs so much as by hopes to rid society of many of drugs' ill effects. This context must be understood when considering new policy initiatives, especially such proposals as drug decriminalization or drug legalization. The concerns of most antiprohibitionists are soaring crime rates, domestic militarization, and abuses of civil liberties and human rights associated with present antidrug laws and their implementation. Antiprohibitionists judge the potential ills of regulated demand to be less grave than the ills of current illegalizing laws and policies. Most antiprohibitionists are therefore certainly not in "favor" of a drugged society and would be quite pleased with a reduction in consumption, supply, and traffic deriving from policies or values that were not as socially and economically costly as those currently in place.

Regardless, reducing demand, curtailing supply, and suppressing traffic are the strategies currently in vogue (see Table 11). We discussed them and their attendant policies in Section B. New proposals from drug prohibitionists call for greater or lesser emphases among these strategic categories, and even among the policy areas within each category. For example, some observers now call for greater efforts in reducing demand than in reducing supply or suppressing traffic. Within *reducing demand*, as an illustration, some call for greater emphasis on *treatment* and less on *general law enforcement*. Many new proposals are therefore simply variations of established themes. Others are quite substantially different.

Table 12 indicates the principal policy variations (in bold) from currently established practices. *Testing in the workplace*, for example, has given way to

Table 11
Distribution of Existing Antidrug Efforts

LOCI OF ACTIVITIES		
To Reduce Demand	**To Reduce Supply**	**To Suppress Traffic**
General Law Enforcement	Crop Eradication	Disruption of Networks
Education	Interdiction	Sequestration of Assets
Testing in the Workplace	Control of Precursor Chemicals	Improvement of Techniques
Civic Action	Crop Substitution	
The Mass Media	Rural Economic Development	Extradition
Treatment		

a much broader set of *workplace initiatives*. *Treatment* as a demand-reduction policy now tends to be focused around an "anticontagion model." And, people are more and more frequently speaking of developing an *antidrug ethos* as a way to reduce illicit drug demand.

In the supply-reduction category of Table 12, the traditional themes of crop eradication, interdiction, control of precursor chemicals, crop substitution, and rural economic development remain and are pursued, but they are now supplemented by vigorous discussions about new initiatives to bring them to fruition. The most radical in the new supply-reduction group is *Americanization of the drug war*.

The *suppression of traffic* strategy of Table 11 has given way in some circles to the *reduction of criminality and AIDS* category in Table 12. The increasing reorientation of some people's philosophy from suppression of traffic to a reduction of the criminality and the transmission of AIDS associated with it has probably been fostered on three counts: law enforcement failure to suppress the traffic; the alarming increase of AIDS among intravenous drug users and their sexual partners; and the discussions of

Table 12
Distribution of Proffered New Solutions

	LOCI OF EMPHASES IN EXISTING AND NEW CATEGORIES OF ACTIVITY		
	To Reduce Demand	**To Reduce Supply**	**To Reduce Criminality and AIDS Transmission**
E X I S T I N G	General Law Enforcement	Crop Eradication	Disruption of Networks
	Education	Interdiction	Sequestration of Assets
	Testing in the Workplace	Control of Precursor Chemicals	Improvement of Techniques
	Civic Action	Crop Substitution	
	The Mass Media	Rural Economic Development	Extradition
	Treatment		
N E W	Anticontagion Model of Treatment	Increased U.S. Funding for Producer Country Drug Enforcement Efforts	Decriminalization
	Antidrug Ethos	Income Alternative for Growers	Legalization
	Workplace Initiatives	Debt Retirement Incentives	
		Additional General Foreign Aid	
		Americanization of the Drug War	

decriminalization and *legalization*. Indeed, policy options that focus on decriminalization and legalization as strategies to reduce organized crime and the transmission of AIDS are currently undergoing vigorous debate in the United States. These options substantially depart from currently fashionable U.S. policy initiatives.

All this notwithstanding, prohibitionists predominate in most consuming countries, except, perhaps, the Netherlands, Spain, and Switzerland. Prohibitionists are concerned about drug-related crime and violence, too; but they tend to view legalization policies as opening the door to more of both, not less. Moreover, they see legalizing laws and policies fostering an increase in drug use. In this they see the social, political, and economic externalities of drug use that exist independent of illegalizing drug laws and their implementation. Thus continued calls are heard to reduce, if not prevent, illicit demand by general law enforcement activities, education, initiatives in the workplace, civic action, the mass media, and anticontagion treatment; to control supply through crop eradication, product interdiction, control of precursor chemicals, crop substitution, and rural economic development with additional international funding and, if necessary, direct U.S. involvement; and to suppress illicit international trafficking through disruption of major trafficking networks, asset forfeitures, controlled deliveries, extradition, and surveillance. Prohibitionists view traffic suppression as the gateway to reducing drug criminality and organized crime.

Demand for illicit drugs may be reduced in one of two ways or by a combination of both: by convincing people to adopt antidrug values, through education and a changing ethos; or, through law enforcement deterrence, by heightening the risk and fear associated with drug use. Many people advocate increasing efforts to convince people to change their drug-taking values or to increase their fear if they do not.

Supplies may be reduced through product interdiction. It is also thought that supplies may be controlled by focusing on growers, putting their incomes constantly at risk (crop eradication or crop confiscation) or by providing them with incentives to engage in alternative income-producing activities (crop substitution or rural economic development). Calls are out to increase efforts in each area.

Traffickers may be suppressed, with an accompanying reduction in criminality and organized crime, by heightening risk (law enforcement) or by eliminating the *crime tax* traffickers collect as their business profits (by decriminalizing or legalizing currently illicit drugs). Both prohibitionists and antiprohibitionists assume that following their preferred policy orientation would reduce criminality and the transmission of AIDS.

In Chapter 7 we review proffered new initiatives to reduce demand; in Chapter 8, to reduce supply; and in Chapter 9, to reduce criminality and the spread of AIDS.

7

Loci of Activities
to Reduce Demand

Since 1989, net consuming countries have given additional attention to reducing demand, a decision made in part because of supplier nations' cajoling them to solve their own domestic problems domestically rather than attempting to do so by externalizing the costs on others through supply-reduction emphases abroad. In addition, the demand emphasis has arisen from the realization—dramatically highlighted in the U.S. Department of State's 1990 *International Narcotics Control Strategy Report*—that global illicit drug supplies are not being significantly reduced (see Figure 3, Ch. 1; Figures 10 and 11, Ch. 2; Figures 15 and 17, Ch. 3).

The proffered demand-reduction methods under discussion in this chapter are innovations and variations associated with general law enforcement, education, initiatives in the workplace, civic action, utilization of the mass media, treatment programs following an anticontagion model, and development of an antidrug ethos.

GENERAL LAW ENFORCEMENT

Law enforcement proposals may be classified by their intended effects on traffickers and their intended effects on consumers. We look at the proposals to deal with traffickers later in this chapter. As for consumer demand-reduction intentions, proposals may be classified as "steady as she goes but improve efficiency and coverage for damage containment," "get tougher," and "look for flexibility."[1] All are intended to reduce demand by heightening risk and imposing costs on existing and potential users, especially those on, or likely to get on, hard drugs such as the opiates and cocaine. It is thought that imposing additional significant costs on drug users will deter them from continued consumption.

There is near consensus that existing law enforcement strategies and tactics are insufficiently successful in reducing demand. To improve coverage and efficiency, changes must be made. Thus calls frequently are made for organizational improvements to unify a command structure, redirect resources, and reduce bureaucratic infighting and therefore improve the efficiency of law enforcement efforts. Accordingly, one proposal calls for the reorganization of several U.S. federal bureaucracies into a single agency to control the country's borders and make integrated decisions about fighting the drug war, including not only interdiction of traffic but "deterrent arrests" among final users. Proposed in this initiative is an independent Border Control Department, perhaps with cabinet status, which would include the U.S. Coast Guard, the Customs Service, the Border Patrol, and the Drug Enforcement Administration. It would be a uniformed agency with a military ethic.[2] It is assumed that in due course military resources dedicated to the drug war would also be integrated into a unified command structure.[3]

"Profit sharing" is also advanced as a means to increase the efficiency of demand-reduction law enforcement efforts. One observer, in a not quite tongue-in-cheek proposal, calls not only for taking drug profits (assets) from drug-dealing convicts and allocating them to law enforcement agencies but also for dividing them among people who turn dealers in to the police.[4]

The proposed organizational changes and profit sharing plans might add not only efficiency but also an element of "toughness on users" to current law enforcement efforts. This would probably be accompanied by an eventual decrease in border interdiction efforts (a failure, anyway, it is said) and an increase in law enforcement at the street level along with a concomitant expansion in prison and court capacities[5] and the military's assumption of police duties. We have already discussed the considerable concern over societal militarization and abuse of civil liberties that could follow such developments.

Regardless, increasing the "toughness" of existing law enforcement efforts and improving their efficiency are vigorously advanced in some circles as ways to reduce consumer demand for illicit drugs.[6] Ranking highest on the list is the proposal to adopt measures similar to Iran's and Malaysia's—the death penalty for traffickers and perhaps users, too.[7] Fallback positions call for new incarceration policies that range from imprisoning all drug users to locking up only the most seriously criminal while mandating compulsory treatment—with confinement if necessary—for the remainder.[8] All this may entail a modification of individual-cell prisons to camp-type prisons,[9] or the creation of supplemental camp-type prisons away from population centers. Already some U.S. political officials are considering action to use closed military bases as prisons for convicted drug dealers. One senator affirms that "the drug prison plan is a creative, inexpensive way to get convicted criminals off the street. During this time of record deficits, there really are few other options when seeking new weapons to fight the war on drugs."[10] Parallel with these arguments, one sees in the United States the development of new drug offence sentencing policies which are distanced from traditional values of rehabilitation and which move toward sentencing based on principles of uniformity and retribution.[11]

Antidrug *motivational* policies are also put forward to influence drug users to curtail their consumption. Aside from the conventional policies of forfeiting one's time (prison), forfeiting one's social network (e.g., imprisonment far away from home),[12] or forfeiting one's assets (fines and sequestration),[13] some new proposals focus on forfeiting privileges. For example, potentially persuasive for drug-using youth with sufficient income either to own or to have access to a car is forfeiture of their drivers licenses,[14] or their privilege to participate in school or community sports. The loss-of-privilege model even holds among principal proponents of legalization. Thus one author who prefers to legalize drugs would nevertheless demand that addicts and other users live productive and noncriminal lives, forfeiting both freedoms and assets if they did not. Moreover, they would not be allowed to ignore their legitimate jobs, the support of their offspring, or the criminal law.[15]

Along these same motivational lines, publishing in an "antisocial registry" the names of certain classes of users who would have much to lose from public notoriety or embarrassment over drug consumption charges (just as is done with solicitors of prostitutes in some communities) could also have a chilling effect on drug demand.[16] However, it is highly problematical that this would have any effect on the majority of drug users.

Increasingly discussed is "situational" law enforcement. Thus one observer wants to get "real" public policy control of the two major legal recreational drugs (alcohol and nicotine) before legalizing anything else, and wants to ease up on enforcement against marijuana importation but increase heroin enforcement, particularly at the retail level.[17] Another calls for more toughness in fighting hard drugs, more compassion in treating addicts, and perhaps more flexibility toward marijuana.[18] Several reviewers consider marijuana to be in a category by itself; they want marijuana-use rules and regulations to be less restrictive, more workable, more administratively and economically sound, and more constitutionally proper than they now are. "Economic due process" is a drug policy code phrase among these people.[19]

Other observers would keep all drugs illegal, but target only the most dangerous ones for vigorous law enforcement (e.g., heroin, cocaine/crack), leaving marijuana as a safety release for people who find it difficult to live without drug support.[20] Still others, who want to achieve a regulatory effect with a prohibition policy toward heroin, recommend both strategies and tactics for law enforcement administration to accomplish this without going through the political trauma of trying to decriminalize drug use.[21]

In a short but far-reaching treatise, Murray Jarvik proposes demand-reduction strategies beyond those which focus on youth and concentrate on changing their values through community and school-based programs, treatment centers, and pharmacological agents. His alternatives are (1) a creation of demonstration pilot projects designed to test the effectiveness of supply vs. demand reduction strategies, clearly supposing, however that demand-reduction strategies will be called for and that these must be premised on sure detection and some coercion; (2) the refining of modern chemical detection techniques, including quick voluntary testing devices; (3) making punishment immediate for using illicit drugs; and (4) searching for an "antagonist" drug (like buprenorphine).[22] Thereafter, he would cause the criminal justice system to accommodate required changes (e.g., making the law enforceable and its enforcement correspond to fiscal reality). Others see such applications possible only if mandatory urine testing is required for all arrestees and their subsequent parole premised on a continued testing clean for drugs. Clearly, the focus here is on users who support the market rather than on traffickers who supply it.[23]

Beyond these permutations, numerous people propose slight to moderate modifications in existing law enforcement practices,[24] including searching for ways within law enforcement to ameliorate some of prohibition's harms in the interest of maintaining a deterrent effect on demand.[25]

Prohibition with an accompanying general law enforcement strategy that is increasingly tough, flexible, and direct on *users* as a means to reduce the demand for illicit drugs is likely to be effective only among two types of people: those who have something of value to lose and those who see themselves as having a future worth sacrificing for. Crack cocaine and heroin users, present and future, might not be much affected.

EDUCATION

In consuming countries, we have seen that antidrug emphases have begun to shift away from suppliers and traffickers and toward user demand at home. In attempting to affect demand materially, some observers want to shift from a law enforcement to an education emphasis. In early 1989 the Bush administration announced its intention to focus its "all-out war on drugs" mainly on educational efforts rather than on a law enforcement crackdown. The context of the president's remarks suggested his agreement that the long-term solution to the drug problem in the United States lies not in suppressing supply or in trying to curb demand by negative deterrence but in convincing people that it is in their own best interest to stop using, or never start using, illicit drugs.[26] The old adage of "teaching people to govern themselves responsibly" is somewhat distant from "forcing" them to do so. But is education up to the task? We have already seen in Section B that the evidence is mixed. So what new proposals are afoot?

The principal shift in new proposals lies in the realization that education within the classroom must be coupled with community-wide integrated efforts that involve peers, family, community, and school, and that these efforts must be combined with explicit antidrug values disseminated with peer and hero modeling at a fairly early age.[27]

Community and school efforts are broached in a later subsection (on civic action). Here it will be useful to draw in some of the literature on peers and family. It has long been established that peer influence *for* drug taking has been substantially effective.[28] The question is, can that same influence be corralled for inducing *antidrug* behavior? As of 1982 the question was hardly ever asked. One author reported that "even a cursory review of current prevention and treatment strategies reveals that the peer friendship network has been all but ignored as a specific target for intervention."[29]

As reported in Section B, a positive response to the potential good that peers may have in reducing demand has been launched in several schools. From the literature in our bibliography, it would appear that considerable latitude yet exists to orchestrate peer-influenced antidrug behavior.

More interest has developed in the family as a means of reducing demand, at least where families, loosely construed, still exist, and where interventions may occur not only to help families come to grips with internal stress over addiction[30] but also to make families a positive influence in its avoidance.[31] This is seen as being especially promising for female children, who appear to be more likely affected by family antidrug socialization than male children.[32] Regardless, it might be said that the new frontier in demand-reduction possibilities is parental involvement in preventing their children's drug dependency.[33] Thus the family is seen as one of the promising community resources that can be utilized for the prevention and reduction of drug abuse.[34] But, clearly, some parents are either incapable of or unwilling to become involved. They may be "burned out," "intimidated," or "resigned." Special ways will have to be found to get them involved if the truly positive demand-reduction possibilities of family interaction with at-risk members is to be realized.[35]

The drawback with these approaches is that education and corollary community and parental development efforts constitute a long-term initiative producing results, if at all, measured in generational, not in political periods of time that may coincide with the reelection schedules of the people's representatives. Politicians sometimes have no better vision of the future than do crack users in America's inner cities. Thus the test for new initiatives in education may lie less in the adequacy of the initiatives than in the political will of a country to sustain them long enough to see results.

INITIATIVES IN THE WORKPLACE

In Section B we reviewed literature showing the effect that employment-contingent satisfactory urine tests have on employee drug use. We explored several related constitutional and morale issues. The fact remains that, among some classes of people, work is more important than drugs; these people will thus forego drugs to preserve an income security. For these people, urine tests have been an effective deterrent to illicit drug use.

However, on occasion, employers discover that some drug users remain valued employees; abruptly dismissing them is not necessarily in the firms' economic interests. Rather than ignore the matter or dismiss people outright, some employers have begun to initiate support arrangements involving employees' families, friends, colleagues, and trusted confidants in a concentrated and reinforcing effort to extract users from the clutches of illicit drugs. The initiatives are frequently successful. This change marks much of the new literature on drugs in the workplace and constitutes a move, however hesitatingly, away from complete reliance on negative deterrence (e.g., urine tests) to a positive interaction with valued employees and their families.[36] The model is an integrated one, somewhat akin, in structure and intent, to the new educational initiatives discussed above.[37]

The drawback to a positive incentive workplace model in the United States and perhaps elsewhere lies in its unlikely demand-reducing effect on the burgeoning number of the nation's inner-city crack users. For effective application, the model presumes that the drug user wants employment and has employment, that the employer values that specific employee, and that both employee and employer have an incentive to work together to accomplish the end of having a drug-free workplace. All these factors are unlikely to coalesce among unskilled, minimum skilled, or minimum wage employees who may be seen as being "quickly replaceable" as soon as a problem arises and who themselves are just as likely to drift from job to job among "replaceable" employers. Nevertheless, among the skilled, the wanted, and the scarce, and among those who really desire to retain their employment, hardly a better opportunity exists than the workplace to initiate positive incentives to accompany the usual array of antidrug deterrents.[38]

CIVIC ACTION

Civic action proposals and experiences are of two general kinds: cooperative and unilateral. Among the former are collaborative initiatives involving communities, schools, industries, and regular law enforcement agencies to encourage, through positive and negative sanctions, a reduction in illicit drug demand. These initiatives are encouraged by reports showing that comprehensive community programs which encourage teenagers to avoid drugs, including cigarettes and alcohol, have been much more successful than antidrug programs relying only on the schools.[39]

Thus, in part, because of the general failure of classroom isolated drug education programs to reduce drug demand and, in part, because a substantial percentage of drug users are either not in school or are of post–high school age, some communities have reached out to embrace a variety of private and religious organizations in a common antidrug cause. One community, for example, collaborated with a religious organization in a comprehensive effort in an abandoned house district, purchasing "crack houses," renovating them, and selling them at low cost (for an average in 1988 of

$18,000) to senior citizens and single-parent families who needed housing the most and who could be relied upon either to withdraw from or not to begin participating in drug trade and drug use.[40] Some observers opine that these collaborative initiatives help build up neighborhoods, the quality of the residents who live in them, and eventually the antidrug socialization of the children being reared there. Community-based comprehensive proposals are advanced more and more frequently.[41]

On the other hand, some civic action proposals and accomplishments are quite unilateral in their initiatives and intent. For example, one author, on the premise that it is difficult to get youth to realize they have a drug problem and to get them into treatment centers, asserts that the community must therefore forcefully intervene on their behalf. Families cannot be involved, for family members are not reliable in dealing with drug-abusing youngsters.[42] Such proposals do pose the classic dilemma of moving the loci of responsibility to higher and more abstract levels in the wake of failure at lower levels. Rather than work to reinforce the will of the individual within the context of family to overcome a difficult problem, this model assumes that the problem can be dealt with authoritatively from above. It hardly ever can.

Another example of unilateral civic action involves American tenants in apartment complexes who object to drug operations in their domain. They alert police, shut off the buildings' water supply before a police raid so that dealers cannot flush their wares down the toilet, and in general make life difficult for both users and pushers. It is noted, by the way, that after tenants themselves have taken these initiatives, muggings and burglaries in their apartment complexes have substantially declined as has the incidence of drug use in them.[43]

A recent initiative in the United States has seen public housing project residents launch aggressive responses against drug dealers. They are creating citywide networks in Washington, D.C., Los Angeles, and Miami, and they are carrying out night patrols in their housing complexes. They are assaulting some suspected drug dealers in order to frighten them out of their neighborhoods.[44]

One perpetual problem of aggressive unilateral civic action is migration. Use and traffic may be reduced in one area while aggregate demand in a whole community remains untouched unless allied civic action operations are under way everywhere. Even under these conditions, dealers simply elect to "find another more tolerant city." Regardless, it is popularly difficult to fault people who, in desperation, resort to extraordinary means to clean up their own neighborhoods.

THE MASS MEDIA

Clearly, the mass media in several consuming nations have for some time targeted selective audiences for antidrug campaigns. Some research has inquired into their success.[45] In some instances, selective audience targeting has appeared to be beneficial. Should more be done? Can more be done?

Advocates of the media answer yes to both queries, and they call for expanding all media efforts, both public and private. They encourage free public-service advertising "which attacks apathy and ignorance of drug dangers."[46]

In the past, media effectiveness (or the lack thereof) was discussed considerably. Then the issue became one of cost. The question was not only air time, which may be acquired gratis as a public service, but the cost of developing effective messages. Perhaps advertising executives, as an element of civic action, already have shown how costs may be contained.[47] However, success in the hardest drug-using areas will likely require the combined services of sociologists, urban anthropologists, and media experts if "apathy" and "ignorance" are to be addressed in an instrumental way. Over the long haul it seems unlikely that this can happen with impromptu civic action, public service grants, and free air time. Governments will need to determine whether the potential for demand reduction via the media does not merit uncommon financial consideration.

Finally, if one may assume that youth are prone to hero worship and that children of the underprivileged are especially attracted to sports, one might conclude that high-profile sports personalities could play an effective role in promoting antidrug values among some youngsters. Some sports personalities apparently now invest time and energy to this end. The trick will be to assure that significant sports heros, themselves, are clean from illicit drugs and therefore have a credible message to give. "Mixed messages" from accorded heroes are not likely to produce any positive end.

ANTICONTAGION TREATMENT PROGRAMS

As we saw in Section B, treatment programs are advanced for a variety of reasons—to reduce criminality, to undercut organized crime, to express humanitarian care, and to reduce ultimate costs to society. Few people speak of treatment programs per se as a means to reduce demand. There is at least one exception; it derives from "anticontagion" addiction theories. The model is the epidemiology of a contagious disease;[48] the underlying assumption is that most people become drug users and perhaps eventual addicts because friends have introduced them to the practice. Some of the friends may have been pushing drugs in order to support their own addictions. Thus success- fully treating addicts removes their economic need to market drugs to acquaintances and therefore removes a large part of the reason for the spread of drug addiction. Accordingly, initiatives are made, even from highly placed law enforcement officers,[49] for considerably more treatment funding for anticontagion purposes[50] as well as others.[51]

Some call for compulsory treatment in order to meet the requisite of adequate demand reduction.[52] Naturally, there are many problems with such an approach. Aside from the legal, civil, constitutional, and ethical questions raised,[53] a principal remaining one, as usual, is the failure of agreement on what produces successful treatment.[54]

ANTIDRUG ETHOS

A strong deterrent to illicit drugs is people's conviction that it is inappropriate to use them. Reasons may be moral or utilitarian. They may derive from fear, economic calculus, or perhaps even from acquisitiveness, greed, and avarice. Regardless, if, for whatever reason, people decline to consume illicit drugs, it seems clear that the demand problem has been dented, at least as far as those specific people are concerned. However, change the calculus, remove the police, elect or appoint drug-disposed leaders, or sell an alternative educational curriculum to the schools, and the problem returns.

But change the disposition, character, or fundamental values peculiar to a specific people, their culture, or their political ideology, and the reduction in demand will likely be more lasting. Clearly, however, the value change must be one of persuasion rather than coercion—something even the Chinese have discovered as drugs emerge once again in their society after drugs were largely eliminated for the better part of two generations.[55]

All this has caused some people to consider that, absent fundamental social change or the development of a pervasive antidrug ethos, contemporary drug consuming nations are essentially lost to drug consumption. Indeed, harking on "rise and fall of civilization" themes, some street talk opines that future historians will look upon the inevitable fall of America and Western Europe in light of the anticivilization values generally associated with drugs.

Thus some observers are not only looking into values but are also wanting to take a longer view of the drug problem than is usually politically expedient, exploring cultural totems and taboos, and concentrating on the relationship of the social context of drug use to drug policy options involving social change.[56] Calls are made for strong mobilization of all positive forces to reestablish damaged social values and therefore turn back the drug onslaught.[57] One device is to present substantial incentives for people to reform their life-styles[58] leading, eventually, to the establishment of antidrug controls that derive not from law but from custom and social pressure.[59] Another is simply to create alternative images worth pursuing. For example, in the United States, there has been in recent years a lowered alcohol use among the American public, and the cause seems to be a change in the public's mood. People have become more interested in health and fitness, and this has led to more moderate consumption. The same has occurred with smoking. Massive value changes altered public thought and transformed society on these issues. It took two generations. It may well be that this approach could be successful with drugs. In the end, it is society's attitude toward drugs that will limit drug use. As one said: "If there has been such a drastic evolution in thought about liquor and tobacco, perhaps the day will come when we can chronicle as dramatic a mental turnabout on drugs."[60] The trends in the United States at least look promising (see Figures 4, 5, 6, 7, and 17).

The magnitude of such a charge is exemplified by one author's reflection on the value terrain that would have to be reversed: "accomplishment, competition, and success; self restraint, self discipline, and the postponement of gratification; the stability of the family; and a belief in certain moral universals" have given way to an ethos that scorns the pursuit of success, tolerates—or even encourages—sensual gratification, and accepts deviant forms of notions about the family and emphasizes ethical relativism.[61] But such a wholesale reversal to yesteryear's values may not be necessary if schools, parents, and communities commit their activities not just to short-term gains but to long-term value change about drugs.

In any event, it seems quite clear that policy makers must face the reality that their domestic drug consumption problem is primarily an internal matter and that the solution for it must ultimately be found within the borders of their own countries.[62]

In summary, we can see that proffered new solutions to reduce illicit drug demand are tactical variations of previous efforts. All of them concentrate on users and suggest that their propensity to indulge in illicit drug taking may be reduced by approaches that invoke fear, self interest, or value change.

So far, a fear premise has underlain America's consumer-focused demand reduction policies—fear of jail, fear of notoriety (with attendant loss of status or employment), fear of property losses. Not surprisingly, fear strategies work as a function of intensity and best on people who have personal freedom, good employment, and property at risk—in America, mostly its middle class. A fear strategy has no proven drug consumption effect on America's economic underclass where much hard-core drug abuse currently transpires.

Regardless (and any effectiveness notwithstanding), as we have seen, a fear strategy plagues nations with an assortment of socioeconomic and political costs. Comparative examples at the extreme are instructive. Singapore, Malaysia, and Saudi Arabia exhibit encouraging drug consumption indicators. But liberal democracies have difficulty both in applying the attendant fear-invoking penalties and in accepting all the enforcement mechanisms' socioeconomic and political consequences. Thus America's *fear regime*, its current principal demand-reduction strategy, is controversial as to philosophy, effectiveness, and appropriateness. The struggle continues.

Self interest, an alternative demand-reduction strategy, may also be driven by a calculus of fear (as in fear of losing one's employment). However, much self-interested behavior is driven less by fear than by a calculus of desires. Thus many drug-treatment centers successfully appeal to addicts' concerns about their health, family, friends, economic well being, and happiness.

More imaginative demand-reduction efforts not requiring coercive laws could be advanced. Some observers argue that micro experiences with "reward-based" systems ought to be explored in great detail, especially among youth. For example, paying children of America's economic underclass to attend a "drug-free" school and successfully complete its curriculum would probably be considerably less costly than the country's current demand-reduction efforts premised principally on fear. Economic incentives appeal to instincts for short-term gratification, which is thought to consume the underclasses anyway and which would therefore keep their attention.[63] At the same time, such economic incentives would foster a higher-horizon vision. Half the "wage" could be disbursed on a weekly basis and half could be banked for lump-sum payment upon successful completion of the requirements. The requirements are simple. Acquire productive skills and be drug free. Youth volunteering for the incentives yet failing their weekly saliva tests[64] would forfeit their banked sums and see all or a portion of them lumped into a cohort pool for eventual payment to successful completers. At some point even recalcitrant youth would get the idea that something of self-interest importance was happening.

Significantly appealing to *self interest* by many means could remove large segments of new underclass generations from a drug-abuse culture. Certainly, there are complex psychological issues here as well as the complications of unstable or defective family structures and few role models. But self interest properly nurtured creates its own role models. On the whole, self-interested youth brushed with pragmatic alternatives are appropriately motivated.

Problems and imponderables abound, of course. Neither present nor future policies are free of this burden. But a substantial public effort on a self-interest strategy would produce demand-reduction results. Moreover, demand-reduction outcomes based on self-interest as opposed to fear have the prospect of being more durable. There is an additional advantage. Many of the costs that fear regimes externalize to the larger society would be eliminated.

Obvious caveats exist. While a voluntary self-interest regime will likely produce quick gains among many children of the present underclass, such gains may not be sustainable *across* generations. New efforts lose enthusiasm as novelty ages, and implementing bureaucracies tend to corrupt their original goals as their work becomes "institutionalized." And, demand-reduction sustainability *within* a generation cohort affected by a regime of self interest will depend on the extent to which nondrug-abusing, educationally prepared children from the underclass ultimately find a society that assimilates them economically, socially, and politically.

Whereas *self interest* is judged favorably as a regime strategy to reduce drug demand, neither it nor a regime based on *fear* will produce desirable long-term drug consumption results in the absence of *value change*—the general development of generations of people who desire to sustain their lives without abusing drugs. The best of prospects will also be the hardest to achieve.

That substantial illicit-drug consumption still exists in America, for example, despite punitive laws is compelling evidence that large numbers of people have adopted strong drug-taking values. As even garrison states (e.g., post-W.W. II China) have not been able to eliminate illicit drugs completely from within their borders, it seems unlikely that other drug-using nations can be made completely drug free. However, attainable, no doubt, are a vast reduction in drug abuse if not use and certainly a substantial reduction in the public's burdens deriving from individual consumption and illegalizing laws. The best long-term prospects lie in value initiatives that are credible.

As the largest net consuming nation in the world, the United States will need to embark on a profound consideration of civilizing values that may be required to sustain it for another century and which therefore ought to be "passed on" to new generations by conscious social and political choice. For one hundred fifty years the country built upon the value strengths of its founders and immigrants, apparently assuming that the chemistry was self renewable. Educators have shied away from "value education" for nearly a half century, and the politicians who replaced the statesmen have ignored it for at least half that long. Thus the political system has been unable to influence America's ethos in ways that augur well for its continuity as a great nation.

"We shouldn't impose our values on others" is now the norm in America's schools and communities. Strange, is it not, that a fear strategy to reduce drug demand is thought to be value free? For long-term success, an aggressive holistic move is required to induce people to distance themselves from pro drug-taking values while simultaneously addressing whatever structural conditions give rise to or sustain such values.

If, in the interest of reducing unacceptable public costs, a relaxation of antidrug laws is to be considered, noteworthy simultaneous if not prior efforts are called for to deal vigorously with drug-taking values on the plausible assumption that politically acceptable ways can be engineered. Because of the public externalities, the people have a legitimate right to their interest here. Thus some consider it time to address community values as a matter of national security[65] if not survival, assuming that altered values on drugs as much as national economic well-being are required for the republic's continuity. This, of course, opens the whole book on normative political philosophy regarding the relationship of the individual to the state.

Both drug-taking and antidrug-taking values will require more public policy scrutiny than they have yet received. The reasons are two-fold: Campaigns among the middle class are more easily undertaken than among the underclass where drug-taking values are thought to be more pervasive; the art of "engineering" social values is unpredictable, whether from induced structural change or from its absence.

It is widely acknowledged that the systemic relationships of engineered value and structural change are inadequately understood. Contradictory examples abound. Thus many observers agree that U.S. civil-rights legislation contributed to a reduction in race-bias values among Americans. On the other hand, collectivization did not endear Eastern Europeans and Soviets to anyone's concept of a united order. "Drug education" has probably increased experimentation and tampering with illicit drugs more than deterred it. Yet, the anti-tobacco crusade appears to have successfully removed large numbers of smokers and prospective smokers from America's tobacco rolls.

On an encouraging side for the United States, there are plausible signs, as we discussed in chapters 1-3, that a change in drug-taking values within certain population segments may already be under way.

NOTES

[1]Charles Paul Freund ["Redefining the Drug Crisis," *The Washington Post*, 1989] speaks of the three "languages" of drug policy initiatives: the language of the drug war, the language of drug legalization, and the language of drug containment (a middle ground). *Containment* suggests that the drug war is unwinnable, a position that some U.S. inner-city mayors are taking.

[2]William E. Odom, "It's Time to Create a Border Control Department," *U.S. News and World Report*, 1988.

[3]See the testimony given in U.S. Congress, Senate Committee on Armed Services, Hearing, "Role of the Department of Defense in Drug Interdiction," 1988.

[4]William Raspberry, "Sharing the Drug Peddlers' Profits," *The Washington Post*, 1988.

[5]John Dillin ["US Wrestles with Drug Strategy," *The Christian Science Monitor*, 1989] briefly mentions Mathea Falco's advocacy of this point within the context of a complex, multifaceted law enforcement, education, and treatment proposal.

[6]See, for example, William Raspberry, "Legalize Drugs? No," *The Washington Post*, 1988.

[7]A pro-con debate on whether the death penalty should be adopted may be found in Mack Mattingly, et al., "Should Congress Authorize use of the Death Penalty for Continuing Criminal Enterprise Drug Offenses?," *Congressional Digest*, 1986.

[8]Bruce D. Johnson et al., survey options discussed for heroin abusers in *Taking Care of Business: The Economics of Crime by Heroin Users*, 1985. Options for control of cannabis are discussed by Frank Logan [*Cannabis: Options for Control*, 1979], one of which is to increase maximum penalties and ensure that they are meted out. He examines the practical problems each policy option would entail, along with its probable consequences, including probable effects on consumption or demand.

[9]This is the logical conclusion of a "toughening" law enforcement trend ["Report from the Field on an Endless War," *The New York Times*, 1989] if one assumes that demand would not be affected by the probability that a user would experience just such a camp.

[10]Harry Reid, U.S. Senator from Nevada, letter on the peace dividend, "Military Bases as Drug Prisons," *The New York Times*, 1990 .

[11]James C. Weissman, "Drug Offence Sentencing Practices in the United States of America," *Bulletin on Narcotics*, 1984.

[12]See Sheldon Ekland-Olson, John Lieb, and Louis Zurcher," The Paradoxical Impact of Criminal Sanctions: Some Microstructural Findings," *Law and Society Review*, 1984.

[13]Most discussions about asset forfeiture relate to traffickers and deal with the sequestration of assets used in a crime. There is some discussion in popular circles about applying forfeiture concepts to users. For example, users' vehicles would be as subject to sequestration as are traffickers' when illicit drugs are found within them. William Raspberry ["Living—and Dying—Like Animals," *The Washington Post*, 1988] wants to take property away from customers and imprison the owners.

[14]Herbert D. Kleber, "Epidemic Cocaine Abuse: America's Present, Britain's Future?" *British Journal of Addiction*, 1988.

[15]Arnold Trebach, *The Great Drug War and Radical Proposals That Could Make America Safe Again*, 1987.

[16]Herbert D. Kleber, "Epidemic Cocaine Abuse: America's Present, Britain's Future?" *British Journal of Addiction*, 1988.

[17]Mark Albert Robert Kleiman, "Vice Policy in a Liberal Society: An Analysis of the Impasse in the War on Drugs," *Nova Law Review*, 1987.

[18]Andrew Kupfer, "What to Do about Drugs," *Fortune*, 1988.

[19]Richard T. Oakes, "Marijuana and Economic Due Process: A Transition from Prohibition to Regulation," *Contemporary Drug Problems*, 1980.

[20]These are among Mathea Falco's proposals which she advanced as part of a comprehensive package. See John Dillin, "US Wrestles with Drug Strategy," *The Christian Science Monitor*, 1989.

[21]Mark Harrison Moore, *Buy and Bust: The Effective Regulation of an Illicit Market in Heroin*, 1977.

[22]Jarvik, Murray E., "The Drug Dilemma: Manipulating the Demand," *Science*, 1990.

[23]John Kaplan, "Taking Drugs Seriously," *The Public Interest*, 1988.

[24]See, for example, C. J. Brink's report [*Cocaine: A Symposium*, 1985] on a 1985 symposium attended by more than 400 professionals in Wisconsin. The conference was a major initiative on the part of the Wisconsin Institute on Drug Abuse. See also Mark Fraser and Nance Kohlert, "Substance Abuse and Public Policy," *Social Service Review*, 1988; Gilbert Levin, Edward B. Roberts, and Gary B. Hirsh, *The Persistent Poppy: A Computer-Aided Search for Heroin Policy*, 1975; and "Too Soon to Back Down on Drugs," *The New York Times*, 1988.

[25]See, for example, John Dillin, "US Wrestles with Drug Strategy," *The Christian Science Monitor*, 1989; Harold M. Ginzburg, Mhairi Graham MacDonald, and James William Glass, "AIDS, HTLV-III Diseases, Minorities and Intravenous Drug Abuse," *Advances in Alcohol and Substance Abuse*, 1987; and Ian D. Leader-Elliott, "Heroin in Australia: The Costs and Consequences of Prohibition," *Journal of Drug Issues*, 1986.

[26]Gerald M. Boyd, "Bush, Citing Cost, Says Drug War will Focus Largely on Education," *The New York Times*, 1989.

[27]See, for example, Kirk J. Brower and M. Douglas Anglin, "Developments, Trends, and Prospects in Substance Abuse," *Journal of Drug Education*, 1987; Valerie A. Brown et al., *Our Daily Fix: Drugs in Australia*, 1986; Harold Ginzburg, Mhairi Graham MacDonald, and James William Glass, "AIDS, HTLV-III Diseases, Minorities and Intravenous Drug Abuse," *Advances in Alcohol and Substance Abuse*, 1987; John Kaplan, "Taking Drugs Seriously," *The Public Interest*, 1988; Herbert D. Kleber, "Epidemic Cocaine Abuse: America's Present, Britain's Future?," *British Journal of*

Addiction, 1988; Stanton Peele, "A Values Approach to Addiction: Drug Policy That Is Moral Rather Than Moralistic," *The Journal of Drug Issues*, 1990; August Pérez, *Cocaína: Surgimiento y Evolución de un Mito*, 1987; William Raspberry, "Legalize Drugs? No," *The Washington Post*, 1988; K. Paul Satinder, *Drug Use: Criminal, Sick or Cultural?*, 1980; Reginald G. Smart, *Forbidden Highs: The Nature, Treatment, and Prevention of Illicit Drug Abuse*, 1983; "Too Soon to Back Down on Drugs," *The New York Times*, 1988; and U.S. Congress, House Select Committee on Narcotics Abuse and Control, Report, "1987 Update on Drugs and Dropouts," 1987.

[28]Kirk J. Brower and M. Douglas Anglin, "Developments, Trends, and Prospects in Substance Abuse," *Journal of Drug Education*, 1987.

[29]Delbert S. Elliott, David Huizinga, and Suzanne S. Ageton, *Explaining Delinquency and Drug Use*, 1982, p. 148.

[30]Don Colburn et al., "Health: Getting Hooked, Getting Helped," *The Washington Post*, 1988.

[31]See, for example, S. K. Chatterjee, "Drugs and the Young: Some Legal Issues," *Bulletin on Narcotics*, 1985; Mark Fraser and Nance Kohlert, "Substance Abuse and Public Policy," *Social Service Review*, 1988; and Reginald G. Smart, *Forbidden Highs: The Nature, Treatment, and Prevention of Illicit Drug Abuse*, 1983.

[32]Jeanette Covington, "Crime and Heroin: The Effect of Race and Gender," *Journal of Black Studies*, 1988.

[33]Kent A. Laudeman, "17 Ways to Get Parents Involved in Substance Abuse Education," *Journal of Drug Education*, 1984.

[34]F. Ruegg, "For an Overall Approach to Prevention: Basic Critical Considerations," *Bulletin on Narcotics*, 1985.

[35]Ibid.; and Justine Picardie and Dorothy Wade, *Heroin: Chasing the Dragon*, 1985.

[36]See, for example, Tom Adams and Barbara West, "The Private Sector: Taking a Role in the Prevention of Drug and Alcohol Abuse for Young People," *Journal of Drug Education*, 1988.

[37]For pro and con discussions about various facets of initiatives in the workplace, see David L. Carter and Darrel W. Stephens, *Drug Abuse by Police Officers: An Analysis of Critical Policy Issues*, 1988; David Lees, "Executive Addicts," *Canadian Business*, 1986; and Lawrence Miike and Maria Hewitt, "Accuracy and Reliability of Urine Drug Tests," *Kansas University Law Review*, 1988.

[38]The logic of such motivation has now filtered into police departments, who now routinely report drug arrests to employers ["Miami Beach's New Approach to Drug Arrests: Tell the Employers," *The New York Times*, 1990].

[39]See Gina Kolata, "Community Program Succeeds in Drug Fight," *The New York Times*, 1989. Others call for community perspectives to be included in policy decisions, but are not so sanguine about communities' solving problems in the absence of a fairly widespread and integrated approach to the drug-abuse problem [Ann F. Brunswick, "Dealing with Drugs: Heroin Abuse as a Social Problem," *The International Journal of the Addictions*, 1986].

[40]Isabel Wilkerson, "Detroit Citizens Join with Church to Rid Community of Drugs," *The New York Times*, 1988.

[41]A. Okasha ["Young People and the Struggle against Drug Abuse in the Arab Countries," *Bulletin on Narcotics*, 1985] chronicles the involvement of young people from all socioeconomic strata in new, nontraditional forms of drug abuse in Egypt. He suggests that comprehensive community-based programs need to be organized to improve

the personal and social functioning of drug-dependent persons, to promote drug education, and to increase understanding between younger and older generations. For the United Kingdom, see Justine Picardie and Dorothy Wade, *Heroin: Chasing the Dragon*, 1985. For a geographically generic discussion, see F. Ruegg, "For an Overall Approach to Prevention: Basic Critical Considerations," *Bulletin on Narcotics*, 1985. See also E. Sackstein, "Drugs and Youth: An International Perspective on Vocational and Social Reintegration," *Bulletin on Narcotics*, 1981.

[42]See, for example, the discussion by Barry Brown et al., "Kids and Cocaine—A Treatment Dilemma," *Journal of Substance Abuse Treatment*, 1989.

[43]"How to Oust a Drug Dealer: Ideas for Embattled Tenants," *The New York Times*, 1987.

[44]Michel Marriott, "And in the Streets, Citizens Fight Dealers," *The New York Times*, 1989.

[45]See, for example, Patricia Bandy and Patricia Alford President, "Recent Literature on Drug Abuse Prevention and Mass Media: Focusing on Youth, Parents, Women and the Elderly," *Journal of Drug Education*, 1983.

[46]John Dillin, "US Wrestles with Drug Strategy," *The Christian Science Monitor*, 1989.

[47]Joseph B. Treaster, "On Toys to TV Shows, Stepping Up Drug Fight," *The New York Times*, 1991.

[48]Justine Picardie and Dorothy Wade, *Heroin: Chasing the Dragon*, 1985.

[49]For example, in December 1989, Washington, D.C. police chief, Isaac Fulwood, Jr., called the U.S. federal government's emphasis on law enforcement "absolutely wrong" and called for increased funding of drug treatment programs [Philip Shenon, "Bush Officials Say War on Drugs in the Nation's Capital Is a Failure," *The New York Times*, 1990].

[50]"Too Soon to Back Down on Drugs," *The New York Times*, 1988; Arnold M. Washton, "Preventing Relapse to Cocaine," *Journal of Clinical Psychiatry*, 1988.

[51]See Frank H. Gawin and Herbert D. Kleber, "Abstinence Symptomatology and Psychiatric Diagnosis in Cocaine Abusers," *Archives of General Psychiatry*, 1986; "Getting Britain Off the Heroin Hook," *The Economist*, 1984; John Holahan, "The Economics of Control of the Illegal Supply of Heroin," *Public Finance Quarterly*, 1973; Herbert D. Kleber, "Epidemic Cocaine Abuse: America's Present, Britain's Future?," *British Journal of Addiction*, 1988; Andrew Kupfer, "What to Do about Drugs," *Fortune*, 1988; Jeremy Laurance, "Shooting up the Desperate," *New Statesman and Society*, 1988; Gilbert Levin, Edward B. Roberts, and Gary B. Hirsh, *The Persistent Poppy: A Computer-Aided Search for Heroin Policy*, 1975; F. Ruegg, "For an Overall Approach to Prevention: Basic Critical Considerations," *Bulletin on Narcotics*, 1985; and E. Sackstein, "Drugs and Youth: An International Perspective on Vocational and Social Reintegration," *Bulletin on Narcotics*, 1981.

[52]John Kaplan, *The Hardest Drug: Heroin and Public Policy*, 1983; U. Khant, "Measures to Prevent and Reduce Drug Abuse among Young People in Burma," *Bulletin on Narcotics*, 1985; Carl Leukefeld and Frank M. Tims, eds., *Compulsory Treatment of Drug Abuse: Research and Clinical Practice*, 1988; and Jerome J. Platt et al., "The Prospects and Limitations of Compulsory Treatment for Drug Addiction," *Journal of Drug Issues*, 1988.

[53]See, for example, the discussion by Christopher D. Webster, "Compulsory Treatment of Narcotic Addiction," *International Journal of Law and Psychiatry*, 1986.

[54]See the discussion by Irving Silverman, "Addiction Intervention: Treatment Models and Public Policy," *International Journal of the Addictions*, 1985; Herbert D. Kleber, "Epidemic Cocaine Abuse: America's Present, Britain's Future?," *British Journal of Clinical Psychiatry,* 1988.

[55]See, for example, Nicholas D. Kristof, "Heroin Spreads Among Young in China," *The New York Times*, 1991.

[56]Valerie A. Brown et al., *Our Daily Fix: Drugs in Australia*, 1986; Bill Hanson et al., *Life with Heroin: Voices from the Inner City*, 1985; Stanton Peele, "A Values Approach to Addiction: Drug Policy that Is Moral Rather than Moralistic," *The Journal of Drug Issues*, 1990; and Linda S. Wong, "Critical Analysis of Drug War Alternatives: The Need for a Shift in Personal and Social Values," *The Journal of Drug Issues*, 1990.

[57]A. Carmi and S. Schneider, eds., *Drugs and Alcohol*, 1986. See also Andrew M. Mecca, "A Cultural Response to Alcohol and Drug Abuse in America," *Contemporary Drug Problems*, 1982; William Raspberry, "Living—and Dying—Like Animals," *The Washington Post*, 1988.

[58]This is discussed as option 4 in Bruce D. Johnson et al., *Taking Care of Business: The Economics of Crime by Heroin Users*, 1985.

[59]T. Asuni and O. A. Pela, "Drug Abuse in Africa," *Bulletin on Narcotics*, 1986; Alexander Cockburn, "Some Radical Notions about Fighting Drugs," *The Wall Street Journal*, 1986; and Steven Wisotsky, "Exposing the War on Cocaine: The Futility and Destructiveness of Prohibition," *Wisconsin Law Review*, 1983.

[60]John Hughes, "Booze Today, Drugs Tomorrow?," *The Christian Science Monitor*, 1989.

[61]Joseph Adelson, "Drugs and Youth, *Commentary*, 1989.

[62]Ted Galen Carpenter, "The U.S. Campaign against International Narcotics Trafficking: A Cure Worse than the Disease," *Cato Institute Policy Analysis*, 1985.

[63]James Q. Wilson and Richard Herrnstein, *Crime and Human Nature* (New York: Simon and Schuster, 1985).

[64]Saliva testing exceeds urine testing's costs but is devoid of many of its philosophical objections [Murray E. Jarvik, "The Drug Dilemma: Manipulating the Demand," *Science* 250(19 October 1990): 390]. Some form of adequate surveillance is unavoidable [John Kaplan, "Taking Drugs Seriously," *The Public Interest* 92(Summer 1988): 32-50].

[65]Aspects of this view are covered by Joseph Adelson, "Drugs and Youth," *Commentary* 87:5(1989): 24-28; A. Carmi and S. Schneider, eds., *Drugs and Alcohol* (New York: Springer-Verlag), 1986; Mark Fraser and Nance Kohlert, "Substance Abuse and Public Policy," *Social Service Review*, March 1988, 103-126; John Hughes, "Booze Today, Drugs Tomorrow?" *The Christian Science Monitor*, 22 March 1989; Rushworth M. Kidder, "Drug Strategy Within an 'Ethical Fairyland,'" *The Christian Science Monitor*, 1989, p. 13; Tom Morganthau and Michael Reese, "Going After Hollywood: Critics Call for the Deglamorization of Drugs," *Newsweek*, 11 August, 1986; William Raspberry, "Living—and Dying—Like Animals," *The Washington Post*, 1988; and James Q. Wilson, "Against the Legalization of Drugs," *Commentary* 89:2(February 1990): 21-28.

8

Loci of Activities
to Reduce Supply

Policies now in place to reduce drug supplies flowing from net producing countries include crop eradication, product interdiction, control of precursor chemicals, crop substitution, and rural economic development (see Chapter 5). As we already have seen, these initiatives have not worked well enough to have had much of an impact on the availability of illicit drugs on the world market. There appears to be increasing discouragement in both net producing and net consuming nations that a successful policy to control supply, without a worldwide reduction in demand,[1] will be forthcoming. That pessimism notwithstanding, what new reduction initiatives are being proposed?

The new initiatives are more tactical than strategic; they include the following options: increasing U.S. government funding for each of the above categories so that domestic governments may more adequately carry out their appropriate tasks; emphasizing income alternatives for peasant growers rather than concentrating on crop eradication; using international debt retirement incentives and general foreign aid to encourage producer governments to more vigorously suppress supplies with the money they now have and with additional funding that may be forthcoming; and having the U.S. government take over in-country control operations outright (frequently termed "Americanizing the drug war").

INCREASED U.S. GOVERNMENT FUNDING

Advocates of increased funding for existing programs are certainly aware of contemporary failures in supply-reduction efforts. But the cause of the failure is viewed as inadequate funding, not any inappropriateness of supply-reducing strategies and tactics. More money is needed.[2]

Within the new financial initiatives, the view apparently still prevails that insufficient law enforcement funding for crop eradication (and, as we later discuss, traffic suppression) is at the root cause of these failures rather than financial inadequacies elsewhere (e.g., crop substitution and rural economic development). The assumption appears to be that the institutional and political fabric of net producer countries is sufficient for the task, lacking only the money for manpower, equipment, and materiel.

Thus more firepower, more intelligence, and more technical support would turn the tide in favor of supply reduction. We have already reviewed in Chapter 5 the calls for herbicides, radar systems, electronic devices to bug and jam traffickers' communications, heat-seeking equipment to detect drug laboratories, more police and more police firepower, and security systems for top-level judges and other members of the judiciary. This costs money; the expenditure of more of it to fill these needs is thought to be needed.

Aside from assistance with technology and materiel, incentives must be improved for producer countries' drug-enforcement personnel. On occasion, therefore, "counterbribes" are talked about to encourage members of law enforcement agencies and the judiciary to remain loyal to the government that pays their nominal salaries rather than to the drug barons who frequently supplement those salaries with "incentive pay."

How well would substantial U.S.–provisioned funding for technology and people be utilized? Not too well, some fear. There are concerns about the reliability of the technical expertise of personnel in net producer countries as well as what drives their career goals. Moreover, substantial problems discussed in Section B will be recalled: the corrosive influence of corruption, the debilitating influence of weak domestic political institutions, and the increasingly intimidating capability of the drug barons and their allies to spread terror with impunity. Profound obstacles are believed to exist. The lack of money is only one of several limiting factors in net producer countries' inability to control supplies.

All this does not detract from the courageous and loyal public servants who daily risk their own lives to sustain supply control policies they are sworn to uphold. Nor does it take away from the several pockets of sophisticated technological expertise that do exist. It does acknowledge that the task is large and that human and institutional weaknesses are great.

The old adage that "you can buy anything with money" may be almost true for drug traffickers' spendable resources, but less likely for consumer nations' resources funneled into an existing socioeconomic and political arrangement that is increasingly difficult and perhaps hostile. U.S. money may not be able to buy incorruptibility, strong institutions, or a pervasively courageous law enforcement system in net producer countries.

INCOME ALTERNATIVES FOR PEASANT GROWERS

Perhaps positive incentives to reduce supply would work.[3] Initiatives to provide income alternatives to peasant growers to wean them from drug cultivation are driven by a pessimistic view of the effectiveness of law enforcement suppression strategies. Peasants and other growers (e.g., marijuana cultivators in California and Kentucky) will make an economic calculus in favor of drug cultivation as long as economic margins are substantially in favor of drug crops, even if present crop loss risks increase somewhat. The proper response is viewed as increased funding, principally from the United States, to reduce the income gap between regular farming and drug farming.

Under some conditions, economic alternatives are known to work. For example, in the late 1970s, after earning significant income from illegal coca growing, several communities in Colombia's Cauca state suffered severe economic depression after drug-enforcement agents targeted them for crop eradication and saw to it that the task was consistently carried out. The community of El Moro responded to a project jointly sponsored by the Colombian government and the United Nations Fund for Drug Abuse Control (UNFDAC) in developing economic alternatives to coca growing. The farmers cleared off their uprooted coca bushes and planted other crops.

The former coca growers' income is not as great now as it used to be, but it is probably as high as one might expect possible outside the coca economy. Moreover, El Moro has regained some of its social integrity. Growers are pleased with that. Adding to that pleasure is a decline in incidences of theft, violence, and crime in the community.[4]

Three conditions prevailed in El Moro's success: destruction of the cocaine-based economy, provisioning of alternative economic opportunities, and community acceptance of both (or the community's inability to do otherwise). Two of the three conditions resulted from the infusion of relatively massive outside resources; the third came from a positive community response. However, as long as a significant price differential exists between the profitability of growing coca and growing other commodities, individuals may be motivated to move back into the drug trade.[5] Someone will need to keep a significant watch.

The strategy of "economic alternatives" is to keep the income differentials between the drug crops and other crops narrow, either by infusing capital into growers' hands through crop price supports or other techniques or by suppressing producer level drug commodity prices. Alternatively, the drug crops must be eradicated by police action. Absent an economic answer, therefore, the risk to growers of crop losses by eradication must remain a credible threat.

All this would appear to require constant vigilance. Not only must the authorities exercise watchfulness over existing drug growers, they must deal with new ones who will not take long to discover an ability to leverage the drug trade to their risk-free favor by soliciting government income to "withdraw" from drug farming, practically before they plant their new drug crops.

Is there enough money in the world or enough political will and energy to generalize the El Moro model and keep it alive indefinitely in tens of thousands of villages as long as high demand exists for illicit drugs? Analytically, the challenge is simple enough. Either governments must strongly repress their drug growers or strongly assist them in finding alternative ways to make a living.[6] Or they must do both.

Alberto Fujimori, Peru's new president, following the advice of one of his chief economic advisers, Hernando de Soto,[7] has embarked on the creation of a free-market agricultural environment to entice farmers into growing food crops. One initiative has been to deed land to squatters on condition that they stay in the legitimate crop business.[8] Since secure land ownership has historically been a prized possession of Peru's peasantry, it will be interesting to watch Fujimori's experiment.

A generalized repression model is not working anywhere. That leaves income incentives as a plausible strategy. It is quite unlikely that sufficient money exists to implement this strategy independent of also putting growers at severe risk of losing crops through eradication. But, the proper mix between repression and income incentives has not yet been discovered in Peru or Bolivia or in most other drug growing regions, although, as we mentioned in Section B, several crop substitution successes have been noted in Thailand as well as in Colombia. The incredible challenge for income alternative initiatives, a proven success in isolated cases, is generalization. At what cost? At what requisite political will? Over what period of time?

INTERNATIONAL DEBT RETIREMENT INCENTIVES AND ADDITIONAL GENERAL FOREIGN AID

Debt retirement[9] and foreign aid advocates[10] appear to view money shortages as being less than the essential limiting factor in producer countries' efforts to control drug supplies. The critical linchpin here is political will. But money certainly has a role. Thus holding out the prospects of a significant reduction in a country's international debt based on its performance in controlling drug supplies is thought to motivate a stiffening of political will. The same effect is thought to occur with generous additional infusions of foreign aid. The additional financial considerations would, of course, also facilitate supply control program developments and operations.

Will money stiffen political will? Has it? One's enthusiasm for either "yes" or "no" to these queries acknowledges acceptance or rejection of essential assumptions in order for these economic initiatives to have a working chance. Whether they will actually work if given that chance is an open empirical question. Debt retirement may provoke something. Additional foreign aid is unlikely to do so.[11]

AMERICANIZE THE DRUG WAR

From a horizon of despair, some people see nothing working to control illicit drug supplies. Money is being wasted, lives lost, the incidence of criminality increasing, public institutions destroyed. The critical limiting factor is the absence of U.S. know-how, resolve, technical expertise, institutional integrity, and political will. The proffered option is simply to move U.S. military forces forthwith into drug growing regions to destroy supplies and to undo drug networks.[12]

Implementation of this option would require U.S. personnel to be involved in at least the following activities: front-line intelligence operations, pursuit and arrest of suspects and engagement with their paramilitary forces, the involuntary removal of suspects to the United States for trial and incarceration, operations against drug labs, deployment of U.S. Navy task forces to producer countries' territorial waters, and U.S. Navy and Air Force interdiction on the high seas and within producer countries' territorial waters and airspace.

This option's limitations relate principally to issues of producer country sovereignty and to U.S. political will to sustain numerous casualties over a prolonged time. In the long term, the corrupting influence of the drug trade on U.S. military personnel would also begin to take its toll.

A taste of sovereignty and anti-American nationalism issues can be seen from a 1990 decision of the Bush administration to station a U.S. Navy task force just off the Colombian coast for interdiction and surveillance work. The flotilla actually set sail from Florida and was some distance into its journey when the outcry and furor in Colombia persuaded President Bush to order its return to port while at the same time trying to assuage the anger of outraged Colombians who were ready to lynch the politicians who had encouraged such an arrangement.[13] Treating a "drug ally" as an occupied country would appear to present significant diplomatic and political obstacles.

Casualties à la Vietnam would likely be sustained for at least several months as U.S. troops worked their way through jungle terrain and confronted well-equipped paramilitary forces protecting clandestine laboratories. One cannot assume that national armies themselves would remain aloof. Invasion of sovereignty does odd things to people. The consequences of "Americanizing the War" could be more problematical than the present war itself.

Past efforts to control supply have not been effective on a global basis. We are left to conclude that, as long as significant demand remains, future supply-control variations are unlikely to be any more so.

NOTES

[1]This is an increasingly strong position taken in net producer countries. See, for example, Asociación Peruana de Estudios 3 Investigación para la Paz, *Cocaína: Problemas y Soluciones Andinos*, 1990.

[2]This clearly was the tenor of the discussion at the high-level antidrug summit in Cartagena, Colombia, among the presidents of Peru, Bolivia, Colombia, and the United States. See Andrew Rosenthal, "3 Andean Leaders and Bush Pledge Drug Cooperation," *The New York Times*, 1990. Such positions are increasingly being criticized, even in the popular press. See, for example, Louis Kraar, "How to Win the War on Drugs,"

Fortune, 1990.

[3]See, for example, Edmundo Morales, "Comprehensive Economic Development: An Alternative Measure to Reduce Cocaine Supply," *The Journal of Drug Issues*, 1990; Charles Stuart Park, "The Coke War," *The Atlantic*, 1987; and Andrew Rosenthal, "3 Andean Leaders and Bush Pledge Drug Cooperation," *The New York Times*, 1990.

[4]See Tyler Bridges, "Colombian Farmers Start Anew after Coca 'Bonanza,'" *The Christian Science Monitor*, 1986; Timothy Ross, "UN Aid Helps Some Colombians Shake Free of Coca Dependency," *The Christian Science Monitor*, 1988; and Mark A. Uhlig, "Colombia's War on Cocaine: Farmers' Fears Help Cause," *The New York Times*, 1989.

[5]See the discussion on prices in the following: John Holahan, "The Economics of Control of the Illegal Supply of Heroin," *Public Finance Quarterly*, 1973; James V. Koch and Stanley E. Grupp, "The Economics of Drug Control Policies," *The International Journal of the Addictions*, 1971; and "Should Cocaine Cost More? Less?," *The New York Times*, 1988.

[6]See, for example, the discussions by the following: Merrill Collett, "Peruvians Flock to Upper Huallaga Valley to Cash in on Expanding Coca Bonanza," *Latinamerica Press*, 1988; Kevin Healy, "Bolivia and Cocaine: A Developing Country's Dilemmas," *British Journal of Addiction*, 1988; Instituto Latinoamericano de Investigaciones Sociales, "La Economía Campesina y el Cultivo de la Coca," *Debate Agrario*, 1987; Enrique Juscamaita, "La Economía Cocalera y su Impacto en la Dinámica Regional: El Caso del Valle del Río Apurímac-Ayacucho," *Socialismo y Participación*, 1983; Rensselaer W. Lee III, "Why the U.S. Cannot Stop South American Cocaine," *Orbis*, 1988; Scott B. MacDonald, *Dancing on a Volcano: The Latin American Drug Trade*, 1988; Scott B. MacDonald, "Slaying the Drug Hydra," *SAIS Review*, 1989; Scott MacDonald, *Mountain High, White Avalanche: Cocaine and Power in the Andean States and Panama*, 1989; and Charles Stuart Park, "The Coke War," *The Atlantic*, 1987.

[7]de Soto is author of one of the most widely read treatises on free-market economics ever published in Latin America. It is now widely consulted in English translation [*The Other Path: The Invisible Revolution in the Third World*, 1989].

[8]James Brooke, "Peruvian with a Vision Gets Power," *The New York Times*, 1990.

[9]The debt reduction option is discussed by Scott B. MacDonald ["Slaying the Drug Hydra," *SAIS Review*, 1989]. In 1991 Peru and the United States announced a joint-venture plan to fight coca leaf cultivation that included debt relief as an essential incentive [James Brooke, "Peru Develops Plan to Work with U.S. to Combat Drugs," *The New York Times*, 1991].

[10]Using additional foreign aid as leverage on drug issues is discussed by Scott B. MacDonald, *Dancing on a Volcano: The Latin American Drug Trade*, 1988; and Kevin Fisher, "Trends in Extraterritorial Narcotics Control: Slamming the Stable Door after the Horse Has Bolted," *New York University Journal of International Law and Politics*, 1984.

[11]See the discussion on the antireform aspects of certain kinds of foreign aid in F. LaMond Tullis, "Food Aid and Political Instability," in *Food, the State, and International Political Economy: Dilemmas of Developing Countries*, 1986, p. 215.

[12]The option is discussed and criticized by the following: Bruce M. Bagley, "Colombia and the War on Drugs," *Foreign Affairs*, 1988; Bruce M. Bagley, "The New Hundred Years War? U.S. National Security and the War on Drugs in Latin America," *Journal of Interamerican Studies and World Affairs*, 1988; and Rensselaer W. Lee III, "Why the U.S. Cannot Stop South American Cocaine," *Orbis*, 1988.

[13]Michael Gordon, "U.S. Postpones Deploying Ships Near Colombia," *The New York Times*, 1990.

9

Loci of Activities
to Reduce Criminality
and the Spread of AIDS

Criminality is reduced by removing from the crime scene the criminals, the people and conditions on which criminals prey, or the profits that drive criminal activities. Removing drug criminals has been the task of traditional law enforcement and newly created drug-enforcement agencies. The conventional categories of disruption of networks, improvement of techniques (for making arrests), and extradition listed in the third column of Table 12 have described these efforts. We discussed past and current practices in Chapter 5.

New proposals to remove drug criminals from circulation simply call for more vigilant and all-encompassing extradition treaties and practices[1] and more police and military personnel to assault drug networks and the people who run them.[2] This thinking was raised to perhaps the highest stakes possible with the U.S. military invasion of Panama in late 1989 and the removal of its head, General Manuel Noriega, to the United States for trial.

Still, new criminals emerge as fast or faster than old ones are removed. Someone always seems ready to step in when a drug leader has fallen or an opportunity to carve out new drug territory for additional productive activity appears.

Removing the people and conditions on which drug criminals prey is more problematical than removing the criminals. In the extreme, this would lead to a massive prison population in net consuming and producing countries (see the discussion on general law enforcement in Chapter 7) into which all drug users and their potential sympathizers would be cast.

Insofar as poverty and despair are contributory to people's falling into drug related activities (whether as growers, pushers, or users), structural intervention in America's ghettos and producing countries' rural villages could help. However, after nearly a half century of trying, hardly anyone now claims to know how to do that across the board, or pretends to have the money it would cost if a proper strategy were known. And, of course, all socioeconomic classes consume illicit drugs.

Finally, one may develop options to reduce drug criminality by attacking the profits that drive drug crime. Sequestering assets (see Table 12) has been the conventional mode; current proposals augur for more international cooperation in tracing and attaching criminal assets, more government-to-government disclosures on international financial transactions and transfers, and an expansion of the sequestration net to include assets beyond those used in any given criminal transaction.[3]

AIDS transmission presents similar options. Absent voluntary restraint either from moral or practical considerations (e.g., no dirty needles; no unsafe, let alone promiscuous, sex), AIDS victims could be isolated like ancient lepers; the people AIDS victims associate with could be removed from circulation; or the principal mechanism by which AIDS is transferred among intravenous drug users could be removed. The first two nonvoluntary options are not acceptable to contemporary civilized societies because of human rights concerns and because most modern civilizations seek to care for rather than destroy their people. That leaves the third option, which, in pragmatic terms, means providing drug users with clean, uncontaminated needles[4] and working hard to educate them, and their friends, about unsafe sex.[5]

This leaves untouched the AIDS problem among another type of carrier and purveyor. There appears to have been a rush into commercial sex in order to raise money for crack cocaine purchases. Crack is inexpensive, but highly addictive, and it pushes its users into frequent use. They quickly expend their resources in support of the habit; females and males sell their bodies just to keep going. Syphilis and gonorrhea are increasing among these people along with the incidence of AIDS. Twenty percent of the 100,000 U.S. AIDS cases come from New York City; 20 percent of those live in just two burroughs, Brooklyn and the Bronx.[6] It would seem that clean needles would do little for these people; perhaps cheaper drugs would not either. That leaves a crack maintenance program as a last resort. It is unlikely to be adopted.

As reviewers survey this panorama of trouble and despair, with failed policies strewn along the landscape like cornstalks after a heavy hailstorm, they look for new options. Among these are drug decriminalization and legalization. It is thought that once implemented, these would have a heavy impact on drug criminality by attacking the profits that drive it, and on health-related consequences of drug abuse by making drug consumption relatively safe.

DECRIMINALIZATION AND LEGALIZATION

Decriminalization (removing penalties, or at least "looking the other way") and legalization (officially sanctioning currently illegal behavior) may occur at the user, producer, or trafficker levels in the drug chain. Most arguments in favor of some kind of liberalizing policy concentrate on decriminalizing or legalizing *consumer* drug use;[7] a few advocate the same policies for *producers*;[8] hardly any are in favor of relieving *traffickers* from a potential confrontation with the law.

Larger moral issues such as reducing crime, enhancing public health and safety, and invigorating a sense of community are appealed to in the proposals.[9] Thus an outright libertarian preference for unfettered freedom to consume psychoactive drugs is hardly ever advanced;[10] most proposals are therefore not necessarily so much in favor of unqualified personal drug liberties as they are against the most feared consequences of illegalizing policies and their implementation—drug-related crime and AIDS. Accordingly, arguments for controls (regulation and taxation, perhaps similar to policies now in vogue for tobacco and alcohol[11]) are frequently advanced. Occasionally, proposals call for tax proceeds from the legitimate sale of drugs to be dedicated to consumer antidrug education and to public entities that deal with the overhead costs of drug use (e.g., hospitals that care for crack babies).[12] The experiences of the Netherlands and Switzerland are appealed to as prototypical examples.[13]

Most proposals for drug user decriminalization focus on marijuana,[14] several on cocaine,[15] a few on heroin.[16] Some do not differentiate policies on the basis of a specific target drug.[17] Some would legalize all but crack cocaine. Thus several kinds of drug-specific decriminalization and legalization options are advanced.

In considering both drug consuming and drug producing countries, several decriminalization or legalization permutations are apparent. For example, production could be legalized in a net producer country, or consumption could be legalized in a net consumer country. A net producer country, if it could recover from international sanctions from unilateral legalization, would probably see crime syndicate assaults decline and probably would enjoy something of an economic boom as drug profits, now "squirreled away" in more or less secure financial repositories abroad, were brought home for investment on native soil.

If net user countries decriminalized consumption, there would be no crime tax for smugglers and pushers to reap, and therefore no reason for them to carry out turf wars, assault police, terrorize neighborhoods, and undermine countries' institutional integrity. Savings from a cutback in law enforcement expenses could be spent elsewhere, such as on drug education. The analogy is the alcohol related crime syndicates in the United States after that country ended alcohol prohibition in 1933. The syndicates faded away, went into other criminal pursuits, or invested their alcohol-acquired resources in legitimate businesses.

On the health issue, clean drugs, clean needles, and a humane environment could reduce the incidence of drug-related AIDS transmission. Other causes of AIDS transmission would not, of course, be affected.

The concerns among those not converted to a legalization position are many and intense. Would demand increase? Probably yes. Would the social, political, and economic externalities that societies suffer independent of illegalizing laws and policies therefore not be as great or worse than the present condition? If the answer is a plausible "yes" and legalization turned out to be both disingenuous and counterproductive, could a country recover? Would these concerns be sufficiently worrisome and empirically verified to make the futility and destructiveness of prohibition later appear less onerous than the futility and destructiveness of legalization? These and related concerns justifiably weigh heavily on the unconverted.[18]

Arguments for and arguments against decriminalization and legalization compel thoughtful engagement with the troubling issues of crime, consumption, and AIDS. There are many imponderables in these policy issues, matters incapable of being evaluated or weighed with precision. Nevertheless, the flurry of events may dictate policy initiatives that produce both helpful and hurtful consequences, intended and unintended. Constant vigilance will be required. In the long term, people voluntarily turning away from drugs that are harmful to self and society would appear to be the only option with consequences that are largely predictable and which international public policy can then address with reasonable precision. Clearly, it is a difficult task.

NOTES

[1]See, for example, J. Richard Barnett, "Extradition Treaty Improvement to Combat Drug Trafficking" *Georgia Journal of International and Comparative Law*, 1985; Steven A. Bernholz, Martin J. Bernholz, and G. Nicholas Herman, "International Extradition in Drug Cases," *North Carolina Journal of International Law and Commercial Regulation*, 1985; James Brooke, "A Report from the Front Lines in Colombia: The Drug War Will Be Long," *The New York Times*, 1989; "Colombian Court Backs Extradition," *The New York Times*, 1989; Robert Linke, *Extradition for Drug-Related Offenses: A Study of Existing Extradition Practices and Suggested Guidelines for Use in Concluding Extradition Treaties*, 1985; Roberta Louise Rubin, "International Agreements: Two Treaties between the U.S. and Italy," *Harvard International Law Journal*, 1985; and U.S. Congress, House Committee on Foreign Affairs, Hearing, "Worldwide Review of Status of U.S. Extradition Treaties and Mutual Legal Assistance Treaties," 1987.

[2]See, for example, Richard L. Berke, "Panel Said to Seek New Military Role in Fight on Drugs," *The New York Times*, 1989; Alan Dixon et al., "Should U.S. Armed Forces Play a Major Role in Interdicting Drug Traffic into the U.S.?," *Congressional Digest*, 1986; and Sara Fritz and John Broder, "Urban Blood Baths Spur Plan for Pentagon War on Drugs," *The Los Angeles Times*, 1988. Peter Reuter, Gordon Crawford, and Jonathan Cave [*Sealing the Borders: The Effects of Increased Military Participation in Drug Interdiction*, 1988] critique proposals for additional military involvement. A U.S. General Accounting Office report to congressional requesters [*Drug Control: Issues Surrounding Increased Use of the Military in Drug Interdiction*, 1988] lays out the fundamental arguments against the proposals.

[3]See, for example, John Dombrink and James Meeker's call for nullification of bills paid by drug money ["Beyond 'Buy and Bust': Nontraditional Sanctions in Federal Drug Law Enforcement," *Contemporary Drug Problems*, 1986]; Paula Dwyer's analysis of overseas bank deposit sequestrations ["Getting Banks to Just Say 'No.'" *Business Week*, 1989]; Catherine Foster's description of the policies in a number of U.S. states that

require drug dealers to pay a stamp tax on their illegal drugs ["'Grass Tax' Aims for Dealers' Wallets," *The Christian Science Monitor*, 1989]; and Andrea M. Grilli's discussion of denying drug dealers a "safe haven" ["Preventing Billions from Being Washed Offshore: A Growing Approach to Stopping International Drug Trafficking," *Syracuse Journal of International Law and Commerce*, 1987].

⁴See, for example, the following: Lawrence K. Altman, "Needle Exchange Programs Hint a Cut in AIDS Virus Transmission," *The New York Times*, 1989; Richard Conviser and John H. Rutledge, "Can Public Policies Limit the Spread of HIV among IV Drug Users?," *Journal of Drug Issues*, 1989; Ernest Drucker, "AIDS and Addiction in New York City," *American Journal of Drug and Alcohol Abuse*, 1986; Ernest Drucker, "The Disease of Ignorance," *New York News Day*, 1988; and C. Schuster and R. Pickens, "AIDS and Intravenous Drug Abuse," in *Problems of Drug Dependence 1988*, Louis Harris, ed., 1988.

⁵See Ernest Drucker, "AIDS and Addiction in New York City," *American Journal of Drug and Alcohol Abuse*, 1986; Josette Mondanaro, *Chemically Dependent Women: Assessment and Treatment*, 1989.

⁶"The AIDS Plague Spreads," *The Economist*, 1989.

⁷For discussions on decriminalizing or legalizing drug consumption (but not necessarily drug trafficking or drug production) see the following: Bruce K. Alexander, "Alternatives to the War on Drugs," *The Journal of Drug Issues*, 1990; Richard Ashley, *Cocaine: Its History, Uses and Effects*, 1975; Marie Andrée Bertrand, "Beyond Antiprohibitionism," *The Journal of Drug Issues*, 1990; Richard J. Bonnie, *Marijuana Use and Criminal Sanctions: Essays on the Theory and Practice of Decriminalization*, 1980; Joel Brinkley, "The War on Narcotics: Can It Be Won?," *The New York Times*, 1984; Amado Canelas and Juán Carlos Canelas, *Bolivia, Coca, Cocaína: Subdesarrollo y Poder Político*, 1983; Greg Chesher and Alex Wodak, "Evolving a New Policy for Illicit Drugs," *The Journal of Drug Issues*, 1990; Alvin W. Cohn, "Drugs, Crime and Criminal Justice: State-of-the-Art and Future Direction," *Federal Probation*, 1984; Michael Cross, "A Case for Legal Heroin," *New Scientist*, 1984; "Drugs: It Doesn't Have to Be Like This," *The Economist*, 1989; Michael Dunham, "When the Smoke Clears," *Reason*, 1983; Anthony Henman, Roger Lewis, and Tim Malyon, *Big Deal: The Politics of the Illicit Drugs Business*, 1985; John M. Kramer, "Drug Abuse in the Soviet Union," *Problems of Communism*, 1988; Eliot Marshall, "Drug Wars: Legalization Gets a Hearing," *Science*, 1988; Chester N. Mitchell, "A Comparative Analysis of Cannabis Regulation," *Queen's Law Journal*, 1983; Stephen J. Morse, "War on Drugs Produces the Crime: Since We're Losing, Why Not Debate the Alternative?" *The Los Angeles Times*, 1988; Ethan A. Nadelmann, "The Case for Legalization," *The Public Interest*, 1988; Ethan A. Nadelmann, "U.S. Drug Policy: A Bad Export," *Foreign Policy*, 1988; Ethan A. Nadelmann, "Drug Prohibition in the United States: Costs, Consequences, and Alternatives," *Science*, 1989; Richard T. Oakes, "Marijuana and Economic Due Process: A Transition from Prohibition to Regulation," *Contemporary Drug Problems*, 1980; Robert C. Petersen, "Toward a Rationally Based Social Policy on Marijuana Usage," *Annals of the New York Academy of Sciences*, 1976; Robert C. Petersen, "Decriminalization of Marijuana—A Brief Overview of Research-Relevant Policy Issues," *Contemporary Drug Problems*, 1981; Susanna Rance, "U.S. Government's Drug Control Strategy Accents Heavy Repression in Third World," *Latinamerica Press*, 1988; K. Paul Satinder, *Drug Use: Criminal, Sick or Cultural?*, 1980; Kurt L. Schmoke, "Decriminalizing Drugs: It Just Might Work—and Nothing Else Does," *The Washington Post*, 1988; James B. Slaughter, "Marijuana Prohibition in the U.S.: History and Analysis of a Failed

Policy," *Columbia Journal of Law and Social Problems*, 1988; Lester C. Thurow, "U.S. Drug Policy: Colossal Ignorance," *The New York Times*, 1988; Arnold S. Trebach, "The Lesson of Ayatollah Khalkhali," *Journal of Drug Issues*, 1983; Arnold S. Trebach, "Tough Choices: The Practical Politics of Drug Policy Reform," *American Behavioral Scientist*, 1989; U.S. Congress, Senate Committee on the Judiciary, Subcommittee to Investigate Juvenile Delinquency, Hearings, "Marijuana Decriminalization," (3 vol., 1975–1977); U.S. Congress, House Select Committee on Narcotics Abuse and Control, Hearing, "Decriminalization of Marihuana," 1977; Henk Jan van Vliet, "Separation of Drug Markets and the Normalization of Drug Problems in the Netherlands: An Example for Other Nations?," *The Journal of Drug Issues*, 1990; Andrew T. Weil, "Observations on Consciousness Alteration: Why Coca Leaf Should Be Available as a Recreational Drug," *Journal of Psychedelic Drugs*, 1977; and Norman Zinberg, *Drugs, Set, and Setting: The Basis for Controlled Intoxicant Use*, 1984.

⁸See, for example, Alvaro Camacho, *Droga, Corrupción y Poder: Marijuana y Cocaína en la Sociedad Colombiana*, 1981; Amado Canelas and Juán Carlos Canelas, *Bolivia, Coca, Cocaína: Subdesarrollo y Poder Político*, 1983; "Drugs: It Doesn't Have to Be Like This," *The Economist*, 1989; Jonathan Hartlyn, "Commentary on Bagley's 'The New Hundred Years War? National Security and the War on Drugs in Latin America,'" *Journal of Interamerican Studies and World Affairs*, 1988; Anthony Henman, Roger Lewis, and Tim Malyon, *Big Deal: The Politics of the Illicit Drugs Business*, 1985; Scott B. MacDonald, *Dancing on a Volcano: The Latin American Drug Trade*, 1988; Ethan Nadelmann, "U.S. Drug Policy: A Bad Export," *Foreign Policy*, 1988; M. Niedergang, "Some See Answer to Colombia's Problems in Legal Drugs," *LeMonde/Manchester Guardian Weekly*, 1987; Ernesto Samper, "Marihuana y la Propuesta de su Legalización," in *La Legalización de la Marihuana*, E. Samper et al., eds., 1980; Elaine Sciolino, "Colombian Official Talks of Legalizing Cocaine," *The New York Times*, 1988; Francisco E. Thoumi, "Colombian Laws and Institutions, Money Dirtying, Money Laundering, and Narco-Businessmen's Behavior," 1989.

⁹Such posturing is probably required for the proposals to be politically acceptable. See Jerome H. Skolnick, "Drugs: More or Fewer Controls?," *The Los Angeles Times*, 1988.

¹⁰Exceptions occur. See Anthony Lewis's arguments and his citing of Milton Friedman and others ["Dose of Reality Will Help Cure Drug Ills," *The Salt Lake Tribune* (Utah), 1989].

¹¹See, for example, John Dillin, "US Wrestles with Drug Strategy," *The Christian Science Monitor*, 1989; Mark Albert Robert Kleiman, "Vice Policy in a Liberal Society: An Analysis of the Impasse in the War on Drugs," *Nova Law Review*, 1987; and Chester N. Mitchell, "A Comparative Analysis of Cannabis Regulation," *Queen's Law Journal*, 1983.

¹²See Lester Grinspoon, "A Proposal for Regulation and Taxation of Drugs," *Nova Law Review*, 1987; Joel Brinkley, "The War on Narcotics: Can It Be Won?," *The New York Times*, 1984; and Ethan A. Nadelmann, "Drug Prohibition in the United States: Costs, Consequences, and Alternatives," *Science*, 1989.

¹³Burton Bollag, "Swiss-Dutch Drug Stance: Tolerance," *The New York Times*, 1989; Richard J. Bonnie, *Marijuana Use and Criminal Sanctions: Essays on the Theory and Practice of Decriminalization*, 1980; Peter Cohen, *Cocaine Use in Amsterdam in Non-Deviant Subcultures*, 1989; Martien Kooyman, "The Drug Problem in the Netherlands," *Journal of Substance Abuse Treatment*, 1984; Andrew Kupfer, "What To Do About Drugs," *Fortune*, 1988; Scott B. MacDonald, *Dancing on A Volcano: The Latin*

American Drug Trade, 1988; Henk Jan van Vliet, "Separation of Drug Markets and the Normalization of Drug Problems in the Netherlands: An Example For Other Nations?," *The Journal of Drug Issues*, 1990; and Govert F. Van de Wijngaart, "A Social History of Drug Use in the Netherlands: Policy Outcomes and Implications," *Journal of Drug Issues*, 1988. See also the discussion in note 23, Chapter 2.

[14]Richard J. Bonnie ["The Meaning of 'Decriminalization': A Review of the Law," *Contemporary Drug Problems*, 1981] reviews the post-1973 decriminalization movement in the United States, finding statutory endorsement in eleven states, at least as far as possession of small amounts of marijuana is concerned. Bonnie [*Marijuana Use and Criminal Sanctions: Essays on the Theory and Practice of Decriminalization*, 1980] has actively sought decriminalization legislation in the United States, and in this book he presents a treatise for the movement and a drafter's guide for doing it. Additionally, he gives a comparative view on decriminalization in Europe. Some people are not too pleased with Bonnie's proposals. See, for example, Walter R. Cuskey, "Critique of Marijuana Decriminalization Research," *Contemporary Drug Problems*, 1981; and Lee I. Dogoloff, "Don't Legalize Marijuana," *The New York Times*, 1987. For additional proposals, see Michael Dunham, "When the Smoke Clears," *Reason*, 1983; Jon Gettman, "Decriminalizing Marijuana," *American Behavioral Scientist*, 1989; Lester Grinspoon, *Marihuana Reconsidered*, 2d ed., 1977; Michael Isikoff, "Legalization of Marijuana Argued on Hill: Schmoke Leads Fight for New Drug Policy," *The Washington Post*, 1988; Eric Josephson, "Marijuana Decriminalization: The Processes and Prospects of Change," *Contemporary Drug Problems*, 1981; Louis Lasagna and Gardner Lindzey, "Marijuana Policy and Drug Mythology," *Society*, 1983; Chester N. Mitchell, "A Comparative Analysis of Cannabis Regulation," *Queen's Law Journal*, 1983; Richard T. Oakes, "Marijuana and Economic Due Process: A Transition from Prohibition to Regulation," *Contemporary Drug Problems*, 1980; Robert C. Petersen, "Toward a Rationally Based Social Policy on Marijuana Usage," *Annals of the New York Academy of Sciences*, 1977; Robert Petersen, "Decriminalization of Marijuana—A Brief Overview of Research-Relevant Policy Issues," *Contemporary Drug Problems*, 1981; James B. Slaughter, "Marijuana Prohibition in the U.S.: History and Analysis of a Failed Policy," *Columbia Journal of Law and Social Problems*, 1988; U.S. Congress, Senate Committee on the Judiciary, Subcommittee to Investigate Juvenile Delinquency, Hearings, "Marijuana Decriminalization," 3 vol., 1975–1977; U.S. Congress, House Select Committee on Narcotics Abuse and Control, Hearing, "Decriminalization of Marihuana," 1977; Richard Vigilante and Richard C. Cowan, "Pot-Talk: Is Decriminalization Advisable?," *National Review*, 1983; and Norman E. Zinberg, "Breaking the Impasse in the War on Drugs: A Search for New Directions," *NOVA Law Review*, 1987.

[15]See, for example, Richard Ashley, *Cocaine: Its History, Uses and Effects*, 1975; Amado Canelas and Juán Carlos Canelas, *Bolivia, Coca, Cocaína: Subdesarrollo y Poder Político*, 1983; Steven Wisotsky, "Exposing the War on Cocaine: The Futility and Destructiveness of Prohibition, *Wisconsin Law Review*, 1983; and Steven Wisotsky, *Breaking the Impasse in the War on Drugs*, 1987.

[16]See, for example, Michael Cross, "A Case for Legal Heroin," *New Scientist*, 1984; and David Hawks, "The Proposal to Make Heroin Available Legally to Intravenous Drug Abusers," *The Medical Journal of Australia*, 1988.

[17]See, for example, Joel Brinkley, "The War on Narcotics: Can It Be Won?," *The New York Times*, 1984; Alvin W. Cohn, "Drugs, Crime and Criminal Justice: State-of-the-Art and Future Direction," *Federal Probation*, 1984; "Drugs: It Doesn't Have To Be Like This," *The Economist*, 1989; Ronald Hamowy, ed., *Dealing With Drugs:*

Consequences of Government Control, 1987; Pat M. Holt, "The U.S. Should Repeal 'Drug Prohibition,'" *The Christian Science Monitor*, 1989; "Hooked on Just Saying No," *The Economist*, 1989; Eliot Marshall, "Drug Wars: Legalization Gets a Hearing," *Science*, 1988; Stephen J. Morse, "War on Drugs Produces the Crime: Since We're Losing, Why Not Debate the Alternative?," *The Los Angeles Times*, 1988; Ethan Nadelmann, "U.S. Drug Policy: A Bad Export," *Foreign Policy*, 1988; K. Paul Satinder, *Drug Use: Criminal, Sick or Cultural?*, 1980; Kurt L. Schmoke, "Decriminalizing Drugs: It Just Might Work—and Nothing Else Does," *The Washington Post*, 1988; Lester C. Thurow, "U.S. Drug Policy: Colossal Ignorance," *The New York Times*, 1988; Arnold S. Trebach, "The Lesson of Ayatollah Khalkhali," *Journal of Drug Issues*, 1983; Arnold S. Trebach, "Tough Choices: The Practical Politics of Drug Policy Reform," *American Behavioral Scientist*, 1989; Norman Zinberg, *Drugs, Set, and Setting: The Basis for Controlled Intoxicant Use*, 1984; and Norman Zinberg, "Breaking the Impasse in the War on Drugs: A Search for New Directions," *NOVA Law Review*, 1987.

[18]These and related concerns may be found in the following: Angela Burr, "A British View of Prescribing Pharmaceutical Heroin to Opiate Addicts: A Critique of the 'Heroin Solution' with Special Reference to the Piccadilly and Kensington Market Drug Scenes in London," *International Journal of the Addictions*, 1986; Richard R. Clayton, "Legalization of Drugs: An Idea Whose Time Has Not Come," *American Behavioral Scientist*, 1989; Lee I. Dogoloff, "Don't Legalize Marijuana," *The New York Times*, 1987; Robert G. Fichenburg, "Legalization May Resurface if Bush's Drug Fight Fails," *The Salt Lake Tribune* (Utah), 1989; Ronald Goldfarb and Robert DuPont, "Avoiding Nostrums and Illusions in the War on Drugs," *The Los Angeles Times*, 1989; James A. Inciardi, "Editor's Introduction: Debating the Legalization of Drugs," *American Behavioral Scientist*, 1989; James A. Inciardi and Duane C. McBride, "Legalization: A High-Risk Alternative in the War on Drugs," *American Behavioral Scientist*, 1989; George de Leon, "The Decriminalization Issue Revisited," *Social Policy*, 1982; James Lieber, "Coping with Cocaine," *Atlantic*, 1986; Tom Morganthau et al., "Should Drugs Be Legal?," *Newsweek*, 1988; David Mutch, "To the Heart of the Drug Problem," *The Christian Science Monitor*, 1989; Gabriel G. Nahas et al., "A Drug Policy for Our Times," *Bulletin on Narcotics*, 1986; William von Raab, "Legalize Drugs? Not Now, Not Ever," *The Washington Post*, 1988; Charles B. Rangel, "'Legalize Drugs?' Not on Your Life," *The New York Times*, 1988; William Raspberry, "Legalize Drugs? No," *The Washington Post*, 1988; "Too Soon to Back Down on Drugs," *The New York Times*, 1988; U.S. Congress, Senate Committee on the Judiciary, Subcommittee on Criminal Justice, Hearing, "Health Consequences of Marihuana Use," 1980; U.S. Congress, House Select Committee on Narcotics Abuse and Control, Hearing, "Drug Legalization—Catastrophe for Black Americans," 1988; U.S. Congress, House Select Committee on Narcotics Abuse and Control, Hearing, "Legalization of Illicit Drugs—Part II," 1988; Richard Vigilante and Richard C. Cowan, "Pot-Talk: Is Decriminalization Advisable?," *National Review*, 1983; John Walsh, "Frank Press Takes Exception to NAS Panel Recommendations on Marijuana," *Science*, 1982; Gordon Witkin and Stephen J. Hedges, "The Coming Cocaine Plague in Europe," *U.S. News and World Report*, 1989; and Margaret Y. K. Woo, "Drug Delusions," *The Christian Science Monitor*, 1988.

10

Summary of Part I

We have reviewed literature on the social, economic, and political consequences of the international trade in illicit drugs. Our principal focus
has been on illicit drugs currently significant in international transactions—cocaine, heroin, and marijuana and other cannabis products. This
handbook, containing 2,058 annotated bibliographical entries, has examined
information on the production, distribution, and consumption of those drugs
and the policy instruments designed to deal with their socioeconomic and
political effects. The handbook has also included literature that evaluates the
intended, and sometimes unintended, consequences of various policies. It has
reviewed consequences of drug consumption independent of the laws and
policies that make them illegal, and it has briefly examined an array of newly
proffered solutions designed to reduce consumption and supply and the
criminality and health consequences associated with traffic and use.

We have noted that, during the past fifteen years, the illicit international
drug trade has grown from cottage export production to highly organized,
international economic exchanges employing hundreds of thousands of
people and earning scores of billions of dollars annually. The political and
socioeconomic consequences to societies and peoples have been substantial.

A strong international demand for psychoactive drugs, coupled with use
illegality, present compelling incentives on two fronts. The first is to supply
the market; the second is to try to impede its operation. Suppliers are motivated by money—lots of it. Impeders' motives are more diverse—moral,
utilitarian, political, ideological, and pragmatic.

Impeders' countervailing efforts are sometimes logical, sometimes irrational, but nearly always intense. In net producer countries, international and
domestic efforts invoke the full spectrum of law enforcement and drug
control strategies, including crop eradication, control of precursor chemicals,
crop substitution, disruption of major trafficking networks, asset forfeitures,
techniques of controlled delivery, facilitation of extradition, and surveillance
of land, water, and air approaches to the frontier, and controls over ships
and aircraft in international space. Sometimes economic incentives are

included to encourage producer-country growers to abandon their coca bushes, opium poppies, and cannabis plants. On occasion, these economic incentives are coupled with integrated rural development strategies.

All internationally invoked strategies within net producer countries are directed toward controlling illicit drug supply and suppressing illicit international trafficking before products ever reach the principal consuming nations. Although supply and demand constitute an integrated international condition, and although many net consuming countries are also producers just as principal producers have increasingly become consumers of their own products, until recently many international policy initiatives have failed to be sensitive to the global integration of the world's illicit drug market. With increasing efforts being made to reduce the demand for illicit drugs, the artificial policy distinctions between producing and consuming nations may be on the wane.

In principal consuming countries, law and drug enforcement efforts are expended to heighten trafficker and user risk—through network disruption, interdiction, asset forfeiture, "stings," surveillance, criminal prosecution, detention—and to implement educational and other programs to convince people to voluntarily reduce their illicit drug use. These *negative* and *positive* sanctions are intended to reduce demand.

The intense efforts to supply drugs and vigorous efforts to control drug supply and consumption in most parts of the world would not exist absent, on the one hand, consumer demand for psychoactive drugs and, on the other, policies that illegalize consumption. The rise of a new genre of organized trafficker to service demand, and the increased implementation of countervailing initiatives to suppress demand and supply, constitute, therefore, the first round of consequences of the twin factors of drug demand and drug illegality.

The international traffic in illicit drugs and the consumer demand that has given rise to it have produced benefits and beneficiaries as well as liabilities and victims. Most of the extant literature concentrates on the latter. Within net producing countries traffickers infiltrate state bureaucracies, corrupt the political and policy process, make alliances with terrorist ideologues, assassinate, maim, and destroy indiscriminately, and create an antistate wholly outside the rule of law. Increasingly these factors are being felt in net consuming countries, in addition to the social, economic, and political externalities of acute and chronic consumption that the public must bear whether illegalizing laws and policies exist or not.

Efforts to implement drug control, law enforcement, and other countervailing initiatives in the wake of all this have produced their own array of consequences, both intended and unintended. The initiatives have included multilateral and bilateral control agreements and national policies designed to reduce demand, control supply, suppress trafficking, and treat and rehabilitate chronic offenders. As supplies have not been reduced significantly, it is therefore the unintended consequences of countervailing measures that much of the literature focuses upon: organized crime, violence, AIDS, corruption, congested judicial and penal systems, law enforcement budgets out of sight, human rights violations, and other kinds of social overhead costs. Reducing demand, curtailing supply, and suppressing traffic nevertheless continue to be the policy applications.

Supply, demand, and the efforts to disrupt or reduce both have all created externalities, both peculiar and expected, which have social, economic, and political consequences. Some are tolerable, some counterproductive, some inadmissable. Is anything yet to be done? A large array of proffered new solutions is found in the literature.

To reduce demand, new initiatives in the workplace, identification of certain treatment models, and the development of an "antidrug ethos" through educational and other efforts are advanced.

To reduce supply, greater funding for crop eradication, product interdiction, control of precursor chemicals, crop substitution, and rural economic development are sought. In the supply reduction category, the new initiatives are more tactical than strategic and include the following: increasing U.S. funding for work in the above categories so that domestic governments may more adequately carry out their appropriate tasks; emphasizing income alternatives for peasant growers rather than concentrating on crop eradication; using international debt retirement incentives and general foreign aid to encourage producer governments more vigorously to suppress supplies with the money they now have and with additional funding that may be forthcoming; and having the U.S. government take over in-country control operations outright. All these initiatives have raised serious public questions, and some have provoked nationalist sensibilities.

The concern over traffickers in most new drug policy proposals has now shifted to criminality and public health issues such as the spread of AIDS. This has led to discussions about decriminalization and legalization, which many people think would disrupt crime by removing the rationale for its existence, and would reduce the spread of AIDS by allowing intravenous addicts access to clean needles with which to pursue their habit.

There are many imponderables in the policy issues raised in the literature on illicit drugs, matters incapable of being evaluated or weighed with precision. Nevertheless, rapidly unfolding events carry a logic of their own, virtually assuring that significant, perhaps radical, new initiatives will be forthcoming.

In the long term, the only apparent sure solutions lie in the decline of demand and the willingness of current net consumer countries to assist current net producer countries in rebuilding their economies, their societies, and their polities on the basis of legitimate international transactions. Reducing demand and building economies are both large tasks. The outcome is uncertain.

PART II

DRUG AND DRUG-RELATED LITERATURE

Annotated Bibliography

Keywords at the end of each bibliographical entry below are found in the index, preceded by a caret (^). These keywords are followed by the number of each corresponding bibliographical entry. To save space, "Proffered Solutions" in the key words has been abbreviated to P\S. Thus *^P\S\Treatment* refers to *^Proffered\Solutions\Treatment* in the index.

Index entries for the main text are not preceded by a caret. Numbers following main text entries correspond to the page numbers in that text.

1. Abarro, P. A. (1983). "The Role of the Drug Advisory Programme of the Colombo Plan Bureau in the Fight against Illicit Drug Traffic." *Bulletin on Narcotics* 35(4): 67–72. The Colombo Plan consists of twenty-six member countries cooperating for socioeconomic development in Asia and the Pacific. The role of the Drug Advisory Programme in helping member states update drug legislation and promote drug law enforcement actions is described. ^Southeast\Asia ^International\Cooperation ^Drug\Control\Policies ^Law\Enforcement

2. ——— (1987). "The Role of an Intergovernmental Regional Organization in Combating Drug Trafficking: A Perspective of the Colombo Plan Bureau." *Bulletin on Narcotics* 39(1): 41–55. The Colombo Plan, established in 1950 as a regional intergovernmental organization for cooperative economic and social development in Asia and the Pacific, comprises twenty-six member states. Its permanent secretariat has a Drug Advisory Programme (DAP) headed by a drug advisor. Description of the activities of the Drug Advisory Programme, particularly its involvement in developing and strengthening cooperation between agencies and member states that deal with drug problems. ^Southeast\Asia ^Drug\Control\Policies ^International\Cooperation

3. Abbasi, Sami M., Kenneth W. Hollman, and Joe H. Murey, Jr. (1988). "Drug Testing: The Moral, Constitutional, and Accuracy Issues." *Journal of Collective Negotiations* 17(3): 221–235. A major concern over drug testing in both public and private institutions is the embarrassment, invasion of privacy, and other "human cost" factors that must be weighed against the value of the information received. These costs are unnecessary. The problem can be deterred by educational programs, the creation of confidence between workers and management, and treatment programs for

affected workers. ^United\States ^Drug\Control\Policies ^Drug\Testing ^Proffered\Solutions ^Consequences\Social

4. Abel, Ernest L. (1979). *A Comprehensive Guide to the Cannabis Literature*. Westport, Conn: Greenwood Press. Bibliography on cannabis and marihuana, indexed and cross-referenced. ^Cannabis ^Bibliographies

5. ———— (1980). *Marihuana, the First Twelve Thousand Years*. New York: Plenum Press. A descriptive history of marijuana and its abuse and a discussion of the relationship of drug policy and drug use to social and economic assumptions and consequences. Regardless of marijuana's past (viewed differentially from various socioeconomic classes over time and among various cultures), "its future will inevitably be that of decriminalization and eventual legalization, subject no doubt to the same regulatory measures as those that apply to alcohol" (p. 271). ^Cannabis ^Drug\Use\History ^Drug\Control\Policies

6. ———— (1983). *Drugs and Sex: A Bibliography*. Westport, Conn: Greenwood Press. Only psychoactive substances (agents whose sites of action are primarily in the brain) affecting sexuality are discussed. The bibliography is indexed but not annotated. Cocaine, marijuana, and opium derivatives such as heroin are included, as are general findings in numerous drug categories relative to sexuality. ^Drug\Use ^Bibliographies ^Sexuality ^Consequences\Sexuality ^Consequences\Social ^Cocaine ^Cannabis ^Opiates

7. ———— (1983). *Marijuana, Tobacco, Alcohol, and Reproduction*. Boca Raton, Fla: CRC Press. Of interest to this bibliography is the potential impact of marijuana consumption on sexual activity and on fetuses. As for sexual activity, marijuana use is unquestionably associated with increased sexual activity for many individuals, but, on the other hand, increased sex may have little to do with marijuana. There is very little reliable information concerning marijuana usage and human sexual function. Contemporary evidence indicates that marijuana usage does not affect testosterone levels, but does adversely affect sperm production. However, the changes in sperm production do not appear to have any biological significance. As for effects on the fetus, pharmacological studies have demonstrated that marijuana and its derivatives freely cross the placenta and might adversely affect the fetus. In general, cannabinoids do not produce gross malformations except at relatively high doses. These conclusions are derived from animal studies. ^ Cannabis ^ Health ^ Sexuality ^ Consequences\Sexuality ^ Consequences\Fetuses ^ Fetuses ^ Consequences\Health ^ Consequences\Reproduction

8. ———— (1983). *Narcotics and Reproduction: A Bibliography*. Westport, Conn: Greenwood Press. Focusing on the effects of narcotic drugs and reproduction, it also includes materials dealing with sexual behavior, sexual function, and sexual physiology. Most of the articles deal with the effects of narcotics on what the author calls "the conceptus" of humans and animals. 1,891 entries are included and organized alphabetically according to author. A subject index cross-references the entries, by number, into numerous categories. ^ Opiates ^ Drug\Use ^ Bibliographies ^ Health ^ Sexuality ^ Consequences\Health ^ Consequences\Fetuses ^ Fetuses ^ Consequences\Sexuality ^ Consequences\Reproduction

9. ———— (1985). *Psychoactive Drugs and Sex*. New York: Plenum Press. Fourteen drugs are surveyed, including tobacco and alcohol. Of interest to this bibliography are the surveys on cocaine, marijuana, and opium derived narcotics. In each drug category, the cities surveyed and clinical reports are referenced, as are the animal studies. Effects on hormones and reproductive tissue are reviewed. With cocaine, effects are dose related. As dose increases, previous experiences of enhanced libido and sexual performance are reversed. There is still little reliable information on how marijuana affects human sexuality. Female reproductive function is probably adversely affected, but

conclusions can only be arrived at after nutritional factors have been properly dealt with. Chronic and acute administration, however, produces measurable and incontrovertible hormonal effects of biological significance in the female. As for opium derived narcotics, among males sperm counts are reduced but fertility appears not to be significantly affected; serum testosterone levels are reduced. Among females, problems in sexual physiology and sexual activity are widely noted. At issue is whether narcotic drugs precipitate the problems or are taken to alleviate them. In general, there is loss of libido and increase in reproductive dysfunction. Reasons developed in the literature are reviewed. A substantial bibliography for each chapter. ^Cannabis ^Cocaine ^Opiates ^Drug\Use ^Health ^Sexuality ^Bibliographies ^Consequences\Health ^Fetuses ^Reviews ^Consequences\Social ^Consequences\Sexuality ^Consequences\Fetuses

10. Abel, Ernest L., and Robert J. Sokol (1988). "Marijuana and Cocaine Use During Pregnancy." In *Drug Use in Pregnancy*, edited by Jennifer R. Niebyl, pp. 223–230. Philadelphia: LEA and Febiger. The authors review and summarize information on cocaine and marijuana use during pregnancy. Suggestions for the clinical management of pregnant patients who use drugs. Many studies with inconclusive correlations are noted. ^Cannabis ^Cocaine ^Health ^Reviews ^Fetuses ^Consequences\Fetuses ^Consequences\Health

11. Abramovsky, Abraham (1986). "Money-Laundering and Narcotics Prosecution." *Fordham Law Review* 54:471–505. Constitutional rights of the travelling public must be balanced against the need to fight narcotics trafficking. It is fine to suppress money laundering, even by extraordinary means, but with due care taken to fourth and fifth amendment protections. The author examines how this fine line may be walked. ^United\States ^Money\Laundering ^Law\Enforcement ^Consequences\Political ^Consequences\Legal ^P\S\Constitutional

12. Abramovsky, Abraham, and Steven J. Eagle (1977). "U.S. Policy in Apprehending Alleged Offenders Abroad: Extradition, Abduction, or Irregular Detention?" *Oregon Law Review* 57:51–93. Historically, nations have sought bilateral extradition treaties to gain physical custody over alleged offenders. Recently, in order to circumvent traditional extradition processes, the United States has resorted to extraordinary means, including abductions and irregular detentions. Abductions are unilateral seizures of alleged offenders. Irregular detentions occur when law enforcement agents bilaterally collaborate, independently of judicial processes, to move alleged offenders into the hands of the state that seeks them. Serious legal issues are associated with these "extraordinary apprehensions." ^United\States ^Extradition ^Drug\Control\Policies ^Consequences\Legal ^Law\Enforcement

13. Abramowitz, Michael (1989). "AIDS Stimulates New Interest in Methadone; Controversial Drug Called a Lifesaver—and a Crutch for Addicts." *The Washington Post*, 20 February, A1. Bring addicts into clinics for "methadone maintenance." This will reduce needle sharing. Various aspects of the controversy are discussed. ^United\States ^Heroin ^Health ^AIDS ^Treatment ^Methadone ^Consequences\AIDS ^Consequences\Health ^Prevention\Methadone

14. ——— (1989). "Need for Hospital Stays by Addicts Questioned." *The Washington Post*, 1 July, 1A. The substantial costs of detoxifying addicts and alcoholics (upwards of $15,000 a month) has caused concern among insurers and employers. ^United\States ^Drug\Use ^Treatment ^Consequences\Economic

15. ——— (1989). "Pregnant Cocaine Users Reduce Risk by Stopping." *The Washington Post*, 24 March, A11. According to recent reports, cocaine-using women who stop taking the drug soon after becoming pregnant might be able to reduce

the risk of physical damage to the fetus. Report issued from the Northwestern University Medical School. ^Cocaine ^Health ^Consequences\Health ^Consequences\Fetuses ^Fetuses ^P\S\Abstinence

16. Abrams, Elliott (1986). "Drug Wars: The New Alliance against Traffickers and Terrorists." *Department of State Bulletin*, April. Abrams' address before the Council on Foreign Relations gives the brief for the administration's findings on the existence of an alliance between drug traffickers and terrorists. ^Drug\Traffic ^United\States ^Drug\Control\Policies ^Consequences\Terrorists ^Terrorists ^Traffickers

17. Adams, Chris (1988). "Funding for Drug War Is Delayed by Red Tape; Complex Procedures and Appeals Hinder Disbursement." *The Washington Post*, 16 August, A2. Vying for money to fund the drug war, various local U.S. government agencies have caused delayed distribution of federal funds. As a result, the funds are locked in court proceedings and cannot be used for their intended purposes. ^United\States ^Drug\Control\Policies ^Drug\Control\Politics

18. —— (1988). "Second Thoughts on the Military as Narcs; Hearings Stress Doubts on Pentagon's Drug-Interdiction Role." *The Washington Post*, 15 June, A21. Reviewing testimony presented before the U.S. Senate Armed Services Committee, senators are reconsidering the involvement of the military in drug interdiction efforts. This testimony follows the 83-6 senate vote on May 13 giving the military a greater role in detecting and tracking drug smugglers, allowing the use of military equipment and personnel in border enforcement programs, and giving the Navy limited powers to arrest outside U.S. waters. ^United\States ^Interdiction ^Military

19. Adams, Edgar H., Joseph C. Gfroerer, Beatrice A. Rouse, and Nicholas J. Kozel (1986). "Trends in Prevalence and Consequences of Cocaine Use." *Advances in Alcohol and Substance Abuse* 6(2): 49–71. Surveys some of the literature relating to the health consequences of cocaine abuse. ^Cocaine ^Health ^Reviews ^Consequences\Health

20. Adams, James (1986). *The Financing of Terror*. London: New English Library. Terrorist groups (Chapter 9) are represented as obtaining considerable funding from narcotics trafficking. Terrorists cannot be combatted if their sources of income are not reduced. Terrorist groups operating in Colombia are given the most coverage. ^Latin\America ^Colombia ^Drug\Traffic ^Consequences\Terrorists ^Traffickers ^Terrorists

21. Adams, Tom, and Barbara West (1988). "The Private Sector: Taking a Role in the Prevention of Drug and Alcohol Abuse for Young People." *Journal of Drug Education* 18(3): 185–199. With increasing employee drug use in the 1960s and 1970s, U.S. employers feared considerable economic costs. As response measures, some companies designed and implemented Employee Assistance Programs, others adopted insurance coverage to support treatment of chemically dependent employees and their families, and others became involved in prevention measures. Furthermore, employee health and fitness centers were developed. Active support of projects designed to prevent drug use among young people were also supported. ^United\States ^Drug\Use ^Prevention ^Youth ^Workplace

22. Adelson, Joseph (1989). "Drugs and Youth." *Commentary* 87(5): 24–28. The author disagrees with the ideological portrayal of young people in much of the academic literature. Genuinely disturbed youngsters constitute only a minority—about 20%—of the total. This is not much different than it has ever been. Therefore, youth cannot generally be seen as revolting against family, conventional values, or social institutions. The so-called doctrines justifying drug use are precisely those justifying both the liberation of schools from coercive authority and people doing their own thing.

"Accomplishment, competition, and success; self restraint, self discipline, and the postponement of gratification; the stability of the family; and a belief in certain moral universals" (p. 27) have given way to an ethos that scorns the pursuit of success, tolerates—or even encourages—sensual gratification, and accepts deviant notions about the family and emphasizes ethical relativism. The current policies of "prohibitionism" will have little success unless parents take upon themselves the task of influencing their children in some very traditional ways. ^United\States ^Drug\Use ^Youth ^Prevention ^Family ^P\S\Values

23. Adler, Jerry, Ginny Carroll, Frank Washington, David L. Gonzalez, Tony Emerson, Lisa Drew, Tessa Namuth, Deborah Witherspoon, Nonny Abbott, Andrew Murr, Michael A. Lerner, Tony Clifton, and Mark Miller (1988). "Hour by Hour Crack." *Newsweek*, 28 November, 64–75. Anecdotal description of real life events in the United States dealing with drug law enforcement, family disintegration, parental neglect, insurance costs of detoxification programs, effects of crack abuse on infants, and the role of the judiciary in the war on drugs. ^United\States ^Cocaine ^Crack ^Drug\Use ^Health ^Family ^Drug\Control\Policies ^Law\Enforcement ^Consequences\Health ^Consequences\Social ^Consequences\Economic ^Consequences\Political

24. Adler, Patricia A. (1985). *Wheeling and Dealing: An Ethnography of an Upper-Level Drug Dealing and Smuggling Community*. New York: Columbia University Press. Study of a community of drug dealers and smugglers at an elite upperlevel and of the social scene they inhabit. The author "penetrated" a drug dealing community for six years and now gives a subjective understanding of how the participants lived, felt, thought, and acted. The study derives from the "existential" branch of sociology, suggesting that hedonism is a motivation for deviance. Air, land, and water smuggling routes and strategies are discussed. Presents evidence, in Chapter 4, against the cocaine "cartel" actually being a monopolistic structure. Examines the personality characteristics and lifestyle preferences of the smugglers and high level dealers. Drug dealers and smugglers did not remove themselves from conventional society and enter a life of deviance because legitimate opportunities for alternative activity were blocked, as others have claimed. Nor did they do so because they were failures within their conventional reference groups. They became deviants because of personality characteristics that craved pleasure and gratification which conventional society repressed through its bureaucratization and impersonality. With this as a base, those individuals who became aware of upper-level dealing and smuggling as a subculture (which signifies that they were drug consumers) were attracted to its free wheeling lifestyle of hedonism and illicit enterprise. ^Cocaine ^Drug\Traffic ^Traffickers ^Consequences\Economic ^Consequences\Social ^United\States

25. Adler, Patricia A., and Peter Adler (1983). "Shifts and Oscillations in Deviant Careers: The Case of Upper-Level Drug Dealers and Smugglers." *Social Problems* 31(2): 195–207. Claims to be the first study of drug trafficking in the United States to penetrate the upper echelons of the marijuana and cocaine business. Examines the typical career paths of the traffickers, specifically, how the traffickers enter the drug business and rise to the top, how they then become disenchanted, and then either voluntarily or involuntarily leave the business. Further, it considers why so many traffickers end up returning to their deviant careers or to other careers within the drug world. Claims that the dealing and smuggling careers are temporary and fraught with multiple attempts at retirement. Nevertheless, retirements are also quite temporary. ^United\States ^Cannabis ^Cocaine ^Drug\Traffic ^Traffickers

26. "After Three Years on the Road to Hell, FBI Arrests 'Angels' in Nationwide Raids" (1985). *Organized Crime Digest*, May, 2–3. Hell's Angels

motorcycle organization is raided on both controlled substance violations and the Rico Act. ^United\States ^Law\Enforcement ^Organized\Crime ^FBI

27. "Agency Intensifies Effort in Anti-Drug Fight" (1988). *USAID Highlights* 5(1). Description, by the United States Agency for International Development, of its efforts to reduce drug consumption and production in developing nations. The agency is trying to wean Latin American farmers from growing coca and Asian farmers from growing opium poppies by encouraging alternative crop cultivation. ^Southeast\Asia ^Latin\America ^United\States ^Opiates ^Coca ^Foreign\Aid ^Crop\Substitution ^Drug\Control\Policies ^Drug\Use ^Production

28. Agreda R., Flores (1986). "Drug Abuse Problems in Countries of the Andean Subregion." *Bulletin on Narcotics* 38(1-2): 27–36. In Bolivia, Colombia, and Peru prevalence of drug abuse, particularly of cocaine paste, is relatively high. For instance, internal surveys in Peru show that 37% of secondary school students use drugs, and over a quarter of the students first get involved by smoking cocaine paste. All social classes are involved. This coincides with the dramatic increase in the cultivation of coca and the production of its alkaloid derivatives. ^Bolivia ^Colombia ^Peru ^Drug\Use ^Youth ^Latin\America ^Coca ^Cocaine\Paste

29. —— (1987). "Basic Elements for a National Comprehensive Plan for Drug Abuse Control in Peru." *Bulletin on Narcotics* 39(2): 37–49. Describes the nature and extent of drug abuse in Peru, with particular reference to the illicit cultivation of the coca plant and the national responses to ensuing problems. Both the problems and national responses are analyzed in the context of historical and current developments that have influenced Peruvian drug abuse control policies. Summarizes the salient points of Peru's new national comprehensive plan for drug abuse control. The plan targets four major sectors of activity—prevention, treatment, and rehabilitation; control and monitoring of substances used for legitimate purposes; suppression of the illicit drug traffic; and the eradication of illicit coca plant growing. Agricultural, agro-industrial, and forestial development are promoted as alternatives to the drug economy. Urges the whole nation to be mobilized in the implementation of the plan. ^Peru ^Coca ^Drug\Use ^Drug\Control\Policies ^Drug\Use\History ^Proffered\Solutions ^Production ^Latin\America

30. Ahmed, Yasmeen, Amechi Anumonye, Dorothy Black, Gerhard Buhringer, Carmen Garcia Linan, Robert Philip Irwin, Richard Lindblad, and Udomisil Srisangnam (1983). "Report of the Expert Group on Drug Abuse Reduction." *Bulletin on Narcotics* 35(3): 3–17. Describes the group's recommendations to better prevent and reduce drug abuse. Argues for an integrated approach rather than isolated or segmented approaches. Specific audience tailoring should be considered in program development. All resources targeted for prevention and reduction of illicit demand for drugs should be allocated for realistic targets. ^P\S\Integrated

31. "AIDS and Drugs: Shooting Up" (1989). *The Economist*, 1 April, 48–49. In Britain, the HIV virus is spreading rapidly among clients of drug-abuse clinics. Public costs are increasing. Statistics are given. ^United\Kingdom ^AIDS ^Statistics ^Consequences\Economic

32. "AIDS Benefit in Methadone Use Is Questioned" (1989). *The New York Times*, 3 August, B6. Two government studies made public on 3 August said that a plan to give heroin addicts greater access to methadone would probably not ease the spread of AIDS. The reports questioned the effectiveness of current treatment programs. Methadone will not solve the problem. The studies are from the U.S. Department of Health and Human Services. ^United\States ^Heroin ^Drug\Use ^Treatment ^Methadone ^Health ^AIDS ^Prevention ^Reviews

33. "The AIDS Plague Spreads" (1989). *The Economist*, 15 July, 23–24. Increasing numbers of crack users in New York City are now shown to be infected by the HIV virus. There seems to have been a rush into commercial sex in order to raise money for crack purchases. While crack is cheap, it is so addictive that users quickly run out of money to support their habits. Syphilis and gonorrhea are also on the increase. Twenty percent of the 100,000 U.S. cases are New Yorkers, and 20 percent of those live in just two boroughs of New York, Brooklyn and the Bronx. ^United\States ^Cocaine ^Crack ^Heroin ^AIDS ^Prostitution ^Consequences\Health ^New\York

34. "AIDS Watch: Mapping the Epidemic" (1988). *Discover*, April, 28–31. Gives worldwide statistics on AIDS in relationship to geographic concentrations. Does likewise for the United States, and for New York City. Whereas in the past the virus was spread mostly by homosexuals, now it is rampant in the drug user community. The rate of new infections in homosexual men has dropped sharply since 1983 but is steadily rising among needle-using addicts at the rate of three percent a year. ^United\States ^Heroin ^Health ^AIDS ^Consequences\AIDS ^Consequences\Health ^New\York

35. Alderman, Michael H., Ernest E. Drucker, Allen Rosenfield, and Cheryl Healton (1988). "Predicting the Future of the AIDS Epidemic and Its Consequences for the Health Care System of New York City." *Bulletin of the New York Academy of Medicine* 64(2): 175–182. Projections from case reports are very limited. One probably needs to take an epidemiological approach and, on the basis of demographic variables and imputed behavioral characteristics, make projections. Making such projections even on a conservative basis shows horrendous implications for the delivery of health services in New York City. ^United\States ^Drug\Use ^Health ^AIDS ^Consequences\Health ^Consequences\AIDS ^Consequences\Economic ^New\York

36. Alexander, Bruce K. (1990). "Alternatives to the War on Drugs." *The Journal of Drug Issues* 20:1(Winter): 1–27. Inasmuch as the war on drugs is ineffective it ought to be altered, although not abandoned. Alteration should be directed towards solving real social problems. The author proposes such an alternative. He advances replacements for three major components of the drug war. First, localized, pragmatic controls should be introduced to replace drug prohibition laws. These would include legal regulation, regional differences consistent with people's culture, controlled distribution and social control. Second, valid information should replace antidrug propaganda. Ultimately, this would reduce the resistance to valid information. Finally, social innovations should replace bureaucratized drug treatment. These would include medical dispensation of prohibited drugs, community support for drug users, the development of nonprofessional support organizations, and the creation of other innovations that would aid the healing process both for society and for individuals. ^P\S\Legalization ^P\S\Drug\Education ^P\S\Culture ^P\S\Controlled\Sales

37. Alexander, Bruce K., and Patricia L. Holborn (1990). "Introduction: A Time For Change." *The Journal of Drug Issues* 20:4(Fall): 509–13. In introducing this special issue of the journal, dedicated to "alternatives to the war on drugs," the authors point out a range of policy alternatives to prohibition that exist, many of which are advanced in this issue. These range from legalization to controlled distribution associated with some kind of user accountability. ^Proffered\Solutions ^P\S\Policies

38. Alexander, Herbert E., and Gerald E. Caiden, eds. (1985). *The Politics and Economics of Organized Crime*. Lexington, Mass: Lexington Books. Edited volume contains individually authored articles on money laundering, cartels, the relationship of drug enforcement to organized crime, organized crime and politics, political corruption in small, machine run cities, and asset forfeiture under the U.S.

federal criminal law. Also includes a policy related article on dealing with organized crime. Peter Reuter is a contributor. ^United\States ^Drug\Traffic ^Organized\Crime ^Money\Laundering ^Drug\Control\Policies ^Asset\Forfeiture ^Consequences\Economic ^Consequences\Political ^Consequences\Corruption

39. Alfonso, Pablo (1989). "Expertos sobre Cuba Dudan que Castro Desconociera Narcotráfico." *El Nuevo Herald*, 25 June, 13A. In a conference held at Harvard University, Jorge Dominguez expressed profound doubts that Fidel Castro knew nothing about the narcotrafficking going on in Cuba under the jurisdiction of some of his high officials. ^Cuba ^Drug\Traffic ^Latin\America

40. Allen, Catherine J. (1988). *The Hold Life Has: Coca and Cultural Identity in an Andean Community*. Washington, D.C.: Smithsonian Institution Press. Another contribution, in the ethnographic tradition of contemporary anthropologists, to show the integration that coca and its associated rituals have with cultural identity in a Peruvian village. The implication, of course, is that insofar as coca use changes (forced or voluntary), so also does culture. ^Latin\America ^Peru ^Coca ^Drug\Use ^Society ^Culture

41. Allen, David, ed. (1985). *The Cocaine Crisis*. Based on the proceedings of the First International Cocaine Symposium, held 21–22 November 1985, in the Bahamas, co-sponsored by the American Embassy and the Bahamas government. Focuses on treatment of cocaine addicts who "freebase"—sometimes known as smoking cocaine in the "rock" or "crack" form. Normative focus is to convince people that cocaine kills, and that the perpetuation of the myth that cocaine is harmless is totally outside reality. While an educational program might convince non-users or infrequent users to abstain from cocaine and marijuana, those who have already become "addicted" have made their choice. Educating addicts would be impossible without concurrent strong enforcement and a concomitant demand by society that cocaine use no longer be tolerated. It is important, therefore, to highlight the medical consequences of cocaine use, which this book sets out to do. Interrelationship of history, society, and economics on the individual who chooses to become a drug abuser is discussed. Data are produced from among individuals in "consumer societies," in "trans-shipment societies," and in "producer societies." ^Cocaine ^Health ^Drug\Control\Policies ^Treatment ^Consequences\Health ^Consequences\Social ^Drug\Use\History ^Proffered\Solutions

42. Allison, Margaret and Robert L. Hubbard (1985). "Drug Abuse Treatment Process: A Review of the Literature." *International Journal of the Addictions* 20(9): 1321–1345. Substantial literature is reviewed on drug abuse treatment in two areas. The first describes three major treatment modalities (out-patient methadone, residential, and out-patient drug-free). The second section covers general studies of drug abuse treatment. Various typologies of treatment are presented, discussed, and critiqued. As no clear, coherent integrated picture of the treatment process has emerged, findings may be idiosyncratic because of their single setting approach. The author notes that all of the studies reviewed failed to take into account the complex relationships among the broad range of variables identified. ^Treatment ^Reviews ^Methadone

43. Altman, Lawrence K. (1989). "Needle Exchange Programs Hint a Cut in AIDS Virus Transmission." *The New York Times*, 7 June, B5. New studies show that needle exchange programs in three cities have reduced needle sharing and therefore the risk of transmitting the AIDS virus, and all this without an increase in drug use. ^Heroin ^Health ^AIDS ^P\S\Needle\Exchange ^Drug\Use ^Prevention\Needle\Exchange ^Consequences\AIDS

44. —— (1989). "US to Ease Methadone Rules for Addicts to Combat AIDS." *The New York Times*, 3 March, 1. The FDA and the National Institute of Drug Abuse now urge that methadone be made available to thousands of heroin addicts independent of their being involved in a comprehensive treatment program. Over fifty percent of intravenous drug users who seek methadone treatment are infected with the AIDS virus. The relaxation of methadone requirements is an effort to halt the spread of AIDS into the remaining fifty percent of the heroin addicted population. ^United\States ^Heroin ^Health ^AIDS ^Treatment ^Methadone ^Drug\Use ^Prevention\Methadone

45. Alvarez, Elena (1983). "Government Policies and the Persistence of Rural Poverty in Peru, 1960-1980." Ph.D. diss. New School for Social Research. Analysis of the effects on various agricultural producers of economic policies in Peru from 1960 to 1980. Policies have differentially impacted some producers, and the author seeks to explain how these policies contribute to the persistence of rural poverty in Peru. In general, agricultural policies did not address rural poverty so much as they fostered urban industrial growth. The lowest producers (*minifundistas*), the bulk of Peru's agricultural producers, were neither helped nor harmed by these transfer policies. The author suggests that the extreme poverty of small agricultural farmers is not due to government measures. Rather, ecological and other constraints prevented small farmers from being integrated competitively into labor and product markets. (All this as a precursor to the expanding coca trade is implied.) ^Latin\America ^Peru ^Coca ^Producers

46. American Council on Marijuana and Other Psychoactive Drugs, Inc. (1982). *Marijuana: The National Impact on Education* (1982). Rockville, Md.: The Council. Marijuana smoking can interfere with the ability to form new memories, it alters sensory and cognitive integrity, and individuals intoxicated from cannabis have reduced motivation and goal direction. These are some of the impact issues discussed, but many of the participants in the conference that gave rise to this volume focus on prevention and treatment. As summarized, the most effective ones first created an atmosphere of intolerance toward drugs within the school, educated teachers about the effects of habitual marijuana use on the adolescents and assisted them in recognizing symptoms, gave students opportunities to help each other and themselves through positive peer counseling programs, and involved a kind of preventive maintenance—education and other materials beginning as early as the seventh grade. Also, in all areas parent groups were heavily involved. The underlying assumption was that "every element of learning is incompatible with either the acute intoxication or the chronic mental changes that marijuana can bring." ^United\States ^Cannabis ^Drug\Use ^Youth ^Consequences\Neurological ^Amotivational\Syndrome ^Prevention\Integrated

47. "Americans in Colombia Fear Reprisals for Lehder's Capture" (1987). *The Los Angeles Times*, 7 February, 4. Not only have Colombian leaders feared reprisals for activities initiated against drug barons, now American citizens living in Colombia fear that they may become indiscriminate targets for terrorism in reprisal for Carlos Lehder's capture and extradition to the United States. ^Colombia ^United\States ^Extradition ^Latin\America ^Drug\Control\Policies ^Consequences\Terrorists ^Consequences\Violence

48. *Analysis of the Domestic Cannabis Problem and the Federal Response* (1986). Washington, D.C.: The National Drug Enforcement Policy Board. During the 1980s the United States has become a significant producer of cannabis. As early as 1984 more than 12% of the marijuana consumed in the United States was thought to be domestically grown. Roughly 22 million Americans have been users of cannabis, within the month prior to publication. In addition, 10 million are thought to have experimented or used it frequently. Social costs of marijuana abuse are born by all

Americans. These include increased motor vehicle and industrial accidents, worker productivity losses, violence, environmental damage, and adverse health consequences for users. Violence associated with cannabis cultivation usually occurs among competing growers and between growers and "patch pirates." Indoor cultivation to avoid detection is noted. Federal response to this increased domestic marijuana production is reviewed, which has mostly been an eradication and intelligence-collection policy. ^United\States ^Cannabis ^Health ^Producers ^Drug\Control\Policies ^Drug\Use ^Consequences\Social ^Consequences\Violence

49. Anderson, Thomas P. (1988). "Politics and the Military in Honduras." *Current History* (December): 425–431. The military continues to rule Honduras behind the scenes, and Honduran army officers are profiting from funnelling arms to the Contras and engaging in drug trafficking. Honduras has become a point for transshipment to the United States. ^Honduras ^Drug\Traffic ^Military ^Latin\America ^Consequences\Political ^Consequences\Corruption ^Consequences\Environmental

50. Anglin, Lise (1985). *Cocaine: A Selection of Annotated Papers from 1980 to 1984 Concerning Health Effects.* Toronto: Addiction Research Foundation. Includes English, French, and German papers dealing with health effects of recreational cocaine use. History, chemistry, and botany may be mentioned in passing, but are not discussed at length in the annotations. Annotations are non-evaluative. Most entries are from scientific journals, but several have been published as book chapters or separate reports. There are 277 entries and an author and subject index. ^Cocaine ^Health ^Bibliographies ^Consequences\Health

51. Anglin, M. Douglas and George Speckart (1988). "Narcotics Use and Crime: A Multisample, Multimethod Analysis." *Criminology* 26(2): 197–233. During an addiction period, addicts commit significantly more property crimes than during periods of curtailed narcotics use produced by treatment. ^Heroin ^Drug\Use ^Crime ^Consequences\Crime

52. Anglin, M. Douglas, George R. Speckart, Mary W. Booth, and Timothy M. Ryan (1989). "Consequences and Costs of Shutting off Methadone." *Addictive Behaviors* 14:307–326. As local communities become strapped for funds and become more fiscally conservative, many have reduced or eliminated public funding for methadone maintenance programs and have permitted private institutions (for fee) to replace them. In a study on two such populations in Southern California, major adverse consequences were found for clients who were either unable or unwilling to transfer to private programs. Consequences were higher crime and narcotics dealing rates, more contact with the criminal justice system, and higher rates of illicit drug use. Savings from reducing the methadone maintenance programs were nearly offset by increased direct costs for incarceration, legal supervision, and other government funded drug treatment. Indirect costs were not assessed. ^United\States ^Heroin ^Drug\Use ^Crime ^Treatment ^Methadone ^Consequences\Crime ^Consequences\Economic ^Drug\Control\Policies ^California

53. "'Anti-Mafia' Law Follows Exposés" (1984). *Latin American Regional Reports,* 14 December, 3. Discussion of the "Venezuelan mafia" and its connections to the drug trade. ^Venezuela ^Drug\Traffic ^Organized\Crime ^Latin\America ^Drug\Control\Policies

54. Anturiano Hurtado, Julio (1986). *La Hiena: Drama Social sobre la Droga, Drogadicción, y Corrupción.* Santa Cruz, Bolivia: Empresa Editora El País. Discussion of the Bolivian cocaine trade and the corruption, sadism, and violation of the peasantry that have resulted. The United States is responsible for Bolivia's drug problems, being "the author of [Bolivia's] disgrace, tearing apart not only [its] society but its authorities, politicians, the military, and the police" (p. 10). The book offers, in its own way, a strong call for the country to struggle against drug addiction. ^Bolivia ^Coca

^Cocaine ^Drug\Traffic ^Consequences\Social ^Consequences\Political ^Latin\America ^United\States ^Drug\Control\Policies ^Prevention\Abstinence ^Drug\Use

55. Appavoo, S. J. (1985). "Addiction—Plague of the Nation." *The Police Journal* (January): 32–48. Discusses the new heroin epidemic sweeping Britain, its causes and consequences, and what should be done about it. Argues for heavier sentences, public awareness so as to be able to detect drug involvement by young children, and revamping of laws so as to deal more effectively with drug pushers. Above all, long mandatory sentences of imprisonment as well as confiscation of all property owned or held by non-dependent drug dealers must be implemented. There must be a new presumption that all property held by people so involved has arisen from their criminal activity. Let the onus rest on the accused to rebut it. ^United\Kingdom ^Heroin ^Drug\Use ^Drug\Control\Policies ^P\S\Law\Enforcement ^P\S\Asset\Forfeiture

56. Applesome, Peter (1987). "Agent's Slaying Points up Rise in Border Drugs." *The New York Times*, 3 January, A5. Increasing arrests of drug traffickers in Texas and Florida are thought to coincide with increased drug traffic in these areas. ^United\States ^Drug\Traffic ^Law\Enforcement ^Texas ^Florida

57. Aramayo, G., and M. Sánchez (1980). "Clinical Manifestations Using Cocaine Paste." In *Cocaine 1980. Proceedings of the Interamerican Seminar on Medical and Sociological Aspects of Coca and Cocaine*, edited by F. R. Jeri. Lima, Peru: Pacific Press, 120–126. (Book is annotated in this bibliography under Jeri, F. Raúl.) Physiological and neurological effects, many severe, of intoxication and chronic use are noted. ^Cocaine\Paste ^Drug\Use ^Health ^Consequences\Health ^Bolivia ^Consequences\Physiological ^Consequences\Neurological

58. Arango Jaramillo, Mario (1988). *Impacto del Narcotráfico en Antioquía.* Medellín, Colombia: Multigráficas Ltda. Examines cultural changes over the last quarter century that have been observed in Medellín, Colombia, and nearby areas in the department of Antioquía as a consequence of the development of the illicit drug trade. The subculture of the narcotrafficker and its association with violence are catalogued, the replacement of the traditional Colombian business enterprise with that of those dealing in drug contraband is discussed, and the cultural/personality characteristic of those so involved is identified. The implications of all this for the regional economy, social mobilization, and cultural change are noted. The final chapter discusses the narcotics trafficking as an economic phenomena of capitalist society. ^Latin\America ^Colombia ^Drug\Traffic ^Consequences\Social ^Consequences\Cultural ^Consequences\Violence ^Traffickers ^Consequences\Economic

59. Arango Jaramillo, Mario, and Jorge Child Vélez (1985). *Los Condenados de la Coca: El Manejo Político de la Droga.* Medellín, Colombia: Editorial J.M. Arango. Discusses, from a Colombian perspective, how the narcotics business works internationally and, in particular, how United States antidrug policies operate with "the Drug Enforcement Agency now substituting for the CIA." Economics of the narcotraffic and the problem of "colonial extradition" are analyzed. Highly critical of the United States and its policies; indicative, Chapter 8 is entitled "Cocaine: Almost Innocuous." In all, the author sees the international political economy of cocaine having deleterious effects on Colombia, not so much because Colombia is a cocaine producer but because of the international pressures being brought to bear on Colombia to stop being a producer. ^Latin\America ^Colombia ^United\States ^Cocaine ^Drug\Traffic ^Drug\Control\Policies ^Extradition ^Consequences\Foreign\Relations ^Consequences\Economic ^Consequences\Social ^Consequences\Political ^DEA

60. Arango J., Mario, and Jorge Child V. (1987). *Narcotráfico: Imperio de la Cocaína.* Mexico: Edivisión Companía Editorial. Aside from a very large

historical backdrop, this volume includes a number of "consequences" issues: Derived fortunes and what is done with them, the connection with organized crime, the relationship, in Colombia, of the drug traffic to the exportation of emeralds, how the trafficking is done in Colombia, who the big consuming nations are and what drives them (United States), and economic interests and political domination in the war on narcotics. ^Latin\America ^Colombia ^United\States ^Cocaine ^Drug\Traffic ^Organized\Crime ^Drug\Use ^Drug\Control\Policies ^Consequences\Social ^Consequences\Political ^Consequences\Economic

61. Arif, A., ed. (1987). *Adverse Health Consequences of Cocaine Abuse.* Geneva, Switzerland: World Health Organization. Aside from summarizing existing knowledge on the problem of cocaine dependence throughout the world, this small booklet reviews current approaches to treatment. Importance is given to prevention programs. The book also summarizes world consumption trends and notes recently developed forms of ingestion, such as coca-paste smoking and cocaine free-base smoking. ^Cocaine ^Health ^Prevention ^Treatment ^Consequences\Health ^Drug\Use

62. Arlacchi, P. (1984). "Effects of the New Anti-Mafia Law on the Proceeds of Crime and on the Italian Economy." *Bulletin on Narcotics* 36(4): 93–100. In 1982 Italy enacted a new law against the mafia allowing for seizure and confiscation of illegally acquired assets. The law, applied more systematically in Southern Italy, had positive results during the two year period following adoption. On 352 occasions property suspected of being derived from crimes was seized. On another 108 occasions illegally acquired property was confiscated. In the wake of these confiscations there is a frantic rush in southern Italy to convert all monies into "legal properties." ^Italy ^Asset\Forfeiture ^Europe ^Consequences\Economic

63. Armstrong, Scott (1987). "New Wave of Narcotics Cases Puts Severe Strain on US Courts." *The Christian Science Monitor*, 9 January, 3. Nationwide war on drugs is congesting the U.S. court system. New judges are being added to state court systems which have been particularly hard hit. ^United\States ^Law\Enforcement ^Consequences\Judiciary

64. ———— (1988). "Crack Reasserts Itself across US; Flak-Jacketed Police Battle Resurging, Violent Drug Tide." *The Christian Science Monitor*, 14 March, 1. Crack addiction produces increasing dilemmas for U.S. police officers and communities. ^United\States ^Cocaine ^Crack ^Drug\Traffic ^Law\Enforcement ^Consequences\Violence ^Drug\Use

65. ———— (1988). "Los Angeles Gangs Go National." *The Christian Science Monitor*, 19 July, 3. Los Angeles gangs are moving their drug operations to other parts of the United States in pursuit of new profits and new territory. ^United\States ^Drug\Traffic ^Organized\Crime

66. ———— (1989). "School Drug Programs: Are They Helping Kids Say 'No?'" *The Christian Science Monitor*, 13 June, 1. Existing school drug programs in the United States are criticized as being ineffective. ^United\States ^Drug\Use ^Prevention\Drug\Education ^Prevention\Critique

67. ———— (1990). "Drug Use Gets Tougher Look on America's Last Frontier." *The Christian Science Monitor*, 11 April, 1. A political backlash against Alaska's permissive marijuana drug policies is described. Alaska therefore joins other states, which had earlier decriminalized marijuana, in reconsidering its position. Policies in Maine, Oregon, Michigan, and Minnesota are discussed. ^Decriminalization\Critique ^United\States ^Alaska ^Maine ^Oregon ^Michigan ^Minnesota

68. ———— (1980). "U.S.–Bolivia Relations Further Strained as Cocaine Smuggling Charges Fly." *The Christian Science Monitor*, 14 August, 5. Embittered relations between the United States and the new military junta in Bolivia show

signs of souring still further. The dispute arises over charges that an international cocaine smuggling operation is bankrolling the military regime that overthrew the country's civilian government in July. ^Bolivia ^United\States ^Cocaine ^Drug\Traffic ^Consequences\Political ^Consequences\Foreign\Relations

69. Arnao, Giancario (1988). "Drug Enforcement Policy as a Factor in Trends of Trafficking and Use of Different Substances." *Journal of Psychoactive Drugs* 20(4): 463–465. Drug enforcement policies have unintended consequences, one of which is law enforcement itself indirectly promoting the evolution of the illegal market rather than undermining it. Analysis of the conditions under which this unfortunate consequence occurs. Many people "need" psychotropic drugs, and as they weigh their own risk management in obtaining them, they influence the market to move toward more pharmacologically concentrated substances that have the unfortunate consequence of causing greater ills than the more bulky "natural" substances they replace. Pakistan, for example, where heroin addiction was unknown until 1979 but opium widely used, now has a major heroin addiction problem since the banning of opium. ^Heroin ^Drug\Use ^Pakistan ^Law\Enforcement ^Opiates ^Consequences\Illegal\Economy ^Consequences\Drug\Concentration ^Golden\Crescent ^Southwest\Asia

70. Aronson, Thomas A., and Thomas J. Craig (1986). "Cocaine Precipitation of Panic Disorder." *The American Journal of Psychiatry* 143(5): 643–645. Case studies are given of patients suffering from "panic disorder" which began during recreational use of cocaine and continued on its own even after drug usage was stopped. Theoretical and practical implications are discussed. (Panic disorders are characterized, among other things, by a rapidly beating heart, faintness, shortness of breath, and extreme nervousness). ^Cocaine ^Health ^Consequences\Health

71. "Arrested DEA Agent May Have Tipped off Major Cocaine Ring" (1989). *The Miami Herald*, 18 August, 22A. The arrest of Edward K. O'Brian has now raised, for the first time, the prospect that DEA headquarters has been penetrated by drug traffickers. Particulars of the case are laid out. ^United\States ^Cocaine ^Law\Enforcement ^Consequences\Corruption ^DEA

72. Ashley, Richard (1975). *Cocaine: Its History, Uses and Effects*. New York: St. Martin's Press. A heavily cited and read handbook that argues against the prohibition of cocaine. The author believes that antidrug laws are historically ineffective and that there is little reason to believe that drug prohibition will ever be effective. Cocaine is nonaddictive and should therefore be legalized. Included are appendices on how to refine, store, and use cocaine. ^Cocaine ^Consequences\Health ^Drug\Control\Policies ^P\S\Legalization ^Drug\Use\History

73. "The Asian Connection: U.S. Forces Too Often Fight Each Other in a Secret War against the Golden Triangle's Heroin Supplier" (1984). *Newsweek*, 25 June, 62–63. Describes the self defeating bureaucratic battles among various U.S. federal agencies responsible for carrying out the "war" against the Golden Triangle's heroin suppliers. ^United\States ^Burma ^Thailand ^Laos ^Southeast\Asia ^Drug\Control\Policies ^Politics ^Bureaucracy ^Golden\Triangle

74. Asociación Peruana de Estudios e Investigación para la Paz (1990). *Cocaína: Problemas y Soluciones Andinos*. Lima, Peru: Asociación Peruana de Estudios e Investigación para la Paz (APEP). Country studies are offered for Bolivia, Colombia, and Peru. These concentrate on the international nature of the illicit drug problem, therefore emphasizing the need for integrated international efforts to resolve it. Ultimately, consuming countries must address the problem of demand if the integrated problems that derive from consumption and production are to be addressed.

Thus, all countries have shared responsibilities that require common efforts for resolution of the problems. ^Latin\America ^Bolivia ^Peru ^Colombia ^Drug\Traffic ^P\S\Demand\Reduction ^P\S\International\Cooperation ^P\S\Integrated ^Cocaine

75. "Asset Forfeiture: Taking the Profit Out of Drug Trafficking" (1987). *The Police Chief* (September): 13-16. Leaders of trafficking organizations come and go. Unless the assets of the drug trade are forfeited, trafficking will persist. ^Drug\Traffic ^Asset\Forfeiture ^P\S\Asset\Forfeiture

76. Astor, David (1984). "'Striking Back' against a U.S. Epidemic." *Editor and Publisher*, 27 October, 32. Discussion of an educational effort by Sue Rushie who, in a newspaper column, twice weekly discusses the harmful effects of drugs and offers help to users and users' parents. ^United\States ^Prevention\Media

77. Asuni, T., and F. Bruno (1984). "Summary of an Eleven-Country Study of Socio-Legal Measures to Combat Drug Abuse and Related Crime." *Bulletin on Narcotics* 36(3): 3–17. Reports a comparative study of experimental and controlled subjects in Argentina, Brazil, Costa Rica, Japan, Jordan, Italy, Malaysia, Singapore, and the United States (state of New York). Also reports on independent studies conducted in Sweden and the United Kingdom. A close association was found to exist between drug abuse, criminal behavior, and social attitudes towards such problems. No correlation was found between the severity of drug laws and the extent of drug abuse and its associated criminality. The study encourages the review, testing, and implementation of alternative measures to penal sanctions, particularly therapeutic approaches to correct the deviant behavior of drug abusers. ^Argentina ^Brazil ^Costa\Rica ^Japan ^Jordan ^Malaysia ^Singapore ^Middle\East ^United\States ^Latin\America ^Southeast\Asia ^Italy ^New\York ^Sweden ^Scandinavia ^United\Kingdom ^P\S\Therapy ^Drug\Use ^Crime ^Law\Enforcement ^Society

78. Asuni, T., and O. A. Pela (1986). "Drug Abuse in Africa." *Bulletin on Narcotics* 38(1–2): 55-64. Aside from cannabis use and khat chewing, drug abuse in Africa is relatively new. It is now escalating to more dangerous drugs and to a wider range of people. While the most available drug of abuse is still cannabis, cocaine and heroin are rapidly invading some African countries. What can be done about this? African countries should strengthen not only formal drug control systems but also informal control mechanisms. Strengthening informal control mechanisms will compensate for insufficient funds and other limiting factors such as the capacity of trained personnel in implementing formal drug control measures. ^Africa ^Cannabis ^Cocaine ^Heroin ^Drug\Use ^Drug\Control\Policies ^Proffered\Solutions ^P\S\Social

79. Auld, John (1981). *Marijuana Use and Social Control.* New York: Academic Press. Study of the social reaction in the early 1970s to marijuana usage. Besides being illegal, marijuana use was thought to pose a considerable challenge to some of society's core values and interests. Clearly, the social reaction to marijuana use had a profound effect upon the kind of meanings that were attached to its use. As the social meanings changed, the attraction of marijuana to different groups changed. Ultimately, usage perception became associated with a subculture of marijuana users who were in a significant personal crisis or state of anomie. The study therefore represents an attempt to explore some of the linkages between objective and subjective social realties and to examine some of the ways in which a highly contentious public issue could simultaneously be reflected in significant numbers of personal troubles. The author suggests a number of possible personal adaptations and reasons, and why some are more likely to be favored than others. All cautions aside, one thing is certain: "No adequate understanding of the effect of marijuana is likely to be achieved until researchers pay at least as much attention to the meaning which its users assign to it as to its pharmacological properties" (p. 188). ^United\States ^Cannabis ^Drug\Use ^Consequences\Social

80. Ausubel, David P. (1983). "Methadone Maintenance Treatment: The Other Side of the Coin." *International Journal of the Addictions* 18(6): 851–62. Methadone maintenance treatment for heroin addiction leaves much to be desired. Unsatisfactory factors are discussed; it is asserted that official evaluation studies have grossly exaggerated the clinical effectiveness of methadone treatment. Furthermore, the maintenance program has inadvertently created many more methadone addicts than it has cured heroin addicts. ^Heroin ^Treatment ^Methadone ^Treatment\Critique

81. Ayres, B. Drummond, Jr. (1990). "Change in Drug Data Brings Hope to Washington." *The New York Times*, February 12, A14. There has been a decline in the number of people testing positive for drug use among those arrested each month in the District of Colombia. Other nearby jurisdictions in Maryland and Virginia report similar findings. ^United\States ^Virginia ^Maryland ^Drug\Use ^Drug\Testing ^Washington\DC

82. Avignolo, Maria Laura (1988). "Bolivia: Coca Control Law Feeds Anti–U.S. Sentiment." *Latinamerica Press*, 15 September, 7. Description of how the new coca eradication law enacted at the behest of the Reagan administration stirred anti-U.S. sentiment in Bolivia. Description of the eradication law and its intended effect. Penalties are somewhat draconian: Peasants who grow coca outside stipulated zones and others who violate the law can be sentenced from two to twenty-five years in prison. ^Latin\America ^Bolivia ^United\States ^Coca ^Crop\Eradication ^Politics ^Consequences\Foreign\Relations ^Drug\Control\Policies ^Consequences\Penal

83. Aznam, Suhaini, and Emily Lau (1986). "Equal under the Law." *Far Eastern Economic Review* 133(17 July): 26–27. Description of two Australians hung by the Malaysian government for drug offenses in Malaysia. These were the first caucasians to die under Malaysia's Dangerous Drugs Act. ^Malaysia ^Drug\Traffic ^Law\Enforcement

84. Bacchetta, Vittoria (1987). "Brazil: Drug Trafficking Gangs Vie for Control of Rio's Impoverished Favelas." *Latinamerica Press*, 24 September, 3. Anecdotal description of the movement of organized drug lords into the outskirts of São Paulo. Description of the Lords' "Robin Hood" drug role. Favela residents defend the traffickers from the police. Brazilian political scientist Helio Jaguaribe views all this in social class terms: "We can't have a modern industrial society that includes a small sector of the population while the majority vegetate on the sidelines." ^Latin\America ^Brazil ^Drug\Traffic ^Organized\Crime ^Consequences\Political ^Consequences\Social

85. Bachman, Jerald G., Lloyd D. Johnston, Patrick M. O'Malley, and Ronald H. Humphrey (1988). "Explaining the Recent Decline in Marijuana Use: Differentiating the Effects of Perceived Risks, Disapproval, and General Lifestyle Factors." *Journal of Health and Social Behavior* 29 (March): 91–112. Marijuana use among high school seniors in the United States has been declining since 1979. How does one account for this trend? Is it because young people have simply become more conservative, or have their views about marijuana changed? Perceived risks and disapproval associated with marijuana use appear to account for much of the actual decline. This has important implications for drug prevention efforts. ^United\States ^Cannabis ^Drug\Use ^Youth ^Prevention

86. Bacon, John (1981). "Is the French Connection Really Dead?" *Drug Enforcement* (Summer): 19–21. Describes the French Connection and those who dominated it, and ponders its possible resurrection. The French Connection—elements of the French criminal underworld—supplied heroin to American addicts from the 1930s until 1973. Its operations were terminated by an international law enforcement effort.

The resulting shortage of heroin enabled Mexican and Asian traffickers to penetrate the American market. ^France ^Heroin ^Drug\Traffic ^Organized\Crime ^Europe ^Traffickers

87. Bacon, Kenneth H. (1989). "Lifelong Struggle: Curtis Eagle's Story Shows How an Addict Can Conquer Cocaine." *The Wall Street Journal*, 2 August. Description of specific therapy experiences used to conquer cocaine addiction in the United States. The continual psychological challenge and the need for long-term positive reinforcement for individuals undergoing treatment are noted. ^United\States ^Cocaine ^Treatment

88. Bagley, Bruce M. (1986). "The Colombian Connection: The Impact of Drug Traffic on Colombia." In *Coca and Cocaine. Effects on People and Policy in Latin America*, edited by Deborah Pacini and Christine Franquemont, pp. 89–100. Boston: Cultural Survival. Analyzes social and economic transformation (e.g. the New Rich) and their impact on politics in Colombia. ^Colombia ^Drug\Traffic ^Latin\America ^Consequences\Economic ^Consequences\Political ^Consequences\Social

89. ———— (1987). "Colombian Politics: Crisis or Community." *Current History* 86(516): 21–41. Describes the legacy that Colombian President Virgilio Barco inherited when he took over the Colombian presidency in 1986: Debt, economic stagnation, insurgency, and an explosive underground economy driven by narcotics. ^Colombia ^Cocaine ^Drug\Traffic ^Latin\America ^Consequences\Economic ^Consequences\Political ^Consequences\Illegal\Economy ^International\Debt

90. ———— (1988). "Colombia and the War on Drugs." *Foreign Affairs* 67(1): 71–92. Describes Colombia's emergence as a key source and trafficking country for cocaine, and the Colombian government's efforts to stop drug trafficking (very little, until recently). Looks at the cocaine cartel's response to drug control efforts in Colombia. What is to be done? Four options are analyzed: United States' financing of Latin American government's drug-fighting capabilities; "Americanization" of antidrug operations in Latin America, with U.S. personnel assuming drug enforcement functions in most countries; U.S. support of efforts to offer viable economic alternatives to the drug trade; and, finally, legalization, or at least decriminalization, of drug consumption. ^Colombia ^United\States ^Drug\Traffic ^Drug\Control\Policies ^Latin\America ^Consequences\Foreign\Relations ^P\S\Legalization ^Proffered\Solutions

91. ———— (1988). "The New Hundred Years War? US National Security and the War on Drugs in Latin America." *Journal of Interamerican Studies and World Affairs* 30(1): 161–182. Illicit drugs will continue to be smuggled into the United States as long as profits are bolstered by a strong domestic demand. This demand must be addressed in narcotics control. However, U.S. policy must recognize that the economies in producing countries will be substantially affected by any effort to decrease demand in the United States, including legalization. Failure to address those options in light of impacts on producing countries will imperil the national security interests of the United States. Several policy options include: Expanding the drug fighting capabilities of Latin American governments, Americanizing Latin American narcotics control policies, supporting Latin American efforts to develop viable economic alternatives to the drug trade, and, finally, abandoning the war on drugs and decriminalizing drug consumption. ^Latin\America ^United\States ^Drug\Control\Policies ^Consequences\Economic ^Consequences\Political ^P\S\Legalization ^Demand ^Proffered\Solutions

92. Bahamas Commission of Inquiry (1984). *Report of the Commission of Inquiry* (Appointed to Inquire into the Illegal Use of the Bahamas for the Trans-shipment of Dangerous Drugs Destined for the United States of America, November 1983–December 1984). Nassau, Bahamas: Government

Printing Department. Focuses on the nature and extent of drug smuggling through the Bahamas. Examines the drug trade's impact on political, judicial, and law enforcement corruption. Discusses money laundering and the general nature of law enforcement activities, including penalties and confiscation. Much anecdotal evidence is given which describes specific locations, people, and organizations involved in the drug trade. ^Bahamas ^Drug\Traffic ^Money\Laundering ^Law\Enforcement ^Asset\Forfeiture ^Consequences\Political ^Consequences\Corruption ^Caribbean

93. Bakalar, James B., and Lester Grinspoon (1983). "Why Drug Policy Is So Harsh." *The Hastings Center Report* (August): 34–39. The metaphors used to describe drug use perpetuate harsh narcotics control policies. These metaphors suggest that recreational drug use is a moral offense endangering the social fabric, an epidemic disease, or an ignorant use of a dangerous instrument like a chain saw. Social attitudes and legal regulations relate to these three analogies in different ways and each serves to reinforce the other in escalating a regime of stricter controls. ^United\States ^Drug\Control\Policies ^Consequences\Social ^Drug\Control\Politics

94. ───── (1984). *Drug Control in a Free Society*. Cambridge, England: Cambridge University Press. Nonpolemical view of the medical, legal, and social status of drugs. Examines the formal and informal controls over drug use employed in modern industrial societies and compares them with other methods that have been or might be used. The approach is historical, sociological, moral, and practical. In the latter categories, the question is how to balance the requirements of health, safety, and social order against the need for individual freedom and diversity of experience. Thus, the authors begin with reflections on old problems of political liberty and their relevance to drug control, moving thereafter to addiction, dependence, and compulsive drug use. They supplement political and medical theories by examining the history and sociology of modern drug control, eventually offering a typology of the forms of drug control, which they then judge on their historical roots, theoretical basis, and comparative advantages and drawbacks. Finally, the authors consider alternative ways of looking at what is usually called the "drug problem." Since neither a drug-using utopia nor a drug-free society is now possible, circumstances are forcing us toward more flexible policies, which the authors then examine. Their commentary on the drug literature is usefully summarized in their own words: "Drug research has produced historical narratives, pharmacological and clinical studies, theories about the nature of addiction and dependence, discussions of practical law enforcement problems, and polemics on drug policy that often combine impassioned certainty about what should be done with ignorance about what is the case. The clinical and pharmacological studies are useful but have a narrow range; the theories about addiction and dependence are inconclusive and rarely relate to larger social issues; the debates on policy tend to be distorted by a lack of historical background and indulgence of passions and prejudices. The sociological and historical studies rarely relate what they say about drug use and drug controls to other tendencies in modern society. Lessons from the vast literature on alcohol and alcoholism are not applied to other drugs. And political theory usually receives too little attention in analyses of drug policy" (p. vii). ^Drug\Control\Policies ^Drug\Use ^Drug\Use\History ^Drug\Use\Theories ^Prevention\Critique

95. Baker, Bob (1988). "Tough Boss Shows Gang Members New Way of Life." *The Los Angeles Times*, 15 April, A1. Description of a pipeline entrepreneur who has hired drug gang members as bona fide employees and has been successful in reforming a number of them. ^United\States ^Treatment ^Prevention ^Private\Initiatives

96. Baker, Bob, and Eric Malnic (1988). "Potent New 'Designer Drug' Seized in Federal Raid on Simi Valley Lab." *The Los Angeles Times*, 4

August, 27. Discussion of pepap, a synthetic heroin that is 36 times more powerful than pure heroin; one ounce of pure pepap produces 20,000 dosage units and makes a profit of about $200,000. The Simi Valley laboratory was raided. ^United\States ^Heroin ^Designer\Drugs ^Drug\Traffic ^Law\Enforcement

97. Ball, John (1976). "A Selective Review of the Crime-Drug Literature with Reference to Future Research Implications." In *Drug Use and Crime: Report of the Panel on Drug Use and Criminal Behavior*, edited by Robert Shellow, 215–29. Washington, D.C.: U.S. Department of Commerce, National Technical Information Service. Reviews the significance of selected studies' findings on the relationship of drug abuse to criminal behavior. Establishes that most heroin addicts are deeply involved in crime; daily opiate use increases criminality several fold; the majority of heroin abusers are not interested in obtaining treatment although drug treatment programs do reduce the criminality of addicts while they are in treatment. Suggests that the criminal justice system ought to differentiate various types of deviant behavior associated with drugs and tailor rehabilitation/penal responses to those typologies. ^Heroin ^Drug\Use ^Crime ^Reviews ^Consequences\Crime

98. Ball, John C., John W. Shaffer, and David N. Nurco (1983). "The Day-to-Day Criminality of Heroin Addicts in Baltimore: A Study in the Continuity of Offense Rates." *Drug and Alcohol Dependence* 12:119–42. Addiction to heroin is associated with a high level of criminality. Theft of property is the most common type of crime, followed by drug sales, other offenses, con-games, and violent offenses. The study's sample included 354 male heroin addicts living in the Baltimore metropolitan area who were traced from onset of opiate use to ascertain any changes in the frequency or type of offenses committed during their years of addiction. Interestingly, criminality decreased over successive non-addiction periods. ^United\States ^Heroin ^Drug\Use ^Crime ^Maryland

99. Ball, John C., Lawrence Rosen, John A. Flueck, and David Nurco (1981). "The Criminality of Heroin Addicts When Addicted and When off Opiates." In *The Drug-Crime Connection*, edited by James A. Inciardi, 29–65. Beverly Hills: Sage. Daily heroin use enhances the probability of criminal behavior among street addicts. The sample group consisted of 243 male opiate addicts. The authors attempted to ascertain the frequency and types of offenses committed by the sample during an 11 year period while on opiates and when off them. When addicted, the subject's average crime-days per year were 248. When not consuming opiates regularly, the average was 40.8 days per year. Thus, there was a 6-fold increase in crime frequency when subjects were addicted. These findings are advanced as having considerable significance for both research and policy implications. ^United\States ^Heroin ^Drug\Use ^Crime ^Consequences\Crime

100. ———— (1982). "Lifetime Criminality of Heroin Addicts in the United States." *Journal of Drug Issues* 12(3): 225–239. The evidence that heroin addicts commit many crimes is overwhelming. Reports the data and methodology associated with studies coming to this conclusion. ^United\States ^Heroin ^Drug\Use ^Crime ^Reviews

101. Bandy, Patricia and Patricia Alford President (1983). "Recent Literature on Drug Abuse Prevention and Mass Media: Focusing on Youth, Parents, Women and the Elderly." *Journal of Drug Education* 13(3): 255-271. Reviews the literature on media campaigns designed to promote drug prevention sentiments among four target audiences: youth, parents, women, and the elderly. Of these four categories, the discussion most germane for this bibliography deals with youth and parents. The role of parents as intermediaries in the delivery system designed to reach

youths is analyzed. The need to segment audiences and design custom presentations appears to be critical across all target populations. ^Drug\Use ^Prevention\Media ^Youth ^Reviews ^Women ^Family

102. Bannister, Shala Mills (1988). "Drug Testing Legislation: What Are the States Doing?" *Kansas University Law Review* 36:919–951. Provides legislative background and history on drug testing in the United States and examines the drug testing statutes of Utah, Iowa, Montana, Vermont, Minnesota, Rhode Island, Connecticut, and Oregon. Also compares and contrasts the statutes from the perspectives of employer interests, employee interests, reasonable suspicion, random testing, rebuttal, confirmatory tests, confidentiality, discipline/discharge, and employee remedies. ^United\States ^Drug\Testing\History ^Drug\Testing\Laws ^Drug\Testing ^Legislation ^Utah ^Iowa ^Montana ^Vermont ^Minnesota ^Rhode\Island ^Connecticut ^Oregon

103. Baratta, Robert Thomas (1987). "Political Violence in Ecuador and the AVC." *Terrorism* 10:165–174. An Ecuadorian terrorist group, which appears to be working in coordination with groups in Colombia and Peru, is also cooperating with regional narcotics traffickers. The government has been unable to uproot the group. ^Ecuador ^Drug\Traffic ^Insurgents ^Terrorists ^Latin\America

104. "Barco Takes on the Private Armies" (1989). *Latin American Weekly Report*, 20 April, 10–11. Depicts the new Colombian president as making a vigorous attack on the private armies of the narcotics traffickers. Information is also given on the weapons the private armies obtain through international arms trafficking. ^Colombia ^Drug\Traffic ^Law\Enforcement ^Latin\America ^Traffickers\Private\Armies

105. Barden, J. C. (1990). "Foster Care System Reeling, Despite Law Meant to Help." *The New York Times*, September 21, A1. Children in distress, injured in the womb by drugs or alcohol (or battered or neglected by parents or guardians) are creating a substantial rise in welfare costs. The tide of abuse and neglect is swollen by increased use of drugs and alcohol. Statistics show a dramatic increase between 1976 and 1988 of reports of child abuse. The matter is complicated for some children because they are also infected with AIDS. ^United\States ^Consequences\Economic ^Consequences\Children ^AIDS

106. Barnea, Zipora (1989). "A Critical and Comparative Review of the Prevention of Drug and Alcohol Abuse in Israel." *Journal of Drug Education* 19(1): 59–81. Concentrates mainly on primary and secondary stages of prevention among youth, and reviews the various programs and intervention strategies of drug abuse prevention in Israel. Looks at school-based prevention programs as well as community-based programs designated or targeted for youth. Israel's prevention methods are compared to those in other Western countries. Discussion also includes recommendations for future development. ^Israel ^Drug\Use ^Prevention ^Youth ^Reviews ^Middle\East

107. Barnes, Deborah M. (1988). "Drugs: Running the Numbers." *Science* 240(24 June): 1729–1731. Criticism of the way most U.S. drug abuse statistics are both extrapolated and used. ^United\States ^Drug\Use ^Statistics\Critique

108. —— (1989). "Breaking the Cycle of Addiction." *Science* 241(26 August): 1029–1030. Aside from discussing a mix of drug therapy, behavioral therapy, and psychotherapy as probably the most effective instruments in treating cocaine addiction, the author discusses specifically the effects of two drugs which, when administered at critical stages of cocaine withdrawal, have proven to be helpful—desipramine and lithium. ^Cocaine ^Treatment

109. Barnes, Mark J., Carrol H. Kinsey, and Ellice A. Halpern (1988). "A Question of America's Future: Drug-Free or Not?" *Kansas University Law*

Review 36:699–754. A drug-free work place became the object of a U.S. government executive order in September 1986. Article focuses on that executive order and the American administration's policies to achieve a drug-free federal workplace in the executive branch. Discusses legislation that governs procedural aspects of the federal strategy, litigation in the courts challenging that strategy, and national initiatives undertaken to combat drug abuse under Ronald Reagan's presidency. ^United\States ^Drug\Testing ^Workplace ^Drug\Control\Policies ^Legislation

110. Barnett, J. Richard (1985). "Extradition Treaty Improvement to Combat Drug Trafficking." *Georgia Journal of International and Comparative Law* 15:285–315. A legal brief that describes the scope of the drug trafficking problem and why improvement in the extradition treaties would help the United States better confront the problem. Argues for broadening of the scope of extraditable offenses by allowing extradition for attempts and conspiracies. Suggests that treaties signed in 1984 with Costa Rica, Jamaica, Thailand, and Italy should become part of a large program of international cooperation. The treaties provide the mechanism for such cooperation. ^United\States ^Extradition ^Drug\Traffic ^International\Cooperation ^Latin\America ^Costa\Rica ^Caribbean ^Jamaica ^Golden\Triangle ^Thailand ^Southeast\Asia ^Europe ^Italy

111. Barol, Bill, Linda R. Prout, Karen Fitzgerald, Susan Katz, and Patricia King (1986). "Cocaine Babies: Hooked at Birth." *Newsweek*, 28 July, 56–57. Describes the hardships that newborns suffer when they are born already addicted to cocaine. ^Cocaine ^Health ^Fetuses ^Consequences\Health

112. Barrón, Marcial (1984). *El Infierno Blanco*. Lima, Peru: Huamán Poma. A journalist's penetration of cocaine traffic in Peru. Principal Peruvian narco-traffickers are identified, the antidrug operations against them are described, the political response of the drug empire, when under siege, is analyzed, and the contribution of all to political corruption in Peru is pointed out. ^Peru ^Cocaine ^Drug\Traffic ^Traffickers ^Drug\Control\Policies ^Latin\America ^Law\Enforcement ^Consequences\Political ^Consequences\Corruption ^Insurgents

113. Bartone, John C. (1987). *Drug Effects on Memory: Medical Subject Analysis with Research Bibliography*. Washington, D.C.: ABBE Publishers. Focuses on chemically induced memory disorders and the effects of drugs on learning. From a bibliography of 225 entries the author has generated a key word or key phrase index. For example, if one is interested in amnesia, the reader will be referred to 14 works within the bibliography that focus on it. ^Drug\Use ^Health ^Consequences\Neurological ^Bibliographies

114. Bascope Aspiazú, René (1982). *La Veta Blanca: Coca y Cocaína en Bolivia*. La Paz: Ediciones Aquí. Focuses on coca and cocaine use in Bolivia, emphasizing the associated economic conditions and politics of drug control. Accordingly, this book is a wide-ranging treatment encompassing the origins of coca and its use in Bolivia, the initiation of coca as an element of economic surplus attached to the agrarian reform movement, and the integration of that economy with cocaine trafficking in the United States. Specific instances are given regarding production and commercialization of cocaine. Other anecdotes highlight the expansion, production, and refinement of cocaine in various village areas. Some discussion about interdiction. ^Bolivia ^Coca ^Cocaine ^Drug\Traffic ^Drug\Control\Policies ^Consequences\Economic ^Consequences\Political ^Latin\America ^Coca\History ^Interdiction

115. Battjes, Robert J. (1985). "Prevention of Adolescent Drug Abuse." *The International Journal of the Addictions* 20(6-7): 1113–1134. Reviews the literature on past efforts to prevent adolescent drug abuse, noting that the results of social

pressures and social skills training on smoking prevention might also prove promising for the prevention of drug abuse. ^Prevention ^Youth ^Reviews ^Tobacco

116. "Battling the Poppy" (1982). *Business Review* (January), 13–18. Discussion of poppy growing in the Golden Triangle and, in particular, Northwestern Thailand where crop substitution programs have been carried out by the United Nations and other agencies. Focuses on the red kidney bean, coffee, and the potato. Coffee and the red bean looked most promising because of the perishability of the potato. To eliminate poppy cultivation thoroughly in Thailand will require further integration of the Hill tribes into the Thai culture, economy, and society. ^Thailand ^United\Nations ^Opiates ^Golden\Triangle ^Southeast\Asia ^Crop\Substitution ^Proffered\Solutions

117. Bauman, Pamela S., and Stephen A. Levine (1986). "The Development of Children of Drug Addicts." *The International Journal of the Addictions* 21(8): 849–863. From a study of 70 methadone-maintained mothers and their preschool-aged children and a matched control group, the authors conclude that there is a tendency for methadone children to have developmental delays, lower IQ scores, and lower heights and weights. ^Heroin ^Treatment ^Methadone ^Health ^Fetuses ^Consequences\Neurological ^Consequences\Physiological

118. Baumrind, Diana, and Kenneth A. Moselle (1985). "A Developmental Perspective on Adolescent Drug Abuse." *Advances in Alcohol and Substance Abuse*. Binghamton, N.Y.: The Haworth Press. Provides a historical and developmental perspective for adolescent drug use, and develops a case against early adolescent drug use due to negative consequences including impairment of attention and memory, developmental lag, and a so-called amotivational syndrome. Also there are problems of social alienation and estrangement. Having presented such a case, however, the authors argue that there is no conclusive evidence in their report, and they call for research to either support or rebut the propositions and thus address the factual claims underlying the socio-moral concerns of social policy planners. As it now stands, there is not enough real evidence to give social policy planners a leg to stand on. ^Drug\Use ^Youth ^Health ^Drug\Use\History ^Amotivational\Syndrome ^Consequences\Critique ^United\States

119. Bayer, I. (1983). "The Monitoring of Trade in and Control of Psychotropic Substances to Guard against Their Diversion." *Bulletin on Narcotics* 35(4): 3–13. Reviews the establishment of international narcotics control and explores the limitations of these controls in preventing the diversion of substances from legal sources to illicit channels. ^Drug\Control\Policies ^International\Cooperation\History

120. Bayer, Ronald (1981). "Heroin Addiction, Criminal Culpability, and the Penal Sanction." In *Criminal Justice and Drugs: The Unresolved Connection*, edited by James C. Weissman and Robert L. DuPont. Port Washington, N.Y.: Kennikat Press. Administration of criminal justice with respect to narcotics offenders. ^Heroin ^Drug\Use ^Law\Enforcement ^United\States

121. Beauchamp, Mark (1987). "Getting Straight." *Forbes*, 1 June, 92–96. Focuses on California's Humbolt county and the marijuana cultivation there. Details California's anti-marijuana drive known as CAMP. Mentions that local residents turned down federal antinarcotics money in the late 1970s because of the extraordinary economic boom from the marijuana trade. Residents turned around, however, when violence came along with economic success and when public lands were becoming inaccessible to the public. ^United\States ^Cannabis ^Drug\Traffic ^Drug\Control\Policies ^California ^Production\Incentives\Economic ^Consequences\Social ^Consequences\Economic

122. Beck, Jerome, and Patricia A. Morgan (1986). "Designer Drug Confusion: A Focus on MDMA." *Journal of Drug Education* 16(3): 287–302. A

specific "designer drug" known as MDMA has now become illegal in the United States. The author proposes that interest in the drug will nevertheless continue, based in part on the fact that it possesses both stimulant and psychedelic properties. ^United\States ^Drug\Use ^Designer\Drugs

123. Beck, Melinda (1985). "The Evil Empire." *Newsweek,* 25 February, 14–23. From the backdrop of the torture assassination of Enrique Camarena Salazar, this article describes the U.S. Drug Enforcement Administration's interdiction efforts and details the money, murder, and politics along the Latin American "cocaine trail." A special issue of *Newsweek.* ^Latin\America ^United\States ^Cocaine ^Drug\Traffic ^Interdiction ^Law\Enforcement ^Consequences\Violence ^Consequences\Political ^Statistics

124. Becker, Thomas H. (1981). "Footnote on the Golden Triangle." *Drug Enforcement* (Summer), 25–26. The Golden Triangle's opiate production quantities and prices per kilogram are given for 1979 and 1980. Statistics on opiate seizures in the United States and Europe for the same years are also given. ^Southeast\Asia ^Europe ^United\States ^Heroin ^Opiates ^Drug\Traffic ^Interdiction ^Golden\Triangle ^Production ^Production\Incentives\Economic

125. Becton, Charles L. (1987). "The Drug Courier Profile: 'All Seems Infected to th' Infected Spy, as All Looks Yellow to the Jandic'd Eye.'" *North Carolina Law Review* 65:417–480. The Drug Courier Profile, developed to aid agents of the Drug Enforcement Agency to curb the rising tide of illegal drugs into the United States, contains characteristics thought to indicate whether a particular airline passenger is carrying drugs. Relying on this profile, airport agents have questioned, detained, and searched such individuals. The author analyzes the inconsistencies and empirical inadequacies in the DEA's profile and critiques the Court's apparent willingness to accept the profile's validity. ^United\States ^Drug\Traffic ^Law\Enforcement ^Drug\Courier\Profile ^DEA

126. Beeching, Jack (1975). *The Chinese Opium Wars.* London, UK: Hutchinson and Co. A blow by blow account–names, places, events– of precursors to the Chinese Opium Wars, of the wars themselves, and of post-war events leading to the burning of the summer palace in 1860. ^Southeast\Asia ^China ^Opiates\History ^United\Kingdom ^Consequences\Sovereignty ^Foreign\Relations

127. "Belize Breeze: An Ill Wind" (1985). *Africa,* December, 56. Belize is the world's second largest exporter of marihuana. United States pressure may force it to resume aerial spraying with the herbicide paraquat. The problem is economics. When the British pulled out in 1981, they left a vacuum into which drug barons moved. ^Belize ^Cannabis ^Production ^Crop\Eradication ^Herbicides ^Consequences\Economic ^Latin\America ^Traffickers

128. Bellis, David J. (1981). *Heroin and Politicians: The Failure of Public Policy to Control Addiction in America.* Westport, Conn.: Greenwood Press. Gives a backdrop on the formulation of heroin control policies up through the Nixon administration, and explores the physiology, politics, and social aspects of methadone maintenance. Concludes that the United States' Federal Government treatment response to heroin addiction is political and shaped by questionable scientific evidence; that rehabilitation of addicts has not generally worked; and that the criminalization of heroin since 1914 has led to a powerful upper and underworld interest group that resists alteration of basic prohibition policy. Thus, neither repression nor rehabilitation have constituted an effective response to heroin addiction in America. Moreover, law enforcement efforts to control heroin abuse by interrupting supply of the drug have not provided a solution to heroin addiction. Can we really legislate behavior? The author, from a vantage of the year 2080, looks back on "the decline of heroin and the rise of new

highs." While addiction treatment and drug law enforcement did not have a very profound impact in this scenario, other, more powerful, factors led to the amelioration of the heroin addiction problem. The author projects, and speculates about, the impact of the declining birth rate, an older population, the appearance of nonaddictive depressant drugs many times more powerful than heroin, and, finally, the advent of electronic remote control brain stimulation devices that supplant mind-altering chemicals altogether. ^United\States ^Heroin ^Drug\Control\Policies ^Drug\Control\Policies\History ^Methadone ^Treatment\Critique ^Proffered\Solutions

129. Belsie, Laurent (1989). "Drugs on the Streets: Fed-up Communities Fight Back." *The Christian Science Monitor*, 20 December, 7. Description of private citizens' drug-fighting strategies in a Chicago neighborhood. Citizens have taken landlords to court and have boarded up "vacant" buildings occupied by drug users. They have organized community picnics and marches in drug areas that disrupt traffickers and dramatize drug movement problems to local politicians. ^United\States ^Private\Initiatives

130. ——— (1989). "Governors Link Anti-Drug Efforts." *The Christian Science Monitor*, 2 August, 7. Description of state initiatives to fight drug abuse (because of the slowness of the Federal government to move ahead) that include interstate cooperation on a broad range of activities. ^United\States ^Drug\Control\Policies

131. Belyea, Michael J. and Matthew T. Zingraff (1985). "Monitoring Rural-Urban Drug Trends: An Analysis of Drug Arrest Statistics 1976–1980." *International Journal of the Addictions* 20(3): 369-380. Statistics indicate the alarming increase in urban drug use. The relatively lower rates of abuse noted for rural areas are now suspect. ^United\States ^Drug\Use ^Statistics ^United\States\Rural\Areas

132. "Bennett Studying Drug Babies" (1989). *The Miami Herald*, 18 June, B7. United States "drug czar" William Bennett calls for forced treatment of cocaine-addicted pregnant women to avoid a generation of offspring with severe learning disabilities. Description of the babies' conditions is given. ^United\States ^Cocaine ^Treatment ^Women ^Fetuses ^P\S\Treatment

133. Bennett, Trevor (1988). "The British Experience with Heroin Regulation." *Law and Contemporary Problems* 51(1): 299–314. Britain, over the years, has experienced rapidly changing drug policies. This change sends mixed messages about drug use to both users and nonusers. The government is seen as not having developed a philosophically and morally sound system for controlling addiction, and this, in the absence of a rational pragmatic approach, gives users and nonusers alike contradictory signals. The article calls for "rational pragmatism." ^United\Kingdom ^Heroin ^Drug\Control\Policies\Critique ^Proffered\Solutions

134. Bensinger, Peter B. (1986). "An Inadequate War against Drugs." *Newsweek*, 28 July, 8. A former head of the Drug Enforcement Administration, under three presidents, points out how difficult it has been to get some U.S. agencies into the war on drugs. ^United\States ^Drug\Control\Policies\Critique

135. Ben-Yehuda, Nachman (1986). "The Sociology of Moral Panics: Toward a New Synthesis." *Sociological Quarterly* 27(4): 495–513. Within the context of a general examination of moral panics from both a moral and interest perspective, the article uses, as illustration, a May 1982 national moral panic about drugs that occurred in Israel. Focus is on a theoretical sociological formulation of moral panics. ^Israel ^Drug\Use ^Society ^Middle\East ^Drug\Use\Theories

136. ——— (1987). "Drug Abuse Social Policy in the United States and Israel: A Comparative Sociological Perspective." *International Journal of the*

Addictions 22(1): 17–45. The United States and Israel have adopted a similar supply/demand reduction model aimed at minimizing illicit drug use in their respective countries. This model has achieved relative success in Israel, and has been a relative failure in the United States. Examining the causes of success and failure from a sociological perspective, the author concludes that it is most efficaciously viewed as a moral-ideological one, not as it has been, a technical-medical problem. The basic explanatory variables relate to the different cultural matrices of the two societies. ^Israel ^United\States ^Drug\Control\Policies ^Supply ^Demand ^Middle\East ^Prevention\Values

137. Berg, Ronald H. (1987). "Sendero Luminoso and the Peasantry of Andahuaylas." *Journal of Interamerican Studies and World Affairs* 28(4): 165–196. To the surprise of many, *Sendero Luminoso* not only has waged a guerrilla campaign against Peru's civilian government, but has done so successfully. It has kept the military on the defensive and has attracted a small but significant national following. ^Peru ^Politics ^Insurgents ^Latin\America

138. Berger, Gilda (1987). *Crack: The New Drug Epidemic!* London: Franklin Watts. A popularized view of crack, who uses it, what its dangers are, how it is manufactured and sold, how the supply and demand may be cut, and how people addicted to it may be treated. ^Cocaine ^Crack ^Drug\Use ^Drug\Traffic ^Drug\Control\Policies ^Prevention ^Treatment ^Proffered\Solutions

139. Berke, Richard L. (1989). "Among Mayors, a Tide of Drugs Brings Forth Desperation and Ideas." *The New York Times*, 12 February, E6. A radical suggestion: devise a vaccine for the U.S. government to administer to young drug users to blunt the euphoria from drugs. That proposition was cited as illustration of the desperate measures city law enforcement agencies consider taking. ^United\States ^Drug\Control\Policies\Critique ^P\S\Antagonists

140. —— (1989). "Bennett Expects 'Frictions' as Leader of Drug War." *The New York Times*, 4 February, 8. Raising the expectations that internal bureaucratic conflicts will also be part of the United States' "war on drugs," William J. Bennett, the Bush administration's "drug czar," intends to focus on both demand and supply. ^United\States ^Drug\Control\Policies ^Drug\Control\Politics ^Demand ^Supply

141. —— (1989). "Capital's Government Denounced by Bennett, Opening Drug Drive." *The New York Times*, 11 April, A1. Bennett accuses the Washington, D.C., government of having failed to serve its citizens in dealing with criminals and, in particular, those associated with the drug trade. Washington, D.C., has yielded more drug-related murders per capita than any other city. ^United\States ^Drug\Traffic ^Consequences\Crime ^Consequences\Violence ^Washington\DC

142. —— (1989). "Capitol's War on Drugs: An Assault on 3 Fronts." *The New York Times*, 7 April, A7. The three-pronged attack by William Bennett in the United States' capital includes expanding court staffs to handle offenders in narcotics cases, efforts to curb the drug trade in public housing projects, and adding prison space to house those who are convicted. ^United\States ^Drug\Control\Policies ^Public\Housing ^P\S\Law\Enforcement

143. —— (1989). "Drug Chief Calls for a Vast Prison Plan." *The New York Times*, 3 August, B6. William J. Bennett has asked the Bush administration to double the projected expenditures for new prisons and to increase drug treatment programs by nearly 50 percent for the next fiscal year. Federal expenditures on jails would therefore increase to $1.2 billion in 1990. ^United\States ^P\S\Treatment ^P\S\Penal

144. —— (1989). "Criminals' Cases Clog U.S. Courts." *The New York Times*, 26 September. Many civil matters are being squeezed out by a surge in drug

cases, which have jumped 270 percent in nine years ending in June 1989. ^United\States ^Law\Enforcement ^Consequences\Judiciary

145. ———— (1989). "Foreign Policy Said to Hinder Drug War." *The New York Times*, 14 April, 1. The tactics and strategies employed by the Reagan administration to achieve its foreign policy goals frequently compromised efforts to curb drug trafficking. Issues relating to Nicaragua, the Bahamas, Honduras, and Panama are discussed. In short, the United States "did not crack down on people who were doing us a favor." ^United\States ^Drug\Control\Policies ^Consequences\Political ^Consequences\Foreign\Policy ^Latin\America ^Nicaragua ^Bahamas ^Honduras ^Panama

146. ———— (1989). "Jamaican Backs off Proposal for Anti-Drug Force." *The New York Times*, 7 November, A4. Jamaica's prime minister, Michael Manley, having earlier proposed an international paramilitary strike force to battle drug traffickers, has now changed his mind. Too many people have criticized him for being a "threat to the sovereignty" of their countries. ^Jamaica ^P\S\International\Cooperation ^Military ^Caribbean ^Sovereignty

147. ———— (1989). "Panel Said to Seek New Military Role in Fight on Drugs." *The New York Times*, 2 July, 1A. Discusses a national security council task force's preparation to recommend that President Bush send military advisors along with economic aid to South American countries where cocaine production flourishes. Ostensibly, the U.S. troops would help train local forces in combatting traffickers. Would there be a combat role? The possibility has not been ruled out. ^Latin\America ^United\States ^P\S\Military

148. ———— (1989). "Seized Assets to Go to Areas Hardest Hit by Drugs." *The New York Times*, 13 April, A25. From the "returns" to the U.S. federal government from drug-related seizures, much will be sent to areas hardest hit by drugs. ^United\States ^Asset\Forfeiture ^Drug\Control\Policies

149. ———— (1989). "Two Admirals Named to Combat Drugs: Pentagon to be Main Agency in Bid to Stop Smugglers." *The New York Times*, 8 February, A23. An integrated agency task force, headed by Coast Guard admirals, will lead joint military efforts to stop drug smuggling on the Atlantic and Pacific coasts of the United States. ^United\States ^Interdiction ^Military ^Drug\Control\Policies ^Coast\Guard

150. ———— (1989). "White House Backs Drug Plan but Shuns a Brawl." *The New York Times*, 12 April, A14. Focus is on Washington, D.C., Mr. Bennett's drug war strategy, and discussions on how comprehensive that strategy should be. Peter Reuter is quoted as saying "there is a curious lack of interest in the treatment system." ^United\States ^Drug\Control\Policies\Critique ^Washington\DC

151. ———— (1990). "Survey Shows Use of Drugs by Students Fell Last Year." *The New York Times*, February 14, A12. The federally financed University of Michigan's annual national survey reports a continued downward trend in the number of high school seniors saying they have used illicit drugs at least once during the year. Seventeen thousand students at 135 public and private high schools across the country were surveyed. According to data in the survey, the use of crack shows no significant reduction. However, there is a reported increase in the use of PCP. Data for cocaine, marijuana, and all illicit drugs combined is given for the years 1975 through 1989. ^Drug\Use ^Statistics ^United\States

152. Bernardo, Mark A. de (1987). *Drug Abuse in the Workplace: An Employer's Guide for Prevention*. Washington, D.C.: U.S. Chamber of Commerce. Designed to assist in practical compliance with federal and state drug abuse regulations. Drug testing is emphasized within the context of a suggestion for a larger

comprehensive drug prevention program. Some discussion of drug-related workplace accidents and the implied economic costs they impose on an enterprise are reviewed. ^United\States ^Drug\Use ^Workplace ^Prevention ^Consequences\Economic ^Drug\Testing ^Prevention\Drug\Testing

153. Bernholz, Steven A., Martin J. Bernholz, and G. Nicholas Herman (1985). "International Extradition in Drug Cases." *North Carolina Journal of International Law and Commercial Regulation* 10:353–82. Within the context of the United States's effort to extradite drug traffickers from foreign countries, much has been written. However, of that, hardly anything derives from the standpoint of the criminal defense bar. This article focuses on the drug defendant and attempts to address that oversight. ^United\States ^Extradition

154. Bernstein, Jonas (1989). "Bitter Convulsions in a Nation under the Influence of Drugs." *Insight*, 25 September, 30–31. The current bloodletting going on between the Colombian government and the country's drug lords is reminiscent of prior chapters in a turbulent history of violence in the country. Key personnel are discussed, including the "Mexican Bandit" Rodríguez Gacha. ^Colombia ^Drug\Traffic ^Traffickers ^Law\Enforcement ^Latin\America ^Consequences\Violence

155. Bertrand, Marie Andrée (1990). "Beyond Antiprohibitionism." *The Journal of Drug Issues* 20:4(Fall): 533–42. Describes the antiprohibition movement. Advances options for decriminalization which range from a "minimalist" to an "abolitionist" position on criminal policy matters. ^P\S\Legalization ^Decriminalization

156. Beschner, George, ed. (1986). *Teen Drug Use*. Lexington, Mass.: Lexington Books. Addresses, essays, and lectures dealing with the physiological effects of youth drug abuse. Also deals with U.S. narcotics laws. A nontechnical book written not only about adolescent drug abusers but for them and their families and for others interested in youngsters who use drugs. Explains adolescent drug use as seen by young drug users and their parents; reveals why some users have problems while others do not; includes information on the effects different drugs have and about dealing in drugs; gives information on legal consequences of illicit drug use and how secondary prevention methods can be applied when youngsters are already using the drug; and includes information conventionally found in many other volumes on drug abuse: sociocultural and demographic breakdowns, theories on the causes of drug abuse, and the relationship between drug abuse and criminality and delinquency. ^United\States ^Drug\Use ^Crime ^Law\Enforcement ^Prevention ^Youth ^Consequences\Physiological ^Drug\Control\Policies ^Drug\Use\Theories ^Consequences\Crime

157. Beschner, George M., and Alfred S. Friedman (1985). "Treatment of Adolescent Drug Abusers." *The International Journal of the Addictions* 20(6–7): 971–993. Reviews a substantial body of literature relating to the correlates of adolescent drug use, such as family situations, multiple drug use patterns, and psychological and socioeconomic factors. Existing data sets are analyzed which evaluate treatment approaches and models directed to youth drug abusers. Concludes that the findings are encouraging, acknowledging that it is important and sometimes even vital to work with the parents of adolescent substance abusers. ^Drug\Use ^Youth ^Family ^Reviews ^Drug\Use\Theories ^Proffered\Solutions

158. Besteman, Karst J. (1989). "War Is Not the Answer." *American Behavioral Scientist* 32(3): 290–94. Rather than declare war on drugs, which has been U.S. policy since President Nixon first announced it, the country ought to piggy back on the prohealth movement and public health approaches to disease control. ^United\States ^Proffered\Solutions

159. Biernacki, Patrick (1986). *Pathways from Heroin Addiction: Recovery without Treatment.* Philadelphia: Temple University Press. Discusses treatment and rehabilitation of heroin addicts. Since the 1920s, a social problems perspective has held sway over drug research and treatment. Opiate addiction has been perceived as a serious problem that has to be controlled, if not totally eradicated. Since the 1960s, research efforts have concentrated on documenting how people have become addicted, on the incidence of addiction, and on how addicts might be treated. This has turned research efforts away from developing a substantive understanding of the natural course of addiction as it might unfold to its termination. This book seeks to understand the "natural processes" and to explain how self-initiated natural recovery occurs and how it could help in the formulation of more thoughtful social policies concerning illicit drug use and addiction. ^Heroin ^Treatment ^Drug\Use\History ^Treatment\History ^Drug\Use\Theories

160. Bird, Kai, and Max Holland (1985). "Paraguay: The Stroessner Connection." *Nation*, 26 October, 401. Short discussion on how Paraguay is apparently a transshipment point for ether, acetone, and hydrochloric acid for use in the refining of cocaine hydrochloride. High-level officials in the Stroessner administration are implicated. ^Paraguay ^Drug\Traffic ^Precursor\Chemicals ^Latin\America ^Consequences\Political ^Consequences\Corruption

161. Bishop, Katherine (1989). "Neighbors in West Use Small Claims Court to Combat Drugs." *The New York Times*, 17 October, A9. Residents in a San Francisco and Berkeley, California, area are fighting crack-house dealers in small claims court. Inasmuch as arrests for possession of drugs seemed not to shut the crack houses down, neighbors sued building owners for health and building code violations. This encouraged owners to rent their properties to a non–drug dealing clientele. ^United\States ^Private\Initiatives

162. Blachly, Paul H. (1976). "Effects of Decriminalization of Marijuana in Oregon." In *Chronic Cannabis Use. Annals of the New York Academy of Sciences*, edited by R. L. Dornbush, A. M. Freedman, and M. Fink, 282: 405–15. From "opinion air" research, the author concludes that medically significant problems from marijuana use decreased coincident with decriminalizing marijuana in Oregon. But there is extreme divergence of opinion, still, regarding the change in the law, and the association of that change with continuing drug problems in the state. ^United\States ^Cannabis ^Decriminalization ^Oregon ^Consequences\Health

163. Blachman, Morris J., and Kenneth E. Sharpe (1989–90). "The War on Drugs: American Democracy under Assault." *World Policy Journal* 7:1 (Winter): 135–163. Reviews the political rationale for the U.S. "war on drugs." While the law enforcement approach to the drug problem is sustained by widespread political support, it is structurally flawed. It erodes basic liberties, contributes to official abuses of power, and militarizes societies in which such power is exercised. These costs are unlikely to be countered by any significant reduction in drug demand. Thus the whole strategy is "fraught with illusion." Is there not a better way? Move well beyond current drug education and treatment programs already advocated to "confront the conditions that have led to drug abuse and addiction among millions of Americans, recognizing that the drug problem arises out of conditions that vary across class, ethnic, and racial lines" (p. 157). Population-specific strategies could therefore include the development of educational programs and treatment centers, improvement of housing and schools, cleaning up streets, addressing the problem of homelessness, and improving local economies. At all stages it is necessary to involve local citizens in finding better solutions. ^United\States ^Drug\Control\Policies\Critique ^Proffered\Solutions

164. Blackwell, Judith (1988). "The Saboteurs of Britain's Opiate Policy: Overprescribing Physicians or American-Style 'Junkies?'" *International Journal of the Addictions* 23(5): 517–26. After giving a brief historical review of opiate users and drug policies in Britain, the article discusses the arrival, in the 1950s, of the British "junkie." Argues that this new underclass was produced by overprescribing physicians. The British medical system is, therefore, responsible for creating a new generation of heroin users. ^United\Kingdom ^Heroin ^Drug\Use ^Drug\Control\Policies\History ^Drug\Control\Policies\Critique

165. Blackwell, Judith C., and Patricia G. Erickson (1988). *Illicit Drugs in Canada: A Risky Business*. Ontario: Nelson Canada. Of interest to this bibliography is Canada's history and legislative response to illicit drugs traffic and consumption, the role of the criminal justice system in arrests and prosecutions, and a section on policy analysis dealing with lessons from the past and proposals for change. Issues dealing with legalization or decriminalization, as discussed in Canada, are raised in this section. ^Canada ^Drug\Control\Policies ^Decriminalization ^Law\Enforcement ^Drug\Control\Policies\History ^P\S\Legalization

166. Blair, Roger D., and Ronald J. Vogel (1973). "Heroin Addiction and Urban Crime." *Public Finance Quarterly* 1(4): 457–66. Should heroin be decriminalized? There is extensive literature revealing that democratic decision making does not necessarily yield socially optimal results. At whatever price, addicts turn to criminal activity to finance their habits. So, can the demand for heroin be evaded? A policy in this direction would require something to prevent potential addicts from becoming actual addicts, as well as reducing existing addicts. Try methadone maintenance programs and other therapeutic communities. ^Heroin ^Drug\Use ^Crime ^Prevention ^Treatment ^Methadone ^P\S\Methadone

167. Blanes, J. (1983). *De los Valles al Chapare: Estrategias Familiares en un Contexto de Cambios*. Cochabamba, Bolivia: Centro de Estudios de la Realidad Económica y Social. While not dealing directly with the narcotics trade, this book gives an intimate anthropological benchmark into patterns of migration, colonization, and community and family survival in the Chapare region of Bolivia, which has come to be dominated by coca/cocaine trafficking. It therefore constitutes an important social benchmark for an understanding of how coca/cocaine became an enticing economic activity in the region. ^Bolivia ^Coca ^Cocaine ^Drug\Traffic ^Economics ^Society ^Latin\America ^Production\Incentives\Economic

168. Blau, Charles W. (1984). "Role of the Narcotic and Dangerous Drug Section in the Federal Government's Fight against Drug Trafficking." *Drug Enforcement* (Summer): 16–20. Description of the participation and activities of the Department of Justice Criminal Division's Section on Narcotic and Dangerous Drugs. This Narcotic and Dangerous Drug Section gives legal support to the United States Attorney's office, the Organized Crime Drug Enforcement Task Force Program, and the Drug Enforcement Administration. The section also plays an important part in the development and shaping of international and domestic drug policies of the Justice Department. ^United\States ^Drug\Control\Policies

169. Blau, Charles W., Amy G. Rudnick, G. Roger Markley, Juan Marrero, John A. Jarvey, and Helene Greenwald (1983). *Investigation and Prosecution of Illegal Money Laundering: A Guide to the Bank Secrecy Act*. Washington, D.C.: Department of Justice, Criminal Division. Discusses the U.S. banking laws, confidential communications among U.S. banks, and records and correspondence

of U.S. banks and banking institutions that have relevance to narcotic and dangerous drug money laundering. ^United\States ^Drug\Control\Policies ^Money\Laundering ^Banking\Regulations.

170. Blumenthal, Ralph (1988). *Last Days of the Sicilians*. New York: Times Books. Documentary description of the billion-dollar heroin pipeline that came to be known as the Pizza Connection, which was "busted" on April 9, 1984. The participants were obscure Sicilian bakers and contractors operating in the United States independently of American mafia counterparts, while, at the same time, masterminding the flow of heroin into the United States and laundering money back to Switzerland. ^United\States ^Heroin ^Drug\Traffic ^Money\Laundering ^Organized\Crime ^Traffickers ^Switzerland ^Europe

171. Blumstein, Alfred, Jacqueline Cohen, and Daniel Nagin, eds. (1978). *Deterrence and Incapacitation: Estimating the Effects of Criminal Sanctions on Crime Rates*. Washington, D.C.: National Academy of Sciences. What is the appropriate role of criminal sanctions in reducing high crime rates of the 1970s (and presumably beyond)? The National Academy of Science's Panel on Research on Deterrent and Incapacitative Effects was established to address this question. The book is its report. The evidence is classified according to noncapital sanctions, capital sanctions, and incapacitation. On noncapital sanctions, the evidence showed, with few exceptions, a negative association between crime rates and noncapital-sanctioned risks. On capital sanctions, the panel concluded that the evidence available at the time did not provide any usable evidence on the deterrent effect of capital punishment. The judgment was that it would take a large increase in the prison population to achieve a noticeable percentage reduction in crime. Considerable "softness" in the data and the analysis were acknowledged, however. ^Law\Enforcement ^Crime ^United\States ^Prevention\Penal

172. Boe, Kathy Smith (1985). "Paraquat Eradication: Legal Means for a Prudent Policy?" *Environmental Affairs* 12(3): 491–526. Paraquat, its application by the U.S. government, and its effects are described. Discussed also are the health risks of marijuana and the Drug Enforcement Agency's efforts to control marijuana both prior to the domestic paraquat program and after it. The paraquat domestic program is assessed under the National Environmental Policy Act and various other federal acts, including the Insecticide, Fungicide, and Rodenticide Acts. Environmental groups sued the DEA and prevented the continuation of its program until an environmental impact statement was prepared and the paraquat label amended. The DEA paraquat program was potentially hazardous to both the public and the environment, and it also violated two federal environmental acts. The recommendation was that the paraquat program be permanently enjoined. ^United\States ^Cannabis ^Crop\Eradication ^Herbicides ^Drug\Control\Policies ^Consequences\Environmental ^DEA

173. Boffey, Philip M. (1988). "U.S. Attacks Drug Suppliers but Loses Battle of the Users." *The New York Times*, 12 April, A1. The U.S. government's policies are failing because they emphasize a crackdown on suppliers (a futile operation) while giving insufficient attention to weaning the American public from its narcotics habits. ^United\States ^Drug\Use ^Drug\Traffic ^Drug\Control\Policies\Critique

174. Bogoliubova, T. A. and K. A. Tolpekin (1988). "Narcotism and Narcomania: Basic Directions of Control and Prevention." *Soviet Law and Government* (Summer), 26–38. Increasingly, the Soviet press has taken up discussion about drug abuse problems in the country. Drug abuse has been intensified, apparently, by *glasnost*. Drug addiction, or narcomania, has become a substantial problem. The disease and its consequences are described, as are current policies and laws directed toward eliminating the problem. ^USSR ^Drug\Use ^Drug\Control\Policies

175. Bohlen, Celestine (1989). "Number of Women in Jail Surges with Drug Sales." *The New York Times*, 17 April, A1.   Greater law enforcement crackdown on drug offenses in the United States is turning many women's prisons into congested areas; many show a fourfold increase since 1981. Crack is a major cause of this, because of its inexpensiveness. Some of the women indicate that they turned to selling crack when they could not keep their families going on welfare alone. ^Consequences\Penal ^United\States ^Cocaine ^Crack ^Drug\Traffic ^Women ^Law\Enforcement ^Consequences\Personal

176. ——— (1989). "Support Groups Are Offering Embrace to Cocaine's Victims." *The New York Times*, 29 January, 1.   Description of how cocaine addicts and their families find solace in self-help groups, which are blossoming virtually everywhere in the United States. Some, such as Cocaine Anonymous, are patterned after holistic rehabilitation programs having a long history of success in alcoholic dependence. ^United\States ^Cocaine ^Treatment

177. Bohning, Don (1989). "Cuba Ties Officers to Drug Ring." *The Miami Herald*, 23 June, 1A.   Further revelations on the involvement of Cuban military officers and government officials in the international trafficking of narcotics. ^Cuba ^Drug\Traffic ^Military ^Caribbean

178. ——— (1989). "General Making War on Drug Traffic." *The Miami Herald*, 8 June, 2A.   Description of the antidrug efforts in Haiti. ^Haiti ^Drug\Control\Policies ^Caribbean

179. "Bolivia Arrests 100 in Attempted Coup; Denies Cocaine Link" (1984). *The New York Times*, 3 July.   A suggestion is raised that there could have been cocaine money or involvement with some officers linked with the narcotics trade in the attempted coup. Two former cabinet ministers and about 100 right-wing military officers, policemen, and politicians were all arrested. ^Bolivia ^Cocaine ^Drug\Traffic ^Latin\America ^Consequences\Political ^Military ^Consequences\Corruption ^Traffickers

180. "Bolivia: Herbicides Used against Coca, Report Says" (1988). *Latinamerica Press*, 14 July, 6.   While the Bolivian government to date has denied charges that herbicides were being used against coca, Bolivia's agricultural affairs minister admitted that herbicides had been used on experimental plots. Experiments were conducted in Villa Tunari, a town where a confrontation between small coca growers and police claimed several lives in June 1988. Critics of the herbicidal experiment refer to these chemical agents as being highly toxic with multiplier effects on water, plant life, and, in general, the ecology of the area where they are used. ^Bolivia ^Coca ^Crop\Eradication ^Herbicides ^Latin\America ^Drug\Control\Policies

181. "Bolivia: Laid-off Miners Survive by Growing Coca" (1988). *Latinamerica Press*, 17 March, 1.   Description of some 1,000 unemployed tin miners and their families who marched 120 kilometers from La Paz to the coca growing region of Chulumani—a two-day march. The effort was a grand-standing parade designed to put political pressure on the government to do something about the plight of recently laid-off miners. ^Bolivia ^Coca ^Producers ^Consequences\Economic ^Latin\America ^Production\Incentives\Economic

182. "Bolivia under Paz Estenssoro" (1988). *Latinamerica Press*, 20 October, 6.   Within the context of discussing general human rights issues in Bolivia and violence associated with the economic decline in the country, mention is made that most of the violence has occurred in the coca growing region of the Chapare where more than a dozen peasants have been killed by police in the past two years. One of the victims was two months old. With the recent passage of the new law limiting coca production, the situation is likely to grow much worse. Accusations are made that antidrug police

routinely attack coca growers, robbing them of money and goods. Still unresolved are the highly publicized 1986 killings of Bolivian scientist Noel Kempff Mercado and two companions who had stumbled upon a giant cocaine factory in the eastern jungle region. ^Bolivia ^Coca ^Drug\Control\Policies ^Latin\America ^Consequences\Violence ^Consequences\Human\Rights

183. "Bolivian Farmers Die in Battle with Drug Police" (1988). *Latin-america Press*, 7 July, 1. Description of a June 1988 confrontation between police and coca growers resulting in the death of several peasant farmers. The peasants have demanded the expulsion of U.S. drug control agents who are assisting Bolivian police and Army officers in suppressing cocaine production. ^Bolivia ^United\States ^Coca ^Drug\Control\Policies ^Latin\America ^Consequences\Violence ^Consequences\Political

184. "Bolivian Farmers Persuaded to Destroy Coca" (1988). *The Herald*, 1 January, 9. An Associated Press report in a regional newspaper (Provo, Utah) asserts that the crop substitution program sponsored by the United States has met with unprecedented success. The program's Bolivian director, Anibal Aguilar, said that in the three-month period from August through December 1987, 2,500 acres of coca had been destroyed, considerably beyond the quota. The program has given farmers an estimated two year's earnings on their land if they eradicate coca and plant something else. The new program foresees a wide range of assistance in the affected areas, including schools, roads, health clinics, and electrical power. ^Bolivia ^Latin\America ^Coca ^Crop\Substitution

185. "Bolivian Leader Starts a Fast" (1984). *The New York Times*, 27 October. Description of Bolivian President Hernán Siles Zuazo's beginning a hunger strike to protest congressional censure of his decision to negotiate with drug traffickers. The inducement for negotiation was drug trafficker Roberto Suárez's offer of $2 billion toward the country's foreign debt if the authorities would allow him to operate freely. ^ Bolivia ^ Cocaine ^ Drug\Control\Policies ^ Latin\America ^ Consequences\Economic ^ Consequences\Political ^ Consequences\Foreign\Debt ^ Traffickers ^ International\Debt

186. Bollag, Burton (1989). "Swiss-Dutch Drug Stance: Tolerance." *The New York Times*, 1 December, A4. A virtually complete tolerance of marijuana and hashish use in the Netherlands has contributed to a reduction in the incidence of heroin addiction. This, coupled with free needle exchanges, has also greatly reduced the spread of the AIDS virus. While the Netherlands keeps heroin dealers off of the streets (allowing them to make "house calls"), Switzerland allows them, as well as marijuana and hashish dealers, to deal in the open. Both Switzerland and the Netherlands view arresting or harassing drug users and small-time dealers as being counterproductive. ^Europe ^Drug\Control\Policies ^Netherlands ^Switzerland

187. Bolton, Ralph (1976). "Andean Coca Chewing: A Metabolic Perspective." *American Anthropology* 78:630–634. Reviews the social use of coca in Andean cultures, and suggests that it is an integral part of the Andean way of life, essential for the people's cultural and physiological well-being. The evidence in favor of the positive functions of coca chewing is mounting. Essentially, it is a general anthropological call to "leave the natives alone." There is extensive reference to the contradictory literature on this issue. ^Latin\America ^Coca ^Drug\Use ^Health ^Society ^Culture ^Coca\History

188. Bonnie, Richard J. (1980). *Marijuana Use and Criminal Sanctions: Essays on the Theory and Practice of Decriminalization*. Charlottesville, V.: Michie Company. The author has been actively involved in the effort to win legislative support for reforming U.S. marijuana laws (decriminalization). The book is a treatise for decriminalization and a drafter's guide about how to go about it. Additionally, a comparative view on decriminalization in Europe—involving France, Italy, Switzerland, the Netherlands, and the United Kingdom—is presented. Since 1977 the face of reform

(towards decriminalization) has waned significantly. The startling increase in the late 1970s in teenage use of marijuana in the United States aroused an alarm that concerned many American people. ^Europe ^United\States ^Cannabis ^Decriminalization ^P\S\Legalization ^Drug\Use ^Drug\Control\Politics ^France ^Italy ^Switzerland ^Netherlands ^United\Kingdom

189. —— (1981). "The Meaning of 'Decriminalization': A Review of the Law." *Contemporary Drug Problems* 10(3): 277–289. Reviews the post-1973 decriminalization movement in the United States, finding statutory endorsement in eleven states, at least as far as possession of small amounts of marijuana is concerned. ^United\States ^Cannabis ^Decriminalization ^Reviews ^Oregon ^Drug\Control\Policies\History

190. Boodman, Sandra G. (1988). "Premarital AIDS Testing Annoying Many in Illinois: Some Couples Head out of State to Say 'I Do.'" *The Washington Post*, 30 July, A1. Faced with mandatory AIDS testing in Illinois, many couples are going to Wisconsin, Indiana, and other surrounding states to circumvent that law. The law has not fulfilled its original purpose of curbing the spread of the AIDS syndrome. Only ten of more than 75,000 marriage license applicants have tested positive for the AIDS virus. ^United\States ^Illinois ^AIDS ^Health

191. —— (1989). "Clean Needles Don't Make More Addicts, Panel Told." *The Washington Post*, 25 April, A9. In an effort to reduce the spread of AIDS, some people have advocated a needle-exchange program in order to cut down on the shared needle transmission of the virus from one drug user to another. Critics claim that this will simply create more addicts. Here testimony is given to the contrary. ^Heroin ^Health ^AIDS ^P\S\Needle\Exchange ^United\States

192. Booth, Cathy (1988). "Tentacles of the Octopus; The Mafia Brings Europe's Worst Drug Epidemic Home." *Time*, 12 December, 48. Description of the extraordinary drug epidemic in Italy that is thought to derive from the mafia's lucrative drug trade that it has shared with crime families in both North and South America. The mafia is characterized as being strong enough to be an "anti-state." ^Italy ^Drug\Traffic ^Organized\Crime ^Europe ^Drug\Use ^Consequences\Political ^United\States ^Latin\America

193. Booth, William (1988). "War Breaks out over Drug Research Agency." *Science* 241(5 August): 648–50. The U.S. National Institute of Drug Abuse (NIDA) is heavily criticized as having grown into an overly bureaucratic agency that has lost sight of its mission. As one might expect, NIDA objects to this characterization. ^United\States ^Drug\Control\Policies ^NIDA ^NIDA\Critique

194. Bordreaux, Richard (1989). "Scandal Spotlights Costa Rica's Battle on Drugs." *The Los Angeles Times*, 19 February, 8. A highly influential Argentine national living in Costa Rica has been arrested and extradited to France on heroin trafficking. Many in his web of protection, including justices and an ambassador, have resigned their positions. Costa Rica, because of its vulnerability, has increasingly become a transit point for drugs. ^Costa\Rica ^Drug\Traffic ^Extradition ^Latin\America ^Consequences\Corruption ^France ^Europe

195. Botvin, Gilbert J., and Thomas A. Wills (1985). "Personal and Social Skills Training: Cognitive\Behavioral Approaches to Substance Abuse Prevention." In *Prevention Research: Deterring Drug Abuse Among Children and Adolescents*, NIDA Research Monograph 63, edited by Catherine S. Bell and Robert Battjes. Rockville, Md.: National Institute on Drug Abuse. Reviews the empirical evidence on the effectiveness of preventing substance abuse through teaching generic personal and social skills. Nine evaluation studies are reported. The

magnitude of their effects generally appears to be large. ^Drug\Use ^Prevention ^Youth ^Reviews ^NIDA

196. Bower, B. (1984). "Cocaine Smoking May Cause Lung Damage." *Science News* 126(3): 37–38. The smoking of cocaine (free-basing) is represented here as a serious health hazard because it can cause a significant reduction of gas exchange in the lungs, even if the practice occurs only over a period of several months. ^Cocaine ^Drug\Use ^Consequences\Health

197. ———— (1984). "Heroin and Crime: A Stronger Link." *Science News* 126(1 December):343. A new study conducted in New York City by Bruce D. Johnson shows that urban heroin users commit crimes in greater number and diversity than has previously been documented. ^United\States ^Heroin ^Drug\Use ^Crime ^New\York

198. ———— (1985). "'Day After' Effects of Pot Smoking." *Science News* 128(16 November): 310. Pilots who get "high" on marijuana the day before taking control of an aircraft may have difficulty landing it safely. ^Cannabis ^Drug\Use ^Consequences\Neurological ^Consequences\Public\Safety ^Aircraft

199. Bowker, Lee Harrington, with contributions by Meda Chesney-Lind and Joy Pollock (1978). *Women, Crime, and the Criminal Justice System*. Lexington, Mass.: Lexington Books. Focuses on female offenders, drugs and women, crimes against women, and administration of criminal justice with respect to women. Chapter 3 discusses women and drugs, including sexual differentiation in their use, the nature of and extension of addiction among women, particular problems among housewives, and a general sociological theory of female drug use. ^Drug\Use ^Law\Enforcement ^Women ^Drug\Use\Theories

200. Boyce, Daniel (1987). "Narco-Terrorism." *FBI Law Enforcement Bulletin* (October): 24–27. There does not appear to be linkages between narcotics traffickers and terrorist groups in the United States. Nevertheless, the author allows for the development of such a possibility in view of events elsewhere in the world. Some speculation is given about the provisional Irish Republican Army's relationship with terrorists. ^United\States ^Drug\Traffic ^Terrorists ^Ireland

201. Boyd, Gerald M. (1989). "Bush, Citing Cost, Says Drug War Will Focus Largely on Education." *The New York Times*, 26 January. The Bush administration intends to focus its "all-out war on drugs" mainly on educational efforts rather than on a law enforcement crackdown. The context of the president's remarks suggests that he agrees with those who argue that the only long-term solution lies in curbing the demand for illegal drugs, not in simply depressing the supply. There is a discussion of supply versus demand. ^United\States ^Demand\Reduction ^Supply ^Prevention\Drug\Education ^Demand

202. Boyd, Neil (1983). "Canadian Punishment of Illegal Drug Use: Theory and Practice." *Journal of Drug Issues* 13(4): 445–59. The Canadian government has not entered strongly the legislative arena in relation to the sentencing of drug offenders. Sentencing has been left to the Canadian judiciary, which enacts policy in the absence of a legislative will. There has been an unhappy legacy in all this, something the author discusses in his socio-legal history of Canadian drug penalties. The focus, until recent years, has been almost exclusively on marijuana. ^Canada ^Law\Enforcement ^Drug\Control\Policies ^Drug\Control\Policies\History

203. Bradley, Barbara (1988). "Cracking the Drug Menace." *The Christian Science Monitor*, 26 February, 1. High-level corruption in foreign countries is making the U.S. war on drugs, already an uphill battle, far steeper. In response to the escalating violence associated with drug trafficking, the FBI and the Drug Enforcement

Agency have agreed to coordinate their efforts in six "core" drug cities—Miami, Los Angeles, San Diego, Chicago, New York, and Houston. Discussion of problems finding witnesses who will testify and locating documents that are reliable when accusing those involved in corruption. Description of the efforts to indict Panama's General Noriega. Names and places, relative to corruption, are mentioned for the following countries: Panama, Haiti, Honduras, Bahamas, Mexico, Colombia, Turks and Caicos Islands, Surinam. ^Latin\America ^Panama ^Haiti ^Honduras ^Bahamas ^Mexico ^Colombia ^Turks\and\Caicos ^Surinam ^Politics ^Consequences\Corruption ^Consequences\Violence ^Drug\Traffic ^Florida ^California ^Illinois ^New\York ^Texas ^Consequences\Judiciary ^Caribbean ^DEA ^FBI

204. —— (1988). "New Drug Strategy Focuses on Cartels." *The Christian Science Monitor*, 26 April, 1. The idea is to go after the drug cartels rather than just drug dealers. A graph depicts manpower devoted to the federal drug program in terms of prosecutors and investigators. Both show a substantial increase in the last decade. ^United\States ^Drug\Control\Policies ^Law\Enforcement ^Organized\Crime

205. —— (1988). "US Agents Target Foreign Outlaws, Porous Borders, and Seller-User Network at Home." *The Christian Science Monitor*, 7 March, 1. Depicts the U.S. war on drugs as a guerrilla war at home and characterizes it consistently with that metaphor. Includes a graph describing budgetary priorities in U.S. narcotics control policy. ^United\States ^Drug\Control\Policies ^Statistics

206. —— (1988). "Users Now Prime Targets in U.S. Antidrug Offensive." *The Christian Science Monitor*, 4 May, 1. Discussion of the U.S. Custom's Services zero-tolerance program, launched on March 21, which allowed confiscation of anyone's property who had even a trace of illegal drugs. Description of new stepped-up enforcement presence on the "demand side" in Miami and New Jersey. ^United\States ^Drug\Use ^Law\Enforcement ^Demand ^Asset\Forfeiture

207. —— (1989). "Formidable Task Awaits Drug Czar." *The Christian Science Monitor*, 4 January, 7. Some of the advice U.S. "drug czar" William Bennett is getting from narcotics experts includes the following: develop core model educational projects and spread them around; focus on the inner city; focus on the criminal justice system; eliminate overlapping programs; and tap the expertise and energies of members of Congress. ^United\States ^P\S\Drug\Education ^P\S\Inner\Cities ^P\S\Law\Enforcement ^P\S\Political

208. Branigin, William (1988). "The Mexican Connection." *The Washington Post Weekly*, 14-20 March, 7. A series of raids in recent weeks by the Mexican police highlight the workings of the Medellín cartel in Mexico. Description of Colombia's two-way trafficking arrangement through Mexico, in which cocaine moves north and weapons and money move back to Colombia. ^Colombia ^Mexico ^Cocaine ^Drug\Traffic ^Organized\Crime ^Latin\America ^Terrorists

209. —— (1989). "Mexicans Arrest Prime Drug Suspect: Felix Gallardo Led DEA's Wanted List." *The Washington Post*, 11 April, A1. Details given of the arrest of Miguel Ángel Félix Gallardo, perhaps the second most notorious Mexican drug trafficker. ^Latin\America ^Mexico ^DEA ^Law\Enforcement ^International\Cooperation ^Traffickers

210. —— (1989). "Panamanians Arrest 5 Accused in Drug Ring; Noriega's Officials, DEA Cooperating." *The Washington Post*, 2 April, A35. In rare cooperation between Panamanian officials and the Drug Enforcement Agency, combined efforts result in the arrest of people involved in a major international drug money laundering ring. ^Panama ^Money\Laundering ^Latin\America ^DEA

211. Braude, Monique C. (1987). "Perinatal Effects of Drugs of Abuse." *Federation Proceedings* 46(7): 2446–2453. Summary of a symposium presented by the American Society for Pharmacology and Experimental Therapeutics in 1986. Among other things, the author discusses the placental transfer of drugs of abuse, endocrine consequences of perinatal methadone exposure, consequences of intrauterine exposure to cocaine, and the effect of marijuana use on neonatal outcome. ^Drug\Use ^Consequences\Fetuses ^Methadone ^Cocaine ^Cannabis

212. Braude, Monique C., and Jacqueline P. Ludford, eds. (1983). *Marijuana Effects on the Endocrine and Reproductive Systems*, NIDA Research Monograph 44. Rockville, Md.:National Institute on Drug Abuse. Individual chapters are annotated under their respective authors. ^Cannabis ^Health ^NIDA ^Consequences\Reproduction

213. Braun, Dick (1988). "Drug Dealers Invade Rural Towns." *Farm Journal* (October): 44–48. Review of the widespread epidemic of alcohol and drug abuse infecting rural areas in the United States. Drug dealers have made a concerted effort to develop markets in rural areas. ^Drug\Traffic ^Alcohol ^Drug\Use ^United\States\Rural\Areas

214. Bresler, Fenton (1980). *The Trail of the Triads; An Investigation into International Crime*. London: Weidenfeld and Nicolson. The author draws a connection between the post-1970 vast increase in the numbers of predominantly young ethnic Chinese, primarily from Hong Kong, coming to Europe and to the United States and the explosion in the international trafficking and consumption of heroin. An examination of the "gangs" (Triads) that the author sees as a major new element in the international drug scene. The author is a British lawyer (barrister) who presents his results after two years of research. ^Hong\Kong ^Heroin ^Drug\Traffic ^Organized\Crime ^Triads ^Europe ^United\States ^Southeast\Asia

215. ——— (1981). *The Chinese Mafia: An Investigation into International Crime*. New York: Stein and Day Publishers. Investigates Southeast Asian Triads, their involvement in the heroin trade, and how they have moved into the international scene with operations in Holland, Great Britain, the United States, Canada, and all of Europe. The author believes there are two distinct kinds of criminal Triad activity. The first is the more loosely organized gangs of Hong Kong and the United States with tendencies to follow secret Triad society traditions. The second is more akin to an organized international conspiracy with a strict hierarchy, "operating from a central base in the Far East, with a Mafia-type control over its members, and almost limitless capacity for criminal evil stretching across the world" (p. 211). ^Canada ^China ^Hong\Kong ^Europe ^United\Kingdom ^United\States ^Heroin ^Drug\Traffic ^Organized\Crime ^Netherlands ^Southeast\Asia ^Triads

216. Brewer, Colin (1988). "The Management of Opiate Abuse: Learning from Other Addictions." *Journal of Drug Issues* 18(4): 679–697. Presents four basic arguments: that opiate dependence is just one example of "excessive appetites," having much in common with other excessive appetites, such as those for alcohol, gambling, sex, and food; that an understanding of opiate dependence and of methods to limit the harm it causes is facilitated by experiences in these related dependencies, especially in those that cause conflict with the law; that management of opiate dependence now has an opiate antagonist (naltrexone), the use of which is based on the same principles as the use of disulfiram in the management of alcohol abuse; that because the results of treating alcohol abuse with techniques that include supervised disulfiram in both voluntary and court-mandated programs are so encouraging, it is to this area, and its analogies in the field of opiate dependence, that treatment should be particularly directed. ^Opiates ^Treatment ^Drug\Use\Theories ^Alcohol ^P\S\Antagonists ^P\S\Treatment

217. Briceño Puente, Carlos Alberto (1983). *Las Drogas en el Peru*. Pueblo Libre, Lima, Peru: Tip. Drug abuse among Peruvian youth; control of narcotics in Peru. Something of a catchall volume, ranging from a listing, in the appendix, of fifteen Peruvian antidrug laws to an action plan for parents of children who are involved in drugs. In between are descriptive chapters on opium, marijuana, barbiturates, tranquilizers, and stimulants (which include amphetamines, caffeine, coca, coca paste, and cocaine). Does drug consumption cause crime? The author reviews several international studies, concluding that the explanation is multidimensional. ^Peru ^Drug\Use ^Drug\Control\Policies ^Latin\America ^Prevention ^Opiates ^Coca ^Cocaine\Paste ^Cocaine ^Crime

218. Bridges, Tyler (1986). "Colombia: Drug Problems at Home." *The Washington Post*, 19 September, F1. Describes how young Colombians have become addicted to smoking bazuco, an intermediary cocaine product. A government-sponsored education program is attempting to arrest the popularity of smoking bazuco. It is highly addictive and deleterious to one's health. Considerable problems with young people's turning to crime to support their bazuco habits. ^Colombia ^Cocaine ^Drug\Use ^Youth ^Crime ^Health ^Prevention ^Latin\America ^Cocaine\Paste ^Prevention\Drug\Education

219. ——— (1986). "Colombian Farmers Start Anew after Coca 'Bonanza.'" *The Christian Science Monitor*, 29 October, 1. In the late 1970s, after earning significant income from illegal coca growing, communities in the Cauca state were hard hit when antinarcotics police destroyed their crops. Describes how El Moro, a community in Cauca state, responded to a joint project of the Colombian government and the United Nations Fund for Drug Abuse Control (UNFDAC) in developing an economic alternative to coca growing. While the economic returns are not as good, farmers cooperate out of fear of another police raid if they return to growing coca. Thus the UN-sponsored program offers these people the only viable hope out of their grinding poverty. Discussion of how, during the coca bonanza, the social integrity of the community collapsed—theft, violence, crime. ^Colombia ^United\Nations ^Coca ^Latin\America ^Law\Enforcement ^Crop\Eradication ^UNFDAC ^Crop\Substitution ^Consequences\Violence ^Consequences\Crime ^Consequences\Economic

220. ——— (1986). "Traffickers Eye Europe; U.S. Market for Cocaine Said to be Flooded." *The Washington Post*, 6 October, A17. Not only are traffickers looking for additional markets in Europe, but Europe appears to have become a transshipment point for drugs being sent to the Middle East and perhaps even to the Far East. ^Europe ^United\States ^Cocaine ^Drug\Traffic ^Economics ^Traffickers ^Middle\East ^Southeast\Asia

221. ——— (1987). "Colombian Antidrug Plan." *The Christian Science Monitor*, 12 January, 23. Describes an official campaign to develop after-school activities for Colombian teenagers both to educate them about and to divert their attention from bazuco, the cocaine paste mixed with tobacco and smoked. Efforts are being implemented to create sports teams, dance clubs, and theater groups. ^Colombia ^Cocaine ^Latin\America ^Prevention\Drug\Education ^Prevention\Recreation ^Youth

222. ——— (1987). "Drug Traffickers, Guerrillas Curtail Peru's Antidrug Efforts." *The Christian Science Monitor*, 28 April, 9. Describes the ongoing war between antidrug efforts and pro trafficker interests in the upper Huallaga Valley of Peru. One analyst views the valley as being totally out of control in terms of criminal activity and drug trafficking. Several specific Peruvian agencies involved in the drug trafficking are mentioned and described. It is believed that Colombian drug traffickers control the entire northern part of the upper Huallaga Valley. Shining Path guerrillas have gained control over a considerable portion of the valley as well. ^Coca ^Cocaine ^Drug\Traffic ^Organized\Crime ^Politics ^Insurgents ^Drug\Control\Policies ^Latin\America ^Consequences\Violence ^Peru ^Terrorists

223. —— (1987). "Resurgence of Bolivia's Drug Trade Sparks New Prevention Push with U.S." *The Christian Science Monitor*, 1 July, 1. Eight months after a major United States antidrug mission in Bolivia, the country's cocaine trade is flourishing again. Discussion of the status of interdiction and eradication programs is given. ^Bolivia ^United\States ^Coca ^Crop\Eradication ^Cocaine ^Interdiction ^Latin\America ^Drug\Control\Policies\Effectiveness

224. Brink, C. J. (1985). *Cocaine: A Symposium.* Madison: Wisconsin Institute on Drug Abuse. A 1985 symposium attended by more than 400 professionals, in Milwaukee, Wisconsin, was the foundation for this volume. The symposium covered the epidemiological aspects of cocaine use, international consequences, local law enforcement issues, and how the supply of cocaine might be controlled. This was a major initiative on the part of a state institute—the Wisconsin Institute on Drug Abuse. ^Cocaine ^Drug\Traffic ^Drug\Control\Policies ^Law\Enforcement ^United\States ^Proffered\Solutions

225. Brinkley, Joel (1984). "Bolivia Drug Crackdown Brews Trouble." *The New York Times*, 12 September, A1. On-site report of efforts by a government, already in turmoil, to come to grips with the extraordinary increase in the cocaine trade. In this instance the Bolivian military occupied the Chapare. There is a general description of the cocaine trade, money laundering, corruption, and U.S. aid. ^Bolivia ^United\States ^Cocaine ^Drug\Traffic ^Money\Laundering ^Law\Enforcement ^Foreign\Aid ^Drug\Control\Policies ^Military ^Latin\America ^Consequences\Political ^Consequences\Corruption

226. —— (1984). "In the Drug War, Battles Won and Lost." *The New York Times*, 13 September, 1. Crop substitution and crop eradication programs are not working. There is no better illustration than Thailand where the United States, other countries, and the United Nations have spent millions of dollars in the last few years setting up pilot crop substitution programs that show peasants how to grow coffee, kidney beans, and Idaho potatoes. Case-study type reports from Burma, Pakistan, Mexico, and Peru. ^Burma ^Mexico ^Pakistan ^Peru ^Thailand ^Cannabis ^Coca ^Opiates ^Crop\Substitution ^Crop\Substitution\Critique ^Crop\Eradication\Critique ^United\Nations ^Golden\Crescent ^Golden\Triangle ^Southeast\Asia ^Middle\East ^Latin\America ^Southwest\Asia

227. —— (1984). "Rampant Drug Abuse Brings Call for Move against Source Nations: Supply Soars as Traffic Corrupts Government." *The New York Times*, 9 September, 1. General description of the international traffic in narcotics and the degree to which its increase has occasioned internal political maneuvering in the United States as well as United States diplomatic maneuvering abroad. The U.S. Department of State is singled out for particular criticism because its agenda is other than the "war on drugs." ^United\States ^Drug\Control\Policies ^Consequences\Foreign\Policy ^Consequences\Political ^Department\of\State ^Production

228. —— (1984). "The War on Narcotics: Can It Be Won?" *The New York Times*, 14 September, A12. Unless the demand for illicit drugs can either be reduced or eliminated, the amount of money is so large that traffickers will continue to take whatever risk is necessary to supply the market. Even if demand cannot be reduced, one way to reduce the corrupting influence of large sums of money is to legalize a drug and then tax it. This idea is less popular than it appeared to have been in the late 1970s. ^Drug\Traffic ^Drug\Control\Policies ^Demand ^P\S\Legalization

229. —— (1985). "Paraguay Pledges Action on Cocaine: Reportedly Tells Congressmen It Will Destroy Chemicals Used to Produce Drug." *The New York Times*, 23 January, A4. When members of Congress visited Paraguay in 1985, the Paraguayan government promised that it would destroy nearly 50,000 gallons of chemicals that were believed to have been intended for the manufacture of cocaine. With that much chemical precursor in hand, it is thought that drug traffickers could make

about eight tons of cocaine, or, by the estimates of Brinkley, about 10 percent of the United States supply for a year. ^Paraguay ^Cocaine ^Drug\Traffic ^Precursor\Chemicals ^Latin\America

230. ——— (1987). "Contra Arms Crews Said to Smuggle Drugs." *The New York Times*, 20 January, A1. In the fall of 1986 federal drug investigators discovered that American flight crews covertly ferrying arms to the Nicaraguan rebels were smuggling cocaine and other drugs on their return trips to the United States. One crew member, when confronted, argued that he had White House protection. U.S. drug officials thought it was strictly a "freelance operation." Others have assumed that high American officials have had intimate knowledge of the trafficking. ^Nicaragua ^United\States ^Cocaine ^Drug\Traffic ^Consequences\Corruption ^Contras

231. ——— (1987). "Drugs and Graft Main Issue in Bahamas Vote." *The New York Times*, 14 June, A1. A single dominant issue emerges from one of the most important national elections in recent history in the Bahamas—drug trafficking and the official government corruption it has spawned. Charges are levied against high-ranking government ministers, including the prime minister himself. It is reported that American intelligence corroborated the charges. Relations between the United States and the Bahamas, on drug-related issues, have become extremely tense. The Bahamas drug controversy began in 1983 after it was discovered that Robert Vesco and the Colombian drug baron Carlos Lehder had converted one tiny Bahamian island into an elaborate transit station for drugs. ^Bahamas ^United\States ^Drug\Traffic ^Politics ^Consequences\Corruption ^Caribbean ^Consequences\Foreign\Relations ^Traffickers

232. Brock, David (1989). "Drug Smuggling Runs Deep in Official Cuban Connection." *Insight*, 14 August, 34–37. Description of the extensive drug scandal that has shaken Cuba. Four top government officials were convicted of and have been executed for their involvement in a drug smuggling ring that brought tons of illicit drugs into Florida. Fidel Castro had long denied any Cuban involvement in drug smuggling, and offered public surprise at the corruption ultimately uncovered. However, it is thought that the executions were designed more to distance Castro from drug operations and to remove political obstacles for his brother Raúl, Cuba's second in command, than as an actual punishment for the trafficking. ^Cuba ^Cocaine ^Drug\Traffic ^Consequences\Corruption ^Law\Enforcement ^Caribbean ^Consequences\Political ^Drug\Control\Policies

233. Broder, David S. (1989). "Fearing Crack Invasion, Europe Steps up Antidrug Efforts." *The Washington Post*, 20 May, A15. Fear that the "saturation" of the United States market will shift traffickers to Europe, high-level authorities are discussing how best to prevent the succumbing of Europe to the crack epidemic. ^Europe ^Cocaine ^Crack ^Drug\Traffic ^Proffered\Solutions

234. Bronstein, Scott (1987). "Study Shows Sharp Rise in Cocaine Use by Suspects in Crimes." *The New York Times*, 19 February, B1. The National Institute of Justice's study, which looked at more than 5,000 men arrested and detained in Manhattan, found arrestees to be substantially more involved in crime if they were drug users. The conclusion was that drug use "is the accelerator to criminal activity." ^United\States ^Cocaine ^Drug\Use ^Crime ^Consequences\Crime

235. Brooke, James (1987). "West Africa Becomes Route for Heroin Trade." *The New York Times*, 26 July, 9. Pakistani heroin is increasingly being transited through West Africa. There is a "Nigerian Connection." Several reasons are given for Nigeria becoming a major staging point: Airport controls are traditionally lax, there is a national wanderlust, and Nigeria's economy is depressed. In the final category, it ought to be noted that, where the minimum wage is $1 a day in Nigeria, a heroin

courier can earn $2,000 on a run to New York City. ^Africa ^Nigeria ^Heroin ^Drug\Traffic ^Traffickers\Incentives\Economic ^Traffickers\Incentives\Political ^United\States ^New\York

236. —— (1989). "In the Drug War, Medellín Is a Reluctant Fighter." *The New York Times*, 25 September, A4. Political resolve in Medellín is decreasing in the wake of the economic downturn that drug-related violence has caused and in light of the intimidation that drug barons have brought upon the city. It appears that a number of political leaders would rather "talk than fight." ^Colombia ^Law\Enforcement ^Organized\Crime ^Consequences\Violence ^Consequences\Political ^Consequences\Economic ^Traffickers ^Latin\America

237. —— (1989). "A Report from the Front Lines in Colombia: The Drug War Will Be Long." *The New York Times*, 18 September, A4. Description of the combat power of the government and the drug cartel in Colombia and how they are moving against each other. On the drug dealers side is their vast wealth and also considerable official corruption. On the government's side is a high-level resolve to get at the drug traders, but the cartel's answer, being more violent, has intimidated a large number of people. The top twelve traffickers remain at large. Interestingly, the public's attitude has shifted to favor extradition to the United States for trial. ^Colombia ^Drug\Traffic ^Organized\Crime ^Extradition ^Law\Enforcement ^Latin\America ^Consequences\Violence ^Traffickers ^Consequences\Corruption ^Consequences\Political ^Consequences\Social

238. —— (1990). "Colombia Presses Drive on Rebels, Smashing Base." *The New York Times*, December 14, A16. The Colombian army has launched a large offensive against the guerilla group known as the Revolutionary Armed Forces of Colombia (FARC), at its jungle headquarters. The FARC had obtained its financing in part by collecting a tax on coca paste from Andean peasants. In an operation last month against the guerrillas, the military seized a small laboratory for converting coca leaves into coca paste. ^Latin\America ^Colombia ^Military ^Insurgents ^Consequences\Economic ^Refining ^Coca ^Cocaine\Paste ^Drug\Control\Policies

239. —— (1990). "Peruvian With a Vision Gets Power." *The New York Times*, November 27, A3. Hernando de Soto's economic planning role under Peru's new president, Alberto Fujimori. De Soto's intends to create a free-market agricultural environment to entice farmers to grow something other than coca leaves. One initiative is to give coca farmers land titles. ^Latin\America ^Peru ^Economics ^Crop\Substitution ^Supply ^Land\Reform ^Drug\Control\Policies ^State\Policies ^Markets

240. —— (1990). "Colombia Abductions Signal Escalation of Drug War." *The New York Times*, September 23, L3. Drug lords have escalated attacks on journalists who oppose their work. ^Latin\America ^Colombia ^Consequences\Terrorists ^Terrorists ^Media

241. —— (1991). "Colombian Kidnappings Are Gagging the Press." *The New York Times*, January 28, A2. The Colombian press, noted for its vigilance and tenacity, is nevertheless being gagged through self-censorship as reporters fear for their lives in the wake of assassinations by drug traffickers. Moreover, many journalists have left Colombia for work in Mexico and Spain or in Spanish-language news media in the United States. ^Latin\America ^Colombia ^Terrorists ^Media ^Consequences\Assassination ^Consequences\Terrorists

242. —— (1991). "Ecuador Fighting to Avoid Drug Link." *The New York Times*, January 27, All. Ecuador may be on the verge of becoming a transhipment country for cocaine bound for the United States. Considerable money laundering also goes on in the country. There is a spill-over effect of the Colombian trade: cash-rich Colombian investors are bidding up prices of farm land in border areas by as much as three hundred percent. In the past, Ecuadorians have moved decisively on drug problems.

They hope to continue to do so even though, in their view, Colombia and Peru have become soft. It is thought that about thirty tons of cocaine per year pass through Ecuadorian ports. ^Ecuador ^Latin\America ^Colombia ^Money\Laundering ^Consequences\Economic ^Traffickers ^Cocaine

243. —— (1991). "Peru Develops Plan to Work With U.S. to Combat Drugs." *The New York Times,* January 25, A2. A joint-venture plan with the United States to fight coca leaf cultivation is announced. The United States will provide military aid, development aid, and debt relief. For its part, the Peruvian government will create a "super ministry" to coordinate crop substitution programs and to attack traffickers and their Guerilla backers. The United States will provide military equipment and counterinsurgency training, along with materiel and provisions. Concomitantly, Peru will enter a free trade agreement with the United States. ^Latin\America ^Peru ^Military ^International\Cooperation ^United\States ^Foreign\Aid ^Crop\Substitution ^Economics

244. —— (1991). "Peru, Its U.S. Aid Imperiled, Plots a New Drug Strategy." *The New York Times,* January 14, A2. With economic pressures intensifying, and with the possible cutoff of $100 million in American antidrug aid, the country has made renewed efforts to cut its cocaine exports. In spite of all efforts, including a large American-built base in the Huallaga Valley, coca crops have grown so fast that prices crashed in 1990. As of January 1991, a kilo of dried leaves was sold for forty American cents in the valley, well below what is thought to be the $1.40 break-even cost for growers. A new agency will be created to circumvent problems of corruption within the Peruvian bureaucracies. ^Latin\America ^Peru ^United\States ^Foreign\Aid ^Coca ^Economics ^State\Policies

245. Brookes, Stephen (1989). "Chinese Mafia Takes Vice Abroad." *Insight,* 24 April, 34–36. New evidence is given that a powerful Chinese mafia, based in Hong Kong, is spreading its network of heroin and other vices to North Atlantic countries and Australia. The judgment is made that, with Hong Kong's facing an uncertain future under Chinese rule, the groups appear to want to expand their markets in any way that would produce income. ^Australia ^Europe ^Hong\Kong ^Heroin ^Drug\Traffic ^Organized\Crime ^Southeast\Asia ^Triads

246. —— (1990). "The Perilous Swim in Heroin's Stream." *Insight,* 5 February, 8–31. Substantial opium flows from the Burmese hills to refineries in Thailand and Laos, orchestrated by Chinese crime syndicates. Shipping points to world markets are out of Bangkok and Hong Kong. Considerable internal competition in the Golden Triangle for supplier markets exists, and insurgent groups are killing each other for control. There is fear that the plentiful availability of heroin will create a flood of addiction in consuming countries such as the United States. ^Southeast\Asia ^Opiates ^Production ^Heroin ^Traffickers ^Triads ^Refining ^Golden\Triangle ^Burma ^Laos ^Thailand ^Organized\Crime ^Consequences\Markets ^Consequences\Violence ^Drug\Traffic ^Supply ^Hong\Kong

247. Broughton, Diane (1986). "Youth Peer Programs Springing up across Country." *Alcoholism and Addiction* (March-April): 55–57. Describes a "network for abstinence groups" that are forming all over the United States at, according to the author, a "rather astonishing rate." Carrying various names (Peer Counselors, Teen Institute, Partners in Prevention, Focus, Natural Helpers, or SADD), the principals and dynamics operate on the assumption that peers helping peers have an enormous influence. Describes the "careers" of several sixteen- and seventeen-year-old "peer counselors" who are influencing their friends away from drugs. ^United\States ^Youth ^Prevention\Peers

248. Brower, Kirk J., and M. Douglas Anglin (1987). "Developments, Trends, and Prospects in Substance Abuse." *Journal of Drug Education* 17(2): 163–180. A number of epidemiological studies of adolescent cocaine use are reviewed

with risk factors identified and prevention strategies implied. The factors associated with initial cocaine use are being male, using marijuana, lacking social connections to family and school, being influenced by peers, and psychopathology. Suggestions are given as to ways parents, educators, and health care providers can become involved in prevention programs to address these critical risk factors. ^Cocaine ^Drug\Use ^Youth ^Society ^Prevention ^Reviews ^Drug\Use\Theories

249. Brown, Barry S. (1985). "Federal Drug Abuse Policy and Minority Group Issues—Reflections of a Participant-Observer." *International Journal of the Addictions* 20(1): 203–15. While many segments of minority communities have been deeply concerned about the penetration of drug use into their communities, they have also been alarmed by, and, in some instances, hostile toward U.S. federal drug abuse policy and program implementation. For example, the methadone maintenance program was viewed with a mixture of hostility and alarm. For many minority groups the "real" motivation in initiating new drug abuse programs, particularly during the Nixon administration, were suspect. ^United\States ^Drug\Control\Policies ^Drug\Control\Politics ^Society ^Minorities ^Methadone ^Drug\Control\Policies\Effectiveness

250. ——— (1988). "Civil Commitment: An International Perspective." *Journal of Drug Issues* 18(4): 663–678. The civil commitment process, treatment services, and reported effectiveness in containing drug abuse is described for several countries. Conditions viewed as necessary for the initiation of civil commitment and appropriate safeguards for commitment procedures are discussed. The special case of AIDS is taken up, with the implication that it may have the potential to encourage civil commitment practices directed toward intravenous drug users. ^Law\Enforcement ^Treatment ^AIDS ^P\S\Compulsory\Treatment ^Reviews

251. Brown, Barry S., Marc R. Rose, William W. Weddington, and Jerome H. Jaffe (1989). "Kids and Cocaine—A Treatment Dilemma." *Journal of Substance Abuse Treatment* 6:3–8. As it is difficult to get youth to realize they have a drug problem or to get them into treatment centers, it must be the responsibility of others to intervene on their behalf. Family members are not reliable in referring their own youngsters. Community resources must intervene. Describes those that might be potential candidates. ^Cocaine ^Drug\Use ^Youth ^Treatment ^Prevention ^P\S\Treatment

252. Brown, David D. (1987). "UN Antidrug Conference Chalks up Significant Firsts." *The Christian Science Monitor*, 26 June, 9. Describes the document emerging from the ten-day meeting of the United Nations International Conference on Drug Abuse and Illicit Trafficking. It was the first-ever meeting of the United Nations member states to discuss and assess both the supply and demand sides of the drug abuse chain. A practical handbook of recommended steps for governmental and nongovernmental organizations to use to combat drug abuse in all of its spectra emerged from the conference. ^United\Nations ^Drug\Control\Policies ^International\Cooperation ^Supply ^Demand ^P\S\Policies

253. Brown, Lee P. (1988). "Strategies for Dealing with Crack Houses." *FBI Law Enforcement Bulletin* (June): 4–7. Crack houses have been opening in Houston with increasing regularity. Simply closing the houses down and arresting the occupants is insufficient to control the problem. The real question is how to keep the drug dealers from reopening the facilities—often within a matter of a few days. The answer is to be found in the forfeiture clauses of the U.S. code dealing with property that has been used to commit or to facilitate the commission of drug law violations. The article describes how the Houston police have implemented these provisions. ^United\States ^Cocaine ^Crack ^Asset\Forfeiture ^Law\Enforcement ^P\S\Asset\Forfeiture ^Texas

254. Brown, Valerie A., Desmond Manderson, Margaret O'Callaghan, and Robyn Thompson (1986). *Our Daily Fix: Drugs in Australia*. Elmsford, N.Y.: Pergamon Press. The book is oriented toward reducing the abuse of drugs by better understanding their use. Consists of briefing papers designed to give participants at an alcohol and drug workshop a basis-in-fact policy regarding drugs. Explores cultural aspects of totems and taboos, and concentrates on the relationship of the social context of drug use to drug policy, politics, and values. For strategies in reducing drug abuse, this article focuses on the control of source, on treatment, on education, and on aspects of social change. With respect to concrete action, it advances a national repertoire of action plans. The thrust is not so "simplistic" as to try to discourage all drug use, but rather seeks to discover how to use drugs well, presumably in moderation. Bibliography on Australian sources. ^Australia ^Drug\Use ^Drug\Control\Policies ^Society ^Culture ^Proffered\-Solutions ^Bibliographies

255. Brule, C. (1983). "The Role of the Pompidou Group of the Council of Europe in Combating Drug Abuse and Illicit Drug Trafficking." *Bulletin on Narcotics* 35(4): 73–77. Description of the Pompidou Group, an international cooperative group set up to combat drug abuse and illicit trafficking in drugs. The group deals with all areas of drug control including suppression, prevention, treatment and rehabilitation, and physiological and other health effects of drug use. In this article the political and technical activities of the Pompidou Group are described, illustrating how it operates to combat drug abuse at the international level. ^Europe ^Drug\Control\Policies ^International\Cooperation ^Pompidou\Group

256. Bruno, Francesco (1984). *Combatting Drug Abuse and Related Crime: Comparative Research on the Effectiveness of Socio-Legal Preventive and Control Measures in Different Countries on the Interaction between Criminal Behaviour and Drug Abuse*. Rome, Italy: Fratelli Palombi Editori. A comparative study of the effectiveness of socio-legal prevention and control measures on the interaction between criminal behavior and drug abuse. Eleven countries are represented—Argentina, Brazil, Costa Rica, Italy, Japan, Jordan, Malaysia, Singapore, Sweden, the United Kingdom, and the United States. Attempts to sort out the causal chain between drug abuse and criminal behavior. Even excluding criminality strictly associated with production, sale, and distribution of illegal drugs, affirms that drug abuse can lead to various groups of crimes that, from a penal point of view, "assume different connotations depending on whether they are committed by a person under the influence of drug, under acute or chronic state of intoxication, or, vice versa, committed by a person with the intention and the scope of providing for his personal need" (p. 13). There is an extensive bibliography. ^Argentina ^Brazil ^Costa\Rica ^Italy ^Japan ^Jordan ^Malaysia ^Singapore ^Sweden ^United\Kingdom ^United\States ^Drug\Use ^Crime ^Law\Enforcement ^Drug\Control\Policies\Effectiveness ^Latin\America ^Scandinavia ^Southeast\Asia ^Bibliographies

257. Brunswick, Ann F. (1986). "Dealing with Drugs: Heroin Abuse as a Social Problem." *The International Journal of the Addictions* 20(11-12): 1773–1791. Operating under the assumption that heroin abuse is a social problem with social costs, this author develops an ecological model to analyze the effects of illicit drugs on neighborhoods. Focuses also on policies aimed at prevention, intervention, and treatment. Community perspectives must be included in policy decisions, and key opinion leaders ought to be relied on as a reliable source of appropriate information regarding policy. ^Heroin ^Drug\Use ^Prevention ^Treatment ^Consequences\Social

258. Bruun, Kettil, and Pia Rosenqvist (1980). "Alcohol and Drug Control Policies in the Nordic Countries." *Journal of Drug Issues* 10(4): 421–33. The

governments' policies aimed at influencing the availability of alcohol and drugs is brought up for review. A comparative analysis of the various Nordic countries is done. Denmark appears to be most out of step with other Nordic countries, especially in alcohol control. The narcotics policies of the various countries tend to support existing international agreements regarding criminal-political measures. Most of the discussion centers on alcohol. ^Europe ^Denmark ^Drug\Control\Policies ^Scandinavia ^Alcohol

259. Bry, Brenna H. (1983). "Empirical Foundations of Family-Based Approaches to Adolescent Substance Abuse." In *Preventing Adolescent Drug Abuse: Intervention Strategies*, NIDA Research Monograph 47, edited by Thomas J. Glynn, Carl G. Leukefeld, and Jacqueline P. Ludford. Rockville, Md.:National Institute on Drug Abuse. Identification of substance abuse precursors, how they combine, and what processes affect them (e.g., poor parent-child relationships, estrangement from parents, depression, low academic motivation, low religiosity, high family misuse of substances, high peer substance use, early cigarette use). Evidence is then presented showing that family involvement can reduce substance abuse precursors and early signs of abuse, and, therefore, can be an effective deterrent to drug abuse. ^Drug\Use\Theories ^Youth ^Prevention\Family

260. —— (1983). "Predicting Drug Abuse: Review and Reformulation." *International Journal of the Addictions* 18(2): 223–233. The author advances a theory stressing the *number* of diverse stresses or risk factors instead of one particular set as accounting for drug abuse. In general, the psychosocial factors considered were perception of distance in the family, psychological distress, low self-esteem, low achievement motivation, disregard for rules, low religiosity, high sensation seeking, misuse of substances within the family, high use of drugs among peers, and early use of tobacco, alcohol, and drugs. ^Drug\Use\Theories ^Society ^Family

261. —— (1988). "Family-Based Approaches to Reducing Adolescent Substance Use: Theories, Techniques, and Findings." In *Adolescent Drug Abuse: Analyses of Treatment Research*, NIDA Research Monograph 77, edited by Elizabeth R. Rahdert and John Grabowski. Rockville, Md.:National Institute on Drug Abuse. Examines two significantly different theoretical viewpoints from which family-based interventions on adolescent substance abuse are currently being pursued. Highlights the accomplishments of the scientists in both models or paradigms by presenting the premises and current concepts of both competing theories, by describing the interventions that each framework elicits, and by reviewing the findings that each area has produced. ^Drug\Use ^Youth ^Treatment ^Family ^Reviews ^Prevention\Family ^Prevention\Theories

262. Bucknell, Patrick (1985). "Some Proposals for Drugs Legislation." *British Journal of Addiction* 80:149–52. Misuse of addictive drugs in the United Kingdom is spreading. A problem exists in the present system of legislation, in particular in the classification of drugs and in the determination of maximum penalties by reference to that classification. Hong Kong has improved its legislative condition, and the United Kingdom might model its efforts on Hong Kong's. That legislation distinguishes between drug traffickers and addicts by reference to the quantity of drugs in an offender's possession. Provision is made in Hong Kong for compulsory treatment of addicts and denies persons possessing a small amount of narcotics a right to elect trial in court. ^United\Kingdom ^Hong\Kong ^Drug\Use ^Drug\Control\Policies ^Southeast\Asia ^Legislation\Critique ^P\S\Compulsory\Treatment

263. Buder, Leonard (1988). "Dealer Must Pay to Treat Addicts; $2 Million Restitution Is Set in Brooklyn Heroin Case." *The New York Times*, 29

March, A1. An unusual application, with heavy economic overtones and potential disincentives to dealers, was handed down by a Brooklyn judge who ordered a convicted heroin dealer to pay more than $2 million in restitution to support drug rehabilitation programs in New York City. The judge had calculated a direct "harm to victims" formula. The judge hoped that this would set a precedent. ^United\States ^Law\Enforcement ^Judiciary ^New\York ^P\S\Fines

264. "Budget Constraints Force Coast Guard to Cut Antismuggling Missions in Half" (1988). *Aviation Week and Space Technology*, 20 June, 24. Decreased fiscal 1988 funding for the Coast Guard caused a significant reduction in the number of flying hours devoted to intercepting illegal drugs being smuggled into the United States. ^United\States ^Interdiction ^Coast\Guard

265. Bullington, Bruce (1977). *Heroin Use in the Barrio*. Lexington, Mass.: Lexington Books. Drug abuse treatment and prevention among California's Mexican Americans. The author claims not to be involved in the intractable ideological positions regarding the magnitude, causes, and solutions to the problem of drug abuse. Describes the "criminal penalty" school and the "involuntary institutional commitment for treatment" school as being ideologically driven. Decries the empirical justification for either school, for the author claims that supporting studies did not relate individuals to the distinctive life-styles or to the cultural setting in which drug use takes place. He attempts to correct for the latter by studying the drug-related behavior of ethnic groups in East Los Angeles. The only way to deal with the drug abuse problem is through identifying the characteristics of users (he identified seven categories in East Los Angeles) and tailoring responses specific to those categories as understood in their social and cultural settings. Drug interdiction programs are doomed to failure as well as is the continuation of criminalization policies. While decriminalization of drug use does not embrace a drug advocacy position, it does allow that the ultimate resolution of the conflict realistically lies in alternative socialization procedures and in nonstigmatizing, nonjudgmental approaches to the problem. ^United\States ^Heroin ^Drug\Use ^Treatment ^Society ^Culture ^Minorities ^California ^Drug\Control\Policies\Critique ^P\S\Legalization

266. *Burma; Extrajudicial Execution and Torture of Members of Ethnic Minorities* (1988). London: Amnesty International Publications. The civil war in Burma and the army's counterinsurgency operations have pushed thousands of ethnic minorities out of the country. Most are from the state of Karen, bordering on Thailand. Summary executions are noted. ^Burma ^Insurgents ^Southeast\Asia ^Golden\Triangle ^Minorities ^Consequences\Human\Rights ^Consequences\Migration

267. Burr, Angela (1986). "A British View of Prescribing Pharmaceutical Heroin to Opiate Addicts: A Critique of the 'Heroin Solution' with Special Reference to the Piccadilly and Kensington Market Drug Scenes in London." *International Journal of the Addictions* 21(1): 83–96. It has been suggested that, in order to solve the "heroin problem" and organized crime's involvement in it, pharmaceutical heroin should be prescribed legally to opiate addicts. Using data from London's drug subculture, the authors examine this premise and conclude that if such a policy were implemented in London it would have numerous unintended negative consequences. Illicitly manufactured heroin on the market would hardly be interfered with and, moreover, a rapid and substantial increase in the number of pharmaceutical heroin users would probably occur. Insofar as these data may be generalized, the authors conclude that the issues discussed ought to be examined before a "heroin solution" is implemented in other countries. ^United\Kingdom ^Heroin ^Decriminalization ^Reviews ^Drug\Control\Policies\Critique ^Consequences\Unintended

268. ———— (1987). "Chasing the Dragon." *The British Journal of Criminology* 27(4): 333–357. Social anthropological discussion of heroin misuse, delinquency, and crime within the context of a South London culture. Supports the idea that heroin use is an extension rather than a cause of delinquent behavior. The need to support their habit could not account for the scope of the criminality or deviancy of the addicts. This does not give strength to the conventional interpretations about the relationship between the rapid rise in crime in Britain and the heroin epidemic there. Includes a reasonable bibliography. ^United\Kingdom ^Heroin ^Drug\Use ^Crime

269. Burstein, Daniel (1982). "The Deadly Politics of Opium." *Maclean's*, 6 December, 10–16. Describes a Thai border patrol attack on the mountain stronghold of the opium warlord Khun Sa. Describes the general nature of the opium trade out of the Golden Triangle and Thailand, and the United States' efforts to interdict it. ^Thailand ^United\States ^Opiates ^Drug\Traffic ^Interdiction ^Insurgents ^Golden\Triangle ^Southeast\Asia ^Consequences\Violence

270. Buruma, Ian, and John MacBeth (1984). "Asia's Organized-Crime Jigsaw and the Western Connection; An East-Side Story." *Far Eastern Economic Review*, 27 December, 34–47. Describes various Asian mafias' role in the drug trade. Discussed, in particular, are the Triads and the Japanese mafia known as the Yakuza. Discussion of how the overseas Chinese have dominated the illicit Asian drug trade since the mid-1880s. ^Southeast\Asia ^Drug\Traffic ^Organized\Crime ^Triads ^Yakuza

271. Busch, Katie A., and Sidney H. Schnoll (1985). "Cocaine—Review of Current Literature and Interface with the Law." *Behavioral Sciences and the Law* 3(3): 282–298. Reviews the epidemiology, history, anu pharmacology of cocaine. Discusses knowledge of the relationship between cocaine and violence, as well as the forensic-psychiatric issues surrounding its use. ^Cocaine ^Drug\Use ^Health ^Reviews ^Law\Enforcement ^Consequences\Violence ^Cocaine\History ^Epidemiology ^Cocaine\Pharmacology

272. Caffrey, Ronald J. (1984). "Counter-Attack on Cocaine Trafficking: The Strategy of Drug Law Enforcement." *Bulletin on Narcotics* 36(2): 57–63. Suppression of cocaine traffic is one of the most important priorities of the Drug Enforcement Administration (DEA) of the United States. The organization is involved in coca plant eradication and in conducting investigation, intelligence, and training programs in cocaine source areas. Domestically, task forces against organized crime have been established in twelve key areas of the United States. Among the matters being monitored are precursor and essential chemicals used for clandestine drug manufacture. ^United\States ^Drug\Control\Policies ^DEA ^Crop\Eradication ^Organized\Crime ^Precursor\Chemicals

273. Cagliotti, Carlos Norberto (1980). "Some Considerations about the Chewing of Coca Leaf in the Argentine Republic." In *Cocaine 1980. Proceedings of the Interamerican Seminar on Medical and Sociological Aspects of Coca and Cocaine*, edited by F. R. Jeri, 137–44. Lima, Peru: Pacific Press. (See Jeri, F. Raúl for an additional annotation). Discusses physiological effects of coca chewing. Some consequences, under chronic use, can be debilitating. ^Argentina ^Coca ^Health ^Latin\America ^Coca\History ^Consequences\Health ^Consequences\Social ^Culture ^Consequences\Physiological

274. ———— (1981). "La Economía de la Coca en Bolivia." *Revista de la Sanidad de las Fuerzas Policiales* 42(2): 161–65. The cultivation of coca in Bolivia is examined from the vantage of its economic value. Statistics on that value and the production levels show that the value exceeds other exports, including petroleum. The principal problem for Bolivian authorities is not the suppression of coca production and the criminal activities associated with it but rather recognizing that the cultivation of coca

is the principal source of income for the Bolivian peasantry. ^Bolivia ^Coca ^Latin\America ^Production\Incentives\Economic ^Production\Statistics ^Drug\Control\Policies\Critique

275. —— (1983). "The Role of the South American Agreement on Narcotic Drugs and Psychotropic Substances in the Fight against Illicit Drug Trafficking." *Bulletin on Narcotics* 35(4): 83–95. Describes the involvement of ASEP (South American Agreement on Narcotic Drugs and Psychotropic Substances) in the suppression of illicit drug trafficking such as the establishment of national drug control coordinating bodies, cooperation between states in the area of legislative measures conducive to drug control, and the operation of a computerized system designed to facilitate contacts between the various drug law enforcement agencies of the state's parties and ASEP. ^Latin\America ^Drug\Control\Policies ^International\Cooperation ^ASEP

276. —— (1987). "Co-operation between South American Countries in the Struggle against Drug Abuse and Illicit Drug Trafficking." *Bulletin on Narcotics* 39(1): 61–67. Describes the South American agreement on narcotic drugs and psychotropic substances (ASEP), which came into force in 1976. Description of the support received for the eradication of coca crops and of cooperation in general. ^Latin\America ^Coca ^Crop\Eradication ^International\Cooperation ^ASEP

277. Cajias, Lupe (1989). "Increased Presence of U.S. Troops Worries Bolivians." *Latinamerica Press*, 5 January, 6. In recent months, small contingents of U.S. soldiers have arrived to undertake "civic action" projects in some of Bolivia's most volatile areas. A number of Bolivians are alarmed, fearing their strategically located nation could become a base for U.S. operations. Aside from cocaine related issues, the rhetoric of sovereignty is raised. ^Latin\America ^Bolivia ^United\States ^Cocaine ^Drug\Control\Policies ^Military ^Consequences\Foreign\Relations ^Consequences\Sovereignty

278. Camacho Guizado, Alvaro (1981). *Droga, Corrupción y Poder: Marijuana y Cocaína en la Sociedad Colombiana*. Colombia: CIDSE, Universidad Del Valle. The Center for Socioeconomic Research (CIDSE) of the University of Del Valle's department of social and economic sciences is the actual publisher of this work. Camacho Guizado is a sociologist. The work focuses on issues of legalization and police control of the production and commercialization of marijuana and cocaine in Colombia during the three years preceding publication. The author sees the drug trade as the heart of a number of social, economic, and political processes now affecting Colombian society. Chapters are directed to the economic significance of the drug traffic, its social significance, its relationship to corruption and power, and the conflict this poses within Colombian society for public policy. ^Colombia ^Drug\Traffic ^Law\Enforcement ^P\S\Legalization ^Latin\America ^Consequences\Social ^Consequences\Political ^Consequences\Economic ^Consequences\Corruption

279. Camargo, Pedro Pablo (1989). "Luchan los Narcos por el Control de las Plazas; Destruyen Centro Comercial y Matan un Alcalde." *Excelsior*, 9 May, 2A. Describes the veritable destruction of the central plaza in the city of Armenia in Colombia as warring gangs fight for the New York cocaine market. It is a struggle between Medellín and Cali. ^Colombia ^Cocaine ^Drug\Traffic ^Latin\America ^Traffickers ^Consequences\Violence ^Consequences\Political

280. Camí, J., and M. E. Rodríguez (1988). "Cocaína: La Epidemia que Viene." *Medicina Clínica* 91(2): 71–76. Examines the factors likely to contribute to Spain's experiencing a substantial cocaine consumption epidemic. Consequences to health are explored. These include physical, psychological, and neurological effects. Treatment modalities are explored as well as advances in the field of drug antagonists. ^Europe ^Spain ^Drug\Use ^Cocaine ^Drug\Use\Theories ^Consequences\Physical ^Consequences\Psychological ^Consequences\Neurological ^Treatment\Antagonists

281. Canelas Orellana, Amado, and Juán Carlos Canelas Zannier (1983). *Bolivia, Coca, Cocaína: Subdesarrollo y Poder Político*. La Paz, Bolivia: Editorial Los Amigos del Libro. Discusses the use of coca and cocaine, the trafficking and control of narcotics, and economic policy in Bolivia. Contains interpretive information about the diverse factors and their interrelationships that explain why coca and cocaine have caught on so extensively in Bolivia. Contains discussions on economic and political history of Bolivia, sociology, pharmacology, medicine, law, and international relations. Assumes that most of the driving force within Bolivia is economic, which could be turned away from cocaine to other matters if an externally funded Marshall Plan were instituted for the country. Also contains discussions about decriminalization of cocaine for recreational use, first in Bolivia and then in the United States and Western Europe. Argues that decriminalization (or legalization) would reduce many negative aspects of the trade and at least make it tolerable for both producing and consuming countries. ^Bolivia ^Coca ^Cocaine ^Drug\Traffic ^Drug\Control\Policies ^P\S\Legalization ^Production\Incentives\Economic ^Latin\America ^Culture ^P\S\Economic

282. Carbajal, C. (1980). "Psychosis Produced by Nasal Aspiration of Cocaine in Hydrochloride." In *Cocaine 1980. Proceedings of the Interamerican Seminar on Medical and Sociological Aspects of Coca and Cocaine*, edited by F. R. Jeri, 127–33. Lima, Peru: Pacific Press. Psychopathological problems caused by cocaine usually do not last long, and therefore most individuals do not seek treatment. In some instances, however, the problems can be serious and long lasting, producing a psychosis similar to paranoid schizophrenia. ^Cocaine ^Health ^Consequences\Psychological

283. Carias S., German (1986). *La Mafia De La Cocaína*. Caracas, Venezuela: Industrial Tipográfica Amazonas, C.A. The author, a reporter for the daily *El Nacional* brings a number of his writings together to serve as a consultative text for those interested in drug problems in general, and in particular, Venezuela. The author, as one of Venezuela's foremost investigative reporters, traces drug trafficking routes, the involvement of the Colombian mafia, Venezuela as a transshipment point, how the United States has been invaded by cocaine, etc. ^Venezuela ^Cocaine ^Drug\Traffic ^Organized\Crime ^Latin\America ^United\States

284. Carley, William (1988). "Losing Battle: U.S. Air War on Drugs So Far Fails to Stem Caribbean Smuggling." *The Wall Street Journal*, 20 October. Smugglers' planes elude radar while cocaine shipments increase and federal forces bicker with each other. ^Caribbean ^Aircraft ^Traffickers ^Bureaucracy ^Cocaine

285. Carlson, B. Robert, and William H. Edwards (1987). "Human Values and Cocaine Use." *Journal of Drug Education* 17(3): 183–95. The results of this study, done among 383 college-aged subjects, support the view that dominant value orientations differ between drug users and nondrug users. Personal values are more important to drug users, whereas social values are more important to nondrug users. This suggests that theories informing educational and treatment arrangements ought to account for people's value structures that discriminate between those who use cocaine and those who do not. ^Cocaine ^Drug\Use ^Treatment\Theories ^Prevention\Theories ^United\States ^Drug\Use\Theories

286. Carmi, A., and S. Schneider, eds. (1986). *Drugs and Alcohol*. New York: Springer-Verlag. The twenty-eight contributors to this volume, which includes discussions on consumption and its consequences of alcohol and drugs, shed light on how societies are deprived of the contribution of many of its members; on how limited resources within a society are necessarily diverted to assist, cure, and rehabilitate drug addicts; how the economics of the drug traffic contribute to strengthening criminal

organizations and give rise to new criminal syndicates; and how "corruption, racketeering, oppression, and illicit influences are among the dreadful elements which unavoidably accompany drug trafficking." The price paid for this by a country is practically incalculable. The volume calls for strong mobilization of all positive forces to counteract the disruptive wave and reestablish the damaged values of society that have permitted the onslaught. Thus the psychological, ethical, and legal aspects of drug abuse are discussed. ^Drug\Use ^Drug\Traffic ^Crime ^Society ^Alcohol ^Consequences\Social ^Consequences\Economic ^Consequences\Crime ^P\S\Values

287. Carpenter, Cheryl, Barry Glassner, Bruce D. Johnson, and Julia Loughlin (1988). *Kids, Drugs, and Crime*. Lexington, Mass.: Lexington Books. Discusses drug use among United States youth and its association with drug abuse, crime, and juvenile delinquency. Authors have adopted a theoretical/methodological orientation that relies on youths' perspectives as being evidentiary in identifying the relationship among drugs, alcohol, and crime among normal adolescents. Their findings are based on a study of 100 youths. Delinquency is situational as well as experiential. Conclusions: "[S]eriously delinquent youths are usually regular users of drugs and alcohol;" "youths relied on conventional wisdom in explaining how drugs and alcohol influence the criminality of others, but not themselves"; "the linkages between drugs/alcohol and criminal activities are complex and take on different meaning for youths depending on time, place, and interactions with others"; "virtually all delinquents state that they do not commit thefts and other property crimes to gain money with which to buy drugs"; "youths who sold drugs on a relatively regular basis were among the most regular users of drugs"; "delinquent youths attempt to legitimate their crimes and to minimize the risk of apprehension and the personal harm they inflict on their victims"; and "fear of criminal sanctions as an adult has a deterrent effect among segments of adolescent delinquents." Extensive bibliography. ^United\States ^Drug\Use ^Youth ^Crime ^Bibliographies ^Alcohol ^Consequences\Crime ^Prevention\Law\Enforcement

288. Carpenter, Ted Galen (1985). "The US Campaign against International Narcotics Trafficking: A Cure Worse than the Disease." *Cato Institute Policy Analysis 63*. Washington D.C.: Cato Institute. The Reagan administration's narcotics diplomacy pursued five objectives: 1) drug-crop eradication projects; 2) crop substitution programs; 3) the interdiction of drug trafficking; 4) the training, equipping, and advising of indigenous antinarcotics units; and 5) financial subsidies to enhance local governmental resources if these were insufficient. "The overall goal is to encourage, persuade, bribe, or coerce foreign governments into joining the U.S. anti-drug crusade" (p. 4). There have been numerous difficulties. As a foreign policy initiative, the U.S. narcotics policy has failed. The policy has accomplished little except to disburse narcotics trafficking across a larger geographic area. There are painful lessons to be learned. Present policies have channeled much of the narcotics activity into the hands of criminal elements rather than honest business entrepreneurs. Also, it is rapidly draining any reservoir of good will that may exist between the United States and the Third World. U.S. policymakers must face the reality that American drug abuse is primarily an internal matter and that the solution for it must be found within the borders of the United States. ^United\States ^Drug\Control\Policies\Critique

289. Carter, David L., and Darrel W. Stephens (1988). *Drug Abuse by Police Officers: An Analysis of Critical Policy Issues*. Springfield, Ill.: Charles C. Thomas. It is acknowledged that drug abuse among some U.S. police departments has become a serious problem; the question, however, is how that problem may be addressed. The contributors to this volume look into drug testing, how one deals with

legal issues in drug testing, and other departmental drug control policies. ^United\States ^Drug\Use ^Drug\Testing ^Workplace

290. Carter, William E., ed. (1980). *Cannabis Use in Costa Rica: A Study of Chronic Marihuana Use.* Philadelphia: Institute for the Study of Human Issues. The easy generalizations so often made about marihuana use tend not to reflect reality. Research increasingly indicates that the reasons for and results of such use are not the same for all groups and are not the same through time; a full understanding of the impact of the drug on human life can come only through knowledge from a wide range of social and cultural settings. Outside the United States, marihuana use has been more widespread, heavier, and of greater duration. In parts of Africa, India, and Central and South America, many individuals have traditionally smoked marihuana in quantities equaling daily tobacco smoking in the United States. This being the case, and with a growing demand for scientific knowledge about the long-range effects of the drug, it is logical to turn to other countries and peoples for answers that cannot be found in the United States setting, where use has been of shorter duration. Heavy use in a society like Costa Rica can help answer many remaining questions regarding the chronic effects of marihuana use. In general, neuropsychological and personality correlates between chronic users and nonusers in the matched sample of forty-one users and forty-one nonusers proved to be nonsignificant. Life-styles were significantly different. However, in areas of personal and social life, marihuana use was not shown to result in behavior that impaired the individuals' ability to function as a regular member of society. The significant differences found between users and nonusers tended to be associated with events antedating marihuana use. Where deviant behavior was encountered, marihuana appeared to be more a correlate than a cause (p. 203). Correlation is not synonymous with cause and effect, and those officials responsible for laws must take great care never to confuse the two. They must realize that any serious attempt at unravelling the drug dilemma will require extreme care in sampling procedures, detailed observations in natural settings, strict controls, and totally appropriate physiological, biochemical, and psychological measures. They must abandon the comfortable position of taking seriously only those scientific results that agree with their particular point of view, and they must consider divergent, even conflicting findings. Then they must exercise their best judgement in determining whether and how laws need to be altered. A critical analysis is given of previous studies in Egypt, Greece, and Jamaica, where effects of smoking marihuana were noted, to a greater or lesser degree, as being significant. ^Costa\Rica ^Cannabis ^Drug\Use ^Crime ^Health ^Society ^Latin\America ^Consequences\Psychological ^Consequences\Social ^Culture ^Reviews ^Middle\East ^Egypt ^Europe ^Greece ^Caribbean ^Jamaica

291. Carter, William E., ed. (1983). *Ensayos Científicos sobre la Coca.* La Paz, Bolivia: Librería Editorial Juventud. The author paints a grave situation for Bolivia with respect to production and consumption of coca and cocaine. The gravity deals, apparently, more with international efforts to destroy Bolivia's coca economy than with additional consequences that other authors may have discussed. Given this grave situation, the purpose of this book is to make accessible basic information with respect to the role of coca in the Andean life of Bolivia. The coca leaf penetrates Andean culture in a way that has no parallel in any other substance or any other class of substance or in any other culture. It serves as cultural identification for a whole race of people. Programs for the control, or substitution of cultivations, or eradication, tend to hurt, more than any others, the small farmer and traditional consumer. Governments of this hemisphere ought to guarantee respect for Andean ethnic traditions, within which the coca leaf plays such an important part. ^Bolivia ^Coca ^Producers ^Production ^Drug\Use ^Drug\Control\Policies ^Society ^Culture ^Latin\America ^Consequences\Economic

292. Carter, William E., and Paul L. Doughty (1976). "Social and Cultural Aspects of Cannabis Use in Costa Rica." *Annals of the New York Academy of Sciences* 282:2–16. The significant differences in behavior found between users and nonusers are highly correlated with different kinds of socialization experiences. The differences appear not to be adequately explained by marijuana use because marijuana use does not appear to have deleterious effects. ^Costa\Rica ^Cannabis ^Drug\Use ^Society ^Culture ^Latin\America ^Drug\Use\Theories

293. Castillo, Fabio (1987). *Los Jinetes de la Cocaína*. Bogotá, Colombia: Editorial Documentos Periodísticos. A reporter for Bogota's *El Espectador* [a paper that has taken an uncompromising position against the drug traffickers and whose editor in chief, Guillermo Cano, was assassinated] chronicles the drug trade in his country, including the birth of the trafficking "families." Included, also, are chapters on money laundering, extradition, and the uncompromising position of the Medellín drug cartel. The degree to which the narcotraffickers have infiltrated law enforcement and judicial administrations is implied. ^Colombia ^Cocaine ^Drug\Traffic ^Organized\Crime ^Traffickers ^Money\Laundering ^Drug\Traffic\History ^Consequences\Political ^Consequences\Corruption ^Latin\America

294. Castro de la Mata, R. (1987). "Farmacodependencia en el Perú." *Psicoactiva* 1(1): 15-53. Lima, Peru. While this article covers several topics, including economic aspects of statutory decrees in Peru, its principal value for this bibliography lies in its review of all epidemiological studies on psychoactive substances carried out in Peru up to the latest one published in 1986. ^Latin\America ^Peru ^Drug\Use ^Reviews ^Epidemiology

295. Castro, Janice (1986). "Battling the Enemy Within." *Time*, 17 March, 52-61. Description of how U.S. companies are working to drive illegal drugs out of the workplace. G.M., for example, hires undercover agents. Another company cut the personal padlocks off 400 employee lockers and examined their contents. ^United\States ^Drug\Control\Policies ^Workplace ^Private\Initiatives ^Consequences\Human\Rights

296. Cavanagh, Jonathan (1984). "Peru Rebels Threaten U.S. Drug Program." *The Wall Street Journal*, 10 August. Describes the entrance of the *Sendero Luminoso* or Shining Path into the upper Huallaga region of Peru and its successfully having turned opinion against a United States–backed coca eradication program into a campaign of antigovernment violence. The U.S.-backed coca substitution and eradication program has had to withdraw, and all government officials in the area surrounding Tingo María have resigned following guerrilla threats. It is reported that the guerrillas encourage the peasants to grow food crops—"food for the revolution"—but don't prohibit coca. Shining Path documents specify punishments for smoking coca paste, but none for growing or marketing the leaf. ^Peru ^Coca ^Drug\Control\Policies ^Insurgents ^Latin\America ^Production ^Consequences\Violence ^Terrorists ^Drug\Control\Policies\Effectiveness

297. Cave, Jonathan A. K., and Peter Reuter (1988). *The Interdictor's Lot: A Dynamic Model of the Market for Drug Smuggling Services*. Santa Monica, Calif.: Rand Corporation. While interdiction efforts have increased, and while quantities of illegal narcotics seized have risen, as have arrests, retail prices of cocaine have nevertheless fallen dramatically and the quantity successfully imported has risen sharply. Conventional static models of smuggling activity cannot reconcile these divergent observations. The authors develop a model that analyzes the evolution of the smugglers' market, integrating smuggler's expectation of the present value of future profits, the lowering of their costs through experience in smuggling, and how law enforcement or interdiction efforts may serve to increase costs or lower perceptions of future profits. Interdiction efforts that focus on experienced smugglers work best when

certain conditions prevail, and efforts on the novice smuggler work best when other conditions prevail. ^Drug\Traffic ^Interdiction ^Drug\Control\Policies\Effectiveness ^Drug\Control\Policies\Theories

298. Cervantes Angulo, José (1980). *La Noche de las Luciérnagas*. 2d ed. Bogotá, Colombia: Plaza and Janes. Documentary narrative of marihuana trafficking and narcotics control in Colombia. ^Colombia ^Cannabis ^Drug\Traffic ^Drug\Control\Policies ^Latin\America ^Drug\Control\Policies\History

299. Chaddock, Gail Russell (1990). "Families Fight Drugs: 'Mad Dads' Take to the Streets." *The Christian Science Monitor*, 12 January, 12. Description of a citizen's effort in Nebraska to bring strong black men into the lives of children of single-parent households. Some success is reported regarding reduction in drug use among youth. ^United\States ^Drug\Use ^Minorities ^Private\Initiatives

300. Chaiken, D. A. (1984). "Commonwealth Initiative in the Tracing, Seizing, Freezing and Forfeiture of Drug Proceeds." *Bulletin on Narcotics* 36(4): 111–14. More than reporting on existence of legislation and experience, this article more generally concentrates on what the Commonwealth Secretariat is formulating by way of creating greater mutual judicial assistance in criminal matters to strengthen the ability of national authorities to investigate, prosecute, and convict international drug traffickers. Work on model legislation is noted. ^United\Kingdom ^Law\Enforcement ^International\Cooperation ^Legislation

301. Chaiken, Jan, and Marcia R. Chaiken with Joyce E. Peterson (1982). *Varieties of Criminal Behavior: Summary and Policy Implications*. Santa Monica, Calif.: Rand Corporation. Creates categories of criminal behavior that identify the serious criminal, and then suggests policy and research implications associated with those categories. Discusses criminal drug use and drug control. Drug use is associated with almost every major kind of crime studied, and the authors argue that information about criminals' drug histories can tell more about the seriousness of their criminal activity than the kinds of crimes they are arrested for. The implication seems to be that one should test for drugs and then make assumptions about correlates of criminal behavior. The authors do allow for recent ethnographic studies which suggest that drug use and crime cannot be discussed in one-dimensional or simplistic terms. ^Drug\Use ^Crime ^Law\Enforcement ^Drug\Testing ^Drug\Control\Policies\Theories

302. Chambers, Carl, James A. Inciardi, David M. Petersen, Harvey A. Siegel, and O. Z. White (1987). *Chemical Dependencies: Patterns, Costs, and Consequences*. Athens: Ohio University Press. Of interest to this bibliography are two sections: "Health Consequences of Use," with their implied social overhead concerns, and "Crime Consequences of Use," focusing on all age levels, and specifically on heroin and crime. The drugs discussed in this volume include, but are not limited to, marijuana, heroin, and cocaine. ^Drug\Use ^Cannabis ^Cocaine ^Heroin ^Crime ^Health ^Consequences\Health ^Consequences\Social ^Consequences\Economic ^Consequences\Crime

303. Chambers, Carl, and Kathryn Pribble (1987). "Gaining Some Understanding of Drugs and Their Effects," in *Chemical Dependencies: Patterns, Costs, and Consequences*, edited by Carl Chambers, James A. Inciardi, David M. Petersen, Harvey A. Siegel, and O. Z. White. Athens: Ohio University Press. See the annotation of the edited volume under Chambers, Carl et al. ^Consequences\Health ^Consequences\Crime ^Drug\Use ^Cannabis ^Heroin ^Cocaine ^Consequences\Misc ^Health ^Crime

304. Chasnoff, Ira J. (1985). "Effects of Maternal Narcotic vs. Nonnarcotic Addiction on Neonatal Neurobehavior and Infant Development." In *Current*

Research on the Consequences of Maternal Drug Abuse, NIDA Research Monograph 59, edited by Theodore M. Pinkert. Rockville, Md.:National Institute on Drug Abuse. The outcome of the studies on nonnarcotic-exposed infants is sparse, but the present study indicates that newborns delivered to women whose primary substance of abuse was sedative/stimulants or PCP demonstrated marked deficits in neonatal behavior. ^Drug\Use ^Health ^NIDA ^Fetuses ^Consequences\Fetuses

305. ——— (1987). *Drug Use in Pregnancy: Mother and Child.* United Kingdom and Europe: MTP Press. Brings together clinicians and researchers who have been active in developing programs for the recognition and management of the chemically dependent pregnant woman and her newborn. All follows from research and treatment programs that have led, in recent years, to a recognition of a full range of psychoactive drugs that affect the developing fetus either somatically or behaviorally. Multiple disciplines are represented among the authors making presentations. ^Drug\Use ^Health ^Women ^Fetuses ^Consequences\Fetuses ^Treatment

306. Chasnoff, Ira J., William J. Burns, Sidney H. Schnoll, and Kayreen A. Burns (1985). "Cocaine Use in Pregnancy." *New England Journal of Medicine* 313(11): 666–669. From a controlled study of twenty-three individuals, the researchers found that cocaine using women had a significantly higher rate of spontaneous abortion than did women in the study's two control groups. The infants carried to term who were exposed to cocaine had significant depression of interactive behavior and "a poor organizational response to environmental stimuli." Other pregnancy complications are also noted. Suggests that cocaine influences not only the outcome of pregnancy but also the neurologic behavior of the newborn infant. ^Cocaine ^Health ^Fetuses ^Consequences\Fetuses

307. Chatlos, Calvin, and Lawrence D. Chilnick (1987). *Crack: What You Should Know about the Cocaine Epidemic.* New York: Putnam. Directed to those who use cocaine and crack, or who are otherwise dependent on illicit drugs. Semipopular discussion, by clinical personnel at a drug treatment center, about crack: what it is, what it does, and what social and economic impacts it has on those who use it. The moral imperative is clear, they argue: "Teach your kids to say no to crack." Helpful comments on referral services and other aids. ^Cocaine ^Crack ^Drug\Use ^Health ^Prevention ^Treatment ^Consequences\Social ^Consequences\Economic ^Consequences\Physiological

308. Chatterjee, S. K. (1981). *Legal Aspects of International Drug Control.* Netherlands: The Hague. The author's revised doctoral dissertation (University of London) in international economic law covers a wide range of topics: a survey of the history of drug use and early moves toward international control; international action for the control of trade and traffic in drugs between 1920 and 1944; discussions about the structure and methods of international drug control through the United Nations; and a description of several intergovernmental and international nongovernmental organizations dedicated to the eradication of illicit trade and traffic in narcotic drugs. ^Drug\Control\Policies ^International\Cooperation ^History ^United\States

309. ——— (1983). "Forfeiture of Proceeds of Drug-Related Crimes: A British Commonwealth Perspective." *Bulletin on Narcotics* 35(2): 3–19. British Commonwealth countries had not, as of this writing, seemed to have given much attention to the forfeiture of proceeds of drug-related offenses or crimes. Other countries have specific legislation; the Commonwealth nations put theirs under the purview of general criminal law. Effective enforcement of forfeiture judgments is not possible as long as the practice of maintaining inviolability of bank secrecy remains. The author wonders if an international convention might offer assistance in the successful implementation of

forfeiture judgments, especially where the ill-gotten gains had been transferred to a foreign jurisdiction. ^United\Kingdom ^Asset\Forfeiture ^P\S\Asset\Forfeiture

310. —— (1985). "Drugs and the Young: Some Legal Issues." *Bulletin on Narcotics* 37(2–3): 157-168. Another in the increasingly long line of arguments for a comprehensive response to drug-related offenses committed by young people, including activities of the community at large, families, parents, and guardians. A review of age of responsibility legislation or statutes in various countries is made. International enterprise in the prevention of juvenile drug culture can be initiated, and is noted. ^Drug\Use ^Youth ^Law\Enforcement ^International\Cooperation ^P\S\Integrated ^Family ^Legislation ^Prevention

311. —— (1987). "Can Demand for Illicit Drugs Be Reduced?" *Bulletin on Narcotics* 39(2): 3–9. Reduction of the illicit demand for drugs, given the pervasive influence of traffickers and the proclivities of consumers, can be achieved only by concurrent implementation of both stringent drug law enforcement measures and effective programs for the prevention of drug abuse and for the treatment, rehabilitation, and social reintegration of drug-addicted persons. ^Drug\Use ^Drug\Control\Policies ^Law\Enforcement ^Prevention ^Treatment ^Demand ^P\S\Law\Enforcement ^P\S\Treatment ^P\S\Rehabilitation

312. —— (1989). *Drug Abuse and Drug-Related Crimes: Some Unresolved Legal Problems*. Boston: Martinus Nijhoff Publishers. Two drug conventions adopted by the United Nations—the Single Convention on Narcotics Drugs of 1961 as amended by the Protocol of 1972, and the Convention on Psychotropic Substances—are mostly concerned with the prevention and eradication of drug problems. Both conventions make provisions for law enforcement measures as well as drug education, rehabilitation, and training of drug addicts. What was not considered at the time—largely because it was of negligible consequence—was dealing with organized crime's involvement in drug trafficking. The relevant U.N. agencies have been involved in considering how best to deal with this new dimension. This book identifies issues and discusses difficulties associated with resolving them in relationship to dealing with drug trafficking by organized crime. The UN conventions are included as appendices to the book. ^United\Nations ^Drug\Traffic ^Organized\Crime ^Law\Enforcement ^International\Cooperation

313. Chávez de Sánchez, María Isabel, Ana Alicia Solís de Fuentes, Gerardo Pacheco Santos, and Olga Salinas de Valle (1977). *Drogas y Pobreza: Estudio Etnográfico del Fenómeno de la Farmacodependencia en una Colonia Suburbana de la Ciudad de México*. México City: Editorial Trillas. The study was triggered by the author's association with a group of addict teenagers; this volume attempts to describe these young people ethnographically. Additionally, the authors give background on theories of drug abuse and dependency, an exposition of the research methodology they employed, a description of the location of their study, and a larger ethnographic consideration of the inhabitants of the area. Included is a socioeconomic description of the families of the addicts. ^Mexico ^Drug\Use ^Youth ^Society ^Family ^Latin\America ^Drug\Use\Theories

314. Chenru, Shen (1984). "Keeping Narcotics under Strict Control: Some Effects in China." *Impact of Science on Society* 34(133): 131–137. Description of Chinese policies toward psychotropic substances. This follows the People's Republic of China's successfully banning opium by 1952. ^China ^Drug\Control\Policies ^Southeast\Asia

315. Chesher, Greg, and Alex Wodak (1990). "Evolving a New Policy for Illicit Drugs," *The Journal of Drug Issues* 20:4(Fall): 555–61. A prudent drug policy ought to minimize the harm that may result from drug consumption. Although drug consumption harms society by inducing antisocial behavior and by causing morbidity and tissue damage, the other social problems, such as crime, violence, and

corruption, derive from the application of the policy of prohibition itself. Because much harm comes from the nature of the illicit drug market, the author proposes to eliminate this harm by employing "market forces" through various kinds of relaxed restrictions on drug use. ^P\S\Legalization ^P\S\Controlled\Sales ^P\S\Partial\Prohibition ^P\S\Policies

316. Chiang, Nora C. and Charles C. Lee, editors (1985). *Prenatal Drug Exposure: Kinetics And Dynamics.* Rockville, MD: U.S. Department of Health and Human Services. Drug abuse by women during pregnancy and the effect of drugs on the fetus. Information on prenatal effects of drug abuse is very limited. In many instances, the available data are confusing or contradictory. Nevertheless, research efforts to determine the concentrations of drugs/chemicals in body fluids of the newborns of maternal drug users have provided valuable information for the assessment of potential adverse effects on the infants. The adverse effects of opiates on the offspring due to maternal drug exposure have been well documented, although the mechanisms of action are not clear. ^Drug\Use ^Health ^Consequences\Fetuses

317. Childress, Anna Rose, A. Thomas McLellan, and Charles P. O'Brien (1985). "Behavioral Therapies for Substance Abuse." *The International Journal of the Addictions* 20(6-7): 947–69. The authors review the considerable research done in the past twenty years regarding behavioral interventions to treat drug and alcohol abuse. Major areas of research activity covered are aversive stimuli (chemical, electrical, and covert), skills training, contingency management, extinction/desensitization, and combined behavioral treatments. Concludes that few of these treatment strategies have been fully explored with properly controlled group studies, although some of the strategies appear to hold promise. ^Drug\Use ^Treatment ^Reviews ^Alcohol ^Treatment\Theories

318. "China Cracks Big Drug Case" (1988). *Beijing Review*, 28 March, 12–13. Short report of the results of a criminal investigation that produced the arrest of numerous drug traffickers. China appears to be serious in its antidrug efforts, even collaborating with Interpol. ^China ^Drug\Traffic ^Law\Enforcement ^Interpol ^International\Cooperation ^Southeast\Asia ^Traffickers

319. "China Vows War on Drug Abuse" (1988). *Beijing Review*, 1 July, 12–13. China, a transit area for smuggling drugs into other countries, has suffered "leakage" to its own population. A government official vows "unremitting efforts to help in the fight." ^China ^Drug\Traffic ^Drug\Use ^Drug\Control\Policies ^Southeast\Asia

320. "China's Attitude towards Narcotics Control" (1987). *Beijing Review*, 16 March, 21-22. The Chinese government's policy prohibits the planting of opium poppy and combats the illegal making, trading, and transporting of illicit narcotic substances. ^China ^Drug\Control\Policies ^Southeast\Asia ^Opiates

321. Chopra, Gurbakhsh S. (1972). "Sociological and Economic Aspects of Drug Dependence in India." *The International Journal of the Addictions* 7(1): 57–63. This study, from a data base of 1,000 cases, attempts to assess the role of narcotic drugs on the social and economic life of habitual users in India. Opium and cannabis are the principal drugs of dependence and, in general, the pattern of drug abuse has changed very little in the previous few decades. ^India ^Cannabis ^Opiates ^Drug\Use ^Consequences\Economic ^Society ^Culture

322. Christensen, Susan J., and Alice Q. Swanson (1974). "Women and Drug Use: An Annotated Bibliography." *Journal of Psychedelic Drugs* 6:4. Extensive annotations of the literature on women and drugs prior to the early 1970s. Over two-thirds of all opiate users in the nineteenth century were women; even up through the 1960s most drugs prescribed licitly were for women. Despite these factors, the literature on drugs and women is quite scant, and this bibliography, somewhat dated,

helps to fill the gap. The focus is on the relationship of women to alcohol, psychotherapeutic drugs, narcotics, smoking, drug advertising, and drug treatment programs. ^Drug\Use ^Treatment ^Women ^Bibliographies ^Drug\Use\History ^Alcohol ^Opiates ^Tobacco

323. Christian, Shirley (1987). "Bolivians Fight Efforts to Eradicate Coca." *The New York Times*, 27 July, A3. Bolivia is the only country in South America where joint Bolivian and American military efforts have been under way to combat cocaine exports and to eradicate the agricultural crop that sustains them. Organized peasant growers of coca are giving strong opposition to these joint efforts. The efforts, their effects, and the peasants' resistance are noted. Options other than military ones are mentioned. ^Bolivia ^United\States ^Coca ^Crop\Eradication ^Military ^Latin\America ^Consequences\Political ^International\Cooperation ^Producers\Unions

324. ——— (1988). "Bolivian Peasants Pin Hopes on Coca; Despite Government Program to Eradicate Plants, Poor Are Increasing Crops." *The New York Times*, 4 May, A11. New plantings of coca bush may be seen in the main growing areas of Bolivia. A severe shortage of money for the government to carry out its crop substitution and relocation programs leaves the peasants with almost no choice. Coca growing is one of the few viable economic enterprises in which they may engage. ^Bolivia ^Coca ^Latin\America ^Production ^Drug\Control\Policies\Effectiveness ^Crop\Substitution ^Production\Incentives\Economic

325. ——— (1988). "Drug Case Raises Doubts in Bolivia." *The New York Times*, 5 May, A3. Several of the best-known names in the drug trade were acquitted in Santa Cruz, Bolivia. Serious questions are raised as to the ability of the criminal justice system to do anything about narcotics kingpins. ^Bolivia ^Cocaine ^Law\Enforcement ^Organized\Crime ^Latin\America ^Traffickers ^Consequences\Political ^Consequences\Corruption ^Consequences\Judiciary

326. ——— (1989). "Bolivia Shifts Tactics in Drug Fight." *The New York Times*, 22 March, A3. With policy failure abounding, Bolivia has now switched its priorities with respect to coca growing and cocaine production to voluntary crop substitution and eradication. Military and police forces alone have not persuaded peasants to quit growing coca. Additional aid is therefore sought to help farmers switch crops. ^Latin\America ^Bolivia ^Coca ^Crop\Substitution ^Foreign\Aid ^Drug\Control\Policies\Effectiveness ^Military ^Law\Enforcement ^P\S\Foreign\Aid

327. Chung, Tan (1978). *China and the Brave New World: A Study of the Origins of the Opium War* (1840–42). Durham, North Carolina: Carolina Academic Press. Examines principal historical perspectives advanced to explain Britain's successful efforts to legalize the opium trade in China. The war, or wars, which accomplished this are, according to Chung, not to be understood either as deriving from cultural conflict or trade. Economic gains for the British were to be had by maintaining China in a condition of decadent culture. Part of this motivation derived from British economic exigencies in India. ^Southeast\Asia ^China ^Opiates\History ^United\Kingdom ^Foreign\Relations ^Theories ^Traffickers\Theories

328. Claiborne, William (1984). "Pakistan Steps up Antidrug Campaign." *The Washington Post*, 30 January, A13. A description of law enforcement efforts in Pakistan that includes the rounding up of suspected dealers. Pakistan is, of course, a major world supplier of heroin. ^Pakistan ^Heroin ^Drug\Traffic ^Law\Enforcement ^Golden\Crescent ^Southwest\Asia ^Traffickers

329. "Clamping down on Marijuana" (1985). *Latin American Weekly Report*, 17 May, 9. Description of a resurgence of marijuana growing in Belize, and the economics that drive that new production. ^Belize ^Cannabis ^Production ^Caribbean ^Production\Incentives\Economic

330. Clayton, Richard R. (1980). "The Delinquency and Drug Use Relationship among Adolescents: A Critical Review." In *Drug Abuse and the American Adolescent*, NIDA Research Monograph 38, edited by Dan J. Lettieri and Jacqueline P. Ludford. Rockville, Md.:National Institute on Drug Abuse. Advances a methodological model that attempts to assess whether delinquency and drug use among adolescents are truly correlated, what the predominant temporal order is, and if the relationship could be spurious. Considerable literature is discussed. A consistent statistical association between delinquency and drug use is noted. There is consensus that onset of delinquency usually precedes involvement with illicit drugs. Analysis of 3,000 adolescents in this study contradicts earlier evidence presented about the spuriousness of delinquency and drug use. These authors provide strong evidence that the delinquency-drug use relationship is not spurious. ^Drug\Use ^Youth ^Crime ^Reviews ^NIDA ^Crime\Theories ^Consequences\Crime

331. —— (1981). "Federal Drugs-Crime Research: Setting the Agenda." In *The Drugs-Crime Connection*, edited by James A. Inciardi, 17–38. Beverly Hills: Sage. Examines the movement of the federal drug bureaucracy in stimulating drugs-crime research. Concerned with the *process* of setting the research agenda at the federal level that addresses the crime-drug linkage. The goals are to describe the key events, actors, and documents that have emerged since early 1975; to analyze the many factors that have made the construction of such an agenda difficult to achieve; and to synthesize what has been learned from a half decade of effort. Much writing on drug- and crime-related activities is an outgrowth of the federal research agenda. A primary task for the federal government is not to develop a master plan but rather to foster interagency collaboration in funding studies dealing with important crime-drug issues and in synthesizing findings from relatively independent research efforts. ^United\States ^Drug\Use ^Crime

332. —— (1985). "Cocaine Use in the United States: In a Blizzard or Just Being Snowed?" In *Cocaine Use in America: Epidemiologic and Clinical Perspectives*, edited by N. J. Kozel and E. H. Adams, 8–34. Rockville, Md.: National Institute on Drug Abuse. See the general annotation under Kozel, Nicholas J., and Edgar H. Adams, *Cocaine Use in America*. ^United\States ^Cocaine ^Drug\Use ^Society ^NIDA ^Consequences\Social ^Consequences\Economic ^Consequences\Health ^Consequences\Psychological ^Treatment

333. —— (1989). "Legalization of Drugs: An Idea Whose Time Has Not Come." *American Behavioral Scientist* 32(3): 316–32. Five short commentaries, by others, are here reviewed by Clayton. ^P\S\Legalization ^Reviews

334. Clayton, Richard R., and Harwin L. Voss (1981). *Young Men and Drugs in Manhattan: A Causal Analysis*. Rockville, Md.: National Institute on Drug Abuse. From a sample survey distinctively different from those used in nationwide surveys (one designed to enhance the probability of selecting men who had used heroin) this study examines the ideology and natural history of drug use with a special focus on heroin. Argues that the primary emphasis in earlier studies in the drug field was descriptive, shifting, in the 1980s to explanation. The studies described in this report reflect this recent change. The best predictor of drug use among adolescents is peer influence. Comments are raised about the difficulties in operationalizing and quantitatively testing the "societal reaction" or "labeling perspective" (p. 168). This focus does not pretend to explain why individuals do or do not commit rule-breaking acts but rather what the process is that leads to secondary confusion. Includes annotated bibliographical

reference to prior theoretical studies. ^United\States ^Heroin ^Drug\Use ^Youth ^Crime ^Society ^Bibliographies ^Reviews ^New\York ^Drug\Use\Theories

335. "Clean-up Campaign Gives Poor Results" (1984). *Latin American Weekly Report*, 18 May, 9. Description of a huge campaign against the Colombian drug mafia, following the assassination of Colombian Minister of Justice Bonilla. Scant results, with the side effect being that fleeing members of the mafia have put up a large amount of real estate for quick sale; this has depressed market prices for luxury homes on the Atlantic coast. ^Colombia ^Law\Enforcement ^Organized\Crime ^Latin\America ^Consequences\Economic ^Consequences\Violence

336. Cloyd, Jerald W. (1982). *Drugs and Information Control: The Role of Men and Manipulation in the Control of Drug Trafficking*. Westport, Conn.: Greenwood Press. Drug abuse, narcotic laws, and control of narcotics in the United States. Presents an understanding of drug issues within an "existential-conflict perspective." The underlying theory is that groups of individuals generate strategies to manipulate the ambiguous social state for their own purposes, and the information feedback loops that develop when this manipulation process is successful serve to reinforce their own position in society as well as to determine the understanding society gives to their work. Thus the book shows how the Federal Bureau of Narcotics manipulates legal ambiguities to increase its organizational power. Special attention is paid to the strategies the bureau uses to control the definition of drug abuse, expand its jurisdiction over other drugs, and use different crises to buttress its image as an effective law enforcement agency. All this control of information and ability to "label" are seen in the practical enforcement procedures used by the criminal justice system to enforce antidrug laws. Focus is given, principally, to work of U.S. customs at the border and the criminal justice system and its plea bargaining operations. ^United\States ^Drug\Control\Policies ^Drug\Control\Politics ^Customs

337. "Cocaine and Heroin: Just Say Buprenorphine" (1989). *The Economist*, 28 October, 95. Buprenorphine, a heroin opiate substitute that is only slightly addictive, is to be tested on 600 cocaine and heroin users in America under the auspices of the National Institute on Drug Abuse. It is thought that medical maintenance on this drug will avoid many of heroin's derivative problems. ^Treatment\Antagonists ^United\States ^NIDA ^Cocaine ^Heroin

338. "The Cocaine Economies; Latin America's Killing Fields" (1988). *The Economist*, 8 October, 21–24. Description of how cocaine is crucial, now, to the economies of Bolivia, Peru. and Colombia. Financial statistics are given. ^Latin\America ^Bolivia ^Peru ^Colombia ^Cocaine ^Drug\Traffic ^Economics ^Statistics

339. "Cocaine Kitchen on the Boil" (1983). *Latin American Weekly Report*, 8 July, 8–9. Report of a substantial drop in the price for Peruvian cocaine paste and the devastating impact this has had on the entire economy of the high jungle around Tingo María. ^Peru ^Coca ^Drug\Traffic ^Latin\America ^Consequences\Economic

340. "Cocaine Mafias Outmanoeuvre the DEA" (1982). *Latin American Weekly Report*, 22 January, 10–11. Short description of law enforcement agencies in Brazil and Colombia having been bought off by the drug barons and having been uncooperative with the U.S. Drug Enforcement Administration. ^Latin\America ^Brazil ^Colombia ^United\States ^Law\Enforcement ^Organized\Crime ^DEA ^Consequences\Political ^Consequences\Corruption

341. "Cocaine Route Turns North" (1985). *Latin American Weekly Report*, 18 January, 5. Paraguay is noted as having become an important transit country of precursor chemicals for the manufacture of cocaine. ^Latin\America ^Paraguay ^Cocaine ^Drug\Traffic ^Precursor\Chemicals

342. "Cocaine Scandal Hits Lima" (1985). *Latin American Weekly Report*, 16 August, 3. Many of the higher officials of the Belaúnde administration are under suspicion of having participated in the cocaine trade. This was brought to light when one cocaine "kitchen" in Lima exploded. ^Latin\America ^Peru ^Cocaine ^Drug\Traffic ^Consequences\Corruption ^Refining

343. "Cocaine 'Snorting' for Fun" (1976). *The Medical Journal of Australia* 2(2):40. Short description of coca and cocaine's use through history, noting that its reemergence as a popular drug of abuse is a matter of concern. Cocaine's physiological and psychological effects are briefly mentioned. ^Cocaine ^Drug\Use ^Cocaine\History ^Consequences\Physiological ^Consequences\Psychological

344. "Cocaine: The Military Connection" (1980). *Latin American Regional Reports*, 29 August, 5–6. For the first time ever the drug mafia has evidently bought itself a government—Bolivia. The new military regime walks hand in glove with the narco mafia. ^Latin\America ^Bolivia ^Cocaine ^Drug\Traffic ^Military ^Consequences\Political ^Consequences\Corruption ^Organized\Crime

345. "Cocaine Traffickers Kill 17 in Peru Raid on Antidrug Team" (1984). *The New York Times*, 19 November. Describes an event in the upper Huallaga Valley in which a band of cocaine traffickers burst into a jungle campsite and opened fire on Peruvian employees of the coca reduction organization known as Umopar, killing at least seventeen. Background information given on the valley and production tendencies and social transformations within it. ^Peru ^Cocaine ^Drug\Traffic ^Crop\Eradication ^Production ^Consequences\Social ^Consequences\Violence ^Latin\America

346. Cockburn, Alexander (1986). "Some Radical Notions about Fighting Drugs." *The Wall Street Journal*, 11 September, 35. Calls for a less punitive policy of social regimentation and a more cooperative, socially transforming policy that could, in the long run, bring about better prospects of a drug-free society in the United States. ^United\States ^Proffered\Solutions

347. Cody, Edward (1986). "Drug Raid Proves Bust; Villagers Lament Jamaican Drive on 'Ganja.'" *The Washington Post*, 21 January, A11. With the arrest of a local drug family in Jamaica, the local economy deteriorates markedly, and the "Robin Hood" behavior of the indicted family is sorely missed. ^Jamaica ^Cannabis ^Drug\Traffic ^Law\Enforcement ^Consequences\Economic ^Consequences\Social ^Caribbean

348. ——— (1988). "Dutch Pull Welcome Mat away from Drug Users; Crackdown Intended to Alter Image That Attracts Tourists Seeking Trouble-free High." *The Washington Post*, 17 November, A35. The Dutch are tired of their reputation of being a country that is soft on drug users and that, therefore, attracts tourists seeking a trouble-free high. ^Netherlands ^Drug\Use ^Law\Enforcement ^Drug\Control\Policies

349. Coffey, John P. (1987). "The Navy's Role in Interdicting Narcotics Traffic: War on Drugs or Ambush on the Constitution?" *The Georgetown Law Journal* 75:1947–66. Using the Navy to interdict drug smugglers raises serious questions about traditional constitutional protection of individual rights. The article is extensively referenced. ^United\States ^Interdiction ^Military ^Drug\Control\Policies\Critique ^Consequences\Constitutional

350. Cohen, Peter (1989). *Cocaine Use in Amsterdam in Non-Deviant Subcultures*. Amsterdam, Netherlands: Instituut Voor Sociale Geografie Universiteit van Amsterdam. Reports an analysis of interviews of 160 experienced cocaine users. Such users showed that they can control cocaine use. Therefore, fears about psychopharmacological consequences that would impose a threat to society are

unfounded. Criminal involvement of this group was found to be low, also. Criminalization or prohibition laws therefore unwarantedly makes users into criminals. It is thought that this remarkable condition—users handling their cocaine well—derived from a relatively low level of police activity directed against them. ^Europe ^Netherlands ^Consequences\Crime ^Consequences\Violence ^Drug\Control\Policies\Critique

351. Cohen, Sidney (1981). *Cocaine Today.* Rockville, Md.:American Council for Drug Education. The short volume explores history and pharmacology of the use of the coca plant, modes of use, pharmacological effects, and dangers. ^Coca ^Cocaine ^Health ^Coca\History ^Cocaine\Pharmacology ^Cocaine\History

352. —— (1981). *The Substance Abuse Problems.* Binghamton, NY: Haworth Press. Of interest to this bibliography is Section 5, "How Drugs Change People and Society." ^Drug\Use ^Health ^Consequences\Social

353. —— (1982). "Cannabis: Effects upon Adolescent Motivation." In *Marijuana and Youth: Clinical Observations on Motivation and Learning.* Rockville, Md.:National Institute of Mental Health. The impact of frequently consumed marijuana appears to diminish drive states and goal direction. The evidence, however, is open to ambiguous interpretations. What may cause cannabis amotivation? Briefly mentioned are eight orientations, views, or theories, including theories about sedation, decadent society, retained THC, "louder music and stronger wine," decreased drive hormone, brain cell change, hemispheric dominance, and psychic depression. ^Cannabis ^Health ^Amotivational\Syndrome\Theories ^Consequences\Personal ^Consequences\Neurological ^Consequences\Psychological ^Youth

354. —— (1984). "Recent Developments in the Abuse of Cocaine." *Bulletin on Narcotics* 36(2): 3–14. Cocaine is a powerful euphoriant and it relieves, though only transiently, depression, dread, and dysphoria. New patterns of cocaine abuse, such as the inhalation of vaporized cocaine base, the intravenous injection of cocaine hydrochloride, and the smoking of coca paste, produce a brief elation that quickly gives way either to a return to the baseline mood or to displeasure, resulting in a strong desire to return to the momentary ecstatic experience—a cycle that leads to compulsive use. The alleged safety in the use of cocaine is a myth. Cocaine can be lethal. The high dosages of cocaine abused today induce physical dependence, but this is less a contributory factor than the intense psychological craving to perpetuate cocaine use. There is no specific way to treat dysfunctional cocaine use. Notes are made on abstinence, detoxification, education, family involvement, group and individual therapy, contingency contracting, pharmacological therapy, and other activities and measures. ^Cocaine ^Drug\Use ^Treatment ^Cocaine\Paste ^Consequences\Personal ^Treatment\Abstinence ^Treatment\Detoxification^Treatment\Education^Treatment\Family^Treatment\Therapy^Treatment\Antagonists

355. —— (1985). "Adverse Effects of Cocaine." *Consumer's Research Magazine* 68(11): 14–16. This is a partial review of the National Institute of Drug Abuse's 1985 study entitled *Cocaine Use in America: Epidemiologic and Clinic Perspectives.* Mostly, however, it is an excerpt from a chapter in the NIDA study that describes the harmful effects of cocaine use and abuse. As defined by Cohen, cocaine is unquestionably addicting, although he wants to cast his understanding more in terms of psychological criteria than physiological criteria such as are frequently used with heroin. ^Cocaine ^Drug\Use ^Epidemiology ^Health ^NIDA ^Consequences\Health ^Consequences\Personal

356. —— (1985). *Cocaine: The Bottom Line.* Rockville, Md.:American Council for Drug Education. Cohen recites the "cocaine story" over the past few years, and concludes that it is indeed very grim. Argues that those who use the drug and contribute to other people's usage should have to pay a substantial price. Prevention programs, interdiction and eradication programs, seizure of assets, and interdiction of

drug money should all be pursued in a harsh way, because the situation drug users and pushers create is also harsh. ^Cocaine ^Proffered\Solutions ^Consequences\Economic ^Consequences\Social

357. Cohn, Alvin W. (1984). "Drugs, Crime and Criminal Justice: State-of-the-Art and Future Direction." *Federal Probation* 48(3): 13–24. Drug laws are puritanical in their zeal, and have had consequences for all taxpayers, not only economically but in terms of civil liberties. It may be time therefore to develop higher social tolerance levels of addiction and look for different means by which to control the massive problem of drug abuse. Discusses the arguments for the involvement of criminal law in prohibiting victimless crimes and the implications of pursuing those arguments. Moralizing citizens have created a vast bureaucracy to eliminate drug usage through relentless enforcement of antidrug laws. This has imposed huge costs on all taxpayers. A call is made for developing alternative methods for controlling the drug abuse problem. Specific categorization of the consequences of "over criminalization." Package programs for decriminalization are suggested. ^United\States ^Drug\Control\Policies\Critique ^Consequences\Economic ^P\S\Legalization ^Consequences\Human\Rights

358. Colburn, Don, Sally Squires, Larry Thompson, Paul Berg, Sandy Rovner, Jay Siwek, Vicor Cohn, Carol Krucoff, Catherine O'Neill, and Abigail Trafford (1988). "Health: Getting Hooked, Getting Helped." *The Washington Post*, Special Report, 27 December, 6–22. A special section of *The Washington Post* includes a miscellany of information—anecdotal and technical—about the medical side of the war on drugs, the dilemma of treatment and recovery, how drugs attack the brain, teenage abusers and the problems parents encounter finding a correct balance between discipline and support, helping families come to grips with internal stress over addiction, drug education, why doctors miss the warning signs, and what is, literally, beyond the reach of medicine. Technical, physiological, and psychological discussions are also included. ^Drug\Use ^Health ^Prevention ^Treatment ^Consequences\Neurological ^Consequences\Family ^Family ^Consequences\Psychological ^Youth ^Consequences\Physiological

359. Cole, Stuart, and Dennis Muirhead (1983). "The Law and Politics of Drug Sentencing in Australia." *Journal of Drug Issues* 13(4): 417–29. The major concern of the Australian courts in dealing with illicit drug activity is to reduce the incidence of large-scale importation and distribution of drugs by applying "virtues of deterrence" sentences and publicizing them regularly. Nevertheless, there is wide disparity in sentencing practices among the various Australian states. Each appears to respond idiosyncratically to political variables. ^Australia ^Law\Enforcement ^Prevention\Penal ^Prevention\Media ^Consequences\Political ^Drug\Control\Policies

360. Collett, Merrill (1987). "'Drug Barons' Tentacles Run Deep in Colombian Society." *The Christian Science Monitor*, 20 November, 1. Describes how the enormous, vertically integrated cocaine industry centered in Medellín has reached into the heart of Colombian society; cocaine industry now involves magistrates and law enforcement officials who are poorly paid and witnesses who are easily bought off. Description also of a number of Colombian politicians who have courageously taken up the antidrug crusade. ^Colombia ^Cocaine ^Drug\Traffic ^Organized\Crime ^Latin\America ^Consequences\Social ^Consequences\Political ^Consequences\Corruption ^Drug\Control\Policies ^Consequences\Judiciary

361. —— (1987). "Venezuela Launches Patriotic War on Growing Drug Traffic." *The Christian Science Monitor*, 4 February, 9. Combine patriotism with a conventional antidrug educational effort and launch it to save a nation. Such is the effort being made by a Venezuelan attorney. ^Latin\America ^Venezuela ^Drug\Traffic ^Drug\Use ^Prevention ^Prevention\Drug\Education

362. —— (1988). "Colombia's Losing War with Drug Kings." *The Christian Science Monitor*, 13 May, 9. Chronicles the drug barons' assault on the political and judicial systems of Colombia. Notes the vertically integrated nature of the Medellín cartel, and how it uses its assets to create a "war chest." The resulting narco armies are, in many instances, better equipped than the Colombian military. There is growing sentiment among some national leaders that Colombia should negotiate with the traffickers and not continue to fight. As for the cartel, it has made clear what it would demand in any negotiations: an ironclad promise not to extradite any drug baron to the United States. ^Colombia ^Cocaine ^Drug\Control\Policies ^Extradition ^Law\Enforcement ^Latin\America ^Traffickers ^Consequences\Political ^Consequences\Judiciary ^Traffickers\Private\Armies ^Consequences\Violence ^P\S\Negotiations

363. —— (1988). "Colombia's Sophisticated Drug Traffickers Trigger Economic Boom, Political Violence." *Latinamerica Press*, 29 September, 3. Describes the way the Medellín Cartel, in particular, has used its "business wizardry" to create an economic boom in Colombia. Describes the efforts made by the cocaine barons to have themselves viewed as successful entrepreneurs rather than as criminals, and how they have launched a propaganda campaign to have themselves identified with creating jobs and generating wealth. Describes the deadly war between the traffickers and the guerrillas of the political left who are forcing the "new entrepreneurs" to keep up the price paid peasants for coca paste in regions under guerrilla control. ^Latin\America ^Colombia ^Coca ^Cocaine ^Drug\Traffic ^Traffickers ^Organized\Crime ^Society ^Consequences\Economic ^Consequences\Political ^Consequences\Social ^Consequences\Violence ^Insurgents ^Producers

364. —— (1988). "Maoist Guerrilla Band Complicates Antidrug War in Peru." *The Washington Post*, 4 June, A21. Reports the irony of a guerrilla movement, *Sendero Luminoso*, reaping badly needed funds in the upper Huallaga Valley from the coca/cocaine enterprise that it abhors and eventually hopes to eradicate. Description of U.S.–supported raids against the coca industry and the guerrilla movement in the area. In the wake of government raids, Shining Path rebels have expanded their influence as peasant growers become more discontent and frustrated. Whenever the Shining Path takes over a village, it cleans up streets, improves public services, and imposes a bloody but effective brand of justice in a region that the central government, as far as municipal services and government are concerned, has largely abandoned. The guerrillas, by protecting the peasants, facilitate the production of drugs, but they prohibit their use in the area. ^Latin\America ^Peru ^Coca ^Production ^Drug\Control\Policies ^Insurgents ^International\Cooperation ^Consequences\Political ^Producers ^Consequences\Violence

365. —— (1988). "The Myth of the Narco-Guerrillas." *The Nation* (August): 1. Decries arguments attempting to show a collaborative relationship between political guerrillas and narcotraffickers. ^Drug\Traffic ^Insurgents ^Traffickers

366. —— (1988). "Peruvians Flock to Upper Huallaga Valley to Cash in on Expanding Coca Bonanza." *Latinamerica Press*, 29 September, 6. Description of general failure of the eradication program in the Upper Huallaga Valley. During the past year *Sendero Luminoso* has become a violent new player in valley politics, having made rapid advances by proclaiming the cause of coca growing peasants against government eradication programs. Peasants, fearful for their assets, have flocked to the guerrillas for protection. As for the government, it concludes that there are only two possible solutions to the coca problem in the valley: either through strong repression or by involving the population in finding another way to make a living. ^Latin\America ^Peru ^Coca ^Drug\Traffic ^Drug\Control\Policies ^Crop\Eradication ^Drug\Control\Policies\Critique ^Consequences\Violence ^Producers ^Insurgents ^Consequences\Political ^Consequences\Economic ^P\S\Law\Enforcement ^P\S\Economic

367. —— (1989). "Collision Course in Colombia: Traffickers Threaten Land Reform." *The Christian Science Monitor*, 24 January, 3. For virtually the first time in Colombian history, an effective land reform law is both on the books and is funded. Legislators passed the law in late 1987 after a bitter battle that culminated in flying fists on the floor of Congress. The government, for the first time, may now force landowners to sell their holdings to the National Land Reform Institute, which resells the land to peasants under favorable terms. The director, Carlos Ossa, is vigorously implementing the provisions of the law. In 1989 it intends to distribute 350,000 acres to 5,600 families. At the same time this reform program is under way, elite cocaine traffickers are buying up large cattle ranches and many small holdings, which they consolidate to turn into cattle ranches. A number of reasons for their doing this are discussed. The question is, what is going to happen when the land reform agency decides to take over the great estates of the drug traffic barons? Already some skirmishes have been noted.
^Latin\America ^Colombia ^Cocaine ^Drug\Traffic ^Organized\Crime ^Land\Reform ^Legislation ^Traffickers ^Consequences\Economic ^Consequences\Political ^Consequences\Violence

368. —— (1989). "Rumors of Drug Money Taint Vote." *The Christian Science Monitor*, 10 May, 4. Discussion of recent elections in Bolivia and of their having been influenced by drug dollars. ^Latin\America ^Bolivia ^Coca ^Cocaine ^Drug\Traffic ^Consequences\Political ^Consequences\Corruption

369. Collier, Robert (1988). "Honduras: Mounting Evidence Implicates Armed Forces in Cocaine Trafficking." *Latinamerica Press*, 9 June, 5. Long-held suspicions exist that Honduran armed forces have been involved in drug trafficking. The arrest of a Honduran official, Rigoberto Regalado, on drug-related charges has added weight to the suspicions. Regalado is Honduras' ambassador to Panama; he was arrested in May in Miami carrying twenty-five pounds of cocaine in his suitcase. The affair has been made more complicated by the presence in Honduras of the U.S.–supported contras who have been supplied arms and ammunition (at a time when U.S. proscribed such) in exchange for allowing contra supply planes to carry South American drugs on return flights to the United States. ^Honduras ^Cocaine ^Drug\Traffic ^Military ^Consequences\Corruption ^Latin\America ^Consequences\Political ^Contras

370. Collins, James J., Robert L. Hubbard, and J. Valley Rachal (1985). "Expensive Drug Use and Illegal Income: A Test of Explanatory Hypotheses." *Criminology* 23(4): 743–764. There is a profound empirical association between heroin use and income-generating crime. The magnitude of that association, when other factors are controlled, is not sufficiently well known nor, necessarily, is the connection causal. This article tests the strength of the heroin use/income-generating crime relationship and examines, as well, the same question for cocaine. Analysis of 3,500 individuals shows that daily use of heroin and weekly and daily use of cocaine are strongly associated with illegal income. On the basis of theoretical interpretation, the author concludes that the addiction/compulsion model is an insufficient explanation, that the life style concept is useful for understanding the expensive drug use/income-generating crime relationship, and, finally, that the concept of addiction needs refinement and elaboration.
^Cocaine ^Heroin ^Drug\Use ^Crime ^Crime\Theories

371. "Colombia; All Fall Down" (1988). *The Economist*, 3 September, 42–43. Description of the internecine war among drug gangs and cartels in Colombia. ^Colombia ^Cocaine ^Drug\Traffic ^Organized\Crime ^Crime ^Latin\America ^Consequences\Violence

372. "Colombia Cartels Tied to Bombing" (1989). *The New York Times*, December 8, A10. A truck loaded with explosives was detonated in downtown Bogotá, Colombia, killing fifty-two people. It was one of the worst attacks that Colombia has suffered. Smaller bombs have exploded throughout the city. Over a thousand people

have been wounded. Most of the bombings are thought to emanate from the orders of murderous drug barons who have chosen this means to make a political statement. They want freedom from prosecution, and they do not want to be extradited to the United States. ^Latin\America ^Traffickers ^Colombia ^Consequences\Violence ^Terrorists ^Extradition

373. "Colombia: The Drug Economy" (1988). *The Economist*, 2 April, 62–63. Colombia is currently Latin America's economic success story, in part because of prudent economic management, and in part because of the underground economy associated with drugs. Specific data are given. ^Colombia ^Cocaine ^Drug\Traffic ^Economics ^Latin\America ^Consequences\Illegal\Economy ^Statistics

374. "Colombian Court Backs Extradition" (1989). *The New York Times*, 4 October. The Colombian Supreme Court has upheld the legality of the president's decree allowing extradition of suspected drug traffickers to the United States. Contrary to earlier rulings, this gives support to the country's campaign against the cocaine cartels. ^Latin\America ^Colombia ^Cocaine ^Extradition ^Judiciary

375. "Colombianization" (1989). *World Press Review* (February): 40. One of the costs of the "drug war" in producing countries is contract killings. Santa Cruz, Bolivia has become a "hit town." ^Latin\America ^Bolivia ^Cocaine ^Drug\Traffic ^Organized\Crime ^Crime ^Consequences\Violence ^Consequences\Crime ^Consequences\Assassination

376. "Colombians Blame Drug Traffickers" (1987). *Latin American Weekly Report*, 2 July, 3. Describes an armed confrontation between Venezuelan national guardsmen engaged in destroying drug plantations along the Colombian border and drug paramilitary forces. Nine Venezuelan soldiers were killed. Venezuela accuses Colombia of not patrolling its borders sufficiently well. ^Latin\America ^Colombia ^Venezuela ^Cocaine ^Consequences\Foreign\Relations ^Traffickers\Private\Armies ^Consequences\Violence

377. "Colombia's Cocaine Overdose" (1989). *The Economist*, 26 August, 29–30. Describes law enforcement and seizure efforts in Colombia following the country's declaration of war on drug barons. Description of the turbulence in the market for cocaine and how this helps to explain the drug barons violence as they face a saturated U.S. market and attempt to energetically open up Europe by way of Spain, where cocaine brings four times the Miami retail price. The whole affair is compounded by the fact that the world price for coffee (Colombia's main legitimate trade produced by 500,000 growers, mostly small holders) has been halved. ^Colombia ^Europe ^Cocaine ^Drug\Traffic ^Latin\America ^Consequences\Violence ^Spain ^Consequences\Economic ^Traffickers ^Consequences\Markets

378. Comitas, Lambros (1976). "Cannabis and Work in Jamaica: A Refutation of the Amotivational Syndrome." *Annals of the New York Academy of Sciences* 282:24–32. The paper's agenda "is an attempt to alleviate unwarranted fears of social collapse by providing examples from a society in which cannabis has been in widespread use among the working class for a long time but where passivity and withdrawal from every day work does not exist and where the amotivational syndrome does not pertain" (p. 25). ^Jamaica ^Cannabis ^Health ^Amotivational\Syndrome ^Caribbean

379. Conger, Lucy (1990). "Mexico: Rights Violations Are on the Rise." *Latinamerica Press*, June 28, p. 1. The antinarcotics unit of Mexico's federal judicial police is accused of being responsible for a substantial increase in human rights violations. ^Latin\America ^Mexico ^Human\Rights

380. Connell, Philip H. (1986). "'I Need Heroin.' Thirty Years' Experience of Drug Dependence and of the Medical Challenges at Local, National, International and Political Levels. What Next?" *British Journal of Addiction* 81:461–72. The thinking behind the Dangerous Drugs Act of 1967 is reviewed, as well

as developments since 1968 in terms of official organizational response to the drug trade. Has anything worked? We may not know satisfactorily because problems in financing, coordination, setting up evaluation procedures, and the paucity of experts in the field militate against good policy review. The new factors of AIDS and "designer drugs" are referred to. ^United\Kingdom ^Heroin ^Health ^AIDS ^Designer\Drugs ^Drug\Control\Policies\History

381. Conover, Kirsten A. (1989). "Defeating Drug Dealers: Drop-a-Dime Project Pays Off." *The Christian Science Monitor*, 18 August, 14. Through an anonymous hotline, a community submerged in illicit drug trafficking and related violence tries to move the traffickers out. Neighborhood residents, who may be fearful to call police (worrying about being betrayed) appear willing to use the anonymous hotline to report drug activities in their neighborhood. Information is then passed on to the police. Police investigate and then report to "Drop-a-Dime" as feedback, which is then circulated around the community. ^United\States ^Drug\Traffic ^Law\Enforcement ^Private\Initiatives

382. Consejo Nacional de Lucha contra el Narcotráfico (1982). *Narcotráfico: Causas y Soluciones*. La Paz, Bolivia. Presents and to some extent analyzes Bolivia's ten-year plan for its fight against narcotrafficking. Bolivia sees itself as being seriously affected by the extent of cocaine trafficking. The country asks consuming nations, in particular the United States, to change not only their own ways but the way in which they relate to Bolivia. Bolivia cannot be expected to solve other people's problems on its own. ^Latin\America ^Bolivia ^United\States ^Cocaine ^Drug\Control\Policies ^Politics ^Consequences\Foreign\Relations ^International\Cooperation\Critique

383. Conviser, Richard, and John H. Rutledge (1989). "Can Public Policies Limit the Spread of HIV among IV Drug Users?" *Journal of Drug Issues* 19(1): 113–28. It is now incontrovertible that intravenous drug users are spreading the AIDS virus in a rapid way. Some of the difficulty appears to be associated with the way society marginalizes the intravenous drug users. Marginalized, they are quite unamenable to policy initiatives to change their behavior. If they were brought into a less socially marginalized state, public policy might have a better chance of influencing them. For example, public policy might move away from the more punitive measures against addicts to requiring that they give up their addictions as the price for public health protection. Liberal needle distribution strategies that ensure a plentiful supply of sterile needles for those who do shoot drugs ought to be implemented. Alternatively, intravenous drug users ought to be provided with information about how to prevent the spread of the AIDS virus by sterilizing needles and syringes between uses. Any innovative health education techniques to motivate the intravenous drug users to change their behavior need to be sensitive culturally so as to be able to function as an accepted outreach program. Given that the heterosexual transmission of the AIDS virus from intravenous drug users is now affecting larger, and in some sense, even innocent populations, policymakers have a greater motivation to address the health of the intravenous drug user. Inasmuch as the addicts themselves will not change behavior unless motivated to do so, greater sympathy and understanding on the part of policymakers could provide an opening to make a serious effort to understand and eradicate the social conditions that give rise to drug addiction in the first place. ^Drug\Use ^Health ^AIDS ^Drug\Use\Theories ^P\S\Health\Protection ^P\S\Needle\Exchange ^Drug\Control\Policies

384. Conybeare, Bruce C., Jr. (1984). "Federal Civil Forfeiture: An Ill-Conceived Scheme Unfairly Deprives an Innocent Party of Its Property Interest." *University of Detroit Law Review* 62:87–108. Describes the current federal civil forfeiture scheme that allows confiscation of any conveyance used in an unlawful activity. Thus, the conveyance is considered to be the offender. This

unjustifiably deprives innocent interest holders of their property. A call is made for congressional action so that innocent claimants will not continue to be deprived of their property interests without just compensation, which violates the fifth amendment. ^United\States ^Asset\Forfeiture\Critique ^Consequences\Constitutional

385. Cook, Royer, Hazel Lawrence, Carolyn Morse, and Janice Roehl (1984). "An Evaluation of the Alternatives Approach to Drug Abuse Prevention." *International Journal of the Addictions* 19(7): 767–87. Since the mid-1960s, approaches to prevent the abuse of drugs have taken many forms. Among the more intriguing prevention efforts developed is the "alternatives approach." An alternatives-oriented, school-based drug abuse prevention program, known as the Positive Alternatives for Youth (PAY), was evaluated over a two-year period. During the first year, significant differences were detected between the studied group and the control group of students. Fewer differences were found in the second year. Reasons for specific results are discussed and implications are drawn for the alternatives approach to drug abuse prevention. ^Drug\Use ^Youth ^Prevention

386. Coombs, Robert H., Felipe O. Santana, and Fawzy I. Fawzy (1984). "Parent Training to Prevent Adolescent Drug Use: An Educational Model." *Journal of Drug Issues* 14(2): 393–402. Assumptions are that drug abuse is a learned behavior, exacerbated in family situations where children have low self-esteem. A model is presented to educate parents to give youth positive reinforcement rather than negative interaction—less parental criticism, complaining, and punishment and more praise, positive involvement, and encouragement. ^Drug\Use ^Prevention ^Youth ^Family ^Prevention\Parental\Training

387. Cooper, James R., et al, eds. (1983). *Research on the Treatment of Narcotic Addiction: State of the Art.* Rockville, Md.:National Institute on Drug Abuse. Focuses specifically on methadone as a drug maintenance strategy and as a detoxification treatment. Also looks at the effects of methadone on offspring and users, as well as factors affecting the outcome of methadone treatment. Critiques are offered on various papers. Extensive bibliographies are attached to many of the papers. ^Heroin ^Treatment ^Methadone ^Reviews ^NIDA ^Prevention\Methadone ^Consequences\Methadone

388. Cooper, Nancy, and Steven Strasser (1986). "We Closed Our Eyes to It." *Newsweek*, 6 October, 34. Description of the drug problem the Soviets now admit to having. ^USSR ^Drug\Use

389. Corcoran, David (1989). "Legalizing Drugs: Failures Spur Debate." *The New York Times*, 27 November, A9. The failure of drug-enforcement policies has encouraged a number of people to speak out in favor of discussing the possibility of legalizing drugs. These include George P. Schultz, Charles Murray, and William F. Buckley. The problem is a trade-off between reduction in crime and probable increase in addiction. ^P\S\Legalization ^United\States

390. Corcoran, William J., and Martin C. Carlson (1983). "Criminal Prosecution of Drug Traffickers under the Continuing Criminal Enterprises Statute in Federal Courts of the United States of America." *Bulletin on Narcotics* 35(2): 77–94. The statute, enacted in 1970 to facilitate suppression of illicit traffic in drugs, contains a mandatory minimum sentencing provision of not less than ten years following conviction. It also contains a provision for forfeiture of profits. When drug traffickers move their assets abroad, however, this statute is not very helpful. Pursuit of those assets under this statute requires cooperation with other countries. This is facilitated by a bilateral mutual judicial assistance treaty, when it exists. ^United\States

^Drug\Traffic ^Law\Enforcement ^Asset\Forfeiture ^Asset\Forfeiture\Critique ^Treaties ^Money\Laundering ^International\Cooperation

391. Corrigan, D. (1986). "Drug Abuse in the Republic of Ireland: An Overview." *Bulletin on Narcotics* 38(1-2): 91–97. Since 1979 there has been an alarming increase in Ireland of young people abusing drugs, perhaps even as much as six fold. Heroin and other opiate addicts seeking treatment have increased alarmingly. Also, increasing numbers of cases of hepatitis B are noted, along with drug-related deaths. One study in the northern part of Dublin suggested that as much as 10 percent of the young people between fifteen and twenty years of age were addicted to heroin. Speculates that disrupted family life, attributable to many factors, appears to be the major risk factor underlying heroin abuse among young people. ^Ireland ^Heroin ^Drug\Use ^Youth ^Family ^Consequences\Personal ^Drug\Use\Theories

392. Corry, James M. and Peter Cimbolic (1985). *Drugs: Facts, Alternatives, Decisions.* Belmont, Calif.: Wadsworth Publishing Company. Gives an overview of drug use today but in the context of social setting and legal implications, the pharmacology of drugs, alternatives to drugs, rehabilitation, and abuse prevention. Written for a college-level reader. References some of the literature relevant to its various sections. Intended to help readers reach informed judgments about the personal effects of recreational drug taking—whether they are essentially innocuous or are illness producing. While a variety of views is presented, including alternatives to drugs with respect to altering consciousness, the volume is quite "a-valuational" (except in its prevention bias), simply giving readers a challenge to explore "his or her values and behaviors related to drug use." Early prevention efforts were unsuccessful because of the style of education, which used a one-dimensional, cognitive approach: lectures about the evils of drugs, having as a goal complete abstinence from psychoactive drugs. These authors hope to help people discover their potential, explore their own sense of being, accept themselves, give young people an accurate account of what drugs do and do not do and a set of natural skills that can help them duplicate or exceed both a drug high as well as the coping mechanisms drugs apparently offer. ^ Drug\Use ^ Prevention ^ Youth ^ Society ^ Cocaine\Pharmacology ^ Heroin\Pharmacology ^ Cannabis\Pharmacology ^ Prevention\Drug\Education\- Critique ^ P\S\Skills ^ P\S\Values

393. Courtwright, David T. (1982). *Dark Paradise: Opiate Addiction in America Before 1940.* Cambridge, Mass.: Harvard University Press. History of the opium habit in the United States, including morphine and heroin, and the therapeutic use of opium. Offers a social-class analysis of drug law development. Several additional themes are developed: Opiate addiction, though mutable, has thus far been intractable; there is an inverse relation between the availability of legal drugs and the amount of crime committed by users; American narcotic laws were passed, interpreted, and defended on the basis of misleading, even fraudulent, information; those groups who, for whatever reason, have had the greatest exposure to opiates have had the highest rates of opiate addiction. Includes an extensive bibliography. ^United\States ^Opiates ^Drug\Use ^Society ^Crime ^Opiates\History ^Bibliographies ^Drug\Control\Policies\History ^Drug\Control\Policies\Critique ^Drug\Use\Theories

394. Covington, Jeanette (1988). "Crime and Heroin: The Effect of Race and Gender." *Journal of Black Studies,* June, 487–506. The literature on traditional theories of crime is reviewed, and against that backdrop the author describes a data sample that examines the impact and traditional explanations of crime on racial subsamples. When all controls are in, are blacks really more prone to crime than are whites in similar socioeconomic categories? Race, the conclusion says, is not nearly so

important as gender. Implications for drug prevention are advanced. ^Heroin ^Drug\Use ^Crime ^Crime\Theories ^Minorities ^Women

395. Cowell, Alan (1987). "For Heroin, Turkey Is Land Bridge to West." *The New York Times*, 14 July, A14. Describes the explosive increase of heroin traffic coming from the East, a portion of which is being transited through Turkey. ^Middle\East ^Turkey ^Heroin ^Drug\Traffic ^Production

396. ——— (1989). "A Poor Land Torn by a Rich Craving." *The New York Times*, 20 May, 4. Describes heroin addiction and the hashish trade in Egypt. Cocaine has made inroads into the country as well; some social and economic data are given. Considers that cocaine, hashish, and opium abuse are threatening Egypt's economy and security. ^Middle\East ^Egypt ^Cannabis ^Cocaine ^Opiates ^Drug\Use ^Consequences\Economic ^Consequences\Social ^Statistics ^Consequences\Sovereignty

397. Cox, Terrence C., et al. (1983). *Drugs and Drug Abuse: A Reference Text*. Toronto, Canada: Addiction Research Foundation. A general reference text dealing with understanding drug use, classifications of drugs and how they affect the central nervous system, specific discussion of thirty-seven psychoactive drugs and twenty-nine "additional drugs of interest." Coverage ranges all the way from "morning glory seeds" to heroin, and includes a wide range of legally prescribed and illegal drugs. ^Cocaine\Pharmacology ^Heroin\Pharmacology ^Cannabis\Pharmacology ^Drug\Use

398. "Crack" (1986). *The Medical Letter on Drugs and Therapeutics* 28:718. Describes how alkaloidal cocaine is precipitated from cocaine hydrochloride, and the physiological effects that occur from smoking it. Treatment of crack addiction is difficult, in part because it is a rapidly addicting form of cocaine. It can readily cause lethal overdosage. ^Cocaine ^Crack ^Health ^Treatment ^Consequences\Physiological

399. "Cracking the Market" (1989). *The Economist*, 21 January, 58. Brief description of drug seizures in Britain, which suggest that increasing amounts of drugs are entering the country. In 1988 officers seized drugs worth a record 185 million pounds, an increase of almost 60 percent on the previous year. Figures are up from 1987 for almost all kinds of drugs: by 162 percent for cannabis, 30 percent for heroin, and 538 percent for opium. As customs barriers come down in 1992 in Britain, there may be an additional surge into the British market. ^United\Kingdom ^Cannabis ^Heroin ^Opiates ^Drug\Traffic ^Interdiction ^Statistics ^Drug\Use

400. Craig, Richard B. (1978). "La Campaña Permanente: Mexico's Antidrug Campaign." *Journal of Interamerican Studies and World Affairs* 20(2): 107–131. Gives a brief history of Mexico's nationwide antidrug effort to halt illicit cultivation, manufacture, and shipping of illicit drugs; looks at the extent of Mexico's drug problem (giving a historical perspective on it) and offers an analysis of the effects of the antidrug campaign. In halting cultivation and processing and in interdicting drug traffic, the results are ambiguous. Nevertheless, some statistical analyses suggest that the results ought to be viewed as impressive. Mexico continues to produce considerable marijuana and heroin annually, the great bulk of which is destined for the American market, and this continues to be a thorn in U.S.–Mexican relations. ^Mexico ^Cannabis ^Heroin ^Crop\Eradication ^Interdiction ^Law\Enforcement ^Drug\Control\Policies\History ^Latin\America ^Refining ^Drug\Control\Policies\Effectiveness ^Consequences\Foreign\Relations

401. ——— (1980). "Human Rights and Mexico's Antidrug Campaign." *Social Science Quarterly* 60(4): 691–701. From the many human rights charges leveled against Mexico in its antidrug campaign, four are analyzed here: the use of defoliant chemicals; failure to protect those who attack drug-related corruption; the abuse of human rights during arrest, detention, and imprisonment for narcotics violations; and the wholesale abuse of peasants during drug-related maneuvers in the countryside.

^Mexico ^Crop\Eradication ^Herbicides ^Law\Enforcement ^Consequences\Human\Rights ^Consequences\Corruption ^Consequences\Violence ^Latin\America

402. ——— (1980). "Operation Condor: Mexico's Antidrug Campaign Enters a New Era." *Journal of Interamerican Studies and World Affairs*, 22(3): 345–363. With Operation Condor, which began in 1976, the antidrug campaign included the use of defoliant chemicals. Describes the accomplishments of Operation Condor, its promise, and problems, some of the latter involving corruption of Mexico's national security forces. ^Mexico ^Drug\Control\Policies ^Law\Enforcement ^Latin\America ^Drug\Control\Policies\Effectiveness ^Consequences\Corruption ^Consequences\Political

403. ——— (1981). "Colombian Narcotics and United States-Colombian Relations." *Journal of Interamerican Studies and World Affairs* 23(3): 243–70. Analysis of Colombian–United States "narco politics" reveals a complex, delicate set of problems at international, national, and subnational levels. With this view in mind, the author examines the Colombian drug scene, Colombia's antidrug campaign, and the puzzlement in Colombia of the inconsistent and even contradictory nature of U.S. drug policies. As for internal politics, concludes that drug traffickers, their political and social liaisons, and their millions of dollars "constitute the greatest single threat to Colombian democracy since *la violencia* of the 1940s" [p. 266]. The problem cannot be solved without addressing the domestic reasons for the trafficker's success. ^Latin\America ^Colombia ^United\States ^Drug\Traffic ^Drug\Control\Policies ^Consequences\Foreign\Relations ^Traffickers ^Consequences\Social ^Consequences\Political ^Consequences\Economic ^Prevention\Development

404. ——— (1983). "Domestic Implications of Illicit Colombian Drug Production and Trafficking." *Journal of Interamerican Studies and World Affairs* 25(3): 325–350. Concentrates primarily on social and political implications of illicit narcotics traffic in Colombia. The explosive mixture of mega dollars and arms with isolation, neglect, poverty, violence, and corruption has brought serious political, economic, and social problems to the country. ^Colombia ^Drug\Traffic ^Society ^Latin\America ^Consequences\Social ^Consequences\Political

405. ——— (1985). "Illicit Drug Traffic and U.S.–Latin American Relations." *Washington Quarterly* 8 (Winter):105–34. Gives a case study of Bolivia, Peru, Colombia, and Mexico. Focuses on the domestic and foreign policy implications of drug production and trafficking. Viewed from a comparative perspective, cooperation between U.S. and Latin American drug officials has improved considerably in recent years. This derives, in part, from Latin American leaders now realizing as never before that drug trafficking and all it implies represent a threat to their own political systems. Inasmuch, however, as the principal reason for the existence of drug trafficking is United States' demand, it is clear that ultimate resolution of the problem will necessarily reside in the United States. ^Latin\America ^Bolivia ^Colombia ^Mexico ^Peru ^United\States ^Drug\Traffic ^Drug\Control\Policies ^International\Cooperation ^Production ^Consequences\Sovereignty ^Demand ^Consequences\Foreign\Relations ^Consequences\Political ^P\S\Demand\Reduction

406. ——— (1987). "Illicit Drug Traffic: Implications for South American Source Countries." *Journal of Interamerican Studies and World Affairs* 29(Summer): 1–35. Focuses on the social, economic, and political effects on producing countries of the illicit cocaine traffic. Case study approach to Bolivia, Peru, and Colombia. Governments at all levels have been corrupted, challenged, assaulted, and destabilized. Economies have been subverted by, or have become dependent upon, narco dollars. Traditional social structures have been threatened by new narcotics elite who seek to buy and intimidate their way into social respectability. Drug abuse has become a serious health problem. National images have been transformed in the eyes of the

outside world (in particular, Colombia). Analysis of the Bolivian case shows the country to be virtually swept through by dependency on drug trafficking. Upwards of half a million people are employed in the coca/cocaine industry. Bolivia, like all source nations, is now plagued by an escalating drug-abuse problem. The country is also heavily subjected to political corruption and social violence. While the Paz administration has attempted to suppress drug trafficking (more so than any other Bolivian government), the results are negligible. This implies, of course, negligible impact on the part of U.S. efforts in Bolivia. In Peru, the negative manifestations of the drug boom are exemplified by violence, corruption, and drug abuse. The Shining Path (*Sendero Luminoso*) figures into all of this in the Upper Huallaga Valley. The economic effects are most vividly seen in the frontier boomtown atmosphere of the coca growing regions. No country better epitomizes the multiple ramifications of drug trafficking for a producing or source nation than does Colombia. Socially, drug trafficking has even affected the nation's psyche. Domestic drug abuse has now become a substantial problem. Some politicians are calling for decriminalization or legalization in Colombia. The proposal has, however, not gained much support. The enormous underground or parallel economy has had multiple effects. Among these, which repeat Bolivian and Peruvian scenarios, are narco boomtowns, conspicuous consumption, no sound investment of earnings, and serious discontent when the illicit market changes, moves, or dries up. In this regard, the drug underground economy has contributed substantially to inflation and growth in Colombia's money supply; jeopardized Colombia's financial institutions and rendered precarious all forms of government economic planning; diverted large sums to suppress drug trafficking which were sorely needed elsewhere; shrunk the pool of money available for legitimate lending and raised credit rates; grossly inflated the value of land, property, goods, and services in trafficking zones and in such major cities as Cali, Barranquilla, Medellín, and Bogotá; and raised the level of corruption throughout the entire economic system to unimagined heights. Thus, the drug traffic has also affected the nation's political processes at all levels: international, national, regional, and local. ^Latin\America ^Bolivia ^Colombia ^Peru ^Coca ^Cocaine ^Drug\Traffic ^Insurgents ^Society ^Consequences\Economic ^Consequences\Political ^Consequences\Corruption ^Consequences\Social ^Consequences\Health ^Consequences\Illegal\Economy ^Consequences\Markets

407. Crawford, G. B., and Peter Reuter with K. Isaacson and P. Murphy (1988). *Simulation of Adaptive Response: A Model of Drug Interdiction.* Santa Monica, Calif.: Rand Corporation. This research note presents a simulation model of the effect of interdiction on smugglers which takes into account smugglers' adaptations to the strategies of interdiction agencies. It traces how this adaptation affects increased interdiction efforts to reduce U.S. drug consumption. It incorporates the so-called soar technique (simulation of adaptive response). ^United\States ^Interdiction ^Interdiction\Theories

408. Cregler, Louis L., and Herbert Mark (1986). "Medical Complications of Cocaine Abuse." *New England Journal of Medicine* 315(23): 1495–1500. Argues that cocaine, earlier simply a minor problem, has now emerged into a relatively major public health threat with important economic and social consequences. Cocaine abuse is addictive and produces chronic disorders with consequences that spill over into the public treasury. Argues for a national campaign to inform the public of the myths surrounding cocaine and its effects. The public should be informed as to the true dangers, which are substantial. ^Cocaine ^Drug\Use ^Health ^Society ^Consequences\Health ^Consequences\Economic ^P\S\Drug\Education

409. Cribb, Robert (1988). "Opium and the Indonesian Revolution." *Modern Asian Studies* 22(4): 701–22. Opium has long been used in the Indonesian Archipelago. In the early part of the century a government opium agency possessed a full

monopoly on the trade in the "Netherlands' Indies." The opium trade helped to fund bureaucratic expenditures. As political instability increased in Indonesia and a rebellion was at hand, the Dutch put up a trade blockade. Unable to sell previous staples such as rubber and sugar, the republic turned to opium. These opium transactions made a significant contribution to the struggle of the Indonesian Republic against the Dutch from 1945 to 1949. Opium therefore contributed to the demise of a European power in Asia. ^Southeast\Asia ^Indonesia ^Opiates ^Drug\Traffic ^Insurgents ^Opiates\History ^Production\History

410. "Crime's Link to Drugs up Steeply in 12 Years" (1988). *The New York Times*, 11 July, A12. Summarizes the Justice Department's Bureau of Justice Statistics report issued July 10, 1988, stating that crime associated with drug use has risen sharply. ^United\States ^Drug\Use ^Crime ^Statistics

411. Crooker, Richard A. (1988). "Forces of Change in the Thailand Opium Zone." *The Geographical Review* 78(3): 241–256. Description of the hill tribes in Thailand which illegally grow opium for cash income. Argues that the economic rewards are insufficient or are unsustainable given the degeneration of physical and environmental resources in the hill areas. An economic plight is impelling the hill tribes toward a "legitimate participation in the Thai economy" (p. 255). "Only pockets of opium production will exist in the near future" (p. 256). This article is developed in ecological terms, both physical and human. ^Thailand ^Opiates ^Production ^Economics ^Consequences\Environmental ^Golden\Triangle ^Southeast\Asia ^Producers ^Consequences\Economic

412. Cross, Michael (1984). "A Case for Legal Heroin." *New Scientist*, 20 September, 10–11. Aside from the addiction itself, the negative ancillary affects to society associated with heroin addiction derive from its illegality rather than from its pharmacological effects. ^Heroin ^P\S\Legalization

413. Crossette, Barbara (1987). "An Opium Warlord's News Conference Spurs Burma and Thailand to Battle Him." *The New York Times*, 22 February, 18. Describes warring opium factions in Thailand, with particular focus on one group whose trafficking has supported an armed rebellion against Burma. Burmese and Thai forces are on the attack. Khun Sa held a news conference in rebel-held territory in January 1987 in which he boasted of a bumper opium crop that was going to reap him a very large fortune. ^Burma ^Thailand ^Opiates ^Drug\Traffic ^Traffickers ^Insurgents ^Consequences\Political ^Golden\Triangle ^Southeast\Asia ^Traffickers\Private\Armies

414. —— (1987). "Thai Officials Say Laos Turns to Marijuana to Help Budget." *The New York Times*, 11 July, 2. The accusation by the Thais that the Laotian government is promoting cultivation and export of marijuana as a means to foreign exchange appears to be seconded by a number of unnamed international narcotics agents who say they believe that American crime syndicates are behind the expanding marijuana trade in the region. Poor areas in Thailand became a focus of international syndicates when some Mexican and South American sources of marijuana were curtailed as a result of crop eradication programs. Thailand denies the accusations. ^Laos ^Thailand ^Cannabis ^Production ^Golden\Triangle ^Southeast\Asia ^Consequences\Corruption ^Consequences\Drug\Control\Policies ^Consequences\Economic ^Foreign\Exchange

415. —— (1988). "Addiction Rising among Vietnamese Youth." *The New York Times*, 20 April, A15. Narcotics addiction has invaded the youth of Vietnam beyond the traditional methods of opiate consumption in Southeast Asia. ^Vietnam ^Heroin ^Opiates ^Drug\Use ^Youth ^Southeast\Asia

416. Cruze, Alvin M., Hendrick J. Harwood, Patricia Kristiansen, James J. Collins, and Dale C. Jones (1981). *Economic Cost to Society of Alcohol and Drug Abuse and Mental Illness—1977*. Research Triangle Park, N.C.:

Research Triangle Institute. Estimates the economic costs, direct and indirect, of alcohol, drug, and mental disorders, placing the combined costs at $106 billion in 1977. Of this, $49.4 billion was due to alcohol abuse and $16.4 billion to drug abuse. ^United\States ^Drug\Use ^Consequences\Economic ^Alcohol ^Statistics

417. Cuban-American National Foundation (1983). *Castro and the Narcotics Connection: The Cuban Government's Use of Narcotics Trafficking to Finance and Promote Terrorism.* Washington, D.C.: The Cuban-American National Foundation. A white paper from the Cuban-American National Foundation which shows the government of Cuba, or at least some of its higher officials, to be directly involved in the production and trafficking of narcotics with the goal of promoting addiction, crime, and corruption in, and obtaining hard currency from, the United States. ^Cuba ^Drug\Traffic ^Consequences\Foreign\Policy ^United\States ^Consequences\Corruption

418. ——— (1983). *Castro's Narcotics Trade.* Washington, D.C.: The Cuban-American National Foundation, Inc. A compilation of articles detailing what some view to be the public history of the Castro government's involvement in smuggling illegal narcotics into the United States. Sixteen articles are reproduced, ranging from *The New York Times* and *The Miami Herald* to *The New Republic. The Miami Herald* has the highest frequency of inclusion. ^Cuba ^Drug\Traffic ^Consequences\Corruption

419. Cushman, John H., Jr. (1989). "Drug Use Ruled a Cause in Plane Crash." *The New York Times*, 2 February. Traces of cocaine were found in a dead pilot's blood and urine, and investigators learned that he probably used the drug the night before the crash. While the pilot may not have used the drug during the flight, it was likely that he was fatigued after a night of drug abuse and that this somehow affected his concentration and hampered his approach to the tricky runway at Durango, Colorado. ^United\States ^Cocaine ^Drug\Use ^Consequences\Public\Safety ^Colorado ^Aircraft

420. ——— (1989). "More Private Workers to Face Drug Tests." *The New York Times*, 18 December, A16. The U.S. transportation department has tested its own employees for illegal drug use for the past two years, affecting approximately 32,000 people. Millions of employees in privately owned transportation companies will now join this group that is routinely tested. Considerable opposition has developed, but opponents do not have much hope of eliminating the testing program. ^United\States ^Drug\Testing

421. Cuskey, Walter R. (1981). "Critique of Marijuana Decriminalization Research." *Contemporary Drug Problems* 10(3): 323–34. Many controversies surround marijuana decriminalization discussions because of possible resulting changes (increase) in marijuana and other drug use following enactment of any enabling legislation. Reviews recent research on decriminalization and marijuana use in light of experiences in those American states where decriminalization statutes have been enacted. The studies show that, among certain demographic sectors, experience with marijuana has markedly increased. There are ambiguous interpretations with respect to the frequency and intensity of marijuana use. According to the studies reviewed, it appears that marijuana use, even in the context of decriminalization, may not escalate to the more serious patterns, and that social-recreational use, which involves lesser risks to the individual and to society, seems to be the rule. Nevertheless, among younger age groups, the research is somewhat indeterminate and the author calls for more precisely gauged studies to weigh the effects of more lenient laws on this group. ^United\States ^Cannabis ^Drug\Use ^Decriminalization ^Reviews ^Decriminalization\Critique ^Oregon ^Youth

422. Cutting, P. D. (1983). "The Technique of Controlled Delivery as a Weapon in Dealing with Illicit Traffic in Narcotics Drugs and Psychotropic

Substances." *Bulletin on Narcotics* 35(4): 15–22. "Controlled delivery" simply means that once a consignment of illicit drugs is detected it is followed through to its ultimate destination in order to secure evidence against organizers of the traffic. The technique merits wider use and does not involve any element of entrapment. The nature of the security required and cooperation viewed as being essential are discussed. Evidence is given of a number of important detections made as a result of speedy international cooperation. ^Law\Enforcement ^International\Cooperation ^Drug\Control\Policies

423. Czechowicz, Dorynne (1988). "Adolescent Alcohol and Drug Abuse and Its Consequences—An Overview." *American Journal of Drug and Alcohol Abuse* 14(2): 189–97. Citing the Research Triangle's report by H. J. Harwood and others entitled *Economic Costs to Society of Alcohol and Drug Abuse and Mental Illness*, the author agrees that the societal costs of drug abuse alone may be as much as $65 billion. This does not, however, take into consideration the personal and social costs of alcohol and drug abuse (including killing self and others). Is there some way that the discipline of psychiatry might intervene in a helpful way? Yes, the author argues, at least in terms of prevention and early intervention of substance-abuse problems. Psychiatrists involved in the treatment of children and youth having abnormal behavioral and emotional problems should particularly be alert to the probability that drug abuse may be a contributing factor. Intervention, however, requires close cooperation between parents, educators, primary health care providers, and drug-abuse counselors. ^Drug\Use ^Youth ^Prevention ^Treatment ^Statistics ^Consequences\Economic ^Alcohol ^Consequences\Personal

424. Dandler, Jorge (1984). "El Desarrollo de la Agricultura, Políticas Estatales y el Proceso de Acumulación en Bolivia." *Estudios Rurales Latino-americanos* 7(2): 81–149. Analysis of the impact of state policy on the development of the agricultural sector after agrarian reform, the role that agriculture and the peasantry play within the global economy, processes of capital accumulation and finance of a middle class in the country, and the ensuing capitalist expansion and social differentiation in the countryside. A small section (pp. 139–140) analyzes coca and cocaine trafficking as part of Bolivia's agricultural crisis. Estimates are given on production, prices, effects on the national economy, and the relationship of all that to the general agricultural crisis in Bolivia. ^Latin\America ^Bolivia ^Coca ^Production ^Cocaine ^Drug\Traffic ^Economics ^Agriculture ^Society ^Statistics

425. Dash, Leon (1989). "A Dealer's Rule: Be Willing to Die." *The Washington Post*, 3 April, 1. Describes the life-style of one young cocaine dealer in Washington D.C., fitting it into the context of a general social psychological orientation that breeds "meaner streets" as young people attempt to assert their manhood via the drug culture. ^United\States ^Cocaine ^Drug\Traffic ^Culture ^Washington\DC ^Consequences\Social

426. Davidson, Jean (1989). "Newborn Drug Exposure Conviction a 'Drastic' First." *The Los Angeles Times*, 31 July, 1. A cocaine-addicted mother is convicted of "delivering cocaine to her unborn child." This is considered a landmark conviction. ^United\States ^Judiciary ^Fetuses ^Women ^Law\Enforcement ^Drug\Control\Policies

427. Davis, Don DeBoau (1985). "Neurobehavioral Functions Among Children Exposed to Narcotics in Utero: A Multivariate Analysis." Ph.D. diss., California School of Professional Psychology, Fresno. Narcotic-exposed children scored significantly lower on several neuropsychological and behavioral tests administered to controlled groups of children. Moreover, these children scored significantly in the more pathological direction on several tests. The inferences from the findings are that "*in utero* narcotic exposure seems to cause pervasive neuropsychological and behavioral results, primarily in the domains of perceptual-motor, memory, spacial

relations, concentration, impulse control, feeling of well being, and general competence to interact with the environment" (p. vi). Interestingly, those children exposed to methadone maintenance programs scored in the more pathological direction than those exposed to heroin. This raises concerns about the societal and ethical implications of methadone treatment. ^Heroin ^Methadone ^Health ^Opiates ^Fetuses ^Consequences\Fetuses ^Consequences\Methadone ^Treatment\Critique

428. Davis, Patricia (1989). "Uneven Scales of Justice Tilt Drug War in Dealers' Favor; Sentences in Fairfax Case Vary Widely." *The Washington Post*, 26 February, A1. Some judges are lenient and others hard in their sentences on drug dealers. The sentencing disparity is causing problems for law enforcement agencies. ^United\States ^Law\Enforcement ^Judiciary

429. Day, Mark (1989). "Peru: Battle Intensifies over Renewed Drug Eradication Plan." *Latinamerica Press*, 7 September, 1. Currently, U.S. drug enforcement administration agents train and advise South American antidrug police. President Bush's war on drugs calls for an expansion of U.S. military aid to Colombia, Bolivia, and Peru. It is feared in the U.S. Congress that the U.S. Drug Enforcement Administration (DEA) might eventually become involved in full-scale battles with terrorist groups operating in Peru, given that the Peruvian police, with DEA funding, have constructed a fortified base at Santa Lucía in the upper Huallaga Valley. Examples of U.S. DEA agent indiscretions are noted. Failure of eradication and interdiction efforts are noted, along with experimental herbicidal applications on coca. Domestic police corruption greatly impedes efficient work. Any U.S. intervention causes the government in power to take a domestic beating from opposition leaders. ^Latin\America ^Peru ^United\States ^Coca ^Cocaine ^Crop\Eradication ^Herbicides ^Interdiction ^Politics ^Consequences\Foreign\Relations ^Insurgents ^Consequences\Corruption ^Military ^Foreign\Aid ^Bolivia ^Colombia ^DEA ^Terrorists ^Drug\Control\Policies\Critique ^Consequences\Political

430. Dealy, Glen Caudill (1977). *The Public Man: An Interpretation of Latin American and Other Catholic Countries*. Amherst: University of Massachusetts Press. Describes Latin American *caudillaje* and resulting ethos that have helped to establish religious foundations for public virtue and vice in Latin America. The relevance for this bibliography is the book's strong emphasis on the constraints that culture imposes on reform activities such as drug control programs. Offers insights into why, for example, drug cartels can be so manipulated by single personalities. ^Latin\America ^Culture

431. "DEA Smashes Leadership of Yakuza: New Wars Predicted" (1985). *Organized Crime Digest* (September): 9-10. Top leaders in the Japanese Yakuza were arrested. The arrests brought to light evidence of increased organized crime by the Japanese mafia in Hawaii and the western United States. ^United\States ^Southeast\Asia ^Japan ^Drug\Traffic ^Law\Enforcement ^Organized\Crime ^Yakuza ^Hawaii

432. *Debate Agrario: La Economía Campesina y el Cultivo de la Coca (II)* (1988). La Paz, Bolivia: Instituto Latino-Americano de Investigaciones Sociales. Summarizes the eleventh *Agrarian Debate* carried out 25 February 1988 regarding Bolivia's peasant economy and coca cultivation, a continuation of a 25 August 1987 session. Peasant producers, directors of the National Peasant Confederation, and professionals participated. The backdrop was the precipitous fall in coca leaf prices to levels at or below production costs. In a major exposition, the government's Division of Rural Development Alternatives was represented by Jorge Salinas, followed by commentaries from José Antonio Quiroga and Antonio Paz. Views of coca producers, government officials trying to reduce coca production, and the role of foreign aid were discussed. Appendices include a three-year plan for anti-narcotraffic control as well as the

final report from the government commission on coca. ^Latin\America ^Bolivia ^Coca ^Consequences\Markets ^Drug\Control\Policies\Critique ^Proffered\Solutions

433. "Decrees Boost Police Capabilities against Kingpins" (1989). *The Miami Herald*, 20 August, 18A. Describes measures that gave the military and police forces considerable capacity for action in Colombia following the assassination of Luís Carlos Galán. ^Colombia ^Law\Enforcement ^Military ^Organized\Crime ^Legislation ^Consequences\Assassination ^Consequences\Political ^Latin\America

434. Del Olmo, Rosa (1986). "Female Criminality and Drug Trafficking in Latin America: Preliminary Findings." *Studies in Third World Societies* 37: 163–178. Discusses how traditional abstinence of females from criminal activity has been compromised by both economic push and pull factors associated with the drug trade. Even in this, women are taken advantage of by men, as both pursue illegal activity in the drug trade. There is a separate section on female drug crime in Venezuela. ^Latin\America ^Venezuela ^Drug\Traffic ^Women ^Crime

435. Delaine, Bernard L. (1979). "El Cultivo de la Coca en el Chapare, una Interpretación Sociológica." La Paz, Bolivia: PRODES. Derives from his Ph.D. dissertation research (Sociology, Saint Louis University). ^Bolivia ^Coca ^Production ^Society ^Culture

436. Dembo, Richard, Max Dertke, Scott Borders, Mark Washburn, and James Schmeidler (1988). "The Relationship between Physical and Sexual Abuse and Tobacco, Alcohol, and Illicit Drug Use among Youths in a Juvenile Detention Center." *International Journal of the Addictions* 23(4): 351–378. From a study of youths in a regional detention center, conclusions permitted the following interpretation: Sexual and physical abuse to youths is significantly and positively related to their use of illicit drugs. The authors were unsure as to why this correlation existed, except to suggest that traumatizing experiences influence young people to become involved in deviant behavior. ^Drug\Use ^Youth ^Society ^Consequences\Violence

437. Deming, Angus, and John Barry (1986). "Reluctant Recruits: Drugs and the Military." *Newsweek*, 28 July, 30–31. Discusses the involvement of the U.S. military in drug interdiction programs. The enormous magnitude of the task and the apparent futility of it are noted. The U.S. military has been involved, also, in cocaine raids in Bolivia and Colombia. ^United\States ^Interdiction ^Military ^Bolivia ^Colombia ^Latin\America ^Drug\Control\Policies ^International\Cooperation ^Consequences\Foreign\Relations ^Cocaine

438. DeMott, John S. (1986). "Striking at the Source." *Time*, 28 July, 12–14. Description of U.S. aircraft carrying American advisors and Bolivian troops to do "drug battle" in Bolivia. Bolivia agreed to support the raids on cocaine processing laboratories provided the United States left the coca fields undisturbed. ^Latin\America ^Bolivia ^United\States ^Cocaine ^Coca ^Interdiction ^Military ^International\Cooperation ^Consequences\Foreign\Relations ^Drug\Control\Policies

439. DeMott, Stephen T. (1985). "Bolivia: Poor Caught between Economic Chaos and Lucrative Cocaine Trade." *Latinamerica Press*, 16 May, 3. Discussion of how hyperinflation in Bolivia in the mid-1980s affected the peasantry and contributed to pushing them into dealing in cocaine-related income activities. Relative dollar figures are given. ^Latin\America ^Bolivia ^Cocaine ^Coca ^Drug\Traffic ^Economics ^Production\Incentives\Economic ^Traffickers\Incentives\Economic

440. Dempsey, Mary (1988). "Butterflies Thwart Cocaine Barons." *New Scientist*, 4 February, 27. Notation that swarms of "scarce butterflies" have destroyed almost 20,000 hectares of illegally grown coca in Peru. The butterflies are voracious

eaters and feed exclusively on the leaves of the coca plant. Antidrug experts are trying to figure out ways to propagate the butterflies, but entomologists know very little about them. ^Latin\America ^Peru ^Coca ^Crop\Eradication ^P\S\Butterflies

441. Denenberg, Tia Schneider, and R. V. Denenberg (1983). *Alcohol and Drugs: Issues in the Workplace.* Washington, D.C.: Bureau of National Affairs. Written to help meet the need for a full discussion of industrial relations issues raised by the invasion of alcohol and drugs into the workplace. Economic losses, impacts on careers, and added economic and social externalities on business enterprises are points of departure in this book. In general, details employers' "legal rights" when they have an alcohol or drug problem on their hands. ^United\States ^Drug\Use ^Drug\Testing ^Workplace ^Alcohol ^Consequences\Economic ^Consequences\Social

442. Dennis, Richard J. (1990). "The Economics of Legalizing Drugs," *The Atlantic Monthly,* November, pp. 126–32. Constitutes a brief for legalizing drugs. Dennis looks at what the drug war costs economically and what could be saved by avoiding the war through legalization. Thus if drug consumption were legal, there would be no need to police it. Considers the most frequently raised objections to legalization and rejects them. ^P\S\Legalization ^Cocaine ^Crack ^Economics ^Drug\Control\Policies\Critique

443. Desmond, David P., and James F. Maddux (1984). "Mexican-American Heroin Addicts." *American Journal of Drug and Alcohol Abuse* 10(3): 317–346. Next to blacks, Mexican-Americans are the largest ethnic minority group among the visible heroin addict population in the United States. The contributory aspects of Mexican-American culture both in terms of addiction and treatment are noted. ^United\States ^Heroin ^Drug\Use ^Treatment ^Society ^Culture ^Minorities ^Drug\Use\Theories

444. Deustua C., Alejandro (1987). *El Narcotráfico y el Interés Nacional: Un Análisis en la Perspectiva Internacional.* Lima, Peru: Centro Peruano de Estudios Internacionales. In light of the dramatic increase in international narcotics trafficking and of the real and probable impacts, both perceptual and physical, of such traffic on Peru's international relations possibilities, what should be done? The author addresses national priorities with respect to setting a standard of international behavior and securing the security of the country in terms of its economy, territory, population, and budgets. While multilateral external relations have their problems, a reasonable multilateral approach should be taken. ^Latin\America ^Peru ^Coca ^Cocaine ^Drug\Traffic ^Drug\Control\Policies ^International\Cooperation ^Consequences\Foreign\Relations ^Proffered\Solutions ^National\Security

445. Dewar, Heather (1989). "Developer Indicted as Drug Dealer." *The Miami Herald,* 14 June, A1. A prominent "developer" in Miami is indicted for drug smuggling. "Money buys legitimacy in this community," and for this reason, no doubt, the developer, Leonel Martinez, had been honored by Dade County six months previously for his "fantastic accomplishments." One of the interesting consequences of contemporary America is that people, at least in Miami, seem to have very few questions about where an individual derives funds. ^United\States ^Drug\Traffic ^Traffickers ^Economics ^Florida ^Consequences\Social ^Consequences\Political

446. Dewar, Heather, and Lori Rozsa (1989). "Cartel Figure Arrested." *The Miami Herald,* 10 June, B1. The ingenious devices being put together by rival Colombian cartels to murder one another's principals became known in Miami when a leader was arrested on a murder plot. ^Latin\America ^Colombia ^United\States ^Drug\Traffic ^Crime ^Traffickers ^Consequences\Assassination

447. DeYoung, Karen (1985). "Britain Coming to Grips with Surge of Drug Abuse." *The Washington Post,* 20 August, A1. With a speed unpredicted and

largely unrecognized, Britain has found itself with a massive drug problem. Heroin is being used in epidemic proportions. ^United\Kingdom ^Heroin ^Drug\Use ^Prevention

448. —— (1985). "British Antidrug Drive Highlights 'Sliding Slope' of Heroin Use." *The Washington Post*, 21 August, A21. Description of Britain's "punchy antidrug drive." The target is British teens. Also, a table is given depicting seizures of heroin, cocaine, and cannabis in Britain from 1975 to 1984. ^United\Kingdom ^Cannabis ^Cocaine ^Heroin ^Interdiction ^Prevention ^Youth ^Statistics

449. Dhawan, B.N. (1987). "Drug Abuse in India: Progress in Research." In *Structure-Activity Relationships of the Cannabinoids*, NIDA Research Monograph 79, edited by Rao S. Rapaka and Alexandros Makriyannis. Rockville, Md.:National Institute on Drug Abuse. Traditionally, drug abuse in India has been different than in most of its neighboring countries. Opium abuse never became a major problem because of a well-defined governmental control policy in 1895. As there has been no ban on or control of cannabis, by definition, the problem has not risen to public purview. Heroin traffic has been low, until recently, because of India's closed borders with Pakistan. Nevertheless, recent studies suggest that there is a movement away from people's considering nonuse of drugs as a cultural norm, even in India's restrictive societies. Those mostly involved in this cultural transition or "deviation" are from the small, affluent upper socioeconomic groups. There does not appear to be counter-culture overtones or symbolic protests as a value set associated with this transformation; such as has happened in many Western societies. ^India ^Drug\Use ^Society ^Culture ^NIDA ^Drug\Use\History ^Pakistan ^Southwest\Asia ^Golden\Crescent ^Consequences\Social

450. Diehl, Jackson (1984). "Model Antidrug Drive Fails in Peru: Cocaine Business Flourishing in Special Target Area." *The Washington Post*, 29 December. Brief discussion of the United States' "model program" for reducing illegal drug supplies by having committed $30 million to an array of eradication, development, and enforcement projects in the Upper Huallaga Valley. The idea was to eliminate 35,000 acres of coca plants. The campaign was paralyzed, however, by violence, mismanagement, corruption, and resistance from the public and local authorities. Its very presence, however, encouraged leftists rebels (*Sendero Luminoso* or Shining Path) to become involved. Brief description also of Peruvian government agricultural policies and commodity prices. ^United\States ^Latin\America ^Peru ^Coca ^Drug\Control\Policies ^Drug\Control\Policies\Critique ^Crop\Eradication ^Law\Enforcement ^Prevention\Development ^Insurgents ^Agriculture ^Statistics

451. —— (1984). "U.S. Drug Crackdown Stalls in Bolivia." *The Washington Post*, 23 January. Discussion of the failure of the Reagan administration's initiative to help Bolivia control illegal cocaine distribution and coca production. The failures have derived from delays, inefficiency, and corruption. ^Bolivia ^United\States ^Latin\America ^Coca ^Cocaine ^Drug\Control\Policies\Critique ^Consequences\Corruption

452. Dillin, John (1989). "Addiction in America: Roots of U.S. Drug Crisis Run Deep." *The Christian Science Monitor*, 26 April, 7. The roots of addiction in America are found in history (a century ago narcotics were found in stores, taverns, patent medicines, and soft drinks), among physicians who constantly prescribed opiates to people (who have learned to expect, and even to demand, immediate pharmacological relief from discomfort), the counterculture movement, prosperity, social expectations of instant gratification, and popular culture (particularly portrayed by movie actors, television programs, and novels). ^United\States ^Drug\Use ^Society ^Culture ^Drug\Use\History ^Drug\Use\Theories

453. ——— (1989). "Drug Crisis Burdens Prison System." *The Christian Science Monitor*, 6 November, 6. Georgia is encountering a desperate need for more prisons because of numerous drug possession and drug trafficking arrests. Statistics are given on the Georgia prison system and its difficulties. ^United\States ^Consequences\Penal ^Georgia

454. ——— (1989). "Drug Use Dropping in Spite of City Woes, Studies Say." *The Christian Science Monitor*, 25 April, 1. In spite of all the horror stories one hears about, some statistical evidence suggests that the current drug crisis may have passed its peak. Consumption among younger people is dropping. Even crack cocaine use is declining. The improvements cut across social, economic, and racial lines. More people are shunning illegal drugs. The current violence, mayhem, and murder is the harvest of the cocaine epidemic of the late 1970s and the crack epidemic of the mid-1980s. There is a time lag between getting on cocaine and society's having to deal with its consequences. ^United\States ^Cocaine ^Crack ^Drug\Use ^Society ^Consequences\Economic ^Consequences\Social ^Statistics

455. ——— (1989). "Narco Economy: Drug Traffic Thrives along Border." *The Christian Science Monitor*, 22 December, 6. Describes the increasing incidence of crime and violence along the United States border with Mexico, associated with the drug trade. Reviews the "McAllen Report" from the United States border patrol in South Texas. Money laundering and the "underground economy" in Texas resulting from the drug trade are also noted. ^United\States ^Mexico ^Texas ^Drug\Traffic ^Consequences\Crime ^Consequences\Violence ^Money\Laundering ^Consequences\Illegal\Economy

456. ——— (1989). "Shock Incarceration, Hardship, Help for Drug Dealers." *The Christian Science Monitor*, 10 November, 7. Describes a military-like boot camp under fairly severe conditions into which young drug dealers in Georgia are placed. It is a kind of "marine-style kick-in-the-face" training that is said to turn two-thirds of offenders in the ninety-day program away from drug use and trafficking. This is a substitute for conventional prison terms. ^United\States ^Georgia ^Prevention ^Treatment\Compulsory ^P\S\Prison\Alternatives

457. ——— (1989). "South Sees Drugs as Security Issue." *The Christian Science Monitor*, 16 October, 7. Southern governors view drugs and illegal immigrants to be a substantial threat to security in their states, and therefore show a rising support for use of the military to protect their borders. This would include mobilization of national guard units where necessary. ^United\States ^Consequences\National\Security ^Drug\Traffic ^P\S\Military

458. ——— (1989). "US Wrestles with Drug Strategy." *The Christian Science Monitor*, 3 July, 8. Drug strategy will involve law enforcement, education, and treatment. Which combination or single area will the White House and Congress decide to pursue? Whatever, they must decide soon. Inasmuch as the failure of law enforcement efforts is quite clear, new approaches must be advanced. One, advanced by Mathea Falco, a former assistant secretary of state who has dealt with international narcotics problems, is outlined. ^United\States ^Drug\Control\Policies ^Law\Enforcement\Critique

459. ——— (1990). "Andeans Hooked on Drug Money." *The Christian Science Monitor*, 7 March, 7. The economic impact of the drug trade in Colombia, Peru, and Bolivia has provided rising incomes, thousands of jobs, and considerable hope in rural areas that residents can ultimately rise above the regions' grinding poverty. Statistics estimating incomes and percentage of populations involved are given. ^Latin\America ^Colombia ^Peru ^Bolivia ^Consequences\Economic ^Statistics

460. "Dirty Money: Closing Down the Launderette." (1990). *The Economist*, October 27, p. 90. It is estimated that approximately $10 billion in drug money is funnelled into Europe's financial system each year. The European Commission has proposed a mechanism that would force European community countries to pass laws against money laundering. The nature of the directive and the political commentary it has evoked are described. ^Europe ^Money\Laundering ^P\S\Legislation

461. Dixon, Alan, Barry Goldwater, Don Edwards, Paula Hawkins, William L. Dickinson, Charles E. Bennett, Dan Daniel, Mario Biaggi, Benjamin Gilman, G. William Whitehurst, Duncan L. Hunter, and Richard Ray (1986). "Should U.S. Armed Forces Play a Major Role in Interdicting Drug Traffic into the U.S.?" *Congressional Digest*, November, 266–79. The essential arguments, from a popular and public policy perspective, are raised by various congressmen who argue both for and against the proposition. ^United\States ^Interdiction ^Military

462. Dodson, Marcida (1989). "Practice Spreads; New Kind of School Test—For Drugs." *The Los Angeles Times*, 2 June, 1. Description of random tests for drugs (urinalysis) among high school athletes. ^United\States ^Drug\Testing ^Prevention\Drug\Testing

463. Doerner, William R. (1989). "The Chemical Connection." *Time*, 20 February, 44–45. Description of a seizure of nearly half a million gallons of precursor chemicals in the Colombian jungle. Where do the chemicals come from? Industrial nations supply them. ^Latin\America ^Colombia ^Cocaine ^Drug\Traffic ^Precursor\Chemicals

464. "Does This War Make Sense?" (1989). *The Economist*, 21 January, 25–27. After reviewing many of the policy issues in the drug war, the article suggests that the economic costs of America's drug habit may be somewhere between $50 and $100 billion a year. There is acknowledgement that alcoholism carries an even higher bill. Discusses the crime and violence associated with narcotics trafficking, but from a unique point of view. Argues that the price of cocaine has declined so vigorously that the supply of cocaine now outstrips demand. In the wake of this, drug dealers battle each other with submachine guns for their turf. Gangs are moving out of traditional drug trafficking centers, such as Miami, New York, and Los Angeles, in pursuit of higher profits in cities where a franchise is still available. The interdiction of cocaine and the reduction of supply are not likely to have much impact, under conditions of oversupply, in reducing associated mafia-like criminal activity. Includes graphs describing socioeconomic characteristics of drug users. ^United\States ^Cocaine ^Drug\Use ^Economics ^Society ^Drug\Control\Policies ^Crime ^Consequences\Economic ^Alcohol ^Consequences\-Crime ^Consequences\Violence ^Consequences\Markets ^Traffickers ^Florida ^New\York ^California ^Drug\Control\Policies\Critique ^Drug\Use\Theories

465. Dogoloff, Lee I. (1987). "Don't Legalize Marijuana." *The New York Times*, 1 December, A26. A letter to the editor from the Executive Director of the American Council for Drug Education points out the deleterious health effects of smoking marijuana. ^United\States ^Cannabis ^Health ^Decriminalization\Critique

466. Dolan, Edward F., Jr. (1985). *International Drug Traffic*. New York: Franklin Watts. Describes contemporary international drug traffic of cocaine, heroin, and marijuana. Where the drugs originate, how they are smuggled, and how they are distributed to users are described. Observed also are the effects of the three drugs on abusers and the social consequences (tragedies) that have resulted from abuse. This book may be described as an educational effort to acquaint people with the international drug traffic and motivate them to make some contribution towards ending it. ^Cannabis ^Cocaine ^Heroin ^Drug\Traffic ^Drug\Use ^Consequences\Social ^Consequences\Personal

467. Dombrink, John, and James W. Meeker (1986). "Beyond 'Buy and Bust': Nontraditional Sanctions in Federal Drug Law Enforcement." *Contemporary Drug Problems* 13:711–740. Discusses not only the standard forfeiture of capital and property used in drug transactions, but also the nullification of bills paid by drug money. Thus, for example, attorneys' fees paid by drug money can be forfeited. This has had some impact on attorney/client relations. ^United\States ^Asset\Forfeiture ^Attorneys

468. Dombrink, John, James W. Meeker, and Julie Paik (1988). "Fighting for Fees—Drug Trafficking and the Forfeiture of Attorney's Fees." *Journal of Drug Issues* 18(3): 421–36. Should narcotics traffickers be allowed to use the proceeds of their trade to hire expensive banks of attorneys to defend them? Government prosecutors say no; attorneys say yes. This article looks at the issues in this debate, their origin, and how they have been articulated in judicial opinions. Particular attention is given to how the impact of these developments will affect the quality of justice in major drug trafficking and organized crime cases. ^United\States ^Asset\Forfeiture ^Attorneys ^Consequences\Judiciary ^Judiciary

469. Domínguez, Jorge I. (1989). "The Crisis in Cuba's Regime." *The Miami Herald*, 9 July. With respect to the drug trafficking crisis in Cuba, what did Castro know and when did he know it? Obviously, one of the executed leaders, General Ochoa, was no minor functionary in the regime. One explanation is that drug trafficking was no issue—it was only a coverup to deal with an attempted coup. Domínguez rejects this explanation. Did Cuba use trafficking to finance arms shipments to Latin American guerrillas? There is some question on this issue. The fact that the "financing of the guerrillas" took a turn for personal enrichment of some major Cuban underlings does not, apparently, implicate Castro himself. ^Caribbean ^Cuba ^Drug\Traffic ^Consequences\Corruption ^Insurgents

470. Doria Medina, Samuel (1986). *La Economía Informal en Bolivia*. La Paz, Bolivia: Editorial Offset Boliviana. Deals with the informal economic sector in Bolivia, which is dominated by cocaine trafficking. Also addresses drug control in Bolivia. The author examines, in Chapter 4, the relationship of coca and cocaine to the underground or "informal" economy of the country. Production tables are given for coca in the Chapare, the production of cocaine, value added to coca, and capital flight associated with cocaine. The author, a Bolivian national, received his education in Bolivia, the University of Arizona, and the London School of Economics. ^Latin\America ^Bolivia ^Coca ^Cocaine ^Drug\Traffic ^Consequences\Illegal\Economy ^Drug\Control\Policies ^Production ^Statistics ^Refining ^Consequences\Economic

471. Dorn, Nicholas, and Nigel South (1986). "Criminology and Economics of Drug Distribution in Britain: Options for Control." *Journal of Drug Issues* 16(4): 523–35. Severe criticism of the explanations within the drug literature and within social policy circles for the increase in drug use in Britain that derive principally from "supply side" and "demand lead" orientations. There is offered an alternative perspective that focuses on the political economics of the irregular economy in Great Britain as the primary motor behind recent expansions in heroin use in the country. If interventions are to be successful, then they must be done in that irregular economy and can be done within the context of new trends in thinking about crime prevention and family responses. ^United\Kingdom ^Drug\Traffic ^Drug\Control\Policies ^Reviews ^Drug\Use\Theories\Critique ^Supply ^Demand ^Drug\Use\Theories ^Consequences\Illegal\Economy ^P\S\Economic

472. Dorn, Nicholas, and Nigel South, eds. (1987). *A Land Fit for Heroin? Drug Policies, Prevention and Practice*. New York: St. Martin's Press. Gives

a general overview of heroin, policies regarding the illicit use of heroin, and the consequences to families and societies resulting from both use and policy application. The empirical setting is Great Britain. Nevertheless, that analysis is placed within a world economy and is related to other Western countries. Includes a ten-page bibliography. ^United\Kingdom ^Heroin ^Drug\Use ^Drug\Control\Policies ^Consequences\Economic ^Family ^Consequences\Family ^Consequences\Social ^Bibliographies

473. Dornbush, Rhea L., and A. Kokkevi (1976). "Acute Effects of Cannabis on Cognitive, Perceptual, and Motor Performance in Chronic Hashish Users." *Annals of the New York Academy of Sciences*, 282:313–333. Describes the acute effects of marijuana in the usual measurable categories of mental functioning and time reaction among those with limited cannabis experience. The effects on chronic users are more unclear; the analysis suggests results that are not exactly parallel to the non chronic user. ^Cannabis ^Health ^Consequences\Neurological

474. Dornbush, Rhea L., Alfred M. Freedman, and Max Fink, eds. (1976). "Chronic Cannabis Use." *Annals of the New York Academy of Sciences*, 282. Explores the current data to determine whether cannabis has any specific capacity for inhibition of motivation, not possessed by other drugs (amotivation syndrome in cannabis users); whether chronic cannabis use affects mental health; whether tolerance and physical withdrawal symptoms develop in humans after chronic use of cannabis; whether, or to what extent, medical complications are associated with cannabis use. Examines behavioral and biologic aspects of marijuana use under controlled laboratory conditions; effects of cannabis on automobile driving and psychomotor tracking; whether brain damage results from long-term cannabis use; and the effects of certain kinds of policy initiatives associated with marijuana use. In this latter category, Paul Blachly discusses "Effects of Decriminalization of Marijuana in Oregon" and Robert Petersen discusses "Rationally Based Social Policy on Marijuana Usage." ^Cannabis ^Health ^Reviews ^Decriminalization ^Amotivational\Syndrome ^Consequences\Public\Safety ^Consequences\Neurological ^Consequences\Physiological ^Consequences\Psychological ^United\States ^Oregon

475. Douglas, Lorraine Jean (1987). "Perceived Family Dynamics of Cocaine Abusers, as Compared to Opiate Abusers and Non-Drug Abusers." Ph.D. Diss., University of Florida. Examines the perceived family dynamics of cocaine abusers as compared to opiate abusers and nondrug abusers. The methodology included a sample of white males, consisting of thirty cocaine abusers, thirty opiate abusers, and thirty nondrug abusers. All three groups were compared as to family history, family life cycles, and family structure. On these variables, cocaine abusers were more similar than different from opiate abusers. Both drug-abusing groups were significantly different from the nondrug-abusing group. Suggestions, based on the information, for counseling and future research are described. ^United\States ^Family ^Proffered\Solutions

476. Dreher, Melanie C. (1989). "Poor and Pregnant: Perinatal Ganja Use in Rural Jamaica." *Advances in Alcohol and Substance Abuse* 8(1): 45–54. In Jamaica, the use of ganja (cannabis) in reducing the physiological symptoms of pregnancy and associated psychological stress is frequent. This author describes the use for that purpose in relation to the sociocultural context of pregnancy in low-income, rural communities. The cultural use of marijuana under some circumstances may actually mitigate its potentially harmful effects. ^Caribbean ^Jamaica ^Cannabis ^Drug\Use ^Women ^Society ^Culture

477. Drucker, Ernest (1986). "AIDS and Addiction in New York City." *American Journal of Drug and Alcohol Abuse* 12(1&2): 165–81. Drug abusers are acquiring AIDS in epidemic proportions due to several factors: Drug users are already highly affected with the HIV virus (approximately 50 percent), and they share

needles, have sexual contact with each other, and transmit the disease to fetuses. The impact of large numbers of new cases of AIDS among addicts on the health care services of a few urban areas is creating havoc. Drucker outlines the projected dimensions of the AIDS epidemic of drug users in New York City, and posits implications for hospital utilization and local health care expenditures. Inasmuch as the present course will cause a breakdown in health care delivery, he raises the urgent need for a rapid expansion of addiction treatment services and a modification of the treatment objectives in vogue. Moral sensitivities ought not to get in the way of explicit educational programs teaching people how to use needles and have sex safely. ^United\States ^Heroin ^Health ^AIDS ^Economics ^Consequences\Health\Care ^P\S\Treatment ^New\York ^Consequences\Economic ^P\S\Needle\Exchange ^P\S\Safe\Sex

478. ——— (1987). "AIDS and Addiction in New York City, the Transformation of a Chronic Social Problem into a Public Health Catastrophe." Paper presented at Colloque SIDA, Droit ET Libertes at medicins du Monde/AIDES, Paris, France 11-12 December. Since the mid-1970s New York City has had more than 200,000 intravenous drug users, mostly poor, black and hispanic, age 25–45, residing in deteriorating inner-city communities of the Bronx, Brooklyn, and Manhattan. Approximately 50 percent of these addicts are infected with the AIDS virus. New AIDS cases can be expected at the rate of 10–15,000 per year. Communities face various consequences. At least $5 billion will be needed for medical care. At least 10,000 additional health care and social services workers will be needed. Health care facilities of some kind will have to be massively increased. Housing and child care services, already totally inadequate, will become even more so. Drug treatment centers will be overwhelmed. Already AIDS is the leading cause of death among New York women age 25–45. There is a high level infection of the HIV virus among intravenous drug users in Europe: Barcelona, 70 percent; Edinburgh, 42 percent; Bologna, 52 percent; Milan, 30 percent; Paris, 65 percent; Vienna, 35 percent; Belgrade, 48 percent. The big fear now is movement of the HIV virus, heterosexually, to wider populations. ^Austria ^France ^Italy ^Scotland ^Spain ^United\States ^Yugoslavia ^Heroin ^Health ^AIDS ^Economics ^Consequences\Health\Care ^Europe ^Women ^New\York

479. ——— (1988). "The Disease of Ignorance." *New York News Day*, 15 September, 1. The most serious AIDS risk to the adolescent population in New York City, especially young women, is related to their heterosexual behavior. Adolescents with AIDS are twice as likely as adults to be female and to have acquired the disease through heterosexual intercourse. Calls for counseling of those found to have AIDS. Wants to discover new ways to bolster young people's ability to make prudent choices about their sexual partners and gain some control over their sexual behavior. ^AIDS ^Women ^Sexuality ^Proffered\Solutions ^New\York ^Consequences\Health ^P\S\Safe\Sex

480. ——— (1989). "New York: Through the Eye of the Needle." *International Journal on Drug Policy* 1(June). Drug addiction is, among other things, a chronic disease. The public health approach to addiction is to treat it as such, and it therefore supports such things as needle-exchange programs in New York City. The law enforcement/public orientation views addiction as a crime, and therefore opposes needle-exchange programs. Describes these conflicting approaches in terms of politics and policy as played out in New York City's virtually failed needle-exchange program for heroin addicts. ^United\States ^Heroin ^Health ^AIDS ^Treatment\Public\Health\Approach ^Prevention\Needle\Exchange ^New\York ^Law\Enforcement\Critique ^Treatment\Theories

481. Drucker, Ernest, Joel Rothschild, Bridget Poust, Anitra Pivnick, Beryl Dunsmoir, and Kathleen Eric (1988). "IV Drug Users with AIDS in New York: A Study of Dependent Children, Housing and Drug Addiction

Treatment." Unpublished paper of the Department of Epidemiology and Social Medicine, Montefiore Medical Center, Albert Einstein College of Medicine, Bronx, New York City, 20 July. Case records of 174 recently diagnosed IV drug-using AIDS patients from five New York City hospitals were reviewed and social workers interviewed. The object was to gather detailed baseline data on the number, age, and custody arrangements for the patient's children, the type and stability of their housing, and their current status in drug addiction treatment programs. The data show that IV drug users with AIDS enter hospital care with profound deficits in social supports, child care arrangements, housing, and treatment of their addiction. Inasmuch as the progression of the disease, as well as more people getting it, is likely to be accentuated in future years, it can only be expected that this will place great stress on New York City's child care, housing, and drug treatment services. ^United\States ^Heroin ^Health ^AIDS ^Treatment ^Society ^New\York ^Consequences\Children

482. *Drug Abuse: The Workplace Issues* (1987). New York: AMA Membership Publications Division, American Management Association. Generally, this is a practical help volume for American business enterprises faced with drug problems and desiring, or needing, to institute drug-testing procedures to combat them. The AMA presents a survey on approaches to drug abuse in the workplace, analyzes the legal issues associated with workplace drug testing, points out the kinds of education and awareness programs commonly used, assesses various kinds of drug-testing technology, and presents a sample of company policies on illicit drugs. ^United\States ^Drug\Testing ^Drug\Testing\Laws ^Workplace

483. "Drug Mafia Could Have Killed Pardo" (1987). *Latin American Weekly Report*, 26 November, 10–11. The drug mafia in Colombia appears to be financing paramilitary death squads responsible for some murders of political leaders and activists who are opposed to the drug trade. Highly sophisticated arms and techniques are being used. ^ Latin\America ^ Colombia ^ Cocaine ^Drug\Control\Policies ^ Organized\Crime ^ Consequences\Political ^ Consequences\Violence ^ Consequences\Assassination ^ Traffickers\Private\Armies

484. "Drug Smuggling: Only Mexicans Need Apply" (1989). *Economist*, 11 March, 44. The new government of Mexico seems to be getting tough with Mexico's drug dealers. Small returns are predicted, given that perhaps one-third of the officials meant to fight drug trafficking in Mexico had, by 1985, been bribed or frightened into collaborating with the traffickers. Still, when Mr. Salinas, the new President, wants to, he can move swiftly and ruthlessly, and in several instances he has imprisoned known traffickers. ^Latin\America ^Mexico ^Drug\Traffic ^Law\Enforcement ^Consequences\Corruption ^Traffickers ^Consequences\Violence

485. "Drug Traffickers Guilty of Felony-Murder" (1985). *The Criminal Law Report*, 2 January, 2232–33. The Virginia Supreme Court held that a defendant who had supplied cocaine to a woman who died as a result of an overdose was properly found guilty of second-degree felony-murder. ^United\States ^Cocaine ^Law\Enforcement ^Judiciary ^Virginia

486. "Drugs: Goodbye, Cocaine." (1990). *The Economist*, September 8, pp. 28–33. According to the Drug Abuse Warning Network (DAWN), cocaine-related admissions to hospitals are falling. Cocaine's price has risen sharply, after having fallen for each of the past ten years. If reports about use are to be believed, demand has apparently dropped. So, how is the increase in wholesale prices to be explained, particularly given the substantial increase (e.g., 23 percent in Miami, 88 percent in Los Angeles)? It is thought that harsher law enforcement efforts account for this, reducing supplies more sharply than demand. This seems probable, given that the price of the coca leaf in

Bolivia and Peru has declined substantially. ^DAWN ^Consequences\Health ^Cocaine ^Economics ^Law\Enforcement ^Drug\Control\Policies\Effectiveness

487. "Drugs: It Doesn't Have to Be Like This" (1989). *The Economist*, 2 September, 21-24. "Colombia is fighting a war against drugs. America is losing one. The rest of the world will lose too, if its weapon is prohibition" (p. 21). ^Drug\Traffic ^P\S\Legalization

488. "Drugs: Who Pays the Bill?" (1989). *Economist*, 18 March. The tremendous costs of fighting the war against drugs are just beginning to strike home. Aside from the massive U.S. federal costs ($3-4 billion in 1988) attention is now shifting to the burden thrust on the states, cities, and counties. Hospitals, schools, public housing estates, even playgrounds are finding themselves in the front line. Schools are discovering that antidrug programs are becoming a big addition to their work. ^United\States ^Drug\Control\Policies ^Society ^Consequences\Economic ^Consequences\Misc

489. Drummond, C., G. Edwards, A. Glanz, I. Glass, P. Jackson, E. Oppenheimer, M. Sheehan, C. Taylor, and B. Thom (1987). "Rethinking Drug Policies in the Context of the Acquired Immunodeficiency Syndrome." *Bulletin on Narcotics* 39(2): 29–35. Presents a policy analysis of suggested responses to problems associated with the AIDS syndrome and drug misuse in Great Britain. Policies must aim at small multiple gains rather than at master strokes. International communication must be strengthened. The AIDS epidemic requires reexamination of the penal handling of drug misusers. Treating more patients earlier may contribute significantly to prevention strategies. Compulsory treatment or testing for the AIDS virus is not favored. The issues raised are of wider relevance than just to Great Britain. ^United\Kingdom ^Heroin ^Health ^AIDS ^Drug\Control\Policies ^Treatment ^Proffered\Solutions ^Treatment\Compulsory\Critique

490. Dunham, Michael (1983). "When the Smoke Clears." *Reason* (March): 33–36. Since marijuana was decriminalized in Alaska in 1975, have any of the dire predictions of the likely consequences been borne out? None of the most dire predictions have. No additional usage, no invasion of teenagers, no increase in automobile deaths, no reduction in study habits or productivity. There might even have been some benefits. One is the belief that casual use of marijuana does not make one a criminal. (Smuggling and sales are still illegal.) ^United\States ^Cannabis ^Decriminalization ^Alaska

491. DuPont, Robert L. (1984). *Getting Tough on Gateway Drugs: A Guide for the Family*. Washington D.C.: American Psychiatric Press, Inc. A how to book advanced as a resource for families troubled with teenage drug abuse. Aside from exploring the drug epidemic and the drug dependency syndrome, the author describes what marijuana, alcohol, and cocaine do to the body. He then explores how families can prevent and treat drug problems. ^Drug\Use ^Prevention ^Treatment ^Youth ^Family ^Proffered\Solutions

492. ——— (1989). "Never Trust Anyone under 40." *Policy Review* (Spring): 52–57. Focuses on the high costs of drug abuse to American employers, and urges a policy of random testing to deter employee use of illicit drugs in the U.S. workplace. ^United\States ^Drug\Use ^Drug\Testing ^Workplace ^Consequences\Economic ^P\S\Drug\Testing

493. DuPont, Robert L., ed. (1987). *Drug Abuse Research, an Agenda for Action*. Rockville, Md.: Institute of Behavior and Health. This report describes an ambitious goal of returning, by the year 2000, to the levels of illicit drug use characteristic of the early 1960s—the pre-epidemic levels. The report contains specific recommendations for research action, including both high-priority and longer term research agenda. The high-priority research agenda includes studies about the negative effects of drug use; treatment research; refinements of survey research to determine how much of

a drug problem there really is; prevention research; drug testing technologies; special population studies (athletes, native Americas, children, etc); evaluation research; supply reduction research; historical and cross-cultural studies; Third World drug dependence; research management. The longer term research agenda includes designer drugs, ultimate causes of substance abuse, and basic psychopharmacology. ^United\States ^Drug\Use ^P\S\Research

494. "Dutch Drug Sellers Getting Too Pushy" (1987). *The Los Angeles Times*, 21 February, 3. Drug pushers in Amsterdam's booming drug market now offer free home delivery. Police say that this is pushing the limits of official tolerance. A local courier service has advertised its wares. ^Netherlands ^Drug\Traffic ^Drug\Control\Policies ^Europe

495. Dwyer, Paula (1989). "Getting Banks to Just Say 'No.'" *Business Week*, 17 April, 16–17. A new federal probe aimed at banks, which causes them to incur substantial internal costs, "signals the start of a new era" in attacking money laundering associated with illicit drugs. For the first time the Justice Department is using the civil forfeiture laws to order banks to return money they are holding in overseas branches. Aside from a Colombian bank, Chicago's Continental Bank is also implicated. ^United\States ^Money\Laundering ^Drug\Control\Policies ^Banking\Regulations ^Asset\Forfeiture

496. Eastwood, D. A. and H. J. Pollard (1986). "Colonization and Cocaine in the Chapare, Bolivia: A Development Paradox for Colonization Theory." *Tijdschrift Voor Economishe en Sociale Geografie* 77(44): 258–68. Gives a historical and physical setting to colonization in the Chapare, where farmers moved from traditional agricultural pursuits into coca cultivation in response to international demand for cocaine. As the production of coca increases, and as the profits derived therefrom continue to become well known, both combine to serve as a stimulus to increased colonization and further coca production. Concludes that the increased production is explainable strictly from economic factors and that, therefore, crop substitution will be effective only insofar as the economics of it are attractive. Coca control measures are also reviewed. ^Latin\America ^Bolivia ^Coca ^Production ^Drug\Control\Policies ^Consequences\Migration ^Colonization ^Crop\Substitution ^P\S\Economic

497. ——— (1987). "The Accelerating Growth of Coca and Colonisation in Bolivia." *Geography* 72:165–66. Production tables are given for the Chapare in Bolivia as well as recent colonization there. ^Latin\America ^Bolivia ^Coca ^Consequences\Migration ^Colonization ^Production ^Statistics ^Production\Incentives\Economic

498. Eckl, Corina (1986). "Deterring Illegal Drug Traffic through the Tax Code." *State Legislatures* (May–June): 7-8. Arizona and Minnesota have enacted legislation that puts excise taxes on illegal drugs. Arizona requires that drug dealers purchase licenses. This allows prosecutions to be carried out on the basis of tax evasion as well as drug trafficking charges. There is concern that such laws would give the appearance of legalizing the transactions. ^United\States ^Drug\Traffic ^Drug\Control\Policies ^Arizona ^Minnesota ^P\S\Taxation

499. Edelson, Edward (1987). *Drugs & The Brain*. New York: Chelsea House Publications. Examines the effects of both beneficial and potentially damaging psychoactive drugs on the brain. Looks at the toxicology of psychotropic drugs. The book is designed for a popular audience. ^Drug\Use ^Health ^Consequences\Health

500. Edwards, Griffith, and Awni Arif, eds. (1980). *Drug Problems in the Sociocultural Context: A Basis for Policies and Programme Planning*. Public Health Papers Number 73. Geneva, Switzerland: World Health Organization. Gives case studies of sociocultural patterns of drug use and offers an analysis of the

commonalities and diversity among drug use patterns in different countries. Case studies come from the Middle East, Africa, Latin America, the Far East, and South East Asia. The degree to which these sociocultural patterns suggest variety in health care approaches is also discussed and analyzed. Finally, strategies for reducing demand for drugs, approached from the vantage of case studies, is given. Specific suggestions are given for clinical programs that treat drug abusers. ^Africa ^Southeast\Asia ^Latin\America ^Drug\Use ^Drug\Control\Policies ^Prevention ^Society ^Culture ^WHO ^United\Nations ^Drug\Use\Theories ^Middle\East ^P\S\Health\Care ^Demand ^Treatment

501. *Efectos del Narcotráfico: Temas de Política Social* (1988). La Paz, Bolivia: Editorial Offset Boliviana Ltda. Four authors contribute to the round table presentation published in this volume: José Valdivia on the social problems attached to narcotics trafficking, Eric Roth on the consumption of cocaine paste, Federico Aguiló on migration and social mobility generated by the narcotraffic, and Daniel Cabezas on the effects of narcotraffic on the health and education of people. The last 35 pages report a debate among the authors on various points raised in their expositions. ^Latin\America ^Coca ^Drug\Use ^Cocaine ^Drug\Traffic ^Drug\Control\Policies ^Migration ^Health ^Consequences\Social ^Cocaine\Paste ^Consequences\Health ^Consequences\Educational

502. Egan, Donald J., and David Owen Robinson (1979). "Cocaine: Magical Drug or Menace?" *International Journal of the Addictions* 14(2): 231–41. Reviews the evidence available as of the late 1970s concerning cocaine's physiological and psychological safety. Use of the drug may result in liver and respiratory problems and may lead to paranoid psychotic conditions. Many deficiencies in the knowledge base of the effects of this drug on the human organism exist. ^Cocaine ^Health ^Reviews ^Consequences\Health ^Consequences\Physiological ^Consequences\Psychological

503. Ehrenfeld, Rachel (1988). "Narco-Terrorism and the Cuban Connection." *Strategic Review* (Summer) 55–63. There is a war being waged against the United States. It is multifaceted, including a merger of international networks of drug traffickers and terrorist organizations. This merger and associated organization depict a well-organized web in the Western Hemisphere that embraces drug cartels and insurgent groups in Colombia; transshipment points for narcotics and arms in Nicaragua, Cuba, and Mexico; and money laundering in Panama. The network's lines of command converge in Havana. The central objective is not simply profits but the undermining of American society. The author has a doctorate in criminology from Hebrew University in Jerusalem, and has been a visiting fellow at Colombia University and the Fletcher School of Law and Diplomacy. ^Latin\America ^Colombia ^Cuba ^Mexico ^Nicaragua ^Panama ^Money\Laundering ^Drug\Traffic ^Insurgents ^Organized\Crime ^Consequences\Political ^Consequences\Social

504. Eisenlohr, L. E. S. (1981). *International Narcotics Control*. New York: Arno Press. For those interested in history and its replication, this book, first published in 1934, rehearses many of the issues and much of the organizational consideration currently in vogue today with respect to international control of narcotics. The focus of the book is, of course, on opium, but its policy ramifications are germane for other drug issues, even today. ^Opiates ^Drug\Control\Policies\History

505. Ek, Poh Geok (1984). "Denial of Passports to Drug Offenders in Singapore." *Bulletin on Narcotics* 36(3): 43–45. The immigration department maintains a register of drug offenders and refuses to issue passports to people who have a drug offense. Designed to curtail illicit drug trafficking. ^Singapore ^Law\Enforcement ^Emigration ^Southeast\Asia ^Drug\Control\Policies

506. Ekland-Olson, Sheldon, John Lieb, and Louis Zurcher (1984). "The Paradoxical Impact of Criminal Sanctions: Some Microstructural Findings."

Law and Society Review 18(2): 159–78. Field data from a longitudinal study of drug dealing reveal the importance of interpersonal networks in determining the impact of criminal sanctions. When arrests were not perceived to disrupt interpersonal networks, they were viewed quite casually. If, on the other hand, interpersonal networks could be disrupted by arrests, arrests were avoided nearly at all costs. Thus the perceived severity of sanctions is in large measure tied to the degree of interpersonal disruption caused by the sanctioning process. Placing criminal sanctions into a social complex and noting network tolerance for them improves the analysis of appropriate law enforcement policies and priorities. Forcing "network closure" reduces some criminal activity that otherwise would occur. Thus one may speak of "situational law enforcement." ^Traffickers ^Law\Enforcement ^Society ^Crime ^Drug\Control\Policies\Effectiveness

507. *El Problema Actual de la Coca en la Sociedad Peruana: Diferentes Enfoques* (1979). Lima: Centro de Investigaciones Socio-Económicas, Taller de Coyuntura Agraria, Universidad Nacional Agraria. Discusses cocaine habits and control of narcotics in Peru. As world attention began to focus on Peruvian coca production, and as the possibility of internationally supported eradication efforts was discussed, intellectuals at various Peruvian universities began to explore the implications of such a move and/or its desirability. This book is a compendium of numerous contributions. ^Latin\America ^Peru ^Coca ^Drug\Control\Policies ^Production ^Crop\Eradication ^Consequences\Social ^Consequences\Political ^Consequences\Economic

508. Elliott, Delbert S., David Huizinga, and Suzanne S. Ageton (1982). *Explaining Delinquency and Drug Use*. Boulder, Colo.: Behavioral Research Institute. Presents an explanatory model that builds upon and synthesizes traditional "strain, social control, and social learning" perspectives, bringing them together into a single model that the authors believe account for delinquent behavior and drug use. While the explanatory model was initially developed to account for delinquent behavior, the authors investigated its utility for explaining drug-using behavior as well. The study also notes implications for treatment and practice. Not surprisingly, the authors found that a critical role is played by adolescent peer group pressure in determining whether one adopts delinquent behavior. They note, however, that "even a cursory review of current prevention and treatment strategies reveals that the peer friendship network has been all but ignored as a specific target for intervention" (p. 148). They thus argue for intervention at the peer group level. ^Drug\Use ^Prevention ^Youth ^Society ^Crime\Theories ^Drug\Use\Theories ^Prevention\Peers ^P\S\Peers

509. Emmelkamp, Paul M. G., and Harry Heeres (1988). "Drug Addiction and Parental Rearing Style: A Controlled Study." *International Journal of the Addictions* 23(2): 207–16. Based on a study of 43 multiple drug addicts and 111 control subjects, a psychometric instrument known as EMBU was used to assess parental attitudes and rearing behaviors. Three variables associated with drug use among adolescents emerged with high correlations: rejection, lack of emotional warmth, and overprotection. The most striking correlations were for paternal rejection and lack of paternal emotional warmth. ^Drug\Use ^Youth ^Society ^Family ^Drug\Use\Theories

510. Engelberg, Stephen (1988). "U.S. Said to Ignore Noriega Drug Role." *The New York Times*, 5 April, A1. Another in the series of articles pointing out the conflict of goals between some foreign policy objectives and drug traffic interdiction. It is said here that General Noriega was seen, by the Reagan administration, as being vital to the Contras, and for that reason was pretty much left alone. ^Panama ^United\States ^Drug\Control\Policies ^Politics ^Consequences\Foreign\Policy ^Contras ^Traffickers

511. Epstein, Edward Jay (1977). *Agency of Fear: Opiates and Political Power in America*. New York: Putnam. Some American politicians (including Nelson Rockefeller and Richard Nixon) both used and manipulated the public's concern over drug-related criminality to advance their own political causes and to increasingly bring into existence what, by Nixon's time, could be termed nothing other than a secret police. The author concludes that this thesis better explains the Nixon crusades than any other extant theory. Copious details are presented. The book is, therefore, more a story about intrigue and influence in U.S. government than it is a focus on narcotics. Narcotics simply was a means to a political end that a number of important politicians used. Epstein documents the catastrophic consequences of some of those means. ^United\States ^Opiates ^Drug\Control\Policies ^Drug\Control\Policies\Critique ^Drug\Control\Policies\Theories ^Consequences\Political

512. Epstein, Nadine (1988). "US Border Agents Charged with Rights Abuse: Customs, INS Forces Walk Legal Tightrope in Bid to Catch Illegals and Drug Smugglers." *The Christian Science Monitor*, 13 April, 1. How much and what kind of interdiction may be done at the borders is a difficult matter to determine in practice. Aside from many opinions about what is proper, any aggressive interdiction efforts open border agents to charges of abuse of authority. ^United\States ^Drug\Traffic ^Law\Enforcement ^Immigration ^Customs ^Consequences\Human\Rights ^Law\Enforcement\Critique ^Consequences\Constitutional

513. Erickson, Patricia G., et al (1987). *The Steel Drug: Cocaine in Perspective*. Lexington, Mass.: Lexington Books. Discusses cocaine habits in the United States and Canada, drug-abuse surveys in the United States and Canada, and control of narcotics in the United States. Gives a historical perspective on cocaine and shows how cocaine has been, and now is, tied up in "popular culture"—music, literature, comics, newspapers, magazines, movies, and television. Explores recent trends and current use of cocaine and then presents an empirical study of cocaine use within a community. Case histories are given. The empirical study included 111 cocaine users. Much of the focus is on Canada. There is an overview of Canada's cocaine laws and the extent of their enforcement. The following policy concerns flow from this study. Legal policy and deterrents: It is highly unlikely that attacks on supply will be successful. We are left, therefore, to consider the problem of demand reduction, which, essentially, boils down to coercion or persuasion. The existence of severe penalties does not, of itself, discourage use. It is only the credibility of their application. That application is not nearly credible enough to be much of a negative persuasive force. Beyond this there are many costs. The criminalization of users and the associated stigma, the financial costs of operating the criminal justice machinery, and the interference with personal rights of freedoms mount up under a system of total prohibition. Education strategies, on the other hand, aimed at reducing the demand for cocaine, involve much lower social costs and fewer adverse individual consequences to users. A basic premise is that the actual risks of infrequent cocaine use have been exaggerated in the media. This appears to be more true for Canada than for the United States. But, the potential risks are serious enough to justify concern without resorting to hyperbole. It is best never to try the drug, and educational efforts ought to be launched in that vein. Educational efforts to reduce demand are the most feasible and financially defensible approaches. The objective would be to increase awareness of the real risks of cocaine and thus counter its image of being safe and glamorous. Extensive bibliography. ^Canada ^United\States ^Cocaine ^Drug\Use ^Drug\Control\Policies ^Drug\Use\Critique ^Bibliographies ^Cocaine\History ^Statistics ^Demand ^Law\Enforcement\Critique ^Consequences\Human\Rights

514. Erlanger, Steven (1988). "Burma's Unrest and Weather Help Opium Flourish." *The New York Times*, 11 December, 21. The Burmese government's preoccupation with internal political dissent, and the best opium growing weather conditions in many years, have combined to produce a bumper crop of opium poppies. Production statistics and involvement of international agencies are listed. ^Southeast\Asia ^Burma ^Production ^Statistics

515. ———— (1989). "In Malaysia and Singapore, a Mixed Drug Picture." *The New York Times*, 15 December, A6. Malaysia and Singapore have intensive antidrug consumption efforts that include education, advertising, testing, rehabilitation, harsh mandatory penalties, and even the death penalty for possession of relatively small amounts. Nevertheless, drug use appears to be increasing in Malaysia and shows only a minor decline in Singapore. Amsterdam, which takes the opposite approach, appears to be experiencing a decline in addiction and related ills. Discussion of whether the "harsh treatment" is really a productive drug control policy. ^Southeast\Asia ^Malaysia ^Singapore ^Drug\Control\Policies\Critique ^Netherlands ^Drug\Use

516. Fahlman, Robert C., Shelley A. Keele, and Rodney T. Stamler (1985). "The Current Drug Situation in Canada." *The Police Chief* (October): 77-79. Description of the demographic and financial statistics associated with heroin, cocaine, cannabis, and other chemical drugs. Notes given on international cooperation, education, and prevention programs. ^Canada ^Cannabis ^Cocaine ^Heroin ^Drug\Use ^Drug\Control\Policies ^International\Cooperation ^Prevention ^Statistics ^Consequences\Economic

517. Faith, Karlene (1981). "Drug Addiction: From a Study of Women and Criminal Justice." Ph.D. diss., University of California, Santa Cruz. The author spent three years interviewing prisoners in the California Institution for Women. Upward of 75 percent of all inmates had a history of drug abuse. Alcohol, marijuana, cocaine, heroin, and prescription drugs are analyzed with respect to the lives of these women. Analysis includes the economics of the legal and illegal drug industries, and considers violence relative to specific drugs. Treatment programs for drug offenders are reviewed, with the conclusion that punishment and rehabilitation are mutually antagonistic approaches to the drug problem. The reasons for drug addiction are global in scope, affected by economic, political, and social factors. Thus individual punishment within the context of a criminal justice system or individual treatment excised from the patient's relationship to society cannot be the solution. ^United\States ^Drug\Use ^Law\Enforcement ^Treatment ^Women ^California ^Alcohol ^Cocaine ^Cannabis ^Heroin ^Consequences\Pharmacological ^Treatment\Critique ^Drug\Use\Theories ^Drug\Control\Policies\Critique

518. Fajardo Sainz, Humberto (1984). *La Herencia de la Coca: Pasado y Presente de la Cocaína: Estudio sobre la Coca y Su Influencia en el Desarrollo Psico-físico, Social y Económico del Hombre de los Andes Bolivianos*. La Paz, Bolivia: Universo. History of coca and cocaine use in Bolivia. The Bolivian author reflects on the influence that coca has had in the physical, psychological, social, and economic development of Andean Bolivians. Views coca and cocaine as being public enemy number one in Bolivia. Considers Bolivia to have been caught up in its embraces innocently. Power and American dollars are what drive the industry in Bolivia, and one of the effects has been a "social decomposition" in the country. ^Latin\America ^United\States ^Bolivia ^Coca ^Cocaine\History ^Drug\Use\History ^Consequences\Economic ^Consequences\Social ^Consequences\Political ^Consequences\Psychological ^Consequences\Physiological ^Demand

519. Farag, Sami Assaad (1980). "The Role of the General Administration in Drug Abuse Control in Egypt." *Bulletin on Narcotics* 32(1): 27–31. Aside from giving a historical backdrop, the author discusses the reduction of illicit drug

demand in Egypt and the specific measures taken to accomplish it. ^Egypt ^Drug\Control\Policies\History ^Middle\East ^Demand

520. Faupel, Charles E. (1986). "Heroin Use, Street Crime, and the 'Main Hustle': Implications for the Validity of Official Crime Data." *Deviant Behavior* 7:31–45. Using intensive live history interviews with thirty hard-core heroin addict-criminals, the author develops a notion of "criminal specialization" with a development of enhanced corollary skills that largely remove the addicts criminal activity from police detection. Occasionally, addicts will drift into nonspecialized criminal activities for which they have reduced skills and it is under these circumstances that the predominant police arrests occur. Accordingly, the validity of official criminal records as indicators of criminal histories among addict populations is heavily called into question. ^Heroin ^Crime ^Statistics\Critique

521. Faupel, Charles E., and Carl B. Klockars (1987). "Drugs-Crime Connections: Elaborations from the Life Histories of Hard-Core Heroin Addicts." *Social Problems* 34(1): 54–68. It has been alleged that crime is related to heroin addiction for two reasons: Heroin addicts are under a heavy financial burden to support their habits, which must be subsidized in ways beyond normal legal means; and, once into the criminal subculture which distributes heroin, criminal solutions are facilitated and encouraged in order to finance heroin addiction. The thirty-two life history interviews reported in this study suggest that both hypotheses are true for only certain periods in addicts' careers, while at other times the causal dynamics or assumed causal dynamics are neutralized or reversed. Research suggests that successful treatment will require provisions for an alternative life structure that gives rewards for conventional behavior and removes individuals from the network of criminality. ^Heroin ^Crime ^Treatment ^Crime\Theories ^P\S\Rehabilitation

522. Fawzy, Fawzy I., Robert H. Coombs, Judith M. Simon, and Mary Bowman-Terrell (1987). "Family Composition, Socioeconomic Status, and Adolescent Substance Use." *Addictive Behaviors* 12:79–83. Children of professionals in the sample were more likely to abstain from drug use than were children of managers or foremen. "A possible explanation for this result is that occupation may somehow be related to parental style. The common sense assumption that parental absence and economic hardship are directly responsible for youth substance use is unsupported by [their] data." ^Drug\Use\Theories ^Youth ^Society ^Family ^Parenting

523. *Federal Strategy for Prevention of Drug Abuse and Drug Trafficking* (1982). Drug Abuse Policy Office, Office of Policy Development, the White House. This document lays out President Ronald Reagan's program. It discusses international cooperation, drug law enforcement, education and prevention, detoxification and treatment, research, and drug and alcohol abuse in the armed forces. ^United\States ^Drug\Control\Policies

524. Fein, Esther B. (1989). "Soviets Confront Growers." *The New York Times*, 5 August, 4. Areas in Southwest Russia where poppy growing has developed into a serious business are Turkmenia and immediately surrounding border provinces. Poppy and hemp growing sites discovered by the authorities in Soviet Turkmenia jumped from approximately 35 in 1985 to over 200 in 1987. A slight decrease was noted for 1988. Describes the antidrug enforcement efforts in the region, including activities in Soviet prisons. ^USSR ^Cannabis ^Opiates ^Production ^Drug\Control\Policies

525. Feldman, Paul (1987). "Drug-Peddling Street Gang Holds Neighborhood in Fear." *The Los Angeles Times*, 16 November. Description of what happens to a neighborhood when street gangs peddling their drugs move in. "I feel like

I'm jailing my tenants to protect them from the kids outside," said one apartment owner who had just doubled the height of his perimeter fence to twelve feet. Despite such precautions, muggings, murders, and other uncivil activities abound. ^United\States ^Drug\Traffic ^Organized\Crime ^Crime ^Consequences\Crime ^Consequences\Social ^Consequences\Violence

526. Feldmann, Linda (1988). "Hearings Tie Noriega to Contras and Drugs; Panamanian Bases Used for Contra Training." *The Christian Science Monitor*, 11 February, 3. Reviews congressional hearings that not only link Noriega to drug trafficking but also show how the drug mafias have penetrated U.S. intelligence and other agencies. Noriega's extravagant life-style is mentioned. ^Panama ^Drug\Traffic ^Traffickers ^Contras ^Consequences\Political

527. —— (1989). "Bush Approach Seen by Many as Best by Default." *The Christian Science Monitor*, 1 September, 1. While the Bush initiative, which also concentrates on demand at home, is given many positive comments, there are several potential pitfalls: The military-oriented approach could enhance the Colombian military's ability to increase human rights violations; some elements of the military are thought to be in league with the drug traffickers; and beefing up the military could further weaken the state and throw the civilian military balance further out of line. Colombia may be pushed into attempting to co-opt the drug lords. ^Colombia ^United\States ^Consequences\Human\Rights^Drug\Control\Policies ^Consequences\Political ^Consequences\Foreign\Relations ^Consequences\Corruption ^Military ^Demand

528. —— (1989). "Multinational Drug Force Proposed." *The Christian Science Monitor*, 19 June, 6. Discusses the proposal from Jamaican Prime Minister Michael Manley to create a multinational antidrug strike force. A Peruvian diplomat's response was: "The only country that could give equipment is the U.S. And if you send in troops for drugs, you could start sending troops for other things." ^Military ^Jamaica ^P\S\Militarization ^Peru ^Caribbean ^Latin\America

529. Felman, James, and Christopher J. Petrini (1988). "Drug Testing and Public Employment: Toward a Rational Application of the Fourth Amendment." *Law and Contemporary Problems* 51(1): 253–297. If mandatory drug testing is upheld as being constitutional, this will represent "an unfortunate chapter in the fourth amendment chronicle." Individual interests will have been subordinated to social interests to a greater degree than ever before. Drug testing is a highly intrusive bodily search that invades reasonable privacy rights. ^United\States ^Drug\Testing\Critique ^Consequences\Constitutional

530. Fialka, John J. (1986). "Death of US Agent in Mexico Drug Case Uncovers Grid of Graft." *The Wall Street Journal*, 19 November, 1. Police at all levels profited from the trade in marijuana, some of them accumulating huge assets. Describes the work of Enrique Camarena and the particulars surrounding his execution by drug traffickers. Describes how trafficker Caro Quintero bought his own release from Mexican custody. ^Mexico ^Cannabis ^Law\Enforcement ^Consequences\Corruption ^Consequences\Violence ^Traffickers ^Consequences\Political

531. —— (1986). "How the Mexican Trail in Drug Agent's Death Yields Cache of 'Crack.'" *The Wall Street Journal*, 20 November, 1. Continuation of details on the Enrique Camarena case in Mexico and the involvement of Caro Quintero in that case as well as in the wholesale corruption of the Mexican law enforcement system. ^Mexico ^Cocaine ^Crack ^Law\Enforcement ^Consequences\Violence ^Consequences\Political ^Consequences\Corruption ^Traffickers

532. Fichenburg, Robert G. (1989). "Legalization May Resurface If Bush's Drug Fight Fails." *The Salt Lake Tribune*, 12 September. Suggests the rationale

that will be used in the event the Bush war on drugs fails to produce reduction in consumption. Argues against an element of that rationale—legalization—because, contrary to our history with liquor, comparisons with prohibition and usage cease when one considers that drugs are not merely automatically addictive, they automatically damage if not destroy the lives of every user. Thus legalization would not solve the underlying problems. ^United\States ^Decriminalization ^Demand ^Decriminalization\Critique

533. Fields, Allen B. (1984). "Slinging Weed." *Urban Life* 13(2-3): 247–70. Discussion of dealers at the lower levels of the illicit market, principally black youth. Examines activities of young black dealers who regularly sell marijuana on the street in low-income black communities. The different levels and types of dealers and their various strategies and tactics are discussed. ^United\States ^Cannabis ^Drug\Traffic ^Youth ^Minorities ^Traffickers

534. *The Fight against the Drug Traffic in Colombia* (1988). Office of the President of the Republic. This volume may be viewed as an official White Paper from the Colombian government regarding that country's antidrug activities and the results that have been attained. The extradition treaty problems are raised for particular review. The focus is on both marijuana and cocaine. ^Latin\America ^Colombia ^Drug\Control\Policies ^Extradition ^Cannabis ^Cocaine

535. "Fighting the Drug War" (1989). *The Christian Science Monitor*, 1 September, 20. Half of homicides are drug related; half of those are related to crack. All of this causes Jack Kemp, secretary of HUD, to argue that the true crisis is not just one of authority, but of values. Harvard's Robert Coles calls it a moral and spiritual crisis brought on by the bleakness and emptiness of a conventional, material sense of life. At some point, the editorial argues, Americans are going to have to end their drug dependency if demand is to be reduced. ^United\States ^Drug\Use ^Society ^Values ^Consequences\Violence ^Demand ^Consequences\Social

536. Fiks, Kathleen B., Helen L. Johnson, and Tove S. Rosen (1985). "Methadone-Maintained Mothers: 3-Year Follow-up of Parental Functioning." *International Journal of the Addictions* 20(5): 651–60. There is a statistically significant relationship showing that methadone mothers require more assistance in parenting, are more isolated socially, and are less likely to pursue vocational and educational activities. There is also high risk exposure to fetuses. ^Heroin ^Treatment ^Methadone ^Women ^Parenting ^Health ^Fetuses ^Consequences\Fetuses

537. Fineman, Mark (1988). "Afghan Accord May Boost Heroin Trade." *The Los Angeles Times*, 16 July, 5. With the withdrawal of Soviet troops from war-torn Afghanistan, and with the accompanying economic decay likely to result, both the growing of opium poppies and the trafficking in heroin through Afghanistan will likely substantially increase. "As long as there is a lack of government control, you'll have a lot of opium." Tonnage estimates are given. ^Middle\East ^Afghanistan ^USSR ^Golden\Crescent ^Heroin ^Drug\Traffic ^Opiates ^Production ^Consequences\Political

538. Finnegan, Loretta P. and Ronald J. Wapner (1988). "Narcotic Addiction in Pregnancy." In *Drug Use in Pregnancy*, edited by Jennifer R. Niebyl, 203–22. Philadelphia: LEA and Febiger. General review of clinical conditions associated with narcotic addiction in pregnancy; designed for use by medical personnel who need to be informed about treatment and recognition of problems. ^Drug\Use ^Women ^Pregnancy ^Reviews ^Consequences\Personal

539. Fischman, Marian W. and Charles R. Schuster (1983). "Cocaine Self-Administration in Humans." *Psychopharmacology Bulletin* 19(4):772–73. "Knowing cocaine to be a potent reinforcer in animals, the authors set up an experiment

to see whether this would also be true for humans. An unspecified number of subjects were allowed to choose between I.V. doses of cocaine and saline during ten two-hour sessions for two weeks. Doses ranged from 4 to 32 mg. Records were kept of drug choice, heart rate, blood pressure, subjective effects, and plasma levels. The majority (percentage unspecified) preferred cocaine, even at the low doses which did not affect heart rate, blood pressure, or measures of subjective effects. The preference for cocaine did not decline over the session. Therefore, cocaine appears to be a potent reinforcer for humans as well as animals." [Quotation is from Anglin, *Cocaine*, entry #105] ^Cocaine ^Drug\Use ^Health ^Consequences\Personal

540. Fisher, Kevin (1984). "Trends in Extraterritorial Narcotics Control: Slamming the Stable Door after the Horse Has Bolted." *New York University Journal of International Law and Politics* 16:353–413. The United States has focused on law enforcement solutions to drug control problems in producing countries. Several approaches to criminal prosecution and crop eradication have resulted. Additional leverage could be acquired by using U.S. foreign aid. Describes the origins of the law enforcement perspective (including the U.S.-Turkey bi-lateral agreements, United Nation's efforts in the 1970s, the Mexican experiments, and efforts in other countries, the transition from aid leveraging to law enforcement in the Carter administration); the escalation of the law enforcement approach during the Reagan Administration (using U.S. laws to prosecute foreign nationals, seizure of assets of foreign traffickers, shifting narcotics control to military and intelligence agencies). The author recommends that U.S. assistance be advanced to foreign governments that enforce their own narcotics laws. Issues discussed include crop substitution and law enforcement assistance. Extensively documented. ^ United\States ^ Drug\Control\Policies ^ Crop\Substitution ^ Law\Enforcement ^ Drug\Control\Policies\History ^ P\S\Foreign\Aid ^ Drug\Control\Policies\Critique ^ Middle\East ^ International\Cooperation\History ^ Turkey ^ Mexico ^ United\Nations ^ Latin\America

541. Fishman, H. Charles (1982). "A Family Approach to Marijuana Use." In *Marijuana and Youth: Clinical Observations on Motivation and Learning.* Rockville, Md.: National Institute on Mental Health. Argues that focusing on marijuana and not the interpersonal difficulties that maintain it as a serious problem is to fall into the trap of seeing the symptom and ignoring the systemic dysfunction (within a family) that accompanies it. ^Cannabis ^Drug\Use ^Treatment ^Society ^Family ^Drug\Control\Policies\Critique

542. Fitzgerald, William M. (1984). "The Constitutionality of the Canine Sniff Search: From Katz to Dogs." *Marquette Law Review* 68(27): 57–92. Discussion of contradictory rulings within the U.S. judicial system regarding the constitutionality of searches for narcotics. ^United\States ^Interdiction ^Politics ^Judiciary ^Consequences\Constitutional

543. Flatte, Michael, and Alexei J. Cowett (1986). "Drugs and Politics: An Unhealthy Mix." *Harvard International Review* (January-February): 29–31. Just as individuals may become addicted to drugs, so also may nations. That is the case of Colombia and Bolivia. Economics, politics, and corruption are discussed. ^Colombia ^Bolivia ^Cannabis ^Cocaine ^Drug\Traffic ^Consequences\Economic ^Consequences\Social ^Consequences\Political

544. Flax, Steven (1985). "The Executive Addict." *Fortune*, 24 June, 24–31. A general description of the involvement of increasing numbers of U.S. company executives in the consumption of illicit drugs. Suggestions are given on "how to help rescue a drug-impaired executive." Significant costs for U.S. business. ^United\States ^Drug\Use ^Workplace ^Consequences\Economic ^Proffered\Solutions

545. Flores, Gonzalo, and José Blanes (1984). *¿Adónde Vá el Chapare?* Cochabamba, Bolivia: CERES. From a social/economic survey on-site in the Chapare, the authors have produced a volume that examines social relations there and the basic structures underlying them. While it is based on social science surveys, it is not written for specialists, but rather for the interested informed citizen who is concerned about what is happening in the Chapare. Examines the phenomenal impact of the coca/cocaine economy on the region and shows how this has transformed the relationship of the region with other valleys and affected processes of population expansion and change, the use of land, migration, and syndicalism. The data gathered are basically from family situations—noting basic socioeconomic characteristics, land use patterns, agricultural production, how agricultural work is organized, the relationship of the population to the various zones of their origin, marketing, and other aspects. Various policy options are discussed respecting what might be done with the Chapare. Given the powerful drug factor, hardly anything but state plans could be implemented. Because the predominant interest of the colonizers is in the cultivation of coca, and given the persistent presence of narcotrafficking, state initiatives will appear less and less viable. The state, pressed between fear and impotence, will see itself obligated to leave a space of land untouched for narcotraffic, giving it, in effect, legitimacy, impunity, and silence.
^Bolivia ^Coca ^Drug\Traffic ^Economics ^Society ^Latin\America ^Consequences\Social ^Consequences\Economic ^Consequences\Political ^Consequences\Migration ^Agriculture ^Consequences\State\Authority ^Drug\Control\Policies ^Colonization ^Consequences\Markets

546. Flynn, Sean, and Padraig Yeates (1985). *Smack: The Criminal Drugs Racket in Ireland*. Ireland: Gill and Macmillan Ltd. Investigative reporters look into the development of the drug traffic in Ireland, the operations of the police and judicial systems in response, and the degree to which institutional interests and societal interests have been compromised by money and violence. ^Ireland ^Drug\Traffic ^Drug\Control\Policies ^Law\Enforcement ^Consequences\Political ^Consequences\Corruption ^Consequences\Social

547. Forno, Joseph J., Richard T. Young, and Cynthia Levitt (1981). "Cocaine Abuse—The Evolution from Coca Leaves to Freebase." *Journal of Drug Education* 11(4): 311–15. The article describes historical and sociological patterns of cocaine use, with people continually experimenting in ways to produce enhanced euphoria. The use of cocaine freebase is described, as are the consequences of its use. ^Cocaine ^Drug\Use\History ^Consequences\Health

548. Foronda, Erick (1988). "Bolivia: Military Exposé Attests Official Protection of Druglords." *Latinamerica Press*, 25 February, 1. A former Bolivian naval officer has given testimony, with extensive documentation, of extensive police and military protection of the country's illegal drug manufacturers. Three days later, six unidentified persons machine gunned the man's home. It has been said that the Bolivian congress now has, for the first time, the documents it needs to "lift the veil that so generously has been provided to protect the drug trafficker's network." ^Latin\America ^Bolivia ^Cocaine ^Drug\Traffic ^Military ^Consequences\Political ^Consequences\Corruption ^Consequences\Violence ^Consequences\Human\Rights

549. ——— (1989). "Number of Street Kids Grows as Bolivian Economy Worsens." *Latinamerica Press*, 2 February. Thousands of children are flocking into La Paz, Bolivia, in search of food and money. A brief description of the economic conditions and incentives for street children are given. A growing concern of those working with street children is their propensity for using drugs. ^Latin\America ^Bolivia ^Drug\Use ^Youth ^Consequences\Migration ^Consequences\Children

550. "43 Nations Sign U.N. Pact on Fighting Drugs" (1988). *The Los Angeles Times*, 21 December, 9. The Convention against Illicit Traffic in Narcotic Drugs and Psychotropic Substances will better enable nations to freeze and confiscate bank accounts and extradite suspects. The convention must now be ratified by respective countries' parliaments. Once ratified, the convention would supplement the 1961 and 1971 UN conventions. ^United\Nations ^International\Cooperation ^Asset\Forfeiture ^Extradition

551. Foster, Catherine (1989). "'Grass Tax' Aims for Dealers' Wallets." *The Christian Science Monitor*, 11 August, 8. Description of the policies in a number of states requiring dealers to pay a stamp tax on their illegal drugs. The ability to expedite property seizures is discussed. ^United\States ^Cannabis ^Drug\Traffic ^Drug\Control\Policies ^P\S\Taxation

552. ——— (1989). "War on Drugs: States Get Tough on 'Casual Users.'" *The Christian Science Monitor*, 21 December, 7. Several states in the United States are devising ways to hold drug users accountable in ways that do not involve placing them in jail. These include suspension of drivers licenses, fines, compulsory specialized outpatient treatment programs, and making public the names of people who are arrested. States discussed are Maryland, Massachusetts, New Jersey, Michigan, and Arizona. ^United\States ^Drug\Control\Policies ^Consequences\Penal ^Maryland ^Massachusetts ^New\Jersey ^Michigan ^Arizona

553. Foster, Harold E. (1989). "The Drug-Debt Link." *The Christian Science Monitor*, 15 November, 19. Producing countries could see their democratic institutions fall victim to the pressures of debt and drugs under conditions in which the drug traffickers themselves could overturn political and social institutions. ^International\Debt ^Production ^Traffickers ^Consequences\Political ^Consequences\Social

554. "4,000 Held in Soviet Union in Drug Crackdown" (1987). *The New York Times*, 7 January, A10. Russia is having its own problems with increased drug abuse. A police sweep resulted in the arrest of 300 drug traffickers and 4,000 narcotics producers. Drug abuse can no longer, one official said, be castigated as an exclusive practice of capitalist countries. ^USSR ^Law\Enforcement ^Drug\Use

555. Frank, Allan Dodds (1986). "See No Evil." *Forbes*, 6 October, 38. Discussion of how the federal reserve system itself may unwittingly be involved in laundering drug money in ways that involve the most respectable banks. Description of how drug dealers hide their cash. ^United\States ^Money\Laundering ^Banking\Regulations

556. ——— (1988). "Unwelcome Side Effects from Peace in Afghanistan." *Forbes*, 8 August, 34. The war in Afghanistan disrupted some of the trade in heroin. It now appears that smokeable heroin is being made available through Afghanistan and may position itself competitively in the market with crack and cocaine. ^Afghanistan ^Heroin ^Drug\Traffic ^Middle\East ^Consequences\Markets ^Golden\Crescent

557. Fraser, Mark and Nance Kohlert (1988). "Substance Abuse and Public Policy." *Social Service Review* (March): 103–126. Evaluation is made of five drug control strategies employed by the United States—foreign crop eradication, border interdiction, deterrence, treatment, and prevention. The authors conclude that U.S. policy is misguided in that it has been directed by long-standing and insupportable beliefs that supply-side intervention such as eradication and interdiction will, in effect, do the job. So what should be done? Policy must be formulated that focuses on eradicating the experimentation with and use of illicit substances. Second, the demand side must be more vigorously attacked. Programs strengthening informal social controls, that build infrastructure in high risk neighborhoods, and that employ teachers with the power to develop new teaching strategies must be undertaken. Children whose parents have chemical

dependencies need special attention so that they will not follow in their parents footsteps. And, psychosocial and environmental conditions that produce substance abuse must be addressed. There are 108 citations. ^United\States ^Drug\Control\Policies ^Reviews ^P\S\Environmental ^P\S\Demand\Reduction ^P\S\Values ^P\S\Social ^Supply ^Interdiction ^Law\Enforcement ^Treatment ^Prevention ^Drug\Control\Policies\Critique ^Crop\Eradication

558. French, Howard W. (1989). "New York City Babies Face Drug Crisis." *The New York Times*, 18 October, A16. Drug-abuse patterns in New York, if continued, will result within five years in up to 5 percent of all newborn babies requiring admission to intensive care hospital wards. AIDS-infected women are giving birth as are drug-addicted women. High costs are associated with providing intensive care to their newborns. Beyond that, many newborns are left with lifelong physical and developmental impairments. ^United\States ^New\York ^Drug\Use ^Consequences\Fetuses ^Consequences\Children ^Consequences\Economic

559. Freudenberger, Herbert J. (1982). "Substance Abuse in the Workplace." *Contemporary Drug Problems* 11(2): 243–250. U.S. corporations have just begun to deal with employees' many personal anxieties, some of which may lead to substance abuse. Companies and organizations must learn to think in terms of prevention in ways that deal with the total human being. Wellness programs, nutritional awareness, and physical fitness are some of the comprehensive approaches that need to be utilized in order to reduce the cost to society of workers who do not perform to their level of expectation. ^United\States ^Drug\Use ^Workplace ^Prevention ^P\S\Integrated

560. Freund, Charles Paul (1989). "Redefining the Drug Crisis." *The Washington Post*, 21 March, A17. The three "tongues" are the language of the drug war, the language of drug legalization, and the language of drug containment (a middle ground). The idea of containment is that the drug war is not winnable. It is a language that some inner-city mayors are adopting. ^United\States ^Drug\Control\Policies ^Drug\Control\Policies\Critique

561. Frey, Bruno S., and Werner W. Pommerehne (1984). "The Hidden Economy: State and Prospects for Measurement." *Review of Income and Wealth* 30(March): 1–23. The authors argue that for economic theory and economic policy it is important to know the size and development of the hidden economy. They show that it can be quantitatively estimated in various ways, using indicators, determinants, and a combination of the two. Although there is no "best" method, the various approaches each highlight different aspects of hidden economy and therefore have specific strengths and weaknesses. Though the range and size estimates of the hidden economy is wide, there is general agreement that the size has been growing for all countries analyzed over recent decades. While no specific reference is made to that portion of the underground economy associated with drug trafficking, the analysis suggests ways by which approaches toward estimates of that economy, as a portion of the hidden economy, might be made. ^Drug\Traffic ^Economics ^Informal\Economy

562. Fried, P. A. (1985). "Postnatal Consequences of Maternal Marijuana Use." In *Current Research on the Consequences of Maternal Drug Abuse*, NIDA Research Monograph 59, edited by Theodore M. Pinkert. Rockville, Md.: National Institute of Drug Abuse. Mothers' prenatal use of marijuana does have neurobehavioral consequences in the offspring of regular maternal marijuana users. This does not seem to express itself in poorer performance in cognitive and motor tests at one and one half and two years of age. However, this conclusion must be viewed cautiously because it is not clear whether the neurological disturbances present at birth are truly transient and overcome, whether they are simply compensated for with

maturity, or whether the tests used at the one and one half and two year ages might have decreased discriminatory sensitivity to settle cognitive differences that actually may exist.
^Cannabis ^Consequences\Fetuses

563. Friedman, Alfred S., Arlene T. Utada, Nita W. Glickman, and Margaret R. Morrissey (1987). "Psychopathology as an Antecedent To, and as a 'Consequence' of, Substance Use, in Adolescence." *Journal of Drug Education* 17(3): 233–244. From a longitudinal study of 232 students, there appears to be an additive or cumulative interaction between psychiatric symptoms (psychopathology) and drug use. Those who exhibit psychiatric symptoms are, to a much higher degree, likely to become drug users, and once having become drug users have a much higher tendency to present deleterious psychiatric symptoms. Nine types of psychic symptoms were measured, including hostility, paranoidism, depression, and obsession-compulsion.
^Drug\Use ^Youth ^Health ^Consequences\Psychological

564. Friedman, Alfred S., Errol Pomerance, Richard Sanders, Yoav Santo, and Arlene Utada (1980). "The Structure and Problems of the Families of Adolescent Drug Abusers." *Contemporary Drug Problems* 9(3): 327–56. Presents nonclinical data on family structure and demographic variables, and on types of family problems as they relate to drug abuse. The national (U.S.) sample consists of adolescents admitted to drug treatment. The degree to which family factors may be considered to predispose, or to "cause" drug abuse is discussed. The article reviews, also, key literature on family structure and family problem factors in drug abuse.
^Drug\Use ^Youth ^Society ^Family ^Reviews ^United\States ^Drug\Use\Theories

565. Friedman, Alfred S., Nita Glickman, and Arlene Utada (1985). "Does Drug and Alcohol Use Lead to Failure to Graduate from High School?" *Journal of Drug Education* 15(4): 353–64. Drug use is found to be positively associated with dropping out of high school in a large sample of Philadelphia adolescents, even when twenty demographic, personal, and family variables were controlled. "While drug use may not be the main cause of dropping out of high school, but only a concomitant effect of earlier, more basic state of disaffection from school, it is nevertheless clear that drug use by adolescents interferes with academic progress in high school" (p. 353).
^United\States ^Drug\Use ^Youth ^Society ^Consequences\Educational ^Family

566. Friedman, Samuel R., Don C. Des Jarlais, and Douglas S. Goldsmith (1987). "An Overview of AIDS Prevention Efforts Aimed at Intravenous Drug Users." *The Journal of Drug Issues* 19(1): 93–112. The article provides a brief overview of some of the drug user-related AIDS prevention and health activities occurring in the United States and other countries in early 1987. Outreach models are examined as well as existing drug treatment program efforts. An analysis of the assumptions and apparent consequences of applying those assumptions in various models is given. ^Heroin ^Health ^AIDS ^Prevention ^Treatment ^Reviews

567. Fritz, Sara (1989). "Cheney, Nunn at Odds over Military's Drug Role." *The Los Angeles Times*, 12 March, 25. Continuation in the on-going debate in the United States over what role the established military institutions should play in the war on drugs. A part of the military's struggle is economic: Whatever it allocates to the war on drugs must be subtracted from its defense weapons systems. ^United\States ^Drug\Control\Policies ^Military ^Economics

568. Fritz, Sara, and John Broder (1988). "Urban Blood Baths Spur Plan for Pentagon War on Drugs." *The Los Angeles Times*, 10 May, 1. The politicians are pushing vigorously to involve the military, assuming that it will reduce both

violence and loss of life. The military, however, continues to resist any role in the war on drugs. ^United\States ^Drug\Control\Policies ^Military

569. Fujii, Edwin T. (1979). "Public Investment in the Rehabilitation of Heroin Addicts." *Social Science Quarterly* 55(1): 39–51. Enormous sums of money are obtained through criminal behavior by drug addicts to support their habits. Effective rehabilitation programs, on a cost/benefit analysis, could save society considerable money even though the programs are somewhat costly. This study attempts to establish criteria for evaluating program effectiveness, identifying the most effective programs. Expanded discussion is developed in seven alternative areas: 1) additional supply restriction, 2) detoxification, 3) civil commitment, 4) imprisonment and parole, 5) methadone maintenance, 6) heroin maintenance, and 7) heroin legalization. ^Heroin ^Treatment ^Economics ^Crime ^P\S\Rehabilitation ^Drug\Control\Policies\Effectiveness ^Drug\Control\Policies\Critique

570. Gabiani, A. A. (1988). "Drug Addiction." *Soviet Sociology*, (Spring): 50–57. Admission that Soviet society, long complacent, is experiencing drug addiction problems. Offers a sociological overview of the Soviet addict. ^USSR ^Drug\Use ^Society ^Drug\Use\Theories

571. Gaertner, Wulf, and Alouis Wenig, eds. (1983). *Studies in Contemporary Economics: The Economics of the Shadow Economy*. New York: Springer-Berlag. Although this volume does not deal directly with drug trafficking, its subject matter is highly germane. Drug trafficking produces a considerable volume of unreported economic activities. This, related with other underground economic activities, implies that important macroeconomic variables are biased in a country's official statistics. The rate of unemployment, for example, may be highly overestimated while production figures, on the other hand, tend to be underrated. Governments could thus be misled to choose inadequate policies. All of this is observed independent of issues of taxation, decline in tax morale, skepticism towards official politics, and considerations that some types of criminal behavior are "normal." Volume contains the proceedings of the International Conference on The Economics of the Shadow Economy held at the University of Bielefeld, West Germany, October 1983. ^Informal\Economy ^Consequences\Social ^Consequences\Political ^Consequences\Economic

572. Gaines-Carter, Patrice (1989). "Crack Sends Some Drug Users Backsliding into Arms of Heroin." *The Washington Post*, 9 January, D1. Crack addicts are now apparently supplementing their highs with heroin. Overdose deaths in Washington, D.C., are increasingly noted from mixtures of heroin and cocaine. ^United\States ^Cocaine ^Crack ^Heroin ^Drug\Use ^Washington\DC ^Consequences\Personal

573. Galanter, Marc (1986). "Social Network Therapy for Cocaine Dependence." *Advances in Alcohol and Substance Abuse* 6(2): 159–75. Another in the increasing number of articles looking at the role immediate family and close friends may play in the rehabilitation of drug abusers. Focuses on the rehabilitation of cocaine users. ^Cocaine ^Treatment ^Family ^Treatment\Family ^Treatment\Peers ^Treatment\Rehabilitation

574. Galizio, Mark, and Stephen A. Maisto (1985). *Determinants of Substance Abuse: Biological, Psychological, and Environmental Factors*. New York: Plenum Press. Discusses biological and psychosocial factors that contribute to substance abuse. Both genes and the environment are analyzed. The editors believe a "biopsycho-social theory of substance abuse" is possible, and make efforts toward pointing the direction that will have to be taken to realize it. ^Drug\Use ^Society ^Drug\Use\Theories

575. Gallagher, Winifred (1986). "The Looming Menace of Designer Drugs." *Discover* 7(8): 24–35. Argues that synthetic opiates are just as dangerous as

crack. Discusses how people, including members of the medical profession, get trapped into the "fentanyl pit," and how phantom chemists everywhere are ready to supply such people's needs. The alarming aspect of designer drugs is that underground chemists working in obscure laboratories can cook up an enormous supply of fentanyl analogs in just a few months. How to deal with designer drugs, from a public policy perspective, is also a focus of the article. ^Drug\Traffic ^Drug\Control\Policies ^Designer\Drugs

576. Gandossy, Robert P., Jay R. Williams, Jo Cohen, and Henrick J. Harwood (1980). *Drugs and Crime: A Survey and Analysis of the Literature.* Washington, D.C.: U.S. Government Printing Office. The development of this bibliography was supported by a grant to the Research Triangle Institute by the National Institute of Law Enforcement and Criminal Justice. In 1976 Congress mandated the Law Enforcement Assistance Administration (LEAA) and National Institute of Law Enforcement and Criminal Justice (NILECJ), to make studies and undertake research programs to determine the relationship between drug abuse and crime. The NILECJ's center for the study of crime correlates and criminal behavior undertook a variety of projects, one of which was to develop a crime/drug research agenda. It was intended that this would be built on work already done by a 1976 National Institute of Drug Abuse (NIDA) drug/crime panel. The literature review and analysis reported in this volume are an outgrowth of that agenda. The review is categorized into methodological issues, patterns of drug use and criminal behavior, life cycles, economic issues, and drug treatment. Concerning the relationship between drugs and crime, there has not been enough research to make any definitive statements. It is shown, however, that a substantial number of violent crimes are associated with alcohol abuse and that there is some evidence indicating a relationship between barbiturates and amphetamines and violent offenses. As for life cycles, most studies reviewed found that contemporary addicts have criminal records prior to drug use. As for economic issues, it was shown that as prices increase, non heroin users frequently exit the drug consumption market. It has long been believed that the commission of income-generating crimes is necessary to maintain a heroin habit. The literature here found that compulsive heroin users do maintain the size of their habits while increasing their expenditures when the price of heroin rises. The resources, however, come as much from family, friends, or dealing in drugs at an elevated price to other consumers as much as from nominal increased theft. ^Drug\Use ^Crime ^Reviews ^Treatment ^Economics ^Bibliographies ^NIDA ^Alcohol ^Heroin

577. Gannon, J. D. (1989). "Tiny Costa Rica Gamely Tackles Drug Trafficking: Nation Finds that Democratic Traditions Are a Boon as Well as a Vulnerability in this War." *The Christian Science Monitor*, 30 January, 1. Costa Rica has little drug addiction, but drug traffickers are attempting to convert the country into "their private air strip." The threat to Costa Rica is in the undermining of the integrity of its judicial and law enforcement systems. Ironically, it is both the open and democratic nature of Costa Rican society that has made it alluring to drug traffickers, and the challenge will be to find a way to use those democratic traditions successfully in a war against invading aliens. ^Costa\Rica ^Drug\Traffic ^Drug\Control\Policies ^Latin\America ^Traffickers ^Consequences\Social ^Consequences\Political ^Consequences\Economic ^Consequences\Judiciary ^Consequences\Law\Enforcement

578. Gardner, Stephen E., ed. (1980). *National Drug/Alcohol Collaborative Project: Issues in Multiple Substance Abuse.* Rockville, Md.: National Institute on Drug Abuse. Concludes that significant medical and psychosocial consequences are associated with substance abuse combinations, including liver damage, increased mortality rates, neuropsychiatric impairment, greater social dysfunction, and a decreased

retention in treatment programs. ^Drug\Use ^Health ^Reviews ^Consequences\Health ^Consequences\Neurological ^Consequences\Social

579. Garfield, Emily F., and Jeanne Gibbs (1982). "Fostering Parent Involvement for Drug Prevention." *Journal of Drug Education* 12(2): 87–96. Given the widespread impression that drug treatment officials have acquired regarding the involvement of parents in drug prevention and treatment programs, this article seeks to foster the formation of parent groups engaged in just such a series of events. Nine models are summarized, with recommendations for professionals who might facilitate the development and positive role implementation of local parents' organizations. ^Drug\Use ^Prevention ^Treatment ^Youth ^Family ^P\S\Parenting

580. Garmon, L. (1983). "Pot-Smokers May Be Imperiled by Paraquat-Spraying Program." *Science News* 124(July 23): 55. Scientists of the Centers for Disease Control reported their disagreement with the U.S. State Department's announcement in December of 1982 that it is "unlikely" that paraquat spraying endangers the health of marijuana smokers in the United States. ^United\States ^Cannabis ^Crop\Eradication ^Herbicides ^Health ^Consequences\Health

581. Garrison, Lloyd (1984). "Let Them Shoot Smack." *Time*, 19 March, 35. Heroin, once considered strictly an illegal export for "weak willed Western cultures," has now caught on at home, and increasing numbers of addicts are causing substantial social overhead costs for countries such as Malaysia, Thailand, and Pakistan. ^Southwest\Asia ^Southeast\Asia ^Malaysia ^Pakistan ^Thailand ^Heroin ^Drug\Use ^Society ^Consequences\Economic ^Consequences\Social ^Golden\Triangle ^Golden\Crescent

582. Gawin, Frank H. and Everett H. Ellinwood, Jr. (1988). "Cocaine and Other Stimulants." *The New England Journal of Medicine* 318(18): 1173. Looks at cocaine use from the vantage of psychiatry, focusing on the historical and epidemiological features of the recent upsurge in cocaine abuse. Examines emerging treatment procedures and describes perceptions of the biologic nature of the stimulant action. Psychiatric complications are noted. Developed also is a discussion on "new avenues of theory and research." 131 references are cited. ^Cocaine ^Drug\Use\History ^Health ^Treatment ^Reviews ^Epidemiology ^Consequences\Psychological ^Drug\Use\Theories

583. Gawin, Frank H., and Herbert D. Kleber (1986). "Abstinence Symptomatology and Psychiatric Diagnosis in Cocaine Abusers." *Archives of General Psychiatry* 43(2): 107–113. Thirty chronic cocaine abusers were studied with respect to withdrawal symptoms when they abstained from cocaine usage. All the cocaine abusers exhibited uniform major depressive-like symptomatology during periods immediately following cocaine use, but these symptoms were usually transient. Less severe symptoms then emerged in some of the patients. All of the symptoms are described and generalizations from the study laid out. Treatment rationales based on the findings are discussed. ^Cocaine ^Drug\Use ^Health ^Treatment ^Consequences\Psychological

584. ——— (1986). "Pharmacologic Treatments of Cocaine Abuse." *Psychiatric Clinics of North America* 9(3): 573–583. It has usually been thought that cocaine dependence is a minor "psychological" addiction without a "physiological" withdrawal syndrome. Thus, treatments for cocaine abuse have usually involved psychological therapeutic efforts aimed at altering addictive behaviors. There is now increasing clinical evidence of intractable addiction and profound deleterious physiological effects of chronic cocaine abuse. Treatment intervention therefore is moving towards pharmacological agents. ^Cocaine ^Treatment ^Reviews ^Treatment\Antagonists ^Consequences\Physiological ^Consequences\Psychological

585. Gee, Marcus, Ken Macqueen, and Michael Rose (1986). "Montreal's Deadly New Traffic in Cocaine." *Maclean's*, 24 March, 24–26. Describes the

ascendancy of Colombians involved in cocaine trafficking in Montreal. ^Canada ^Cocaine ^Drug\Traffic ^Traffickers ^Latin\America ^Colombia

586. Gehrke, Donna, and Aaron Epstein (1989). "Lawyers Dealt Setback in Drug-Case Defenses." *The Miami Herald*, 23 June, 1A. The U.S. Supreme Court has narrowly ruled that the government can freeze defendant's assets intended for legal fees in cases involving drugs. It is thought that this will deter some lawyers from wanting to represent clients accused of drug-related activities. ^United\States ^Asset\Forfeiture ^Attorneys

587. Gemoules, Craig (1989). "Metro: No Dealers in Public Housing." *The Miami Herald*, 7 June, B1. Evicting drug dealers from public housing projects and running checks before tenancy on drug users is now a matter of course in Miami. ^United\States ^Drug\Control\Policies ^Public\Housing

588. Germani, Clara (1984). "Efforts Renewed to Put Marijuana Growers out of Business." *The Christian Science Monitor*, 30 August, 3. Description of the largest eradication program in the United States as being underway in Northern California. ^United\States ^Cannabis ^Crop\Eradication ^California

589. ——— (1987). "Drug Corruption Is Main Issue in Bahamian Election." *The Christian Science Monitor*, 18 June, 9. The government of the Bahamas has been charged with official conniving in the international drug trade. Drug charges have become an extremely volatile issue in the 1987 political campaign, heavily involving the Prime Minister, Lynden Pindling, who is something of a national hero and has been the Bahamian Prime Minister for twenty years. ^Bahamas ^Drug\Traffic ^Caribbean ^Consequences\Political ^Consequences\Corruption

590. ——— (1988). "Coca Addiction Hits Home—Among Rural Children of Drug-Producing Bolivia." *The Christian Science Monitor*, 30 September, 1. Brief description of Bolivian children selling coca paste on the streets. Because of the lack of education about drug abuse, most Latin Americans (Bolivians included) do not see drug abuse as a health problem. A lot of this is economically related. The poor economic and social conditions that have made alcoholism the largest addiction problem also encouraged the growing use of coca paste. Many Bolivian officials are involved in the trafficking; however, it is unlikely that any concerted government effort will be made to deal with children on the streets who supplement their income by selling narcotics while at the same time becoming addicted to their use. ^Bolivia ^Coca ^Drug\Use ^Youth ^Economics ^Latin\America ^Cocaine\Paste ^Consequences\Children ^Drug\Use\Theories ^Consequences\Corruption

591. ——— (1988). "Combating the Drug Menace: Environment Is the Latest Coca Victim." *The Christian Science Monitor*, 31 August, 1. Description of the destruction of vegetation and trees in the Amazon Basin as growers burn the forest in preparation for planting coca. The erosion and chemical pollution consequences are described. ^Latin\America ^Consequences\Environmental ^Peru ^Bolivia

592. ——— (1988). "In Bolivia, the Hard Reality of Coca; Even Bold Anti-drug Measures Can't Beat the Economic Facts." *The Christian Science Monitor*, 12 August, 7. The hard reality is that antidrug measures cannot beat the economic facts. There is hardly any other source of income for hundreds of thousands of peasants other than coca. Thus, they will continue to grow coca regardless of antidrug efforts made in the country. The crop substitution programs are not working because monies promised are not paid. ^Bolivia ^Coca ^Drug\Control\Policies ^Economics ^Producers ^Latin\America ^Production\Incentives\Economic

593. Gerth, Jeff (1990). "2 Foreign Bank Units Plead Guilty to Money Laundering." *The New York Times*, 17 January, A8. The U.S. federal government has brought a money-laundering case against two large international banks headquartered in Luxembourg. A first case of its kind. ^Law\Enforcement ^Money\Laundering ^Europe ^Luxembourg

594. Gerth, Jeff (1991). "Report Says Mercenaries Aided Colombian Cartels." *The New York Times*, February 28, A20. British and Israeli mercenaries have provided paramilitary assistance to Colombian drug-trafficking organizations. Former Israeli military officials have been involved. The retired Israeli military officer, Yairg Klein is mentioned. ^Latin\America ^Colombia ^Terrorists ^Traffickers ^Israel ^Military ^Consequences\Violence

595. "Getting Britain off the Heroin Hook" (1984). *The Economist*, 30 June, 49. Heroin addiction is growing in Great Britain, imports are increasing, dealers are becoming more numerous, and users are substantially increasing. Suggestions are made for treatment and rehabilitation. ^United\Kingdom ^Heroin ^Drug\Use ^Drug\Traffic ^Treatment ^P\S\Treatment ^P\S\Rehabilitation

596. Gettman, Jon (1989). "Decriminalizing Marijuana." *American Behavioral Scientist* 32(3): 243–48. Many of the conventional reasons for decriminalization are briefly stated. Some mention is made of decriminalization experiences in several American states. ^United\States ^Decriminalization ^Oregon ^Alaska

597. Ghodse, A. Hamid (1986). "Cannabis Psychosis." *The British Journal of Addiction* 81:473–78. Evidence from countries where heavy use of cannabis is common shows that heavy use can cause a short-lived toxic psychosis characterized by confusion, delusions, hallucinations, and emotional instability. The exact nature of this psychosis is reviewed from clinical and psychiatric bases. ^Cannabis ^Health ^Consequences\Psychological

598. Gieringer, Dale (1986). "Inside the DEA." *Reason* (December): 23–29. Within the bureaucracy, behavior is murky and agents "lie, cheat, and steal in the name of the law." The focus is on intelligence, informants, and strikes. Searches and seizures carried out without legal authorization are discussed. ^United\States ^Law\Enforcement ^DEA ^DEA\Critique

599. ——— (1988). "Marijuana, Driving and Accident Safety." *Journal of Psychoactive Drugs* 20(1): 93-101. While alcohol is the leading drug-related accident factor in automobiles, evidence shows that marijuana produces secondary impairments and therefore constitutes a safety risk. Reliable verification tests are also discussed. ^Cannabis ^Drug\Use ^Alcohol ^Consequences\Public\Safety

600. Gill, Lesley (1987). *Peasants, Entrepreneurs, and Social Change. Frontier Development in Lowland Bolivia*. Boulder, Colo.: Westview Press. An anthropological study of peasants and entrepreneurs in the frontier of eastern Bolivia, specifically in the west-central Santa Cruz department. Chronicles the expansion and decline of communities, the transformation of cropping patterns and commodities, and the way in which both peasants and capitalists dealt with crises. One crisis led to the formation of the powerful agro-industrial bourgeoisie and, through the cocaine traffic, to the development of an alliance with a military dictatorship. Expansionist tendencies in Bolivia following the agrarian reform allowed both the traditional upper-class and a new group of entrepreneurs to invest in agriculture and in commercial activities in the cities. When hit by a world recession in commodity exports, many of these turned to cocaine traffic, which offered a lucrative alternative to sugar cane and cotton cultivation. Thus the author sees the emergence of a cocaine industry as being a product of social

relations of production established well before. Explores, in the last chapter, the impact of cocaine and the economic crisis on the rural population. When cocaine manufacturers relocated their operations to more remote sites, legitimate agro-industries continued to decline and the whole region entered a serious economic crisis. This crisis led to peasant and worker group reorganization under a new democratic government, and the process of "proletarianization" began to reverse itself, as peasants pressed vigorously their demands for land, higher wages, and technical assistance. Book based on doctoral dissertation at Columbia University. ^Bolivia ^Coca ^Production ^Economics ^Society ^Latin\America ^Military ^Consequences\Corruption ^Consequences\Economic ^Consequences\-Social ^Producers\Unions

601. Gillgannon, Michael J. (1988). "Drugs, Debt and Dependency." *America* 159(12): 310–14. The drug trade distorts and destroys the national economies of producing nations such as Peru and Bolivia. The more technical term may be "Dutch disease." The shadow economy of drugs offers no incentive for change to such governments. ^Latin\America ^Bolivia ^Peru ^Cocaine ^Drug\Traffic ^Economics ^Informal\Economy ^Consequences\Political ^Consequences\Economic ^International\Debt

602. Ginzburg, Harold M., Mhairi Graham MacDonald, and James William Glass (1987). "AIDS, HTLV-III Diseases, Minorities and Intravenous Drug Abuse." *Advances in Alcohol and Substance Abuse* 6(3): 7–21. The alarming increase of AIDS and HTLV-III diseases now being observed among minorities and women who engage in high-risk activities is attributable to the high incidence of drug abuse in the respective communities. Suggestions are made on ways to reach such groups with education programs. Such approaches will likely not be traditional. ^Heroin ^Drug\Use ^Health ^AIDS ^Women ^Minorities ^Prevention ^P\S\Education

603. Girardet, Edward (1988). "In Afghanistan, Drug Trade Is Blooming." *The Christian Science Monitor*, 28 December, 1. As refugees from the civil war return to northeastern Afghanistan and begin to reclaim and replant their terraced fields, many are planting opium poppies. Economics of the trade are discussed. A map is included. Connections with Pakistan and Iran are noted. ^Afghanistan ^Iran ^Pakistan ^Opiates ^Production ^Economics ^Golden\Crescent ^Southwest\Asia

604. ——— (1989). "Helping Farmers Shake Poppy Habit." *The Christian Science Monitor*, 12 January, 6. Poppy substitution programs in Pakistan have persuaded some Pakistani tribesmen to change their crops. Only selected districts are affected. A regional map is included. ^Pakistan ^Southwest\Asia ^Golden\Crescent ^Opiates ^Crop\Substitution ^Middle\East

605. Giuliani, Rudolph W. (1985). "Organizing Law Enforcement as Well as Organized Crime." *Public Administration Review* (November): 712–17. In attempting to combat organized crime, President Ronald Reagan established the Organized Crime Drug Enforcement Task Force (OCDETF). One of its principal architects was the author of this article who, here, surveys the organization of law enforcement and the history of drug enforcement in the United States. Noting the problems of coordinating law enforcement agencies in combatting drug trafficking, Guiliani turns to assess the success and the problems associated with OCDETF programs. ^United\States ^Law\Enforcement ^Organized\Crime ^Drug\Control\Policies\History ^Bureaucracy

606. Gladwell, Malcolm (1988). "Plan to Curb Drug Trade in Peru Set Back: Eli Lilly Refuses to Sell Herbicide." *The Washington Post*, 1 June, A1. A planned herbicidal campaign against coca growers in Peru has been thwarted, temporarily at least, by Eli Lilly's refusing to sell the herbicide required to do it. Eli Lilly is the sole manufacturer of the requisite chemical. The intended target was the Huallaga Valley. Factors involved in the refusal: Environmentalists have protested wildly against

the company because of health risks; Eli Lilly was worried about inviting reprisals from guerrilla groups against its operations in Central America. ^Latin\America ^Peru ^Coca ^Crop\Eradication^Herbicides^Consequences\Environmental^Consequences\Health^Consequences\Political ^Consequences\Violence

607. Glantz, Meyer D., ed. (1984). *Correlates and Consequences of Marijuana Use.* Rockville, Md: U.S. Department of Health and Human Services, National Institute of Drug Abuse. Provides researchers with an up-to-date survey of the recent literature on the psychological and social correlates and consequences of marijuana use. Robert Petersen first reviews the literature and provides an integrative summary of what is currently known. The second part of the volume contains 127 abstracts of both representative and significant research and theory. Most of these are drawn from the American empirical human research literature published between 1974 and 1981. There is also an extensive bibliography. ^Cannabis ^Drug\Use ^Health ^Society ^Reviews ^Bibliographies ^NIDA ^Consequences\Social ^Consequences\Psychological ^Drug\Use\Theories ^Consequences\Theories ^United\States

608. *The Global Legal Framework for Narcotics and Prohibitive Substances* (1979). Washington, D.C.: U.S. Department of State. This volume describes and analyzes the response to a State Department request, given to U.S. embassies worldwide in the late 1970s, to supply a broad range of information on narcotics and prohibitive substances and legislation or laws governing their use in the countries in which the United States has representation. 153 countries are reported in this survey. ^Drug\Control\Policies ^Legislation

609. Glynn, Thomas J. (1984). "Adolescent Drug Use and the Family Environment: A Review." *Journal of Drug Issues* 14(2): 271–95. Broad-based review of the literature on the relationship between adolescent drug use and the family. Offers methodological critiques of numerous variables used in the studies (e.g., birth order, family size, family makeup). Concludes that family dynamics hold much promise for study with respect to an understanding of adolescent drug behavior and that variables such as parental roles and parent-child relationships, especially in terms of distance regulation and over involvement, are promising ones for study. ^Drug\Use ^Youth ^Society ^Family ^Reviews ^Drug\Use\Theories\Critique ^Drug\Use\Theories ^Parenting ^P\S\Parenting

610. Glynn, Thomas J., ed. (1983). *Drug Abuse Prevention Research.* Research Issues 33. Rockville, Md.: National Institute on Drug Abuse. Summarizes the literature on drug-related prevention research. The literature surveyed is more concentrated on theory and issues development than it is on data-based research because of the relative paucity of the latter. However, some data-based studies are included. 155 studies are summarized. Contains 95 summaries of research conducted on drug use in countries other than the United States. Many of the studies are purely epidemiological; others focus on specific issues involved in drug use, such as personality or background characteristics of users, crime, and law enforcement. Cannabis is heavily represented because, at the time, it was the most widely abused illicit drug. ^Drug\Use ^Prevention ^Reviews ^NIDA ^Cannabis ^Drug\Use\Theories ^Crime

611. Glynn, Thomas J., Carl G. Leukefeld, and Jacqueline P. Ludford, editors (1983). *Preventing Adolescent Drug Abuse: Intervention Strategies.* Rockville, Md.: National Institute on Drug Abuse. Reviews prevention strategies that have been used with a degree of success in the tobacco smoking area and evaluates their applicability to drug abuse prevention strategies. ^Drug\Use ^Prevention ^Youth ^Reviews ^NIDA ^Tobacco

612. Godwin, Bernard (1983). "An Economic Analysis of the Illicit Drug Market." *The International Journal of the Addictions* 18(5): 681–700. Previous

studies of heroin addiction have tended to follow a unilinear analysis between increases in heroin price and criminal conduct. The assumption is made that as price increases occur, heroin addicts must increase their criminal behavior in order to support their habits. This article identifies variables of complements and substitutes and their effects upon price, supply and demand, criminality, and possible implementation of treatment procedures.   ^Heroin ^Drug\Use ^Crime ^Treatment ^Drug\Use\Theories\Critique ^Consequences\Crime ^Consequences\Economic

613. Gold, Mark S. (1989). *Marijuana.* New York: Plenum Medical Book Company. A general handbook on marijuana use and abuse. Of interest to this bibliography are chapters on treatment and prevention of marijuana abuse. ^Cannabis ^Drug\Use ^Prevention ^Treatment

614. Goldfarb, Ronald, and Robert DuPont (1989). "Avoiding Nostrums and Illusions in the War on Drugs." *Los Angeles Times,* 22 January, 3. Legalization? "Increasing the availability and social acceptance of drugs not only condones but inevitably increases drug use. Since the major costs of drug abuse are not law enforcement, but health, safety and productivity costs, making drugs more available inevitably increases society's burdens." The author then cites the experience of two legal drugs—alcohol and tobacco—which raise substantial tax revenue but which also are the leading causes of preventable death and illness in the United States, costing the nation more than all illegal drugs put together. Interdiction? An illusory policy. Tough criminal penalties on drug sellers? This will make only a dent in the problem. Several solutions suggested.   ^United\States ^Drug\Control\Policies ^Decriminalization\Critique ^Alcohol ^Tobacco ^Taxation

615. Goldstein, Paul J. (1979). *Prostitution and Drugs.* Lexington, Mass.: Lexington Books. Examines social scientific knowledge about the relationship between female drug use and prostitution. What is the role of drug use in becoming a prostitute; what are the functions and dysfunctions of drug use for prostitutes; and how does the nature and scope of drug use serve to differentiate socially the subculture of prostitution? The author interviewed sixty women, all of whom were or had been drug abusers. Forty-three had also been prostitutes. Drug use was shown to have both functional and dysfunctional effects on prostitution careers. ^Drug\Use ^Women ^Prostitution

616. Golwyn, Daniel H. (1988). "Cocaine Abuse Treated with Phenelzine." *International Journal of the Addictions* 23(9): 897–905. Argues that cocaine abuse can be controlled effectively and inexpensively by employing phenelzine. When phenelzine is taken, subsequent use of cocaine produces very disagreeable results. Beyond that, phenelzine appears to reduce the craving for cocaine. It is even thought that phenelzine corrects biochemical defects caused by chronic cocaine use. Analysis of treatment failures regarding cocaine abuse that use other pharmacological agents is also presented. ^Cocaine ^Treatment ^P\S\Antagonists

617. Gomez, Linda (1984). "Cocaine: America's 100 Years of Euphoria and Despair." *Life* (May): 57-68. Description, with accompanying photographs, of America's love affair with cocaine from the late eighteenth century to contemporary times. ^United\States ^Cocaine ^Drug\Use\History

618. Gonzales-Carrero, A., and A. Mancilla (1980). "Considerations about the Problem of Coca and Cocaine in Venezuela." In *Cocaine 1980. Proceedings of the Interamerican Seminar on Medical and Sociological Aspects of Coca and Cocaine,* edited by F. R. Jeri, 206–12. Lima, Peru: Pacific Press. Pervasive drug abuse is potentially destructive, as evidence in jails, hospitals, and cemeteries attests. Legal restrictions seem not to be sufficiently effective in curbing illicit drug

consumption, a kind of social disease. While in Venezuela coca chewing is not a pervasive habit, increased evidence of consumption intranasally or in conjunction with smoking tobacco is found. The best prevention are educational efforts coupled with value forming attitudinal change. ^Society ^Latin\America ^Tobacco ^Prevention\Drug\Education ^P\S\Values ^Venezuela

619. González, Guadalupe, and Marta Tienda, eds. (1989). *The Drug Connection in U.S.– Mexican Relations.* Volume 4 of the *Dimensions of the United States–Mexican Relations* series, edited by Rosario Greene and Peter H. Smith. San Diego, Calif.: Center for U.S.– Mexican Studies, University of California, San Diego. Articles in this volume address the drug demand patterns in the United States that affect supply incentives for Mexican growers and traffickers. As both supply and traffickers have increased, the United States has elaborated a narcotics policy toward Mexico that has uncertain implications for the two countries' bilateral relationships. Observations are raised on how the United States and Mexican drug markets might be controlled in ways that would not hurt the bilateral relationships of the two countries. ^United\States ^Drug\Control\Policies ^Consequences\Drug\Control\Policies ^Demand ^Consequences\Foreign\Relations

620. Goodman, Ellen (1988). "Needles for Addicts? No." *The Washington Post*, 2 July, A23. The argument from Europe is that needle exchange-programs do not increase drug use, yet the same evidence disputes how effective these programs are in controlling AIDS infection. ^Europe ^Heroin ^Drug\Use ^Health ^AIDS ^P\S\Needle\Exchange

621. Goodman, Louis W., and Johanna S. R. Mendelson (1988). "Whose Drug War Is It, Anyway?" *The Christian Science Monitor*, 22 July, 12. A multilateral approach to the war on drugs, led by civilian government leaders from throughout the Western Hemisphere, constitutes the best hope for dealing with the interdiction and eradication programs in the illicit narcotics trade. Offering U.S. military assistance to foreign militaries to encourage them to fight the drug war can only tip the balance of power toward the return of military governments in the Western Hemisphere. ^United\States ^Latin\America ^Crop\Eradication ^Interdiction ^International\Cooperation ^Military ^Military\Critique

622. Goodstadt, Michael S., Margaret A. Sheppard, and Godwin C. Chan (1982). "Relationships between Drug Education and Drug Use: Carts and Horses." *Journal of Drug Issues* 12(4): 431–42. From longitudinal survey data from large samples of students at intervals two years apart, the conclusion is that alcohol and other drug use are positively related to reported drug education, especially among the younger age groups. This has the curious effect of calling into question the "benign" effect of "drug education" in schools reported by other reviewers. More systematic analyses need to be carried out to see what forms of drug education, if any, are effective in reducing the incidence of drug abuse. What are the critical variables? What are the mediating variables? Current drug education programs tend to ignore the powerful influence of the family, peers, nonschool education, and other societal norms and support systems. All these have got to be brought into a general drug education system. ^Drug\Use ^Prevention ^Youth ^Prevention\Drug\Education\Critique ^Family ^Prevention\Family ^Prevention\Peers ^Society

623. Gooi, Kim (1986). "Just a Freedom Fighter." *Far Eastern Economic Review*, 20 February, 28–29. Khun Sa does not view himself as being so much an opium warlord as a freedom fighter for the independence of the Shan states. Khun Sa implied that the opium trade could be stopped if his people and region could become independent and free from "Burmese oppression." The matter is strictly economic for poor farmers, he says. Given the Burmese oppression, the only thing the Shan people can

do is grow opium which they then barter for rice and other basic necessities from Thailand. ^Southeast\Asia ^Burma ^Golden\Triangle ^Opiates ^Production ^Drug\Traffic ^Traffickers ^Economics ^Insurgents ^Production\Incentives\Economic

624. Gooi, Kim, and John McBeth (1986). "High-Priced High." *Far Eastern Economic Review*, 20 February, 28–29. As Khun Sa consolidates trade on the Thai-Burmese border, he is able to dictate supplier conditions for the market and therefore raise prices. Prices more than doubled within six months. ^Southeast\Asia ^Burma ^Golden\Triangle ^Opiates ^Drug\Traffic ^Organized\Crime ^Economics ^Insurgents ^Production\Incentives\Economic ^Consequences\Markets ^Traffickers ^Statistics

625. Gordon, Michael (1990). "U.S. Postpones Deploying Ships Near Colombia." *The New York Times*, January 17, A1. In an effort to suppress cocaine supplies entering the United States, the U.S. Navy planned to deploy an aircraft carrier battle group off the coast of Colombia. The task force began its journey. Colombian public opinion was so fiercely opposed to this idea–an attack on its sovereignty–that the Colombian government was forced to object officially, thereby scuttling the plan. The deployment was intended to be a U.S. centerpiece in the expanded use of its military to stop drug shipments from Latin America. The cancellation was viewed as a setback for the U.S. administration. ^Latin\America ^Colombia ^United\States ^Military ^Supply ^Interdiction ^Drug\Control\Policies ^International\Cooperation\Critique ^Consequences\Foreign\Policy ^Sovereignty

626. Goshko, John M. (1985). "U.S. Prods Paraguay on Cocaine." *The Washington Post*, 4 January, A18. Paraguay is a substantial source of precursor chemicals required for the manufacturing of cocaine. The United States has urged the country to control trafficking in those chemicals to a greater degree. ^Latin\America ^United\States ^Paraguay ^Cocaine ^Drug\Control\Policies ^Precursor\Chemicals ^Consequences\Foreign\Relations

627. Gotschlich, G. D. (1983). "Action by the Customs Co-Operation Council to Combat Illicit Drug Trafficking." *Bulletin on Narcotics* 35(4): 79–81. Since its establishment in 1953, the Customs Co-Operation Council (CCC) has been actively involved in combatting illicit drug trafficking. It has adopted legal measures designed to meet the requirements of states in a joint effort to promote the prevention, investigation, and repression of customs offenses, including drug smuggling. ^Drug\Control\Policies ^International\Cooperation ^Customs\Cooperation\Council

628. Gottheil, Edward (1986). "Cocaine Abuse and Dependence: The Scope of the Problem." *Advances in Alcohol and Substance Abuse* 6(2): 23–30. There has been a dramatic increase in the use of cocaine over the past twenty years; and, because of cocaine's properties, usage is likely to expand. The problem is that there is little or no knowledge about the degree to which increased use translates into a need for treatment. Additional research is needed, along with preventive and treatment approaches specifically tailored to cocaine. ^Cocaine ^Drug\Use ^Treatment

629. Grabowski, John, and Steven I. Dworkin (1985). "Cocaine: An Overview of Current Issues." *The International Journal of the Addictions* 20(6-7): 1065–88. Reviews a respectable body of literature in areas dealing with behavioral and neurobiological effects of the use of cocaine, risks, dosage, routes of administration, and treatment. On the basis of these "medical" kinds of studies, it is especially necessary for the future of public policy to develop an integrated policy view for the study of the behavioral effects of drug agents from interdisciplinary physiological, behavioral, and social perspectives. ^Cocaine ^Health ^Treatment ^Reviews ^P\S\Integrated

630. Graham, Bradley (1986). "Bolivian Barometer: Coca Price Falls." *The Washington Post*, 27 July, A22. Describes the public anxiety about what Americans

may be doing next in the eradication procedures under way in Bolivia. Major population movements are associated with the activities. Slackened demand has forced a substantial reduction in the price of coca. Prices have fallen from 65 cents to 25 cents per pound. Keeping the price down will encourage peasants to seek alternative employment opportunities. ^Bolivia ^Coca ^Drug\Traffic ^Crop\Eradication ^Economics ^Latin\America ^Consequences\Social ^Consequences\Political ^Consequences\Foreign\Relations ^Consequences\Migration ^P\S\Economic

631. ——— (1988). "Impact of Colombian Traffickers Spreads: Corrupted Officials Said to Undercut Hemispheric Security." *The Washington Post*, 24 February, A1. The spreading power of Colombia's narco mafia is undermining governments throughout Latin America and is beginning to pose a threat to U.S. security interests. This derives from the Colombian drug lords having secured the allegiance of many officials in various governments and armies through bribes and other forms of corruption. ^Latin\America ^Colombia ^Cocaine ^Drug\Traffic ^Consequences\Political ^Consequences\Corruption ^Military

632. Gray, Denis D. (1987). "Hailed US Herbicide Campaign Comes under Attack." *The Nation*, 21 February, 5. While American officials praise Burma's aerial spraying of herbicide over thousands of acres of opium in the Golden Triangle, critics charge that it is supplying dangerous chemicals to an authoritarian government that uses it mostly for military purposes against rebellious tribesmen. ^Southeast\Asia ^Burma ^Opiates ^Crop\Eradication ^Herbicides ^Insurgents ^Golden\Triangle ^Consequences\Political ^Military

633. ——— (1989). "A Deluge from the Golden Triangle." *Nation*, 2 February. The hills of Burma have produced a bumper crop of heroin destined for dealers around the world. Why? The cutoff of a controversial U.S. herbicide spraying program contributed to some additional tonnage; Burma's military rulers, who suppressed prodemocracy movements a year ago, are doing nothing to improve a wrecked economy; the United States, outraged by Burma's abuses, stopped all aid, including an antinarcotics program; and an apparent pact has been forged between one opium war lord (Khun Sa) and the Burmese government. ^Burma ^United\States ^Heroin ^Drug\Traffic ^Opiates ^Crop\Eradication ^Herbicides ^Economics ^Consequences\Foreign\Relations ^Consequences\Corruption ^Consequences\Political ^Traffickers ^Consequences\Unintended

634. Greenhaw, Wayne (1984). *Flying High: Inside Big-Time Drug Smuggling*. New York: Dodd, Mead and Company. A journalist penetrates both law enforcement agencies and the underworld to discover who smuggles drugs into the United States, how they are organized, where they buy their drugs, how much they pay, and how individuals get started in the business. In answering the questions, the author discovered an organization called *The Company*, a loosely knit group making money by smuggling marijuana into the United States. It was this company that law enforcement agents penetrated and from which they collected the largest ever in terms of number of defendants, size of forfeitures, and the area covered by the law enforcement authorities covert operations. ^United\States ^Cannabis ^Drug\Traffic ^Traffickers ^Law\Enforcement ^Asset\Forfeiture ^Organized\Crime

635. Greenhouse, Linda (1989). "Court Backs Tests of Some Workers to Deter Drug Use." *The New York Times*, 22 March, 1. The U.S. Supreme Court has upheld drug testing programs begun in the railroad industry. Some of the more far-reaching programs the federal government is putting into effect to assure a "drug-free workplace" may not pass the court's test. ^United\States ^Drug\Testing ^Workplace ^Drug\Testing\Critique ^Consequences\Constitutional

636. ——— (1989). "High Court Backs Airport Detention Based on 'Profile': Drug War Tactic Upheld, but Brennan and Marshall Say That Use of a List

of Traits Is Dangerous Method." *The New York Times*, 4 April, A1. A "drug courier profile" based on patterns of behavior of known narcotics traffickers may be sufficient justification for detaining people in airports. These brief detentions give police an opportunity to use their trained sniffer dogs to determine if cocaine is present. ^United\States ^Interdiction ^Law\Enforcement ^Drug\Courier\Profile

637. —— (1990). "Justices Back Property Searches of Foreigners in Foreign Nations." *The New York Times*, 1 March, 1. The U.S. Constitution does not protect foreigners in foreign countries from "unreasonable searches" by U.S. agencies. Justice Brennan's dissenting opinion was particularly severe. ^United\States ^Judiciary ^Consequences\Human\Rights ^Consequences\Constitutional

638. Greve, Frank (1989). "U.S. Weighs Drug-Boss Assassinations." *The Miami Herald*, 9 June, 1A. The assassination of major international drug traffickers is now a discussible policy option. The National Security Council convened a team to discuss "military operations," including assassinations. U.S.-sponsored official hit teams would move abroad for covert action against drug lords and their operations. ^United\States ^Drug\Control\Policies ^Consequences\Assassination ^P\S\Assassinations

639. Grichting, Wolfgang L., and James G. Barber (1988). "Fighting Drug Abuse in Australia." *International Journal of the Addictions* 23(5): 491–507. Three types of drug control programs operate in North Queensland, Australia: education, rehabilitation, and social control (law enforcement). Education is the most favored policy initiative; rehabilitation (treatment) is the least favored. ^Australia ^Drug\Control\Policies

640. Grier, Peter (1988). "Congress, Pentagon Dispute Armed Forces' Role in Drug Fight." *The Christian Science Monitor*, 24 May, 3. Antidrug personnel are stationed aboard regular U.S. ships and with military forces. Pentagon officials are resigned to a forced cooperation, but many are clearly unhappy about it. They worry about money being siphoned away from their regular operations and about the impact on the military forces. ^United\States ^Drug\Control\Policies ^Military ^Bureaucracy ^Consequences\Political

641. —— (1989). "Pentagon's Support Role Increases." *The Christian Science Monitor*, 1 September. While U.S. law prohibits using the military as a police force, the military nevertheless is now tracking shipments and supplies equipment to law enforcement endeavors. Description of some of those activities. ^United\States ^Interdiction ^Military

642. —— (1990). "Drug War Diplomacy: No Carrier Off Colombia—For Now." *The Christian Science Monitor*, 16 January, 6. The carrier task force that steamed from Florida toward the Colombian coast has been halted at mid-trip. Latin American nations, and particularly Colombia, have scorned this new U.S. surveillance mission. Description of additional U.S. military and coast guard drug control efforts is given. ^United\States ^Military ^Coast\Guard ^Latin\America ^Colombia ^Consequences\Foreign\Relations

643. Griffin, Keith (1989). "Observations on Possible Coca Policies in Bolivia." Unpublished paper, Department of Economics, University of California, Riverside. The coca economy is a significant contributor to Bolivia's overall economic condition. If the coca sector were to decline, the consequent fall in average incomes that inevitably would result would not be distributed uniformly. The brunt would fall on Bolivia's poor. Thus, "poverty, inequality and social discontent would increase." (p. 2). Discussion is advanced regarding the relationship of these observations to specific policy measures—crop eradication, product interdiction, crop substitution, and rural development. ^Latin\America ^Bolivia ^Economics ^Consequences\Economic ^Crop\Eradication ^Interdiction ^Crop\Substitution ^Proffered\Solutions ^P\S\Development

644. —— (1990). "The Coca Economy and Alternative Development in Bolivia." Unpublished Paper, Department of Economics, University of California, Riverside. The "coca economy" has become significantly important to Bolivia's whole economy. Serious consequences could result if the coca economy were eliminated without some form of compensation. A Bolivian report dealing with this issue is reviewed. It includes a detailed analysis of the coca economy in 1987. Suggestion is made that a strong case could be advanced arguing that Bolivia's best interests would be served by decriminalizing its coca economy. ^Latin\America ^Bolivia ^Economics ^P\S\Legalization ^Decriminalization

645. Griffin, Margaret L., and Steven M. Mirin (1989). "A Comparison of Male and Female Cocaine Abusers." *Archives of General Psychiatry* 46:122–26. Female cocaine abusers were diagnosed more often as having major depression, and their depressive symptoms improved much more slowly than men's when drug free. The findings suggest that women cocaine abusers may initially experience more problems with depression and job dissatisfaction, as well as other difficulties, than men after they have gone through a drug treatment program. Drug treatment centers ought, therefore, to be sensitive to these potential difficulties. ^Cocaine ^Health ^Treatment ^Women ^Consequences\Psychological ^P\S\Treatment

646. Grilli, Andrea M. (1987). "Preventing Billions from Being Washed Offshore: A Growing Approach to Stopping International Drug Trafficking." *Syracuse Journal of International Law and Commerce* 14(65): 65–88. The United States, following a supply-based approach, spends billions of dollars attempting to suppress the narcotics trade. Producing countries argue that the solution is to be found in a demand-oriented model. A third avenue of thought is now emerging, one that focuses on how money relates both to supply and to demand. Hence the current interest in attaching illegal profits and enacting seizure laws. "Seizing a drug operation's profits and assets has proven to be more effective in shutting down the operation than simply putting the trafficker in jail" (p. 66). Reviews legislation addressing money schemes, and examines how traffickers work to avoid the application of that legislation. The concept of "safe haven" is discussed. Various legal devices for obtaining information are reviewed. ^United\States ^Drug\Control\Policies ^Money\Laundering ^Asset\Forfeiture ^Supply ^Demand ^Legislation

647. Grinspoon, Lester (1977). *Marihuana Reconsidered.* 2d ed. Cambridge, Mass: Harvard University Press. As he did in the 1971 volume, Grinspoon here covers the waterfront on marijuana, including a chapter on the question of legalization where he urges that laws be changed to make the social use of marijuana legal. He claims that much less damage would be done to young people than by keeping the present course. In this edition Grinspoon attempts, even more vigorously, to educate the public about the "paranoid ideas" that conventional wisdom has about acute anxiety reaction and psychotic responses to marijuana use, to crime and violence and its use, and to the effects on cognition and motor coordination. There is a selected bibliography. ^Cannabis ^Health ^Reviews ^Consequences\Psychological ^P\S\Legalization ^Consequences\Critique ^Crime ^Consequences\Violence ^Consequences\Neurological

648. —— (1987). "A Proposal for Regulation and Taxation of Drugs." *Nova Law Review* 11:927–30. Grinspoon wants to legalize and tax current illegal drugs. He would use the taxes for drug education and for paying the medical and social costs of drug abuse. The trade-off? Less public expense, corruption, chaos, and terror. ^United\States ^P\S\Legalization ^Taxation

649. Grinspoon, Lester, and James B. Bakalar (1981). "Adverse Effects of Cocaine: Selected Issues." *Annals of the New York Academy of Sciences* 362:125–31. Controlled experimental work on human beings from the mid-1970s through 1981 constitute the review base for this article. For recreational cocaine users, undesired effects are rare and not serious. Yet reports of undesirable effects persist, including irritability and lassitude. In high doses cocaine can cause depression and even death. Contrary to some forms of amphetamines, cocaine tends not to produce aggressive behavior. Animal studies are also included in this article. Chronic cocaine abuse does not commonly appear as a medical problem. ^Cocaine ^Health ^Reviews ^Consequences\Misc ^Consequences\Critique

650. —— (1985). *Cocaine: A Drug and Its Social Evolution*. Rev. Ed. New York: Basic Books. History of use of cocaine in the United States and the development of the cocaine habit. This edition of Grinspoon and Bakalar's 1976 volume contains a new chapter summarizing the major developments in cocaine research and cocaine use since the first edition was published. Cocaine use and abuse have spread much more widely than anticipated on the basis of the 1976 study. Cocaine use is a greater social problem now than at any time in its previous history, with ramifications in all areas of American life. Review of new findings on coca leaf chewing and the effects of chronic cocaine use, and a discussion on the "new and dangerous practice of smoking cocaine," or free basing. The viability of certain treatment patterns is noted, and an updated bibliography is offered. Addressed mainly to the nonspecialist but does include material on neurophysiology and pharmacology. The authors provide a bibliographical essay. ^United\States ^Cocaine ^Drug\Use ^Health ^Bibliographies ^Drug\Use\History ^Consequences\Social ^Coca ^Consequences\Misc ^Cocaine\Pharmacology ^Consequences\Neurological ^Consequences\Physiological

651. —— (1990). "Arguments for a Harmfulness Tax." *The Journal of Drug Issues* 20:4(Fall): 599–604. All legal and illegal drugs should be taxed on the basis of the harm they impose on society. This tax should be imposed on alcohol, tobacco and marijuana to begin with, and thereafter extended to other drugs, including cocaine. Such a tax regime would ultimately replace current prohibition laws. ^P\S\Taxation ^P\S\Policies

652. Groedidler, Camille (1984). "Mexico Becoming Center of Drug Traffic Despite Anti-Drug Drive." *The Christian Science Monitor*, 11 January, 9. Brief description of how Mexico is becoming a key transshipment state for drugs from Latin America to the United States. Interestingly, cocaine factories that have never been there before are moving into Mexico and are processing coca paste. Petrochemical ingredients needed are more available and less controlled in Mexico than in conventional countries that produce narcotics (i.e., Colombia). ^Mexico ^Cocaine ^Drug\Traffic ^Precursor\Chemicals ^Latin\America ^Refining ^Cocaine\Paste ^Colombia

653. Gropper, Bernard A. (1985). "Probing the Links Between Drugs and Crime." *National Institute of Justice: Research in Brief* (February): 1–6. The nature and extent of linkages between drugs and crime are far from being fully understood, yet the belief continues that they are linked in fundamental ways, and this guides efforts to control crime through the prevention and control of drug abuse. Summary of findings from recent research that examines the nature and extent of the drug-crime relationship at the individual offender level. There is a growing body of evidence suggesting that drug abusers are at high risk for violence. Discusses direct and indirect relations among drugs, crime, and the longer term effects of addiction on complex causal mechanisms at work. Strikingly, even among hard-core heroin addicts, reducing the level of drug use reduces the level of criminal activity, as is also the reverse when drug usage

increases. The average daily heroin user gained over $18,000 in economic value (cash and drugs received without payment) from crime. Citing B. Johnson and others (*Taking Care of Business: The Economics of Crime By Heroin Abusers*, Lexington Books, 1985), comments are made about the economic impacts on victims and society. Freeloading, drug distribution crimes, and nondrug crimes are assessed with dollar figures appended. ^Drug\Use ^Crime ^Economics ^Society ^Consequences\Violence ^Drug\Use\Theories ^Crime\Theories ^Consequences\Social ^Consequences\Economic ^Statistics

654. Gross, Jane (1988). "Speed's Gain in Use Could Rival Crack, Drug Experts Warn." *The New York Times*, 27 November, 1. Speed, or methamphetamine, a powerful stimulant to the nervous system, is manufactured in clandestine laboratories in the United States and is seeing its use increased astronomically. ^United\States ^Drug\Use ^Designer\Drugs

655. Grosse, Robert (1990). "The Economic Impact of Andean Cocaine Traffic on Florida." *Journal of Interamerican Studies and World Affairs* 32:4 (Winter): 136–59. Examines the impact of Latin America's cocaine trade on law enforcement, medical expenses, lost production (due to employee work indisposition) and opportunity costs associated with investment and consumption. ^United\States ^Florida ^Cocaine ^Consequences\Economic ^Consequences\Law\Enforcement ^Consequences\Health\Care ^Workplace

656. "Growing Concern over the Drug Scene" (1986). *The Current Digest of the Soviet Press* 38(34): 1–20. Interviews with various named official sources about the extent of drug usage in the Soviet Union. ^USSR ^Drug\Use

657. "The Guaraní Connection" (1985). *Latin American Regional Reports*, 2 August, 6. Describes Paraguay's role in providing chemicals essential to the production of cocaine and the facilitation by government authorities of its transit to Peru. ^Latin\America ^Peru ^Paraguay ^Cocaine ^Drug\Traffic ^Precursor\Chemicals ^Politics ^Consequences\Corruption

658. "Guatemala: International Pressure on Drug Traffickers Opens a New Frontier." (1989). *Latinamerica Press*, November 23, p. 5. In response to antidrug pressures elsewhere in South America and the Caribbean, Guatemala has become an important transhipment point in the trade. It is estimated that about 1000 kilos of cocaine pass through Guatemala every week. Beyond this, however, Guatemala is also developing into a major opium poppy producing country. Opium poppies have now overtaken marijuana in economic importance there. ^Latin\America ^Guatemala ^Traffickers ^Opiates ^Cannabis

659. "Guess Which Country Has Legalized Pot" (1983). *Newsweek*, 1 August, 40. Announcement that Spain, in July 1983, became the first nation in Europe to legalize the use of marijuana. ^Europe ^Spain ^Cannabis ^Decriminalization

660. Gugliotta, Guy (1989). "Bennett Urges Aid to Divert Coca Economy." *The Miami Herald*, 27 May, 6A. William Bennett is now talking of the need for integrated aid to Latin America—to persuade the politicians and the military to participate, and the peasants to grow alternative crops, as a means of cutting back supplies of coca. ^United\States ^Coca ^P\S\Foreign\Aid ^Military ^Crop\Substitution

661. —— (1989). "Castro Learns Tough Lesson about the Business of Drugs." *The Miami Herald*, 1 July, A1. High-ranking elements in the Cuban government, including General Ochoa, were subverted by money associated with international traffic in narcotics. ^Cuba ^Drug\Traffic ^Consequences\Political ^Consequences\Corruption ^Caribbean

662. —— (1989). "Costa Rica Drug Probe Taints Elite with Scandal." *The Miami Herald*, 25 June, 12A. The Costa Rican Legislative Commission on Drug Trafficking has uncovered a scandal involving three supreme court justices, one leading presidential contender, and the homicide chief of the judicial police. Other reputations have been sullied. ^Costa\Rica ^Drug\Traffic ^Latin\America ^Consequences\Corruption

663. —— (1989). "Cuba Accuses U.S. of Withholding Drug Information." *The Miami Herald*, 4 July, 1A. Cuba, claiming that it did not know its own people were trafficking in drugs, now criticizes the United States for withholding information about that trafficking for over two years. ^Cuba ^Caribbean ^United\States ^Drug\Control\Policies ^International\Cooperation ^Consequences\Foreign\Relations

664. —— (1989). "Cuban Court Sentences 4 to Death." *The Miami Herald*, 8 July, 1. Description of the outcome, in Cuba, of the court proceedings against Major General Arnoldo Ochoa and his coconspirators in the international drug trade. ^Cuba ^Caribbean ^Drug\Traffic ^Law\Enforcement ^Consequences\Foreign\Relations ^Traffickers ^Consequences\Corruption

665. —— (1989). "Drug Scandal Widens; Cuba Jails Four More." *The Miami Herald*, 1 August, A1. The interior ministry has been virtually "decapitated" in recent weeks in the Cuban government's continuing purge of functionaries stained by a seven-week drug scandal. Earlier three top-level functionaries were executed. Names involved in subsequent personnel shuffles are given. In less than a month, Cuba has purged four out of the six top-ranking officials of the interior ministry and three of the five top-ranking members of the ministry's central political directorate. ^Cuba ^Drug\Traffic ^Law\Enforcement ^Caribbean ^Consequences\Political ^Consequences\Corruption

666. —— (1989). *Kings of Cocaine: Inside the Medellín Cartel—An Astonishing True Story of Murder, Money, and International Corruption*. New York: Simon and Schuster. Investigative reporters review the names, places, and events associated with the rise of the Colombian drug traffickers' operations and networks in the United States, in transiting countries, and in Colombia. The saga of their internal wars, assaults on government and people, conflicts among themselves, and success in marketing their product are noted. An epilogue gives recent biographical sketches on numerous personalities in the trade. Connections with Panama, Cuba, Nicaragua, and the Bahamas are explored. ^Drug\Traffic ^Latin\America ^Colombia ^Traffickers ^Consequences\Corruption ^Consequences\Violence ^United\States ^Florida ^Law\Enforcement ^Cuba ^Bahamas ^Panama ^Nicaragua

667. Gujral, B. B. (1983). "Forfeiture of Illegally Acquired Assets of Drug Traffickers: The Position in India." *Bulletin on Narcotics* 35(2): 41–48. Traditional enforcement techniques aimed only at carriers and confiscation of seized contraband no longer provide sufficient deterrents. In 1976, India enacted specific legislation providing for the forfeiture of the property and assets of smugglers, including traffickers and foreign exchange manipulators. Described are the essential features of this act which has enabled forfeiture action in over 2,000 cases, covering property valued in excess of 40 million U.S. dollars. ^India ^Asset\Forfeiture ^Law\Enforcement ^Legislation ^Drug\Control\Policies\History

668. Gunn, P. C. (1984). "Forfeiture of Narcotics-Generated Wealth in the United States of America Pursuant to the Comprehensive Forfeiture Act of 1984." *Bulletin on Narcotics* 36(4): 61–89. In 1984 the United States Congress enacted the Comprehensive Forfeiture Act. This article discusses the act's parts and its relationship to the RICO (Racketeer Influence and Corrupt Organization) statutes. Also, the author discusses implementation of provisions for the 1984 act. ^United\States ^Asset\Forfeiture ^Drug\Control\Policies\History ^Legislation

669. Gylys, Julius A. (1988). "Cocaine Industry and Demographic Patterns of Consumption." *International Social Science Review* 63(2): 78–83. Recent cocaine abuse surveys suggest that major demographic changes are occurring among American cocaine users. The increased supply and eventual decline of price not only created a market glut but also made cocaine and its derivatives affordable to lower income groups. The result is that, with increased use, a serious public health problem of major proportions could be upon the United States. ^United\States ^Cocaine ^Drug\Use ^Economics ^Society ^Supply ^Consequences\Markets ^Consequences\Social ^Consequences\Health ^Consequences\Economic

670. Hackett, George (1988). "Saying 'No' to Crack Gangs." *Newsweek*, 28 March, 29. Description of Moslem brotherhoods working to take back the neighborhoods in which they live from the drug traders. ^United\States ^Law\Enforcement ^Private\Initiatives

671. Hackett, George and Michael A. Lerner (1987). "L.A. Law: Gangs and Crack." *Newsweek*, 27 April, 35–36. Gangs are fighting for market shares in Los Angeles, and violence and mayhem are the order of the day. A staggering abundance of crack and cocaine are available in the L.A. area. ^United\States ^Cocaine ^Crack ^Drug\Traffic ^Organized\Crime ^California ^Consequences\Violence

672. Hager, Philip (1987). "Air Searches for Marijuana in Open Fields Ruled Legal." *Los Angeles Times*, 1 January, 32. The California Supreme Court has upheld the constitutionality of warrantless aerial surveillance over open fields as police search for illegal marijuana cultivations. ^United\States ^Cannabis ^Law\Enforcement ^Surveillance ^California ^Judiciary ^Consequences\Human\Rights

673. Haislip, Gene R. (1982). "International Traffic in Methaqualone." *Drug Enforcement* (Summer): 11-13. Discussion of a synthetic sedative-type drug which can be addictive and which can cause seizures. This drug is being traded internationally, excessively, and, in some instances, illegally. ^Drug\Traffic ^Designer\Drugs

674. ———— (1984). "Commerce in Drugs and Chemicals and the Detection of Clandestine Laboratories." *Bulletin on Narcotics* 36(1): 25–31. Numerous clandestine laboratories operate in the United States producing methamphetamines, PSP, and LSD. The number in operation appears to be increasing. When drugs are seized, it is necessary to determine whether they have been clandestinely manufactured. Special techniques are used, involving detailed physical and chemical examinations. Describes the nature of these examinations and how they are used. Describes undercover techniques for detecting clandestine laboratories. Chemicals used in these laboratories are often diverted from legitimate sources through international commerce as well as clandestine sources. This is an international problem requiring monitoring through international cooperation. ^United\States ^Law\Enforcement ^Designer\Drugs

675. Hakim, Peter (1987). "Debt and Drugs: Deadly Partnership." *The Christian Science Monitor*, 1 May, 18. In the wake of massive Latin American debt came collapsing domestic economies. And in the wake of the collapsing economies came the development of drug supply capabilities that offer incentive, employment, and security for hundreds of thousands of people. The flow of drugs to the United States will continue so long as economic crisis blocks the alternatives to jobs, income, and foreign exchange that drugs now provide and the Latin American people seek. All this nourishes guerrilla movements and makes people more readily available for recruitment into the drug trade. Governments, pressed hard to find additional sources of hard currency that have been upset by existing debt arrangements, have been led into a certain tolerance for the drug trade. ^Latin\America ^Drug\Traffic ^Economics ^International\Debt ^Consequences\Social

^Consequences\Political ^Consequences\Economic ^Production\Incentives\Economic ^Insurgents
^Foreign\Exchange

676. Halikas, James A., Ronald A. Weller, Carolyn L. Morse, and Raymond G. Hoffmann (1985). "A Longitudinal Study of Marijuana Effects." *The International Journal of the Addictions* 20(50): 701–11. In the early 1970s 100 regular marijuana users volunteered to be extensively interviewed and their experiences assessed in 105 areas. Six to eight years later 97 of these informants were relocated, and a time series comparison was done on the groupings. Reports of appetite effects, sex effects, and intoxication effects on sleep remained stable. Reports of cognitive effects, mood effects, and aftereffects on sleep appeared to be shifting from desirable to undesirable.   ^Cannabis ^Health ^Consequences\Misc ^Consequences\Sexuality ^Consequences\Physiological ^Consequences\Neurological ^Consequences\Psychological

677. Hallgrimsson, Olafur (1980). "Methadone Treatment: The Nordic Attitude." *Journal of Drug Issues* 10(4): 463–75. Methadone maintenance treatment programs, in America and England, particularly England, have not given scientific proof that it is a legitimate treatment of drug addicts, and this 15 years after the development of the maintenance programs. The degree of skepticism about methadone maintenance is strong in the Nordic countries and only to a limited extent has it been used there. Specific discussion is undertaken for Norway, Denmark, Sweden, Finland, and Iceland. ^Norway ^United\States ^United\Kingdom ^Scandinavia ^Denmark ^Sweden ^Finland ^Iceland ^Heroin ^Treatment ^Methadone ^Treatment\Critique

678. Hamm, Mark Steven (1985). "Heroin Addiction, Anomie and Social Policy in the United States and Britain." Ph.D. diss., Arizona State University. What predisposes people to become heroin addicts? Is it the nature of a country's social control policy, or is it a country's general social and cultural ambience? This dissertation attempts to explain the role of *both* policy and social-economic background and processes as explanatory factors in heroin addiction. The rates of heroin addiction are correlated against social factors related to the concept of anomie—suicide, family disorder, unemployment, crime, and mental illness. Both U.S. and British rates of heroin addiction have increased several times greater than national rates of social disturbance. There is an inverse relationship among rates of heroin addiction and suicide, homicide, and mental illness. Thus the findings point toward the "policy thesis" as being the best explanation of the dimensions of heroin problems noted in the United States and in Britain.   ^United\Kingdom ^United\States ^Heroin ^Drug\Use ^Law\Enforcement ^Society ^Drug\Use\Theories ^Consequences\Misc

679. Hammer, Signe, and Lesley Hazleton (1984). "Cocaine and the Chemical Brain." *Science Digest* 92(10): 58. From the vantage of a pharmacologist, the alkaloids of cocaine are studied, and a hypothesis is advanced as to how they alter the action of delicate neurons in the brain. ^Cocaine ^Health ^Consequences\Neurological ^Cocaine\Pharmacology

680. Hamowy, Ronald, ed. (1987). *Dealing with Drugs: Consequences of Government Control.* Lexington, Mass.: Lexington Books. Drug abuse and narcotic laws in the United States. This is a wide-ranging, edited volume, including individually authored chapters by some of the principal scholars/advocates on drugs (e.g., Lester Grinspoon, Arnold Trebach). The focus is on the effects of prohibition (Part 1), medical research concerning illicit substances (Part 2), and discussions about policy reform (Part 3). Within the whole, discussions are developed regarding the history of legislative control over opiates, cocaine, and their derivatives; the harmful side effects of legal prohibition of certain kinds of drugs; the need for reform of international narcotics laws; the relationship of drugs to United States foreign policy; a study of heroin

markets before and after legalization; and a moral philosophy discussion on drug controls. With respect to medical research, discussions are raised about the medical uses of illicit drugs, the meaning of addiction with respect to cocaine and marijuana, and factors involved in the development of controlled use of intoxicants so as not to misuse them. There is an extensive bibliography. ^United\States ^Drug\Control\Policies ^Reviews ^Bibliographies ^Consequences\Law\Enforcement ^Consequences\Drug\Control\Policies ^Drug\Control\Policies\History ^Consequences\Foreign\Relations ^Consequences\Markets ^Heroin ^Decriminalization ^Consequences\Misc

681. Hannon, Timothy H. (1981). "On the Optimality of Legalizing Heroin Sales." In *Research in Urban Economics*, edited by J. Vernon Henderson. Greenwich, Conn.: Jai Press Inc. A technical paper, employing econometric theory, formally presents conditions governing the effect of antisupply enforcement against heroin which could argue for the legalization of heroin sales. Concludes that legalization in a dynamic framework in which less costly availability of heroin could produce additional addicts would make the "legalization of heroin sales . . . far from optimal." On the other hand, if antisupply enforcement were found to have no effect on the creation of additional addicts (or the maturation of existing addicts), legalization of sales could be dictated regardless of other considerations. ^Heroin ^Drug\Traffic ^Economics ^Decriminalization\Critique ^Supply ^Demand ^Consequences\Social

682. Hanreich, H. (1984). "Drug-Related Crime and Sentencing Policies from the Perspective of the United Nations Crime Prevention and Criminal Justice Programme." *Bulletin on Narcotics* 36(3): 49–57. Due, in part, to the incompleteness of available data, no conclusive evidence exists on the effectiveness of sentencing policies in various countries. This deficiency relates especially to drug-related infractions. Regardless, drug legislation in the respective countries reflects the sociocultural, religious, and other values of a nation. There is a growing tendency to move toward treatment and social reintegration of offenders rather than continual application of punitive sanctions. There is also a growing tendency to decriminalize the simple use of drugs and to provide more severe penalties for drug trafficking. In some countries, however, there is a trend toward increased penalties for illicit drug use as well. ^Drug\Use ^Law\Enforcement ^Drug\Control\Policies ^Reviews

683. Hanson, Bill, George Beschner, James M. Walters, and Elliott Bovelle (1985). *Life with Heroin: Voices from the Inner City*. Lexington, Mass.: Lexington Books. Focuses on the social relationships and roles of addicts outside of treatment settings. This book is about inner-city, black, male heroin users, and, following a modified ethnographic methodology, relies on the users' own words to describe lives that revolve around the use of heroin. In-depth interviews were conducted with 124 men in ghettos of Chicago, New York, Washington, D.C., and Philadelphia. The interviews, conducted by former heroin addicts, reveal a wide range of skills and adaptive strategies that enable addicts to survive and be part of a daily routine in their neighborhoods. One striking finding is that "it is the pursuit of normalcy rather than of euphoria which propels these heroin users to continue to use the substance. In a society which has relegated them to a lowly status, which they reject, the achievement of normalcy is an accomplishment that these men value" (p. 177). The picture painted of the black, inner city, male, regular heroin user who has never been in treatment reveals the existence of a unique and culturally complex group of users. The existence of such groups implies significant consideration of policy decisions regarding how best to cope with, prevent, and treat heroin use. One implication of this study deals with heroin use and crime. Significant findings include: (1) the volume of crime the men needed to support their habit was lower than previously attributed to inner-city heroin users; (2) their heroin

intake was adjusted to their economic circumstances—they used or did not use it depending on their success of generating income, from whatever source; (3) their volume of crime is volitional rather than compulsive (only 18% of the men reported involvement in armed robbery or stickups); and (4) the antidote for heroin-related volitional crime is probably not the administration of treatment but rather the administration of justice (p. 181). Insofar as these findings are accurate, it would seem that development of effective early-prevention and early-intervention strategies would provide the opportunity for youthful heroin experimenters to discontinue drug use by stressing, among other things, their need to understand and manage their social and cultural system (which the addicts prided themselves in being able to do). Contains a methodological appendix. ^United\States ^Heroin ^Crime ^Society ^Culture ^Prevention ^Minorities ^Consequences\Social ^Illinois ^New\York ^Washington\DC ^Pennsylvania ^Consequences\Personal ^Drug\Use ^P\S\Law\Enforcement

684. Hanson, David J. (1982). "The Effectiveness of Alcohol and Drug Education." *Journal of Alcohol and Drug Education* 27(2): 1–13. In a review of a large number of studies, most find no effects of drug education on drug use. A few have found drug use to be reduced as a consequence of drug education; others have found it to actually increase following such education. Over 120 studies are cited. ^Drug\Use ^Reviews ^Drug\Control\Policies\Effectiveness ^Prevention\Drug\Education\Critique

685. Hanson, F. Allan (1988). "Some Implications of Drug Testing." *Kansas University Law Review* 36:899–917. Approached anthropologically, the author explores the economic and social conditions that make drug testing an acceptable social convention as well as the general consequences the testing has for society. As for consequences, he sees a possible contribution to a growing schism in American society. He gives substantial consideration to the implications of confidentiality associated with drug testing. ^United\States ^Drug\Testing ^Economics ^Society ^Consequences\Social

686. Haqqani, Husain (1986). "Poppy-Bloom Boom." *Far Eastern Economic Review*, 10 July, 42. Description of the substantial increase in the growing of poppies in Pakistan. ^Pakistan ^Golden\Crescent ^Opiates ^Production ^Southwest\Asia ^Production\Statistics

687. Harden, Blaine (1985). "Marijuana is Not a Jamaican Staple Crop, Seaga Says." *The Washington Post*, 2 February, A12. The Jamaican Prime Minister, Edward Seaga, says that the United States statistics on the importance of his country's marijuana production for the country's economy have been grossly exaggerated. ^Jamaica ^Caribbean ^Cannabis ^Drug\Traffic ^Economics ^Statistics\Critique

688. Harrison, Carlos (1989). "Kids on Crack: 880 Crimes Each in a Year." *The Miami Herald*, 3 August, 1. A study of 254 Dade County 12 to 17-year-olds using or selling crack illustrates the stunning association of criminality with drugs. By their own estimates, the youth were responsible for 223,000 crimes—about 880 each, involving drug dealing, prostitution, robberies, and burglaries. Many of the crimes were done to sustain drug habits. Almost all the youngsters started their abuse careers by drinking alcohol. James Inciardi is quoted as saying, "What we are seeing in this data is really the destruction of a whole generation of youth." The data were collected by Inciardi, who counters conventional wisdom about the rapidly debilitating and almost instantly addictive properties of crack. People who start on crack very likely will continue, but for reasons other than its immediate addictiveness. And what is the solution? Drugs will go away when economic, social, and environmental conditions in inner cities are improved. ^United\States ^Cocaine ^Crack ^Drug\Use ^Youth ^Crime ^Society ^Florida ^Statistics ^P\S\Economic

689. Hart, Roy Hanu (1980). *Bitter Grass: The Cruel Truth about Marijuana*. Shawnee Mission, Kansas Psychoneurologia Press, in cooperation with

American Academy of Psychiatry and Neurology. Physiological effects and toxicology of marijuana. This is the work of a clinical psychiatrist. He distances himself from a "research" psychiatrist but argues that clinical studies can provide extraordinary insights. From his clinical practice he concludes that there is only one public policy response to marijuana: Figure out how to reduce or eliminate its use. ^Cannabis ^Health ^Consequences\Physiological

690. Hartlyn, Jonathan (1988). "Commentary on Bagley's 'The New Hundred Years War? National Security and the War on Drugs in Latin America.'" *Journal of Interamerican Studies and World Affairs* 30(1): 183–86. The author reviews Bagley's work favorably, but wants to concentrate more on the legalization question. Rather than accept, as Bagley has, the fact that legalization is not currently politically viable, this author wants to focus research on the development of more detailed options of legalization, along with their potential costs, modes of implementation, and methods of enforcement. ^P\S\Legalization

691. Hartnoll, R. L. (1986). "Current Situation Relating to Drug Abuse Assessment in European Countries." *Bulletin on Narcotics* 38(1-2): 65–80. Since the mid-1970s substantial increases in heroin abuse have occurred in most European countries. The reliability of the reported statistics is reviewed and questioned, but without arguing that there is anything other than a serious drug problem in Europe. Calls for improved cooperation among European countries in elaborating, as a minimum, common criteria and definitions, along with instruments to gather data. The entire level of intercountry cooperation on drug issues needs to be improved. ^Europe ^Drug\Use ^Drug\Control\Policies ^Reviews ^Heroin ^Statistics\Critique ^P\S\International\Cooperation

692. Harwood, Henrick J., Robert L. Hubbard, James J. Collins, and J. Valley Rachal (1988). "The Costs of Crime and the Benefits of Drug Abuse Treatment: A Cost-Benefitting Analysis Using TOPS Data." In *Compulsory Treatment of Drug Abuse: Research and Clinical Practice*, NIDA Research Monograph 86, edited by Carl G. Leukefeld and Frank M. Tims. Rockville, Md.: National Institute on Drug Abuse. Discussed are the economic impacts of drug abuse and perspectives on the social costs of that abuse. The economic measures employed show that crime is lower after treatment than before. Reduction magnitudes differ considerably depending on what economic measures are used. Treatment comparisons and economic measures need to be scrutinized. Statistical tables include data on criminal activity in the year before and after treatment of over 2,000 clients, economic impacts of drug abusers one year before treatment and one year after discharge of the same number of clients, and the average economic impact of abusers in the year before treatment and the year after discharge. Significant benefits derive to law-abiding citizens, in economic terms, from drug-abuse treatment. ^Drug\Use ^Crime ^Treatment ^Economics ^NIDA ^Consequences\Economic ^Treatment\Compulsory ^Statistics

693. Hauge, Ragnar (1985). "Trends in Drug Use in Norway." *Journal of Drug Issues* 15(3): 321–31. Heated debates occur in Norway with respect to the social problems associated with drug abuse. Some say problems are increasing; others say they are not. The incidence of new users seems to be stable, but the number of older users who continue their drug use in adult age is increasing. Inasmuch as older groups tend to have more personal and social problems than younger ones, drug problems in Norway can be said to be increasing. ^Scandinavia ^Norway ^Drug\Use ^Society ^Consequences\Social

694. Havemann, Judith (1988). "Report Rejects Penalizing Panama; Certification as Drug Fighter Urged for U.S. Security Reasons." *The Washington*

Post, 21 February, A27. Politics and international foreign policy are interfering with the "drug war" again. A state department draft report recommends that Panama, whose military leader is under federal indictment on drug-related charges, be certified as cooperating in the worldwide U.S. fight against illegal drugs. This is in the interest of "other national interests." ^Latin\America ^Panama ^United\States ^Drug\Control\Policies ^Consequences\Foreign\Policy

695. ———— (1989). "Drug Tests Catch 203 in Sensitive Jobs: U.S. Officials Say Policy's Value Proven." *The Washington Post*, 8 March, A1. The government's program of random drug testing has caught 203 federal employees using illegal drugs. Among these are 60 air traffic controllers and 42 employees in the nuclear and chemical weapons security program. Still, the controversy as to whether this is an appropriate method for creating a "drug-free work place" is pertinent. ^United\States ^Drug\Testing ^Workplace ^Consequences\Public\Safety ^Drug\Testing\Laws

696. ———— (1989). "Rulings Force Agencies to Reevaluate Test Policies." *The Washington Post*, 22 March, A14. Discusses the recent ruling of the Supreme Court allowing mandatory testing of employees in law enforcement and public safety occupations for illegal drugs. This will force federal agencies to reexamine plans for their random testing. Discussion of the difficulty of deciding who should be tested. ^United\States ^Drug\Testing ^Drug\Testing\Laws

697. Haverkos, Harry W. (1988). "Overview: HIV Infection among Intravenous Drug Abusers in the United States and Europe." In *Needle Sharing among Intravenous Drug Abusers: National and International Perspectives*, NIDA Research Monograph 80, edited by Robert J. Battjes and Roy W. Pickens. Rockville, Md.: National Institute on Drug Abuse. Data are given on AIDS cases among intravenous drug users in the United States and in Europe. Various studies are reviewed. It is apparent that once AIDS or HIV is introduced into a group of intravenous drug users, it can spread readily among the users, to their sexual partners, and to their children yet unborn. The magnitude of HIV prevalence rates and AIDS cases is expected to continue to increase among intravenous drug users worldwide for at least the next several years. ^Europe ^United\States ^Heroin ^Drug\Use ^AIDS ^NIDA ^Statistics ^Fetuses ^Consequences\Fetuses

698. Hawkes, Nigel (1988). *The International Drug Trade*. Vero Beach, Fla.: Rourke Enterprises Inc. This is an example of a drug literature book that attempts to swing people away from narcotics consumption. Amply endowed with photographs and simple language, the book is, nevertheless, reasonably accurate in its discussion of addiction, how drugs are produced, how they are smuggled and trafficked, how the law enforcement agents attempt to stop the trade, and what the international response has been. ^Prevention\Drug\Education

699. Hawkins, J. David, and Richard F. Catalano, Jr. (1985). "Aftercare in Drug Abuse Treatment." *International Journal of the Addictions* 20(6-7): 917–45. Summarizes the literature on the effectiveness of various kinds of post-treatment care to prevent relapse among treated drug abusers. Limitations in this literature are noted, and promising directions for policy development are described. ^Drug\Use ^Treatment ^Drug\Control\Policies\Effectiveness ^Reviews

700. Hawks, David (1988). "The Proposal to Make Heroin Available Legally to Intravenous Drug Abusers." *The Medical Journal of Australia* 149:455–456. Inasmuch as it seems unlikely that drug dependence will be reduced, the target now should be to render drug dependence safer. This at least would be a positive step toward dealing with AIDS. The pitfalls, in terms of making heroin available legally,

are discussed. The intent is to force upon public policymakers a consideration of the implications of a change in heroin policy before prematurely embarking on change. ^Australia ^Heroin ^Drug\Use ^Health ^AIDS ^P\S\Legalization ^Decriminalization\Critique

701. Haworth, A. (1983). "Reactions to Problems of Drug Abuse in Zambia." *Bulletin on Narcotics* 35(1): 1–9. Apart from cannabis, other illicit drugs had not been much of a problem in Zambia. When UNESCO initiated a study, however, it became apparent that a drug-abuse problem was beginning to develop in Zambia. Preventive efforts should be implemented and should include drug education, information, and research components. The proposed components are described in this article. ^Zambia ^Africa ^Drug\Use ^Drug\Control\Policies ^Proffered\Solutions ^UNESCO

702. Hayes, Janice S., Melanie C. Dreher, and J. Kevin Nugent (1988). "Newborn Outcomes with Maternal Marihuana Use in Jamaican Women." *Pediatric Nursing* 14(2): 107–10. In Jamaica, marijuana use in pregnancy carries social overtones of reinforcement, mutual aid and help, and conviviality. Newborn babies are cared for and are stimulated. Marijuana used in pregnancy under these cultural and social environmental conditions must be viewed differently from marijuana used under other circumstances when examining newborn outcomes. The care-giving environment may have a greater effect on the positive development of the infant than the single effects of marijuana use during pregnancy. ^Jamaica ^Cannabis ^Drug\Use ^Women ^Health ^Society ^Culture ^Caribbean ^Consequences\Social ^Fetuses ^Pregnancy

703. Hayes, Monte (1987). "Peru Rebels Profit from Drug Ties." *Los Angeles Times*, 27 December, 32. Argues that since early 1987 the rebels of the Maoist guerrilla movement Shining Path have worked in a "deadly alliance" with drug dealers and peasants involved in the drug trade. Description of the associated violence in the upper Huallaga Valley. The motivation, it is alleged, is economic because the coca trade has become a source of income for the terrorists. ^Latin\America ^Peru ^Coca ^Drug\Traffic ^Insurgents ^Consequences\Violence ^Traffickers\Incentives\Economic ^Terrorists

704. Hazarika, Sanjoy (1987). "Heroin Addiction Big New Problem in India." *The New York Times*, 15 February, 25. From an anecdotal statement about two 13-year-olds in New Delhi, the author briefly explores the swiftly growing number of Indians, estimated at between a half million and one million, who have become heroin addicts in the country within the last five years. All of this is challenging cultural traditions and family life and, it is said, is fragmenting the social fabric of India's cities. It has moved beyond the affluent neighborhoods to rootless migrants. The drug is easily available in New Delhi and in other Indian cities. ^India ^Heroin ^Drug\Use ^Society ^Consequences\Social ^Consequences\Family

705. Headley, Bernard D. (1988). "War In 'Babylon': Dynamics of the Jamaican Informal Drug Economy." *Social Justice* 15(3-4): 61–86. The author's basic aim is to show how "dependent development" in Jamaica has produced such a scarcity of socially acceptable work that a substantial part of the Jamaican population has been economically marginalized. To extricate itself from the result of that marginalization, some Jamaicans join gangs, become expatriots, and become involved in the international drug traffic. Violence, crime, and terror are a partial result in the mainland United States. The author sees the pursuit of the drug trade as just "normal" capitalistic goals and values (primarily accumulation and market monopoly) which produce terror and crime. ^Jamaica ^United\States ^Drug\Traffic ^Organized\Crime ^Economics ^Informal\Economy ^Traffickers\Theories

706. "Heads Roll in Trafficking Saga" (1985). *Latin America Weekly Report*, 15 February, 3. Description of a growing scandal over cocaine shipment through Colombia's Madrid embassy, which has occasioned head rolling in Colombia's foreign

ministry. Colombia's presidential press secretary and others are now jailed on charges of participating in those shipments via the ministry's foreign diplomatic pouch. ^Colombia ^Spain ^Cocaine ^Drug\Traffic ^Europe ^Latin\America ^Consequences\Corruption ^Consequences\Political

707. Healy, Kevin (1986). "The Boom Within the Crisis: Some Recent Effects of Foreign Cocaine Markets on Bolivian Rural Society and Economy." In *Coca and Cocaine, Effects on People and Policy in Latin America*, edited by D. Pacini and C. Franquemont, 101–43. Cambridge, Mass.: Cornell University and Cultural Survival. (See the entry under Pacini, Deborah, and Christine Franquemont) ^Latin\America ^Bolivia ^Cocaine ^Drug\Traffic ^Consequences\Social ^Consequences\Economic

708. ——— (1988). "Bolivia and Cocaine: A Developing Country's Dilemmas." *British Journal of Addiction* 83:19–23. Amidst Bolivia's worst economic crisis of the century, the illicit cocaine business during the 1980s has generated much needed foreign exchange along with income and employment for tens of thousands of poor farmers and traders. While these economic benefits have been highly visible, they have been accompanied by a long list of social ills ranging from corruption and drug abuse to decreasing food production and superfluous, if not luxury, consumption, particularly among the *narcotraficantes*. These problems present Bolivia with a difficult dilemma between economic survival and the well-being of its society. The effective opposition to coca leaf eradication programs from well-organized peasant unions tied closely to the national labor movement is noted. Solutions must provide attractive prices for alternate crops via preferential export markets in the U.S. and Western Europe. ^Bolivia ^Cocaine ^Drug\Traffic ^Economics ^Society ^P\S\Economic ^Traffickers ^Producers\Unions ^Latin\America ^Foreign\Exchange ^Consequences\Economic ^Consequences\Social ^Consequences\Corruption ^Drug\Use ^Consequences\Misc

709. ——— (1988). "Coca, the State, and the Peasantry in Bolivia, 1982–1988." *Journal of Interamerican Studies and World Affairs* 30, nos. 2 & 3 (Summer, Fall):105–26. Chronicles the development of Bolivian coca producers as an interest group and their affiliation with formal peasant labor organizations. Examines the political conflicts between the government and its peasantry over the production and distribution of coca during the 1980s. Efforts to reduce coca production have been largely unsuccessful. Political and economic explanations are given. Bolivia's anti–coca leaf law of 1987 is examined. The dynamics are placed in the context of Bolivia's political culture. Prospects for eradication of coca crops in Bolivia's Chapare are reviewed. ^Latin\America ^Bolivia ^Production ^Coca ^Producers\Unions ^Consequences\Political ^Drug\Control\Policies\Critique ^Legislation ^Consequences\Cultural ^Crop\Eradication

710. ——— (1989). "The Political Ascent of Bolivia's Peasant Coca Leaf Producers." Paper Presented at the Fifteenth International Congress of the Latin American Studies Association, Miami, Florida, 3 December. Chronicles and analyzes the efforts of coca leaf producers, principally in the Chapare region, to protect their economic interests from national and international efforts to eradicate their crops. The effect of the exchange between national policy and producer interest on Bolivia's political system is analyzed. The effect of this exchange on the ability of the producer unions to improve their political skills, forge alliances with other groups, and prosecute legal positions is discussed. ^Latin\America ^Bolivia ^Coca ^Production ^Producers\Unions ^Consequences\Political ^Crop\Eradication

711. Hebert, L. Camille (1988). "Private Sector Drug Testing: Employer Rights, Risks, and Responsibilities." *Kansas University Law Review* 36:823–68. Employers implementing drug screening programs have met with challenges from several

fronts, and this article discusses the methods that private employers use and the issues such methods raise with respect to invasion of privacy, defamation, infliction of emotional distress, wrongful discharge, and discrimination against the handicapped. Extensively documented. ^United\States ^Drug\Testing ^Workplace ^Consequences\Political ^Consequences\Human\Rights

712. Heffernan, Ronald, John M. Martin, and Anne T. Romano (1982). "Homicides Related to Drug Trafficking." *Federal Probation* 42(3): 3–7. Examines whether the significantly increased homicides in the United States are drug related. Concludes that drug-related homicides do indeed exist on an increasing basis, and are a by-product of the violence inherent in trafficking the drugs. ^United\States ^Drug\Traffic ^Crime ^Consequences\Violence

713. Heineke, J. M., ed. (1978). *Economic Models of Criminal Behavior.* Amsterdam; Netherlands: North-Holland. Although not related directly to drug usage, this book draws together studies, which for economists have been rather new, in the economic analysis of illegal behavior. A portion of this volume summarizes, reviews, and critiques this literature. Insofar as the econometric models of the economists may have general application, it gives an important entry into ideas that may be applicable to understanding people's involvement in the narcotics trade as a subset of larger issues of illegal behavior. ^Drug\Traffic ^Economics ^Reviews ^Crime\Theories

714. Hendin, Herbert (1987). *Living High: Daily Marijuana Use among Adults.* New York: Human Sciences Press. Most past studies of marijuana usage have included subjects who use the drug minimally or only occasionally, and have been correlated with diverse variables such as peer pressure, "youth culture," poor academic performance, precocious sexual activity and antisocial behavior, anxiety and depression, low self-esteem, social difficulties, "amotivational" personality characteristics, and so forth. This study focuses on the adaptation of adults who, despite heavy marijuana use, appear, at least outwardly, to be leading productive lives. The goal was to obtain psychological understanding of the adaptive significance and consequences of long-term daily marijuana usage. The data collection methodology included a number of in-depth face-to-face interviews, a questionnaire, and psychological tests. Among the functions of marijuana are the following: related to self awareness—marijuana usage permitted the individuals they studied to lead an unexamined life strikingly free of introspection; work—marijuana reduced aggressiveness among hyper achievers and permitted them to relax and to enjoy social relationships, or to put aside responsibilities of the adult world; personal relationships—heavy usage made social involvement possible while keeping an emotional distance from others, including parents from their children. Marijuana maintained certain adults in a troubled adaptation, reinforcing their tendency not to look at, understand, or attempt to master their difficulties. "It served to detach them from their problems and allowed them to regard even serious difficulties as unimportant. Marijuana provided a buffer zone of sensation that functioned as a barrier against self-awareness and closeness to others" (pp. 172). ^Cannabis ^Health ^Drug\Use\Theories ^Amotivational\Syndrome ^Consequences\Psychological ^Workplace ^Consequences\Personal

715. Henkel, Ray (1982). "The Move to the Oriente: Colonization and Environmental Impact." In *Modern-Day Bolivia: Legacy of the Revolution and Prospects for the Future*, edited by J. R. Ladman, 277–301. Tempe: Center for Latin American Studies, Arizona State University, 277-301. Explores the Bolivian government's promotion, in the first half of the twentieth century, of colonization in the eastern lowlands as a means of solving many national development problems. Although it does not focus on the spontaneous colonization deriving from the drug trade into the areas of eastern Bolivia, the author nevertheless focuses on environmental

impacts that surely have been aggravated by enhanced colonization in recent years.
^Latin\America ^Bolivia ^Coca ^Economics ^Colonization ^Consequences\Environmental ^Consequences\Migration

716. ——— (1988). "The Bolivian Cocaine Industry." *Studies in Third World Societies* 37:53–80. Examines the origin and development of the Bolivian cocaine industry and looks at its economic value to the country. Traces where the money went, and what, in macro categories, was bought with it—land, other real estate, consumer goods, and legitimate business enterprises. With respect to the social impact of the cocaine industry, looks at coca-paste smoking and the politics of coca and cocaine control (and related corruption). Concludes that controlled cocaine production in Bolivia probably cannot be achieved as long as production of the coca leaf itself remains legal. Regardless, the cocaine economy has so permeated the entire political, economic, and social structures of the country that it will be difficult for Bolivia to gain much national autonomy until the government gains control over the coca and cocaine industry. ^Latin\America ^Bolivia ^Coca ^Cocaine ^Drug\Traffic ^Drug\Control\Policies ^Culture ^Cocaine\History ^Consequences\Economic ^Consequences\Social ^Cocaine\Paste ^Consequences\Corruption ^Drug\Control\Policies\Critique ^Consequences\Political ^Consequences\Sexuality

717. Henman, Anthony, and Osvaldo Pessoa, Jr. (1986). *Diamba Sarabamba*. São Paulo, Brazil: Ground. Cannabis use is traced in Brazil historically. Medical, juridical, and anthropological observations are made. Controlling cannabis use is much more feasible by utilizing cultural aspects of users rather than by imposing rules, regulations, and sanctions by some "outside authority." ^Latin\America ^Brazil ^Cannabis ^Drug\Use\History ^Drug\Control\Policies ^Prevention ^Society ^Culture ^P\S\Culture

718. Henman, Anthony, Roger Lewis, and Tim Malyon (1985). *Big Deal: The Politics of the Illicit Drugs Business*. London: Pluto Press. Political aspects of the control of narcotics, focusing on heroin, cocaine, and marijuana. The authors, stridently representing themselves as almost beyond the pale of conventional journalistic scholarship, have a clear agenda in mind. It is to encourage people to come to a realization that the economic contradictions and political costs generated by the illicit narcotics trade are totally unacceptable, and that the only apparent way out is to legalize drug trafficking. Thereafter governments can work at minimizing any eventual harm resulting from indiscriminate use of drug substances through educational and other policies. This would create conditions that would cease victimization of coca growers and others resulting from eradication and suppression policies aimed at suppliers. The basic methodology is to report experiences of the actual participants in the trade—the producers, traffickers, and users—"rather than reiterating received wisdoms." It is a book that looks at capitalist economies in general to examine whether the enormous sums of money generated in the illicit drug business are likely to constitute a real threat to their orthodoxy. Subjects addressed deal with heroin, cannabis, and cocaine, along with "style and money." Politics and economics internal to producing and consuming countries are treated, along with international politics and economics associated with narcotics trafficking. ^Drug\Traffic ^Economics ^Consequences\Political ^Consequences\Economic ^Consequences\Markets ^Proffered\Solutions

719. Henry, James S. (1980). "How to Make the Mob Miserable." *Washington Monthly* (June): 54–61. Currency demand in the United States is abnormally high, and one-hundred-dollar bills now make up over a third of the cash currency in circulation. A response? Invalidate large bills and give a selected period of time for them to be exchanged for smaller bills. When the bills come in for exchange, the Internal Revenue Service could ask appropriate questions. ^United\States ^Drug\Control\Policies ^P\S\Currency

720. "Heroin Availability Remains Stable Despite Enforcement Efforts of World's Police" (1985). *Organized Crime Digest* (March): 2-3. Supply remains up, made possible in part by the inability of police to enter inaccessible source areas, a lack of diplomatic relations with some of the major opium producing nations (such as Iran), political tensions in relationships between Mexico and the United States (along with the wide-open borders between the two countries), and a general period of bounteous agricultural production of poppies. ^Iran ^Latin\America ^Mexico ^Middle\East ^Opiates ^Heroin ^Production ^Supply ^Drug\Control\Policies\Effectiveness

721. "Heroin Brings More Trouble" (1986). *The Economist*, 20 December, 51–52. Pakistan is now the world's biggest exporter of heroin. ^Southwest\Asia ^Pakistan ^Golden\Crescent ^Heroin ^Drug\Traffic ^Refining

722. "Heroin Sale That Results in Death May Constitute Murder, Manslaughter" (1984). *The Criminal Law Reporter*, 17 October, 2049–50. A Tennessee Supreme Court held that "A heroin seller who is shown to have acted with such conscious indifference to the consequences of his unlawful actions as to constitute malice may be liable for murder when a customer dies from the effects of the heroin" (p. 2049). ^Heroin ^Law\Enforcement ^Judiciary ^United\States ^Tennessee ^Traffickers ^Consequences\Personal

723. Hey, Robert P. (1986). "Nations Unite to Fight Drugs: Combating Foreign Supply and US Demand." *The Christian Science Monitor*, 21 July, 1. Joint U.S.–Bolivian efforts to destroy drug supplies and production laboratories in Bolivia are viewed as a positive step toward international cooperation required to suppress the drug trade. ^Bolivia ^United\States ^Cocaine ^Interdiction ^International\Cooperation ^Demand ^Supply ^Latin\America

724. ——— (1989). "City Officials Fault Bush's Strategy Against Drugs." *The Christian Science Monitor*, 24 August, 1. Local leaders say they lack funding to combat urban drug problems and that they must have flexibility to attack those problems locally. They insist that this requires more federal funds to come directly to them, and in more than token amounts. In 153 cities with relatively successful antidrug programs, sponsored through local initiatives, four common themes emerged. The programs emphasized strengthening families and neighborhoods; they operated in a cooperative way with all neighboring cities and towns; they pushed aside normal bureaucratic inertia; and they had a balance between enforcement, treatment, and prevention. ^United\States ^Drug\Control\Policies ^Prevention\Family ^Bureaucracy ^Prevention\Integrated

725. ——— (1989). "City Under Siege: Nation's Capital Fights Drug War." *The Christian Science Monitor*, 22 March. The new "drug czar," William Bennett, plans a strategy to cope with Washington's increasing narcotics problem. ^United\States ^Drug\Control\Policies ^Washington\DC

726. ——— (1989). "Drug Traffickers Outgunning Police, A Mayor Laments." *The Christian Science Monitor*, 17 March. Throughout the United States, drug pushers and their cohorts have far more effective guns than do the police who are trying to control them. ^United\States ^Traffickers\Private\Armies ^Law\Enforcement ^Consequences\Violence

727. ——— (1989). "Public Girds for Long-Term Battle." *The Christian Science Monitor*, 21 November, 8. Discusses public strategies for dealing with the drug epidemic in the United States, noting that private business initiatives are increasing. This derives from the economic cost to business in theft, absenteeism, accidents, and deaths. An estimate is given that America's business enterprises pay around $100 billion a year in costs associated with drug and alcohol abuse. Awareness is growing that broad-brush

approaches are unsatisfactory. Some progress is seen in educational efforts. ^United\States ^Workplace ^Consequences\Economic

728. —— (1990). "U.S. Targets Maternal Drug Abuse as Costs of Problem Escalate." *The Christian Science Monitor*, 22 May, 7. Substantial personal, social, and financial costs derive from pregnant women taking drugs. The nature and extent of these costs are mentioned. Among these costs are drug-addicted infants who cost society roughly "$134,000 annually." ^United\States ^Drug\Use ^Women ^Fetuses ^Consequences\Economic ^Consequences\Social ^Consequences\Personal

729. Highfield, Roger (1986). "Designer Drugs." *World Health* (June). Discusses the kinds of drugs that are now being marketed from chemists' laboratories and the apparent difficulty in legislating against the expansion of this market. ^Designer\Drugs ^Legislation

730. Highland Agricultural Project (1981). *Developmental Research on Economic Ferns as Cash Crop for the Hilltribes of Northern Thailand.* Bangkok, Thailand: Kasetsart University. Research was carried out on experimental plots in the highlands of Thailand. The standard agronomic tests and experiments were conducted. Some attention was given to export market possibilities and to the shipping and transport requirements that would be associated with it. Thus, both economic feasibility of fern cultivation as well as the technology of handling and processing the fern products are considered. Both the technology that could be developed and demonstrated and the economics of fern cultivation argue for the ferns' functioning as a good substitute or replacement for opium production. ^Thailand ^Opiates ^Golden\Triangle ^Southeast\Asia ^Crop\Substitution

731. —— (1984). *Research on Dried Ornamental Plant Materials as a Substitute for Opium Poppy Production.* Bangkok, Thailand: Kasetsart University. While the technology and some marketability are shown to have been developed by this research, by its own acknowledgement the report calls for encouragement of local markets and assistance in identification of additional export market potential. Nevertheless, some attention was given to artifact production and packaging for appropriate market considerations. ^Thailand ^Opiates ^Crop\Substitution ^Golden\Triangle ^Southeast\Asia

732. —— (1984). *Research on Identification and Production of Diosgenin Produced Plants for Opium Poppy Substitute in the Highland of Northern Thailand.* Bangkok, Thailand: Kasetsart University. Identifies the appropriate plants and the horticultural information required to support them in a new region. ^Southeast\Asia ^Thailand ^Golden\Triangle ^Opiates ^Crop\Substitution

733. —— (1984). *Research on Small Fruit Production as Substitute Crops for Opium Poppy.* Bangkok, Thailand: Kasetsart University. Grapes, kiwi fruits, passion fruits, raspberries, blackberries, blueberries, and the cape gooseberry were investigated. All of the research was technical agronomic showing how yields could be improved. ^Southeast\Asia ^Thailand ^Golden\Triangle ^Opiates ^Crop\Substitution

734. —— (1985). *Exotic Fruit Production as a Substitute for Opium Poppy in the Highlands of Thailand.* Bangkok, Thailand: Kasetsart University. After three years of fieldwork and testing, pomegranate was confirmed as having a good replacement potential for the opium poppy. Figs also showed promise as an important substitute crop. Interestingly, the pomegranate is now accepted by the hill tribe people and thousands have begun to grow them with a hope that good commercial results will be obtained in the near future. ^Southeast\Asia ^Golden\Triangle ^Thailand ^Opiates ^Crop\Substitution

735. ———— (1986). *Appropriate Technologies for Horticultural Crops in the Highlands: Production, Handling and Utilization to Replace Opium Based Agriculture.* Bangkok, Thailand: Kasetsart University. A technical agronomic study showing that a number of fruits *could* be produced. Using vegetable matter as an alternative fuel for home cooking is also discussed. ^Thailand ^Southeast\Asia ^Golden\Triangle ^Opiates ^Crop\Substitution

736. ———— (1986). *Weed Control Research on Upland Rice and Potatoes to Replace Opium Based Agriculture.* Bangkok, Thailand: Kasetsart University. Herbicides of various varieties were experimented with in minimum tillage systems. The experimentation was conducted to determine weed control efficacy and the effect of the herbicides on yields of different rice varieties. The objective is to find a suitable combination to replace opium cultivation. ^Southeast\Asia ^Golden\Triangle ^Thailand ^Opiates ^Crop\Substitution

737. Himmelstein, Jerome L. (1983). "From Killer Weed to Drop-Out Drug: The Changing Ideology of Marihuana." *Contemporary Crises* 7:13–38. Documents the early 1980s shift in public attitude about marijuana, which saw it gaining more acceptance and less opprobrium within American society. ^United\States ^Cannabis ^Drug\Use\History ^Society

738. ———— (1983). *The Strange Case of Marijuana: Politics and Ideology of Drug Control in America.* Westport, Conn.: Greenwood Press. Examines the history of marijuana laws in the United States, attempting to account for both their change and their orientation. Before the 1960s, marijuana laws were to be understood by the "anslinger hypothesis" and the "Mexican hypothesis." In summary, the anslinger hypothesis suggests that the Treasury Department's Bureau of Narcotics furnished most of the enterprise that produced the marijuana tax act and initial federal control on marijuana matters. It is a "bureaucratic politics" orientation. The Mexican hypothesis basically argues an "ethnic bias" orientation (marijuana was associated with Mexican/Chicanos; they were part of the underclass; it wouldn't be nice to have part of the under class generalized into American society). Explanations for the drug laws since the 1960s include the "embourgeoisement hypothesis" and the "hippie hypothesis." The embourgeoisement hypothesis basically argues that the large-scale spread of marijuana use to the middle class youth in 1960s led to a reevaluation of the drug's dangers and to pressure for marijuana law reform. The politics are therefore symbolic. The same holds true for the hippie hypothesis. As marijuana became associated with the political and cultural rebellion of its youthful users in the late 1960s, disapproval of marijuana use came to reflect not so much what the drug did, but what it represented. More stringent laws were therefore reemployed. In this context, condemning marijuana use became a symbolic way of condemning the counterculture. Today the ideology of control is associated with one's belief as to whether marijuana is a dangerous weed or a mild euphorium. Which camp of "experts" should ideology follow? The answer to this question is influenced heavily by the structure of information control and through the predispositions of policymakers, the media, and the general populous. ^United\States ^Cannabis ^Drug\Control\Policies\History ^Drug\Control\Policies\Critique ^Culture ^Society

739. ———— (1986). "The Continuing Career of Marijuana: Backlash . . . Within Limits." *Contemporary Drug Problems* 13(Spring): 1–21. A sociological study operating on the presupposition that the social status of the actor determines the moral status of the act. Marijuana, increasingly used by middle- and upper-class citizens, is now associated with a decrease in the intensity of a tax against it. ^United\States ^Cannabis ^Drug\Use ^Society ^Culture ^Drug\Control\Policies\Critique

740. Hingson, Ralph, Barry Zuckerman, Hortensia Amaro, Deborah A. Frank, Herbert Kayne, James R. Sorenson, Janet Mitchell, Steven Parker, Suzette Morelock, and Ralph Timperi (1986). "Maternal Marijuana Use and Neonatal Outcome: Uncertainty Posed by Self-Reports." *American Journal of Public Health* 76(6): 667–69. The accuracy of self-reported marijuana use during pregnancy is questioned, given an experimental intervention described in this article. Inasmuch as the self-reports establish the foundation for correlational studies on effects, the conclusions of other studies may also be opened to question. ^Cannabis ^Drug\Use ^Health ^Fetuses ^Consequences\Fetuses ^Consequences\Critique

741. Hinton, Peter (1983). "Why the Karen Do Not Grow Opium: Competition and Contradiction in the Highlands of North Thailand." *Ethnology* 22(1): 1–16. How is it possible that a certain people in a region where cultivation of the opium poppy would offer the highest cash returns for any crop do not, in fact, cultivate the poppy? The author approaches his answers from the vantage of complex systems analysis which give insights on forces that promote social change and establish the rationality of social systems. The target is "the areas of disorder"—parts of social systems that the outsiders perceive to be out of tune with the socioecological structure as a whole rather than on the parts which appear to be in harmony with one another. In doing this researchers look for stress in the system that can, in the particular case of poppy growing, serve to help explain why some systems are unable to take advantage of substantial economic incentives. The author employs the case study method. ^Southeast\Asia ^Golden\Triangle ^Thailand ^Opiates ^Production ^Society ^Culture ^Minorities ^Production\Theories

742. Hirn, Richard J. (1988). "Drug Tests Threaten Employers, Too." *The New York Times*, 12 November, 27. Employees may sue employers for invasion of privacy and, in any event, expose the employers to considerable costs. All of this says nothing about the general morale problem that random drug testing imposes. ^United\States ^Drug\Testing ^Workplace ^Consequences\Drug\Control\Policies

743. Hodgson, Jim (1988). "Dominican Republic, Haiti Struggle against Smuggling of Basic Food Items, Narcotics." *Latinamerica Press*, 30 June, 6. Smuggled food imports are driving domestic producers out of the market. For example, smuggled Dominican rice (into Haiti) sells for less than its Haitian counterpart because it is subsidized by the Dominican government. There is much official complicity in the food contraband, as there is also in drug transshipments from Latin America destined for markets in the United States. The Duvalier regime was shot through with corruption on drug issues. Since Duvalier's departure, the drug trade has continued to grow. Influential members of the army and the government continue to be involved. The army has been unhappy with the new civilian government's attempts to limit its power—especially in the sensitive area of narcotics trading. ^Dominican\Republic ^Haiti ^Caribbean ^Drug\Traffic ^Consequences\Corruption

744. Hoge, Warren (1982). "Bolivians Find Patron in Reputed Drug Chief." *The New York Times*, 15 August, 1. On-site description of drug barons in Bolivia taking on the "Robin Hood" role among peasants in remote villages associated with the cocaine trade. The man in question is Roberto Suárez. Description of his operations, his paramilitary mercenaries, his connections with Nazis, and the extent of his economic empire. ^Bolivia ^Cocaine ^Drug\Traffic ^Traffickers ^Latin\America ^Traffickers\Private\Armies ^Consequences\Economic

745. Holahan, John (1973). "The Economics of Control of the Illegal Supply of Heroin." *Public Finance Quarterly* 1(4): 467–77. Efforts are made to control the supply of heroin by large-scale purchases of opium crops, by enforcement of

direct controls on opium production, or by increasing the probability of arrest and severity of penalties. On the whole, efforts to control supply raise the price of heroin and are therefore likely to be ineffective. Since the demand for heroin is most likely price inelastic, it would be better to operate directly on demand by affecting such factors as tastes, prices, and availability of alternative drugs, treatment, and so forth. ^Heroin ^Drug\Control\Policies ^Economics ^Supply

746. Hollister, Leo E. (1988). "Cannabis—1988." *Acta Psychiatrica Scandinavia Supplement* 78:108–18. Updates a review of research on Cannabis and pays additional attention to increasing numbers of studies on how the components of Cannabis are distributed in the human system, as well as their possible effects on health. Despite widespread use of Cannabis in virtually all parts of the world, no catastrophic effects on health have been noted. Cannabis appears to be relatively safe when compared to other current social drugs. It is too early to tell, however, as to whether possible bad effects might simply have been overlooked. ^Cannabis ^Health ^Reviews ^Consequences\Health ^Drug\Use\Critique

747. ——— (1988). "Marijuana and Immunity." *Journal of Psychoactive Drugs* 20(1): 3–8. This article reviews the controversial evidence on the effect of marijuana on immune defenses. The matter is still unsettled. ^Cannabis ^Reviews ^Consequences\Health

748. Holmes, Steven A. (1990). "A Dealer Finds Many Eager to Launder His Drug Money." *The New York Times*, 24 January, 1. A New York City dealer finds merchants eager to launder his cash derived from illegal drug sales. Description of how that laundering is done, along with statistics. ^United\States ^New\York ^Money\Laundering ^Statistics

749. Holt, Pat M. (1989). "The U.S. Should Repeal 'Drug Prohibition.'" *The Christian Science Monitor*, 1 February, 18. Nothing has worked with respect to interdiction and suppression of the drug trade. Young people in numerous countries are being destroyed. It is money that drives the drug trade, and the money was put there by the war on drugs. The money needs to be taken out. This would remove much of the incentive to deal in drugs, and would also take away the means of corrupting public officials. The analogy with prohibition is appropriate. The repeal of prohibition did not end alcoholism, but it did end gang warfare. Legalizing drugs will not end drug addiction, but it will end a great deal of the crime associated with drugs. Legalization does not mean decontrol; drugs could be handled in the same way that tobacco and alcohol are now handled. ^United\States ^P\S\Legalization

750. "Honduras: Et Tu?" (1988). *The Economist*, 16 April, 51–52. A notorious drug trafficker in Honduras was kidnapped, apparently by the Americans, and flown to the United States where he was placed in jail. Wide-eyed protests in Honduras. ^Honduras ^United\States ^Extradition ^Consequences\Foreign\Relations ^Latin\America ^Drug\Control\Policies

751. "Hooked on Just Saying No" (1989). *The Economist*, 21 January, 19. Criminalizing drugs compounds the problems such a policy was meant to solve. So end it. Legalize, control, discourage; those are the weapons for Mr. Bennett's war, not a continuation of his present course. ^United\States ^Drug\Control\Policies ^P\S\Legalization

752. Horgan, John (1988). "Ignorance in Action." *Scientific American* 259(5): 17. Science, mostly consensually, has been arguing for a move away from an adversarial approach with respect to drugs to a therapeutic model. This does not necessarily imply legalization. The government has not listened to this scientific counsel, and the adversarial approach has prevailed. The politicians want to focus on interdiction and law enforcement; the scientists, on therapeutic responses. Scientists view the politicians as "ignorance in action." ^United\States ^Drug\Control\Policies\Critique ^P\S\Therapy

753. Hoskin, Gary (1988). "Colombia's Political Crisis." *Current History* (January): 9-38. Colombia has been experiencing a political crisis that has been accompanied, paradoxically, by a strong economic recovery. While some of the violence is associated with the drug trade, and therefore contributory to the political crisis, both are rooted firmly in the Colombian political culture and are not restricted solely either to insurrectionary activity of guerrilla movements or to the drug trade. ^Latin\America ^Economics ^Colombia ^Drug\Traffic ^Consequences\Theories ^Consequences\Political ^Consequences\Violence ^Culture

754. Hosty, Robert E., and Francis J. Elliott (1985). "Drug Abuse in Industry: What Does It Cost and What Can Be Done?" *Security Management* (October): 53-58. The report shows that, spread out over the entire work force, drug abuse in the United States during 1980 cost $472 per employee (averaged over 100,000,000 employees in 1980). Of this, 81 percent was attributed to lost productivity, 12 percent to crime costs, 3 percent to medical expenses, 2 percent to victims cost, and 1 percent to social programs. Property damage was .2 percent of the total cost. ^United\States ^Drug\Use ^Workplace ^Consequences\Economic ^Statistics

755. House, Richard (1984). "Mafia Boss' Arrest Reveals Brazilian Cocaine Connection." *The Washington Post*, 22 November, E1. Pushed out of Colombia and pressed in Peru and Bolivia, traffickers have moved to Brazil, which has become a new growth pole for transshipment of drugs. The focus is on the European and U.S. markets. ^Latin\America ^Brazil ^Cocaine ^Drug\Traffic ^Consequences\Markets

756. Houser, Arthur (1988). "Colombia: Lessons in Language and Violence." *Los Angeles Times*, 10 April, 3. Personal reflection by a school teacher in Colombia about how the current scene is teaching youth to be violent and to behave without principle. ^Colombia ^Drug\Traffic ^Society ^Culture ^Latin\America ^Consequences\Social

757. Houston, Paul (1988). "201 in U.S., Italy Charged in Drug Trade." *Los Angeles Times*, 2 December, 4. Report of a massive international crackdown resulting in the arrest of 68 persons in the United States and 133 in Italy, including several in the "Sicilian mafia." This is a result of international cooperation. ^Italy ^United\States ^Law\Enforcement ^Organized\Crime ^Europe ^International\Cooperation

758. Hovius, B. (1980). "Hauser: Narcotic Drugs, Criminal Law, and Peace, Order and Good Government." *University of Wisconsin Law Review* 18(2): 505-19. Describes the evolution of Canadian law, in reference to the Supreme Court of Canada's decision in Hauser, which may have far-reaching consequences on the scope of criminal law power, particularly as applied to possession of and trafficking in illegal narcotics. ^Canada ^Law\Enforcement ^Judiciary

759. "How to Oust a Drug Dealer: Ideas for Embattled Tenants" (1987). *The New York Times*, 1 March, 38. Description of American tenants, who object to drug operations, attempts to evict drug dealers from their apartments. Among these are getting the building's water supply shut off before a police raid so that dealers cannot flush their wares down the toilet. Other suggestions are given. After tenants themselves had taken these initiatives, muggings and burglaries substantially declined. ^United\States ^Law\Enforcement ^Private\Initiatives ^Proffered\Solutions

760. Hoyt, Les Leanne (1981). "Effects of Marijuana on Fetal Development." *Journal of Drug and Alcohol Education* 26(3): 30-36. Moves well beyond simply analyzing the effects of marijuana on fetal development, presenting, as it does, a historical perspective of the public view of marijuana and exploring, based on a 1979 survey, respondents' knowledge about the effects of marijuana and the relationship this has had to the mass media. It is, therefore, mostly a study of social perceptions

about the effects of marijuana as opposed to the actual effects of marijuana. ^Cannabis
^Health ^Fetuses ^Society ^Consequences\Fetuses ^Prevention\Media ^Consequences\Social

761. Hubbard, Robert L., et al (1986). *Drug Abuse Treatment, Client Characteristics, and Pretreatment Behaviors.* Rockville, Md.: U.S. Department of Health and Human Services. Data are reported from 11,750 clients entering forty-one different drug-abuse treatment programs from 1979 to 1981, before the federal government moved, in 1981, to block grant funding to the states for community-based drug-abuse treatment. Documents the changing "demographics" among the population of clients entering the treatment centers. The population is much more heterogenous than before; it suffers from complex patterns of drug abuse including use of secondary drugs (particularly cocaine, marijuana, and alcohol) in conjunction with heroin and an associated, broad range of social, family, and economic drug-related problems. References to the relationship of drug abuse and involvement with the criminal justice system are noted. ^United\States ^Drug\Use ^Treatment ^Society ^Statistics ^Consequences\Social ^Crime ^Alcohol

762. Hughes, John (1989). "Booze Today, Drugs Tomorrow?" *The Christian Science Monitor*, 22 March. There has been, in recent years, lower alcohol use among the American public, and the cause seems to be a change in the public's mood. People are more interested in health and fitness, which has led to more moderate consumption. The same goes for smoking. Massive value changes altered public thought and transformed society on these issues. It very well may be that this approach will need to be taken toward drugs. In the end, it is society's attitude toward drugs that will limit their use. "If there has been such drastic evolution in thought about liquor and tobacco, perhaps the day will come when we can chronicle as dramatic a mental turnabout on drugs." ^United\States ^Drug\Use ^Society ^Culture ^Values ^Alcohol ^Tobacco ^Consequences\Values
^P\S\Values

763. Hughes, Patrick H. (1977). *Behind the Wall of Respect: Community Experiments in Heroin Addiction Control.* Chicago, Ill.: University of Chicago Press. Drug-abuse treatment in Chicago, including discussion of halfway houses. The book describes how a mobile epidemiological team penetrated Chicago's heroin subculture and succeeded in reducing the number of addicts in several neighborhoods, reduced the incidence of new cases, and worked in other areas to contain a heroin epidemic. They advance a model for researching and intervening in heroin epidemics. Authors distance themselves from dealing with solutions to the drug addiction problem that are based upon highly emotional or ideological debates, and advance their findings and results as a consequence of clinical research and program evaluation which they believe offer good prospects for implementation. ^United\States ^Heroin ^Prevention ^Treatment
^Illinois

764. Hull, Jennifer (1987). "Shooting up under a Red Star." *Time*, 19 January, 46. Short discussion on the extent to which narcotics have invaded Eastern Europe. ^Europe ^Drug\Use

765. "Human Rights Watch—August" (1988). *Latinamerica Press*, 8 September, 7. Brief allegation that an antidrug police squad in the coca growing region of the Chapare attacked peasants and robbed them of money and goods. Twelve peasants have been killed in confrontations with antidrug police during the past year. ^Latin\America
^Bolivia ^Coca ^Law\Enforcement ^Consequences\Human\Rights ^Consequences\Law\Enforcement
^Consequences\Political

766. "Human Rights Watch—May" (1099). *Latinamerica Press*, 9 June, 7. Brief description of the kidnapping of a Colombian politician, allegedly by a narco hit squad that demanded the release of prisoners accused of drug trafficking in exchange for the politician. ^Latin\America ^Colombia ^Law\Enforcement ^Consequences\Violence

767. Hunt, Dana E., Douglas S. Lipton, and Barry Spunt (1984). "Patterns of Criminal Activity among Methadone Clients and Current Narcotics Users Not in Treatment." *Journal of Drug Issues* 14(4): 687–702. From an apparent assumption that criminal activity and heroin addiction go hand in hand, the question arises as to what changes in criminal activity of narcotics addicts occur when they enter methadone maintenance treatment programs. Methadone clients are not only less involved in criminal activity than addicts not in treatment, but among clients continuing their criminal activity there is less involvement in the more serious crimes. These differences are not explained as a function of a lower level of criminal activity prior to treatment, but relate to being in treatment. In accounting for the individuals on methadone maintenance programs who continue to commit crimes, they either continue to use heroin and/or cocaine or are individuals for whom crime is an income or an income supplement. ^Heroin ^Crime ^Treatment ^Methadone

768. Hunt, Frances A. (1987). "Are the National Forests Going to Pot?" *American Forests* (March/April): 37. Description of reported cannabis cultivation in the United States, with a principal focus on where it is occurring in the nation's national forests. Social transformations in growing areas have seen a move away from the "left-over hippie generation" to marijuana cultivations being worked by hired growers. This is suggestive of organized crime. Forest service efforts are being made to suppress the illegal cultivations. ^United\States ^Cannabis ^Production ^Organized\Crime ^Drug\Control\Policies ^Society

769. Husain, M. (1984). "Provisions in the Laws of Pakistan to Combat Serious Drug–Related Offences." *Bulletin on Narcotics* 36(3): 15-17. British drug laws were enforced in Pakistan until 1979. Then, more severe penalties were prescribed for violators of the importation, exportation, manufacturing, or processing of any intoxicants—referring mainly to products of cannabis, opiates, and cocaine. In 1983 even more punitive sanctions for offenders were instituted. The article gives a description of these measures. ^Pakistan ^Southwest\Asia ^Golden\Crescent ^Drug\Traffic ^Law\Enforcement

770. Husain, S., and I. Khan (1985). "An Update on Cannabis Research." *Bulletin on Narcotics* 37(4): 3–13. Describes the results of the symposium of over 125 scientists, held in August 1984 at the campus of Oxford University, which considered the latest developments concerning cannabis research. ^Cannabis ^Health ^Reviews

771. Hymes, Donna J. (1987). "New Reasons to 'Keep off the Grass.'" *Current Health*, March, 18. A report popularly summarizing new research showing that marijuana damages the lungs; causes brain damage; impairs learning, memory, and intellectual development; impedes personality development and psychological functioning; lowers resistance to disease; aggravates heart disease; adversely affects glands and hormones involved in growth and reproduction; harms the unborn; is deceptive as to its harmful effects; and affects moral judgment and behavior. ^Cannabis ^Health ^Reviews ^Consequences\Health ^Consequences\Fetuses ^Consequences\Neurological ^Consequences\Physiological ^Consequences\Misc ^Consequences\Reproduction

772. Ibginovia, Patrick Edobar (1983). "The Prevention, Treatment and Rehabilitation of Drug-Dependent Persons in Africa." *International Journal of Offender Therapy and Comparative Criminology* 27(3): 235–42. Analyzes governmental efforts and programs targeted to drug-abuse prevention, treatment, and rehabilitation in Africa. It both describes existing policies and prescribes changes. ^Africa ^Drug\Use ^Prevention ^Treatment ^Proffered\Solutions

773. Ibrahim, Youssef M. (1989). "Iran Puts Addicts in Its Labor Camps." *The New York Times*, 22 July, 3. In its current antidrug campaign, Iran has rounded

up 55,000 drug addicts and plans to send them to labor camps in several provinces. One hundred fifty thousand registered drug addicts may soon follow. Members of the neighborhood Islamic revolutionary committees took over the drug fighting effort from the police. Labor camp work to be required until habits cease. Previous vigorous antidrug attempts in Iran have failed in the past ten years. Some have observed that Iran is using its capital punishment campaign (nearly 1,000 smugglers executed this year) against its political opponents rather than smugglers. ^Middle\East ^Iran ^Drug\Use ^Law\Enforcement ^Drug\Control\Policies ^Consequences\Human\Rights

774. "Ice Overdose" (1989). *The Economist*, 2 December, 29. Description of a smokeable form of methamphetamine now available in Hawaii and thought to be penetrating the West Coast of the United States. Described is its fearful impact on users' neurological systems. It is, apparently, extremely addictive, and gives a much greater "push" than crack cocaine. ^United\States ^Drug\Use ^Designer\Drugs

775. Ifill, Gwen (1989). "Cities Seek to Emulate Alexandria on Evictions." *The Washington Post*, 30 March, A25. The public nuisance eviction criteria employed by the city of Alexandria, Virginia, is viewed as a model for public housing projects in other American cities. The public nuisance device is used to clear suspected drug pushers and consumers from public housing premises. ^United\States ^Drug\Control\Policies ^Public\Housing ^Virginia

776. Ikleinman, Paula H., Eric D. Wish, Sherry Deren, Gregory Rainone, and Ellen Morehouse (1988). "Daily Marijuana Use and Problem Behaviors among Adolescents." *International Journal of the Addictions* 23(1): 87–107. The level of marijuana use does not make a significant independent contribution to school problems if certain control factors are introduced into the outcomes. These control factors are lifetime cigarette smoking, lifetime multiple drug use, rebelliousness, gender, and whether a respondent has ever used an illicit drug. Marijuana use is only one element in a large and complex picture of interrelated problems and behaviors. ^Cannabis ^Drug\Use ^Youth ^Society ^Consequences\Educational ^Tobacco ^Consequences\Theories

777. Imran, M., and T. B. Uppal (1979). "Opium Administration to Infants in Peshawar Region of Pakistan." *Bulletin on Narcotics* 31(3-4): 69–75. Opium is used for sedating infants in a frontier province of Pakistan, and this is a matter of grave public health concern. Infants are hospitalized for opium overdosage. It is thought that all this contributes to infant mortality. Calls for a preventive program to educate parents otherwise ignorant of opium's danger to infants. ^Southwest\Asia ^Pakistan ^Golden\Crescent ^Opiates ^Drug\Use ^Health ^Society ^Culture ^Consequences\Children

778. Inciardi, James A. (1979). "Heroin Use and Street Crime." *Crime and Delinquency* 25(July): 335–46. From a sample of 356 active heroin users from Miami, Florida, for which the author investigated both known criminal offenses and self-reported ones, he concludes that heroin users are involved extensively in crime, and that their criminality is largely for the purpose of supporting their drug intake. Moreover, both substance abuse and criminal activity occur at a relatively early age. What is not clear, however, is whether criminal behaviors are altered at the onset of drug use, or at the onset of initial criminal justice processing; whether drug use results in an increase or decrease in criminal activity; or whether a drug-taking career places adolescents into a criminal career path that biases them away from more law-abiding pursuits as they approach young adulthood. A more comprehensive model is needed which moves away from the simple discussion of whether drugs cause crime or crime causes drug use. ^Heroin ^Crime ^Reviews

779. ——— (1980). "Youth, Drugs, and Street Crime." In *Drugs and the Youth Culture*, edited by Frank Scarpitti and Susan K. Datesman, 175–204.

Beverly Hills, Calif.: Sage. A chronological view of experimentation by American youth cultures with drugs: from "a decade of repression" (the 1950s), through "a decade of revolution" (the 1960s), to the 1970s and beyond which are characterized by "the war on drugs." The author investigated crime and drugs within the campus setting and crime and drugs within the street setting. Drug use and crime are concomitant aspects of the youth scene. Nevertheless, among students, only those who were dealers or who used drugs on a regular basis evidenced a widespread prevalence of criminality. By contrast, within the street population studied, high-volume drug use and widespread criminality went hand in hand, regardless of whether the users were involved with heroin or not. A simple cause and effect assumption of an enslavement theory cannot, however, be supported by the data of this study, as the authors are quick to point out. Nevertheless, the patterns suggest that the initiation of drug use occurs perhaps a year prior to the onset of criminal activity. The ambiguousness of the data suggest the possibility of a socio-cultural matrix to be the cause of criminality as opposed to simple drug abuse. ^United\States ^Drug\Use ^Youth ^Crime ^Drug\Use\History ^Statistics

780. ———— (1981). "Crucial Variables in Marijuana Decriminalization Research." *Contemporary Drug Problems* 10(4): 383–90. Stiff criminal penalties imposed on people who may have only one marijuana cigarette clearly have long-term consequences for society as a whole when large portions of the otherwise law-abiding population consume the drug for its euphoric effects. An examination of the application of various laws and what they produce in terms of arrests are reviewed. By implication, there is notation regarding the economic costs of enforcing marijuana laws. ^Cannabis ^Decriminalization ^Law\Enforcement ^Consequences\Economic ^Society

781. ———— (1981). *The Drugs-Crime Connection.* Beverly Hills, Calif.: Sage. Even though much has been said about the relationship between illegal drug use and criminal behavior, an overview of the scholarly, scientific, and popular literature to date, with few exceptions, has provided only minimal useful information or conclusions. A variety of schools of thought, academic postulations, political rhetoric, and popular belief systems have also come and gone, serving only to confuse our understanding of the issue even further. The standard questions, repeated over the years, remain: Is crime the result of, or perhaps some response to, a special set of life circumstances brought about by addiction to narcotic drugs? Or, conversely, is addiction per se some deviant tendency characteristic of individuals already prone to offensive behavior? In a nutshell, which came first in the offender's career—crime, or drugs? Befitting the earlier statement above, findings in the literature have led to a series of peculiar and contradictory per-spectives. "Medical" and "criminal" models of explanation are discussed within the context of a historical perspective. While the perspectives offered in this volume clearly do not provide all the answers, they nevertheless contribute in three of the most signifi-cant areas of inquiry: They reflect a higher level of thinking in perspective and methods; they offer new data on which other research can solidly rely; they suggest how to ask the right questions. ^Drug\Use ^Crime ^Crime\Theories ^Drug\Use\Theories

782. ———— (1981). "Marijuana Decriminalization Research." *Criminology* 19(1): 145–59. The article calls for a model that would examine, with cost-benefit analysis, criminalization of marijuana laws versus their decriminalization. While there may be no benefits, necessarily, to decriminalization, there are huge costs to a continua-tion of the criminalization of marijuana use. Decriminalization should be taken within some sort of cost-benefit perspective. While there may be hardly any benefits to mari-juana, aside from the euphoric states of feelings and well-being, there are certainly huge human, social, and economic costs that could be eliminated by decriminalizing its use.

^Cannabis ^Economics ^Society ^Decriminalization ^Consequences\Social ^Consequences\Economic
^P\S\Legalization ^Decriminalization\Theories

783. —— (1986). *The War on Drugs. Heroin, Cocaine, Crime and Public Policy*. Palo Alto, Calif.: Mayfield. Reflects on a wide variety of issues relating to drug production, trafficking, and consumption. Much is based on street research in Miami and New York City and on interviews with heroin and cocaine users, dealers, and traffickers who live there, and with law enforcement agents and government officials charged with controlling drug use and crime. The data are anecdotal, mostly, and to some extent systematic. Some interviews were also carried out in South America. The reflections are intended to provoke an examination of American drug policy against the backdrop of social and cultural change. Chapter 6 is devoted to the domestic and international implications of drug trafficking. Economic, social, and political implications in Colombia, Peru, and Bolivia are discussed in this chapter. The epilogue reviews a number of scholars taking one or another position on current U.S. drug policy. Various scenarios associated with legalization and decriminalization are reviewed. ^Latin\America
^United\States ^Drug\Traffic ^Drug\Control\Policies ^Economics ^Politics ^Society ^Florida ^New\York
^Peru ^Colombia ^Bolivia ^Decriminalization ^Consequences\Theories

784. —— (1987). "Beyond Cocaine: Basuco, Crack, and Other Coca Products." *Contemporary Drug Problems* 14(3): 461–92. Historical summary of the nineteenth-century transfer of coca products to Europe and America, bringing the matter up through the 1980s when cocaine began to be "free based" and coca paste and other products began to be smoked. Describes the preparation of cocaine products and their distribution to consumers. How far have these products penetrated the population? As an extension of other Miami street studies reported elsewhere, the data for this study were gathered through the traditional "snowball sampling" technique derived through the use of a sociometrically oriented model. The research method is described and the results of the interviews of over 300 informants are discussed. Crack, the drug of the moment, appears to be so because it is relatively inexpensive and produces a quick response. The author opines that if the war on drugs in the United States is successful, it will probably drive more people to use crack because increased cocaine prices would move that drug beyond normal consumption abilities. The author speculates on new drug fads that may soon emerge. ^Cocaine ^Crack ^Drug\Use\History ^Cocaine\Paste ^Cocaine\History ^Consequences\Unintended

785. —— (1989). "Editor's Introduction: Debating the Legalization of Drugs." *American Behavioral Scientist* 32(3): 233–42. Inciardi briefly reviews American drug policy and considers the nature of its impact and effectiveness. He then moves on to present a backdrop for the current debate on legalization (or decriminalization) of drugs. Inciardi reviews the literature of those who have argued that federal prohibition of drugs since 1914 has been not only been costly, but also an abject failure. The January/February 1989 issue of the *American Behavioral Scientist* is a special issue concerning the debate over the legalization of drugs. ^United\States ^Legalization ^Reviews
^Drug\Control\Policies\Effectiveness^Decriminalization^Drug\Control\Policies\History^P\S\Legalization
^Decriminalization\Theories

786. —— (1990). "HIV, AIDS and Intravenous Drug Use: Some Considerations." *The Journal of Drug Issues* 20:2(Spring): 181–94. Intravenous drug users are preceded only by homosexual and bisexual men as the largest risk group for HIV and AIDS. However, as a group, intravenous drug users have not responded well to AIDS prevention messages. Statistical information, including patterns of epidemiology, are given for countries and regions of the world. ^Prevention\Drug\Education\Critique ^AIDS
^Statistics ^Drug\Use ^Consequences\Health

787. Inciardi, James A., and Duane C. McBride (1989). "Legalization: A High-Risk Alternative in the War on Drugs." *American Behavioral Scientist* 32(3): 259–89. Presents a wide-ranging analysis of the cost-benefit variety regarding drug use and its legalization. On balance, Inciardi argues that the costs of legalization would exceed the benefits of so doing. Thus, according to him, existing data do not support a utilitarian benefit of legalization. Inciardi, given his acknowledgement that the "war" on drugs is problematic, would nevertheless strengthen supply-side programs aimed at keeping drugs out of the country. But the matter would have to be dealt with from an awareness of a much more complex pattern of cause and effect than current policy allows. Accordingly, more attention must be focused on the demand side of the equation. This includes issues of treatment and education. Inciardi reviews a substantial body of literature. ^United\States ^Drug\Control\Policies\Critique ^Reviews ^Bibliographies ^Decriminalization ^Treatment ^Prevention\Drug\Education ^Supply ^Demand ^Drug\Use\Theories

788. "Increased Concern over Trafficking" (1986). *Latin American Weekly Report*, 18 December, 2. With increased pressure on cocaine traffickers in Peru and Colombia, it appears that some traffickers are moving into Venezuela. Furthermore, it appears that more of the drug is being home grown and used in Venezuela. ^Peru ^Colombia ^Latin\America ^Venezuela ^Cocaine ^Drug\Use ^Drug\Traffic

789. "India's Drug Byways" (1989). *World Press Review*, January, 45. India's location between the Golden Crescent (Afghanistan, Pakistan, and Iran) and the Golden Triangle (Burma, Thailand, and Laos) places it in a position to be a major transit country for movement of opium-derived drugs to the West. ^India ^Opiates ^Drug\Traffic

790. Ingwerson, Marshall (1987). "Authorities Target the Profits of Crime." *The Christian Science Monitor*, 21 September, 3. Does confiscation of property associated with trafficking in narcotics violate people's constitutional rights? A case is described where property was forfeited with no crime having been established. ^United\States ^Asset\Forfeiture\Critique ^Human\Rights

791. ——— (1987). "Jamaican Drug Gangs Stake out Turf in US." *The Christian Science Monitor*, 13 August, 1. Closely knit, heavily armed groups are emerging from Jamaica and residing in the United States, mostly in South Florida, and are now extending their operations to such unlikely cities as Kansas City, Missouri, and Newport News, Virginia. They make higher profits than other drug distributors because they have cut out middlemen. The Jamaicans have been particularly adept at moving crack into northern cities. They also have extended their operations and coverage into southern cities. ^United\States ^Jamaica ^Caribbean ^Florida ^Kansas ^Virginia ^Cocaine ^Crack ^Drug\Traffic ^Organized\Crime

792. ——— (1988). "Rise in Drug Offenses Crams Prisons; Inmates Getting Released Earlier—in Florida, After Just One-Third of Term." *The Christian Science Monitor*, 13 December, 3. In Florida some inmates are getting released much earlier, usually after fulfilling just one-third of their term. This is happening in spite of the state's adding the equivalent of five large prisons a year. Tougher sentences and more drug convictions are cramming the system. This is a nationwide phenomenon. ^United\States ^Law\Enforcement ^Consequences\Penal ^Florida

793. Instituto Latinoamericano de Investigaciones Sociales (1987). "La Economía Campesina y el Cultivo de la Coca." *Debate Agrario*. La Paz, Bolivia: Imprenta EDOBOL. Presents a debate about coca cultivation, which has become decisive not only for the agricultural sector but for the entire national economy. This is one of the first meetings of agricultural economists intent on reducing rather than increasing the cultivation of an exportable crop. Discussed was not only the regional and

national effects of the incorporation of coca into peasant economies but the possible consequences—favorable and pernicious—of continuing with its production, with crop substitution, or with crop eradication. All of this has implications for political and social stability and international relations, which are noted. Fragments from the UN international conference on the abuse and traffic of illicit drugs (Vienna 1987) are included. Most perspectives raised are from the vantage point of the peasant economy. ^Bolivia ^Coca ^Production ^Crop\Substitution ^Crop\Eradication ^Economics ^Consequences\Economic ^Consequences\Social ^Consequences\Political ^Consequences\Foreign\Relations ^United\Nations ^Producers ^Latin\America

794. Inter-American Dialogue, Report (1988). *The Americas in 1988: A Time for Choices.* Washington D.C.: The Inter-American Dialogue. Chapter 3 is the relevant discussion for this bibliography. Entitled "Drugs: A Shared Tragedy," the chapter reviews public policy in the United States and in Latin America, and the international hemispheric relations associated with those policies. Suggests narcotics control policies for both the United States and Latin America. These policies should be designed to contain U.S. demand and reduce counterproductive pressure on foreign suppliers. ^Latin\America ^United\States ^Drug\Control\Policies ^Consequences\Foreign\Relations ^P\S\Demand\Reduction ^Demand ^Supply

795. "Inter-Parliamentary Conference on Drug Abuse and Illicit Trafficking in the Western Hemisphere" (1988). *Inter-Parliamentary Bulletin* 1:5–32. The conference, organized by the Inter-Parliamentary Union in cooperation with the United Nations and with the support of the World Health Organization and the Latin American Parliament, was held in Venezuela. Twenty-four Western Hemispheric nations attended (including the United States) and also the United Kingdom. The report gives a final declaration keyed to issues of prevention of drug abuse, reduction of illicit demand, strengthening control over supply, and fostering treatment and rehabilitation. ^Latin\America ^United\Nations ^Drug\Control\Policies ^International\Cooperation ^WHO ^Latin\American\Parliament ^Proffered\Solutions ^Demand ^Supply

796. Iosub, S., M. Fuchs, N. Bingol, R. K. Stone, D. S. Gromisch, and E. Wasserman (1985). "Incidence of Major Congenital Malformations in Offspring of Alcoholics and Polydrug Abusers." *Alcohol* 2:521–23. In comparing the offsprings of mothers who abused only alcohol with those who abused alcohol in conjunction with opiates during pregnancy, it was shown that alcohol alone produced a higher incidence of fetus malformation than did alcohol in conjunction with opiates. The incidence of the "fetal alcohol syndrome" was higher in blacks than in hispanics. ^Heroin ^Drug\Use ^Health ^Alcohol ^Consequences\Fetuses ^Fetuses

797. "Iran's Drug Crackdown Stirs Concern in Gulf" (1989). *The Christian Science Monitor,* 12 April. Mention is made of at least 356 drug smugglers having been executed, a matter that has caused other Gulf states to be worried for fear that most of the drug trade will be shifted into their countries. ^Iran ^Middle\East ^Golden\Crescent ^Drug\Traffic ^Law\Enforcement ^Economics ^Consequences\Foreign\Relations ^Traffickers ^Consequences\Personal

798. Irusta Medrano, Gerdo, and J. Poirot (1986). *Los Adoradores de la Diosa Blanca: Relatos Verídicos del Narcotráfico en Bolivia.* La Paz, Bolivia: Editorial Calama. From journalistic and police reports, these authors construct numerous episodes of narcotics trafficking in Bolivia, which they trace with a literary flare and reportorial elegance. Their view is best described by their dedicatory phrase for this volume: "We dedicate this book to all honest generals, chiefs, officials, and other members of the national police who have clear conscience about the dramatic situation through which this country is now going and who do what they can to take a direct

resolve to correct it, even knowing that the task is colossal." ^Latin\America ^Bolivia
^Cocaine ^Drug\Traffic ^Consequences\Political ^Consequences\Corruption

799. Irwin, Don (1984). "Mexico Seizure Points to Greater Pot Use." *Los Angeles Times*, 24 November. The United States government affirmed that it would need to revalue previous estimates of the traffic of marijuana from Mexico to the United States in view of the record 10,000 tons of marijuana seized and destroyed earlier in northern Mexico. The seizure suggested a 70 percent increase in earlier estimates that total U.S. consumption of the drug was around 14,000 tons. ^Latin\America ^Mexico ^United\States ^Cannabis ^Drug\Traffic ^Statistics ^Statistics\Critique ^Production ^Interdiction

800. Irwin, Michael H. K. (1985). *The Cocaine Epidemic*. New York: Public Affairs Committee. General treatment on virtually all notable issues associated with the illicit use of cocaine, ranging from the facts about drug production to physiological consequences. There is a section on the link between cocaine and crime which deals with the matter on a macro "illicit transaction" basis rather than a personal cause/effect motivation basis. In general, the work is intended to inform people about the particulars of cocaine use and to enlist their cooperation in preventing that use. It is, therefore, a good example of an agency document intended for a social purpose. ^Cocaine ^Crime ^Prevention ^Consequences\Misc ^Crime\Theories

801. Irwin, Victoria (1986). "Drugs and Police: Cities Probe the Corruption Connection." *The Christian Science Monitor*, 30 September. Describes problems of corruption of law enforcement agents in New York City and Miami over drug trafficking issues. Drug-dealer "shakedowns" are noted. ^United\States ^Law\Enforcement ^Consequences\Corruption ^New\York ^Florida

802. Isikoff, Michael (1988). "The Drug Bill and Decriminalization." *The Washington Post*, 28 October, A3. The author, in reviewing the bill passed by Congress in October of 1988 that was hailed as a tough escalation in the war on drugs, points out that some experts say the bill opens the door to federal decriminalization of narcotics possession. The discussion appears to involve the payment of civil fines for personal drug possession rather than being subjected to alternative, more severe, felony convictions. ^United\States ^Legislation ^Decriminalization

803. —— (1988). "30 Nations Join in Attacks on Drug Cartels." *The Washington Post*, 31 August, A4. The United States and twenty-nine other countries in Latin America and Europe have secretly coordinated military and police operations aimed at destroying clandestine cocaine laboratories and disrupting the operations of Colombian drug cartels. ^Europe ^Latin\America ^Colombia ^Cocaine ^Drug\Control\Policies ^Organized\Crime ^Interdiction ^International\Cooperation ^Military

804. —— (1988). "Drug Testing Ferrets out Few Users; Critics Cite Low Figures as Proof Program Is Costly, Fruitless." *The Washington Post*, 19 July, A17. An attack on generalized drug testing, citing low detection figures as proof that the program is too costly and therefore fruitless for its intended purpose. ^United\States ^Drug\Testing\Critique

805. —— (1988). "Drugs Allegedly Shipped in Army Planes' Mail." *The Washington Post*, 2 June, A3. Eight people, including three former soldiers, have been arrested and charged with using U.S. military mails, aircraft, and pouches to ship cocaine from Panama to the United States. ^Latin\America ^Panama ^Military ^Consequences\Corruption ^Aircraft

806. —— (1988). "Fighting the Drug War: From Arizona to Fairfax." *The Washington Post*, 6 November, A1. Looking at the flotilla of tethered balloons to interdict drug traffickers, Peter Reuter is cited as comparing them with the Maginot Line.

As the balloons went up, traffickers began increasing their land shipments. The technique now is to conceal shipments inside cargo containers. ^United\States ^Interdiction ^Drug\Control\Policies\Effectiveness

807. —— (1988). "Informer Ties Top Mexican to Drug Deals; Allegations Revealed in DEA Affidavit." *The Washington Post*, 4 June, A3. Mexico's Defense Secretary, General Juán Arévalo, is said to have taken payoffs from drug traffickers. There is question about the validity of the informers' reports. ^Latin\America ^Mexico ^Drug\Traffic ^Consequences\Corruption

808. —— (1988). "Legalization of Marijuana Argued on Hill: Schmoke Leads Fight for New Drug Policy." *The Washington Post*, 30 September, A4. Description of Baltimore Mayor Kurt L. Schmoke's testimony before a congressional hearing on legalization of drugs. Other mayors and politicians testified as well. Some argued that drug abuse should be treated as a medical problem, a position committee members scorned. This was billed as the first congressional hearing ever held on drug legalization. ^United\States ^Cannabis ^Decriminalization ^Legalization

809. —— (1988). "Medellín Cartel Leaders Offered U.S. a Deal; Officials Rebuffed Plan That Sought Amnesty for Ending Drug Trade, Providing Data on Leftists." *The Washington Post*, 20 July, A4. Colombia's drug cartel, the world's largest, offered in the fall of 1986 to abandon its trade and to provide sensitive intelligence about guerrilla movements in Colombia in return for amnesty from prosecution. The U.S. refused, saying "we don't do business with international outlaws." ^United\States ^Cocaine ^Law\Enforcement ^Drug\Control\Policies ^Insurgents ^Traffickers

810. —— (1988). "Paraquat Spraying to Resume at Suspected Marijuana Fields; Opponents Threaten to Block DEA Plan in Court." *The Washington Post*, 14 July, A3. As the plans for resumption were announced, environmentalists struck with vigorous objections. ^United\States ^Cannabis ^Crop\Eradication ^Herbicides ^DEA

811. —— (1988). "Seeds of Success or Budding 'Police State'?; California Drive against Marijuana Growers Hailed as Model, Hit as Insensitive to Civil Rights." *The Washington Post*, 25 September, A3. California's drive against marijuana growers, including those operating on public lands, is reviewed in light of the substantial intervention in "human liberties" that the campaign requires. The conventional dilemma between law enforcement and individual freedom is raised for discussion vis-à-vis marijuana growers. ^United\States ^Cannabis ^Law\Enforcement ^California ^Consequences\Human\Rights ^Drug\Control\Politics ^Consequences\Constitutional

812. —— (1988). "Soviets Suggest Trading Facts on Drug Traffic; U.S. Weighing Moscow's Unusual Proposal." *The Washington Post*, 20 July, A13. The Soviet Union, admitting to a problem far more serious than ever before, has proposed a formal agreement with the United States Drug Enforcement Administration to cooperate in the struggle against international narcotics traffickers. ^USSR ^United\States ^Drug\Control\Policies ^International\Cooperation ^DEA

813. —— (1988). "Drug Fighters Resist Unifying, Senators Say." *The Washington Post*, 16 September, A25. Description of a two-year-old custom's service program set up to centralize federal drug interdiction efforts that has been hindered by agency rivalries and other problems. Questions are raised as to whether Congress should continue funding it. ^United\States ^Interdiction ^Bureaucracy ^Drug\Control\Politics

814. —— (1988). "U.S. Anti-Drug Effort Criticized; Cultivation of Coca Booming in South America, GAO Reports." *The Washington Post*, 12 November, A15. A description of a General Accounting Office report that strongly

contrasts with State Department claims that programs being funded through its Bureau of International Narcotics Matters are achieving some success in Latin America. ^United-ed\States ^Latin\America ^Drug\Control\Policies\Critique

815. —— (1989). "Cuba Seeks U.S. Cooperation in Curbing Drug Flights." *The Washington Post*, 19 July, A3. Cuba has, in private, made overtures to U.S. officials, offering to work with the United States in curbing a surge of drug smuggling flights over Cuban territory. ^Cuba ^United\States ^Caribbean ^Interdiction ^International\Cooperation

816. —— (1989). "DEA in Bolivia: 'Guerrilla Warfare,' Coca Traffic Proves Resistant." *The Washington Post*, 16 January, A1. Describes the conflicts in Bolivia's Chapare where U.S. drug enforcement agents function as "advisors" to Bolivia's U.S.–trained antinarcotics militia—the "Leopards." In fact, they serve as the Leopards' de facto commanders, blowing up airstrips, raiding jungle laboratories, searching village markets, and burning primitive factories. The economic and political impacts of the drug trade, including corruption, are substantial. Description also of peasant resistance to the destruction of their coca operations. All the efforts, however, appear to have made no serious dent in the Chapare's coca traffic. Crop substitution programs? "For most of these farmers, the government's offer to pay nearly $5,000 for the destruction of one acre of coca is not even tempting." Growing coca is "the only way to survive." ^Latin\America ^Bolivia ^United\States ^Coca ^Production ^Drug\Control\Policies ^International\Cooperation ^DEA ^Economics ^Crop\Substitution ^Producers\Incentives\Economic ^Military ^Consequences\Corruption ^Consequences\Political ^Consequences\Economic ^Statistics ^Producers\Unions ^Drug\Control\Policies\Effectiveness

817. —— (1989). "Domestic Marijuana Crop Growing." *The Washington Post*, 18 May, A5. In spite of U.S. efforts to destroy domestically grown marijuana crops, production increased 38 percent last year, now virtually tying Mexican growers as the world's second largest producer behind Colombia. While marijuana prices for high-quality products continue to rise in spite of increased production, cocaine prices continue their precipitous fall, amid signs of a worldwide glut. In 1985 cocaine sold for $30,000 per kilogram; in 1988 it fell to around $11,000. These data derived from the National Narcotics Intelligence Consumers Committee report issued in May 1989. ^United\States ^Cannabis ^Production ^Economics ^Statistics ^Producers\Incentives\Economic

818. —— (1989). "Drug Flights Unabated over Cuba." *The Washington Post*, 28 June, A20. Despite the Cuban government's breakup of a major narcotics trafficking ring and the execution of some of the principal Cuban people involved, drug smuggling flights over Cuba continue at a steady pace. It is suggested that complicity between Colombian drug traffickers and Cuban officials may extend well beyond the original Ochoa ring. ^Latin\America ^Colombia ^Cuba ^Drug\Traffic ^Traffickers ^Consequences\Corruption

819. —— (1989). "Escalating Violence in Peru Thwarting U.S. War on Drugs." *The Miami Herald*, 30 May, A1. Isikoff suggests there is a near breakdown of the U.S. antidrug policy throughout Latin America as evidenced by increasing production of coca and by increasing violence associated with it. ^Latin\America ^United\States ^Drug\Control\Policies

820. —— (1989). "Home-Grown Coca Plagues Colombia." *The Washington Post*, 9 January, A1. The article describes the highly toxic cocaine derivative called basuco (in Colombia) that has spread rapidly in Colombia and has given the country one of the highest rates of drug addiction in the world. The drug is made from low-grade coca paste. The method is to smoke it. There is considerable concern that the drug, or the contaminants in it, cause brain damage. The drug traffickers themselves issue basuco

as part compensation to underlings involved in the drug trade. While the drug cartels have worked to develop a basuco market in Colombia, there is no evidence, yet, that they have worked to develop one in the United States. ^Latin\America ^Colombia ^Coca ^Drug\Use ^Cocaine\Paste

821. —— (1989). "Jamaican Urges Anti-Drug Force." *The Washington Post*, 10 June, A6. Jamaican Prime Minister Michael Manley has proposed an international antinarcotics force that could interdict drugs, eradicate crops, and mount paramilitary-style attacks against traffickers. This may be the first proposal in the Western Hemisphere outside the United States for the concept of a multilateral paramilitary strategy against the drug traffickers. ^Drug\Control\Policies\Critique ^Drug\Control\Policies\Effectiveness ^P\S\Military

822. —— (1989). "Los Angeles Bank Surplus Linked to Drug Trade; Region Emerges as Money-Laundering Center." *The Washington Post*, 29 March, A3. A $3.8 billion cash surplus in Los Angeles' federal reserve bank, a 2,200 percent jump since 1985, is thought to confirm the region's emergence as a drug and money laundering center. ^United\States ^Money\Laundering

823. —— (1989). "Peruvian Coca Fields Sprayed in Test of Plan." *The Washington Post*, 22 March, A16. A seventy-acre test, the final one before massive aerial eradication begins, was carried out. Soil samples will be evaluated over a period of months. Environmentalists are outraged. Eli Lilly has refused to sell its Spike to the State Department. ^Latin\America ^Peru ^Coca ^Crop\Eradication ^Herbicides ^Drug\Control\Politics

824. —— (1989). "Reagan Aides Accused of Hampering Drug War; Contra Aid Had Priority over Fighting Traffickers, Hill Report Says." *The Washington Post*, 14 April, A20. The mixture of politics regarding foreign aid and international diplomacy create a caldron of institutional discontent and conflicting organizational outcomes. A congressional report, in this instance, points out that Reagan's aid to the Nicaraguan Contras had priority over fighting drug traffickers. ^United\States ^Drug\Control\Policies ^Drug\Control\Politics ^Foreign\Aid ^Contras

825. —— (1989). "Rural Drug Users Spur Comeback." *The Washington Post*, 20 February, A1. Crank has been used illegally for decades and is now enjoying a comeback. "This is [U.S.] domestically produced cocaine." Argument that the users are social-class specific (cocaine for the yuppies, crank for those who drive a Harley Davidson). ^United\States ^Drug\Use ^Designer\Drugs

826. —— (1989). "Survey of Student Drug Abuse Finds Lowest Levels in Decade." *The Washington Post*, 1 March, A1. This "federally financed survey represents the strongest evidence yet that efforts to educate young people about the dangers of drug abuse are starting to pay off." ^United\States ^Drug\Use ^Youth ^Prevention\Drug\Education ^Drug\Control\Policies\Effectiveness

827. —— (1989). "U.S. Suffering Setbacks in Latin Drug Offensive; Violence Mounting as Coca Production Soars." *The Washington Post*, 27 May, A1. Escalating violence in Peru as coca production soars. The economic foundation of the traffic as well as activities in producing areas by growers, terrorists, and interdiction agents supported by the United States are described. ^Latin\America ^Peru ^United\States ^Coca ^Drug\Control\Policies ^Politics ^Terrorists ^Interdiction ^Consequences\Violence ^Production

828. —— (1989). "Users of Crack Cocaine Link Violence to Drug's Influence." *The Washington Post*, 24 March, A11. In one of the first studies clearly linking violent behavior and crack cocaine use, a survey reports that nearly half of the callers to a nationwide cocaine hotline said they have committed violent crimes or aggressive acts, including murder, robbery, rape, child abuse, and physical assaults; two-

thirds of those reporting such behavior said they did so while using crack rather than during withdrawal. ^Cocaine ^Crack ^Drug\Use ^Crime ^Consequences\Violence

829. ———— (1989). "Warriors against Cocaine: It's Guerrilla Warfare for DEA Agents on the Bolivian Front Lines." *The Washington Post Weekly*, 23-29 January, 17-18. An on-site description of a U.S. Drug Enforcement Agency-sponsored strike in an area of Bolivia. The author likens it to guerrilla warfare. Although the U.S. agents are technically "advisors" to Bolivia's U.S.-trained antinarcotics militia, they have in fact moved to the front lines. In the past year, about 100 DEA agents have been flown into this Chapare region of Bolivia, yet nearly everyone is of the opinion that the heart of the struggle is economic, not military. Pervasive corruption within Bolivia's military and police. The degree to which all these efforts have produced deep anti-U.S. sentiments is explored. ^ Latin\America ^ Bolivia ^ United\States ^ Cocaine ^ Law\Enforcement ^ DEA ^ Military ^ Economics ^ Consequences\Political ^ Consequences\Corruption ^ Consequences\Foreign\Relations ^ Consequences\Economic

830. Isikoff, Michael, and Eugene Robinson (1989). "Colombia's Drug Kings Becoming Entrenched; Cocaine Profits Penetrating Economy." *The Washington Post*, 8 January, A1. As the cocaine profits penetrate large segments of Colombia's economy, people begin to wonder whether the drug cartels will now necessarily be accepted as a permanent fixture in Colombian life. A consensus appears to be emerging among the country's political and business elites: The drug traffickers are too big and too powerful to be destroyed. A mood of fatalism appears to be sweeping the land. This becomes more apparent as some of the notorious and key traffickers begin to move into grass-roots politics. ^Latin\America ^Colombia ^Cocaine ^Drug\Traffic ^Consequences\Economic ^Consequences\Political ^Organized\Crime ^Traffickers

831. "Island in a Stew" (1985). *The Economist*, 23 March, 42. The Turks and Caicos Islands, southeast of the Bahamas, have become a stepping stone for drug importation into the United States. A chief minister is indicted and jailed in Miami. ^Turks\and\Caicos ^Drug\Traffic ^Consequences\Corruption

832. Isner, Jerry M., Mark Estes III, Paul D. Thompson, María Rosa Costanzo-Nordin, Ramiah Subramanian, Gary Miller, George Katsas, Kristin Sweeney, and William Q. Sturner (1986). "Acute Cardiac Events Temporally Related to Cocaine Abuse." *The New England Journal of Medicine* 315(23): 1438–43. A misconception exists that recreational use of cocaine is not associated with serious medical complications. Here the authors report clinical and pathological findings in seven people in whom nonintravenous recreational use of cocaine was temporally related to acute myocardial infarction and other heart attack complications, including sudden death. Nineteen previously reported cases are added to the data base and an analysis is given of twenty-six patients. Findings: Cocaine induced cardiac disorders can occur in healthy hearts; the consequences are not limited to massive doses of the drug; the drug does not need to be taken intravenously to produce these disorders. ^Cocaine ^Drug\Use ^Health ^Consequences\Health

833. Iyer, Pico (1985). "Fighting the Cocaine Wars: Drug Traffic Spreads and the U.S. Finds Itself Mired in a Violent Losing Battle." *Time*, 25 February, 26–35. On-site description of a major Drug Enforcement Agency–Colombian narcotics police raid on a hidden laboratory in the heart of Colombia's Amazon basin along the Yari River. The agents dumped almost fourteen tons of pure cocaine into the river. General description of processing, trafficking, interdiction, and eradication efforts both in Latin America and in the United States. ^Colombia ^Latin\America ^United\States ^Cocaine ^Drug\Traffic ^Drug\Control\Policies ^Interdiction ^Crop\Eradication

834. Jacobs, James B. (1990). "Imagining Drug Legalization." *The Public Interest* 101(Fall): 28–42. Legalization advocates are criticized for not presenting concrete proposals about how their plans would work. Jacobs does this for them, he says, by proposing "to advance the drug-legalization debate by focusing on the costs of legalization *in practice*, rather than in principle" (p. 29). Three practical models are advanced and critiqued: "Treating all drugs like alcohol and cigarettes," "A government-regulated system," "a public health system." He argues that any change toward legalization implies profound cultural changes that, in the case of alcohol, have taken millennia to evolve but which, in the case of drugs, would occur chaotically and rapidly. "Cultural Revolution," he terms it. He sees hardly anything good about that. ^Legalization ^Decriminalization\Theories ^P\S\Legalization\Critique

835. Jackson, Robert L. (1988). "Drug Battle Targets Private Planes." *Los Angeles Times*, 25 November, 4. Securing aircraft ownership certificates from the U.S. Federal Aviation Administration is, apparently, "easier than getting a driver's license." With the license in hand, planes can be retrofitted and then used for drug transport. ^United\States ^Drug\Traffic ^Drug\Control\Policies\Critique

836. Jacoby, Tamar, Mark Miller, and Richard Sandza (1988). "A Choice of Poisons." *Newsweek*, 19 December, 62. The illegal coca bush economy in the Huallaga Valley of Peru has devastated the region by slash-and-burn farming. The effects: eroding soil, diminished soil nutrients, and increased risk of landslides. ^Peru ^Coca ^Production ^Crop\Eradication ^Herbicides ^Consequences\Environmental ^Latin\America

837. Jacquemart, C. (1984). "An Assessment of Legal Measures to Trace, Freeze and Confiscate the Proceeds of Drug Crimes in France: The Customs Viewpoint." *Bulletin on Narcotics* 36(4): 43–50. In France, it is the French customs officials who deal with drug crimes in the sense of profiting from the proceedings derived from them. They alert the police, who can make house searches anywhere in the country, even if no court procedure has been initiated. The confiscation of property, however, must be ordered by a court of law. Generally limited effects of the provisions in France are noted. ^Europe ^France ^Asset\Forfeiture ^Legislation

838. Jaffe, Jerome H. (1987). "Footnotes in the Evolution of the American National Response: Some Little Known Aspects of the First American Strategy for Drug Abuse and Drug Traffic Prevention. The Inaugural Thomas Okey Memorial Lecture." *British Journal of Addiction* 82:587–600. Gives a historical review of the development of a national drug strategy in America. Suggests that heroin use in Vietnam not only precipitated major initiatives to combat drug abuse, but perhaps also resulted in a more advanced infestation in American society. ^United\States ^Heroin ^Drug\Use ^Drug\Control\Policies\History ^Vietnam ^Southeast\Asia ^Consequences\Misc

839. "Japan's Gangsters: Honourable Mob" (1990). *The Economist*, 27 January, 19–22. Description of the Japanese Yakuza which is so heavily involved in drug trafficking. ^Traffickers ^Yakuza ^Southeast\Asia

840. Jarlais, Don C. des (1988). "Policy Issues regarding AIDS among Intravenous Drug Users: An Overview." *AIDS and Public Policy Journal* 3(2): 1–5. Functioning as the special editor on this issue's focus on "AIDS and Intravenous Drug Use," Jarlais sets the stage for the articles by focusing on minorities, prostitutes, methadone, drug users' organizations, HIV infections in prison, women, and the AIDS phenomenon in Australia, San Francisco, and Germany. ^Australia ^United\States ^California ^Germany ^Europe ^Minorities ^Prostitution ^Methadone ^Women ^Consequences\Health ^Heroin ^Drug\Use ^Health ^AIDS ^Reviews

841. Jarlais, Don Des, and Dana E. Hunt (1988). "AIDS and Intravenous Drug Use." *National Institute of Justice AIDS Bulletin* (February). Intravenous drug users have been the dominant source of heterosexual and perinatal transmission of the HIV virus up to the writing of this paper. The fear of death and the occurrence of deaths around those who are intravenous drug users is nothing new to them. They always have routinely risked death from overdoses, violence, or a variety of related ailments. AIDS poses a new fear for this group, and many are responding to the threat by changing their needle-sharing behavior and, to a lesser extent, their sexual behavior. ^Heroin ^Drug\Use ^Health ^AIDS ^Consequences\Sexuality ^Consequences\Health ^Consequences\Personal

842. Jarvik, Murray E. (1990). "The Drug Dilemma: Manipulating the Demand." *Science* 250(19 Oct): 387–92. Drug abuse is a substantial public policy dilemma in the United States. The challenge is to reduce drug abuse without endangering civil liberties. Campaigns to reduce supply have not—will not—be successful. Efforts to reduce demand should command the highest priority. Murray reviews the etiology of drug abuse. He gives arguments for and against legalization and examines the conditions under which a society would tolerate it. Such conditions would necessarily entail a low incidence of use deriving from either a fear of toxicity or a moral objection to use, whichever would cause people successfully to resist the temptation to experiment. Numerous problems exist with continuation of prohibition. Strategies for reducing demand in order to avoid problems of prohibition and legalization are recommended. Existing demand-reduction strategies concentrate on the youth (changing their values through community and school-based programs), treatment centers, and pharmacological agents (antagonists). Murray proposes alternative strategies: 1) create a demonstration pilot project designed to test effectiveness of supply vs. demand reduction strategies; 2) Refine modern chemical detection techniques, including quick voluntary testing devices; 3) make punishment immediate for using illicit drugs; and 4) search for an "antagonist" drug (like buprenorphine). Thereafter, cause the criminal justice system to accommodate required changes (e.g., make law enforceable and cause it to correspond to fiscal reality). ^ Drug\Use ^ Demand ^ P\S\Demand\Reduction ^ P\S\Drug\Testing ^ P\S\Antagonists ^ P\S\Law\Enforcement ^ Supply

843. Jayasuriya, D. C. (1984). "Penal Measures for Drug Offences: Perspectives from Some Asian Countries." *Bulletin on Narcotics* 36(3): 9–13. Reviews the variety of penal measures in the Asian region against drug offenses. Severe punitive sanctions, including the death penalty, exist in Iran, Malaysia, the Philippines, Singapore, Sri Lanka, and Thailand. Several countries have made provisions for compulsory treatment and rehabilitation of offenders. There is a shortage of research studies on the efficiency of penal measures and approaches in drug control. The call is for such studies to be done. ^Southeast\Asia ^Iran ^Malaysia ^Philippines ^Singapore ^Sri\Lanka ^Thailand ^Law\Enforcement ^Golden\Triangle ^Drug\Control\Policies ^Consequences\Penal ^Treatment\Compulsory ^Treatment\Rehabilitation ^Drug\Control\Policies\Effectiveness

844. —— (1985). "Law and the Treatment of Alcohol- and Drug-Dependent Persons in South-East Asia." *Medicine and Law* 4:251–63. Deals with the legal framework relating to drug and alcohol treatment in Southeast Asia—Bangladesh, Bhutan, Burma, the Democratic People's Republic of Korea, India, Indonesia, Maldives, Mongolia, Nepal, Sri Lanka, and Thailand. ^Southeast\Asia ^Bangladesh ^Bhutan ^Burma ^Korea ^India ^Indonesia ^Maldives ^Mongolia ^Nepal ^Sri\Lanka ^Thailand ^Treatment ^Alcohol ^Consequences\Legal

845. Jehl, Douglas (1981). "U.S. Enlisting Guard in Drug Fight; California among 12 States Involved in New Border Patrol Roles." *Los Angeles Times*, 31 March, 4. The United States has now moved for the first time to enlist the National

Guard in its war on drugs, granting special funds to California and eleven other states to allow guardsmen to inspect goods and man borders along the nation's southern and western perimeter. This is a fundamentally new role for many guard units. It also marks the first military involvement in the antidrug effort. ^United\States ^Drug\Control\Policies ^Military ^California ^National\Guard

846. ———— (1989). "Surge Reported in Health Emergencies Tied to Cocaine." *Los Angeles Times*, 23 May, 23. A huge surge in cocaine-related hospital emergencies is being reported from hospitals across the United States. ^United\States ^Cocaine ^Consequences\Health

847. ———— (1989). "U.S. Ends Seizures of Vessels under 'Zero Tolerance' Policy." *Los Angeles Times*, 16 February, 18. Under revised procedures, fishing vessels will not be seized in which only "personal use amounts" of illicit drugs are found. The 113 vessels seized under zero-tolerance policies brought heated criticism by boat owners who claimed they were being punished for violations over which they had no control. Among commercial fishermen, concern was raised that the livelihood of an entire crew could be endangered by one crew member. ^United\States ^Law\Enforcement ^Asset\Forfeiture ^Consequences\Economic

848. ———— (1989). "U.S. Waives Tenant Laws to Aid Virginia Battle against Drugs in Public Housing." *Los Angeles Times*, 30 March, 4. Note that the Bush administration has officially exempted Virginia from federal tenant protection laws in order to allow it to pursue its aggressive eviction policies against drug dealers. ^United\States ^Drug\Control\Policies ^Public\Housing

849. Jeri, F. Raúl, et al. (1978). "Further Experiences with the Syndromes Produced by Coca Paste Smoking." *Bulletin on Narcotics* 30(3): 1–11. The authors studied patients admitted to four hospitals in Lima, Peru, because coca-paste smoking had become a serious problem for their health or for social adjustment. The main symptoms were anxiety mingled with euphoria and a rapidly developing compulsion to continue smoking. Other symptoms included irritability, illusions, and hallucinations. ^Coca ^Drug\Use ^Cocaine\Paste ^Consequences\Health ^Consequences\Neurological ^Consequences\Social

850. Jeri, F. Raúl, ed. (1980). *Cocaine 1980: Proceedings of the Interamerican Seminar on Medical and Sociological Aspects of Coca and Cocaine*. Lima, Peru: Pacific Press. Reviews the state of research, the data regarding consumption patterns, and revisionist views about cocaine's effects on both health and public policy. In a sense, therefore, the contributions cover production and consumption of cocaine (effects and impacts) and also the social, economic, family, and labor factors implicated in production, consumption, and distribution. Some tentative conclusions: Coca-leaf chewing as practiced by Bolivian and Peruvian inhabitants is not shown to produce any ill effects on intelligence, growth, reproduction, nutrition, behavior, or inheritance. Excessive chewing may be detrimental to health in other areas. The effects of coca-paste smoking are due to cocaine. Coca-paste smoking is therefore potentially harmful. More definite knowledge would need to be brought by research before governments would be necessarily obligated to review their laws and regulations concerning coca growing, substitution, and eradication. Only the Argentinean delegation firmly objected to the above, insisting that their position was firmly abolitionist. ^Coca ^Health ^Drug\Traffic ^Economics ^Society ^Reviews ^Drug\Use ^Family ^Consequences\Health ^Consequences\Misc ^Consequences\Social ^Consequences\Economic ^Cocaine\Paste ^Tobacco ^Consequences\Reproduction

851. Jeri, F. Raúl (1984). "Coca-Paste Smoking in Some Latin American Countries: A Severe and Unabated Form of Addiction." *Bulletin on Narcotics* 36(2): 15-31. Coca paste, the intermediary product between coca leaves and cocaine,

may be dried, and then mixed with tobacco and smoked. This pattern of drug abuse is said to be at epidemic proportions in Bolivia, Colombia, and Peru. It is an addictive form of abuse and has serious health, social, and economic consequences. Mental disorders such as euphoria, dysphoria, hallucinosis, and paranoid psychosis are noted. Excessive coca-paste smoking is often resistant to therapeutic interventions. ^Coca ^Drug\Use ^Health ^Cocaine\Paste ^Tobacco ^Consequences\Neurological ^Consequences\Health ^Consequences\Economic ^Consequences\Social ^Latin\America ^Bolivia ^Peru ^Colombia

852. Jeri, F. Raúl, C. C. Sanchez, T. del Pozo, and M. Fernández (1978). "The Syndrome of Coca Paste." *Journal of Psychedelic Drugs* 10(4): 361–70. This is one of the first systematic studies that analyzes both the contents of coca paste as well as its rapid toxic effects and the degree to which it has been disseminated among young people in Peru, as of the late 1970s. Aside from chronic intoxication, coca paste is capable of producing acute intoxication and therefore death. Furthermore, grave social effects exist, associated with coca-paste usage, including people dedicating themselves to robbery, swindling, and going into debt in order to buy the drug. Such people became unreliable at their jobs, were frequently absent or neglected their duties, and even smoked paste during work hours. University students often abandoned their studies or failed their courses. ^Coca ^Drug\Use ^Health ^Cocaine\Paste ^Cocaine\Pharmacology ^Consequences\Social ^Consequences\Personal ^Consequences\Educational

853. Jeri, F. Raúl, C. C. Sánchez, T. de Pozo, M. Fernández, and C. Carbajal (1980). "Further Experience with the Syndromes Produced by Coca Paste Smoking." In *Cocaine 1980. Proceedings of the Interamerican Seminar on Medical and Sociological Aspects of Coca and Cocaine*, edited by F. R. Jeri, 76–85. Lima, Peru: Pacific Press. The effects on health and social interaction are noted among 108 patients treated in a Lima, Peru, hospital for coca-paste addiction. The specific effects are described. ^Coca ^Drug\Use ^Cocaine\Paste ^Peru ^Consequences\Sexuality ^Consequences\Personal ^Consequences\Psychological ^Consequences\Neurological

854. Johnson, Bruce D. (1984). "If You Can Incarcerate Local Heroin Abusers, You Can Cut Back on Property Crimes." *Crime Control Digest*, 17 December, 6–8. How much crime do heroin users actually commit? A report of a systematic study by the National Institute on Drug Abuse and the National Institute of Justice show that abusers commit a large number and variety of serious crimes. ^United\States ^Heroin ^NIDA ^Consequences\Crime

855. Johnson, Bruce D., et al. (1985). *Taking Care of Business: The Economics of Crime by Heroin Users*. Lexington, Mass.: Lexington Books. Drug abuse and crime in the United States, particularly among heroin users, is explored, as are also the economic aspects of heroin use in the United States. From extensive reviews of scientific and social scientific literature and from a substantial field research project carried out in east and central Harlem, the authors explore what is known and what is not known about the relationship of heroin use to crime rates and certain kinds of economic consequences. On the whole, heroin abusers have a "multi-problem life-style," and the heroin-distribution system is central to this life-style. With respect to a countering social policy, such policies must attempt to undermine the heroin-distribution system at the retail level if they are to be successful at all. Interestingly, the federal government places its emphasis on preventing the importation of heroin and cocaine, while state and local police attempt to make major buys and prosecute upper-level dealers. But little is done to disrupt the low-level heroin-distribution system (in part because there are hardly any places left to put people who may be arrested). Interestingly, heroin abusers are economically productive. Probably the most important implication of Chapter 12 lies in the jarring realization that, from a truly economic standpoint, heroin abuser criminality

is not all "bad." Nevertheless, the central concern remains: "What should be done with heroin abusers?" The authors suggest five policy alternatives and consider the benefits and drawbacks associated with each. These are (1) incarcerating all heroin abusers, (2) incarcerating the most seriously criminal, (3) mandating treatment of convicted heroin abusers, (4) providing incentives to reform life styles, and (5) maintaining the status quo. The authors seem more inclined toward "maintaining the status quo" as far as their judgment of feasibility and consequences on reform seem to be. The book contains a methodological appendix. ^United\States ^Heroin ^New\York ^Consequences\Crime ^Reviews ^Law\Enforcement ^Proffered\Solutions ^Consequences\Social ^Consequences\Economic

856. Johnson, Bruce, Kevin Anderson, and Eric D. Wish (1988). "A Day in the Life of 105 Drug Addicts and Abusers: Crimes Committed and How the Money Was Spent." *Sociology and Social Research* 72(3): 185–191. Reports on crime committed in a previous twenty-four hours by a sample of 105 drug addicts. The study notes how the illegal gains were spent, and in particular what portion of it was spent for alcohol and specific drugs. ^Heroin ^Crime ^Alcohol ^Consequences\Crime ^Consequences\Economic

857. Johnson, Charles (1983). "The Marijuana Invasion." *Farm Journal*, Mid-March, 9. U.S. farm lands are being appropriated for marijuana growing. The economics of marijuana growing place profits as high as $3,500 a plant, with total receipts for the 1982 crop being around $10.4 billion. Two factors hurdled the marijuana industry to the forefront: Spraying of paraquat on Mexican marijuana and a truly astounding agronomic revolution in marijuana production that made it possible to grow marijuana anywhere in the United States. ^United\States ^Cannabis ^Production ^Production\Incentives\Economic

858. Johnson, Julie (1989). "Drug Gangs Are Now Operating in Rural States, Justice Department Says." *The New York Times*, 4 August, A1. Ohio and Wyoming are noted particularly for expansion activities of drug trafficking organizations. Rural Georgia and South Carolina are also mentioned. There is some speculation that drug organizations may actually have coalesced around a chief executive officer and a disciplined central bureaucracy. ^United\States\Rural\Areas ^Ohio ^Wyoming ^Georgia ^South\Carolina ^Drug\Traffic ^Organized\Crime

859. Johnson, Sally Hope (1983). "Treatment of Drug Abusers in Malaysia: A Comparison." *The International Journal of the Addictions* 18(7): 951–58. Two forms of treatment for heroin abusers in Malaysia are examined—traditional medicine and institutional modern medicine. An evaluation of which form is the most effective indicated that "traditional medicine was better for some abusers, but institutional treatment was better for others." The critical intervening variables were personality and an individual's felt needs. ^Malaysia ^Heroin ^Treatment ^Society ^Culture ^Southeast\Asia ^Drug\Control\Policies\Effectiveness

860. Johnston, David (1989). "119 Seized in Drive to Halt Indoor Marijuana Growing." *The New York Times*, 27 October, A10. One hundred nineteen people in retail stores in forty-six states in the U.S. which sell specialized equipment to grow marijuana indoors were arrested. Business documents, shipping records, and customer lists were confiscated. Only Hawaii, Nebraska, North Dakota, and West Virginia escaped the net. ^United\States ^Cannabis ^Drug\Control\Policies ^Law\Enforcement

861. Johnston, Lloyd D., Patrick M. O'Malley, and Jerald G. Bachman (1988). *Illicit Drug Use, Smoking, and Drinking by America's High School Students, College Students, and Young Adults, 1975–1987*. Washington, D.C.: Department of Health and Human Services. Presents basic survey information

on the prevalence of drug use among high school seniors and college students. The results are broken down into the usual demographic indicators, suggesting trends and attitudes. ^United\States ^Drug\Use ^Youth ^Statistics ^Alcohol ^Tobacco

862. Johnston, Lloyd D., Patrick M. O'Malley, and Jerald G. Bachman, editors (1987). *National Trends in Drug Use and Related Factors among American High School Students and Young Adults, 1975–1986*. Rockville, Md.: National Institute on Drug Abuse. Between 1975 and 1986 there was an appreciable decline in the use of a number of illicit drugs among the populations surveyed (high school seniors, college students, young adults). Cocaine use, however, increased. While the trends are encouraging, American high school students and other young adults consume more illicit drugs than do their cohorts in any other industrialized nation in the world. ^United\States ^Drug\Use ^Youth ^NIDA ^Statistics

863. Jonas, Steven (1989). "Is the Drug Problem Soluble?" *American Behavioral Scientist* 32(3): 295–315. This wide-ranging article deals with epidemiology, interrelationships among drugs, the economic cost of consuming them, drugs and crime, foreign policy considerations, what legalization would do, the causes of drug abuse, and the politics of changing current U.S. policy regarding drugs. ^United\States ^Drug\Control\Policies ^Reviews ^Epidemiology ^Consequences\Economic ^Consequences\Crime ^Consequences\Foreign\Policy ^Decriminalization ^Drug\Use\Theories ^Drug\Control\Politics

864. Jones, Helen C., and Paul W. Lovinger (1985). *The Marijuana Question and Science's Search for an Answer*. New York: Dodd, Mead. Physiological effects and social aspects of marijuana use. A major motivation behind this volume is that however little is known for certain about the effects of marijuana on human health, all that one has reason to suspect justifies serious national concern. This volume contains an astonishing array of anecdotal, clinical, survey, and other information about an equally astonishing array of topics including the lungs and respiratory system; sex, reproduction, and offspring; the heart and circulatory system; immunity and resistance; cells and chromosomes; the brain; the mind; the changing scene within society; driving, aviation and other transportation; the nonsmoker; dependence; crime; other drugs; military; and medicine. On the whole, warns that the weight of evidence shows that marijuana smoking is dangerous to one's health and to one's society. It would not come down on the side, therefore, of speaking of marijuana activity as a victimless crime, but rather sees society as the victim. The book is intended to affect public opinion. Extensively documented and referenced to the scientific and social scientific literature. ^Cannabis ^Drug\Use ^Reviews ^Consequences\Physiological ^Consequences\Social ^Consequences\Health ^Consequences\Sexuality ^Consequences\Fetuses ^Consequences\Neurological ^Consequences\Public\Safety ^Consequences\Crime ^Military ^Consequences\Reproduction

865. Jones, Patricia A. (1989). "Cocaine and Violence: A Marriage Made in Hell!" *Crisis* (March): 17. Innocent bystanders now fall as a consequence of the contemporary drug wars. Terrorist activities associated with drug use are at the root of this new phenomenon. Discussion is raised about terrorist connections with the drug industry both in the United States and in South America. ^United\States ^Latin\America ^Cocaine ^Drug\Traffic ^Consequences\Violence ^Insurgents ^Consequences\Social ^Terrorists

866. Jordan, Rosa (1987). "Hair Analysis: RIAH[sm] Detects Drug Use Patterns." *Alcoholism and Addiction* (September-October): 47. Urinalysis cannot be relied upon because the test is so easy to evade or even avoid. A better technology has arrived. Based on the application of radioimmunoassays to hair, the test promises to be useful in both drug detection and drug rehabilitation because it can measure quantitatively, distinguishing between light or occasional use and chronic or

heavy use of drugs. Moreover it can be done on a small snippet of hair, and it cannot therefore be evaded. ^Drug\Testing

867. Josephson, Eric (1981). "Marijuana Decriminalization: The Processes and Prospects of Change." *Contemporary Drug Problems* 10(3): 291–322. When marijuana consumption, particularly among adolescents, sky rocketed in the 1960s and early 1970s, possession of the drug was a felonious offense under federal and all state laws. Subsequently penalties were reduced to a misdemeanor in nearly all states and the federal government adopted a policy that, while not making possession licit, eliminated penalties for possession of small amounts. This article looks into factors contributing to decriminalization of marijuana and also factors that may block further liberalization of that policy. The focus is on the processes of change and prospects for further change, not with the impact of decriminalization on use of the drug or on the costs of law enforcement. ^United\States ^Cannabis ^Society ^Decriminalization ^Drug\Control\Politics ^Drug\Control\Policies\History

868. Junguito, R., and C. Caballero (1982). "Illegal Trade Transactions and the Underground Economy of Colombia." In *The Underground Economy in the United States and Abroad*, edited by V. Tanzi, 285–313. Lexington, MA: Lexington Books. (Book is annotated under Tanzi, Vito) ^Colombia ^Drug\Traffic ^Economics ^Informal\Economy

869. Jurich, Anthony P., Cheryl J. Polson, Julie A. Jurich, and Rodney A. Bates (1985). "Family Factors in the Lives of Drug Users and Abusers." *Adolescence* 20(77): 143–59. What factors, among identifiable family matters, have an impact on drug use? These are parental absence, discipline, scapegoating, hypocritical morality, parent-child communication gap, parental divorce, mother-father conflicts, family breakup, and the use of "psychological crutches" to cope with stress. Each of these issues is discussed. ^Drug\Use ^Youth ^Society ^Family ^Drug\Use\Theories

870. Juscamaita, Enrique (1983). "La Economía Cocalera y Su Impacto en la Dinámica Regional: El Caso del Valle del Río Apurímac-Ayacucho." *Socialismo y Participación* 24:37-58. Discusses the historical and geographical context of the social economy around Ayacucho, the influence of the Tambo-Rio Apurímac highway which brought jungle area into the local economy, the economic exchange from the highland and coca growing regions, the increasing production of coca around the Rio Apurímac, and the coca micro economy. The coca economy has engulfed an entire peasant population, and simple eradication will not be a solution. The author advances economic solutions that must take into consideration the welfare of the peasant producer. ^Peru ^Coca ^Drug\Traffic ^Economics ^Consequences\Economic ^P\S\Economic ^Drug\Control\Policies\Critique

871. Kadish, Mark J., Rosalyn Suna Kadish, and Alan J. Baverman (1983). "A Powerful Weapon for Federal Prosecutors." *Trial* (October): 66–109. Describes the "continuing criminal enterprise" statute, 21 U.S.C. paragraph 848, which forces courts to impose minimum mandatory sentences on people involved in certain kinds of drug crimes. ^United\States ^Law\Enforcement ^Legislation ^Judiciary

872. Kagan, Daniel (1989). "How America Lost Its First Drug War." *Insight*, 20 November, 8–17. Reviews the history of drug epidemics and drug use in the United States and the official and public responses to those epidemics. The relationship of the response to the first drug epidemic in the United States to the drug boom of the 1960s is reviewed. David Musto's work is reviewed. The history of political and public opinion about drugs in the United States is also reviewed. ^United\States ^Drug\Use\History ^Drug\Control\Policies\History

873. Kagel, John H., Raymond C. Battalio, and C. G. Miles (1980). "Marijuana and Work Performance: Results from an Experiment." *The Journal of Human Resources* 15(3): 373–95. This study, from an experimental micro economy involving resident volunteer human subjects, explores the effects of marijuana availability and consumption on production, hours of work, and output per hour in the workplace. No effect of consumption on total output or total hours worked is noted. ^Cannabis ^Drug\Use ^Economics ^Workplace

874. Kalant, Oriana Josseau (1972). "Report of the Indian Drugs Commission, 1893–94: A Critical Review." *The International Journal of the Addictions* 7(1): 77–96. As have many other writers who have commented on this massive set of volumes, this author also applauds the thoroughness and rationality applied to the analysis of the data, and the lucid and consistent manner with which the social philosophy of the commission was related to the issues and recommendations made in its document. This amply justifies admiration for the commission's approach, but does not warrant the uncritical acceptance of all its conclusions which some modern writers have shown. Among other things, the potentially harmful effects of marijuana must be looked at in terms of contemporary scientific and medical standards. Also, it must be borne in mind that the social and legal issues involve political and moral rather than scientific considerations, and that there are substantial differences in all these areas today as there was in the situation in India at the end of the nineteenth century. ^India ^Cannabis ^Drug\Use\History ^Health ^Society ^Reviews ^Culture ^Consequences\Critique

875. Kalant, Oriana Josseau, Kevin O'Brien Fehr, Diana Arras, and Lise Anglin (1983). *Cannabis: Health Risks. A Comprehensive Annotated Bibliography (1844–1982)*. Bibliographic Series No. 16. Toronto, Canada: Alcoholism and Drug Addiction Research Foundation. This bibliography contains 1,718 annotated entries cross-referenced, by number, in numerous categories. Criteria for inclusion were simply anything that "dealt with, claimed, or clearly demonstrated adverse effects of cannabis on health," regardless of quality. The bibliography does not include papers from the social sciences, or papers dealing with legal or political issues. The abstracts are nonevaluative. ^Cannabis ^Health ^Bibliographies

876. Kamas, Linda (1987). "Dutch Disease Economics and the Colombian Export Boom." *World Development* 14(9): 1177–98. Examines the effects on the Colombian economy of large increases in foreign exchange earnings from coffee and illegal drug exports. As predicted by Dutch disease models, the relative price of non-traded goods rose, and the real exchange rate appreciated. After the boom subsided, neither the price of home goods nor the real exchange rate depreciated significantly. It was not until 1984 that such depreciation began. ^Latin\America ^Colombia ^Drug\Traffic ^Economics ^Foreign\Exchange ^Consequences\Economic ^Consequences\Markets

877. Kamen, Al (1989). "Court Curbs Use of Criminals' Assets to Pay Lawyers." *The Washington Post*, 23 June, A9. The decision to not allow criminals to use their assets to pay lawyers is considered a victory for the government in its fight against drug dealers and racketeers. Understandably, lawyers are objecting to the Supreme Court decision. ^United\States ^Asset\Forfeiture ^Attorneys ^Judiciary

878. ——— (1989). "Court Upholds Conrail Policy on Drug Tests." *The Washington Post*, 20 June, A14. The Supreme Court ruled on 19 June 1989 that federal law does not require the railroad industry to negotiate with unions before imposing mandatory drug testing for employees. It is not thought that this ruling will necessarily affect other firms. ^United\States ^Drug\Testing ^Workplace ^Judiciary

879. Kamiya, Gary (1989). "The Crack Epidemic: The Season of Hard Choices." *Crisis* (March): 11. In the astonishing short space of only three years, crack has overwhelmed the criminal justice system. Crack has also had a devastating impact on minority communities and, in many instances, turned inner cities into battle-grounds. Thousands of lives have been ruined; and numerous police officers have been killed during drug-enforcement activities. The social costs of the invasion of crack are incalculable, running all the way from spreading syphilis and AIDS to overburdening criminal justice and social welfare systems. The problem affects every class and race, and there appears to be no ready solution to the problem. Interdiction of the trafficking is not working. Suppression of the production in Bolivia, Peru, and Colombia has also failed, for a simple reason—those countries can't afford to quit. The economic travail is compounded by Latin America's national debt. ^United\States ^Cocaine ^Crack ^Drug\Traffic ^Consequences\Law\Enforcement ^Consequences\Judiciary ^Consequences\Penal ^Consequences\Social ^Consequences\Personal ^Consequences\Economic ^AIDS ^Drug\Control\Policies\Critique ^Latin\America ^Bolivia ^Peru ^Colombia ^International\Debt

880. Kamm, Henry (1988). "Afghan Opium Yield up as Pakistan Curbs Crop." *The New York Times*, 14 April, A16. There is a bumper crop of opium poppies in the mountains on both sides of the rugged border of Pakistan and Afghanistan. Poppies prove a quick source of money for poor people, and there are not many income alternatives right now. ^Afghanistan ^Opiates ^Production ^Golden\Crescent ^Pakistan ^Produc-ers\Incentives\Economic ^Southwest\Asia

881. ——— (1990). "U.S. and Laos Are Getting Friendlier." *The New York Times*, 31 January, A3. The communist leaders of Laos desire improved relations with the United States and are therefore willing to cooperate in a drug eradication program. The program is linked to a development aid project. ^Southeast\Asia ^Laos ^Prevention\Development ^Crop\Eradication ^United\States ^Drug\Control\Policies ^Conse-quences\Foreign\Relations ^International\Cooperation

882. Kandel, Denise B. (1980). "Drugs and Drinking Behavior among Youth." *Annual Review of Sociology* 6:235–85. This is a substantial review of the literature on alcohol and other drug (particularly marijuana) abuse by adolescents and young adults. The literature is classified into various approaches: trends, theoretical orientations, and conceptual frameworks. It deals with longitudinal drug research as a methodology and with socialization theory. More than 100 articles and books are cited in the review. ^Cannabis ^Drug\Use ^Youth ^Society ^Reviews ^Alcohol ^Drug\Use\Theories

883. Kandel, Denise B., ed. (1978). *Longitudinal Research on Drug Use: Empirical Findings and Methodological Issues*. Washington, D.C.: Hemis-phere-Wiley. Studies where respondents are followed over time constitute one of the most powerful approaches available to social scientists in answering questions about social behavior. This book brings together eight drug researchers who have carried out substantial empirical, longitudinal investigations, and it attempts to integrate their sub-stantive findings on antecedents and consequences of drug use in various populations. The objective, of course, is to move toward a theoretical synthesis of these findings. The book also offers detailed methodological critiques of the eight longitudinal drug studies included in it. These studies illustrate the role of social context in the initiation of drug usage and document that many of the factors that have been found to be related to drug usage (such as low academic performance, crime, depression, or rebelliousness) precede the use of drugs. The authors deal with peer influence and maturational effects on drug behavior, and they develop the idea of stages as a strategy in identifying specific factors in developmental transitions or changes. Kandel's synthesis of the results of the research related to patterns of involvement in drug use, antecedents of drug use, and consequences

of drug use are organized in the form of nineteen propositions (15ff), including the following: The period of risk of initiation into illicit drug use is over by the mid-20s; a high proportion of youths who have tried marijuana will eventually go on to experiment with other illicit drugs; later age of onset is associated with lesser involvement and the greater probability of stopping; there are clear-cut developmental steps and sequences in drug behavior, so that use of one of the legal drugs almost always precedes use of illegal drugs; addiction to heroin is not necessarily a permanent state; occasional use of heroin does not necessarily lead to addiction; although stages of drug use are identifiable, a wide variety of factors is involved in the transitions into those stages; personality factors, indicative of maladjustment, precede the use of marijuana and other illicit drugs; a constellation of attitudes and values favorable to deviants precedes involvement in illicit drugs; there is a process of anticipatory socialization in which youths who will initiate the use of drugs develop attitudes favorable to their use prior to initiation; drug behavior and drug-related attitudes of peers are among the most potent predictors of drug involvement; parental behaviors, parental attitudes, and parental closeness to their children have differential importance at different stages of involvement of drugs; sociodemographic variables hold little predictive power for initiation into marijuana; age of onset of drug use declines as degree of proneness to deviance increases; a social setting favorable to drug use reinforces and increases individual predisposition to use; nonaddiction illicit drug use has not been shown to lead to increased criminality; and drug use has not been shown to lead to amotivational syndrome. ^Youth ^Society ^Reviews ^Drug\Use\Theories ^Consequences\Theories ^Parenting ^Crime ^Consequences\Critique ^Amotivational\Syndrome

884. Kantor, Glenda Kaufman (1984). "Treatment Outcomes of Narcotic-Dependent Women: A Study of the Effects of Affiliations, Support Systems, Presence of Children and Sex-Role Perceptions." Master's thesis, University of Illinois at Chicago. From a study of forty-five women in drug treatment programs, the author found no significant sex differences in treatment outcomes, and offers that this finding refutes the stereotypical conceptions of greater emotional pathology for female addicts than for male addicts. ^Drug\Use ^Treatment ^Women ^Consequences\Critique

885. Kaplan, Elaine, and Lois G. Williams (1988). "Will Employees' Rights Be the First Casualty of the War on Drugs?" *Kansas University Law Review* 36:755–85. Discussion of all the privacy issues associated with drug testing, particularly urine testing, for evidence of drug use. Extensively documented. ^United\States ^Drug\Testing ^Workplace ^Consequences\Human\Rights

886. Kaplan, Howard B. (1981). "Conceptual Issues in Marijuana Decriminalization Research." *Contemporary Drug Problems* 10(4): 365–82. In considering relevant theoretical orientations in decriminalization research, these authors give primary emphasis to social-psychological theories, assuming that other orientations (economics, political science) are easily translatable into social-psychological ones. The intent here is to illustrate the range of theoretical models leading to different expectations regarding marijuana use. Which models best reflect reality? Researchers need to make proper applications, given the social contexts. ^Cannabis ^Society ^Decriminalization\Theories

887. Kaplan, John (1983). *The Hardest Drug: Heroin and Public Policy*. Chicago, Ill.: University of Chicago Press. Studies in crime and justice, focusing on the United States government's policy in the control of narcotics. Examines the costs and benefits of different public policies toward heroin. Any heroin policy will benefit some people while hurting others; it is clear that the United States' present policy hurts U.S. institutions of criminal justice, those who are addicted, and those upon whom addicts prey—at least to the extent of any additional depredation caused by their heroin

addiction. After examining these consequences of heroin prohibition, the author explores a policy of "free availability." This policy would, in many ways, improve the lives of present addicts and of those they victimize, as well as the integrity of criminal justice processes. On the other hand, it would hurt those who would then become addicted and who would not otherwise have encountered heroin. It would also hurt those who, in one way or another, would suffer more from the public health and personal aspects of a greatly increased addiction rate than they do from the many ramifications of the present U.S. heroin policy. If "free availability" does not hold sufficient benefits to warrant implementation, what about "heroin maintenance?" Implementation of this policy in the United States would injure those who would have to foot the bill, those who live in the vicinity of a heroin distribution center, and those who become addicted through diversion from the system; it would improve the lot of prison addicts and those whom they victimize. The author then presents an extensive discussion on "the law and the user," arguing that decriminalizing use (as opposed to decriminalizing supply), if coupled with coerced treatment for those who cannot "handle their drug," would constitute a least offensive option and one that would produce greater benefits than any of the current policies extant or variations that he examined. ^United\States ^Heroin ^Drug\Control\Policies\Effectiveness ^Decriminalization\Theories ^P\S\Legalization

888. —— (1983). "Not the Answer: Heroin for Addicts." *Stanford Lawyer* (Fall): 5–66. Looks at the British heroin substitution program experience and concludes that neither it, nor any of its variants, is likely to have productive applicability in the United States. ^United\States ^United\Kingdom ^Heroin ^Drug\Control\Policies\Critique

889. —— (1987). "The War on Drugs: Predicting the Status Quo." *Nova Law Review* 11:931–32. If hardly anything can change trends in America today, then one might only look forward to a new synthetic drug that will come on the scene following cocaine and marijuana. ^United\States ^Drug\Control\Policies\Effectiveness ^Consequences\Drug\Concentration ^Designer\Drugs ^Consequences\Drug\Control\Policies

890. —— (1988). "Taking Drugs Seriously." *The Public Interest* 92(Summer): 32–50. Present drug-control efforts have bogged down. None of the policy options advanced is attractive. The point is to choose the policy that is "least bad." Should that be a repeal of drug prohibition? Comparisons with alcohol prohibition and repeal are given. A cost-benefit analysis raises serious questions about such a move. Should we adopt a "prescription system"? That would be inappropriate. Firm declaration of a "no surrender" policy? A cost-benefit analysis on cocaine and heroin (but not marijuana) suggests the need to continue viable policies that reduce demand and limit supply. Explored are educational approaches (not very effective), peer counseling (effective), putting pressure on the retailing of cocaine and heroin, and building an incentive system to behavior that would unclog the courts. Mandatory urine testing would be required for all arrestees; subsequent parole would be premised on a continued testing clean for drugs. The focus is on those (users) who do the most to support the illegal market. ^ Drug\Control\Policies\Effectiveness ^ Drug\Control\Policies\Critique ^ Supply ^ P\S\Demand\Reduction ^ P\S\Education ^ P\S\Peers ^ P\S\Drug\Testing ^ P\S\Law\Enforcement ^ Cocaine ^ Heroin

891. Kaslow, Amy (1990). "New Lebanese Plan Would Fight Hashish in the Bekaa Valley." *The Christian Science Monitor*, 7 March, 7. Hashish production in the war-torn Bekaa Valley is extraordinarily important economically. Indeed, the Lebanese newspapers routinely list tables displaying prices of hashish, opium, and cocaine on world markets. "It's like a commodity report." Described here is Lebanon's plan to try to wean the Bekaa Valley from its dependence on illegal narcotics. ^ Middle\East ^ Lebanon ^ Statistics ^ Production ^ Opiates ^ Drug\Control\Policies ^ Economics

892. Kaufman, Edward (1985). "Family Systems and Family Therapy of Substance Abuse: An Overview of Two Decades of Research and Clinical Experience." *International Journal of the Addictions* 20(6-7): 897–916. Following in the growing tradition of involvement of the entire family, particularly parents, in substance abuse treatment for family members, this article adds additional information regarding family treatment methods developed to motivate substance abusers, to detoxify them, and to work with the family when the drug abuser is not involved in treatment. ^Drug\Use ^Treatment\Family ^Reviews

893. ——— (1986). "A Contemporary Approach to the Family Treatment of Substance Abuse Disorders." *American Journal of Drug and Alcohol Abuse* 12(3): 199-211. Family therapy may be used to treat substance abuse. Several "family factors" or variables are discussed, including motivating the entire family to participate in the treatment of one of its members. ^Drug\Use ^Treatment\Family ^Treatment\Therapy

894. Kaufman, Victoria (1988). "United Nations: International Conference on Drug Abuse and Illicit Trafficking." *Harvard International Law Journal* 29(2): 581–86. The 1987 conference held in Vienna adopted two independent documents. While the conference addressed the long-standing issues of supply in the illicit trafficking of drugs, it also emphasized the need to reduce demand and increase the quality and number of rehabilitative centers. This note describes the documents and places them into historical context. ^United\Nations ^Drug\Control\Policies ^International\Cooperation\History ^Supply ^Demand ^P\S\Rehabilitation

895. Kawell, JoAnn (1988). "Bolivia: Coca Trade Employs 15 Percent of Labor Force." *Latinamerica Press*, 29 September, 4. A Cochabamba research group argues that coca trade is the country's number one employer, providing jobs to 15 percent of the labor force. More than 70,000 farmers and their families—5 percent of the total population—grow coca. ^Latin\America ^Bolivia ^Coca ^Drug\Traffic ^Economics ^Consequences\Economic ^Statistics

896. Kellner, Leon B. (1987). "The National Strategy—An Overview." *Nova Law Review* 11:933–38. The article summarizes briefly America's national strategy for prevention of drug abuse and drug trafficking which was promulgated in 1984. ^United\States ^Drug\Control\Policies

897. Kelly, Neil (1982). "Southeast Asian Raids Pinch World Heroin Trade." *The Christian Science Monitor*, 1–3 March. A three-part series explores heroin production in Southeast Asia and efforts to prevent its export to other regions such as Western Europe and the United States. ^Southeast\Asia ^Heroin ^Drug\Traffic ^Drug\Control\Policies ^Production ^Interdiction

898. Kendall, John (1988). "Drugs, Money Add up to Temptation for Police." *Los Angeles Times*, 20 December, 3. Signs of corruption among narcotics law enforcement officers are cropping up in New York, Washington, and Miami, among rural sheriffs in Georgia, federal prosecutors in Boston, and government agents and customs officials in California. ^United\States ^Law\Enforcement ^Consequences\Corruption ^New\York ^Washington ^Florida ^Georgia ^Massachusetts ^California ^Customs

899. Kennedy, Joseph (1985). *Coca Exotica: The Illustrated Story of Cocaine*. Madison, New Jersey: Fairleigh Dickinson University Press. Looks at humanity's historical experience with coca, from ancient beginnings among the Incas through coca's migration to Europe, the refining of its alkaloids in the 1890's in Europe and America, the resulting addiction of thousands of people, its use in patent medicines, the creation of anticocaine laws and movements to exterminate it, and the present day

wherein cocaine has been reinserted into the human experience. ^Coca\History ^Cocaine\History

900. Kennedy, J. Michael (1989). "Aerial Drug War Has Its Ups, Downs." *Los Angeles Times*, 7 March, 1. Discussion of the radar-detecting blimps on the southern border of the United States which are both costly and arguably ineffective. ^United\States ^Interdiction ^Surveillance

901. Kerr, Peter (1987). "Chasing the Heroin from Plush Hotel to Mean Streets." *The New York Times*, 11 August, B1. Description of undercover drug buys in New York City as part of a general surveillance of Chinese drug rings transporting heroin along "the China White Trail," from Thailand to Hong Kong's secret societies, to Chinese neighborhoods in Queens, New York. This is an anecdotal account in the life of "group 41," the Federal Drug Enforcement Administration's unit assigned to break up the Chinese drug rings in New York City. ^United\States ^Heroin ^Drug\Traffic ^Law\Enforcement ^Organized\Crime ^Triads ^Thailand ^Southeast\Asia ^Golden\Triangle ^Hong\Kong ^New\York

902. ———— (1987). "Chinese Now Dominate New York Heroin Trade." *The New York Times*, 9 August, 1. Further description of the new heroin connection known as the "China White Trail." The multi billion dollar New York City heroin industry has suddenly been taken over by Chinese criminals. Chinese organized crime is on the rise around the country, and it is connected to the Southeast Asian heroin trafficking. Penetration of the Chinese into the New York heroin trade has been made possible by the weakening of traditional organized crime there due to generational divisions and a series of major prosecutions. In other words, a vacuum developed, and the Chinese filled it. ^China ^United\States ^Heroin ^Drug\Traffic ^Organized\Crime ^Triads ^New\York ^Law\Enforcement

903. ———— (1987). "Crack Addiction: The Tragic Toll on Women and Their Children." *The New York Times*, 9 February, B1. Crack has arisen as a heroin replacement in poor neighborhoods with the increasing incidence of use among women, particularly single mothers. Explores the relationship of its use among this population segment to child abuse, neglect, and death linked to drug use by parents. Also discussed is the phenomenon of infants neglected or abandoned by their parents, and who languish in New York's hospitals awaiting foster homes. The rising number of women involved with crack is striking. ^United\States ^Cocaine ^Crack ^Drug\Use ^Women ^Society ^Parenting ^Consequences\Children

904. ———— (1987). "War on Drugs Puts Strain on Prisons, U.S. Officials Say." *The New York Times*, 25 September, 1. Estimates are made that the federal jail capacity needs to double if the legislation enacting the war on drugs is to be carried out to its ultimate conclusion. Otherwise the ability of federal agencies charged with making arrests will be jeopardized by a backup in the judicial system and a reluctance of judges to send convicts to overcrowded prisons. ^United\States ^Law\Enforcement ^Consequences\Penal ^Legislation ^Consequences\Judiciary

905. ———— (1988). "Bolivia, with U.S. Aid, Battles Cocaine at the Root." *The New York Times*, 17 April. Bolivia is working with the United States in order to put an end to cocaine production. ^Latin\America ^Bolivia ^United\States ^Coca ^Crop\Eradication ^International\Cooperation ^Foreign\Aid ^Drug\Control\Policies

906. ———— (1988). "Citizen Anti-Crack Drive: Vigilance or Vigilantism?" *The New York Times*, 23 May, B1. Description of citizen patrols begun in drug-infested areas where government has been ineffectual. They have made citizens' arrests without the help of police. ^United\States ^Law\Enforcement ^Private\Initiatives

907. —— (1988). "U.S. Says Laos Government Is Deeply Involved in Drugs." *The New York Times*, 11 May, B3. Evidence given that the Laotian government is officially involved in the production and exportation of heroin. ^South-east\Asia ^Golden\Triangle ^Laos ^Heroin ^Drug\Traffic ^Consequences\Corruption

908. —— (1990). "Anti-Drug Agents Castigate U.S. Policy as Inadequate." *The New York Times*, 1 March, A16. Describes the critical comments of two retiring drug agents regarding the U.S. focus on supply reduction as its principal drug control policy. Arrests of traffickers in the United States have been compromised for "political reasons." ^United\States ^Drug\Control\Policies\Critique

909. Kesler, Ronald (1983). "Cheaper Heroin Resulting in More Deaths." *The Washington Post*, 14 June, A6. As prices of heroin have fallen, and as purity has increased, emergency room admissions (and associated deaths) for heroin overdoses have dramatically increased in the United States. ^United\States ^Heroin ^Consequences\Personal ^Consequences\Economic

910. Khant, U. (1985). "Measures to Prevent and Reduce Drug Abuse among Young People in Burma." *Bulletin on Narcotics* 37(2-3): 81–89. After the early 1970s, marijuana and opium were replaced by heroin as an addictive substance, which spread rapidly among young people, reaching epidemic proportions. The social and health problems deriving from that epidemic have been serious, and have resulted in legislation invoking compulsory treatment and severe penalties, including the death sentence for certain categories of drug trafficking. Various forms of drug-abuse preventive programs, for which compulsory registration as well as treatment and rehabilitation are carried out, are described. ^Southeast\Asia ^Golden\Triangle ^Burma ^Drug\Use ^Prevention ^Treatment ^Youth ^Law\Enforcement ^Epidemiology ^Consequences\Social ^Consequences\Health ^Legislation ^Treatment\Compulsory ^Prevention

911. Khavari, Khalil Akhtar, and Teresa McCray Harmon (1982). "The Relationship Between the Degree of Professed Religious Belief and Use of Drugs." *International Journal of the Addictions* 17(5): 847–57. From a study of nearly 5,000 respondents, those who viewed themselves as "very religious" tended to drink less and use fewer psychoactive drugs when compared to individuals who considered themselves "not religious at all." Significantly elevated use of drugs was noted among those with "not religious at all" preferences. ^Drug\Use ^Society ^Values

912. Kidder, Rushworth M. (1989). "Drug Strategy within an 'Ethical Fairyland.'" *The Christian Science Monitor*, 18 September, 13. The gravest domestic threat is not drugs but the cave-in of values that makes drugs attractive. In this "war" we will have to talk about ethics—not the ethics of the street people and the traffickers—the ethics of the society that tolerates them. Society and its institutions, education and all others, must simply rise to say "that's wrong." But what's wrong must not only be drugs, but alcohol, tobacco, sexual license, greed, and violence. ^United\States ^Drug\Control\Policies ^Society ^Values ^P\S\Values ^Tobacco ^Alcohol

913. Kirk, Robin (1987). "Peru: Ayacucho Relief Work Faces Multiple Obstacles." *Latinamerica Press*, 28 May, 3. Describes the "home country" of *Sendero Luminoso* (the Shining Path), a guerrilla force, and the extension of its operations into Peru's upper Huallaga Valley where coca is grown extensively. ^Latin\America ^Peru ^Coca ^Drug\Traffic ^Insurgents ^Terrorists

914. Kleber, Herbert D. (1988). "Cocaine Abuse: Historical, Epidemiological, and Psychological Perspectives." *Journal of Clinical Psychiatry* 49(2): 3–6. This article, which introduces a special issue of *Clinical Psychiatry* on cocaine use,

focuses on the historical development of cocaine use and the epidemiology of its abuse.
^Cocaine ^Drug\Use\History ^Epidemiology

915. —— (1988). "Epidemic Cocaine Abuse: America's Present, Britain's Future?" *British Journal of Addiction* 83:1359–72. Reviews the historical setting in which cocaine first became prevalent in America in the late nineteenth century as well as its recent reemergence. Possible reasons for this reemergence are reviewed and explained, including counterproductive myths (exaggerations) as to safety, relationship to prior marijuana use, celebrity endorsements and the role of the media, changes in the route of administration, and the reinforcing effects of the drug itself. Heavy cocaine use is now acknowledged to cause physiologic as well as psychologic dependence, and may therefore be amenable to pharmacologic prevention. Preventing relapses in treatment methods is discussed. Lists possible interventions that might lessen the problem if adopted, including steps that can be taken in the realms of education, law enforcement, and treatment. This is a substantial effort by an observer of the British scene to see what can be learned from U.S. experiences to help Britain prevent as severe an epidemic or to manage it better once it has occurred. The author predicts that most, if not all, educational efforts will fail in stemming the problem for Britain, and so therefore people must look to alternative devices. ^United\Kingdom ^United\States ^Cocaine ^Drug\Use\History ^Society ^Drug\Use\Theories ^Consequences\Critique ^Consequences\Physiological ^Consequences\Psychological ^P\S\Antagonists ^Drug\Control\Policies\Critique

916. Kleiman, Mark Albert Robert (1985). "Allocating Federal Drug Enforcement Resources: The Case of Marijuana." Master's thesis, Harvard University. A considerable reduction in resources currently allocated to federal marijuana enforcement programs would be accompanied by only a small increase in drug abuse and would be associated with fewer illicit market spinoff crimes. Thus, less enforcement appears to be better for public policy. Does this mean that legalization of marijuana would be the best policy? While it might, the author admits that his arguments do not establish that it is, and is therefore unwilling to advance such a proposition. "The effect of legalization on marijuana consumption is subject to enormous uncertainties, and the legalization decision, if it proved to be a mistake, would be very costly to reverse" (p. 195). How about "decriminalization"? This, the author maintains, creates a worse illicit market problem then either legalization or continued prohibition. It presumably would increase demand for a drug whose production and distribution would continue to be left entirely in illicit hands. ^United\States ^Cannabis ^Drug\Use ^Drug\Control\Policies\Critique ^Decriminalization\Critique ^P\S\Legalization\Critique ^Demand ^Crime ^Economics ^Society

917. —— (1987). "Vice Policy in a Liberal Society: An Analysis of the Impasse in the War on Drugs." *Nova Law Review* 11:919–25. Discusses principles on which a liberal society ought to found its drug policies. These principles must take into consideration, of course, the fact that the essential problem is failure of individual self-control. In making a critique of liberal policy, the author shows that "none of your business" and "you can't stop it, anyway and you'll only make things worse by trying" lack logical applicability. Yet, the horrible side effects of existing drug policy remain. He offers three concrete suggestions: "Before we legalize anything else, get control of the two major legal recreational drugs, alcohol and nicotine"; "ease up on enforcement against marijuana importation"; and "increase heroin enforcement, particularly at the retail level" (pp. 923–24). ^United\States ^Drug\Control\Policies\Theories ^Drug\Control\Policies\Critique ^Reviews ^Proffered\Solutions

918. —— (1988). "Dead Wrong." *The New Republic* (September): 14–16. Argument against capital punishment for narcotics dealers and drug lords. ^United\States ^Drug\Traffic ^Law\Enforcement ^Drug\Control\Policies\Critique

919. Kleinman, Paula H., Eric D. Wish, Sherry Deren, and Gregory Rainone (1988). "Daily Marijuana Use and Problem Behaviors among Adolescents." *International Journal of the Addictions* 23(1): 87–107. Some researchers have found daily marijuana use to affect adversely behavior among high school students. This research finds that when independent contribution to school problems of such factors as lifetime cigarette smoking, lifetime multiple drug use, rebelliousness, and gender are taken into account, the level of marijuana use does not make a significant independent contribution. Marijuana is, therefore, only one factor in a complex arena of interrelated problems associated with adverse behavior of high school students. ^Drug\Use ^Youth ^Cannabis ^Consequences\Theories

920. Kline, David (1982). "From a Smugglers' Paradise Comes Hell." *Maclean's*, 8 November, 14. A reporter's graphic description of the entrance of the Pakistani hill tribes into the heroin market in the early 1980s. In the early 1980s somewhere between 55 and 70 percent of the heroin entering North America and as much as 90 percent of the narcotics smuggled into Europe and Great Britain came from Southwest Asia, mostly form Pakistan. The Russian invasion of Afghanistan disrupted normal traffic there, convulsions in Iran disturbed its opium markets, and the hill tribes imported chemists from Asia to teach them how to convert opium into heroin. Description of the economics of the transactions and the delicate reasons why the Pakistani central government has difficulty imposing central authority among the hill tribes. ^Pakistan ^Afghanistan ^Southwest\Asia ^Iran ^Opiates ^Production ^Heroin ^Drug\Traffic ^Drug\Control\Policies ^Economics ^Politics ^Golden\Crescent

921. ——— (1982). "The Khyber Connection." *The Christian Science Monitor*, 9-11 November. A three-part series on the origin of the dramatic increase in the flow of heroin into Europe and the United States from tribal areas of Northwest Pakistan and Afghanistan, and what government officials are doing about it. ^Southwest\Asia ^Afghanistan ^Pakistan ^Opiates ^Production ^Heroin ^Drug\Traffic ^Drug\Control\Policies ^Europe ^United\States

922. ——— (1987). "How to Lose the Coke War." *The Atlantic* 259(5): 22–27. An anecdotal treatment of political and judicial corruption in Bolivia associated with that country's U.S.–assisted war on narcotics traffickers. The whole effort, as far as U.S. involvement is concerned, is criticized in that the antinarcotics operations have avoided the underground narcotics bosses and have focused instead on the mass of the impoverished peasants that make up the empire's work force. ^Bolivia ^Cocaine ^Drug\Control\Policies\Critique ^Consequences\Corruption ^Latin\America ^Consequences\Political

923. Koch, Edward I. (1989) "For Anti-Drug Boot Camps." *The New York Times*, 24 May, A31. Discussion of the advisability of turning U.S. military bases scheduled for closing into boot camps to treat and discipline first-time drug offenders and to punish repeat offenders. ^United\States ^Law\Enforcement ^P\S\Military\Bases

924. Koch, James V., and Stanley E. Grupp (1971). "The Economics of Drug Control Policies." *The International Journal of the Addictions* 6(4): 571–84. Examines the economic effects of drug law enforcement within the context of supply and demand analysis. Enforcement policies designed to restrict supply are usually undesirable because they increase the price of the drug in question and consequently increase criminal activities. Moreover, because of almost infinite price elasticity (particularly with heroin), policies and enforcement against supply will not greatly decrease the quantity consumed. On the other hand, policies and enforcement activities designed to restrict demand (through education, rehabilitation, substitute drugs) are preferable from an a priori standpoint because they decrease both the quantity consumed and the drug

price. Lesser crime results. Finally, legal drug substitution programs have desirable results in terms of lowering the price and lessening criminal activity. ^Drug\Control\Policies ^Economics ^Supply ^Demand ^Consequences\Economic

925. Kohn, Marek (1987). *Narcomania on Heroin.* London: Faber and Faber. This book is about perceptions of the British drugs epidemic and the panic associated with it. It is a polemic, in the sense that it presents an amoral discussion about the significance of heroin and what it is or is not doing to British society. The author wants to "cut through" received wisdom on a subject that is ill informed. He is a neuro-biologist who wrote his dissertation on the endorphins, the natural chemicals whose proper place in the nervous system opiates usurp. He presents himself as one for whom heroin addiction—"a monomaniac dependency which threatens an individual's intricate and multiple relationships of the world"—is dreadful. But the dread need not be absolute, and it certainly can be ended. He is in favor neither of punishment of drug users by the criminal law nor of the drugs' free availability. Drugs must, in the final analysis, be controlled by culture, by customs and conventions for which the law weights as a "recourse of last resort." In many ways the book is an examination of the rhetoric of drug usage and drug campaigns in Britain. The focus is on heroin. ^United\Kingdom ^Heroin ^Drug\Control\Policies\Critique ^Culture

926. Kolata, Gina (1989). "Community Program Succeeds in Drug Fight." *The New York Times*, 11 June, 33. Report on a new study showing that a compre-hensive community program that encourages teenagers to avoid drugs, including ciga-rettes and alcohol, has been much more successful than programs relying only on the schools. ^United\States ^Prevention\Integrated ^Youth ^Alcohol ^Tobacco

927. —— (1989). "Drug Addicts among the Homeless: Case Studies of Some 'Lost Dreams.'" *The New York Times*, 30 May, A16. Drug and alcohol abuse contributes to homelessness. Addicts constitute a higher proportion of the homeless than do other identifiable subgroups, such as the mentally ill. The human cost and the cost to society are substantial. ^United\States ^Drug\Use ^Society ^Alcohol ^Consequences\Misc ^Consequences\Personal ^Consequences\Economic

928. —— (1989). "Experts Finding New Hope on Treating Crack Addict." *The New York Times*, 24 August, 1. Until recently it was thought that the physical aspects of crack were responsible for the extreme difficulties users had in removing themselves from its influence. Now, drug experts are treating crack addiction more in relationship to the setting and circumstances of the users than to the biochemical reaction that the drug produces. Crack addiction, under the right conditions, can be successfully treated. ^Cocaine ^Crack ^Treatment ^Society ^Culture ^Consequences\Physical ^Consequences\Physi-ological ^Consequences\Critique

929. —— (1989). "In Cities, Poor Families Are Dying of Crack." *The New York Times*, 11 August, A1. In poor urban neighborhoods, mothers are increasingly becoming addicted and children are selling crack in greater numbers than ever before. Description of wholesale family breakdown and the extraordinary impact this is having on females is described. In many cases, mothers and brothers procure sex for the young women in their families to raise money to buy crack. Some teenagers have to support extended families through drug selling. ^United\States ^Cocaine ^Crack ^Drug\Use ^Women ^Youth ^Drug\Traffic ^Society ^Family ^Consequences\Children ^Parenting ^Consequences\Family ^Prostitution

930. —— (1989). "Twins of the Streets: Homelessness and Addiction." *The New York Times*, 22 May, A1. However bad the problem was in the past, it became infinitely more grave for the homeless, and therefore for social agencies charged with dealing with them, when crack became readily available. Some people even longed for

the "good old days" when the agencies were dealing only with heroin addicts. Discusses new policies that some agencies for the homeless have begun to adopt to try to impose greater responsibility on addicts in exchange for treatment privileges. ^United\States ^Cocaine ^Crack ^Drug\Use ^Treatment ^Consequences\Misc ^Consequences\Social ^Consequences\Economic

931. ―――― (1989). "Virus That May Cause Leukemia Is Spreading among Drug Addicts." *The New York Times,* 2 February. A troubling virus that was thought to be very rare is now spreading widely among groups of intravenous drug users in the United States. The virus may cause leukemia and other serious diseases. The article describes the findings, possible links to other viruses, and the frightening prospects that all this suggests. ^United\States ^Heroin ^Health ^Consequences\Health ^Drug\Use

932. ―――― (1990). "Study Finds Cocaine in Many Motorists Killed in New York." *The New York Times,* 12 January, A1. Nearly 25 percent of drivers between sixteen and forty-five years of age killed in New York City traffic accidents from 1984–1987 tested positive for cocaine use. The presumption is that cocaine-using drivers are driving impaired. ^United\States ^New\York ^Cocaine ^Drug\Use ^Consequences\Public\Safety ^Consequences\Personal

933. Komisar, Lucy (1988). "Burmese Connection." *News Analysis,* 30 August. Due to Burma's growing of opium poppies, the United States has a major stake there. Description of the political turmoil that may affect poppy crops is laid out. ^Burma ^Southeast\Asia ^Golden\Triangle ^Opiates ^Production ^Politics

934. ―――― (1988). "Solving Burma's Guerrilla War Would End the Opium Trade." *The Christian Science Monitor,* 30 March, 13. If peace could be brought to the region, then crop substitution programs could take place, therefore reducing poppy growing. The civil war has disrupted the transport system for cash crops other than opium in many of the hill regions. ^Burma ^Southeast\Asia ^Golden\Triangle ^Opiates ^Production ^Politics ^Insurgents

935. Kooyman, Martien (1984). "The Drug Problem in the Netherlands." *Journal of Substance Abuse Treatment* 1:125–130. Gives a historical backdrop to the drug problem in the Netherlands, including a number of assumptions, which the author calls "illusions," underlying the country's permissive policy. The illusions are that all addicts can be treated successfully, that they will choose treatment after contact with professionals, that dispensation of methadone on a large scale will control the problem, and that heroin distribution to addicts will cure failures in the above. Disillusionment here. Now, several experimental projects within family therapy have been started. However, the current policy is to accept the fact that drug addiction cannot be solved and that a country may only make efforts to diminish the negative side effects of drug abuse. ^Netherlands ^Drug\Use ^Drug\Control\Policies ^Europe ^Drug\Control\Policies\Effectiveness ^Drug\Control\Policies\Critique ^Treatment\Family ^Treatment\Therapy ^Drug\Use\History

936. Koplan, Jeffrey P., Ann M. Hardy, and James R. Allen (1985). "Epidemiology of the Acquired Immunodeficiency Syndrome in Intravenous Drug Abusers." *Advances in Alcohol and Substance Abuse* 5(1-2): 13–23. Describes the epidemiology of AIDS in intravenous drug users and explores questions, yet apparently unanswered, that arise from a consideration of the limited data now available. ^Heroin ^Health ^AIDS ^Epidemiology ^Drug\Use

937. Kozel, Nicholas J., and Edgar H. Adams, eds. (1985). *Cocaine Use in America: Epidemiologic and Clinical Perspectives.* Department of Health and Human Services. Washington, D.C.: U.S. Government Printing Office. One of the social impacts of cocaine abuse is, of course, the costs on society to deal with chronic users either in outpatient programs or in other ways that deal with health

problems. This volume describes new trends in cocaine use and deals with psychological and other consequences that must, for those who desire, be treated, and usually at a social cost. Although the prevalence of cocaine use in the general population appears to have leveled off since 1979, the adverse consequences have continued to increase dramatically. Increased combination-drug use appears to be partially responsible. A shift to more dangerous routes of administration also appear to explain some of the problems. The various contributors to this volume give not only an introduction and overview to this increased problem but also examine in some detail the deleterious consequences that now impose externalities on society. Specific research areas necessitating attention are discussed. ^United\States ^Cocaine ^Drug\Use ^Society ^NIDA ^Consequences\Social ^Consequences\Economic ^Consequences\Health ^Consequences\Psychological ^Treatment

938. Kraar, Louis (1988). "The Drug Trade." *Fortune* 20(June): 27–38. The drug trade should be viewed as a highly sophisticated agribusiness producing an internationally traded commodity enjoying a fast-moving top management, a widespread distribution network, and price-insensitive customers. Description of some of the "men behind the drug trade." The economics of the trade are referenced, including prices. Both cocaine and heroin are discussed. ^Cocaine ^Heroin ^Drug\Traffic ^Traffickers ^Economics

939. ——— (1990). "How to Win the War on Drugs." *Fortune*, March 12, pp. 70–79. Criticizes supply-reduction strategies abroad and calls for programs that reduce demand in the United States. Advocates providing more medical help for addicts and allowing courts to commit hard-core users to treatment. Suggests converting surplus military bases to drug treatment sites. Schools, educators, companies, and others should join in prevention efforts. As for drug law enforcement, the criminal justice system must be unclogged, alternative forms of punishment must be employed, and police must circulate in troubled neighborhoods. Drug profits ought to be more vigorously seized. Internationally, the economic roots of the supply problem need to be addressed, not just the supply. ^ P\S\Demand\Reduction ^ Law\Enforcement\Critique ^ P\S\Military\Bases ^ P\S\Law\Enforcement ^ P\S\Asset\Forfeiture ^ P\S\Development

940. Kramer, John M. (1988). "Drug Abuse in the Soviet Union." *Problems of Communism* (March-April): 28–40. Since the 1960s there has been evidence of a far more widespread drug problem in the Soviet Union than publicly acknowledged. The scope of the problem is assessed and its perplexing impact on Soviet ideology and criminal justice behavior is reviewed. One outcome has been an increased cooperation of the USSR with capitalist countries as well as other communist states to combat drug abuse. Also, there are efforts in the Soviet Union to decriminalize the casual use of (especially nonnarcotic) drugs. Overall, however, the efforts in the USSR have been limited and mostly ineffectual. ^ USSR ^ Drug\Use ^ Drug\Control\Policies ^ International\Cooperation ^ Consequences\Penal ^ Consequences\Political ^ Consequences\Law\Enforcement ^ Decriminalization

941. Kraus, J. (1981). "Juvenile Drug Abuse and Delinquency: Some Differential Associations." *British Journal of Psychiatry* 139:422–30. Is there a relationship between drug abuse and delinquency. The findings presented in this study do not shed direct light on any sequential relationship, or on the popular hypotheses of progression from cannabis to hard drugs. The study does suggest that juvenile delinquency precedes the use of opiates. ^Drug\Use ^Crime ^Youth ^Drug\Use\Theories\Critique

942. Krauss, Clifford (1990). "Anti-Drug Effort Drags Outside U.S." *The New York Times*, November 25, L9. Two years' efforts to control the supply of drugs coming into the United States has produced little consequence. Although traffick has been deterred from entering Florida from the Caribbean, it has simply been redirected through Central America and Mexico into the American southwest. Panamanian banking laws continue to be a problem with respect to money laundering. The antisupply

efforts undertaken in Peru are described. ^Drug\Control\Policies\Critique ^Drug\Control\Policies\Effectiveness ^United\States ^Traffickers ^Florida ^Caribbean ^Latin\America ^Mexico ^Panama ^Money\Laundering

943. —— (1991). "Colombian Leader is Hailed by Bush." *The New York Times*, February 27, A8. Describes Colombia's policy of aggressive police action against narcotics activities which is coupled with judicial leniency for traffickers who turn themselves in and confess to at least one drug-related crime. President George Bush is quoted as being highly supportive of this policy. Those who turn themselves in are immune from extradition. ^Latin\America ^Colombia ^State\Policies ^Law\Enforcement ^Judiciary ^Extradition

944. "Kremlin Admits Drug Use Is Spreading in USSR" (1987). *The Christian Science Monitor*, 7 January, 2. Short statement acknowledging that there has been an eighteen-fold increase in two years among drug users in the USSR. Some marijuana production and organized trafficking is also acknowledged. ^USSR ^Drug\Use ^Cannabis ^Drug\Traffic

945. Kristof, Nicholas D. (1987). "Hong Kong Program: Addicts without AIDS." *The New York Times*, 17 June, 1. Describes Hong Kong's drug treatment program, which is the use of methadone as a heroin substitute. Speculates that this is responsible for the low incidence of AIDS among Hong Kong addicts. As methadone is taken orally, there is no risk of spreading AIDS by sharing needles. ^Southeast\Asia ^Hong\Kong ^Heroin ^Health ^AIDS ^Treatment ^Methadone

946. —— (1991). "Heroin Spreads Among Young in China." *The New York Times*, March 21, A1. Among Chinese youth who are bored and unhappy, drug addition is spreading rapidly, particularly in Yunnan province in southwest China. The source is Burma, largely from overland shipments destined to Hong Kong. Draconian law enforcement responses have been applied. Drug use frightens many Chinese because it reminds them of their humiliation under the British in the nineteenth century. ^Southeast\Asia ^China ^Drug\Use ^Heroin ^Traffickers ^Youth ^Hong\Kong

947. Kristol, Irving (1988). "War on Drugs? Then Get Serious and Use the Military." *The Washington Post*, 28 March, A15. Why fetter the military? Look at the British precedent with regard to the slave trade in the nineteenth century. Give the military extraterritoriality and don't ask so many questions. ^United\States ^P\S\Military

948. Krivanek, Jára (1988). *Heroin: Myths and Reality*. Sydney, Australia: Allen and Unwin. This overview of heroin in Australia, by an Australian, explores the use of the drug in history (Britain and America), its pharmacology and toxicology, its transaction as a commodity in commodity markets, and how those markets may be controlled. Suggestions are raised on suppressing heroin use, including "managing the addict, managing the drug, and managing the system." Practical suggestions are given for policy consideration. ^Australia ^United\Kingdom ^United\States ^Heroin ^Drug\Traffic ^Drug\Control\Policies ^Drug\Use\History ^Heroin\Pharmacology ^Consequences\Markets ^Proffered\Solutions

949. Kumarasingha, D. P. (1988). "Drugs—A Growing Problem in Sri Lanka." *Forensic Science International* 36:283–84. Heroin, infiltrated into Sri Lanka by tourists, is now the most widely abused drug. Separatist terrorists in Sri Lanka have engaged in drug trafficking in order to finance their purchasing of arms and ammunition. ^Southeast\Asia ^Sri\Lanka ^Heroin ^Drug\Use ^Drug\Traffic ^Insurgents ^Terrorists ^Consequences\Political

950. Kupfer, Andrew (1988). "Is Drug Testing Good or Bad?" *Fortune*, 19 December, 133–40. Before joining the burgeoning ranks of drug testers, executives ought to train their supervisors to spot problems, to promote employee assistance

programs, and to communicate clearly and sympathetically with employees about drug problems on the assumption that then companies won't have them. "Managers might want to consider the two companies that make the fancy mass spectrometers—Perkin-Elmer and Hewlett-Packard. Neither uses drug tests. They say that they know their employees so they don't need to" (p. 140). The many drawbacks and ambiguities of drug testing are also noted. ^United\States ^Workplace ^Drug\Testing ^Proffered\Solutions ^Drug\Testing\Critique

951. ——— (1988). "What to Do about Drugs." *Fortune*, 20 June, 39–41. Description of the flaws in existing policy, and some comparisons about how other countries, in particular the Netherlands, are dealing with their drug problems. The prescription for the United States is that it needs a new policy: more toughness in fighting hard drugs, more compassion in treating addicts, and perhaps more flexibility toward marijuana. ^Netherlands ^United\States ^Drug\Control\Policies\Critique ^Proffered\Solutions

952. Kurisky, George A., Jr. (1988). "Civil Forfeiture of Assets: A Final Solution to International Drug Trafficking?" *Houston Journal of International Law* 10:239-273. Focuses on the ultimate reward of criminal activity—illegal profits—and how to remove the economic incentives associated with those profits. Conventional methods of fighting drug trafficking, such as crop substitution, interdiction, and foreign aid, are not getting anywhere. Statutory forfeiture of drug-related assets is the most effective method of attacking traffickers. Thus, specifically, this legal comment focuses on Title 21 of the United States Code, Section 881, and explores its superior potential to deter the importation and trafficking of illicit drugs in the United States. ^United\States ^Asset\Forfeiture ^Drug\Control\Policies\Critique ^Legislation

953. Kurtz, Howard (1989). "Across the Nation, Rising Outrage." *The Washington Post*, 4 April, A1. Authorities often feel overwhelmed by what they term an increase in drug-driven crime. The man on the street sees drug users involved in crime to an ever increasing extent and assumes a causal relationship. The criminal justice system is "breaking down." ^United\States ^Drug\Use ^Consequences\Crime ^Consequences\Law\Enforcement ^Consequences\Judiciary ^Consequences\Penal

954. Kwitny, Jonathan (1987). *The Crimes of Patriots: A True Tale of Dope, Dirty Money, and the CIA*. New York: W. W. Norton and Company. This book, by a respected investigative journalist, exposes, by the author's claim, "crimes committed against American citizens in pursuit of [our anticommunist foreign] policy." In exposing the workings of a small Australian bank, the author draws a network of U.S. generals, admirals, and CIA men, including a former director of the CIA, into operations that promote the heroin trade, tax evasion, and gun running. ^United\States ^Heroin ^Drug\Traffic ^Consequences\Corruption ^CIA ^Consequences\Misc

955. Kwitny, Jonathan (1987). "Money, Drugs and the Contras." *The Nation*, 29 August, 1. In spite of congressional hearings finding no evidence linking contras to drug smuggling, there is, in fact, much evidence. That evidence is reviewed. ^United\States ^Drug\Traffic ^Contras

956. Labaton, Stephen (1989). "Banking Technology Helps Drug Dealers Export Cash." *The New York Times*, 14 August, A1. $100 billion a year from selling cocaine in the United States is being sent from the United States via electronic transfer from American banks to accounts in foreign countries. While elaborate reporting procedures exist, there is hardly any accountability or tracking capability. ^United\States ^Cocaine ^Money\Laundering

957. ——— (1989). "Canada Seen as Major Haven for Laundering Drug Money." *The New York Times*, 28 September. Hundreds of millions of dollars are

being moved annually to Canadian banks to avoid U.S. banking laws, which are more strict, and which are intended to curb money laundering. ^Canada ^Money\Laundering

958. ——— (1989). "Federal Judge Urges Legalization of Crack, Heroin and Other Drugs." *The New York Times*, 13 December, A1. Given that the current war on illicit drugs is "bankrupt," and given the futility of sentencing drug criminals who have been convicted of violating drug laws, and given that the justice system is now overwhelmed by drug-related cases, there appears to be only one way out—legalization. ^P\S\Legalization

959. ——— (1989). "Unassuming Store Fronts Believed to Launder Drug Dealer's Profits." *The New York Times*, 25 September, 1. Describes the store fronts, how they are linked to legitimate banks, and how money is moved about so as to hide its original source. Tracking money launderers is metaphorically stated as being akin to "fighting windmills." ^United\States ^Money\Laundering

960. ——— (1989). "US, In Drug Drive, to Regulate Shift of Funds Abroad." *The New York Times*, 5 October, 1. The Bush administration has now decided to regulate international money transfers for American banks. As much as $110 billion is laundered through banks, many of which are legitimate. To monitor these transactions, the government will open a financial crimes center with high-level computer capabilities. ^United\States ^Money\Laundering ^Drug\Control\Policies ^Banking\Regulations

961. Ladouceur, Patricia, and Mark Temple (1985). "Substance Use among Rapists: A Comparison with Other Serious Felons." *Crime and Delinquency* (April): 269–94. In assessing the relationship between substance abuse and crime among rapists as compared to offenders whose crimes involved different levels of sex and violence, no significant differences were found. These findings did not appear to be modified by race, age, or social context. ^Drug\Use ^Crime ^Consequences\Critique ^Consequences\Crime

962. LaFranchi, Howard (1988). "Mexican Heroin, Upgraded, Reenters US." *The Christian Science Monitor*, 16 March, 3. Mexican heroin, which in the early 1980s lost its heroin market share to Asian varieties, is now reappearing. This seems to derive from Mexicans producing a more highly refined product (more potent). ^Latin\America ^Mexico ^Heroin ^Drug\Traffic ^Production ^Refining

963. Lait, Matt (1989). "At the Border, Deep Concern about a Shallow Ditch." *The Washington Post*, 2 March, A3. The dry mesa near San Ysidro, California, where thousands of smugglers have, for years, driven their profitable cargos into the United States from Mexico is the subject of this article. The cable that stretches across the area, marking the U.S.–Mexico line is routinely destroyed or rendered useless. The U.S. Immigration and Naturalization Service has decided to dig a ditch fourteen feet wide and four feet deep to replace it. Description of the controversy this decision has created. ^United\States ^Interdiction ^Drug\Control\Policies\Critique

964. ——— (1989). "Heroin Traffic Shifts to the West; Mexican, Asian Smugglers Dominate; Seizures Rise Dramatically." *The Washington Post*, 4 January, A4. Most heroin entering the United States now comes from the western United States. The destination is largely for addicts in New York. Street prices and values are given, with specific reference to the "China white" Asian variety that is increasingly being found in the United States. Asian traffickers now replace traditional criminal organizations in the United States. Heroin ranked second to cocaine as a problem drug in hospital emergency rooms in 1987. ^United\States ^Heroin ^Drug\Traffic ^Organized\Crime ^Statistics ^Traffickers ^Consequences\Personal

965. Lamanna, Michael (1981). "Marijuana: Implications of Use by Young People." *Journal of Drug Education* 11(4): 281–310. From seven problem areas discussed, two are of significance to this bibliography: Use of marijuana impairs learning; use of marijuana leads to schooling problems. With respect to learning, as reported by users, most agreed that considerable difficulty was not in areas of concentration of a single subject or idea, but in the temporal sequencing of information and in the incorporation of peripheral or intruding ideas into a thought sequence. And, with respect to schooling, most of this study's informants argued that it is the user, not the drug, that causes school problems—negative attitudes, lack of involvement, poor motivation. Nevertheless, marijuana users recorded higher delinquency scores than did alcohol users. There is a significant statistical relationship between social deviance and marijuana use, regardless of what causes what. ^Cannabis ^Drug\Use ^Youth ^Crime ^Health ^Consequences\Neurological ^Consequences\Educational

966. Lamar, Jacob V. (1988). "Where the War Is Being Lost." *Time*, 14 March, 21–22. The crack business has so far been largely immune to suppression, and it also has led to unprecedented violence by dealers fighting for their share of the market. ^United\States ^Cocaine ^Crack ^Drug\Control\Policies ^Consequences\Violence ^Consequences\Markets ^Traffickers

967. Lambert, Bruce (1987). "New York City Maps Deadly Pattern of AIDS." *The New York Times*, 13 December, 1. Nationally, 27 percent of the AIDS cases reported in the United States are in New York City, and within New York City the concentration is on Manhattan Island and the Bronx. Thus both demographic and behavioral approaches to prevention are required. In the South Bronx, the AIDS virus infects as many as one in five sexually active men. Ernest Drucker's work is noted. ^AIDS ^New\York ^United\States

968. —— (1988). "AIDS Danger Rises for Cocaine Users; Virus Is Spreading Faster than with Heroin—Peril Is in Contaminated Needles." *The New York Times*, 28 November, A22. The AIDS virus appears to be spreading faster among people who inject cocaine than among those who inject heroin. This confirms public health official's worst fears. The reason for the higher rate among cocaine users is that they often inject several times an hour. ^Cocaine ^Consequences\Health ^AIDS ^Drug\Use

969. —— (1988). "Ethics and Needles; Proponents of Free Distribution Say Data Show No Rise in Drug Abuse." *The New York Times*, 13 August, 29. Discussion of the black market in needles and its contribution to AIDS, on the one hand, and, on the other, contemplation of distributing needles in ways that may promote drug abuse. ^Heroin ^Health ^AIDS ^Drug\Control\Policies ^Needle\Exchange\Programs

970. —— (1989). "Hospitals Seen Near Limit in AIDS Crisis." *The New York Times*, 3 March, B3. New Yorkers run the risk of losing access to medical care unless the overcrowded health care system is expanded quickly to deal with the rising number of AIDS patients. There are 1,800 AIDS patients in hospitals in New York City, and most hospitals there are filled to near capacity. ^Heroin ^Health ^AIDS ^United\States ^New\York ^Consequences\Economic

971. Land, Thomas (1988). "Soviet Drug War." *The New Leader*, 14 November, 4. The Soviet Union, having long denied that it has a problem with drugs, is expected to make a formal bid to join Interpol, the 140-nation global police organization. A principal motivation deals with illicit drugs pedaled by crime syndicates which are invading the Soviet Union. In the Asian regions of the USSR, opium poppies have been used for many generations. Heroin is now being smuggled in from Pakistan, Afghanistan,

and Iran. ^USSR ^Drug\Use ^Drug\Traffic ^Organized\Crime ^Drug\Control\Policies ^Opiates ^Pakistan ^Afghanistan ^Southwest\Asia ^Iran ^Middle\East ^Golden\Crescent ^Interpol

972. Landrigan, Philip J., Kenneth E. Powell, Levy M. James, and Philip R. Taylor (1983). "Paraquat and Marijuana: Epidemiologic Risk Assessment." *American Journal of Public Health* 73(7): 785–89. In the late 1970s, over one-fifth of the marijuana samples from the Southwestern United States were contaminated with paraquat. Aerial spraying had been done in Mexico. Smoking marijuana was judged to be a health hazard. ^Cannabis ^Crop\Eradication ^Herbicides ^Consequences\Health

973. Lane, Charles (1985). "Coke Basket of America." *New Republic*, 30 December, 10. An on-site report from Peru's upper Huallaga Valley. Discussion of the extent of coca production in the valley, the economic incentive it offers to peasant growers, the efforts by the United States to eliminate or reduce the growing of coca, involvement of *Sendero Luminoso* (Shining Path) in the politics of eradication, and the violence associated with efforts to eradicate. ^Latin\America ^Peru ^Coca ^Drug\Traffic ^Drug\Control\Policies ^Insurgents ^Production ^Producers\Incentives\Economic ^Drug\Control\Politics ^Crop\Eradication ^Consequences\Violence ^National\Security

974. Lang, John S., and Ronald A. Taylor (1986). "America on Drugs." *U.S. News and World Report*, 28 July, 48–50. Describes how narcotics, once only a street menace, have now turned into a national security threat. The U.S. borders have become indefensible: U.S. troops are attacking foreign cocaine; and Americans are wondering about how they can fight this invasion into their homes. ^United\States ^Drug\Use ^Consequences\Sovereignty

975. Langer, John H. (1986). "Recent Developments in Drug Trafficking: The Terrorism Connection." *The Police Chief* 53(April): 44–51. Places the connection of drugs and terrorism into an international perspective that takes into account various kinds of terrorist activities. Gives details on the "Cuban involvement" and other involvements in Latin America that combine drug trafficking with destabilizing elements. Prognosticates that as the financial rewards of drug trafficking increase so also will drug related terrorist activities. ^Cuba ^Caribbean ^Latin\America ^Drug\Traffic ^Politics ^Terrorists ^Economics

976. Lanter, Ingrid L. (1982). "Marijuana Abuse by Children and Teenagers: A Pediatrician's View." In *Marijuana and Youth: Clinical Observations on Motivation and Learning*. Rockville, Md.: National Institute on Mental Health. There is a relationship between marijuana use and complaints about persistent fatigue, inertia, and occasional sleeping during class. The evidence is anecdotal or clinic specific. Several patients came from families with absolutely no significant dysfunction as a causal agent contributing to teenage marijuana abuse. ^Cannabis ^Health ^Youth ^Consequences\Health ^Consequences\Children

977. Lapham, Lewis H. (1989). "A Political Opiate: The War on Drugs Is a Folly and a Menace." *Harper's Magazine* (December): 43–48. A principal problem with the war on drugs is that it is a political war, waged by police officers and politicians rather than by scientists and doctors who would be best qualified to deal with illicit drug use. Thus much drug policy grandstanding is postured by politicians making moves for votes but having no sense of obligation about the consequences of their political rhetoric or the policies that derive therefrom. Current policies are therefore heavily criticized as is the position taken by United States drug czar William Bennett. The current policy undermines civil liberties, corrupts the judiciary, and enhances criminal activity. ^United\States ^Drug\Control\Policies\Critique ^Politics

978. Larkin, Ralph W. (1979). *Suburban Youth in Cultural Crisis*. New York: Oxford University Press. This scholarly treatise needs to be read as a composite *ethnography* of an American middle-class suburb and its high school. It has many themes not directly related to drug issues (e.g., impact of monopoly capitalism on student employment and functional utility, the relationship of schools and media to the teaching of youth and adults to want degrading products, arguments for the restructuring of society). Chapter 4, "Sex and Drugs," is important for the development of "routinization of pleasure" and its impact on the social fabric and social interaction of young people. Students "engage in pleasureful activities—both sex and drugs are sources of pleasure. Yet it is the rare student who feels joyful. . . . Pleasure comes easy to them but joy does not" (p. 122). ^United\States ^Drug\Use ^Society ^Youth ^Culture ^Consequences\Sexuality ^Consequences\Social

979. Larmer, Brook (1988). "Honduran Drug Kingpin Poses Dilemma for US Pursuers: While a Honduran Cocaine Connection Flourished, US Attention Focused on Honduras's Backing for the Nicaraguan Contras." *The Christian Science Monitor*, 7 March, 9. While Honduras was supporting the United States' foreign policy initiative with the Contras against the Nicaraguan Sandinista regime, the U.S. turned a blind eye to cocaine connections flourishing in Honduras. It is now difficult to do much, because the key Honduran drug figure has close ties to the Honduran military. ^Latin\America ^Honduras ^United\States ^Cocaine ^Drug\Traffic ^Politics ^Consequences\Corruption ^Consequences\Foreign\Relations ^Consequences\Political ^Bureaucracy ^Contras

980. ——— (1988). "Mexican Drug Case Frustrates US." *The Christian Science Monitor*, 12 January, 7. Continuation of the discussion on the Camarena case, which still remains unresolved in Mexican courts. The United States indicted nine Mexican citizens in 1985. The popular mood in Mexico appears to be that it is not a bad thing to grow marijuana and sell it in the United States. ^Latin\America ^Mexico ^Cannabis ^Drug\Traffic ^Society ^Values ^Culture

981. ——— (1989). "Colombians Take Over 'Coke' Trade in Mexico." *The Christian Science Monitor*, 9 January, 1. At least five major Colombian drug rings now operate freely out of Mexico. The proliferation of these "mafias" poses serious challenges for the new Mexican government, particularly because President Salinas has promised to purge corrupt officials and expand the power of his Attorney General's office. ^Latin\America ^Colombia ^Mexico ^Cocaine ^Drug\Traffic ^Organized\Crime ^Law\Enforcement ^Traffickers

982. ——— (1989). "Mexico's Corruption Clampdown; Arrest of Corrupt Officials Along with Drug Baron May Root out Graft." *The Christian Science Monitor*, 13 April, 1. While arresting one of Mexico's notorious drug barons (Angel Felix Gallardo), the new Mexico regime also arrested a number of corrupt governmental officials. It is thought that Gallardo's operations accounted for around 75 percent of the cocaine passing through Mexico to the United States. Nearly a dozen police officers and an official in the Attorney General's office were also arrested. The United States and Mexico hope this will put a dent in the drug trade. ^Latin\America ^Mexico ^Cocaine ^Drug\Traffic ^Organized\Crime ^Law\Enforcement ^Consequences\Corruption ^Consequences\Political ^Traffickers

983. ——— (1990). "US Targets Guatemalan Opium." *The Christian Science Monitor*, 7 March, 6. Opium poppies are being grown in small plots in Guatemala. Description of a spraying program designed to destroy them. Critics say the program is aimed less at opium poppies than at political rebels operating in the countryside. In the process, the spraying damages legitimate crops. Corruption is rampant. ^Latin\America

^Guatemala ^Opiates ^Production ^Herbicides ^Crop\Eradication ^Consequences\Drug\Control\Policies ^Consequences\Unintended

984. Larrazábal, Hernando, et al (1986). *El Sector Informal en Bolivia.* La Paz, Bolivia: Producciones Cima. In general, the Bolivian authors represented in this volume are attached to various Bolivian agencies or institutions. For example, Larrazábal is a developmental economist with an adjunct position with the Center for Labor and Agrarian Studies (CEDLA). There is, apparently, no institutional affiliation for the book itself, and the copyright is held by "the authors." The improbable provenance of this volume notwithstanding, it focuses in a responsible academic and practical way on the informal economy in Bolivia. Theoretical and methodological discussions are raised along with several rounds of commentaries. Astonishingly, the empirical, theoretical, and methodological discussions are raised as if, in Bolivia, there were not an "informal economy" attached to drug trafficking. ^Latin\America ^Bolivia ^Coca ^Drug\Traffic ^Economics ^Informal\Economy

985. Lasagna, Louis (1985). "Is the Social Use of Marijuana Dangerous or Addictive?" *Advances in Alcohol and Substance Abuse* 5(1-2): 77–81. While marijuana and hashish are not innocent or harmless materials, the exaggeration of the risks of using them, and the loss of credibility that scientists and regulatory officials suffer when they fall into a "reefer madness" mode, does everyone a great disservice. The best policy is to be both concerned and honest. ^Cannabis ^Health ^Proffered\Solutions ^Drug\Use\Critique

986. Lasagna, Louis, and Gardner Lindzey (1983). "Marijuana Policy and Drug Mythology." *Society* (January-February): 67–80. The discussion of choices to be made between prohibiting and regulating marijuana supply is advanced. Louis Lasagna (chair) and Gardner Lindzey, member, of the Committee on Substance Abuse and Habitual Behavior of the National Research Council and the National Academy of Sciences argue for a change in current U.S. policy. This is based on the ineffectiveness of the present federal policy of complete prohibition to prevent use. Current policies directed at controlling marijuana supply should therefore be seriously reconsidered. Although specific alternatives cannot be determined with confidence, they must be reviewed. Some jurisdiction must therefore try a regulatory policy, even though this is likely to result in increased marijuana use. Marijuana regulation would permit systematic provision of comprehensive, clearly communicated health warnings on package inserts or covers, in public health education, and elsewhere. In a follow-up statement, Frank Press, chairman of the National Research Council distances himself from this recommendation, arguing that it is value laden and cannot be attached to the scientific evidence absent a consideration of the values associated with the recommendation. He accepts it, therefore, as a committee report but not one that commits the National Research Council to a policy position on marijuana. ^United\States ^Cannabis ^Society ^Values ^Drug\Control\Policies\Effectiveness ^Drug\Control\Policies\Critique ^Decriminalization ^P\S\Legalization ^P\S\Legalization\Critique

987. "The Last Tango in Paraguay" (1989). *U.S. News and World Report,* 13 February, p. 14. Smuggling accounts for more than 50 percent of Paraguay's gross national product, and the new president, Andrés Rodríguez, is unlikely to change any of the previous regime's policies. ^Latin\America ^Paraguay ^Cocaine ^Drug\Traffic ^Economics ^Politics ^Consequences\Corruption

988. Lau, Emily (1984). "Brotherhood of Extortion." *Far Eastern Economic Review,* 27 December, 49–53. Discussion of the Triads and their operations out of Hong Kong in the drug trade. The Triads are depicted as extremely closely knit brotherhoods, difficult to penetrate. Aside from involvement in narcotics, they have become

associated with much other organized crime. ^Southeast\Asia ^Hong\Kong ^Heroin ^Drug\Traffic ^Organized\Crime ^Triads

989. Laudeman, Kent A. (1984). "17 Ways to Get Parents Involved in Substance Abuse Education." *Journal of Drug Education* 14(4): 307–14. The "new frontier" of the anti-drug campaign is parental involvement in the prevention of chemical dependency of their children. However, several kinds of parents are unwilling, or unable, to become involved. They are described as "apathetic," "burned out," "intimidated," and "resigned." Strategies are advanced to involve these kinds of parents in an antidrug dependency campaign. ^Prevention ^Youth ^Family ^Prevention\Family ^Parenting ^P\S\Family

990. "Laundering Drug Money: Whitewash—or Crackdown?" (1989). *The Economist*, 4 March, 76. On *The Economist's* list are eighteen cities or countries wherein drug laundering is facilitated. Four of the laundry cities are in America—Houston, Los Angeles, Miami, and New York. Foreign governments have been reluctant to cooperate with drug busting at a money-laundering level, although the Bahamas and Hong Kong are cooperating more. Panama is not cooperating at all. ^Southeast\Asia ^Caribbean ^Latin\America ^Hong\Kong ^Bahamas ^Panama ^United\States ^Texas ^California ^Florida ^New\York ^Money\Laundering ^Drug\Control\Policies ^International\Cooperation

991. Laurance, Jeremy (1988). "Shooting up the Desperate." *New Statesman and Society*, 23 September, 8–9. If addicts are going to simply face imprisonment, become gangsters, or carry AIDS, why not prescribe injectable heroin for them to be dispensed at clinics? The proposal is discussed. The setting is Liverpool, England. ^United\Kingdom ^Heroin ^P\S\Drug\Maintenance

992. Leader-Elliott, Ian D. (1986). "Heroin in Australia: The Costs and Consequences of Prohibition." *Journal of Drug Issues* 16(2): 131–52. From a brief historical backdrop, the author examines the use of heroin in Australia as estimated by the Australian Royal Commission. Argues that the estimates are fundamentally misleading. All of this is presented in order to advance two principal arguments: First, the contemporary patterns of heroin supply, use, and dependence in Australia are, for the most part, the products or the consequences of the stringent criminal prohibitions affecting the opiates (prohibition has caused enormously severe social problems, which is not to argue that prohibition should be abandoned). Second, accepting existing prohibitions does not argue that they become more stringent. Rather than tightening them still further, the author argues that public policy ought to seriously consider ways in which the harms that prohibition gives rise to can be ameliorated. Among those harms are the injury to the legal system and the abandonment of principle in pursuit of enemies. Finally, for a small minority among users, illicit heroin use is a stimulant to theft. The extravagant expenditure of resources in pursuit of drug traffickers, combined with a lack of any comparable effort to control the stolen property market, only accelerates the slide towards catastrophe. The article is heavily documented. ^Australia ^Heroin ^Drug\Control\Policies ^Consequences\Social ^Consequences\Economic ^Statistics\Critique ^Consequences\Judiciary ^Consequences\Law\Enforcement

993. Leamy, W. J. (1981). "International Co-Operation through the Interpol System to Counter Illicit Drug Trafficking." *Bulletin on Narcotics* 35(4): 55–60. One hundred fifty-three countries are members of Interpol. It has a drugs subdivision that responds to incoming communications on drug-enforcement matters, conducts intelligence analysis of information, and produces tactical and strategic intelligence reports. Other activities of this division of Interpol are described. ^Drug\Control\Policies ^International\Cooperation ^Interpol

994. Lee, Rensselaer W. III (1985). "The Latin American Drug Connection." *Foreign Policy* 61(Fall): 142–160. In spite of U.S. efforts and U.S. money, the drug industry in Latin America continues to grow. The author examines the drug trafficking chain and the economics associated with it, and he looks at the political and social impacts in areas of coercion, bribes, and political campaigns. There is a drugs-insurgency nexus, although the author argues that even if the guerrillas and traffickers do collaborate, they probably do not share a common political or ideological agenda, even though certain economic factors may contribute to collaboration. Difficulties in the conventional means governments employ to try to reduce cultivation, interdict traffic, and reduce demand are reviewed. ^Latin\America ^Drug\Traffic ^Drug\Control\Policies\Critique ^Economics ^Politics ^Society ^Consequences\Economic ^Consequences\Political ^Consequences\Social ^Insurgents

995. —— (1987). "The Drug Trade and Developing Countries." *Policy Focus* 4(May): 2–10. For the world's relatively poor countries, the economic and political costs of antidrug campaigns are high—the narcotics industry is a source of jobs, income, and foreign exchange. All of this is compounded by pressure from narcotics lobbies, lack of strong public support, weak central governments, and tensions between civilian and military authorities. U.S. narcotics control programs should stress reasonable and attainable objectives, including new income sources and stimulation for self-sustaining growth. Negotiation with chief executives of the narcotics industry should not be ruled out. ^United\States ^Drug\Control\Policies ^Economics ^Consequences\Economic ^Consequences\Political ^Foreign\Exchange ^P\S\Economic ^P\S\Political

996. —— (1988). "Why the U.S. Cannot Stop South American Cocaine." *Orbis* 32(Fall): 499–519. The cocaine industry's enormous wealth, its large popular base and substantial employment source, and its formidable organization combine to give it great political influence in the Andean countries. The farmers defend their right to cultivate coca, and cocaine dealers exert a range of influences over the criminal justice system and state generally. The profits are enormous, and the economic incentives are so high that ways will be found to circumvent any programs aimed at suppression. The author discusses the U.S. policy dilemma with respect to enhancement of drug fighting capabilities in producer countries, Americanization of the war on drugs, income replacement, sanctions, and negotiating cutbacks in drug production. ^Latin\America ^United\States ^Cocaine ^Drug\Traffic ^Drug\Control\Policies ^Economics ^Politics ^Drug\Control\Policies\Theories ^Production\Incentives\Economic

997. —— (1989). *The White Labyrinth: Cocaine and Political Power.* New Brunswick, N.J.: Transaction Publishers. Study focuses on the South American cocaine industry and traffic through the 1980s. The book is informed by the author's having access to Spanish-language materials, U.S. government reports (including internal cables and memoranda), and transcripts of congressional hearings. Field trips were conducted in Colombia, Bolivia, and Peru. Approaching the drug control problem with supply-side efforts is given extensive discussion, with focus on the enormous economic and political costs to producing countries. Policy issues are dealt with throughout. The relationship of cocaine and coca to South American economies is reviewed as is the political clout of the "coca lobbies." Relationship of the trade to organized crime and terrorist groups is examined. The following sections are discussed in reference to U.S. policy options or "dilemmas": enhancement of drug fighting capabilities in producer countries, Americanization of the war on drugs, income replacement, sanctions, negotiations of cutbacks and drug production, reduction of demand, and legalization. ^Latin\America ^Cocaine ^Colombia ^Peru ^Bolivia ^Supply ^Demand ^Drug\Control\Policies\Critique

^Consequences\Economic ^Consequences\Political ^Drug\Control\Policies ^Drug\Traffic ^P\S\Critique ^Legalization

998. Leen, Jeff (1989). "Bush Lauds Colombia Drug Battle." *The Miami Herald*, 20 August, 1. Description of the Colombian policy, following the assassination of Luís Carlos Galán, to renew the war on the cocaine traffickers. One of the policies, warmly received by the United States, was extradition. Prominent cartel murders are listed, along with short biographical paragraphs of the top four "extraditables"—Pablo Escobar Gaviria, Jorge Ochoa, González Rodríguez Gacha, and Gilberto Rodríguez Orejuela. ^Latin\America ^Colombia ^Drug\Traffic ^Traffickers ^Extradition ^Drug\Control\Policies ^Consequences\Violence

999. —— (1989). "Cuba, U.S. Had Informal Talks about Drugs." *The Miami Herald*, 9 July, 1. Cuban and U.S. officials had unofficial discussions and contacts in relationship with two Miami drug cases that contained allegations against the Cuban military nearly a year before Castro ordered the arrests of several of his high-ranking military officers on drug charges. The article describes in detail the contacts, those who were involved, and the chronology of events. ^Cuba ^United\States ^Drug\Control\Policies ^Consequences\Corruption ^Consequences\Foreign\Relations

1000. Lees, David (1986). "Executive Addicts." *Canadian Business* (February): 52. Cocaine has reached the Canadian workplace. Cocaine has seduced ambitious executives, helping them to stay awake to work longer, eat less, keep lean, and become confident enough to feel like Superman; although most users can afford it at first, many later turn to fraud to support their habit. The biggest cost, however, is absenteeism from the workplace, not crime. Description of ways by which drug use in the workplace might be reduced. ^Canada ^Drug\Use ^Workplace ^Consequences\Economic ^Consequences\Crime

1001. Leger, Kathryn (1986). "Bolivians Awaken to Tragedy of Child Drug Addiction." *The Christian Science Monitor*, 8 September. Large numbers of young people, including some only six years of age, are becoming addicted to raw cocaine paste mixed with tobacco and smoked in tinfoil pipes. All of the normal difficulties of growing up are extremely exacerbated among these individuals, who get drugged and then want to rob in order to be able to do it again. Bolivia now recognizes that the "drug problem" is just not a matter for consumers in the United States. ^Latin\America ^Bolivia ^Coca ^Drug\Use ^Youth ^Consequences\Children ^Cocaine\Paste ^Tobacco ^Consequences\Crime ^Consequences\Misc

1002. —— (1986). "For Many Bolivians, Growing Coca Leaves Is a Means of Survival." *The Christian Science Monitor*, 30 July. Considerable concern among Bolivian peasants in the Chapare region about United States–sponsored eradication efforts. The unemployment rate of 30 percent would be increased substantially if the drug trade were to be suppressed. Hundreds of thousands of Bolivians would be thrown out of work. Thus, "the cocaine problem has gone beyond all limits of the country to solve it." ^Latin\America ^Bolivia ^Coca ^Production ^Economics

1003. —— (1987). "Bolivia No Longer Dancing for President Paz." *The Christian Science Monitor*, 21 December, 9–11. Description of catastrophic economic circumstances in Bolivia that have led to a withdrawal of political support to President Paz Estenssoro (who has been vigorous in the antinarcotic traffic operations) and that have also driven many Bolivians to the single most attractive economic option in Bolivia—coca growing and cocaine production. ^Latin\America ^Latin\America ^Bolivia ^Cocaine ^Drug\Traffic ^Drug\Control\Policies ^Economics ^Politics ^Production\Incentives\Economic ^Traffickers\Incentives\Economic ^Production ^Refining

1004. —— (1987). "US Faces Uphill Battle in Eradicating Cocaine in Bolivia." *The Christian Science Monitor*, 28 October, 25. Describes the crop eradication and crop substitution programs in Bolivia, acknowledging that, even with the $2,000 per hectare that peasants receive in compensation, and even in spite of their eligibility for low-interest loans, the economics go against the programs. The implications are substantial: Coca production accounts for some 30 to 45 percent of Bolivia's agricultural production. ^Latin\America ^Bolivia ^United\States ^Coca ^Production ^Crop\Eradication ^Crop\Substitution ^Economics

1005. —— (1989). "Peru Rebels Flourish in Drug Zone." *The Christian Science Monitor*, 12 May, 3. Description of how the upper Huallaga Valley in Peru has become a major stronghold for the Maoist rebels known as *Sendero Luminoso*. Description of some of the violence and terrorism invoked by the guerrilla group. Some residents who have left the area because of the violence are now, out of economic necessity, returning. In effect it appears that the *Sendero Luminoso* protects coca growing peasants from the national government and from local police—for a price. ^Latin\America ^Peru ^Coca ^Production ^Politics ^Insurgents ^Terrorists ^Consequences\Violence ^Migration

1006. Leon, George de (1982). "The Decriminalization Issue Revisited." *Social Policy* (Fall): 46–48. The move for decriminalization basically centers around the contention that the move would minimize costs and abuses of enforcement in the criminal justice system. The evidence in support of that idea was substantial, from both historical and empirical sources. The history of alcohol regulation in America gave support to such views. The assumptions underlying all this imply that people are prepared to exercise informed free choice. Socially disadvantaged and young people in particular are not well prepared to exercise informed free choice. The decriminalization solution has proven to be an inadequate response, given that marijuana is now an accepted part of the social scene among adolescents and young adults who also use other substances in a widespread way. Any current social policies will need to take into consideration the changed social and cultural view in America today. ^United\States ^Society ^Decriminalization\Critique

1007. —— (1984). *The Therapeutic Community: Study of Effectiveness.* Rockville, Md.: National Institute on Drug Abuse. Research findings show that the success—in terms of removing people from crime and drug use—of the therapeutic community approach toward rehabilitation has been rather impressive. After a lengthy longitudinal study, 31 percent of dropouts from the program remained successes (no crime and no drug use) compared with 75 percent of the graduates; 56 percent of the dropouts and 93 percent of the graduates improved over their pretreatment status. A drug-free residential therapeutic community is contrasted with other modalities of treatment, including detoxification, methadone maintenance, and drug-free outpatient treatment. ^Drug\Use ^Treatment\Therapeutic\Community ^Crime ^NIDA ^Drug\Control\Policies\Effectiveness

1008. Leong, J. H. K. (1980). "Beating the Gong and Chasing the Dragon in the Lion City." *Journal of Drug Issues* 1091:229–40. Gives a historical perspective on the emergence of the three distinct products of the opium poppy—smokeable extract of opium, morphine, and heroin—with their three distinctive modes of administration—smoking, injection, and inhalation. Treatment and rehabilitation observations are made along with noting a number of unanswered questions. Among these are questions about the social costs including lost work days and other debilitating effects, how far controls must or are able to go, and how much one can rely on statistics of drug abuse. ^Heroin ^Opiates ^Drug\Traffic ^Drug\Control\Policies ^Consequences\Drug\Concentration ^Drug\Use\History ^Consequences\Economic ^Consequences\Social ^Statistics\Critique

1009. Lerner, William D., and James M. Raczynski (1988). "The Economic Shaping of Substance Abuse." In *Learning Factors in Substance Abuse*, NIDA

Research Monograph 84. Rockville, Md.: National Institute on Drug Abuse. Discussed are economic relationships in drug marketing, economic relationships in drug selection, and drug effects on user's economics. Discussed also are economic effects on drug addicts' social relationships and economic relationships to psychopathology. ^Drug\Use ^Economics ^NIDA ^Consequences\Markets ^Consequences\Economic ^Consequences\Social ^Consequences\Psychological

1010. Lernoux, Penny (1988). "Colombia Can't Kick Drugs Alone." *The Nation*, 5 March, 1. Description of assassinations for hire, kidnappings, and the general impact of the Colombian drug cartel on the politics of Colombia. ^Latin\America ^Colombia ^Drug\Traffic ^Organized\Crime ^Consequences\Political ^Consequences\Violence ^Consequences\Assassination

1011. —— (1989). "Playing Golf While Drugs Flow." *The Nation*, 13 February, 188–92.p The cocaine business is booming in Riberalta, Bolivia, although the area has three military bases built at U.S. instigation and has U.S. army personnel and Drug Enforcement Administration agents frequently in the area. Corruption of the political and judicial system is rampant because the cocaine industry has brought unprecedented prosperity to the area. The Colombian cartel that sets prices in Bolivia wields enormous power as well, which is described. ^Bolivia ^United\States ^Cocaine ^Drug\Traffic ^Drug\Control\Policies ^Military ^Latin\America ^Consequences\Corruption ^Production ^Drug\Control\Policies\Effectiveness ^Drug\Control\Politics ^Traffickers

1012. Lesser-Katz, Miriam (1982). "Some Effects of Maternal Drug Addiction on the Neonate." *International Journal of the Addictions* 17(5): 887–96. The effect of fetus' exposure to drugs of abuse was studied in ten infants of drug-dependent mothers. A control set of fourteen newborns was established. Infants exposed to drugs of abuse during fetal life exhibited high levels of arousal and irritability and extreme muscle tone fluctuations. They were also highly active, tremulous, and immature with respect to their motor muscles, and they displayed near-constant crying and disturbed sleep patterns. However, their orientation to external stimuli and the findings on neurological examination were similar to those of the control group. ^Drug\Use ^Health ^Fetuses ^Consequences\Fetuses

1013. Leukefeld, Carl G. (1985). "The Clinical Connection: Drugs and Crime." *The International Journal of the Addictions* 20(6-7): 1049–64. Examines the relationship, as reported in the literature, between drugs and crime. There is particular emphasis given to combining, in a treatment program, clinical procedures in collaboration with criminal justice authority. Selected studies are reviewed and historical patterns are noted. ^Drug\Use ^Crime ^Reviews ^Treatment

1014. Leukefeld, Carl G. and Frank M. Tims, eds. (1988). *Compulsory Treatment of Drug Abuse: Research and Clinical Practice.* NIDA Research Monograph 86. Rockville, Md.: National Institute on Drug Abuse. In the NIDA research monograph dedicated to examining compulsory treatment, three questions were examined by the various contributors: When is legal coercion therapeutically useful? What is legal coercion's value in reducing the "contagious" aspects of the drug-using lifestyle? Where and how has compulsory treatment and civil commitment/legal coercion been used in the past? ^Drug\Use ^Treatment\Compulsory ^NIDA ^Drug\Control\Policies\Effectiveness

1015. Levin, Ann (1987). "Some Children, Turned off to Drugs, Turn In Their Parents." *The Christian Science Monitor*, 7 January, 5. Some frustrated American children have begun to turn in their drug addict parents, accusing them of neglect. ^United\States ^Drug\Use ^Family ^Parenting ^Consequences\Children

1016. Levin, Gilbert, Edward B. Roberts, and Gary B. Hirsh (1975). *The Persistent Poppy: A Computer-Aided Search for Heroin Policy.* Cambridge, Mass.: Ballinger Publishing Co. Offers a method for examining forces, thought to be systemic, that encourage and discourage the growth of heroin use in cities and suburbs of the United States. The authors' theorizing has been aided by a mathematical model that embodies generally agreed upon facts as well as informed opinions of social scientists, treatment program directors, drug-enforcement officials, addicts, and victims. Incorporates the language of system dynamics, presents policy experiments and recommendations, and alternative heroin futures based on modeling techniques. Aside from the policy model itself, the book gives important background information about the heroin trafficking system, about how people become addicted, the role of law enforcement agencies in dealing with them, and alternatives for coping, including methadone treatments. ^Heroin ^Drug\Use\Theories ^United\States ^Drug\Traffic ^Law\Enforcement ^Prevention ^Methadone

1017. Levine, Richard (1988). "More Infants Showing Signs of Narcotics; Withdrawal Symptoms Surge in New York City." *The New York Times*, 1 April, B1. The number of infants born in New York City with symptoms of drug withdrawal doubled in 1987 and continued to climb sharply. The social overhead imposed on society is implied. ^United\States ^Drug\Use ^Women ^Consequences\Fetuses ^Consequences\Children ^Consequences\Economic

1018. Levinthal, Charles F. (1985). "Milk of Paradise/Milk of Hell—The History of Ideas about Opium." *Perspectives in Biology and Medicine* 28(4): 561–77. The author gives a historical perspective on the use of the opium poppy, its relationship to the China trade, its use in England and in America, and the advent of heroin via morphine and the syringe. ^Opiates\History

1019. Lewin, Tamar (1990). "Drug Use during Pregnancy: New Issue before the Courts." *The New York Times*, 5 February, A1. Description of the first U.S. woman ordered to stand trial on a charge of delivering cocaine "to a minor"—her fetus. Other cases eliciting differential legal and judiciary responses are reviewed. The issue is whether the public can control the extent to which a woman may freely impair her unborn child. ^United\States ^Drug\Control\Policies ^Women ^Fetuses ^Judiciary ^Law\Enforcement

1020. Lewis, Anthony (1989). "Dose of Reality Will Help Cure Drug Ills." *The Salt Lake Tribune*, 28 September. Presentation of the libertarian argument for decriminalization of drugs. Quotes Milton Friedman and others. ^P\S\Legalization

1021. Lewis, Flora (1988). "Two U.S. Wars." *The New York Times*, 14 May, 14. Washington has a conflict of interest in Honduras. On the one hand, it wants to use Honduras as a base for attacking the Sandinista regime; on the other, the Honduran military is actively involved in the drug trade, and the United States wants to turn its head. ^Latin\America ^Honduras ^United\States ^Consequences\Foreign\Policy ^Military ^Consequences\Corruption

1022. Lewis, Neil A. (1990). "Drug Lawyers' Quandary: Lure of Money vs. Ethics." *The New York Times*, 9 February, A1. Discusses the "ins and outs" of defending drug clients. Some view lawyers' involvement with drug clients as simply an attempt to make big money. Others view lawyers having responsibility not to refuse cases simply because the subject matter is unpopular. Either way, the debate over ethics and the public good is increasing. Description of the kinds of lawyers who defend drug clients. ^United\States ^Judiciary ^Traffickers ^Attorneys

1023. Lewis, Peter (1983). "Legal Heroin in Holland?" *Maclean's*, 11 July, 35. Amsterdam city hall has petitioned the Dutch government for permission to dispense free heroin to addicts in order to combat the rising tide of drug addiction in the city. The Dutch government agreed to study the issue. ^Netherlands ^Heroin ^P\S\Drug\Maintenance

1024. Lewis, Roger, Richard Hartnoll, Susan Bryer, Emmanuelle Daviaud, and Martin Mitcheson (1985). "Scoring Smack: The Illicit Heroin Market in London, 1980–1983." *British Journal of Addiction* 80:281–90. The rising and falling prices of heroin in London during 1980–1983 are discussed in terms of heroin availability, its dilution, and how the distribution system and price fluctuations affected consumption. Retail and wholesale heroin prices provide a useful indicator of market conditions. The evidence points to a flourishing and expanding market in illicit heroin in London. ^United\Kingdom ^Heroin ^Drug\Traffic ^Economics ^Statistics ^Consequences\Markets

1025. Liappas, J. A., F. A. Jenner, B. Vincente (1988). "Literature on Methadone Maintenance Clinics." *International Journal of the Addictions* 23(9): 927–40. Review of the principal literature on the impact of methadone maintenance clinics relative to their goals of treating heroin addicts. On the basis of the evidence, there is little justification to maintain the clinics. Society has gained little advantage from the expense of the clinics in terms of removing people from heroin addiction, while at the same time the clinics have served to spread methadone addiction. ^Heroin ^Treatment ^Methadone ^Reviews ^Drug\Control\Policies\Effectiveness ^Treatment\Critique

1026. Lidz, Charles W., and Andrew L. Walker (1980). *Heroin, Deviance, and Morality*. Beverly Hills, Calif.: Sage Publications. Focus on drug-related deviant behavior in the United States and the moral conditions that surround it. The main emphasis is on the sociology of deviance, and the exploration of heroin (considerable empirical evidence) is intended to offer ramifications for the sociology of deviance. The presentation of theory, evidence, and argument, therefore, are more intent upon the examination of sociological theory than on policy ramifications. Orienting research questions for the volume were: Why was drug use apparently increasing so rapidly in the 1960s and early 1970s? Why had society suddenly become so concerned about drugs? Why did the United States resurrect the program of medical intervention, abandoned a half-century earlier to supplement law enforcement efforts? None of the extant theories of deviance and control (e.g., "labeling theory") proved satisfactory answers to the question. Drug use and control in "crisis" times were different than in other times. The key to the understanding of crisis, and therefore to the understanding of accelerated deviance and control regarding heroin, lies in a dynamic concept of morality—that is, in the socially based schema operating at the time that determines the rightness and wrongness of acts, actors, interactions, and settings. By analyzing the general social crisis of the 1960s and early 1970s within a dynamic concept of morality, the authors show that drugs were nothing other than a "normal" social episode that played an integral role in the ongoing and dynamic process of cultural integration. A review of the sociological literature is given as well as the evidence. From the short policy perspective that is given, the authors provide a simple conclusion from their findings: "The crisis was a phony creation of a variety of powerful people who felt threatened by the growth of expressive pacifist beliefs in the youth culture and revolutionary politics among blacks. It seems that there was little reality to the belief that large sectors of the American population were about to become addicted to heroin, rather, the Drug Crisis was a smoke screen for the repression of political and cultural groups" (p. 252). Extensive bibliography. ^United\States ^Heroin ^Drug\Control\Policies ^Politics ^Bureaucracy ^Society ^Culture ^Values ^Reviews ^Bibliographies ^Crime ^Drug\Use\Theories ^Drug\Control\Policies\Theories ^Drug\Control\Policies\Critique

1027. Lieber, James (1986). "Coping with Cocaine." *Atlantic* (January): 39. There are four ways to make cocaine less available to confirmed and potential users. First, "go to the source" and try to inhibit coca cultivation in foreign lands; second, try to prevent the importation of the drug—"interdiction"; third, once on our shores, try to disrupt or destroy the dealing and money-laundering operations that make the trade profitable; and, fourth, punish those who use cocaine, doing what can be done to break their habits and try to persuade everyone else not to use it in the first place. Aside from these issues, the author discusses the physiological effects—"rush"—of cocaine usage and the risk to those who have become addicted to the drug. Argues that suppression and interdiction not only have not worked satisfactorily, they are unlikely to, because of the multitudinous ways that traffickers can subvert narcotics control efforts. The real problem is "demand." Reviews Steven Wisotsky's often quoted argument for decriminalization as an effort to reduce demand. He, in turn, analyzes the many reasons why decriminalization would have unfortunate side effects. He sees one hope for diminishing the demand for cocaine lying in education, both in and out of school with respect to drug prevention programs aimed at young people. He cites a report from the Rand Corporation suggesting that antidrug education will have the best chance of success if it employs techniques borrowed from antismoking campaigns that are known to have worked. Discusses drug treatment programs for those who are already "hooked" on the drug. Because the traffic in cocaine is one of the most corruptive and corrosive forces in American society, Washington has an obligation to fight it intelligently. Doing so requires that the government cease to virtually ignore the demand side of the cocaine traffic—the side that is somewhat more susceptible to government influence. The government has invested a great deal of money in supply-side enforcement, and that, unfortunately, may very well have made the problem worse. ^United\States ^Cocaine ^Drug\Use ^Drug\Control\Policies\Critique ^Reviews ^Consequences\Misc ^Drug\Control\Policies\Effectiveness ^Demand ^Decriminalization\Critique ^P\S\Education ^Tobacco ^Treatment ^Supply ^Consequences\Drug\Control\Policies

1028. Lifschultz, Lawrence (1988). "Inside the Kingdom of Heroin." *The Nation*, 14 November, 1. The United States, in the interest of foreign policy goals, has done business with narcotraffickers. Particular discussion of President Zia of Pakistan and George Bush. ^Pakistan ^United\States ^Heroin ^Drug\Traffic ^Consequences\Foreign\Policy ^Consequences\Corruption ^Southwest\Asia ^Consequences\Political

1029. Lindblad, R. A. (1983). "A Review of the Concerned Parent Movement in the United States of America." *Bulletin on Narcotics* 35(3): 411–52. Reviews the rapidly increasing number and size of parent groups whose common goal is to prevent drug use among young people. More than 4,000 formal parent organizations now exist. This nationally unified group has had substantial influence on public laws, policies, and attitudes. This article describes the movement, the leaders, and the policies affected. The recent decline in drug abuse among teenagers has, to a certain extent, been attributed to the movement. ^United\States ^Prevention ^Youth ^Family ^Reviews ^Private\Initiatives ^Prevention\Family

1030. Ling, George M. (1984). "The Global Problem of Drug Abuse: Analysis and Perspectives." *Impact of Science on Society* 34:133: 11–21. Reviews the multitude of drugs which societies, down through the ages, have used to alter mood, thought, and behavior. The problems these drugs have created for individuals and societies are reviewed, along with a discussion of the prospects "of dealing with them intelligently" (p. 11). ^Drug\Use ^Consequences\Misc ^Drug\Use\History

1031. Linke, Robert (1985). *Extradition for Drug-Related Offenses: A Study of Existing Extradition Practices and Suggested Guidelines for Use in Concluding Extradition Treaties*. New York: United Nations, Division of Narcotic

Drugs. Studies existing extradition practices with particular reference to their application in connection with drug-related offence. Designed to assist government officials and jurists in interpreting existing laws and regulations governing extradition cases. It is thought that the volume also may be of assistance to drafters of domestic legislation in matters relating to extradition and mutual assistance in criminal matters. ^United\Nations ^Extradition ^International\Cooperation ^Bibliographies ^Legislation

1032. Linn, Shai, Stephen C. Schoenbaum, Richard R. Monson, Richard Rosner, Phillip C. Stubblefield, and Kenneth J. Ryan (1983). "The Association of Marijuana Use with Outcome of Pregnancy." *American Journal of Public Health* 73(10): 1161–64. The relationships of low birth weight, short gestation, and major malformations occurring among offspring of marijuana users were not statistically significant in the more than 12,000 women sampled. ^Cannabis ^Health ^Fetuses ^Consequences\Fetuses ^Drug\Use\Critique

1033. Lintner, Bertil (1984). "Orchards and Opium." *Far Eastern Economic Review*, 6 September, 30–31. The remnants of the Chinese Kuomintang, who entered Thailand as a defeated army, are now less interested in practicing military matters than in doing business in opium. "In these mountains, the only money is opium." ^Thailand ^Opiates ^Drug\Traffic ^Organized\Crime ^Southeast\Asia ^Golden\Triangle

1034. ——— (1987). "The Deadly Deluge." *Far Eastern Economic Review*, 12 November, 54–55. The Burmese government, in a program sponsored by the United States, has attempted to eradicate poppy fields in its sector of the Golden Triangle by aerial spraying. A massive influx of hill tribe refugees into Thailand, as a consequence of the crop destruction, has alarmed human rights organizations. ^Burma ^Southeast\Asia ^Golden\Triangle ^Opiates ^Crop\Eradication ^Herbicides ^Migration ^Minorities ^Consequences\Economic ^Consequences\Human\Rights

1035. ——— (1987). "Tax Revenue from Opium Helps Finance the Party." *Far Eastern Economic Review*, 4 June, 31–33. Describes the travails of rural peasants who find that governmental crop substitution programs have produced only famine and crisis for them. So they have reverted to growing opium poppies. A dominant Burmese political party helps to finance itself by taxing the opium trade. In areas dominated by the Chinese-sponsored CPB party, opium is the only cash crop. ^Southeast\Asia ^Burma ^Golden\Triangle ^Opiates ^Production ^Crop\Substitution ^Consequences\Corruption ^Producers\Incentives\Economic ^Drug\Control\Policies\Critique

1036. Lips, J. Alan, and Michael C. Lueder (1988). "An Employer's Right to Test for Substance Abuse, Infectious Diseases, and Truthfulness versus an Employee's Right to Privacy." *Labor Law Journal* (August): 528–34. While an employer is justified in testing employees, the prudent employer will base testing decisions on reasonable needs, rather than on economic power to require tests, and will, in any event, keep the information confidential. ^United\States ^Drug\Testing ^Workplace

1037. Lipton, Douglas S., and Michael J. Maranda (1982). "Detoxification from Heroin Dependency: An Overview of Method and Effectiveness." *Advances in Alcohol and Drug Abuse* 2(1): 31–55. Discusses, briefly, the history of opiate detoxification, and reviews methods and procedures currently in place for detoxification from heroin dependency. Detoxification fails as a treatment procedure because it does not produce satisfactory retention rates of detoxified conditions. Detoxification should be viewed as a preliminary step only. ^Heroin ^Treatment\Detoxification ^Treatment\Critique ^Treatment\History

1038. "Literature on the Drug Issue" (1988). *Journal of Interamerican Studies and World Affairs* 30:2 & 3(Summer/Fall): 213–31. Lists entries from the congressional research service of the Library of Congress in two categories: narcotics trafficking and U.S. law enforcement policies, and narcotics interdiction and the use of the military. These entries are annotated. They include books, articles from journals and the responsible press, and public documents. ^Bibliographies ^Drug\Traffic ^Law\Enforcement ^United\States ^Drug\Control\Policies ^Interdiction ^Military

1039. Liu, Hsien Chou (1979). *The Development of a Single Convention on Narcotic Drugs: A Historical Survey for the International Cooperation in Solving the Crucial Problem of Narcotic Drugs.* A brief historical survey on the development of documents relating to international cooperation in solving problems of narcotic drugs. Bangkok, Thailand: Academy of New Society. ^United\Nations ^Drug\Control\Policies ^International\Cooperation\History

1040. Liverpool, N. (1983). "The Seizure and Forfeiture of Property Associated with Criminal Activity." *Bulletin on Narcotics* 35(2): 21–39. Simply imprisoning criminals, particularly those associated with international criminal organizations, does not deter criminality. Other people simply rise to the vacated positions. Attacking the earnings of crime, however, can put a dent in criminal activity. Legislation needs to be enacted that would allow confiscatory action to be taken against property associated with criminal activity, and facilitate the seizure of property prior to a criminal trial and the forfeiture of property directly related to or involved in the crime. None of the present legislative models within the British Commonwealth is wholly adequate. The author gives specific recommendations. ^United\Kingdom ^Asset\Forfeiture ^Drug\Control\Policies\Critique ^P\S\Asset\Forfeiture

1041. Lockwood, R. S. (1977). "The United States Drug Problem and International Trafficking. Part I. The Need for More Rigorous Controls." *International Journal of the Addictions* 12(5): 633–50. Discusses remedies in international law for obtaining prosecutional jurisdiction over illicit drug traffickers. Examines extradition, expulsion, exclusion, and reconduction as means by which one state may obtain control of an offender. ^United\States ^Extradition ^International\Cooperation ^Drug\Control\Policies

1042. ——— (1977). "The United States Drug Problem and International Trafficking. Part II. Denial of Safe-Havens to Illicit Drug Traffickers." *International Journal of the Addictions* 12(8): 1007–46. Argues that excessive reliance on extradition as a means of acquiring prosecutional control over illicit drug traffickers is short sighted. Informal arrangements such as expulsion should be given more consideration. A method for developing and implementing an expulsion policy through existing diplomatic channels is advanced, principally through the use of safe haven denial. Focus is on drug traffickers. ^United\States ^Drug\Control\Policies ^Extradition ^International\Cooperation ^Drug\Control\Policies\Critique

1043. Loeper, Stephen (1989). "20 Tons of Cocaine Confiscated in Los Angeles." *The Salt Lake Tribune*, 30 September, 1. Describes the discovery of cocaine at a warehouse in a quiet section of the city; officials call it the biggest drug haul in history. ^United\States ^California ^Cocaine ^Interdiction

1044. Logan, Frank (1979). *Cannabis: Options for Control.* London: Quartermaine House Ltd. Four options are discussed in this volume: changes in maximum penalties, decriminalization, licensing systems, and legalization. The volume examines the practical problems each policy option would entertain, along with their probable consequences, including the effects of the options on consumption (without addressing the issue of health). ^United\Kingdom ^Cannabis ^Drug\Control\Policies ^Decriminalization\Critique

1045. Lohrmann, David K., and Stuart W. Fors (1986). "Can School-Based Educational Programs Really Be Expected to Solve the Adolescent Drug Abuse Problem?" *Journal of Drug Education* 16(4): 327–39. In 1984 a Rand Corporation report stated that the most effective way to prevent adolescent drug abuse was through preventive education. The underlying assumptions of this report are examined within the context of theories about the causes of drug abuse. Many variables contribute to adolescents' beginning use of psychoactive substances, and a good many of those variables are not within the purview of schools. Such a drug prevention program as suggested by Rand can work only if there is a consistent antidrug governmental policy, if there are special education intervention programs for high-risk children, and if specific supplemental strategies are developed that involve social institutions besides the schools. ^Drug\Use ^Prevention ^Youth ^Reviews ^Drug\Use\Theories ^Prevention\Drug\Education\Critique ^Prevention\Integrated

1046. Long, Janice (1987). "House Approves Chemical Diversion Bill." *Chemical and Engineering News* 66(38): 19. Efforts are afoot to force chemical companies to keep closer track of what happens to certain chemicals that are needed to make illegal drugs. ^United\States ^Drug\Control\Policies ^Precursor\Chemicals

1047. "The Long, Losing Battle against Drugs" (1988). *The Economist*, 5 March, 23–24. Aside from noting the substantial increase in drug usage in America and its deleterious effects (hospital admissions, etc.), the article opines that a sad failure in American drug policy is to starve prevention and treatment programs while funding fairly adequately drug fighting and interception programs. ^United\States ^Drug\Use ^Drug\Control\Policies\Critique ^Society

1048. Long, William R. (1987). "Drug Lords Rule over Rio's Slums." *Los Angeles Times*, 16 October. Description of how the "Robin Hood" activities of drug lords in slum areas have won over the people in patterns of loyalty and dedication that protect them from the authorities. ^Latin\America ^Brazil ^Drug\Traffic ^Traffickers ^Consequences\Political

1049. ———— (1988). "Bolivia's U.S.–Aided Attack on Cocaine; an Uphill Struggle." *Los Angeles Times*, 13 May, 8. Description of a Bolivian raid on a market where cocaine paste was being sold, only to have hundreds of peasants come back to pelt the raiders with rocks and sticks of dynamite. The raiders were overcome and beat a hurried retreat. ^Latin\America ^Bolivia ^Coca ^Law\Enforcement ^Politics ^Consequences\Violence ^Cocaine\Paste ^Producers\Unions

1050. ———— (1989). "Colombia Girds to Face Drug Lords' Hired Guns." *Los Angeles Times*, 23 April. Description of the internal war going on in Colombia between national authority and law enforcement agents and hired gunmen directed by the cocaine traffickers and other right-wing groups. Description of the activities of the paramilitary groups as well as operations to shut them down. ^Latin\America ^Colombia ^Law\Enforcement ^Organized\Crime ^Consequences\Violence ^Traffickers ^Traffickers\Private\Armies

1051. López Espinoza, W. Homero (1984). *La Droga: Los Estupefacientes en el Ecuador "Consumo, Tráfico y Control."* Quito, Ecuador: Juan Carlos. General treatise for Ecuadorian lawyers, judges, magistrates, justice administrators, teachers, and students. It addresses the pharmacological and psychopharmacological aspects of the drug, but also concentrates on drug enforcement administrators, including Interpol, and police procedures. Clearly, its motive is to discourage drug consumption and trafficking among Ecuadorian youth. ^Ecuador ^Drug\Use ^Drug\Traffic ^Drug\Control\Policies ^Prevention ^Consequences\Misc ^Interpol ^Law\Enforcement ^Latin\America

1052. "Losing the War against 'Narcos'" (1983). *Latin American Regional Reports*, 29 July, 7–8. Bolivia's Drug Enforcement Agency admits that the illegal cocaine industry has overwhelmed the capacity of the country's security forces; there appears to be no end in sight. Economic data are given. ^Latin\America ^Bolivia ^Cocaine ^Law\Enforcement ^Economics ^Statistics ^Consequences\Political

1053. Lowinger, Paul (1977). "The Solution to Narcotic Addiction in the People's Republic of China." *American Journal of Drug and Alcohol Abuse* 4(2): 165–78. A two-front attack was made in China. On the one hand, addiction was dealt with as a political problem; as people were given hope, food, shelter, work, and land instead of opium, addiction lost much of its appeal. On the other hand, large-scale opium distributors were imprisoned. A mass campaign against addiction mobilized the entire nation. ^China ^Opiates ^Drug\Control\Policies

1054. Luaderdale, Pat, and James Inverarity (1984). "Regulation of Opiates." *Journal of Drug Issues* 14(3): 567–77. Focusing on recent historical efforts in the regulation of opiates, the author looks at the Harrison Act and the San Francisco ordinances relating to drug usage in the United States. The author attempts to analyze why drug laws are created and why regulation of individual behavior occurs. Argues that the explanation of drug regulation can be fully explained only through reference to the social context, namely, a structure of society characterized by increasingly regulated international and national economies, the rationalization of bureaucratic agencies, and the expansion of formal, rational legal procedures. ^United\States ^Heroin ^Opiates ^Drug\Control\Policies\History ^Society ^Drug\Control\Policies\Theories

1055. Lucchini, R. (1985). "Young Drug Addicts and the Drug Scene." *Bulletin on Narcotics* 13(2 & 3): 135–48. Analysis of the "sociology of addiction" among young people. The social consequences for the individual drug user are noted. There appears to be a distinct addict subculture associated with each type of drug consumed. In time, multiple drug abuse takes over, and this frequently aggravates drug addicts' medical and social problems. ^Drug\Use ^Consequences\Social

1056. Lupsha, Peter A. (1981). "Drug Trafficking: Mexico and Colombia in Comparative Perspective." *Journal of International Affairs* 35(1): 95–115. Aside from giving a general orientation to the trafficking of drugs in Mexico and Colombia, including drug trafficking patterns, the article focuses on the effects of the traffic on the financial structure of Colombia. The "underground economy" is examined. As for U.S. policy, Mexico and Colombia are sufficiently different in the impact of the number of political and economic variables as to make it appear that the policy of eradication will not work in Colombia (although it has had better success in Mexico). Reasons are given. The geographical and political dissimilarities of Mexico and Colombia will make it impossible for the same U.S.-sponsored drug policy to work in both countries. In particular, the author shows how paraquat and herbicide spraying policy with respect to Mexico could not be used in Colombia. A multi-dimensional global strategy must be called for if an impact is to be had in Colombia. The article is heavily documented. ^Latin\America ^Colombia ^Mexico ^United\States ^Drug\Traffic ^Crop\Eradication ^Herbicides ^Consequences\Economic ^Informal\Economy ^Drug\Control\Policies\Critique ^Proffered\Solutions

1057. Lupsha, Peter A., and Kip Schlegel (1980). *The Political Economy of Drug Trafficking: The Herrera Organization (Mexico and the United States)*. Latin American Institute. Albuquerque: University of New Mexico. Examines the effects of contraband drug traffic between Mexico and the United States, and in particular on the political economy of both. More particularly, the focus is on the border lands of the two countries. The specific focus is on the trafficking in heroin and a narcotics organization specializing in it. Some forms of border lands drug trafficking appear to provide an illicit and untaxed form of foreign aid for Mexico, aid that reaches into very different sectors and levels within an economy than does the regular foreign aid program. Law enforcement, whether federal or local, cannot be expected ever fully to accomplish its mission so long as such grand political and economic incentives to trafficking that positively affect so many people continue to exist. ^Mexico ^Heroin ^Drug\Traffic ^Traffickers ^Consequences\Economic ^Consequences\Foreign\Aid ^Consequences\Political ^Drug\Control\Policies\Critique ^Latin\America

1058. Luxner, Larry (1989). "Island Bids to Seal Its Ports from Drugs." *The Miami Herald*, 14 July, 2A. Description of an elaborate and accelerated response to Jamaica's being used as a transshipment point for illegal drugs. The response includes fiber-optic seals on outgoing containers and an elite 300-man security force at Jamaican air and sea ports. $200 million in fines against three shipping lines has caused them to lend considerable attention. ^Caribbean ^Jamaica ^Drug\Traffic ^Law\Enforcement ^Interdiction

1059. Lyman, Michael D. (1987). *Narcotics and Crime Control*. Springfield, Ill.: Charles C. Thomas Publishing. Comprises four parts. The first is a historical look at drug use, giving classes of drugs and their source nations. The economics of trafficking are discussed. The second part focuses on manufacturers, traffickers, distributors, dealers, users, and agents. Organized crime and outside informers are also discussed. The third part concerns drug enforcement. Drug laws, drug investigations, interagency cooperation and coordination, investigative techniques and the kind of equipment agents use in their investigations to detect how people smuggle drugs are presented. The relationship between drugs and crime is explored. The fourth section deals with drugs on the job, drug testing, and treatment and prevention programs. The book presents itself as a comprehensive sourcebook which provides reliable information about the illicit business of drugs, drug trafficking, and enforcement practices. It is written for a nontechnical audience. ^Drug\Use\History ^Drug\Traffic ^Traffickers ^Organized\Crime ^Law\Enforcement ^Drug\Testing ^Workplace ^Prevention ^Treatment ^Crime ^Economics ^Refining ^Bureaucracy ^Reviews

1060. ―――― (1989). *Gangland: Drug Trafficking by Organized Criminals.* Springfield, Ill.: Charles C. Thomas Publishing. The single conduit linking the origin of illicit drugs with the numerous problems associated with their use (deterioration in the quality of neighborhoods, destruction of families, health problems, AIDS and hepatitis, reduction of GNP through untaxed dollars) is organized crime. Hundreds of organized criminal groups flourish in the United States. Of all the activities in which they engage, drug trafficking offers the largest and quickest form of revenue . A university professor/gang investigator couples his knowledge and experiences with insights of others whom he interviewed to produce a treatise on gangs and drug trafficking in the United States. It describes several of the most influential gangs who control the flow of drugs into and within the United States and seeks to generate interest in different methods of investigating their criminal activities. The Latin American connection is discussed as is also that of Asia. ^United\States ^Drug\Traffic ^Organized\Crime ^Traffickers ^Latin\America ^Southeast\Asia

1061. McAllister, Donald R. (1988). *1987 Drug-Related Costs in the County of Los Angeles*. Los Angeles: Department of Health Services. There are enormous costs attached to drug abuse in America—costs of the criminal justice system's involvement with arrest and prosecution, costs of drug-related crime and its costs to victims, costs of short- and long-term medical expenses, lost productivity, and the costs of drug abuse prevention and treatment. Many, if not all of these costs are born by industry; federal, state, and local governments; and ultimately by the general public.

Details some of those costs with respect to the county of Los Angeles. The costs identified during the calendar year 1987 totaled 1.2264 billion dollars. A number of direct or indirect drug-related costs could not be estimated and were therefore not included. These included the costs of hospitalization, physicians, and medication for individuals suffering from drug-related diseases; and the cost to the state and federal prison and parole system for Los Angeles county residents convicted of drug offenses while not in the county; the costs of increased accident, property, and health insurance for all residents, industries, and governmental units that could be attributed to the result of drug use. ^United\States ^Drug\Traffic ^Consequences\Economic ^Consequences\Crime ^Consequences\Fetuses ^Statistics

1062. McBee, Suzanne (1985). "Flood of Drugs—A Losing Game." *U.S. News and World Report*, 25 March, 53–57. In spite of increased efforts to suppress the international trade in illicit drugs, all has been thwarted by ruthless and elusive traffickers who wield incredible power and money. Corruption, global politics, and nature conspire to hamper the drive to cut off the flow of narcotics at the source. Increasing numbers of young men are opting for the "fast-buck" trafficking in illicit drugs. While Burma, the world's largest illicit opium producer, has moved forcefully to halt growth and traffic, it has hardly been able to because of the remote area where the growing goes on and because the government has little control in remote, rural areas. With coca, the matter is compounded by the fact that it grows "like a weed" because it is a weed. "Stamping out illicit drugs is like trying to control a glob of mercury." Survey of current events in Colombia. ^Southeast\Asia ^Latin\America ^Burma ^Colombia ^Drug\Traffic ^Traffickers ^Drug\Control\Policies\Effectiveness ^Consequences\Corruption ^Production ^Consequences\State\Authority ^Politics

1063. McBeth, John (1984). "The Opium Laws." *Far Eastern Economic Review*, 29 March, 40–43. The Thai government is studying a $1 million crop-substitution plan proposed by the United States. The Thai government is still wary, because it was the destruction of opium fields that allowed Communist cadres to infiltrate and win over many hill tribesmen. The United Nations Fund for Drug Abuse Control (UNFDAC) has for years carried out a substitution demonstration project in the area. No crop substitution is likely to bring an equivalent income to the tribesmen. Crop substitution, taken alone, is not enough. ^Thailand ^United\Nations ^Opiates ^Crop\Substitution ^Economics ^UNFDAC ^Crop\Substitution\Critique

1064. McBride, Duane C., and Clyde B. McCoy (1982). "Crime and Drugs: The Issues and Literature." *Journal of Drug Issues* 12(2): 137–52. Examines major research issues associated with the relationship of crime and drugs. Classifies the relationship of crime and drugs, and discusses the whole problem of causal priority and direction of causal effects. The authors find considerable disagreement and inconclusiveness in the studies they have examined, at least taken as a whole. They thus call for additional research for a more systematic, analytical approach to study, longitudinally, the relationship between all types of crime and types of drug use. ^Drug\Use ^Crime ^Reviews

1065. McBride, Nicholas C. (1988). "Marijuana: Latest US Agribusiness." *The Christian Science Monitor*, 2 November, 1. Description of the increasing share of the U.S. market that U.S. marijuana is gaining. The effects of this growth industry on forest lands (environmental and their availability to recreationists) is noted. Statistics are given regarding production and eradication in the United States. ^United\States ^Cannabis ^Production ^Crop\Eradication

1066. ———— (1988). "'Zero Tolerance': Zero Effect? Prosecutors See Few Results from Crackdown on Drug Users." *The Christian Science Monitor*, 23 August, 3. Prosecutors see few results from crackdown on drug users, in part because judges are reluctant to impose draconian penalties on people they believe do not merit them. ^United\States ^Drug\Use ^Drug\Control\Policies\Effectiveness

1067. McBride, Robert B. (1983). "Business as Usual: Heroin Distribution in the United States." *Journal of Drug Issues* 13(1): 147–66. The heroin industry is a stable system in the United States, deeply rooted in its economy and far reaching in its organization. Substantial social and economic change would be necessary if heroin transactions were to be reduced significantly. This derives from heroin's being not so much a social aberration as a product distribution and utilization scheme within the normal structure and functioning of U.S. capitalism which generates both the market for the drug and the industry that supplies it. An underground economy operates parallel to a legal goods economy, but with distinctive features that provide reduced risk for dealers and long-term stability for the industry as a whole. The key role of syndicates in the expansion of the industry is analyzed. ^United\States ^Heroin ^Drug\Traffic ^Organized\Crime ^Economics ^Informal\Economy ^Society

1068. McCallion, Gail (1988). "Drug Testing in the Workplace: An Overview of Employee and Employer Interests." *CRS Issue Brief*, 12 December. General discussion of the issues associated with drug testing in the workplace. Points raised by proponents and opponents are considered. The author also gives an analysis of what drug tests are, and what they can and cannot do. Notes on legislation on this issue are also included. ^United\States ^Drug\Testing ^Workplace ^Reviews ^Drug\Testing\Critique

1069. McCartney, Robert J. (1985). "The Gold in Mexico's Hills: Drugs." *The Washington Post*, 12 May, 1. Local farmers are now planting opium poppies and marijuana in the bottoms of deep ravines and canyons where they are difficult to see from the air. Crops are also being planted at large farms. The drug trade is clearly flourishing in Mexico. Specific names of those involved, operations against them, and economic statistics regarding the trade are given. ^Latin\America ^Mexico ^Heroin ^Drug\Traffic ^Traffickers ^Economics ^Production ^Cannabis ^Producers ^Statistics

1070. McClintick, David (1988). "The Drug War—Losing While Winning; Frustrated at Home, the DEA Is Mounting a Secret and Dangerous Worldwide Offensive." *The Washington Post*, 21 February, B1. Measured by usual standards of law enforcement effectiveness (arrests and convictions), the DEA is a success. But when judged against whether it is winning the war on drugs, the agency must be rated a failure. The article describes the DEA's worldwide enforcement and interdiction efforts, and the degree to which they are successful. America's previous drug habit, which it broke in the 1920s, was more easily contained than this one. Today the drugs are more numerous and varied; the criminals are better organized and they have more money. ^United\States ^Law\Enforcement ^DEA ^Drug\Control\Policies\Effectiveness ^Interdiction ^Organized\Crime ^Drug\Use\History

1071. McClintock, Cynthia (1988). "The War on Drugs: The Peruvian Case." *Journal of Interamerican Studies and World Affairs* 30:2 & 3(Summer/Fall): 127–42. Describes what is known about Peru's coca production and its conversion to cocaine paste. Antidrug efforts undertaken by the U.S. and Peruvian governments are explained. Considerable statistical material is reported regarding production and trafficking patterns and the repatriation and utilization of drug profits. Eradication, interdiction, and herbicidal programs are examined. Domestic politics and economics have contributed to "shotgun marriages" in the upper Huallaga Valley between traffickers and guerrilla organizations, principally Sendero Luminoso. Also involved is the guerrilla group known as Movimiento Revolucionario Túpac Amaru. But Sendero's ability to draw on income from the drug trade has allowed it to triumph over its Túpac

Amaru rival. All the efforts to interdict, eradicate, and otherwise attack drug supplies have fared very badly in Peru. The U.S. and Peruvian governments are losing this war; however, the war has created conditions for an alliance between coca growers and Sendero Luminoso in the upper Huallaga Valley. ^Latin\America ^Peru ^Coca ^Production ^Drug\Control\Policies ^International\Cooperation ^United\States ^Statistics ^Money\Laundering ^Crop\Eradication ^Interdiction ^Herbicides ^Traffickers ^Terrorists ^Insurgents

1072. McClintock, Cynthia, Abraham F. Lowenthal, and Gabriela Tara-zona-Sevillano (1989). "Peru's Harvest of Instability and Terrorism." *The Christian Science Monitor*, 16 March, 19. Discusses the drug trade in Peru, and how it has created power bases within Latin America that threaten the United States because they provide support for a drug industry and generate insurgent activities that threaten Latin American democracies. This may be one of the interesting aspects of the "death knell" to Latin American democracies as they are undone by the international trade in narcotics. Specifically discussed is the upper Huallaga Valley. ^Latin\America ^Peru ^Cocaine ^Drug\Traffic ^Insurgents ^Consequences\Political ^Consequences\Sovereignty

1073. McConahay, Mary Jo, and Robin Kirk (1989). "Over There." *Mother Jones* (February/March): 37–42. America's drug war abroad is a "bust." Opium production in Burma has doubled, Pakistan is undergoing a poppy boom, and increased acreage is devoted to coca cultivation in Latin America. More marijuana is produced in Mexico than ever. We can't win this war because of the economics associated with the trade against the backdrop of economic chaos in the country. Accusations are made that the United States is using its drug campaign as a cover for waging anti-insurgency campaigns in Latin America and elsewhere. The State Department denies, of course, any counter insurgency intent to spraying and other eradication procedures. General broadside against indiscriminate herbicidal spraying. ^Burma ^Pakistan ^United\States ^Cannabis ^Coca ^Opiates ^Production ^Crop\Eradication ^Herbicides ^Drug\Control\Policies ^Economics ^Politics ^Consequences\Foreign\Policy ^Insurgents ^Golden\Triangle ^Southeast\Asia ^Golden\Crescent ^Middle\East ^Mexico ^Latin\America ^Drug\Control\Policies\Critique ^Southwest\Asia

1074. McCoy, John (1987). "Bolivia: Promised Economic Recovery Program Fizzles." *Latinamerica Press*, 11 June. General discussion of the extraordinary economic difficulties in Bolivia that have made traffic in cocaine one of the few profitable options for Bolivians of all social classes. Description of the degree to which Bolivians have actively entered this industry. ^Latin\America ^Bolivia ^Cocaine ^Drug\Traffic ^Economics

1075. —— (1987). "Cocaine Business Booms in Bolivia and Peru Despite U.S. Eradication Efforts." *Latinamerica Press*, 10 September, 5. Description of the general ineffectiveness of U.S. eradication efforts in the Chapare area of Bolivia. Assertion that the efforts in Peru have proven to be equally as ineffective. Discussion focuses on U.S.-sponsored drug police forces in Peru and Bolivia. ^Latin\America ^Bolivia ^Peru ^United\States ^Coca ^Crop\Eradication ^Law\Enforcement ^Drug\Control\Policies\Effectiveness

1076. —— (1988). "The Cocaine Boom: A Latin American Perspective." *Latinamerica Press*, 29 September. General description of the production of coca and trafficking in cocaine and its economic impact—including thousands of jobs—for Latin American economies. Suggests that in Colombia the new rich drug barons have arisen to replace the coffee oligarchy of the late nineteenth century. Far from destabilizing the old social order, drug money has reenforced it. ^Latin\America ^Colombia ^Cocaine ^Drug\Traffic ^Traffickers ^Production ^Consequences\Economic ^Consequences\Social

1077. McCuen, Gary E. (1989). *The International Drug Trade*. Hudson, Wis.: Gary E. McCuen Publications Inc. This edited volume, designed as a reasonably sophisticated public education effort, presents materials in a "point" and "counterpoint" format. Topics include financing the drug trade, the political corruption associated with it, various ways to control the drug epidemic (including various current policies that are failures), and a discussion on drug legalization. The pedagogical thrust is to develop reasoning skills through the examination of complex and competing materials. ^Drug\Traffic ^Drug\Control\Policies ^Legalization ^Drug\Control\Policies\Critique ^P\S\Education ^Economics ^Consequences\Corruption

1078. **Macdonald, Donald Ian** (1988). "Marijuana Smoking Worse for Lungs." *Journal of the American Medical Association* 259(23): 3384. Brief summary of a study claiming that smoking one marijuana "joint" is approximately four times more hazardous to health than smoking a single tobacco cigarette. ^Cannabis ^Consequences\Health

1079. **Macdonald, John Marshall, and Jerry Kennedy** (1984). *Criminal Investigation of Drug Offenses: The Narcs' Manual.* Springfield, Ill.: Charles C. Thomas Publishing. Focuses on dealers, laws, enforcement agencies, and control of narcotics trafficking in the United States. Deals also with narcotics-trafficking crime in the United States. "This book provides police officers, narcotics detectives and special agents with information not readily available within a single book, on the world of the drug dealer and his clients. It reviews the drug dealers' methods of operation; the motives of informants and problems likely to be encountered in working with them; the techniques of surveillance including electronic and aerial surveillance; the complexities of search warrants; the profiles of drug couriers, drug-smuggling planes, and mother ships; the investigation of prescription fraud, clandestine laboratories, and major drug dealers; as well as the perils of drug raids and under cover operations" (p. v). Mac-Donald is a professor of psychiatry at the University of Colorado, and Kennedy is a police officer with the Denver Police Force. Bibliography. ^United\States ^Drug\Traffic ^Law\Enforcement ^Reviews ^Drug\Control\Policies ^Drug\Use ^Traffickers ^Surveillance

1080. **Macdonald, Patrick T.** (1985). "Prime Time Drug Depictions." *Contemporary Drug Problems* 12(3): 419–38. Assuming that the media affect people's attitudes about many things, including drug use, this study examines how drugs are being shown on prime time television in the United States. The media rather uniformly depicts users of illegal drugs to be abusers, while users of legal drugs rarely experience any untoward effects in their drug use. The most startling finding is the phenomenal amount of inconsequential drug use on television. With respect to illicit drugs, the substances are shown as almost always producing negative consequences, frequently with dire results. ^United\States ^Drug\Use ^Society ^Media

1081. **MacDonald, Scott B.** (1988). *Dancing on a Volcano: The Latin American Drug Trade.* New York: Praeger. Based on a substantial bibliography and numerous personal contacts and interviews, the author explores the nature and extent of the Latin American drug trade, including Caribbean producers—Jamaica and Belize—and the Cuban and Nicaraguan connections. The author has attempted to bring scholarly research up to the pace of current events. Are there any solutions to the drug trade? Any considered must be viewed in the context of history. After all, the current narcotics epidemic is not unique. Consider China under various dynasties. China's approach in the 1700s and 1800s was prohibition and interdiction. Neither was successful. Eradication, done under the communists after 1949, was done with repressive techniques. Malaysia and Singapore have death penalties for traffickers. Singapore also imposes stiff penalties on users (the demand side). While drug use has declined, Singapore is still not completely free. While the Singaporian model, which allowed for enforced incarceration to detoxify users (cold turkey) worked relatively well for Singapore, does it offer a model for the United States and Latin American nations? No. Prohibition, interdiction, and targeting the user for particular applications are not applicable to the Americas. Should, therefore, drugs such as cocaine and marijuana be legalized? This is an approach that the Netherlands has taken. Yet, even here, the problems of drug use have not been resolved. Historically, antidrug campaigns have never been entirely successful; some people will always take drugs: There is a need for governments to recognize that a scorched-earth policy against all users is beyond any government's capabilities. Thus, under certain circumstances, marijuana should be prescribed and be made available. The circumstances would include the terminally ill and patients with certain diseases. Beyond that, however, both hard and soft drugs should not be decriminalized or legalized. Both supply and demand approaches to drug control are required, ranging from crop eradication to greater public awareness. As far as the supply side is concerned, one possible option not yet attempted is to link debt and drugs together in one antinarcotic package. ^Latin\America ^Drug\Traffic ^Drug\Control\Policies\History ^Reviews ^Bibliographies ^Jamaica ^Caribbean ^Belize ^Cuba ^Nicaragua ^Netherlands ^Europe ^Malaysia ^Singapore ^Southeast\Asia ^Crop\Eradication ^Treatment\Compulsory ^Decriminalization\Critique ^Supply ^Demand ^P\S\International\Debt

1082. —— (1989). *Mountain High, White Avalanche: Cocaine and Power in the Andean States and Panama.* New York: Praeger Publishers. The contribution of the cocaine trade to a possible deterioration of the political environment in the Andean states has the potential to create a most severe security threat to the United States and allied democratic governments in the Western Hemisphere. Already the continuing problems of narcoterrorism present significant threats to Colombia's national security. It may be that the problem in Colombia is uncontainable now, but, although Bolivia and Peru are being swept down the slopes in an avalanche of cocaine, the danger can be contained. Venezuela and Ecuador increasingly attract cocaine trafficking as well as production. There is potential for major national security problems in these countries. In terms of consequences of drug trading, Panama perhaps is one of the worst cases of involvement in the trade (as far as small nations are concerned). Unless a more coherent U.S. policy gives the Andean states of South America higher priority, the tremors already developing in the region will trigger the ultimate avalanche. ^ Panama ^Latin\America ^ Peru ^ Bolivia ^ Colombia ^ Venezuela ^ Ecuador ^ United\States ^ Cocaine ^ Drug\Traffic ^ Drug\Control\Policies ^ Insurgents ^ Consequences\Political ^ Consequences\Foreign\Policy ^ Terrorists ^ Consequences\National\Security ^ Drug\Control\Policies\Critique

1083. —— (1989). "Slaying the Drug Hydra." *SAIS Review* 9(1): 65–85. Suppressing or otherwise interfering with drug trafficking/consumption is essential if America is to overcome the interrelated health, societal, and national security problems fostered by it. This article discusses the scope of the problem, and its interrelatedness, and offers elements of a drug policy for the Bush administration. The author makes specific recommendations for the U.S. "drug czar," discusses the legalization issue and notes both specific and broad policy options in the area of foreign policy and also in the management of international debt. The general orientation is to use every policy now in the Drug Enforcement Administration's handbag and also to develop coordinated foreign policy initiatives. ^ United\States ^ Drug\Control\Policies ^ Proffered\Solutions ^ P\S\Legalization\Critique ^ Consequences\Misc ^ Consequences\Foreign\Policy ^ P\S\International\Debt

1084. McDonnell, Patrick (1988). "Odds Still with Smugglers in U.S. Air War against Drugs." *The Los Angeles Times*, 18 July, 3. The judgment is made by a director of Customs Aviation Operations that an experienced smuggling pilot is unlikely to be caught entering the United States from Mexico. ^United\States ^Interdiction ^Customs ^Drug\Control\Policies\Effectiveness

1085. McFadden, Robert D. (1989). "Federal Drug Agency Takes Center Stage." *The New York Times*, 10 March. The federal Drug Enforcement Administration now finds itself in a national spotlight as U.S. President Bush has kicked off an antidrug crusade, listing the DEA as the nation's primary agency in its war against cocaine, heroin, and other illegal drugs. ^United\States ^Drug\Control\Policies ^DEA

1086. McGlothlin, W. H. (1980). "The Singapore Heroin Control Programme." *Bulletin on Narcotics* 32(1): 1–14. Following a sudden and precipitous increase in 1975 of heroin use (involving up to 3 percent of the young males in the country), the government responded in 1977 with an all-out enforcement strategy aimed at rapid containment. To reduce demand, large-scale maneuvers were implemented to arrest suspected users and commit those with positive tests to mandatory rehabilitation centers. This article describes the rehabilitation emphasis (instilling discipline, social responsibility, and sound work habits), the release policy, and so forth. With respect to supply reduction, the programs were not immediately successful. While new heroin cases are minimal, there is some evidence of increased use of cannabis, psychotropic drugs, and alcohol. Overall the epidemic appears to have been controlled. ^Southeast\Asia ^Singapore ^Heroin ^Law\Enforcement ^Treatment ^Demand ^Rehabilitation ^Supply ^Alcohol

1087. McGlothlin, William H., Kay Jamison, and Steven Rosenblatt (1981). "Marijuana Criminal Justice and the Use of Other Drugs." In *Criminal Justice and Drugs: The Unresolved Connection*, edited by James C. Weissman and Robert L. DuPont. Point Washington, N.Y.: Kennikat Press. From questionnaire data and other sources, the authors examine the degree to which cannabis regulation (reduced availability) results in people's increasing their consumption of both alcohol and other illicit intoxicants. While marijuana use is a "gateway" to other drugs, a matter established by much research, there is a need to consider how reducing the supply of marijuana might also cause people to turn to more injurious competing intoxicants. ^Cannabis ^Law\Enforcement ^Drug\Use ^Drug\Control\Policies ^Drug\Control\Policies\Critique

1088. McGovern, Thomas L. III (1987). "Employee Drug-Testing Legislation: Redrawing the Battlelines in the War on Drugs." *Stanford Law Review* 39:1453–517. Argument for using drug testing in "safety-only" conditions so that testing could not be used as a weapon against social malaise or "impurity." Thus a certain amount of limited drug testing is not only acceptable but legally justified. Moreover, a "safety-only approach" will protect the majority of employees who would otherwise be vulnerable because they have little to shield them from incorrect testing or inappropriately applied procedures. ^United\States ^Drug\Use ^Workplace ^Public\Safety ^Drug\Testing ^Consequences\Human\Rights

1089. McGuire, Phillip C. (1988). "Jamaican Posses: A Call for Cooperation Among Law Enforcement Agencies." *The Police Chief* (January): 20. Discussion of the development of "Jamaican posses" (gangs) and their current involvement in drug trafficking and associated violence and murder. Six hundred of these murders are thought to have occurred in the United States at their hands. ^United\States ^Drug\Traffic ^Organized\Crime ^Consequences\Violence ^Jamaica ^Caribbean

1090. McKinley, James C., Jr. (1989). "Friendships and Fear Erode a Will to Fight Drugs in Brooklyn." *The New York Times*, 18 September, A13. Describes the activities of isolated residents in drug neighborhoods to move traffickers out, as well as the fear and intimidation for the whole neighborhood that results. Residents in a New York neighborhood applauded the efforts but will not join in the campaign against drug dealers. Description of how some cope with this psychological trauma. The economics that bring young people into the drug trade are discussed, along with other demographic features associated with low-income neighborhoods. ^United\States ^Drug\Traffic ^Economics ^Law\Enforcement ^Private\Initiatives ^New\York ^Traffickers\Incentives\Economic ^Consequences\Social

1091. McNicoll, Andre (1983). *Drug Trafficking; A North-South Perspective.* Ottawa, Canada: The North-South Institute. This study seeks to shed additional light on the relative roles of supply and demand in the dangerous drug trade. Up to its publication, most discussions tended to concentrate on supply and prosecution as opposed to demand and prevention. The author focuses also on producer societies and their economies as contributors to the international flow of illegal narcotics. The drug trade is a huge economic factor in some developing economies. Insofar as economics are an explanatory variable, can rural development be an antidote? Can crop substitution provide some solutions? The author is not very optimistic. ^Drug\Traffic ^Drug\Control\Policies ^Economics ^Reviews ^Supply ^Demand ^Producers ^Drug\Control\Policies\Critique ^Consequences\Economic ^P\S\Economic ^Crop\Substitution ^P\S\Critique

1092. McWeeney, Sean M. (1987). "The Sicilian Mafia and Its Impact on the United States." *FBI Law Enforcement Bulletin* (February): 1–9. Reviews the historical development of organized crime in Italy and its transplantation, by immigration, to the United States. The Sicilian mafia is reviewed, in particular, its relationship to criminal activities associated with heroin and cocaine trafficking. The Sicilian mafia has had a substantial impact on crime in the United States since the turn of the century. Currently it is in control of a worldwide heroin distribution network. ^United\States ^Heroin ^Drug\Traffic ^Organized\Crime

1093. Mabry, Donald (1988). "The US Military and the War on Drugs in Latin America." *Journal of Interamerican Studies and World Affairs* 30:2 & 3(Summer/Fall): 77–86. The U.S. Military has been under pressure and constraint to deal with the supply of drugs coming into the United States. This article examines the military's current efforts in drug interdiction, the demands for its increased participation, and the efforts by the Department of Defense to distance the military from drug engagements. The author analyses implementation problems of the new demands: logistical difficulties of maritime and border interdiction, problems of corruption within the military if faced with the drug trade, assault on civil liberties because militaries are not trained for police work, and the cost effectiveness of the policies. Ten policy recommendations are given. ^United\States ^Drug\Control\Policies ^Military ^Department\of\Defense

1094. Machalaba, Daniel (1989). "Shipping Lines Fall Prey to Drug Dealers." *The Asian Wall Street Journal,* 22 May, 9. Discusses the pervasive extent to which legitimate shipping has become a target for smuggling, aided in part by organized narcotics criminals, but also by corrupted shipping lines employees and dockyard guards. Signaled out for particular criticism is the port at Kingston, Jamaica. Some companies, consequently, have boycotted making further deliveries from Kingston to the United States, a factor that has hit Kingston hard. The port has seen its business fall by 50 percent in the past twelve months. ^Jamaica ^Drug\Traffic ^Consequences\Corruption ^Caribbean ^Private\Initiatives ^Consequences\Economic ^Consequences\Political

1095. Maitland, Derek (1981). "Once Again, a Golden Triangle." *Maclean's,* 26 January, 33. Production problems in the Golden Triangle in the late 1970s and in 1980 radically reduced opium supplies. Prices skyrocketed: a block of raw opium rose from $85 to $850 in just twelve months. Good weather returned, some political arrangements were made, and the Golden Triangle began once again to export massive amounts of opium and heroin products. ^Southeast\Asia ^Opiates ^Drug\Traffic ^Golden\Triangle ^Statistics ^Consequences\Economic ^Production

1096. Malcolm, Andrew H. (1990). "Weapon in Drug War: Imagination." *The New York Times,* February 2, A15. Describes changing tactics among many urban American police departments in dealing with drug use and traffic in the inner cities. The change is motivated by police dissatisfaction with the criminal justice system.

Police arrest users and traffickers only to see them reappear on the streets as they emerge from a judicial system that cannot handle the strain. The new police tactic-imagination-is a psychological offensive that involves intimidation and high-visibility police presence on the street. The police appear in force in notorious neighborhoods and make drug customers highly uncomfortable. ^Drug\Control\Policies ^Law\Enforcement ^Prevention\Law\Enforcement ^United\States

1097. Malloy, James (1987). "Bolivia's Economic Crisis." *Current History* (January): 9–38. In 1987 Bolivia was in a state of crisis, perhaps the worst in the nation's history. After thirty years of authoritarian rule, the country attempted to reestablish a mass-based civil democratic rule. Imposition of an austerity program contributed to economic destabilization and forced upon the new administration additional internal pressures even as its policy options became more limited. Brief mention of the drug trade. The growing economic and political power of the cocaine barons has reduced the policy options in Bolivia for recovery. The Bolivian government has therefore petitioned the United States for $100 million in direct aid to sustain the anticocaine effort and to maintain the economy. ^Latin\America ^Bolivia ^Cocaine ^Drug\Traffic ^Economics

1098. Manatt, Marsha (1983). *Parents, Peers and Pot II: Parents in Action*. Rockville, Md.: National Institute on Drug Abuse. Description of various citizen groups, with individuals coming from a wide variety of religious, political, and ethnic backgrounds, who have begun a movement for drug-free youth that has become national in scope and long range in aim. The intent in this publication is to introduce the movement as a potential replicable model for others to follow in the war on drugs. ^United\States ^Prevention ^Youth ^Family ^NIDA ^Private\Initiatives

1099. Mandel, Jerry (1988). "Is Marijuana Law Enforcement Racist?" *Journal of Psychoactive Drugs* 20(1): 83–91. Marijuana felony arrests for Latinos and to a lesser extent blacks soared from 1980 to 1985, when it plunged for whites. The economic options that drive minorities into the trade, therefore making them more vulnerable to arrest, are discussed. A call is made to reverse the arrest procedures. ^United\States ^Cannabis ^Drug\Traffic ^Minorities ^Law\Enforcement ^Traffickers\Incentives\Economic ^Drug\Control\Policies\Critique

1100. Manning, Peter K. (1980). *The Narcs' Game: Organizational and Informational Limits on Drug Law Enforcement*. Cambridge, Mass.: MIT Press. Describes the informational and organizational constraints on drug policing, which are not included in official claims. Shows the gap that exists between police rhetoric designed for administrative self-assurance and public relations and what police drug control units can do or are now doing. ^Law\Enforcement ^Bureaucracy ^Drug\Control\Policies\Critique

1101. Maranto, Gina (1985). "Coke: The Random Killer." *Discover* (March): 16–21. General survey for a popular audience of the current scientific findings showing that cocaine is unsafe at almost any dose. ^Cocaine ^Drug\Use ^Consequences\Health

1102. Marcus, Ruth (1988). "Assault on Cartel Fails to Halt Drugs; Prosecutors Say Leader of Colombian Group Smuggled Tons of Cocaine into the U.S." *The Washington Post*, 15 February, A4. Describes the prosecution of Carlos Lehder in a Florida court. Pulling together the Colombian cartel, in Lehder's absence, is also discussed. ^ United\States ^ Latin\America ^ Colombia ^ Cocaine ^ Drug\Traffic ^ Organized\Crime ^ Law\Enforcement ^ Traffickers ^ Drug\Control\Policies\Critique ^ Supply

1103. Mardon, Mark (1988). "The Big Push." *Sierra* (November-December): 67–75. A journalist's description of coca/cocaine activities in the Upper Huallaga Valley of Peru. Included are impressionistic discussions about drug-enforcement activities, crop eradication efforts, substitution programs, and coca/cocaine trafficking. The author discusses these issues with particular reference to the environmental impact on the Upper Huallaga Valley's rain forests and rivers. ^Latin\America ^Peru ^Coca ^Drug\Traffic ^Drug\Control\Policies ^Consequences\Environmental ^Cocaine ^Law\Enforcement ^Crop\Eradication

1104. Marek, Andzej E., and Shawomir Redo (1978). "Drug Abuse in Poland." *Bulletin on Narcotics* 30(1): 43–53. Because drug abuse in Poland has been a lesser problem than alcoholism, only recently have drugs become a subject of interest. Describes events as they existed in the 1970s as well as provisions of Polish criminal law to fight drug abuse. ^Europe ^Poland ^Drug\Use ^Law\Enforcement ^Drug\Control\Policies

1105. Margolia, Mac (1986). "Bolivian Economy Hooked on Cocaine." *The Christian Science Monitor*, 14 May, 1. In spite of Bolivia's official statistics showing it to be economically straight jacketed, Bolivians survive, and some even flourish. Many economists call it a full-employment economy, due, mostly, to the clandestine trade in illegal drugs. As the successful people accumulate wealth and organize, they bring armed groups around them which pose a risk for the newly constituted government. ^Latin\America ^Bolivia ^Cocaine ^Drug\Traffic ^Economics ^Informal\Economy ^Consequences\Illegal\Economy ^Consequences\Social ^Consequences\Political ^Consequences\Sovereignty ^Traffickers\Private\Armies

1106. "Marijuana Crop: Moonshine Again" (1990). *The Economist*, October 20, p. 25. Kentucky has a thriving marijuana industry. State authorities are working vigorously to destroy it. The socioeconomic base of production (in eastern Kentucky's poorest counties) and official efforts to destroy the crop are described. ^United\States ^Kentucky ^Economics ^Cannabis ^Production\Incentives\Economic

1107. "Marijuana More Harmful than Tobacco" (1987). *New Scientist*, 17 December, 15. A summary of a report in the *British Medical Journal* that people who smoke marijuana run a greater risk of damaging their lungs than those who smoke tobacco. ^Cannabis ^Health ^Consequences\Physiological ^Tobacco

1108. Marks, Robert (1990). "A Freer Market for Heroin in Australia: Alternatives to Subsidizing Organized Crime." *The Journal of Drug Issues* 20:1(Winter): 131–76. Australia has had stringent enforcement policies against heroin importation, manufacture, distribution, possession, and use. The author describes the laws and social attitudes toward heroin use in Australia and then, from an economic framework for analyzing black markets, examines various policy options, including an increased tightening of prohibition on heroin supply and a reduction in demand for the drug. Supply restrictions have increased the costs that society must bear, as evidenced in criminality and police corruption. Freer availability of heroin would impose fewer costs on society than do failed prohibition policies. ^Australia ^Drug\Control\Policies\Critique ^Heroin ^Theories ^Informal\Economy ^P\S\Partial\Prohibition ^P\S\Controlled\Sales ^Consequences\Crime ^Consequences\Corruption

1109. Marquand, Robert (1989). "Fatal Attraction for Inner-City Teens: An Honor Student Done in by Drugs." *The Christian Science Monitor*, 22 March. From a specific case, the discussion moves on to examine ghetto culture and the attraction, within that culture, of narcotics for the youth. ^United\States ^Drug\Use ^Youth ^Society ^Culture ^Minorities ^Consequences\Personal

1110. Marriott, Michel (1989). "After Three Years, Crack Plague in New York Only Gets Worse." *The New York Times*, 20 February, 1. Despite more than $500 million spent by New York City in the previous year on drug-related enforcement alone, more than twice the amount than in 1986, crack is more pervasive and prevalent than ever before, and its effects are more violent and insidious on poor people in New York City. Crack has contributed to a soaring homicide rate (up over 10 percent); it has more than tripled the number of cocaine users since 1986; it has contributed to a tripling of the cases in which parents under the influence of drugs abuse or neglect their children; and it has accounted for much of the surge in prisoners entering the city's prison system. ^United\States ^Cocaine ^Crack ^Drug\Use ^Law\Enforcement ^New\York ^Drug\Control\Policies\Effectiveness ^Consequences\Violence ^Parenting ^Consequences\Family ^Consequences\Crime

1111. ——— (1989). "And in the Streets, Citizens Fight Dealers." *The New York Times*, 14 August, A1. Public housing project residents stand up to drug dealers. It is thought that this is a part of a trend beginning to emerge in other major urban centers such as Washington, D.C., Los Angeles, and Miami. Citywide networks are being created. Night patrols are being carried out. Some assaults are made on suspected drug dealers. ^United\States ^Law\Enforcement ^Public\Housing ^Private\Initiatives ^Consequences\Violence Washington\DC ^California ^Florida

1112. ——— (1989). "Drug Needle Exchange Is Gaining but Still under Fire." *The New York Times*, 7 June, B1. For the first half of 1989 and latter part of 1988, New York City has had a program to give intravenous drug addicts new hypodermic needles to help stem the spread of AIDS. The program has begun to attract more participants, but remains under attack. In fact, only 160 addicts have enrolled in a program intended for 400. Part of the purpose of the program is to conduct research to learn whether intravenous drug users can change their behavior and not share hypodermic syringes. ^United\States ^Heroin ^Health ^AIDS ^Drug\Control\Policies ^Needle\Exchange\Programs

1113. ——— (1989). "Latest Drug of Choice for Abusers Brings New Generation to Heroin." *The New York Times*, 13 July, A1. A highly addictive mixture of cocaine/crack and smokeable heroin has now emerged as a drug of choice among some New York chronic drug abusers, precisely at a time when it was thought that heroin use was winding down. The combination mixes the physical addiction of heroin with the intense high of crack. ^United\States ^Cocaine ^Crack ^Heroin ^Drug\Use ^New\York ^Consequences\Physiological

1114. ——— (1989). "New York Alters Needle Plan for Addicts to Combat AIDS." *The New York Times*, 30 January, 1. More discussion about the needle-exchange program, in this case institutionalized (supported by city government), in an attempt to determine if the spread of AIDS among addicts who share their needles can be slowed. ^United\States ^Heroin ^Health ^AIDS ^Drug\Control\Policies ^Needle\Exchange\Programs

1115. ——— (1989). "A Pioneer in Residential Drug Treatment Reaches Out." *The New York Times*, 13 November, A4. Describes the work of Daytop Village in New York, "The oldest and largest drug-treatment program in the United States." The Strategy is to use drug-free long-term residential treatment, assisted by reformed addicts. ^United\States ^Treatment

1116. Marsh, Jeanne C., and Nancy A. Miller (1985). "Female Clients in Substance Abuse Treatment." *The International Journal of the Addictions* 20(6-7): 995–1019. Women who are addicted are likely to be helped best by receiving programs of ancillary services designed to meet their particular needs, such as child care. ^Drug\Use ^Women ^Treatment\Integrated

1117. Marshall, Eliot (1988). "Drug Wars: Legalization Gets a Hearing." *Science* 241(2 September): 1157–59. Discussion of the evolution of thinking among a small number of politicians and academics that has led to open discussion and hearings about legalization. Peter Reuter is cited. Comparison with the Dutch and American experiences is made. ^United\States ^Netherlands ^Legalization

1118. ———— (1988). "Flying Blind in the War on Drugs." *Science* 240(17 June): 1605–07. Large amounts of money are being both expended and prepared to be expended, but hardly any strategy has emerged that would direct the spending. ^United\States ^Drug\Control\Policies ^Consequences\Economic ^Drug\Control\Policies\Effectiveness

1119. ———— (1988). "Testing Urine for Drugs." *Science* 241(8 July): 150–52. Urine tests to detect drugs are fast and reasonably accurate. Their use is still controversial. ^United\States ^Drug\Testing

1120. ———— (1988). "A War on Drugs with Real Troops?" *Science* 241(1 July): 13–15. Continuation of the discussion on the controversy over involvement of military forces in the war on drugs. ^United\States ^Drug\Control\Policies ^Military

1121. Martin, David (1984). "Victory on the High Seas." *Policy Review* 28: 72–74. Description of U.S. Navy policies aimed at motivating Navy personnel to avoid drug use. The consequences of the application of those policies are discussed. ^United\States ^Drug\Use ^Military ^Prevention ^Prevention\Critique

1122. Martin, Everett G. (1983). "A Little Cattle Town in Bolivia Is Thriving as a Financial Center." *The Wall Street Journal*, 17 February. On-site description of the general cocaine/coca traffic around Trinidad, Bolivia, the role of small aircraft in the transit of cocaine, and the economic impact of narcotics derived dollars on people and their community. ^Latin\America ^Bolivia ^Cocaine ^Drug\Traffic ^Consequences\Economic ^Coca

1123. ———— (1984). "High Drama in the Jungles of Peru: Fight against Cocaine Is a Tangled-up Affair." *The Wall Street Journal*, 20 March, 1. On-site description of the general traffic in coca and cocaine in Peru's upper Huallaga Valley and an analysis of why crop substitution programs have not been favorably received by the valley's peasants. ^Latin\America ^Peru ^Coca ^Production ^Cocaine ^Drug\Traffic ^Crop\Substitution ^Drug\Control\Policies\Critique

1124. Martz, Larry, et al. (1986). "Trying to Say No." *Newsweek*, 11 August, 14–19. Notes, with pessimism, the proffered solutions to the drug crisis that focus on cutting into the availability of the supply of drugs. If the supply cannot be shut off, perhaps demand can—by somehow persuading drug users to turn off, or even not to turn on in the first place. Notes the efforts of Muslims to have an impact on demand. Gives results of a poll regarding people's opinions about drug tests and dealing with narcotics traffickers. Notes Nancy Reagan's efforts, as the chief advocate of the Reagan administration, to reduce demand. ^United\States ^Prevention ^Supply ^Demand ^Private\Initiatives

1125. Mashberg, Tom (1990). "Drugs in Europe: Signs of a Spreading Plague." *The New York Times*, November 18, L21. The Colombians are looking at European integration in 1992 and at the integration of Eastern Europe into Western Europe. They are moving to create, if not supply, cocaine markets. The Europeans seem less concerned about these possibilities than do the Americans. ^Drug\Use ^Europe ^Traffickers ^Markets ^Cocaine ^Latin\America ^Colombia

1126. Massing, Michael (1989). "Don't Just Throw Money at the Drug Problem." *The Christian Science Monitor*, 6 November, 19. Criticizes the law enforcement approach to drug control. ^Law\Enforcement\Critique

1127. ———— (1990). "In the Cocaine War, the Jungle Is Winning." *The New York Times Magazine*, March 4, pp. 26, 88–91. Describes efforts of the Drug Enforcement Administration to destroy coca production in Peru. Coca exports earn more than $1 billion annually and provide employment for more than one million of Peru's twenty-one million people. The real enemy is not coca, however, but guerrillas, poverty, and the jungle. Describes the secure military base at Santa Lucía and how its antidrug operations are carried out. Economic incentives and relative prices are discussed. Incentives for bush pilots may amount to $15,000 per flight. The U.S. government's antidrug aid program is described. ^Latin\America ^Peru ^DEA\Critique ^Production ^Producers\Incentives\Economic ^Foreign\Aid ^Consequences\Economic

1128. Mathews, Jay (1988). "Cocaine Seizures up in California; Big Rise Attributed to Rerouting of Drug Traffic from Florida." *The Washington Post*, 2 January, A3. The large increase in cocaine seizures in California is attributed to the rerouting of the drug traffic from Florida where clampdowns have been successful. There may also be a relationship between increased seizures, greater resources available to drug enforcement agencies, and heavier cocaine production in South America. ^United\States ^Cocaine ^Drug\Traffic ^Interdiction ^Florida ^California ^Production

1129. ——— (1989). "Cities Target Drug Dealers for Eviction; N.Y. Renters Ousted before Criminal Trial." *The Washington Post*, 12 February, A15. Top officials in New York and Los Angeles, the nation's two largest cities, are evicting people arrested for drug dealing from public housing, before any criminal trials. ^United\States ^Drug\Control\Policies ^Public\Housing ^New\York ^California

1130. Mattingly, Mack, Peter W. Rodino, Jr., Harold L. Volkmer, Bill McCollum, Robert W. Kastenmeier, George W. Gekas, William Clay, and John Conyers (1986). "Should Congress Authorize Use of the Death Penalty for Continuing Criminal Enterprise Drug Offenses?" *Congressional Digest* (November): 280–87. A pro-con debate by representative Mack Mattingly and Peter W. Rodino on whether the death penalty amendment, proposed by Mattingly, should be adopted. Several other congressmen add their views both in favor of and opposed to the amendment. ^United\States ^Law\Enforcement ^P\S\Death\Penalty

1131. Mauer, Richard (1990). "Alaskans to Vote on Marijuana Use." *The New York Times*, October 25, A16. Fifteen years after the Alaskan supreme court legalized possession of small amounts of marijuana, voters have chosen, through an initiative for the November ballot, to test whether that law should stand. Described is the antidrug crusade and the positions various interest groups have taken on this ballot initiative. ^United\States ^Alaska ^Legislation ^Drug\Control\Politics

1132. Maugh, Thomas H. (1982). "Marijuana 'Justifies Serious Concern.'" *Science* 215(19 March): 1488–89. Review of a new report on marijuana issued in February 1982 by the Institute of Medicine of the National Academy of Sciences (marijuana and health) which suggests that cannabis has some potentially harmful effects, as well as some possible therapeutic uses. ^Cannabis ^Consequences\Health

1133. Maugh, Thomas H., II (1989). "Drug Seems to Block Users' Cocaine Need." *The Los Angeles Times*, 25 August, 1. A report on the work of two Harvard scientists published in August in the *Journal of Science* suggesting that a pain-killing drug dramatically reduces the craving for both cocaine and heroin. If successful, this would be the first medication that effectively blocks the craving for cocaine (as opposed to current use of antidepressants to help wean cocaine addicts from their addiction). The drug is buprenorphine. It is already being studied for use in treating heroin addiction. The drug appears not to be addictive. ^Cocaine ^Heroin ^Treatment\Antagonists

1134. Maykut, Madelaine O. (1984). *Health Consequences of Acute and Chronic Marijuana Use*. New York: Pergamon Press. Deals with the metabolism, toxicology, and pharmacodynamics of cannabis. Looks at the physiological effects and complications associated with cannabis abuse. The author has done a search of original literature to try to find out why certain alleged controversies exist about the consequences of the use of marijuana. She looks into the conditions of reported investigations such as subject studied; materials used, including potency, dose, route and/or mode of administration; frequency and duration of doses used; previous drug use; and state of health of the subjects studied. Representative papers have been reviewed depicting only part of the available massive literature. The author stressed clinical investigations and, where these were lacking, basic and animal research noting clinical implications which should be watched in future clinical studies. The study includes a short discussion on the chemistry and metabolism of marijuana, followed by more detailed study of the cellular metabolic effects in the body. There is also a discussion on the effects of marijuana on the reproductive and central nervous systems. ^Cannabis ^Reviews ^Consequences\Physiological ^Consequences\Pharmacological

1135. Mecca, Andrew M. (1982). "A Cultural Response to Alcohol and Drug Abuse in America." *Contemporary Drug Problems* 11(1): 159–67. The author's intent is to provide a context within which people may consider the underlying reasons why humankind ingests psychoactive substances, noting that, particularly in America, it is done on a huge scale—laxatives, coffee, tea, cigarettes, tranquilizers, soft drinks, alcoholic beverages. He advances that the only viable response to abuse is a cultural transformation emphasizing independence, assertiveness, and responsibility. ^United\States ^Drug\Control\Policies ^Society ^Culture ^Drug\Use\Theories ^P\S\Culture

1136. Mecham, Michael (1989). "Drug Smugglers Prove Elusive Targets for Interdiction Forces." *Aviation Week and Space Technology*, 30 January, 34–36. Contains a series of stories on airborne drug interdiction which highlight the difficulty of interdicting airborne drug traffic. ^United\States ^Interdiction ^Drug\Control\Policies\Effectiveness

1137. Mechoulam, Raphael (1984). "Research on Cannabis: An Overview." *Impact of Science on Society* 34(133): 23–31. Discussion of the typical structure of some of the natural cannabinoids, their synthesis, metabolism, and toxicity. Several behavioral and clinical impacts are noted, as well as the effects of cannabis on biological systems such as the reproductive system. ^Cannabis ^Health ^Reviews

1138. *Medicinal Plants as Economic Replacement Crops for Opium Poppy in Northern Thailand* (1981). 2 vols. Chiang Mai, Thailand: Chiang Mai University. Domestically consumed medicinal plants were selected for experimentation during a three-year period. Attention was given not only to the plants but to developing markets for their commercialization. It was not thought that an export market would be found. In particular, medicinal plants that could be used by domestic pharmaceutical industries were investigated. Promising plants were identified. ^Thailand ^Opiates ^Crop\Substitution

1139. Meier, Berry (1989). "Police Using New Tests to Stop the Drugged Driver." *The New York Times*, 25 September, 1. Describes a new test that police officers are being trained to use to identify quickly drug-impaired drivers. The test combines physical and toxicological procedures and is thought to be fairly accurate in discriminating the kinds of drugs that a driver may have taken, prior to a more formal medical examination. ^United\States ^Drug\Use ^Public\Safety ^Law\Enforcement ^Drug\Testing

1140. Mellinger, Glen D., Robert H. Somers, Susan T. Davison, and Dean I. Manheimer (1976). "The Amotivational Syndrome and the College Student." In *Chronic Cannabis Use. Annals of the New York Academy of Sciences*, 282:37–55. People go to college, usually, to find self-fulfilling and socially useful roles in society. Does drug use impair the process that produces such people, producing instead what is called an "amotivational syndrome" of apathy, mental confusion, and lack of goals? As measured by the incidence of dropping out, as well as grades and career indecision, the authors' analysis, in all their cases, suggest that sociocultural factors account for most of the relation of drug use to adverse outcomes *in this normal population*. There is, however, a small residual relation that may be due to the amotivational syndrome, to other personality factors, or to some idiosyncratic combination of factors. Particularly is this true among multiple drug users and not those who use only marijuana. ^Cannabis ^Health ^Amotivational\Syndrome

1141. Melton, R. H. (1989). "Virginia National Guard Enlisted in Drug War." *The Washington Post*, 23 June, C1. National Guardsmen, acting as volunteers, are enlisted to do undercover work. ^United\States ^Drug\Control\Policies ^Military ^National\Guard ^Virginia

1142. Méndez Asensio, Luís (1985). *Caro Quintero al Trasluz.* Mexico City: Plaza and Janes. A biography, of sorts, of one of Mexico's most noted narcotraffickers. Within the context of the biography, Mexico's antidrug efforts and the limitations placed on those by the corrupting influence of the narcotraffickers is noted. Because Caro Quintero's operations are intimately associated with the abduction and brutal slaying of U.S. DEA agent Enrique Camarena, his name appears throughout the pages. ^Latin\America ^Mexico ^Drug\Traffic ^Traffickers ^Consequences\Corruption ^Drug\Control\Policies\Effectiveness ^DEA

1143. Mendhiratta, Sarbjit S., Vijoy K. Varma, Ravinder Dang, Anil K. Malhotra, Karobie Das, and Ritu Nehra (1988). "Cannabis and Cognitive Functions: A Re-Evaluation Study." *British Journal of Addiction* 83:749–53. A matched-pair, systematic study shows significant additional deterioration among chronic users of cannabis on a number of psychological measures, which are specified in the article. Thus, the article corroborates the findings of others on impairment of cognitive functions associated with long-term heavy cannabis use. ^Cannabis ^Health ^Consequences\Neurological ^Consequences\Psychological

1144. Mendis, N. (1985). "Heroin Addiction among Young People: A New Development in Sri Lanka." *Bulletin on Narcotics* 37(2-3): 25–29. Heroin addiction is a recent phenomenon in Sri Lanka, and it has been on the increase in recent years. This article summarizes the results of a study of 100 heroin addicts treated in the psychiatry unit of the general hospital at Colombo in 1983 and 1984. The generalized estimates vary from 2,000 to 10,000 addicts in Sri Lanka. Heroin seems to be freely available in most major urban centers and tourist areas in the country. ^Southeast\Asia ^Sri\Lanka ^Heroin ^Drug\Use ^Youth

1145. Mendoza, Ramon (1984). "Prevention of Drug Abuse among Students: A Spanish Approach." *Impact of Science on Society* 34(133): 97–109. Discussion of Spain's new drug education program and its new drug legislation. Spaniards view the problem as having sociocultural and economic roots, with heroin addicts building on the psychology of habitual smokers of tobacco, alcoholics, users of legally prescribed drugs, and habitual smokers of cannabis. ^Europe ^Spain ^Drug\Use ^Prevention ^Youth ^Society ^Prevention\Drug\Education ^Legislation ^Drug\Use\Theories

1146. Merrick, Joav (1985). "Addicted Mothers and Their Children: Research Results from Denmark." *International Journal of Rehabilitation* 8(1): 79–84. Reviews the effects of alcohol and drug abuse on fetuses in four Danish cities. The extent of maternal drug abuse is correlated with obstetric complications and developmental characteristics of the fetus. The effects of an unstable fetal life carry over into childhood. With proper care, many of those effects can be overcome. ^Scandinavia ^Denmark ^Drug\Use ^Alcohol ^Consequences\Fetuses ^Consequences\Children

1147. Messick, M. James (1985). "Postal Interdiction of Marijuana." *The Police Chief* (October): 72–95. Description of how postal authorities in Alaska, following a precedent set in Hawaii, set about to determine if the mails were being used substantially for the shipment of marijuana. A "package profile" was developed for detecting suspected shipments. The U.S. mails represent a significant conduit for illegal drugs. ^United\States ^Cannabis ^Interdiction ^Alaska ^Drug\Traffic

1148. *Mexican Topics: Questions Involving Mexico That Have Aroused International Public Interest* (1986). Mexico, D.F.: Government of Mexico. This Mexican government white paper, which presents the de la Madrid administration in its arguably most favorable light regarding a number of domestic and international issues, is of interest to this bibliography for its section on Mexico's "permanent campaign against drug trafficking." The discussion fully admits to Mexico's involvement in drug traffic, but suggests that international demand factors, principally in the United States, are an important factor that has made Mexico a victim in the trafficking enterprise. ^Latin\America ^Mexico ^Drug\Traffic ^Drug\Control\Policies ^Supply ^Demand

1149. "Mexico—A Profile" (1985). *Drug Enforcement* (Summer): 11-18. Describes marijuana, opium, and cocaine trafficking, including the economics of that trafficking. Land smuggling routes, utilization of Mexican airstrips, and the drug-enforcement situation in Mexico are discussed. ^Latin\America ^Mexico ^Cannabis ^Opiates ^Cocaine ^Drug\Traffic ^Law\Enforcement ^Traffickers\Incentives\Economic

1150. Meyer, Roger E. (1975). "Psychiatric Consequences of Marihuana Use: The State of the Evidence." In *Marijuana and Health Hazards: Methodological Issues in Current Marijuana Research*, edited by J. R. Tinklenberg. New York: Academic Press. As of the writing of this paper, a question that persisted regarding marijuana and health concerns the psychiatric consequences of different degrees of marijuana use. Acknowledging that the literature is a "crazy quilt of clinical descriptions occasionally backed by the 'implications' of laboratory investigation," the author examines the question in several discrete categories, including acute adverse reactions, flashbacks, prolonged reactions, triggering of schizophrenic reactions, cannabis psychosis, nonpsychotic prolonged adverse reactions, and the relationship of marijuana-induced behavior as a function of toxicity. Within the context of tremendous changes in values and life style that have occurred through 1975, it might be extremely difficult to sort out a specific etiological role for marijuana. While the data are not definitive, marijuana use is likely to be one aspect of social change rather than the responsible agent. ^Cannabis ^Reviews ^Consequences\Psychological ^Consequences\Social ^Society ^Consequences\Critique

1151. ——— (1986). "Psychobiology and the Treatment of Drug Dependence: The Biobehavioral Interface." *American Journal of Drug and Alcohol Abuse* 12(3): 223–33. With respect to the etiology of compulsive drug consumption, there appears to be an interface of drugs, brain function, and behavior. Among humans, linkages are embellished by effective states, interpersonal relationships, and the environment. The paper provides an overview of research on the psychobiology of drug dependence with implications for the clinician. ^Drug\Use ^Treatment ^Reviews ^Consequences\Physiological ^Consequences\Psychological

1152. "Miami Beach's New Approach in Drug Arrests: Tell the Employers" (1990). *The New York Times*, November 23, B21. In a move that has upset the American Civil Liberties Union, police in Miami Beach are now required to report drug arrests to employers. It is thought that this will deter drug abuse. ^United\States ^Florida ^Drug\Control\Policies ^Workplace

1153. Michel, James H. (1983). "Cuban Involvement in Narcotics Trafficking." *Department of State Bulletin* 83(2077): 86. A State Department white paper describing the apparent sanctioning by Cuba of narcotics trafficking and its profiting from that trafficking as a means to finance political subversion in Latin America. ^Latin\America ^Cuba ^Drug\Traffic ^Insurgents ^Consequences\Foreign\Relations

1154. Miike, Lawrence, and Maria Hewitt (1988). "Accuracy and Reliability of Urine Drug Tests." *Kansas University Law Review* 36:641–81. The physical intrusion increasingly required to collect reliable urine samples, and the fact that drugs are detectable in urine for a substantial amount of time, raises fundamental questions as to whether requiring urine testing as a condition of employment is reasonable. In an extensively annotated article, the authors examine the drugs for which urine screening is done, how urine drug screening tests work, and confirmatory testing done by some laboratories and the accuracy or reliability of the tests that they do. All of this is compromised by the fact that there is considerable chance for error in mass testing, and even a small error rate will represent large numbers of people. Alternatives to urine testing are mentioned. ^Drug\Testing\Critique

1155. Mikuriya, Tod H. (1968). "Physical, Mental, and Moral Effects of Marijuana: The Indian Hemp Drugs Commission Report." *The International Journal of the Addictions* 3(2): 253–70. In 1894 a volume by the Indian Hemp Drugs Commission was published, comprising seven volumes and 3,281 pages. That was a landmark study and summarized virtually all of the evidence available to date regarding the effects attributed to hemp drugs. This article reviews the substance of those seven volumes and the conclusions to which the commission came. As for physical effects, the moderate use of hemp drugs is practically attended by no evil results at all; as for mental effects, no injurious effects on the mind were noted; as for moral effects, there is no moral injury whatever. On the other hand, excessive consumption, it was noted, had moral, mental, and physical effects that were negative. ^Cannabis ^Reviews ^Consequences\Physiological^Consequences\Critique^Consequences\Neurological^Values^Consequences\Social

1156. Mikuriya, Tod H., and Michael R. Aldrich (1988). "Cannabis 1988: Old Drug, New Dangers; The Potency Question." *Journal of Psychoactive Drugs* 20(1): 47–55. There has been a "new marijuana" scare alleging that the potency in newly marketed varieties is anywhere from four to ten times higher than in the past. Beware, therefore. The scare tactics of the new marijuana proponents are not only inaccurate but irrelevant. All of it is a product of a disinformation campaign. This will have the effect of reducing the legitimacy and credibility of drug counselors. ^Cannabis ^Health ^Consequences\Critique ^Refining

1157. "Milestones in the War on Drugs" (1987). *Nova Law Review* 11:1041–48. Gives a chronological breakdown, since 1914 through October 1986, of the legal and statutory war on drugs. Also included are dates and places of major events, such as drug seizures. ^United\States ^Law\Enforcement ^Legislation ^Drug\Control\Policies\History ^Interdiction

1158. Miller, Dave (1988). "Drug Mafia Arms Campesinos." *Latinamerica Press*, 14 July, 6. It is believed that drug traffickers are creating a potential battlefield in Bolivia's Chapare region by arming peasant coca growers. The region's peasants recently had demanded that U.S. drug control advisors be expelled from the country. ^Latin\America ^Bolivia ^Coca ^Drug\Traffic ^Traffickers\Private\Armies ^Producers\Unions ^Consequences\Political ^Consequences\Foreign\Relations

1159. Miller, George W., Jr. (1985). "The Cocaine Habit." *American Family Physician* 31(2): 173–76. Alerts physicians to psychosocial effects of cocaine addiction, the physical effects that are manifested, and the characteristics of withdrawal or the "withdrawal syndrome." ^Cocaine ^Health ^Consequences\Physiological ^Consequences\Social ^Consequences\Psychological

1160. Miller, Marjorie (1989). "Mexicans Furious over Helms' Drug Allegations." *The Los Angeles Times*, 19 March, 5. The Bush administration certified Mexico as cooperating fully in the war on drugs. Jesse Helms wants to reverse that. Mexicans are infuriated. This is because the Salinas administration has attempted vigorously to pursue the drug war, at least in the eyes of Mexicans. The whole issue is over the degree to which the Mexican law enforcement system has been corrupted by drug traffickers. ^Latin\America ^Mexico ^United\States ^Drug\Control\Policies ^Politics ^Consequences\Corruption ^Consequences\Foreign\Relations ^Consequences\Political

1161. ——— (1989). "U.S. Officials Worry about Mexico Police Appointees." *The Los Angeles Times*, 7 January, A1. New Mexican police appointees, including a fugitive from the United States, are viewed as signaling a lack of commitment by Mexico's new president to crack down on narcotics trafficking and improve law enforcement. ^Latin\America ^Mexico ^Law\Enforcement ^Consequences\Corruption ^Consequences\Political

1162. Millman, Doris H. (1982). "Psychological Effects of Cannabis in Adolescence." In *Marijuana and Youth: Clinical Observations on Motivation and Learning*. Rockville, Md.: National Institute of Mental Health. The amotivation syndrome is there, but to what extent is it determined by cannabis, by intrinsic adolescent instability, or by preexisting personality factors? The answers are still open. ^Cannabis ^Health ^Youth ^Amotivational\Syndrome\Theories ^Consequences\Psychological

1163. Millman, R. B. (1982). "Adverse Effects of Cocaine." *Hospital and Community Psychiatry* 33(10): 804. Discusses the effects of cocaine in relation to the route of administration. Psychiatric complications are noted. ^Cocaine ^Consequences\Psychological

1164. Milloy, Courtland, and Edward D. Sargent (1983). "U.S. Crime Wave Linked to Flood of Heroin, Cocaine." *The Washington Post*, 30 January, A12. The citizens of America have come to believe that increased heroin and other traffic in illicit drugs have enhanced crime and their own vulnerability to criminal behavior. The result has been a burgeoning of private anticrime efforts, including security guards, guard dogs, bars and alarm systems, self-defense classes, and handgun sales. ^United\States ^Cocaine ^Heroin ^Drug\Use ^Drug\Traffic ^Crime ^Consequences\Economic ^Private\Initiatives

1165. Mills, James (1986). *The Underground Empire: Where Crime and Governments Embrace*. Garden City, N.Y.: Doubleday and Company. In this volume, which the author claims is true, with no names having been changed and no composite characters invented in scenes or dialogue, this one-time reporter for *Life* magazine offers an inside account of investigations by the Drug Enforcement Administration's now dismantled Centac operation, a global antidrug strike force. Mills holds the U.S. government responsible for not bringing to closure operations that would, in fact, dismantle drug trafficking and the corruption that it creates. Clearly, according to Mills, the indulgence of the U.S. government allows the underground empire to exist. He paints a picture of an underground conspiracy that works in the embrace of government even though half-hearted, public media attempts are made to suggest otherwise. ^United\States ^Law\Enforcement ^Consequences\Corruption ^DEA ^Media

1166. Mirante, Edith T. (1987). "Burma—Frontier Minorities in Arms." *Cultural Survival Quarterly* 11(4): 14–17. Discusses the history of the minorities' conflict with the central government and how trade is largely controlled by the insurgent groups bordering on China and Thailand. Much of the trade is in opium. Trade in opium has allowed insurgent groups to obtain better weapons than those of the Burmese army. ^Burma ^Opiates ^Drug\Traffic ^Insurgents ^Consequences\Political ^Minorities ^Southeast\Asia ^Golden\Triangle ^China ^Thailand ^Consequences\Violence

1167. —— (1988). "Burma Update: Urban Uprising and Frontier Rebellion." *Cultural Survival Quarterly* 13(1): 52–54. Aside from analyzing the internal political situation in Burma, the author mentions how fierce combat between Karen and Mon ethnic minorities in Burma ended up destroying a lucrative trade route for the two of them (presumably including trade in opium and its products). ^Burma ^Opiates ^Drug\Traffic ^Consequences\Political ^Consequences\Violence ^Minorities ^Southeast\Asia ^Golden\Triangle ^Traffickers

1168. —— (1989). "Burma: Indigenous People Mired in 'Foreign Mud.'" Paper presented at Symposium on Drugs, National Security and U.S. Public Policy, Tufts University, Medford, Mass., 2 March. Caught between eradication programs, military dictatorships, poor economies, and few economic options, tribal opium growers are profiting little. ^Southeast\Asia ^Burma ^Golden\Triangle ^Opiates ^Drug\Traffic ^Economics ^Politics ^Consequences\Economic

1169. —— (1989). "How Opium Became Burma's Cash Crop." *The New York Times*, 13 January. In this letter, Mirante argues that it is the presence of the Burmese army as an occupying force in the frontier that has made the country the world's foremost opium producer, not urban uprisings that have diverted the army's attention. The army's abuse has forced the people to flee into remote mountain areas where opium is the only valuable trade crop. ^Southeast\Asia ^Burma ^Golden\Triangle ^Opiates ^Drug\Traffic ^Economics ^Politics ^Consequences\Drug\Control\Policies ^Production\Incentives\Economic ^Production\Incentives\Political ^Migration

1170. —— (1989). "A Rare Look at America's Opium War—From the Ground Up." *Earth Island Journal* (Winter): 30. Consists of excerpts from Mirante's fifty-nine page report following her investigation, in Burma, of the herbicidal spaying program that reportedly killed a number of elderly women. She was deported by the military regime for "illegally entering Burma." She chronicles how food crops were destroyed, animals died, and children and old people were made sick, some of whom died, after touching the spray or the plants that had been sprayed. ^Southeast\Asia ^Burma ^Golden\Triangle ^Opiates ^Crop\Eradication ^Herbicides ^Consequences\Environmental ^Consequences\Health

1171. —— (1989). "The Shan Frontier: Exploitation and Eradication." Paper presented at Symposium on Drugs, National Security and U.S. Public Policy, Tufts University, Medford, Mass., 3 March. In Burma's Shan state (bordering Laos and Thailand), opium production soars under the supervision of regional "warlords." The growers themselves profit little from their "arduous labor," for it is a buyers market. Description of the major trafficking groups (placed in three categories): Burmese Communist party, Kuomintang, and Burmese military. ^Southeast\Asia ^Burma ^Golden\Triangle ^Opiates ^Drug\Traffic ^Economics ^Traffickers ^Production ^Producers ^Laos ^Thailand ^Consequences\Economic

1172. Mitchel, Margaret E., Teh-Wei Hu, Nancy S. McDonnell, and John D. Swisher (1984). "Cost-Effectiveness Analysis of an Educational Drug Abuse Prevention Program." *Journal of Drug Education* 14(3): 271–92. From a reasonably well controlled experimental research design, students were more or less randomly assigned to specific courses in their school, designed to influence their drug taking behavior. The courses were in health, social studies, and religion. Only the religion course appeared to alter significantly subsequent drug taking behavior. ^Drug\Use ^Prevention ^Youth ^Society ^Values ^Prevention\Drug\Education\Critique

1173. Mitchell, Chester N. (1983). "A Comparative Analysis of Cannabis Regulation." *Queen's Law Journal* 9(1): 110–42. The alcohol control model, while not ideal, does exhibit the basic features recommended in this article for the regulation of cannabis. Cannabis should be regulated and not prohibited by express policy preference. Legislators and policy makers, once having a more comprehensive view of alternative forms of control for harmful drugs, would well opt for control as opposed to prohibition. Features of a control policy are discussed in their social and economic terms. ^Cannabis ^P\S\Legalization ^P\S\Taxation

1174. Mohan, D., Adityanjee, S. Saxena, and S. Lal (1985). "Changing Trends in Heroin Abuse in India: An Assessment Based on Treatment Records." *Bulletin on Narcotics* 37(2-3): 19–23. Through 1984, especially for the period measured beginning 1981, there was a steady increase in the number of heroin addicts who sought treatment in facilities of the India Institute of Medical Sciences. ^India ^Heroin ^Drug\Use

1175. Mohan, D., H. S. Sethi, and E. Tongue (1981). *Current Research in Drug Abuse in India*. New Delhi: Gemini Printers. Includes epidemiological studies, attitudinal studies, and treatment studies. Of more particular interest to this bibliography is Section 5: "Supply and Demand Reduction." Reviewed are implications of international treaties on demand reduction of drugs, national control policy for drug-abuse prevention as a component of demand-reduction programs, current laws and national policies in India, history of narcotics control in India, and the social consequences of drug abuse. In this last category, briefly mentioned are automobile driving and work efficiency, capability of doing schoolwork, and the relationship between drug use and crime. Additionally, mention is made of the strain imposed on various elements in the community health service both in terms of personnel and care facilities. Drug overdose problems do indeed inflict social overhead. Then, of course, there is the general problem of an underground or parallel economy. ^India ^Drug\Use ^Drug\Control\Policies\History ^Economics ^Crime ^Consequences\Social ^Consequences\Public\Safety ^Informal\Economy ^Consequences\Health\Care ^Consequences\Educational ^Supply ^Demand

1176. Mohr, Charles (1988). "Experts Question Drug Bill's Impact." *The New York Times*, 30 October. Discussion of the new drug bill Congress passed in October 1988, with informants unsure as to whether the new tools to curb illicit drugs would be clearly effective. There was some ambiguity with respect to civil penalties for occasional use, for example. Criticism is rendered on government agencies having failed to cooperate or coordinate their drug programs fully. ^United\States ^Drug\Control\Policies ^Legislation ^Bureaucracy

1177. Mohun, Janet (1988). "Amsterdam Targets Its Drug Users." *New Scientist*, 18 August, 27. About one-third of Amsterdam's estimated 3,000 intravenous drug users are suspected of being HIV carriers. A needle-exchange program has been introduced. Amsterdam has long had liberal attitudes toward drugs and sex. It has a high incidence of homosexual men, drug users, and prostitutes. ^Netherlands ^Heroin ^Health ^AIDS ^Drug\Control\Policies ^Needle\Exchange\Programs ^Consequences\Misc

1178. Moller, Richard Jay (1981). *Marijuana: Your Legal Rights*, edited by Ralph Warner. Reading, Mass.: Addison-Wesley Publishing Company. The author advocates legalization of marijuana usage, but recognizes that its current status, however unfortunate, makes a user a criminal. If one desires to use marijuana, understanding that doing so is a crime, how may he or she do so in ways that allow asserting and protecting fourth and fifth amendment rights to privacy? The book tells how. ^United\States ^Cannabis ^Drug\Use ^Politics ^Consequences\Human\Rights ^P\S\Avoid\Sanctions ^P\S\Legalization

1179. Mondanaro, Josette (1989). *Chemically Dependent Women: Assessment and Treatment*. Lexington, Mass.: Lexington Books. A clinical discussion of why some women become chemically dependent, how this affects pregnancy and parenting, how AIDS infections may be reduced through "safe sex," common coexisting disorders in chemically dependent women such as depression and eating disorders, and, finally, a discussion of cocaine as being the perfect trap for women. In each case, the focus is on appropriate treatment strategies. ^Drug\Use ^Treatment ^Women ^Pregnancy ^Consequences\Parenting ^P\S\Safe\Sex ^AIDS

1180. "Money Laundering: Who's Involved, How It Works, and Where It's Spreading" (1985). *Business Week*, 18 March, 74. Graphic description, with many anecdotes, of how money derived from illicit narcotics sales is laundered. Panama figures prominently in the discussion, in part because its bank secrecy laws prevent U.S. investigators from determining who owns the accounts in Panama to which money from the United States is sent. The economics of the transactions and the various individual and corporate levels of involvement are discussed. In 1985, the most startling increase in apparent money laundering occurred in the cities of El Paso, Los Angeles, Philadelphia, and San Francisco. ^Latin\America ^Panama ^United\States ^Money\Laundering ^Economics ^Banking\Regulations ^California ^Texas

1181. Montalbano, William D. (1985). "Cash Crop, Curse: Latins Push Belated War on Cocaine." *The Los Angeles Times*, December 1, A1. Governments throughout South America have begun to attack coca production and cocaine processing not so much from being beholden to the U.S. government as from a realization that producer countries' own social and economic problems are worsening as a consequence of the drug trade. The countries now view illicit drugs as a threat to their national security because the traffic subverts political and social institutions, which are already fragile. ^Drug\Control\Policies ^Latin\America ^Coca ^Production ^Refining ^Consequences\Social ^Consequences\Economic

1182. ——— (1987). "Colombia's Press Pays in Blood for Anti-Drug Stand." *The Los Angeles Times*, 5 February, 14. Description of the campaign that drug traffickers have taken in Colombia against editors and newspaper owners who have dared to speak out against them. One paper, in particular, *El Espectador*, has launched investigative efforts into police corruption, reporting on a police captain who assigned his whole small-town force to protect cocaine kingpins as they attended a party. The owner of the paper was gunned down. The tenor of the article is to applaud the extraordinary courage of some press owners and editors in the wake of increasing amounts of intimidation and threats against not only themselves but also their families. ^Latin\America ^Colombia ^Cocaine ^Drug\Traffic ^Consequences\Corruption ^Consequences\Violence ^Consequences\Political ^Media

1183. Montaner, Carlos Alberto (1989). "El Cartel de la Habana." *El Nuevo Herald*, 25 June, 12A. Gives evidence and speculation that Fidel Castro was lying when he asserted that he knew nothing about the drug trading that some high officials in his government and military forces were undertaking and for which they were recently executed. ^Caribbean ^Cuba ^Drug\Traffic ^Politics ^Consequences\Corruption

1184. Moore, John W. (1987). "No Quick Fix." *National Journal*, 21 November, 2954–59. Focus on the interagency squabbling that impeded U.S. drug efforts in the middle 1980s. ^United\States ^Drug\Control\Policies ^Bureaucracy

1185. Moore, Mark Harrison (1977). *Buy and Bust: The Effective Regulation of an Illicit Market in Heroin*. Lexington, Mass.: Lexington Books. This book limits its analysis to a single strategy designed to reduce the supply of heroin—the activities of state and local enforcement agencies on domestic distribution systems. A major purpose of the analysis is to design a strategy for *regulating* the distribution of heroin under a policy that *prohibits* all uses of heroin. In effect, the author wants to achieve a regulatory effect with a prohibition policy. The book sets objectives of law enforcement in the context of an overall policy toward heroin use, recommends both strategies and tactics, and identifies major bureaucratic obstacles to implementation of the proposed strategies. The geographic focus is on New York City. Includes an extensive bibliography. ^United\States ^Heroin ^Law\Enforcement ^P\S\Law\Enforcement ^Bibliographies ^New\York ^Supply

1186. Moore, Molly (1989). "Coast Guard to Coordinate Drug Interdiction Effort." *The Washington Post*, 10 February, A25. In its first step toward becoming the nation's leading agency on drug interdiction, the Defense Department has established a command network to coordinate military surveillance of drug smuggling. Two top-level Coast Guard officials have been given major responsibilities, and the U.S. Customs Service is complaining that it has been bypassed. ^United\States ^Interdiction ^Coast\Guard ^Bureaucracy ^Department\of\Defense ^Customs

1187. Morales Anaya, Rolando (1985). *La Crisis Económica en Bolivia y Su Impacto en las Condiciones de Vida de los Niños*. La Paz, Bolivia: Papiro. Chronicles the worst economic crisis in Bolivia's history, beginning in about 1978, augmenting considerably in 1981, and continuing on through 1983. While the issue of drugs is not raised, and while the nature of the crisis is integrated into the international economy and the recession of the period, the fact that such a devastating economic deterioration in Bolivia existed lays foundation for the views of others that the drug crisis grew on economic catastrophe. ^Latin\America ^Bolivia ^Cocaine ^Drug\Traffic ^Economics ^Production\Incentives\Economic

1188. Morales, Armando (1984). "Substance Abuse and Mexican American Youth: An Overview." *Journal of Drug Issues* 14(2): 297–311. The author advances six separate viewpoints as points of departure for explaining substance abuse by Mexican-American youth. He then evaluates extant literature on the basis of these viewpoints. His own conclusion is that Mexican-American youths' drug use patterns may well be less related to cultural factors than they are to poverty factors. In terms of a practical policy response, intervention in the cycle of poverty and deprivation would seem to be a critical necessity. ^United\States ^Drug\Use\Theories ^Youth ^Minorities ^Economics ^Society ^Culture ^Reviews ^Drug\Use\Theories\Critique ^P\S\Economic

1189. Morales, Edmundo (1983). "Land Reform, Social Change, and Modernization in the National Periphery: A Study of Five Villages in the Northeastern Andes of Peru." Ph.D. diss., City University of New York. An anthropological/sociological study of a Peruvian highland district comprising five villages in Peru's northeastern Andes. While the study focuses on history, household economy, and the politics of land reform at the local and regional levels, it also includes a chapter on the "underground economy." In this chapter, the author shows how Peru's opening of its jungle to colonization efforts (in which initial agriculture expectations failed), which opened the country to coca growing, has created an enormous interrelationship between highland communities such as in and around Paras and the eastern uplands of the Amazon where the coca plant flourishes. The chapter describes "food energy outflow from Paras" to coca growing regions in exchange for both coca and cocaine. It shows how the peasants of the highlands facilitate the narcotics traffic by becoming commercial providers of the food-stuffs required for it to continue. Argues that the "caloric exchange ratio," that is, the ratio of food exported to benefits received, is quite deleterious to the highland peasant. For reasons the author does not explain, the peasants feed the cocaine entrepreneurs and their families before they take care even of their own. "The direct economic relationship between peasants, the urban poor and the underworld brings a plethora of negative effects that disturb the traditional life in the countryside" (p. 136). There is a direct relationship between *Sendero Luminoso* and narcotics trafficking, suggesting that the guerrilla movement exploits income from narcotic transactions to finance its own activities. As for changes in behavior as well as economy, robbery and crime have become problems, all of which correlate with coca and cocaine traffic. Every horse, mule, or whatever stolen from the area is sold in the jungle without any proof of possession. "Thievery perpetrated to supply transportation and food to cocaine centers and crime motivated by robbery and drug traffic have plagued the whole province, not to mention the rest of the Andes" (p. 143). ^Latin\America ^Peru ^Coca ^Cocaine ^Drug\Traffic ^Economics ^Informal\Economy ^Politics ^Insurgents ^Society ^Colonization ^Producers ^Consequences\Misc ^Consequences\Crime ^Land\Reform

1190. —— (1986). "Coca and Cocaine Economy and Social Change in the Andes of Peru." *Economic Development and Cultural Change* 35(1): 143-161. Describes the author's ethnographic fieldwork, reported earlier in his Ph.D. dissertation from the City University of New York. The focus is anthropological/sociological, and the article includes information on economics, cocaine entrepreneurship, and politics within the five communities studied. ^Latin\America ^Peru ^Coca ^Cocaine ^Drug\Traffic ^Economics ^Politics ^Society

1191. —— (1986). "Coca Culture: The White Cities of Peru." *The Graduate School Magazine* 1, no. 1 (Fall):4–11 CUNY. A general discussion of the coca culture in Peru. The focus is on the recent changes in the upper Huallaga Valley where the "coca-paste mafia" has developed a rigid hierarchy with five social groups. The groups are described, named, and analyzed. Their relationships and the economic transactions among them are noted. The activities of the Peruvian law enforcement agencies are noted, with observations that the nature of their activities gives them ample opportunities for shakedowns. The U.S–sponsored programs for eradication and crop substitution are mentioned. ^Latin\America ^Peru ^Coca ^Drug\Traffic ^Drug\Control\Policies ^Economics ^Society ^Culture ^Traffickers ^Organized\Crime ^Law\Enforcement ^Consequences\Corruption ^Crop\Substitution ^Crop\Eradication

1192. —— (1986). "Coca Paste and Crack: A Cross–National Ethnographic Approach." *Drugs in Latin America: Studies in Third World Societies* 37:179–200. From field research in Peru, the author examines coca paste. From his position as an employee with the New York State Division of Substance Abuse Services, he obtained information on street dealings and the urban drug ethnographic characteristics of those involved. Coca-paste smoking is having extraordinarily deleterious effects in Peru, particularly among young people. Killings and street gangs run amuck. With respect to crack, the author, as he did with coca paste, describes the procedures for producing it. Both in source countries and consumer centers, production of coca paste and its variations, crack and cocaine, and their distribution are creating an economic dependence among low-income and marginal groups. ^Latin\America ^Peru ^United\States ^Coca ^Cocaine ^Crack ^Drug\Use ^Youth ^Economics ^Consequences\Economic ^Consequences\Violence ^Consequences\Health ^Cocaine\Paste

1193. —— (1989). *Cocaine: White Gold Rush in Peru.* Tucson: University of Arizona Press. Discusses the social, political, and economic transformation of Peruvians in response to the American demand for cocaine. The growing of coca and the processing of its derivative alkaloids have become major Peruvian growth industries. The ramifications of these activities have not only settled in the backwater regions of the eastern Amazonic uplands where coca is grown, but also have reached into the heart of Peru's political, law enforcement, and judicial systems. The effect of this new commerce has been corrosive of traditional society and of modern institutions, has placed the country in even more onerous conditions of international dependency, and has solidified new kinds of social class exploitation. The cocaine industry, largely vertically integrated through intimidation and terror by international narcotics cartels centered mostly in Colombia, is likely to create even more socially and politically impoverishing conditions for Peru. The deleterious effects will unlikely be satisfactorily addressed by any current policy applications (e.g., U.S.-supported crop eradication and crop substitution programs, drug interdiction and other law enforcement efforts, U.S. aid, currently advocated alternative forms of economic development, and so forth). The book is a social and political ethnography, developed in large part by the participant-observer methods of social anthropology. Its subjects therefore are wide ranging, from discussions about the coca leaf in Andean traditional life, to coca culture, to the cocaine economy, and to the politics of control and eradication. ^Latin\America ^Peru ^Coca ^Cocaine ^Drug\Traffic ^Consequences\Economic ^Consequences\Social ^Consequences\Political ^Consequences\Cultural ^Consequences\Judiciary ^Consequences\Law\Enforcement ^Drug\Control\Policies\Critique ^Drug\Control\Politics ^Traffickers

1194. —— (1990). "Comprehensive Economic Development: An Alternative Measure to Reduce Cocaine Supply." *The Journal of Drug Issues* 20:4(Fall): 629–37. Reduction of drug supplies cannot be obtained by policies now in force. Supply reduction can only occur through ways that counter the political and economic conditions that promote production efforts in the first place. Peasants, if they are to be weaned from their dependence on an illicit cocaine economy, must be given an economic alternative. That alternative is comprehensive economic development in the areas where they live. Statistics on drug production, trafficking, and supply reduction policies are reviewed. ^Supply ^Cocaine ^P\S\Development ^Latin\America ^Drug\Traffic ^Production ^Statistics

1195. Morales-Vaca, Mercedes (1984). "A Laboratory Approach to the Control of Cocaine in Bolivia." *Bulletin on Narcotics*, 36:2: 33–44. A report of 4,196 samples of drugs seized and analyzed at the toxicology laboratory of the National Bureau for the Control of Dangerous Substances (Bolivia) during the period 1975-1982. Ninety percent contained coca paste, cocaine hydrochloride, or related substances. Most of these originated in the Bolivian cities of La Paz, Santa Cruz, and Cochabamba. Coca paste was found to have been adulterated with calcium (or sodium) carbonate, flour, sodium bicarbonate, procaine, and benzocaine. The most common adulterant detected was sodium carbonate, followed by flour. ^Latin\America ^Bolivia ^Cocaine ^Cocaine\Paste ^Drug\Use

1196. Moran, Richard (1988). "When Drug Laws Are Too Harsh to Work." *The Christian Science Monitor*, 9 August, 12. Harsh mandatory sentences apparently are not an effective deterrent because one may punish only the offenders who are arrested, indicted, and convicted, and getting convictions on harsh penalties is exceedingly difficult. ^United\States ^Law\Enforcement ^Drug\Control\Policies\Critique

1197. Morello, Ted (1984). "Hooking Them Young." *Far Eastern Economic Review*, 23 February, 26. In an arc running from Pakistan through South Asia to Japan, narcotics abuse by young people is increasing at an explosive rate. This coincides with a substantial regional rise in the cultivation and refining of opium poppies. ^Southeast\Asia ^Pakistan ^Japan ^Opiates ^Drug\Use ^Youth ^Southwest\Asia

1198. Morgan, John P. (1988). "The 'Scientific' Justification for Urine Drug Testing." *Kansas University Law Review* 36:683–97. The rationale used for drug testing via urinary analysis is justified more from religious than from scientific language. The author examines justification statements and examines their accuracy. ^United\States ^Drug\Testing\Critique

1199. Morganthau, Tom, and Mark Miller (1988). "Getting Tough on Cocaine; The U.S. Is Losing the War—And the Best Way to Fight Back is with Aggressive Law Enforcement." *Newsweek*, 28 November, 64–75. General discussion of the drug prices in America today and policy options that may be open, including the "gamble" of legalization. ^United\States ^Drug\Control\Policies\Critique ^Legalization

1200. Morganthau, Tom, and Michael Reese (1986). "Going after Hollywood: Critics Call for the Deglamorization of Drugs." *Newsweek*, 11 August, 20. A general call to the television networks and others to design and broadcast major national campaigns against drug abuse. It is noted that it would probably be necessary to somehow undermine Hollywood's own drug mores if any antidrug message generated could be promulgated with credibility. ^United\States ^Drug\Use ^Society ^P\S\Values ^Media

1201. Morganthau, Tom, Peter McKillop, Gregory Cerio, and Richard Sandza (1988). "Should Drugs Be Legal?" *Newsweek*, 30 May, 36–38. The author claims that proponents are logical, sincere, and well intended, but wrong. ^United\States ^P\S\Legalization\Critique

1202. Morganthau, Tom, Mark Miller, Janet Huck, and Jeanne DeQuine (1986). "Kids and Cocaine." *Newsweek*, 17 March, 58. An epidemic of cheap, deadly "crack" exposes a generation of American children to the nightmare of cocaine addiction. Anecdotes on personal battles are given. Involvement of narcotics law enforcement agencies in high school is described. ^United\States ^Cocaine ^Crack ^Drug\Use ^Youth ^Law\Enforcement ^Consequences\Personal ^Prevention\Schools

1203. Morganthau, Tom, Michael A. Lerner, Richard Sandza, Nonny Abbott, David L. Gonzalez, and Patricia King (1988). "The Drug Gangs." *Newsweek*, 28 March, 20–27. "Spurred on by the flourishing narcotics trade, they're waging war in cities across the country. As crime rates rise, can the cops battle back?" (p. 20). ^United\States ^Drug\Traffic ^Organized\Crime ^Law\Enforcement

1204. Morningstar, Patricia J. (1985). "Thandai and Chilam: Traditional Hindu Beliefs about the Proper Uses of Cannabis." *Journal of Psychoactive Drugs* 17(3): 141–65. Discusses the history of cannabis use in the Hindu tradition, current use patterns in North India, beliefs concerning amotivational syndrome, and beliefs concerning the effects of cannabis on sexual functioning. All of these imply a historic condition wherein a belief system orders a cultural system in such a way as to direct the appropriate use of a drug to enhance complex phenomenal events. ^India ^Cannabis ^Drug\Use ^Society ^Culture ^Amotivational\Syndrome ^Consequences\Sexuality ^Values

1205. Morrison, David C. (1986). "The Pentagon's Drug Wars." *National Journal*, 6 September, 2104–109. Description of the Defense Department's expanding role in the United States' "war on drugs," and the degree to which this poses questions of civil liberties as well as whether the new mission helps or hurts military readiness. Several sides of the prevailing arguments on these issues are presented. ^United\States ^Drug\Control\Policies\Critique ^Military ^Department\of\Defense ^Consequences\Human\Rights

1206. Morse, Stephen J. (1988). "War on Drugs Produces the Crime: Since We're Losing, Why Not Debate the Alternative?" *The Los Angeles Times*, 8 April, 7. Argument that one of the consequences of the war on drugs is to create conditions conducive to criminal activity; and, since we're losing, why not debate? ^United\States ^Consequences\Drug\Control\Policies ^Crime ^P\S\Legalization

1207. Moses, Jonathan M. (1988). "High-Tech Helps Drug Dealers Evade the Law; Cellular Car Phones Are Hard to Tap, Give Traffickers Mobility." *The Washington Post*, 30 July, A1. Cellular car phones, being hard to tap, give traffickers mobility and secretiveness that they would not normally have. To counteract these developments would cost an enormous amount of money. The cellular telephone technology follows on the electronic paging device enthusiasm that has become a staple of drug trafficking. ^United\States ^Drug\Traffic ^Law\Enforcement

1208. Moskowitz, Joel M., Janet Malvin, Gary A. Schaeffer, and Eric Schaps (1983). "Evaluation of a Junior High School Primary Prevention Program." *Addictive Behaviors* 3:393–401. In a controlled study of two junior high schools, an intervention educational program produced positive effects for females on several drug-related variables, but few effects on males. Again, it is a question of there being a small correlation between knowledge of drugs and interest in not becoming involved with them. Studies that do not focus on social and psychological factors influencing drug use and training students in relative resistive competencies appear to have no effect. ^Youth ^Prevention\Drug\Education\Critique

1209. Mott, Joy (1980). "Opiate Use and Crime in the United Kingdom." *Contemporary Drug Problems* 9(4): 437–51. A brief historical account of the development of drug control policies in the United Kingdom is given. The prevalence of opiate addiction is reviewed and the results of treatment are indicated. What is the relationship between opiate use and crime? All the evidence so far available suggests, for nontherapeutic addicts at least, that addiction and criminals' histories tend to run a parallel course. The major effect of opiate use on the criminal history is the increase in the number of convictions for drug offenses, and in the number of individuals convicted of such offenses. Criminal activity would not be an economic necessity for opiate users in the U.K. because of the treatment policy and because of the availability of social security benefits for those who are unable to work. Thus, opiate addiction has never been regarded as a major source of criminal behavior in the United Kingdom. It is apparent that the relationship between opiate use and crime cannot be simply ascribed to the type of control policy. It is more likely to be the result of a complex interaction between treatment practice, the availability of licit and illicit supplies, and the social security legislation. Relevant also are the individual social and criminal characteristics of the user. ^United\Kingdom ^Heroin ^Drug\Use ^Drug\Control\Policies ^Crime ^Opiates ^Economics ^Crime\Theories ^Drug\Control\Policies\History

1210. Mouat, Lucia (1990). "Nations More Willing to Concede 'Rights' to Fight International Drug War." *The Christian Science Monitor*, February 27, p. 5. In an effort to curb supply and demand of illicit drugs, historical sensitivities regarding sovereign "rights" are declining slightly in favor of wider international cooperation. This includes aircraft overflights and banking practices wherein one country technically "invades" the sovereignty of another. Cooperation is thought to enhance the national security of all countries. ^Sovereignty ^National\Security ^International\Cooperation

1211. ——— (1990). "UN Session Plots a Global Antidrug Strategy." *The Christian Science Monitor*, February 27, p. 5. Describes the agreements obtained in the special session of the United Nations General Assembly held in mid February 1990 dedicated to finding an effective way for the UN to expand its antidrug efforts. The session called for vigilance over precursor chemicals, money laundering, and arms transfers. Considerable burden was placed on consuming countries to reduce their drug demand. Developing countries were clearly pleased to see a shift in emphasis from almost exclusive supply reduction policies to an incorporation of demand reduction policies on the agenda. This is a historic moment, because most of the fourteen international narcotics agreements that have been reached in the last three quarters of a century focus on curbing drug supplies. Multilateral, as opposed to bilateral agreements, are emphasized. ^United\Nations ^Drug\Control\Policies ^Precursor\Chemicals ^Money\Laundering ^P\S\Demand\Reduction ^Supply

1212. Moynihan, M. (1983). "Law Enforcement and Drug Trafficking Money: Recent Developments in Australian Law and Procedure." *Bulletin on Narcotics* 35(2): 49–55. Argues that the most effective action against drug traffickers will be to destroy the financial basis of their activities. Makes specific recommendations about how this might be done. ^Australia ^Asset\Forfe:ture ^Money\Laundering ^P\S\Economic

1213. Mufti, K. A. (1986). "Community Programme in Pakistan Aimed at Preventing and Reducing Drug Abuse." *Bulletin on Narcotics* 38(1-2): 121–27. Chronicles the growth and development of the Green December Movement, established in 1983, to catalyze community and provincial resources in North Western Pakistan to treat and rehabilitate drug addicts. Two centers have been established to provide free treatment. Emphasis has been placed on the involvement of religious leaders in drug-abuse prevention strategies, particularly in an educational sense for the broad population not yet addicted. They also give spiritual and psychological support for addicts. The Green December Movement also functions as an educational organ for various target groups, and it urges youth to participate in community activities aimed at preventing drug abuse. In the evaluation section of this article, it appears that the Green December Movement activities carried out have produced positive results. [One word of derivational caution: K. A. Mufti is the founder of the Green December Movement.] ^Pakistan ^Southwest\Asia ^Drug\Use ^Prevention ^Private\Initiatives ^Treatment ^Rehabilitation ^Treatment\History

1214. Mugford, Stephen K. (1986). "Drug Policies in Australia: Alternatives to Prohibitionism." *Journal of Drug Issues* 16(2): 153–69. Gives an overview of Australia's policies regarding drugs and the nature of the Australian drug problem. Five arguments frequently raised to justify prohibitionist stances are reviewed and shown to be inadequate. Conditions under which a successful prohibition policy might be attempted are discussed, and it is suggested that the underlying conditions do not exist in Australia. Thus, it seems highly unlikely that any prohibitionist stance adopted in the face of these conditions could be successful. Several possible alternatives are examined without suggesting that any would be acceptable. Basically, the author proposes to explore alternatives via economic strategies. Among these would be a government monopoly with some restrictions on sale. ^Australia ^Legalization ^Drug\Control\Policies\Critique ^P\S\Controlled\Sales

1215. Muir, Jim (1987). "Syria Gets Tough on Lebanon's Drug Trade." *The Christian Science Monitor*, 16 April, 9. Syrian troops occupying Lebanon's eastern Bekaa Valley have decided to put an end to the drug business that has been such a lucrative trading commodity for the country, having made it a major world source of drugs. Hashish has been cultivated openly in the northern regions of the Bekaa for decades. Marijuana was earlier tolerated, but poppies discouraged. Recently, poppies have been planted extensively. So now the authorities are simply burning the crops. ^Middle\East ^Lebanon ^Syria ^Cannabis ^Opiates ^Drug\Traffic ^Drug\Control\Policies ^Production

1216. Muller, B. (1985). "The Drug Problem in the Federal Republic of Germany." *Drug and Alcohol Dependence* 15:335–39. West Germany's newly adopted (mid-1980s) narcotic drugs law is analyzed from the viewpoint of punishment vs. treatment. The author pushes for alternatives to sentences and other harsh sanctions. While the new federal drug law permits the principle of therapy to be invoked, those means have to be put to more and better use. ^Europe ^Germany ^Drug\Control\Policies ^Law\Enforcement ^Drug\Use ^Treatment ^Reviews ^P\S\Therapy

1217. Murphy, Cait (1987). "High Times in America; Why Our Drug Policy Can't Work." *Policy Review* 39(Winter): 46–50. As long as a substantial demand for drugs exists, it seems inconceivable that supplies will be substantially affected by law enforcement efforts. In 1974, when Turkey stopped growing opium at the behest of the United States, Mexico and Pakistan proceeded to fill the market that was left. Drug-enforcement agents seize more drugs than ever before, every year, but street prices seem not to be affected. Hardly any program, however sensible it may be, "can stop Americans from doing what they want to do." What they want to do is consume narcotics. ^United\States ^Turkey ^Mexico ^Pakistan ^Middle\East ^Golden\Crescent ^Drug\Control\Policies\Critique ^Supply ^Demand ^Consequences\Markets ^Latin\America ^Southwest\Asia

1218. Murphy, Jack W. (1983). "Implementation of International Narcotics Control: The Struggle against Opium Cultivation in Pakistan." *Boston College International and Comparative Law Review* 6(1): 199–241. This research note examines illicit opium production and trade in Pakistan and the efforts that the United Nations, Pakistan, and other countries have made to control that trade. International conventions, obligations of Pakistan regarding those conventions, international aid, and political and other difficulties in enforcing the antinarcotics laws in the tribal areas of Pakistan are reviewed. ^Pakistan ^United\Nations ^Southwest\Asia ^Opiates ^Production ^Drug\Control\Policies ^Golden\Crescent ^International\Cooperation

1219. Murphy, Kim (1987). "Seizure of Pot Grower's Property Upheld." *The Los Angeles Times*, 11 July, 33. The courts have upheld the seizure laws, even to the extent that, in this particular case, a marijuana grower forfeited his entire property even though he used only a small portion of it for illegal activities. The U.S. 9th Circuit Court of Appeals reversed a lower court's judgment that only the land on which the marijuana had actually been grown was subject to forfeiture. The extent of the application of the forfeiture statutes, by the appeals court, startled many observers. ^United\States ^Cannabis ^Asset\Forfeiture ^Judiciary

1220. Murphy, Sheigla (1987). "Intravenous Drug Use and AIDS: Notes on the Social Economy of Needle Sharing." *Contemporary Drug Problems* 14(3): 373–95. It is apparent that large numbers of I.V. drug users throughout the United States and Europe are infected with the AIDS virus. Male I.V. drug users can transmit the virus to noninfected female sexual partners. The risks are very high. What motivates addicts to take the risks, and what do they know about AIDS? What strategies could help prevent the spread among these people? This article offers discussion and findings relative to these questions. Suggestions for AIDS education are raised. ^Europe ^United\States ^Heroin ^Health ^AIDS ^Prevention ^Consequences\Health ^Proffered\Solutions ^Drug\Use\Theories

1221. Murray, David M., and Cheryl L. Perry (1985). "The Prevention of Adolescent Drug Abuse: Implications of Etiological, Developmental, Behavioral, and Environmental Models." In *Etiology of Drug Abuse: Implications for Prevention*, NIDA Research Monograph 56, edited by Coryl LaRue Jones and Robert J. Battjes. Rockville, Md.: National Institute on Drug Abuse. Reviews models of causation with respect to adolescents' adopting drug abuse behavior. Etiological work (causation) has, the authors argue, been crucial in shaping current prevention efforts. Thus many prevention efforts now have moved away from simple knowledge dissemination programs to dealing with social skills and environmental concerns. ^Drug\Use\Theories ^Prevention\Integrated

1222. Murray, John B. (1986). "An Overview of Cocaine Use and Abuse." *Psychological Reports* 59:243–64. Considerable literature is reviewed in this article. Cocaine is a more toxic compound than heroin when unlimited access is possible, and therefore is not a safe recreational drug. If the high cost of cocaine is reduced, even greater usage can be expected. Cocaine leads human subjects to abnormal behavior and adverse social consequences. Psychological dependency develops very quickly. ^Cocaine ^Health ^Reviews ^Consequences\Social ^Consequences\Economic ^Consequences\Psychological ^Drug\Use ^Heroin

1223. Musto, David I. (1987). *The American Disease: Origins of Narcotic Control.* New York: Oxford University Press. How is it possible to understand the current epidemic of drug use and abuse in the United States? Only through knowing its history in America will we be able to make wise decisions concerning drug abuse now and in the future. There are definite parallels in drug use and abuse today which peaked around the turn of the century in the United States. We need to have a public awareness of this in order to understand both the limitations and the possibilities of current and future public policy. The 1987 edition contains the 1973 text with corrections and added chapters that cover more recent events. ^United\States ^Drug\Use\History ^Drug\Control\Policies

1224. Mutch, David (1989). "To the Heart of the Drug Problem; Noted Social Psychologist Cites Spiritual Emptiness, Self-Preoccupation as Underlying Causes." *The Christian Science Monitor*, 24 May, 12–13. Noted social psychologist Robert Coles views America's problem as being one of spiritual emptiness and a self-preoccupation or, in other words, an egocentrism. Legalization is an act of moral surrender. ^United\States ^Drug\Use ^Society ^Values ^Legalization

1225. Mydans, Seth (1989). "Powerful Arms of Drug War Arousing Concern for Rights." *The New York Times*, 16 October, 1. Examples are given of law-abiding citizens who have become victims of drug enforcement operations. The Supreme Court's position on civil rights issues associated with drug control policies is reviewed. ^Law\Enforcement ^Consequences\Human\Rights

1226. ——— (1991). "6 Los Angeles Officers Charged in Drug Cases." *The New York Times*, January 11, A18. In a grand jury investigation of police brutality against prisoners, six former members of the Los Angeles county sheriff's department elite narcotics unit were convicted of twenty five counts (arising from a theft of $1.4 million seized from traffickers in drug raids). The officers also had planted cocaine in ways that would incriminate victims they intended to rob. ^United\States ^California ^Law\Enforcement ^Corruption

1227. Nadelmann, Ethan (1985). "International Drug Trafficking and U.S. Foreign Policy." *Washington Quarterly* 8(Winter): 87–102. Within the U.S. government, increased attention and resources have been devoted to controlling international drug production and trafficking. These efforts, and the obstacles which confront them, are the subject of this article. The broad objectives of the policy can be described as two pronged: elimination of the drugs themselves before they reach the borders of the United States and elimination of the traffickers who produce the drugs for the U.S. market. Both prongs clearly aim at not only reducing the amount of drugs entering the United States but also increasing their cost to the consumer. Different agencies focus on these two prongs. They are listed. As for producing country motivation to participate with U.S. international foreign policy initiatives on drug trafficking, their focus on traffickers as opposed to producers constitutes a less costly, if less effective way of appeasing U.S. demands. Beyond this, such activities help producing country governments maintain control of their own populations. The strong caveat, of course, is basically in Latin America, where politicians, judges, military and police figures, and even cabinet ministers, as well as their friends and relatives are deeply involved in profiting from the traffic in drugs. Drug trafficking control efforts in numerous countries are listed, including Latin America and Asia. Distinctions are made between foreign policy issues associated with cocaine and marijuana production on the one hand, and opium and heroin production on the other. The Mexican case, until recently touted as a substantial success, fell on hard times when the entire governmental apparatus was penetrated by officials on the take. However, the country reacted when the narcotraffickers appeared to be taking over substantial sections of it. This part of the analysis suggests that many governments in drug-producing countries will tolerate extensive drug activity, even given the resources to curtail it, until the traffickers push them too far. At that point, their interests coincide with U.S. pressures and action will occur. Many traditional attitudes are in flux now as both producing countries and transshipment countries begin to suffer many debilitating consequences of drug abuse among their own populations. Questions are raised as to whether the whole governmental apparatus associated with illegal drugs (suppression, interdiction, control) is worth it. A cost-benefit analysis is presented. Comparisons are made with the imposition and lifting of prohibition in the United States. Thus the author concludes, on a mixed basis, that, on the one hand, there is no reason not to continue to pursue and prosecute the criminals who profit from the drug trade, particularly insofar as they are involved in all sorts of other criminal activities. On the other hand, there is a strong need to be more honest and open minded about the drug problem. For starters, one needs to recognize that alcohol and tobacco are each responsible for more economic loss, physical suffering, and death than all of the illegally consumed drugs combined. Greater efforts could be made to distinguish the costs of drug abuse from the many costs which arise from the illegality of the drugs. These include the untold effects on the millions of nonabusing drug consumers; the existence of powerful and violent drug trafficking organizations; the loss of tens of billions of dollars into untaxed, underground economies; and the billions of taxpayers' dollars spent on catching, prosecuting, and imprisoning drug traffickers as well as mere drug consumers. ^Latin\America ^Southeast\Asia ^Mexico ^United\States ^Drug\Control\Policies ^Consequences\Sovereignty ^Proffered\Solutions ^Alcohol ^Tobacco ^Consequences\Illegal\Economy ^Crime ^Supply ^Consequences\Corruption ^Consequences\Foreign\Policy ^Drug\Control\Policies\Critique ^Opiates ^Cocaine ^Cannabis ^Consequences\State\Authority

1228. —— (1987). "The DEA in Latin America: Dealing with Institutionalized Corruption." *Journal of Interamerican Studies and World Affairs* 29(Winter): 1–39. Examines how the U.S. government has dealt with drug-related corruption in Latin America and the Caribbean, specifically how DEA agents deal with obstacles created by in-country corruption. In examining U.S. efforts to deal with drug-related corruption in foreign governments, this analysis contributes to two areas of public policy studies that rarely intersect: corruption reform, and foreign policy. This approach to the problem of corruption in government is unique in two respects; it focuses on the role played by an outsider, one lacking any sovereign power, in trying to influence the nature and impact of government corruption; and it is primarily concerned, not with how corrupt agencies are reformed, but rather with how they are made to perform their designated tasks despite that corruption. Among the police services, those agencies and units that specialize in drug enforcement tend to have the most notorious reputations for corruption. Discusses means by which DEA agents establish lines of trust with their in-country counterparts, how they work around corruption, and how, through the processes of extradition, they get foreign drug traffickers into U.S. courts. Discusses cases of U.S. DEA involvement in torturing drug traffickers. So long as consumers in the United States continue to demand psychoactive substances produced abroad, and so long as the market for those substances continues to be a criminal one, drug-related corruption promises to persist. ^Latin\America ^United\States ^Drug\Control\Policies ^DEA ^Politics ^Consequences\Foreign\Policy ^Consequences\Human\Rights ^Consequences\Corruption ^Extradition

1229. ——— (1988). "The Case for Legalization." *The Public Interest* 92(Summer): 3–31. What can be done about the "drug problem?" Current "war" strategies (domestic and international) are not producing the desired outcomes; and, the current strategies are highly costly and some of them are producing counter-productive results. Among these are crime, corruption, and physical and moral costs. Many of the drug laws should therefore be repealed. The results would not be as bad as the critics maintain, and many positive consequences would result. Nadelmann downplays the idea that demand (drug consumption) would increase in the wake of legalization. Several of the ideas developed here are expanded with extensive notations in Nadelmann's 1989 article in *Science* ("Drug Prohibition in the United States: Costs, Consequences, and Alternatives"). ^P\S\Legalization ^Decriminalization\Theories

1230. ——— (1988). "U.S. Drug Policy: A Bad Export." *Foreign Policy* 70(Spring): 97–108. When thinking about an optimal drug policy, one must be concerned not only with minimizing drug abuse but also with the societal costs that are imposed by drug control measures. The article reviews the measures introduced so far, critiques them, compares the risks associated with various policies, including governmental subversion, and draws up a list of drug policy alternatives for consideration. The failure of prohibition laws is reviewed, and their application to the current drug situation is considered. Voices for legalization are given coverage. ^United\States ^Drug\Control\Policies\Critique ^Legalization ^Consequences\Economic ^Consequences\Social

1231. ——— (1989). "Drug Prohibition in the United States: Costs, Consequences, and Alternatives." *Science* 245(1 September): 939–47. Drug prohibition policies are severely limited in their ability to control drug abuse and mitigate its consequences. They have not controlled consumption nor have they materially affected the supply of drugs on the market. The costs and consequences of those failed policies are therefore enormous. Legalization (or decriminalization), at least at some "middle ground," is preferable, including legal availability of some or all illicit drugs but with vigorous efforts to restrict consumption by voluntary means. Such legalization (or decriminalization) would reduce crime, violence, corruption, personal tragedies deriving from consuming unregulated drugs, allow for moral consistency in America's drug laws (vis-à-vis tobacco and alcohol), reduce the spread of AIDS, and recover funds (through drug taxation and reordering of law enforcement activities) that could be spent in publicly beneficial ways. It is unlikely that consumption would increase materially or that, if it did, the consequences would be as great as now exist. Legalized drugs could also be used for helpful and legitimate medical purposes (e.g., to reduce the nausea that accompanies chemotherapy, to treat glaucoma, and to reduce pain in some victims of multiple sclerosis). A lengthy discussion is given on the drug-crime nexus and how legalization could ameliorate whatever causal and associational connections exist. Numerous alternatives to drug prohibition policies are discussed and their hypothesized consequences are set forth. ^Drug\Control\Policies ^United\States ^Drug\Control\Policies\Critique ^P\S\Legalization ^Decriminalization ^Crime\Theories

1232. ——— (1990). "Global Prohibition Regimes: The Evolution of Norms in International Society." *International Organization* 44:4(Autumn): 479–526. The author examines how prohibition norms have evolved in international and national society and gives a comparative analysis of piracy, slavery, drug trafficking, prostitution, and the killing of whales and elephants. He analyzes the fate and future of global prohibition regimes. Certain kinds of prohibition regimes can be highly effective in "suppressing threats to the safety, welfare, and moral sensibilities of international society. Nonetheless, there are, as Herbert Packer argued persuasively, inherent limits to what the criminal sanction can accomplish, particularly in international society" (p. 526). ^Values ^International\Cooperation ^Drug\Control\Policies\Critique ^Drug\Traffic ^Prostitution

1233. Nagler, N. A. (1984). "Forfeiture of the Proceeds of Drug Trafficking." *Bulletin on Narcotics* 36(4): 21–30. A committee in Britain issued a report with recommendations regarding confiscation orders for property derived from drug trafficking. The author comments on those recommendations and suggests three possible ways of developing international cooperation to secure the tracing or confiscation of illegally acquired assets held abroad. Alternatives include extending national laws to deal with the problems, following Canada's example where possession of criminal money is assumed to be a crime regardless of whether the crime took place in Canada, or developing some alternative extensive extra-territorial jurisdiction. Following the developments of international law on terrorism might offer a model. ^Asset\Forfeiture ^United\Kingdom ^Canada ^P\S\International\Cooperation

1234. —— (1987). "The Council of Europe Co-operation Group to Combat Drug Abuse and Illicit Trafficking in Drugs (The Pompidou Group)." *Bulletin on Narcotics* 39(1): 31–39. In 1971, the Pompidou Group was set up to exchange views in Western Europe in response to the growing drug problem. In 1980 the group became part of the Council of Europe. Now it has sixteen members. A description of the topics it has considered is reviewed. Among these are those dealing with drug trafficking on the high seas, the role of the criminal justice system in responding to the needs of drug misusers, methods of reaching young people particularly at risk, problems concerning women and drugs, control services at major airports, and AIDS. ^Europe ^Drug\Control\Policies ^International\Cooperation ^Pompidou\Group

1235. Nahas, Gabriel G. (1979). *Keep off the Grass: A Scientific Enquiry into the Biological Effects of Marijuana.* New York: Pergamon Press. Physiological effects and toxicology of marijuana. Research findings on marijuana use. This is a book of a crusader. Nahas and others of his view who have conducted well-controlled investigations conclude that the chronic use of marijuana in certain concentrations is hazardous, both to the user and to the society exposed to the consequences of the user's judgment during his "high." This is the personal story of a crusade, written for a semi-popular audience. ^Cannabis ^Health ^Consequences\Health ^Consequences\Social ^Consequences\Psychological

1236. —— (1985). "Critique of a Study on Ganja in Jamaica." *Bulletin on Narcotics* 37(4): 15–27. Criticizes the study by Vera Rubin and Lambros Comitas on Ganja in Jamaica—the methodological limitations in the sampling technique, the small number in the sample, and the philosophical premises that dispose the authors to view cannabis smoking as having socially beneficial properties. ^Jamaica ^Caribbean ^Cannabis ^Drug\Use ^Society ^Reviews

1237. —— (1985). "Hashish and Drug Abuse in Egypt during the 19th and 20th Centuries." *Bulletin New York Academies of Medicine* 61(5): 428–44. Gives a chronology of the Egyptian experience, including the heroin epidemic of the mid-1930s. The use of hashish was culturally sanctioned and repressive measures were unable to remove it from society. On the other hand, heroin and cocaine had no cultural sanction within traditional society; thus, repressive measures succeeded in removing them from significant use. ^Middle\East ^Egypt ^Cannabis ^Drug\Use\History ^Drug\Control\Policies\History ^Society ^Culture ^Cocaine ^Heroin

1238. Nahas, Gabriel G., and H.C. Frick II, eds. (1981). *Drug Abuse in the Modern World: A Perspective for the Eighties.* New York: Pergamon Press. Included in this volume are papers delivered at an international symposium, at the College of Physician and Surgeons, Columbia University, New York City, in 1981. It was sponsored by the National Federation of Parents for a Drug Free Youth, the American Council on Marihuana, and other research and drug prevention organizations. Of interest to this bibliography are articles dealing with the effect of drugs on children and adolescents (Milman), drug use's contribution to "fashionable nihilism" (Tyrmand), successes and pitfalls with respect to drug law enforcement (Langer), and some comparative country data on drug use as, for example, in the Soviet Union (Segal), the eastern block and China (Rosinsky), and several Third World countries (Khan). ^Drug\Use ^Law\Enforcement ^Society ^Youth ^Consequences\Values ^Consequences\Social ^Drug\Control\Policies\Critique ^Europe ^Southeast\Asia ^USSR ^China

1239. Nahas, Gabriel G., Phillip Zeidenberg, and Claude Lefebure (1975). "Kif in Morocco." *The International Journal of the Addictions* 10(6): 977–93. Chronic cannabis intoxication still prevails in a significant fraction of the male population on Morocco. Cultivation occurs principally in the mountains of northern Morocco, where it constitutes the main cash crop of the local farmers. Moroccan health authorities claim that cannabis intoxication represents a major health hazard. The article details some of the history and the nature of the cultivation zones and how kif is prepared and consumed in Morocco. ^Morocco ^Cannabis ^Drug\Use ^Production ^Consequences\Health

1240. Nahas, Gabriel G., David J. Harvey, Michel Paris, and Henry Brill (1984). *Marihuana in Science and Medicine.* New York: Raven Press. This volume is an entirely revised and updated edition of the scientific volume *Marijuana—Deceptive Weed.* Summarizes the information from thousands of scientific papers and dozens of monographs and reports published in the decade prior to 1984 that analyze chemical, botanical, and biomedical effects of marihuana. The volume was especially written for the scientific and medical community. The historical, social, and cultural aspects of marihuana use are published in a companion volume entitled *The Escape of the Genie: A History of Hashish Throughout the Ages.* ^Cannabis ^Health ^Reviews

1241. Nahas, Gabriel G., H. C. Frick II, T. Gleaton, K. Schuchard, and O. Moulton (1986). "A Drug Policy for Our Times." *Bulletin on Narcotics* 38(1-2): 3–14. Raises and vigorously argues against three underlying assumptions influencing many people's orientation to illicit drug abuse, and, indeed, some aspects of drug-abuse control policy. The first is that dependence-producing drugs are little different from other substances that people consume, and that there is no greater inherent danger in consuming them. The second is that young persons may learn to use psychotropic drugs in a reasonable and responsible fashion and in ways that would not damage their health. The third is that social acceptance and commercial availability of illicit drugs would eliminate the social costs associated with their illegal traffic, principally crime and corruption. The authors systematically argue against these assumptions, showing that of those who are generally attached to alcohol consumption, only about 9 percent drink in amounts that damage their health. On the other hand, where cannabis is socially accepted and easily available, more than half of the consumers use cannabis enough to damage their health. The most damaging data are for cocaine and heroin, where approximately 90 to 95 percent of those who use the drug do so on a daily basis, and therefore in an amount that would have between seven and fourteen times greater dependence-producing potential than that of alcohol. It is thought that this is damaging to society and to individual health. Policies therefore must curtail the illicit supply and reduce demand. The arguments herein are based on pharmacological and epidemiological studies of dependence-producing drugs, and the assumptions are based on opposition to slavery of the mind by the consumption of dependence-producing drugs. ^Drug\Use\Theories\Critique ^Drug\Control\Policies ^Reviews ^Proffered\Solutions ^P\S\Legalization\Critique ^Alcohol ^Consequences\Health ^Supply ^Demand

1242. "Narcoespías Infiltran Gobierno Colombiano" (1989). *El Nuevo Herald*, 4 June, 1A. Allegations that a mole is at work in the U.S. Embassy in Bogota and is in collaboration with infiltrators into the most important Colombian state agencies which, in collaboration, have given the drug barons access to decisions of the National Security Council, the Supreme Court, the armed forces, the secret police, and the United States Embassy. ^Latin\America ^United\States ^Drug\Control\Policies ^Colombia ^Drug\Traffic ^Consequences\Corruption

1243. *Narcotráfico y Política: Militarismo y Mafia en Bolivia* (1982). Madrid, Spain: LAB—Iepala. Iepala is the Institute of Political Studies for Latin America and Africa, with headquarters in Madrid. The book itself was written by a team of American investigators put together by the Latin American Bureau of London. The volume is a translation from an English text (of origin unknown to this reviewer). The translators were fearful that the "yellow and sensationalist press" nature of the original would be lost in translation. They tried to preserve it. In substance, the powerful organizations of narcotics traffickers operating within Bolivia would be unable to work as they do were it not for the direct complicity of the Bolivian armed forces, or at least the Bolivian armed forces command. The book documents and analyzes how the trafficking of narcotics grew, protected by the military dictatorship. The United States is portrayed both as being responsible for and as a victim of the troubles in Bolivia. There is a discussion about the impossibility of coca eradication or of using herbicides. The authors argue for a cautious investigation of ways by which legalization in the United States might occur. ^Latin\America ^Bolivia ^Coca ^Cocaine ^Drug\Traffic ^Drug\Control\Policies\Critique ^Politics ^Consequences\Corruption ^Military ^Drug\Traffic\History ^Legalization

1244. *Narcotráfico y Política II: Bolivia 1982–1985* (1985). Cochabamba, Bolivia. Who are the authors of this volume (they remain unnamed, as does the publishing house)? Fears of retribution? The volume describes the narcotic mafia's hiding within obscure zones of the national economy which affects Bolivia internationally. It chronicles the internal subversion of the state and its economy as a consequence of international and national pressures and decision making which, on the whole, have gone against Bolivia's national interests. In some sense, Bolivia's entrance into the international political economy of coca/cocaine constitutes one more evidence of its "cursed role of periphery" that international capitalism has assigned it. ^Latin\America ^Bolivia ^Coca ^Cocaine ^Drug\Traffic ^Consequences\Political ^Consequences\Economic ^Consequences\Social ^Consequences\Drug\Control\Policies

1245. National Academy of Sciences, Institute of Medicine (1982). *Marijuana and Health* (1982). Washington, D.C.: The Institute of Medicine. Contains the results of a fifteen-month study of the health-related effects of marijuana. Five National Academy of Sciences' committees contributed, collectively, to the conclusions derived. The effort was to provide reliable and detailed information about the effects of marijuana use on health both in the long and short terms. Regarding effects on the nervous system and on behavior, marijuana produces acute effects on the brain, including chemical and electrophysiological changes. These are directly related to dosage. Marijuana impairs motor coordination and affects tracking ability in sensory and perceptual functions important for safe driving and the operation of other machines. It impairs short-term memory and slows learning. There is no conclusive evidence as to whether prolonged use of marijuana causes permanent changes in the nervous system or sustained impairment of brain function and behavior in human beings. Chronic, relatively heavy use of marijuana is associated with behavioral dysfunction and mental disorders, but it is not known whether these are the cause or effect of the mental condition. The long-term effects on the human brain and on human behavior therefore remain to be defined.

Effects on the cardiovascular and respiratory systems usually cause acute changes in the heart circulation that are characteristic of stress, but no evidence exists to indicate that a permanently deleterious effect on normal cardiovascular system functions occurs. There is some evidence that prolonged heavy smoking of marijuana, like tobacco, will lead to cancer of the respiratory tract and to serious impairment of lung function. Regarding the effects on the reproductive system and on chromosomes, there appears to be a modest reversible suppression on sperm production in men, but no evidence that it affects male fertility. Evidence presented on human female hormonal functioning is not convincing. However, there is convincing evidence that marijuana interferes with ovulation in female monkeys. While marijuana is known to cross the placenta readily and, in large doses, cause birth defects when administered to experimental animals, no clinical studies have been carried out to determine if its use can harm the human fetus. Thus while problems may exist, the effects of marijuana on reproductive function and on the fetus are unclear and may prove to be negligible, but further research is required. The academy's major conclusion is that "what little we know for certain about the effects of marijuana on human health—and all that we have reason to expect—justifies serious national concern" (p. 5). ^Cannabis ^Public\Safety ^Reviews ^Consequences\Health ^Consequences\Physiological ^Consequences\Neurological ^Consequences\Psychological ^Consequences\Sexuality ^Consequences\Fetuses

1246. National Institute on Drug Abuse (1982). *Marijuana and Health. Ninth Report to the U.S. Congress from the Secretary of Health and Human Services.* Rockville, Md.: NIDA. This year's report, based primarily on two major 1981 scientific reviews of the issues, causes the department to continue to believe that marijuana use is a major public health problem in the United States. Acute intoxication interferes with many mental health aspects and impedes classroom performance. It has deleterious effects on perception and performance in certain skills, including driving. Chronic effects include impaired lung functioning, decreased sperm counts and sperm motility, interference with ovulation and prenatal development, impaired immune response, and possible adverse effects on heart function. Among children, there is considerable concern over the drug's behavioral and physiological effects. Marijuana is now much more potent. ^Cannabis ^Health ^Reviews ^NIDA ^Consequences\Children

1247. —— (1985). *Epidemiology of Heroin: 1964–1984.* Rockville, Md.: NIDA. Data from eight selective cities is presented, focusing on indicators of heroin use such as morbidity, mortality, and other health consequences. Focuses also on use changes and drug combination use. Notes that heroin use had become epidemic and that it was part of a broader picture of a number of drug epidemics developing since 1964. Also discussed are the dynamics of heroin abuse, including changing supply sources, parts of the country affected, demographic characteristics of users, and frequency of use patterns. ^United\States ^Heroin ^Drug\Use ^Epidemiology ^NIDA ^Consequences\Health

1248. —— (1985). *Patterns and Trends in Drug Abuse: A National and International Perspective.* Rockville, Md.: NIDA. Statistics are given on the incidence of drug use, including polydrug users. Statistics regarding heroin and cocaine from both Europe and Southeast Asia generally parallel the U.S. experience—heroin usage has appeared to peak with users belonging to an aging cohort. There is an increase in adverse health consequences several years after initiation of cocaine use. Survey information is presented for various United States cities. The following foreign countries are represented: Thailand, France, Mexico, West Germany, and Italy. ^NIDA ^Statistics ^Drug\Use ^Southeast\Asia ^Europe ^United\States ^Cocaine ^Heroin ^Consequences\Health ^Thailand ^France ^Mexico ^Germany ^Italy

1249. —— (1987). *National Household Survey on Drug Abuse: Population Estimates 1985.* Washington, D.C.: Department of Health and Human

Services. This is the eighth study in a series of national surveys to measure the prevalence of drug use among the American household population age twelve and over. ^United\States ^Drug\Use ^Statistics ^NIDA

1250. ―――― (1987). *Trends in Demographic Characteristics and Patterns of Drug Use of Clients Admitted to Drug Abuse Treatment Programs for Cocaine Abuse in Selected States: Cocaine Client Admissions 1979–1984.* Washington, D.C.: Department of Health and Human Services. Contains state-specific statistics showing trends in client admissions with a cocaine problem to state-monitored drug-abuse treatment programs. ^United\States ^Cocaine ^Drug\Use ^Treatment ^Society ^NIDA ^Consequences\Health\Care ^Consequences\Social ^Consequences\Economic ^Statistics

1251. ―――― Statistical Series (published annually). *Annual Data* Series I. Washington D.C.: Department of Health and Human Services. This annual report presents drug-abuse information collected through the Drug Abuse Warning Network (DAWN). Statistics are given (DAWN). Statistics are given of hospital emergency room activities involving drug abuse and medical examiner facilities reporting deaths. Types of drugs, their classification, and certain metropolitan area profiles are given. ^United\States ^Drug\Use ^Health ^Statistics ^NIDA ^DAWN ^Consequences\Health\Care

1252. ―――― Statistical Series (1987). *Trends in Drug Abuse Related Hospital Emergency Room Episodes and Medical Examiner Cases for Selected Drugs: DAWN 1976–1985* Series H, Number 3. Rockville, Md.: Department of Health and Human Services. This report presents trends in drug-abuse data collected through the Drug Abuse Warning Network (DAWN) for the ten-year period from 1976 to 1985. Based on drug-abuse-related cases reported by 564 hospital emergency rooms and 62 medical examiner facilities that participated consistently in DAWN throughout the entire period. ^United\States ^Drug\Use ^Health ^Statistics ^NIDA ^DAWN ^Consequences\Health\Care

1253. National Narcotics Intelligence Consumers Committee (1981). *The Supply of Drugs to the U.S. Illicit Market from Foreign and Domestic Sources in 1980 (with Projection through 1984).* Washington D.C.: NNICC. As usual, this report is a composite of information from the NNICC's member agencies. As of the writing of this report the committee membership included the U.S. Coast Guard and Custom Services, the Department of Defense, Drug Enforcement Administration, the Federal Bureau of Investigation, Immigration and Naturalization Service, Internal Revenue Service, National Institute on Drug Abuse, Department of State, Department of the Treasury, and the White House. Specific indicators are given and source countries, with tonnage, are identified. ^United\States ^Drug\Use ^Production ^Drug\Traffic ^Statistics ^NNICC ^Coast\Guard ^Customs ^Department\of\Defense ^DEA ^FBI ^Department\of\State ^NIDA ^Drug\Control\Policies

1254. ―――― (1983). *Narcotics Intelligence Estimate: The Supply of Drugs to the U.S. Illicit Market from Foreign and Domestic Sources in 1982 (with Projections through 1983).* Series began in 1978. Washington, D.C.: NNICC. The committee's 1983 report on production and trafficking trends in cannabis, cocaine, opiates, and other dangerous drugs. Also included is a chapter on "drug money." In general, the committee found that as of 1983 the use of marijuana among young people had continued to decline gradually since 1979, although there was no indication of decline among other age groups. Cocaine use levels among high school seniors were unchanged during 1983, but the committee estimated that use among the general population grew approximately 12 percent. Heroin consumption remained stable, rising only 1 percent in 1983 following increases of 5 percent and 4 percent in 1982 and 1981, respectively. As for source countries, the committee's report included, for marijuana, Colombia, Jamaica, Mexico, Belize, Thailand, Brazil, Panama, Venezuela, Costa Rica, Laos, Indonesia, and Nigeria. The major marijuana producers for the United States market are Colombia, Jamaica, and Mexico. As for hashish, the major producers are Lebanon, Pakistan, and Afghanistan, with lesser amounts supplied by Morocco, Nepal, and India. As for cocaine, production and refining data are included for Colombia, Bolivia, and Peru. The committee suggested that its data for Peru and Bolivia were much more speculative than were its data for Colombia. Heroin producers for the U.S. market are Mexico (about 33 percent), Southwest Asia (48 percent), and Southeast Asia (19 percent). In 1983 opium production in Southwest Asia increased sharply, primarily as a result of the rise in cultivation in Afghanistan. Production in Iran probably remained stable. Opium poppy cultivation in Pakistan declined. There is a description of the major banking centers where drug money-laundering goes on. ^United\States ^Drug\Use ^Production ^Drug\Traffic ^Statistics ^NNICC ^Cocaine ^Heroin ^Cannabis ^Opiates ^Latin\America ^Colombia ^Caribbean ^Jamaica ^Mexico ^Belize ^Thailand ^Southeast\Asia ^Golden\Triangle ^Brazil ^Panama ^Venezuela ^Costa\Rica ^Laos ^Indonesia ^Nigeria ^Lebanon ^Middle\East ^Pakistan ^Afghanistan ^Golden\Crescent ^Morocco ^Nepal ^India ^Bolivia ^Peru ^Iran ^Money\Laundering ^Supply ^Southwest\Asia ^Africa

1255. —— (1985). *Narcotics Intelligence Estimate 1984*. Washington, D.C.: NNICC. Discusses source country trends and trafficking operations with respect to cannabis, cocaine, opiates, and other dangerous drugs. Also includes a chapter on drug money laundering. Marijuana consumption in the United States dropped an estimated 3 percent in 1984, primarily as a result of continuing decline among young people. Cocaine use remained widespread, with overall U.S. consumption rising 11 percent. Heroin consumption decreased an estimated 1 percent in 1984. Source countries remained largely unchanged from 1983. With respect to cocaine, the seizure of three cocaine laboratories in Mexico, one in Canada, major complexes in Panama and Venezuela, and twenty-one laboratories in the United States is indicative of increased smuggling of cocaine base to the United States and other countries where essential chemicals for refinement are more readily available. In July 1984, more than one metric ton of cocaine base was seized from a single air cargo shipment to South Florida. ^United\States ^Drug\Use ^Production ^Drug\Traffic ^Statistics ^NNICC ^Cocaine\Paste ^Cannabis ^Cocaine ^Opiates ^Money\Laundering ^Interdiction ^Refining ^Mexico ^Latin\America ^Canada ^Panama ^Venezuela ^Law\Enforcement

1256. —— (1987). *The NNICC Report 1985–1986*. Washington, D.C.: Drug Enforcement Administration. This is the ninth of the NNICC reports providing estimates of the supply of illicit drugs. This document, based on data currently available and on the combined available expertise of NNICC member agencies, "is the most comprehensive assessment prepared for the federal government on the worldwide illicit drug situation in 1985 and 1986." A primary source for production estimates and drug control efforts in foreign countries is the Department of State's *International Narcotics Control Strategy Report*. In general, the report notes that marijuana consumption in the United States declined from 1982 to 1985; cocaine became more readily available throughout the country, with a 24 percent increase in hospital-related emergencies. Also, the use of heroin in combination with other drugs remained a serious problem. In 1985, opium production increased in Southwest Asia and Mexico while a decrease was reported in the Golden Triangle (Burma, Laos, and Thailand). But increases in both areas were noted for 1986. ^United\States ^Drug\Use ^Production ^Drug\Traffic ^Statistics ^NNICC ^Supply ^Department\of\State ^Golden\Triangle ^Burma ^Laos ^Thailand ^Latin\America ^Mexico ^Opiates ^Southeast\Asia

1257. —— (1988). *The National Narcotics Intelligence Consumer Committee Report 1987*. Washington, D.C.: NNICC. Discusses, as customary for this series, sources of and trafficking in cannabis, cocaine, opiates, and other dangerous drugs. Includes a chapter on drug money laundering. Contributing agencies to the report are the Central Intelligence Agency, U.S. Coast Guard, U.S. Custom's Service, Department of Defense, Drug Enforcement Administration, Federal Bureau of Investigation, Immigration and Naturalization Service, Internal Revenue Service, National Institute on Drug Abuse, Department of State, Department of the Treasury, and the White House Drug Abuse Policy Office. A primary source for production estimates and drug control efforts in foreign countries is the Department of State's International Narcotics Control Strategy Report, prepared annually. Marijuana was readily available in the United States during 1987, because the supply increased. Increases were noted from Mexico and Colombia (the principal sources) as well as an increased domestic U.S. supply in spite of the eradication of about 2.7 million more cultivated cannabis plants in 1987 than in 1986. Successful eradication efforts in Jamaica and Belize decreased the supply of marijuana from those countries. Cocaine hydrochloride was also readily available. Colombia trafficking groups remained the principal producers and distributors for the United States. While purity levels remained high, wholesale prices were the lowest ever reported. Crack continued to be a problem in 1987. Heroin was generally available in most metropolitan areas of the United States. Based on heroin signature samples, it appears that Mexican heroin was the predominate variety, although Southeast Asian heroin has increased since 1985. The use of needles/syringes to administer heroin and the connection of that to AIDS remained a serious health concern. As for money laundering, southern Florida, northern and southern California, New York, and the Southwest were the centers for the collection and laundering of moneys associated with the importation and distribution of illegal drugs. In 1987 the government of Pakistan made additional efforts to bring to trial and punishment those involved in committing narcotic offenses. These include an amendment to an earlier drug act to include a provision for asset seizure. The government also, in 1987, sprayed opium poppy fields with the herbicide 2-4-D. The Indian government continued to implement its seizure provisions of its 1985 narcotic drugs and psychotropic substances act. Turkish law enforcement officers became more vigilant, and in the spring of 1987 the Syrians conducted an operation in the Bekaa Valley designed to eradicate opium poppies there. The results were negligible. ^United\States ^Drug\Use ^Drug\Traffic ^Production ^Money\Laundering ^Statistics ^NNICC ^Department\of\State ^Mexico ^Latin\America ^Colombia ^Jamaica ^Belize ^Caribbean ^Crop\Eradication ^Traffickers ^Heroin ^Cocaine ^Cannabis ^Syria ^Middle\East ^Turkey ^India ^Herbicides ^Legislation ^Law\Enforcement ^Asset\Forfeiture ^Pakistan ^Southwest\Asia ^Florida ^California ^New\York ^Southeast\Asia ^AIDS

1258. ———— (1989). *The NNICC Report 1988: The Supply of Illicit Drugs to the United States.* Washington D.C.: NNICC. The National Narcotics Intelligence Consumers Committee report brings together information from the collaborative efforts of all federal agencies with drug-related functions. The 1988 report shows that available marijuana increased, and that it remained the most widely used illegal drug in the United States. Despite record seizures, cocaine continued to be readily available in the United States. Colombian nationals continued to be the principal producers and distributors. Wholesale and retail prices fell to the lowest reported for any year. As for heroin, Southeast Asian heroin was the predominant variety available in the eastern United States while Mexican black tar heroin predominated in the West. Southern Florida continued to be a major money-laundering center. ^United\States ^Drug\Use ^Production ^Drug\Traffic ^Money\Laundering ^Statistics ^NNICC ^Cannabis ^Drug\Control\Policies\Effectiveness ^Economics ^Heroin ^Cocaine ^Florida ^Mexico ^Latin\America

1259. National Research Council (1982). *An Analysis of Marijuana Policy.* Washington D.C.: National Academy Press. Insofar as marijuana is a potentially hazardous psychoactive substance—and most observers now view it to be, especially for heavy users and for youth—policy options for legal control may be divided into three classes—prohibition of supply and use, partial prohibition of supply only, and regulation of supply. The National Commission on Marijuana and Drug Abuse recommended, in 1972, a policy of partial prohibition as the best approach. This report analyzes the evidence acquired since 1972 in terms of economic costs, social effects, and incidence of use. Eleven states adopted the partial prohibition option, and their experience suggests that such an option is as effective in controlling marijuana use as complete prohibition, but it offers substantially reduced social and economic costs. Insufficient information is available to assess the costs of regulatory policy options. ^United\States ^Cannabis ^Drug\Control\Policies ^Reviews ^P\S\Partial\Prohibition ^Consequences\Economic

1260. Nebelkopf, Ethan (1987). "Herbal Therapy in the Treatment of Drug Use." *The International Journal of the Addictions* 22(8): 695–717. This article reviews the use of herbal therapy, a relatively new phenomenon in modern days, although the practice of herbalism goes back many centuries in the treatment of drug abusers. The concern is to develop programs that utilize a holistic approach in dealing with mental, physical, emotional, and spiritual problems accompanying substance abuse. An annotated bibliography is included. ^Drug\Use ^Treatment\Therapy ^Bibliographies ^Treatment\Integrated

1261. Negrete, Juan C. (1978). "Coca Leaf Chewing; A Public Health Assessment." *British Journal of Addiction* 73(3): 283–90. Although coca leaf production is increasing, the total number of traditional chewers seems to be diminishing. Socioeconomic progress and better educational opportunities are largely responsible for this tendency. Some health problems are noted among habitual chewers. ^Latin\America ^Coca ^Drug\Use ^Consequences\Health ^Culture

1262. —— (1988). "What's Happened to the Cannabis Debate?" *British Journal of Addiction* 83:359–72. A professor of psychiatry laments that the public debate on cannabis is showing signs of extinction. Politicians have not talked much about it in recent years, and the scientific community appears to be losing interest. This derives, perhaps, from social complacency, the emergence of other drug habits that are potentially more serious or at least interesting, and also from the rather limited progress made in answering some major cannabis research questions. Unfortunately, scientific work is frequently prompted by expressed social needs, or at least by expressed political attention to those needs. When such social pressure diminishes, scientific interest tends to fade away. Warns against repetition of such historical episodes with respect to cannabis and lists the many research issues that remain unanswered as of 1988. ^Cannabis ^Consequences\Theories ^Drug\Control\Policies\Critique

1263. "The New Guerrilla Front" (1984). *The Andean Report* (August): 146–53. *Sendero Luminoso* is successfully resisting government attempts to contain it. A front has opened in Tingo María, fueled by a three-pronged thirty-million-dollar U.S. effort to eradicate the region's coca, promote alternative crops, and enforce law and order. ^Latin\America ^Peru ^Coca ^Crop\Eradication ^Politics ^Insurgents ^Consequences\Drug\Control\Policies

1264. "New Report Shows 'Startling' Use of Cocaine by Young Adults" (1985). *Narcotics Control Digest,* 2 October, 3. A new survey shows that more than a quarter of young adults aged eighteen to twenty-five have used cocaine. ^United\States ^Cocaine ^Drug\Use ^Statistics

1265. Newcomb, Michael D. and Peter M. Bentler (1988). *Consequences of Adolescent Drug Use: Impact on the Lives of Young Adults.* Beverly Hills, Calif.: Sage Publications. Seeks, through scientific evidence, to explore consequences of drug abuse in relatively normal and unselected populations. The book is represented as a pioneering attempt to evaluate the effects of general and specific drug use during adolescence on young adult functioning. Research was funded by the National Institute on Drug Abuse. Specifically, what is the impact or consequences of teenage drug use on the transition into young adulthood? Four "domains of consequences" are discussed: biological (such as physiological processes), intrapersonal (within the individual), interpersonal (social), and sociocultural (community system). Theories of drug use consequences are presented as well as information about the study design, sample, and methodological considerations. Specific topics include impacts on family formation and stability, criminality and deviant behavior, sexual behavior and involvement, educational pursuits, livelihood pursuits, mental health, and social integration. ^United\States ^Drug\Use ^Youth ^NIDA ^Consequences\Physiological ^Consequences\Psychological ^Consequences\Social ^Consequences\Cultural   ^Consequences\Theories   ^Consequences\Family   ^Consequences\Crime   ^Consequences\Sexuality ^Consequences\Educational

1266. Ng, B. C. (1984). "Treatment and Rehabilitation of Drug Addicts in Singapore 1977-1982." *The Annals of the Academy of Medicine* 13(1): 66–68. The treatment and rehabilitation of drug addicts consists of detoxification, recuperation and orientation, indoctrination, physical training, and work programs. A follow-up through a day-release program is made to bridge the gap between the disciplinary regimen of the treatment program and the relative freedom of the outside world. Addicts are given opportunities to pursue academic studies. Here, two review committees monitor the progress. It is significant that from 1977 to 1982 there was a notable decrease in the total number of admissions to treatment and rehabilitation programs. There also appeared to be a drop in the number of youths recruited into drug abuse. ^Southeast\Asia ^Singapore ^Drug\Use ^Treatment ^Rehabilitation

1267. Ng, Handrick W. K. (1985). "Drug Demand Reduction Programmes for Young People in Hong Kong." *Bulletin on Narcotics* 37(2-3): 91–97. Description of community involvement projects, preventive drug education, and the production of educational and publicity materials designed to reduce the attraction of drugs for young people. Description of a program called "Youth against Drugs Scheme," which provides youths an opportunity to develop and implement antinarcotics publicity projects in their own way with limited supervision. ^Hong\Kong ^Drug\Use ^Youth ^Southeast\Asia ^Prevention\Drug\Education ^Private\Initiatives

1268. Nichols, Henry (1988). "Narcotics Anonymous." *Journal of Substance Abuse Treatment* 5:195–96. Description of the development of Narcotics Anonymous, modelled after Alcoholics Anonymous. Narcotics Anonymous can be a useful resource for professionals working in the field of addiction treatment. Particularly is it helpful in terms of social reinforcement. ^Drug\Use ^Treatment\Therapeutic\Community ^Private\Initiatives

1269. Niedergang, M. (1987). "Some See Answer to Colombia's Problems in Legal Drugs." *LeMonde/Manchester Guardian Weekly*, 11 January. Should trafficking in narcotics be legalized? Some see that the Colombian Supreme Court's ruling of "unconstitutional" on a 1980 law that ratified an extradition treaty with the United States as, in effect, approaching a legalization policy. This is because the extradition treaty has been fiercely opposed by the Colombian crime syndicate which, having won this round, is now pressing for legalizing drug traffic. The United States is pressing Colombia to extradite forty-nine people. The drug barons' private armies, their methods of recruitment, and the "cheapness" of life are discussed. ^Latin\America ^Colombia ^Extradition ^Traffickers\Private\Armies ^Consequences\Social ^P\S\Legalization ^Consequences\Violence

1270. Nietschmann, Bernard (1987). "Drugs-for-Guns Cycle Produces Bitter Ironies." *The New York Times*, 28 August. A short discussion on how U.S. aid to grower countries to eradicate narcotics plants provides those governments with arms that they then turn on their own citizens, which encourages frantic narcotics products growing in order for the people to buy military weapons to defend themselves. ^United\States ^Drug\Control\Policies ^Consequences\Foreign\Aid ^Consequences\Unintended ^Crop\Eradication ^Consequences\Human\Rights

1271. Nirenberg, Ted D., and Stephen A. Maisto, eds. (1987). *Developments in the Assessment and Treatment of Addictive Behaviors.* Norwood, N.J.: Ablex Publishing Corporation. Previous failures in treating addictive behavior have resulted, in part, because researchers and clinicians have studied such behavior independently of available information on other addictive behaviors (e.g., alcohol, tobacco). New evidence presented here suggests a number of commonalities among the addictions. Reviews recent treatment advances for each of the addictions and highlights similarities among those addictions in etiology and maintenance. ^Drug\Use ^Treatment ^Reviews ^Alcohol ^Tobacco ^Treatment\Theories

1272. Noble, Kenneth B. (1987). "Infighting Hampers Anti-Drug War." *The New York Times*, 9 August, 4. Describes the bureaucratic infighting during the Reagan administration relative to the antidrug war. Offers the kind of information that critics frequently cite to argue that the drug war has more to do with internal politics in the United States than it does with anything relating to narcotics. ^United\States ^Drug\Control\Policies ^Bureaucracy ^Consequences\Political

1273. Norwood, Glenda R. (1985). "A Society That Promotes Drug Abuse." *Child Education*, March/April, 267–71. In America not only are illicit drugs abused, but licit ones as well in the form of prescription drugs. Looks into the social and other reasons as to why drugs are abused, the societal messages that promote drug abuse, and the probable impact all this has on preadolescent children. ^United\States ^Drug\Use ^Youth ^Society ^Culture ^Drug\Use\Theories ^Consequences\Children

1274. Novick, D. M., I. Khan, and M. J. Kreek (1986). "Acquired Immunodeficiency Syndrome and Infection with Hepatitis Viruses in Individuals Abusing Drugs by Injection." *Bulletin on Narcotics* 38(1-2): 15–25. Drug injection has long been associated with the hepatitis D virus that attacks the liver. Additional viruses are now noted among drug users. More than a quarter of the individuals acquiring the AIDS virus in the United States are homosexual or heterosexual males who are also needle-using drug abusers. It is this population that is implicated in the spreading of the AIDS virus to the general population. The authors call for intensive international cooperation in trying to develop effective measures to deal with needle-using drug abusers and the complications that derive from their habits. ^Heroin ^AIDS ^Consequences\Health ^Proffered\Solutions

1275. "Now Let's Slay the Other Dragon" (1988). *The Economist*, 30 July, 42–43. Describes Bolivia's new law restricting the cultivation of coca. Immediately after implementation, Roberto Suárez was escorted from his ranch by policemen and has already begun to serve the twelve-year jail term to which he had been sentenced. In return for suppressing the livelihood of substantial numbers of Bolivians, the country's president is hoping for United States aid. This will finance Bolivia's crop eradication and crop substitution programs. ^Latin\America ^Bolivia ^Coca ^Drug\Control\Policies ^Traffickers

1276. Nurco, David N., and Robert L. DuPont (1977). "A Preliminary Report of Crime and Addiction within a Community-Wide Population of Narcotic Addicts." *Drug and Alcohol Dependence* 2:109–21. Discusses the criminal behavior of narcotic addicts based on a sample of males identified as narcotics abusers by a large U.S. urban police department over a twenty year period. The records of 252 subjects were analyzed. The findings generally support previous ones in regard to the increase of criminal activity after the onset of narcotic addiction. ^United\States ^Heroin ^Consequences\Crime ^Drug\Use

1277. Nurco, David N., John C. Ball, John W. Shaffer, and Thomas E. Hanlon (1985). "The Criminality of Narcotic Addicts." *The Journal of Nervous and Mental Disease* 173(2): 94–102. Consistent with most studies on the relationship between crime and narcotic addiction (primarily heroin), this study shows that narcotic addicts commit a vast amount of crime, with much of it directly related to their need to purchase drugs. In order to detect causal relationships, addicts must be classified according to different types. When addicts are treated for narcotics addiction successfully, their criminality is reduced. In treatment programs, extensive prior criminal involvement is associated with negative treatment outcomes. ^Heroin ^Treatment ^Consequences\Crime ^Drug\Use

1278. Nurco, David N., Thomas E. Hanlon, Timothy W. Kinlock, and Karen R. Duszynski (1988). "Differential Criminal Patterns of Narcotic Addicts over an Addiction Career." *Criminology* 26(3): 407–423. Do criminals engage in crimes and drug addiction, or does drug addiction lead to crime? Those previously involved in crime increase their criminal activities when they become addicted. Those not involved in preaddiction crime become much more sharply involved in criminal behavior. ^Heroin ^Drug\Use ^Consequences\Crime

1279. Nurco, David N., John W. Shaffer, Timothy W. Kinlock, and John Langrod (1986). "A Comparison by Race/Ethnicity of Narcotic Addict Crime Rates in Baltimore, New York, and Philadelphia." *American Journal of Drug and Alcohol Abuse* 12(4): 297–307. Crime rates are higher during the period of active addiction (suggesting then that drugs may be said to "drive" crime), and there are distinctive differences among black, white, and hispanic addicts. Blacks had higher rates than either whites or hispanics with respect to all crime indices. This may derive from a lack of legitimate employment opportunities for blacks. ^United\States ^Heroin ^Minorities ^Consequences\Crime ^Crime\Theories

1280. Nurco, David N., Norma Wegner, Philip Stephenson, Abraham Makofsky, and John W. Shaffer (1983). *Ex-Addicts' Self-Help Groups: Potentials and Pitfalls.* New York: Praeger. Rehabilitation of narcotic addicts in the United States through self-help groups. This volume is advanced as another resource for drug treatment specialists as well as addicts themselves, concentrating on self-help concepts that have in recent years gained more and more attention. The authors claim that this volume represents the first documented attempt to utilize self-help concepts and techniques in the treatment of narcotic addiction. The method of presentation is the case study. ^Drug\Use ^Treatment\Therapeutic\Community

1281. Oakes, Richard T. (1980). "Marijuana and Economic Due Process: A Transition from Prohibition to Regulation." *Contemporary Drug Problems* 9(4): 401–35. Up to the early 1980s, criminal law was the principal tool of social control over marijuana. This article traces the history of prohibition and discusses some of the untoward results and social costs. The current system is viewed as being nonrational, sending conflicting signals within the family and the criminal justice system. Not surprisingly, the author concludes that prohibition does not work. The balance of the article explores and then rejects prohibition arguments, legal and social, based upon privacy or an extrapolated right to alter one's consciousness. If prohibition does not work, and if legal rights to substance abuse are not obtained, what is to be done? One starts with a careful examination of the police power and economic due process. Exercising economic due process, marijuana regulation ought to be viewed, or the controls associated with it ought to be derived, from the economic system as protected by the constitution, not as a constitutional right. The underlying assumptions are that prohibition is unworkable, perhaps even damaging, and that therefore an alternative means of acceptable control must be presented. It must be constitutionally proper, less restrictive, workable, and administratively and economically sound. ^Cannabis ^Drug\Control\Policies\History ^Legalization ^Consequences\Economic ^Consequences\Social ^Drug\Control\Policies\Critique ^P\S\Constitutional

1282. Oblitas Fernández, Edgar (1982). *Narcotráfico, Decreto Ley No. 18714 de Control y Lucha Contra Sustancias Peligrosas de 25 de Noviembre de 1981: Estudio Crítico Jurisprudencia.* Sucre, Bolivia: Editorial "Tupac Katari." A brief discussion is given about the political/social/economic backdrop to the passage of decree law #18714 of November 25, 1981. The law, intended to give Bolivia legal clout with respect to dealing with narcotic trafficking, is given in its entirety. The appendix includes previous statutes on drug trafficking. A large portion of the book is dedicated to an examination of specific court cases and their disposition by appeals courts. ^Latin\America ^Bolivia ^Drug\Control\Policies ^Legislation ^Judiciary ^Consequences\Social ^Consequences\Economic ^Consequences\Political

1283. O'Connell, David F. (1989). "Treating the High Risk Adolescent: A Survey of Effective Programs and Interventions." *Journal of Chemical Dependency Treatment* 2(1): 49–69. Strong efforts at early identification of vulnerable adolescents and the design of appropriate prevention and intervention programs by clinicians needs to be made. All of this is complicated by the fact that adolescents at risk come from a highly diversified group in terms of age, background, and levels of psychopathology, life adjustment, and coping skills. ^Drug\Use\Theories ^Youth ^Prevention ^Treatment

1284. Odom, William E. (1988). "It's Time to Create a Border Control Department." *U.S. News and World Report,* 5 December, 22. The author calls for reorganization of federal bureaucracies to create a single agency to control U.S. borders and make integrated decisions about fighting the drug war. He proposes the creation of a Border Control Department. It would be an independent agency, perhaps with cabinet status, and would include the Coast Guard, the Customs Service, the Border Patrol, and the Drug Enforcement Administration. It would be a uniformed agency with a military ethic. ^United\States ^Interdiction ^Bureaucracy ^P\S\Military

1285. O'Hara, Charles P. III (1987). "Behavioral Effects of Phencyclidine and Cocaine on Infants Exposed in Utero, as Measured by the Neonatal Behavioral Assessment Scale." Ph.D. diss., California School of Professional Psychology. This dissertation examines the usefulness of the Neonatal Behavioral Assessment Scale in identifying significant behavioral differences among infants who are exposed to PCP or to cocaine during fetal development. The analysis shows that the test can discriminate among neonates whose mothers abused PCP or cocaine during pregnancy. The differences between the user group and the control group indicate that the infant whose mother abused PCP is most at risk for difficult bonding with a care giver. The cocaine infant is also at risk during this early bonding period. ^Cocaine ^Health ^Consequences\Fetuses ^Consequences\Children ^Consequences\Parenting

1286. O'Hara, J. L. and M. Zawawi Salleh (1987). "Recent Developments in Legislative and Administrative Measures in Countries of the Association of Southeast Asian Nations to Counter the Illicit Trafficking in Drugs." *Bulletin on Narcotics* 39(1): 51–56. ASEAN member states, in order to achieve the common goal of suppressing illicit trafficking in drugs, have adopted various legislative and administrative measures aimed at establishing uniform methods. Describes some of the latest developments in the adoption of these measures. The authors are senior advisers in the Attorney General's office of Malaysia. ^Southeast\Asia ^Drug\Control\Policies ^International\Cooperation ^ASEAN

1287. Ojeda, Roseliano (1987). *Como se Desangra un País*. Carácas, Venezuela: Vadell Hermanos Editores. Foremost, this book articulates the ways by which a country bleeds itself to death. Included are discussions about debt, capital flight, political corruption, and internal political conflict. Of interest to this bibliography is the discussion on drugs, more specifically, the traffic, consumption, and laundering of dollars associated with drugs. The thesis is that the traffic in and consumption of drugs is a problem created externally but imposed and imported into the country and done so in ways that threaten the national integrity of the country. ^Drug\Traffic ^Economics ^Politics ^Demand ^Consequences\Social ^Consequences\Economic ^Consequences\Political ^National\Security ^International\Debt

1288. Okasha, A. (1985). "Young People and the Struggle against Drug Abuse in the Arab Countries." *Bulletin on Narcotics* 37(2-3): 67–73. Chronicles the involvement of Egyptian youth from all socioeconomic strata in new, nontraditional forms of drug abuse. Suggests that comprehensive community-based programs need to be organized to improve the personal and social functioning of drug-dependent persons, to promote drug education, and to increase understanding between younger and older generations. ^Middle\East ^Egypt ^Drug\Use ^Youth ^P\S\Integrated

1289. Olivares, Gilbert J., Ramesh C. Gupta, George D. Lundberg, and S. H. Montgomery (1977). "Street Cocaine 1971–1975: Nature, Cost and Effects." *Veterinary and Human Toxicology* 19(3): 169–72. Reports on a laboratory examination of 270 street drug samples alleged to be, or tested as, cocaine. Considerable adulteration, including other drugs, is noted. ^Cocaine ^Health

1290. "Omnibus Drug Legislation" (1986). *Congressional Digest* (November): 259–88. Description of the legislation intended to strengthen the hand of law enforcement in dealing with the drug trade. There is a death penalty provision as well as increased sanctions. The evolution of current drug legislation (1965–1982) is discussed, federal agencies involved are indicated, and various commentaries are included. ^United\States ^Drug\Control\Policies ^Legislation

1291. "On-the-Job Drug Use Increasing" (1985). *Narcotics Control Digest*, 17 April, 3. A survey reports that people are increasingly using drugs at work, and it is judged that this has affected their job performance. Alarmingly, many would become heavier users if given a promotion or a raise. ^United\States ^Drug\Use ^Workplace ^Consequences\Economic

1292. Onís, Juan de (1985). "Brazil's Role in Cocaine Trade Is Expanding." *The Los Angeles Times*, 24 February, 8. Describes the sudden rise of a wealthy businessman who was killed in the crash of his own cocaine-carrying plane in Brazil. The aircraft, apparently, had been serving cocaine traffickers in Bolivia. ^Latin\America ^Brazil ^Cocaine ^Drug\Traffic ^Traffickers

1293. "Open Palms among the Palm Trees" (1986). *The Economist*, 11 October, 47. Continuing involvement of the Turks and Caicos Islands in the drug trade. Britain has virtually reimposed direct rule on these dependencies. Comments made, also, about the Cayman Islands, Jamaica, and Panama. ^Turks\and\Caicos ^Drug\Traffic ^Cayman ^Jamaica ^Panama ^Caribbean ^Latin\America

1294. Oreskes, Michael (1988). "Castro Tells Group from Congress He Wants to Assist in Drug Fight." *The New York Times*, 16 December, A18. Fidel Castro, long accused by the United States of aiding drug traffickers, told congressional visitors that he wanted to begin joint efforts to halt the flow of drugs. The question of how much "official complicity" Cuba has had in the drug traffic moving through its territory has long been debated. ^Cuba ^Caribbean ^United\States ^International\Cooperation ^Drug\Control\Policies

1295. Ortíz Pinchetti, Francisco, Miguel Cabildo, Federico Campbell, and Ignacio Rodríguez (1981). *La Operación Cóndor.* Mexico City: Proceso. This small volume (77 pages) lays out the decision, and means to implement it, undertaken by the Mexican government to reduce drug traffic within its borders—suppressing the planting, cultivation, harvesting, production, exportation, importation, distribution, and the use and possession of psychotropic drugs. A specific focus is on opium poppy and marijuana plants. To address growth in these areas, the Mexican government launched its Operation Condor. The book chronicles the excesses of the police force (torture, rape, abuse) involved in the operation. It includes an article on the herbicide paraquat and its danger to humankind. ^Latin\America ^Mexico ^Crop\Eradication ^Herbicides ^Drug\Control\Policies\Critique ^Supply ^Consequences\Human\Rights

1296. Overend, William (1987). "Cocaine Floods Southland via Colombia–Mexico Link." *The Los Angeles Times*, 31 December. A partnership has developed between Colombian cocaine cartels and "seven major drug families of Mexico," and the effect is to facilitate a flood of cocaine into southern California. The Drug Enforcement Agency estimates that up to 40 percent of all cocaine entering the United States now enters through Mexico. ^Latin\America ^Colombia ^Mexico ^United\States ^Cocaine ^Drug\Traffic ^Traffickers

1297. —— (1987). "Failure to Share Funds Could Cripple War on Drugs, Gates Says." *The Los Angeles Times*, 5 November, 28. Part of the motivation of U.S. drug enforcement agencies and local police forces to engage in their own drug interdiction efforts is that they have been able to share in the proceeds of whatever property and material they confiscate. There has been some discussion that this sharing would cease, and this article cites Los Angeles Police Chief Daryl F. Gates as saying that such a policy shift would produce negative consequences. ^United\States ^Asset\Forfeiture ^Politics

1298. —— (1988). "Chaotic DEA Office Ripe for Problems in the Early 1980s." *The Los Angeles Times*, 19 December, 3. Discusses personnel problems within the agency, including some corruption in spite of the vast majority of the agents being honest. ^United\States ^DEA ^Consequences\Corruption ^Bureaucracy

1299. —— (1988). "Violence Feared as Asian Heroin Influx Soars." *The Los Angeles Times*, 25 February, 3. A replication of the "cocaine cowboy" wars which plagued Florida in the 1970s when rival drug dealers engaged in shootouts in the streets, is considered to be a possibility for California's West Coast as record amounts of heroin land there. Asian gangs in Los Angeles (Triads) are extremely active. Ethnic battles among Asian, Mexican, and black gangs are increasing. ^United\States ^Heroin ^Drug\Traffic ^Organized\Crime ^Crime ^Consequences\Violence ^Triads ^Minorities

1300. Overend, William, and John Kendall (1988). "Drug Agents' Tips to Dealers Alleged; Officials Say Activities of 3 Suspects May Have Involved Arrest Warnings." *The Los Angeles Times*, 24 November, 1. Three former federal drug agents have been charged in a cocaine corruption case in which they allegedly gave tips to dealers. There appears to be some collusion, also, in money-laundering schemes. ^United\States ^Consequences\Corruption

1301. Pacini, Deborah, and Christine Franquemont, eds. (1986). *Coca and Cocaine: Effects on People and Policy in Latin America*. Proceedings of the

Conference on the Coca Leaf and Its Derivatives—Biology, Society and Policy. Sponsored by the Latin American Studies Program, Cornell University, April 25–26, 1985. Cambridge, Mass.: Cultural Survival. This colloquium of papers from a Cornell University conference dealing with the coca leaf and its derivatives as they relate to biology, society, and public policy, covers an extraordinary array of topics. These range from the botanical origins of coca in South America to coca as a symbol of cultural identity in Andean communities, to coca production in the Bolivian yungas in the colonial period, to the international narcotics control system as related to coca and cocaine, to foreign politics of cocaine as exemplified in the United States' plan to eradicate the leaf in Peru, to the Colombian connection, and, in particular, to the impact of the drug traffic on Colombia, on Bolivian rural society and economy, and on tribal Amazonian Indians. ^Latin\America ^Coca ^Cocaine ^Drug\Traffic ^Drug\Control\Policies\History ^Economics ^Politics ^Society ^Culture ^Drug\Use\History ^Colombia ^Bolivia ^Consequences\Social ^Consequences\Economic

1302. Page, J. Bryan, Jack Fletcher, and William R. True (1988). "Psychosociocultural Perspectives on Chronic Cannabis Use: The Costa Rican Follow-Up." *Journal of Psychoactive Drugs* 20(1): 57–65. These authors returned to the population sample used by Vera Rubin and Lambros Comitas in their 1973-1975 NIDA sponsored study of chronic cannabis use in Costa Rica. New tests were applied on the subjects. The principal problem in assessing the relationship between marijuana use and the human condition of marijuana users is, in the case of Costa Rica, the pervasive influence of the general social disapproval of marijuana smoking. Marijuana smokers, on the whole, are lodged in the bottom strata of Costa Rican society. Under these circumstances, marijuana smokers really have a tough time in Costa Rica. They have greater problems with kin and family; they are more vulnerable to arrest and imprisonment; they are viewed as being untrustworthy and undesirable; and they have difficulty both obtaining and retaining employment. ^Latin\America ^Costa\Rica ^Cannabis ^Drug\Use ^Society ^Reviews ^NIDA ^Consequences\Misc

1303. Page, Richard C., and Sam Mitchell (1988). "The Effects of Two Therapeutic Communities on Illicit Drug Users between 6 Months and 1 Year after Treatment." *International Journal of the Addictions* 23(6): 591–601. From a relatively small sample (thirty), former residents of two drug treatment communities were studied. It was found that the amount of time they spent in treatment was associated with fewer arrests (the longer in treatment, the fewer the arrests) once they graduated from the programs. Also, less subsequent drug use was noted as a function of time spent in treatment and a fact that graduation occurred. ^Drug\Use ^Treatment\Therapeutic\Communities ^Crime

1304. Painter, James (1989). "Bolivia Struggles in War on Drugs." *The Christian Science Monitor*, 6 September, 6. The new government in Bolivia and its antidrug police force are convinced that to turn the tide in the cocaine war they need substantial foreign aid, more logistical support, and a better shared intelligence—but no United States troops. The Bolivians have vintage Korean War fire-arms, inferior communications, and only one radar station based in La Paz (which does not cover the eastern departments of the Beni and Santa Cruz where most of the ferrying of cocaine takes place). José Ali Parada, one of Bolivia's five most wanted traffickers, was just arrested and, because he was sentenced in absentia two years ago, immediately began serving his prison term in La Paz. Bolivia is now producing increasing amounts of cocaine hydrochloride, not just cocaine paste and the coca leaf. ^Latin\America ^Bolivia ^Cocaine ^Production ^Drug\Control\Policies ^Law\Enforcement ^Refining ^Traffickers ^International\Cooperation ^Foreign\Aid

1305. ———— (1989). "Bolivia to Crack Down on Coca." *The Christian Science Monitor*, 21 July, 4. Description of how peasants in certain areas of the Chapare have been pushed or convinced to eradicate their coca plants. A number of peasant protests have been noted. ^Latin\America ^Bolivia ^Coca ^Crop\Eradication ^Producers\Unions

1306. ———— (1989). "Bolivia's New President Faces an Old Problem: How to Control Coca Growing." *Latinamerica Press*, 24 August, 3. Describes the resistance of coca growers, who have become unionized, to the forced eradication of coca plants in areas now defined as illegal for coca growing. The U.S.-funded coca eradication program has fallen far short of its goals. There are positive economic incentives: Peasants who pull up their coca plants receive about $810 in compensation for every acre. However, this has not been sufficient to bring large numbers of peasants into compliance. Part of the problem is a lack of institutional support for alternative crops including credit for a reasonable length of time. ^Bolivia ^Coca ^Crop\Substitution ^Crop\Eradication ^Producers\Unions ^Economics ^Latin\America

1307. ———— (1990). "Andean Leaders Respond to Bush." *The Christian Science Monitor*, November 29, p. 3. Previews some of the issues that will be discussed at the summit of the five presidents of the Andean pact countries. An effort is being made to set up a regime of regional cooperation among Peru, Bolivia, Colombia, Venezuela, and Ecuador. With new presidents in Peru and Bolivia, a joint strategy appears to be more feasible. Colombia, Bolivia, and Peru, especially, insist that consumer countries should provide considerable economic aid. ^Latin\America ^Peru ^Bolivia ^Colombia ^Ecuador ^Venezuela ^International\Cooperation ^P\S\Foreign\Aid

1308. ———— (1990). "Bolivia Resists Drug Role for Army." *The Christian Science Monitor*, 7 May, 6. Considerable political opposition has arisen in Bolivia, among unions representing coca producers and politicians, about Bolivia's armed forces becoming involved in any coca eradication program. A comparison of military operations in Peru and Colombia is given. Statistics on supply reduction programs are noted. ^Latin\America ^Bolivia ^Peru ^Colombia ^Military ^Crop\Eradication ^Statistics ^Consequences\Political ^Producers\Unions

1309. ———— (1990). "Bolivia Resists U.S. on Antidrug Fight." *The Christian Science Monitor*, November 29, p. 3. The United States insists that Bolivia order its army to join in the country's antidrug fight, but Bolivia's president stoutly resists. Coca union leaders in the Chapare region threatened to march on the nation's capitol if the government sent in its army. Bolivia continues to work in nonmilitary ways to eradicate its coca crop. About 20,000 acres, equivalent to one-fifth of the coca growing areas of the Chapare, were eradicated in 1990. ^Latin\America ^United\States ^Bolivia ^International\Cooperation\Critique ^Military ^Producers\Unions ^Drug\Control\Politics ^Production ^Coca

1310. ———— (1990). "Bolivia Tries to Break Its Economic Addiction." *The Christian Science Monitor*, May 24, p. 5. There is a glut of coca leaves on the market, and farmers are hard pressed to find alternative crops from which they can make a living. Some 6000 peasants have eradicated all or some of their coca bushes in the previous five months, and some have obtained a $2,000 grant to uproot coca bushes from each hectare of their land. Prices are motivating. A one-hundred pound bag of leaves has dropped from $60 to $10, although production costs are estimated to be about $30. Statistics are given regarding estimated numbers of producers, numbers of people who depend on the coca market for their living (about 20% of the Bolivian population), and the desperate economic straits in which the peasantry now finds itself. ^Latin\America ^Bolivia ^Coca ^Production ^Consequences\Economic ^Crop\Substitution ^Crop\Eradication ^Economics

1311. ———— (1990). "Bolivian Coca Growers Voluntarily Eradicate Crops as Price Drops." *The Christian Science Monitor*, 21 February, 3. Colombia's war against its own cocaine traffickers has had a considerable effect in Bolivia. Movement of coca leaves and coca paste has drastically dropped, there is a surplus on the market, and the price paid coca growers has crashed. Peasants increasingly are desirous of eradicating their crop in exchange for the $2,000 per hectare promised by the country's eradication program. ^Latin\America ^Consequences\Markets ^Production ^Coca ^Bolivia ^Crop\Eradication ^Consequences\Political

1312. Pakistan Narcotics Control Board (1986). *National Survey on Drug Abuse in Pakistan.* Islamabad, Pakistan: PanGraphics Ltd. Drug abuse in Pakistan in recent years has reached epidemic proportions. What has been the extent and ramifications of its impact on Pakistani society? A survey was undertaken under the auspices of the Pakistan Narcotics Control Board in 1982 to answer the question. The analysis of the results of that survey is the subject of this volume. 1.3 million regular drug abusers live in Pakistan. This does not include the casual user. Nearly half the total number of abusers are literate, and they are relatively young. As much as 20 percent of a wage earner's income is spent on satisfying his drug desires. For heroin abusers, unemployment poses a particularly great problem. The amount spent represents as much as 1.1 percent of Pakistan's gross national product. Heroin, virtually unknown and unavailable until 1980, assumed seventh place in 1982 and fifth at the end of 1983. In all opiate categories, some 175 tons were consumed in 1982 in Pakistan. ^Pakistan ^Southwest\Asia ^Drug\Use ^Statistics ^Consequences\Economic

1313. "Pakistan Tribes a Big Hurdle in Drive to Limit Heroin Trade" (1985). *Narcotics Control Digest,* 10 July, 5–6. Fierce tribal chieftains and a rugged, unguarded border combine to make Pakistan's northwest frontier province a conduit for more than half of America's heroin. Tough suppression measures have failed to make much of a dent. Some of the labs have moved to Afghanistan. ^Pakistan ^Southwest\Asia ^Afghanistan ^Heroin ^Drug\Traffic ^Law\Enforcement ^Golden\Crescent ^Drug\Control\Policies\Effectiveness

1314. "Panama: Corruption, Drug Charges Hurt but Fail to Unseat Noriega" (1988). *Latinamerica Press,* 3 March, 1. Discussion of how General Noriega has played "both sides" in the drug accusation war. ^Latin\America ^Panama ^Drug\Traffic ^Politics ^Consequences\Corruption

1315. "Paraguay Officials Blamed for Condoning Drug Trade" (1988). *Latinamerica Press,* 24 March, 1. The U.S. ambassador to Paraguay heightened tension between the two countries by accusing high-level officials in the Stroessner regime of involvement in drug trafficking. Ambassador Taylor named human rights infractions and drug trafficking as the two thorns in U.S.–Paraguayan relations. The Paraguayan official posture is to fight the illegal drug trade. ^Latin\America ^Paraguay ^United\States ^Drug\Control\Policies ^Politics ^Consequences\Corruption ^Consequences\Foreign\Relations

1316. "Paraguay Refuses to Destroy Cocaine Production Chemicals" (1985). *Narcotics Control Digest,* 9 January, 10–11. Paraguayan officials seized nearly 50,000 gallons of ether, acetone, and hydrochloric acid—precursor chemicals for processing cocaine hydrochloride—obviously destined for the drug traffic, but refused a U.S. solicitation to destroy them. Paraguayan officials stated that orders would need to come from President Stroessner. ^Latin\America ^Paraguay ^Cocaine ^Drug\Traffic ^Precursor\Chemicals

1317. "Paraquat Is Sprayed on Marijuana in Texas" (1988). *The New York Times,* 20 July, A14. Sixteen acres of private land were sprayed, involving the DEA in such activity, on private land, for the first time. ^United\States ^Cannabis ^Crop\Eradication ^Herbicides ^Texas

1318. Park, Charles Stuart (1987). "The Coke War." *The Atlantic* (August): 6. A brief letter to the editor arguing against David Kline's previous *Atlantic* article on "How to Lose the Coke War." Park sees the solution to the eradication of coca and cocaine production not in high-visibility, high-speed strikes, but in long-term programs of essential rural development and crop substitution. ^United\States ^Cocaine ^Production ^P\S\Economic

1319. Parker, Howard, Keith Bakx, and Russel Newcomb (1988). *Living with Heroin*. Philadelphia, Penn.: Open University Press. A social-scientific study laced with anecdotes about what happened to a community in northwest England when, suddenly and unexpectedly, within the course of about three years several thousand of its younger and poorest residents became regular heroin users. The sociological and medical literature proved to be surprisingly unhelpful in understanding what was happening. Praise is given to Americans' willingness to combine medical and sociological perspectives to explain widespread heroin use in their inner cities. The consequences on individuals, their families, the community, and the political decision makers (who were paralyzed) are documented. The move of the youths to deviant behavior in order to finance their addiction is noted. ^United\Kingdom ^Heroin ^Drug\Use ^Youth ^Society

1320. Pascale, Pietro J. (1988). "Trend Analyses of Four Large-Scale Surveys of High School Drug Use 1977–1986." *Journal of Drug Education* 18(3): 221–64. Four large-scale surveys were conducted at three-year intervals beginning in 1977; the most recent one was implemented in 1986. The standard demographic variables were employed. The analysis confirms some of the speculations found elsewhere in the literature—that although education appears to increase a student's drug-related knowledge, it does little to change his or her attitudes about substance abuse. Interestingly, however, this study shows that when peer groups are the primary sources of instruction about drug abuse, larger attitude changes are more likely to take place. Also, when students volunteered for the education programs, greater change was noted in behavior. By implication, required courses in drug education seemed not to produce a positive outcome. ^United\States ^Drug\Use ^Prevention ^Youth ^Society ^Prevention\Drug\Education\Critique

1321. Passell, Peter (1988). "Faulty U.S. Logic in Cocaine Policy." *The New York Times*, 9 March, D2. Rising cocaine production and smuggling comes as no surprise to economists who study markets for illicit drugs. The war, they say, is fought on the front with the wrong weapons. Interdiction and destruction are irrelevant to long-term prospects for victory. The authority cited is Peter Reuter. Mark Kleiman, a researcher at Harvard's Kennedy School of Government, is cited as arguing that even large changes in smuggling costs are unlikely to affect American consumption very much. Tighter drug controls at the border that caused prices to rise would have the perverse effect of increasing the drug importers' revenues. ^United\States ^Cocaine ^Drug\Control\Policies\Critique ^Economics ^Drug\Traffic

1322. Pasternack, Peter F., Stephen B. Colvin, and F. Gregory Baumann, (1985). "Cocaine-Induced Angina Pectoris and Acute Myocardial Infarction in Patients Younger Than 40 Years." *The American Journal of Cardiology* 55(1 March): 847–48. Describes three patients in their thirties who were referred for coronary angiography after having angina pectoris or acute myocardial infarction, or both, coincident with an increase in frequency of cocaine use. The clinical observations suggest that there is a clear relation between increased cocaine abuse, onset of angina, and occurrence of acute myocardial infarction. ^Cocaine ^Consequences\Health

1323. Pasto, M. E., L. J. Graziani, S. L. Tunis, J. M. Deiling, A. B. Kurtz, B. Goldberg, and L. P. Finnegan (1985). "Ventricular Configuration and Cerebral Growth in Infants Born to Drug-Dependent Mothers." *Pediatric Radiology* 15:77–81. Report on ultrasound images on fifteen control infants and fifteen infants exposed to neonatal substance abuse (who demonstrated "neonatal abstinence syndrome"). In the drug-exposed infants, the "intracranial hemidiameter" was significantly smaller. "Whether or not the ventricles remain small and brain growth remains parallel after the period of abstinence awaits further investigation" (p. 77). ^Drug\Use ^Consequences\Fetuses ^Consequences\Children

1324. Pear, Robert (1988). "Draft Treaty Seeks to Take the Profit out of Drugs." *The New York Times*, 2 October, 11. The United States and more than 100 nations have negotiated a draft treaty that would require them to outlaw money laundering and also to pass laws enabling them to confiscate drug smuggling proceeds along with the physical equipment used to engage in smuggling practices. Detailed records would be required regarding precursor chemicals. ^Money\Laundering ^Drug\Control\Policies ^Precursor\Chemicals ^International\Cooperation

1325. ——— (1989). "Cubans Disclose a Drug Network." *The New York Times*, 24 June, A1. Having denied a "Cuban connection" for years, Castro is now condemning the existence of such a connection among senior military officers who had been accused of helping the Colombian cartels move drugs to the United States. ^Caribbean ^Cuba ^Drug\Traffic ^Law\Enforcement

1326. ——— (1989). "U.S. Praises Haitian on Drug Efforts." *The New York Times*, 11 April, A3. The president of Haiti has received praise for his efforts to combat narcotics, but this effort may have been a factor in bringing about the recent coup attempt against him. ^Haiti ^Drug\Control\Policies ^Insurgents ^Consequences\Political ^Caribbean

1327. ——— (1990). "Jamaican Criticizes Panama Invasion." *The New York Times*, 30 January, A15. However horrible the Panamanian government had become, the invasion to dislodge it from power was unjustified. Description of Jamaican president Michael Manley's position on drugs and politics in Latin America. ^Jamaica ^Panama ^United\States ^Drug\Control\Policies\Critique ^Latin\America ^Consequences\Foreign\Relations

1328. Pearson, Geoffrey (1987). "Social Deprivation, Unemployment, and Patterns of Heroin Use." In *A Land Fit for Heroin? Drug Policies, Prevention and Practice*, edited by Nicholas Dorn and Nigel South. London: Macmillan. There is an incontrovertible association between unemployment and heroin use. The relationships are over various kinds of factors and are complex. Here, the author "unpacks" them with respect to some of Britain's rundown working-class neighborhoods and housing estates. ^United\Kingdom ^Heroin ^Drug\Use\Theories ^Economics

1329. Pearson, Geoffrey, Mark Gilman, and Shirley McIver (1987). *Young People and Heroin: An Examination of Heroin Use in the North of England.* London, England: Gower Publishing Company. Heroin use in the north of England has recently become a matter for serious public concern. This volume identifies the extent of heroin use and comments about the social contexts within which health education must operate. Because of the highly variegated population groups involved in heroin usage, it was not thought that a nationally devised strategy could respond meaningfully and effectively to the local variations. Decentralization and tailoring for regional needs was emphasized. It was not known whether it would be possible to aim for an outright preventive strategy which hopes to reduce the demand for drugs, or simply to provide "harm minimization" advice where drug users can be helped to reduce the health risks associated with that use. It is not so much the heroin "pusher" who is responsible for the spreading of the drug in Britain as it is contexts of "friendship" within which heroin changes hands at its lowest level of distribution. ^United\Kingdom ^Heroin ^Drug\Use ^Youth ^Prevention ^Society

1330. "Peasants Agree on Coca Eradication" (1989). *Latin American Weekly Report* 89 no. 11 (16 March):9. In exchange for 70 million U.S. dollars, in March 1989, the Bolivian government signed with representatives of the National Peasant Confederation program to eradicate 5,000 hectares of coca plantations. This would be, according to the representations, about one-tenth of the area currently estimated to be planted in coca. Two-thirds of the funds will be coming from the United States and other North Atlantic countries. ^Latin\America ^Bolivia ^Coca ^Crop\Eradication ^Producers\Unions

1331. "Peasants Protest at Coca Plan" (1987). *Latin American Weekly Report*, 11 June, 2. Peasants in Bolivia have begun protesting again against the government's decision to begin a new three-year U.S.-backed coca eradication program. ^Latin\America ^Bolivia ^Coca ^Crop\Eradication ^Politics ^Producers\Unions

1332. Peat, Marwick, Mitchell and Company (1977). *Marijuana: A Study of State Policies and Penalties*. Prepared for the National Governors' Conference, Center for Policy Research and Analysis. Washington, D.C.: The Center. Research and case studies on marijuana, law and legislation in the United States relating to drugs, and control of narcotics in the United States. The volume gives a conventional historical overview and profile of current trends, along with a discussion of medical, health, and legal features. Legislative, legal, and law enforcement practices are presented for nine states (in case studies): California, Ohio, Texas, Colorado, Iowa, Louisiana, Maine, Minnesota, and New Jersey. ^United\States ^Cannabis ^Drug\Control\Policies ^Legislation ^Drug\Control\Policies\History ^California ^Ohio ^Texas ^Colorado ^Iowa ^Louisiana ^Maine ^Minnesota ^New\Jersey

1333. Peele, Stanton (1990). "A Values Approach to Addiction: Drug Policy That is Moral Rather Than Moralistic." *The Journal of Drug Issues* 20:4(Fall): 639–46. The most successful antidotes to addiction are social values and behavior that encourage people to avoid experimentation with drugs. Thus, approaches that concentrate on values, skills, and the environment will be more effective than approaches, currently popular, that focus on medical and moralistic approaches to drug abuse. The deficiencies of the current war on drugs are reviewed. Suggestions are given on inculcating constructive values which involve people in work and social institutions, and on strengthening community norms. ^P\S\Values ^P\S\Skills ^P\S\Environmental ^P\S\Culture ^Workplace ^P\S\Demand\Reduction ^P\S\Integrated ^P\S\Peers ^P\S\Social

1334. Pela, A. Ona, and Jerome J. Platt (1989). "AIDS in Africa." *Social Science and Medicine* 28(1): 2–8. In discussing an African origin of AIDS and its cluster distribution in Africa, intravenous drug abuse and changing patterns of sexual and drug abuse behavior are noted as contributing to its expansion. ^Africa ^Heroin ^Health ^AIDS

1335. Penning, Margaret, and Gordon E. Barnes (1982). "Adolescent Marijuana Use: A Review." *International Journal of the Addictions* 17(5): 749–91. The authors identified personality-specific and social-specific variables that might account for the increased use of marijuana among high school students and high school dropouts, with special notes made on the increasing number of female users. As for social-specific variables, mixed support has been found for family situations that are predictive. Parents of marijuana users are generally characterized as being less supportive and more inclined toward the use of drugs themselves. They also tend to be more permissive. Peer and sibling use of marijuana also seem to be particularly important predictors of adolescent marijuana use. Findings on personality characteristics of marijuana users are not extensive and are somewhat contradictory. ^United\States ^Cannabis ^Drug\Use\Theories ^Youth ^Society ^Reviews

1336. Pérez Gómez, August (1987). *Cocaína: Surgimiento y Evolución de un Mito.* Bogotá, Colombia: Catálogo Científico. A Colombian national, educated in Belgium with advanced degrees in psychology, gives an overview of cocaine. Of specific interest to this bibliography are his suggestions about preventing cocaine abuse. He places almost absolute confidence in the function of information and education to attack the difficulties (apparently as he has encountered them in his own country). ^Latin\America ^Colombia ^Cocaine ^Prevention ^Prevention\Drug\Education

1337. Perl, Raphael F. (1990). "United States International Drug Policy: Recent Developments and Issues." *Journal of Interamerican Studies and World Affairs* 32:4(Winter): 123–36. Reviews the comprehensive antidrug program advanced by George Bush on 5 September 1989. Takes issue with the plan, arguing that resources for its implementation would be insufficient. Moreover, it would militarize the drug war and hinder continued cooperation of the United States with producer countries. ^United\States ^Drug\Control\Policies\Critique ^Military\Critique ^International\Cooperation

1338. "Peru Begins Spraying of Aerial Coca Killer" (1989). *Latinamerica Press*, 6 April, 1. Despite heavy criticism, Peru has, in collaboration with the United States, begun aerial testing of herbicides to kill coca plants. The herbicide is known as "spike," a chemical that has U.S. approval for use only on nonfood crops. It destroys not only coca, but everything else that photosynthesizes. A forty-acre ravine near Tingo María was selected for spraying. ^Latin\America ^Peru ^Coca ^Crop\Eradication ^Herbicides

1339. "Peru: 'Coca-Dollars' Keep Economy Afloat but Offer No Long-Term National Gain" (1988). *Latinamerica Press*, 29 September, 5. Brief description of coca/cocaine transactions in Peru and the increasing acreage devoted to the coca crop (land devoted to coca plants doubles every three years). There are important notes on widespread deforestation as a consequence of the coca industry, and also on the protective role of *Sendero Luminoso* (the Shining Path) in the upper Huallaga Valley. ^Latin\America ^Peru ^Cocaine ^Drug\Traffic ^Economics ^Consequences\Environmental ^Consequences\Political ^Insurgents

1340. "Peru: Meese Visit Signals New U.S. Resolve to Eradicate Coca Plant" (1988). *Latinamerica Press*, 28 April, 1. Description of latest methods the United States is pursuing in its campaign to halt Peruvian and Bolivian coca leaf production. Describes the visit by U.S. Attorney General Edwin Meese to South America, with his paying special attention to Peru's upper Huallaga Valley and Bolivia's Chapare region. The United States wants to see aerial spraying, and Meese won assurances from Peru's Alán García to allow use of U.S.-supplied herbicides beginning in 1989. Effects of the chemical now being tested by the U.S. State Department (tebuthiuron) may have deleterious environmental consequences. It kills all vegetation (food crops along with coca), and its effects on the ecosystem and on the human organism are still not known. ^Latin\America ^Peru ^United\States ^Coca ^Crop\Eradication ^Herbicides ^Bolivia ^Drug\Control\Policies ^Consequences\Environmental

1341. "Peruvians Operate on Cocaine Addicts' Brains" (1983). *New Scientist*, 1 December, 640. Brain surgery is being performed on a number of Peruvian "paste addicts." The whole affair is very controversial. ^Latin\America ^Peru ^Coca ^Treatment ^Treatment\Critique

1342. Petchel, Jacquee (1989). "Crece la Inmigración Peruana en la Florida." *El Nuevo Herald*, 30 May, 1A. Political and economic crises in Peru are sending thousands of Peruvians toward considering emigrating to the United States, and insofar as they are successful, up to 75 percent of them will arrive in South Florida. Peru has become a country of fear, and citizens uncomfortable with a cocaine economy want out. ^Peru ^Coca ^Drug\Traffic ^Economics ^Politics ^Emigration ^United\States ^Florida ^Latin\America

1343. Petersen, Robert C. (1976) "Toward a Rationally Based Social Policy on Marijuana Usage." In *Chronic Cannabis Use, Annals of New York Academy of Sciences* 282: While proof is difficult to come by, there is good reason for believing that social controls represented by custom and patterns of usage in one's social reference group are much more significant than are legal restraints in governing use of recreational drugs. Decriminalizing the possession of marijuana for personal use ought, therefore, to be undertaken. ^Cannabis ^Drug\Control\Policies\Critique ^Society ^Culture ^P\S\Legalization

1344. —— (1981). "Decriminalization of Marijuana—A Brief Overview of Research-Relevant Policy Issues." *Contemporary Drug Problems* 10(3): 265–75. A series of twelve questions (e.g., what impact do changes in the laws governing possession have on the seller and the general acceptance of illicit drug traffic?) which fairly well cover the gamut of issues that might be researched in dealing with decriminalizing marijuana and, by implication, other drugs. ^Cannabis ^Decriminalization ^Reviews

1345. —— (1984). "Marijuana Overview," in *Correlates and Consequences of Marijuana Use*, edited by Meyer D. Glantz. Rockville, MD.: National Institute on Drug Abuse, pp. 1–17. Reviews the epidemiology, psychosocial correlates, acute psychological effects, and physiological effects of marijuana use and intoxication. Effects from chronic use which are associated with respiratory ills, reproductive outcomes, behavior, and neurological disturbances are reviewed. ^Drug\Use ^Consequences\Personal ^Consequences\Health ^Consequences\Public\Safety

1346. Petersen, Robert C., and Richard C. Stillman, eds. (1977). *Cocaine: 1977*. Rockville, Md.: National Institute on Drug Abuse. This first major NIDA report on cocaine describes what was known and not known about the drug and its implications for health in the mid-1970s. The authors agreed that they were, to a large extent, still ignorant of the actual and potential health hazards posed by cocaine, even though it had been used by about 2 million Americans in 1977. But they agreed that they did know that cocaine could, for example, kill—not commonly but occasionally and perhaps not predictably. Death sometimes occurs even when the drug is snorted rather than injected. They also agreed that cocaine was among the most powerfully reinforcing of all abused drugs. Although not physically addictive in the sense that some other drugs are (e.g., opiates), there is good evidence of a remarkably strong desire to continue use when the drug is available. While the accumulated evidence did not justify the claim that the American public was suffering greatly as a consequence of cocaine use, the authors did agree that much more needs to be known before actions are taken that might result in a wider availability of the drug at lower costs. There is an author and subject index. ^Cocaine ^Health ^Reviews ^NIDA

1347. Petersen, Robert C., Sidney Cohen, F. R. Jeri, David E. Smith, and Lee I. Dogoloff (1983). *Cocaine: A Second Look*. Rockville, Md.: American Council for Drug Education. The short volume is structured (giving historical, botanical, pharmacological, and epidemiological evidence) so as to lead to the conclusion that both coca and cocaine are disasters for society. Society must be influenced, and it must have an accurate portrayal of cocaine. The entertainment industry needs to be convinced that it is in the public interest to refrain from portraying cocaine as chic and therefore inadvertently encouraging or sanctioning its use. Unless something is turned around, we run the risk of relearning some of the painful lessons of history and fostering a climate in which cocaine epidemics, like those in Peru, can flourish. ^United\States ^Cocaine ^Drug\Use ^Society ^Consequences\Misc

1348. Peterson, Ruth D. (1985). "Discriminatory Decision Making at the Legislative Level." *Law and Human Behavior* 9(3): 243–69. In 1970 President Richard Nixon signed into law the Comprehensive Drug Abuse Prevention Control Act. The act made numerous changes in how the federal government approaches drug control, including establishing new and complex sets of penalties for violations of federal drug laws. This paper looks at the development of that legislation in light of "liberal" and "coercive" provisions, each based on the sociological assumption that Congress enacts coercive laws when a minority's behavior becomes threatening, and liberalizing laws when the interests of dominant groups are being attacked by existing legislation. The 1970 legislation had both liberalizing elements (so as not to stigmatize middle-class and upper-middle-class white drug users) and criminalizing aspects (so as to get at drug pushers). In this article the discriminatory features of the 1970 act are identified and explained. The implications of the act for race- or class-based decisions in applying sanctions are also discussed. ^United\States ^Law\Enforcement ^Politics ^Legislation ^Drug\Control\Policies\Theories

1349. Peyrot, Mark (1985). "Narcotics Anonymous: Its History, Structure, and Approach." *International Journal of the Addictions* 20(10): 1509–22. Narcotics Anonymous is the oldest and largest self-help group for those desiring to leave the drug culture. This paper looks at its history, structure, philosophy, and activities. It views Narcotics Anonymous as both an underground social movement and a major treatment mechan' 1 for drug abusers. ^Drug\Use ^Treatment\Therapeutic\Community ^Treatment\History

1350. Philip, George (1984). "Belize: Marijuana and the British Connection." *World Today* 41(3): 50. Evidence given of the impact on local politics and society of marijuana trade in a country. The party in power suffered both from allegations of corruption and from the unpopularity of its limited efforts to do something about the marijuana trade. ^Belize ^Cannabis ^Drug\Traffic ^Drug\Control\Policies ^Caribbean ^Consequences\Political ^Consequences\Social ^Consequences\Economic

1351. Phillips, J. L., and R. W. Wynne (1980). *Cocaine: The Mystique and the Reality.* New York: Avon Books. Wynne, a research psychologist, and Joel Phillips, a free-lance historian and consultant on criminal justice, combine to provide a comprehensive summary of historical, scientific, and popular information on cocaine and coca, statistical information regarding the use and abuse of cocaine, an overview of relevant federal and state laws and legal developments extant as of the late 1970s, and the results of their field study of street myths and rituals involving cocaine. Departing, in a sense, from conventional scholarly work, the authors include a chapter on consumer practicalities, from pricing, cutting, and purification techniques to a variety of tests consumers can use to protect themselves. The historical parts trace coca from its origin in South America into Europe, and discuss the popularizing and counterpopularizing reactions to it. The technical section attempts to summarize much of what was known, as of the late 1970s, about the pharmacology, physiology, biochemistry, and toxicology of cocaine. The core of the book, at least in terms of the primary purpose of the authors' contract with the National Institute of Drug Abuse, focuses on the sociopsychological aspect of cocaine use and abuse. The authors are inclined to discount much of the evidence advanced by others that chronic use of cocaine is deleterious to health and society. ^Cocaine ^Drug\Use ^Health ^Society ^Cocaine\History ^Coca\History ^Legislation ^Statistics ^Consequences\Critique

1352. Phillips, Joel L., and Ronald D. Wynne (1975). *A Cocaine Bibliography—Nonannotated.* No. 8 in the National Institute on Drug Abuse's Research Issue Series. Rockville, Md. This bibliography includes over 1,800 references from some 350 scientific and popular articles gleaned from around the world. Deals with sociopsychological, biomedical, political, and economic aspects of cocaine and, to a lesser extent, coca, from 1585 to 1974. ^Cocaine ^Coca ^Health ^Economics ^Politics ^Bibliographies

1353. Picardie, Justine, and Dorothy Wade (1985). *Heroin: Chasing the Dragon.* Harmondsworth, Middlesex, England: Penguin Books Ltd. Description of events in Britain that led to a heroin-use crisis in the late 1970s and early 1980s. Description also of the governmental response that launched a new antiheroin strategy, recruiting more customs officers and pledging considerable money to the UN fund to help the Pakistani government reduce its opium crops. Police moved in on big dealers instead of individual addicts. Grants were made to regional health authorities. Lessons learned? Neither draconian prohibition nor legalization is the correct solution for a crisis of the magnitude that Britain has experienced with heroin. A community must treat drug abuse as a disease from which no segment or individual is immune. There must be cooperation between governments, law enforcement agencies, professionals, schools, and families. The price of ultimate failure is unthinkable. ^United\Kingdom ^Heroin ^Drug\Use ^Drug\Control\Policies\Critique ^Treatment\Theories

1354. Pickens, Keith (1985). "Drug Education: The Effects of Giving Information." *Journal of Alcohol and Drug Education* 30(3): 32–44. Giving young people information about drugs does, in fact, make them more knowledgeable about drugs. However, more information does not necessarily mean that young people will adopt an antidrug perspective; in fact, sometimes it is the reverse. Giving them no information is not an option. The struggle is to discover the complex of variables that will combine with more information to produce less drug usage. ^Drug\Use ^Prevention ^Youth ^Prevention\Drug\Education\Critique

1355. Pilon, Juliana Geran (1987). "The Bulgarian Connection: Drugs, Weapons and Terrorism." *Terrorism* 9(4): 361–71. Allegations are made and evidence given that the Bulgarian government, intent on subverting Western governments in ways that to be appear orchestrated in Moscow, is dealing in drugs, weapons, and terrorism. The allegations prompted one U.S. senator to introduce a bill that would direct the president to conduct a comprehensive review of U.S. policy toward Bulgaria. This article analyzes that legislative initiative as well as the degree to which drugs and terrorism are connected in Bulgaria. ^Bulgaria ^United\States ^Drug\Traffic ^Politics ^Consequences\Foreign\Relations ^Europe ^Legislation

1356. Pincus, Walter (1982). "Aid to Bolivia Tied to Progress in Cocaine War." *The Washington Post,* 8 November. Describes early U.S. government efforts to induce Bolivia to engage in an eradication and interdiction program against drug trafficking. Description of high-level Bolivian traffickers operating with impunity. ^Latin\America ^Bolivia ^United\States ^Cocaine ^Drug\Control\Policies ^Politics ^Foreign\Aid ^Traffickers ^Consequences\Corruption

1357. Pinkert, Theodore M., ed. (1985). *Current Research on the Consequences of Maternal Drug Abuse.* Rockville, Md.: National Institute on Drug Abuse. Focuses attention on recent studies on the effects of maternal substance abuse on offspring. Includes reviews of animal data, as well as the results of large interdisciplinary clinical studies. Methodological difficulties in conducting the research and contradictory outcomes, relative to prior clinical studies, are noted. ^Drug\Use ^Health ^Reviews ^Consequences\Fetuses ^NIDA

1358. Pisani, Robert L. (1983). "International Efforts to Reform Cannabis Laws." *Journal of Drug Issues* 13(4): 401–15. Describes international efforts to control cannabis in the twentieth century, including a discussion on The Single Convention on Narcotic Drugs with respect to its provisions on cannabis. Advances a discussion of alternative ways that cannabis could be legally regulated and taxed both within the framework of the convention and by modifying it. Inasmuch as efforts already have been made to reform international cannabis laws, the author reviews these and analyzes potential possibilities for change. A portion of the discussion is focused on the United Nations Commission on Narcotic Drugs. ^United\Nations ^Cannabis ^International\Cooperation ^Drug\Control\Policies\History ^Treaties ^P\S\Partial\Prohibition

1359. Pitt, David E. (1989). "Bogotá Journalists Reveal Fears on the Frontline of the Drug War." *The New York Times*, 2 November, A15. Colombian journalists informed their American counterparts of the extreme dangers that a free press publishing on the issue of drugs faces in Colombia. ^Latin\America ^Colombia ^Media ^Consequences\Violence

1360. ———— (1989). "Surge in New York Drug Arrests Sets off Criminal-Justice Crisis." *The New York Times*, 4 April, B1. In the wake of the killing of a rookie policeman in Queens, New York City set off a major effort to deal with drug traffickers. So many people are being processed through the criminal justice system now that there is considerable speculation that it is "swamped." The newly organized Tactical Narcotics Teams (TNTs) are making most of the arrests. ^United\States ^Law\Enforcement ^Consequences\Judiciary ^Consequences\Violence

1361. Plant, Martin (1985). "The Real Problem with Drugs." *New Society*, 7 June, 350–52. Details the increased consumption of drugs, including alcohol and tobacco, in Britain during the last decade. The increase in all categories has been striking as also has the number of noted adverse reactions that impose some costs on society (e.g., drug-related automobile deaths). A call is made for a national network of agencies to help support those who have drug problems. ^United\Kingdom ^Drug\Use ^Alcohol ^Tobacco ^Statistics ^Consequences\Social ^Consequences\Economic

1362. Plant, Martin A., David F. Peck, Elaine Samuel, and Ray Stuart (1985). *Alcohol, Drugs, and School-Leavers*. New York: Travistock Publications. Longitudinal studies of substance use and school dropouts in Great Britain. This book is about a group of young people whose use of alcohol and other psychoactive or mind-altering drugs was followed up for four years. The central focus is the pattern of alcohol use among "normal" young people from a variety of backgrounds. These young people are examined before and after they graduate from school or otherwise leave it in order to shed light on some of the influences upon the use and misuse of alcohol, as well as of tobacco and illicit drugs. This is one of the few sociological studies to link alcohol and tobacco and illicit drugs to a common discussion. Reasons are discussed as to why users fall into patterns of misuse (evidence extremely inconclusive) and include the relationship of availability of alcohol, tobacco, and drugs to their levels of use and misuse, and the degree that health education has an impact on use or misuse. The consequences of misuse are sufficiently deleterious that an anti-alcohol, tobacco, and drug-related policy should be advanced for young people. While most people use alcohol or illicit drugs in moderation, the price to be paid for widespread moderate use (made possible, for example, by decriminalization and enhanced availability) posits a greater level of harm for a minority of people. This situation demands a rational, balanced response. ^United\Kingdom ^Drug\Use ^Youth ^Society ^Alcohol ^Tobacco ^Drug\Use\Theories ^P\S\Critique

1363. Platt, Jerome J., Gerhard Buhringer, Charles D. Kaplan, Barry S. Brown, and Daniel O. Taube (1988). "The Prospects and Limitations of Compulsory Treatment for Drug Addiction." *Journal of Drug Issues* 18(4): 505–25. Reviews the pressures within the legal, social, and treatment systems of the United States and the Federal Republic of Germany with respect to getting drug addicts into treatment programs. Concludes that the present lack of knowledge about the effectiveness of compulsory treatment raises ethical as well as practical questions. Does not hold out much hope for compulsory treatment as an answer, in part because coercive pressure undermines generally understood norms of human freedom. ^Germany ^United-ed\States ^Treatment\Compulsory ^Politics ^Treatment\Critique ^Consequences\Constitutional ^Europe

1364. Plowman, Timothy (1984). "The Origin, Evolution and Diffusion of Coca (*Erythroxylum spp.*) in South and Central America." In *Pre-Columbian Plant Migration*, edited by Doris Stone. Cambridge, Mass.: Papers of the Peabody Museum of Archaeology and Ethnology 76, 126–63. The origin and dissemination of the huánuco and ipadú coca plant varieties are discussed. Extensive reference is made to the literature. ^Coca\History ^Latin\America

1365. ———— (1986). "Coca Chewing and Botanical Origins of Coca (*Erythroxylum spp.*) in South America." In *Coca and Cocaine. Effects on People and Policy in Latin America*, edited by Deborah Pacini and Christine Franquemont. Boston: Cultural Survival, 5–33. [See Pacini, Deborah, and Christine Franquemont, eds., for annotation.] ^Latin\America ^Drug\Use ^Culture

1366. Pollack, Mark H., Andrew W. Brotman, and Jerrold F. Rosenbaum (1989). "Cocaine Abuse and Treatment." *Comprehensive Psychiatry* 30(1): 31–44. Although cocaine abuse has been leveling off, the drug will likely continue as a significant problem for some time. This article is designed to help clinicians become cognizant of the psychodynamic, behavioral, and psychological correlates of cocaine use. Also, it alerts them to the problems of dual diagnosis and dual dependence, and to the effects of drug use on family, employment, and social systems. Suggests chemical agents useful in the fighting of cocaine abuse. There is an extensive bibliography. ^Cocaine ^Drug\Use ^Treatment ^Consequences\Family ^Consequences\Social ^Treatment\Antagonists ^Bibliographies

1367. Ponce Caballero, A. Gastón (1983). *Coca, Cocaína, Tráfico.* La Paz, Bolivia: Empresa El Diario. Another Bolivian author's contributions to "global studies" of coca and cocaine. This short volume gives a history of its use and botanical ingredients, including nutritional and medicinal properties, international conventions on narcotics, production data from Bolivia, the history of cocaine usage, escalation in market prices, antidrug campaigns in the United States and in Bolivia, Bolivian legislation against narcotics trafficking, numerous anecdotes regarding public legislative and judicial documents, and a page or two of possible solutions. ^Latin\America ^Bolivia ^Coca\History ^Cocaine\History ^Drug\Traffic ^Drug\Control\Policies ^Production ^Consequences\Markets ^Legislation ^Proffered\Solutions

1368. Pooley, Eric (1989). "Fighting Back against Crack." *The New York Times*, 23 January, 30–39. It takes a lot to mobilize New Yorkers to become involved in social campaigns involving personal risk. Describes how a number of groups took on crack dealers in their neighborhoods. ^United\States ^New\York ^Cocaine ^Crack ^Drug\Traffic ^Law\Enforcement ^Private\Initiatives

1369. Popolizio, Emmanuel P. (1988). "At Long Last, a Victory over the Drug Dealers." *The New York Times*, 21 May, 31. Description of New York's housing authority's invoking new eviction laws for drug dealers. ^United\States ^Drug\Control\Policies ^Public\Housing ^New\York

1370. Poshyachinda, Vichai (1984). "Indigenous Treatment for Drug Dependence in Thailand." *Impact of Science on Society* 34(133): 67–77. Indigenous medications used, mock funerals held, methods of administration, social reinforcement. These things undertaken by Buddhist temples have been a major social service to otherwise unmet needs of a population dependent on drugs. ^Thailand ^Treatment\Therapeutic\Community ^Southeast\Asia

1371. Post, R. M. and N. R. Contel (1983). "Human and Animal Studies of Cocaine: Implications for Development of Behavioral Pathology." In *Stimulants: Neurochemical, Behavioral, and Clinical Perspectives*, edited by I. Creese, 169–203. New York: Raven Press. Virtually covers the waterfront in terms of physical and behavioral responses to cocaine administration and usage. ^Cocaine ^Health ^Consequences\Misc

1372. Potas, Ivan, and John Walker (1983). *Sentencing the Federal Drug Offender: An Experiment in Computer-Aided Sentencing.* Canberra: Australian Institute of Criminology. Other Australian studies have noted extremely disparate sentencing practices in the various regions. This is an effort to devise ways by which Australia could implement the principle that offenders against the laws of the commonwealth should be treated as uniformly as possible. ^Australia ^Law\Enforcement ^P\S\Law\Enforcement

1373. "President Turns Right for Support" (1984). *Latin American Weekly Report*, 8 June, 5. Description of the political effect of the murder of Justice Minister Lara Bonilla in Colombia. ^Latin\America ^Colombia ^Drug\Traffic ^Politics ^Consequences\Violence

1374. President's Commission on Organized Crime (1984). *The Cash Connection: Organized Crime, Financial Institutions, and Money Laundering.* Interim Report to the President and the Attorney General. Washington D.C.: The commission. This report, the first of the Commission's, reviews the means by which individuals or groups conceal the existence, illegal source, or legal application of income, and then disguise the income to make it appear legitimate. Not only do criminals, such as drug traffickers, seek to launder their money, but also Fortune 500 companies. The Bank Secrecy Act is the principal tool now utilized to detect, measure, and punish money laundering. The volume discusses the efficacy of the act and makes recommendations about how its provisions could be more amply applied. ^United\States ^Drug\Control\Policies ^Money\Laundering ^Organized\Crime ^Banking\Regulations

1375. —— (1984). *Organized Crime and Money Laundering.* Record of Hearing II, March 14, 1984, New York. Washington D.C.: The Commission. Since the passage of the Bank Secrecy Act, money launderers have become increasingly sophisticated in devising ways to hide vast sums of money from narcotics trafficking and other sources. At this hearing the commission sought to understand the magnitude of this problem, and collected information and testimony from witnesses about it. This is the second on the commission's hearings on the subject. ^Money\Laundering ^Organized\Crime ^Banking\Regulations

1376. —— (1984). *Organized Crime of Asian Origin.* Record of Hearing III, October 23–25, 1984, New York. Washington D.C.: The Commission. This third hearing of the commission solicited testimony from numerous law enforcement officials and police officers in foreign jurisdictions who could give information about organized crime of Asian origin operating in the United States. Using powers of its enabling legislation, the commission also compelled a testimony from a number of other witnesses. Three elements were exposed: Triad societies, a Japanese organized crime group known as the Yakuza, and an emerging problem of Vietnamese gangs. The criminal activities of these groups have created enclaves of terror in various parts of the United States; the commission desired to lay out information so that law enforcement agencies could better understand how to deal with the groups. Much of the extortion, corruption, and protection rackets fostered by these groups are associated with illegal narcotics. ^Southeast\Asia ^Drug\Traffic ^Organized\Crime ^Triads ^Yakuza ^Consequences\Social ^Consequences\Corruption ^Consequences\Violence

1377. —— (1984). *Organized Crime and Cocaine Trafficking.* Record of Hearing IV, November 27–29. Washington, D.C.: The Commission. This hefty tome (726 pages) contains a presentation of facts, theories, and opinions from a wide variety of perspectives: the ability of cocaine networks to merchandise their product through domestic organized crime groups, new research pointing to a relationship between cocaine abuse and crime in New York City, factors that affect the demand for and supply of cocaine and who is victimized. Major cocaine networks are identified; their occasional alliance with countergovernment movements in other countries, and sometimes with the complicity of foreign governments, is set forth. The commission also explored the entire cocaine marketing cycle, including cultivation, refining, importation, distribution, and money laundering. A description is also given about efforts to reduce the supply through raids on Colombian refineries, interdiction by air and sea, abroad as well as at home. Finally, the commission explored the sophisticated electronic countermeasures routinely used by cocaine networks to thwart investigation by law enforcement. ^ United\States ^ Cocaine ^ Drug\Traffic ^ Traffickers ^ Organized\Crime ^ Crime ^ Politics ^ Consequences\Corruption ^ Money\Laundering ^ Law\Enforcement ^ Interdiction ^ Traffickers\Theories ^ New\York ^ Demand ^ Supply ^ Insurgents ^ Consequences\Markets

1378. —— (1985). *Organized Crime and Heroin Trafficking.* Record of Hearing V, February 20–21. Washington D.C.: The Commission. While heroin is the best understood of illegal drugs in terms of its addictive properties and pernicious effects, it is ironic that this reputation appears to be declining. Heroin is now being used in combination with other drugs, and it is being ingested by middle-class and upper-middle-class people. The purpose of the hearings reported in this volume was to examine these and other trends in heroin consumption and trafficking. The commission took depositions not only from federal and local law enforcement agencies, but also from private individuals who were in a position to provide first-hand information. ^Heroin ^Drug\Traffic ^Organized\Crime ^Drug\Use

1379. —— (1986). *America's Habit: Drug Abuse, Drug Trafficking, and Organized Crime.* Washington D.C.: U.S. Government Printing Office. The commission's report includes discussions about the impact of the drug trade, portraits of drug production and use (including cocaine, heroin, marijuana, and synthetic drugs), drug trafficking and organized crime, the federal drug strategy, and the roles of current drug enforcement agencies in reducing demand and supply. Seven appendices include related documents. Recommendations are given in areas of interdiction, intelligence, domestic investigations and prosecutions, foreign assistance, source country crop control, and reduction in the demand for drugs. The commission concluded that although efforts to reduce the supply of drugs in the United States by interdiction and source country crop controls would perhaps be helpful, efforts to reduce the demand for drugs had the greatest prospect for making a contribution. Concluded that the nation's drug policy must emphasize more strongly efforts to reduce the demand for drugs. Also concluded that because drug trafficking and abuse are the most serious organized crime problems in

America today, that issue must receive attention from the highest levels of the national government. It urged that the cost of the nation's antidrug efforts be subsidized by the seizure and forfeiture of drug traffickers' assets. ^United\States ^Drug\Traffic ^Drug\Control\Policies ^Organized\Crime ^Demand ^Supply ^Drug\Use ^Production ^Proffered\Solutions ^Foreign\Aid ^Drug\Control\Policies\Critique

1380. ———— (1986). *The Impact: Organized Crime Today.* Report to the President and the Attorney General. Washington D.C.: The Commission. The Commission's report describes La Cosa Nostra, outlaw motorcycle gangs, prison gangs, the Mexican mafia, the Aryan Brotherhood, the Texas syndicate, Chinese organized crime (Triads), Vietnamese Gangs, Cuban interests, Colombian cocaine rings, and so forth. It discusses the roles of state and local law enforcement agencies in combatting organized crime, including drug dealers. Included are "minority reports" from various members of the President's Commission. Also included are five case studies of mob connected lawyers and organized crime. ^United\States ^Drug\Traffic ^Law\Enforcement ^Organized\Crime ^Triads ^Crime ^Judiciary

1381. "Pro and Con: Free Needles for Addicts, to Help Curb AIDS?" (1989). *The New York Times*, 23 May. The conventional arguments are given on each side of this question, some factual, some ideological. ^Heroin ^Health ^AIDS ^Drug\Control\Policies ^Needle\Exchange\Programs

1382. "Probing into the Underworld" (1983). *Latin American Regional Reports*, 4 March, 3–4. Short note about drug barons smuggling arms into Bolivia for their own paramilitary forces. The government fears that they are preparing to destabilize the Bolivian political system. ^Cocaine ^Drug\Traffic ^Politics ^Insurgents ^Traffickers\Private\Armies ^Traffickers ^Bolivia ^Latin\America ^Consequences\Political ^National\Security

1383. Proto, Neil T. (1989). "Illicit Plans Threatening Sovereignty at Home and Abroad." *The Christian Science Monitor*, 6 September, 19. Sovereignty is in jeopardy in Colombia today as it was in Mexico in the 1970s. The question is not whether a legislature can enact a law or a judiciary interpret it but whether the executive can, in fact, enforce the law within the confines of the nation. The counterforces in Colombia threaten to overwhelm the institutional fabric of the country. ^Latin\America ^Colombia ^Law\Enforcement ^Consequences\Sovereignty ^Consequences\Political ^National\Security

1384. "Purga en la Policía Colombiana" (1989). *El Nuevo Herald*, 2 June, 3A. Notice is given of twenty-eight officers and agents of the police who were accused of being in the service of narcotraffickers. Many are in very high places in the Colombian police. ^Latin\America ^Colombia ^Consequences\Corruption

1385. Pyes, Craig, and Laurie Becklund (1985). "Inside Dope in El Salvador." *The New Republic*, 15 April, 15–20. Right-wing business circles attached to Roberto d'Aubuisson are discussed as having attachments to the cocaine trade. D'Aubuisson himself is implicated. ^El\Salvador ^Cocaine ^Drug\Traffic ^Consequences\Political ^Consequences\Corruption ^Latin\America

1386. Qazi, Qutub H., Evelyn Mariano, Doris H. Milman, Eva Beller, and William Crombleholme (1985). "Abnormalities in Offspring Associated with Prenatal Marihuana Exposure." *Developmental Pharmacology and Therapeutics* 8:141–48. On the basis of five cases of newborn infants with mothers who acknowledged steady use of marijuana, symptoms of retardation of growth, neurological problems, and abnormal morphogenesis were noted. These findings give substance and support to experimental studies and surveys indicating that cannabis products have a teratogenic potential; however, rigorous proof must await further information because of the reduced number of human cases that have or can be surveyed. ^Cannabis ^Health ^Consequences\Fetuses ^Drug\Use

1387. Quejas, S. Q. (1983). "The Role of Non-Governmental Organizations in the Prevention and Reduction of Drug Abuse: The Philippine Experience." *Bulletin on Narcotics* 35(3): 53–62. Describes a government coordinating body's facilitating efforts with non-governmental organizations to make drug-abuse prevention programs more viable and relevant. ^Philippines ^Prevention ^Private\Initiatives

1388. Raab, Selwyn (1988). "Links to 200 Murders in New York City Last Year; The Ruthless Young Crack Gangsters." *The New York Times*, 20 March, E9. Crack peddling gangs are implicated in murders. Most slayings remain unsolved. It is not clear whether it is the crack, or the gangs that is the causal agent. ^United\States ^Cocaine ^Crack ^Drug\Traffic ^Organized\Crime ^Crime ^Consequences\Violence ^New\York

1389. Raab, William von (1988). "Legalize Drugs? Not Now, Not Ever." *The Washington Post*, 20 July, A15. The writer, the commissioner of the United States Customs Service, presents a brief editorial outlining why people ought not to feel so desperate and afraid that they would consider drug legalization. ^United\States ^Legalization

1390. Rance, Susanna (1986). "Bolivia: Coca Trade Warps Economy, Way of Life." *Latinamerica Press*, 5 June, 5. Describes the degree to which the cocaine trade has influenced the society and economy of Bolivia. Specific focus on peasant producers in the Chapare zone and of the economic returns to producers and traffickers operating there. ^Latin\America ^Bolivia ^Coca ^Drug\Traffic ^Consequences\Economic ^Consequences\Social

1391. ———— (1988). "Bolivia: New Coca Control Law Aggravates Tense Situation." *Latinamerica Press*, 28 July, 6. A new coca law that disavows earlier agreements between the government and coca growers has aggravated an already tense political and social situation. The new law ignores agreements established making a clear difference between growing coca, which has been done for centuries, and the production and illegal trafficking of cocaine. Several areas are targeted for traditional growing and consuming purposes and everything else is targeted for eradication. Labor and peasant groups have strongly protested the new law, arguing that Bolivia has caved in to pressure from the United States and has therefore lost its nationality. All of this follows in the wake of increased violence, in particular the June 1988 confrontation in Villa Tunari, the Chapare's principal town, where several thousand small coca growers confronted anti-drug police and demanded an end to the experimental use of herbicides for eradicating coca plants. Ten peasants died and seven disappeared after they were arrested by police. ^Latin\America ^Bolivia ^Coca ^Crop\Eradication ^Herbicides ^Drug\Control\Policies ^Consequences\Violence^Consequences\Law\Enforcement^Consequences\Foreign\Relations^Consequences\Political ^Producers\Unions

1392. ———— (1988). "U.S. Government's Drug Control Strategy Accents Heavy Repression in Third World." *Latinamerica Press*, 29 September, 7. Brief article describing "education" for consumers and "reprisals" against producers in the coca/cocaine controversies. The author is inclined to believe that the effectiveness of all these efforts, past and present, is open to strong doubt. She advances conventional arguments on decriminalizing drugs although she suggests that it is not likely to occur in the foreseeable future. Notes the complicity of international financial institutions in the maintenance of the trafficking industry's ability to finance itself. ^United\States ^Drug\Control\Policies\Critique ^P\S\Legalization ^Banking\Regulations

1393. Randal, Jonathan C. (1980). "In Britain, Drug Kills Are Rarity." *The Washington Post*, 11 March, A18. Compares the extremely low homicide rate in Great Britain with that of the District of Columbia. As guns are difficult to obtain in the

United Kingdom, and as their entry into the country is closely guarded, their use in violence associated with drug activity is relatively low. Nevertheless, specialists expressed fears that if the cocaine derivative, crack, made serious inroads into Great Britain, the prevailing absence of violence could end because crack, unlike heroin, tends to make addicts aggressive. ^United\Kingdom ^Drug\Traffic ^Crime ^United\States Washington\DC ^Consequences\Violence ^Cocaine ^Crack

1394. Rangel, Charles B. (1988). "Legalize Drugs? Not on Your Life." *The New York Times*, 17 May, A25. As Americans begin to fatigue in their war against drugs, the subject of legalization increasingly is talked about. Too many questions are unanswered. Those questions are raised in this short article. ^United\States ^Legalization ^P\S\Legalization\Critique

1395. Rao, M. V. N. (1984). "Forfeiture of Properties in Respect of Economic Offences: The Indian Experience." *Bulletin on Narcotics* 36(4): 101–09. India has laws providing for seizure and forfeiture of illegally acquired property. The article describes numerous parts of various legislative acts that make such forfeiture possible. In an effort to fight the greater ingenuity and sophistication in methods of drug trafficking, India not only goes against the drug trafficking chains but also against the organizers and financiers of such trafficking, including international drug traffickers. ^India ^Asset\Forfeiture ^Drug\Control\Policies

1396. Rasheed, Jamal (1984). "A Deadly Export Comes Home to Roost among the Youth of Pakistan." *Far Eastern Economic Review*, 29 March, 48. Pakistan is one of the world's largest sources of heroin and hashish. Less well known is the huge increase of drug taking inside the country, especially among students. Information is given on the number of addicts and who is using the drugs and why. Description of drug smuggling as having become a way of life for many of Pakistan's elite who holiday in Europe. ^Pakistan ^Southwest\Asia ^Drug\Use ^Youth ^Golden\Crescent ^Consequences\Social ^Consequences\Political

1397. Rashke, Richard (1983). "The Amsterdam Connection." *The Washingtonian* (May): 67-116. Washington, D.C., police, the FBI, and the Drug Enforcement Agency trailed the capital's largest heroin smuggling gang between Holland and Washington, D.C. As the noose closed, the gang's leader, Big Boy Gray, was able to beat drug smuggling charges. This documented discussion, by a veteran investigative writer, tells the story. ^Netherlands ^United\States ^Heroin ^Drug\Traffic ^DEA ^FBI ^Washington\DC

1398. Raspberry, William (1988). "Legalize Drugs? No." *The Washington Post*, 14 May, A27. This is an argument against Baltimore's mayor Schmoke's favorable view on decriminalization. It is too risky to attempt to take the profits out of illegal drugs by decriminalizing them. User-targeted law enforcement should be used more vigorously. Try better education, also. ^United\States ^Legalization ^Proffered\Solutions

1399. —— (1988). "Living—and Dying—Like Animals." *The Washington Post*, 2 November, A21. Despairing about the lawlessness, violence, and homicides associated with drug traffic, is anything to be done? Take property away from the customers and throw them in jail. Beyond that, a whole generation of children must be taught that there is a future and that one can have a good life. ^United\States ^Drug\Traffic ^Crime ^P\S\Values ^P\S\Education ^P\S\Law\Enforcement

1400. —— (1988). "The Second Cocaine War." *The Washington Post*, 4 May, A23. Cocaine use was thought to have developed epidemic proportions back in 1909 when there was no prohibition against its use. Go back to the earlier lessons of how we resolved the difficulty, the author argues. The whole question has to do much less with legal sanctions than it does with popular revulsion. ^United\States ^Cocaine ^Drug\Control\Policies\History ^Society ^Culture ^Drug\Use\History

1401. ——— (1988). "Sharing the Drug Peddlers' Profits." *The Washington Post*, 21 March, A11. The not quite so tongue-in-cheek proposal is made not only to take the profits (assets) from those convicted of dealing in drugs, but also to split those profits with the person who turns the dealer in. "The point is, if greed is what makes people deal drugs, why not use that same greed to bust up the drug traffic?" ^United\States ^Asset\Forfeiture ^Proffered\Solutions

1402. Raufer, Xavier and Pierre Rigoulot (1988). "Lifting the Veil on Crime." *World Press Review* (June): 16. Drug addiction and crime associated with it are spreading in the Soviet Union. ^USSR ^Drug\Use ^Crime

1403. *Reflections on Drug Abuse* (1984). Islamabad: Pakistan Narcotics Control Board. Twenty-four contributors discuss virtually the entire range of relevant topics regarding drug abuse in Pakistan. ^Pakistan ^Southwest\Asia ^Drug\Traffic ^Drug\Control\Policies ^Drug\Use ^Middle\East ^Golden\Crescent

1404. Reid, Harry (1990). "Military Bases as Drug Prisons." *The New York Times*, 3 April, A18. A letter to the editor suggests using surplus military bases as drug prisons to handle drug-related cases that otherwise would occasion jail sentences. The plan would provide a place for "discipline and treatment" with expectations that prisoners could reenter society as productive citizens. It is thought that this plan would be less expensive than conventional prison terms. ^P\S\Prison\Alternatives

1405. Reid, Michael (1989). "Peru and US Squabble over Base." *The Christian Science Monitor*, 7 November, 4. Description of the drug-enforcement military base in Santa Lucía. While the base has been developed to play a key role in the United States' "Andean initiative" against drugs, it remains uncompleted. Description of insurgent activity around the base. Conflicts between Peru and the United States have resulted in limited operations (which include helicopter raids on laboratories and airstrips) designed to destroy professional traffickers but avoid coca farmers. ^Latin\America ^Peru ^United\States ^Consequences\Foreign\Relations ^Military ^Drug\Control\Policies ^Insurgents

1406. ——— (1989). "Public Support for Barco Wanes." *The Christian Science Monitor*, 11 October, 1. Many Colombians have begun to question the economic and political costs of the war; their enthusiasm for continuing current policies therefore is declining. They note that the traffickers' bombs undermine business, drive away tourists, and create additional economic costs for their country. All this is complicated by a breakdown in the international coffee agreement that will cost Colombia $400 million a year in lost exports. The implication, for Colombians, is that they need the cocaine trade in order to maintain their export income. ^Latin\America ^Colombia ^Economics ^Consequences\Political

1407. Reinarman, Craig, Dan Waldorf, and B. Murphy (1988). "Scapegoating and Social Control in the Construction of a Public Problem: Empirical and Critical Findings on Cocaine and Work." *Research in Law, Deviance and Social Control* 9:37–62. Presents empirical findings designed to argue against cocaine's role of being as evil in terms of its consequences as some make it out to be. The focus is on cocaine and the workplace. The data base consists of sixty users who reported using cocaine at work. A modest body of literature is reviewed. ^United\States ^Cocaine ^Drug\Use ^Workplace ^Reviews ^Drug\Use\Theories\Critique

1408. Reinhold, Robert (1987). "U.S. Drug Searches Snarl Border Traffic and Vex Businesses." *The New York Times*, 16 February, A1. Description of the enormous delays incurred at the Mexican–U.S. border when the United States elected to show its displeasure at Mexican drug enforcement efforts by strictly following customs procedures. ^Latin\America ^Mexico ^United\States ^Consequences\Foreign\Relations

1409. "Release of Trafficker Shakes Hope in Colombian Drug Plan" (1991). *The New York Times,* January 25, A2. A Colombian judge has released a notorious drug trafficker after a short term in prison. The judge then promptly resigned his office. Considerable discussion is raised in Colombia and the United States about whether this is how the Colombian government's new "amnesty program" for traffickers will work. ^Latin\America ^Colombia ^Judiciary ^Consequences\Corruption ^Drug\Control\Policies ^Traffickers

1410. Remos, Ariel (1985). "Cuba's Drug-Trafficking Bank." *Washington Times,* 13 December, 5. Not only are Cubans financing international drug trafficking, they are also known for their loyalty to the Castro brothers, and have served them since the beginning of the Cuban revolution. The article describes "the bank" and its branches in Nicaragua and Peru. ^Cuba ^Money\Laundering ^Banking\Regulations

1411. "Report from the Field on an Endless War" (1989). *The New York Times,* 12 March. Interview with Francis C. Hall, commander of New York City's Police Department's 1,300-member narcotics division. The war cannot be won under existing demand conditions, and therefore measures for prevention must be pursued. The demand is so high because people despair (in the inner cities) and they find a drug high to be the only high they can expect. Synthetic drugs are a potential threat beyond most people's imagination. Individual cell prisons will have to be modified to camp-type prisons (work camps?). Police cannot eliminate drugs any more than they can eliminate murder or robbery. ^ United\States ^ Law\Enforcement ^ Drug\Control\Policies\Critique ^ Drug\Use\Theories ^ Consequences\Penal

1412. *Research on Carnation as a Replacement Crop for Opium Poppy* (1981). Chiang Mai, Thailand: Chiang Mai University. The first of many studies authorized and paid for by the Thai government searching for a substitute for the opium poppy economy within its borders. This, as others, is technical-agronomic almost exclusively, although this report does have a section on economic feasibility. When economic feasibility is considered, the attractiveness of carnations as a crop substitute decline. For one thing, carnations require insect proof houses to preserve the flowers for the most profitable export opportunities. ^Southeast\Asia ^Thailand ^Opiates ^Crop\Substitution

1413. Resnick, Richard B., and Elaine B. Resnick (1984). "Cocaine Abuse and Its Treatment." *The Psychiatric Clinics of North America* 7(4): 713–28. A survey of established knowledge as of the mid-1980s regarding routes of administration, patterns of cocaine abuse, and effects of cocaine. Laboratory studies report the physiological, psychological, and behavioral effects, and clinical interviews give insight into sexual effects, tolerance, depression, and "crashing." Treatment of cocaine abuse, including family treatment and psychological treatments, is discussed. ^Cocaine ^Drug\Use ^Health ^Treatment ^Reviews ^Consequences\Sexuality ^Consequences\Misc

1414. Restak, Richard (1988). "Drug Deaths and Pavlov's Dogs." *The Washington Post,* 23 October, C3. Discussion about ways in which drug treatment may be undertaken, with the suggestion that taking a purely medical curative approach—substituting one drug for another—seems less promising than approaches based on learning and conditioning. ^Treatment\Theories

1415. Retterstol, Nils (1980). "Models for the Treatment of Young Drug Dependents in Scandinavia." *Journal of Drug Issues* 10(4): 433–441. Description of Scandinavia's response to the new wave of drug dependence among youth surfacing in the area from the mid-1970s on. These include psychiatric clinics and hospitals, new types of out-patient clinics and field work, treatment programs in collectives, programs initiated by idealistically oriented organizations, and coercive treatment measures. The coercive measures are used, in Scandinavia, much less frequently than are other approaches. Hopeful outcomes are reported. ^Europe ^Scandinavia ^Treatment ^Youth

1416. Reuter, Peter (1984). "The (Continued) Vitality of Mythical Numbers." *The Public Interest* 75:135–47. Examines assumptions lying behind estimates of the number of heroin addicts in the United States. The author is not very impressed with current estimates nor with analyses of addicts' crimes that derive from those estimates. Concludes that some of the figures are "patently absurd." Nor is he pleased with estimates of the size of the illegal drug market. Why are these mythical numbers allowed to circulate without criticism? There is no constituency for keeping the numbers accurate, although there is one for keeping them high. The lack of systematic scholarly interest in the whole issue allows for wide circulation of the estimates. Finally, the numbers have almost no policy consequence. Whether high or low, the size of government's expenditures on drug treatment or law enforcement is not much driven by these numbers. ^United\States ^Drug\Traffic ^Statistics\Critique

1417. ——— (1985). "Eternal Hope: America's Quest for Narcotics Control." *The Public Interest* 75:80–81. The United States has based its principal drug control efforts on suppressing the availability of drugs in source countries, and therefore in reducing the ability of traffickers to move them to the United States. Examines the data, places the information into the context of experience and procedures, and concludes, from the vantage of a political economy analysis, that the victories have been small and the failures substantial. Drying up the supply in one country affects the pricing structure such as to occasion production increases in another country. Operations in Asia and Latin America are discussed. ^United\States ^Drug\Control\Policies ^Economics ^Supply ^Drug\Control\Policies\Effectiveness ^Consequences\Markets

1418. ——— (1987). "Coda: What Impasse? A Skeptical View." *Nova Law Review* 11:1025–40. To some extent, drugs have always been with America. America's policy, currently a mix of prohibition and regulation, is largely determined by historical factors. Reuter discusses the shifting balance between prohibition and regulation within the context of historical social trends, exploring the issues associated with each. Specific drugs raised for review are marijuana, cocaine, and heroin. Measures to address drug demand are explored. ^United\States ^Drug\Control\Policies\History ^Cocaine ^Heroin ^Cannabis

1419. ——— (1988). *Can the Borders Be Sealed?* Santa Monica, Calif.: Rand Corporation. Increased interdiction efforts have resulted in more cocaine seizures. However, at the same time, prices have fallen. The recent past suggests that interdiction, even if it produces a high rate of seizures, will do little to decrease cocaine imports. Thus it appears that interdiction cannot affect the consumption of cocaine in the United States because it appears to have no significant impact on price. There are too many experienced smugglers and too many ways to smuggle cocaine. The reasons why risk factors associated with smuggling introduce such negligible increases in costs is discussed. Experienced smugglers can benefit from interdiction, since it catches the potential competition. Thus, the profits of the cartels rise without a corresponding increase in risk. Interdiction will also increase the earnings of source country producers. They are thus more inclined to stay in the business. This is because, with seizures, total export demand goes up. The porousness of the Mexican border is an important part of the problem. The nation would be better off putting more money into treatment and less into interdiction. ^United\States ^Cocaine ^Interdiction ^Economics ^Traffickers\Incentives\Economic ^Drug\Control\Policies\Critique

1420. —— (1988). "Intercepting the Drugs: Big Cost, Small Results." *The Washington Post*, 16 May, A15. Interdiction will not limit the amount of drugs brought into the United States. There are too many ways to get the drugs in. The demand for cocaine is probably insensitive to changes in smugglers' costs, and all that prohibition does is assure that exporting countries will receive a lot of dollars. Interdiction efforts should remain, but increasing them substantially will not offer much promise. "We must look inside our borders, rather than beyond them, if we are to solve the U.S. cocaine problem." ^United\States ^Cocaine ^Interdiction ^Economics ^Drug\Control\Policies\Critique

1421. —— (1988). "Quantity Illusions and Paradoxes of Drug Interdiction: Federal Intervention into Vice Policy." *Law and Contemporary Problems* 51(1): 233–52. The federal government, of necessity, has taken a highly visible interventionist role in the control of drugs. As a measure of the effectiveness of drug enforcement procedures, much emphasis has been placed on the quantity of drugs seized. It is clear that federal officials have seized large quantities of drugs. However, the replacement cost of drugs seized at the border is small in comparison to replacement cost of drugs seized at other points closer to the consumer. The use of unweighted seizure quantities as the measure of drug enforcement effectiveness, therefore, overstates the impact of federal agencies. A more appropriate measure of drug enforcement effectiveness is the cost of replacing the seized drugs. One must concentrate on the role of prices and how the importance of quantities must be differentiated in light of relative prices. ^United\States ^Interdiction ^Statistics\Critique ^Economics ^Drug\Control\Policies\Critique

1422. —— (1989). "An Economist Looks at the Carnage." *The Washington Post*, 26 March, D7. How does one account for so many drug-related homicides in Washington, D.C.? There is a market imbalance, with supply exceeding demand. Battles over market shares therefore ensue. ^United\States ^Drug\Traffic ^Crime ^Economics ^Crime\Theories ^Supply ^Demand

1423. Reuter, Peter, and John Haaga (1989). *The Organization of High-Level Drug Markets: An Exploratory Study.* Santa Monica, Calif.: Rand Corporation. Cocaine and marijuana are distributed through mass markets involving many thousands of participants. The degree to which these markets may be suppressed is affected by how the markets are organized and the nature of how people enter them. This study explores a method for learning about careers and organizations in the upper levels of the cocaine and marijuana markets. Data collection consisted principally of interviews with inmates convicted on narcotics crimes. The barriers to entry into the higher levels of the drug markets are minimal; successful operation does not require the creation of a large or enduring organization; it is possible to function as a high-level dealer without recourse to violence; the wholesale market is national rather than regional. ^Drug\Traffic ^Economics ^Consequences\Markets

1424. Reuter, Peter, and Mark A. R. Kleiman (1986). "Risks and Prices: An Economic Analysis of Drug Enforcement." *Drug Enforcement*. The federal government's campaign against marijuana and cocaine during the past several years has not led to a significant reduction in the availability of the two drugs, though relatively high prices, such as these drugs have commanded, historically are a consequence of enforcement. Why have the law enforcement pressures provoked such a lack of appropriate response? The answer may lie in structural characteristics of the markets rather than in failure of law enforcement efforts. The federal effort aims at importation and high-level distribution, which, in the case of marijuana and cocaine, account for a modest share of the retail prices of these drugs. Moving against importers or high-level distributors is thus likely to have only a modest effect on the retail price, and it is unlikely to have any other effect on the conditions of use. Street level enforcement is, of course, hindered by the sheer scale of the market. Many of the risks associated with drug trafficking come from the actions of other participants in the trade themselves, and this also limits the ability of law enforcement agencies to act in ways that will cause prices to precipitously increase or alter market conditions. It is noted that law enforcement efforts directed at heroin have been much more effective at restricting drug use. ^Law\Enforcement ^Economics ^Drug\Control\Policies\Effectiveness ^Consequences\Markets

1425. Reuter, Peter, Gordon Crawford, and Jonathan Cave (1988). *Sealing the Borders. The Effects of Increased Military Participation in Drug Interdiction.* Santa Monica, Calif.: Rand Corporation. Rising concern with drug use in the United States has led to increased emphasis on the interdiction of drugs before they reach this country. The military services are now being asked to assume a substantial share of the burden of this interdiction. Increased drug interdiction efforts are not likely to greatly affect the availability of cocaine in the United States. The involvement of the military may create greater effectiveness in interdiction programs; however, the efforts are likely to fail anyway, strongly suggesting that military services cannot be primary interdiction agencies and that a major increase in military support is unlikely to significantly reduce drug consumption in the United States. ^United\States ^Cocaine ^Interdiction ^Military ^Drug\Control\Policies\Critique

1426. Rexed, Bror, et al (1984). *Guidelines for the Control of Narcotic and Psychotropic Substances: In the Context of the International Treaties.* Geneva, Switzerland: World Health Organization. Drug abuse, narcotic habits, and laws and legislation on illegal drugs. Efforts to provide an international legal framework for the control of psychoactive drugs, begun by the International Opium Commission of Shanghai in 1909, have resulted in a number of international treaties. These include the 1961 Single Convention on Narcotic Drugs, its 1972 amending protocol, and the 1971 Convention on Psychotropic Substances. This volume contains guidelines for member states as they promote the rational use of psychoactive drugs and as they direct their administrations to areas where action for control may be required. The guidelines explain the obligations of member states and clarify how they should formulate their national drug policies and legislation to conform with the international conventions. It is hoped that these guidelines will help to promote the rational utilization of the controlled substances and the prevention of their abuse and to counteract illicit international traffic. Specific guidelines are associated with policies and regulations for drug control, surveillance of supply, and use of psychoactive drugs. ^Drug\Control\Policies\History ^International\Cooperation\History ^Legislation

1427. Rhodes, Jean E., and Leonard A. Jason (1988). *Preventing Substance Abuse among Children and Adolescents.* New York: Pergamon Press. Provides practitioners with a developmental framework for a better understanding of factors that contribute to substance abuse. Critiques campaigns, curricula, and related efforts designed to prevent substance abuse among children and adolescents. It is an example of the substantially increasing number of "help" books for people trying to make a difference in other people's lives on the drug issue. Identifies risk factors in terms of their occurring in early or late childhood or adolescence. ^Prevention\Critique ^Youth ^Society ^Drug\Use\Theories

1428. Riberdahl, S. (1984). "Forfeiture of the Proceeds of Drug-Related Crimes: A Swedish Point of View." *Bulletin on Narcotics* 36(4): 51–59. Sweden's narcotic laws provide for extensive legal means to trace, sequestrate, and forfeit the proceeds of drug crimes. This article discusses the difficulty of doing that with, in particular, individuals who have neither domicile nor property in Sweden, have transferred the proceeds of their drug crimes abroad, or are able, by various means, to frustrate the application of the Narcotics Drugs Act. The author proposes remedies for all these difficulties. ^Scandinavia ^Sweden ^Asset\Forfeiture ^Drug\Control\Policies

1429. Rich, Spencer (1989). "Aiding Needle Exchange Is Illegal, Rangel Says: Experts Dispute Drug Panel Chairman." *The Washington Post*, 10 March, A3. United States Secretary of Health and Human Services Louis W. Sullivan had said that the U.S. government would be "supportive" of local communities wanting to institute a needle-exchange program to help stop the spread of AIDS by drug addicts. He was severely criticized. ^United\States ^Heroin ^Health ^AIDS ^Drug\Control\Policies ^Needle\Exchange\Programs

1430. Richards, David A. J. (1982). *Sex, Drugs, Death and the Law: An Essay on Human Rights and Overcriminalization.* Totowa, N.J.: Rowman and Littlefield. The principal interest of this volume for this bibliography is Chapter 4, "Drug Use and the Rights of the Person." After exploring anthropological, historical, and pharmacological perspectives on drugs, arguments are reviewed for the criminalization of drug use, the morality of drug use and the rights of the person, drug use and constitutional privacy, and further positions regarding decriminalization and policies against prohibition. On the whole it is a "law teacher's approach" blessed by a sensitivity to moral philosophy. It is therefore highly interdisciplinary, involving moral, legal, and political arguments brought to bear on a moral criticism of overcriminalization of drug use. ^Consequences\Human\Rights ^Decriminalization ^Values ^Consequences\Constitutional

1431. ――― (1987). "Towards New Perspectives on Drug Control: A Negotiated Settlement to the War on Drugs." *NOVA Law Review* 11:909–13. Drug prohibition policies are morally wrong and remarkably ineffective. Calls for a "negotiated settlement" on the war on drugs. Regulatory policies would replace prohibition and would thus shape drug use in ways less violative of decent respect for persons. ^United\States ^Drug\Control\Policies\Critique ^P\S\Legalization

1432. Richards, Louise Greene (1980). "Drugs and Crime: Theory Engagement after a Forced Marriage." *Contemporary Drug Problems* 9(4): 461–73. Purpose is to summarize briefly the state of research findings on drug use and crime and suggest potential future departures worth pursuing. While research on drug use and crime have been substantial, generalizations have not been satisfying. Describes the nature and degree of that dissatisfaction. ^Drug\Use ^Crime ^Reviews

1433. Richards, Nancy Louise (1980). "Erythroxylon Coca in the Peruvian Highlands: Practices and Beliefs." Ph.D. diss., University of California, Irvine. Of interest to this bibliography, this dissertation in social anthropology concludes that the international pressure for the eradication of coca has failed to take into consideration cultural beliefs of local populations, which are remarkably acceptable to the use of coca. Beyond this, however, crop substitution programs have been unsuccessful, due in part to the economics and cultural superiority of coca over other crops. Concludes that there will likely be considerable resistance to any change in planting and harvesting practices in the Peruvian highlands. ^Peru ^Coca ^Crop\Eradication\Critique ^Society ^Culture ^Crop\Substitution\Critique ^Drug\Use\History ^Latin\America

1434. Richburg, Keith B. (1988). "More Heroin Said to Enter U.S. from Asia; Chinese Gangs Replacing Traditional Organized Crime Networks." *The Washington Post*, 16 March, A16. Further discussion on allegations that Chinese gangs are replacing traditional organized crime networks and are, with respect to the drug trade, overpowering them. Trade routes for entry into the United States are noted. ^Southeast\Asia ^United\States ^Heroin ^Drug\Traffic ^Organized\Crime ^Triads

1435. Richey, Warren (1985). "Cocaine Connection: Wealth, Violence, Drugs and Colombia." *The Christian Science Monitor*, 20 December, 3. Colombian drug traffickers are emerging among organized crime groups operating in the United States as a new and powerful force. "Many of these organizations are doing business in the area of $200 million to $1 billion a year." These organizations are not as structured as the traditional Sicilian mafia. ^Latin\America ^Colombia ^United\States ^Cocaine ^Organized\Crime ^Traffickers

1436. ——— (1985). "Teamwork to Fight Drugs." *The Christian Science Monitor*, 22 August, 3. There is increasing cooperation among Latin American governmental officials in dealing with the drug trade. There is less attempt to assess blame over whether one is a producer or consumer and a move to cooperative efforts to protect "our citizens from the plague of narcotics trafficking." The new Latin American attitude is thought to derive from problems of increasing drug addiction among young people in Latin America, a growing internal security threat deriving from drug trafficking, and, finally, a recognition that the United States is deadly serious about its antidrug campaign. ^United\States ^Latin\America ^Drug\Control\Policies ^International\Cooperation ^Drug\Use ^Consequences\National\Security

1437. ——— (1986). "Critics Charge US Is Doing Too Little to Halt Drug Trade at Source." *The Christian Science Monitor*, 9 September. Following the, by now, conventional wisdom of commenting about whether the drug problem is demand driven or supply driven, this author focuses on experts who argue that the cutting of supplies must be vigorously increased in addition to easing demand, and that the United States has probably not been tough enough in slashing coca production in the Andes. ^United\States ^Drug\Control\Policies\Critique ^Crop\Eradication ^Interdiction ^Supply ^Demand

1438. ——— (1986). "Despite Treaty Most Colombian Drug Dealers Escape US Hands." *The Christian Science Monitor*, 13 March, 5. Discussion of the failure of the U.S.–Colombian extradition treaty, even before Colombia declared it null and void. Notably, however, while the major traffickers lived relatively visible lives prior to 1982, as soon as the extradition treaty was signed, and appeared to be in force, the big dealers either fled to the jungles or left the country. ^Latin\America ^Colombia ^Extradition ^Drug\Control\Policies\Effectiveness ^Traffickers

1439. Ricks, Thomas E. (1986). "The Cocaine Business: Big Risks and Profits, High Labor Turnover." *The Wall Street Journal*, 30 June. How supply meets demand, and at what clearing prices, and for whom and where, constitute the general discussion of this marketing/pricing analysis. ^Cocaine ^Drug\Traffic ^Economics ^Consequences\Markets ^Supply ^Demand

1440. Riding, Alan (1984). "Drug Region in Peru Booming Again." *The New York Times*, 29 December, 1. On-site report from Peru's Upper Huallaga Valley describing the booming cocaine industry and its social and economic consequences. ^Latin\America ^Peru ^Coca ^Cocaine ^Drug\Traffic ^Production ^Consequences\Social ^Consequences\Economic

1441. ——— (1984). "Shaken Colombia Acts at Last on Drugs." *The New York Times*, 11 September, 1. Describes the murder on April 30, 1984 of Justice Minister Rodrigo Lara Bonilla by hired narcotics gunmen and the effect this had on mobilizing the Colombian political system to address narcotics trafficking more vigorously. Background on eradication efforts that have developed in the wake of growing drug trade operations in Colombia and surrounding regions. The collaboration of the United States in all this is noted. The effect on the narcotics traffickers was sufficient to motivate them to appeal for negotiations with the government. Mainly, the traffickers wanted the extradition treaty with the United States revised or dropped. ^Latin\America

^Colombia ^Drug\Control\Policies ^Extradition ^Politics ^Consequences\Violence ^Crop\Eradication ^Traffickers

1442. —— (1987). "Brazil Acting to Halt New Trafficking in Cocaine." *The New York Times*, 7 June, 19. South American drug trafficking rings have moved into Brazil, which has good airline connections and easy access to the vital chemicals required to process coca and coca paste into cocaine. Brazil is the only South American country where the required chemicals—ether and acetone—are manufactured in industrial quantities. ^Latin\America ^Brazil ^Cocaine ^Drug\Traffic ^Precursor\Chemicals

1443. —— (1987). "Cocaine Billionaires: The Men Who Hold Colombia Hostage." *The New York Times*, 8 March. Description of the cocaine empires built on terror and bribery that are under increasing challenge. The focus is on Colombia, and it deals with Carlos Lehder, the Escobars, the Ochoas, and others who are the mainstream cocaine barony. Description of the impact that the drug trafficking has had on Colombian society, economy, and politics. ^Latin\America ^Colombia ^Cocaine ^Drug\Traffic ^Organized\Crime ^Traffickers ^Consequences\Economic ^Consequences\Political ^Consequences\Social

1444. —— (1987). "Cocaine Finds a New Route in Venezuela." *The New York Times*, 18 June, A15. Colombian traffickers have been moving their cocaine product across the Venezuelan/Colombian frontier and loading it for U.S. ports from Venezuelan ports. The new cocaine route has left in its wake the corrupting influence of drug money on police officers, customs officials, judges, and military officers. All of this follows Colombia's having begun an antidrug campaign in 1984 and creating conditions that made direct trafficking through Miami more difficult. Venezuela was drawn in after Colombia tightened control on imports of ether and acetone. ^Venezuela ^Cocaine ^Drug\Traffic ^Consequences\Corruption ^Colombia ^Latin\America ^Traffickers ^Consequences\Law\Enforcement ^United\States ^Florida ^Precursor\Chemicals

1445. —— (1987). "Colombia Effort against Drugs Hits Dead End." *The New York Times*, 16 August, 1. Chronicles the declining "will," judicial and law enforcement, to make a dent in the drug trading organizations of Colombia. The declining will is associated with the furious response of the cocaine mafia to the extradition of Carlos Lehder to the United States. ^Latin\America ^Colombia ^Law\Enforcement ^Consequences\Violence ^Consequences\Political

1446. —— (1987). "Colombia's Drugs and Violent Politics Make Murder a Way of Life." *The New York Times*, 27 August, 3. Description of the wholesale murdering of politicians and drug trafficking personnel as a way of life in Colombia. Long known for its "culture of violence," Colombia has now exceeded even its own cultural limits. ^Latin\America ^Colombia ^Drug\Traffic ^Consequences\Violence ^Culture

1447. —— (1987). "Colombia's Press Unites to Fight Drugs." *The New York Times*, 18 January, L3. Even in the wake of severe terrorist attacks on Colombia's press, including the killing of thirty journalists in apparent retaliation for their reporting on drug activities, the Colombian press have vowed to form a united front to demand that the government, political parties, and society take effective measures to defeat the cocaine business. ^Latin\America ^Colombia ^Drug\Control\Policies ^Media ^Terrorists

1448. —— (1987). "Peru's Two Complex Battles: Drugs and Terror." *The New York Times*, 23 August, 8. Presents evidence of the relationship between drug trafficking and the terrorist activities of the Shining Path or *Sendero Luminoso*. In one area of the Huallaga Valley where both had been dislodged, it appeared that the guerrillas had imposed a strict political regime, but had made no move to discourage cultivation of coca plants. This seemed to endear growers who, in particular, have been subject to some exploitation by foreign drug cartels. ^Latin\America ^Peru ^Coca ^Drug\Traffic ^Politics ^Insurgents ^Terrorists ^Consequences\Political

1449. ——— (1988). "Brazil Now a Vital Crossroad for Latin Cocaine Traffickers." *The New York Times*, 28 August. Brazil has emerged as the most important new player in the international narcotics trade. Those pushed from other regions are infiltrating a relatively unprotected area of Brazil. Stepped-up antidrug efforts in Colombia, Peru, and Bolivia have driven the cocaine mafias to look to Brazil as a more open and "tolerant" base of operations. The Brazilian government apparently felt, for a long time, that drugs would not become a significant internal or domestic problem. All this occurred while coca plantations were being established in northwestern Brazil. ^Latin\America ^Brazil ^Coca ^Production ^Cocaine ^Drug\Traffic ^Traffickers ^Emigration

1450. ——— (1988). "Colombia Uses Army in Cocaine Raids." *The New York Times*, 5 May, A3. Describes the first-time involvement of Colombia's armed forces in raids on two large cocaine processing complexes. The seizure of the complexes and destruction of four and a half tons of cocaine are the most important gains for the government since the destruction of a complex in Tranquilandia in 1984. ^Latin\America ^Colombia ^Cocaine ^Interdiction ^Military

1451. ——— (1989). "Colombian Cocaine Dealers Tap European Market." *The New York Times*, 29 April, 1. Colombian cocaine dealers, using Spain as the principal port of entry, have set up highly profitable trafficking networks to feed Western Europe's rising demand for cocaine. They are supplying Europe with over fifty tons of the drug each year. As overproduction saturated the American market, Colombians turned their attention to Europe. While Europe still is awash in heroin, cocaine is rapidly gaining ground. ^Latin\America ^Colombia ^Europe ^Spain ^Cocaine ^Drug\Traffic ^Organized\Crime ^Consequences\Markets

1452. ——— (1989). "Paraguay's Leader Denies Ties to Drugs." *The New York Times*, 7 February. Rumors of Paraguay's drug connections continue, and its president, General Andrés Rodríguez, tries to dispel the rumors. ^Latin\America ^Paraguay ^Drug\Traffic ^Consequences\Corruption

1453. ——— (1989). "Rebels Disrupting Coca Eradication in Peru." *The New York Times*, 26 January, A10. A surge of leftist guerrilla activity is bringing new difficulties to a U.S.-backed campaign to eradicate coca production and break up drug trafficking gangs in Peru's main coca growing region in the upper Huallaga Valley. The guerrillas are entrenched in the region, and the coca growing communities are in rebel hands. Some traffickers pose as rebels, and, in any event, the rebels are thought to benefit from trade in coca/cocaine substances. There is thus considerable emphasis to change the eradication program to an aerial application of an herbicide known as "Spike." There is concern that programs be developed to soften the social and political effects of eradication on the livelihood of tens of thousands of peasants. Otherwise, it is thought that the guerrillas will never be shut out from the region. ^Latin\America ^Peru ^Coca ^Crop\Eradication ^Herbicides ^Insurgents ^Consequences\Political ^Consequences\Social

1454. "Riding High on Cocaine" (1983). *Latin American Regional Reports*, 24 June, 7–8. The peasant unions have forced the Bolivian government to reassess the U.S.-backed coca eradication programs in the Andes. It is increasingly less likely, therefore, that armed intervention will occur in areas where peasant unions are strong, or that herbicide spraying will occur there. All this is happening, however, while sharply declining prices for coca leaves and semirefined cocaine base are developing. ^Latin\America ^Bolivia ^Coca ^Crop\Eradication ^Consequences\Political ^Producers\Unions ^Economics ^Consequences\Markets

1455. Riley, Norman (1989). "The Crack Boom Is Really an Echo." *Crisis* (March): 26. In the past, outside groups have targeted the black community as a dumping ground for drugs, and the current move with crack is simply a repeat of that historical experience. Just as in the mid-1940s organized crime recognized a potential gold mine in the mass sale and distribution of heroin in America, now also they recognize the profits to be realized in the sale of crack to increase the mass distribution of cocaine derivatives, which may be done at a relatively lower per unit cost to the consumer. ^United\States ^Cocaine ^Crack ^Drug\Traffic ^Organized\Crime ^Minorities ^Drug\Traffic\History ^Consequences\Markets

1456. Ring, Wilson (1989). "Opium Production Rises in Guatemala Mountains." *The Washington Post*, 30 June, A25. There has been a meteoric rise in opium production in the mountains of western Guatemala and a concomitant increase in the activities of and power of drug traffickers there. Thousands of acres along the Mexican border have been transferred from traditional agricultural production into poppy fields. Enough is being produced to supply three times the yearly need of the estimated 500,000 U.S. addicts. All of this complicates the fact that the eastern portion of the country is used for cocaine transshipment and marijuana production. Aerial spraying has been suspended because of ground fire. Peasants are able to triple their incomes. The poppy growing is protected by leftist insurgents, who reap a financial reward. In order to avoid corrupting influences, army personnel are not sent to the zone. The highest levels of the civilian government appear already to have been corrupted. ^Latin\America ^Guatemala ^Cocaine ^Opiates ^Production ^Drug\Traffic ^Consequences\Corruption ^Insurgents ^Cannabis ^Production\Incentives\Economic ^Consequences\Political

1457. "The Risk of Telling the Whole Truth" (1989). *Inside*, 2 October, 24–25. As more crimes become drug related, intimidation of witnesses increases. Description of the dilemma of eyewitnesses risking their lives to serve justice administration. Law enforcement protection for such witnesses sometimes works, sometimes does not. ^United\States ^Law\Enforcement ^Consequences\Judiciary

1458. Rivier, L. and J. G. Bruhn, eds. (1981). "Coca and Cocaine 1981." *Journal of Ethnopharmacology* 3(2-3): 1-200. Extensive survey (200 pages) of what is known about coca and cocaine from both a historical and scientific orientation. Sundry episodes in the history of coca and cocaine are reported as well as the use of coca and cocaine as medicines from the vantage of historical experience and the social functions of coca and its various varieties. There is also a chapter on the therapeutic value of coca in contemporary medicine. ^Coca ^Cocaine ^Drug\Use ^Culture ^Reviews ^Coca\History ^Cocaine\History ^Consequences\Misc

1459. Robertson, Frank (1977). *Triangle of Death: The Inside Story of the Triads—The Chinese Mafia*. London: Routledge and K. Paul. A story of the criminal offshoots of a once vast patriotic organization formed to rid China of the Manchu overlords, the Ching Dynasty, and establish a republic—China's Triad Society. Represents the original Triad Society as still existing, in fragmented form, in Hong Kong and every sizable Chinese community overseas. While the overwhelming majority of its members are lawful and hardworking citizens, there is a criminal minority, organized into some 1,500 gangs, which trafficks in narcotics and is engaged in protection rackets, illegal gambling, prostitution, and homicide. ^Southeast\Asia ^China ^Drug\Traffic ^Organized\Crime ^Triads ^Hong\Kong ^Consequences\Violence

1460. Robertson, Roy (1987). *Heroin, AIDS and Society*. London: Hodder and Stroughton. Based on the author's experience as a general medical practitioner in Scotland, looks at the social consequences of heroin dependence including illness and death, in particular, AIDS. Advocates a new perception of heroin from the basis of knowledge of nondependent use, controlled use, and risk reduction. The real issues of preventing damage and passing on information should take precedence over efforts of trying to cure an individual of an "evil influence or disease." Attitudes would therefore be changed from punitive to palliative. This would be a first vital step in helping drug users. Much heroin use is "victimless" and society should not intervene. Five pages of references are given. ^Heroin ^AIDS ^Drug\Control\Policies ^Values ^Consequences\Social ^Consequences\Personal ^Consequences\Health ^P\S\Partial\Prohibition

1461. Robinette, Jeff (1989). "South American Farmers' Drug Dependency." *The Christian Science Monitor*, 18 August, 19. If the cocaine market disappeared overnight, some countries would experience an unprecedented economic and political upheaval because much of their economic foundation is tied to the "alternative economy" of cocaine trafficking. Failure of the United States to perceive this and provide economic options for farmers either forced off or weaned from the drug trade does a disservice. ^Latin\America ^Cocaine ^Drug\Traffic ^Drug\Control\Policies ^Consequences\Economic ^Consequences\Drug\Control\Policies ^Consequences\Illegal\Economy ^Drug\Control\Policies\Critique

1462. Robinson, Carl (1988). "The Day of the Triads: Hong Kong's Gangs Move in on Australia." *Newsweek*, 7 November, 72. Relatively substantial numbers of young Hong Kong criminals have infiltrated Australia and have hurt the Chinese community's image there. The resident Chinese, nevertheless, have not been willing to inform on the infiltrators. The Triad agents are infiltrating heroin into Australia. ^Southeast\Asia ^Triads ^Australia ^China ^Heroin ^Drug\Traffic ^Organized\Crime

1463. Rodríguez, Enrique Vélez (1985). "La Persecución de Narcóticos en Alta Mar: Su Efecto sobre los Principios Jurisdiccionales del Derecho Internacional." *Revista Jurídica de la Universidad Interamericana* 19(2): 397–408. Discussion of the evolving considerations relating to jurisdictional principles in international law as a consequence of the pursuit of narcotics traffickers on the high seas. ^Drug\Control\Policies ^Interdiction ^Consequences\Constitutional

1464. Roehrich, Herb, and Mark S. Gold (1988). "800-COCAINE: Origin, Significance, and Findings." *Yale Journal of Biology and Medicine* 61:149–55. Describes the national cocaine hotline and indicates that the information gathered from it corroborates other studies documenting the psychosocial and medical consequences of addiction. Because of the educational track it takes, the hotline is viewed as a preventive measure. ^United\States ^Cocaine ^Drug\Use ^Prevention\Drug\Education ^Consequences\Misc

1465. Rohrer, Glenn E., Ruth Handley, Gilbert J. Riordan, Richard Stock, and Melville Thomas (1987). "Crack Cocaine Education in the Public Schools." *Journal of Alcohol and Drug Education* 32(3): 65–68. Describes a crack cocaine education project carried out in a Florida school system. Ten patients being treated for cocaine addiction were used as members of a crack awareness team to present information to Florida school students. A before and after test was administered on a self-esteem index, and the experiment showed that seven of the ten patients being treated for cocaine addiction improved, and also that they had a constructive impact on the students. ^United\States ^Cocaine ^Crack ^Prevention\Schools ^Youth ^Consequences\Educational ^Florida

1466. Rohter, Larry (1987). "Mexico Battles Drugs Anew; Says War Is Far from Over." *The New York Times*, 15 June, A1. Anecdotal description of activities in the heart of Mexico's drug country and of Mexican operations to suppress the traffic. Moves and countermoves by government forces and narcotics traffickers are mentioned, along with a pessimistic observation that any success will be forthcoming. ^Latin\America ^Mexico ^United\States ^Drug\Traffic ^Drug\Control\Policies\Effectiveness ^Law\Enforcement

1467. ——— (1987). "Mexico Challenging U.S. on Drugs." *The New York Times*, 17 July, A3. In mid 1987, Mexico presented its arguments that the United States ought to shoulder more responsibility and blame for the drug problem. The United

States had accused Mexico of being a drug haven, something that has become a major irritant in relations between the two countries. Mexico's President de la Madrid is quoted as saying that "the narcotics traffic is a crime that originates in, is fed by and benefits from the large industrialized markets, principally those of the United States." ^Latin\America ^Mexico ^United\States ^Drug\Control\Policies ^Politics ^Consequences\Foreign\Relations ^Supply ^Demand

1468. —— (1989). "As Mexico Moves on Drug Dealers, More Move In." *The New York Times*, 16 April, E2. Continued discussion of the capture of Félix Gallardo and the implications of that capture on improved interdiction and law enforcement efforts by Mexican authorities. Traffickers appear to simply shift the arena of operations to other locales, using different people. ^Latin\America ^Mexico ^Drug\Traffic ^Law\Enforcement ^Drug\Control\Policies\Effectiveness ^Emigration ^Traffickers

1469. —— (1989). "In Mexico, an Annual Ritual to Lobby the U.S. Congress." *The New York Times*, 1 March. The congressional "certification" that countries are doing their best to eradicate the drug trade brings heated discussions between Mexico and the United States. ^Latin\America ^Mexico ^United\States ^Drug\Control\Policies ^Drug\Control\Politics ^Consequences\Foreign\Relations ^Foreign\Aid

1470. —— (1989). "Mexicans Arrest Top Drug Figure and 80 Policemen." *The New York Times*, 11 April, A1. Making good on his promises, the new president of Mexico has facilitated the arrest of Miguel Ángel Félix Gallardo, reputed to be head of the narcotics ring that makes shipments to the United States. ^Latin\America ^Mexico ^Law\Enforcement ^Organized\Crime ^Traffickers ^Drug\Control\Policies\Effectiveness

1471. —— (1989). "Mexico Using Special Squad in Drug War." *The New York Times*, 13 April, A11. Mexico is training about 1,200 police officers, engineers, doctors, teachers, and former soldiers to be deployed across Mexico in "special groups" to function as the "shock troops" commanded by the Mexican attorney general's newly created antinarcotics investigation and operations division. The problem of corruption in Mexico poses a problem with respect to the effectiveness of drug campaigns. It is hoped that this limiting element can be avoided in this particular program. ^Latin\America ^Mexico ^Law\Enforcement ^Politics ^Consequences\Corruption

1472. —— (1990). "Mexico Is Accusing a Slain U.S. Agent." *The New York Times*, 16 January, A7. Diplomatic tensions continue to grow between the United States and Mexico over U.S. accusations of corruption in the 1985 killing in Mexico of U.S. drug agent Enrique Camarena. The Mexican government went to unprecedented lengths to attack a U.S. NBC series on Mexican corruption related to the drug case. ^Mexico ^United\States ^Consequences\Foreign\Relations

1473. Roman, Ivan (1989). "Drug Den Turned into Livable Units." *The Miami Herald*, 1 July, 1B. Description of a municipal policy and a developer's money combining to produce not only livable accommodations but policies to maintain them, turning a "drug den into a drug-free building." The urban league will house seventy-five single mothers in the complex as the first step toward getting them off welfare. The property is located in Dade County. ^United\States ^Drug\Control\Policies ^Public\Housing ^Private\Initiatives ^Florida

1474. Romano, Ruggiero (1982). "Problemi della Coca nel Peru del secolo XX." *Nova Americana* 4:67–106. Discusses, over the very long term of the twentieth century, production of coca, its exportation (even data on arrivals in Amsterdam from 1905–1913), and consumption of coca, offering survey data on internal consumption in producing countries among peasants, laborers, and miners. Concentrates principally on traditional uses. Based on field and archival research in Peru. ^Latin\America ^Peru ^Coca ^Drug\Use\History ^Society ^Culture ^Coca\History

1475. Rootman, I., and P. H. Hughs (1980). *Drug-Abuse Reporting Systems.* Geneva, Switzerland: World Health Organization. Reviews the technical, administrative, and financial aspects of drug-abuse reporting systems among developing countries. Based on published and unpublished documents, correspondence, discussions with professionals in the field, and visits to selected countries to examine their reporting systems. Statistics are given involving national programs of drug-abuse prevention, treatment, and rehabilitation. Drugs abused and the abuse rates are also listed for various countries. ^Drug\Use ^Statistics\Critique ^Statistics ^Prevention ^Treatment ^Rehabilitation

1476. Ropp, Steve (1986). "General Noriega's Panama." *Current History* (December): 421–32. Aside from general details about Panama's internal politics and the surprising residual strength of General Noriega, discusses the cocaine trade in relationship to the Panama Canal and to the "Cuban connection." ^Panama ^Cuba ^Cocaine ^Drug\Traffic

1477. Rosecan, Jeffrey S., and Barbara F. Gross (1986). "Newborn Victims of Cocaine Abuse." *Medical Aspects of Human Sexuality* (November): 30-35. There is a belief—pending conclusive studies—that cocaine use by pregnant women may have deleterious effects on their fetuses and the newborn. There appear to be more spontaneous abortions and lower birth weights among the children of chronic cocaine users. ^Cocaine ^Health ^Consequences\Fetuses ^Fetuses ^Consequences\Children ^Pregnancy

1478. Rosen, Tove S., and Helen L. Johnson (1985). "Long-Term Effects of Prenatal Methadone Maintenance." In *Current Research on the Consequences of Maternal Drug Abuse*, NIDA Research Monograph 59, edited by Theodore M. Pinkert. Rockville, Md.: National Institute on Drug Abuse. There are no uniform long-term effects of prenatal methadone maintenance on the children revealed in this study. In the short term (the first thirty-six months of life), however, methadone-maintained children have a higher incidence of minor neurological abnormalities and lower scores on developmental evaluations. ^Heroin ^Treatment\Methadone ^NIDA ^Consequences\Children ^Consequences\Fetuses ^Consequences\Methadone

1479. Rosenbaum, Marsha (1979). "Difficulties in Taking Care of Business: Women Addicts as Mothers." *American Journal of Drug and Alcohol Abuse* 6(4): 431-446. If a woman has adequate financial support and is available for her children, she may combine addiction and mothering with some success. If, however, she must work outside the home (usually in criminal pursuits), the general chaos of her life greatly impinges on her ability to fulfill mothering duties. There are conditions of extreme guilt and remorse, mistreatment of children, and a sense of failure. When an addict's children and her role as mother are in jeopardy, this presents substantial motivation to seek treatment. ^Drug\Use ^Women ^Parenting ^Consequences\Children

1480. ——— (1981). "When Drugs Come into the Picture, Love Flies out the Window: Love Relationships among Women Addicts." *International Journal of the Addictions* 16(7): 1197–1206. Heroin use undermines a love relationship, producing arguments over money and drugs, with bitterness, resentment, and often violence as a result of perceived inequalities on the part of one partner or the other. The woman addict gradually becomes embittered with the man. With such embitterment, she occasionally gives up men completely and, in so doing, relinquishes one of the few roles open to her—that of homemaker. ^Heroin ^Drug\Use ^Women ^Consequences\Personal

1481. ——— (1981). *Women on Heroin.* New Brunswick, N.J.: Rutgers University Press. Mental health, crime, law, and deviance among women heroin addicts. Prior to 1914, drug addiction was not defined as a crime, and addiction was most often supported by physician's prescriptions. In consequence, most addicts were women, diagnosed by their physicians as weak, fragile, and in need of medical treatments such as opiates. After opiates became illegal, addiction became a male form of deviance. Lately, women addicts have been increasing relative to men at an alarming rate. Who are these women? What is the nature of their experience in the world of illegal opiates? How do they fare in the heroin life? The author attempts to answer these questions, and on the basis of her analysis (extensive review of extant literature), offers nominal prescriptions. She lays considerable credibility on affirmative action in preparing women for work through developing job skills and formal education, in giving incentives to employers for hiring women ex-addicts, and in punitive treatment centers that make allowance for women to continue a positive relationship with their children. "In the absence of these changes in occupational and parenting roles, the outlook for women addicts is dismal." Methodological appendix, extensive bibliography. ^Heroin ^Drug\Use\History ^Treatment ^Women ^Health ^Crime ^Proffered\Solutions ^Bibliographies

1482. Rosenberg, Mark B. (1988). "Narcos and Politicos: The Politics of Drug Trafficking in Honduras." *Journal of Interamerican Studies and World Affairs* 30:2 & 3 (Summer/Fall): 143–67. Honduras has become a transhipment point for drugs between Colombia and the United States. The political arrangements in Honduras that facilitate this are discussed. The incompatibility of U.S. support of the Contras as opposed to all other policy objectives is examined. ^Latin\America ^Honduras ^Corruption ^Traffickers ^Drug\Traffic ^Consequences\Foreign\Policy

1483. Rosenberg, Tina (1986). "Miami South." *The New Republic* 194, no. 3717 (14 April):10. This short journalistic piece notes the landing of Rafael Caro Quintero, the chief of the Guadalajara drug ring, into Costa Rica and his settlement there without any problems. The article then develops a discussion about the ease of immigration into Costa Rica and how drug lords avoid any problems. Costa Ricans rarely investigate anyone's "story." ^Latin\America ^Costa\Rica ^Drug\Traffic ^Traffickers ^Organized\Crime ^Law\Enforcement ^Immigration

1484. —— (1988). "Murder City." *Atlantic* 262(5): 20–30. Description of the "cheapness" of life in Medellín, Colombia, where "contract killings" are carried out for as little as ten dollars. ^Latin\America ^Colombia ^Drug\Traffic ^Crime ^Consequences\Violence ^Consequences\Assassination

1485. Rosenblatt, Roger, and Evan Thomas (1986). "The Enemy Within: A Nation Wrestles with the Dark and Dangerous Recesses of Its Soul; America's Crusade: What Is behind the Latest War on Drugs." *Time*, 15 September, 58–73. A general description of the evolution of Americans' love affair with cocaine. Description of its impact on children and its association with crime. Description of law enforcement efforts to reduce the trafficking, including border interdiction, general police crackdowns, drug testing, drug treatment, and education. ^United\States ^Cocaine ^Drug\Traffic ^Drug\Control\Policies ^Drug\Use\History ^Consequences\Children ^Law\Enforcement ^Treatment ^Prevention\Drug\Education

1486. Rosenthal, Andrew (1990). "3 Andean Leaders and Bush Pledge Drug Cooperation." *The New York Times*, February 16, A1. From the high-level antidrug summit in Cartagena, Colombia, the presidents of Peru, Bolivia, Colombia, and the United States met. Their joint statement appeared to reduce the emphasis that the United States wanted to place on military involvement in favor of other orientations such as crop substitution programs and economic alternatives for growers. The statement concluded, however, that narcotics control "is essentially a law-enforcement matter" (p. A12). U.S. State Department estimates of coca leaf production for Bolivia, Colombia, Ecuador, and Peru are given. ^Latin\America ^United\States ^Peru ^Bolivia ^Colombia ^Ecuador

^Military^International\Cooperation^P\S\Development ^Law\Enforcement ^Drug\Control\Policies^Coca ^Production ^Proffered\Solutions ^Crop\Substitution

1487. Ross, John (1986). "Colombia: Judge's Murder Linked to Drug Mafias." *Latinamerica Press*, 4 September, 6. The assassination of Supreme Court Justice Hernando Baquero, who was one of only ten surviving hostages taken from last November's bloody guerrilla takeover of the Colombian Supreme Court, was in apparent revenge for controversial extraditions of Colombian citizens to the United States to stand trial for narcotics charges. Under the existing treaty, seventeen drug traffickers on a list of seventy indicted in absentia in the United States had been sent to the United States; most were serving long sentences in federal prisons. Description of how all of this violence has weakened the rule of law and weakened the resolve of politicians. ^Latin\America ^Colombia ^Drug\Traffic ^Organized\Crime ^Extradition ^Consequences\Violence ^Consequences\Political

1488. —— (1987). "Mexican Youth Make Folk Hero out of Drug Lord." *Latinamerica Press*, 18 June, 7. Description of the "Robin Hood" syndrome again, this time in reference to Rafael Caro Quintero from Costa Rica who had been charged with the murder of U.S. drug enforcement agent Enrique Camarena. The popular ballads and films glorifying Caro Quintero are of concern to the authorities. Some have wondered if the man has become a "legitimate anti-hero for Mexico's restless masses." ^Latin\America ^Mexico ^Drug\Traffic ^Traffickers ^Consequences\Political ^Consequences\Social

1489. —— (1988). "Mexico: Chimalapas Forest Falls to Loggers, Oil Pipelines, Poppy and Marijuana Fields." *Latinamerica Press*, 21 July, 5. Another in a series of brief articles demonstrating a relationship between drug trafficking/production and the deforestation of important rain forests. The impact of drug trafficking on the forest runs in tandem with illegal logging and clearing for rangeland. ^Latin\America ^Mexico ^Drug\Traffic ^Consequences\Environmental

1490. —— (1989). "Mexico: Drug Bosses Achieve Growing Political Influence." *Latinamerica Press*, 9 February, 4. The Mexican climate has been kind to drug traffickers. This article discusses why, where, and in what way. Discussion of corruption within the Mexican government. ^Latin\America ^Mexico ^Drug\Traffic ^Consequences\Corruption ^Traffickers ^Consequences\Political ^Drug\Control\Policies\Effectiveness

1491. Ross, Timothy (1987). "Colombia Goes after Drug Barons." *The Christian Science Monitor*, 12 January, 9. The Colombian administration mounted a belated offensive to halt killings of newsmen, judges, and police. The effect of this campaign on drug prices and general law enforcement efforts is noted. It is alleged that drug traffickers pay rebel groups, such as M-19 guerrillas, to protect their laboratories and to kill their opposition. ^Latin\America ^Colombia ^Law\Enforcement ^Organized\Crime ^Insurgents ^Consequences\Violence ^Consequences\Law\Enforcement ^Consequences\Markets

1492. —— (1987). "Colombian Media Take on the Drug Lords." *The Christian Science Monitor*, 20 February, 11. Another article among many discussing how the Colombian press have been welded into almost a united front against the drug lords in response to the drug barons having murdered the respected newspaper editor, Guillermo Cano. This is thought to be a courageous campaign, given the knowledge that traffickers do not hesitate to have their opponents gunned down. ^Latin\America ^Colombia ^Drug\Control\Policies ^Media ^Consequences\Violence ^Private\Initiatives

1493. —— (1987). "Colombia's Bid to Cut off Drug-Processing Chemicals Backfires." *The Christian Science Monitor*, 4 May, 20. Moving away from a failed campaign to interdict the raw materials that produce cocaine, the authorities have begun a clampdown on the processing chemicals required in the industry. The underground cocaine "cooks" simply are now using more dangerous chemicals and creating new major health hazards. One result has been that prices continue to decrease for cocaine and coca base because of overproduction and the use of cheaper precursor chemicals. Benzene, a carcinogen, is noted. ^Latin\America ^Colombia ^Drug\Control\Policies ^Precursor\Chemicals ^Consequences\Environmental ^Consequences\Health ^Consequences\Markets ^Drug\Control\Policies\Effectiveness ^Cocaine\Paste

1494. ——— (1988). "UN Aid Helps Some Colombians Shake Free of Coca Dependency." *The Christian Science Monitor*, 5 January, 7. Description of how villagers in Colombia's Cauca Province voluntarily eradicated coca plants and stopped taking drugs. This was done with the help of a UN program. Participation in the project has created "evangelical zeal among former self proclaimed 'bandits.'" ^Latin\America ^Colombia ^United\Nations ^Coca ^Crop\Substitution ^Treatment ^International\Cooperation

1495. Rowen, Carl T. (1988). "The New Lynch Mobs: Drug Vigilantes." *The Washington Post*, 27 April, A21. Brief description of the Muslim patrols in several black communities that are pursuing both drug users and drug pushers. Argument against Americans surrendering their rights and protections to "rag tag" vigilantes. ^United\States ^Law\Enforcement ^Private\Initiatives

1496. Rubin, Roberta Louise (1985). "International Agreements: Two Treaties between the U.S. and Italy." *Harvard International Law Journal* 26: 601–607. Discussion of an extradition treaty and a treaty on mutual assistance in criminal matters between the United States and Italy. ^Europe ^Italy ^United\States ^Extradition ^International\Cooperation ^Treaties

1497. Rubin, Vera (1975). *Cannabis and Culture*. The Hague, Netherlands: Mouton. Contains many of the papers presented at the Ninth International Congress of Anthropological and Ethnological Sciences. Under the general editorship of Sol Tax, this volume is one in a series on world anthropology. This volume may be the first exploration of any drug that bears not only on the complexity of the substance but its multiple uses in a broad range of societies, particularly as informed by the discipline of anthropology. Looks at the botany and pharmacology of cannabis, the history of its diffusion and use, and differential effects in diverse social and cultural contexts. Numerous case studies from many parts of the world constitute a particular virtue of this volume. An emphasis is to understand the sociocultural differences in reactions to cannabis. ^Cannabis ^Culture ^Drug\Use\History ^Cannabis\Pharmacology ^Cannabis\History ^Consequences\Misc ^Consequences\Cultural ^Consequences\Social

1498. Rubin, Vera, and Lambros Comitas (1975). *Ganja in Jamaica: Medical Anthropological Study of Chronic Marihuana Use*. The Hague, Netherlands: Mouton. While Americans are concerned with what is thought to be the very negative "amotivational" and drug escalation effects of marijuana, ganja in Jamaica serves to fulfill values of the work ethic. The use of ganja is simply a traditional practice that has not resulted in drug escalation. There is little correlation between the use of ganja and crime. There are no indications of organic brain or chromosomal damage among the subjects studied, and no significant clinical (psychiatric, psychological, or medical) differences between the smokers and the control group. They did find some indication of functional "hypoxia" among heavy, long-term chronic smokers, but could not differentiate the cause of that from marijuana use as opposed to tobacco use. Suggests that ganja is smoked without deleterious social or psychological consequences. The findings shed new light on the cannabis question, particularly that the relationship between user and marijuana is not simply pharmacological, and suggests the need for new approaches. ^Jamaica ^Cannabis ^Drug\Use ^Health ^Society ^Culture ^Amotivational\Syndrome ^Caribbean ^Consequences\Misc ^Crime ^Consequences\Critique

1499. Ruegg, F. (1985). "For an Overall Approach to Prevention: Basic Critical Considerations." *Bulletin on Narcotics* 37(2-3): 177-184. Pleads for a comprehensive approach to the prevention of drug abuse. Such a comprehensive approach necessarily involves individuals throughout their lives and takes account of their psychosocial characteristics and spiritual values. Given this as an assumption, certain drug abuse prevention programs are identified as being counterproductive. Argument raised that the family is one of the promising community resources that can be utilized for the prevention and reduction of drug abuse. ^Drug\Use ^Prevention ^Family ^P\S\Integrated ^Prevention\Critique

1500. Rumrrill, Roger (1986). *Narcotráfico y Violencia Política en la Amazonia Peruana*. Lima, Peru: Privately published by Roger Rumrrill. Describes the historic agro-industrial integration of the upper and lower Peruvian Amazon into the national economy and how this has been disrupted by guerrilla warfare and the introduction of coca/cocaine trafficking. Calls for an elimination of coca, cocaine, and political violence so that the process of economic integration may continue. ^Latin\America ^Peru ^Cocaine ^Drug\Traffic ^Consequences\Economic ^Agriculture

1501. "Rural Property Is Targeted by Narcos" (1988). *Latin American Weekly Report* 88, no. 49 (15 December):10-11. In figuring out how to launder their money, many narcotics traffickers are investing in Colombian real estate. Popular at the moment are large cattle ranching investments protected by hired guns. ^Latin\America ^Colombia ^Money\Laundering ^Consequences\Economic ^Traffickers

1502. Russel, George (1983). "Battle of the Warlords." *Time*, 17 January, 32. Description of the internal battles in the Golden Triangle involving Khun Sa and other warlords jousting for control over the opium poppies. ^Southeast\Asia ^Burma ^Opiates ^Golden\Triangle^Drug\Traffic^Traffickers^Consequences\Political^Consequences\Violence^Insurgents

1503. Russell, John S. (1978). "Discussion of Legal Heroin Distribution." Vancouver, British Colombia, Canada: Province of British Columbia, Ministry of Health, Alcohol and Drug Commission. Establishes criteria for evaluating the desirability of heroin maintenance and legal distribution, including nonmedical assumptions underlying such a policy direction. Analyzes the likely effectiveness of such a policy in reducing illegal heroin use or problems associated with such use. Some of the anticipated major advantages, such as attracting most addicts into treatment, eliminating the black market, and making productive citizens out of the addict population, are questionable. Crime would probably be reduced, but the present level of enforcement of drug control legislation in Canada would probably have to be maintained. Beyond this the heroin program would have significant problems—how to control the drug, the danger of more people becoming involved in heroin use, and the legitimizing of an activity that many people would like to discourage. ^Canada ^Heroin ^P\S\Drug\Maintenance

1504. Ruttenber, A. James, and James L. Luke (1984). "Heroin-Related Deaths: New Epidemiologic Insights." *Science* 226(October): 14–20. In attempting to assess or to explain an epidemic of heroin-related deaths in the District of Columbia between 1979 and 1982, post mortem analysis suggested that the increased casual use of heroin in combination with ethanol and quinine was the epidemic's probable cause. ^United\States ^Heroin ^Health ^Consequences\Personal ^Washington\DC^ Epidemiology

1505. Ryser, Jeffrey, et al (1986). "Can South America's Addict Economies Ever Break Free?" *Business Week*, 22 September, 40–44. Short description of how Bolivian, Peruvian, and Colombian economies are closely tied to the drug trade, especially Bolivia's. Would there be any hope for that country, particularly if the drug trade were to cease? There is discussion on the laundering of drug money and the

510 *Annotated Bibliography*

consequences of corruption on the local political and judicial systems. ^Latin\America ^Drug\Traffic ^Money\Laundering ^Bolivia ^Colombia ^Peru ^Consequences\Economic ^Consequences\Corruption

1506. S., Vichai (1983). "Warlords of the Poppy Fields." *Bangkok Post*, 24 February, 60. Warlords, of the type abundant in the China of old, are alive and well in Burma. Discussion of Khun Sa and his Golden Triangle exploitations. Other warlords are also noted. ^Southeast\Asia ^Burma ^Opiates ^Drug\Traffic ^Traffickers ^Golden\Triangle

1507. Sackstein, E. (1981). "Drugs and Youth: An International Perspective on Vocational and Social Reintegration." *Bulletin on Narcotics* 33(4): 33–45. There is positive outlook, the author argues, for reintegration of drug-dependent users into a normal social and employment atmosphere. Describes the vocational rehabilitation processes that can serve well for most drug rehabilitation programs. Innovative approaches that have demonstrated some measure of positive outcome are reviewed. Stresses the need for compassionate and direct involvement of communities in the rehabilitation and reintegration of drug-dependent youth. Programs for employed drug-dependent persons are also cited as a preventive and highly effective approach. ^Drug\Use ^Treatment\Rehabilitation ^Youth

1508. Sage, Colin (1987). "The Cocaine Economy in Bolivia: Its Development and Current Importance." *Corruption and Reform* 2:99–109. Reviews the economic and political circumstances leading to coca's unprecedented importance in the Bolivian economy. Gives a historical background on the way traffickers took advantage of expanding market demand. Production, refining, and trading statistics, as well as income estimates are listed. Given the importance that the coca economy now plays in Bolivia's macro economy, and given the social and economic intertwining of those two economies, a policy of repression (e.g., crop eradication) will not be an effective solution to the supply problem. The economic conditions in Bolivia will have to be addressed simultaneously with or before the country can be weaned from its coca income. ^Latin\America ^Bolivia ^Economics ^Cocaine ^Coca ^Production\History ^Statistics ^Consequences\Economic ^Drug\Control\Policies\Critique

1509. ——— (1989). "Drugs and Economic Development in Latin America: A Study in the Political Economy of Cocaine in Bolivia." In *Corruption, Development and Inequality*, edited by Peter Ward. London: Routledge. Gives background to the development of a narcotics industry in Latin America as well as the consequences of this industry on a systematic undermining of the fiscal, judicial, and political credibility of the state and its institutions. Gives background on the traditional role of coca in Bolivia and its evolution to an international commodity. Examines the rise of a Bolivian "narcocracy." The integration of coca into the international and domestic capital markets is discussed. Repressive measures have proved to be ineffective because the producers simply move their operations into frontier areas outside the reach of the state. ^Latin\America ^Production ^Consequences\Political ^Consequences\Judiciary ^Coca\History ^Traffickers ^Consequences\Markets ^Drug\Control\Policies\Effectiveness ^Consequences\Migration

1510. Salazar, Luís Suárez (1987). "El Narcotráfico en las Relaciones Interamericanas: una Aproximación Estructural." *Cuadernos de Nuestra América* 4(8): 24–64. Analysis of drug trafficking within the context of capitalist markets. Discussions about price, demand, and supply. How all this operates to produce extraordinary gain for the traffickers is placed within a market analysis. This economic analysis is given a political economy overlay, all of which is placed into a social transformation context. In this context, the Reagan administration is criticized for using drug issues to mask larger international political economy initiatives. ^Latin\America ^United\States

^Drug\Traffic ^Economics ^Politics ^Society ^Consequences\Markets ^Demand ^Supply ^Consequences\Social ^Consequences\Political ^Consequences\Foreign\Relations

1511. Samper Pizano, Ernesto (1979). *Marihuana: Legalización o Represión*. Bogotá, Colombia: Biblioteca ANIF. Colloquium of papers and observations dealing with the principal themes discussed in the Asociación Nacional de Instituciones Financieras (ANIF) annual symposium. The overall theme of the conference is expressed in the title of this book—legalization or repression. In addition to the conventional topics on the relationship of marijuana to health and to law enforcement, the volume discusses the social and economic implications within Colombia of marijuana production and trade, and also discusses how consumption within the United States affects the public policy climate in Colombia. ^Latin\America ^Colombia ^Cannabis ^Drug\Traffic ^Drug\Control\Policies ^Legalization ^Consequences\Economic ^Consequences\Social ^Law\Enforcement ^Consequences\Health

1512. ——— (1980). "Marihuana y la Propuesta de su Legalización." In *La Legalización de la Marihuana*, edited by E. Samper et al. Bogota, Colombia: ANIF, Fondo Editorial. In this opening address to an ANIF symposium in Bolivia, the author reviews the social structure of marijuana production, presents data affirming that internal consumption is growing, and also that consumption is growing in the United States. After examining the economics of marijuana, he suggests that two of the consequences of the current drug control program are internal repression and corruption. Rather than either of the two, he suggests that the country study the legalization of marijuana as an alternative to its repression. ^Latin\America ^Colombia ^Cannabis ^Drug\Use ^Consequences\Drug\Control\Policies^Consequences\Corruption^Consequences\Human\Rights^P\S\Legalization

1513. Samper Pizano, Ernesto, ed. (1980). *La Legalización de la Marihuana*. Bogotá, Colombia: ANIF, Fondo Editorial. Addresses, essays, and lectures dealing with marijuana use in Colombia; addresses, essays, lectures, and law and legislation associated with marijuana in the United States. Colombian authors, in a semipopular way, range the gamut in their discussions about marijuana, including production and commerce in Colombia, consumption in the United States, the relationship of marijuana to health, aspects of the war on marijuana, and the "legal reality" of marijuana. The value premise underlying the book is that the current criminalization of marijuana consumption in the United States imposes unacceptable consequences on Colombia, and that, therefore, the United States ought to change its laws (decriminalize) as an act of conscience in favor of Colombia. The current arrangements create conditions wherein Colombia receives 20 percent of the income and pays out 100 percent in terms of bad reputation, Colombia destroys the agricultural plots of its peasantry without giving them anything else to cultivate simply to satisfy electoral aspirations of politicians in the United States; Colombia pays with corruption and with the corrosion of its institutions by its armed forces, and with its moral posture, as it relates to the United States; and Colombia supports the disequilibrium promoted by a strong underground economy to which all of the rents from exports of the drug accrue while the country as a whole receives no income. Within a regional context, there is considerable discussion about the impact of marijuana activity on social, economic, and political institutions. ^Latin\America ^Colombia ^United\States ^Cannabis ^Drug\Traffic ^Legalization ^Economics ^Informal\Economy ^Politics ^Consequences\Corruption ^Demand ^Supply ^Drug\Use ^Consequences\Drug\Control\Policies ^Consequences\Political^Consequences\Economic ^Consequences\Social^Drug\Control\Policies\Critique

1514. Sampler, Daniel (1987). "Who Created the Drug Trafficking Monster?" *The New York Times*, 25 January, 3. Drugs are strictly an American vice, and too many Colombians are paying too high a price for the consequences of it. The war against narcotics is undermining institutions, killing respectable public figures, disrupting society, and ruining the political system. Colombia has become a hostage to powerful and rich American markets for drugs. ^Latin\America ^Colombia ^United\States ^Drug\Traffic ^Consequences\Drug\Control\Policies ^Consequences\Social ^Consequences\Economic ^Consequences\Political

1515. San Pedro, R. M., and E. G. Ponce (1988). "School Programmes in Drug Rehabilitation and Social Reintegration in the Philippines." *Bulletin on Narcotics* 40(1): 63–66. Describes the Philippine government's three rehabilitation centers and analyzes the outcome with respect to 500 individuals who have graduated from the school programs. ^Philippines ^Drug\Use ^Treatment\Rehabilitation ^Youth

1516. Sanabria, Harry (1988). "Coca, Migration, and Differentiation in the Bolivian Lowlands." *Studies in Third World Societies* 37:81–124. While, because of serious economic considerations, migration of Bolivians to the eastern lowlands of their country had taken place much earlier than the late 1970s and early 1980s, all of this has been vastly intensified by the spectacular increase in the demand for cocaine. A process of socioeconomic differentiation is rapidly spreading in Bolivian colonization zones where the production and commercialization of coca is the primary economic activity of lowland settlers. A geographic focus is on the community of Sacaba, about 35 kilometers east of the city of Cochabamba. The author gives a background of out-migration and coca production (with labor requirements and associated differentiation), and shows how a sharp decline in the price of key export crops and short-fall of capital transfers through official governmental channels prompted the agro-industrial capitalists of Santa Cruz to turn to the illegal cocaine industry, which they have done in ways that now support large-scale operations as well as peasant cottage industries. The expansion and the consolidation of the cocaine market has come about as a consequence of high-level capital interests. As the demand for cocaine increased, the demand for coca leaves was also intensified. In Bolivia this heightening demand and rising price for the leaves was paralleled by the worst economic crisis in recent memory, which reached its peak by mid-1985. Both factors were, by the early 1980s, fueling a massive migration of highland-based peasants to the eastern lowlands, especially around Cochabamba. ^Latin\America ^Bolivia ^Coca ^Drug\Traffic ^Economics ^Migration ^Colonization ^Consequences\Migration ^Consequences\Social ^Consequences\Economic ^Production ^Demand ^Supply ^Consequences\Markets

1517. ——— (1989). "Social and Economic Change in a Bolivian Highland Valley Peasant Community: The Impact of Migration and Coca." Ph.D. diss., University of Wisconsin—Madison. Explains social, political, and economic changes occurring in a Bolivian peasant community as a consequence of its having been drawn into intimate economic relationships with the coca growing lowlands. The stress or emphasis is on social and economic ramifications at the community and household level occasioned by the massive flow of migrants from the village of Pampa to the eastern coca growing lowlands. The data are used to examine the utility of several abstract theories about social change. The author concludes, under the circumstances of coca migration, that these theories are insufficient. The thesis is sensitive to the historical process of modernization and development policies following the agrarian reform of 1952 which instituted the development of a wealthy and powerful agrarian class in the eastern lowlands where coca later became a principal export commodity. Consequences in land tenure, labor availability, and migration are noted. The social consequences of an increasingly wealthy and prominent group of "cocaine migrants" are examined. What economic prosperity has derived is likely to be illusory. "Little if any of the resources generated by the cocaine market are reinvested in productive activities, basic crop production is on the decline, economic polarization is on the rise, and the differential accumulation of land and wealth is a likely outcome" (p. 301). ^Latin\America ^Bolivia ^Consequences\Economic ^Consequences\Political ^Consequences\Social ^Migration

1518. Sanctis, Michael T. De (1985). "Nigerians Becoming More Active in the Smuggling of Southwest Asian Heroin in the U.S., Europe." *Narcotics Control Digest*, 20 March, 2–4. Describes the increased heroin traffic and gives a pricing structure. Notes corruption, fraud, currency problems, and how the smuggling groups operate within the context of U.S. distribution networks. Groups are operating in many U.S. cities. ^Africa ^Nigeria ^United\States ^Heroin ^Drug\Traffic ^Organized\Crime ^Politics ^Consequences\Corruption

1519. Saphos, Charles S., Michael Zeldin, Harry Harbin, Gary Schneider, and Thomas M. Hollenhorst (1987). *Handbook on the Anti-Drug Abuse Act of 1986*. Washington, D.C.: U.S. Department of Justice. This handbook describes the provisions of the act that bear on law enforcement practice relating to control of narcotics and drug trafficking. There are now three levels of penalties for such offenses, which vary in severity according to the kind and quantity of controlled substance involved in any offense and depending on the defendant's prior record of drug-related convictions. They also depend on whether death or serious bodily injury resulted from the use or distribution of the drug. The discussion, annotation, and explanation deals with the three levels of penalties: Those involving ten-year or greater mandatory jail terms, those involving five-year or greater mandatory jail terms, and those involving primarily nonmandatory jail terms. The Anti-Drug Abuse Act of 1986 substantially increased the maximum penalties—terms of imprisonment, fines, and special parole terms—in the new penalty statutes that may be imposed for offenses of the Controlled Substance Act. This handbook was prepared to assist federal prosecutors and investigators, as well as other persons with federal criminal justice responsibilities, in their review and implementation of this new major law. ^United\States ^Law\Enforcement ^Legislation

1520. Satchell, Michael (1987). "Narcotics: Terror's New Ally." *U.S. News and World Report*, 4 May, 30–37. Narcotics traffickers are using their ill-gotten gains to force agendas on governments, destabilize democracies, spawn anarchy, and export revolution. Examples are given of a Tamil atrocity in Sri Lanka, of the activities of the drug baron Khun Sa in the Golden Triangle, of Cuba's involvement in the Sandinista connection, and of the Kremlin's role. The predictions for the future are gloomy. ^Southeast\Asia ^Sri\Lanka ^Cuba ^Golden\Triangle ^Insurgents ^Traffickers ^Consequences\Political ^Consequences\Violence

1521. Satinder, K. Paul (1980). *Drug Use: Criminal, Sick or Cultural?* Roslyn Heights, N.Y.: Libra Publishers, Inc. There is "no valid reason to consider drug use a crime" (p. 64). Thus, the author proposes the removal of legal restraints on drug use and considers probable consequences that would result. In the final chapter a host of reasons is advanced not to suppress drug use, based principally on utilitarian concerns (e.g., drug suppression strategies are used as an instrument for harassment of unpopular elements in society; the harassment, that is, the application of the laws, creates a need to increase expenditures in order to deal with their mounting consequences). Drug regulation is the key; the author advances mechanisms by which that could be done. Campaigns also ought to be advanced that would encourage people not to use dangerous drugs. Education should be employed; he advances suggestions as to what needs to be done to make drug education effective. The author is a professor of psychology, Lakehead University, Ontario, Canada. ^Drug\Use ^Prevention ^P\S\Legalization ^P\S\Education ^Drug\Control\Policies\Critique

1522. Schachter, Jim (1987). "Customs Service Cleans House in a Drive on Drug Corruption." *The Los Angeles Times*, 16 June, 3. The degree to which the

U.S. Customs Service has succumbed to the temptation of personal gain from trafficking in narcotics is noted. Though not widespread, drug-related improprieties among border inspectors are serious and increasing. However, the extent of corruption is not viewed as being extensive. A few spectacular excesses have, nevertheless, hurt the good image of the U.S. Customs Service. ^United\States ^Customs ^Consequences\Corruption

1523. Schanche, Don A. (1989). "Bahamas Leader Denies Drug Ties; Pindling Blames U.S. Officials for Accusations of Payoff." *The Los Angeles Times*, 5 March, 16. The prime minister of the Bahamas is incensed over suggestions that he might be indicted on drug charges in the United States. He has launched a counter diplomatic campaign. ^Caribbean ^Bahamas ^Drug\Traffic ^Politics ^Consequences\Corruption

1524. Schaps, Eric, Joel M. Moskowitz, Janet H. Malvin, and Gary A. Schaeffer (1986). "Evaluation of 7 School-Based Prevention Programs: A Final Report on the Napa Project." *International Journal of the Addictions* 21(9-10): 1081–1112. Describes characteristics of the prevention programs under study, the populations treated, and treatment settings. Examines the research methods and the evaluation reports themselves. Overall, hardly any of the programs produced more than minor effects on drug use behaviors and attitudes. When a subset of programs was taken for intensive review, however, some encouraging observations about efficacy were able to be made. Only the drug education course showed any pattern of significant effects, and these were short term and obtained only for girls. (The studies dealt with programs delivered to elementary or junior high students.) "The findings call into question the efficacy of generic prevention programs, at least as such programs are commonly implemented" (p. 1082). ^Prevention\Drug\Education\Critique ^Prevention\Schools ^Youth ^Treatment ^Drug\Control\Policies\Effectiveness ^Drug\Use

1525. Schatzman, Morton, Andrea Sabbadini, and Laura Forti (1976). "Coca and Cocaine: A Bibliography." *Journal of Psychedelic Drugs* 8(2): 95–128. This bibliography is presented in two sections covering coca and cocaine. Each section consists of two parts: annotated works and works that are simply referenced. The emphasis is more on sociology, psychology, and clinical features than on pharmacology and biochemistry. Insofar as the article may contain a certain bias, one might reflect on the following: "We have come across no author who self administered coca or cocaine and regretted it" (p. 100). Most regular cocaine users—if the drug is ingested by nose or mouth—have been able to stop their use easily when they chose to, without returning to it. "The authors believe that those who inject will find it harder to stop using cocaine than those who employ other routes of administration, and that injection of high doses is most likely to produce dangerous effects like violence, paranoia and psychosis" (Anglin, *Cocaine*, entry #216). ^Coca ^Cocaine ^Drug\Use ^Bibliographies ^Consequences\Misc

1526. Schioler, P. (1981). "Information, Teaching and Education in the Primary Prevention of Drug Abuse among Youth in Denmark." *Bulletin on Narcotics* 33(4): 57-65. Briefly describes new approaches to drug-abuse prevention as developed in the early 1980s in Denmark. Moving well beyond the "risk-oriented teaching method" (teaching young people about the pharmacological properties of drugs to produce aversion, fear, and anxieties among them—largely a failure), and "person-oriented teaching methods" (focusing on unfavorable family conditions, genes, bad housing, insufficient education—also a failure) the article discusses "situation-oriented teaching methods." This method places the individual in a social, psychological, and cultural setting and looks at situations that can be affected within those settings. Describes such an approach, acknowledging, nevertheless, that no prevention of drug abuse is possible without a broad spectrum of concerted action involving information, teaching, education (such as the kind that is prescribed here), as well as the activities of the police and customs officials and services provided by medical and social institutions. Absent education programs integrated into the very heart and soul of the community, however, it is unlikely that the programs will be successful. ^Denmark ^Youth ^Prevention\Integrated ^Prevention\Drug\Education\Critique ^Scandinavia

1527. Schlesinger, H. L. (1985). "Topics in the Chemistry of Cocaine." *Bulletin on Narcotics* 37(1): 63–78. Reviews substantial literature concerning the taxonomy and alkaloidal contents of coca plants. Describes how cocaine alkaloids are extracted from the plant and gives chemical formulae associated with cocaine processing. Describes how forensic scientists may trace cocaine when called upon to give legal testimony. ^Cocaine ^Reviews

1528. Schmidt, William E. (1989). "Crack Epidemic Missing Chicago in Urban Sweep." *The New York Times*, 10 February, A14. Crack has not invaded Chicago as much as some other urban centers; suspicion is raised that the gangs themselves may be holding down crack because they don't want the exposure of problems associated with it. There is, on the other hand, rather heavy consumption of cocaine. ^United\States ^Cocaine ^Crack ^Drug\Traffic ^Illinois ^Consequences\Markets ^Organized\Crime

1529. Schmoke, Kurt L. (1988). "Decriminalizing Drugs; It Just Might Work—And Nothing Else Does." *The Washington Post*, 15 May, B1. Nothing else has worked, so why not try decriminalizing drugs. Three basic arguments in favor of decriminalization are raised: libertarianism, economics, and health. Basically, the argument is to take the profit out of drug dealing. ^United\States ^P\S\Legalization ^Decriminalization

1530. Schreier, James W. (1983). "A Survey of Drug Abuse in Organizations." *Personnel Journal*, June, 478–84. More than 80 percent of the organizations surveyed have had to deal directly with drug problems. The data developed for this research suggest that antidrug efforts over the last five to ten years have largely been ineffective. Drug abuse has increased in organizations. ^United\States ^Drug\Use ^Workplace

1531. Schroeder, Richard C. (1980). *The Politics of Drugs: An American Dilemma*. Washington, D.C.: Congressional Quarterly. Covers the conventional questions about marijuana and other drugs, and then focuses on international drug traffic, international control of the drug traffic, and domestic drug-abuse law enforcement, along with public policy issues. The conventional questions deal with many of the same facts about drug abuse, shifts in attitudes toward drug use, and whether drugs should be criminalized or legalized. ^United\States ^Drug\Traffic ^Drug\Control\Policies ^Legalization ^Drug\Use

1532. Schuster, C., and R. Pickens (1988). "AIDS and Intravenous Drug Abuse." In *Problems of Drug Dependence, 1988*, NIDA Research Monograph 90, edited by Louis S. Harris. Rockville, Md.: National Institute on Drug Abuse. Gives basic information on the HIV infection, its epidemiology, how infection occurs among intravenous drug abusers, and the National Institute of Drug Abuse's AIDS program. Concludes that control of AIDS will be a difficult public health problem. Insofar as intravenous drug abusers contribute to the problem—and they most certainly do—efforts will require a focus on treatment and prevention of intravenous drug abuse. ^Drug\Use ^Heroin ^Health ^AIDS ^NIDA ^Epidemiology ^Treatment ^Prevention

1533. Schwartz, Richard H. (1985). "Frequent Marijuana Use in Adolescence: What Are the Signs, Stages?" *NASSP Bulletin*, December, 103–108. The precursor signs placing adolescents at risk are estrangement from family, moodiness, deterioration in moral values, apathy, shift in peer group allegiance to a drug using clique, academic underachievement, school attendance problems, and defense of drugs and drug culture. The impact of abuse on the adolescent's family is noted. ^Cannabis ^Drug\Use ^Youth ^Society ^Family ^Values ^Drug\Use\Theories

1534. Schwarz, Michael (1987). "Deadly Traffic." *The New York Times*, 22 March, 54. To be caught with drugs in Malaysia is to be jailed and perhaps hanged. The question is, do such draconian measures work to suppress or subdue the drug trade? Clearly, fear is one of the main elements in Malaysia's enforcement efforts. There is controversial evidence on the degree to which the measures, including whipping, are having with respect to suppression of the trade. What seems to be clear is that the draconian measures, which in turn derive from draconian laws, have had an impoverishing effect on what little democracy the country has enjoyed. The economic incentives to be involved in the drug trade, draconian measures notwithstanding, are discussed. Focusing on the government's perception, there is clear enthusiasm that these measures work to suppress the trade. ^Southeast\Asia ^Malaysia ^Law\Enforcement ^Judiciary ^Consequences\Penal ^Consequences\Personal ^Consequences\Constitutional

1535. Sciolino, Elaine (1988). "Colombian Official Talks of Legalizing Cocaine." *The New York Times*, 25 February, A11. Colombia's Attorney General has given up. The war on drugs, he says, is useless and the government might have to consider negotiating with drug barons as well as legalizing cocaine. ^Latin\America ^Colombia ^Cocaine ^Legalization ^Drug\Control\Policies\Effectiveness

1536. ——— (1989). "Drug Production Rising Worldwide, State Department Says; U.S. Control Is Limited; War and Economic Need Said to Curb American Leverage in Eradicating Crops." *The New York Times*, 2 March, A1. Synopsis of a State Department report that global production of coca, marijuana, opium poppies, and hashish increased sharply in 1988. The increasing relationship of the drug trade to the viability of producing country economies is discussed. ^Cannabis ^Coca ^Opiates ^Production ^Consequences\Economic ^Statistics

1537. ——— (1989). "U.S. Study Praises Mexico's Drug Moves." *The New York Times*, 1 March, A8. The new government in Mexico has received resounding praise for its commitment to substantially increase its antinarcotics efforts. ^Latin\America ^Mexico ^United\States ^Law\Enforcement ^Consequences\Foreign\Relations

1538. ——— (1989). "U.S. Urging Afghan Rebels to Limit Opium." *The New York Times*, 26 March, 4. The United States has asked the Afghan rebel government in exile to curb the soaring production of opium poppies in areas of Afghanistan controlled by guerrillas. ^ Afghanistan ^ Middle\East ^ Golden\Crescent ^ United\States ^ Opiates ^ Production ^ Politics ^ Consequences\Foreign\Relations

1539. ——— (1990). "World Drug Crop up Sharply in 1989 Despite U.S. Effort." *The New York Times*, 2 March, A1. Reviews the March 1990 *International Narcotics Control Strategy Report* from the U.S. Department of State. Gives statistics from major drug producers, and assails the corruption within their governments. Notes the shifts in strategy for crop reduction. ^Production ^Statistics ^Supply ^Drug\Control\Policies ^Consequences\Corruption

1540. Scorzelli, James F. (1988). "Assessing the Effectiveness of Malaysia's Drug Prevention Education and Rehabilitation Programs." *Journal of Substance Abuse Treatment* 5:253–62. The multifaceted nature of Malaysia's drug prevention education and rehabilitation system is reviewed. It was evaluated to have contributed to the steady decrease of a number of identified drug abusers in the country. Examined here are those components in the Malaysian system that might be applicable to Southeast Asian Americans who have become involved in drug abuse. ^Southeast\Asia ^Malaysia ^Drug\Use ^Prevention ^Treatment ^Reviews ^Drug\Control\Policies\Effectiveness

1541. Scott, David Clark (1989). "Surging Sales for Golden Triangle: Many Drug-Enforcement Officials Believe Hong Kong Crime Syndicates Are Responsible." *The Christian Science Monitor*, 6 January, 4. The aggressive growth of heroin traffic out of the Golden Triangle, fostered, many believe, from Hong Kong crime syndicates, is now startling law enforcement agencies worldwide. ^Burma ^Laos ^Thailand ^Southeast\Asia ^Hong\Kong ^Heroin ^Drug\Traffic ^Organized\Crime ^Golden\Triangle ^Production

1542. "Secret Drug Talks Hamper Amnesty" (1984). *Latin American Weekly Report*, 20 July, 3. Description of Colombia's attorney general's meeting with three of Colombia's leading narcotics traffickers in Panama City just three weeks following the death of Justice Minister Rodrigo Lara Bonilla. A number of people are outraged. ^Latin\America ^Colombia ^Drug\Control\Policies ^Traffickers

1543. "Secret Report on Drugs Is Leaked" (1987). *Latin American Weekly Report*, 19 February, 3. An internal report from the government of Trinidad and Tobago discloses the link of top governmental officials to drug transiting operations. Drug abuse in Trinidad and Tobago has increased alarmingly. ^Trinidad\and\Tobago ^Drug\Traffic ^Politics ^Consequences\Corruption ^Drug\Use ^Caribbean

1544. Segal, Bernard, ed. (1986). *Perspectives on Drug Use in the United States*. New York: The Haworth Press. Desires to present critical review essays on contemporary issues that provide directions for additional research. Authors make scathing conclusions on the effect of contemporary drug control policies and procedures, take issue with "the deviance model of drug taking behavior," look at women's issues in relationship to drug taking, and examine drug use in the United States in a cultural-anthropological context (thus departing from traditional psychosocial discussions of drug abuse). ^United\States ^Drug\Use ^Women ^Drug\Control\Policies\Critique ^Society ^Culture ^Consequences\Social ^Consequences\Economic ^Consequences\Political

1545. Seligmann, Jean (1986). "Crack: The Road Back." *Newsweek*, 30 June, 52–53. Description of how rehabilitation centers are straining under the load that the new drug epidemic has caused. ^United\States ^Cocaine ^Crack ^Treatment ^Consequences\Economic ^Treatment\Rehabilitation

1546. Selser, Gregorio (1982). *Bolivia: El Cuartelazo de los Cocadólares*. Mexico City: Mexsur. Relationship of cocaine trafficking to politics, government, and corruption in Bolivia. In July 1980 the civilian government of Bolivia suffered a coup d'état and was replaced by a dictatorship that specialized in narcotics trafficking. For more than two years this military dictatorship facilitated international trafficking in cocaine, finally being pushed out of power in October 1982. A large part of the history of this period, with its sordid mess, corruption, and intrigue, is told in this book. It consists mainly of reprints of newspaper articles published by the author, a Bolivian newsman. ^Latin\America ^Bolivia ^Cocaine ^Drug\Traffic\History ^Politics ^Consequences\Corruption ^Military ^Consequences\Political

1547. Semlitz, Linda, and Mark S. Gold (1986). "Adolescent Drug Abuse." *Psychiatric Clinics of North America* 9(3): 455–73. Describes drug use as being progressive. Drug use begins with cigarettes and alcohol, develops into the use of marijuana and eventually cocaine, hallucinogens, and other drugs. Drug users experience dysfunctional development, poor interpersonal skills, learning deficits, and concurrent psychiatric illnesses. Also discusses the treatment and prevention of adolescent drug abuse, emphasizing the social pressures model for prevention and the family involvement model for treatment. Calls for more research into the biological and behavioral consequences of marijuana, cocaine, and other drugs. ^Drug\Use ^Prevention ^Treatment ^Youth

^Tobacco ^Alcohol ^Consequences\Misc ^Family ^Consequences\Psychological ^Consequences\Neuro-
logical ^Consequences\Physiological ^Treatment\Peers

1548. Senay, Edward C. (1985). "Methadone Maintenance Treatment." *The International Journal of the Addictions* 20(6-7): 803–21. Reviews the world literature on methadone. There are positive relationships with respect to reduction in use of opiates, criminality, and improvements in general health. Despite these positive data, public opinion remains negative. ^Heroin ^Treatment ^Methadone ^Reviews ^Treatment\Methadone ^Drug\Control\Policies\Effectiveness

1549. Serdahely, William J. (1980). "A Factual Approach to Drug Education and Its Effects on Drug Consumption." *Journal of Alcohol and Drug Education* 26(1): 63–68. Some studies on drug education suggest that the more you teach young people about drugs, the more they are inclined to use them (the "factual approach to drug education"). This author reports that, based on his statistical analysis, no significant changes were found in drug consumption patterns as a consequence of students having received factual information. ^Drug\Use ^Youth ^Prevention\Drug\Education

1550. "17 Reported Hanged in Iran Anti-Drug Campaign" (1989). *The New York Times*, 8 January, A14. From among 1,000 people arrested in a drug sweep in Iranian cities, 17 were hanged. The country has draconian execution laws with respect to drug traffickers, including a mandatory death sentence for anyone caught with more than an ounce of heroin, morphine, codeine, or methadone. ^Middle\East ^Iran ^Law\Enforcement ^Golden\Crescent ^Drug\Control\Policies

1551. Shafer, Jack (1985). "Designer Drugs." *Science* 6(2): 60–67. Discusses how, by altering the molecular structures of compounds, underground chemists are able to create substitutes for heroin and other drugs. It is difficult for legal provisions to be elaborated against each drug as quickly as the drugs themselves may be changed. An "inset discussion" in this issue of *Science* discusses the connection between MPTP, the contaminant discovered in new heroin, and Parkinson's disease. This, insofar as the connection has proved valid, adds to the hazards of taking the drug as well as to society's grief in dealing, collectively, with its consequences. ^United\States ^Drug\Traffic ^Designer\Drugs ^Drug\Control\Policies ^Society ^Consequences\Health

1552. Shaffer, Howard, and Milton Earl Burglass, eds. (1981). *Classic Contributions in the Addictions*. New York: Brunner/Mazel. Addresses, essays, and lectures associated with drug abuse and the narcotic habit. The volume is an effort to bring together the major contributions to the addiction treatment theory literature. Attempts to identify and organize into a single text the body of work that guides several orientations. Orientations toward addictions are rooted in a multitude of disciplines: History, sociology, psychology, medicine, physiology, pharmacology, philosophy, politics, witchcraft, and religion. Each spawns a "school," and it is not surprising that advocates' orientations are highly consistent with their own background. Thus, "some physicians offer a theory of opiate addiction based on metabolic deficiency; some sociologists contribute perspectives dealing with social/cultural environmental influences; several psychoanalysts present evidence regarding functioning of the mind; and behavioralists offer a behavioral orientation" (p. 483). Offers perspectives on history and related social policy, on the psychodynamics of addiction, on psychosocial perspectives of addiction, on behavioral approaches to addiction, and on physiological formulations of addiction. Research issues and themes are identified. The editors have provided an annotated bibliography. ^Drug\Control\Policies ^Reviews ^Treatment\Theories ^Drug\Use\Theories ^Bibliographies ^Drug\Use\History

1553. Shain, Martin, William Riddell, and Heather Lee Kilty. (1977). *Influence, Choice, and Drugs: Towards a Systematic Approach to the*

Prevention of Substance Abuse. Lexington, Mass.: Lexington Books. Drug abuse and prevention among United States youth. Written as a conceptual aid for community workers, educators, and consultants who work or wish to work in drug and alcohol abuse prevention. Mostly, it illustrates the experiences of two community consultants and a researcher (Canada) who took a broad philosophy of community development and attempted to draw it into a theory and practice for prevention. It is therefore not strictly a "how to do it" manual. The focus is upon influences that affect adolescent decision making about the use of psychoactive substances. The approach is systemic and integrationalist. The viewpoint, therefore, is that drug use is promoted or deterred by conditions in family, school, and peer group, and cannot be understood as a result of individual intrapsychic processes. Authors are therefore suspicious of studies that simply report on the characteristics of drug users without reference to the social conditions that affect them. ^United\States ^Drug\Use ^Prevention\Theories ^Youth ^Family ^Society

1554. Shannon, Don (1989). "High-Level Drug Case Rocks Cuba." *The Los Angeles Times*, 26 June, 5. Cuba has been shocked by Raúl Castro's admission that Cuban higher-ups have been involved in international narcotics trafficking. It was Raúl Castro, in a June 15 rambling speech, who officially changed Cuba's statements about complicity in the transportation of drugs through its territory. All of this flies in the face of Cuba's having proudly proclaimed that one of the accomplishments of its revolution was the eradication of drugs, gambling, and prostitution in Havana. The larger issue may be that some military officers, including General Ochoa, are descending politically. ^Caribbean ^Cuba ^Law\Enforcement ^Drug\Traffic ^Politics

1555. Shannon, Elaine (1986). "The Eastern Connection: Coke Was a Frequent Flyer." *Newsweek*, 24 February, 63. Discusses the degree to which Eastern Airlines has been a conduit for illegal shipments of cocaine worth billions of dollars. ^United\States ^Cocaine ^Drug\Traffic ^Aircraft

1556. ———— (1988). *Desperados: Latin Drug Lords, U.S. Lawmen, and the War America Can't Win.* New York: Viking. This book is about the politics of drugs, and, in particular, about the tensions and contradictions created by United States domestic political priorities, its economic and national security interests, its geopolitical agenda, and its law enforcement responsibilities. The author, an investigative reporter, bases the book on hundreds of interviews and a point of view that assumes conflict among bureaucratic entities. In effect it is a chronicle of how, if not why, United States government agencies cannot, or will not, act in concert on drug suppression issues. ^United\States^Drug\Control\Policies^Bureaucracy^Drug\Control\Politics^Consequences\Foreign\Policy

1557. ———— (1988). "Why We're Facing a World of Noriegas." *The Washington Post*, 23 October, C1. Description of the enduring conflict between foreign policy goals and drug suppression goals. A good many "friends" of the United States appear to be involved in drug dealings in countries such as Mexico, Panama, Colombia, Peru, Bolivia, Chile, the Bahamas, Thailand, and Pakistan. ^United\States ^Drug\Control\Policies ^Politics ^Consequences\Foreign\Policy ^Bureaucracy ^Consequences\Corruption ^Mexico ^Panama ^Colombia ^Peru ^Bolivia ^Chile ^Bahamas ^Thailand ^Pakistan ^Latin\America ^Caribbean ^Southeast\Asia ^Middle\East ^Golden\Triangle ^Golden\Crescent ^Southwest\Asia

1558. Shapiro, Arthur M. (1988). "Drugs and Politics in Latin America: The Argentine Connections." *The New Leader*, 27 June, 9. A connection is made between right-wing military interests in Argentina and the international drug trade. The former military dictatorship in Argentina helped to install the drug trafficking García Mesa regime in Bolivia in return for an agreement that he would not sell cocaine in Argentina. But that is all changing as the far right appears to be financing itself

through drug dealing. ^Latin\America ^Argentina ^Cocaine ^Drug\Traffic ^Politics ^Conse-
quences\Corruption ^Military ^Consequences\Political

1559. Shenon, Philip (1990). "Bush Officials Say War on Drugs in the Nation's Capital Is a Failure." *The New York Times*, 5 April, A1. Illegal drugs are still relatively easily obtained and reasonably inexpensive on the nation's capital's streets. Consistent with that trend is a deterioration in everything else—"more murders, more drug abuse, more crime." ^United\States ^Washington\DC ^Drug\Control\Policies\Effectiveness

1560. Sherman-Peter, A. M. (1987). "Co-ordinated Countermeasures of Caribbean Countries against the Illicit Drug Traffic: Recent Developments and Prospects." *Bulletin on Narcotics* 39(1): 69–71. Describes the efforts that Caribbean governments have taken, legal and administrative, to prevent and eradicate illicit cultivation of narcotic crops, as well as to prevent and reduce illicit demand for drugs, and also to reduce the degree to which their countries are used as transshipment points. There is a limited availability of trained professional manpower and of the technical and economic resources required to combat drug trafficking effectively. A call is given to provide technical and financial assistance to help overcome constraints and therefore enable the countries to cope with the increasing drug problems in the subregion. ^Latin\America ^Caribbean ^Drug\Control\Policies ^International\Cooperation ^Demand ^Supply ^P\S\Foreign\Aid

1561. "Should Cocaine Cost More? Less?" (1988). *The New York Times*, 28 July. Policies that lead to higher prices induce more crime. Policies must focus on demand, which would lower prices and reduce crime. ^Cocaine ^Drug\Control\Policies\Critique ^Crime ^Economics ^Demand ^Supply ^Consequences\Markets

1562. Shulgin, A. T. (1975). "Drugs of Abuse in the Future." *Clinical Toxicology* 8(4): 405–56. In addition to comments about cocaine, Shulgin has a section on opiates, exploring them within the same dimensional framework, that is, the ease and facility with which they may be synthesized and therefore become part of a new horror story based on the American drug market. ^Cocaine ^Opiates ^Designer\Drugs

1563. Shultz, George (1984). "The Campaign against Drugs: The International Dimension." U.S. Department of State, Bureau of Public Affairs, *Current Policy #611*. An address given before the Miami Chamber of Commerce, Miami, Florida, 14 September 1984. Shultz discusses strategies that must be employed both within the United States and within producing countries to reduce, if not eliminate, the challenge of narcotics trafficking. Within the United States there must be programs concentrating on prevention, which includes educating youth about the dangers of drugs; detoxification and treatment for drug abusers; research aimed at understanding the causes and consequences of drug abuse; drug law enforcement to destroy drug networks and interdict drug supplies before they reach the consumers; and development of an internal capacity capable of initiating international cooperation to control the production and shipment of narcotics. With respect to the international dimension, Shultz reveals the role that Cuba and Nicaragua have had in transhipment of drugs to the United States, and their utilization of both the proceeds and capacity to funnel arms to terrorist groups. He considers that the diplomatic and program efforts of the Reagan administration, together with the increasing awareness in producer countries of the disastrous effects on them of the drug trade, have to combine to improve the prospects of narcotics control. ^United\States ^Drug\Control\Policies ^Cuba ^Nicaragua ^Terrorists ^Latin\America ^Caribbean

1564. Siddle, John (1982). "Anglo-American Co-Operation in the Suppression of Drug Smuggling." *International and Comparative Law Quarterly* 31(October): 726–47. In 1981 an agreement was reached between the United States and the United Kingdom which allowed the United States to board private British vessels on the high seas in the Gulf of Mexico, the Caribbean, and on the eastern seaboard to search for drugs. If drugs were found, the vessel could be seized and forcibly taken to the United States where it was subject to forfeiture and the crew to trial. Examines the problem that gave rise to an exchange of diplomatic notes, then reviews the agreement in detail. ^United\Kingdom ^United\States ^Interdiction ^Asset\Forfeiture ^International\Cooperation

1565. Siegel, Ronald K. (1979). "Cocaine Smoking." *New England Journal of Medicine* 300(7): 373. This short correspondence asserts that smoking coca leaves, cigars, and cigarettes, and even mixing cocaine hydrochloride (street cocaine) with tobacco or marijuana cigarettes seems to provoke little or no intoxication except for large doses (50 to 100 mg), which result in mild mood elevation. However, users now experimenting with smoking cocaine alkaloid or base, known in street terms as "free base," present conditions highly deleterious to personal health, and are involved in excesses unlike those who simply tend to use intranasal doses. Depending on dose and personality, the syndrome described may progress to a manic-like euphoria, depressive-like dysphoria, or schizophrenic-like paranoid psychosis. The rarity of such findings among intranasal cocaine users and the increasing appeal of smoking among this population present a potential medical hazard. ^Cocaine ^Drug\Use ^Tobacco ^Consequences\Health

1566. ———— (1980). "Long-Term Effects of Recreational Cocaine Use: A Four Year Study." In *Cocaine 1980. Proceedings of the Interamerican Seminar on Medical and Sociological Aspects of Coca and Cocaine*, edited by F. R. Jeri, 11–16. Lima, Peru: Pacific Press. The study of ninety-nine young adult cocaine users on which this report is based lasted four years. Tables are given outlining users' reported positive and negative acute and long-term effects. ^Cocaine ^Drug\Use ^Consequences\Health ^Consequences\Misc ^Consequences\Sexuality ^Consequences\Psychological

1567. ———— (1982). "Cocaine and Sexual Dysfunction: The Curse of Mama Coca." *Journal of Psychoactive Drugs* 14(1–2): 71-74. The author's judgment is clear: "Taken together, these cases illustrate that the positive rewards derived from cocaine use—the stimulation and euphoria—overshadow the negative effects, even when such effects are dysfunctional to appetite, sleep, or sexual activities. The continuing appeal of cocaine as an aphrodisiac, despite apparent sexual disinterest or dysfunction, goes beyond the psychopharmacological considerations of central nervous system excitation, arousal and pleasure. It also goes beyond the drug's unique properties of delaying orgasm while facilitating performance. The appeal can be understood only in the context of cocaine's association with status, glamour and power" (p. 73). ^Cocaine ^Consequences\Sexuality

1568. Sigler, Robert T. (1987). "Social Disorganization on Bimini: Impact of the Drug Trade." *International Journal of Comparative and Applied Criminal Justice* 11(1): 133–42. A social anthropological model was used to examine the impact of the drug trade on Bimini, an island in the Bahamas. The drug trade constituted a nontechnological new element that increased economic resources controlled by people who had relatively low status. There was thus a shift in power or a reduction in the authority of community leaders; the consequence has been increased social disorganization. ^Bahamas ^Drug\Traffic ^Caribbean ^Consequences\Social ^Consequences\Economic ^Consequences\Political

1569. Silverman, Irving (1985). "Addiction Intervention: Treatment Models and Public Policy." *International Journal of the Addictions* 20(1): 183–201. Reviews several kinds of treatment models, including the therapeutic community (inspired by Alcoholics Anonymous), hospitalization, detoxification programs, methadone maintenance treatment programs, methadone to abstinence programs, and law enforcement programs. Briefly discusses the successes and failures of these models and argues for a movement toward a more coherent system that is holistic in its orientation. ^Drug\Use ^Reviews ^Treatment\Theories ^P\S\Integrated ^Treatment\Critique ^Treatment\Therapeutic\Community ^Treatment\Public\Health\Approach ^Treatment\Detoxification ^Treatment\Abstinence ^Methadone

1570. Silverman, Lester P., and Nancy L. Spruill (1977). "Urban Crime and the Price of Heroin." *Journal of Urban Economics* 4:80–103. Examines the relationship between a price index for retail heroin and monthly crimes reported to the police. Price elasticity of demand for heroin and the elasticity of crime with respect to price are factored into the model. Based on data from Detroit, the author estimates that a 50 percent increase in the price of heroin would result in a 14 percent increase in the total property crime and a 13 percent decrease in the quantity of heroin consumed. The largest effects would be on burglaries and robberies in poor, nonwhite neighborhoods. ^Heroin ^Crime ^Economics

1571. Silverstein, Josef (1988). "Foreign Mediation Could Help End Burma's Civil War." *Far Eastern Economic Review*, 19 May, 28–29. Discussion that the ongoing civil war in Burma has less to do with competing interests regarding smuggling and opium trading than with basic issues of democracy. Describes the erratic herbicidal spraying program and how it has gone awry in the minority regions. ^Southeast\Asia ^Burma ^Opiates ^Drug\Traffic ^Crop\Eradication ^Herbicides ^Politics ^Insurgents ^Consequences\Violence

1572. Simon, Carl P., and Ann D. Witte (1982). *Beating the System: The Underground Economy*. Boston: Auburn House. Of interest to this bibliography is an entire section on the production and distribution of drugs, including chapters on heroin, cocaine, and marijuana. ^Drug\Traffic ^Economics ^Informal\Economy

1573. Simons, Marlise (1984). "Cocaine Means Cash in Bolivia Bank." *The New York Times*, 21 July. On-site report from La Paz describing the economic impact of the coca/cocaine trade on the Bolivian economy. ^Latin\America ^Bolivia ^Coca ^Cocaine ^Drug\Traffic ^Consequences\Economic

1574. ———— (1987). "Bolivia Cocaine Trade Revives After G.I.'s Go." *The New York Times*, 3 January, A1. Describes the United States' efforts, by landing its own troops in July 1987, to combat the cocaine trade in Bolivia. Yet within two months after the American troops left, the cocaine business had returned to normal, as had coca prices. Discussion of methods by which international transactions occur, noting the fact that no important cocaine bosses have been jailed in Bolivia. Some people who allegedly collaborated with the military forces were found shot to death. ^Latin\America ^Bolivia ^United\States ^Cocaine ^Drug\Control\Policies ^Military ^International\Cooperation ^Drug\Control\Policies\Effectiveness ^Consequences\Violence ^Drug\Traffic

1575. Simpson, D. Dwayne, and S. B. Sells (1982). "Effectiveness of Treatment for Drug Abuse: An Overview of the DARP Research Program." *Advances in Alcohol and Substance Abuse* 2(1): 7–29. The DARP program simply refers to the Drug Abuse Reporting Program that, for the reports summarized here, contained almost 44,000 admissions between 1969 and 1973 attached to fifty-two treatment programs located in the United States and in Puerto Rico. Based on a longitudinal study, nearly 5,000 interviews were conducted. Overall, findings offer hope for methadone maintenance, therapeutic communities, and outpatient drug-free programs as effective means to improve post-treatment reduction or elimination of drug abuse, criminality, and associated activities. Not much hope was given for outpatient detoxification programs. ^Heroin ^Treatment ^Methadone ^Reviews ^United\States ^Puerto\Rico ^Treatment\Critique ^Treatment\Therapeutic\Community

1576. "Singapore Declares War on International Drug Traffickers" (1985). *Narcotics Control Digest*, 10 July. Gives data on the number of people arrested in Singapore and sentenced to death by hanging for drug trafficking. As of the publication date, twenty-one people, including two women, had been convicted and sentenced to death; eighteen of them have been hanged. ^Southeast\Asia ^Singapore ^Law\Enforcement ^Consequences\Penal ^Judiciary

1577. Singh, Kedar Man (1986). "A Taste of Smack." *Far Eastern Economic Review*, 1 May, 36–37. While marijuana has long been used in Nepal, harder drugs have only recently come to the country. Now, there is widespread heroin addiction by Nepalese school children. One out of every ten homes in some areas is affected. ^Southeast\Asia ^Nepal ^Heroin ^Drug\Use ^Youth

1578. Sitomer, Curtis (1986). "Drugs, Drink, and Youth Crime." *The Christian Science Monitor*, 18 November. From the vantage of judges, there is a clear relationship between substance abuse and crime. Many of the jurists surveyed considered that mandatory (coercive) treatment of juvenile drug abusers would be an effective approach to coping with juvenile drug-related crime. ^United\States ^Drug\Use ^Youth ^Consequences\Crime

1579. Skolnick, Jerome H. (1988). "Drugs: More or Fewer Controls?" *The Los Angeles Times*, 22 June, 7. To be acceptable, decriminalization would need to be grounded in a larger moral purpose such as reducing crime, enhancing public health and safety, invigorating a sense of community, and so forth. Few current proposals for decriminalization view the matter within this important moral context. ^United\States ^Decriminalization ^P\S\Legalization\Critique

1580. Skrlj, M. (1986). "Programme Base for the Prevention of Drug Abuse in Yugoslavia." *Bulletin on Narcotics* 38(1-2): 105–112. Yugoslavia, along the main road between the Middle East and Western Europe, finds itself as a country involved in the illicit transit of heroin, cannabis, and other drugs. Estimates suggest that huge quantities of drugs transit through Yugoslavia. Some of these spill over into use in Yugoslavia. Summarizes policies and strategies adopted by Yugoslavia's federal government to deal with the problem. Theirs is a comprehensive approach, involving communities, parents, other members of families, schools, and workplaces. The police are intensifying their efforts, and community service agencies are trying to create "healthy activities" for youth. ^Middle\East ^Europe ^Yugoslavia ^Drug\Use ^Prevention ^Drug\Traffic ^Prevention\Integrated

1581. "Slaughter in the Streets; Crack Touches off a Homicide Epidemic" (1988). *Time*, 5 December, 32. A substantial increase in homicide rates in New York City, Houston, and Washington, D.C., are thought, by some police personnel, to be directly correlated with the use of crack. It appears that turf wars between rival dope gangs posturing for market shares is partly responsible for increased homicide. ^United\States ^Cocaine ^Crack ^Drug\Traffic ^Crime ^Washington\DC ^Consequences\Violence ^Traffickers ^Consequences\Markets

1582. Slaughter, James B. (1988). "Marijuana Prohibition in the U.S.: History and Analysis of a Failed Policy." *Columbia Journal of Law and Social Problems* 21(417): 417–74. Prohibition in the United States has failed to control the use of marijuana, and the government's accelerating pursuit of a prohibition model causes society to incur a price far exceeding the harm of this "mild intoxicant." The origins and development of marijuana prohibition are explored; and subsequent "waves of reform" are reviewed, including decriminalization in some states in the 1970s, and the public health and policy debate over cannabis in the 1980s. Discusses public health questions. The article, heavily annotated, clearly comes down on the side of decriminalizing marijuana. ^United\States ^Cannabis ^Drug\Control\Policies\History ^P\S\Legalization ^Drug\Control\Policies\Critique

1583. "Slice of Vice: More Miami Cops Arrested" (1986). *Time,* 8 January, 72. Discusses corruption within the Miami, Florida, police force, and notes that more Miami policemen have been arrested on drug-related charges. ^United\States ^Law\Enforcement ^Consequences\Corruption ^Florida

1584. Smart, Carol (1984). "Social Policy and Drug Addiction: A Critical Study of Policy Development." *British Journal of Addiction* 79:31–39. A general review of the consequences in Britain of developing social policy in the field of drug addiction by treating social problems as medical problems. This is unfruitful. A more broadly gauged understanding of contemporary drug-related events (rational knowledge) is required to underpin policy shifts. ^United\Kingdom ^Drug\Control\Policies\History ^Drug\Control\Policies\Critique

1585. Smart, Reginald G. (1983). *Forbidden Highs: The Nature, Treatment, and Prevention of Illicit Drug Abuse.* Toronto, Canada: ARF Books. Presents a historical perspective on drug use in Canada, including cannabis, heroin and other narcotic drugs, stimulants, cocaine, LSD, glue, solvents, and vasodilators. An assessment is made of the degree of effectiveness of efforts at abuse control and prevention, including national laws, drug education, the role of parents, and the role of treatment centers. Canada has experienced overdependency on legal controls as the response to drug-abuse problems. Whether or not legal controls are relaxed, initiatives should be made in treatment and education. A problem is that the available evidence on the value of education and preventive efforts is not encouraging. ^Canada ^Drug\Use ^Law\Enforcement ^Drug\Control\Policies\Critique^Drug\Use\History^Drug\Control\Policies^Prevention\Critique^Prevention\Drug\Education\Critique

1586. —— (1986). "Cocaine Use and Problems in North America." *Canadian Journal of Criminology* 28(2): 109–28. This review examines the epidemiology of cocaine use, especially the characteristics of users and heavy users, their patterns of use, and the problems they have from cocaine use. All of this is painted against a historical backdrop that includes aggregate statistics summarized from a number of surveys. ^United\States ^Canada ^Cocaine ^Drug\Use ^Health ^Consequences\Health ^Consequences\Misc ^Drug\Use\History ^Statistics ^Epidemiology

1587. —— (1988). "'Crack' Cocaine Use in Canada: A New Epidemic?" *American Journal of Epidemiology* 127(6): 1315–17. Describes the first studies of crack use in Canada. Crack use among students and adults has increased remarkably. Nevertheless, it still involves only a small proportion of adults and students, but a much larger proportion of those already using cocaine. ^Canada ^Cocaine ^Crack ^Drug\Use

1588. Smart, Reginald G., and H. D. Archibald (1980). "Intervention Approaches for Rural Opium Users." *Bulletin on Narcotics* 32(4): 11–27. Opium addiction among adults in opium growing areas varies between 3 and 10 percent. Supply reduction efforts have been largely unsuccessful, and concurrent programs aimed at reducing demand are now being initiated. Among the efforts to reduce demand are programs dealing with socioeconomic development. The role of this in reducing demand for opium has not been fully explored. Article explores additional demand-reduction approaches including health education and treatment strategies appropriate for a rural people. ^Opiates ^Drug\Use ^Prevention ^Treatment ^Demand ^Drug\Control\Policies

1589. Smart, Reginald G., and Glenn F. Murray (1985). "Narcotic Drug Abuse in 152 Countries: Social and Economic Conditions as Predictors." *International Journal of the Addictions* 20(5): 737–49. In general, the best thing that can be said is that social and economic conditions do not predict well across countries, unless one is willing to accept a relationship that is extremely complex. ^Drug\Use ^Drug\Use\Theories

1590. Smart, Reginald G., Glenn F. Murray, and Awni Arif (1988). "Drug Abuse and Prevention Programs in 29 Countries." *International Journal of the Addictions* 23(1): 1–17. Based on reports submitted by each country to the World Health Organization's project on Guidelines for Drug Abuse Prevention, the authors review and summarize drug prevention programs in twenty-nine countries. The most common types of primary prevention programs are legal control measures and school-based, mass media, and professional education programs. ^Prevention ^Reviews ^WHO

1591. Smith, David E. (1988). "The Role of Substance Abuse Professionals in the AIDS Epidemic." *Advances in Alcohol and Substance Abuse* 7(2): 175–95. With the development of the AIDS epidemic, drug treatment professionals are increasingly involved in dealing with the HIV carriers. Factors contributing to the AIDS epidemic are discussed as well as several prevention programs. Drug-abuse treatment programs may be compromised unless treatment personnel develop an AIDS treatment component within their program. ^AIDS ^Treatment

1592. Smith, David E., and D. R. Wesson (1978). "Cocaine." *Journal of Psychedelic Drugs* 10(4): 351–60. This is a general study focusing on cocaine as a central nervous system stimulant of moderately high abuse potential. Focuses on the pharmacological aspects of cocaine, the methods of administration, and the drug's reaction on live tissue. Several case studies are presented, as well as notes on the medical uses of cocaine. ^Cocaine\Pharmacology ^Drug\Use ^Health

1593. Smith, David E., Steven M. Anderson, Millicent Buxton, Nancy Gottlieb, William Harvey, and Tommy Chung (1977). *A Multicultural View of Drug Abuse: Proceedings of the National Drug Abuse Conference, 1977.* Boston: G. K. Hall and Company. In addition to addressing issues related to cocaine, marijuana, and heroin, the papers also focus on drug-abuse policy, regulatory and law enforcement issues, prevention and training issues, and treatment and evaluation issues. Particularly germane to this bibliography is a section on vocational rehabilitation and industrial issues, for these pose impact consequences on consuming societies. Particular emphasis is given to addressing both an understanding of drug use and treatment for its abuse in the context of different cultures requiring different kinds of approaches. ^Drug\Control\Policies ^Drug\Use\Theories ^Society ^Culture ^Consequences\Economic ^Treatment ^Treatment\Theories

1594. Smith, James F. (1989). "Peruvian Guerrillas Unite Peasants, Set Social Order." *The Los Angeles Times*, March 5, 1. *Sendero Luminoso* has been methodically efficient at organizing thousands of peasants into local communities and imposing its own social order on those communities, particularly in the Huallaga Valley. Ordinary crime has virtually been wiped out, but all of the enforcement mechanisms are "above the law." Shining Path's three primary rules are: "Do not mistreat prisoners; do not steal 'so much as a needle or a thread'; and return what you borrow." ^Latin\America ^Peru ^Politics ^Insurgents ^Consequences\Political ^Consequences\Social

1595. Smith, M. O., and I. Khan (1988). "An Acupuncture Programme for the Treatment of Drug-Addicted Persons." *Bulletin on Narcotics* 40(1): 35–41. At Lincoln Hospital in New York City, acupuncture is the primary method of treatment for drug addiction. Acupuncture relieves withdrawal symptoms, prevents the craving for drugs, and increases the rate of participation of patients in long-term treatment programs. ^Cocaine ^United\States ^New\York ^Treatment\Acupuncture

1596. Smith, Michael L. (1988). "Peru Calls for U.S. to Join in Tougher Anti-Coca Effort." *The Washington Post*, 5 August, A26. Astonishing virtually everyone, Peru's President Alan García said that he is willing to use herbicides in the eradication of coca leaf products if UN scientists certify that the ecological impact will be minimal. ^Latin\America ^Peru ^Coca ^Crop\Eradication ^Herbicides

1597. Smith, Thomas Edward (1984). "Reviewing Adolescent Marijuana Abuse." *Social Work* 29(January-February): 17–21. Presents a mini review of existing research and gives practical directions for social workers. Salient among these are "sermons against use are likely to result in adolescents' dismissing the information" (p. 19). In summary, social workers need to be credible—not attempt to scare—actively involve the students, and help adolescents learn to understand when use becomes abuse. There is a dearth of social work literature on marijuana abuse. ^Cannabis ^Drug\Use ^Youth ^Reviews ^Prevention\Theories

1598. Smolowe, Jill (1988). "The Drug Thugs." *Time*, 7 March, 28–37. Narcotics traffickers are moving in on legitimate governments and undermining the legitimacy of their existence. Costa Rica is noted. ^Drug\Traffic ^Traffickers ^Consequences\Corruption ^Consequences\Political ^Latin\America ^Costa\Rica

1599. Sneider, Daniel (1987). "How the Eliot Ness of Japan's Drug World Gets the Job Done." *The Christian Science Monitor*, 23 July, 1. Describes the operations of Japan's Yakuza, a mafia-like drug trafficking organization. Two key elements in the Japanese war on illegal drugs are an unwavering police force and a closely knit society which readily cooperates with the police. Their main strategy is aimed at suppliers of the drugs. This particular combination has proven fairly effective in Japan. ^Southeast\Asia ^Japan ^Law\Enforcement ^Organized\Crime ^Yakuza ^Drug\Control\Policies

1600. Sokalska, Maria E. (1984). "Legal Measures to Combat Drug-Related Problems in Poland." *Bulletin on Narcotics* 36(3): 19–25. Drug abuse, mainly among young people, has been on the increase in Poland. This article discusses the penal sanctions that the state may apply and reviews a new comprehensive drug law being drafted. ^Europe ^Poland ^Law\Enforcement ^Drug\Use ^Consequences\Penal ^Legislation

1601. Solomon, Joel, and Kim A. Keeley, eds. (1982). *Perspectives in Alcohol and Drug Abuse: Similarities and Differences*. Boston: J. Wright-PSG. A historical review of drug and alcohol use, sociocultural aspects of drug use and abuse, pharmacology of addictive drugs, personality and psychopathology, treatments for drug and alcohol addiction, prevention of alcoholism and drug abuse, and research relating to alcohol and opiate dependence. Also discusses the political aspects of alcoholism and drug abuse. ^Drug\Use\History ^Health ^Society ^Culture ^Prevention ^Drug\Use\Theories ^Treatment ^Reviews ^Consequences\Misc ^Alcohol ^Politics

1602. Solomon, R., and M. Green (1982). "The First Century: The History of Nonmedical Opiate Use and Control Policies in Canada, 1870–1970." *University of Western Ontario Law Review* 20(2): 307–36. For its historical interest, this review, heavily noted, explores Canada's experience with opium and the federal response to it both in terms of penalties and alternative treatments. ^Canada ^Opiates ^Drug\Use\History ^Drug\Control\Policies\History

1603. Solomon, Robert (1979). "The Development and Politics of the Latin American Heroin Market." *Journal of Drug Issues* (Summer): A21. In Latin America, political and economic conditions provide an ideal setting for contraband markets, including those of heroin and other drugs. When these conditions were coupled with the changing patterns of illicit international supply, Latin America emerged as the primary source and a major transshipment center for United States–bound heroin. Responding slowly, the United States only in the late 1970s succeeded in stemming the Latin American heroin trade, doing so by exerting considerable economic and diplomatic pressure on the countries involved. However, as the underlying conditions which spawn the heroin trade continue to exist, the author makes the prescient prediction that "progress made to date may ultimately prove to be temporary." [While heroin remained considerably suppressed, cocaine walked into the void.] In this article, the Mexican heroin trade is targeted for considerable review and, to a lesser extent, the heroin trade in Central and South America. ^Latin\America ^Mexico ^Guatemala ^Heroin ^Drug\Traffic ^Politics ^Economics

1604. "Some Plain Talk about Drug Addiction" (1986). *The Current Digest of the Soviet Press* 38(22): 1. The Soviet press is increasingly opening its coverage to the rise in drug problems in the USSR. Reviewed here is traffickers' easy access to Soviet poppy fields, thus creating a ready supply of heroin and lucrative opportunities for those engaged in the trade. Improved countermeasures and antidrug training are urged. ^USSR ^Heroin ^Drug\Traffic ^Drug\Control\Policies

1605. Soto, Hernando de (1989). *The Other Path: The Invisible Revolution in the Third World*. New York, Harper and Row. A best-seller in Latin America that explains how the economic underground in Peru operates. The economic underground that services legitimate economic needs emerged because of government incompetence and the red tape it uses to clutter legitimate economic activity. The book's value for this bibliography is its insights into how illegitimate informal economy may work. ^Latin\America ^Peru ^Informal\Economy

1606. Soueif, M. I. (1976). "Differential Association between Chronic Cannabis Use and Brain Function Deficits." In *Chronic Cannabis Use. Annals of the New York Academy of Sciences*, 282: 323–43. In a series of impressive tests on 850 male regular cannabis users and 839 nonusers, the authors were able, in most cases, to identify significant differentiation between consumers of cannabis and nonconsumers in such areas as speed of psychomotor performance, distance estimation, time estimation, immediate memory, and visual-motor coordination. ^Cannabis ^Drug\Use ^Health ^Consequences\Neurological ^Consequences\Psychological ^Consequences\Public\Safety ^Consequences\Physiological

1607. Soueif, M. I., F. A. Yunis, and H. S. Taha (1986). "Extent and Patterns of Drug Abuse and Its Associated Factors in Egypt." *Bulletin on Narcotics* 38(1-2): 113–20. Large-scale field surveys conducted by the authors since 1957 provide the basis for the integrated picture of the drug-abuse situation in Egypt presented in this article. Cannabis remains the most widely abused drug, aside from alcohol and tobacco. Cocaine and heroin have made inroads. The social matrix is a reinforcing one, in the sense that drug users are those who hear about new drugs, see drugs, and have personal friends and relatives who themselves abuse drugs. ^Egypt ^Drug\Use ^Society ^Cannabis ^Alcohol ^Tobacco ^Cocaine ^Heroin

1608. Southerland, Daniel (1988). "Smugglers Using Routes in China to Move Heroin; Police Say Flow of Drug Is Increasing." *The Washington Post*, 6 December, A33. As Hong Kong police have become more effective in interdicting drug transports out of the Golden Triangle that arrive by sea, smugglers have secured land routes to transport the heroin through China to Hong Kong. Half of the heroin that smugglers ship out of Hong Kong arrives on the U.S. market. Drug smuggling became a problem for China following the country's opening of its borders to tens of thousands of tourists and businessmen in 1981. All of this follows the 1988 bumper crop in opium production in the Golden Triangle. ^Southeast\Asia ^Hong\Kong ^China ^Heroin ^Opiates ^Production ^Drug\Traffic ^Golden\Triangle ^Consequences\Markets

1609. Souza, Percival de (1981). *Society-Cocaína*. São Paulo, Brazil: Traço Editora. Explores cocaine habits and drug control in Brazil. The author is a well-known Brazilian journalist who has spent much of his life reporting on Brazilian law enforcement matters. In this volume he lays out the extent of the drug traffic in Brazil and, by showing that the production, trafficking in, and consumption of cocaine is a question of corruption—the police at all levels are those principally responsible for the distribution of cocaine in Brazil—initiates a call for modification of the Brazilian government's policies on cocaine. ^Latin\America ^Brazil ^Cocaine ^Drug\Traffic ^Traffickers ^Drug\Control\Policies ^Law\Enforcement ^Politics ^Consequences\Corruption ^Consequences\Law\Enforcement ^Proffered\Solutions

1610. "Soviet Drug Scene Gets Heavy Coverage" (1987). *The Current Digest of the Soviet Press* 39(2): 1–14. The Soviet Union now acknowledges that it has a drug problem. The figures given for the number of addicts (46,000) is about one-third of what other sources have given. Commentaries and special features from correspondents to various Soviet publications are featured. ^USSR ^Drug\Use

1611. Spain, James W. (1975). "The United States, Turkey, and the Poppy." *The Middle East Journal* 29(3): 395–09. Historical discussion of U.S. efforts to encourage Turkey to suppress poppy growing. Turkey's ambiguous early response and ultimate rejection of the proffered policies is discussed. "Poppy meant at least as much as tobacco to Kentucky" (p. 305). ^United\States ^Turkey ^Opiates ^Drug\Control\Policies\History ^Drug\Control\Policies\Effectiveness

1612. "Special Issue on Cocaine" (1984). *Bulletin on Narcotics* 36, no. 2 (April-June). Describes recent developments in the abuse of cocaine, the advent of coca-paste smoking in some Latin American countries, the utilization of drug law enforcement as a counterattack on cocaine trafficking, and a study of the herbicide 2-4-D on coca plants. Makes observations about the residual chemical left. ^Coca ^Cocaine ^Drug\Use ^Drug\Control\Policies ^Cocaine\Paste ^Law\Enforcement ^Herbicides ^Health

1613. Speckart, George (1984). "Narcotics and Crime: A Multisample Multimethod Approach." Ph.D. diss., University of California, Los Angeles. Attempts to identify causal relationships between narcotic use and crime. The results are consistent with previous literature in showing that criminality often precedes narcotic addiction, and that criminality shows a strong common positive relationship with levels or rates of narcotics use. His "structural equation models," however, do not support a direct causal relationship between narcotics use and crime over time. It is methodological shortcomings that preclude the identification, he affirms, rather than anything inherent in the expected relationship. The most reasonable conclusion from studies reviewed for this dissertation and the data presented here "is that the great preponderance of crime committed by addicts is engendered by high levels of narcotics use, i.e., that in general narcotics use causes crime" (p. xi). ^Heroin ^Crime\Theories ^Consequences\Crime

1614. Speckart, George, and M. Douglas Anglin (1986). "Narcotics Use and Crime: An Overview of Recent Research Advances." *Contemporary Drug Problems* 13(4): 741–69. The principal controversy regarding narcotics use and crime is the nature and "direction" of causation. Does narcotics use cause crime, crime cause narcotics use, or are narcotics use and crime simply spuriously related as a consequence of their derivation from common antecedent causes? No definitive resolution of this controversy has been forthcoming. Findings of recent projects derived from studies using multiple samples and a variety of statistical techniques nevertheless provide some

additional perspectives on the causal dynamics relating narcotics use and the economic cost to support property crime. Among the conclusions or statistical generalizations are the following: Both arrest and minor property crime precede addiction for most addicts; narcotics use levels facilitate and multiply the amount of property crime activity; there is a qualitative shift in the types of crime as addiction levels increase; dealing in illicit narcotics is a major intervening factor in narcotics use; there is an inverse relationship between dealing and property crime; along with additional noted relationships between the stability of property crime, dealing in narcotics, and narcotics use. The authors note that legal interventions "can reduce criminality among most addicts by making 'choice' of addiction, and the crime required to support it, less desirable" (p. 766). By the same token, "excessive reliance on a medical model of addiction-related behaviors can be theoretically fallacious as well as inefficient from a social cost perspective" (p. 766).
^Heroin ^Reviews ^Drug\Use ^Crime\Theories ^Drug\Control\Policies\Critique

1615. "Speedway to Euphoria" (1986). *The Economist*, 21 June, 63. Description of the invasion of Britain and Europe by the cocaine barons because the market in America was becoming saturated. ^Europe ^United\Kingdom ^Cocaine ^Drug\Traffic ^Consequences\Markets

1616. Spencer, C. P. and V. Navaratnam (1981). *Drug Abuse in East Asia*. New York: Oxford University Press. This volume is presented as a survey of the history of drug production and use in East Asia and of contemporary patterns of abuse among adults and teenagers. Of particular interest to this bibliography is the discussion on preventive education and information campaigns in the various countries of East Asia. Additionally, legal and enforcement responses to drug abuse in each country are discussed. A country-specific bibliography is given for Malaysia, Thailand, Singapore, Indonesia, the Philippines, Laos, Hong Kong, China, Japan, India, Pakistan, Sri Lanka, Burma, and Bangladesh. ^Southeast\Asia ^Malaysia ^Thailand ^Singapore ^Indonesia ^Philippines ^Laos ^Hong\Kong ^China ^Japan ^India ^Pakistan ^Sri\Lanka ^Burma ^Bangladesh ^Drug\Use ^Prevention ^Bibliographies ^Drug\Use\History ^Production\History ^Prevention\Drug\Education ^Golden\Crescent ^Golden\Triangle ^Southwest\Asia ^Law\Enforcement

1617. Spencer, Christopher (1985). "Tradition, Cultural Patterns and Drug Availability as Predictors of Youthful Drug Abuse: A Comparison of Malaysia with Post-Revolutionary Iran." *Journal of Psychoactive Drugs* 17(1): 19–24. Explanations and generalizations regarding precursor characteristics and risk factors may well not have validity in cross-cultural settings. Article attempts to illustrate how usage patterns may relate to differences in the availability of drugs, in historical, geographical, and economic factors, and in campaigns for prevention and control as well as to cultural factors. ^Iran ^Malaysia ^Drug\Use\Theories ^Youth ^Society ^Culture

1618. Spolar, Chris (1988). "An Off-Duty User's Fate; Firing Reflects Reach of Company Policies." *The Washington Post*, 4 December, A1. Discussion of how company policies on illegal drugs reach beyond the job into the private lives of individuals. Data given on local Washington companies and their drug testing policies. ^United\States ^Drug\Testing ^Workplace ^Consequences\Human\Rights

1619. ——— (1988). "How Lab Results Can Change Lives; Technology and Accuracy Improve, but Growing Pains Apparent." *The Washington Post*, 6 December, A1. Mistakes occurring in drug testing laboratories are causing substantial problems. Some people have had considerable difficulty reestablishing their reputations. There must be safeguards for employees so that procedures for finding and acknowledging testing errors may be institutionalized. ^United\States ^Drug\Testing ^Workplace ^Drug\Testing\Critique

1620. ——— (1988). "When Privacy and Company Prerogatives Clash." *The Washington Post*, 5 December, A1. Description of how one company in Albuquerque, New Mexico, conducted a private raid on its employees, and what constitutional and practical issues emerged. Discussion, also, on the larger question of drug testing in American businesses. ^United\States ^Drug\Testing ^Workplace ^Drug\Testing\Critique ^New\Mexico

1621. Spotts, James V., and Franklin C. Shontz (1985). "A Theory of Adolescent Substance Abuse." *Advances in Alcohol and Substance Abuse*, 117–38. A theory is presented that adolescent substance abuse is rooted in dysfunctional relationships with parental figures that block or delay the normal individuation process. ^Drug\Use\Theories ^Youth ^Family ^Parenting

1622. Spunt, Barry, Dana E. Hunt, Douglas S. Lipton, and Douglas S. Goldsmith (1986). "Methadone Diversion: A New Look." *Journal of Drug Issues* 1694: 569–83. Methadone provided through a treatment program is, apparently, diverted to street usage. An approach is advanced to help reduce diversion in ways that would not simply contain it on the surface, but drive the activity underground. ^Heroin ^Treatment ^Methadone ^Drug\Control\Policies ^Consequences\Unintended

1623. Sricharatchanya, Paisal (1987). "Beating a Retreat." *Far Eastern Economic Review*, 16 April, 29. Description of the Thai armies forcing Khun Sa from his mountain stronghold. Burma may not be so cooperative. ^Burma ^Thailand ^Drug\Control\Policies ^Organized\Crime ^Insurgents ^Southeast\Asia ^Golden\Triangle

1624. Stamler, Rodney T. (1983). "The Profits of Organized Crime: The Illicit Drug Trade in Canada." *Bulletin on Narcotics* 35(2): 61–70. Description of the laundering of monies derived from street-level crime into criminal organizations for the benefit of top-level members. The economic and risk-taking features associated with the drug trade are examined as principal attractions to crime syndicates. Problems in applying Canadian legislation permitting tracing of proceeds of crime and prosecuting those who possess the assets are discussed. ^Canada ^Money\Laundering ^Organized\Crime ^Asset\Forfeiture ^Consequences\Economic ^Traffickers\Incentives\Political

1625. ——— (1984). "Forfeiture of the Profits and Proceeds of Drug Crimes." *Bulletin on Narcotics* 36(4): 3–19. Drug trafficking is controlled by well-organized international criminal syndicates. At the highest levels in these syndicates, risk is relatively low. The task, then, is to figure out ways to interdict laundering of the proceeds of drug crimes as they occur through sophisticated international transactions often covered by legitimate operations. Current legislative provisions at both national and international levels are inadequate to this task. Discusses the inadequacies and raises recommendations. ^Drug\Traffic ^Asset\Forfeiture ^Drug\Control\Policies\Critique ^Money\Laundering^

1626. Stamler, Rodney T., and Robert C. Fahlman, eds. *RCMP National Drug Intelligence Estimate 1984/85 with Trend Indicators through 1987* (1987). Royal Canadian Mounted Police. Ottawa, Canada: Royal Canadian Mounted Police for the Drug Enforcement Directorate. These RCMP trend indicators are designed to present a comprehensive annual review of the origin, volume, trafficking routes, modes of transport, and smuggling methods of all drugs on the illicit Canadian market. This is the fourth in the annual series. ^Canada ^Drug\Traffic ^Statistics

1627. Stamler, Rodney T., Robert C. Fahlman, and G. W. Clement (1987). "Co-operation between Canada and Other Countries and Territories to Promote Countermeasures against Illicit Drug Trafficking." *Bulletin on Narcotics* 39(1): 79–85. Reviews the late 1980s program and legislation relating to drug control and cooperation in drug law enforcement between Canada and other countries. Proposes measures to promote worldwide cooperation in controlling illicit traffic. Among these are the following: no safe haven for organized crime, in order to reduce profits associated with it; full cooperation in all investigations and inquiries concerning organized crime; new treaties; cooperation in effective prosecution of individuals and removing them from their illegally accumulated profits. ^Canada ^Drug\Control\Policies\History ^International\Cooperation ^Legislation ^P\S\International\Cooperation

1628. Stamler, Rodney T., Robert C. Fahlman, and S. A. Keele (1983). "Recent Trends in Illicit Drug Trafficking from the Canadian Perspective." *Bulletin on Narcotics* 35(4): 23–32. Discusses the increased supply of heroin and cocaine to the Canadian markets and identifies their points of origin. An illicit demand has also been created for the more potent preparations of cannabis. The dramatic increase in armed robberies perpetrated by criminal groups to procure manufactured drugs is a relatively new and alarming trend. Together with "natural drugs" and activities associated with them, these trends are largely controlled, in Canada, by organized criminal syndicates. ^Canada ^Drug\Traffic ^Organized\Crime ^Heroin ^Cannabis ^Consequences\Crime

1629. ——— (1984). "Illicit Traffic and Abuse of Cocaine." *Bulletin on Narcotics* 36(2): 45–55. Special issue on cocaine. Discusses cocaine related problems in Canada, including increase in use, seizures, and recent trends in smuggling methods and trafficking routes that have Canada as a destination. The main ports of entry in Canada are Montreal, Toronto, and Vancouver. ^Canada ^Cocaine ^Drug\Traffic ^Drug\Use ^Interdiction

1630. Stamler, Rodney T., Robert C. Fahlman, and H. Vigeant (1985). "Illicit Traffic and Abuse of Cannabis in Canada." *Bulletin on Narcotics* 37(4): 37-49. In 1984 cannabis derivatives, in particular marijuana, hashish and liquid hashish, continued to be the most readily available drugs of abuse in Canada. Description of their availability, prices, trends in trafficking, and origin of supply. ^Canada ^Cannabis ^Drug\Use ^Drug\Traffic ^Economics

1631. Stangeland, Per, ed. (1987). *Drugs and Drug Control.* Scandinavian Studies in Criminology 8. Oxford, U.K.: Norwegian University Press. The topic is specific: illicit drug control policy in the Nordic countries. Focuses on the effects of regulations upon society rather than upon drug use's effects on the individual drug user. Gives few hints as to how the war on drugs can be brought to any satisfactory conclusion. Neither victory nor defeat is very likely, the authors assert. Some of the contributing authors do advocate legalization of some or all drugs, and press us to learn to live with them. Others view this as not being realistic in political terms. Since the war cannot be brought to an end, what about diminished damage done on both sides? Many of the contributing authors attempt to answer this question. Norway, with the most vigorous control policies, also has the highest street drug market prices, the lowest number of hard drug addicts, and the lowest public acceptance of drug use. That country's moralistic drives against drug use are thought to be an effective deterrent strategy. Finland has more repressive penal traditions, and drug consumption has never become a major issue in Finnish public debate. The authors suggest that Finland may be the most interesting model of all Nordic countries. ^Scandinavia ^Finland ^Norway ^Drug\Control\Policies ^Drug\Use ^Prevention ^Legalization ^Society ^Consequences\Drug\Control\Policies ^Drug\Control\Policies\Effectiveness ^Proffered\Solutions

1632. Stanton, M. Duncan, Thomas C. Todd, et al (1982). *The Family Therapy of Drug Abuse and Addiction.* New York: Guilford Press. Drug-abuse therapy as a subset of family psychotherapy. Book premised on the authors' view that the theory and practice of many programs for drug abusers that focus on self-responsibility, proximity, group cohesion, and symmetry, are basically unproductive. The authors emphasize the mutual responsibility of family members in family functioning, and they develop a therapeutic method that focuses on hierarchical restructuring and distancing. Attempts to balance scholarly erudition with practicality ranging from a review of the literature to a focus on the minutia of a therapeutic session. This book is one specific treatment program's efforts to evaluate its own effectiveness and to assess the utility of the theory that underlies its practice. Extensive bibliography. ^Drug\Use ^Treatment\Family ^Reviews ^Bibliographies ^Treatment\Critique

1633. "State Asset Forfeiture Laws Can Help Stop Drug Traffic, Beef up Police Budgets." (1985). *Crime Control Digest*, 4 November, 2–3. Forty-seven states permit the seizure of conveyances used to transport, conceal, or facilitate a crime. Some ambiguities remain. Examples are given, along with policy recommendations. ^United\States ^Asset\Forfeiture

1634. Stefanis, Costas, Rhea Dornbush, and Max Fink, eds. (1977). *Hashish: Studies of Long-Term Use.* New York: Raven Press. Physiological effects and psychological aspects of the use of hashish. This volume is part of a series of studies on the health consequences of chronic cannabis use sponsored by the U.S. National Institute on Drug Abuse (NIDA). The organization had initiated three studies in foreign countries where cannabis use is more traditional and/or has a longer history than in the United States. These were a study of ganja use in Jamaica, hashish use in Greece, and, more recently, marijuana use in Costa Rica. Important to keep in mind the social and cultural matrices of the countries where cannabis is used. Attempts are made to explore and indicate the nature of this social matrix in Greece. Beyond that the authors have demonstrated some important pharmacological consequences of hashish. The conclusions in terms of long-term health consequences are that, while hashish is a relatively potent form of cannabis, it is not found to produce brain damage, at least as evidenced by the relatively sophisticated techniques of electroencephalography, echo-encephalography, and psychological testing. The authors found no evidence of deleterious organic effects or motivational effects in their working-class subjects. Their subjects, however, did exhibit a higher incident of psychopathology, although this study could not determine whether it was related to hashish use. In any event, the medical findings were largely indistinguishable from those in the control population. Nevertheless, the users had a higher incidence of arrests and imprisonments, and a lower incidence of satisfactory military service. They thus were alienated from the native culture, where cannabis is proscribed but tobacco and alcohol accepted. Smoking cannabis, even in large quantities, seems less dangerous to users or to society than the penalties meted out to users who are judged guilty of violating cannabis proscriptions (p. 156). The principal limitation of the NIDA-supported studies of long-term users in Greece, Jamaica, and Costa Rica is the small sample size in each study. The study in Greece, for example, had only twenty users. It is therefore quite possible that the samples are biased, not reflecting those users who may have suffered the most significant effects. What is not known, therefore, is anything about subjects who may have happened to discontinue their use of cannabis and why, or whether they died as a result of its use, or if the incidents of medical complications for them is or was similar to the incidents among tobacco users, and so forth. At the time of this study the effects on chromosomes, sex hormones, and the development of neoplasms were still indeterminate. If it is true that the most important issues, therefore, relate to the social and cultural factors that lead people to use cannabis and sustain its use, combined sociological and psychological studies of which governments may make use as they consider cannabis proscription to control their populations requires intensive political and sociological study. ^Greece ^Cannabis ^Drug\Use ^Society ^Culture ^Consequences\Drug\Control\Policies   ^Consequences\Physiological   ^Consequences\Psychological   ^NIDA

^Consequences\Health ^Jamaica ^Costa\Rica ^Amotivational\Syndrome ^Consequences\Crime ^Consequences\Law\Enforcement ^Caribbean ^Latin\America

1635. Stein, Jeff (1984). "Free-Market Magic: Jamaica Has Gone to Ganja." *The Washington Post*, 11 November, D1. A market is available, and marijuana is filling it. "The marijuana crop is tended so carefully that it looks like a Japanese rice paddy." A substantial question for Jamaica is how to replace income derived from the Drug traffic if the country successfully suppresses it. "The ganja trade is the one, foolproof means to make enough money to get off the island and secure some kind of future." ^Caribbean ^Jamaica ^Cannabis ^Production ^Drug\Traffic ^Economics ^Supply ^Demand

1636. Stein, Mark A. (1989). "Recriminalization: Lenient Pot Laws Going up in Smoke." *The Los Angeles Times*, 29 August, 1. Reversing freethinking trends of the 1970s, state legislatures and antidrug activists in a number of states are reexamining the once popular movement to reduce penalties for simple possession of personal-use quantities of marijuana. Even Oregon, which pioneered marijuana decriminalization in 1973, has reversed its position. States discussed are Washington, Alaska, Oregon, Nebraska, North Carolina, Maine, and California. ^United\States ^Cannabis ^Legislation ^Oregon ^Washington ^Alaska ^Nebraska ^North\Carolina ^Maine ^California ^Decriminalization

1637. Stein, S. D. (1985). *International Diplomacy, State Administrators, and Narcotics Control: The Origins of a Social Problem*. Brookfield, Vt.: Gower Press. Control of narcotics in the United States and Great Britain. Gives a broad historical sweep of the development of the current "social problem"—from the Far Eastern opium traffic of 1820-1906, the Shanghai conference and its aftermath, the Hague conferences, the impact of World War II, and the role of the medical profession in the dispensing of dangerous drugs. Two chapters deal with theories of addiction and with addiction treatment. Extensive Bibliography. ^United\Kingdom ^United\States ^Drug\Control\Policies\History ^Bibliographies ^Treaties ^Drug\Use\Theories ^Treatment\Theories

1638. Steinitz, Mark S. (1985). "Insurgents, Terrorists, and the Drug Trade." *The Washington Quarterly* 8(4): 141–56. Examines the evidence of terrorist involvement in the drug trade in Latin America, Southeast Asia, the Middle East, and Europe. Also examines factors behind the linkages, and in particular changing patterns of the international drug scene that have brought insurgency, terrorism, and the drug trade into closer geographical proximity. Examinations for government policy vis-à-vis terrorism are made. ^Drug\Traffic ^Politics ^Insurgents ^Southeast\Asia ^Latin\America ^Middle\East ^Europe ^Consequences\Violence ^Consequences\Political ^Consequences\Terrorists

1639. Stevens, Amy (1988). "State Balks at Paraquat Use on Marijuana Fields." *The Los Angeles Times*, 16 July, 31. The federal government has proposed to spray herbicides on the nation's burgeoning marijuana crop. California officials balk, preferring to chop down the plants and remove them by helicopter for burning. ^United\States ^Cannabis ^Crop\Eradication ^Herbicides ^California ^Consequences\Political

1640. Stewart, Alva W. (1986). *Drug Smuggling: The Problem and Efforts to Curb It*. Monticello, Ill.: Vance Bibliographies. A substantial sampling of books, newspaper articles, periodicals, and U.S. government publications prior to 1986 are given. ^United\States ^Drug\Traffic ^Drug\Control\Policies ^Bibliographies

1641. Stimmel, Barry (1987). "AIDS, Alcohol and Heroin: A Particularly Deadly Combination." *Advances in Alcohol and Substance Abuse* 6(3): 1–5. Narcotic addiction enhances the transfer of the AIDS virus. AIDS transferred as a consequence of addiction is of particular concern because it is also then transferred to innocent heterosexual, nondrug-using people. Innocent children are also affected. Up to a million people may already have been infected by the AIDS virus, with an estimated annual attack rate of from 1 to 2 percent. The degree to which alcohol may affect the immune system in relationship to AIDS infection and drug abuse is still unclear. ^Heroin ^Health ^AIDS ^Society ^Consequences\Misc ^Consequences\Children ^Alcohol

1642. Stimmel, Barry, Judith Brook, Dan Lettieri, and David W. Brook, eds. (1985). *Alcohol and Substance Abuse in Adolescence.* New York: The Haworth Press. Why do American youth turn to drugs, what are the most efficacious ways to manage those so afflicted, and how might youth be educated so as to prevent their initial involvement which leads to severe psychological and physiological dysfunctions? The various papers of this volume treat one or more of those questions. ^United\States ^Drug\Use\Theories ^Prevention\Theories ^Treatment\Theories ^Youth

1643. Stimson, Gerry V., and Edna Oppenheimer (1982). *Heroin Addiction: Treatment and Control in Britain.* New York: Tavistock Publications. This book is about what happens to heroin addicts in Britain, based on the lives of 128 people who were heroin addicts in the 1960s. People were followed for ten years to see what kind of lives they led, how they led them, and how they died. The major part of the work was conducted by the Addiction Research Unit of the Institute of Psychiatry in London. In light of the findings, the authors comment on the historical experience in Great Britain. ^United\Kingdom ^Heroin ^Drug\Use ^Treatment\History ^Consequences\Misc ^Drug\Use\History

1644. "Stirring the Pot" (1985). *The Economist,* 17 August, 24–25. America's biggest cash crop, after corn, is marijuana, which brought in nearly 17 billion dollars in 1984. Description of who the modern "grass growers" are. ^United\States ^Cannabis ^Production ^Economics ^Producers

1645. Stone, Karen, and Judith R. Thompson (1989). "Drug Testing: A National Controversy." *Journal of Alcohol and Drug Education* 34(3): 70–79. Discusses the historical background of drug testing and what the different tests are, outlines some national statistics and opinions on drug testing, and deals with the controversial issues associated with it. Reports the results of a survey taken of a Louisiana population dealing with this issue. ^United\States ^Drug\Testing\History ^Society ^Statistics ^Louisiana

1646. Stoneburner, Rand L. (1988). "A Larger Spectrum of Severe HIV-1–Related Disease in Intravenous Drug Users in New York City." *Science* 242: 916–19. There is a large underestimation of the impact of AIDS on IV drug users, blacks, and hispanics. Details are noted. ^United\States ^Heroin ^Health ^AIDS ^Minorities

1647. Storm, Daniel (1987). *Marijuana Hydroponics: High-Tech Water Culture.* Berkeley, Calif.: And/Or Books. Example of a new genre of books dedicated to showing how marijuana plants can be grown artificially [and by implication, more clandestinely], although no value statement was made that would encourage either the consumption or growing of marijuana. ^Cannabis ^Producers

1648. Strauss, Richard H., ed. (1987). *Drugs and Performance in Sports.* Philadelphia, Pa.: W.B. Saunders. A handy reference treatise giving medical and scientific information about which kinds of drugs enhance athletic performance and under what conditions, what their harmful side effects are, the ethical implications of their use, and which drugs impair performance. Both legal and illegal drugs are discussed. ^Drug\Use ^Consequences\Athletic

1649. "Stronger than the State" (1987). *The Economist,* 28 November, 43. Superficially, life goes on normally in Colombia. Beneath the surface, cocaine is invading every aspect of it and is destroying it. ^Colombia ^Cocaine ^Consequences\State\Authority ^Consequences\Political ^Latin\America ^Consequences\Social ^Drug\Control\Policies\Effectiveness

1650. Strug, David (1983). "The Foreign Politics of Cocaine: Comments on a Plan to Eradicate the Coca Leaf in Peru." *Journal of Drug Issues* 13, no. 1 (Winter): 135–45. Focusing on the Peruvian case, the author illustrates that a complex web of economic, political, and social factors operate within Peru and between Peru and the United States, making it possible for a U.S. initiative to eradicate the coca leaf in Peru to be accepted. In spite of the disagreeable nature of intervention in Peru, there are sufficient trade-offs to make the policy marginally attractive. On the other hand, the policy, it was thought, would silence congressional criticism that U.S. narcotics agencies have been ineffectual in stopping trafficking. The article is based on anthropological fieldwork carried out in Peru in 1979, and on conversations with government officials in the United States and Peru. ^Latin\America ^Peru ^United\States ^Coca ^Crop\Eradication ^Politics ^Consequences\Foreign\Relations

1651. *Substance Abuse in Mining* (1987). Washington, D.C.: U.S. Department of Labor, Mine Safety and Health Administration. Describes relationship of drugs to mine safety in the United States. ^United\States ^Drug\Use ^Workplace ^Consequences\Public\Safety

1652. Suggs, David L. (1981). "A Qualitative and Quantitative Analysis of the Impact of Nebraska's Decriminalization of Marijuana." *Law and Human Behavior* 5(1): 45–71. In 1979, Nebraska decriminalized first offense possession of an ounce or less of marijuana. This article assesses the effectiveness of Nebraska's new law in allowing the state to nevertheless control deviant behavior, clarifies general issues regarding the decriminalization of marijuana, and offers insight into issues related to the legal theory of decriminalizing a broad range of "victimless crimes." ^United\States ^Nebraska ^Cannabis ^Decriminalization

1653. Sullivan, Cheryl (1986). "Cocaine in the Workplace Alarms Silicon Valley." *The Christian Science Monitor*, 21 July, 3. More companies appear to view cocaine as a health problem that cuts into their profit margins. Specific examples from Silicon Valley, the "gold work force," are noted. ^United\States ^Cocaine ^Drug\Use ^Workplace ^Consequences\Economic

1654. "Supply-Side Failures" (1988). *The Economist*, 17 December, 32. An organization financed by forty of the city's largest firms and entitled the Citizens Crime Commission of New York strongly criticizes the city's TNTs (Technical Narcotic Teams) for their mass arrests, saying that saturating enforcement in one area simply shifts drug dealing to others. ^United\States ^Law\Enforcement ^New\York ^Drug\Control\Policies\Critique

1655. Suro, Roberto (1987). "Italy's Heroin Addicts Face New Challenge: AIDS." *The New York Times*, 28 December, B12. An alarmingly high incidence of AIDS is noted among drug addicts in Italy, although there is not a clear understanding of why the incidence is so high. Description of a Catholic community of brothers who is attempting to help arrest the spread of AIDS and, in general, rehabilitate drug addicts. ^Europe ^Italy ^Heroin ^Health ^AIDS ^Private\Initiatives

1656. Suwanela, Charas, and Vichai Poshyachinda (1986). "Drug Abuse in Asia." *Bulletin on Narcotics* 38(1-2): 41–53. Southeast Asia is seriously affected by traffic in and abuse of opium and its derivatives. When opium use and sale were prohibited in Burma, Hong Kong, Malaysia, Singapore, and Thailand, many opium addicts switched to heroin. This trend, developing over at least two decades, is accelerating. Heroin abuse has spread geographically, involving such countries as India and Sri Lanka, which had no prior experience with the problem. China and Japan are also discussed. ^Southeast\Asia ^Burma ^Hong\Kong ^Malaysia ^Singapore ^Thailand ^India ^Sri\Lanka ^China ^Japan ^Heroin ^Opiates ^Drug\Use ^Golden\Triangle ^Consequences\Drug\Concentration ^Drug\Use\History

1657. Suwanwela, Charas, Somsong Kanchanahuta, and Yupha Onthaum (1979). "Hill Tribe Opium Addicts: A Retrospective Study of 1,382 Patients." *Bulletin on Narcotics* 31(1): 23–40. Discussion of a retrospective study of patients admitted to a treatment center for hill tribes in Thailand underwritten, in part, by the World Health Organization, the UN, and the Thai Program for Drug Abuse Control. The study revealed widespread opium addiction among the hill tribes, of whom the Karen were the largest group. Among the Hmong, the second largest tribe, the addiction problem was also revealed as serious. Within the context of the society, being an addict did not cause one to be downgraded. Discussion of the economic losses associated with opium addiction. ^Southeast\Asia ^Thailand ^Golden\Triangle ^Opiates ^Drug\Use ^Economics ^Society ^Culture ^WHO ^United\Nations ^Consequences\Economic ^Minorities

1658. "Suspect Tied to Medellín Cartel Leadership Becomes 3rd to Surrender" (1991). *The New York Times*, February 17, L3. Announcement is made that Juan David Ochoa has surrendered to Colombian government authorities. This makes three Ochoas having surrendered. Discussion is raised about whether the main trafficker, Pablo Escobar, will turn himself in under Colombia's modified amnesty law for drug traffickers. ^Latin\America ^Colombia ^Traffickers

1659. Suwanela, Charas, Vichai Poshyachinda, Prida Tasanapradit, and Ayut Dharmkrong-At (1980). "Opium Use Among the Hill Tribes of Thailand." *Journal of Drug Issues* 10(1): 215–20. While there are a number of contexts in which opium is socially used among the hill tribes of Thailand, for the most part it is a drug used to treat illnesses; it is also used as a psychotropic substance. The reasons for use differ among the various tribes. ^Southeast\Asia ^Thailand ^Golden\Triangle ^Opiates ^Drug\Use ^Society ^Culture ^Minorities

1660. Swisher, John D., and Teh-Wei Hu (1984). "A Review of the Reliability and Validity of the Drug Abuse Warning Network." *International Journal of the Addictions* 19(1): 57–77. Briefly describes the government-funded Drug Abuse Warning Network (DAWN) which is used extensively by governments at all levels in policy formulation and program evaluation with respect to its being an indicator of changing trends in substance abuse. Examines reviews of the DAWN system and assesses the strengths and limitations of the data that it produces. Research and policy initiative areas are pointed out. ^United\States ^Drug\Use ^Health ^Statistics ^Reviews ^DAWN ^Statistics\Critique

1661. "Synthetic Heroin Seen as Cause in 18 Deaths" (1988). *The New York Times*, 25 December, 43. A clandestine laboratory in Pittsburgh has put drugs on the street that have caused the deaths of a number of people. ^United\States ^Designer\Drugs ^Drug\Use ^Health ^Consequences\Personal ^Pennsylvania

1662. Tanzi, Vito (1983). "The Underground Economy." *Finance and Development* 20 no. 4 (December): 10–13. "Underground economy" relates to activities ranging from relatively legal to totally criminal that escape official attention and may distort official statistics and lead to erroneous policies. While the underground drug economy is not given explicit discussion here, the categories reviewed (e.g., "bureaucratic corruption") raise issues germane for analytical consideration. ^Drug\Traffic ^Politics ^Consequences\Corruption ^Economics ^Informal\Economy ^Consequences\Illegal\Economy

1663. Tanzi, Vito, ed. (1982). *The Underground Economy in the United States and Abroad.* Lexington, Mass.: Lexington Books. Contributors review the general aspects of hidden or "underground economies" and then direct their attention to the underground economies in the United States, some European countries, and selected other countries, which include Canada, Colombia, Australia, and Israel. For the purpose of this bibliography, the chapter by Roberto Junguito and Carlos Caballero is most interesting, for it includes a discussion of illegal trade and the underground drug economy. ^Drug\Traffic ^Economics ^Informal\Economy ^United\States ^Europe ^Canada ^Colombia ^Australia ^Israel ^Middle\East ^Latin\America

1664. Tapp, Nicholas (1986). *The Hmong of Thailand: Opium People of the Golden Triangle*. London: Anti-Slavery Society. The Hmong and other minorities in the Golden Triangle, particularly those in Thailand, have been under a "pernicious and iniquitous" attack. All has been justified by the Hmong's being "opium producers," "insurgents," and "destroyers of the environment." The Hmong are not to blame for the narcotics problems of the West, but have been abused and treated as cannon fodder in the service of other people's causes of which they have had no real understanding. This book is about the Hmong, opium, the political situation in which minorities reside, forestry, farming, and change. ^Southeast\Asia ^Thailand ^Opiates ^Golden\Triangle ^Drug\Traffic ^Politics ^Insurgents ^Minorities ^Agriculture

1665. Tarpy, Cliff (1989). "Straight: A Gloves-off Treatment Program." *National Geographic* 175, no. 1 (January): 48–51. Description of a no-nonsense confrontational, group-oriented approach to dealing with teenage drug addicts. ^United\States ^Treatment\Therapeutic\Community ^Youth

1666. Tashkin, D. P., B. J. Shapiro, Y. E. Lee, and C. H. Harper (1976). "Subacute Effects of Heavy Marihuana Smoking on Pulmonary Function in Healthy Men." *New England Journal of Medicine* 294:125-29. Suggests that heavy marijuana smoking for 47 to 59 days causes mild but definite narrowing of both large and medium-sized airways (as reflected by the increases in airway resistance and decreases in specific conductants) and of small airways (as reflected by the changes in maximal midexpiratory flow rate and closing volume). Serial lung-function tests performed in the small number of subjects who were restudied after sensation of smoking for one week and, again, for one month after discharge from the hospital indicate that the mild impairment in airway dynamics resulting from several weeks of heavy daily smoking was reversible. However, the significant correlation between the quantity of marijuana smoked, the degree of functional impairment, and the lack of complete reversibility of the functional changes after one week of no smoking suggest that heavy marijuana smoking over a much longer period might lead to clinically important and less readily reversible impairment. ^Cannabis ^Consequences\Physiological ^Consequences\Health

1667. Tasker, Rodney (1987). "Chasing the Red Dragon." *Far Eastern Economic Review*, 13 August, 28–31. Representations are made that Communist Laos is condoning drug production. Opium production has risen from 50 tons a year to somewhere between 100 and 200 tons. Production figures are given for Burma (1,000 tons) and Thailand (15–30 tons). The struggle between Khun Sa and Thai military troops is noted. ^Southeast\Asia ^Laos ^Burma ^Thailand ^Opiates ^Production ^Drug\Traffic ^Politics ^Insurgents ^Statistics ^Golden\Triangle

1668. Taylor, Clyde D. (1985). "Links Between International Narcotics Trafficking and Terrorism." *Department of State Bulletin*, August, pp. 69–74. Consists of Taylor's testimony, including summaries of country reports, before a joint session of the senate committees on foreign relations and the judiciary, on May 14, 1985. Describes the difficulties of implementing drug control policies, particularly as they are impeded by terrorist activities. All this is made more difficult because political criminals are now associating with the drug trade in order to finance their operations. Summary statements are given on these and related issues for Bolivia, Colombia, Cuba, Nicaragua, Peru, Bulgaria, Turkey, Lebanon, Syria, Burma, and Thailand. ^United\States ^Bolivia

^Drug\Control\Policies\Effectiveness ^Latin\America ^Colombia ^Cuba ^Nicaragua ^Peru ^Middle\East ^Bulgaria ^Turkey ^Lebanon ^Syria ^Southeast\Asia ^Burma ^Thailand

1669. Taylor, Ronald A., Adam Paul Weisman, and Ted Gest (1986). "Uncovering New Truths about the Country's no. 1 Menace." *U.S. News and World Report* 101, no. 4 (28 July): 50–54. A "perception-reality" point and counterpoint dealing with the dangers of drugs, eluding the law, testing for drug abuse, addiction, rehabilitation, law enforcement, and smuggling. For example, on smuggling, the point is that "drug smuggling can be stopped at the U.S. border if only we would commit more money, manpower and equipment" (p. 54). The counterpoint is that in spite of increased crackdowns, more illegal narcotic shipments than ever before have been seized by U.S. authorities. ^United\States ^Drug\Traffic ^Drug\Control\Policies ^Drug\Use ^Treatment\Rehabilitation ^Law\Enforcement

1670. Tefft, Sheila (1989). "Bhutto Battles the Drug Trade." *The Christian Science Monitor,* 28 September, 3. While Pakistan's prime minister, Benazir Bhutto, has pleased the United States by pledging to halt the heroin trade that has tarnished her country's international reputation and that poses a major threat at home, so far her "war" is still just a skirmish. Pakistani authorities say they are doing all they can. The United States is giving aid. ^Pakistan ^United\States ^Heroin ^Drug\Control\Policies\Effectiveness ^Consequences\Foreign\Relations ^Golden\Crescent ^Southwest\Asia

1671. ——— (1989). "Pakistan's Leader Holds On . . . Just." *The Christian Science Monitor,* 6 November, 5. Internal political feuding in Pakistan has caused the country's president, Benazir Bhutto, to ignore economic issues which, of course, have implications for drug control activities as well. ^Pakistan ^Economics ^Politics ^Southwest\Asia

1672. Teichman, Meir, Giora Rahav, and Zipora Barnea (1988). "A Comprehensive Substance Prevention Program: An Israeli Experiment." *Journal of Alcohol and Drug Education* 33(3): 1–10. Based on the assumptions that Israeli adolescents increase their use of drugs as a function of peers' positive attitudes about them, peers' and their own parents' use of alcohol and drugs, certain personality variables, and the availability of drugs at home and in the community, these authors report on the development of a comprehensive alcohol and drug prevention program that was experimentally implemented. The authors are pessimistic that any school-based substance prevention programs relying on a single method of approach will be successful. ^Middle\East ^Israel ^Drug\Use\Theories ^Prevention ^Youth ^Prevention\Schools ^Prevention\Critique

1673. "Telltale Tapes: Torture and Death" (1986). *Newsweek,* 24 February, 26. Brief note on the death of U.S. Drug Enforcement Administration agent Enrique Camarena. The "telltale tapes" suggest official Mexican police involvement in the drug trafficking. ^Latin\America ^Mexico ^Law\Enforcement ^Consequences\Corruption ^Consequences\Violence

1674. Teltsch, Kathleen (1990). "In Detroit, A Drug Recovery Center That Welcomes the Pregnant Addict." *The New York Times,* 20 March, A8. Hospital treatment centers discourage low-income pregnant drug users from seeking care from them. The Eleonore Hutzel Recovery center admits these pregnant addicts. Description of the care they receive and the social and value education given to mother and child alike. ^United\States ^Treatment ^Women ^Fetuses

1675. Tempest, Rone (1987). "Drugs, Murder Attempt, Corruption Rob Peaceful Nepal of Its Innocence." *The Los Angeles Times,* 16 August, 5. The peaceful kingdom of Nepal has been rocked by the arrest of high-ranking aids and authorities, including a national police superintendent, on charges of corruption and drug smuggling. The integrity of even the Gurkha troops has been impugned. ^Southeast\Asia ^Nepal ^Drug\Traffic ^Consequences\Corruption

1676. Tennes, Katherine (1983). "Effects of Marijuana on Pregnancy and Fetal Development in the Human." In *Marijuana Effects on the Endocrine and Reproductive Systems*, NIDA Research Monograph 44, edited by Monique C. Braude and Jacqueline P. Ludford. Rockville, Md.: National Institute of Drug Abuse. Early studies on human pregnancies suggest that marijuana could alter the delivery process, reduce the infant's weight gain, or affect visual and neurological processes. This author concludes that confirmation of these findings is lacking, as is evidence for the effect of direct action of marijuana. ^Cannabis ^Pregnancy ^Consequences\Fetuses

1677. Terry, Don (1989). "Drug Riches of the Capital Luring Poor Youth down a Bloody Path." *The New York Times*, 2 April, 1. Description of the turf wars among young people dealing for drugs in the nation's capital. Crack has poisoned families, housing projects, and many young people. ^United\States ^Cocaine ^Crack ^Drug\Traffic ^Youth ^Society ^Consequences\Family ^Public\Housing ^Consequences\Violence ^Consequences\Markets

1678. "Thailand: Antidrug Success Story" (1988). *The Christian Science Monitor*, 26 June, 9. A decade ago 200 tons of opium were illegally produced in Thailand; in 1988, the figure was 20 tons and falling. Crop substitution programs are hailed as the key to reduction. ^Southeast\Asia ^Thailand ^Golden\Triangle ^Opiates ^Crop\Substitution ^Production ^Drug\Control\Policies\Effectiveness

1679. Thomas, Jon R. (1985). "International Narcotics Control: The Challenge of Our Decade." *The Police Chief* (October): 42-46. To be successful at narcotics control, international cooperation will be required. The Bureau of International Narcotics matters of the U.S. State Department has been working with other countries for some time. Description of the consequences of that work in Asia, Latin America, and other nations. ^Southeast\Asia ^Latin\America ^Drug\Control\Policies ^United\States ^Department\of\State ^International\Cooperation

1680. ——— (1986). "Narcotics Control in Latin America." *Department of State Bulletin* 86(2109): 77–81. State Department white paper on activities in Colombia, Peru, Bolivia, Ecuador, Belize, Panama. Some discussion on the use of herbicides. Some discussion about the relationship of drug trade to national security is viewed not only from the vantage of the United States but also several Latin American countries. ^Latin\America ^Colombia ^Peru ^Bolivia ^Ecuador ^Belize ^Panama ^Drug\Control\Policies ^Herbicides ^Consequences\National\Security

1681. Thomas, Owen (1988). "Citizen Patrols: Self-Help to an Extreme? Many Residents Praise Them, but Critics Warn of Possible Excesses." *The Christian Science Monitor*, 5 July, 3. The irony is that while citizen patrols are effective in removing drug traffic from the neighborhoods they patrol, the tactics they employ often strike against civil liberties. Several of the patrols "definitely tend toward vigilantism." ^United\States ^Drug\Control\Policies ^Private\Initiatives ^Consequences\Human\Rights

1682. Thompson, Tracy (1989). "26 Charged in Cartel Linked to Big Drug Shipments Here." *The Washington Post*, 17 May. In describing a series of drug arrests, evidence is presented regarding the massive invasion of the drug mafia into Washington, D.C. ^United\States ^Drug\Traffic ^Organized\Crime ^Washington\DC

1683. ——— (1989). "Ruling Clears Way for Drug Tests of Workers with Top Clearances." *The Washington Post*, 1 July, A9. A federal appeals court ruled that the Justice Department may begin random drug testing of some employees who hold top secret security clearances. ^United\States ^Drug\Testing ^Workplace ^Judiciary

1684. Thornburgh, Richard (1990). "Worldwide Alliance against Drugs." *The Christian Science Monitor*, 1 March. Recounts the United States' signing of the United Nations Drug Law Enforcement Convention Ratification Papers. Provisions of the agreement are summarized. ^International\Cooperation ^United\Nations ^Treaties

1685. Thornton, Mary (1983). "Sales of Opium Reportedly Fund Afghan Rebels." *The Washington Post*, 17 December, A32. Allegation is made that Afghanistan rebels have financed their battle against the Soviet Union, at least partially, through the sale of opium. Some of that ends up in the United States as heroin. ^Middle\East ^Afghanistan ^United\States ^Opiates ^Drug\Traffic ^Politics ^Insurgents

1686. Thornton, Mary and Zeynep Alemdar (1986). "Lawmakers Ask TV Networks to Aid Drug Fight." *The Washington Post*, 6 August, A4. With recognition that the drug boom in the United States is fueled by the "demand of our children," congressional representatives have urged U.S. television networks to begin a campaign against illegal drug use. Description, also, of a bill that senate democrats had introduced to fight the powerful drug crack. ^United\States ^Media ^Demand ^Legislation

1687. Thoumi, Francisco (1987). "Some Implications of the Growth of the Underground Economy in Colombia." *Journal of Interamerican Studies and World Affairs* 29, no. 2 (Summer): 35–53. Surveys the impact on Colombia of the growth of the underground economy, mainly that of the illegal drug industry. While illegal drugs have contributed to a substantial increase in national income, they have also generated many negative effects. The drug boom has hurt the development of agricultural and manufacturing activities because of its "Dutch disease" effects; it has lowered the quality of investments as these have become increasingly oriented to the short term; it has weakened the institutions of government by eroding public respect for their efficacy; and, finally, it has undermined the ability of the country either to continue on a path of stable growth, or to compete in international markets in the future. These effects have caused profound changes in Colombian society which will be hard to reverse if the drug boom passes. All of this is made inherently more complicated by the appearance of a population of young adults who have learned to view their social environment as inherently hostile, one which has not prepared them to assume the role of responsible citizen. In some, Colombia has fallen into a trap of widespread dishonesty throughout its society and from which it will be very difficult to extricate itself. Any solution to the problem, given the nature of the drug market, will require joint action by both the Colombian and U.S. governments. Such action is likely not to be forthcoming given the impediments that exist in the United States—the U.S. system of government is geared to the safeguard of personal freedom and to the minimizing of police abuse, and therefore is largely unable to control demand or consumption; the Colombian government does not have full control over all regions of its country and therefore cannot control supply. ^Latin\America ^Colombia ^United\States ^Drug\Traffic ^Drug\Control\Policies ^Economics ^Politics ^Society ^Culture ^Consequences\Illegal\Economy ^Consequences\Economic ^Agriculture ^Consequences\Misc ^Consequences\Social ^Consequences\State\Authority

1688. ——— (1989). "Colombian Laws and Institutions, Money Dirtying, Money Laundering, and Narco-Businessmen's Behavior." Unpublished manuscript, California State University, Chico (September). While a substantial portion of the profits accruing to Colombian narcotic traffickers has remained abroad, that which has returned to the Colombian economy has been large enough to generate significant economic distortions and to completely alter the domestic power structure. The best extended discussion of this, by Americans, is, Thoumi asserts, by Guy

Gugliotta and Jay Leen, *Kings of Cocaine* (Simon and Schuster, 1989). Whatever the economic consequences, the narcotraffickers' economic behavior is highly influenced and largely explained by the economic institutions of the environment in which they operate, the nature of their business, their need to legitimize their assets, and whether they are consumers of the products they sell. The legal and illegal income and capital and the incentives that narcotraffickers have to operate in the legal and underground sectors of the economy are discussed. Risk factors are assessed and analyzed with respect to traffickers' behavior. In particular, this is related to the laundering of capital. One important implication, given the widespread acceptance of economic illegality throughout Colombian society, is that there is no practical way to differentiate between "moral" and "immoral" illegal capital so as to implement confiscation policies. Beyond this, much of the illegally gotten gains from both narcotics and other activities are outside Colombian jurisdiction (in Switzerland). Repatriation of and utilization of domestically contained illegally gotten gains is a serious policy consideration for Colombian governments in the future. In any event, a prerequisite for asset legalization to work in Colombia is the elimination of the high profits obtained from the international narcotics trade. The argument, therefore, is for legalization of drugs. ^Latin\America ^Colombia ^Drug\Traffic ^Traffickers ^Money\Laundering ^Asset\Forfeiture ^Economics ^Politics ^Society ^Values ^P\S\Economic ^P\S\Legalization

1689. Thurow, Lester C. (1988). "U.S. Drug Policy: Colossal Ignorance." *The New York Times*, 8 May, E29. The only way to get at criminals is to deprive them of large profits from selling drugs. The only way to do that is to legalize the drugs. ^United\States ^P\S\Legalization ^Economics ^Crime

1690. Timmer, Doug (1982). "The Productivity of Crime in the United States: Drugs and Capital Accumulation." *Journal of Drug Issues* 12(4): 383–97. Under some kinds of conditions, an underground economy provides a mechanism for capital accumulation that may be more readily achieved and, indeed, preferable to legal or licit capital formation. The author discusses at least four reasons for this: The underground economy harboring an illegal industry is oftentimes in a growth situation; the activities are unregulated and therefore untaxed, which means that high profit margins are available; there are significant linkages with the licit economy; and there is a transformation of labor-market conditions that are increasingly favorable to the sale of illicit and illegal goods and services. The author examines propositions associated with each of these categories, illustrating their applicability to the production and distribution of illegal drugs—primarily heroin—in the United States. Ironically, the author finds that the advanced capitalist economy of the United States is "not only crisis-ridden, but crisis-dependent, it is also not only crime-ridden, but crime-dependent" (p. 394). The dependencies relate to the interrelationship between the illegal underground economy and the licit "above ground" economy. The linkages produce a "criminal-legal" economy that drives much of the capitalist system. ^United\States ^Drug\Traffic ^Economics ^Informal\Economy ^Crime

1691. Tobler, Nancy S. (1986). "Meta-Analysis of 143 Adolescent Drug Prevention Programs: Quantitative Outcome Results of Program Participants Compared to a Control or Comparison Group." *Journal of Drug Issues* 16(4): 537–67. What are the most effective programs for reducing teenage drug use? "Meta-Analysis techniques" are advanced as providing a systematic approach to accumulate, quantify, and integrate the numerous research findings around answers to this question. Of the programs reviewed, the "Alternatives Programs" were shown to be highly successful for adolescents such as drug abusers, juvenile delinquents, or students having school problems. A second effective program was within the category of Peer Programs.

These were the only two intervention programs noted as being successful. A substantial bibliography is attached to this article. ^Drug\Use ^Prevention\Theories ^Youth ^Reviews ^Prevention\Peers ^Drug\Control\Policies\Effectiveness

1692. Toit, Brian M. du (1978). *Drug Use and South African Students.* Ohio University Center for International Studies, Africa Program. Discusses use of cannabis by high school and college students in South Africa. Funded by the National Institute on Drug Abuse, the study looks at chronic cannabis use in its natural setting. This is one of several studies, this one looks at drug use in the normal social context rather than among persons who have been institutionalized or incarcerated. The study expected to find that African students (as opposed to coloreds or whites) would smoke more cannabis and view it more naturally than the other several ethnic groups. While all student groups had members using cannabis, among the Africans the study found strong continuities of ritual, medicinal, and contextual uses of the drug. ^Africa ^South\Africa ^Cannabis ^Drug\Use ^Youth ^Society ^Culture ^NIDA

1693. —— (1980). *Cannabis in Africa: A Survey of its Distribution in Africa, and a Study of Cannabis Use and Users in Multi-Ethnic South Africa.* Gainesville, Fl.: A. A. Balkema, Published for the African Studies Center, University of Florida. Includes social aspects of cannabis use in South Africa, informed by social surveys. Presents the findings of an investigation of cannabis use in Africa, with field study conducted between 1972 and 1974. Gives a history of diffusion of cannabis in Africa and its use among aboriginals. In contemporary South Africa, its use is investigated among blacks (urban and rural, long term and short term), the "coloreds," the Indians, and whites. Based on information from earlier studies (which are cited) the author developed a research interview design that included questionnaires administered to a random sample of various populations. Statistical tables are given in connection with crimes and cannabis use, church membership and attendance patterns of rural African cannabis users, income and employment patterns of rural African cannabis users, cannabis use and protein content of meals, physical and emotional effects of first cannabis use, social effects of cannabis use, and physical and emotional effects of regular cannabis use. The territorial focus is in the district of Natal, South Africa. Both the African and Indian samples have a long tradition of cannabis use, with associated social and economic behavior that extends throughout the society. In contrast to the African and Indian ethnic samples, the colored and white samples were characterized by an absence of a drug tradition. Drug use among African and Indian samples was not viewed in nearly the negative terms (by the respective peoples) as among coloreds and whites. The basic aim of the study was to report on cannabis use in vivo through observation. Rather than dealing in isolation with the drug and its use or its effects, the author views the drug in its total social setting, recording all interconnections and studying both behavior and attitudinal aspects. ^Africa ^South\Africa ^Cannabis ^Drug\Use ^Society ^Culture ^NIDA ^Cannabis\History ^Drug\Use\History ^Statistics ^Crime ^Economics ^Consequences\Misc ^Values

1694. Tokatlian, Juan G. (1988). "National Security and Drugs: Their Impact on Colombian–US Relations." *Journal of Interamerican Studies and World Affairs* 30(1): 133–60. Looks into the impact that the "drug problem" has had on the bilateral relations between Colombia and the United States. An issue-oriented article, it looks at different objectives and divergent interests of the two countries. Regardless of the differential views held within the two countries, there are potential policy initiatives, both domestic and international, that could be taken to address the dilemma drug trafficking poses for the future of democracy, inter-American relations, and domestic/regional peace. Some discussion is included on the controversial extradition treaty and its abrogation in Colombia by the country's supreme court. The author includes extensive notes and a bibliography. ^Latin\America ^Colombia ^United\States ^Drug\Traffic^Consequences\Political^Consequences\Foreign\Relations^Extradition^Proffered\Solutions ^Consequences\National\Security

1695. Tolchin, Martin (1989). "Kemp Vows to Oust Tenants over Drugs." *The New York Times*, 8 March. Efforts will now be made to remove drug traffickers, or families of those involved in drug trafficking, from public housing projects. ^United\States ^Drug\Control\Policies ^Public\Housing

1696. Tomeh, N. (1979). "Drug Situation in Lebanon." *Toxicomanies* 13:237–41. Gives a brief historical sketch of the spread of drugs in Lebanon and the institutional response to that spread. ^Middle\East ^Lebanon ^Drug\Traffic ^Drug\Control\Policies ^Drug\Use\History

1697. Tongue, E., and D. Turner (1988). "Treatment Options in Responding to Drug Misuse Problems." *Bulletin on Narcotics* 40(1): 3–19. Supply-reduction efforts will not have much effect unless demand-reduction efforts are successful. Demand reduction is made possible by national strategies that integrate approaches to drug users and potential users, and that maintain contact and successfully assist the individuals either through a successful treatment program or in a preventive educational program. This article summarizes the more common approaches to treatment, rehabilitation, and social reintegration of drug dependent persons. ^Drug\Use ^Treatment ^Reviews ^Supply ^Demand ^Prevention

1698. "Too Soon to Back Down on Drugs" (1988). *The New York Times*, 14 April. Legalization or decriminalization is premature. Several promising approaches should be tried to reduce demand. Suggestions are made for law enforcement agents, treatment programs, and public education. ^United\States ^Decriminalization\Critique

1699. "Tráfico de Drogas desde Cuba" (1989). *El Nuevo Herald*, 12 June, 2A. Speculation that the Castro regime is involved in the increase of contraband flights of drugs from South America. ^Caribbean ^Cuba ^Drug\Traffic

1700. Tragen, I. G. (1987). "Co-operation of Countries within the Organization of American States to Combat Drug Problems." *Bulletin on Narcotics* 39(1): 57–59. The Organization of American States, comprising thirty-one member nations, adopted in 1984 a resolution recognizing drug trafficking as a crime affecting all of mankind. It targeted a conference on traffic and narcotic drugs that took place in Brazil in April 1986. That conference focused on drug trafficking and on ways to deal with it, and on public education programs. The conference adopted specific measures to promote effective inter-American cooperation on drug-related issues. Particularly, the conference worked to find means to take the profit out of drug trafficking operations. ^United\States ^Canada ^Latin\America ^Drug\Control\Policies ^International\Cooperation ^OAS

1701. Traub, James (1982). *The Billion-Dollar Connection: The International Drug Trade*. New York: Julian Messner. Directed toward teenage drug users, intended to influence them to withdraw from the drug trade. Informative description given about growers and processors, distributors and pushers, with everyone making a profit except "the ultimate customer, the drug user—often a teenager." ^Society ^Prevention

1702. Treaster, Joseph B. (1984). "Jamaica, Close U.S. Ally Does Little to Halt Drugs." *The New York Times*, 10 September. At the same time that Jamaica was becoming one of the United States' closest political allies, it was also contributing heavily to the worsening American drug problem. The paradox lies basically at the feet of the Reagan administration, which sees Jamaica as a symbol of democracy on the one hand and on the other as seeing itself unable to apply pressure on that "democracy" to do anything about drugs. A country where half the people consume marijuana is not likely to be extremely alert to U.S. drug sensitivities. Recently, however, fears of rampant cocaine abuse in the country have triggered official anxiety. ^Caribbean ^Jamaica ^United\States ^Drug\Control\Policies ^Politics ^Consequences\Foreign\Relations

1703. —— (1989). "Colombia Turns Drug War into a Long Chase." *The New York Times*, 10 November, A6. Short biographical description on two Colombian drug lords, José Gonzalo Rodríguez Gacha and Pablo Escobar Gaviria, and the political and economic stakes for the country. Description of law enforcement efforts to hunt down and capture or kill these men. ^Latin\America ^Colombia ^Traffickers ^Law\Enforcement

1704. —— (1989). "Colombians, Weary of the Strain, Are Losing Heart in the Drug War." *The New York Times*, 2 October, A1. After six weeks of bombings and shootings, many Colombians are now suggesting that the government abandon its campaign against the powerful cocaine barons. ^Latin\America ^Colombia ^Law\Enforcement ^Consequences\Political ^Consequences\Violence

1705. —— (1989). "Colombia's Cali Drug Cartel: The Less Flamboyant Competitor of Medellín." *The New York Times*, 19 September, A6. Discussion of the differing psychological profiles of drug traffickers in Medellín and Cali. The Medellín cartel leaders are rough cut, mainly uneducated street criminals who found the road to riches and have put much of their money into ranches and farms, creating a small army of gunmen to protect their properties and wipe out leftist guerrillas. The Cali leaders, on the other hand, favor bribery over gunplay, stay out of politics, and try not to embarrass the government. They blend with society, particularly in terms of middle-class appearances. These people have tried to become part of the establishment and quietly assimilate themselves into society. When they find it necessary to kill people, they do so with some discretion. ^Latin\America ^Colombia ^Drug\Traffic ^Organized\Crime ^Traffickers ^Society ^Consequences\Social

1706. —— (1989). "On Front Line of Drug War, U.S.–Built Base Lags in Peru." *The New York Times*, 31 October, A1. Describes difficulties in placing into operation the Santa Lucía military base. Description of supply control activities carried out from this base. ^Latin\America ^Peru ^United\States ^Consequences\Foreign\Relations ^Military ^Drug\Control\Policies

1707. —— (1989). "Rebels in Peru Step up the Killings of Politicians to Disrupt the Elections." *The New York Times*, 26 October, A6. Statistics on the killings are given, one political consequence is that more than 400 candidates for various public offices have resigned in fear. The military's response to this violence has also created its own abuses. ^Latin\America ^Insurgents ^Consequences\Violence ^Peru ^Military

1708. —— (1989). "Uneasy Exile for Ex-Aide of Colombia." *The New York Times*, 29 September. Describes the former Colombian justice minister, Monica De Greiff, in her U.S. exile after having resigned and joined her husband and three-year-old son in the United States. She had been under death threats from the cocaine barons. ^Latin\America ^Colombia ^Law\Enforcement ^Politics ^Consequences\Violence ^Consequences\Political

1709. —— (1990). "'Arsenal' in Trunks Linked to a Colombian Drug Gang." *The New York Times*, September 25, B2. The Colombian cartel known as Cali, which apparently controls most of the cocaine market in New York City, is thought to have shipped steamer trunks filled with submachine guns and explosives to a Manhattan building. ^Latin\America ^United\States ^Colombia ^Traffickers ^Consequences\Violence ^New\York

1710. —— (1990). "Bush Sees Anti-Drug Gain, Others See Flawed Data." *The New York Times*, December 20, A16. President George Bush's optimism about declining drug use, based on a National Institute on Drug Abuse survey, is countered by others who believe the data to be flawed. This survey showed a 45 percent decrease in casual cocaine use among all age groups and a 49 percent decline among adolescents (since 1988). Casual use is understood as that occurring at least once a month. A 12 percent drop in marijuana use among all age groups was also noted. The use of crack, cocaine, and heroine remains unchanged. Heavier cocaine and heroine use appears to be rising among a larger population cohort. Mark A. R. Kleiman is quoted as saying: "A lot of people who used cocaine heavily found that it wasn't good for them and they figured out ways to quit." ^United\States ^Statistics ^Drug\Use

1711. ——— (1990). "Cocaine Prices Rise, and Police Efforts May Be Responsible." *The New York Times*, 14 June, A1. The wholesale price of cocaine has risen sharply, the first such rise in almost ten years, and this may herald the effect of extensive law enforcement efforts both in the United States and in Latin America. Prices have jumped approximately 40 percent; heavily diluted cocaine is now turning up in the marketplace. Cocaine use seems to be declining among the poor (including crack) in ways that follow trends earlier noted among high school students of middle-class families. Drug price statistics are given. ^Cocaine ^Consequences\Markets ^Drug\Control\Policies\Effectiveness ^Drug\Use ^Statistics

1712. ——— (1990). "Drug Traffickers' Peace Offer Divides Colombians." *The New York Times*, 9 February, A5. Describes Colombian traffickers' offer to cease their violence against society in exchange for amnesty. That amnesty would derive, in effect, from eliminating the extradition treaty with the United States. Several hostages were freed. ^Latin\America ^Colombia ^Traffickers ^Proffered\Solutions

1713. ——— (1990). "Eager for Good Press, Drug Bosses Sacrifice Laboratory in Colombia." *The New York Times*, 15 February, A1. Discusses preparations for the drug summit in Colombia as well as gestures from the drug bosses to that initiative. The traffickers are, of course, interested in a "settlement" that would allow them to continue their trade absent the violence associated with it. ^Latin\America ^Colombia ^Proffered\Solutions ^Traffickers

1714. ——— (1990). "A Peruvian Peasant Fails to See Bush." *The New York Times*, 16 February, A9. The president of Peru's large peasant confederation (200,000 members) was taken to the "drug summit" in Colombia by Peru's president, Alan García. García wanted the representative to talk with President Bush. The effort failed. The intent was to impress President Bush with the need to have an economic alternative to growing drug crops. ^Producers\Unions ^Latin\America ^Peru ^Politics

1715. ——— (1991). "Bush Proposes More Anti-Drug Spending." *The New York Times*, February 1, A12. The president indicated there would be an eleven percent increase in federal spending on the drug war. Stung by some criticism on overemphasis on law enforcement initiatives, Bush indicated that new health approaches were included as well as money for treatment and prevention. Critics note that the dominant emphasis remains on keeping supplies from coming into the country. U.S. representative Charles B. Rangel tendered an acerbic criticism. Budgetary statistics for the period 1981 to 1992 are given. The budget has grown from approximately $1.5 billion in 1981 to nearly twelve billion in 1992. The proportion of the budget dedicated for domestic enforcement has increased relative to treatment, prevention, and interdiction. ^United\States ^Drug\Control\Policies ^Legislation ^Drug\Control\Policies\Critique ^P\S\Legislation

1716. ——— (1991). "Drop in Youth's Cocaine Use May Reflect a Societal Shift." *The New York Times*, January 25, A14. Self-reported use of cocaine and crack dropped dramatically in 1990 among high school seniors, as reported in the

University of Michigan's annual federally financed study. Drop of crack and cocaine use were most dramatic in the middle class. Total drug use "appears to be dropping down the social scale," according to Mark A. R. Kleiman, cited in this report. Commensurate with the decline in usage, hospital emergency room cases have also been declining. The administration claimed the survey indicated a marked change in attitude toward drugs. Others were less certain. Data on cocaine use in high schools is given for the years 1980 through 1990. Crack cocaine use, added to the questionnaire in 1986, is also reported. ^United\States ^Drug\Use ^Statistics

1717. —— (1991). "Surrender of Cocaine Smuggler Isn't Expected to Have Large Effect." *The New York Times*, January 21, A15. Jorge Luís Ochoa, a leading cocaine smuggler in Colombia has surrendered to the government under a plan that traffickers who surrender and confess to at least one crime will receive reduced sentences. Most importantly for them, they receive immunity from extradition to the United States. Fabio Ochoa surrendered to authorities on December 18. ^Latin\America ^Colombia ^Traffickers

1718. —— (1991). "On Toys to TV Shows, Stepping Up Drug Fight." *The New York Times*, March 16, A8. In the United States a volunteer group of advertising executives has persuaded a diversity of product manufacturers—of toy cars and trucks, videos that play as motorists pump gasoline, television dramas, and school supplies—to join them in an antidrug crusade—albeit subtle—using the mass media. In 1990 the executives' advertising agencies contributed thousands of hours in creating what they hoped would be influential spots for newspapers, magazines, radio, and television. In turn, TV networks, independent stations, and other media gave $365 million worth of advertising space and time to carry the agencies' donated work. A scholarly assessment of the effectiveness of this campaign has not been done. However, the assumption is that if a clever advertisement can persuade one to buy a specific product, an equally clever advertisement may persuade one to avoid illegal drugs. ^United\States ^Media ^Private\Initiatives

1719. Trebach, Arnold S. (1982). *The Heroin Solution*. New Haven, Conn.: Yale University Press. Discusses United States and British public policy regarding the heroin habit. Also discusses the therapeutic use of heroin. Heroin addiction has become a worldwide epidemic and is worsening. Current criminalizing policies are not in any way counteracting this epidemic. So, what is to be done? First, one must realize that there can be no total, unconditional old-fashioned American style victory in a war on heroin. Nor, on the other hand, need people conclude that no solution is possible. The solution must be a "middle-level" type, aimed at creating a social balance between complete repression and allowance of use under some circumstances. Proposes a heroin maintenance or opium maintenance program for addicts, arguing that it should be made available by new laws or court decisions to all patients under the care of a doctor, not only to the terminally ill. Medical doctors, therefore, should be those who decide the application of a more relaxed social policy, in specific instances. In the future, social policy "should devise methods to help people both to use drugs in beneficial ways and to create a new ethos of higher consciousness that goes beyond drugs" (p. 294). The ultimate goal is to create "rational legal and medical policies" not only toward addicts, but also toward recreational users. ^ United\Kingdom ^ United\States ^ Heroin ^Drug\Control\Policies ^ P\S\Drug\Maintenance ^ P\S\Legalization

1720. —— (1983). "The Lesson of Ayatollah Khalkhali." *Journal of Drug Issues* 1394:379–400. After noting the increase in the drug epidemic and the millions of people involved in helping to supply the demand for drugs, the author focuses on the rigid support of prohibition and harsh criminal sanctions, including even the death penalty, in thirteen countries, which seems to be the preferred policy response. Critical of international drug control organizations such as the UN Commission on Narcotic Drugs, which the author sees as blindly supporting the existing system of harsh domestic laws and punishments. Argues that compromises and adjustments must be made to meet new realities, and that unless these adjustments are made soon—liberalization—"the entire structure of international drug control may collapse completely" (p. 379). ^United\Nations ^Law\Enforcement ^Legalization ^Drug\Control\Policies\Critique ^Politics

1721. —— (1987). *The Great Drug War and Radical Proposals That Could Make America Safe Again*. New York: Macmillan. This book is a foray, frequently anecdotal, into America's drug culture. The culture includes both those who use drugs and those who fight against them. Out of it all, the saddest victims are those who are denied legal medicines who really need them, and this is done because people are afraid of addictions. Beyond legal medicines, we sacrifice our sick by banning their using "hated medicines," such as heroin, which can be good. Calls for "drug peace." Advances the following propositions: 1) Drug wars cannot be won; 2) all drugs, including alcohol, tobacco, and the currently proscribed ones, are dangerous; however, all can be used in relatively nonharmful ways by many people; 3) think about drugs and abusers in new ways; drug abusers can be nice neighbors with a distressing problem, but still nice; 4) legalize drugs, but in return for this demand that addicts live productive and noncriminal lives; if some addicts continue to ignore their legitimate jobs, their loves ones, and the law, the deal, for them, is off; 5) provide affordable treatment for addicts, and protect people from the drug war by declaring no war; 6) "[g]ive the police the financial, legal, and moral backing to escalate their courageous work against major organized-crime syndicates. If we reform drug laws, these social jackals will turn their attention to other illegal activities where they will continue to be major threats" (p. 385). ^United\States ^Drug\Control\Policies\Critique ^P\S\Legalization ^Proffered\Solutions

1722. —— (1989). "Tough Choices: The Practical Politics of Drug Policy Reform." *American Behavioral Scientist* 32(3): 249–58. Argues for carefully guided experiments of limited legalization to see if benefits would not outweigh costs. ^P\S\Legalization ^Drug\Control\Politics

1723. Trebach, Arnold S., ed. (1978). *Drugs, Crime, and Politics*. New York: Praeger Publishers. Three contributed chapters of interest to this bibliography deal with how organizational ambiguities and narcotics law enforcement contribute to a working base for corruption, the role of buying and selling in illicit drug use, and the potential impact of "legal" heroin in America. ^United\States ^Heroin ^Law\Enforcement ^Politics ^Bureaucracy ^Consequences\Corruption ^Consequences\Drug\Control\Policies ^Legalization

1724. Tullis, F. LaMond (1987). "Cocaine and Food: Likely Effects of a Burgeoning Transnational Industry on Food Production in Bolivia and Peru, 247-83." In *Pursuing Food Security: Strategies and Obstacles in Africa, Asia, Latin America, and the Middle East*, edited by W. Ladd Hollist and F. LaMond Tullis. Boulder, Colo.: Lynne Rienner Publishers. Examines agricultural production trends in basic food stuffs, patterns in foreign food aid, labor costs, migration, and food prices in assessing the likely impact of the drug trade on food production in Peru and Bolivia. Concludes that the evidence is strong for adverse effects on production and prices of basic foods. ^Latin\America ^Bolivia ^Peru ^Cocaine ^Drug\Traffic ^Economics ^Agriculture ^Consequences\Misc ^Consequences\Economic ^Consequences\Political

1725. —— (1985). "The Current View on Rural Development: Fad or Breakthrough in Latin America?" *In an International Political Economy*, pp. 223–54, edited by W. Ladd Hollist and F. LaMond Tullis. Boulder,

Colorado: Westview Press. Examines rural development models applied in, or contemplated for Latin America. Analyzes national and international socioeconomic and political implications of these models, pointing out the political constraints that impoverish their implementation. By implication, the article shows the structural dilemma of advocating rural development as an antidote for illicit drug production in Latin America. ^Latin\America ^P\S\Development ^P\S\Critique ^Theories

1726. ———— (1970). *Lord and Peasant in Peru: A Paradigm of Political and Social Change.* Cambridge, Mass.: Harvard University Press, 1970. Examines the socioeconomic and political structure of Andean villages and the market-based economics that drive them. Focuses on peasant solidarity movements and national economic integration initiatives at the village level. Relevance for this bibliography is its examination of peasant initiatives in pursuit of economic gain, an essential precursor to grower involvement in the drug trade. ^Latin\America ^Peru ^Producers\Unions ^Markets

1727. Tunving, K. (1985). "Psychiatric Effects of Cannabis Use." *Acta Psychiatrica Scandinavica* 72:209–17. Focusing on the Scandinavian experience, discusses three risk groups with respect to cannabis use. For all risk groups, the consequences of cannabis use are deleterious. First, teenage cannabis users tend to lose some of their cognitive capacities. They also tend to flee from reality to a world of dreams. Second, heavy daily users often cannot cope with depression or their life circumstances. Finally, psychiatric patients who use cannabis have a diminished resistance to psychosis relapse. ^Cannabis ^Scandinavia ^Consequences\Neurological ^Consequences\Psychological ^Consequences\Health

1728. Tunving, Kerstin, and Kerstin Nilsson (1985). "Young Female Drug Addicts in Treatment: A Twelve Year Perspective." *Journal of Drug Issues* 15(3): 367–82. Women drug addicts enter treatment programs earlier (by age) than do men and, when they leave, have longer periods of abstinence in connection with that treatment or during their child-bearing experiences. However, women seem disproportionately prone to relapses and they appear to need family and therapeutic support for considerable periods after the initial treatment period. ^Drug\Use ^Treatment ^Women

1729. Turner, Carlton E., Beverly S. Urbanek, G. Michael Wall, and Coy W. Waller (1988). *Cocaine: An Annotated Bibliography.* Volume 1. Jackson: University Press of Mississippi. The annotated section of the bibliography (which is prefaced by an introductory statement giving a perspective on cocaine and cocaine-related chemistry) includes 4,055 annotated citations covering technical and scientific publications from 1950 to 1986. An author index with extensive cross-referenced subject indices is contained in Volume 2. While the citations are mostly technical, numerous entries are of interest to this bibliography, including health effects of cocaine use. ^Cocaine ^Bibliographies ^Consequences\Health

1730. Uelmen, Gerald F. (1983). "Punishing Drug Offenders: An International and Comparative Perspective." *Journal of Drug Issues* 13(4): 373–77. Gives comparative analysis for cannabis, cocaine, and opium with respect to drug possession penalties and drug trafficking penalties. The authors note the escalation of penalties, following the lead of America, and make no hesitation to note that they consider this to be a failed policy. "The failure of this policy has been well documented in our literature. But apparently our literature isn't being exported. Our policy of failure is" (p. 377). ^Law\Enforcement ^Consequences\Penal ^Drug\Control\Policies\Critique ^Law\Enforcement\Critique

1731. Uhlig, Mark A. (1989). "As Colombian Terror Grows, the Press Becomes the Prey." *The New York Times,* 24 May, A1. Discussion of the efforts by narcotics traffickers and drug barons to silence the press in Colombia relative to its criticism of trafficking. Specific instances are elaborated. ^Colombia ^Drug\Traffic ^Politics ^Consequences\Violence ^Media ^Latin\America

1732. —— (1989). "Colombia's War on Cocaine: Farmers' Fears Help Cause." *The New York Times*, 3 July, 1-2. Describes the relationship of political corruption and terrorist activity, focusing on the peasant coca grower, that produces resistive violence. The "shimmering promise of wealth" has evaporated, and only violence and social debris have emerged. Describes how some farmers, trying to extricate themselves, have joined the government-sponsored crop substitution program. Focuses on the Cauca region of Colombia. ^Colombia ^Latin\America ^Coca ^Crop\Substitution ^Terrorists ^Consequences\Corruption ^Consequences\Violence ^Consequences\Social ^Consequences\Economic

1733. Ungerleider, J. Thomas, and Therese Andrysiak (1984). "Changes in the Drug Scene: Drug Use Trends and Behavioral Patterns." *Journal of Drug Issues* 14(2): 217–22. Aside from reviewing drug scene trends since 1965, the article's interest for this bibliography is its discussion of drug problems relating to free basing cocaine, and in its discussion of the interface of adolescent development issues and family dynamics as important variables to consider in regard to potential underlying reasons for adolescent drug abuse. ^Drug\Use\Theories ^Youth ^Family ^Consequences\Health

1734. "U.N. Striving for Tact in Its Fight on Drugs" (1987). *The New York Times*, 26 July, 18. Discussion about how the neutrality of the United Nations gives it influence in some places but limits its effectiveness in others. For example, in publishing in 1967 a report linking drug smuggling to terrorism and arms trafficking, it declined to name names. Perhaps a new level of international cooperation is called for. ^United\Nations ^Drug\Control\Policies ^International\Cooperation\Critique ^Terrorists

1735. United Nations (1982). *International Strategy and Policies for Drug Control.* New York: United Nations. Discussion of the UN's December 1981 resolution 36/168 entitled "International Drug Abuse Control Strategy." The general assembly had approved the international drug control strategy and policies prepared by the division of narcotic drugs and finalized by the commission on narcotic drugs in response to the general assembly's request. ^United\Nations ^Drug\Control\Policies ^International\Cooperation

1736. —— (1984). *Summary of Annual Reports of Governments Relating to Narcotic Drugs and Psychotropic Substances 1979–1984.* New York: United Nations Economic and Social Council. Annually, the United Nations Economic and Social Council's Commission on Narcotic Drugs issues a report related to conditions in 105 or more reporting countries. A comparative summary is given on laws and regulations; administrative arrangement; efforts at control and which agencies are involved; where lawful manufacturing of drugs that internationally are viewed as illicit is done; what the domestic trade is and the controls associated with it; the degree to which those controls are associated with, or are bypassed, in international trade; prohibitions; and legal and social measures that are taken to deal with drugs trafficking and a list of responsible country agencies. ^Drug\Control\Policies ^Legislation ^United\Nations ^Statistics

1737. —— (1987). *The United Nations and Drug Abuse Control.* New York: United Nations. Gives a general overview of the UN's historic position on prevention and reduction of illicit demand, control of supply and suppression of illicit trafficking, along with treatment and rehabilitation of drug abusers. Considerable background is given on international cooperation in drug control, including international conventions and the present position of the United Nations system in the control apparatus. The work of specialized agencies is mentioned. ^United\Nations ^Drug\Control\Policies\History ^International\Cooperation ^Demand ^Supply

1738. United Nations, Division of Narcotic Drugs (1988). *Declaration of the International Conference on Drug Abuse and Illicit Trafficking and Comprehensive Multidisciplinary Outline of Future Activities in Drug Abuse Control.* New York: United Nations. Included are the declaration of the international conference on drug abuse and illicit trafficking and a comprehensive multidisciplinary outline of activities in drug abuse control. Within the second category are included strategies to reduce demand and prevent use, control supply, suppress trafficking, and develop treatment and rehabilitation programs. The index consists of key words targeted to paragraphs. ^United\Nations ^Drug\Control\Policies ^International\Cooperation ^Demand ^Supply

1739. United Nations, Economic and Social Council (1987). *Interim Report of the United Nations Fund for Drug Abuse Control.* Vienna, Austria: United Nations. Reviews the status of current master plans and country programs in Latin America and the Caribbean, Asia and the Pacific, the Near and the Middle East, and Africa with respect to UNFDAC's activities. Specific projects are outlined. ^United\Nations ^Drug\Control\Policies ^International\Cooperation ^UNFDAC

1740. ——— (1987). *Quarterly Summary of Reports of Significant Seizures of Narcotic Drugs and Psychotropic Substance Received by the Secretary-General from 1 January to 31 March 1987.* Vienna, Austria: United Nations. Lists seizures by region and country for the period 1 January–31 March 1987. ^Interdiction ^statistics ^United\Nations

1741. ——— (1988). *Situation and Trends in Drug Abuse and the Illicit Traffic.* Sub-Commission on Illicit Drug Traffic and Related Matters in the Near and Middle East Report on the Twenty-Third Session. Vienna, Austria: United Nations. Notes recommendations for action by the commission on narcotic drugs and reviews recent trends in the illicit traffic. A follow-up review is also given to the international conference on drug abuse and illicit trafficking. ^United\Nations ^Drug\Control\Policies ^International\Cooperation

1742. United Nations, General Assembly (1987). *International Campaign against Traffic in Drugs.* New York: United Nations General Assembly, 42nd Session (2-4 November). Agenda item 104 on the International Campaign against traffic and drugs was continued through four sessions of the 42nd General Assembly. Contained are the reports of the Secretary General of the International Conference on drug abuse and illicit trafficking, the draft convention against illicit traffic and narcotic drugs and psychotropic substances, and implementation of the general assembly resolution 41/127 regarding international traffic in illicit drugs. Various delegates rose to make comments from the floor. ^United\Nations ^Drug\Control\Policies ^International\Cooperation

1743. ——— (1987). Report of the Economic and Social Council. *International Co-operation in Drug Abuse Control.* Vienna, Austria: United Nations. Describes the activities carried out by the United Nations' bodies and entities and by the specialized agencies and programs in preparation for and follow up to the 1987 international conference on drug abuse and illicit trafficking. Emphasizes coordination among agencies within the United Nations system, particularly focusing on the Division of Narcotic Drugs, International Narcotics Control Board, United Nations Fund for Drug Abuse Control, the Center for Social Development and Humanitarian Affairs, United Nations Social Defense Research Institute, United Nations Development Program, International Labor Organization, Food and Agricultural Organization of the United Nations, United Nations Educational, Scientific, and Cultural Organization, International Civil Aviation Organization, World Health Organization, Universal Postal Union, International Maritime Organization, and United Nations Industrial Development

Organization. ^United\Nations ^Drug\Control\Policies ^International\Cooperation ^INCB ^UNFDAC ^WHO ^UNESCO

1744. —— (1988). *International Campaign against Traffic in Drugs.* Letter Dated 3 March 1988 from the Permanent Representative of Panama to the United Nations Addressed to the Secretary General. Vienna, Austria: United Nations. In this communication to the U.N. Secretary General, Jorge Eduardo Ritter, Panama's permanent representative and ambassador to the U.N., takes exception to the United States government having declared Panama an uncooperative nation in 1987 relative to cooperative drug control efforts. He calls the United States government's attitude "inconceivable, incongruous, and immoral; we denounce it as such today and will do so in all international forums." ^ Panama ^ United\States ^ Drug\Control\Policies\Critique ^ Politics ^ Consequences\Foreign\Relations ^ Latin\America

1745. —— (1988). *International Campaign Against Traffic in Drugs.* Letter Dated 18 January 1988 from the Permanent Representative of Colombia to the United Nations Addressed to the Secretary General. Vienna, Austria: United Nations. In a letter to the Secretary General, the Colombian Ambassador and Permanent Representative to the UN, Enrique Peñalosa, takes exception to the United States' criticism of his country's judiciary's having released a number of individuals charged with drug trafficking and the subsequent "anti-Colombian" acts relative to the tourist industry that the United States has, apparently, fostered. ^Colombia ^United\States ^Drug\Control\Policies\Critique ^Politics ^Consequences\Foreign\Relations ^Latin\America

1746. United Nations Governing Council of the United Nations Development Programme (1988). *Programme Implementation.* Implementation of Decisions Adopted by the Governing Council at Previous Session. Geneva, Switzerland: United Nations. Mention is made of the United Nations Development Program (UNDP) having funded, in 1986, under its global programme, a research project, jointly financed with the United Nations Social Defense Research Institute (UNSDRI) on drug abuse in the context of development: Prevention, treatment, and rehabilitation. This was intended to give a background to the Vienna International Conference (1987) on drug abuse and illicit trafficking. Mention that efforts would be made to distribute the report more widely as a joint publication of the two agencies. ^United\Nations ^International\Cooperation ^Drug\Use ^Prevention ^Treatment

1747. United Nations, International Narcotics Control Board (1981–1985). *Comparative Statement of Estimates and Statistics on Narcotic Drugs.* New York: United Nations. Each issue of this annual statistical compendium includes country-specific information as reported by the respective governments in accordance with international treaties. ^Production ^Statistics ^United\Nations ^Southeast\Asia ^Latin\America ^Caribbean ^Africa ^Middle\East ^INCB

1748. —— (1981–86). *Statistics on Narcotic Drugs,* Annual Publication. Furnished by Governments in Accordance with the International Treaties. New York: United Nations. In general, the featured discussions focus on the raw materials, their alkaloids and the derivatives of alkaloids, more particularly opium and opiates, cannabis and cannabis resin, and coca leaf and cocaine. Also synthetic narcotic drugs are featured. Gives country-specific statistics. ^Production ^Statistics ^United\Nations ^Southeast\Asia ^Latin\America ^Caribbean ^Africa ^Middle\East ^INCB

1749. —— (1985–88). International Narcotics Control Board. *Report of the International Narcotics Control Board,* Annual Publication. New York: United Nations. The International Narcotics Control Board is the successor to drug control bodies first established more than a half century ago by international treaty. The board's mandate is to "endeavor to limit the cultivation, production, manufacture and use of drugs to an adequate amount required for medical and scientific purposes" (p. i). The board also is charged to prevent illicit cultivation, production, and manufacture of, and illicit trafficking in and use, of drugs. Each annual report includes an analysis of the world situation broken into regional categories. ^Drug\Control\Policies ^United\Nations ^Southeast\Asia ^Africa ^Middle\East ^Latin\America ^Caribbean ^INCB

1750. United Nations Laws and Regulations (1987). *United Kingdom.* Communicated by the Government of the United Kingdom of Great Britain and Northern Ireland. Vienna, Austria: United Nations. The United Kingdom reports the 1985 modifications to the Misuse of Drugs Act 1971. ^United\Kingdom ^Law\Enforcement ^Legislation ^United\Nations

1751. United Nations Laws and Regulations Promulgated to Give Effect to the Provisions of the International Treaties on Narcotic Drugs and Psychotropic Substances (1987). *Adopting the National Narcotic Drugs Statute and Enacting Other Provisions.* Communicated by the Government of Colombia. New York: United Nations. Colombia reports its 1986 draft law to the U.N. Secretariat. It is intended to be a comprehensive law covering all relevant issue areas in drug production, trafficking, and consumption. ^Latin\America ^Colombia ^Drug\Control\Policies ^Treaties ^United\Nations ^Legislation

1752. United Nations Secretariat (1983). "Measure to Assess Drug Abuse and the Health, Social and Economic Consequences of Such Abuse: Summary of Information from 21 Countries." *Bulletin on Narcotics* 35(3): 19–32. This article summarizes the replies received from twenty-one governments to a survey undertaken in 1982 of measures to assess drug abuse and its consequences. In many of the replies it was affirmed that drug abuse imposes a considerable burden on society in terms of health impairment and disabilities, as well as in terms of its social and economic consequences. Drug abusers had reduced ability and motivation to engage in the complex tasks required in modern society; they dropped out of school and performed their work poorly. It was also reported that drug abuse played an important role in the development of criminal, delinquent, and antisocial behavior. ^Drug\Use ^United\Nations ^Consequences\Social ^Consequences\Economic ^Consequences\Political ^Workplace ^Consequences\Crime ^Amotivational\Syndrome

1753. United Nations Secretariat, Division of Narcotic Drugs (1987). "Review of Drug Abuse and Measures to Reduce the Illicit Demand for Drugs by Region." *Bulletin on Narcotics* 39(1): 3–29. The United Nations Commission on Narcotic Drugs noted at its February 1987 session that the drug abuse situation continued to worsen in most parts of the world. The most striking features were the escalation of heroin and cocaine abuse. The injection of drugs contributed significantly to the increasing spread of AIDS and hepatitis B. The age of first users was falling from adolescents to preadolescents and even earlier. In most countries, drug abuse had spread to all social strata, and the proportion of female abusers was growing. The regions considered in this review are Africa, the Americas, Asia and the Far East, Europe, and Oceania. ^Africa ^Southeast\Asia ^Europe ^Latin\America ^United\States ^Drug\Use ^Drug\Control\Policies ^Reviews ^AIDS ^Consequences\Personal

1754. United Nations Social Defense Research Institute (1988). *Drugs and Punishment: An Up-to-Date Interregional Survey on Drug-Related Offences.* Publication No. 30. Rome, Italy: UNSDRI. Surveys drug-related penal measures in Europe, Asia, Africa, and Latin America. ^Africa ^Southeast\Asia ^Europe ^Latin\America ^Law\Enforcement ^Consequences\Penal

1755. "US Ambassador Starts a Row" (1985). *Latin American Regional Reports*, 22 March, 3. Describes U.S. Ambassador John Gavin's attack on the Mexican government as he "spills the beans" about the drug trade originating in or transiting through Mexico. The Mexicans are incensed. ^Mexico ^United\States ^Consequences\Foreign\Relations

1756. U.S. Comptroller General (1988). *Controlling Drug Abuse: A Status Report.* Washington, D.C.: United States Government Accounting Office. Gives a brief overview of the persistence of drug problems in the United States, notes the federal drug control efforts aimed at reducing supply and demand, and raises observations about managing the federal drug control efforts. The appendix discusses nationwide estimates of the drug problem. ^United\States ^Drug\Traffic ^Drug\Control\Policies ^Drug\Use\History ^Supply ^Demand ^Statistics

1757. U.S. Congress, House Committee on Banking, Finance and Urban Affairs (1988). Hearing. "Money Laundering Control Act Amendments of 1988." *One Hundredth Congress, Second Session.* Washington, D.C.: U.S. Government Printing Office. In spite of the efforts to control money laundering, flaws in policy as well as practice necessitated consideration of amendments. Testifiers came from the Department of the Treasury and the Department of Justice. ^United\States ^Drug\Control\Policies ^Money\Laundering ^Legislation

1758. U.S. Congress, House Committee on the District of Columbia, Subcommittee on Fiscal Affairs and Health (1985). Oversight Hearing. "Drug Trafficking in the Washington Metropolitan Area." *Ninety-Ninth Congress, First Session.* Washington, D.C.: U.S. Government Printing Office. Focus on the scope and pattern of interstate drug trafficking in the metropolitan area of the District of Columbia, Maryland, and Virginia. The trafficking is huge, yielding an estimated annual nontaxable income of $1.5 billion. Washington suburban communities have become the centers for the manufacturing, slicing, and cutting of heroin and cocaine, and the packaging of marijuana. The disparity between the sentences handed down by the federal courts in the District of Columbia and federal courts in the surrounding jurisdictions is huge. This disparity is widely known among drug dealers and may well be a major contributing factor to the use of the streets of the District of Columbia as drug distributing locations. It was revealed that a major source of raw cocaine and heroin may be international sources (diplomats?) located in the nation's capital. ^United\States ^Drug\Traffic ^Washington\DC ^Judiciary

1759. U.S. Congress, House Committee on Foreign Affairs (1974). "Turkish Opium Ban Negotiations." *Ninety-Third Congress, Second Session.* Washington, D.C.: U.S. Government Printing Office. Discussion of the development of legislation and laws in Turkey designed to reduce the opium trade; considerations of how U.S. economic assistance might help to improve matters of illicit drug control within Turkey. ^Middle\East ^Turkey ^Legislation ^Opiates ^Drug\Control\Policies

1760. ——— (1982). "International Narcotics Control, Report of Staff Study Missions to Latin America, Southeast Asia, and Pakistan." *Ninety-Seventh Congress, Second Session.* Washington, D.C.: U.S. Government Printing Office. An effort is made to clarify United States policy and to advance recommendations vis-à-vis that clarification. The committee noted that narcotics control is an instrument of American foreign policy, and it is formulated to meet a variety of objectives, of which illicit narcotics control is only one. This, in itself, creates some confusion. The status of cooperation among various countries is given, including Mexico, Jamaica, Colombia, Peru, Bolivia, Thailand, Burma, and Hong Kong. ^Latin\America ^Southeast\Asia

^Mexico ^Jamaica ^Colombia ^Peru ^Bolivia ^Thailand ^Burma ^Hong\Kong ^United\States
^Drug\Control\Policies ^International\Cooperation ^Consequences\Foreign\Policy ^Golden\Triangle

1761. —— (1985). Hearing. "Developments in Latin America in Narcotics Control." *Ninety-Ninth Congress, First Session.* Washington, D.C.: U.S. Government Printing Office. Focus, in particular, on Colombia and Peru. Discouraging trends are noted. Summarizing statements, in addition to countries of principal focus, are made regarding Bolivia, Ecuador, Belize, and Panama. ^Latin\America ^Drug\Control\Policies ^Colombia ^Peru ^Bolivia ^Ecuador ^Belize ^Panama ^Drug\Control\Policies\Effectiveness

1762. —— (1985). Hearing. "Narcotics Production and Transshipments in Belize and Central America." *Ninety-Ninth Congress, First Session.* Washington, D.C.: U.S. Government Printing Office. The committee met to examine the increased narcotics production and trafficking in Belize and Central America. Belize has become the fourth largest supplier of marijuana to the United States, production having increased six fold since 1982. It appears that the narcotics crackdown in Colombia has led Colombian traffickers to seek new areas for production and transshipment, and Belize and Central America apparently have been selected. Testimony was received relative to the degree to which these observations are essentially correct. As usual, contradictory testimony was presented. ^Latin\America ^Belize ^Cannabis ^Drug\Traffic ^Production ^Consequences\Law\Enforcement

1763. —— (1986). Report. "Compilation of Narcotics Laws, Treaties, and Executive Documents." *Ninety-Ninth Congress, Second Session.* Washington, D.C.: U.S. Government Printing Office. Includes federal statutes of interest to the committee along with related documents. The related documents include international treaties and executive branch papers. The appendix includes federal laws on the control of narcotics and other dangerous drugs, enacted between 1961 and 1985. Brief summaries are also given. ^United\States ^Drug\Control\Policies ^International\Cooperation ^Treaties ^Legislation

1764. —— (1986). Hearing. "Issues in United States–Panamanian Antinarcotics Control." *Ninety-Ninth Congress, Second Session.* Washington, D.C.: U.S. Government Printing Office. The committee met to establish whatever facts it could on the current situation regarding drug trafficking, money laundering, and other ancillary issues related to narcotics that involve Panama. ^Latin\America ^Panama ^United\States ^Money\Laundering ^Drug\Traffic ^Drug\Control\Policies

1765. —— (1986). Hearing. "Nicaraguan Government Involvement in Narcotics Trafficking." *Ninety-Ninth Congress, Second Session.* Washington, D.C.: U.S. Government Printing Office. The committee met to examine allegations of Nicaraguan government involvement in narcotics trafficking. Numerous allegations had surfaced, and the committee sought expert testimony. In general, the evidence presented was fairly damaging to Nicaragua. Testimony was received from representatives of the Bureau of International Narcotics Matters, Department of State; the Drug Enforcement Administration; and a former governmental officer in the previous Nicaraguan government. Newspaper reports were submitted for the record. The report suggests that members of the Sandinista government have not only condoned but actually participated in narcotics trafficking activities. ^Latin\America ^Nicaragua ^Drug\Traffic ^Politics ^Consequences\Corruption ^DEA

1766. —— (1986). Hearing. "Review of United States Narcotics Control Efforts in the Middle East and South Asia." *Ninety-Ninth Congress, Second Session.* Washington, D.C.: U.S. Government Printing Office. At this hearing representatives from the Bureau of International Narcotics Matters, Department of State;

Drug Enforcement Administration, Department of Justice; Bureau of Near Eastern and South Asian Affairs, Department of State; Agency for International Development; and the Policy Bureau of the Department of State testified. Among other issues, within the various testimonies, the following emerged: The U.S.-financed narcotics control program for heroin production in Pakistan is apparently bogged down; India is becoming a major transshipment point; allegations of Syrian involvement in trafficking and Soviet tolerance and/or involvement in Afghanistan. Nepal has been added to the list of countries suffering from the effects of narcotics trafficking. ^Southeast\Asia ^United\States ^Drug\Control\Policies\Effectiveness ^DEA ^Department\of\State ^Pakistan ^Heroin ^India ^Syria ^Afghanistan ^Nepal ^Southwest\Asia ^Middle\East

1767. —— (1986). Hearing. "The Role and Activities of the National Drug Enforcement Policy Board." *Ninety-Ninth Congress, Second Session.* Washington, D.C.: U.S. Government Printing Office. Testimony in this brief hearing was in response to questions concerning an update on the extradition treaties in effect between the United States and other countries and also the relationship of the National Drug Enforcement Policy Board to carrying out "Operation Blast Furnace" in Bolivia. As a general statement, the committee met to review the role and the mission of the National Drug Enforcement Policy Board in coordinating U.S. drug enforcement efforts. The board had been responsible for coordinating the activities of Operation Alliance (designed to tighten security and interdict drugs along the southwest border of the United States) as well as Operation Blast Furnace in Bolivia. ^United\States ^Drug\Control\Policies ^Treaties ^Extradition ^Bolivia ^Latin\America

1768. —— (1986). Hearing. "United States–Mexican Cooperation in Narcotics Control Efforts." *Ninety-Ninth Congress, Second Session.* Washington, D.C.: U.S. Government Printing Office. Witnesses discussed the investigation into the assassination of drug enforcement agent Enrique Camarena, and Mexico's efforts and accomplishments in eradication and interdiction. The eradication programs in Mexico were funded by the U.S. State Department. ^Mexico ^United\States ^Drug\Control\Policies\Effectiveness ^International\Cooperation ^Crop\Eradication ^Interdiction

1769. —— (1987). Hearing. "Narcotics Issues in the Bahamas and the Caribbean." *One Hundredth Congress, First Session.* Washington, D.C.: U.S. Government Printing Office. The Bahamas and the Caribbean continue to be major transit points for drugs coming into the United States; the purpose of the hearing was to review narcotics control issues in that area. Additionally, the committee desired to explore some of the serious allegations of high-level drug-related corruption in some of the region's countries. ^Bahamas ^Caribbean ^Drug\Traffic ^Drug\Control\Policies ^Politics ^Consequences\Corruption

1770. —— (1987. Hearing. "Review of the International Narcotics Control Strategy Report: Mid-Year Update." *One Hundredth Congress, First Session.* Washington, D.C.: U.S. Government Printing Office. The purpose of the hearing was to review the State Department's mid-year update on the international narcotics control situation. Statements were taken from Ann B. Wrobleski, assistant secretary of state, Bureau of International Narcotics Matters, and David L. Westrate, assistant administrator, Drug Enforcement Administration, Department of Justice. Additionally, the Department of State has included documents on coca production and eradication in 1985 and 1986 for Bolivia, Brazil, Colombia, Ecuador, and Peru. The Drug Enforcement Agency's eradication programs in Mexico, Burma, Colombia and other countries are discussed. ^United\States ^Drug\Control\Policies ^Bolivia ^Brazil ^Colombia ^Ecuador ^Peru ^Mexico ^Burma ^Latin\America ^Southeast\Asia ^Golden\Triangle ^Production ^Coca ^Crop\Eradication

1771. ——— (1987). Hearing. "Review of Latin American Narcotics Control Issues." *One Hundredth Congress, First Session*. Washington, D.C.: U.S. Government Printing Office. A general review of United States operations in Latin America to reduce production and transport of illegal drugs. In particular, the committee wanted to get a complete assessment of the 1986 "Operation Blast Furnace" in Bolivia. Assessments were also given regarding extradition proceedings in Colombia and aerial spraying programs in Mexico. What cooperation is the United States getting from various Latin American countries? The response from some who testified was sobering. ^United-ed\States ^Latin\America ^Bolivia ^Drug\Control\Policies\Effectiveness ^International\Cooperation ^Supply ^Drug\Traffic

1772. ——— (1987). Hearing. "The Role of Intelligence in International Narcotics Control." *One Hundredth Congress, First Session*. Washington, D.C.: U.S. Government Printing Office. One purpose of the hearing was to learn how the administration had organized the various agencies and coordinated their differing roles in narcotics intelligence production and dissemination. ^United\States ^Drug\Control\Policies ^Bureaucracy

1773. ——— (1987). Hearing. "U.S. Narcotics Control Efforts in Southeast Asia." *One Hundredth Congress, First Session*. Washington, D.C.: U.S. Government Printing Office. In addition to the usual material covered in these hearings, this one adds the testimony of Lt. Colonel James "Bo" Gritz, U.S. Army retired, who also inserted in the record a number of supplemental documents, including news reports from various international networks. ^Southeast\Asia ^United\States ^Drug\Control\Policies\Critique

1774. ——— (1987). Hearing. "The Worldwide Drug Situation and International Narcotics Control Programs." *One Hundredth Congress, First Session*. Washington, D.C.: U.S. Government Printing Office. These hearings were held amidst the general frustration with the lack of drug-enforcement cooperation among Latin American governments. Some of the reports presented were required under the new procedures created by PL 99-570, the Anti-Drug Abuse Act of 1986. Such hearings are held prior to the United States president's being able to certify certain countries as cooperating with America or having taken adequate steps on their own to control production, traffic, or money laundering. The representations made at this hearing were targeted to satisfy that requirement. There is some discussion about the integrity of the U.S. certification effort. ^United\States ^Latin\America ^Drug\Control\Policies\Critique ^Legislation

1775. ——— (1987). Hearing. "Worldwide Review of Status of U.S. Extradition Treaties and Mutual Legal Assistance Treaties." *One Hundredth Congress, First Session*. Washington, D.C.: U.S. Government Printing Office. The committee met to review extradition treaties as they relate to narcotics violations. Given the bleak prospects in most countries for domestic prosecution of drug traffickers, having an effective extradition treaty is thought to be a potent weapon to get traffickers to the United States to face effective justice. Likewise, mutual assistance treaties would pierce the veil of bank secrecy and allow drug enforcement agents to get at the money launderers. Testimony was received from the legal office of the Department of State; from the criminal division of the Department of Justice; and from the Bureau of International Narcotics Matters, Department of State. ^United\States ^Extradition ^Money\Laundering ^Drug\Control\Policies ^International\Cooperation ^Treaties

1776. ——— (1988). Hearing. "Narcotics Review in the Caribbean." *One Hundredth Congress, Second Session*. Washington, D.C.: U.S. Government Printing Office. Testimony was from representatives of the Bureau of International

Narcotics Matters, Department of State; the Bureau of InterAmerican Affairs, Department of State; and the Office of Intelligence, Drug Enforcement Administration, Department of Justice. Various materials from the Bahamas are also inserted in the record. For the purposes of this record, the Caribbean is to be understood as the Bahamas, the Dominican Republic, Haiti, and Jamaica. All these countries have opened traffic for drug lords, with only Jamaica producing any significant amount of the illicit narcotics. The difficulty in Jamaica and elsewhere is related almost exclusively to interdiction and attempts to curb insidious corruption within the country deriving from the drug trade. Considerable discussion on internal corruption. Specific instances or anecdotes are given. Analysis of the narcotics control situation in each country. ^Latin\America ^Caribbean ^Drug\Traffic ^Consequences\Corruption ^Bahamas ^Haiti ^Jamaica

1777. ——— (1988). Hearing. "Narcotics Review in Central America." *One Hundredth Congress, Second Session.* Washington, D.C.: U.S. Government Printing Office. This focus followed in the wake of the United States having taken "the remarkable step" of decertifying Panama for its noncooperation on narcotics control. Two of the foci of this report were the growing power of the traffickers on the one hand, and the corruption among government officials in many Central American countries on the other. Statements were made by Assistant Secretaries Ann Wrobleski and Elliott Abrams from the State Department, and Deputy Assistant Administrator Tom Byrne from the Drug Enforcement Administration. ^Latin\America ^Drug\Traffic ^Consequences\Corruption ^Traffickers ^Consequences\Political

1778. ——— (1988). Hearing. "Narcotics Review in South America." *One Hundredth Congress, Second Session.* Washington, D.C.: U.S. Government Printing Office. As hearings usually go, this one also covers the gamut. However, the initial focus is on Mexico, with the judgment being made that roughly 40 percent of the heroin entering the United States comes from Mexico and that Mexico also has become a major transit point for cocaine and marijuana. Mention is made that a critical limiting factor for the United States in international cooperation with Mexico is the level of official corruption in the Mexican government. Alarming figures are given. In addition to Mexico, aspects of the drug trafficking, production, and consumption equations are mentioned for Argentina, Bolivia, Brazil, Colombia, Ecuador, Paraguay, Peru, Venezuela. Topics discussed are the effectiveness of the U.S. certification process, use of herbicides, eradication programs, paramilitary units supporting the cocaine trade, and corruption everywhere. Extensive discussion on Paraguay and, to a lesser extent, on the upper Huallaga project. ^Latin\America ^Drug\Traffic ^Organized\Crime ^Drug\Control\Policies ^International\Cooperation ^Mexico ^Consequences\Corruption ^Statistics ^Argentina ^Bolivia ^Brazil ^Colombia ^Ecuador ^Paraguay ^Peru ^Venezuela ^Herbicides ^Crop\Eradication ^Traffickers\Private\Armies

1779. ——— (1988). Hearing. "Narcotics Review in Southeast/Southwest Asia, the Middle East, and Africa." *One Hundredth Congress, Second Session.* Washington, D.C.: U.S. Government Printing Office. Statements are given by representatives from the Bureau of International Narcotics Matters, Department of State; and the Drug Enforcement Administration, Department of Justice. Materials submitted for the record include a statement by the Department of State regarding extradition treaties to which the United States is a party and the status of extradition treaties being negotiated or that have been negotiated. Country summaries are given of twenty-eight countries. ^Africa ^Southeast\Asia ^United\States ^Middle\East ^Drug\Control\Policies ^Extradition ^International\Cooperation ^Treaties

1780. ——— (1988). Hearing. "Recent Developments in Colombia." *One Hundredth Congress, Second Session.* Washington, D.C.: U.S. Government

Printing Office. This hearing took place in the wake of the assassination of a number of Supreme Court justices in Colombia and the general ascendancy of the country's cocaine warlords. There is a focus on a "cocaine mafia" and the Medellín cartel. There is general outrage at the inability of the United States, in collaboration with Colombia, to put the kingpins away. Thus, the judiciary and extradition policies in Colombia come up for review. In general, many economic and political impact issues are raised in this volume. ^Latin\America ^Colombia ^Drug\Traffic ^Organized\Crime ^Consequences\Economic ^Consequences\Political ^Consequences\Judiciary ^Extradition

1781. —— (1989). *Drugs and Latin America: Economic and Political Impact and U.S. Policy Options.* Washington D.C.: US Government Printing Office. Proceedings of a seminar held by the congressional research service of the Library of Congress, April 26, 1989. Describes some of the drug trafficking organizations in Latin America and how they are working to affect public opinion–through their own newspapers, television, and radio stations–in the countries in which they operate. Ties between producers and political insurgents at the growers level are discussed. The cocaine trade constitutes a serious threat to public confidence in democratic institutions. The trade, unless curtailed, will undermine governments' capacity to function. All this occurs under conditions of severe economic distress in Peru and Bolivia. Colombia, because of its more diverse and healthy economy, is less negatively affected. Coordinated, multilateral approaches to international drug control will be more effective than existing unilateral of bilateral efforts, which, on the whole, have not been successful. ^Latin\America ^Traffickers ^Media ^Economics ^Peru ^Bolivia ^Colombia ^Consequences\Economic ^P\S\International\Cooperation

1782. —— (1988). Hearing. "Worldwide Narcotics Review of the 1988 International Narcotics Control Strategy Report." *One Hundredth Congress, Second Session.* Washington, D.C.: U.S. Government Printing Office. This hearing was initiated by a task force on international narcotics control, House of Representatives, Committee on Foreign Affairs, chaired by Lawrence J. Smith, representative from Florida. Smith opens with a scathing attack on both the process or procedure and the outcome of presidential certification to Congress each year, pursuant to the 1986 omnibus drug bill, that each major drug producing or trafficking country "has fully cooperated with U.S. drug enforcement efforts or taken steps on its own to reduce the flow of drugs into the United States." For other "national interests" we cannot say "no" to drugs at home and yet say "yes" to drug-infected politics overseas. The balance of the report consists of prepared statements and transcriptions of dialogue for or against the scathing initial salvo from the task force chairman. Prepared statements are inserted from the Bureau of International Narcotics Matters, Department of State; from the Drug Enforcement Administration; and responses to questions submitted to the Drug Enforcement Administration by the task force. Also included are questions submitted to the Department of State by the task force and responses from the state. In general, the executive branch defended both certification and the drug enforcement programs, whereas the task force was exceedingly critical. ^United\States ^Drug\Control\Policies\Critique ^Consequences\Foreign\Policy

1783. U.S. Congress, House Committee on Government Operations (1983). "Commercial Production and Distribution of Domestic Marijuana." *Ninety-Eighth Congress, First Session.* Washington, D.C.: U.S. Government Printing Office. Discusses history of marijuana supply in the United States, the increase in domestic production for commercial transactions, the associated violence and organization among traffickers, including organized crime, and the nature of law enforcement on public lands. There has been a marked increase in the amount of marijuana grown in the

United States in the past five years. A much more potent form of the drug is being grown because of improvements in plant genetics and horticultural techniques. Marijuana is produced as a commercial crop in the majority of states and has exceeded commercial food crops in cash value in many agricultural areas. Producers are often highly organized and sophisticated. Local law enforcement officers and prosecutors are overwhelmed. The DEA has not been active in domestic marijuana enforcement and, therefore, lacks any reliable data base from which to project its programming. Rural areas where marijuana is produced have very little official oversight or coverage. Federal and state lands are commonly used by marijuana growers. This poses disruptive and threatening consequences to national and state park employees and recreational and logging activities. The illicit activity is increasing. ^United\States ^Cannabis ^Production\History ^Drug\Traffic ^Traffickers ^United\States\Rural\Areas ^Organized\Crime ^Law\Enforcement ^Producers ^DEA ^Consequences\Political ^Consequences\Economic

1784. U.S. Congress, House Committee on Government Operations, Government Activities and Transportation Subcommittee (1987). Hearing. "Dealing with Drugs and Alcohol in the Rail and Airline Industries." *One Hundredth Congress, First Session.* Washington, D.C.: U.S. Government Printing Office. It is stated that from 10 to 20 percent of adult Americans have been classified as problem drinkers, and that 10 percent of those over twenty-one years of age are regular users of illegal drugs. What effect is this having on the nation's rail systems and its airline industry? Answers were attempted. ^United\States ^Drug\Use ^Consequences\Public\Safety ^Alcohol ^Aircraft

1785. U.S. Congress, House Committee on Government Operations, Government Information, Justice, and Agricultural Subcommittee (1983). "The Federal Role in Suppressing the Cultivation and Trafficking of Domestic Marijuana." Hearing. *Ninety-Eighth Congress, First Session.* Washington, D.C.: U.S. Government Printing Office. The committee examined the domestic commercial cultivation and trafficking in high-grade marijuana. It has become big business, perhaps having become America's fourth largest cash crop. What should the federal role be in the eradication of this high-quality domestic marijuana? The hearing received testimony on these issues and this question. ^United\States ^Cannabis ^Crop\Eradication ^Production

1786. ——— (1985). Hearing. "The Clandestine Manufacture of Illicit Drugs." *Ninety-Ninth Congress, First Session.* Washington, D.C.: U.S. Government Printing Office. The technology of illegal drug manufacturing has become more widely available and understood; the problems created are substantial. By implication, there is some discussion on "designer drugs." ^Designer\Drugs

1787. U.S. Congress, House Committee on International Relations, Subcommittee on Future Foreign Policy Research and Development (1975). "The Effectiveness of Turkish Opium Control." *Ninety-Fourth Congress, First Session.* Washington, D.C.: U.S. Government Printing Office. A substantial array of opinions is expressed both on the effectiveness (or lack thereof) of Turkish opium control and the prospects of improving that effectiveness in the future. ^Middle\East ^Turkey ^Opiates ^Drug\Control\Policies\Effectiveness

1788. U.S. Congress, House Committee on the Judiciary, Subcommittee on Crime (1982). Hearing. "Forfeiture in Drug Cases." *Ninety-Seventh Congress, First and Second Sessions.* Washington, D.C.: U.S. Government Printing Office. Narcotics laws, organized crime, and forfeiture as a means of deterrence in the United States. Three bills dealing with forfeiture in drug cases were before the committee. Both the bills and the hearings were designed to deal with perceived problems with forfeiture and with important initiatives in dealing with drug cases. There were three issues: the degree to which profits or proceeds from criminal conduct should not be allowed to be available for enterprises, criminal or otherwise; the degree to which the federal government should demonstrate a greater commitment to the use of forfeiture as a tool in its war on crime; and the degree to which the specific bills in committee, or laws on the book, dealt adequately with legal and constitutional issues posed by forfeiture legislation and practice. ^United\States ^Asset\Forfeiture ^Drug\Control\Policies ^Organized\Crime ^Legislation

1789. —— (1985). Hearing. "Defining Customs Waters for Certain Drug Offenses." *Ninety-Ninth Congress, First Session.* Washington, D.C.: U.S. Government Printing Office. Discusses the provisions of the Marijuana on the High Seas Act, which enables the Coast Guard to interdict vessels trafficking in drugs even if outside territorial waters. ^United\States ^Cannabis ^Interdiction ^Legislation ^Coast\Guard

1790. —— (1985). Hearing. "Designer Drugs." *Ninety-Ninth Congress, First Session.* Washington, D.C.: U.S. Government Printing Office. A new comprehensive crime control act (of 1984) gave the Drug Enforcement Agency greater discretion in prosecuting drug substances that, at any given moment, may not be on a "controlled list." Convictions have been obtained of chemists under this emergency authority. The product in question is "fentanyl analogs." The contributors to the hearing discuss the incidence of and problems associated with the distribution of such analogs, and law enforcement efforts to control that distribution. ^United\States ^Drug\Traffic ^Designer\Drugs ^Law\Enforcement

1791. —— (1985). Hearing. "Military Cooperation with Civilian Law Enforcement." *Ninety Ninth Congress, First Session.* Washington, D.C.: U.S. Government Printing Office. The committee met to examine one of the United States' newest strategies to fight drug traffickers, namely, the cooperative efforts of the country's armed forces. The chairman noted that despite the involvement of almost every branch of the armed services, the supply of illegal narcotics continues. Should the military role be expanded? Solicited testimony sought to give an answer. ^United\States ^Law\Enforcement ^Military ^Drug\Control\Policies\Effectiveness

1792. —— (1986). Hearing. "Narcotics Assistance to State and Local Law Enforcement." *Ninety-Ninth Congress, Second Session.* Washington, D.C.: U.S. Government Printing Office. In spite of the Drug Enforcement Administration's forfeiting drug assets valued at $137 million in fiscal year 1985, there still appears to be no appreciable decrease in drug trafficking in the country. The committee met to consider "every conceivable approach within our capacity with the hope, as it springs eternal, that we can someday come upon the right key to this cancer called drug trafficking" (p. 1). Two members of Congress had raised new proposals; the committee met to consider them. Testimony received was quite diverse. ^United\States ^Asset\Forfeiture ^DEA ^Drug\Control\Policies\Effectiveness ^Proffered\Solutions

1793. U.S. Congress, House Committee Report (1986). "Reorganization to Combat Drug Trafficking and Drug Abuse." *Ninety Ninth Congress, Second Session.* Washington, D.C.: U.S. Government Printing Office. The House, finding that the federal government's efforts to combat drug abuse had been hampered by divided responsibility among numerous entities within the executive branch, wished to require the president to submit recommendations for legislation to reorganize the executive branch's drug-related activities. Discussion of that mandate, with sectional analyses, and a proposed amendment. ^United\States ^Drug\Control\Policies ^Bureaucracy ^Legislation

1794. U.S. Congress, House Report of a Staff Study Mission to Peru, Bolivia, Colombia, and Mexico, November 19 to December 18, 1988 to the Committee on Foreign Affairs (1989). "U.S. Narcotics Control Programs in Peru, Bolivia, Colombia, and Mexico: An Update." *One Hundred First Congress, First Session.* Washington, D.C.: U.S. Government Printing Office. From a staff study mission in 1988 to the countries mentioned, the report briefly summarizes existing conditions. Peru, the largest coca producer in the world, is sliding into economic and political chaos; its efforts in all drug related programs are insufficient and, usually, largely ineffective. The roles of the various U.S. agencies involved in Peru's antidrug efforts are reviewed. Bolivia's new "coca law" is discussed. Some hopeful signs emerge. In Colombia, "the narcotics trade pervades and impacts on the entire Colombian system. It has not only paralyzed the judicial system, it has permeated all levels of society" (p. 22). Mexico remains the largest single source of marijuana and heroin entering the United States. Cocaine transshipments are also increasing. A major new trend is the involvement of Colombians in the drug trade through Mexico. In each country's case, the respective U.S. agencies operating therein are discussed. Policy recommendations are tendered. ^United\States ^Latin\America ^Peru ^Producers ^Bureaucracy ^Bolivia ^Economics ^Legislation ^Colombia ^Consequences\Social ^Consequences\Political ^Consequences\Economic ^Mexico ^Drug\Control\Policies\Effectiveness

1795. U.S. Congress, House Select Committee on Narcotics Abuse and Control (1977). Hearing. "Decriminalization of Marihuana." *Ninety-Fifth Congress, First Session.* Washington, D.C.: U.S. Government Printing Office. As expected, the testimony given is wide ranging and contradictory. More than fifty statements are recorded. Comparisons are made with laws and regulations of other countries, and specific federal decriminalization proposals are advanced. Note is made of the California law that gives partial decriminalization. ^United\States ^Cannabis ^Legalization ^Decriminalization

1796. ——— (1979). Hearing. "Health Implications of Paraquat-Contaminated Marihuana." *Ninety-Sixth Congress, First Session.* Washington, D.C.: U.S. Government Printing Office. Toxicology of paraquat-sprayed marihuana. Testimony from staff members from the Select Committee on Narcotics Abuse and Control, the Center for Disease Control, the Department of Agriculture, the Research Triangle Institute, Mitre Corporation, Chevron Chemical Corporation, and the Imperial Chemical Industries of the United Kingdom. Medical research personnel also testified. The purpose of the hearing was to ascertain the health consequences of the herbicide paraquat in domestic agricultural use and its implications as the principal substance for the eradication of marijuana in the United States' international narcotics control program. A National Institute of Drug Abuse Final Report is cited: If a person smokes five marijuana cigarettes every day for one year, with each cigarette containing 500 parts per million of paraquat, permanent lung fibrosis could develop (p. 5). ^Cannabis ^Crop\Eradication ^Herbicides ^Health

1797. ——— (1979). Hearing. "The Scope of Drug Abuse in Puerto Rico—Supply and Demand Reduction." *Ninety-Sixth Congress, First Session.* Washington, D.C.: U.S. Government Printing Office. Many spontaneous and prepared testimonies are given in this volume. The meetings were held in the Commonwealth of Puerto Rico, and were designed to examine questions about the supply of narcotics and the U.S. federal government's response to the demand for them. Many of the testifiers concentrated principally on questions of law enforcement, narcotics trafficking, and the availability of dangerous drugs on the island. Additionally, issues of treatment and prevention of drug abuse were raised. ^Caribbean ^Puerto\Rico ^Drug\Traffic ^Drug\Control\Policies ^Drug\Use ^Supply

1798. ———— (1980). Hearing. "Is Paraquat-Sprayed Marihuana Harmful or Not?" *Ninety-Sixth Congress, Second Session.* Washington, D.C.: U.S. Government Printing Office. Harmful physiological effects of paraquat on humans? The answer has been yes and no, depending on source and, apparently, vested interest. Totally contrary statements had been made by the United States Department of Health Education and Welfare and the World Health Organization. Disturbed by the seemingly contradictory conclusions of these two groups (HEW suggesting there was no need for alarm and WHO arguing the opposite), this committee was convened to discuss the two separate judgments. Part of the purpose of the hearing was to suggest that the World Health Organization's model created overconcern for possible side effects of paraquat-sprayed marihuana. ^Cannabis ^Crop\Eradication ^Herbicides ^Health ^WHO

1799. ———— (1980). House Select Committee on Narcotics Abuse and Control. Report. "The Use of Paraquat to Eradicate Illicit Marihuana Crops and the Health Implications of Paraquat-Contaminated Marihuana on the U.S. Market." *Ninety-Sixth Congress, Second Session.* Washington, D.C.: U.S. Government Printing Office. The hearing was held to determine the health implications of paraquat-contaminated marijuana (potentially resulting from aerial marijuana crop eradication programs) to persons who may use or consume the sprayed drug. While great concern was raised in the United States that the U.S. government was sponsoring a program that would be deleterious to its citizens (the spraying of marijuana by paraquat), none of that concern was sufficient to convince the Mexican government that it should cease spraying its fields. Thus, efforts were made to develop a "marker" so that sprayed marijuana would be detectable by those who smoked it. The efforts to develop a marker have not been successful. In general, testimony confirmed that when ingested or inhaled in concentrated form, paraquat is a potent pulmonary toxin. Inhalation is a significantly greater health risk than ingestion. When inhaled in this form, minute quantities (in the microgram range) can cause fibrosis of the lung. No suitable alternative herbicide for marijuana has been developed and, in any event, it is likely that any health effects associated with paraquat would also be potentially associated with any new herbicide. Inasmuch as the Mexican government will continue to spray with paraquat, this committee thought that it ought to recommend further efforts to develop a marker agent which, when available, should be accompanied by broad education programs designed to assist users in identifying sprayed marijuana. ^United\States ^Cannabis ^Crop\Eradication ^Herbicides ^Health

1800. ———— (1981). Hearing. "Impact of Federal Budget Cuts on Local Narcotics Law Enforcement." Hearing. *Ninety-Seventh Congress, First Session.* Washington, D.C.: U.S. Government Printing Office. The hearing was triggered by concern that the budgetary cuts of Congress would have a serious adverse impact on the enforcement of federal law. Withdrawal of federal assistance to local and state governments might also have more serious impact on the enforcement of local laws. All of this could adversely affect the country's ability to stem the influx of drugs into communities. ^United\States ^Law\Enforcement ^Economics

1801. ———— (1982). "Health Questions about Marihuana." *Ninety-Seventh Congress, Second Session.* Washington, D.C.: U.S. Government Printing Office. The two articles in this document were prepared in response to solicitations for information about marijuana hazards. The first article, "Answering Questions about Marijuana Use," first appeared in the May 30, 1980, issue of *Patient Care*, a journal circulated to more than 108,000 physicians. It was written by Rana Rottenberg with the assistance of Drs. Ingrid L. Lantner, James E. O'Brien, and Harold M. Voth. The second article, "Marijuana: Its Health Hazards and Therapeutic Potentials," was published on October 16, 1981, in the *Journal of the American Medical Association*, under the signature of the AMA's council of scientific affairs. It is based on three council reports that were adopted by the AMA House of Delegates. Both articles relate the status of current research to statistical probabilities of marijuana's deleterious effect of psychosocial and psychomotor performance. There are technical discussions on the effects of the drug on the brain, on its use with other drugs, and on its therapeutic potentials. Guidelines are given on how to help the chronic user. Includes a bibliography. ^Cannabis ^Reviews ^Bibliographies ^Consequences\Health ^Treatment ^Consequences\Neurological ^Consequences\Psychological

1802. —— (1983). Hearing. "Domestic Cultivation of Marihuana." *Ninety-Eighth Congress, First Session*. Washington, D.C.: U.S. Government Printing Office. This hearing consisted of two days of testimony from representatives ranging from the Select Committee on Narcotics Abuse and Control to the Bureau of Land Management. Numerous state officials from Oregon and California also testified. The issue was the significant and increasing share of domestically grown cannabis being consumed in the United States and the questions about the roles of the federal, state, and local agencies in attacking this problem. ^United\States ^Cannabis ^Production ^Drug\Control\Policies

1803. —— (1983). Hearing. "Effects of Drug Trafficking and Drug Abuse in the South Florida Community." *Ninety-Eighth Congress, First Session*. Washington, D.C.: U.S. Government Printing Office. While bulk marijuana trafficking through South Florida was down at the time of this hearing, it was noted that the traffickers had simply shifted operations up the east and along the gulf coast. Record seizures were noted as far north as Maine. The committee met to gauge the continuing effects of drug trafficking and abuse in South Florida and to learn what needed to be done to prevent dangerous drugs from reaching the Florida shores. Focus on interdiction. ^United\States ^Florida ^Drug\Traffic ^Interdiction ^Society

1804. —— (1984). Hearing. "Drugs—The Effects on the Black Community." *Ninety-Eighth Congress, Second Session*. Washington, D.C.: U.S. Government Printing Office. Drug use among Afro-Americans and control of narcotics in the United States. The U.S. Congressional Black Caucus urged a hearing on the effect of drugs on the black community. Testimony is received from church and school officials. Arguments are presented for continued vigorous enforcement against supply on the assumption that lack of efforts there and/or legalization would cause the number of cocaine users among the black community to rise. Deleterious health effects are noted. Negative impacts on school performance are described. Costs to employers are discussed, with the Northrop Corporation reporting a savings of nearly $20,000 a year on each employee that has gone through its alcohol abuse and drug addiction program (p. 31). The effect on violence is noted among the black community (p. 31ff). Considerable discussion of economic impact on life-time earnings and other factors of those who drop out of school in part for drug addiction (pp. 37ff). Social distortions within the black community as a consequence of drug dealing are catalogued (pp. 45ff). ^United\States ^Drug\Use ^Minorities ^Economics ^Society ^Decriminalization\Critique ^Consequences\Economic ^Workplace ^Consequences\Educational ^Consequences\Social

1805. —— (1984). "International Narcotics Control Study Missions to Latin America and Jamaica (August 6-21), 1983 and Hawaii, Hong Kong, Thailand, Burma, Pakistan, Turkey, and Italy (January 4-22, 1984)." *Ninety-*

Eighth Congress, First Session. Washington, D.C.: U.S. Government Printing Office. Within Latin America, the group visited Mexico, Peru, Bolivia, Colombia, and Jamaica. The publication describes the field visits and the findings, and outlines the recommendations that were derived from those findings. Considerable production and distribution data on cocaine, marijuana, and heroin, as well as interdiction and eradication information, are included for each country. ^Latin\America ^Southeast\Asia ^Turkey ^Italy ^United\States ^Drug\Control\Policies ^Production\Statistics ^Pakistan ^Burma ^Thailand ^Hong\Kong ^Hawaii ^Jamaica ^Mexico ^Peru ^Bolivia ^Colombia ^Caribbean ^Golden\Triangle ^Southwest\Asia ^Europe

1806. ———— (1984). Report. "Issues Affecting Federal, State, and Local Efforts to Combat Drug Trafficking and Drug Abuse." *Ninety-Eighth Congress, Second Session*. Washington, D.C.: U.S. Government Printing Office. There has been a large dichotomy between local perspectives on drug problems and the federal government's response to local needs. Federal government representatives are satisfied with the job they are doing, but local officials are highly frustrated and critical. This committee attempts to sort through the issues and find ways by which the gap or the dichotomy may be reduced. Specifically, it examines findings and recommendations gathered from numerous hearings, and proposes concrete actions that must be taken if the federal strategy is to work. ^United\States ^Drug\Control\Policies\Critique ^Politics

1807. ———— (1985). "Cocaine Abuse and the Federal Response." *Ninety-Ninth Congress, First Session*. Washington, D.C.: Government Printing Office. There appeared before the Select Committee a panel of former cocaine users who testified in a frank and candid way about their problem. Professionals also testified; and testimony was received from the administration. Focus: "How to get people off drugs." ^United\States ^Cocaine ^Treatment ^Prevention

1808. ———— (1985). Hearing. "The Effect of Drug Abuse on the Black Community." *Ninety-Ninth Congress, First Session*. Washington, D.C.: U.S. Government Printing Office. In earlier reports the committee had received "shocking testimony" of the relationship between the drug problem and the educational and social "dropout problem." This was focused on students. This volume continues that discussion with a specific ethnic focus on the black community. ^United\States ^Drug\Use ^Youth ^Minorities ^Consequences\Educational

1809. ———— (1985). Hearing. "Heroin and Cocaine Trafficking and the Relationship Between Intravenous Drug Use and AIDS." *Ninety-Ninth Congress, First Session*. Washington, D.C.: Government Printing Office. Congressmen, medical doctors, and treatment analysts and practitioners testify in this hearing. Noting that 34 percent of all AIDS cases in New York City involved intravenous drug users, the document shows that New York and New Jersey account for approximately 80 percent of the drug-abusing AIDS cases. A disproportionate share of those involved are minorities. The description of the dilemma and what should and can be done about it are the subjects of this volume. ^United\States ^Cocaine ^Heroin ^Health ^AIDS ^New\York ^New\Jersey

1810. ———— (1985). Hearing. "International Narcotics Control." *Ninety-Ninth Congress, First Session*. Washington, D.C.: U.S. Government Printing Office. The various contributors (testifiers) at this brief hearing concentrate on a review of programs internationally, in particular those sponsored by the United States, to control drug trafficking. ^United\States ^Drug\Control\Policies

1811. ———— (1986). House Select Committee on Narcotics Abuse and Control. Hearing. "Drug Abuse and Trafficking Along the Southwest Border

(El Paso)." *Ninety-Ninth Congress, Second Session*. Washington, D.C.: U.S. Government Printing Office. This is another in the series of hearings held by the committee in the Southwest (El Paso, Tucson, San Diego) and in Mexico about drug trafficking problems. Mexico is a significant source of illicit narcotics entering the United States, and the hearings were held to try to determine if additional detection and interdiction procedures or policies could be devised. Testimony was received by witnesses from the El Paso police department, officials from Mexico, and from the Drug Enforcement Administration. Several private citizens also testified. ^United\States ^Latin\America ^Mexico ^Drug\Traffic ^Drug\Control\Policies\Effectiveness ^Supply

1812. ———— (1986). "Drug Abuse and Trafficking along the Southwest Border (Tucson)." *Ninety-Ninth Congress, Second Session*. Washington, D.C.: U.S. Government Printing Office. This hearing was conducted as part of the committee's eight-day mission covering the border and going into Mexico. Testimony was received from local police, from the Drug Enforcement Administration, from the Border Patrol, the Customs Service, officials of public high schools, the Arizona Department of Education, and others. In general, things are getting worse and are not likely, in the short term, to get better. There is a description of how the trafficking occurs, and who does it. ^Latin\America ^Mexico ^United\States ^Drug\Control\Policies\Effectiveness ^Drug\Traffic ^Law\Enforcement ^Supply

1813. ———— (1986). Hearing. "Drug Abuse in the Workplace." *Ninety-Ninth Congress, Second Session*. Washington, D.C.: U.S. Government Printing Office. U.S. law and legislation regarding drugs and international cooperation for the control of narcotics. The committee, through its hearings, was trying to find out how the public and private sectors were dealing with drug abuse in the workplace, especially as it related to the controversial issue of urine testing. It is stated that drug abuse in the workplace is burgeoning as never before, and that its impact on society is not only growing but is deleterious. There are no uniform federal guidelines or federal strategies available to deal with the matter, even though many companies have formulated their own response. Perceptions of issues and policy options. ^United\States ^Drug\Use ^Drug\Testing ^Workplace ^Consequences\Economic

1814. ———— (1986). Hearing. "Drug Education, Part II." *Ninety-Ninth Congress, Second Session*. Washington, D.C.: U.S. Government Printing Office. The star witness was the Reverend Jesse Jackson. This follows on the previous day's hearing that starred Secretary of Education William Bennett. Unless demand is turned off, the future looks bleak. ^United\States ^Prevention ^Youth ^Consequences\Educational ^Demand

1815. ———— (1986). Hearing. "Drug Trafficking and Abuse along the Southwest Border (San Diego)." *Ninety-Ninth Congress, Second Session*. Washington, D.C.: U.S. Government Printing Office. The borders with Mexico are out of control, and inquiries need to be made about rectifying possibilities, including making demands on the president of Mexico. The goal was to try to find out how to get a more cooperative working relationship with the government of Mexico and how better to support the law enforcement officials in California. Testimony was received from California's attorney general, from San Diego County's district attorney, from Drug Enforcement Administration officers, and from other official and private individuals. ^United\States ^Latin\America ^Mexico ^Drug\Control\Policies\Effectiveness ^Drug\Traffic ^Law\Enforcement ^Supply

1816. ———— (1986). Hearing. "The Federal War on Drugs: Past, Present, and Future." *Ninety-Ninth Congress, Second Session*. Washington, D.C.: Government Printing Office. Those who testified came from the Department of State's Bureau of International Narcotics Matters, the Department of the Treasury's

Southwest Border Committee on Drug Policy, the Department of Defense's Task Force on Drugs, the Attorney General's Office of the Department of Justice, the U.S. Coast Guard, the National Institute on Drug Abuse, the Department of Education, the National Governor's Association, the National Organization of Black Law Enforcement Executives, the Addiction Research and Treatment Corporation, and others. There is a general description of the problem, and a call for greater work in both supplying and consuming countries. ^United\States ^Drug\Control\Policies\History ^Demand ^Supply

1817. —— (1986). Report. "Latin American Study Missions Concerning International Narcotics Problems." *Ninety-Ninth Congress, Second Session.* Washington, D.C.: U.S. Government Printing Office. The investigating committee reports on its visits to seven countries: Colombia, Ecuador, Peru, Bolivia, Brazil, Argentina, and Uruguay. The narcotic production and the trafficking infrastructures in Colombia, Peru, and Bolivia are expanding into Ecuador, Brazil, and Argentina. Wild coca in the Amazon jungles of Brazil is now being cultivated. Brazil and Argentina are the sources for much of the industrial chemicals used in cocaine production. Argentina has cocaine laboratories in the northeast section of the country. Information on planting, production, and politics are included for each country. ^Latin\America ^Colombia ^Ecuador ^Peru ^Bolivia ^Brazil ^Argentina ^Uruguay ^Coca ^Cocaine ^Production ^Precursor\Chemicals ^Drug\Traffic ^Politics

1818. —— (1986). Hearing. "Panama." *Ninety-Ninth Congress, Second Session.* Washington, D.C.: U.S. Government Printing Office. A continuation of the discussion on General Noriega's involvement in drugs and illicit money and the degree to which that is fostered officially and unofficially in Panama. There is some focus on corruption in this hearing. ^Latin\America ^Panama ^Money\Laundering ^Drug\Traffic ^Politics ^Consequences\Corruption

1819. —— (1986). Hearing. "Southwest Border Hearings El Paso, Texas—Tucson, Arizona—San Diego, California and Mexico Trip Report Nogales—Mexico City—Culiacán." *Ninety-Ninth Congress, Second Session.* Washington, D.C.: U.S. Government Printing Office. From January 12–19, 1986, this committee carried out hearings and conducted a study mission along the U.S.-Mexican border and in Mexico City. Competence in the Mexican government's narcotics control program has been diminishing. There has been a lack of progress in the investigation to the kidnapping, brutal torture, and murder of DEA special agent Enrique Camarena. The committee encouraged enhanced detection and eradication efforts in Mexico. The inability to make a dent in the traffic has caused law enforcement officers both to call for additional help and to intensify demands that federal efforts be made to educate the American people on the dangers of drug abuse and thus to decrease demand for the substances. ^ Latin\America ^ Mexico ^ United\States ^ Drug\Control\Policies ^ Drug\Control\Policies\Effectiveness ^ Law\Enforcement\Critique

1820. —— (1986). "Trafficking and Abuse of 'Crack' in New York City." *Ninety-Ninth Congress, Second Session.* Washington, D.C.: Government Printing Office. Discussion of trafficking and abuse of crack in New York. Numerous entities, private and public, are represented. ^United\States ^Cocaine ^Crack ^Drug\Use ^Drug\Traffic ^New\York

1821. —— (1986). Hearing. "U.S. Narcotics Control Efforts in Mexico and on the Southwest Border." *Ninety-Ninth Congress, Second Session.* Washington, D.C.: U.S. Government Printing Office. Testimony not only by representatives of the Bureau of International Narcotics Matters and the Drug Enforcement Administration, but also the Coast Guard, the Custom's Service, the Border Patrol, the Army

National Guard, and the Department of Defense Task Force on Drug Enforcement. The background for this hearing was a 1986 select committee study mission on the southwest border to the cities of El Paso, Tucson, and San Diego. The commission also met with officials in Mexico. The conclusion was that drug trafficking from Mexico to the United States is out of control; U.S. borders are out of control. ^Latin\America ^Mexico ^United\States ^Drug\Traffic ^Drug\Control\Policies\Effectiveness

1822. —— (1987). Hearing. "Cocaine Babies." *One Hundredth Congress, First Session.* Washington, D.C.: U.S. Government Printing Office. What impact is the cocaine epidemic sweeping the United States having on newborn children of drug abusers? The matter is serious, testifiers concluded, and they addressed means by which counteractive measures could be taken. Rapid increases in the numbers of cocaine-addicted babies being seen in intensive care units in the hospitals are noted, and discussions of the costs of this problem are viewed as being staggering. For example, $100,000 per baby is viewed as not being an unreal figure for care in a new-born intensive care unit. Related to the problem are subsequent child abuse (and the costs to society for dealing with this), the need for and the costs of providing family counseling, and so forth. Also discussed is the nature of cocaine addiction in infants. ^United\States ^Cocaine ^Crack ^Health ^Consequences\Fetuses ^Fetuses ^Consequences\Economic ^Parenting ^Consequences\Children ^Consequences\Family

1823. —— (1987). Hearing. "Colombian Drug Trafficking and Control." *One Hundredth Congress, First Session.* Washington, D.C.: U.S. Government Printing Office. Discusses the difficult situation in Colombia wherein the government had been compromised by narcotrafficking into declaring a "truce" in a so-called FARC or rebel territory. ^Latin\America ^Colombia ^Drug\Traffic ^Politics ^Insurgents

1824. —— (1987). Hearing. "Drug Abuse Prevention in America's Schools." *One Hundredth Congress, First Session.* Washington, D.C.: U.S. Government Printing Office. A principal witness at this hearing was Education Secretary William Bennett [later to become the U.S. "drug czar"], who testified about the Department of Education's role in drug-abuse education. The focus was on "turning off the demand," which responds to several people's observations that it is the only route left open to America. ^United\States ^Drug\Use ^Prevention ^Youth ^Demand

1825. —— (1987). Hearing. "Drug Interdiction." *One Hundredth Congress, First Session.* Washington, D.C.: U.S Government Printing Office. Representatives are heard from the Attorney General's Office, the National Drug Policy Board, U.S. Customs, and a minority statement from the House Select Committee on Narcotics Abuse and Control. ^United\States ^Interdiction

1826. —— (1987). Hearing. "Intravenous Drug Use and AIDS: The Impact on the Black Community." *One Hundredth Congress, First Session.* Washington, D.C.: U.S. Government Printing Office. Testimony at this hearing is from representatives from the National Institute on Drug Abuse, the Public Health Service's AIDS coordinator, the President's Commission on HIV epidemic, the Federal Bureau of Prisons, and various congressmen and private citizens. Among the victims of AIDS, the black community seems to be overrepresented. It is generally believed that through the common sharing of needles, syringes, swabs, and other drug-related instruments contaminated with AIDS–infected blood that the virus is being rapidly transmitted through drug users and AIDS victims. Is this observation valid? And, if so, what might be done about these circumstances? Testifiers attempt to get at these and related questions. ^United\States ^Heroin ^AIDS ^Minorities ^NIDA ^Consequences\Health

1827. ——— (1987). Hearing. "Narcotics Control in Mexico." *One Hundredth Congress, First Session*. Washington, D.C.: U.S. Government Printing Office. In this hearing the committee wanted to know from the executive branch about the amount of drugs being produced in Mexico, the amount being processed, the amount of cocaine being transshipped into the United States, the amount being interdicted, trends in all of the above, and whether there had been an increase in corruption in Mexico. If so, had that affected the ability of the countries to deal with drug traffickers? Is there a plan? Does anyone have a plan? If so, what is it? ^Mexico ^Drug\Traffic ^Production ^Latin\America ^Refining ^Interdiction ^Drug\Control\Policies\Effectiveness ^Consequences\Corruption

1828. ——— (1987). Hearing. "Narcotics Trafficking through John F. Kennedy Airport." *One Hundredth Congress, First Session*. Washington, D.C.: U.S. Government Printing Office. There has been an explosion of both heroin and cocaine trafficking through the Kennedy Airport, and it appears that there were a number of lapses in airport security, perhaps some even intentional, that facilitated the use of Kennedy as a point of entry. What should be done? Recommendations were made. Most of the testifiers direct their attention to answering this question. ^United\States ^Drug\Traffic ^Aircraft

1829. ——— (1987). Report. "1986 Major City Survey on Drug Arrests and Seizures." *One Hundredth Congress, First Session*. Washington, D.C.: U.S. Government Printing Office. The House Committee on Narcotics Abuse and Control had completed a survey of thirty-nine major cities indexed concerning narcotics arrests and seizures in 1986 to determine the severity of the drug problem throughout the United States. Their findings, despite assertions frequently voiced to the contrary, demonstrate that the drug problem is exceedingly severe. Most arrests in the thirty-nine cities for 1986 were for cocaine sale or possession. Second was marijuana, and third was heroin. There is some discussion about the cost of this to society in addition to the individuals using the drug. It is suggested that drugs and crime go hand in hand. Also, their use is associated with the advance of the deadly disease AIDS (involved in intravenous drug use). Statistics from the cities studied are reviewed. ^United\States ^Law\Enforcement ^Statistics ^Drug\Use ^Consequences\Economic ^Crime ^AIDS

1830. ——— (1987). Report. "1987 Update on Drugs and Dropouts." *One Hundredth Congress, First Session*. Washington, D.C.: U.S. Government Printing Office. Elementary and secondary schools are confronted with a serious drug problem. The dropout problem is particularly serious among minority students. There is a definite correlation between drugs and dropping out, but the line of causation is unclear. Gangs are emerging, and they are involved in narcotics trafficking. There is increasing drug abuse by pregnant teenagers. And, despite the clear evidence of drug abuse among teenagers and the relationship between that use and dropping out, some school officials and especially parents deny there is a problem. Prevention and education are the keys to demand reduction, and greater effective communication between state and local officials and the private sector is required. ^United\States ^Drug\Use ^Youth ^Prevention ^Consequences\Educational ^Consequences\Fetuses ^Proffered\Solutions

1831. ——— (1988). Report. "Annual Report for the Year 1988." *One Hundredth Congress, Second Session*. Washington, D.C.: U.S. Government Printing Office. An update on drug trafficking and abuse in 1988, including a discussion of AIDS. The Anti-Drug Abuse Act of 1988 is reviewed, and the committee's activities for the year are chronicled. Considerable discussion related to the committee's legalization hearings held in September 1988. ^United\States ^Drug\Traffic ^AIDS ^Drug\Use ^Legislation ^Legalization

1832. ——— (1988). Hearing. "Drug Legalization—Catastrophe for Black Americans." *One Hundredth Congress, Second Session*. Washington, D.C.: U.S. Government Printing Office. In this hearing testimony was received from political and law enforcement personnel from the president of the AIDS Commission and from the Council of Churches. Those who propose that drugs be legalized have focused on only one part of the problem: the assumption that law enforcement has failed. There is, therefore, a general call for better law enforcement measures as well as a discussion of many of the ills that could befall a society that legalizes what are now illegal drugs. ^United\States ^Society ^Minorities ^P\S\Legalization\Critique

1833. ——— (1988). Hearing. "Legalization of Illicit Drugs—Part II." *One Hundredth Congress, Second Session*. Washington, D.C.: U.S. Government Printing Office. Impromptu statements from members of Congress and testimony from academicians, medical clinicians, and members of drug treatment centers. The whole range of viewpoints on this issue is presented. ^United\States ^Legalization

1834. ——— (1988). Hearing. "National Drug Policy Board Strategy Plans." *One Hundredth Congress, Second Session*. Washington, D.C.: U.S. Government Printing Office. In 1987 the Policy Board had under review federal drug-abuse prevention and enforcement strategies being proposed by various agencies. It had prepared, for this hearing, strategy documents that included recommendations to the Congress for policy, regulatory, and statutory changes as well as resource adjustments or enhancements. International, intelligence, investigation, interdiction, prosecution, education, prevention, and treatment are discussed. ^United\States ^National\Drug\Policy\Board ^Proffered\Solutions

1835. ——— (1988). Report. "Study Mission to Korea, Thailand, Burma, Singapore, Malaysia, Indonesia, and Hawaii (January 14–25, 1988)." *One Hundredth Congress, Second Session*. Washington, D.C.: U.S. Government Printing Office. The Select Committee on Narcotics Abuse and Control (SCNAC) conducted a study mission of opium, heroin, and marijuana producing and trafficking nations in Southeast Asia in January 1988. Progress in interdiction and eradication notwithstanding, the cultivation, processing, and trafficking of narcotic drugs remains at critical levels in Southeast Asia. Additional means will have to be undertaken, for example, in the control of money laundering. The committee urged forfeiture of assets and legislation against conspiracies. Specific findings and recommendations are given for each of the countries listed. ^Southeast\Asia ^Drug\Traffic ^Production ^Money\Laundering ^Drug\Control\Policies\Effectiveness

1836. ——— (1988). Hearing. "U.S. Foreign Policy and International Narcotics Control." *One Hundredth Congress, Second Session*. Washington, D.C.: U.S. Government Printing Office. This hearing followed on the heels of Panama's General Noriega's having been indicted for drug trafficking. Testimony was received from the U.S. Attorney General from the southern district of Florida and also from the District of Columbia. ^Panama ^United\States ^Latin\America ^Traffickers ^Consequences\Foreign\Policy

1837. ——— (1988). Hearing. "U.S. Foreign Policy and International Narcotics Control—Part II." *One Hundredth Congress, Second Session*. Washington, D.C.: U.S. Government Printing Office. In this hearing, testimony was received from representatives of the National Security Council, the Secretary of State for InterAmerican Affairs, the U.S. Customs Service, the Bureau of International Narcotics Matters, and the Drug Enforcement Administration. The committee convened this session at a time when many people were saying that drugs are a more serious threat to the national security of the United States than is Communism. There was considerable concern that U.S. foreign policy was counterproductive with respect to the drug problem. A general review of many countries being held hostage by drug trafficking is entered. ^United\States ^Drug\Control\Policies\Effectiveness ^Politics ^Consequences\Foreign\Policy ^Consequences\National\Security

1838. ——— (1987). Hearing. "Federal Antidrug Abuse Policies, 1987." *One Hundredth Congress, First Session.* Washington, D.C.: U.S. Government Printing Office. Another in the numerous hearings held on the federal government's antidrug abuse efforts. This hearing focused on the National Drug Policy Board—its functions and operations. The board, created in 1985, was to oversee the federal government's drug-enforcement activities. Subsequently it was expanded to include drug-abuse prevention and health programs as well. Every cabinet level department except commerce is represented on the drug policy board. Has the board been effective in its task? The hearing was held to examine that question. ^United\States ^Drug\Control\Policies\Effectiveness ^National\Drug\Policy\Board

1839. ——— (1988). Hearing. "HUD Programs to Combat Drug Abuse in Public Housing." *One Hundredth Congress, Second Session.* Washington, D.C.: U.S. Government Printing Office. Widespread drug abuse has rendered much public housing a "war zone." Projects have become unsafe, unsanitary, and unwanted because of, among other things, the drug traffickers. The hearing examines the nature of the difficulty that public housing residents have with respect to drug issues and how the federal government could help. ^United\States ^Drug\Use ^Public\Housing

1840. U.S. Congress, House Subcommittee on Coast Guard and Navigation of the Committee on Merchant Marine and Fisheries (1988). Hearing. "'Zero Tolerance' Drug Policy and Confiscation of Property." *One Hundredth Congress, Second Session.* Washington, D.C.: U.S. Government Printing Office. Efforts to cut off the supply of drugs cannot be abandoned, but the United States cannot rely primarily on this defense to solve the drug abuse problem. The question of drug demand must be addressed. It is time to make users accountable for all the havoc being created by the trade. This is the aim of "zero tolerance," "a rigorous enforcement policy recently adopted by federal law officers to combat illicit drug use and its source." The hearings looked into the implementation of the policy. Discussions of a policy of "constructive seizure" were made for the protection of the innocent owner or captain of a vessel subject to seizure. ^United\States ^Law\Enforcement ^Asset\Forfeiture\Critique ^Coast\Guard ^Supply ^Demand

1841. U.S. Congress, House Subcommittee on Crime of the Committee of the Judiciary (1983). Hearing. "Drug Production and Trafficking in Latin America and the Caribbean." *Ninety-Eighth Congress, First Session.* Washington, D.C.: U.S. Government Printing Office. Country information on Bolivia, Peru, and Colombia; comments are made on Brazil, Jamaica, Belize, and Cuba. The U.S. role in international narcotics control is outlined and the consequences of certain policies (e.g. eradication) for producing countries are considered. ^Latin\America ^United\States ^Drug\Traffic ^Drug\Control\Policies ^Consequences\Drug\Control\Policies ^Bolivia ^Peru ^Colombia ^Brazil ^Jamaica ^Belize ^Cuba ^Caribbean

1842. ——— (1984). Hearings. "Use of Casinos to Launder Proceeds of Drug Trafficking and Organized Crime." *Ninety-Eighth Congress, Second Session.* Washington, D.C.: U.S. Government Printing Office. Have New Jersey's casinos been appropriated by organized crime and drug traffickers to launder the profits of their activities? No fingers were being pointed or accusations made against the casinos, but it appeared that they were, nevertheless, being appropriated to the advantage of criminal elements. It is noteworthy that the casino industry declined to testify, even though New Jersey's Casino Control Commission provided their facilities for the hearing. ^United\States ^Money\Laundering ^Organized\Crime

1843. —— (1986). Hearing. "Mail Order Drug Paraphernalia Control Act." *Ninety-Ninth Congress, Second Session.* Washington, D.C.: U.S. Government Printing Office. Aside from discussing the act itself, this document includes extensive information about the kinds of paraphernalia available through mail-order catalogues. ^United\States ^Drug\Control\Policies ^Legislation ^Drug\Traffic

1844. U.S. Congress, House Subcommittee on Financial Institutions Supervision, Regulation and Insurance of the Committee on Banking, Finance and Urban Affairs (1986). Hearing. "Tax Evasion, Drug Trafficking and Money Laundering as They Involve Financial Institutions." *Ninety-Ninth Congress, Second Session.* Washington, D.C.: U.S. Government Printing Office. A principal witness for the prosecution and a former money launderer, Herb Friedberg, presented a statement followed by a statement from a host of institutional representatives and politicians. The two-day hearing produced a document of nearly 1,300 pages. ^United\States ^Money\Laundering ^Taxation

1845. U.S. Congress, House Subcommittee on Fiscal Affairs and Health of the Committee on the District of Columbia and the Select Committee on Narcotics Abuse and Control (1988). Joint Oversight Hearing. "National Capital Area—Drug Trafficking." *One Hundredth Congress, Second Session.* Washington, D.C.: U.S. Government Printing Office. The Washington metro area-wide problem of illicit narcotics has increased substantially (allegedly amounting to a nontaxable income of $1.5 billion). Addictive and recreational drug use has increased. There needs to be an intense, long range drug prevention and education program. Criminal organizations also have invaded the area. ^United\States ^Drug\Traffic ^Washington\DC

1846. U.S. Congress, Office of Technology Assessment (1987). *The Border War on Drugs.* Washington, D.C.: U.S. Government Printing Office. Efforts and success of United States narcotic enforcement agents to interdict smuggling and control trafficking in narcotics in the United States. Includes bibliographical references. This report, by the U.S. Government's Office of Technology Assessment, analyzes federal drug interdiction efforts and reports on technological opportunities for future improvement. The study characterizes the drug smuggling problem and the interdiction efforts now in place. Describes technologies potentially available for countering smuggling by various modes—private vessels, private aircraft, land vehicles, commercial carriers, and through official ports of entry. The report also highlights OTA's principal findings: the need for comprehensive design of integrated technological systems, the need for long-range planning for employing technologies, the need for integrated strategies, and the need for data and methods to measure effectiveness. Among the issues not examined are the demand side of the drug problem, international initiatives to control production, investigation and prosecution of drug traffickers, domestic production and distribution of drugs, civil liberty concerns about law enforcement activities, and impacts of drug law enforcement on legitimate commerce or private use of border areas. The key findings include: There is no clear correlation between expenditure levels or efforts devoted to interdiction and the long-term availability of illegal imported drugs in the domestic market; the size, scope, and diversity of the smuggling challenge exceeds current dedication of human and equipment resources; data on smuggling and trafficking and interdiction are inadequate for effective planning and management; responsibilities of the federal drug interdiction agencies are fragmented and overlapping; the value of intelligence is very high for all aspects of drug interdictions; no single technology has been identified that by its addition would solve the drug interdiction problem; and there is a serious lack of support for research, development, tests, and evaluation of new or transferred technologies within all of the drug interdiction agencies. ^United\States ^Interdiction ^Drug\Control\Policies\Critique

1847. U.S. Congress, Senate Caucus on International Narcotics Control and the Congressional Research Service (1987). Report. "Combating International Drug Cartels: Issues for U.S. Policy." *One Hundredth Congress, First Session*. Washington, D.C.: U.S. Government Printing Office. Working document prepared by the Senate Caucus on International Narcotics Control and the Congressional Research Service. Reports seminar proceedings in which participants addressed the characteristics of drug cartels, money laundering and sting operations, domestic drug cultivation and production, efforts in Mexico to combat drug trafficking, and economic analysis regarding prices and programs. Transcription of the discussion period reviews a wide range of subjects. Peter Reuter, senior economist of the Rand Corporation, is featured in special comments as well as a formal paper in the appendix. ^United\States ^Money\Laundering ^Drug\Control\Policies ^Law\Enforcement ^Organized\Crime ^Production ^Economics

1848. _____ (1987). Hearing. "National and International Security Threat of Narcotics Trafficking." *One Hundredth Congress, First Session*. Washington, D.C.: U.S. Government Printing Office. Is it possible that law enforcement officers are being corrupted in the United States, that drug related terrorist activities will become increasingly present there, that Chinese heroin organizations will multiply, that the judicial system will be compromised? Is it possible that an effective response to these imponderables may be given. Many sides of these questions are examined in this brief hearing report. ^United\States ^Drug\Traffic ^Consequences\National\Security ^Consequences\Corruption ^Terrorists

1849. _____ (1987). Report. "The U.N. Draft Convention against Illicit Traffic in Narcotic Drugs and Psychotropic Substances." *One Hundredth Congress, First Session*. Washington, D.C.: U.S. Government Printing Office. The draft convention is a multinational agreement designed to increase the effectiveness of law enforcement efforts against illicit drug trafficking. The means by which this is to be done are a facilitation of eradication, monitoring of chemicals, identifying and seizing illicitly generated proceeds, improving international cooperation, imposing certain requirements on commercial carriers, and preventing illicit traffic. As of the publication (September 1987), the agreement had not been ratified, but was moving along. Some agreement was looked for by late 1988 or early 1989. The United States was keenly pressing for adoption. ^United\Nations ^Drug\Control\Policies ^International\Cooperation ^Treaties

1850. _____ (1987). Report. "Legislation Aimed at Combating International Drug Trafficking and Money Laundering." *One Hundredth Congress, First Session*. Washington, D.C.: U.S. Government Printing Office. Provides an analysis of U.S. statutes aimed at stemming the flow of illicit drugs on the international market. The statutes range from the Agency for International Development's prioritizing development programs linked to narcotics control efforts, to forfeiture provisions that allow sharing of proceeds with foreign governments who cooperate with the U.S. ^United\States ^Drug\Control\Policies ^Legislation ^Supply ^Asset\Forfeiture

1851. U.S. Congress, Senate Committee on Appropriations (1986). "International Narcotic Control Programs and Policies." *Ninety-Ninth, Second*

Session. Washington, D.C.: Government Printing Office. Focus on international cooperation in the control of narcotics. ^United\States ^Drug\Control\Policies ^International\Cooperation

1852. U.S. Congress, Senate Committee on Armed Services (1988). Hearing. "Role of the Department of Defense in Drug Interdiction." *One Hundredth Congress, Second Session*. Washington, D.C.: U.S. Government Printing Office. Can the military be more usefully and responsibly involved in the war against drugs in the United States? A large diversity of response can be anticipated, some of which is evident in these hearings. A House bill under consideration, and on which this hearing was being held, contained a broad, sweeping mandate to the military to substantially halt the flow of narcotics in the United States "within 45 days." Under the House bill the military would seal the borders to narcotics traffickers using whatever search, seizure, and arrest powers would be necessary. A Senate version of a similar bill expanded the role of the military, but in a substantially different way. From this vantage the Department of Defense would detect and monitor all aerial and maritime potential threats to national security. Carefully prescribed designation of certain armed forces personnel to use civil law enforcement powers beyond the country's borders would be articulated. ^United\States ^Interdiction ^Military ^Legislation ^Department\of\Defense

1853. U.S. Congress, Senate Committee on Foreign Relations (1988). Report. "International Narcotics Control and Foreign Assistance Certification: Requirements, Procedures, Timetables, and Guidelines." *One Hundredth Congress, Second Session*. Washington, D.C.: U.S. Government Printing Office. Another in the mandatory reporting of whether a nation is a major illicit drug producing or transiting country and, if so, whether it is making satisfactory progress toward controlling the traffic. Countries failing the test are "sanctioned." This volume lists the sanctions on specific countries. ^United\States ^Drug\Control\Policies ^Politics ^Foreign\Aid ^Consequences\Foreign\Policy

1854. U.S. Congress, Senate Committee on Foreign Relations, Subcommittee on Terrorism, Narcotics and International Operations (1988). "Drugs, Law Enforcement and Foreign Policy." *One Hundredth Congress, Second Session*. Washington, D.C.: U.S. Government Printing Office. This is the Subcommittee on Narcotics, Terrorism and International Operations' report regarding links between foreign policy, narcotics, and law enforcement in connection with drug trafficking from the Caribbean and Central and South America to the United States. Past policies were reviewed as well as practices in handling foreign policy and the war on drugs. Contained are the findings and conclusions based on the subcommittee's investigation, including a country-by-country analysis of the drug problem as it has affected U.S. foreign policy in Latin America, a review of drug links to the Contra movement and the Nicaraguan war, of money laundering, and of issues involving conflicts between law enforcement and national security. Appendices in the report detail allegations of how the committee's initial investigation in 1986 may have been interfered with politically. ^Latin\America ^United\States ^Drug\Traffic ^Consequences\Foreign\Policy ^Terrorists ^Consequences\Political ^Caribbean ^Contras ^Nicaragua ^Bureaucracy ^Politics

1855. U.S. Congress, Senate Committee on Foreign Relations and the Committee on the Judiciary (1985). Joint Hearing. "International Terrorism, Insurgency, and Drug Trafficking: Present Trends in Terrorist Activity." *Ninety-Ninth Congress, First Session*. Washington, D.C.: U.S. Government Printing Office. Continued discussion of how terrorists have invaded the illegal drug market in order to finance their operations. It is not alleged that all terrorist activity is drug-related, only that there now appears to be substantial links being developed between major drug trafficking organizations and terrorist groups in ways that threaten to provide well organized, highly skilled terrorist organizations a consistent source of financing. What policies should be undertaken in light of all this? Testifiers address these issues. ^Drug\Traffic ^Terrorists

1856. U.S. Congress, Senate Committee on Governmental Affairs (1988). "Border Management Reorganization and Drug Interdiction." *One Hundredth Congress, Second Session*. Washington, D.C.: U.S. Government Printing Office. History of Border Patrol policies and procedures, and in particular those associated (at least since 1948) with drug control efforts. Numerous organizational initiatives are reported, including the 1988 proposal to consider merging all federal narcotics interdiction agencies into a single department. Six congressional research service reports are included and seven outside studies are reproduced. ^United\States ^Interdiction ^Drug\Control\Policies\History

1857. U.S. Congress, Senate Committee on Governmental Affairs, Permanent Subcommittee on Investigations (1986). Hearing. "'Crack' Cocaine." *Ninety-Ninth Congress, Second Session*. Washington, D.C.: Government Printing Office. For several years the Subcommittee on Investigations has focused its attention on trying to find ways to reduce the demand for drugs. The growing use of crack is a clear indication of the need for greater attention to that portion of the problem. Testimony given about what the government and the private sector are doing, what all people should be doing, and what many people hope yet to do about the use of crack on the nation's streets and in its schoolyards. ^United\States ^Cocaine ^Crack ^Drug\Control\Policies ^Demand ^Private\Initiatives

1858. U.S. Congress, Senate Committee on the Judiciary, Subcommittee on Criminal Justice (1980). Hearing. "Health Consequences of Marihuana Use." *Ninety Sixth Congress, Second Session*. Washington, D.C.: U.S. Government Printing Office. Physiological effects of marihuana use. The Judiciary Committee has been attempting to recodify federal criminal law. Some aspects of the proposed statute dealt with drug use and abuse, including marijuana. It had been proposed that the Congress decriminalize 30 grams of marijuana. The hearings were held to determine whether that would be a good idea. Testimony was given by people on the following panels: Panel of doctors, panel on overview of the problem, panel on effects to female reproductive system, panel on male reproductive system, panel on effects on cellular function. ^United\States ^Cannabis ^Consequences\Physiological ^P\S\Legalization

1859. U.S. Congress, Senate Committee on the Judiciary, Subcommittee on Security and Terrorism (1983). Hearing. "Impact of the South Florida Task Force on Drug Interdiction in the Gulf Coast Area." *Ninety-Eighth Congress, First Session*. Washington, D.C.: U.S. Government Printing Office. Testimony given concerning the use of the U.S. Gulf Coast area for smuggling narcotics and the ways by which that smuggling is done; the marijuana eradication program in the United States; a statement by William Stewart of the U.S. Coast Guard, coordinator for the National Narcotics Border Interdiction System, Gulf Coast Region, regarding their interdiction activities; the Coast Guards' cooperation with military agencies in Gulf Coast interdiction programs; a statement on behalf of the FBI regarding its work; a statement on behalf of the U.S. Customs Service; discussion of the economics of the drug trade in Gulf Coast areas. ^United\States ^Interdiction ^Drug\Traffic ^Cannabis ^Crop\Eradication ^Military ^Coast\Guard ^FBI ^Customs ^Traffickers\Incentives\Economic

1860. U.S. Congress, Senate Committee on the Judiciary, Subcommittee to Investigate Juvenile Delinquency (1975–1977). Hearing. "Marijuana Decriminalization." *Ninety-Fourth Congress, First Session*. 3 vols. Washington, D.C.: U.S. Government Printing Office. United States law and legislation regarding marijuana and its relationship, in the United States, to drug abuse and crime. A principal focus of the investigation was into juvenile delinquency in the United States. At the time of the hearings, 67 percent of all drug arrests were for marijuana. A large percentage of these were arrested for the possession of small amounts of marijuana. Basically, the committee addressed the question: "Is this a good thing to be doing?" A very large response was had. Should not drug enforcement efforts, and their costs, be apportioned to more consequential matters? ^United\States ^Cannabis ^Legalization ^Legislation ^Drug\Use ^Crime ^Consequences\Economic

1861. U.S. Congress, Senate Committee on Labor and Human Resources (1988). Hearing. "Drug Abuse—Prevention, Education, and Treatment." *One Hundredth Congress, Second Session*. Washington, D.C.: U.S. Government Printing Office. Testimony is given about available treatments that work and what needs to be done both practically and scientifically in search for cures and appropriate treatment for addicts. With respect to the relationship of education to prevention, testimony was given regarding what kinds of approaches are being taken and what could be done more effectively to make a difference with children. It is acknowledged that many current strategies to reduce demand were not effective. ^United\States ^Drug\Use ^Prevention ^Treatment ^Prevention\Drug\Education ^Reviews

1862. U.S. Congress, Senate Committee on Labor and Human Resources, Subcommittee on Alcoholism and Drug Abuse (1984). Hearing. "Drugs and the Juvenile Justice System." *Ninety-Eighth Congress, Second Session*. Washington, D.C.: U.S. Government Printing Office. The hearing was convened to examine how the drug-addicted or drug-troubled juvenile offender was treated within the Florida juvenile justice system. Florida had set up special procedures designed to help such individuals, and the question was to examine whether that help was useful. ^United\States ^Law\Enforcement ^Youth ^Florida

1863. —— (1984). Hearing. "Impact of Drugs on Crime, 1984." *Ninety-Eighth Congress, Second Session*. Washington, D.C.: U.S. Government Printing Office. The hearing started with the "self-evident truth" that there is a relationship between drugs and crime. The panel received a wide range of testimony from politicians, psychiatrists, and from the private sector. ^United\States ^Drug\Traffic ^Crime ^Drug\Use

1864. —— (1984). Hearing. "Role of the Media in Drug Abuse Prevention and Education." *Ninety-Eighth Congress, Second Session*. Washington, D.C.: U.S. Government Printing Office. Testimony is given from a significant cross-section of the "influencers" of American perceptions. These range from a producer of children's cartoons, to a celebrity from an adult prime-time show, and to a network executive committed to "waging war against drugs." The apparent intention of the hearing was to "demonstrate that we, together as a nation, have the will, the drive, and the commitment to end the ravaging effect of drugs, particularly as the problem affects younger and younger people." ^United\States ^Drug\Use ^Prevention ^Media

1865. —— (1985). Senate Subcommittee on Alcoholism and Drug Abuse of the Committee on Labor and Human Resources. Hearing. "Drugs and Terrorism, 1984." *Ninety-Eighth Congress, Second Session*. Washington, D.C.: U.S. Government Printing Office. The link between drugs and terrorism is the focus of this hearing, particularly because it is thought that drug-driven terrorist activities are now affecting U.S. citizens. Observations are made about drug-related terrorist groups in Colombia, Peru, Malaysia, and Burma. They are heavily financed by the sale of illegal drugs. In terms of the economic relationship, the marshalling of a drug market provides terrorists with access to hard currency and therefore to the possibility of purchasing arms that are critical to their needs as they attempt to impose their will. Narcotics have become the currency of international arms trafficking and terrorism. ^Drug\Traffic ^Politics ^Insurgents ^Terrorists ^Colombia ^Peru ^Malaysia ^Burma ^Latin\America ^Southeast\Asia ^Consequences\Economic ^Consequences\Terrorists

1866. U.S. Congress, Senate Committee on Labor and Human Resources, Subcommittee on Children, Family, Drugs, and Alcoholism (1985). Hearing. "Designer Drugs, 1985." *Ninety-Ninth Congress, First Session*. Washington, D.C.: U.S. Government Printing Office. The subcommittee investigated the threat of designer drugs and efforts to stop their distribution. Description of the "analog game," and the difficulties this posed for maintaining an up-to-date "controlled substances" law. ^United\States ^Drug\Traffic ^Law\Enforcement ^Designer\Drugs

1867. —— (1985). Hearing. "Role of Nicaragua in Drug Trafficking." *Ninety-Ninth Congress, First Session*. Washington, D.C.: U.S. Government Printing Office. Evidence of the involvement of brothers of the dictators of Cuba and Nicaragua are mentioned. Additional testimony given regarding "the real inside story" of who planned and carried out the operations that were hatched by Cuba and Nicaragua to run cocaine from South America through Nicaragua to the United States. The goals, as given in the report, were to raise hard cash for the "revolution," and to purposefully destroy American youth and cripple American society. ^Latin\America ^Caribbean ^Cuba ^Nicaragua ^Cocaine ^Drug\Traffic ^Politics ^Consequences\Foreign\Policy

1868. —— (1986). Hearing. "Impact of Drug Education." *Ninety-Ninth Congress, Second Session*. Washington, D.C.: U.S. Government Printing Office. Congress was anticipating expanding funding for drug education programs, and contributors to the hearing attempted to address what curriculum would effectively teach children to say "no" to drugs. It came as no surprise that there was no firm agreement. General concern was expressed that "we need to get more serious." ^United\States ^Prevention ^Youth ^Prevention\Schools ^Prevention\Drug\Education\Critique

1869. U.S. Congress, Senate Committee on Labor and Public Welfare, Subcommittee on Alcoholism and Narcotics (1974). Hearing. "Marihuana Research and Legal Controls." *Ninety-Third Congress, Second Session*. Washington, D.C.: U.S. Government Printing Office. United States law and legislation on marihuana; psychological aspects of and physiological effects of marihuana use. A lengthy list of statements, position papers, and cited exogenous information from legal scholars, medical researchers, and narcotics task force personnel. Problems of drug education are noted. ^United\States ^Cannabis ^Law\Enforcement ^Legislation

1870. U.S. Congress, Senate Permanent Subcommittee on Investigations of the Committee on Governmental Affairs (1987). Hearing. "Federal Drug Interdiction: Command, Control, Communications, and Intelligence Network." *One Hundredth Congress, First Session*. Washington, D.C.: U.S. Government Printing Office. A wide variety of witnesses testified at this hearing on both the philosophy and effectiveness of federal drug interdiction efforts. The chairman noted that, despite a doubling of federal expenditures on interdiction over the five years between 1982 and 1987, the quantity of drugs smuggled into the United States was greater than ever. There appeared to be no clear correlation between the level of expenditures for interdiction purposes and the availability of illegally imported drugs in the domestic market. Federal drug interdiction agencies are fragmented and overlapping, and there is a lack of an overall direction. Should new things be tried? Several were pointed out. ^United\States ^Interdiction ^Drug\Control\Policies\Effectiveness ^Drug\Traffic ^Bureaucracy ^Proffered\Solutions

1871. —— (1988). Hearing. "Drugs and Money Laundering in Panama." *One Hundredth Congress, Second Session.* Washington, D.C.: U.S. Government Printing Office. Focus is on General Manuel Noriega and his alleged involvement in drug trafficking and drug money laundering. ^Latin\America ^Panama ^Money\Laundering ^Drug\Traffic ^Traffickers

1872. U.S. Congress, Senate Select Committee on Narcotics Abuse and Control (1984). Report. "Cultivation and Eradication of Illicit Domestic Marihuana." *Ninety-Eighth Congress, First Session.* Washington D.C.: U.S. Government Printing Office. Marijuana plants cultivated in the United States and their association with drug abuse in the United States. ^United\States ^Drug\Use ^Cannabis ^Production

1873. U.S. Congress, Senate Subcommittee on Children, Family, Drugs, and Alcoholism (1985). "Scope and Impact of Narcotic Trafficking in Alaska." Hearing. *Ninety-Ninth Congress, First Session.* Washington, D.C.: Government Printing Office. The committee chairman, Senator Frank H. Murkowski, from information submitted to the committee prior to the hearing, stated that "the use of every type of illegal drug, from heroin to LSD in Alaska far exceeds the national average." Their surveys showed that cocaine use in Alaska high schools is three times the national average, marijuana use about 25 percent higher. The U.S. Coast Guard views Alaska as becoming increasingly vulnerable as a transshipment point for smuggling drugs from the Orient. This point was reinforced by Robert Sundberg, Alaska's commissioner of public safety, who considered that the Alaska atmosphere was susceptible to clandestine laboratories for producing cocaine and methamphetamines and also as a transshipment point for large quantities of drugs from the Orient that were destined for Canada and the lower forty-eight states. Considerably more evidence was presented in the hearing regarding the availability of drugs in Alaska than upon their impact, social, political, or economic. Of the impact it was thought that usage among Alaska youth would be particularly high because of the generally higher level of disposable income that Alaska youth have relative to their peers in the lower forty-eight states. ^United\States ^Drug\Traffic ^Drug\Use ^Alaska ^Coast\Guard ^Consequences\Psychological ^Consequences\Physiological ^Prevention\Drug\Education\Critique

1874. U.S. Congress, Senate Subcommittee on Security and Terrorism of the Committee on the Judiciary and the Subcommittee on Western Hemisphere Affairs of the Foreign Relations Committee and the Senate Drug Enforcement Caucus (1983). Joint Hearing. "The Cuban Government's Involvement in Facilitating International Drug Traffic." *Ninety-Eighth Congress, First Session.* Washington, D.C.: U.S. Government Printing Office. A select list of witnesses appeared before the panel and gave testimony. Included also in the appendix are exhibits ranging from transcripts of court trials to miscellaneous memorandum. ^Caribbean ^Cuba ^Drug\Traffic

1875. U.S. Department of Commerce (1976). *Drug Use and Crime: Report of the Panel on Drug Use and Criminal Behavior,* Research Triangle Institute. Springfield, Va.: National Technical Information Service. The various panels precursor to this report as well as those involved in this report (which were impaneled by the National Institute on Drug Abuse) considered three essential methodological and conceptual questions: How should crime and criminal behavior be defined and measured? How should types of drugs and drug use be defined and measured? What patterns of drug use and criminal behavior exist and how can they be identified? Summaries, data analysis, and research recommendations focus on one or more of these three questions. All of them, of course, hope to focus on the essential relationship between drug use and crime. Specifically, in terms of policy application, the volume addresses the degree to which demand reduction and supply curtailment will reduce crime. Clearly, there is a strong statistical association between drug use and crime. The causal relationship, however, is not clearly established. The panel recommended guidelines for identifying causal relationships. ^Drug\Use ^Crime ^Reviews

1876. U.S. Department of Health and Human Services, National Institute of Alcohol Abuse and Alcoholism (1986). *Acquired Immune Deficiency Syndrome and Chemical Dependency.* Rockville, Md.: The Institute. A report of a symposium sponsored by the American Medical Society on Alcoholism and Other Drug Dependencies and the National Council on Alcoholism, with papers emerging from their joint/national meeting in San Francisco in April 1986. Discussed are the nature of AIDS, chemical dependency and AIDS, barriers to the recognition of links between drug and alcohol abuse and AIDS, alcohol and the immune system, AIDS and alcoholism, counseling gay men about substance abuse and AIDS (don't take a value position), alcohol abuse, suicidal behavior, and AIDS. ^Heroin ^Health ^AIDS ^Alcohol

1877. U.S. Department of Health, Education, and Welfare (1976). *Cocaine—Summaries of Psychosocial Research.* Research Issue 15. Rockville, MD: National Institute on Drug Abuse. Sixty-nine studies, ranging from Ashley's general treatise on cocaine to more specialized works on the psychopharmacology of cocaine are reviewed. Selections are included from both the scientific and popular literature on the psychosocial aspects of human use of cocaine, and, to a lesser extent, coca. The documents represent a time span from the turn of the century to the mid-1970s. ^Coca ^Cocaine ^Reviews ^Consequences\Psychological ^Consequences\Social

1878. U.S. Department of Justice (1985). *The Illicit Drug Situation in the United States and Canada.* Washington, D.C.: Drug Enforcement Administration. Focusing on marijuana, heroin, and cocaine, this volume gives country-specific information about the extent to which these drugs have penetrated the respective societies and also offers a comparative analysis on the drug situation in the United States. ^Canada ^United\States ^Drug\Traffic ^Drug\Use

1879. ——— (1986). *Liquid Hashish.* Los Angeles: Drug Enforcement Administration. This brief document (appearing in 1986) from the U.S. Department of Justice describes the relatively recent appearance in the market of a form of hashish oil, which is a concentration, rather sophisticatedly derived, of the basic active ingredient in marijuana—tetrahydrocannabinol (THC). Liquid hashish appeared first in the early 1970s; the reports of seizures throughout the world have increased substantially. The basic production principle, similar to that of percolating coffee, is always carried out clandestinely. Only simple equipment is required. The THC potency in this oil may be as high as 90 percent. ^Cannabis ^Drug\Traffic ^Consequences\Drug\Concentration

1880. ——— (1986). *Quarterly Statistical Report 1st Half Fiscal Year 1986.* Washington, D.C.: Drug Enforcement Administration, Planning and Inspection Division. Summarizes arrests and convictions. ^United\States ^Law\Enforcement ^Statistics

1881. —— (1987). "From the Source to the Street: Current Prices for Cannabis, Cocaine, and Heroin." *Intelligence Trends* 14:3, Special Report. Prices are given for domestic marijuana, hashish, foreign source marijuana (originating in Mexico, Colombia, Thailand, and Jamaica), cocaine (originating in Bolivia, Colombia, and Peru), and heroin (originating in Mexico, Southwest Asia, and Southeast Asia). Prices at successive stages of trafficking, along with notes on purity, are given. ^United\States ^Drug\Traffic ^Economics ^Statistics ^Cannabis ^Cocaine ^Heroin ^Mexico ^Colombia ^Thailand ^Jamaica ^Bolivia ^Peru ^Southeast\Asia ^Latin\America ^Consequences\Markets

1882. U.S. Department of Justice, Cannabis Investigations Section, Drug Enforcement Administration (1987). *1987 Domestic Cannabis Eradication/Suppression Program*. Washington, D.C.: Drug Enforcement Administration. The Drug Enforcement Administration's domestic cannabis eradication/suppression program was instituted to coordinate efforts between federal, state, and local United States agencies involving the eradication of domestically cultivated cannabis. This report notes an increase of about 72 percent in the amount of plants having been destroyed in 1987 over previous years. There was also an increase of approximately 60 percent in the number of cultivated plants eradicated. Increases were also noted in the number of arrests, greenhouse operations detected, and weapons and assets seized. In 1987 it was noted that the first undisputed evidence of an organized group involved in the multistate cannabis cultivation and distribution was observed. This was uncovered in Minnesota when forty-eight tons of marijuana were seized on a farm. Eradication and suppression statistics are given. ^United\States ^Cannabis ^Crop\Eradication ^DEA ^Minnesota ^Statistics ^Production ^Organized\Crime ^Traffickers

1883. —— (1988). *1988 Domestic Cannabis Eradication Program*. Washington, D.C.: Drug Enforcement Administration. Relative to 1987, seizures were down, eradication was down, and arrests were down. On the other hand, indoor greenhouse operation seizures increased, as they have in each of the past several years. The booklet describes the Drug Enforcement Administration's program management, funding, and expenditures. ^United\States ^Cannabis ^Crop\Eradication ^DEA

1884. U.S. Department of Justice, Drug Enforcement Administration (issued annually). *Project DAWN Annual Report*. Washington, D.C.: National Institute on Drug Abuse. Project DAWN, cosponsored by the U.S. Drug Enforcement Administration and the National Institute on Drug Abuse, gathers, interprets, and disseminates data on drug abuse from selected locations within the continental United States. It seeks to identify drugs being used and the patterns of their use, and to assess the relative hazards to health, both physiological and psychological. Annual reports. ^United\States ^Drug\Use ^Health ^Statistics ^DAWN

1885. —— (1985). "Cannabis Eradication on Non-Federal and Indian Lands in the Contiguous United States and Hawaii." Draft Environmental Impact Statement. Washington, D.C.: U.S. Department of Justice, Drug Enforcement Administration. Environmental impact statement that examines potential impacts on soils, vegetation, wildlife, endangered and threatened species, water quality and aquatic systems, human health and worker safety, air quality, socioeconomic conditions, historic and cultural resources, visual resources, and noise levels with respect to various combinations of manual, mechanical, and herbicidal methods of eradicating cannabis. ^United\States ^Cannabis ^Crop\Eradication ^Consequences\Environmental

1886. U.S. Department of Justice, Drug Enforcement Administration, Office of Intelligence (1986). *Black Tar Heroin in the United States*. Washington, D.C.: U.S. Department of Justice. Discusses the relatively new form of

Mexican heroin—black tar—that has become increasingly available in United States' domestic traffic. It has high purity, low price, and widespread availability. With the purity, tolerance levels among addicts have risen, requiring ever more daily heroin consumption. With the introduction of black tar, the Mexican share of the heroin market has increased from about 32 percent to 38 percent. ^Mexico ^United\States ^Heroin ^Drug\Use ^Drug\Traffic ^Consequences\Markets ^Consequences\Physiological ^Latin\America ^Production

1887. U.S. Department of Justice, Federal Bureau of Investigation (1984). *Financial Investigative Techniques: Money Laundering.* Washington, D.C.: U.S. Government Printing Office. This is a "hands on" handbook on financial transactions and tax haven countries showing how drug money is laundered and repatriated. ^Money\Laundering ^Taxation

1888. U.S. Department of State, Bureau of International Narcotics Matters (1985). *International Narcotics Control Strategy Report*, Midyear Update, August. Washington, D.C.: U.S. Department of State, Bureau of International Narcotic Matters. Programmatic developments in specific geographic areas of drug production and diplomatic initiatives (including multilateral approaches). ^United\States ^Drug\Control\Policies ^Production ^Statistics ^Latin\America ^Southeast\Asia ^Middle\East ^Golden\Crescent ^Golden\Triangle ^Caribbean ^Europe ^Africa ^Drug\Traffic ^Production\Statistics

1889. ———— (1985). *International Narcotics Control Strategy Report 1985.* Washington, D.C.: U.S. Department of State, Bureau of International Narcotic Matters. Reviews international programs and gives country reports from Latin America, the Caribbean, Southeast Asia, Southern Europe, Southwest Asia, Africa, and Europe. ^United\States ^Drug\Control\Policies ^Production ^Statistics ^Latin\America ^Southeast\Asia ^Middle\East ^Golden\Crescent ^Golden\Triangle ^Caribbean ^Europe ^Africa ^Drug\Traffic ^Production\Statistics

1890. ———— (1986). *International Narcotics Control Strategy Report 1986*, 21 February. Washington, D.C.: U.S. Department of State, Bureau of International Narcotic Matters. Surveys regional events relating to narcotics and the internationalization of the war against their illicit trafficking; gives production estimates throughout the world for illicit drugs. Also, a review is given of the United States' involvement in international programs designed to counteract development of drug trafficking. ^United\States ^Production ^Drug\Control\Policies ^Statistics ^Latin\America ^Southeast\Asia ^Middle\East ^Golden\Crescent ^Golden\Triangle ^Caribbean ^Europe ^Africa ^Drug\Traffic ^Production\Statistics

1891. ———— (1987). *International Narcotics Control Strategy Report* (March). Washington, D.C.: U.S. Department of State, Bureau of International Narcotic Matters. The first annual report prepared pursuant to the U.S. Anti-Drug Abuse Act of 1986. Provides information required by the Congress, and gives a factual basis for the president's initial certifications under the revised law. Includes policy and program developments in 1986 in all countries of the world in which drug trafficking and/or production occurs with the United States as ultimate destination. ^United\States ^Drug\Control\Policies ^Production ^Statistics ^Latin\America ^Southeast\Asia ^Middle\East ^Golden\Crescent ^Golden\Triangle ^Caribbean ^Europe ^Africa ^Drug\Traffic ^Production\Statistics

1892. ———— (1988). *International Narcotics Control Strategy Report* (midyear update). Washington, D.C.: U.S. Department of State, Bureau of International Narcotics Matters. Six months into 1988, the United States Bureau of International Narcotics Matters believed that the international strategy described in its 1988 International Narcotics Control Strategy Report was working. The program called for eradication, enforcement, development assistance, public diplomacy, and international cooperation. The mid-year report notes positive movement in all of these areas, although admittedly there was a mix of progress and frustration. Country-specific data are given for the entire world. ^United\States ^Drug\Control\Policies ^Production ^Statistics ^Latin\America ^Southeast\Asia ^Middle\East ^Golden\Crescent ^Golden\Triangle ^Caribbean ^Europe ^Africa ^Drug\Traffic ^Production\Statistics

1893. ———— (1989). *International Narcotics Control Strategy Report* (March). Washington, D.C.: U.S. Department of State, Bureau of International Narcotic Matters. The third annual report prepared pursuant to the Anti-Drug Abuse Act of 1986. Its purpose, principally, is to offer a statement on certification that countries are making efforts to reduce or control narcotics trafficking. Discusses U.S. policy and program developments in 1988, including personnel and material contributions to operations of various Latin American and other countries. Specific discussion of cocaine and heroin. The herbicide issue is discussed. A table on worldwide production totals is offered. Salient country points are as follows: Afghanistan, denied certification last year, still offers problems; Argentina is of increasing concern as a refining and transit center for cocaine; the Bahamas continues to be a major transit country for cocaine and marijuana entering the U.S., and is an important laundering center; Belize is no longer a major source country for cannabis, however, it is becoming an important transit country for cocaine from South America and marijuana from Guatemala; in Bolivia, additional ground is being planted for coca; Brazil has become vital in the cocaine trade as a transit country for Andean traffickers, as a producer of precursor chemicals, and as an emerging coca cultivator; Bulgaria is a vital transit country for drugs smuggled along the Balkan route; Burma's political turmoil has grounded its large-scale aerial eradication program; there is growing concern, with respect to China, about the transshipment of Golden Triangle heroin through southern China to Hong Kong and traffic in precursor chemicals into the Triangle; Costa Rica is increasingly important as a cocaine transit country; Colombia has made increasing interdiction efforts but is hampered by a judicial system that is intimidated by violence; Cuba continues to function as an important transshipment country; Cyprus is central to the drug trade in the Middle East and especially from Lebanon; the Dominican Republic has become an ideal staging area and refueling stop for traffickers in cocaine; in Ecuador, coca production has fallen but the country is a transit point for cocaine; each is an important consumer of opium, heroin, and hashish, supporting production in Asia and the Middle East, and increasingly is important as a transit point for drugs intended for the European and U.S. markets; Greece remains an important transit point; Guatemala has increased its importance to the U.S. drug situation as larger amounts of opium and marijuana were produced during the past year; Haiti improved its drug interdiction efforts but Haitian waters are used for transshipment of cocaine; Honduras is a transshipment point for Colombian cocaine; Hong Kong is both the financial and money-laundering center of the Far East narcotics trade and an important transit center for Golden Triangle heroin destined for Australia, Canada, the United States, and Europe; India has become of increasing concern over diversion of licit production into illicit trade; Indonesia is a transit site for heroin, opium, hashish, precursor chemicals; Iran, denied certification last year on grounds of non cooperation, continues not to cooperate; Jamaica has reduced marijuana production dramatically; Kenya is of increasing importance as a transit point for Southwest Asian heroin; Laos facilitates narcotics trafficking via its corrupt government; Lebanon continues to be a major narcotics producing and trafficking country; Malaysia is an important heroin conversion and transit center, exporting primarily to Europe and Australia; Mexico expanded its eradication programs but has so many inhibiting effects of corruption throughout the program as to nullify much of the gain; Morocco is a source of cannabis and hashish and is a transit point for heroin and cocaine; Nepal is an increasingly used transit point for heroin produced in Pakistan and the Golden Triangle; Nicaragua continues as a cocaine transit point; Nigeria is a major heroin transit country; Pakistan opium production remained high; Panama continues as a transshipment and money-laundering country; Paraguay, after years of indifference to narcotics control, took several significant steps to improve its performance; Peru conducted vigorous manual eradication programs and tested herbicides, but it continues as the largest cultivator of coca; the Philippines exports locally grown and Thai marijuana; Singapore is a transshipment point for Southeast Asian heroin and has high potential for money laundering, although it cooperates with the United States in monitoring and intercepting international drug traffic; Syria is a transit point for illicit narcotics as well as a heroin refining center, with heavy involvement of the government; Thailand has reduced opium cultivation but remains significant as a refiner of heroin and conduit for opium/heroin from other sources in the Golden Triangle; Turkey traffickers smuggle heroin and hashish; and Venezuela has become an important port for the transit of precursor chemicals and cocaine. ^United\States ^ Drug\Control\Policies ^Production ^Statistics ^Latin\America ^Southeast\Asia ^Middle\East ^Southwest\Asia ^Golden\Crescent ^Golden\Triangle ^Caribbean ^Europe ^Africa ^Drug\Traffic ^Drug\Control\Policies\Effectiveness ^Herbicides ^Afghanistan ^Argentina ^Bahamas ^Money\Laundering ^Guatemala ^Bolivia ^Brazil ^Precursor\Chemicals ^Bulgaria ^Burma ^Crop\Eradication ^China ^Hong\Kong ^Costa\Rica ^Colombia ^Consequences\Judiciary ^Cuba ^Cyprus ^Lebanon ^Dominican\Republic ^Ecuador ^Greece ^Consequences\Markets ^Haiti ^Honduras ^Australia ^Canada ^India ^Iran ^Jamaica ^Kenya ^Laos ^Consequences\Corruption ^Mexico ^Morocco ^Nepal ^Nicaragua ^Nigeria ^Pakistan ^Panama ^Paraguay ^Peru ^Philippines ^Singapore ^Syria ^Thailand ^Turkey ^Venezuela ^Production\Statistics

1894. —— (1990). *International Narcotics Control Strategy Report*, March. Washington, D.C.: BINM. Offers an overview of policy and program developments in 1989, listing worldwide illicit-drug production as well as summarizing drug-control activities in all the relevant countries. A functional activity budget is given, and a special discussion of "financial crimes" is raised. ^Opium ^Cannabis ^Coca ^Production ^Crime ^Drug\Control\Policies ^International\Cooperation ^Afghanistan ^Argentina ^Bahamas ^Bolivia ^Bulgaria ^Burma ^Brazil ^China ^Colombia ^Cuba ^Cyprus ^Dominican\Republic ^Ecuador ^Egypt ^Guatemala ^Haiti ^Honduras ^Hong\Kong ^India ^Indonesia ^Iran ^Ivory\Coast ^Jamaica ^Pakistan ^Kenya ^Laos ^Lebanon ^Malaysia ^Mexico ^Morocco ^Nepal ^Nigeria ^Panama ^Paraguay ^Philippines ^Senegal ^Singapore ^Syria ^Thailand ^Turkey ^Venezuela ^United\States ^USSR ^Production\Statistics

1895. —— (1991). *International Narcotics Control Strategy Report*, March. Reviews policy and program developments in 1990 dealing with efforts to reduce cocaine, opium and heroin supplies. Looks, also, into money laundering, U.S. international drug control strategies, and the work of international organizations to reduce illicit drug demand. Production charts for all major producer countries are given. Qualitative analysis is made for each country. Plans for future drug control activities in Latin America, the Caribbean, Asia and Africa, are indicated. Budgetary summaries are noted. ^United\States ^Drug\Control\Policies ^Production ^Statistics ^Money\Laundering ^Cocaine ^Opiates ^Cannabis ^Southwest\Asia ^Southeast\Asia ^Africa ^Middle\East ^Latin\America ^Argentina ^Bolivia ^Brazil ^Colombia ^Ecuador ^Paraguay ^Peru ^Venezuela ^Belize ^Costa\Rica ^El\Salvador ^Guatemala ^Honduras ^Mexico ^Nicaragua ^Panama ^Bahamas ^Cuba ^Dominican\Republic ^Haiti ^Jamaica ^Afghanistan ^India ^Iran ^Nepal ^Pakistan ^Burma ^China ^Hong\Kong ^Indonesia ^Laos ^Malaysia ^Philippines ^Singapore ^Thailand ^Bulgaria ^Cyprus ^Egypt ^Greece ^Lebanon ^Syria ^Turkey ^Ivory\Coast ^Kenya ^Morocco ^Nigeria ^Senegal ^Productions\Statistics

1896. "U.S. Drug Dilemma: Punishment or Legalization?" (1985). *Inside Drug Law* (May). Severe negative sanctions on users will curtail demand. Alcohol prohibition failed in the 1920s because while prohibition banned the production and sale of alcohol, it left drinkers alone. The result was that crime flourished. So it is with drugs. Put sanctions on the users, and the demand will decrease. Absent that, drugs and their associated criminality can be reduced by legalizing them. The choice has to be made on the basis of values that a society has. Once the choice is made, it must be enforced. "We cannot continue to have things both ways." ^United\States ^Drug\Control\Policies\Critique ^Alcohol ^Crime ^Legalization

1897. U.S. General Accounting Office (1984). *Additional Actions Taken to Control Marijuana Cultivation and Other Crimes on Federal Lands*. Report to the Chairman, Subcommittee on Public Lands and National Parks, Committee on Interior and Insular Affairs, House of Representatives. Washington, D.C.: General Accounting Office. General description of the increasing difficulty that Forest Service personnel have in policing illicit drug growing on federal lands, and, additionally, the danger to private citizens who, unaware, stumble into a marijuana growing area. Booby traps are rigged up, violent incidents are reported, and land users are threatened or harassed. Additionally, considerable resource damage is done by marijuana growers. ^United\States ^Cannabis ^Production ^Consequences\Environmental ^Law\Enforcement ^Consequences\Violence

1898. ——— (1984). *Investigations of Major Drug Trafficking Organizations*. Report to the Honorable Joseph R. Biden, Jr. United States Senate. Washington, D.C.: General Accounting Office. Mid-1980s review of the Drug Enforcement Administration's efforts to immobilize high-level drug traffickers. The report assessed DEA's violator classification system, and looked into its targeting methods and investigative techniques designed to immobilize major drug violators and their organizations. The report discusses the need for better measurements of these efforts. ^United\States ^Law\Enforcement ^Organized\Crime ^DEA ^Drug\Control\Policies\Critique

1899. ——— (1987). *AIDS: Information on Global Dimensions and Possible Impacts*. Fact Sheet to the Honorable Jesse Helms, U.S. Senate. Washington, D.C.: U.S. General Accounting Office. A fact sheet on the extent of the AIDS infection worldwide, particularly in Zaire, and the United States' and the World Health Organization's programs to prevent its advance. ^AIDS ^Statistics ^WHO ^United\States ^Africa ^Zaire ^Prevention

1900. ——— (1987). *Drug Law Enforcement: Military Assistance for Anti-Drug Agencies*. Report to the Congress. Washington, D.C.: U.S. General Accounting Office. A short assessment of the Department of Defense's compliance with Section 3057 of the Anti-Drug Abuse Act of 1986. ^United\States ^Military ^Department\of\Defense ^Legislation

1901. ——— (1988). *Border Control: Drug Interdiction and Related Activities Along the Southwestern U.S. Border*. Fact Sheet for the Chairman, Subcommittee on Government Information, Justice, and Agriculture, Committee on Government Operations, House of Representatives. Washington, D.C.: U.S. General Accounting Office. A fact sheet discussing drug seizures and increased use of personnel and equipment in the drug interdiction program. ^United\States ^Interdiction ^Statistics

1902. ——— (1988). *Controlling Drug Abuse: A Status Report*. Special Report from the Comptroller General of the United States. Washington, D.C.: U.S. General Accounting Office. This is a "slick copy" production, complete with color photographs, that discusses the persisting U.S. drug problem, the federal drug control efforts aimed at reducing supply and demand and criticizes the management of federal drug control efforts: measures of program effectiveness are needed, organizational changes are insufficient to resolve interagency conflicts, and leadership and central oversight need to be strengthened in spite of recent efforts to do so. ^United\States ^Drug\Traffic ^Drug\Control\Policies\Critique ^Proffered\Solutions ^Reviews

1903. ——— (1988). *Drug Control: Issues Surrounding Increased Use of the Military in Drug Interdiction.* Report to Congressional Requesters. Washington, D.C.: U.S. General Accounting Office. Drug interdiction, which has consumed about 35 percent of the $4 billion allocated in fiscal year 1987 to control drugs, has been the responsibility of law enforcement agencies. In recent years the Department of Defense has been increasingly called upon by the U.S. government (Congress and the White House) to provide more assistance. Neither the Department of Defense nor law officials support a significant change in the Defense Department's role. There is no agreement among experts that increased federal interdiction efforts, with or without the Department of Defense's assistance, will significantly affect the amount of drugs entering the United States. It is not additional personnel resources and intelligence information that the law enforcement agents need, they say. It is the removal of legal and practical constraints on their inspections and border patrols. Both law enforcement and Department of Defense officials would rather that law enforcement agencies be funded directly rather than indirectly through U.S. military involvement. While the Government Accounting Office makes no policy recommendations, it does, in this report, provide an overview of information and opinions concerning the issues. ^United\States ^Interdiction ^Military ^Reviews ^Department\of\Defense

1904. ——— (1988). *Drug Control: River Patrol Craft for the Government of Bolivia.* Fact Sheet for the Chairman, Task Force on International Narcotics Control, Committee on Foreign Affairs, House of Representatives. Washington, D.C.: U.S. General Accounting Office. High-tech speed boats were provided to Bolivia to patrol its rivers. This appears to have occurred before any specific river interdiction strategy or an operational plan to govern the use of the boats was implemented. The boats were purchased without a systematic evaluation of their capabilities in the Bolivian rivers or the expertise of the Bolivians to operate and maintain the boats. ^United\States ^Bolivia ^Interdiction ^Foreign\Aid ^Drug\Control\Policies\Effectiveness ^Latin\America

1905. ——— (1988). *Drug Control: U.S. International Narcotics Control Activities.* Report to the Congress. Washington, D.C.: U.S. General Accounting Office. This is another in the annual reports that analyze the global effectiveness of narcotics control programs and identifies impediments that countries face as they attempt to deal with the problem of narcotics production and trafficking. A principal finding is that vast quantities of narcotics are produced in countries where the central government has little control over producing areas or the crops being grown, and where there is little expectation that central government's role will increase. The GAO has specific recommendations that would alter, to some extent, the Department of State's operations. ^United\States ^Drug\Control\Policies\Effectiveness ^Drug\Control\Policies\Critique

1906. ——— (1988). *Drug Control: U.S.-Mexico Opium Poppy and Marijuana Aerial Eradication Program.* Report to the Congress. Washington, D.C.: U.S. General Accounting Office. The GAO concluded that maintaining aerial eradication at current levels would not eliminate Mexico as a major source of heroin and marijuana. Additional cultivations will be forthcoming which will exceed the eradication efforts. Organizational and programmatic goals of the various agencies are criticized. The agencies comment. ^Mexico ^United\States ^Opiates ^Crop\Eradication ^Reviews ^Latin\America ^Drug\Control\Policies\Critique

1907. ——— (1988). *Drug Control: U.S. Supported Efforts in Burma, Pakistan, and Thailand.* Report to the Congress. Washington, D.C.: U.S. General Accounting Office. U.S.-supported crop control, enforcement, and interdiction efforts in the named countries have not produced a substantial reduction in opium availability.

Crop control programs were not effectively managed, and development efforts were not set up to support narcotics reduction goals. The criticized agencies respond. ^Burma ^Pakistan ^Thailand ^United\States ^Opiates ^Drug\Control\Policies ^Crop\Eradication ^Reviews ^Interdiction ^Golden\Triangle ^Drug\Control\Policies\Effectiveness ^Southeast\Asia ^Southwest\Asia

1908. ——— (1988). *Drug Interdiction: Operation Autumn Harvest: A National Guard–Customs Anti-Smuggling Effort.* Report to Congressional Requesters. Washington, D.C.: U.S. General Accounting Office. In September 1987, National Guard units from four states and the U.S. Custom's Service conducted a cooperative drug interdiction effort along the U.S.–Mexican border. The objective was to detect and apprehend smugglers coming across the border in aircraft. While the operation did provide valuable war time readiness training, it did not meet its primary objective of interdicting drug smugglers. The GAO analyzed the causes of the failures. Several agencies respond. ^United\States ^Interdiction ^Military ^Customs ^National\Guard ^Drug\Control\Policies\Critique

1909. ——— (1988). *Drug Interdiction: Should the Customs Command and Control Program Be Continued as Currently Evolving?* Report to Congressional Requesters. Washington, D.C.: U.S. General Accounting Office. Analyzed was the development of a command, control, communications, and intelligence centered program coordinated among federal agencies with the Customs Bureau as the lead agency required by the Anti-Drug Abuse Act of 1986. This new orientation did, according to GAO, enhance customs command and control capabilities and could, it believed, lead to more rational use of resources. ^United\States ^Interdiction ^Customs ^Drug\Control\Policies\Critique

1910. ——— (1988). *Employee Drug Testing: Information on Private Sector Programs.* Report to the Honorable Charles Schumer, House of Representatives. Washington, D.C.: U.S. General Accounting Office. This is a basic fact sheet that gives information on the extent of drug testing, who receives testing and why, which testing methods are used most often, reasons for having drug testing programs, and what happens to individuals who test positive. ^United\States ^Drug\Testing ^Workplace ^Statistics

1911. ——— (1988). Report to the Chairman, Committee on the Judiciary, U.S. Senate. *National Drug Policy Board: Leadership Evolving, Greater Role in Developing Budgets Possible.* Washington, D.C.: U.S. General Accounting Office. The Comprehensive Crime Control Act of 1984 made provisions for a drug enforcement policy board that would coordinate federal drug law enforcement efforts. This article reviews the activities of the policy board to determine if it has fulfilled its responsibilities under the Act. GAO had a generally positive review of the Board. ^United\States ^Drug\Control\Policies ^Legislation ^National\Drug\Policy\Board

1912. ——— (1988). *Seized Conveyances: Justice and Customs Correction of Previous Conveyance Management Problems.* Report to the Subcommittee on Crime, Committee on the Judiciary, House of Representatives. Washington, D.C.: U.S. General Accounting Office. The problem is one of managing seized assets. The Custom's Bureau, among all agencies, has made the best progress in resolving problems of program fragmentation and insufficient management information. ^United\States ^Asset\Forfeiture ^Customs

1913. ——— (1989). *Drug Smuggling: Capabilities for Interdicting Private Aircraft Are Limited and Costly.* Report to Congressional Requesters. Washington, D.C.: U.S. Government Accounting Office. Customs and Coast Guard air interdiction programs have resulted in the seizure of substantial amounts of drugs.

These have been small, however, relative to the amounts of drugs passing through to the United States. Gaps exist in the radar coverage, and, in any event, there are inherent difficulties in having radar work sufficiently well to detect small aircraft. GAO is not convinced that spending additional millions of dollars on air interdiction programs is the most effective use of the limited resources Congress is willing, apparently, to provide. In general, GAO's analysis shows that air and other interdiction programs have not reduced drug supply, that the impact of additional radar facilities cannot yet be determined, and that congress should not make decisions about providing additional funds for air interdiction efforts without considering whether the funds could be put to more effective use on some other aspect of the nation's efforts against illegal drugs.
^United\States ^Interdiction ^Aircraft ^Reviews

1914. "U.S. Has 43 Big Drug Groups" (1989). *The Miami Herald*, 4 August, 5A. The UPI released comments that the first federal reports on the corporate structure of the illegal drug trade identified forty-three major groups operating in the United States, ranging from salaried operatives of Colombian cartels to one-time moonshiners of the "Dixie Mafia." They now involve rural operatives and Los Angeles street gangs. New York mafia families "have strong ties" to Colombian and Cuban dealers in the Miami area and also work with Asian groups and motorcycle gangs. The so-called Jamaican Posses, with around 10,000 members, are also trafficking in Colombian cocaine and appear to be developing relationships with Los Angeles gangs. There are four Colombian drug cartels; the best known ones are Medellín and Cali. They are large, vertically integrated groups. They are a state within a state, "owning a 12th of Colombia's farmland." ^ United\States\Rural\Areas ^ Jamaica ^ Colombia ^ Latin\America ^ Drug\Traffic ^ Organized\Crime ^ Consequences\State\Authority ^ Caribbean

1915. "U.S. Interdiction Efforts Forcing Coke Shipments to Europe, OC Commissioners Report" (1985). *Crime Control Digest*, 21 October, 2–3. Seizures of cocaine have increased dramatically in European countries, where the Colombian cocaine trafficking networks are in the process of opening the European market, primarily through Spain. Italy has noted increasing problems. ^Europe ^United\States ^Cocaine ^Drug\Traffic ^Interdiction ^Spain ^Italy

1916. "U.S. Plans 4-Mile Ditch on Border to Stem Drug Flow to California" (1989). *The New York Times*, 26 January, A12. Discussion of a proposal to build a four-mile-long ditch for a stretch of the United States–Mexican border in an effort to stem the flow of illegal drugs into California. Discussion of the particulars of the program is given, as well as criticisms associated with it. Some have called it "our buried Berlin wall." It would separate San Ysidro in California from Tiajuana. In effect, the effort would be to stop vehicle traffic across the desert in ways that bypass customs offices. ^United\States ^Interdiction

1917. "US Suspends All Aid to the Navy" (1988). *Latin American Weekly Report* 88, no. 45 (17 November): 3. Because of the involvement of high-ranking Bolivian naval officers in the drug trade, the United States has suspended all aid to the Bolivian Navy. It appears that the navy, in one village, pitted itself against Bolivia's drug enforcement agency Umopar. ^Latin\America ^Bolivia ^United\States ^Foreign\Aid ^Consequences\Foreign\Relations ^Consequences\Corruption

1918. Van Dyke, C., and R. Byck (1982). "Cocaine." *Scientific American* 246:128–46. Gives a general overview of what cocaine does, where it comes from, how it gets into the United States, the pharmacology of its alkaloids and its effects under differing intake methods. As for public policy, the writers seem to assume that the potential for the abuse of cocaine does not justify the intensity of eradication, interdiction, and other law enforcement efforts. While the main threat to North American and

European society from cocaine is the waste of human potential that could result from widespread consumption, it is not at all clear that, if legalized, or at least decriminalized, such widespread consumption would in fact occur. ^Cocaine ^Drug\Use ^Health ^Drug\Traffic ^Drug\Control\Policies\Critique ^Legalization ^Demand ^Cocaine\Pharmacology

1919. Van Pelt, Diana (1989). "New Ways to Crack a Cocaine Addiction." *Insight*, 31 July, 54–55. Describes new therapeutic drugs designed to reduce an addict's frantic craving for cocaine. It is not known whether the therapeutic drugs will help users maintain abstentions. ^Cocaine ^Treatment\Antagonists

1920. Van Tuyl, Laura (1989). "City Enlists Students against Drugs." *Christian Science Monitor*, 12 June. Description of how Columbus, Ohio, involved young citizens for their views and got a successful response in the war on drugs. ^United\States ^Drug\Control\Policies ^Youth ^Private\Initiatives

1921. Van Wert, James (1982). "U.S.-Mexican Aerial Opium Eradication Program: A Summative Evaluation." Ph.D. diss., University of Southern California. This doctoral dissertation (Public Administration) is authored by a former employee of the Department of State (international narcotics matters). The author's intent was to evaluate the success of the joint United States government–government of Mexico opium poppy herbicidal eradication program during 1976–1980. Gives a substantially important overview of drug control efforts in Mexico. With the United States' successful efforts to control the trafficking of Turkish heroin in the 1970s (thereby disrupting the "French Connection"), Mexico became an important producer of "substitute heroin." By the mid-1970s Mexican heroin comprised 87 percent of the U.S. market. The fundamental objective of the Mexican government–United States government drug supply reduction strategy was to make illicit drugs "inconvenient, expensive and risky to consume." Fewer people would experiment with them, it was assumed. The study draws on macroeconomic theory and indirect indicators to assess the effectiveness of efforts to reduce heroin supplies originating in Mexico and destined for the United States. The Mexican program, the author concludes, was quite successful. Also gives information about the internal political decision making within Mexico on its poppy eradication program. ^Latin\America ^Mexico ^United\States ^Heroin ^Interdiction ^Opiates ^Crop\Eradication ^Politics ^Aircraft ^Herbicides ^Drug\Control\Policies\History ^Production\History ^Migration ^Drug\Control\Policies\Effectiveness ^Reviews

1922. Varon, Miguel (1987). "Colombia: Labyrinthine Bureaucracy Generates Burgeoning Informal Sector." *Latinamerica Press*, 1 October, 6. Endless government red tape has forced half of Bogota's would-be merchants into the black market—or the "informal sector." This adds to the existence of a substantial informal sector dealing with narcotics. ^Latin\America ^Colombia ^Drug\Traffic ^Economics ^Bureaucracy ^Consequences\Illegal\Economy

1923. ——— (1987). "Drug Trade Brings in $2 Billion Annually: Despite Crackdown, Colombian Drug Barons Control Economy." *Latinamerica Press*, 26 November, 6. A raid in Colombia's remote Putumayo region in July 1987 revealed fifty-three cocaine laboratories and more than 120,000 acres of land planted with coca. Although the antinarcotics team destroyed the laboratories, there was only a slight reversal in Colombia's ability to export drugs. Traffickers simply moved their operations to more remote regions where low-income farmers are willing to work with the drug gangs because coca is the only cash crop giving a reasonable return. Mention is made of specific Colombian drug barons and how they deal with their riches socially. ^Colombia ^Latin\America ^Coca ^Cocaine ^Drug\Traffic ^Economics ^Production ^Refining ^Consequences\Economic ^Producers\Incentives\Economic ^Traffickers ^Consequences\Social

1924. ——— (1988). "Colombia: Drug Bosses Wage War against Extradition." *Latinamerica Press*, 10 March, 3. While the Colombian government has forced Colombia's drug kings underground, the drug bosses have forced the authorities to back off on their plans to extradite narcotics suspects to the United States. Last year, the Colombia Supreme Court, clearly intimidated by the traffickers, struck down the country's 1979 extradition treaty with the United States. Lawyers representing the cartel's ring leaders have, therefore, filed a suit claiming that there is no current provision in Colombian law that permits extraditions. In cases where judges cannot be bought, the dealers resort to intimidation. And if this fails, assassins are sent to take care of "uncooperative" jurists. ^Colombia ^Latin\America ^Extradition ^Consequences\Violence ^Consequences\Political ^Consequences\Judiciary

1925. ——— (1988). "Colombia: Many Flee Abroad as Violence, Death Threats Increase." *Latinamerica Press*, 24 November, 1. Death threats have forced leading journalists and dozens of other prominent Colombians to flee the country. Particularly is this so for those who may in some way resist the drug barons. A listing of prominent Colombians abroad for this reason is given. ^Latin\America ^Colombia ^Drug\Control\Policies ^Consequences\Violence ^Consequences\Personal ^Consequences\Migration

1926. ——— (1988). "Uncontrolled Violence Embroils Smugglers, Narcos, Army in Colombian Emerald Fields." *Latinamerica Press*, 18 February, 3. Colombia is the world's leading emerald producer, and in the past has accounted for as much as 90 percent of the high-grade international grade output. There has always been considerable violence in the emerald fields, particularly since the 1970s when rival emerald barons, backed by private armies, started to fight for control of the region in which the fields are located. All of this has become measurably more problematic now that narcotics traffickers and guerrillas are moving into the emerald field region to expand both their control and their field of operations. Thousands are undeterred by the "wild west" violence surrounding the emerald mines; a single stone can still change the course of a prospector's life. ^Latin\America ^Colombia ^Drug\Traffic ^Economics ^Consequences\Violence

1927. Veatch, Chauncey L. III (1988). "The Response of the State Agencies to AIDS, Addiction, and Alcoholism." *Advances in Alcohol and Substance Abuse* 7(2): 117–41. Intravenous drug abusers account for a substantial percentage of AIDS cases in the United States. If drug using cannot be eliminated, then the risk of AIDS contagion may be reduced by minimizing or eliminating "high-risk activities." Education programs for this group regarding the hazards of sharing needles, enrolling such people in treatment programs to reduce drug use, promoting the use of sterilized needles, and discouraging high-risk sexual activity are options discussed. Developments along these lines in California are noted. The considerable social overhead costs are given in table form. ^United\States ^AIDS ^Consequences\Social ^Proffered\Solutions

1928. *Vegetable Breeding: Breeding and Selection of Improved Cultivars of Tomato, Lettuce, and Cucumber as Substitute Crops for the Opium Poppy in the Highlands* (1984). Chiang Mai, Thailand: Maejo Institute of Agricultural Technology. This research project reports on technical developments of tomato varieties, lettuce, and cucumber cultivars that can withstand adverse weather conditions in the highland tropics. ^Southeast\Asia ^Thailand ^Opiates ^Golden\Triangle ^Crop\Substitution

1929. Vigilante, Richard, and Richard C. Cowan (1983). "Pot-Talk: Is Decriminalization Advisable?" *National Review* 35(April 29): 485–89. Cast in a debate setting, Richard Vigilante argues the negative, and Richard Cowan argues the affirmative response to this question. Within the two responses, many of the relevant policy issues are broached. ^United\States ^Cannabis ^Decriminalization

1930. Vliet, Henk Jan van (1990). "Separation of Drug Markets and the Normalization of Drug Problems in the Netherlands: An Example For Other Nations?" *The Journal of Drug Issues* 20:3(Summer): 463–71. Dutch policies have, on the whole, been diametrically opposed to policies in other countries which advocate a "war on drugs." Two basic elements of the Dutch policy are presented in this article. The first, decriminalization of use and retail trade in marijuana and hashish, is designed as a "separation of markets" to keep young people from experimenting with drugs such as heroin and cocaine. This approach is viewed as having been quite successful. Recently, a concept of "normalization of drug problems" aims at reducing the recrimination that drug users feel by integrating them into society in order to minimize harm to them and to society. It is thought that this policy has played a significant role in the prevention of AIDS. ^Netherlands ^Europe ^AIDS ^Drug\Control\Policies ^Decriminalization ^Cannabis ^Heroin ^Cocaine ^Drug\Control\Policies\Effectiveness

1931. Vohrah, K. C. (1984). "Forfeiture of the Profits and Proceeds Derived from Drug Trafficking: Thoughts on Future Action in Malaysia." *Bulletin on Narcotics* 36(4): 31–41. Gives a brief account of the existing law on forfeiture of the proceeds from drug crimes in Malaysia, notes their inadequacy, and reviews an impending bill in parliament to meet changing patterns of drug trafficking involving criminal syndicate leaders. ^Malaysia ^Asset\Forfeiture ^Organized\Crime ^Legislation ^Southeast\Asia

1932. Volsky, George (1987). "Jamaican Drug Gangs Thriving in U.S. Cities." *The New York Times*, 19 July, 17. Mostly working as illegal aliens, large numbers of Jamaicans are in the United States and Canada and are involved in widespread criminal organizations involved in the distribution of narcotics. It is thought that so far the gangs had not established working relations with regular organized crime organizations in the various cities in which they operate. ^Canada ^United\States ^Drug\Traffic ^Organized\Crime ^Jamaica ^Caribbean

1933. Voss, Harwin L. (1981). "Drugs, Crime, and Occupational Prestige." *Journal of Psychoactive Drugs* 13(3). Illicit drug use is much more extensive among men who report various criminal acts than among those who do not. One may conclude that there is a strong association between crime and drugs, but these data do not argue either that drug use leads to criminal activity or that involvement in crime leads to drug use. The causal chain is left undetermined. The findings, therefore, do not support the popular American belief that drug use leads to criminal behavior. It is to be noted that samples of arrestees and incarcerated offenders have serious limitations, which the author discusses. ^Drug\Use ^Crime

1934. Voth, Harold M. (1982). "The Effects of Marijuana on the Young." In *Marijuana and Youth: Clinical Observations on Motivation and Learning.* Rockville, Md.: National Institute on Mental Health. This author comes down on the side of affirming that marijuana is harmful, especially to the young. He views it leading to maladjustment and to reinforcing rebellious, negativistic behavior, and to lowering young people's motivation for effective social adaptation. ^Cannabis ^Consequences\Health ^Consequences\Psychological ^Youth ^Consequences\Social

1935. Waal, Helge (1980). "Unconventional Treatment Models for Young Drug Abusers in Scandinavia." *Journal of Drug Issues* 10(4): 441–51. The theoretical premises associated with unconventional treatment projects in Denmark, Sweden, and Norway are discussed. The development of collectives is a common nontraditional approach that gives meaningful experiences to young people who otherwise are not involved in the social mainstream wherein they may experience positive social interaction. The author generally views the results as being positive. ^Scandinavia ^Treatment\Therapeutic\Community ^Denmark ^Norway ^Sweden ^Youth

1936. Wagner, Diane (1986). "The Drug Dependency Dilemma: Managers Weigh Privacy versus Productivity in the Quest for a Drug Free Work Place." *California Business*, August, 30-37. As industries try to address the problem of use and abuse of drugs in the workplace through urine tests, drug-sniffing dogs, and desk searches, the problem is becoming California's most hotly debated employment issue. It is one that pits workers' rights to privacy against employers' interests in providing safe—and productive—drug-free work environments. Problems for management arise when workers fight back with lawsuits. ^United\States ^Drug\Control\Policies ^Drug\Testing ^Workplace ^Consequences\Human\Rights ^Consequences\Economic

1937. Wagstaff, Adam, and Alan Maynard (1988). *Economic Aspects of the Illicit Drug Market and Drug Enforcement Policies in the United Kingdom.* Home Office Research Study 95. London: Her Majesty's Stationery Office. Reviews the international economics literature on the cost effectiveness of law enforcement strategies aimed at reducing drug abuse of controlled drugs. Also explores the costs and benefits of the drug enforcement work of Britain's customs office and of its police. Where, in effect, would the government be best advised to put its money in the efforts to suppress drug trade and usage? Considerable measurement efforts are made along with attempts to quantify the welfare function of a number of social variables. A bibliography in excess of fifty items is appended to the publication. ^United\Kingdom ^Law\Enforcement ^Economics ^Reviews

1938. Waller, Coy W., and Jacqueline J. Denny (1972). *Annotated Bibliography of Marihuana, 1964–1970.* University, Miss.: University of Mississippi: Research Institute of Pharmaceutical Sciences, School of Pharmacy. Annotates 1,112 scientific reports. Focuses principally on the chemistry of plant constituents and the use of new analytical tools to identify them. Numerous biological studies are also included. These focus on violence, health, amotivational syndrome, adverse reactions, and so forth. ^Consequences\Health ^Cannabis ^Bibliographies ^Cannabis\Pharmacology ^Amotivational\Syndrome ^Consequences\Violence

1939. Waller, Coy W., Jacqueline J. Denny, and Marjorie Ann Walz (1971). *Annotated Bibliography of Marijuana, 1971 Supplement.* University, Miss.: University of Mississippi: Research Institute of Pharmaceutical Sciences, School of Pharmacy. Includes 467 annotated references on technical knowledge about marijuana. ^Cannabis ^Bibliographies ^Cannabis\Pharmacology ^Consequences\Health

1940. Waller, Coy W., Jacqueline J. Johnson, Judy Buelke, and Carlton E. Turner (1976). *Marihuana: An Annotated Bibliography.* New York: Macmillan. Contains 3,045 entries covering international scientific literature published since 1964 and to about 1975. While the principal focus is on the specialized nature of the chemistry of marijuana, numerous annotated entries of interest to this bibliography are also included. These deal with the relationship of marijuana to adolescents, its adverse effects on users, the relationship of cannabis and alcohol, amotivational syndrome, aggressive behavior, marijuana laws, legal and economic aspects of marketing, and cannabis control measures in various countries. ^Cannabis ^Bibliographies ^Cannabis\Pharmacology ^Youth ^Amotivational\Syndrome ^Consequences\Violence ^Legislation ^Drug\Control\Policies

1941. Waller, Coy W., Rashmi S. Nair, N. F. McAllister, Beverly S. Urbanek, and Carlton E. Turner (1982). *Marihuana: An Annotated*

Bibliography, Volume 2. New York: Macmillan. This volume continues the publication of annotations involving all published research that has been done on marijuana worldwide since 1964. Volume 2 contains 2,669 entries covering international scientific publications from 1975 to 1979. As with Volume 1, the principal focus is on the technical and scientific literature, although numerous entries are of interest to this bibliography. ^Cannabis ^Bibliographies ^Cannabis\Pharmacology ^Youth ^Amotivational\Syndrome ^Consequences\Violence ^Legislation ^Drug\Control\Policies

1942. Waller, Coy W., Kathleen P. Baren, Beverly S. Urbanek, and Carlton E. Turner (1983). *Marihuana: An Annotated Bibliography, 1980 Supplement.* University, Miss.: University of Mississippi: Research Institute of Pharmaceutical Sciences, School of Pharmacy. As with previous volumes listed under Coy W. Waller, this one extends the Research Institute of Pharmaceutical Sciences (at the University of Mississippi) publication of all published research that has been done on marijuana worldwide. This 1980 supplement contains 433 references. ^Cannabis ^Bibliographies ^Cannabis\Pharmacology ^Youth ^Amotivational\Syndrome ^Consequences\Violence ^Legislation ^Drug\Control\Policies

1943. Walsh, John (1982). "Frank Press Takes Exception to NAS Panel Recommendations on Marijuana." *Science* 217(June 11): 228–29. The National Academy of Science's president, Frank Press, took the unusual step of publicly stating his personal disagreement with the central recommendations of an academy report on marijuana policy (an analysis of marijuana policy) and suggested that the committee may have exceeded its charge and introduced "value-laden" judgments in its recommendations. The committee had expressed preference for ending criminal penalties for possession of small quantities of marijuana, and apparently Press took particular exception to this, arguing that the data were insufficient to justify the committee's judgment. "My own view is that the data available to the Committee were insufficient to justify on scientific or analytical grounds changes in current policies dealing with the use of marijuana." ^United\States ^Cannabis ^Decriminalization\Critique ^Reviews

1944. Walsh, Kenneth T., Ronald A. Taylor, and Ted Gest (1988). "The New Drug Vigilantes." *U.S. News and World Report*, 9 May, 20–22. Discussion of citizens' taking matters into their own hands, marching on drug houses, and carrying out vigilante raids. Particular discussion of the Muslims. Some police in Washington, D.C. have been working with these groups. ^United\States ^Law\Enforcement ^Private\Initiatives ^Washington\DC

1945. Walsh, Mary Williams (1986). "Many Mexican Police Supplement Low Pay with 'Tips' and 'Fines.'" *The Wall Street Journal*, 25 November, 1. Describes the generalized corruption of the Mexican police force, with reference to its current involvement in the trafficking of illicit drugs. ^Mexico ^Law\Enforcement ^Consequences\Corruption ^Latin\America

1946. Walsh, Miguel D. (1981). "Impact of the Iraqi-Iranian Conflict." *Drug Enforcement* (Summer): 7-12. Iran has long had an opium addiction problem. It continues so to have. Iraq functions mostly as a transit area. Smuggling routes are pointed out among Iranian and Iraqi minorities (e.g. Kurds). Iran, as well as Pakistan, continues to produce opium products. ^Middle\East ^Iran ^Pakistan ^Iraq ^Opiates ^Production ^Drug\Traffic ^Minorities ^Golden\Crescent ^Southwest\Asia

1947. "War on Drugs Held Burdening Justice" (1988). *The New York Times*, 5 December, B11. The war on drugs is "overwhelming" the criminal justice system, which lacks resources to counterbalance the legal protections afforded accused criminals. ^United\States ^Consequences\Judiciary

1948. "The War on Drugs Should Begin at Home" (1986). *The Economist,* 7 June, 23–24. Description of the invasion of crack into the narcotics consumers market. Financing terrorist activities is frequently not only expensive, but difficult. Linking up with the drug trade helps provide the required resources for terrorist activities to occur. Description of international connections with various terrorist groups and the "Cuban involvement." ^Cuba ^Cocaine ^Crack ^Drug\Traffic ^Politics ^Insurgents ^Terrorists ^Caribbean

1949. Wardlaw, Grant (1986). "The Realities of Drug Enforcement." *Journal of Drug Issues* 16(2): 171–82. Discusses and critically evaluates conventional drug-enforcement strategies such as reduction in supply overseas, dramatic increases in customs and domestic law enforcement resources, forfeiture of proceeds of drug trafficking, harsher penalties, and targeting high-level drug distributors. Argues the limitations and advantages of each approach. Law enforcement strategies, as a principal mechanism by which to control illegal drug use, must necessarily fail. There is a role for law enforcement strategy, however, and the author discusses its proper place, assigning it a lower priority in the complex of policies designed to reduce drug abuse. Such a change would create an atmosphere making it more acceptable to experiment with alternative models, techniques, and systems. "Given that our current efforts produce such poor results, we should not be reluctant to try bold and novel approaches merely because of the fear of failure. The reality is that we fail already" (p. 181). ^Drug\Control\Policies\Critique ^Reviews

1950. ——— (1988). "Linkages Between the Illegal Drugs Traffic and Terrorism." *Conflict Quarterly* (Summer): 5–26. Brief overview of the groups involved in terrorist activities who are also linked to drug traffickers. Wardlaw suggests that the indiscriminate application of the term "narcoterrorism" is unfortunate. The word should be eliminated from our vocabulary. Because others have failed to recognize important distinctions between drug trafficking and political violence, we have failed to assess adequately the threat posed by the drug/political violence linkages. Furthermore, eliminating terrorist links will have little impact on the flow of drugs. Drug connections are for practical economic reasons rather than ideological ones. ^Drug\Traffic ^Politics ^Insurgents ^Terrorists

1951. Wark, Mike (1989). "Texas Begins Selling Drug Stamps with Theme 'Drugs, Death, Taxes.'" *The Salt Lake Tribune,* 9 September, A1. Texas is one of twelve states that tax illicit drugs, and among those is Utah with a law passed in April 1988. The theme is the same, to bring an economic hardship on traffickers, fining them not only for trafficking in illicit drugs but for tax evasion. ^United\States ^Law\Enforcement ^Taxation ^Texas ^Utah

1952. Warner, Roger (1986). *Invisible Hand: The Marijuana Business.* New York: Beech Tree Books. A journalist goes to the streets where "grass-roots" marijuana trading occurs. There he examines not only the various scenarios in which smugglers work, but the economics that drive the trade. He looks also into "the new agrarians" in California as they direct their attention to the growing of marijuana. All sides are losing. The laws and their applications meant to suppress the trade are much weaker than the "laws of economics" that drive it. ^United\States ^Cannabis ^Drug\Traffic ^Economics ^Traffickers\Incentives\Economic ^Producers ^Drug\Control\Policies\Effectiveness

1953. Washton, Arnold M. (1988). "Preventing Relapse to Cocaine." *Journal of Clinical Psychiatry* 49(2): 34–38. Most cocaine addicts easily stop using the drug for a short period of time, but find long-term abstinence extremely difficult. This article describes the problems of relapse and proposes a multivariate prevention program. Principally, treatment must not focus exclusively on simply maintaining abstinence. There must be greater networking of reinforcing factors. ^Cocaine ^Treatment\Integrated ^P\S\Integrated

1954. Washton, Arnold (1989). *Cocaine Addiction: Treatment, Recovery, and Relapse Prevention*. New York: W. W. Norton and Company. Describes techniques for treating cocaine addiction successfully. Practical suggestions and specific guidelines are presented wherever possible for the benefit of clinicians, program administrators, family members of cocaine addicts, and for cocaine addicts themselves. Points to current knowledge about treatment and seeks to expand upon it. An entire chapter is devoted to "Cocaine and the Family." ^Cocaine ^Treatment ^Family

1955. Washton, Arnold M., and Mark S. Gold (1984). "Chronic Cocaine Abuse: Evidence for Adverse Effects on Health and Functioning." *Psychiatric Annals* 14(10): 733–43. Cocaine-related deaths and hospital emergency room visits have increased sharply. Aside from these effects on individuals and society, an often overlooked consequence of cocaine abuse is its tendency to foster the abuse of other drugs or alcohol. ^Cocaine ^Health ^Consequences\Personal ^Consequences\Health ^Alcohol

1956. ——— (1986). "Recent Trends in Cocaine Abuse: A View from the National Hotline, '800-COCAINE.'" *Advances in Alcohol and Substance Abuse* 6(2): 31-47. Extrapolating from data collected from the National Cocaine Hotline over the past three years, the analysis shows that usage is spreading to virtually all parts of the country, increasingly among women, adolescents, minorities, and lower socioeconomic groups. The amount of cocaine individuals consume has also increased, freebase smoking has become popular, and cocaine is used with other drugs. Cocaine-related automobile accidents are noted. ^United\States ^Cocaine ^Drug\Use ^Women ^Minorities ^Youth ^Consequences\Public\Safety ^Statistics

1957. ——— (1987). *Cocaine: A Clinician's Handbook*. New York: The Guilford Press. This book is written primarily for health care professionals—psychologists, psychiatrists, physicians, social workers, nurses, drug- and alcohol-abuse counselors, and other medical or mental health clinicians. Nevertheless, it includes sections of "social impact" importance in that it deals with treatment centers and techniques, cocaine in the workplace, and the consequences of cocaine and other drug use during pregnancy. ^Cocaine ^Health ^Pregnancy ^Drug\Use ^Workplace ^Treatment ^Consequences\Social

1958. Washton, Arnold M. and Nannette S. Stone (1984). "The Human Cost of Chronic Cocaine Use." *Medical Aspects of Human Sexuality* 18(11): 122-130. Abstinence must be the treatment goal because abusers stand to lose family, friends, money, and possibly their lives. All of this does, of course, also impose substantial costs on society. ^Cocaine ^Drug\Use ^Treatment\Abstinence ^Consequences\Personal ^Consequences\Family ^Consequences\Economic

1959. Washton, Arnold M., Mark S. Gold, and A. Carter Pottash (1985). "Opiate and Cocaine Dependencies." *Postgraduate Medicine* 77(5): 293–300. Discusses measures primary care physicians may take, when viewing treatment options, that involve promising developments in drug treatment of opiate dependencies. The authors outline current understandings of cocaine-related problems and their management. They acknowledge that cocaine dependency may be difficult to treat because of the drug's powerful reinforcing qualities. ^Cocaine ^Opiates ^Treatment

1960. Watters, John K. (1989). "Observations on the Importance of Social Context in HIV Transmission among Intravenous Drug Users." *Journal of Drug Issues* 19(1): 9–26. The AIDS virus is perhaps the most significant health consequence associated with intravenous drug use. Needle sharing is the principal culprit. The study explores AIDS-affected communities in San Francisco and New York, and notes considerable disparities. The social contexts and conditions in which risk behavior takes place are discussed. There follows discussion about community-based intervention programs in behalf of public health initiatives, including the efficacy of needle-exchange programs. ^Heroin ^Consequences\Health ^AIDS ^Society ^United\States ^California ^New\York ^Needle\Exchange\Programs ^Treatment

1961. Wayne, E. A. (1988). "Militias Cooperate on Drug Trade to Pay for War—Against Each Other." *Christian Science Monitor*, 9 March, 1. Warring militias in Lebanon each get a cut in the expanding heroin and cocaine trade, as well as the traditional hashish industry. It is thought that up to 20 percent of Lebanon's gross national product may derive from narcotics trade. ^Middle\East ^Lebanon ^Cannabis ^Cocaine ^Heroin ^Drug\Traffic ^Economics ^Politics ^Consequences\Violence ^Traffickers\Private\Armies

1962. ——— (1988). "US Dilemma with Laos: Protect the Living—or Dead?" *Christian Science Monitor*, 18 March, 3. Laos is now a world-class producer and exporter of opium. The Laotian government is giving official sanction to the booming drug trade. The Reagan administration cannot crack down on Laos and still hope to extract the remains of servicemen lost there during the Vietnam war. ^Laos ^United\States ^Opiates ^Drug\Traffic ^Politics ^Consequences\Foreign\Relations ^Production ^Southeast\Asia

1963. Wayne, E. A. and Linda Feldman (1988). "Panamanian Leader Linked in Testimony to Drug Trafficking." *Christian Science Monitor*. 29 January, 3. Inside testimony links Panama's military ruler, General Manuel Noriega, to drug trafficking. ^Latin\America ^Panama ^Traffickers ^Corruption

1964. Weatherford, Jack M (1987). *Narcóticos en Bolivia y los Estados Unidos*. La Paz, Bolivia: Editorial "Los Amigos Del Libro" Werner Guttentag. In a wide-ranging discussion, the author looks into the coca/cocaine economy in Bolivia and to the distortions it has created in Bolivian economic and social life. Among these are the out-migration of the labor force from traditional Andean villages to the Chapare and the subsequent insufficiency of manpower in those areas to maintain conventional food planting and harvesting routines. Thus nutritional deficiencies mount for women and children who are either unable (because of location) or unwilling (because of moral constraints) to enter into the coca/cocaine trade at whatever level. ^Bolivia ^Coca ^Cocaine ^Drug\Traffic ^Agriculture ^Migration ^Latin\America ^Consequences\Social ^Consequences\Economic ^Consequences\Misc ^Women ^Consequences\Children

1965. Webster, Christopher D. (1986). "Compulsory Treatment of Narcotic Addiction." *International Journal of Law and Psychiatry* 8:133–59. Addict populations are extremely heterogeneous. Because of this disparity, neither the prison view nor the hospital view is satisfactory for all addicts. Aside from the problem of heterogeneity of the addict population, there is also extensive disparity in legislative proposals. The problem is further complicated by disparity in policing and sentencing practices. The problem of legislating treatment without legislating evaluation is also noted. ^Drug\Use ^Treatment\Critique ^Drug\Control\Policies\Critique

1966. Weil, Andrew T. (1977). "Observations on Consciousness Alteration: Why Coca Leaf Should Be Available as a Recreational Drug." *Journal of Psychedelic Drugs* 9(1): 75–78. With marijuana decriminalization well under way, why shouldn't decriminalization be extended to coca? The author, in some kind of position in Peru wherein he could prescribe coca as a treatment for various ailments, confirmed some of its folk medicinal applications, particularly in relieving gastrointestinal symptoms and as an adjunct in programs of weight reduction and physical fitness. The chewing of coca leaves would be greatly preferred to the ingestion of cocaine, so why not make it legal? ^Coca ^P\S\Legalization

1967. Weiner, Eric (1989). "Mexico Shooting down Drug Planes, Officials Say." *The New York Times*, 8 December, A11. Description of the Mexican federal police having shot down four drug-laden planes in November and early December. ^Latin\America ^Mexico ^Drug\Control\Policies ^Law\Enforcement ^Aircraft

1968. Weinraub, Bernard (1989). "Money Bush Wants for Drug War Is Less than Sought by Congress." *The New York Times*, 30 January, 1. President Bush has sought only a small increase in money for drug enforcement over Ronald Reagan's final budget. This would hardly give credence to Bush's inaugural address to end the affliction of drugs in the United States. ^United\States ^Drug\Control\Policies ^Politics

1969. Weinstein, Adam K. (1988). "Prosecuting Attorneys for Money Laundering: A New and Questionable Weapon in the War on Crime." *Law and Contemporary Problems* 51(1): 367–86. Description of the money-laundering control act, the amount of monies believed to be involved in money laundering, the legislative history associated with the act, the right of those accused to be defended by competent attorneys, and the implications of placing that relationship in jeopardy if money laundering is discovered. This is viewed as being a constitutional infringement on defendant's rights. ^United\States ^Money\Laundering ^Drug\Control\Policies ^Legislation ^Consequences\Constitutional

1970. Weintraub, Richard M. (1986). "Pakistani Drug Drive Seen in 2 Major Hauls; Military Officers Held in Seizure of Heroin." *The Washington Post*, 31 July, A27. With obvious complicity and evidence of corruption, two Pakistani military officers have been placed under arrest in connection with two seizures of heroin totaling more than 800 pounds. Description of how Pakistan is a major supply route for heroin marketed in the West. ^Pakistan ^Heroin ^Drug\Traffic ^Consequences\Corruption ^Middle\East ^Golden\Crescent ^Southwest\Asia

1971. ——— (1988). "Bhutto Says Drug Fight Is Top Priority; New Premier Frees Political Prisoners." *The Washington Post*, 4 December, A33. Pakistan's prime minister, Benazir Bhutto, on her first day in office, vowed to fight the growth of illicit narcotics distribution and production in Pakistan. ^Pakistan ^Drug\Control\Policies ^Middle\East ^Golden\Crescent ^Southwest\Asia

1972. Weisskopf, Michael (1983). "South China Is Channel for Heroin." *The Washington Post*, 20 September, A10. Major drug syndicates have opened a new transit route through China to facilitate smuggling of heroin from the Golden Triangle to markets in Hong Kong and the West. Interruption of traffic by sea forced traffickers to look for an overland connection to Hong Kong through China. ^China ^Heroin ^Drug\Traffic ^Hong\Kong ^Southeast\Asia ^Golden\Triangle

1973. Weissman, James C. (1984). "Drug Offence Sentencing Practices in the United States of America." *Bulletin on Narcotics* 36(3): 27–41. The U.S. criminal justice system makes available a range of options with respect to sentencing or otherwise disposing of cases of accused narcotic offenders. New drug offense sentencing policies are emerging, and traditional values of rehabilitation are less favored than is sentencing, based on principles of uniformity and retribution. Specific recommendations are offered for revision of drug offense sentence policies to incorporate the emerging penal values. ^United\States ^Law\Enforcement ^Judiciary ^Values ^Consequences\Penal

1974. Weissman, James C., and Karen N. File (1976). "Criminal Behavior Patterns of Female Addicts: A Comparison of Findings in Two Cities." *International Journal of the Addictions* 11(6): 1063–77. Many studies undertaken to describe the relationship between crime and addiction in females have generally concluded that addicted females either become prostitutes or they commit crimes against property. This study developed results forcing a classification into four criminal behavior patterns of female arrestees. These were prostitutes without a history of serious crimes, females with a history of serious crimes who were not prostitutes, females who were both prostitutes and committed serious crimes, and females who were not prostitutes and who committed only minor offenses. ^Drug\Use ^Crime ^Women ^Prostitution

1975. Weissman, James C. and Robert L. DuPont, editors (1981). *Criminal Justice and Drugs: The Unresolved Connection.* Port Washington, N.Y.: Kennikat Press. Multidisciplinary studies in the law: Drug abuse treatment in the United States; drug abuse and crime in the United States; rehabilitation of narcotics addicts; administration of criminal justice with regard to narcotics offenders; and law and legislation in the United States relating to drugs. ^United\States ^Drug\Use ^Crime ^Drug\Control\Policies ^Legislation

1976. Welch, Mary Ellen (1988). "The Extraterritorial War on Cocaine: Perspectives from Bolivia and Colombia." *Suffolk Transnational Law Journal* 12:39–81. Discusses the failure of interdiction, eradication, and extradition. Operation Blast Furnace is discussed as well as the Colombian extradition treaty. A principal drawback in the application of policy so far is the ignoring of the dynamic of market forces that drive "the world's most lucrative industry." Speculation that in the end, the market that drives the cocaine industry may fuel its own destruction from oversupply and a domestic abuse crisis in Bolivia and Colombia. The article is copiously noted (230 annotated footnotes). ^United\States ^Cocaine ^Drug\Control\Policies ^Bolivia ^Colombia ^Economics ^Latin\America ^Consequences\Markets ^Demand ^Traffickers\Incentives\Economic

1977. Werch, Chudley E. (1987). "Rethinking Critical Issues in Drug Programming." *Journal of Alcohol and Drug Education* 32(3): 19–24. Drug education programs have not worked well, and part of the reason is that health educators and other professionals in the development of such programs have not thought clearly about their goals, development of policies, students' rights and protection, and clarification of drug-related terminology and evaluation procedures. This author hopes to correct those deficiencies. ^United\States ^Drug\Use ^Prevention\Drug\Education\Critique ^Reviews

1978. Werlich, David P. (1987). "Debt, Democracy and Terrorism in Peru." *Current History* 86(516): 29–37. Of interest to this bibliography is the discussion of the drug trade. However else Peru's President Alan García has been criticized for his observations about and work with his country's foreign debt problems, he has won the praise of United States officials for his vigorous war on drugs. ^Latin\America ^Peru ^United\States ^Cocaine ^Drug\Control\Policies\Effectiveness ^Consequences\Foreign\Relations ^Politics ^Terrorists ^International\Debt

1979. —— (1988). "Peru: García Loses His Charm." *Current History*, January, 13–16. For almost two years of his five-year term President Alan García had overwhelming support in Peru. During 1987, however, his popularity declined as did the economy. The business community became disenchanted; Peru's unions staged the first general strike of García's administration; and dissonance arose from within the president's own party, the center-left American Popular Revolutionary Alliance (APRA). At the root of the crisis lay economic mismanagement and a spade of bad luck inherited from the military dictatorship of 1968–1980, which bequeathed Peru's former president, Fernando Belaúnde, a heavy $9 billion debt. Then the recession of the early 1980s in the developed world produced a 38-percent drop in prices for Peru's principal exports—petroleum, copper and other nonferrous metals, fish meal, and iron ore—and a severe trade deficit. Among the many consequences emerging were Peru's guerrilla activity (Shining Path or *Sendero Luminoso*), subsequent human rights abuses, and a drug connection. As demand for cocaine increased in the United States and production incentives grew in Peru, an alliance with the United States dedicated resources to interdiction and eradication. But many of Peru's resources were diverted to counter-insurgency activities against the Shining Path. From the early days of the insurgency, Peruvian and U.S. officials suspected that Peru's drug lords, benefitting from the Shining Path's diversion of police resources away from themselves, provided money and weapons to the guerrillas. But neither Lima nor Washington could demonstrate a connection between the Shining Path and the cocaine industry. Then in August 1986 a Shining Path document contained the party's first significant statement concerning the matter. It asserted that cocaine addiction was a problem confined to the capitalist world, and praised the chewing of coca leaves (the source of cocaine) as an ancient and beneficial practice among the Andean peoples. Such a stance permitted an alliance with the international drug network, while indicating the Shining Path's desire to build support among coca farmers, who deeply resent the government's program to eradicate the crop. ^Peru ^Coca ^Cocaine ^Drug\Traffic ^Politics ^Insurgents ^Economics ^Latin\America ^Consequences\Terrorists ^International\Debt

1980. Werner, Leslie Maitland (1988). "Panama Drug Ring Said to Be Broken." *The New York Times*, 2 June, A8. A drug ring in Panama specialized in forging requests to board military aircraft and sending people along who pretended to be active servicemen returning home on leave. They carried drugs with them. An accidental arrest broke into the ring and, apparently, has destroyed it. ^United\States ^Drug\Traffic ^Military ^Consequences\Corruption ^Panama

1981. Wert, Renee C., and Michael L. Raulin (1986). "The Chronic Cerebral Effect of Cannabis Use. II. Psychological Findings and Conclusions." *International Journal of the Addictions* 21(6): 629–42. This literature review article, drawing on evidence from both American and cross-cultural studies, concludes that there is little evidence that marijuana produces structural cerebral changes or that it leads to functional impairment, although subtle impairment cannot be ruled out. ^Cannabis ^Reviews ^Consequences\Neurological

1982. Wesson, Donald R. (1988). "Revival of Medical Maintenance in the Treatment of Heroin Dependence." *Journal of the American Medical Association* 259(22): 3314–15. Physicians in the United States, as opposed to those in England, are highly constrained in the degree to which they may treat narcotic addiction by prescribing narcotics. This short piece is a review of and criticism of several articles in this issue of *JAMA*. ^United\States ^Heroin ^Treatment\Critique ^Treatment\Drug\Maintenance

1983. Westermeyer, Joseph (1976). "The Pro-Heroin Effects of Anti-Opium Laws in Asia." *Archives of General Psychiatry* 33(September): 1135–39. When anti-opium laws were enacted by three Asian governments in countries where opium use was traditional, heroin suddenly appeared. Within a decade, heroin addiction surpassed opium addiction. The article notes that the laws increased the price of narcotics drugs, promoted the black market heroin industry, corrupted law enforcement officials, and produced a major health problem for the countries. The general policy implications of these findings are noted. ^Southeast\Asia ^Opiates ^Drug\Control\Policies ^Heroin ^Drug\Use ^Consequences\Drug\Concentration ^Consequences\Drug\Control\Policies ^Consequences\Unintended

1984. —— (1980). "Treatment for Narcotic Addiction in a Buddhist Monastery." *Journal of Drug Issues* 10(1): 221–27. Describes the treatment and evaluates the treatment outcome of approximately 3,000 narcotics addicts from Laos who were sent to a Buddhist monastery in Thailand to undergo treatment. The data are presented, along with mortality associated with the treatment. ^Laos ^Thailand ^Opiates ^Treatment\Therapeutic\Community ^Treatment\Critique ^Southeast\Asia

1985. —— (1987). "Cultural Patterns of Drug and Alcohol Use: An Analysis of Host and Agent in the Cultural Environment." *Bulletin on Narcotics* 39(2): 11–27. Cross-cultural studies of drug problems show that certain social strategies concerning drug use hinder the development of such problems and help to reduce and prevent the abuse of drugs and alcohol, while certain other strategies are liable to add to drug problems, and these are culturally specific in their effects. It is necessary to develop an understanding of the sociopsychological relationships within a host culture regarding influences leading to drug abuse and public policy measures that might be taken to combat those influences. ^Drug\Use\Theories ^Society ^Culture

1986. —— (1989). "National and International Strategies to Control Drug Abuse." *Advances in Alcohol and Substance Abuse* 8(2): 1–35. Since drug problems continue to produce health problems in consuming societies, how might these be addressed? Attacking the problem from a producer's vantage is one way, from a consumer's vantage another. Whichever, it is important to understand the issues that favor a continued existence of drug abuse and bring national decisions to bear on those issues (because international factors are very strong and overwhelming). The author discusses the financial aspects of production and smuggling, sociocultural factors that favor drug production and commerce (including the question of national minorities, expatriates and refugees, drug lords). There are also political causes and consequences, including the funding of political movements, the raising of private armies and police forces, internal corruption, and confused international relations. From this vantage, political and economic forces can wipe away any developmental changes overnight that might favor crop replacement or other substitution programs. In sum, the best strategy is to suppress the trade through a global effort that would raise the costs to traffickers and consumers for dealing in illicit drugs. Extensive citation. ^Drug\Control\Policies ^Economics ^Politics ^Reviews ^Production\Theories ^Minorities ^Traffickers\Private\Armies ^Consequences\Misc ^Consequences\Corruption ^Consequences\Foreign\Relations

1987. Westrate, David L. (1985). "Drug Trafficking and Terrorism." *Drug Enforcement* (Summer): 19–24. Various terrorist and insurgence groups are either explicitly or implicitly involved in drug trafficking. Reviews of various groups in Colombia and Peru. The *Sendero Luminoso* is specifically discussed. ^Drug\Traffic ^Insurgents ^Terrorists ^Colombia ^Peru ^Latin\America

1988. —— (1985). "How Are Drug Trafficking and Terrorism Related?" *Narcotics Control Digest* 15(11): 1–4. Details the interrelationships in Colombia and Burma. ^Burma ^Colombia ^Drug\Traffic ^Terrorists ^Latin\America ^Southeast\Asia

1989. Wetli, C. V. and Wright, R. K. (1979). "Death Caused by Recreational Cocaine Use." *Journal of the American Medical Association* 241(23): 2519–22. The authors attempt to identify the particular characteristics or features of individuals who were among sixty-eight deaths associated with recreational use of illicit cocaine, and which could help to explain why the drug acted sufficiently strongly to kill them. Rates of absorption, peak blood concentrations, and prior use of cocaine all appear to contribute to the possibility of a fatal reaction. Despite the prevailing belief in the late 1970s, the authors opined that cocaine could not be considered a safe recreational drug. ^Cocaine ^Drug\Use ^Consequences\Health ^Consequences\Personal

1990. Wexler, Harry K., Douglas S. Lipton, and Bruce D. Johnson (1988). *A Criminal Justice System Strategy for Treating Cocaine-Heroin Abusing Offenders in Custody*. Washington, D.C.: U.S. Department of Justice. Based on the firm assumption that there is a positive relationship between drug abuse and crime, this short booklet proposes interventions, based in the research literature and other experiences, for reducing drug abuse and therefore the tendency for criminal behavior of those so involved. A substantial bibliography is included. ^Drug\Use ^Crime ^Proffered\Solutions

1991. Wheeler, Linda (1989). "Crack Houses Are Torched in NW Area; Neighborhood Official Doubts Vigilantism." *The Washington Post*, 2 March, A1. Vacant buildings, used as crack houses, are becoming the target of arsonists who are assuming that burning them down will eliminate the activity conducted in them. ^United\States ^Cocaine ^Crack ^Private\Initiatives

1992. "Where Heroin Is King." (1984). *The Economist*, 28 July, 35. Description of how Chiang Kai-shek's third army, retreating from the Communists in 1949, set up business in Burma, Thailand, and Laos and has come to dominate the opium trade. Description of internecine conflict between this group of Chinese and Khun Sa. ^Southeast\Asia ^Burma ^Laos ^Thailand ^Opiates ^Drug\Traffic\History ^China ^Golden\Triangle

1993. "Where Poppies Once Stood." (1984). *Far Eastern Economic Review*, 29 March, 42–43. Description of an anti-opium crop substitution program in northern Thailand. ^Southeast\Asia ^Thailand ^Opiates ^Crop\Substitution

1994. Whitaker, Ben (1987). *The Global Connection: The Crisis of Drug Addiction*. London: Jonathan Cape Ltd. The aim of this book is to "diagnose correctly" the current drug problem, and then offer suggestions for changes in national and international policy. Thus, after tracing the evolution of the drug-abuse problem throughout the world, after looking into the character of the drugs themselves, after examining reasons why people abuse drugs, and after exploring national and international efforts to cope with drug abusers both by treatment and by control, the author advances his recommendations. The recommendations are sensitive to the whole issue of multinational traffickers, the mafia, and source country politics in the Golden Triangle and Latin America. Arguments are advanced for and against legalization and public and private facilitating efforts on both sides of that question (e.g., private self-help groups in housing units). The arguments employ the benefit of classical philosophers. ^Drug\Traffic ^Drug\Control\Policies ^Legalization ^Reviews ^Proffered\Solutions

1995. White House (1989). *National Drug Control Strategy* (September). Washington, D.C.: The White House. The long-awaited Bennett Plan, authorized by George Bush to be promulgated as his policy. Focuses on national priorities in the criminal justice system, drug treatment, education, international initiatives, interdiction efforts, research, and intelligence. The White House promises to increase funding and aggressive law enforcement activity not only against traffickers but occasional users of illicit drugs as well. ^United\States ^Drug\Control\Policies

1996. *White House Conference for a Drug-Free America* (1988). Washington, D.C.: U.S. Government Printing Office. In 1986 President Ronald Reagan's Anti-Drug Abuse Act was implemented. One requirement was the establishment of a White House Conference for a Drug-Free America, which would hold regional hearings and issue a final report. The idea was to share information, to bring to public attention approaches to drug-abuse education and prevention strategies that had been successful, to highlight dimensions of the drug-abuse crisis, and to examine the essential role of parents and family members in creating a drug-free America. This final report gives concrete recommendations in areas of prevention, education, criminal justice, treatment, workplace, transportation, sports, public housing, media and entertainment, international drug control, federal reorganization, and system-wide integration of antidrug efforts. Throughout the recommendations and the report are to be found the concerns for the consequences deriving from illegal drug use—the federal deficit, family violence and child abuse, increased cost of health care, diminished public safety, impaired national defense, loss of productivity, decline of social and moral value systems, loss of individual freedom, decreased learning, political corruption, increased victimization, and AIDS. ^United\States ^Drug\Traffic ^Drug\Control\Policies ^Proffered\Solutions ^Consequences\Misc

1997. White, Michael D., and William A. Luksetich (1983). "Heroin: Price Elasticity and Enforcement Strategies." *Economic Inquiry* 21(October): 557–64. Many economists have argued that reducing the supply of heroin through harassment of sellers is counterproductive. This simply results in greater property crime and higher revenues for the sellers of heroin. This relationship is made possible by virtue of heroin demand by addicts being relatively "inelastic." And, because many heroin addicts necessarily finance their habit through criminal activity, one sees the relationship. This author contends the preceding argument to be valid only in a special case—when a market for heroin is not effectively monopolized and in which the intensity of enforcement against both the sellers and users of heroin is low, resulting, therefore, in a relatively low price for heroin. In terms of public policy, whether the trend toward reduced user harassment and increased seller harassment is appropriate depends on the elasticity of the demand for heroin at existing prices. ^Heroin ^Law\Enforcement ^Crime ^Economics ^Drug\Control\Policies\Critique

1998. White, Peter T. (1985). "The Poppy." *National Geographic* 107: 142–89. Verbal and visual depiction of the entire range of poppy growing/opium refining/narcotics trafficking. The report is that of a journalist/photographer who visits all of the major poppy growing and transiting areas in Asia and Mexico. ^Heroin ^Opiates ^Drug\Traffic ^Demand ^Supply ^Production ^Consequences\Misc ^Southeast\Asia ^Golden\Triangle ^Mexico ^Latin\America

1999. —— (1989). "Coca." *National Geographic* 175(1): 2–47. Evidence from Colombia, Peru, Bolivia, and South United States dealing with many coca/cocaine–related issues: demand problems in the United States, supply issues in Latin America, marketing strategies, interdiction and eradication efforts, political corruption and intimidation, processing technology, economic incentives, markets, devices and strategies used by couriers, implications of social value changes, demand-reduction strategies in the United States, including stings, prosecution, education, and discussion of issues associated with legalization of cocaine. ^Coca ^Cocaine ^Drug\Traffic ^Drug\Control\Policies ^Peru ^Bolivia ^Colombia ^Latin\America ^Demand ^Supply

2000. White, Terence (1985). "The Drug-Abuse Epidemic Coursing through Pakistan." *Far Eastern Economic Review*, 13 June, 97–99. Description of "Tribal Areas within Pakistan," a legacy of British colonial days, which have facilitated the drug trade. Before 1980, heroin was virtually unknown and unavailable in Pakistan. Today Pakistan is recognized as the world's leading heroin exporter. And a considerable quantity of it is being consumed internally. ^Pakistan ^Heroin ^Drug\Use ^Drug\Traffic ^Minorities ^Consequences\Drug\Concentration ^Southwest\Asia

2001. Whitehead, John (1986). "U.S. International Narcotics Control Programs and Policies." *Department of State Bulletin* 86(October): 37–40. The highest U.S. government priority is reducing production of coca, opium, and cannabis. In 1981, only two countries were eradicating illicit narcotic crops. In 1985, there were eradication programs in fourteen countries. There are efforts currently in Colombia to identify environmentally safe herbicides for the hearty coca plant. The United States and Mexico have begun collaboration on an intensive spraying program of opium poppy in the infamous tristate area. Countries discussed, either as producers of or conduits for illicit narcotics, are Colombia, Bolivia, Peru, Mexico, Pakistan, Thailand, Morocco, Iran, Afghanistan, Laos, India, Malaysia, the Bahamas, Lebanon, Turkey, Panama,

Belize, Ecuador, and Burma. ^United\States ^Drug\Control\Policies ^Crop\Eradication ^Herbicides ^Colombia ^Bolivia ^Peru ^Mexico ^Pakistan ^Thailand ^Morocco ^Iran ^Afghanistan ^Laos ^India ^Malaysia ^Bahamas ^Lebanon ^Turkey ^Panama ^Belize ^Ecuador ^Burma ^Latin\America ^Southeast\Asia ^Middle\East ^Southwest\Asia

2002. Whitney, Craig R. (1989). "Crack Use Starts in Fearful Europe." *The New York Times*, 27 July, A7. Europe, especially Britain, is fearful that the "American disease" will spread to its shores. British police and customs officers have added more than 1,000 people to drug detection and intelligence operations in anticipation of a crack problem deriving from Europe's now being opened as a substantial market for cocaine. Almost all Western European countries are making coordinated planning. ^Europe ^Cocaine ^Crack ^Drug\Use ^Drug\Control\Policies ^Law\Enforcement

2003. "Who Are Soviet Drug Users, Dealers?" (1986). *The Current Digest of the Soviet Press* 38(32): 1–7. The studies reported in this article, concentrating on Georgia, indicate that users are largely young and frequently well off economically. They tend to be the better educated. The dealers, among whom respectable people are found, are seldom caught. ^USSR ^Drug\Use ^Society ^Drug\Traffic ^Traffickers

2004. Wiant, Jon A. (1985). "Narcotics in the Golden Triangle." *The Washington Quarterly* 8(4): 125–40. The Golden Triangle of Southeast Asia produces approximately one-third of the heroin consumed by addicts in the United States. The author examines the geographical and ethnographic landscape associated with opium production and correlates that with the political environment prevailing in the region. Considerable anarchy has been spawned by narcotics trafficking. Thus countering narcotics production and trafficking will pose significant, and in some cases unique, policy responses. The author discusses opium eradication, anti trafficking operations, and border or customs issues. ^Southeast\Asia ^Opiates ^Heroin ^Drug\Traffic ^Drug\Control\Policies ^Golden\Triangle ^Politics ^Consequences\Political ^Crop\Eradication

2005. Wiener, Eric (1989). "Mexican Police Shooting Down Drug Planes, Officials Declare." *The New York Times*, December 8, A10. In the past three months Mexican federal police are said to have shot down four drug laden planes. The police have announced they will continue to fire at suspicious planes if those planes do not obey orders to land. ^Latin\America ^Mexico ^Drug\Control\Policies ^Aircraft

2006. Wijngaart, Govert F. Van de (1988). "A Social History of Drug Use in the Netherlands: Policy Outcomes and Implications." *Journal of Drug Issues* 18(3): 481–95. Both the geography of and the liberal political climate in the Netherlands are conducive to trading and transporting illegal psychotropic substances. This article takes a broad view of these two factors in suggesting their relevance for understanding why the Netherlands are quite different in their drug policy applications. Reviewed are the social welfare and health care systems, the history of drug use in the Netherlands, the provision of methadone, and the governmental policy on aid and prevention. The author suggests that the Dutch, in trying to cope with new and extended drug-abuse problems, are looking for ways to "normalize" their response. ^Netherlands ^Drug\Use\History ^Drug\Control\Policies ^Politics ^Society

2007. Wilbur, Robert (1986). "A Drug to Fight Cocaine." *Science* (March): 42. Wilbur, a pharmacologist, describes how some psychiatrists prescribe anti-depressants and amino acids to cocaine addicts to relieve their craving. The treatment is represented as "working." The implication is that drug therapy works when other treatments fail. ^Cocaine ^Treatment\Antagonists

2008. Wilkerson, Isabel (1987). "Urban Homicide Rates in U.S. up Sharply in 1986." *The New York Times*, 15 January, A14. In the wake of increased urban homicides, observations are made that they are occurring among teenagers linked to cocaine and crack. Almost all the increase (highest now since the 1970s) seems to be associated with drug related slayings. ^United\States ^Cocaine ^Crack ^Drug\Traffic ^Youth ^Crime ^Consequences\Violence

2009. ——— (1988). "Detroit Citizens Join with Church to Rid Community of Drugs." *The New York Times*, 29 June. Description of a community effort in an abandoned-house district of Detroit to purchase crack houses, renovate them, and sell them at low cost (for an average of $18,000) to senior citizens and single-parent families who need housing the most and who can be relied upon not to participate in the drug trade. Considerable volunteerism, including church volunteers and unemployed neighbors hired temporarily, do most of the renovation work. Many people get their down payments through "sweat equity." ^United\States ^Michigan ^Cocaine ^Crack ^Drug\Control\Policies ^Private\Initiatives

2010. Wilkins, Allen J. (1984). "The Economics of Heroin Addiction and Criminal Activity." Ph.D. diss., University of Wisconsin-Madison. This doctoral dissertation, in economics, addresses the economic relationship between heroin addiction and criminal activity. The usefulness of information on the magnitude of the correlation between heroin addiction and crime depends on how causal forces operate. Definitive evidence here has not yet been established. This work attempts to identify new factors that affect consumers' demand for heroin; thus, it provides an analytic framework for structuring policy. Policy implications, given various assumptions regarding the data, are noted. In sum, the approach into the economics of heroin addiction and crime is to identify how economic factors operate to promote such a high correlation as obviously exists. ^Heroin ^Crime ^Economics ^Reviews ^Crime\Theories

2011. Willette, Robert E. (1986). "Drug Testing Programs." In *Urine Testing for Drugs of Abuse*, NIDA Research Monograph 73, edited by Richard L. Hawks and C. Nora Chiang. Rockville, Md.: National Institute on Drug Abuse. Basic survey of the programs already introduced into various government agencies, public utility companies, large industrial corporations, and even some small companies. Successful programs are noted for their having a clear communication to all employees and applicants as to the nature of the drug program and the consequences of detected drug use. Reasonableness and fairness are emphasized as important variables contributing to a successful program. ^United\States ^Drug\Testing ^Workplace

2012. Williams, Alan F., Michael A. Peat, Dennis J. Crouch, Joann K. Wells, and Bryan S. Finkle (1985). "Drugs in Fatally Injured Young Drivers." *Public Health Reports* 100(1): 19–25. Eighty-one percent of 440 male drivers investigated in fatal accidents had one or more drugs in them, mostly alcohol. However, marijuana was found in 37 percent and cocaine in 11 percent. Usually, cocaine and marijuana were found in combination with high blood alcohol concentrations. While alcohol's contribution to the crashes was determinable, the role of other drugs could not be adequately determined. ^Drug\Use ^Consequences\Public\Safety ^Consequences\Economic ^Consequences\Personal

2013. Williams, Dan (1985). "2 Nations Stymied in Efforts to Shut Off Flow: Mexico a Funnel for U.S.–Bound Cocaine." *The Los Angeles Times*, 3 December, 17. Describes the development of the "Mexican connection" for cocaine transiting from South America to the United States, and the degree to which the narcotics traffickers have been able to buy off law enforcement agents in Mexico. ^Mexico ^Cocaine ^Drug\Traffic ^Consequences\Corruption ^Latin\America

2014. ——— (1988). "Drug-Fighting and Diplomacy Mix Like Oil and Water, U.S. Discovers." *The Los Angeles Times*, 27 February, 18. The very officials the United States must frequently deal with in drug producing countries are those "on the take" in the very drug trade the United States is trying to suppress. ^United\States ^Politics ^Consequences\Corruption ^Consequences\Foreign\Relations

2015. Williams, Frank P. III (1985). "Deterrence and Social Control: Rethinking the Relationship." *Journal of Criminal Justice* 13:141–51. Of interest to this bibliography is the conclusion that extra-legal factors are far more important in determining marijuana use than are traditional legal deterrent measures. ^Cannabis ^Drug\Use\Theories

2016. Williams, I. M. G. (1979). "UN/Thai Programme for Drug Abuse Control in Thailand—A Report on Phase I: February 1972–June 1979." *Bulletin on Narcotics* 31(2): 1-44. The article describes the UN/Thai programme for drug-abuse control carried out from 1972 to 1979. It was a pilot program that included crop replacement and community development, treatment and rehabilitation, and drug information and education. The article concludes that the results are sufficiently positive to merit general application. ^Thailand ^United\Nations ^Drug\Control\Policies ^International\Cooperation ^P\S\Integrated ^Southeast\Asia

2017. Williams, Nick B., Jr. (1987). "Smugglers, Thai Agents Play a Cat-and-Mouse Game." *The Los Angeles Times*, 25 May, 14. Smuggling is the number one business in southern Thailand, which borders on Malaysia. Description of the economics of smuggling and efforts made to interdict smuggling traffic. ^Thailand ^Drug\Traffic ^Interdiction ^Traffickers\Incentives\Economic ^Southeast\Asia

2018. Williamson, Richard S. (1983). "International Illicit Drug Traffic: The United States Response." *Bulletin on Narcotics* 35(4): 33–45. Describes the various activities of official U.S. agencies to lower demand, interdict supply, and eradicate crops. ^United\States ^Drug\Control\Policies ^Demand ^Interdiction ^Crop\Eradication ^Supply

2019. ——— (1988). "The United Nations: Some Parts Work." *Orbis* 32(Spring): 187–97. Of interest to this bibliography is the brief discussion of the UN drug agencies. Three UN organizations in Vienna deal with narcotic and psychotropic drug control. The author judges that these make a substantial contribution. These include the Commission on Narcotic Drugs (CND), the International Narcotics Control Board (INCB), and the United Nations Fund for Drug Abuse Control (UNFDAC), which aims to reduce the supply and demand of illicit drugs. ^United\Nations ^Drug\Control\Policies ^UNFDAC

2020. Willis, David K. (1983). "Waking Up to the Dramatic Rise in Drug Use." *The Christian Science Monitor*, 15-19 December. A five part series presenting the results of a three month, ten country investigation by the London correspondent, David K. Willis. Willis focuses on the global challenge, how families and parents in both rich and poor countries are trying to deal with the drug culture, drug substitute or designer drug activities, crop eradication and substitution experiments, and interdiction and law enforcement pressures. ^Drug\Use ^Drug\Control\Policies ^Drug\Traffic ^Family ^Designer\Drugs ^Crop\Eradication ^Interdiction ^Law\Enforcement

2021. Wilson, George C., and Molly Moore (1988). "Pentagon Warns of a No-Win Mission; Military Says Offensive against Drugs Would Overstretch Resources." *The Washington Post*, 13 May, A4. A continuation of reasons given by military leaders to try to thwart Congress' drafting them into the war on drugs. The principal argument is an economic one: the military says that their involvement against drugs would overstretch their resources. ^United\States ^Drug\Control\Policies ^Military

2022. Wilson, James Q. (1990). "Against the Legalization of Drugs." *Commentary* 89:2(February): 21-28. Public policy on cocaine ought to take a lesson from that on heroin. In the 1970s Wilson chaired the National Advisory Council for Drug Abuse Prevention, set up mainly to focus on the "heroin epidemic." The Council resisted arguments for legalization then; heroin addiction was contained. The same policies ought to be continued for cocaine, for otherwise cocaine consumption will increase dramatically. Wilson compares policies in England and the United States on heroin. He notes the psychopharmacological properties of crack cocaine that are conducive to violence, damaged fetuses, and broken families. Criticizes Ethan Nadelmann on a logical fallacy and factual errors (use of illegal cocaine says nothing of use of legal cocaine; Nadelmann's data derive from a survey done in 1985, *before* crack had become a problem). All things considered, the "war" has not been lost except among cocktail partying intellectuals. Moreover, there are continuing benefits of illegality: treatment programs are more effective than they would otherwise be; drug-prevention programs are more credible; a position of moral significance is established (nicotine does not destroy users' humanity; crack does). Analogies are made with America's alcohol problems. Wilson wants to "buy time" to give scientists a longer period in which to work on promising results in treating (or blocking) addiction. He does not want to run the risk of incurring consumption uncertainties if drugs were legalized. The article provoked a long round of replies, published in the May and June issues of *Commentary*, in which standard arguments of legalizers and illegalizers are further portrayed. ^P\S\Legalization\Critique ^Decriminalization\Critique

2023. Wilson, James Q., and Richard J. Herrnstein (1985). *Crime and Human Nature*. New York: Simon and Schuster. Sets forth a theory of criminal behavior that advances associations, causes, and controls. Reviews extensive literature on crime relationships and causes (e.g., genetic or "constitutional" factors [gender, age, intelligence, personality]; developmental factors [families, schools]; social context [community, labor markets, TV, alcohol and heroin]. While causes are complex and multifaceted, behavior, including criminal behavior, is controlled by its consequences, implying, of course, that if institutions can change that alter those consequences, then the incidence of crime will be altered. "Altering the social context" comes to mind, with attendant "deterrence, opportunity, and rehabilitation" activities. Complex interaction of social, psychological, and utilitarian variables are studied. Altering the subjective state of individuals is also discussed. "[T]he intimate connection between how we think and what we experience may suggest that the most efficacious ways of altering behavior are those that link programs designed to alter subjective states with those designed to alter contingencies" (p. 402). Ultimately, people must be responsible for their behavior, including criminal behavior. Of particular interest to this bibliography is the discussion on the relationship of alcohol and heroin to crime (pp. 355-373). With alcohol, the relationship is direct, but with heroin it is indirect. ^Drug\Use ^Crime ^Crime\Theories

2024. Wines, Michael (1989). "Law Enabled U.S. to Seize Proceeds of Drug Money Scheme." *The New York Times*, 31 March, A11. The new 1988 law enacted by the U.S. government allows the Justice Department to seize all funds and assets funneling through operations intended to disguise the source of ill-gotten money, not just the profits as allowed by 1986 law. Nearly a half billion dollars were seized recently. ^United\States ^Asset\Forfeiture ^Legislation

2025. ———— (1989). "Poll Finds Public Favors Tougher Laws against Drug Sale and Use." *The New York Times*, 15 August, A16. The survey by George Gallup found that nearly eight in ten Americans want tougher laws against users of illicit drugs. Even tougher responses were made when the sanctions were related to drug pushers. ^United\States ^Law\Enforcement ^Society

2026. ——— (1989). "Traffic in Cocaine Reported Surging Weeks after Colombian Crackdown." *The New York Times*, 1 November, A10. Smuggling has returned to near normal levels, with Mexico becoming a favored route for smugglers inasmuch as traditional Caribbean routes are becoming increasingly difficult for smugglers to deal with. ^Cocaine ^Drug\Traffic ^Supply ^Latin\America ^Colombia ^Mexico ^Caribbean

2027. Wirpsa, Leslie (1989). "Colombian Mafia Hurt by Testimony of Key Deserter." *The Miami Herald*, 12 June, 4A. The narco mafia has placed a $300,000 price tag as a reward for the execution of a Colombian deserter from one of the mafia's most sinister paramilitary organizations. The informant implicates a number of Colombian front organizations in massacres and terrorist acts. The drug traffickers have even funded an "academy for killers." A grizzly series of murders and assassinations are reported. The organizations began as self-defense forces fighting the Communist guerrillas, but were taken over by drug traffickers as financiers. Today the network has approximately 2,000 contract killers and perhaps 20,000 soldiers of fortune. ^Colombia ^Drug\Traffic ^Organized\Crime ^Consequences\Violence ^Latin\America

2028. ——— (1989). "Colombians Brace for Drug War." *The Christian Science Monitor*, 28 August, 3. Describes measures being taken by the judiciary in Colombia to protect its members from assassination by drug traffickers. Judges in Cali, for example, have spent hours practicing at a police shooting range after many received mock funeral announcements. General description of the vulnerability of the judiciary in Colombia. ^Colombia ^Latin\America ^Politics ^Consequences\Violence ^Consequences\Political ^Consequences\Social

2029. Wisotsky, Steven (1983). "Exposing the War on Cocaine: The Futility and Destructiveness of Prohibition." *Wisconsin Law Review* 6:1305–26. On the basis of a heavily footnoted review, Wisotsky argues that the war on cocaine cannot succeed, that it worsens the drug-abuse problem by nurturing international parasites, and that the secondary effects of the cocaine black market pose a more serious long-term threat to our institutions than does the wider availability of the drug itself. It thus considers alternatives. One alternative is to respect the privacy of the home but disallow public use of drugs. The law would punish individuals for specific acts of wrong doing (such as driving while intoxicated) and not use per se. Rationing would be pursued by taxation just low enough to discourage the entry of black marketeers. Controls would come not from law, but from custom and social pressure. For example, in the market place, job termination would provide a source of discipline to those who use drugs in the workplace. Within this context, major categories of discussion include the role of the law in the black market in cocaine, the structure of the cocaine industry, the law enforcement and control system associated with cocaine, the costs of the institutionalized black market (including economic effects of the black market, balance of payments and inflation), and the social and political effects of the black market. ^United\States ^Cocaine ^Drug\Control\Policies ^Reviews ^Drug\Control\Policies\Effectiveness ^Drug\Control\Policies\Critique ^Consequences\Drug\Control\Policies ^P\S\Legalization ^Culture ^Consequences\Economic ^Consequences\Political

2030. ——— (1987). *Breaking the Impasse in the War on Drugs.* Westport, Conn.: Greenwood Press. America is losing the war on drugs, the author argues, as he examines the black market in cocaine and the structure and the economics of the cocaine industry, along with legal and law enforcement responses. He looks at corruption and violence in the black market and at the international pathology associated with the war on drugs which produces corruption, instability, and narcoterrorism. The war on drugs is premised on the ignorance and foolishness of the individual. We ought to have a higher regard for the practical wisdom of humankind, he argues. It is the war on drugs' fanatic insistence on total abstinence rather than reasonable regulation that has endangered the lives of those who defy the laws as well as innocent bystanders. There should be a gradual transition from where we are now to a regime of drug regulation "premised on the centrality of individual responsibility and accountability." The author sets forth the goals and specific agenda of such a regulatory approach (p. 259). A bibliography is included. ^United\States ^Cocaine ^P\S\Legalization ^Drug\Control\Policies\Critique ^Consequences\Violence ^Consequences\Corruption ^Consequences\Terrorists ^Bibliographies

2031. —— (1987). "Introduction: In Search of a Breakthrough in the War on Drugs." *NOVA Law Review* 11:891–900. The volume, for which Wisotsky's contribution is an introduction, derives from a symposium the author convened to pursue his conviction that the war on drugs is a serious mistake. It inflicts on society ills from two worlds: A rapidly rising tide of drug abuse and the parasitical nature of international drug trafficking. He quickly chronicles why interdiction has proved to be unproductive, and what the consequences of corruption deriving from prohibition have been in the United States. All this, not to mention the cost to government. Isn't there a better way? A discussion of the alternatives that ought to be considered. ^United\States ^Drug\Control\Policies\Critique ^P\S\Legalization ^Consequences\Corruption ^Consequences\Misc ^Consequences\Drug\Control\Policies

2032. Witkin, Gordon (1988). "Hitting Kingpins in Their Assets." *U.S. News and World Report*, 5 December, 20–22. A new strategy has federal officials going after drug lords' bank accounts and other properties, which has caused defense lawyers to scramble for new defensive tactics. The incentive for police is that the proceeds are plowed back into their law enforcement programs. The federal government shares with local crime fighters. Many people besides civil libertarians have concerns about these seizures. ^United\States ^Asset\Forfeiture ^Asset\Forfeiture\Critique

2033. —— (1989). "The New Midnight Dumpers; Illegal Labs Are Creating a Toxic-Waste Nightmare." *U.S. News and World Report*, 9 January, 57. Chemical drums from illegal drug labs are being dumped almost anywhere, including in schoolyard playgrounds. Additionally, the waste goes down the bathtub drains, seeps in backyard pits, and is placed along roads and creeks, contaminating dwellings and polluting soil and water. Oddly, any enforcement agency raiding a lab then becomes responsible for its waste! ^United\States ^Consequences\Environmental

2034. Witkin, Gordon, and Stephen J. Hedges (1989). "The Coming Cocaine Plague in Europe." *U.S. News and World Report*, 20 February, 34–36. Demand is up, seizures are increasing, and frightening parallels exist with the American experience. The cocaine glut has become substantial in the United States, dropping a kilogram to $15,000. In Europe, by contrast, dealers ask up to $65,000 a kilo. The cocaine problem in Spain may be the worst in all Europe, and Spain has legalized drugs. ^Europe ^Spain ^Cocaine ^Drug\Traffic ^Legalization ^Consequences\Markets

2035. Wolinsky, Leo C. (1988). "Assembly OKs Wiretap Bill for Drug Fight." *The Los Angeles Times*, 15 April, 24. After a long struggle, California has passed a bill to allow state police to eavesdrop electronically on suspected drug dealers. The measure has been derided by civil libertarians as an affront to privacy rights. This bill overturns California's long-held prohibition against wiretapping. ^United\States ^Law\Enforcement ^Surveillance ^California ^Consequences\Human\Rights ^Legislation

2036. Wolman, Karen (1989). "Europe's Cocaine Boom Confounds Antidrug War." *The Christian Science Monitor*, 19 June, 1–2. Drug traffic into Italy has burgeoned, and Italian mobsters are increasingly working in tandem with South American drug narcotics barons. Italy has become a gateway for the rest of Europe. Prices, victims, and internal politics regarding the drug trade are discussed. ^Europe ^Italy ^Cocaine ^Drug\Traffic ^Organized\Crime ^Consequences\Political ^Consequences\Misc

2037. ———— (1989). "Italy Takes Aim at Money Laundering." *The Christian Science Monitor*, 10 May, 1–2. Organized crime is moving its money into legitimate businesses such as banking, insurance, brokerage houses, and financial companies outside the underworld's own strongholds. The Italian police and investigative units are accelerating their own investigations. ^Italy ^Money\Laundering ^Drug\Control\Policies ^Organized\Crime ^Consequences\Economic ^Europe

2038. Wong, Linda S. (1990). "Critical Analysis of Drug War Alternatives: The Need for a Shift in Personal and Social Values." *The Journal of Drug Issues* 20:4(Fall): 679–88. People have core psychosocial needs which, if unmet in natural ways, will be met artificially. Many alternatives to the drug war that are advanced would, if implemented, simply perpetuate social values that frustrate human needs and therefore would continue to incline people toward artificial satisfaction of them as, for example, by using drugs. A successful conclusion to the war on drugs will be accompanied by a change in people's personal and eventually social values in order to satisfy their needs in ways that do not require drugs. Demand reduction through value change is therefore the key. ^P\S\Demand\Reduction ^P\S\Values ^Drug\Control\Policies\Critique

2039. Woo, Margaret Y. K. (1988). "Drug Delusions." *The Christian Science Monitor*, 20 June, 12. A law teacher, who taught law in China, argues that just as opium worked to hinder the judgment and destroy the health of the imperial bureaucracy, leaving China crippled for more than 100 years, so also will it in the United States. To legalize drugs is only to hasten our undoing. In particular, legalizing drugs does not address the issue of addiction. ^United\States ^P\S\Legalization\Critique ^Consequences\Misc

2040. Wood, Chris (1989). "A Deadly Plague of Drugs." *Maclean's*, 3 April, 44–47. Description of the increasing amount of drugs available to Canadian drug users in ways that produce high risks and considerable misery among the user population. Description of the trials of one addict who disengaged. ^Canada ^Drug\Use ^Consequences\Misc

2041. Woodbury, Richard (1986). "The Rio Grande's Drug Corridor." *Time*, 17 November, 31. Describes Starr County, Texas, and the stress between lawmen on opposite sides of the U.S.–Mexican border. ^United\States ^Drug\Traffic ^Texas ^Consequences\Foreign\Relations ^Law\Enforcement

2042. Wrobleski, Ann B. (1988). "Presidential Certification of Narcotics Source Countries." *Current Policy*, 1061(April). U.S. Department of State, Bureau of Public Affairs. Through this report, President Reagan certified that the following major narcotics producing and/or major narcotics transiting countries had cooperated fully with the United States, or had taken adequate steps on their own to control narcotics production, trafficking, and money laundering: The Bahamas, Belize, Bolivia, Brazil, Burma, Colombia, Ecuador, Hong Kong, India, Jamaica, Malaysia, Mexico, Morocco, Nigeria, Pakistan, Peru, and Thailand. For other reasons the president determined it to be in the vital national interests to certify Laos, Lebanon, and Paraguay. The president denied certification to Afghanistan, Iran, Panama, and Syria. The special considerations attached to the certifications of Mexico, Colombia, Laos, and Paraguay are discussed in the report. Despite improvements in eradication programs in several countries, programs failed to overcome increases in production in most countries. Countries' specific programs and policies are discussed for all those listed. ^United\States

^Drug\Control\Policies ^Politics ^Foreign\Aid ^Bahamas ^Belize ^Bolivia ^Brazil ^Burma ^Colombia ^Ecuador ^Hong\Kong ^India ^Jamaica ^Malaysia ^Mexico ^Morocco ^Nigeria ^Pakistan ^Peru ^Thailand ^Laos ^Lebanon ^Paraguay ^Afghanistan ^Iran ^Panama ^Syria ^Middle\East ^Southwest\Asia ^Latin\America ^Africa ^Southeast\Asia

2043. Yablonsky, Lewis (1989). *The Therapeutic Community: A Successful Approach for Treating Substance Abusers*. New York: Gardner Press, Inc. The "therapeutic community" is one orientation directed toward rehabilitation of drug abusers. The book traces the history and development of therapeutic communities as a treatment orientation and delineates the concepts and methods that are thought to make such communities work across various cultures. ^Drug\Use ^Treatment\Therapeutic\Community ^Treatment\History

2044. Yamaguchi, Kazuo, and Denise B. Kandel (1985). "Dynamic Relationships Between Premarital Cohabitation and Illicit Drug Use: An Event-History Analysis of Role Selection and Role Socialization." *American Sociological Review* 50(August): 530–46. Use of marijuana and other illicit drugs increases the probability of cohabitation for men and for women, while cohabitation reduces the use of marijuana among women. Among drug users, premarital cohabitation is more likely to end in separation than in marriage. The implication of the dramatic increases in cohabitation and illicit drug use during the last two decades are discussed, along with refinements about probable causal connections. ^United\States ^Drug\Use ^Society

2045. Yelin, Yev (1985). "Why the 'Golden Crescent' Still Flourishes." *The New York Times*, July, 28–31. Describes the booming heroin traffic out of Pakistan, and traces its success to its having been infiltrated by the international narcotics mafia. Why is heroin so easily smuggled through Pakistani customs? Corruption. Even Pakistani diplomats work as couriers. And, there is mafia protection involving intimidation and threat. The U.S. CIA has knowledge of the poppy fields among the hill tribes of Pakistan. So why is nothing done? Could it be the U.S. foreign policy interests in counter-revolutionary operations in Afghanistan that are sustained in this part of Pakistan? On the wide outside, the CIA is thought to be involved in ways that earn it money to facilitate its own activities, financing, for example, Nicaraguan "freedom fighters." ^Afghanistan ^Pakistan ^United\States ^Heroin ^Drug\Traffic ^Politics ^Consequences\Corruption ^Consequences\Foreign\Policy ^Organized\Crime ^CIA ^Contras ^Bureaucracy ^Nicaragua ^Latin\America ^Southwest\Asia

2046. Yerkey, Gary (1986). "Europe Heads up Its War on Drugs." *The Christian Science Monitor*, 21 October, 1. While Amsterdam, Holland, has been noted for its tolerance of drug use, even it has intensified its crackdown on trafficking in hard drugs such as heroin. Heroin in Western Europe, over the past decade, has reached "epidemic" proportions. The British government has drafted an action plan. Some Socialists are calling for decriminalizing drug use. It is with the arrival of cocaine, however, that Europe has agreed that it must take note. ^Europe ^Drug\Control\Policies ^Netherlands ^United\Kingdom ^Decriminalization

2047. Yesavage, Jerome A., Von Otto Leirer, Mark Denari, and Leo E. Hollister (1985). "Carry-over Effects of Marijuana Intoxication on Aircraft Pilot Performance: A Preliminary Report." *American Journal of Psychiatry* 142(11): 1325–29. Under experimental conditions, trained and experienced pilots were each given a marijuana cigarette containing nineteen mg of THC. Twenty-four hours later when they were put through a series of performance tasks, the mean showed trends toward impairment on all variables. Significant impairment was noted in several critical safety areas. ^Cannabis ^Drug\Use ^Consequences\Public\Safety ^Aircraft

2048. Yodmani, Chavalit (1983). "The Role of the Association of South-East Asian Nations in Fighting Illicit Drug Traffic." *Bulletin on Narcotics* 35(4): 97–104. Member states of the Association of South-East Asian Nations (ASEAN) have concerted their efforts to overcome drug-related problems and illicit trafficking. They view trafficking as a threat to national security, stability, and integrity. The activities of each member state demonstrate their role in combatting illicit drug traffic. ^Southeast\Asia ^Drug\Control\Policies ^International\Cooperation ^ASEAN

2049. Yost, Paul A. (1988). "Coast Guard Activities, Performance Increase Despite Budget Difficulties." *Sea Technology* 29(1): 16–18. Description of what the Coast Guard does, the technology it uses, and the resources it makes available to detect illegal shipments of anything. ^United\States ^Interdiction ^Coast\Guard

2050. Zaki, M. S. (1983). "Egyptian Law on the Sequestration and Confiscation of Property Acquired through Smuggling and Trafficking in Drugs." *Bulletin on Narcotics* 35(2): 103–6. Egyptian drug control legislation allows for the confiscation of property used in the commission of a drug-related crime. The legislation also provides for the sequestration of property illegally acquired through illicit drug traffic. ^Egypt ^Asset\Forfeiture ^Legislation

2051. Zealey, Philip (1981). "United Nations/Burma Programme for Drug Abuse Control, the First Phase: 1976–1981." *Bulletin on Narcotics* 33(3): 1–21. Described are the UN-assisted provisions in Burma of its wide-ranging drug-abuse control program. Included are measures dealing with law enforcement, crop substitution, treatment and rehabilitation, and education. Preliminary assessments on the outcome of the program are given. ^Burma ^United\Nations ^Drug\Control\Policies ^International\Cooperation ^Crop\Substitution ^Treatment ^Rehabilitation ^Southeast\Asia

2052. Zelnick, C. Robert (1988). "Missing the Boat on Drugs." *The Christian Science Monitor*, 20 June, 12. In the wake of the drug indictment against Panama's General Manuel Noriega, this columnist considers that transferring our wrath to foreigners who supply drugs to meet our demand or who would enlist the military for a task alien to their tradition are peddling illusions. ^United\States ^Drug\Control\Policies\Critique

2053. Zentner, Joseph L. (1982). "Book Review of *Flowers in the Blood: The Story of Opium*." *Contemporary Drug Problems* 11(1): 169–77. This review not only gives a faithful account of the content of the book being reviewed, but also is itself an important summary of the place of opium in history. ^Opiates\History

2054. Zimmerman, Carita (1989). "Urine Testing, Testing-Based Employment Decisions and the Rehabilitation Act of 1973." *Columbia Journal of Law and Social Problems* 22:219–67. In the wake of a developing perception that drug abuse is costing billions of dollars each year to American businesses (decreased productivity and increased error, theft, absenteeism, and accident rates), the federal government in 1986 mandated a "drug-free federal workplace." Testing programs now in place screen millions of employees. Among the most common device for screening is mass and random urine testing programs. The tests have evoked severe criticism for their inaccuracy and irrelevance. Most claims against such testing rest on the Rehabilitation Act of 1973. In relationship to these factors, this article examines problems commonly involved in the implementation of mass employee urine testing programs, discusses objection issues to employee drug screening as an unreasonable invasion of privacy, and advances the argument that positive drug testing results as the sole basis for employment decisions, without regard to an individual's actual capabilities, constitutes a violation of the 1973 rehabilitation act. ^United\States ^Drug\Testing ^Workplace ^Legislation ^Drug\Testing\Critique

2055. Zimmerman, Steven (1984). "A Windfall in Recovered Assets." *Drug Enforcement* (Summer): 31–32. Describes the application of the RICO laws (Racketeer Influenced Corrupt Organization) in the general confiscation (not to mention recovery) of dealer's assets. ^United\States ^Asset\Forfeiture ^Legislation

2056. Zinberg, Norman (1984). *Drugs, Set, and Setting: The Basis for Controlled Intoxicant Use.* New Haven, Conn.: Yale University Press. Makes a case for increased medical prescription of narcotics. Results are based on experiments that took place in 1968. Emphasizes that "social settings" must be taken into consideration in determining whether it is appropriate to prescribe narcotics medically. Laws should therefore be relaxed to allow people, encouraged in moderation, to experiment with mind altering drugs. There are benefits as well as liabilities to drug use. ^Drug\Use ^Legalization ^Drug\Use\Theories

2057. ——— (1987). "Breaking the Impasse in the War on Drugs: A Search for New Directions." *NOVA Law Review* 11:901–7. The historical logic for decriminalizing marijuana is presented. The way "drugs" have been held hostage by internal politics in the United States is reviewed. What is to be done? Decriminalize marijuana; make heroin available for the terminally ill; impose appropriate medical education at both the undergraduate and continuing education levels for all professionals and paraprofessionals. ^United\States ^Cannabis ^P\S\Legalization ^Decriminalization

2058. Zweben, Joan Ellen, and Kathleen O'Connell (1988). "Strategies for Breaking Marijuana Dependence." *Journal of Psychoactive Drugs* 20(1): 121–27. Although marijuana dependence is less dramatic in its effects than other drugs, trace elements remain in the tissues long after use. Consequently, attempts to terminate marijuana use require a sustained and often difficult effort. ^Cannabis ^Treatment ^Consequences\Misc ^Drug\Use

Index

Keywords corresponding to entry numbers in the annotated bibliography are preceded by a caret (^). Other entries correspond to page numbers in the main text.

A

Abstinence: 138.

Acetone: 127.

Acupuncture: 138.

Addiction: xix; 17, n. 25, n. 26; 18, n. 36; 21, n. 51; 25-28; ; 31, n. 20; 31, n. 22; 113; 117; 137; 155, n. 12; 159, n. 169; 178, n. 348; 181, n. 377; relationship of to drug control policies, 28; to cocaine, 182, n. 383.

^Addiction: (See ^Drug\Use; ^Consequences\Personal; ^Consequences\Psychological; ^Consequences\Physiological; ^Consequences\Health)

Aerial spraying: 124; resistance to, 125.

Afghanistan: 25; 51; 53; 58; hashish production in, 36-37.

^Afghanistan: 537; 556; 603; 880; 920; 921; 971; 1254; 1313; 1538; 1685; 1766; 1893; 1894; 1895; 2001; 2042; 2045.

Africa: 38; 51.

^Africa: 78; 235; 500; 701; 772; 1254; 1334; 1518; 1692; 1693; 1747; 1748; 1749; 1753; 1754; 1779; 1888; 1889; 1890; 1891; 1892; 1893; 1895; 1899.

^Agriculture: 424; 450; 545; 1500; 1664; 1687; 1724; 1964.

AIDS: xxvi, n. 23; 211; impact of on health delivery services, 114; proffered solutions transmission of related to drug control policies, 111–14.

^AIDS: 13; 31; 32; 33; 34; 35; 43; 44; 105; 190; 191; 250; 380; 383; 477; 478; 479; 480; 481; 489; 566; 602; 620; 697; 700; 786; 840; 841; 879; 936; 945; 967; 968; 969; 970; 1112; 1114; 1177; 1179; 1220; 1257; 1274; 1334; 1381; 1429; 1460; 1532; 1591; 1641; 1646; 1655; 1753; 1809; 1826; 1829; 1831; 1876; 1899; 1927; 1930; 1960. (*See also* ^Consequences\AIDS).

Aircraft: drug impaired piloting of, 191–92.

^Aircraft: 198; 284; 419; 805; 1555; 1784; 1828; 1913; 1921; 1967; 2005; 2047.

^Alaska: 67; 490; 596; 1131; 1147; 1636; 1873.

Alcohol: 203, n. 31; 221; 241.

^Alcohol: 213; 216; 258; 286; 287; 317; 322; 416; 423; 441; 464; 517; 576; 599; 614; 761; 762; 796; 844; 856; 861; 882; 912; 926; 927; 1086; 1146; 1227; 1241; 1271; 1361; 1362; 1547; 1601; 1607; 1641; 1784; 1876; 1896; 1955.

Americanization of drug war: 234–35.

^Amotivational\Syndrome: 46; 118; 378; 474; 714; 883; 1140; 1204; 1498; 1634; 1752; 1938; 1940; 1941; 1942. (*See also* ^Amotivational\Syndrome\Theories).

^Amotivational\Syndrome\Theories: 353; 1162. (*See also* ^Amotivational\Syndrome).

Amsterdam: 27.

Andean Drug Conference: 56.

Consumers: illicit drug, demand reduction proposals focusing on, 215–16; social char-

acteristics of, 43, n. 20. (*See also* ^Drug\Use).

Consumption: illicit drug, accepted and disputed conclusions about personal consequences of, 186–89; association of with criminality, 151, n. 81 and 154, n. 106; historical in America, 20, n. 44; historical trends in, xix; public safety aspects of, 190–92; worldwide patterns of, 28; personal values associated with, 19, n. 42. (*See also* ^Drug\Use).

Contras: 16, n. 23; 52–53; 66.

Controlled delivery: supply suppression strategy of, 134.

Convention for the Suppression of Illicit Traffic in Dangerous Drugs: 99.

Convention on Psychotropic Substances: 99.

Cooperation, international: effectiveness of, 54–55. (*See also* ^International\Cooperation)

Corruption: 64–71; relationship of to drug control policies, 111–18.

Costa Rica: 109; 135; 38; 51; corruption in, 67; illicit drug consumption in, 41, n. 11.

Council of Europe: provisions of for controlling illicit narcotics, 100.

Crack: 9; 216; association of with violence, 198–99; theories of consumption of, 21, n. 51.

Crime: 49–72; relationship of to drug control policies, 112–13.

^ Society: 40; 77; 135; 167; 187; 248; 249; 254; 260; 265; 286; 290; 291; 292; 313; 321; 332; 334; 363; 392; 393; 404; 406; 408; 424; 435; 436; 443; 449; 452; 454; 464; 476; 481; 488; 500; 506; 508; 509; 522; 535; 541; 545; 564; 565; 570; 574; 581; 600; 607; 609; 618; 622; 653; 669; 678; 683; 685; 688; 693; 702; 704; 708; 717; 737; 738; 739; 741; 756; 760; 761; 762; 768; 776; 777; 780; 782; 783; 850; 859; 867; 869; 874; 882; 883; 886; 903; 911; 912; 915; 916; 927; 928; 929; 937; 978; 980; 986; 994; 1006; 1026; 1047; 1054; 1067; 1080; 1109; 1135; 1145; 1150; 1172; 1188; 1189; 1190; 1191; 1200; 1204; 1224; 1236; 1237; 1238; 1250; 1273; 1301; 1302; 1319; 1320; 1329; 1335; 1343; 1347; 1351; 1362; 1400; 1427; 1433; 1474; 1498; 1510; 1533; 1544; 1551; 1553; 1593; 1601; 1607; 1617; 1631; 1634; 1641; 1645; 1657; 1659; 1677; 1687; 1688; 1692; 1693; 1701; 1705; 1803; 1804; 1832; 1960; 1985; 2003; 2006; 2025; 2044.

Solutions (*See* Proffered solutions)

Soto, Hernando de: 234.

South American Agreement on Narcotic Drugs and Psychotropic Substances (ASEP): 100; 124. (*See also* ^ ASEP)

South Pacific Commission: provisions of for controlling illicit narcotics, 101.

^ South\Africa: 1692; 1693.

^ South\Carolina: 858.

^ Southeast\Asia: 1; 2; 27; 73; 77; 110; 116; 124; 126; 214; 215; 220; 226; 245; 246; 256; 262; 266; 269; 270; 314; 318; 319; 320; 327; 409; 411; 413; 414; 415; 431; 500; 505; 514; 515; 581; 623; 624; 632; 730; 731; 732; 733; 734; 735; 736; 741; 838; 839; 843; 844; 859; 881; 897; 901; 907; 910; 933; 934; 945; 946; 949; 988; 990; 1033; 1034; 1035; 1060; 1062; 1073; 1081; 1086; 1095; 1144; 1166; 1167; 1168; 1169; 1170; 1171; 1197; 1227; 1238; 1248; 1254; 1256; 1257; 1266; 1267; 1286; 1370; 1376; 1412; 1434; 1459; 1462; 1502; 1506; 1520; 1534; 1540; 1541; 1557; 1571; 1576; 1577; 1599; 1608; 1616; 1623; 1638; 1656; 1657; 1659; 1664; 1667; 1668; 1675; 1678; 1679; 1747; 1748; 1749; 1753; 1754; 1760; 1766; 1770; 1773; 1779; 1805; 1835; 1865; 1881; 1888; 1889; 1890; 1891; 1892; 1893; 1895; 1907; 1928; 1931; 1962; 1972; 1983; 1984; 1988; 1992; 1993; 1998; 2001; 2004; 2016; 2017; 2042; 2048; 2051.

^ Southwest\Asia: 69; 226; 328; 449; 581; 603; 604; 686; 721; 769; 777; 880; 920; 921;

971; 1028; 1073; 1197; 1213; 1217; 1218; 1254; 1257; 1312; 1313; 1396; 1403; 1557; 1616; 1670; 1671; 1766; 1805; 1893; 1895; 1907; 1946; 1970; 1971; 2000; 2001; 2042; 2045.

Sovereignty: 235.

^ Sovereignty: 146; 625; 1210. (*See* ^ Consequences\Sovereignty; and, also, ^ Consequences\National\Security; ^ Consequences\State\Authority.)

Soviet Union: xxvi, n. 27; 38; 51; 53; 101; 106; 107; drug control policies in, 107. (*See also* ^ USSR)

Spain: 51; 211; drug control policies in, 108.

^ Spain: 280; 377; 478; 659; 706; 1145; 1451; 1915; 2034.

Sri Lanka: 27; 28; 52; 68.

^ Sri\Lanka: 843; 844; 949; 1144; 1520; 1616; 1656.

^ State\Policies: 239; 244; 943. (*See also* ^ Drug\Control\Policies; ^ Law\Enforcement; ^ Treatment; ^ Prevention.)

Statistics: xx, n. 9; xxiv, n. 14; xxiv, n. 15; xxv, n. 18; xxv, n. 18; xxv, n. 19; xxv, n. 21; Chapters 1-3, *passim*.

^ Statistics:31; 123; 131; 151; 205; 338; 373; 396; 399; 410; 416; 423; 424; 448; 450; 454; 459; 470; 497; 513; 514; 516; 624; 653; 688; 692; 697; 748; 754; 761; 779; 786; 799; 816; 817; 861; 862; 891; 895; 964; 1024; 1052; 1061; 1069; 1071; 1095; 1194; 1248; 1249; 1250; 1251; 1252; 1253; 1254; 1255; 1256; 1257; 1258; 1264; 1308; 1312; 1351; 1361; 1475; 1508; 1536; 1539; 1586; 1626; 1645; 1660; 1667; 1693; 1710; 1711; 1716; 1736; 1740; 1747; 1748; 1756; 1778; 1829; 1880; 1881; 1882; 1884; 1888; 1889; 1890; 1891; 1892; 1893; 1895; 1899; 1901; 1910; 1956. (*See also* ^ Production\Statistics; ^ Statistics\Critique.)

^ Statistics\Critique: 107; 520; 687; 691; 799; 992; 1008; 1416; 1421; 1475; 1660. (*See also* ^ Statistics; ^ Production\Statistics.)

Suárez, Roberto: 55.

Sulfuric acid: 127.

Supply: 46–48; consequences of, 46; control of, 102–103, 123–37 and 168, n. 271; proffered solutions to reduce, 231–35; reduction of, 210–11; U.S. funding of reduction of, 124–25.

^ Supply: 136; 140; 201; 239; 246; 252; 471; 557; 625; 646; 669; 681; 720; 723; 745;

V

Values: relationship of to cocaine con-
sumption, 19, n. 42.
Venezuela: 51; corruption of judiciary in,
67.
Vietnam: 235.
Villages: economic linkages among in drug
trade, 57–60.
Violence: 198–99; 68–69.

About the Author

LAMOND TULLIS is Professor of Political Science and a Fellow of the David M. Kennedy Center for International and Area Studies at Brigham Young University. His previous books include *Lord and Peasant in Peru: A Paradigm of Political and Social Change*; *Politics and Social Change in Third World Countries*; *Modernization in Brazil*; and *Mormons in Mexico: Dynamics of Faith and Culture*.

CPSIA information can be obtained at www.ICGtesting.com
Printed in the USA
BVOW08*2013250215

389227BV00007B/119/P